WEST'S LAW SCHOOL ADVISORY BOARD

INTELLECTUAL PROPERTY

CASES AND MATERIALS

By

Margreth Barrett
Professor of Law,
University of California,
Hastings College of Law

AMERICAN CASEBOOK SERIES®

WEST PUBLISHING CO.
ST. PAUL, MINN., 1995

610 Opperman Drive
P.O. Box 64526
St. Paul, MN 55164–0526
1–800–328–9352

Printed in the United States of America

Library of Congress Cataloging-in-Publication Data

Barrett, Margreth, 1951–
Cases and materials on intellectual property / by Margreth Barrett.
p. cm. — (American casebook series)
Includes index.
ISBN 0–314–06126–6
1. Intellectual property—United States—Cases. I. Title.
II. Series.
KF2978.B35 1995
346.7304'8—dc20
[347.30648] 95–18565
CIP

ISBN 0–314–06126–6

TEXT IS PRINTED ON 10% POST CONSUMER RECYCLED PAPER

PRINTED WITH SOY INK

For Ken

*

Preface

This book is designed for use in a three or four-hour law school survey course in intellectual property. It can easily be adapted to a two-hour course dedicated to selected intellectual property doctrines. The book should be used with a statutory supplement containing the federal Patent, Copyright and Trademark Acts, such as Roger Schechter's SELECTED INTELLECTUAL PROPERTY AND UNFAIR COMPETITION STATUTES, REGULATIONS AND TREATIES, which is published by West Publishing Company.

While the book places greatest emphasis on the federal law of patents, copyrights, trademarks, and unfair competition, it also provides substantial coverage of state trade secret, unfair competition and right of publicity doctrines. I haven chosen what I consider to be the most logical, straightforward organization. However, recognizing that reasonable minds may differ on the issue of organization, I have designed the book to have self-contained chapters, sections, and subsections that can readily be reorganized in a syllabus to suit the tastes of the instructor.

The book begins with an introductory chapter that explores the basic themes, concepts and policies underlying the whole of intellectual property law. This sets the stage for the subsequent chapters, which demonstrate how these themes, concepts and policies have influenced the development of the individual substantive intellectual property doctrines.

The book then addresses the three intellectual property doctrines that provide rights in ideas and information. Chapter Two reviews the state law of trade secrets. Chapter Three provides a thorough overview of federal patent law. The cases in the patents chapter are specifically selected to be accessible to students of all educational backgrounds, featuring inventions, whose technical aspects do not obscure the courts' discussions of the relevant legal concepts. Chapter Four concludes this portion of the book with a short discussion of how familiar common-law doctrines addressing contracts, unjust enrichment, and confidential relationships may be used to provide legal rights in ideas and information when trade secret and patent doctrines do not apply.

Chapter Five reviews federal copyright law, which provides rights in original forms of expression. The chapter first examines copyright eligibility limitations, then explores the difficulties courts have encountered in applying these limitations to particular categories of copyrightable subject matter, such as factual compilations, computer programs, and the designs of useful articles. The chapter then turns to the rights conveyed by copyright law, and issues of copyright ownership and duration. The chapter discusses copyright formalities, including notice of copyright, but recognizes their shrinking importance under recent amendments to the Copyright Act.

The next three chapters examine legal protection of business good will and related trade values. Chapter Six addresses trademark law, focusing primarily on federal statutory law, but noting points at which statutory rights depart from the underlying common-law trademark cause of action. Chapter Seven examines the unfair competition doctrines preventing passing off, false advertising, product disparagement, misappropriation, and trademark dilution. In the case of the first three of these doctrines, it compares the federal cause of action under Lanham Act § 43(a) with the traditional common-law claim. This portion of the book winds up, in Chapter Eight, with a discussion of state rights of publicity, which protect an individual's interest in the publicity value in his or her identity.

The final chapter addresses the relationship of all the various state and federal intellectual property doctrines under the supremacy clause of the United States Constitution, and the effect of Copyright Act section 301 on state intellectual property causes of action.

In recognition of the increasingly international nature of intellectual property protection, the book integrates discussion of international issues throughout. Several of the chapters describe relevant multinational intellectual property treaties, and analyze their influence on domestic intellectual property law. They also discuss key differences between United States intellectual property practices and those of other countries, both as a vehicle for evaluating existing domestic doctrines and for anticipating future amendments, as nations continue their attempts to harmonize international intellectual property rules.

The book incorporates most, if not all, of the seminal Supreme Court and federal appellate decisions that are generally recognized as the bedrock of intellectual property doctrine. Otherwise, the reported case opinions are very recent, selected to reflect the most current views and trends. In the patents chapter, most of the reported opinions emanate from the United States Court of Appeals for the Federal Circuit, which, since 1982, has exercised exclusive jurisdiction over all intermediate appeals in patent cases. I have made every attempt to select cases with interesting, accessible facts. Text and notes between the reported case opinions provide background information, freeing the class and instructor to move beyond the basics during class. Recognizing that a survey course case book can only go so far on any topic, I have provided references to more in-depth treatments of a wide array of issues.

I have edited the cases and other reported materials. Three asterisks (* * *) indicate that text has been omitted. Inserted material is enclosed in brackets. I have deleted citations and footnotes without indication. Footnotes retained in the case opinions reflect their original numbers.

I would like to thank the Hastings College for its support in this project, and Linda Weir, Hastings librarian extraordinaire. Thanks also to

Eric Ethington, Kimberley Davis-Marks, Sunil Kulkarni, and David Rapallo for their invaluable research assistance. I am very grateful to the numerous authors and copyright owners who graciously permitted me to reprint their materials. They are identified in footnotes associated with the materials they contributed. Finally, I would like to thank my colleagues, and my husband, Ken Louden, for their tolerance and support.

M.B.

San Francisco, 1995

*

Summary of Contents

Table of Contents

PART THREE. RIGHTS IN ORIGINAL FORMS OF EXPRESSION

PART FOUR. RIGHTS IN CONSUMER GOOD WILL AND RELATED TRADE VALUES

Table of Cases

The principal cases are in bold type. Cases cited or discussed in the text are roman type. References are to pages within this book. Cases cited in principal cases and within other quoted materials are not included.

*

Table of Statutes

UNITED STATES

UNITED STATES CONSTITUTION

UNITED STATES CODE ANNOTATED

5 U.S.C.A.—Government Organization and Employees

UNITED STATES CONSTITUTION

7 U.S.C.A.—Agriculture

15 U.S.C.A.—Commerce and Trade

UNITED STATES CODE ANNOTATED
15 U.S.C.A.—Commerce and Trade

Sec.	This Work Page
1064 (Cont'd)	618
	630
	791
1064(3)	656
	784
1064(3)—(5)	792
1065	777
	778
	787
	791
	792
1067	627
1070	627
1071	628
1071(a)	628
1071(b)	628
1072	776
1091(a)	631
1092	631
1094	631
1111	798
1115(a)	777
	792
1115(b)	778
	788
	791
	792
	793
1115(b)(4)	761
1115(b)(5)	777
1116	797
1116(d)	797
1116(d)(1)	724
1117	806
1117(a)	797
1117(b)	724
	797
1118	724
1125(a)	452
	523
	631
	768
	794
	797
	801
	805
	828
1126	803
1126(d)	632
1126(e)	632
	633
1127	605
	606
	607
	610
	611
	616
	617
	625
	723
	784
	786

UNITED STATES CODE ANNOTATED
17 U.S.C.A.—Copyrights
Copyright Act of 1909

Sec.	This Work Page
4	354
10	567
12	567
19—21	567
21	567

Copyright Act of 1976

Sec.	This Work Page
101	360
	363
	396
	397
	404
	415
	416
	437
	438
	439
	456
	513
	525
	553
	556
	565
	571
	576
	581
	582
	583
101 et seq.	354
102	22
	358
	359
	407
	432
	435
	964
102(a)	360
	416
	456
102(a)(8)	456
102(b)	360
	964
103	407
	964
104	355
104A	569
	572
	573
	582
104A(a)(1)(B)	573
104A(d)(1)	573
104A(h)(2)(A)	573

UNITED STATES CODE ANNOTATED
Copyright Act of 1976

UNITED STATES CODE ANNOTATED

Copyright Act of 1976

18 U.S.C.A.—Crimes and Criminal Procedure

19 U.S.C.A.—Customs and Duties

UNITED STATES CODE ANNOTATED

19 U.S.C.A.—Customs and Duties

28 U.S.C.A.—Judiciary and Judicial Procedure

35 U.S.C.A.—Patents (Patent Act)

UNITED STATES CODE ANNOTATED

35 U.S.C.A.—Patents (Patent Act)

UNITED STATES CODE ANNOTATED

35 U.S.C.A.—Patents (Patent Act)

42 U.S.C.A.—The Public Health and Welfare

STATUTES AT LARGE

POPULAR NAME ACTS

FEDERAL FOOD, DRUG AND COSMETICS ACT

FEDERAL INSECTICIDE, FUNGICIDE AND RODENTICIDE ACT

LANHAM ACT

TARIFF ACT

UNIFORM DECEPTIVE TRADE PRACTICES ACT

Sec.	This Work Page
2(a)(8)	835
	852
3	833
3(a)	852

UNIFORM TRADE SECRETS ACT

Sec.	This Work Page
1	37
	39
	43
1(1)	43
	66
1(2)	43
1(4)	38
2(a)	70
3(a)	70
3(b)	71
4	71

STATE STATUTES

WEST'S ANNOTATED CALIFORNIA BUSINESS AND PROFESSIONS CODE

Sec.	This Work Page
16600	61

WEST'S ANNOTATED CALIFORNIA CIVIL CODE

Sec.	This Work Page
980(a)(1)	364
987	523
987(a)	524
987(c)	524
990	895
1797.8—1797.86	754
3344	895
3344(b)	915

WEST'S ANNOTATED CALIFORNIA LABOR CODE

Sec.	This Work Page
2870—2872	84

WEST'S ANNOTATED CALIFORNIA PENAL CODE

Sec.	This Work Page
653h	930

WEST'S FLORIDA STATUTES ANNOTATED

Sec.	This Work Page
540.08	895

LOUISIANA STATUTES ANNOTATED—REVISED STATUTES

Sec.	This Work Page
23:921	61

MASSACHUSETTS GENERAL LAWS ANNOTATED

Ch.	This Work Page
214, § 3A	895

MICHIGAN COMPILED LAWS ANNOTATED

Sec.	This Work Page
445.774A	61

MINNESOTA STATUTES ANNOTATED

Sec.	This Work Page
609.52	71

NEVADA REVISED STATUTES

Sec.	This Work Page
598.984	921

NEW YORK, MCKINNEY'S ARTS AND CULTURAL AFFAIRS LAW

Sec.	This Work Page
14.03	524
14.03(1)	524
14.03(2)	524

NEW YORK, MCKINNEY'S CIVIL RIGHTS LAW

NEW YORK, MCKINNEY'S PENAL LAW

OKLAHOMA STATUTES ANNOTATED

TENNESSEE CODE ANNOTATED

V.T.C.A., BUSINESS & COMMERCE CODE

V.T.C.A., PROPERTY CODE

CODE OF FEDERAL REGULATIONS

FEDERAL REGISTER

*

Table of Secondary Sources

Baxter, J.W. & J.P. Sinnott, World Patent Law and Practice (1993), 96
Becker, S.A., Patent Applications Handbook (1993), 211
Berne Convention Implementation Act of 1988, H.R. Rep. No. 609, 100th Cong., 2d Sess. 33-34 (1988), 523
Best, Controlling False Advertising: A Comparative Study of Public Regulation, Industry Self-Policing, and Private Litigation, 20 Ga. L. Rev. 1 (1985), 832
BeVier, Competitor Suits for False Advertising Under Section 43(a) of the Lanham Act: A Puzzle in the Law of Deception, 78 Va. L. Rev. 1 (1992), 823, 828
Beyer, Internationalism, Art, and the Suppression of Innovation: Film Colorization and the Philosophy of Moral Rights, 82 N.W. U. L. Rev. 1011 (1988), 527
Bilder, The Shrinking Back: The Law of Biography, 43 Stan. L. Rev. 299 (1991), 380
Blake, Employee Agreements Not To Compete, 73 Harv. L. Rev. 625 (1960), 61
Blommer, Washington Letter, AIPLA Bull., 455 (April-May-June, 1992), 235
Boland, Wrongful Assult on the Trademark System, 1987 Colum. Bus. L. Rev. 153, p. 752
Boorstyn, N., Copyright Law (1981 and Supp.), 358
Braga, The Economics of Intellectual Property Rights and the GATT: A View from the South, 22 Vand. J. Transnat'l L. 243 (1989), 27
Breitenfeld, Collective Marks--Should They Be Abolished? 47 Trademark Rep. 1 (1957), 618
Breyer, Copyright: A Rejoinder, 20 U.C.L.A. L. Rev. 75 (1972), 20
Breyer, The Uneasy Case for Copyright: A Study of Copyright in Books, Photocopies, and Computer Programs, 84 Harv. L. Rev. 281 (1970), 20
Bronckers, The Impact of TRIPs: Intellectual Property Protection in Developing Countries, 31 Common Mkt. L. Rev. 1245 (1994), 27
Brown, Advertising and the Public Interest: Legal Protection of Trade Symbols, 57 Yale L.J. 1165 (1948), 760, 881
Brown, Design Protection: An Overview, 34 U.C.L.A. L. Rev. 1341 (1987), 324, 454
Brown, Publication and Preemption in Copyright Law: Elegiac Reflections on Goldstein v. California, 22 U.C.L.A. L. Rev. 1022 (1975), 936
Bruzzone, The Research Exemption: A Proposal, 21 AIPLA Q. J. 52 (1993), 248
Bussert & Davis, Calculating Profits under Section 35 of the Lanham Act: A Practitioner's Guide, 82 Trademark Rep. 182 (1992), 800
Butler, Pragmatism in Software Copyright: Computer Associates v. Altai, 6 Harv. J. L. & Tech. 183 (1992), 431

Callmann, He Who Reaps Where He Has Not Sown: Unjust Enrichment in the Law of Unfair Competition, 55 Harv. L. Rev. 595 (1942), 870
Callmann, R., The Law of Unfair Competition, Trademarks and Monopolies (L. Altman 4th ed. 1981 & Supp.), 803, 849
Carstens & Ward, Conception and the "On Sale" Bar, 34 Wm. & Mary L. Rev. 393 (1993), 165
Cartiglia, The Patent Cooperation Treaty: A Rational Approach to International Patent Filing, 73 J. Pat. & Trademark Off. Soc. 261 (1994), 208
Casey, Marthinsen & Moss, The Economic Impact of the Freedom of Information Act, 12 AIPLA Q. J. 76 (1984), 85
Casey, Jr., W., J. Marthinsen & L. Moss, Entrepreneurship, Productivity and the Freedom of Information Act (1983), 85
Chavez, The Standard for Determining Infringement of a Design Patent, 73 J. Pat. & Trademark Off. Soc. 843 (1991), 324
Chisum, Foreign Activity: Its Effect on Patentability Under United States Law, 11 IIC 26 (1980), 207
Chisum, Patent Law and the Presumption of Moral Regularity: A Critical Review of Recent Federal Circuit Decisions on Inequitable Conduct and Willful Infringement, 69 J. Pat. & Trademark Off. Soc. 27 (1987), 277
Chisum, Sources of Prior Art in Patent Law, 52 Wash. L. Rev. 1 (1976), 179
Chisum, The Patentability of Algorithms, 47 U. Pitt. L. Rev. 959 (1986), 120
Chisom, D.S., Patents: A Treatise on the Law of Patentability, Validity, and Infringement, 96, 119, 135, 149, 167, 168, 210, 211, 251, 277, 279, 280, 324
Clark, Animal Invention Protection, 16 AIPLA Q. J. 442 (1988-89), 106
Closius & Schaffer, Involuntary Nonservitude: The Current Judicial Enforcement of Employee Covenants Not To Compete--A Proposal for Reform, 57 S. Cal.L. Rev. 531 (1984), 61
Cohen, Duration, 24 U.C.L.A. L. Rev. 1180 (1977), 581
Comment, Television Formats, the Search for Protection, 58 Cal. L. Rev.. 1169 (1970), 346
Comment, The Copyrightability of Nonliteral Elements of Computer Programs, 94 Colum. L. Rev. 242 (1994), 431
Comment, Trademark Parody: A Fair Use and First Amendment Analysis, 72 Va. L. Rev. 1079 (1986), 885

Nailing the Jellyfish, 68 Iowa L. Rev. 35 (1982), 851

Filardi, The Adequacy of Compensation for Patent Infringement--An Analysis of Monetary Relief Under 35 U.S.C. § 284, 3 Fordham Ent. Media & Intell. Prop. L. F. 56 (1992), 276

Final Report of the Commission on New Technological Uses of Copyrighted Works (1978) 432, 485, 494

Fiorito, The WIPO "Basic Proposal" for Harmonization of Patent Laws Viewed from the U.S. Practitioner's Point of View, 19 AIPLA Q. J. 24 (1991), 295

Fiorito, The "Basic Proposal" for Harmonization of U.S. and Worldwide Patent Laws Submitted by WIPO, 73 J. Pat. & Trademark Off. Soc. 83 (1991), 209

Fisher, Reconstructing the Fair Use Doctrine, 101 Harv. L. Rev. 1659 (1988), 546

Folsom & Teply, Surveying "Genericness" in Trademark Litigation, 78 Trademark Rep. 1 (1988), 655

Fowler, When Are Surnames Registrable?, 70 Trademark Rep. 66 (1980), 677

Freedman, Reverse Passing Off: A Great Deal of Confusion, 83 Trademark Rep. 305 (1993), 819

Frost, The 1967 Patent Law Debate—First-To-Invent Vs. First-To-File, 1967 Duke L. J. 923 (1967), 153

Fryer, Industrial Design Protection in the United States of America--Present Situation and Plans for Revision, 70 J. Pat. & Trademark Off. Soc. 820 (1988), 324

Fryer, International Review of Pending U.S. Design Legislation: Is it on the Right Track?, 73 J. Pat. & Trademark Off. Soc. 905 (1991), 328

Gable & Leaheey, The Strength of Patent Protection for Computer Products: The Federal Circuit and the Patent Office Refine the Test for Determining which Computer-Related Inventions Constitute Patentable Subject Matter, 17 Rutgers Computer & Tech. L. J. 87 (1991), 119

Gaines, J., Contested Culture (1991), 922

Geller, P., International Copyright Law and Practice (1988 and Supp.), 356

General Agreement on Tariffs and Trade (GATT) Intellectual Property Provisions: Joint Hearing before the Subcomm. on Intellectual Property and Judicial Administration of the House Committee on the Judiciary, and the Subcomm. on Patents, Copyrights and Trademarks of the Senate Comm. on the Judiciary, 103d Cong., 2d Sess. (1994), 218, 573

Gilson, A Federal Dilution Statute: Is It Time?, 83 Trademark Rep. 108 (1993), 883

Gilson, J., Trademark Protection and Practice (1991), 605, 803

Ginsburg, No "Sweat"? Copyright and Other Protection of Works of Information after Feist v. Rural Telephone, 92 Colum. L. Rev. 339 (1992), 378

Ginsburg, Reproduction of Protected Works for University Research or Teaching, 39 J. Copyright Soc. 181 (1992), 544

Ginsburg, Sabotaging and Reconstructing History: A Comment on the Scope of Copyright Protection in Works of History after Hoehling v. Universal City Studios, 72 J. Copyright Soc. 647 (1982), 414

Goldman, Evolution of the Inequitable Conduct Defense in Patent Litigation, 7 Harv. J. L. & Tech. 37 (1993), 284

Goldstein, Copyright and the First Amendment, 70 Colum. L. Rev. 983 (1970), 358

Goldstein, Kewanee Oil Co. v. Bicron Corp: Notes on a Closing Circle, 1974 Sup. Ct. Rev. 81, 945

Goldstein, P., Copyright Principles, Law and Practice (1989), 347, 356, 358, 381, 395, 431, 448, 455, 469, 531, 567, 597, 922, 967

Goodman, Marlette & Trzyna, The Alappat Standard for Determining that Programmed Computers Are Patentable Subject Matter, 76 J. Pat. & Trademark Off. Soc. 771 (1994), 127

Gordon, A Property Right in Self-Expression: Equality and Individualism in the Natural Law of Intellectual Property, 102 Yale L. J. 1533 (1993), 19

Gordon, Fair Use as Market Failure: A Structural and Economic Analysis of the Betamax Case and its Predecessors, 82 Colum. L. Rev. 1600 (1982), 546

Gordon, On Owning Information: Intellectual Property and the Restitutionary Impulse, 78 Va. L. Rev. 149 (1992), 16, 870

Gordon, Reality as Artifact: From Feist to Fair Use, 55 L. & Contemp. Probs. 93 (1992), 380

Gore, Planning a New Biotechnology Policy, 5 Harv. J. L. & Pub. Pol'y 19 (1991), 106

Gorman, The Feist Case: Reflections on a Pathbreaking Copyright Decision, 18 Rutgers Computer & Tech. L. J. 731 (1992), 378

Gorman, Visual Artists Rights Act of 1990, 38 J. Copyright Soc. 233 (1991), 967

Grogan, Decompilation and Disassembly: Undoing Software Protection, 1 The Computer Lawyer 1 (1984), 39

Gullette, State Legislation Governing Ownership Rights in Inventions Under Employee Invention Agreements, 62 J. Pat. Off. Soc. 732 (1980), 82, 84

Hahm, Gray Market Goods: Has a Resolution Been Found?, 81 Trademark Rep. 58 (1991), 754

*

INTELLECTUAL PROPERTY

CASES AND MATERIALS

*

Part One

INTRODUCTION

Chapter One

INTRODUCTION TO INTELLECTUAL PROPERTY LAW

I. THE NATURE OF UNITED STATES INTELLECTUAL PROPERTY LAW

"Intellectual property law" encompasses a number of distinct legal doctrines: patent law, copyright, trademarks and unfair competition, trade secrets, the right of publicity, and common-law protection for ideas. Federal law governs patents, copyrights, trademarks and some unfair competition causes of action. Other unfair competition causes of action, trade secrets, the right of publicity and idea law are the product of state common law and statutes.

While each of the intellectual property doctrines is distinct, they all have characteristics in common. Each provides limited property rights in intangible products of investment, intellect and/or labor, whether they be inventive ideas, accumulations of information, original means of expression, business good will, or the "persona" of a celebrity. Moreover, as discussed below, each doctrine has been shaped by much the same set of critical public policy concerns.

The primary purpose of intellectual property law is to ensure a rich, diverse and competitive marketplace. To achieve this purpose, intellectual property doctrines all provide property rights as incentives to individuals who create new products, services or works of art or literature. Property rights in the fruits of creativity increase the chances that the creator can recoup his investment in the creation process and make a profit from his work. By making creative endeavors financially feasible and potentially rewarding to large numbers of people, intellectual property laws facilitate provision of a variety of creative products and services to the public.

In addition to economic incentives, however, a competitive marketplace requires free access to innovation: Competitors need the freest possible use of others' intellectual creations in order to copy and improve on them. Requiring competitors to "re-invent the wheel" is highly inefficient. The ability to copy results in still greater variety and lower prices in the marketplace. Moreover, since the general public is meant to be the ultimate beneficiary of this bounty of products and services, it is important that the general public have as much access to the products of creativity as possible.

Obviously, the goals of giving creators property rights in their works and ensuring that competitors and the public have free use of those works can conflict. Each intellectual property doctrine seeks to achieve the optimal balance between provision of private property rights and retention of public access to the products of creativity, in order to enhance the competitive marketplace to the fullest possible extent. Each intellectual property doctrine grants property rights to provide an incentive to create, but limits those rights, seeking to provide the greatest public access possible without undermining that incentive.

INTERNATIONAL NEWS SERVICE v. ASSOCIATED PRESS

Supreme Court of the United States, 1918.
248 U.S. 215, 39 S.Ct. 68, 63 L.Ed. 211.

MR. JUSTICE PITNEY delivered the opinion of the Court.

The parties are competitors in the gathering and distribution of news and its publication for profit in newspapers throughout the United States. The Associated Press, which was complainant in the District Court, is a cooperative organization, incorporated under the Membership Corporations Law of the state of New York, its members being individuals who are either proprietors or representatives of about 950 daily newspapers published in all parts of the United States. * * * Complainant gathers in all parts of the world, by means of various instrumentalities of its own, by exchange with its members, and by other appropriate means, news and intelligence of current and recent events of interest to newspaper readers and distributes it daily to its members for publication in their newspapers. The cost of the service, amounting approximately to $3,500,000 per annum, is assessed upon the members and becomes a part of their costs of operation, to be recouped, presumably with profit, through the publication of their several newspapers. Under complainant's by-laws each member agrees upon assuming membership that news received through complainant's service is received exclusively for publication in a particular newspaper, language, and place specified in the certificate of membership, that no other use of it shall be permitted, and that no member shall furnish or permit anyone in his employ or connected with his newspaper to furnish any of complainant's news in advance of publication to any person not a member. And each member is required to gather the local news of his district and supply it to the Associated Press and to no one else.

Defendant is a corporation organized under the laws of the state of New Jersey, whose business is the gathering and selling of news to its customers and clients, consisting of newspapers published throughout the United States, under contracts by which they pay certain amounts at stated times for defendant's service. It has widespread news-gathering agencies; the cost of its operations amounts, it is said, to more than $2,000,000 per annum; and it serves about 400 newspapers located in the various cities of the United States and abroad, a few of which are represented, also, in the membership of the Associated Press. The parties are in the keenest competition between themselves in the distribution of news throughout the United States; and so, as a rule, are the newspapers that they serve, in their several districts.

Complainant in its bill, defendant in its answer, have set forth in almost identical terms the rather obvious circumstances and conditions under which their business is conducted. The value of the service, and of the news furnished, depends upon the promptness of transmission, as well as upon the accuracy and impartiality of the news; it being essential that the news be transmitted to members or subscribers as early or earlier than similar information can be furnished to competing newspapers by other news services, and that the news furnished by each agency shall not be furnished to newspapers which do not contribute to the expense of gathering it. * * *

The bill was filed to restrain the pirating of complainant's news by defendant * * * by copying news from bulletin boards and from early editions of complainant's newspapers and selling this, either bodily or after rewriting it, to defendant's customers.

The District Court, upon consideration of the bill and answer, with voluminous affidavits on both sides * * * refused at that stage to restrain the systematic practice admittedly pursued by defendant, of taking news bodily from the bulletin boards and early editions of complainant's newspapers and selling it as its own. The court expressed itself as satisfied that this practice amounted to unfair trade, but as the legal question was one of first impression it considered that the allowance of an injunction should await the outcome of an appeal. Both parties having appealed, the Circuit Court of Appeals * * * remanded the cause, with directions to issue an injunction against any bodily taking of the words or substance of complainant's news until its commercial value as news had passed away. The present writ of certiorari was then allowed.

The only matter that has been argued before us is whether defendant may lawfully be restrained from appropriating news taken from bulletins issued by complainant or any of its members, or from newspapers published by them, for the purpose of selling it to defendant's clients. Complainant asserts that defendant's admitted course of conduct in this regard both violates complainant's property right in the news and constitutes unfair competition in business. And notwithstanding the case has proceeded only to the stage of a preliminary injunction, we have deemed it proper to consider the underlying questions, since they go to the very merits of the action and are presented upon facts that are not in dispute. As presented in argument, these questions are: (1) Whether there is any property in news; (2) Whether, if there be property in news collected for the purpose of being published, it survives the instant of its publication in the first newspaper to which it is communicated by the news-gatherer; and (3) whether defendant's admitted course of conduct in appropriating for commercial use matter taken from bulletins or early editions of Associated Press publications constitutes unfair competition in trade.

The federal jurisdiction was invoked because of diversity of citizenship, not upon the ground that the suit arose under the copyright or other laws of the United States. Complainant's news matter is not copyrighted. It is said that it could not, in practice, be copyrighted, because of the large number of dispatches that are sent daily; and, according to complainant's contention, news is not within the operation of the copyright act. Defendant, while apparently conceding this, nevertheless invokes the analogies of the law of literary property and copyright, insisting as its principal contention that, assuming complainant has a right of property in its news, it can be maintained (unless the copyright act be complied with) only by being kept secret and confidential, and that upon the publication with complainant's consent of uncopyrighted news of any of complainant's members in a newspaper or upon a bulletin board, the right of property is lost, and the subsequent use of the news by the public or by defendant for any purpose whatever becomes lawful.

* * *

In considering the general question of property in news matter, it is necessary to recognize its dual character, distinguishing between the substance of the information and the particular form or collocation of words in which the writer has communicated it.

No doubt news articles often possess a literary quality, and are the subject of literary property at the common law; nor do we question that such an article, as a literary production, is the subject of copyright by the terms of the act as it now stands. * * *

But the news element—the information respecting current events contained in the literary production—is not the creation of the writer, but is a report of matters that ordinarily are *publici juris*; it is the history of the day. It is not to be supposed that the framers of the Constitution, when they empowered Congress "to promote the progress of science and useful arts, by securing for limited times to authors and inventors the exclusive right to their respective writings and discoveries," (Const. art. 1, § 8, par. 8), intended to confer upon one who might happen to be the first to report a historic event the exclusive right for any period to spread the knowledge of it.

We need spend no time, however, upon the general question of property in news matter at common law, or the application of the copyright act, since it seems to us the case must turn upon the question of unfair competition in business. And, in our opinion, this does not depend upon any general right of property analogous to the common-law right of the proprietor of an unpublished work to prevent its publication without his consent; nor is it foreclosed by showing that the benefits of the copyright act have been waived. We are dealing here not with restrictions upon publication but with the very facilities and processes of publication. The peculiar value of news is in the spreading of it while it is fresh; and it is evident that a valuable property interest in the news, as news, cannot be maintained by keeping it secret. Besides, except for matters improperly disclosed, or published in breach of trust or confidence, or in violation of law, none of which is involved in this branch of the case, the news of current events may be regarded as common property. What we are concerned with is the business of making it known to the world, in which both parties to the present suit are engaged. That business consists in maintaining a prompt, sure, steady, and reliable service designed to place the daily events of the world at the breakfast table of the millions at a price that, while of trifling moment to each reader, is sufficient in the aggregate to afford compensation for the cost of gathering and distributing it, with the added profit so necessary as an incentive to effective action in the commercial world. The service thus performed for newspaper readers is not only innocent but extremely useful in itself, and indubitably constitutes a legitimate business. The parties are competitors in this field; and, on fundamental principles, applicable here as elsewhere, when the rights or privileges of the one are liable to conflict with those of the other, each party is under a duty so to conduct its own business as not unnecessarily or unfairly to injure that of the other.

Obviously, the question of what is unfair competition in business must be determined with particular reference to the character and circumstances of the business. The question here is not so much the rights of either party as against the public but their rights as between themselves. And, although we may and do assume that neither party has any remaining property interest as against the public in uncopyrighted news matter after the moment of its first publication, it by no means follows that there is no remaining property interest in it as between themselves. For, to both of them alike, news matter, however little susceptible of ownership or dominion in the absolute sense, is stock in trade, to be gathered at the cost of enterprise, organization, skill, labor, and money, and to be distributed and sold to those who will pay money for it, as for any other merchandise. Regarding the news, therefore, as but the material out of which both parties are seeking to make profits at the same time and in the same field, we hardly can fail to recognize that for this purpose, and as between them, it must be regarded as quasi property, irrespective of the rights of either as against the public.

In order to sustain the jurisdiction of equity over the controversy, we need not affirm any general and absolute property in the news as such. The rule that a court of equity concerns itself only in the protection of property rights treats any civil right of a pecuniary nature as a property right; and the right to acquire property by honest labor or the conduct of a lawful business is as much entitled to protection as the right to guard property already acquired. It is this right that furnishes the basis of the jurisdiction in the ordinary case of unfair competition.

* * *

Not only do the acquisition and transmission of news require elaborate organization and a large expenditure of money, skill, and effort; not only has it an exchange value to the gatherer, dependent chiefly upon its novelty and freshness, the regularity of the service, its reputed reliability and thoroughness, and its adaptability to the public needs; but also, as is evident, the news has an exchange value to one who can misappropriate it.

The peculiar features of the case arise from the fact that, while novelty and freshness form so important an element in the success of the business, the very processes of distribution and publication necessarily occupy a good deal of time. Complainant's service, as well as defendant's, is a daily service to daily newspapers; most of the foreign news reaches this country at the Atlantic seaboard, principally at the city of New York, and because of this, and of time differentials due to the earth's rotation, the distribution of news matter throughout the country is principally from east to west; and, since in speed the telegraph and telephone easily outstrip the rotation of the earth, it is a simple matter for defendant to take complainant's news from bulletins or early editions of complainant's members in the eastern cities and at the mere cost of telegraphic transmission cause it to be published in western papers issued at least as early as those served by complainant. Besides this, and irrespective of time differentials, irregularities in telegraphic transmission on different lines, and the normal consumption of time in printing and distributing the newspaper, result in permitting pirated news to be placed in the hands of defendant's readers sometimes simultaneously with the service of competing Associated Press papers, occasionally even earlier.

Defendant insists that when, with the sanction and approval of complainant, and as the result of the use of its news for the very purpose for which it is distributed, a portion of complainant's members communicate it to the general public by posting it upon bulletin boards so that all may read, or by issuing it to newspapers and distributing it indiscriminately, complainant no longer has the right to control the use to be made of it; that when it thus reaches the light of day it becomes the common possession of all to whom it is accessible; and that any purchaser of a newspaper has the right to communicate the intelligence which it contains to anybody and for any purpose, even for the purpose of selling it for profit to newspapers published for profit in competition with complainant's members.

The fault in the reasoning lies in applying as a test the right of the complainant as against the public, instead of considering the rights of complainant and defendant, competitors in business, as between themselves. The right of the purchaser of a single newspaper to spread knowledge of its contents gratuitously, for any legitimate purpose not unreasonably interfering with complainant's right to make merchandise of it, may be admitted; but to transmit that news for commercial use, in competition with complainant—which is what defendant has done and seeks to justify—is a very different matter. In doing this defendant, by its very act, admits that it is taking material that has been acquired by complainant as the result of organization and the expenditure of labor, skill, and money, and which is salable by complainant for money, and that defendant in appropriating it and selling it as its own is endeavoring to reap where it has not sown, and by disposing of it to newspapers that are competitors of complainant's members is appropriating to itself the harvest of those who have sown. Stripped of all disguises, the process amounts to an unauthorized interference with the normal operation of complainant's legitimate business precisely at the point where the profit is to be reaped, in order to divert a material portion of the profit from those who have earned it to those who have not; with special advantage to defendant in the competition because of the fact that it is not burdened with any part of the expense of gathering the news. The transaction speaks for itself and a court of equity ought not to hesitate long in characterizing it as unfair competition in business.

The underlying principle is much the same as that which lies at the base of the equitable theory of consideration in the law of trusts—that he who has fairly paid the price should have the beneficial use of the property. It is no answer to say that complainant spends its money for that which is too fugitive or evanescent to be the subject of property. That might, and for the purposes of the discussion we are assuming that it would furnish an answer in a common-law controversy. But in a court of equity, where the question is one of unfair competition, if that which complainant has acquired fairly at substantial cost may be sold fairly at substantial profit, a competitor who is misappropriating it for the purpose of disposing of it to his own profit and to the disadvantage of complainant cannot be heard to say that it is too fugitive or evanescent to be regarded as property. It has all the attributes of property necessary for determining that a misappropriation of it by a competitor is unfair competition because contrary to good conscience.

The contention that the news is abandoned to the public for all purposes when published in the first newspaper is untenable. Abandonment is a question of intent, and the entire organization of the Associated Press negatives such a purpose. The cost of the service would be prohibitive if the reward were to be so limited. No single newspaper, no small group of newspapers, could sustain the expenditure. Indeed, it is one of the most obvious results of defendant's theory that, by permitting indiscriminate publication by anybody and everybody for purposes of profit in competition with the news-gatherer, it would render publication profitless, or so little profitable as in effect to cut off the service by rendering the cost prohibitive in comparison with the return. The practical needs and requirements of the business are reflected in complainant's by-laws which have been referred to. Their effect is that publication by each member must be deemed not by any means an abandonment of the news to the world for any and all purposes, but a publication for limited purposes; for the benefit of the readers of the bulletin or the newspaper as such; not for the purpose of making merchandise of it as news, with the result of depriving complainant's other members of their reasonable opportunity to obtain just returns for their expenditures.

It is to be observed that the view we adopt does not result in giving to complainant the right to monopolize either the gathering or the distribution of the news, or, without complying with the copyright act, to prevent the reproduction of its news articles, but only postpones participation by complainant's competitor in the processes of distribution and reproduction of news that it has not gathered, and only to the extent necessary to prevent that competitor from reaping the fruits of complainant's efforts and expenditure, to the partial exclusion of complainant. * * *

It is said that the elements of unfair competition are lacking because there is no attempt by defendant to palm off its goods as those of the complainant, characteristic of the most familiar, if not the most typical, cases of unfair competition. But we cannot concede that the right to equitable relief is confined to that class of cases. In the present case the fraud upon complainant's rights is more direct and obvious. Regarding news matter as the mere material from which these two competing parties are endeavoring to make money, and treating it, therefore, as *quasi* property for the purposes of their business because they are both selling it as such, defendant's conduct differs from the ordinary case of unfair competition in its trade principally in this that, instead of selling its own goods as those of complainant, it substitutes misappropriation in the place of misrepresentation, and sells complainant's goods as its own.

Besides the misappropriation, there are elements of limitation, of false pretense, in defendant's practices. The device of rewriting complainant's news articles, frequently resorted to, carries its own comment. The habitual failure to give credit to complainant for that which is taken is significant. Indeed, the entire system of appropriating complainant's news and transmitting it as a commercial product to defendant's clients and patrons amounts to a false representation to them and to their newspaper readers that the news transmitted is the result of defendant's own investigation in the field. But these elements, although accentuating the wrong, are not the essence of it. It is something more than the advantage of celebrity of which complainant is being deprived.

* * *

The decree of the Circuit Court of Appeals will be Affirmed.

MR. JUSTICE HOLMES, dissenting.

When an uncopyrighted combination of words is published there is no general right to forbid other people repeating them—in other words there is no property in the combination or in the thoughts or facts that the words express. Property, a creation of law, does not arise from value, although exchangeable—a matter of fact. Many exchangeable values may be destroyed intentionally without compensation. Property depends upon exclusion by law from interference, and a person is not excluded from using any combination of words merely because some one has used it before, even if it took labor and genius to make it. If a given person is to be prohibited from making the use of words that his neighbors are free to make some other ground must be found. One such ground is vaguely expressed in the phrase unfair trade. This means that the words are repeated by a competitor in business in such a way as to convey a misrepresentation that materially injures the person who first used them, by appropriating credit of some kind which the first user has earned. The ordinary case is a representation by device, appearance, or other indirection that the defendant's goods come from the plaintiff. But the only reason why it is actionable to make such a representation is that it tends to give the defendant an advantage in his competition with the plaintiff and that it is thought undesirable that an advantage should be gained in that way. Apart from that the defendant may use such unpatented devices and uncopyrighted combinations of words as he likes. The ordinary case, I say, is palming off the defendant's product as the plaintiff's but the same evil may follow from the opposite falsehood—from saying whether in words or by implication that the plaintiff's product is the defendant's, and that, it seems to me, is what has happened here.

Fresh news is got only by enterprise and expense. To produce such news as it is produced by the defendant represents by implication that it has been acquired by the defendant's enterprise and at its expense. When it comes from one of the great news collecting agencies like the Associated Press, the source generally is indicated, plainly importing that credit; and that such a representation is implied may be inferred with some confidence from the unwillingness of the defendant to give the credit and tell the truth. If the plaintiff produces the news at the same time that the defendant does, the defendant's presentation impliedly denies to the plaintiff the credit of collecting the facts and assumes that credit to the defendant. If the plaintiff is later in Western cities it naturally will be supposed to have obtained its information from the defendant. The falsehood is a little more subtle, the injury, a little more indirect, than in ordinary cases of unfair trade, but I think that the principle that condemns the one condemns the other. It is a question of how strong an infusion of fraud is necessary to turn a flavor into a poison. The dose seems to me strong enough here to need a remedy from the law. But as, in my view, the only ground of complaint that can be recognized without legislation is the implied misstatement, it can be corrected by stating the truth; and a suitable acknowledgment of the source is all that the plaintiff can require. * * *

MR. JUSTICE BRANDEIS, dissenting.

* * *

No question of statutory copyright is involved. The sole question for our consideration is this: Was the International News Service properly enjoined from using, or causing to be used gainfully, news of which it acquired knowledge by lawful means (namely, by reading publicly posted bulletins or papers purchased by it in the open market) merely because the news had been originally gathered by the Associated Press and continued to be of value to some of its members, or because it did not reveal the source from which it was acquired?

* * *

News is a report of recent occurrences. The business of the news agency is to gather systematically knowledge of such occurrences of interest and to distribute reports thereof. The Associated Press contended that knowledge so acquired is property, because it costs money and labor to produce and because it has value for which those who have it not are ready to pay; that it remains property and is entitled to protection as long as it has commercial value as news; and that to protect it effectively, the defendant must be enjoined from making, or causing to be made, any gainful use of it while it retains such value. An essential element of individual property is the legal right to exclude others from enjoying it. If the property is private, the right of exclusion may be absolute; if the property is affected with a public interest, the right of exclusion is qualified. But the fact that a product of the mind has cost its producer money and labor, and has a value for which others are willing to pay, is not sufficient to ensure to it this legal attribute of property. The general rule of law is, that the noblest of human productions—knowledge, truths ascertained, conceptions, and ideas—became, after voluntary communication to others, free as the air to common use. Upon these incorporeal productions the attribute of property is continued after such communication only in certain classes of cases where public policy has seemed to demand it. These exceptions are confined to productions which, in some degree, involve creation, invention, or discovery. But by no means all such are endowed with this attribute of property. The creations which are recognized as property by the common law are literary, dramatic, musical, and other artistic creations; and these have also protection under the copyright statutes. The inventions and discoveries upon which this attribute of property is conferred only by statute, are the few comprised within the patent law. There are also many other cases in which courts interfere to prevent curtailment of plaintiff's enjoyment of incorporeal productions; and in which the right to relief is often called a property right, but is such only in a special sense. In those cases, the plaintiff has no absolute right to the protection of his production; he has merely the qualified right to be protected as against the defendant's acts, because of the special relation in which the latter stands or the wrongful method or means employed in acquiring the knowledge or the manner in which it is used. Protection of this character is afforded where the suit is based upon breach of contract or of trust or upon unfair competition.

The knowledge for which protection is sought in the case at bar is not of a kind upon which the law has heretofore conferred the attributes of property; nor is the manner of its acquisition or use nor the purpose to which it is applied, such as has heretofore been recognized as entitling a plaintiff to relief.

* * *

Plaintiff * * * contended that defendant's practice constitutes unfair competition, because there is "appropriation without cost to itself of values created by" the plaintiff; and it is upon this ground that the decision of this court appears to be based. To appropriate and use for profit, knowledge and ideas produced by other men, without making compensation or even acknowledgment, may be inconsistent with a finer sense of propriety; but, with the exceptions indicated above, the law has heretofore sanctioned the practice. Thus it was held that one may ordinarily make and sell anything in any form, may copy with exactness that which another has produced, or may otherwise use his ideas without his consent and without the payment of compensation, and yet not inflict a legal injury; and that ordinarily one is at perfect liberty to find out, if he can by lawful means, trade secrets of another, however valuable, and then use the knowledge so acquired gainfully, although it cost the original owner much in effort and in money to collect or produce.

Such taking and gainful use of a product of another which, for reasons of public policy, the law has refused to endow with the attributes of property, does not become unlawful because the product happens to have been taken from a rival and is used in competition with him. The unfairness in competition which hitherto has been recognized by the law as a basis for relief, lay in the manner or means of conducting the business; and the manner or means held legally unfair, involves either fraud or force or the doing of acts otherwise prohibited by law. * * *

* * * He who follows the pioneer into a new market, or who engages in the manufacture of an article newly introduced by another, seeks profits due largely to the labor and expense of the first adventurer; but the law sanctions, indeed encourages the pursuit. He who makes a city known through his product, must submit to sharing the resultant trade with others who, perhaps for that reason, locate there later. * * *

The means by which the International News Service obtains news gathered by the Associated Press is also clearly unobjectionable. It is taken from papers bought in the open market or from bulletins publicly posted. No breach of contract such as the court considered to exist in *Hitchman Coal & Coke Co. v. Mitchell*, 245 U.S. 229, 254, 38 Sup. Ct. 65, 62 L.Ed. 260, L. R. A. 1918C, 497 Ann. Cas. 1918B, 461; or of trust such as was present in *Morrison v. Moat*, 9 Hare, 241; and neither fraud nor force is involved. The manner of use is likewise unobjectionable. No reference is made by word or by act to the Associated Press, either in transmitting the news to subscribers or by them in publishing it in their papers. Neither the International News Service nor its subscribers is gaining or seeking to gain in its business a benefit from the reputation of the Associated Press. They are merely using its product without making compensation. That they have a legal right to do, because the product is not property, and they do not stand in any relation to the Associated Press, either of contract or of trust, which otherwise precludes such use. * * *

STANLEY v. COLUMBIA BROADCASTING SYSTEM, INC.

Supreme Court of California, in Bank, 1950.
35 Cal.2d 653, 221 P.2d 73, 86 U.S.P.Q. 520.

* * *

TRAYNOR, JUSTICE (dissenting).

Abstract ideas are common property freely available to all. What men forge out of these ideas with skill, industry, and imagination, into concrete forms uniquely their own, the law protects as private property. It gives the special form the stamp of recognition; it does so to stimulate creative activity. It does something more to stimulate creative activity: it assures all men free utilization of abstract ideas in the process of crystallizing them in fresh forms. For creativeness thrives on freedom; men find new implication in old ideas when they range with open minds though open fields. They would indeed be stifled in their efforts to create forms worth protecting, if in the common through which they ranged they were diverted from their course by one enclosure after another. "We must take care to guard against two extremes equally prejudicial: The one that men of ability, who have employed their time for the service of the community, may not be deprived of their just merits and the reward of their ingenuity and labor; the other, that the world may not be deprived of improvements, nor the progress of the arts be retarded. The act that secures copyrights to authors guards against the piracy of the words and sentiments, but does not prohibit writing on the same subject." (Lord Mansfield, in *Sayre v. Moore*, 1 East 361, 101 Eng.Rep. 140.)

It would be ironic if copyright law, designed to encourage creative activity, became the instrument of its destruction. The very function of creative activity is to keep the common field in continuous germination; it is not for copyright law to render it barren by a succession of enclosures denying access to those who would cultivate it. "The object of copyright is to promote science and the useful arts. If an author, by originating a new arrangement and form of expression of certain ideas or conceptions, could withdraw these ideas or conceptions from the stock of materials to be used by other authors, each copyright would narrow the field of thought open for development and exploitation, and science, poetry, narrative, and dramatic fiction and other branches of literature would be hindered by copyright, instead of being promoted. A poem consists of words, expressing conceptions of words or lines of thoughts; but copyright in the poem gives no monopoly in the separate words, or in the ideas, conception, or facts expressed or described by the words. A copyright extends only to the arrangement of the words. A copyright does not give a monopoly in any incident in a play. Other authors have a right to exploit the facts, experiences, field of thought, and general ideas, provided they do not substantially copy a concrete form, in which the circumstances and ideas have been developed, arranged, and put into shape." *(Eichel v. Marcin,* D.C., 241 F. 404, 408–409.) To insure free trade in ideas, therefore, the monopoly created by copyright is limited to "the arrangement and combination of the ideas * * * the form, sequence, and manner in which the composition expresses the ideas." *(Bowen v. Yankee Network, Inc.* D.C., 46 F.Supp. 62, 64.)

* * *

SEARS, ROEBUCK & CO. v. STIFFEL CO.

Supreme Court of the United States, 1964.
376 U.S. 225, 84 S.Ct. 784, 11 L.Ed.2d 661.

MR. JUSTICE BLACK delivered the opinion of the Court.

* * *

The grant of a patent is the grant of a statutory monopoly. * * * Patents are not given as favors, as was the case of monopolies given by the Tudor monarchs, but are meant to encourage invention by rewarding the inventor with the right, limited to a term of years fixed by the patent, to exclude others from the use of his invention. During that period of time no one may make use, or sell the patented product without the patentee's authority. 35 U.S.C. § 271. But in rewarding useful invention, the "rights and welfare of the community must be fairly dealt with and effectually guarded." *Kendall v. Winsor*, 21 How. 322, 329 (1859). To that end the prerequisites to obtaining a patent are strictly observed, and when the patent has issued the limitations on its exercise are equally strictly enforced. To begin with, a genuine "invention," or "discovery" must be demonstrated "lest in the constant demand for new appliances the heavy hand of tribute be laid on each slight technological advance in an art." *Cuno Engineering Corp. v. Automatic Devices Corp.*, 314 U.S. 84, 92 (1941). Once the patent issues, it is strictly construed, it cannot be used to secure any monopoly beyond that contained in the patent, the patentee's control over the product when it leaves his hands is sharply limited, and the patent monopoly may not be used in disregard of the antitrust laws. Finally, and especially relevant here, when the patent expires the monopoly created by it expires, too, and the right to make the article—including the right to make it in precisely the shape it carried when patented—passes to the public.

Thus the patent system is one in which uniform federal standards are carefully used to promote invention while at the same time preserving free competition. Obviously a State could not, consistently with the Supremacy Clause of the Constitution,[8] extend the life of a patent beyond its expiration date or give a patent on an article which lacked the level of invention required for federal patents. To do either would run counter to the policy of Congress of granting patents only to true inventions, and then only for a limited time. * * *

8. U.S. Const., Art. VI.

In the present case the "pole lamp" sold by Stiffel has been held not to be entitled to the protection of either a mechanical or a design patent. An unpatentable article, like an article on which the patent has expired, is in the public domain and may be made and sold by whoever chooses to do so. What Sears did was to copy Stiffel's design and to sell lamps almost identical to those sold by Stiffel. This it had every right to do under the federal patent laws. That Stiffel originated the pole lamp and made it popular is immaterial. "Sharing in the goodwill of an article unprotected by patent or trade-mark is the exercise of a right possessed by all—and in the free exercise of which the consuming public is deeply interested." *Kellogg Co. v. National Biscuit Co.*, 305 U.S., at 122. To allow a State by use of its law of unfair competition to prevent the copying of an article which represents too slight an advance to be patented would be to permit the State to block off from the public something which federal law has said belongs to the public. * * *

* * *

Notes and Questions

1. *What is "property?"* The key issue in International News Service v. Associated Press ("*I.N.S.*") was whether the news gathered by Associated Press constituted "property," in which Associated Press could assert rights. What is "property?" Does the Court say? As one court has put it, "property rights" are "rights which are recognized and protected by the courts by excluding others therefrom. The designation is therefore more in the nature of a legal conclusion than a description." Metropolitan Opera Association, Inc. v. Wagner–Nichols Recorder Corp., 199 Misc. 786, 101 N.Y.S.2d 483 (1950), *affirmed*, 279 App.Div. 632, 107 N.Y.S.2d 795, 87 U.S.P.Q. 173 (1951). Was the court saying, essentially, that "property" exists whenever a legislative body or court, acting in its proper capacity, says that a person has enforceable rights against others in something (regardless of whether that something is tangible or intangible)? Does that appear to be the *I.N.S.* Court's understanding of the "property" designation?

To what do legislative bodies and courts look in deciding whether to recognize rights (and thus designate "property")? Public policy, or the lawmaker's perception of the public good, is often the guiding principle. What public policy leads the majority in *I.N.S.* to find that Associated Press had property rights in the news it gathered, at least vis-a-vis *I.N.S.*? Did the majority merely base its finding of property rights on its determination that the news had value to Associated Press, as Justice Holmes suggests, or was there more involved? Was it merely that the defendant, *I.N.S.*, got a free ride?

Is "reaping where one has not sown," or "taking a free ride" inherently immoral? Should it be discouraged in all cases? In any case? Why does Justice Brandeis believe that the existence of free riding should not give rise to a property right in the "ridee?" Consider the following:

> [T]he potential free riders—the users, copyists, and adapters—are not mere parasites. Many are creators themselves. They may reach markets different than those reached by the original creators, or they may

> bring new perspective, reduced cost, special expertise, deeper insights, or innovative technology to the exploitation and adaptation of established works. It is true that very often such putative defendants would be able to obtain licenses to utilize the valuable work and that, in those cases, giving the creator protection would not inhibit the flowering of derivative works and new uses. But, at other times complications, such as transaction costs, strategic maneuvering, and income effects—or the perceived inappropriateness of using a market to mediate certain qualitative judgments—will leave us less than satisfied that the grant of a property right to an initial creator will lead to optimal economic development or to optimal opportunities for cultural and individual expression.
>
> * * *
>
> * * * A culture could not exist if all free riding were prohibited within it. Every person's education involves a form of free riding on his predecessor's efforts, as does every form of scholarship and scientific progress. Further, a bedrock proposition of the common law is that persons ordinarily should not be required to pay for the benefit of others' labor unless they have agreed in advance to do so, by contract. Although exceptions to this proposition exist, it has yet to be repudiated in the wholesale way that the adoption of an unlimited reap/sow principle would require.

Gordon, *On Owning Information: Intellectual Property and the Restitutionary Impulse,* 78 VA. L. REV. 149, 157–58, 167–68 (1992).[1] As you will see, the "free rider" issue arises often in the field of intellectual property. Notwithstanding the considerable influence of the *I.N.S.* majority opinion (*I.N.S.* was decided as "federal common law" prior to the decision in Erie Railroad Co. v. Tompkins, 304 U.S. 64, 58 S.Ct. 817, 82 L.Ed. 1188 (1938), and thus is not binding on the states), the existence of free riding on the part of the defendant does not always lead to a finding for the plaintiff. What was the Supreme Court's attitude toward free riding in *Sears?*

What public policy concerns led the Supreme Court to deny protection for the lamp design in the *Sears* opinion excerpt? What public policy concern motivated Justice Traynor in arguing that there should be no property in the idea at issue in the *Stanley* case?

In *Sears,* the Court notes that Congress deliberately limited the availability, duration and scope of patent protection for inventions. It did so in order to balance the conflicting public interests in granting an incentive to invent and making inventive concepts available to competitors, to stimulate competition. Likewise, in his dissent in *Stanley*, Justice Traynor notes that copyright protection for works of authorship is limited to an author's particular means of expressing an idea, and never gives rights in the underlying idea itself. This limitation, he indicates, is meant to balance the competing interests in giving an incentive to authors and leaving as much in the public domain for other authors' use as possible. Is the majority in *I.N.S.* also concerned with this balance? If so, how does the majority accommodate the conflicting interests? In your opinion, does it reach the right balance?

1. ©1992 by Wendy J. Gordon. Reprinted by permission of the copyright owner.

2. *The balance.* As noted above, each of the intellectual property doctrines seeks to obtain a proper balance between the provision of enforceable rights to creators and the retention of public and competitor access to intellectual creations. Thus, the property rights granted in intellectual property are always limited and conditional.

Patent law grants inventors of new and useful processes, machines, articles of manufacture or compositions of matter the right to prevent others from making, using, selling, offering to sell, or importing their invention in the United States—a strong monopoly. But utility patents are available only for those inventions that are worth the inconvenience of a monopoly from the public's standpoint—those that meet the standards of novelty, nonobviousness, and usefulness. Moreover, the law conditions granting a patent on the inventor's fully disclosing the invention and the best mode of practicing it to the public, so that the public will have use of the knowledge underlying the invention. The patent monopoly is limited in duration. After it ends, the invention enters the public domain, and all are free to exploit it. They are assisted in doing so by the inventor's earlier mandatory disclosure.

Trade secret law provides property rights in a business' invention or other proprietary information if the invention or information is valuable, gives the business a competitive advantage, and is kept secret. These property rights, however, fall far short of a monopoly. The trade secret owner may only prevent others from taking or using the secret when the others have obtained it through a breach of confidence, industrial espionage, or some other improper conduct. Competitors obtaining the secret through proper means, such as independent discovery or reverse engineering, are free to use it. Moreover, the business loses its trade secret rights once the invention or information becomes public.

The common-law idea doctrines recognize enforceable property rights in ideas, but in most cases only enable the idea "owner" to enforce her rights against parties who are in a direct contractual or quasicontractual relationship with her, so that the general public's ability to use the idea is unaffected. In most cases, even this modest protection is limited to ideas that meet standards of novelty and concreteness.

Copyright law grants "authors" (including artists, architects, choreographers, cinematographers, etc.) a number of exclusive rights in their works of authorship: The right to reproduce, adapt, publicly distribute, publicly display and publicly perform the work, or authorize others to do so. As Justice Traynor noted in his *Stanley* dissent, however, these rights only extend to the author's particular mode of expressing his or her ideas. The author obtains no rights in the underlying ideas or facts being expressed. Moreover, the Copyright Act imposes a number of exceptions to the author's rights, permitting a wide variety of public uses deemed harmless or in the public interest. Again, like patents, copyrights are limited in duration, usually lasting only fifty years after the author's death.

Trademark and unfair competition laws recognize limited property rights in trademarks, service marks, trade names, and trade dress (words, devices or symbols indicating a product or service's origin) in order to encourage investment in their development. These indicia of origin play an important role in the marketplace because of the information they convey about the products and services they identify, enabling consumers to exercise their preferences among competing brands. They provide the means by which business persons can develop and maintain consumer good will. But the law imposes limits on the types of words, symbols or devices that can be claimed as property, in order to insure that competitors are not deprived of essential means of expression. In addition, the property rights granted in indicia of origin are limited: usually owners may only enjoin others' use of similar indicia when that use causes a likelihood of consumer confusion about the source of goods or services.

Finally, the right of publicity encourages persons such as actors, sports figures, and singers to develop their talents and make them available to the public by giving them the exclusive right to commercially exploit their identities. Publicity law only enables such persons to control *commercial* uses of their identities, however, so that others may use their identities for purposes of political, educational, artistic or other expression. And again, the exclusive rights of commercial exploitation are generally limited in duration.

3. *The pragmatic approach vs. natural rights.* As the case opinions and note 1 suggest, United States legislative bodies and courts traditionally have taken a pragmatic approach to the definition, application and justification of intellectual property rights. They generally have not viewed authors, inventors and other creators as possessing an inherent, natural property right in their intangible creations. In those instances in which the law grants them property rights, it does so for pragmatic reasons, to obtain an overall social benefit, such as greater creative output. This pragmatic view is reflected in the language of the Constitution itself: Article 1, section 8, clause 8 of the U.S. Constitution, known as the Copyrights and Patents Clause, gives Congress the power to grant copyrights and patents in order "[t]o promote the Progress of Science and Useful Arts."

An alternative view is that authors, inventors and other creators have "natural," inherent rights in the products of their labor and intellect, for such products are extensions of the creators' own personalities and selves. This view, greatly influenced by John Locke and Georg Wilhelm Friedrich Hegel, has been more readily embraced in civil law nations, such as France and Germany, and has shaped their law, particularly with regard to the fine arts. Some important differences between the United States' intellectual property laws and those of other nations today arise as the result of this basic difference in philosophy. Does the majority opinion in *I.N.S.* implicitly embrace the notion that one has a natural right in the product of his labor and creativity?

For philosophical and historic approaches to intellectual property rights, see *Symposium on Law and Philosophy*, 13 HARV. J. L. & PUB. POL'Y 757–947 (1990); *Symposium, Property: The Founding, the Welfare State, and Beyond,* 13 HARV. J. L. & PUB. POL'Y, 97–124 (1990); Hughes, *The Philosophy of Intellectual Property,* 77 GEO. L. J. 287 (1988); Vukmir, *The Roots of Anglo–American Intellectual Property Law in Roman Law,* 32 IDEA 123 (1992). For interesting discussions concerning the doctrinal intersection between intellectual property law and the first amendment, see Zimmerman,

Information as Speech, Information as Goods: Some Thoughts on Marketplaces and the Bill of Rights, 33 WM. & MARY L. REV. (1992); Gordon, *A Property Right in Self-Expression: Equality and Individualism in the Natural Law of Intellectual Property,* 102 YALE L.J. 1533 (1993).

4. *Why have a separate law for intellectual property?* Why is it necessary to have a separate body of law to protect intangible intellectual creations? Is the long-established common law of personal property inadequate to protect the interests at stake? Assume that after many years of research and effort an engineer develops a better mousetrap. First, she conceives of the principle on which the mousetrap will operate and the proper method of construction. Then she actually builds a prototype of wood, metal, cheese and other tangible materials. Before she can market the mousetrap, a thief steals the prototype. The laws of personal property should apply. The engineer may seek a court decree requiring the thief to return the prototype and pay the value of the engineer's lost use. (Amounts paid to Acme cat rental service for interim protection?) Is the engineer made whole?

What if, having had brief possession of the prototype, the thief was able to discover the concept underlying the mousetrap? That inventive concept is probably much more valuable to the engineer than the physical manifestation of it. Most likely the concept took more time, effort and resources to develop than the prototype, and offers greater commercial opportunities. Could a court order the thief to return the concept to the engineer? Indeed, has the thief "stolen" the concept if the engineer still has it herself? Information, unlike physical objects, is not diminished when shared. The laws of replevin and conversion were designed with physical objects in mind, and may be difficult to adapt to the theft of a concept.

Suppose that the engineer mass produces copies of the mousetrap and puts them on the market. X buys one, takes it home, and figures out how it works. He then uses that knowledge to make his own copies of the mousetrap and sell them in competition with the engineer. Since X has no research and development investment to recoup, he can sell cheaper than the engineer, and ultimately drive her out of the market. Would the laws of conversion and replevin as we know them offer the engineer any relief against X?

Should the engineer be able to obtain relief against X?

5. *The need for an incentive.* Judicial, legislative and academic authorities routinely justify granting inventors, artists, and business people property rights in their intangible creations on the ground that they need an incentive to engage in the creative process. The theory is that without the assurance of an exclusive right to exploit the creation commercially (enhancing their chance of recouping their investment and making a profit), creators might not consider it worth their while to make new inventions or create new works of art and literature and make them available to the public. In your opinion, is this assumption warranted? If so, how extensive must the property rights be in order to give the needed stimulus? In fact, there is little hard data to prove or disprove the assumption that property rights are needed as an incentive or that the amount of creative output in the United States would significantly decrease if property rights were reduced or denied.

For an interesting and lively argument about the necessity for copyright protection for authors and publishers, see Breyer, *The Uneasy Case for Copyright: A Study of Copyright in Books, Photocopies, and Computer Programs,* 84 HARV. L. REV. 281 (1970); Tyerman, *The Economic Rationale for Published Books: A Reply to Professor Breyer*, 18 U.C.L.A. L. REV. 1100 (1971); Breyer, *Copyright: A Rejoinder,* 20 U.C.L.A. L. REV. 75 (1972).

6. *Jurisdiction.* The United States Constitution expressly authorizes Congress to provide for patents and copyrights in article 1, section 8, clause 8, which provides:

> The Congress shall have power * * *
>
> (8) To promote the Progress of Science and useful Arts, by securing for limited Times to Authors and Inventors the exclusive Right to their respective Writings and Discoveries * * *.

Congress draws its power to regulate trademarks and unfair competition from the commerce clause, article I, section 8, clause 3:

> The Congress shall have power * * *
>
> (3) To regulate Commerce with foreign Nations, and among the several States, and with the Indian Tribes * * *.

The states retain the power to regulate intellectual property under the tenth amendment. However, the U.S. Constitution's supremacy clause (article VI) imposes some limitations. The states may not act if Congress has acted in the field and intended to preempt the field, or if the state law stands "as an obstacle to the accomplishment and execution of the full purposes and objectives of Congress" in enacting the federal law. Hines v. Davidowitz, 312 U.S. 52, 67, 61 S.Ct. 399, 404, 85 L.Ed. 581, 586 (1941).

As you might expect, a number of defendants in state intellectual property causes of action have challenged the state intellectual property doctrines as preempted by federal patent and copyright laws under the supremacy clause. The Supreme Court's standards for evaluating such claims have tended to shift over the years and have created some confusion about the extent to which the states may create or enforce intellectual property rights. The tensions between state and federal laws are addressed at length in Chapter Ten.

II. INTERNATIONAL CONSIDERATIONS

Given today's global economy, American intellectual property lawyers are likely to become involved in international transactions. Each year large numbers of foreign inventors, authors and businesses apply for United States patents [2] and seek United States registration of trademarks and copyrights. They require the assistance of American lawyers in this process and in exploiting their intellectual property rights in the

2. According to one source, in the last quarter of the century, the percent of American patents awarded to foreigners more than doubled. In 1988, 47.1 percent of all American patents awarded were granted to foreign applicants. The highest number of these patents went to Japanese applicants. The second highest number went to West Germans. 37 PAT. TRADEMARK & COPYRIGHT J. (BNA) No. 923 at 529 (March 23, 1989).

United States. American businesses, in turn, are exporting large quantities of goods and services that are protected by United States intellectual property laws. These United States businesses turn to their domestic attorneys for advice about ways to obtain equivalent intellectual property protection in the foreign nations for which the products and services are bound.

Of course, the laws of each nation, including the United States, apply only within the boundaries of that nation. Thus, for example, a United States patent owner seeking to market its invention world-wide and to assert exclusive rights in the invention in each foreign nation it enters must obtain a patent in each nation. While the company undoubtedly will rely on lawyers in the nation of application to assist in the application process and appear in that nation's courts, the company's United States lawyers may be called upon to coordinate its application and enforcement strategies abroad. Accordingly, it is useful not only to understand United States intellectual property laws but also to be familiar with the United States' international intellectual property relations.

The United States is a party to numerous bilateral treaties regarding intellectual property protection, and to several multinational intellectual property conventions. Two multinational conventions which are particularly relevant are the Berne Convention for the Protection of Literary and Artistic Works ("Berne Convention"), regarding copyright protection, and the Paris Convention for the Protection of Industrial Property, ("Paris Convention"), regarding patent, trademark and unfair competition protection. Each has approximately 100 members, and is founded on the notion of national treatment. In essence, these conventions provide that each member nation must give as great protection to nationals of other member nations as it gives to its own nationals. Thus, for example, if countries X and Y are both members of the Paris Convention, a national of X may apply for a patent in Y, and Y must treat his application and resulting patent as favorably as it would the application and patent of a national of Y.

While the conventions do mandate minimum standards of intellectual property protection, members retain significant discretion in determining the nature and scope of protection they will afford, particularly in the case of patent and trademark protection. Thus, even among convention members, the availability and scope of patents, trademark registrations, and other forms of intellectual property protection may differ considerably from one nation to the next. For example, under the Paris Convention, a member may choose not to provide patent protection for a particular type of invention, such as new medications, for its own nationals. Under the rule of national treatment, that nation is not obligated to provide patents for new medications to nationals of other member nations, either, even though these applicants' home nations may afford them protection. Another problem is that even when nations enact comprehensive intellectual property protection, some are lax in enforcing their laws. The following article describes the international situation from the perspective of some American businesses.

THE NEW ERA OF PIRATES

Frank Viviano and John Eckhouse.
San Francisco Chronicle.[3]
February 11, 1991, at 1.

Armed with modern technology and emboldened by the rapid expansion of worldwide trade, a lethal new breed of pirates and counterfeiters is at work in the shadows of the global economy.

No longer satisfied merely to copy Madonna tapes or peddle imitation Levis, these pirates are literally killing people with bogus drugs, dangerously shoddy machinery and fake chemicals bearing the labels of major U.S. companies.

They preside over what is fast becoming one of the largest, most profitable industries on Earth. The new piracy, says one international trade lawyer, "is growing geometrically," and the U.S. International Trade Commission says the problem is looting an estimated $60 billion per year from the American economy.

Contemptuous of the laws on intellectual property—laws designed to protect such intangibles as patented and copyrighted ideas or processes * —the pirating industry has ballooned an astounding 1,100 percent since 1982, when it was worth an estimated $5.5 billion, according to the International Trade Commission.

"If it were reported that a foreign country had expropriated $60 billion from American factories, the public would go bananas," said James Enyart, director of international affairs at the Monsanto Co., which has been hard-hit by chemical counterfeiters.

"But piracy isn't well understood by most people," he said. "They don't understand that the dollars generated by ideas and innovations are just as real—that the intellectual property ripped off by pirates is actually property."

* * *

Already, business interests of the new pirates range from the massive sale of fraudulent agricultural pesticides and unlicensed pharmaceutical products to the manufacture of substandard equipment essential to the U.S. Defense Department.

"I hope this doesn't sound too cynical, but after 24 years in this business, I believe that any product is subject to counterfeiting nowadays," said Bob Merson, managing trademark counsel for the corporate

3. © San Francisco Chronicle, 1991. Reprinted by permission of the copyright owner.

* [By the editor: applications of inventive ideas and processes can be patented, 35 U.S.C. § 101, but they cannot be copyrighted. 17 U.S.C. § 102.]

law department of San Francisco-based Chevron, which has had severe problems with pirated versions of its agricultural chemicals.

Across the industrial spectrum, experts share that grim assessment:

• Law enforcement authorities predict that drugs will soon become the No. 1 pirated product worldwide. "Pharmaceuticals are clearly the area of greatest concern right now," said James Warren, a leading intellectual property attorney with San Francisco-based Pillsbury Madison & Sutro.

Annual losses due to the unlicensed production of medications are running at more than $5 billion, according to the U.S. Pharmaceutical Manufacturers Association. In some countries, more than half of all pharmaceuticals on the shelves are now believed to be counterfeits or unlicensed copies.

• The widespread sale of cheap, counterfeit automobile parts has put a major dent in the legitimate U.S. auto parts industry—at the expense of an estimated 210,000 jobs, according to sources in the Federal Trade Commission.

Subject to no quality control or guarantees, the counterfeit auto parts have a high rate of failure, sometimes with fatal effects. A General Motors investigation of an auto accident in Saudi Arabia revealed that a counterfeit GM brake lining—manufactured from wood chips—was responsible for a brake failure. The accident resulted in the death of a mother and child.

• "Piracy is absolutely making its way into the Defense Department. It's having a major impact on military equipment and on the aerospace industry," said Johannes von Schilcher, executive director of the Washington-based International AntiCounterfeiting Coalition (IACC), an organization that represents 120 North American and European industrial groups. "There are propellers plowing off helicopters because of counterfeit nuts and bolts."

• The U.S. Chemical Manufacturers Association places its members' piracy-related losses at $330 million annually on agricultural chemicals alone. In one dramatic case, a fake fungicide bearing the label of the San Francisco-based Chevron Corp. was responsible for the destruction of thousands of acres of Kenya's coffee crop, the country's chief export commodity.

• The U.S. computer industry reckoned its annual losses in pirated software at more than $2 billion in 1989.

Despite a welter of international laws and agreements designed to curb piracy, industrial leaders are deeply pessimistic about possible remedies. They point out that the very fluidity of world trade, much of which now involves unregulated brokers selling to clients in dozens of nations, makes policing nearly impossible.

Experts predict that enforcement difficulties will worsen as pirate manufacturers migrate away from their bases in newly industrialized countries like South Korea and Taiwan, which have begun to crack down on their activities. Increasingly, they are moving to less developed East Asian and Latin American nations that are more openly hostile toward international intellectual property laws. Many such countries do not even recognize patents.

The problem is compounded because the licensing of patented products for manufacture overseas is a critical component in the U.S. trade picture. In 1987, the United States had a $6.1 billion surplus in licensing exchanges, helping "to offset the much larger deficit in merchandise trade," notes Marjory Searing, director of the International Trade Administration's Office of Multilateral Affairs.

Nothing more epitomizes the reasons why the new piracy is booming—and why it is so difficult to control—than the problems of the pharmaceutical industry.

The unlicensed production and sale of patented drugs has expanded to $5 billion a year, say industry officials, because the demand for cut-rate products is enormous, and it takes very little money to get into the business.

A back street laboratory in Asia or Latin America, where many countries refuse to recognize pharmaceutical patents, may be capable of manufacturing large amounts of a sophisticated drug. Such labs "can be set up for less than $250,000," said Harvey Bale, senior vice president of the Washington-based Pharmaceutical Manufacturers Association.

"We're talking about the production of something that may have cost an American manufacturer $250 million and a decade of research and testing to develop," he said.

Adds attorney Warren: "The pirate manufacturers are extraordinarily mobile, because they don't have research facilities. If a lawsuit threatens, they can pick up and move at a moment's notice."

Executives at Palo Alto-based Syntex Corp., the largest pharmaceutical company on the West Coast, with $1.5 billion in annual sales, said that almost all of their company's drugs are now being reproduced by unlicensed manufacturers in Brazil, which abolished patent protection on drugs two decades ago.

"We employ 2,000 scientists and spend $270 million a year on research and development," said Alan Drubiner, Syntex vice president for international property law. Brazilian firms, he says, "are riding our coattails. They manufacture the same products, with no R & D costs at all—so obviously they can sell them much more cheaply than we can."

Virtually every major pharmaceutical company has similar complaints.

The leading anti-arthritic treatment marketed by New York-based Pfizer Laboratories is being copied for international distribution by at least a dozen pirate operations in Thailand alone, according to industry sources.

In the mid–1980's, more than 1 million counterfeit, improperly formulated birth control pills were sold in the United States under the name of a product of Chicago-based G. D. Searle & Co., according to officials of Monsanto, Searle's parent corporation. The pills, which Monsanto investigators believe were produced in a Latin American factory, resulted in hundreds of unwanted pregnancies before Searle officials realized what was happening.

Many other companies are reluctant to publicize the problem, fearing that it would result in a loss in sales of their legitimate medications. Lawyers for several major drug firms told the Chronicle that their clients were unwilling to go public.

"If consumers hear scare stories that there are dangerous copies of a name-brand drug on pharmacy shelves, they'll avoid it," said one attorney.

In fact, the evidence suggests that most dangerous, badly copied or entirely fraudulent pharmaceuticals do not wind up on American shelves. But they are becoming a deadly feature of life in developing countries.

"A lot of the counterfeit medications sold abroad are grossly understrength, because the object is to make money, not to heal, and there are no regulatory agencies watching their production," said Monsanto's Enyart. "If the product concerned is, say, an antibiotic, the consequences can be appalling."

"In places like Nigeria and the South Asian countries, these drugs are almost certainly killing people," said Bale.

It is also in developing countries that most pirate pharmaceutical manufacturing occurs.

Far from hiding their activities, some of the most active of these manufacturers claim that they have a duty to copy patented drugs.

The issue came to a head recently with an expensive advertising campaign in the pages of U.S. newspapers. The fullpage ads were purchased by the Centro Industriel de Laboratorios Farmaceuticos Argentions, an Argentinean firm, which charged that multinational pharmaceutical manufacturers were out to "monopolize production and sales of life-saving drugs in poor countries."

Countries such as Argentina and Brazil argue that their refusal to recognize pharmaceutical patents is justified on moral grounds, because consumers in developing nations cannot afford the prices set by manufacturers in Europe and North America.

The ad enraged some U.S. pharmaceutical officials. "My response is that it was absolute baloney," said Monsanto's Enyart. "That lab is pirating for its own profit, not to help the poor and downtrodden."

Latin American leaders say that the multinational drug companies are waging an unfair commercial war against the region's own fledgling pharmaceutical industries—and against Latin American consumers.

The tactics, they say, include attempts to halt the production of some drugs on patent grounds, and large increases in the prices of other drugs that Latin American manufacturers lack the technology to duplicate.

"They accuse us of promoting piracy on the international market," Brazilian Health Minister Alceni Guerra said in a December press conference. "I accuse them of promoting piracy in our national economy."

The Pharmaceutical Manufacturers Association points out that only six of the 250 drugs identified by the World Health organization as essential to maintaining care in the Third World are currently patented. The rest can be legally manufactured anywhere without license.

* * *

Notes and Questions

1. *Piracy.* Note that the preceding article lumps several different types of activities together under the term "piracy." Assume that X Company is an American manufacturer of pharmaceutical products and has a United States patent for a new drug. It sells the new drug under the trademark "Xana," which it has registered in the United States. X Co. sells the drug under its trademark throughout the world, and has obtained a patent and registered its trademark in every country that would allow it to do so. The term "piracy" might be applied loosely to any of the following situations:

(a) Y manufactures the same drug and sells it under the name Xana without X Co's permission in countries in which X Co. has both a patent and registered trademark protection.

(b) Y manufactures a different drug and sells it without X Co.'s permission under the name Xana in countries in which X has a trademark registration.

(c) Y manufactures the same drug without X Co.'s permission in countries in which X Co. has a patent, but sells the drug under another trademark.

(d) Y manufactures the same drug without X Co.'s permission and sells it under the name Xana in countries in which X Co. has neither a patent (because the countries afford no patent protection for drugs) nor a valid trademark registration.

(e) Y manufactures the same drug without X Co.'s permission and sells it under another name in countries in which X Co. has no patent (because the countries afford no patent protection for drugs).

Are the ramifications of Y's activity the same in each case? In your opinion, should the term "piracy" be applied to situations (d) and (e)?

2. *Developed vs. Developing Nations.* What are the respective costs and benefits of maintaining a strong system of intellectual property protection? Assuming that the benefits outweigh the costs in the United States, would the same be true in developing countries? On what basis might the governments of developing nations conclude that a strong intellectual property system would not be beneficial? See R. SHERWOOD, INTELLECTU-

AL PROPERTY AND ECONOMIC DEVELOPMENT (1990); Oddi, *The International Patent System and Third World Development: Reality or Myth?*, [1987] DUKE L. J. 829; Braga, *The Economics of Intellectual Property Rights and the GATT: A View from the South,* 22 VAND. J. TRANSNAT'L L. 243 (1989); Pretnar, *Industrial Property and Related Trade Policy in Less–Developed Countries: Economic Appraisal of Legal Concepts*, 21 IIC 782 (1990).

3. *The General Agreement on Tariffs and Trade, Agreement on Trade–Related Aspects of Intellectual Property Rights.* On December 8, 1994, the United States accepted the Uruguay Round of multilateral trade negotiations under the auspices of the General Agreement on Tariffs and Trade ("GATT"), and its Agreement on Trade–Related Aspects of Intellectual Property Rights, Including Trade in Counterfeited Goods ("TRIPs"). The comprehensive TRIPs provisions incorporate existing international standards for intellectual property protection, including those set forth in the Berne and Paris Conventions, and impose a number of new substantive standards for copyrights, trademarks, geographical indications, industrial designs, patents, semiconductor chip designs, and trade secrets. Nations accepting the Uruguay Round Agreements must bring their intellectual property laws into compliance with these substantive standards, and must satisfy the TRIPs standards for enforcing intellectual property rights, both internally and at international borders. The Uruguay Round provides dispute resolution mechanisms to resolve disputes among member nations over compliance with TRIPs intellectual property protection standards. When member nations are determined to be in violation of their TRIPs obligations, other members may impose trade sanctions against them, when other measures fail.

Assuming wide-spread adherence to the Uruguay Round, the situation described in the *Pirates* article should improve. The improvement will be gradual, however. Under the terms of TRIPs Article 65, developing nations and ex-communist nations adopting free-enterprise economies have until the year 2000 to conform their domestic intellectual property laws. Developing countries have an additional five years to extend product patent protection to technologies that were not formerly eligible for protection. Under TRIPs Article 66, "least developed" nations accepting the Uruguay Round may delay TRIPs compliance until 2006, and may be granted further extensions of time.

For additional information about the United States' battle against foreign intellectual property piracy, as well as discussion of the TRIPs provisions, see U.S. GENERAL ACCOUNTING OFFICE, INTERNATIONAL TRADE: STRENGTHENING WORLDWIDE PROTECTION OF INTELLECTUAL PROPERTY RIGHTS (1987); Oman, *Intellectual Property After the Uruguay Round,* 42 J. COPYRIGHT SOC. 18 (1994); Reichman, *The TRIPs Component of the GATT's Uruguay Round: Competitive Prospects for Intellectual Property Owners in an Integrated World Market,* 4 FORDHAM INTELL. PROP. MEDIA & ENT. L.J. 171 (1993); Bronckers, *The Impact of TRIPs: Intellectual Property Protection in Developing Countries,* 31 COMMON MKT. L. REV. 1245 (1994); Leaffer, *Protecting United States Intellectual Property Abroad: Toward a New Multilateralism,* 76 IOWA L. REV. 273 (1991).

*

Part Two

RIGHTS IN IDEAS AND INFORMATION

To assist in learning intellectual property law, it is useful conceptually to divide the various intellectual property doctrines into three groups: 1) those doctrines that provide property rights in ideas and information; 2) those that protect original means of expressing ideas and information; and 3) those doctrines that are designed to protect consumer good will and related trade values.

Part Two, consisting of Chapters Two, Three and Four, will focus on the doctrines that fall within the first group, providing property rights in ideas and information. Chapter Two will address the state law of trade secrets. Chapter Three will examine the federal law of patents. Chapter Four will wind up Part Two with a look at a small collection of state common-law doctrines sometimes referred to collectively as "idea law," or the "law of undeveloped ideas."

The third Part, consisting of Chapter Five, will examine federal copyright law. Copyright provides rights in original ways of expressing ideas and information.

Part Four, consisting of Chapters Six, Seven and Eight, will focus on the state and federal trademark and unfair competition laws, and the state right of publicity, respectively. All of these doctrines recognize limited property rights as a means of protecting economic interests in consumer good will and related intangible trade values.

The final Part, consisting of Chapter Nine, will examine the status of state intellectual property doctrines in light of the United States Constitution's supremacy clause and section 301 of the Copyright Act of 1976, which preempts state causes of action that duplicate federal copyright infringement claims.

Chapter Two

TRADE SECRETS

I. THE THEORY OF TRADE SECRET PROTECTION

CYBERTEK COMPUTER PRODUCTS, INC. v. WHITFIELD

California Superior Court, 1977.
1977 WL 22730, 203 U.S.P.Q. 1020.

TITLE, JUDGE.

* * *

I.

In this action for injunctive relief and damages arising out of alleged misappropriation by defendants of confidential information and trade secrets in connection with plaintiff's computer software system, the Court has bifurcated the issue of liability from that of damages pursuant to stipulation of the parties, and has now concluded the trial of the liability issue. * * *

[T]he dispute essentially arises out of the prior employment of defendant Whitfield by plaintiff, and his subsequent employment by defendant Tracor in the same field of endeavor. Plaintiff was formed in 1969 for the purpose of engaging in the business of furnishing computer related services to the life insurance industry. Defendant Whitfield was one of the founding officers of plaintiff, and had a substantial background and expertise in computer software, as specifically related to its use in the life insurance business. He purchased shares in plaintiff, and in his capacity as an employee of plaintiff, directly participated in the design and development of plaintiff's on-line new business computer system known as the Auto/Issue System, his responsibilities including the specific design of some major portions of the system. For a time he had management responsibility for this system, and subsequently was a senior analyst involved in its design, programming and testing.

In connection with his employment, defendant Whitfield executed an Employee Nondisclosure Agreement, dated December 2, 1970, which provided among other things that the techniques and methods relating to plaintiff's products were trade secrets and confidential, and that he would not at any time disclose to anyone outside of plaintiff any information about plaintiff's products which related to the design, use or development of such products. The agreement specifically made reference to the Auto/Issue System. He voluntarily terminated his employment and relationship with plaintiff on March 31, 1971, at which time he acknowledged in writing that he understood his agreement with plaintiff not to disclose confidential information, and that he had returned all confidential material to plaintiff. He thereafter did some consulting work for defendant Tracor between July and October, 1971, commenced full-time employment with said defendant on November 15, 1971, and ever since that time has remained in said defendant's employ. His duties with defendant Tracor have included responsibility for the development of an insurance on-line new business system, which would provide substantially the same capabilities as plaintiff's Auto/Issue System, and which was to be marketed in direct competition to plaintiff's Auto/Issue System.

Plaintiff developed its Auto/Issue System over a period of approximately two years, from November, 1969 through approximately November, 1971. Since that time it has been marketing the system. Defendant's similar system, which it has named Trac/70, has been substantially though not completely developed, but is nevertheless being marketed at the present time in competition with plaintiff's Auto/Issue System. It was stipulated by the parties that plaintiff and defendant Tracor have each expended in excess of $500,000 in the development of their respective systems.

II.

Plaintiff has at all times maintained and enforced a corporate policy which requires its employees to execute Employee Nondisclosure Agreements such as that executed by defendant Whitfield, and which further requires its potential and actual licensees to execute nondisclosure agreements prior to receiving Auto/Issue documentation other than marketing material. Plaintiff also at all times material herein maintained additional reasonable measures of security which clearly demonstrate plaintiff's intention to keep information concerning its products, including the Auto/Issue System, confidential, such as the marking of documentation relating to its products as confidential, the use of registration numbers in connection with copies of its documentation, and permitting only authorized personnel to have access to its Auto/Issue documentation other than marketing materials. Defendant Tracor has likewise taken similar steps relating to security in order to protect the confidentiality of its on-line new business system known as Trac/70.

III.

It is plaintiff's contention that during defendant Whitfield's consultations and employment with defendant Tracor, he has been substantially and directly involved in the design of said defendant's Trac/70 System, in connection with which he has utilized and disclosed plaintiff's trade secrets and confidential information in violation of his duty to plaintiff, and in breach of his specific Nondisclosure Agreement with plaintiff. Both defendants deny any responsibility to plaintiff, and contend that the alleged trade secrets and confidential matter claimed by plaintiff are in fact not trade secrets or confidential, but rather are well known concepts in the computer industry, that they are, therefore, not confidential, and that defendant Whitfield has merely utilized his substantial degree of skill and experience in his employment by defendant Tracor which he had developed prior to his employment with plaintiff and which he has the right to so utilize.

IV.

There are a number of basic threshold issues to be determined by the Court, which appear to involve mixed questions of law and fact. Among these are the following: Do any or all of the 12 items set forth in plaintiff's Exh. 1A (said exhibit purports to enumerate the areas of design and development of the Auto/Issue System which constitute the confidential information and trade secrets concerning which plaintiff is entitled to protection), or any combination thereof, constitute confidential information or trade secrets? * * * What was the intention of the parties under said nondisclosure agreement? Was any of said alleged confidential matter or trade secrets disclosed by defendant Whitfield to defendant Tracor in connection with the development of the Trac/70 System?

V.

While there may have been a question in the past as to whether or not computer software is susceptible of protection under the trade secret doctrine, it is clear that such protection is available today in practically all jurisdictions. See 38 George Washington Law Review 909, and cases cited by both plaintiff and defendants in their respective trial briefs, all of which make it amply clear that computer software is protectible under the trade secret doctrine, given appropriate facts and circumstances.

[In the next several sections of the opinion, the court finds, among other things, that the confidentiality agreement Whitfield signed is valid, and that the existence of such a contractual agreement, while not essential to a finding of trade secret misappropriation, is an important factor for consideration.]

X.

Simply stated, plaintiff's position is that some 12 areas of development and design in its Auto/Issue System set forth in extremely technical language in Exh. 1A constitute trade secrets, or at least highly confidential matter which should be protected either on the theory that defendant Whitfield breached his confidential duty to plaintiff or breached his express covenant of nondisclosure. To determine this issue, it is necessary to attempt to glean a definition of a trade secret from the authorities and case law, and that examination of the authorities and cases makes it immediately obvious that while the simplistic definitions found therein are easily understood, the application thereof to a highly technical area such as computer software programs is extremely difficult. Section 757 of the Restatement of Torts, Comment b, generally defines a trade secret as any formula, pattern, device or compilation of information which is used in one's business, and which gives him an opportunity to obtain an advantage over competitors who do not know or use it. In spite of this simple definition, it further states that an exact definition of a trade secret is not possible, and lists some factors to be considered in determining the existence or nonexistence of a trade secret. Briefly stated, these include the extent to which the information is known by others outside of the business or employees of the business, the extent of measures taken to guard the secrecy of the information, the value of the information, the effort and expense involved in developing it, and lastly the ease or difficulty with which the information could be properly acquired or duplicated by others. As to some of the latter factors, plaintiff clearly comes within their ambit, as the evidence is virtually uncontradicted that reasonably strict security measures were taken to guard the secrecy of the Auto/Issue System, in excess of $500,000 was expended by plaintiff to develop it, license fees of somewhere between $100,000 and $200,000 are charged plaintiff's customers for the right to use the system, and a formidable and expensive task is faced by any competitor who might desire to properly acquire or duplicate it. The serious conflict in the evidence arises, however, in connection with the factor dealing with the issue as to the extent to which the information is known to others outside of plaintiff's business. Defendants essentially contend that we are not dealing with trade secrets, nor for that matter even confidential matter to any degree, because all the alleged items set forth in Exh. 1A are not secret or confidential information but rather consist of well known concepts in the computer and data processing industry, and consequently cannot by any stretch of the imagination be considered confidential or secret. This issue was joined in the traditional battle of the experts, with Dr. Gilbert and others testifying on behalf of plaintiff to the effect that Exh. 1A indeed did include unique and confidential approaches not known to the computer industry in general, and Mr. Shafto and others testifying on behalf of defendants to the contrary. The technical nature of their testimony would be mind-boggling to the average lay person, as it was to the court, and this is amply demonstrated by the fact that Mr. Shafto, an obviously well qualified expert in the computer field, testified that he had great difficulty in even understanding the meaning of the descriptive language of the alleged trade secrets found in Exh. 1A. The Court has carefully considered all of the testimony, and has concluded that at least to some degree, defendants' position is correct in that some of the approaches utilized in the Auto/Issue System, standing separately, are general concepts known to experts in the computer industry. The cases indicate, and plaintiff concedes that general concepts are not protectible, per se, as trade secrets. However, the cases further indicate that while general concepts are not protectible, the specific implementation involving a particular combination of general concepts may well amount to a trade secret. See Winston Res. Co. v. Minnesota Mining & Mfg. Co., supra, involving the manufacture of a tape recording device, supporting this theory. That court pointed out that the same general concepts had been used in developing defendants' machine as had been used in plaintiff's machine, that such development involved the use of general concepts and approaches which were known in the industry, and were, therefore, not in and of themselves susceptible of trade secret protection. However, the court further pointed out that while the general approach and the basic mechanical elements thereof were not trade secrets, that the specifications of these basic mechanical elements and their relationship to each other embodied in plaintiff's machine were not publicly known, were arrived at only after painstaking research and extensive trial and error, and therefore, constituted a trade secret entitled to protection. In other words, the court found that the specific embodiment of the general concepts and approach into a combination of parts was protectible, even though all or some of them might well be known to the industry. The Court believes that the principle annunciated in these cases applies to our case, and that while some of the concepts set forth in Exh. 1A are general concepts not susceptible of protection, that the entire bundle or combination of these concepts as developed and utilized by plaintiff in its Auto/Issue System do constitute trade secrets which are protectible under the circumstances. As pointed out in the above mentioned Restatement of Torts, as well as in 80 Harvard Law Review 1432, at page 1452, any information which provides a competitive advantage over competitors may well constitute a trade secret, and in the Court's view it is obvious that the combination of factors involved in the Auto/Issue System must give the plaintiff its protection under this doctrine.

XI.

Having concluded that the confidential matter in question should not have been disclosed by defendant Whitfield, the next issue which must be determined is whether in fact there was such a disclosure by him in connection with his work on the development of Tracor's Trac/70 System. Defendant Whitfield contends that since he took away no actual documentation or physical material relating to the Auto/Issue System, it must follow that he did not disclose or use any confidential information relating thereto, but rather merely made use of his expertise and general know-how in the development of Trac/70. Putting it in another way, defendants contend that Trac/70 was independently developed, and was not copied from plaintiff's Auto/Issue System. This presents an extremely close question of fact for the Court to determine, and the Court is not unmindful of the classic confrontation in the law of the policy which strives to extend some protection to an employer from the breach of confidence of a former employee in taking away and utilizing trade secrets with the policy of the law which protects an employee in his right to carry on his trade or profession after he leaves his employer. The Court also has considered the well recognized principle that where a defendant in a trade secret case claims independent development, that the burden then shifts to the defendant and places upon the defendant a heavy burden of persuasion to show that the production was a result of independent development and not from the use of information confidentially secured during the prior employment. * * *

Looking to the evidence, it is not seriously controverted, and the Court finds that there are in fact substantial similarities in the Auto/Issue System and the Trac/70 System. Such similarity, while not determinative of the issue, is of obvious importance, and must be given weight. Granted that the systems are not identical, many cases indicate that such identity is not required, and that trade secrets need not be exactly copied in order to impose liability. Likewise, the conceded difference in terminology utilized in the systems is not significant.

Defendants have also argued that many of the similarities are purely coincidental, since there were relatively few options which every expert in the field would consider in arriving at methods of approach for a new business on-line system. However, plaintiff presented evidence to the effect that there were in fact significant design choices, and that similar choices utilized by defendants would, therefore, indicate copying rather than independent development. This again is a question of fact, and the Court accepts Dr. Gilbert's testimony to the effect that there were significant design choices, and not as indicated by defendants, choices only as to insignificant details. Furthermore, even if the Court resolves the conflict in the evidence regarding whether or not defendant Whitfield took away with him documentation concerning the Auto/Issue System in favor of defendant Whitfield, the cases are clear that documentation need not be taken in order to establish liability, since appropriation by memory alone is proscribed. As pointed out in 38 George Washington Law Review, page 909 at pages 938 and 939, the weight of authority indicates that appropriation by memory will be proscribed under the same circumstances as an appropriation via more tangible means.

When the Court considers all of the above factors, and adds thereto the ingredient sustained by the evidence that defendant Whitfield had complete knowledge and understanding of plaintiff's system, and in addition supervised and oversaw the development of defendants' system, the Court concludes and finds that defendant Whitfield did disclose and utilize substantial aspects of plaintiff's Auto/Issue System in the development of the Trac/70 System.

XII.

Defendant Whitfield's liability having been established, the Court must finally determine whether defendant Tracor also has liability under the circumstances. The cases indicate, as does Section 757 of the Restatement of Torts, that a new employer may also be liable for misappropriation of trade secrets, provided that he utilizes the information with notice of the secret nature thereof and with notice that the employee has disclosed it in breach of his duty to the former employer. The evidence indicates that before any substantial development of the Trac/70 System was begun, defendant Whitfield had been placed on notice by plaintiff by letter concerning a possible trade secret violation, and defendant Tracor was apprised of said demand by defendant Whitfield. In addition, it is conceded by defendants that the instant lawsuit was actually filed before any substantial development of the Trac/70 system. Under these circumstances, the Court finds that defendant Tracor was on notice of the potential liability in this matter, and consequently the Court finds that defendant Tracor has liability herein along with defendant Whitfield.

Notes and Questions

1. *Key influences on the law of trade secrets.* Trade secret doctrine developed in the common law and, since 1939, has been greatly influenced by sections 757 and 758 of the first Restatement of Torts. Restatement of Torts section 757 provides:

> One who discloses or uses another's trade secret, without a privilege to do so, is liable to the other if
>
> (a) he discovered the secret by improper means, or
>
> (b) his disclosure or use constitutes a breach of confidence reposed in him by the other in disclosing the secret to him, or
>
> (c) he learned the secret from a third person with notice of the facts that it was a secret and that the third person discovered it by improper means or that the third person's disclosure of it was otherwise a breach of his duty to the other, or
>
> (d) he learned the secret with notice of the facts that it was a secret and that its disclosure was made to him by mistake.[1]

Restatement section 758 provides:

> One who learns another's trade secret from a third person without notice that it is a secret and that the third person's disclosure is a breach of his duty to the other, or who learns the secret through a mistake without notice of the secrecy and the mistake,
>
> (a) is not liable to the other for a disclosure or use of the secret prior to receipt of such notice, and
>
> (b) is liable to the other for a disclosure or use of the secret after the receipt of such notice, unless prior thereto he has in good faith paid value for the secret or has so changed his position that to subject him to liability would be inequitable.[2]

Courts' frequent reliance on these Restatement provisions, (as exemplified in *Cybertek* and in the *duPont* opinion, *supra*) led to greater uniformity among the states than might otherwise have occurred. When the American Law Institute undertook to draft the Restatement (Second) of Torts in 1977, it omitted provisions regarding trade secret protection on the ground that trade secret doctrine is "no more dependent upon Tort law than it is on many other general fields of the law * * *." RESTATEMENT (SECOND) OF TORTS vol. 4, at 1 (1977). Nonetheless, the first Restatement provi-

sions continued to be quite influential. In the late 1980's, the American Law Institute began proceedings to draft a new Restatement of Unfair Competition, which would include provisions on trade secret law. These provisions can be found in RESTATEMENT (THIRD) OF UNFAIR COMPETITION §§ 39–45 (Tentative Draft No. 4, 1993).

Another important development in trade secret law occurred in 1979, when the National Conference of Commissioners on Uniform State Laws published the Uniform Trade Secrets Act. The Uniform Act was designed to be enacted by individual state legislatures, and indeed, as of 1994, 39 jurisdictions have adopted it or its 1985 revised version.[3] Key provisions of the Uniform Act are quoted in the notes below. As its title suggests, the Uniform Act was intended to codify and further unify state trade secret provisions. In many respects the Uniform Act codified common-law rules that had already been established by the courts, with the influence of Restatement of Torts sections 757 and 758. Thus, the Uniform Act and the Restatement of Torts are similar in many respects and the Restatement provisions continue to be influential in interpreting the law, even in jurisdictions that have adopted the Uniform Act. For a detailed discussion of the Uniform Act and a comparison with Restatement of Torts sections 757 and 758, see Klitzke, *The Uniform Trade Secrets Act*, 64 MARQ. L. REV. 277 (1980).

Under either the Restatement or the Uniform Act, analysis of most trade secret claims breaks down into two basic inquiries: 1) does the information or idea at issue qualify as a trade secret?; and 2) if it does, is the defendant's acquisition, disclosure or use of it prohibited under one of the theories set forth in Restatement of Torts sections 757 and 758 or their counterpart, section 1 of the Uniform Trade Secrets Act?

2. *The definition of "trade secret."* The court in *Cybertek* refers to the Restatement of Torts definition of trade secret information, which is set forth in section 757, comment b:

> A trade secret may consist of any formula, pattern, device or compilation of information which is used in one's business, and which gives him an opportunity to obtain an advantage over competitors who do not know or use it. It may be a formula for a chemical compound, a process of manufacturing, treating or preserving materials, a pattern for a machine or other device, or a list of customers. It differs from other secret information in a business * * * in that it is not simply information as to single or ephemeral events in the conduct of the business, as, for example, the amount or other terms of a secret bid for a contract or the salary of certain employees, or the security investments made or contemplated, or the date fixed for the announcement of a new policy or for bringing out a new model or the like. A trade secret is a process or device for continuous use in the operation of the business.

Section 757, comment b, provides six factors which should be considered in determining whether given information constitutes a trade secret:

3. California adopted the Uniform Trade Secrets Act in 1985, eight years after the decision in *Cybertek*.

> (1) the extent to which the information is known outside of [plaintiff's] business; (2) the extent to which it is known by employees and others involved in his business; (3) the extent of measures taken by him to guard the secrecy of the information; (4) the value of the information to him and to his competitors; (5) the amount of effort or money expended by him in developing the information; (6) the ease or difficulty with which the information could be properly acquired or duplicated by others.[4]

The Uniform Trade Secrets Act, section 1(4), provides:

> "Trade secret" means information, including a formula, pattern, compilation, program, device, method, technique, or process, that
>
> (i) derives independent economic value, actual or potential, from not being generally known to, and not being readily ascertainable by proper means by, other persons who can obtain economic value from its disclosure or use, and
>
> (ii) is the subject of efforts that are reasonable under the circumstances to maintain its secrecy.[5]

Why does Restatement of Torts section 757 comment (b) require that the plaintiff use the secret continuously in his business? This is one of the points at which the Uniform Trade Secrets Act differs from Restatement section 757. The drafters of the Uniform Act deliberately deleted the requirement. Likewise, the Tentative Draft of the Restatement (Third) of Unfair Competition deletes the requirement. RESTATEMENT (THIRD) OF UNFAIR COMPETITION § 39 (Tentative Draft No. 4, 1993). In your opinion, which approach makes more sense? See Uniform Trade Secrets Act § 1, Commissioners' Comment (1979).

3. *The secrecy requirement.* Why should protection be limited to information that is secret? What factors did the *Cybertek* court find relevant in determining that the secrecy requirement was satisfied in that case?

(a) The extent to which the information is known outside of the plaintiff's business. Information that is widely known by the public or by others in the plaintiff's field of business will not qualify as a trade secret. However, the secrecy need not be absolute. Restatement of Torts section 757, comment b, provides that "[o]thers may also know of the information independently, as, for example, when they have discovered the process or formula by independent invention and are keeping it secret. Nevertheless, a substantial element of secrecy must exist, so that, except by the use of improper means, there would be difficulty in acquiring the information."

(b) The ease or difficulty with which the information could be acquired properly by others. If the information is available in trade journals or other published sources, it is not likely to qualify. Likewise, if the information can be ascertained by simply examining the claimant's finished product, trade

4. © 1939 by The American Law Institute. Excerpts from section 757 comment b are reprinted with the permission of The American Law Institute.

5. The Act has been reprinted through the permission of the National Conference of Commissioners on Uniform State Laws, and copies of the Act may be ordered from them at a nominal cost at 676 North St. Clair Street, Suite 1700, Chicago, Illinois 60611.

secrecy status will be destroyed as soon as the product is publicly distributed. The fact that the information can be learned through complex "reverse engineering" of the product, however, generally will not negate trade secrecy status, as long as the defendant learned the information by some other means. See Uniform Trade Secrets Act, § 1, Commissioners' Comment.

Computer programs are originally written in "source code," a language comprised of words and mathematical notations that trained humans can read. When a program is completed, it is transformed into "object code," which directs the electrical impulses that operate the computer. Object code is impossible for most humans to read. It is the object code that is placed on the disk, chip, or other medium distributed to program users. Assume that a software company mass-produced and distributed disks containing its program to the public, but kept its source code in confidence, locked away in the company safe. Would the program be deemed sufficiently "secret" to merit trade secret protection? See Q–Co. Industries, Inc. v. Hoffman, 625 F.Supp. 608, 228 U.S.P.Q. 554 (S.D.N.Y.1985); Grogan, *Decompilation and Disassembly: Undoing Software Protection,* 1 THE COMPUTER LAWYER 1 (1984).

(c) The extent to which the trade secret is known by employees and others connected with the plaintiff's business. Clearly, the owner of a trade secret must be able to use it, and to use it effectively, she must be able to disclose it to some of her employees. Likewise, she may need to share the trade secret with certain of her business' distributors, licensees, joint venturers and others in a close working relationship. This is permissible, as long as the owner limits the information to those who actually need to know it, and takes reasonable precautions to ensure that they keep it confidential. See RESTATEMENT OF TORTS, § 757, comment b (1939).

(d) The measures the plaintiff takes to guard the secrecy of the information. A plaintiff must anticipate ways that competitors might obtain her trade secret and take reasonable steps to prevent them from doing so. Her duty, however, is limited to what is reasonable under the circumstances. See E. I. duPont deNemours & Co., Inc. v. Christopher, 431 F.2d 1012, 166 U.S.P.Q. 421 (5th Cir.1970), *cert. denied* 400 U.S. 1024, 91 S.Ct. 581, 27 L.Ed.2d. 637, 168 U.S.P.Q. 385 (1971). Some courts have suggested that a cost-benefit analysis should be used to evaluate the reasonableness of requiring the plaintiff to take a particular precaution. Will the benefit of added security outweigh the cost of the precaution? If not, the plaintiff will not be required to take the precaution. This approach recognizes that absolute security may not be economically efficient. The court's reasoning in In the Matter of Innovative Construction Systems, Inc., 793 F.2d 875, 230 U.S.P.Q. 94 (7th Cir.1986), is instructive. In that case the U.S. Court of Appeals for the Seventh Circuit, applying Wisconsin law, found that there was sufficient evidence to uphold (against a motion for judgement n. o. v.) a jury verdict for Innovative, granting it trade secret protection in its formulae for producing simulated brick paneling:

> Innovative did not require its employees to sign nondisclosure agreements. Employee guidelines posted within the production area did not mention the confidential nature of the formulas. Furthermore, employees were not given exit interviews concerning the confidential

nature of the formulas. Bowen Supply contends that this establishes "as a matter of law that [Innovative] did not take the steps necessary to impress upon its employees the need to keep its formulas secret." We disagree.

* * * [T]he relevant question is whether, under the circumstances, the measures adopted were reasonable.

For us to require written non-disclosure statements or exit interviews as a matter of law would overlook the nature of the special verdict interrogatory. In asking whether particular efforts were reasonably adequate under the circumstances, the jury is called upon in part to exercise their common-sense judgment in determining whether additional measures were necessary to guard the secrecy of the formulas. In essence, this requires an assessment of the size and nature of Innovative's business, the cost to it of additional measures, and the degree to which such measures would decrease the risk of disclosure. What may be reasonable measures in one context may not necessarily be so in another. Under the facts of this case, it is sufficient that the employees were apprised of the secret nature of the formulas, and were told, and agreed, to keep that information confidential.

Innovative also did not employ security personnel, and the plant was not locked during working hours. Suppliers, job applicants, and personal friends of employees were not denied entry into the manufacturing area. Bowen Supply argues that this establishes as a matter of law that Innovative failed to take reasonably adequate steps to guard the secrecy of its formulas. We disagree.

Innovative introduced testimony that, because of the wet cement generated in the production of Panel Brick, nonemployees would not enter the manufacturing area to an extent sufficient to closely observe the process. We must be mindful also that on appeal Innovative is not claiming trade secret status for the entire production process, but for the formulas only. These formulas, aside from that for the slurry coat, were kept in a notebook in the plant manager's office, and hence out of view. There is no indication in the record that the amount of time such nonemployees were allowed in the plant was substantial, and there is certainly no reason to think that they were in a position to glean the information contained in the formulas from the causal observation of the manufacturing process.

As to the slurry formula, which was posted in the dye shed, the jury was shown a diagram of the plant area, and one of Innovative's witnesses marked on the diagram the area that visitors entered. Hence, the jury was given sufficient evidence from which it could determine the probability whether someone other than an employee could have seen the slurry formula, and whether additional security measures were necessary under the circumstances. We find that there is sufficient evidence to support the inference that the measures adopted by Innovative to guard the secrecy of its formulas from non-employees were reasonably adequate.

Finally, Bowen Supply argues that Innovative took inadequate steps to guard the secrecy of its formulas when discussing the possible sale of

> its business to others. Several companies, including Bowen Supply, had expressed an interest in acquiring Innovative. Representatives from some of these companies would inspect the manufacturing plant. Innovative did not require either the companies or their representatives to sign non-disclosure agreements.
>
> Innovative introduced evidence, however, that written non-disclosure agreements were not normally used in the industry, at least during the preliminary stages of acquisition relevant here. Innovative also introduced testimony that it either obtained oral pledges of confidentiality from interested parties or did not divulge confidential information to them. In regard to representatives of Bowen Supply who occasionally visited the production facility, Innovative introduced testimony that it would hide some of the raw materials used in the process and bring out others in their stead to prevent these representatives from learning the formulas. One such representative testified that, although he was allowed to observe the production line, he was unable to determine how the final product was made. Another representative of Bowen Supply stated that the plant was not in operation at the time he visited it. Yet another Bowen Supply official testified that he learned very little about the production process during his visits, and did not indicate that he had either learned or had access to the formulas.
>
> A representative of another company expressing an interest in acquiring Innovative prepared a report that contained a general description of Panel Brick, including a list of the gross proportions of raw materials used to produce it. Innovative subsequently sent a copy of this report to Bowen Supply. Innovative offered testimony that the representative who compiled the report was pledged to secrecy. The report did not disclose the exact proportions of raw materials used to produce Panel Brick, nor did it indicate the proportions of these materials relative to the three layers in which they were applied. After a thorough examination of this document and of the Panel Brick formulas, we hold that a reasonable jury could find that Innovative did not compromise the secrecy of those formulas by sending the report to Bowen Supply. Furthermore, we find that the evidence as a whole, together with all reasonable inferences drawn therefrom, supports the jury's finding that Innovative took reasonably adequate steps to ensure the secrecy of its formulas.

Id., 793 F.2d at 884–86, 230 U.S.P.Q. at 101–02.

What precautions would you advise your clients to take as a routine matter in order to maintain the secrecy of their "know-how" and proprietary information?

Some clients go to much greater lengths to protect their valuable trade secrets than the plaintiff in *Innovative Construction*. According to report, only two executives of the Coca–Cola Company know the formula for Coke, and they are not allowed to fly together on the same airplane. There is only one written version of the formula, and it is kept in the vault of an Atlanta bank. It can be removed only by resolution of the Coca–Cola Board of Directors. In 1985, during the course of litigation between the Coca–Cola Company and some of its bottlers, a federal district judge ordered Coca–Cola to disclose its formulas for old Coke, new Coke, diet Coke and caffeine-free Coke in discovery. The court provided that the disclosure would be made pursuant to a protective order which would prevent the formulas being made available to anyone outside of the litigation. The Coca–Cola Company flatly refused to comply with the order, risking contempt-of-court charges and a possible default judgement in the litigation. "Coca–Cola Is Told To Disclose Secret of Coke Formula," Wall St. J., Aug. 21, 1985, at 8, col. 2. In a letter to the court, Coca–Cola stated: "The Company has concluded that disclosure of its secret formulae, regardless of the terms of any protective order, could well lead ultimately to public disclosure. In that event, the gravity of the harm to the Company and its bottling system would be incalculable and irreparable." 32 PAT. TRADEMARK & COPYRIGHT J. (BNA) No. 783 at 123 (June 5, 1986). Fortunately for Coca–Cola, the judge decided merely to enter a preclusion order in the litigation, giving the bottlers "the advantage of every possible inference that fairly could be drawn from the formulae evidence sought," and ordered Coca–Cola to pay the bottlers' expenses and fees attributable to the Company's failure to obey the court's discovery order. Coca–Cola Bottling Co. of Shreveport, Inc. v. The Coca–Cola Bottling Co., 110 F.R.D. 363, 369, 230 U.S.P.Q. 1, 4 (1986).

4. *The competitive value requirement.* Information must have "competitive value"—that is, it must derive value from the fact that the owner has it and his competitors do not—in order to qualify as a trade secret. Why impose this requirement? What evidence did the *Cybertek* court rely on to find that the plaintiff's computer program had the requisite value?

Most courts have understood the "competitive value" requirement to indicate that the alleged trade secret must give economic, or commercial benefits to its owner. In Religious Technology Center v. Wollersheim, 796 F.2d 1076 (9th Cir.1986), *cert. denied* 479 U.S. 1103, 107 S.Ct. 1336, 94 L.Ed.2d 187 (1987), a religious group developed materials to be used in the course of its religious practices, and maintained them in secrecy. Another religious group obtained a copy of the materials and threatened to publish them. The first group brought an action for trade secret infringement. The U.S. Court of Appeals for the Ninth Circuit, applying California law, held that the plaintiffs' materials did not constitute trade secrets:

> [t]o be protectible as a trade secret under either Restatement section 757 or the new California statute [the Uniform Trade Secrets Act], the confidential material must convey an actual or potential *commercial* advantage, presumably measurable in dollar terms. We do not accept that a trade secret can be based on the *spiritual advantage* the Church believes its adherents acquire over non-adherents by using the materials in the prescribed manner.

Id. at 1090. In a later opinion in the same case, the Court of Appeals clarified that its opinion in *Wollersheim* did not preclude recovery if the plaintiff alleged and proved that its materials had economic, as well as spiritual value. The plaintiffs, returning to district court after the *Wollersheim* opinion, alleged that "Defendant will obtain an economic advantage that they would not otherwise possess which will be used to divert parishioners, the value and goodwill of which cannot be monetarily measured."

5. *The trade secret cause of action.* Assuming that the plaintiff has a valid trade secret, his property rights are by no means absolute. Trade secret law only enables the owner to prevent others' acquisition, disclosure or use of the secret if their actions involve a breach of confidential duty or other improper behavior. Restatement of Torts section 757, set forth above, prohibits disclosure or use of trade secrets under four scenarios, each involving a breach of confidence or other improper behavior either on the part of the defendant himself or on the part of the person who supplied the trade secret to the defendant.[6] The Uniform Trade Secrets Act, section 1 (1) and (2), provides as follows:

(1) "Improper means" includes theft, bribery, misrepresentation, breach or inducement of a breach of a duty to maintain secrecy, or espionage through electronic or other means;

(2) "Misappropriation" means:

- (i) acquisition of a trade secret of another by a person who knows or has reason to know that the trade secret was acquired by improper means; or
- (ii) disclosure or use of a trade secret of another without express or implied consent by a person who
  - (A) used improper means to acquire knowledge of the trade secret; or
  - (B) at the time of disclosure or use, knew or had reason to know that his knowledge of the trade secret was
    - (I) derived from or through a person who had utilized improper means to acquire it;
    - (II) acquired under circumstances giving rise to a duty to maintain its secrecy or limit its use; or
    - (III) derived from or through a person who owed a duty to the person seeking relief to maintain its secrecy or limit its use; or
  - (C) before a material change of his position, knew or had reason to know that it was a trade secret and that knowledge of it had been acquired by accident or mistake.[7]

Compare the language of section 757 with section 1 of the Uniform Act, above. Is there any material difference in their coverage? On what basis does the *Cybertek* court justify granting relief to the plaintiff? Can you pinpoint the precise subdivision of Restatement of Torts section 757 and Uniform Act section 1 under which the *Cybertek* fact situation would fall?

The meaning of "improper means" other than breach of confidence will be considered in a later section. Breaches of confidence are considered in note 6.

6. *Breaches of Confidence.* There are several different approaches to finding a duty of confidentiality, or duty to maintain secrecy, on the part of defendants in trade secret cases.

6. With regard to Restatement section 757(d), using a trade secret with notice that it was obtained by mistake can be viewed as "improper" behavior because it is unethical.

7. Reprinted with the permission of the National Conference of Commissioners on Uniform State Laws.

First, the defendant may have a duty by virtue of her relationship to the plaintiff. For example, an agent owes a duty of loyalty to her principal which includes a duty to refrain from disclosing the principal's confidential information which she learned within the scope of the agency relationship. RESTATEMENT (SECOND) OF AGENCY § 395 (1958). When an employer gives an employee a trade secret to use in the course of her duties, for example, and the employee has notice that it is a secret, her duty of loyalty to the employer dictates that she refrain from using or disclosing the trade secret without the employer's permission. This is true even if there is no express contractual agreement to this effect between them. Other relationships in which a duty of confidentiality exists include the traditional "fiduciary" relationships such as partnership and joint venture relationships, and attorney-client relationships.

Second, courts often imply a duty of confidentiality on contract-implied-in-fact and contract-implied-in-law theories. A contract implied in fact is simply a contractual agreement between the parties whose existence is proven through the parties' actions, which manifest a meeting of minds, rather than through their express words. Did the parties, through their actions, indicate agreement that if the plaintiff revealed the trade secret to the defendant, the defendant would refrain from disclosing or using it without the plaintiff's permission? A contract implied in law, or quasi-contract, in contrast, is not based on evidence of the parties' intent. Rather, courts imply a contractual duty of confidence in order to avoid an injustice. Would permitting the defendant to make free use of the trade secret under the circumstances result in unjust enrichment? If so, the court may impose a duty on the defendant to maintain the trade secret in confidence and refrain from exploiting it.

A court might rely on either of the implied contract theories to find a duty of confidentiality in a given case. For example, assume that X Company approaches Y, a wealthy person, about investing a large sum of money in the business. In the course of his pitch, the president of X Company tells Y that the investment will be a good one because X Company has a special "top secret" manufacturing process. Y asks what it is, and the president tells her. Note that under these circumstances, Y had notice that the process was confidential and asked to hear it. In doing so, she could be characterized as impliedly acknowledging the secrecy and agreeing to retain it as a condition of disclosure, regardless of whether she ultimately invests in X Company. She might also be characterized as agreeing that her use of the secret will be limited to the purpose for which it was disclosed: making an investment decision. This characterization would result in a contract implied in fact. A court unwilling to find agreement on Y's part might still justify imposing a duty of confidentiality on the grounds that Y would be unjustly enriched if permitted to use the X Company's trade secret. This would result in a contract implied in law.

What if the president, in the course of making his pitch, specifically asked Y if she wanted to hear the process, and she said yes? Same result? What if the president simply revealed the process (without any express discussion about whether y wanted to hear it) and Y listened without protest? Should Y still owe a duty of confidentiality? What if Y protested, but the president told her anyway? See RESTATEMENT OF TORTS,

§ 757, comment j (1939); I R. MILGRIM, MILGRIM ON TRADE SECRETS, §§ 4.02–4.03 (1991).

Finally, a duty of confidentiality may arise from an express contractual provision. Express employee nondisclosure agreements, such as the one in *Cybertek*, are widely used in the United States. In addition to employees, trade secret owners frequently ask suppliers, distributors, purchasers, licensees and others associated with the business who might have access to confidential information to sign express nondisclosure agreements. Why should businesses resort to such express contractual agreements to maintain information in confidence when their employees and business associates are likely already to be subject to a duty of confidentiality under the common law, as described above?

Should it matter which of the above bases the court relies on to find a duty?

7. *Licenses*. A license is a contract in which the owner of a trade secret or other intellectual property permits another party (the "licensee") to use the intellectual property without liability, generally in return for payment. Licensing a trade secret gives an owner flexibility and the opportunity to capitalize more fully on the trade secret.[8] As a general matter, persons who retain title to property and merely license others to use it have greater leeway under the law to control the recipients' use than do persons who sell the title to the property outright. Software manufacturers and distributors, in particular, have seized upon the license mechanism in an attempt to retain trade secrecy in the computer programs they market. In the case of custom-made programs or programs disseminated to a limited number of users, software companies may license their customers to use the program, rather than sell the program outright. In the license agreement, the software company requires the customer to retain the program in confidence and act in a manner that will preserve secrecy. (For example, the customer may be required to promise not to reverse engineer the program to learn how it works.)

It is not feasible for software companies to negotiate individual licenses in the case of mass-marketed programs. Accordingly, they have devised the "shrink-wrap license." Here is an example: On the outside of the package of its mass-marketed word processing program, in prominent print directly under the cellophane wrapping, X Company instructs persons buying the program to read the accompanying "legal agreement." The "agreement" states that the act of opening the sealed package and using the software will indicate the buyer's consent to the terms and conditions of the agreement, and will bind him. If he doesn't agree, he should return the unused program for a refund. The agreement then goes on, among other things, to say that while payment of the price of the software transfers full title to the disk in which the software is embodied, it merely creates a perpetual license

8. Of course, licensing also exposes the owner to greater risk. The more people who know and use the trade secret, the more risk there is that the information will reach competitors or the general public, compromising its status as a trade secret. While the licensing process may give rise to an implied duty of confidentiality under the common law, licensors generally include express confidentiality provisions in the license agreement, and require the licensee to undertake specific precautions to protect the secret.

to use the computer program itself, title to the program remaining in the manufacturer. The agreement then provides that the program is the manufacturer's trade secret and that the purchaser may not reverse engineer, decompile, disassemble or translate the object code. Doing any of these things will terminate the license and subject the buyer to liability. Should shrink-wrap agreements of this sort be enforceable? If you were challenging the validity of such an agreement in court, what arguments would you raise? For a discussion of shrink-wrap licenses and their vulnerabilities, see, e.g., Kemp, *Mass Marketed Software: The Legality of the Form License Agreement*, 48 LA. L. REV. 87 (1987); Rice, *Trade Secret Clauses in Shrink–Wrap Licenses*, 2 COMPUTER LAWYER 17 (1985).

8. *Use of the trade secret.* Is it relevant to a trade secret misappropriation claim that the defendant altered the trade secret, adapting it to his own needs, or perhaps greatly improving it? In such a case, can the defendant be deemed to be "using" the plaintiff's trade secret? Should there be a point at which the defendant's alterations are so great that he escapes liability altogether?

9. *Liability of persons receiving the trade secret from someone other than the plaintiff.* The *Cybertek* court held both Whitfield and his new employer, Tracor, liable for trade secret misappropriation. Under which of the Restatement of Torts section 757 or 758 theories can Tracor's liability be justified? Under which of the subsections of Uniform Trade Secrets Act section 1? To be liable under either the Restatement or the Uniform Act, persons obtaining a trade secret through an intermediate source, rather than directly from the plaintiff, must have notice, or reason to know, that the information is a trade secret and was obtained or is being disclosed through improper conduct or a breach of confidence. Under what circumstances should recipients be deemed to have notice of these facts? See RESTATEMENT OF TORTS, § 757, comments l, m (1939). What is the earliest point at which Tracor may have had the requisite notice?

Assume that A Company manufactures carbonated drinks. A Company and B Company enter into negotiations for B to become a bottler and distributor of A's carbonated drinks. During negotiations, A's representative tells the B Company representative that A will want B to use its (A's) trade secret bottling method, because it preserves the "fizz" better than other methods. B Company agrees to use the method and also to keep it in confidence. After the agreement is finalized, A reveals the bottling method to B. B uses the method in bottling and distributing A's carbonated drink for three years. Then B Company goes out of business. A finds another bottler/distributor to replace B.

The following year, C Company, which makes and distributes its own carbonated drinks, buys the assets of the now defunct B Company. When it takes an inventory, it finds a set of written instructions for bottling which, while not labeled as such is A Company's secret method. C finds the method useful and implements it in its bottling plant.

Two years later, A Company learns that C is using the secret method and demands that C cease all further use. C refuses and continues to use the method. Six months later, A files a lawsuit against C Company for trade secret misappropriation.

Assuming that the method is in fact A Company's trade secret, should A prevail? On what grounds?

10. *Acquisition of trade secret by mistake.* Assume that D Company and E Company are competitors. One day an executive of D prepares a letter to the president of E, and instructs his secretary to attach some documents to it and put it in the mail. While the secretary is assembling the attachments, a copy of D Company's trade secret customer list, which is also on the secretary's desk, accidentally gets mixed in and is sent along with the letter to the president of E Company. The list is marked "confidential." Is E Company free to use the list under Restatement section 757 or the Uniform Trade Secrets Act?

11. *Treatises.* For comprehensive treatment of trade secret issues, see R. MILGRIM, MILGRIM ON TRADE SECRETS (1991); M. JAGER, TRADE SECRETS LAW (1988); and M. EPSTEIN, MODERN INTELLECTUAL PROPERTY (2d ed. 1991).

A. THE SPECIAL PROBLEMS OF CUSTOMER LISTS AND RELATED INFORMATION, GENERAL EMPLOYEE KNOWLEDGE AND SKILL

FLEMING SALES COMPANY, INC. v. BAILEY

United States District Court, Northern District of Illinois, 1985.
611 F.Supp. 507.

SHADUR, DISTRICT JUDGE.

[Fleming Sales Company, Inc. ("Fleming") charges Joseph Bailey ("Bailey") and his company, Unlimited Sales of America, Inc. ("Unlimited") with trade secret misappropriation. Defendants have moved for summary judgment.]

FACTS[1]

Fleming, a family-owned manufacturers' representative business, has an original equipment manufacturers ("OEM") division headquartered in Elkhart, Indiana. Through its OEM division, Fleming is engaged by recreational vehicle ("RV") component manufacturers ("Fleming's principals") to market their products to RV manufacturers ("Fleming's customers"). Bailey was hired as a salesman in the OEM division in March 1977. In July 1980 Bailey was made General Manager of the OEM division, and in August 1983 he was placed on the Fleming Board of Directors. In the meantime he had turned the OEM division into a substantially better business operation for Fleming.

Despite Bailey's relatively rapid rise at Fleming, he had for some time been dissatisfied over what he perceived as his limited freedom to run the OEM division without oversight by Fleming management (he

1. Rule 56 principles impose on the party moving for summary judgment the burden of establishing the lack of a genuine issue of material fact. For that purpose the court must, in viewing the evidence, draw all reasonable inferences in the light most favorable to the nonmovant. * * *

had been promised a "free hand" in that respect) and his limited future prospects in its family-owned structure. On April 27, 1984 Bailey wrote to Fleming Board Chairman Jack Grady ("Grady") explaining his dissatisfactions and announcing his decision to resign from Fleming and the Board of Directors effective May 1, 1984. In fact Bailey continued as OEM division head until May 18 and continued to receive his salary and benefits until the end of May. Bailey had entered into no written employment contract with Fleming, nor had he signed a restrictive covenant of any kind in Fleming's favor.

In late 1983, several months before his resignation from Fleming, Bailey joined with James Clipp ("Clipp") to form Unlimited for the manufacture of a rigid blind product to be sold as an accessory for RVs. Though formed in January 1984, Unlimited did not begin substantial operations before June 1984. It has yet to begin manufacture of the rigid blind product.

In late June Bailey and Clipp formed a second company, Unified Sales of America, Inc. ("Unified"), to compete with Fleming's OEM division in the representation of RV component manufacturers. Bailey hired several Fleming salesmen to work with him at Unified and began to develop Unified's business with Fleming's principals and customers. Soon thereafter (in August 1984) Fleming initiated this lawsuit.

Trade Secrets Claim

Fleming contends Bailey has misappropriated several kinds of information, learned in the course of his employment and protectible as trade secrets, that he is now using to compete with the OEM division:

(1) the names and addresses of Fleming's customers;

(2) other information about customers, including the names of contact people and the customers' prior purchasing and payment histories, projected needs and buying procedures; and

(3) information as to Fleming's principals and other sources of supply, including the terms of principals' contracts with Fleming.

* * *

In 1982 Indiana adopted the Uniform Trade Secrets Act, Ind. Code §§ 24–2–3–1 to 24–2–3–8 (the "Act"), which authorizes injunctive relief, damages and recovery for unjust enrichment in trade secret misappropriation cases. Where the misappropriation was willful and malicious, the Act also allows an award of exemplary damages. * * *

What the parties' dispute really boils down to is whether or not the items of information defendants allegedly misappropriated qualify as "trade secrets" under the Act. If they do not, Fleming has no action against defendants for their use of the information, for Fleming did not elect to bind Bailey by a restrictive covenant of any kind.

After extensive discovery defendants assert there is no reasonable predicate for inferring the information (1) derives independent economic value by virtue of its confidentiality or (2) was the subject of efforts reasonably calculated to maintain its secrecy. Defendants contend each item of information was rather (1) general business knowledge bred of experience (and consequently lacking "independent economic value") or (2) information "readily ascertainable by proper means" or (3) both. In addition defendants say Fleming did not make reasonable efforts to maintain the secrecy of the information. Fleming retorts genuine fact issues exist as to each of those contentions.

This opinion will consider the parties' arguments as to each item of information in turn, but it is first worth taking a step backward to gain a perspective that might otherwise get lost in the welter of citations to cases, affidavits and depositions the parties have set out against one another. Trade secrets law in general and the Act in particular were never intended "to act as a blanket *post facto* restraint on trade." *Steenhoven v. College Life Ins. Co. of America*, 460 N.E.2d 973, 975 n. 7 (Ind.App.1984). Thus the identity of a business' customers is no doubt a legitimate business interest protectible by a restrictive covenant, and the same may perhaps be true of other knowledge a company has amassed simply by virtue of having been in a particular line of business for a long period of time. But that right to impose contractual restraints does *not* render the same knowledge "trade secrets" in the absence of such restraints. Knowledge derived from experience does not automatically carry with it the ability to forestall others who have shared that experience (and thus that knowledge).

In other words, a court called on to define boundaries in this area must take care to strike a balance between (1) the underlying purposes of trade secrets law (to maintain standards of commercial ethics and to encourage research and innovation) and (2) the equally strong policy against inhibiting competition in the marketplace.[4] Analysis of Fleming's claims discloses it has sought to stifle legitimate competition rather than to resist unwarranted encroachment on its property rights.

1. Customer Lists

Fleming says Bailey, through his employment as general manager of its OEM division, had access to a comprehensive list of Fleming's customers. While there is no allegation—and no evidence—Bailey took a copy of the list with him when he left his employment,[5] Fleming does assert he took with him knowledge of the customers' names—knowledge he later used to compete (unfairly) against Fleming. Defendants do not deny Bailey came away from Fleming with a knowledge of who its customers were, but defendants argue (1) Fleming did not exert reasonable efforts to maintain the secrecy of that information and (2) the information was readily ascertainable by other means.

4. Fleming Surreply Mem. 6 is simply wrong in contending the distinction between "confidential information" and "trade secrets" is purely "semantic."

5. In fact Bailey swears:

> In connection with my resignation and leaving Fleming I did not take with me any Fleming business records.

Fleming offers no affirmative evidence to the contrary, with one exception discussed later in this opinion.

Fleming has offered affidavit and deposition evidence indicating a policy of maintaining the confidentiality of the customer list and virtually all other business information. Grady Aff. p. 11 says he "has given directions and established the policy that as much information as possible of Fleming is to remain confidential." Each Fleming employee received a "Rules and Regulations" letter specifying as one basis for termination "[c]ommunication or action detrimental to Fleming Sales Company, including but not limited to, exposing confidential information". As for customers' identity in particular, Fleming has tendered a showing its complete list of customers was available to only a few top Fleming employees, though OEM division salesmen and office personnel had access to lists identifying all of Fleming's Elkhart customers and some, but not all of, its customers outside Indiana. Fleming claims no other employee had access to the list.

Defendants acknowledge there is at least a fact issue as to how widely the customer lists were distributed within Fleming. Defendants point out, however, (1) account lists were provided to Fleming's *principals* from time to time and (2) Fleming has no written policy and no clearly articulated procedures to ensure the confidentiality of the customer lists. For example the lists are not kept under lock and key or marked "confidential," and salesmen routinely keep copies in their offices. Moreover customer list information necessarily appeared on shipping documents stored in Fleming's warehouses.

Of course the absence of specific confidentiality procedures (whether written or unwritten) does not itself negate the existence of "reasonable" efforts to maintain secrecy—all the Act requires. Fleming's OEM division was, after all, a *sales* organization. Constant dealings with its customers—whether by phone, letter or in person—was the essence of the business. Naturally Fleming employees whose business it was to maintain that contact needed ready access to customer information. By the same token, distribution of account list information to principals or on occasion to other customers may well have been necessary to the pursuit of Fleming's business. Fleming was plainly not required to shoot itself in the foot to meet the "reasonable efforts" requirement of the Act. So long as Fleming scrupulously limited distribution of customer list information to employees and outsiders whose access was necessary to Fleming's successful pursuit of its business, it must be deemed to have satisfied the "reasonable efforts" requirement, particularly if those given access to the information were also advised to preserve its confidentiality, as Fleming indicates they were.[6] Were that the critical issue, the factual dispute as to Fleming's efforts in that regard (a dispute defendants acknowledge) would compel denial of defendants' motion.

6. No matter how scrupulous Fleming may have been in handling the customer lists, they might nevertheless not qualify as trade secrets if the demands of Fleming's business required so broad a distribution (either inside or outside the company) as to make it impossible as a practical matter to maintain confidentiality. That question need not be resolved in light of the text analysis.

But there is more to the story. All the efforts in the world to preserve confidentiality of information will not suffice if the information is not secret in the first place—if it is "readily ascertainable" by other proper means. Defendants point to several pieces of evidence demonstrating the customer list information could be procured by such other means:

> 1. Grady stated that as a rule Fleming's principals know "the customers purchasing its products, the amount of product purchased, and the prices paid for those products."
>
> 2. Many of Fleming's customers are listed either in telephone directory Yellow Pages or in the trade publication *RV Business*.
>
> 3. Others in the business testified (a) competing sales companies generally know who each other's customers are and (b) it is generally easy for a principal's competitor to find out who that principal's customers are.

Fleming counters only by arguing defendants are unlikely to be able to reproduce Fleming's customer list from those sources. Not all principals will necessarily be willing to identify their existing customers to new sales companies. Similarly *RV Business* and the Yellow Pages list only a relatively small proportion of the customers on Fleming's list. So, too, a general knowledge of a competitor's customers is something significantly less than access to the customer list itself.

Those assertions may perhaps create a factual issue as to defendants' ability to reproduce the entire customer list precisely from other sources. But what Rule 56 requires is a "material" (that is, outcome-determinative) factual issue. Here it is undisputed that substantial information as to the identity of Fleming's customers is available from other sources. And Fleming has come forward with no evidence at all showing defendants have sought to pursue customers they would not have discovered even without Bailey's exposure to the Fleming list.[7] Especially in a market where customers did business with more than one sales company or were open to the possibility of shifting business from one company to another, it is simply unreasonable to construe the Act's "readily ascertainable" standard as requiring exact duplication of the information on the customer list.

One other aspect of the problem bears mentioning—an aspect that bears not only on the customer-list issue but on each of the other claimed "trade secrets" categories. Fleming Mem. 5 (emphasis in original) urges "Bailey alone could not have taken Fleming's principals from it; he had to have the help of *Fleming's* salesmen." [8] But absent some

7. Eli Magee, an individual with wide experience in the RV business, testified that even customer companies new to the business become generally known in the industry within six months to a year via advertising and exhibitions at trade shows.

8. Fleming Mem. 15–16 says in a pejorative tone:

> In fact, Defendant Bailey has assigned Fleming's former salesmen to exactly the same territories they had previously covered for Fleming. In Indiana, this means

independent tort (such as actionable interference with advantageous relationships) or extraordinary circumstances * * *, it is perfectly permissible to build an organization by hiring a competitor's personnel. And if the consequence is that the individual employees' knowledge of pieces of the competitor's business is aggregated to provide a more comprehensive view of the total picture, that too can legitimately serve as the source of "readily ascertainable" information in the sense of the Act. Even the proverbial six blind men, if they pooled their information, might well produce a reasonably good description of the elephant.

Thus no genuine issue of *material* fact exists as to the availability of the substance of Fleming's customer list from other legitimate sources. Defendants are part way home on their motion.

2. Other Information As to Customers

Fleming also claims trade secret protection for other types of customer information including:

> knowledge of the individual persons at these customers to contact in order to effectuate sales; the prior purchasing history of the customers; the product and service requirements; their present and future projected needs; the packages that Fleming must put together in order to sell particular products; their payment histories; and their buying procedures.

Fleming does not assert any of that information was systematically recorded or compiled in any way, though it says much of the information was supplied to Fleming salesmen in the course of their training. Again Fleming claims to have exerted reasonable efforts to maintain its confidentiality.

Once more that represents only part of the story, and a skewed version at that. Fleming seeks to make the "trade secrets" label carry too much baggage. All the information it tries to wrap in the Act's mantle is nothing more than the kind of knowledge any successful salesman necessarily acquires through experience. In the Act's terms, it is information "readily ascertainable by proper means" over the course of time without efforts beyond those ordinarily exerted by salesmen in developing customers.

That is not to say Bailey may not have derived some benefit from his access to the collective experience of Fleming's OEM division (experience to which Bailey himself doubtless contributed significantly during the course of his employment). It is rather to say such information comprises general skills and knowledge acquired in the course of employment. Those are things an employee is free to take and to use in later pursuits, especially if they do not take the form of written records, compilations or analyses.

the exact same customers as they previously have visited as Fleming salesmen. In particular, they are now soliciting Fleming's customers for Fleming's former principal Vernco.

Any other rule would force a departing employee to perform a prefrontal lobotomy on himself or herself. It would disserve the free market goal of maximizing available resources to foster competition. Or to frame the issue in the way discussed earlier in this opinion, it would not strike a proper balance between the purposes of trade secrets law and the strong policy in favor of fair and vigorous business competition.

All this does not render helpless an employer worried that the skills and knowledge an employee acquires during the course of employment will give him or her an undue competitive advantage. Nothing prevents such an employer from guarding its interests by a restrictive covenant.[10] But it would really be unfair competition to allow the employer *without* such a covenant to obtain trade secret status for the fruits of ordinary experience in the business, thus compelling former employees to reinvent the wheel as the price for entering the competitive market. Once again defendants must prevail.

3. Information As to Principals

Fleming Mem. 16 concedes the identity of its principals is widely known and therefore not a trade secret, but it says other principal-related information is: the identity of the contact people, the sales volumes for particular products, the existence of "minor" items provided by principals or other suppliers for use with a principal's products or necessary to permit use of the products, and the terms of Fleming's contracts with principals. No elaboration is required here: All the earlier analysis as to customer-related information applies with equal force. Once more the information is part and parcel of a salesman's experience in the RV business. Bailey naturally carried away from his years at Fleming a familiarity with the contracts, products and personnel of the principals he did business with, not to mention an awareness of what products sold best. For reasons already surveyed the Act's "trade secret" definition simply does not embrace that kind of information.

Fleming tries to bolster its claim by pointing to defendants' possession of some papers containing information about Fleming's relationship with its principals and other suppliers. Bailey discovered those documents, all from the 1981–83 period, in his garage well after this litigation began, and he produced them in response to a Fleming document request. Bailey has explained he periodically carried papers home during the course of his employment and at one point, well before his resignation, stored them all in a box in his garage. Fleming has offered nothing to contradict that explanation. What really controls, however,

10. Of course the concern about inhibiting fair competition also informs the law of restrictive covenants. In Indiana, as in most jurisdictions, *Licocci v. Cardinal Associates, Inc.*, 445 N.E.2d. 556, 561 (Ind.1983):

> All such covenants as this are in restraint of trade and are not favored by the law. They will be enforced only if they are reasonable with respect to the covenantee, the covenantor, and the public interest.

But if an express covenant were nonenforceable because of overbreadth, the employer could scarcely expect protection from the common law (or the codified common law) of trade secrets.

is that the specific documents Fleming points to do not—even with all inferences in Fleming's favor as Rule 56 requires—create a *material* fact issue. One of them compiles basic information about a number of Fleming principals, including the commissions each pays to Fleming. But because that information is of the sort Bailey was likely to know anyway, and because there is no evidence to indicate defendants made use of the document, Bailey's mere possession is insufficient to raise a genuine issue of fact.

Also among the papers in the box Bailey found in his garage were invoices with the names of two suppliers who provide Fleming with products for resale. Fleming argues the identity of those suppliers is secret, yet Bailey approached one of them—Runglin International ("Runglin")—in an effort to obtain goods for his new sales company. Fleming says that shows Bailey was making use of information gleaned from the documents he had retained. Defendants, however, point to Grady's own deposition testimony that he and Bailey traveled to the Orient in 1984 with a Runglin representative to explore foreign supplier sources. Bailey thus knew of Runglin independently of the documents. Again there is nothing to suggest Bailey's retention of the documents was anything but the oversight he claims it was.

4. Conclusion

There is a telling passage at Fleming Mem. 17:

> [T]he RV Business Directory reveals a most important fact concerning Defendants' actions relative to Fleming. The directory lists several hundred manufacturers of equipment utilized by the RV industry. Bailey could easily have undertaken to represent these other manufacturers. Furthermore, Bailey could have solicited the many thousands of manufacturers of equipment not currently involved with the RV business to bring them into that industry as did Ken Lail. However, Bailey chose not to follow this course of action; rather, he went after those principals whom he had personal contact with because of his position with Fleming, that is, Fleming's principals.

Fleming unconsciously reveals something of itself: Its desire to attach a "trade secrets" label to its own generalized business skills, and to the skills acquired by Bailey while in its employ, simply to prevent competition by its former employee.

But as the Indiana Court of Appeals stated in *Steenhoven*, 460 N.E.2d at 975 n. 7:

> Insofar as College Life attempts to merely restrain Steenhoven's competition, we believe the Uniform Trade Secrets Act to be an improper vehicle therefor. The fact that Steenhoven possesses certain knowledge acquired within the course of his employment does not mandate that, upon his departure, Steenhoven must wipe clean the slate of his memory.

So here Fleming may not look to the Act to restrain competition from Bailey, especially given the nature of the information in issue here. Fleming has come forward with nothing to indicate that the allegedly misappropriated information rose to the "trade secrets" level. Business experience and knowhow as reflected in that information, however valuable, are not something the law protects from the rigors of the marketplace. Defendants' motion is granted as to Count I and its trade secrets claims.

[The Court granted summary judgement to the defendants.]

Notes and Questions

1. *Customer lists as trade secrets.* What leads the *Fleming* court to find that the customer list fails to qualify as a trade secret?

Compare Webcraft Technologies, Inc. v. McCaw, 674 F.Supp. 1039 (S.D.N.Y.1987). In that case, Webcraft, a custom printer engaging in "in-line finishing," sought relief against McCaw, its former sales representative. McCaw had signed a Webcraft employment agreement which, among other things, barred disclosure of Webcraft's "trade secrets," which the agreement defined as including the names and needs of Webcraft customers and pricing information and "any other confidential information or data relating to the business of Webcraft which is not publicly known." *Id.*, at 1043. The agreement also required McCaw to return any documents regarding Webcraft's business upon termination of her employment. After approximately three years of employment with Webcraft, McCaw decided to move to Tech Web, a competitor of Webcraft's which also engaged in in-line finishing. While discussing prospective employment with Tech Web, McCaw gave a Tech Web representative a list of her fifteen or twenty best known customers and customer prospects at Webcraft. After agreeing to take the position at Tech Web, but before notifying Webcraft of her resignation, McCaw passed other confidential Webcraft information to Tech Web, including job specifications on accounts sought by Webcraft, pricing information, and a sketch of a proposed Webcraft product. Upon leaving Webcraft, McCaw took her rolodex, which contained customer names and contacts, eight pages of Webcraft quotes and pricing sheets relating to three jobs she had pursued while at Webcraft. Notwithstanding an exit interview and subsequent letter from Webcraft reminding her of her obligations under the employment contract, upon arriving at Tech Web, McCaw contacted most of her former Webcraft customers and viable prospects to solicit their business. She also gave her Webcraft customer and prospective customer information to her new employer, which entered it into its computer data base.

In considering the merits of Webcraft's claims against McCaw, the court found that the Webcraft customer list was likely to be found a trade secret under both New Jersey and New York law, but that the list of prospective customers probably was not:

> The list of prospects is put together from easily available sources. Although considerable work goes into compilation of the list, which includes some 10,000 names, McCaw may be correct that it would not be considered a trade secret.

The list of Webcraft's customers is a completely different matter. Although it may be self-evident that Company A is a prospective customer for any seller of printing services, Webcraft sells the unusual in-line finishing process. The evidence shows it is a long, difficult process to educate and convert a prospective customer to the benefits of the process. Thus the confidential value of Webcraft's customer list lies not only in its identification of *someone's* customers for printing, but more importantly, especially for competitors in the in-line process like Tech Web, in that it identifies customers who have learned and have bought the benefits of in-line finishing.

McCaw testified that developing a customer is an "arduous" process, that took between two months and two years to accomplish. The sales representative would first attempt, generally through a series of telephone calls, to identify the proper contact at the prospect. Then, the telephone contact would be followed-up by letters, the sending of samples, attendance at meetings, development of presentations, and attempts to learn customer preferences and demands, and pricing information. As McCaw testified, "[i]t would take follow-up calls monthly or bi-weekly to keep in touch and develop a rapport with a customer." Ultimately, Webcraft might be asked to quote a job, which might or might not result in the placement of an order.

The long time needed to develop a customer was largely because "[t]he specialized nature of Webcraft's business was not useful to many people, many kinds of advertising or direct mail customers," and because "[t]o utilize Webcraft's technology, a lot of development takes place on the creative side, on the marketing side." "[E]ducating those people as to what in-line finishing is, is a very difficult, tedious and long process. Most people are intimidated by technology, not understanding it."

* * *

The evidence shows that Webcraft's customer lists took enormous time and effort to develop, including the development of a specialized knowledge of the customer's operations and needs; that the identity of customers for in-line finishing was by no means available to a stranger, but was confidential and a valuable trade secret. It was of particular value to Tech Web, whose own list coincided with McCaw's Webcraft list as to only two names.

In addition, * * * McCaw physically removed the portion of her customer and prospect list represented in her rolodex. Although she maintains that she could have remembered the names and contacts of her few customers and only took the rolodex for convenience, the fact remains that she took the list and no doubt it helped her remember far more than she could have remembered without it.

Finally, * * * McCaw signed an agreement including a non-solicitation provision and a trade secrets provision which expressly included customer lists within its protection.

I find that Webcraft is likely to succeed on the merits in demonstrating that the customer lists qualify as a trade secret, and that it is

> entitled to a preliminary injunction by reason of McCaw's misappropriation of it.

Id., at 1045–46.

How would you reconcile the result in *Fleming* with the result in *Webcraft*?

2. *Other "customer-related" and business information.* In *Fleming*, the plaintiff also alleged trade secret rights in such information as the contact person at each customer's office, the prior purchasing history of customers and projections of their future purchases, customer service requirements, customer payment histories and purchasing procedures. Why does the court reject the claim? Could such information ever qualify as a trade secret? Again, consider Judge Leval's opinion in *Webcraft* with regard to the plaintiff's claim that the contacts at each of its customers and the pricing information McCaw took were trade secrets:

> McCaw acknowledged that it could easily take several telephone calls over a period of time, and perhaps a meeting, to identify the proper contact. Babiuk testified that it takes "extensive work to identify" the proper contact.
>
> In support of her contention that the identity of such contacts is not subject to trade secrets protection, McCaw relies on *Great Lakes Carbon Corp. v. Koch Industries, Inc.*, 497 F.Supp. 462, 471 (S.D.N.Y.1980). But she reads too much into that case. Although the friends and acquaintances acquired in the course of a history of business dealings in an industry are not generally considered a trade secret, different considerations apply where a list of useful and influential contacts among customers and prospects is accumulated with considerable effort for the benefit of the employer.
>
> Although some of McCaw's contacts are apparently friends, and in one case a relative, in general the list represents the names which she discovered through substantial research for sales purposes at the expense of her employer. Many of these names were recorded in the rolodex which McCaw brought with her to Tech Web.
>
> This is data collected on behalf of and at the expense of Webcraft. It is not generally available information; it is maintained in confidence and is valuable to a competitor. Webcraft is likely to succeed on the merits in showing that the contacts list qualifies as a trade secret. * * *
>
> There is little doubt that information which McCaw learned while employed at Webcraft concerning customer preferences and Webcraft's pricing is protectible.

Webcraft Technologies, Inc. v. McCaw, 674 F.Supp at 1046.

Again, how might you reconcile *Fleming* and *Webcraft*?

3. *Striking a balance.* The *Fleming* court justifies limiting the reach of trade secret protection in that case on policy grounds, stating, "a court called on to define boundaries in this area must take care to strike a balance between (1) the underlying purposes of trade secrets law (to maintain standards of commercial ethics and to encourage research and innovation

* * *) and (2) the equally strong policy against inhibiting competition in the marketplace." 611 F.Supp. at 511–12. In your opinion, how would extending trade secret protection to the customer names and information in the *Fleming* case affect that balance? Does the court, in deciding that trade secret protection should not be afforded, strike the right balance?

We have considered the general policy "balance" that exists throughout intellectual property law: providing property rights as an incentive to create vs. assuring free access to information and ideas to enhance competition. Note that the court identifies a second policy goal for the right-hand side of that contest in trade secret law: in addition to providing an incentive to create, trade secret law undertakes to maintain standards of commercial ethics. How does the existence of that second goal affect the mix? How might its existence influence the outcome of a given case? Can you discern any influence in the outcomes in *Fleming* and *Webcraft*, discussed above?

4. *Simple memory vs. the physical taking of documents.* In *Cybertek* and *Fleming*, both courts discussed whether the defendant had physically taken documents from his prior employer or had merely relied on his memory of the employer's trade secrets. In *Webcraft*, discussed above, the court made a point of mentioning that the defendant had in fact taken documents from her prior employer. Why should it matter whether or not the former employee took documents containing the alleged trade secret, as long as he used the trade secret without permission after leaving the plaintiff's employ? See the majority and dissenting opinions in Allen v. Johar, Inc., 308 Ark. 45, 823 S.W.2d 824, 21 U.S.P.Q. 2d 1854 (1992).

NOTE: PROTECTION FOR INFORMATION THAT DOES NOT QUALIFY AS TRADE SECRET

The *Fleming* court observed that its denial of trade secret protection would not render an employer helpless to protect itself against the competition of former employees using the skills and knowledge they acquired in its employ. According to the court, the employer could protect itself through use of a restrictive covenant. 611 F.Supp. at 514. In footnote 10, however, the court acknowledged that "the concern about inhibiting fair competition also informs the law of restrictive covenants," and observed that all such covenants "are in restraint of trade and are not favored by the law. They will be enforced only if they are reasonable with respect to the covenantee, the covenantor, and the public interest." *Id.* In *Cybertek*, the court suggested that nondisclosure agreements may protect information that does not constitute a trade secret, but ultimately did not rely on that principle in finding for the plaintiff. As a practical matter, what additional rights do contractual provisions give an employer beyond what it would obtain under the common law of trade secrets?

For our present purposes, two types of covenants are relevant: the nondisclosure agreement, in which the employee agrees not to disclose trade secret or other confidential information of the employer during and after her employment, and the covenant not to compete, in which the employee agrees not to compete with the employer after leaving its employ. Many employment agreements contain both a nondisclosure covenant and a covenant not to compete.

a. Covenants not to compete. Employers often rely on covenants not to compete to prevent employees from using information obtained on the job to compete with them, as occurred in *Fleming*. They often are unsuccessful in enforcing them, however. While state laws vary, consider Illinois case law as an example. The Appellate Court of Illinois described that State's general rule regarding covenants not to compete in Morrison Metalweld Process Corporation v. Valent, 97 Ill.App.3d 373, 52 Ill.Dec. 825, 422 N.E.2d 1034 (1981):

> Because agreements not to compete are, to at least some extent, restraints of trade, courts scrutinize such agreements carefully to ensure that they do not injure the public by impeding competition. Courts also consider the promisor's right to pursue his livelihood without undue constraints. Where the limitation as to time and territory is not unreasonable, however, injunctive relief is customary and proper. Therefore, when a party to an employment contract agrees, in exchange for certain benefits, to refrain from competing with his or her employer, that agreement should be enforced where equitable. The basic test for enforcing such a covenant is whether it is "reasonably necessary to protect the employer from improper or unfair competition." (*Iroquois Industries Corp. v. Popik* (1980), 91 Ill.App.3d 505, 507, 47 Ill.Dec. 279, 281, 415 N.E.2d 4, 6.) Implicit in this standard are two separate inquiries: (1) Does the employer have a legitimate business interest needing protection? (2) Is the restrictive covenant reasonable in scope?
>
> Not every alleged business interest will be deemed protectible through a covenant not to compete. (*Nationwide Advertising Service, Inc. v. Kolar* (1975), 28 Ill.App.3d 671, 329 N.E.2d 300.) In *Nationwide* we recognized two general situations in which an employer's interest in its customers is "proprietary," that is, legally protectible. First, we noted that "[a] covenant not to compete will be enforced if the employee acquired confidential information through his employment and subsequently attempted to use it for his own benefit." (*Nationwide* at 673, 329 N.E.2d at 302.) Second, we stated that "[a]n employer's interest in its customers also is deemed proprietary if, *by the nature of the business, the customer relationship is near-permanent and but for his association with plaintiff, defendant would never have had contact with the clients in question*." (*Id.*) (Emphasis added.)

Id. at 375–76, 52 Ill.Dec. at 827–28, 422 N.E.2d at 1036–37.

In Iroquois Industries Corp. v. Popik, 91 Ill.App.3d 505, 47 Ill.Dec. 279, 415 N.E.2d 4 (1980), the plaintiff, Iroquois, was a distributor of paper products and packaging materials. Defendant Popik was hired as a regular salesman and required to sign an employment agreement containing a nondisclosure covenant and a covenant not to compete. The agreement explicitly stated that the company's customer information was confidential and that for two years following his employment, Popik could not compete with Iroquois with respect to "actual or prospective accounts, clients or customers of [Iroquois] upon whom [Popik] called during the time he was employed." *Id.*, 91 Ill.App.3d at 506, 47 Ill.Dec. at 280, 415 N.E.2d at 5.

The business was a competitive one, which required that salesmen get to know their clients well. Popik was to sell the company's products to any account in the metropolitan Chicago area. The number of potential customers amounted to "tens of thousands." Popik generated 90% to 95% of the 209 customers he called upon while employed by Iroquois. He did this by "cold calling" businesses whose names he acquired from the telephone book or industrial directories available to all salesmen in the industry. Iroquois gave Popik about a dozen accounts, which were customers who had either not made recent purchases or had made small purchases. After about five years, Popik left Iroquois and went to work for a competitor. He disclosed the names of customers he had called upon while employed by Iroquois to his new employer and made calls upon some of those accounts, soliciting their business and making sales. Iroquois sought a preliminary injunction.

The court noted that the injunction was dependent upon the enforceability of the restrictive covenant, which in turn depended upon whether the covenant was reasonably necessary to protect a legitimate business interest on Iroquois' part. The court noted that the "prevention of competition per se * * * is an unreasonable purpose which renders the covenant unenforceable." *Id.*, 91 Ill.App.3d at 507, 47 Ill.Dec. at 281, 415 N.E.2d at 6. The court pointed out that notwithstanding the assertion in the employment agreement, the customer names were not confidential information. The names of the customers were readily ascertainable from publicly available sources. Moreover, it could not be said that Popik learned of the customers from the plaintiff, since he developed 90% to 95% of them himself. Thus, Iroquois lacked a protectible business interest. "Absent evidence of a protectible business interest in the 209 customers, enforcement of the restrictive covenant would be an effort to prevent competition per se." *Id.*, 91 Ill.App.3d at 509, 47 Ill.Dec. at 282, 415 N.E.2d at 7. The court denied relief.

Of course, covenants not to compete are used to protect more than just customer information. For example, see Modern Controls, Inc., v. Andreadakis, 578 F.2d 1264 (8th Cir.1978). In that case the Eighth Circuit noted that under Minnesota law,

> confidential business information which does not rise to the level of a trade secret can be protected by a properly drawn covenant not to compete. * * * An employer need only show that an employee had access to confidential information and a court will then determine the overall reasonableness of the covenant in light of the interest sought to be protected.

Id., at 1268. The court then found that the defendant/employee's access to the following "confidential business information" justified a preliminary injunction to enforce his covenant not to compete, even though the information had not been proved to be trade secret: a method of laying a thin glass layer over conductors, the manner of making electrical connections to the conductors, the methods followed in creating channels in a glass cover plate that fit over the conductors, the manner of bonding the cover plate and the processes used in exhausting the air within the bonded plate.

A number of states have enacted statutes addressing the validity of noncompetition agreements. See, e.g., CAL. BUS. & PROF. CODE § 16600 (West 1987); LA. REV. STAT. ANN. § 23:921 (West 1985); MICH. COMP. LAWS ANN. § 445.774a (Callaghan 1989); TEX. BUS. & COM. CODE ANN. § 15.50 (West Supp. 1991). On covenants not to compete generally, see D.J. ASPELUND & C.E. ERIKSEN, EMPLOYEE NONCOMPETITION LAW (1993); Closius & Schaffer, *Involuntary Nonservitude: The Current Judicial Enforcement of Employee Covenants Not To Compete—A Proposal for Reform*, 57 S. CAL. L. REV. 531 (1984); Blake, *Employee Agreements Not To Compete*, 73 HARV. L. REV. 625 (1960).

b. Nondisclosure agreements. The courts in *Cybertek* and *Fleming* both indicated that a nondisclosure contract may protect information that does not qualify as a trade secret. Contract law exists separately from the law of trade secrets. One might argue that parties should be able to contract for nondisclosure of information regardless of the nature of the information. Courts have indicated, however, that nondisclosure agreements that unreasonably restrain competition or unduly hinder an individual from pursuing his chosen livelihood will be unenforceable. Courts are unlikely to permit parties to do by nondisclosure contract what they are prohibited from doing by covenant not to compete. See, e.g., Gary Van Zeeland Talent, Inc. v. Sandas, 84 Wisc.2d 202, 267 N.W.2d 242 (1978). In *Van Zeeland Talent*, the employee signed an employment agreement providing, among other things, that he agreed that the employer's customer list was a valuable, special, and unique asset of the employer's business and that he would not disclose it during or after his employment. The employee later left his employment, taking a copy of the customer list with him and using it to compete with his former employer. The customer list consisted of names only, without accompanying information about customer needs, preferences, etc. Upon suit, the court found that the list could be recreated from other publicly available sources and that it did not constitute a trade secret. The court rejected the suggestion that the agreement created enforceable rights in the customer list even so, stating:

> [I]t is contrary to public policy to afford special protection to a restraint-of-trade mechanism where to do so does not give a special incentive for creativity that will inure to the benefit of the public at large. Accordingly, it is contrary to public policy to afford protection to material which is generated in the ordinary course of a business. * * *
>
> [I]t is the public's right to have reasonable competition, irrespective of what self-serving declarations the employer may insist upon.

Id., 84 Wisc.2d at 217, 267 N.W.2d at 250.

Given the constraints on enforcement of covenants not to compete and nondisclosure agreements described above, what are the advantages of having them? See I R. MILGRIM, MILGRIM ON TRADE SECRETS, § 3.02[1] (1991). Are there any disadvantages in having a written agreement? See *Id.* at § 3.02[2].

B. IMPROPER CONDUCT OTHER THAN BREACH OF CONFIDENCE

E.I. duPONT deNEMOURS & COMPANY v. CHRISTOPHER

Unites States Court of Appeals, Fifth Circuit, 1970.
431 F.2d 1012, 166 U.S.P.Q. 421, 167 U.S.P.Q. 1, *cert. denied* 400 U.S. 1024, 91 S.Ct. 581, 27 L.Ed.2d 637 (1971).

GOLDBERG, CIRCUIT JUDGE:

This is a case of industrial espionage in which an airplane is the cloak and a camera the dagger. The defendants-appellants, Rolfe and Gary Christopher, are photographers in Beaumont, Texas. The Christophers were hired by an unknown third party to take aerial photographs of new construction at the Beaumont plant of E. I. duPont deNemours & Company, Inc. Sixteen photographs of the DuPont facility were taken from the air on March 19, 1969, and these photographs were later developed and delivered to the third party.

DuPont employees apparently noticed the airplane on March 19 and immediately began an investigation to determine why the craft was circling over the plant. By that afternoon the investigation had disclosed that the craft was involved in a photographic expedition and that the Christophers were the photographers. DuPont contacted the Christophers that same afternoon and asked them to reveal the name of the person or corporation requesting the photographs. The Christophers refused to disclose this information, giving as their reason the client's desire to remain anonymous.

Having reached a dead end in the investigation, DuPont subsequently filed suit against the Christophers, alleging that the Christophers had wrongfully obtained photographs revealing DuPont's trade secrets which they then sold to the undisclosed third party. DuPont contended that it had developed a highly secret but unpatented process for producing methanol, a process which gave DuPont a competitive advantage over other producers. This process, DuPont alleged, was a trade secret developed after much expensive and time-consuming research, and a secret which the company had taken special precautions to safeguard. The area photographed by the Christophers was the plant designed to produce methanol by this secret process, and because the plant was still under construction parts of the process were exposed to view from directly above the construction area. Photographs of that area, DuPont alleged, would enable a skilled person to deduce the secret process for making methanol. DuPont thus contended that the Christophers had wrongfully appropriated DuPont trade secrets by taking the photographs and delivering them to the undisclosed third party. In its suit DuPont asked for damages to cover the loss it had already sustained as a result of the wrongful disclosure of the trade secret and sought temporary and permanent injunctions prohibiting any further circulation of the photographs already taken and prohibiting any additional photographing of the methanol plant.

The Christophers answered with motions to dismiss for lack of jurisdiction and failure to state a claim upon which relief could be granted. Depositions were taken during which the Christophers again refused to disclose the name of the person to whom they had delivered the photographs. DuPont then filed a motion to compel an answer to this question and all related questions.

On June 5, 1969, the trial court held a hearing on all pending motions and an additional motion by the Christophers for summary judgment. The court denied the Christophers' motions to dismiss for want of jurisdiction and failure to state a claim and also denied their motion for summary judgment. The court granted DuPont's motion to compel the Christophers to divulge the name of their client. Having made these rulings, the court then granted the Christophers' motion for an interlocutory appeal under 28 U.S.C.A. 1292(b) to allow the Christophers to obtain immediate appellate review of the court's finding that DuPont had stated a claim upon which relief could be granted. Agreeing with the trial court's determination that DuPont had stated a valid claim, we affirm the decision of that court.

This is a case of first impression, for the Texas courts have not faced this precise factual issue, and sitting as a diversity court we must sensitize our Erie antennae to divine what the Texas courts would do if such a situation were presented to them. The only question involved in this interlocutory appeal is whether DuPont has asserted a claim upon which relief can be granted. The Christophers argued both at trial and before this court that they committed no "actionable wrong" in photographing the DuPont facility and passing these photographs on to their client because they conducted all of their activities in public airspace, violated no government aviation standard, did not breach any confidential relation, and did not engage in any fraudulent or illegal conduct. In short, the Christophers argue that for an appropriation of trade secrets to be wrongful there must be a trespass, other illegal conduct, or breach of a confidential relationship. We disagree.

It is true, as the Christophers assert, that the previous trade secret cases have contained one or more of these elements. However, we do not think that the Texas courts would limit the trade secret protection exclusively to these elements. On the contrary, in Hyde Corporation v. Huffines, 1958, 158 Tex. 566, 314 S.W.2d 763, the Texas Supreme Court specifically adopted the rule found in the Restatement of Torts which provides:

> "One who discloses or uses another's trade secret, without a privilege to do so, is liable to the other if (a) he discovered the secret by improper means, or (b) his disclosure or use constitutes a breach of confidence reposed in him by the other in disclosing the secret to him * * *."

Restatement of Torts 757 (1939).

Thus, although the previous cases have dealt with a breach of a confidential relationship, a trespass, or other illegal conduct, the rule is much broader than the cases heretofore encountered. Not limiting itself to specific wrongs, Texas adopted subsection (a) of the Restatement which recognizes a cause of action for the discovery of a trade secret by any "improper" means.

* * *

The question remaining, therefore, is whether aerial photography of plant construction is an improper means of obtaining another's trade secret. We conclude that it is and that the Texas courts would so hold. The Supreme Court of that state has declared that "the undoubted tendency of the law has been to recognize and enforce higher standards of commercial morality in the business world." Hyde Corporation v. Huffines, *supra* 314 S.W.2d at 773. That court has quoted with approval articles indicating that the *proper* means of gaining possession of a competitor's secret process is "through inspection and analysis" of the product in order to create a duplicate. K & G Tool & Service Co. v. G & G Fishing Tool Service, 1958, 158 Tex. 594, 314 S.W.2d 782, 783, 788. Later another Texas court explained:

> "The means by which the discovery is made may be obvious, and the experimentation leading from known factors to presently unknown results may be simple and lying in the public domain. But these facts do not destroy the value of the discovery and will not advantage a competitor who by unfair means obtains the knowledge *without paying the price expended by the discoverer*." Brown v. Fowler, Tex.Civ.App.1958, 316 S.W.2d 111, 114, writ ref'd n.r.e. (emphasis added).

We think, therefore, that the Texas rule is clear. One may use his competitor's secret process if he discovers the process by reverse engineering applied to the finished product; one may use a competitor's process if he discovers it by his own independent research; but one may not avoid these labors by taking the process from the discoverer without his permission at a time when he is taking reasonable precautions to maintain its secrecy. To obtain knowledge of a process without spending the time and money to discover it independently is *improper* unless the holder voluntarily discloses it or fails to take reasonable precautions to ensure its secrecy.

In the instant case the Christophers deliberately flew over the DuPont plant to get pictures of a process which DuPont had attempted to keep secret. The Christophers delivered their pictures to a third party who was certainly aware of the means by which they had been acquired and who may be planning to use the information contained therein to manufacture methanol by the DuPont process. The third party has a right to use this process only if he obtains this knowledge through his own research efforts, but thus far all information indicates that the third party has gained this knowledge solely by taking it from DuPont at a time when DuPont was making reasonable efforts to preserve its secrecy. In such a situation DuPont has a valid cause of action to prohibit the Christophers from improperly discovering its trade secret and to prohibit the undisclosed third party from using the improperly obtained information.

We note that this view is in perfect accord with the position taken by the authors of the Restatement. In commenting on improper means of discovery the savants of the Restatement said:

> "f. *Improper means of discovery.* The discovery of another's trade secret by improper means subjects the actor to liability independently of the harm to the interest in the secret. Thus, if one uses physical force to take a secret formula from another's pocket, or breaks into another's office to steal the formula, his conduct is wrongful and subjects him to liability apart from the rule stated in this Section. Such conduct is also an improper means of procuring the secret under this rule. But means may be improper under this rule even though they do not cause any other harm than that to the interest in the trade secret. Examples of such means are fraudulent misrepresentations to induce disclosure, tapping of telephone wires, eavesdropping or other espionage. A complete catalogue of improper means is not possible. In general they are means which fall below the generally accepted standards of commercial morality and reasonable conduct." Restatement of Torts 757, comment f at 10 (1939).

In taking this position we realize that industrial espionage of the sort here perpetrated has become a popular sport in some segments of our industrial community. However, our devotion to free wheeling industrial competition must not force us into accepting the law of the jungle as the standard of morality expected in our commercial relations. Our tolerance of the espionage game must cease when the protections required to prevent another's spying cost so much that the spirit of inventiveness is dampened. Commercial privacy must be protected from espionage which could not have been reasonably anticipated or prevented. We do not mean to imply, however, that everything not in plain view is within the protected vale, nor that all information obtained through every extra optical extension is forbidden. Indeed, for our industrial competition to remain healthy there must be breathing room for observing a competing industrialist. A competitor can and must shop his competition for pricing and examine his products for quality, components, and methods of manufacture. Perhaps ordinary fences and roofs must be built to shut out incursive eyes, but we need not require the discoverer of a trade secret to guard against the unanticipated, the undetectable, or the unpreventable methods of espionage now available.

In the instant case DuPont was in the midst of constructing a plant. Although after construction the finished plant would have protected much of the process from view, during the period of construction the trade secret was exposed to view from the air. To require DuPont to put a roof over the unfinished plant to guard its secret would impose an enormous expense to prevent nothing more than a school boy's trick. We introduce here no new or radical ethic since our ethos has never given moral sanction to piracy. The market place must not deviate far from our mores. We should not require a person or corporation to take unreasonable precautions to prevent another from doing that which he ought not do in the first place. Reasonable precautions against predatory eyes we may require, but an impenetrable fortress is an unreasonable requirement, and we are not disposed to burden industrial inventors with such a duty in order to protect the fruits of their efforts. "Improper" will always be a word of many nuances, determined by time, place, and circumstances. We therefore need not proclaim a catalogue of commercial improprieties. Clearly, however, one of its commandments does say "thou shall not appropriate a trade secret through deviousness under circumstances in which countervailing defenses are not reasonably available."

Having concluded that aerial photography, from whatever altitude, is an improper method of discovering the trade secrets exposed during construction of the DuPont plant, we need not worry about whether the flight pattern chosen by the Christophers violated any federal aviation regulations. Regardless of whether the flight was legal or illegal in that sense, the espionage was an improper means of discovering DuPont's trade secret. The decision of the trial court is affirmed and the case remanded to that court for proceedings on the merits.

Notes and Questions

1. *Improper means.* What standard does the *duPont* court provide to determine whether a defendant's conduct was "improper?" What sorts of factors are courts likely to deem relevant in applying that standard? Why did the court find the defendants' conduct improper in the *duPont* case? Does the concept of "reaping where one has not sown," or "taking a free ride," discussed in Chapter 1, figure into the court's analysis?

The Uniform Trade Secrets Act defines "improper means" as follows: " 'Improper means' includes theft, bribery, misrepresentation, breach or inducement of a breach of a duty to maintain secrecy, or espionage through electronic or other means." UNIFORM TRADE SECRETS ACT § 1(1) (1985). Note that the Uniform Act categorizes breaches of confidential duty as one form of improper conduct, while Restatement of Torts section 757 categorizes improper conduct and breaches of confidential duty separately. RESTATEMENT OF TORTS § 757(a) & (b) (1939). Compare the Uniform Act provision with comment f of the Restatement, set forth in the *duPont* court's opinion. Is the determination of a claim likely to differ depending on whether the court applies the Uniform Act or the Restatement section 757 standard for improper conduct? See RESTATEMENT (THIRD) OF UNFAIR COMPETITION §§ 40, 43 (Tentative Draft No. 4, 1993).

2. *Proper means.* If the defendant's (or its source's) means of obtaining the trade secret are "proper," and there is no duty of confidentiality, the defendant is free to use or disclose the trade secret with impunity. The *duPont* court observes that proper means include independent discovery and

reverse engineering. Why should discovery through reverse engineering be deemed proper? Could the defendants in *duPont* argue that their activities only constituted reverse engineering? How might their activities be distinguished from the type of reverse engineering the court had in mind? What if the defendants had waited and taken aerial photographs of the fully completed duPont plant and tried to learn the plaintiff's secret process from those photographs? Would their conduct still be improper?

CORPORATE SPYING, THE RIGHT WAY

Kathleen Pender.
San Francisco Chronicle.[9]
May 30, 1985, at 27.

Companies that want to snoop on the competition don't have to rifle through trash bins, ply competitors with drinks and run phony help-wanted adds just to interview competitor's employees.

There are plenty of "legally and ethically acceptable ways" to spy on competitors, said Leila Kight, president of a Washington-based research firm that is conducting a seminar in San Francisco this week on corporate intelligence gathering.

Kight's firm, Washington Researchers Ltd., once had a client who wanted to know the plant production of a gelatin capsule manufacturer.

"We had two days to do it. We placed two strategic phone calls. The first was to the plant's union representative. We asked about the number and length of shifts, down-time and who supplied the equipment. Then we called the equipment supplier and asked him about the number of machines (he had sold to the plant) and machine capacity," Kight said.

With that information, estimating the plant's production was a simple calculation. Kight simply took shift length, subtracted down-time and multiplied by the number of shifts per day, the number of machines and the machine capacity per hour.

"If we had asked the union representative directly, 'How much of this do you manufacture?' I am not sure we would have gotten the answer," she said.

Kight believes such tactics are ethical as long as the researchers identify themselves, their companies and their general areas of interest. Many corporate information-seekers go beyond Kight's ethical bounds.

For three years, Kight polled seminar participants about seven hypothetical research strategies, all of which assumed varying degrees of misrepresentation or manipulation. The results imply that business ethics are taking a beating.

While only 30 percent said they would pose as a student job seeker to gain information about a competitor, 70 percent said they would buy

9. © San Francisco Chronicle, 1985. Reprinted by permission.

drinks for competitors at an industry meeting to solicit sensitive information.

The respondents attributed far more ruthless behavior to their competitors—62 percent said other companies would send in undercover job seekers and 87 percent believed others would take advantage of tipsy competitors.

Corporate intelligence gatherers "are under a great deal of pressure," Kight said, "and the longer somebody is involved in intelligence gathering, the more adventuresome he may become."

Not all intelligence experts have abandoned ethics. "At the other end of the spectrum, I have had two people who wouldn't give their company information they found that had been over-disclosed (by a competitor) in a federal document," she said.

Some companies are so afraid of Securities and Exchange Commission regulations that they disclose more information than is required. Kight took advantage of over-disclosure to sleuth out information about Airsignal, a small division of MCI Telecommunications Corp.

"We knew MCI had bought Airsignal from Xerox, which had bought it from Western Union International. We went back to the Western Union documents and found out a lot of information about Airsignal. It was two years old, but it was a base," she said.

The best source of leaks is not published sources, but people. "Often, by being very direct and very bold, you can get people to cough up things you wouldn't believe," Kight said.

Ignorance and intrigue lead many people to let corporate secrets out of the bag. "Some just aren't thinking that the information may be damaging, especially if you ask for it innocuously. A lot of people will talk to you because they are interested in the topic of the conversation. Most people are more personally loyal to their own product, their own advancement, than they are to the company."

Kight's firm was founded in 1973 as an independent information service, which currently researches information for $85 an hour. Most of its clients are Fortune 500 companies who call when their own research staffs get overloaded or when they want to keep their identity confidential.

* * *

In 1978, Kight's firm was the only one offering corporate intelligence seminars. Today, she has several competitors, including McGraw–Hill. "In the last few years there has been a huge rush of companies trying to pin down information about the competitors," she said.

Most companies have been slow to develop defenses against this build-up in intelligence forces. Kight said she once offered a seminar on how to prevent prying, "but it bombed."

Companies "have a right to protect themselves. A company that does it well is admirable," Kight said. "But I look at this as a sporting event. The cleverest players come out ahead."

WHAT RESEARCHERS WILL DO FOR INFORMATION[10]

Research strategies	Affirmative responses: Researcher's own company would use this technique.	Researcher would use this technique.	Researcher believes other companies use this technique.
1. Researcher poses as graduate student working on a thesis. Researcher tells source that dorm phones are very busy, so researcher will call back rather than have phone calls returned. This way, researcher's real identity is protected.	39.6%	42.6%	75.6%
2. Researcher calls the V.P. while s/he is at lunch, hoping to find the secretary who may have some information but is less likely to be suspicious about researcher's motives.	60.6%	68.7%	81.7%
3. Researcher calls competitor's suppliers and distributors, pretending to do a study of the entire industry. Researcher poses as a representative of a private research firm and works at home during the project so that the company's identity is protected.	46.1%	54.6%	81.0%
4. The competitor's representative is coming to a local college to recruit employees. Researcher poses as a student job-seeker to learn recruiting practices and some other general information about competitor.	30.1%	35.4%	62.0%
5. The researcher is asked to verify rumors that the competitor is planning to open a new plant in a small southern town. The researcher poses as an agent from a manufacturer looking for a site similar to the one that the competitor supposedly would need. Researcher uses this cover to become friendly with local representatives of the chamber of commerce, newspapers, realtors, etc.	42.4%	49.1%	75.5%
6. Researcher corners a competitor employee at a national conference, such as American Marketing Association, and offers to buy drinks at the hotel bar. Several drinks later, the researcher asks the hard questions.	70.6%	67.1%	86.8%
7. Researcher finds an individual who works for the competitor to serve as an informant to researcher's company.	39.1%	39.1%	73.8%

KEY ■ Researcher's own company would use this technique. □ Researcher would use this technique. □ Researcher believes other companies use this technique.

Source: Washington Researchers Ltd.

Notes and Questions

1. *Misappropriation of trade secrets?* Assume that the researcher was successful in eliciting trade secrets in each of the seven scenarios described in the chart, and apply the standards set forth in the *duPont* opinion. In your opinion, might the researcher be liable for trade secret misappropriation? Did Ms. Kight's firm's efforts to learn the plant production of the gelatin capsule manufacturer exceeded the bounds?

10. © Washington Researchers, 1985. Graph reprinted by permission of Washington Researchers, Washington, D.C.

2. *Protecting trade secrets in litigation.* A business suspecting that a competitor has misappropriated its trade secret faces a dilemma: in order to litigate, the business will probably have to disclose the trade secret in its court filings or through discovery. While the court may grant protective orders to seal the record, bind parties obtaining access to the information to secrecy, or agree to hear sensitive information *in camera*, the risks involved may nonetheless convince the trade secret owner that it stands to lose more than it may gain in the litigation. For a discussion of these and related considerations, see M. JAGER, TRADE SECRETS LAW, § 5.06 (1989).

3. *Remedies for trade secret misappropriation.* Both injunctive relief and damages are available to trade secret plaintiffs. As in other contexts, the plaintiff must demonstrate irreparable injury and an inadequate remedy at law in order to obtain an injunction. This is relatively easy in many trade secret cases because a defendant's disclosure or use of a trade secret may significantly reduce its value or utterly destroy it, and the monetary loss to a trade secret owner may be difficult to measure.

Assuming that an injunction is warranted, how long should it last? Should it be perpetual, prohibiting the defendant from ever disclosing or using the plaintiff's information, or should it be shorter? If the latter, how should its duration be measured? Compare Valco Cincinnati, Inc. v. N & D Machining Serv., 24 Ohio St.3d 41, 492 N.E.2d 814 (1986) (court uses perpetual injunction as a means of penalizing particularly reprehensible conduct) with K–2 Ski Co. v. Head Ski Co., 506 F.2d 471, 183 U.S.P.Q. 724 (9th Cir.1974) (injunction should be granted for the period of time it would have taken the defendant to reverse engineer the trade secret or obtain it through independent development). See UNIFORM TRADE SECRETS ACT § 2(a) (1985) ("Upon application to the court, an injunction shall be terminated when the trade secret has ceased to exist, but the injunction may be continued for an additional reasonable period of time in order to eliminate commercial advantage that otherwise would be derived from the misappropriation."). With regard to the scope, or breadth, of injunctions against use of trade secrets, see M. JAGER, TRADE SECRETS LAW, § 7.02[4] (1989); RESTATEMENT (THIRD) OF UNFAIR COMPETITION § 44 (Tentative Draft No. 4, 1993).

Courts have employed several different means of measuring damages in trade secret cases. The Uniform Trade Secrets Act, as revised in 1985, provides that damages may include "both the actual loss caused by misappropriation and the unjust enrichment caused by misappropriation that is not taken into account in computing actual loss." *Id.*, § 3(a). Thus, to the extent that the defendant's wrongfully gained profit exceeds the plaintiff's actual loss, that excess is added to the amount of plaintiff's loss. Under what kinds of circumstances might the defendant's gain exceed the plaintiff's loss?

In lieu of damages measured by actual loss and unjust enrichment, the Uniform Act permits a plaintiff to recover the equivalent of a reasonable royalty payment for the defendant's use of the trade secret. *Id.* In that case, the court seeks to determine what a reasonable licensee would have been willing to pay and a reasonable licensor would have been willing to accept in arm's length negotiations for a license to use the trade secret.

The Uniform Act also authorizes an award of exemplary damages of up to twice the amount of compensatory damages in cases of "willful and malicious misappropriation." UNIFORM TRADE SECRETS ACT, § 3(b) (1985). Moreover, in a distinct departure from the common law, the Uniform Act provides for an award of attorney's fees in cases of willful and malicious misappropriation and in certain cases of bad faith. *Id.*, § 4. For a more thorough discussion of damage awards in trade secrets cases, see Michael A. Rosenhouse, Annotation, *Proper Measure and Elements of Damages for Misappropriation of Trade Secret*, 11 A.L.R.4th 12 (1982); M. JAGER, TRADE SECRETS LAW § 7.03 (1988).

A number of states have enacted criminal penalties for theft of trade secrets. *See, e.g.,* MINN. STAT. § 609.52 (1990); N.Y. PENAL LAW § 165.07 (McKinney 1991). For a discussion of criminal prosecution of trade secret theft, see Lederman, *Criminal Liability for Breach of Confidential Commercial Information*, 38 EMORY L. J. 921 (1989); Donald M. Zupanek, Annotation, *Criminal Liability for Misappropriation of Trade Secret*, 84 A.L.R.3d 967 (1976).

4. *Protecting trade secrets abroad.* Assume that your client wishes to engage in international business transactions in which it will use its trade secrets in foreign countries or will license others to do so. How will you advise the client with regard to the risks and proper precautions to protect the secrets? While the majority of nations presently have patent, copyright and trademark laws, trade secret provisions are not so universal. The United States International Trade Commission recently reported on the results of a survey completed by 431 U.S. companies regarding their experiences with international protection of a variety of types of intellectual property. These companies named twenty-six countries which provided no trade secret protection at all. Among foreign nations that did provide some protection, many only went so far as to enforce nondisclosure contracts, declining to provide relief against persons outside of contract who induce others to breach their nondisclosure contract, or take trade secrets by theft or other forms of industrial espionage. Moreover, among those countries that would enforce nondisclosure contracts, a number placed very short time limits on their enforceability. The surveyed U.S. companies also complained about the inadequacy of the remedies afforded when foreign trade secret laws were violated. For example, some countries provided no preliminary or final injunctive relief. See UNITED STATES INTERNATIONAL TRADE COMMISSION, FOREIGN PROTECTION OF INTELLECTUAL PROPERTY RIGHTS AND THE EFFECT ON U.S. INDUSTRY AND TRADE, REPORT TO THE UNITED STATES TRADE REPRESENTATIVE, INVESTIGATION NO. 332–245, UNDER SECTION 332(g) OF THE TARIFF ACT OF 1930 (1988).

The Agreement on Trade–Related Aspects of Intellectual Property Rights, Including Trade in Counterfeit Goods ("TRIPs"), incorporated in the Uruguay Round of multilateral trade negotiations under the auspices of the GATT, may improve the situation. TRIPs Article 39 requires member nations to protect natural and legal persons' "undisclosed information" against unauthorized acquitition or use in a manner contrary to honest commercial practices so long as such information in question

—is secret in the sense that it is not, as a body or in the precise configuration and assembly of its components, generally known among or readily accessible to persons within the circles that normally deal with the kind of information in question;

—has commercial value because it is secret; and

—has been subject to reasonable steps under the circumstances, by the person lawfully in control of the information, to keep it secret.

II. OWNERSHIP OF TRADE SECRETS

STRUCTURAL DYNAMICS RESEARCH CORP. v. ENGINEERING MECHANICS RESEARCH CORP.

United States District Court, E.D. Michigan, 1975.
401 F.Supp. 1102.

FEIKENS, DISTRICT JUDGE.

I.

Structural Dynamics Research Corporation (SDRC) brought this action against three former employees, Kant Kothawala, Karan Surana and Robert Hildebrand, for unfair competition, misappropriation and misuse of confidential and trade secret material, breach of confidential disclosure agreements and interference with SDRC's customer relations, and against Engineering Mechanics Research Corporation (EMRC) for conspiring with the individual defendants to accomplish the above purposes. It seeks both damages and a permanent injunction.

* * *

* * * This case was tried before the court sitting without a jury.

Both SDRC and EMRC are engaged in the business of structural analysis and testing. They are also engaged in the development of computer programs for such purposes for use in their business and for lease to other users.

Kothawala, Surana and Hildebrand were all formerly employed by SDRC in various technical capacities. Kothawala was employed by SDRC between August 3, 1972 and December 31, 1972 as a member of its Technical Staff.[2] Surana worked for SDRC from February of 1970 to January of 1973, initially as a project leader in the computer operations department and later as a member of the Technical Staff. Hildebrand was employed by SDRC as a project manager between August of 1972 and December 31, 1972. Each signed an Employee Patent and Confi-

2. The Technical Staff is comprised of employees having significant technical expertise in the various areas of interest to SDRC. These employees provide technical assistance to project engineers and engage in research and development.

dential Information Agreement while so employed and, in addition, Kothawala executed an Employment Agreement.

These three individuals are now employed by EMRC. Kothawala is the President and sole shareholder. Surana is Vice–President of Engineering. Hildebrand is Manager of Applications.

Structural analysis involves, generally speaking, the prediction of how a physical structure will react when forces are applied to it. One of the methods used to solve structural analysis problems is a finite element computer program. The technical part of this dispute concerns two such programs. These computer programs are used to obtain an approximation of the reaction of a physical structure when forces are applied to it. This approximation is termed a mathematical model. It simulates actual conditions.

[In 1971, after attending a conference in which isoparametric elements were discussed, Surana began to investigate isoparametric technology. He concluded that an isoparametric program would be useful to SDRC in measuring stress on curved surfaces, and notified SDRC management of his conclusion. The management encouraged Surana to continue his efforts, though it required him to continue devoting time to other projects.]

In April, 1972 SDRC gave formal recognition to Surana's isoparametric research by the establishment of a time charge account. By that time Surana had reduced to writing certain preliminary equations, computations and sketches necessary to the development of a program. He continued preliminary development work as time permitted until August.

[In August, 1972, Kothawala and Hildebrand came to work at SDRC. Shortly thereafter, Surana met with the technical staff and explained what he had been doing with regard to the isoparametric program. The group gave Surana authority to devote all his time to developing the program, and assigned Surana and Kothawala responsibility for drafting a formal written proposal. Kothawala was eventually assigned supervisory responsibility for the project.]

On August 23, 1972 Kothawala and Surana submitted a formal proposal. It stressed the importance of the proposed program to SDRC, the advantages and superiority of isoparametric elements, the significance of Surana's technical work to date and the uniqueness of the program. It also contained cost estimates and a timetable for completion. SDRC relied on these representations since no one employed by SDRC at this time other than Surana had any significant knowledge of isoparametric element theory or application.

On October 25, 1972 Kothawala and Surana issued a technical status report. Surana had developed the program to the point of running test problems. Kothawala stated that the program would "revolutionize" SDRC's problem solving ability. SDRC management felt this report established the feasibility of the program. Surana continued his work on the program throughout the rest of the year. He named the program "NIESA", an acronym for "Numerically Integrated Elements for System Analysis".

[In December 1972, Kothawala, who was dissatisfied with his opportunities at SDRC, requested to be released from his contract. SDRC released him from the contract except for the provisions pertaining to post-termination activities. Kothawala went to Detroit and established EMRC. Hildebrand also gave SDRC notice and went to Detroit to work for EMRC as Manager of Applications. Shortly thereafter, Surana gave his notice, staying only long enough to prepare a handwritten description of the program's status and explain the program to other SDRC employees. In March, 1973, Surana began to work for EMRC as Vice President of Engineering.]

Shortly after Kothawala arrived back in Detroit, he called upon American Motors Corporation (AMC). He had learned of its interest in acquiring structural analysis programs while employed by SDRC. On January 10, 1973 he proposed to develop for AMC a conventional, non-isoparametric, finite element program.

Then, on February 27, 1973, before AMC had acted on this proposal, Kothawala and Surana, who had now joined EMRC, submitted a new proposal for an isoparametric program substantially the same as NIESA in design, element library, solver and basic capabilities. Their proposal repeated the representations made to SDRC as to the uniqueness, superiority and value of an isoparametric element program. The written materials contained a number of paragraphs and a drawing taken from Kothawala's and Surana's August 23, 1972 formal proposal to SDRC.

In order to prepare a recommendation to its management, AMC personnel asked questions regarding specifics of the proposal. Kothawala responded by an undated letter. It is apparent from a comparison of the undated letter with the recommendation of Joseph Balnave, manager of AMC's computer center, written in mid-March, that the undated letter was written between February 27 and mid-March, since Balnave's recommendation of mid-March contains many of the specifics set out in the undated letter. In the undated letter Kothawala stated that the program being offered to AMC was partially finished, 1200 hours having been spent on it already and only 500 hours remaining for completion. Since defendants had not commenced working on the program at that time, it is clear that Kothawala offered American Motors the benefit of the time spent by him and Surana at SDRC. The partially finished program thus is SDRC's NIESA.

In March of 1973 EMRC commenced program development under an informal arrangement. In June formal approval for the funding of the program was obtained from AMC management. The program was completed about November 1, 1973. At that time Kothawala furnished AMC with certain program documentation which he stated was confidential and the property of EMRC. He instructed AMC to keep all aspects of the program in confidence in order to prevent any copying of the documents or program. He also refused AMC's request for a copy of the program code on grounds of confidentiality.

EMRC continued development of the program and added additional capabilities. In February of 1974 EMRC began marketing its program under the name "NISA", an acronym for "Numerically Integrated Elements for System Analysis".

SDRC, previously unaware of defendants' development activity, speeded up its own development work on NIESA. NIESA, renamed SUPERB, was placed on the market in April of 1974.

NISA and NIESA–SUPERB are very similar programs. The basic difference between them is that NISA is more fully developed, having the additional capacity to perform dynamic and heat conduction analysis. These additional capacities were included in Kothawala's and Surana's plan for the development of NIESA at SDRC. Thus, NISA is in a sense the implementation of the plan for development of NIESA.

* * *

II.

Plaintiff SDRC makes three basic arguments.

(a) Breach of trust on the part of the individual defendants (formerly employees of plaintiff) who used for their own advantage trade secrets owned by plaintiff and acquired by the individual defendants in a confidential relationship with plaintiff;

(b) Breach of contractual duty not to use or disclose confidential information;

(c) Unfair competition.

* * *

In this case Surana and Kothawala did not obtain the claimed trade secrets through improper means. In substantial measure they were the developers and innovators of a general purpose isoparametric computer program. They were hired by SDRC for research and development activity in this very field, and the manner of their acquisition of knowledge of this technology can in no sense be said to have been obtained improperly.

Does their subsequent use or disclosure of this technology, assuming it to be a trade secret, breach a duty of trust owed by these individual defendants to plaintiff? The *Restatement [of the Law of Torts]*, at 4, suggests this question by its comment: "apart from breach of contract, abuse of confidence or impropriety in the means of procurement, trade secrets may be copied as freely as devices which are not secret".

The relationship giving rise to a duty is not necessarily dependent upon contract; it may be based on agency principles or on specific dealings between parties in which a situation of trust arises and out of which sought-to-be-protected knowledge is acquired. Vital to a consideration of the creation of duty in such situations is the key question as to how the person acquiring such trade secret knowledge obtained it. If the subject matter of the trade secret is in being and an employee learns about it in the course of his employment in a relationship of confidence, the duty not to use or disclose trade secret knowledge adversely to his employer arises. On the other hand, if the subject matter of the trade secret is brought into being because of the initiative of the employee in its creation, innovation or development even though the relationship is one of confidence, no duty arises since the employee may then have an interest in the subject matter at least equal to that of his employer or in any event, such knowledge is a part of the employee's skill and experience. In such a case, absent an express contractual obligation by the employee not to use or disclose such confidential information acquired during his employment adverse to his employer's interest, he is free to use or disclose it in subsequent employment activity.

In *Wexler v. Greenberg*, 399 Pa. 569, 160 A.2d 430 (1960), the Pennsylvania Supreme Court held that in the absence of a contractual obligation not to use or disclose, no duty arose from the employment relationship itself that would prevent a chemist from using and disclosing secret chemical formulae developed by him in the course of his former employment. The court distinguished the cases in which an employer discloses to his employee a preexisting trade secret from those in which the employee himself develops the trade secret sought to be protected. A further distinction was then drawn within the category of employee-developed secrets. Where the employer assigns the employee to a specific development task and commits considerable resources and supervision to the project, a confidential relationship arises that prevents the employee from using or disclosing the fruits of his research. When, on the other hand, the developments are the product of the application of the employee's own skill, "without any appreciable assistance by way of information or great expense or supervision [the employer], outside of the normal expenses of his job", 160 A.2d at 436, he has "an unqualified privilege" to use and disclose the trade secrets so developed. 160 A.2d at 437. *Accord, New Method Die & Cut–Out Co. v. Milton Bradley Co.*, 289 Mass. 277, 194 N.E. 80, 82 (1935) (defendant employee not required to maintain secrecy where he "took part to a substantial extent in developing the process", but "was not employed specifically for this purpose".)

While the question is concededly a close one, the court holds that the isoparametric program developed on the initial encouragement—and under the supervision—of Surana and Kothawala falls within the latter category.

Surana and Kothawala do not owe SDRC a duty not to use or disclose its trade secrets by reason of a relationship of confidence in employment. As the substantial developers and innovators of this technology they have an interest in it and unless they expressly contracted with SDRC not to use or disclose such knowledge or information in future employment activity, there is no duty imposed upon them by reason of their employment relationship with SDRC. Nor is such a duty created by any equitable doctrine of quasi-contract; i. e., a contract implied in law.

Accordingly, the court turns to the remaining question. Are there obligations imposed on the individual defendants not to use or disclose confidential information acquired in and during the course of their employment at SDRC because of express contractual agreements into which they entered?

III.

Here, all three individual defendants entered into an Employee Patent and Confidential Information Agreement. In it they agree:

> "(d) At no time either during his employment, on either a part or full-time basis with the Company or subsequent to termination of such employment will Employee divulge to any person, firm or corporation, or use (other than as required by the Company in the course of his employment) any privileged or confidential information, trade secret or other proprietary information including but not limited to information relating to the experimental and research work of the Corporation, its methods, processes, tools, machinery, formulae, drawings, or appliances imparted or divulged to, gained or developed by or otherwise discovered by Employee during his employment with the Company." * * *

Kothawala also executed a separate employment contract. He himself drafted some of its terms. SDRC had submitted a proposed contract to him. He found it unacceptable, insisted on modifications and then submitted his draft which was executed. It contains the following provisions:

> * * *
>
> "4. Neither during the period of employment nor at any time thereafter will Kothawala disclose to anyone any confidential information or trade secrets concerning the business affairs of SDRC, including but not limited to information relating to the experimental and research work of SDRC, their methods, processes, tools, machinery, formulae, drawings, or appliances imparted or divulged to, gained or developed by or otherwise discovered by Kothawala during his employment with SDRC. Upon termination of his employment, Kothawala will return to SDRC all objects, materials, devices or substances including notes, records, drawings, sketches, recordings, descriptions, samples, specimens, prototypes, models, blueprints, analyses, programs, or the like, and including any facsimile, replica, photograph or reproduction thereof, belonging to SDRC or relating to their respective business."
>
> * * *

The agreements not to disclose confidential information impose obligations by their clear terms since these undertakings do not exclude information, technology or knowledge which the employee himself discovers, develops or contributes. Thus, if the contracts are valid and enforceable, defendants are under obligations not to use or disclose confidential information gained while employed at SDRC.

Some courts have held that such express contracts create a confidential relationship between employer and employee, breach of which results in liability. They use the doctrine of trade secrets in the decisional process. This court finds such an approach too restrictive, especially in an area of knowledge and rapid technological change such as the computer field.

The express contracts in issue apply not only to trade secrets but also to privileged, proprietary and confidential information. In this they are analogous to the breadth of coverage recognized under agency principles. In *Shwayder Chemical Metallurgy Corp. v. Baum*, 45 Mich. App. 220, 206 N.W.2d 484 (1973) it was held that while the process plaintiff sought to protect was not a trade secret, defendant stood in a fiduciary and confidential relationship to plaintiff, that he breached the duties and obligations arising from that relationship and was therefore liable for damages. *See Restatement (Second) of Agency* §§ 395 and 396.

These considerations apply to the express contracts in issue. Defendants are liable for breach of their contracts and are answerable in damages if they used or disclosed confidential information, knowledge or technology gained while employed at SDRC. This is so even though such information, knowledge or technology is not itself a trade secret.

[The court determines that Ohio law applies in the interpretation and enforcement of the contractual provisions.]

This brings the court to the issue of breach.

It is true that initial recognition of the importance of isoparametric elements in a new program, and the feasibility of development of such a program, must be credited to Surana and, to a lesser extent, to Kothawala. However, this information was acquired in the course of their employment and a fulfillment of their specific assigned responsibilities. This information had business value and SDRC had the sole right because of the express contracts to exploit the advantage. SDRC's possession of this information gave it an opportunity to gain an advantage over its competitors who did not have the information. The August 23, 1972 proposal by Kothawala is a significant compilation of marketing and technical planning for the program and this document was therefore proprietary and confidential. The court finds that SDRC relied on the representations of Kothawala and Surana including those contained in the August 23, 1972 document in its decision to devote its resources to the program. SDRC reasonably anticipated that part of its business advantage would flow from its early entry in the market—an advantage recognized by both sides. SDRC did not anticipate that the very employees who extolled the merits of the program and caused SDRC to undertake its development would use the same information to develop a competitive product and achieve the advantage of being first in the market. These actions by defendants breached their contractual obligations not to use or disclose confidential information.

The technical planning and development of NIESA to its stage of development in January, 1973, including the selection of elements, solver routine, organization of sub-routines, coding, and other factors contributing to the efficiency and effectiveness of the program, constituted important and confidential information, particularly prior to public release of the program. The technical accomplishments of Surana and Kothawala reflected in their work on NIESA amounted to a compilation of information which gave SDRC a competitive advantage. The existence or availability of abstract technical data does not detract from the confidentiality of the combination of such parts and data into a program of the type under consideration. This was conceded by Kothawala and confirmed by defendants' actions in dealing with the trade when great emphasis was placed by the defendants on the confidential nature of the NISA program and the competitive importance to EMRC in protecting such confidentiality.

The status report prepared for SDRC by Kathawala and Surana in October includes such information and it is likewise confidential and proprietary. This information had value and was confidential to SDRC. Surana's use of this information for defendants' benefit was a breach of his contract. This also holds true with respect to Kothawala, who hired Surana and participated in the unlawful use of information obtained at SDRC, and who, as sole shareholder of EMRC, is presently the primary beneficiary of the illicit information.

Confidentiality of information can be determined from the manner in which defendants themselves treated the information prior to the litigation. Here the record is replete with statements by the defendants both to SDRC and to AMC as to the value, uniqueness and confidentiality of the program.

A quantity of documents belonging to SDRC were also found in possession of defendants when this action was commenced. These included:

* * *

> Internal SDRC documents pertaining to the NIESA program including the August 23 and October 25 documents, customer information and prospective research and development activities.
>
> Surana's notes prepared as part of his development work on NIESA. The court finds these notes to have significant value both in the case of NIESA and NISA.

The court does not credit defendant's explanation that these documents were permitted to be taken from SDRC's office. The court finds that they were taken without permission.

At a pretrial conference the court directed defendants to make a copy of the static portion of the NISA code available to plaintiff's counsel and experts pursuant to a protective order. The code which was furnished was dated December, 1974, and reflected many revisions made subsequent to defendants' initial code. Defendants have represented that no prior version of the NISA code remained. Portions of the NISA code were compared to the NIESA code as it existed in January, 1973. On the basis of this comparison, plaintiff's experts, Dr. Anderson of the Department of Aerospace Engineering at the University of Michigan, and Michael Coble, a computer programmer also affiliated with the University, concluded that defendants must have copied from the NIESA code. They made a careful analysis of the two programs and found not only similarity in the overall structure and organization (some of which might be explainable on functional grounds) but they found identical segments of code which were solely arbitrary and, most significantly, deviations or quasi-mistakes which, in their judgment, could only be explained by copying. Victor Nicholas, who completed the development of NIESA–SUPERB at SDRC, testified that the input data cards prepared by Surana for NIESA were taken verbatim into NISA. Except for cross-examination, defendants did not address these specifics relied on by the experts, but attributed such similarities as existed to Surana's memory. The court does not accept this explanation. Memory alone cannot explain the specifics which according to the experts do not make sense but are explainable only by copying. The court finds that defendants copied from the physical NIESA code.

The technical and business information which the court has found to have been misappropriated by defendants was treated by SDRC in a manner consistent with the preservation of its confidentiality. Although SDRC did not use the ultimate in policing measures, the professional calibre of its employees, and the nature of its development work made heavy-handed measures unnecessary. Moreover, the confidential nature of development work was specifically called to each employee's attention in his individual confidential disclosure agreement. The court finds that defendants Kothawala and Surana knew that information pertaining to NIESA was confidential and proprietary to SDRC.

SDRC did not disclose confidential information to outside parties in a manner inconsistent with preservation of confidentiality. To the extent that limited disclosure may have been made to representatives of United States Steel Corporation, that company's relationship to SDRC as its largest shareholder and a business partner was not inconsistent with the preservation of confidentiality.

* * *

The court has held that the NISA program of EMRC was developed through the use of the plaintiff's confidential information regarding the NIESA–SUPERB projects. The fact that the NISA program is at a later stage of completion that the status of NIESA at the time that Surana left SDRC or the fact that EMRC may have modified and added additional capabilities than those existing at the time that Surana left is not a defense to this action. There is no requirement that the defendants use the information in exactly the form in which they received it. Furthermore, the court finds that the later state of development of NISA is directly attributable to the head start that the use of SDRC's confidential information gave to EMRC in its pursuit of the NISA project.

* * *

Finally, the court finds that EMRC, the corporation of which defendant Kothawala is sole shareholder, is the entity through which this confidential information is being purveyed in the marketplace; it is liable with the individual defendants for agreeing with them to carry out this improper purpose. In view of these findings, it is unnecessary to consider plaintiff's contention as to unfair competition.

* * *

Notes and Questions

1. *Ownership of trade secrets created by employees.* The *Structural Dynamics* court set forth the common-law rule about ownership of trade secrets created by employees:

> Where the employer assigns the employee to a specific development task and commits considerable resources and supervision to the project, a confidential relationship arises that prevents the employee from using or disclosing the fruits of his research. When, on the other hand, the developments are the product of the application of the employee's own skill, "without any appreciable assistance by way of information or great expense or supervision [from the employer], outside of the normal expenses of his job," 160 A.2d at 436, he has "an unqualified privilege" to use and disclose the trade secrets so developed.

Structural Dynamics, 401 F.Supp. at 1112 (quoting Wexler v. Greenberg, 399 Pa. 569, 582–83, 160 A.2d 430, 436–37, 125 U.S.P.Q. 471 (1960)).

One practitioner-scholar has approached the issue of ownership by dividing employee inventors into three groups: "specific inventive," "general inventive," and "non-inventive."

> "Specific inventive" employment applies to an employee who is either (1) hired to invent a specific invention or (2) is assigned the task of making a specific invention or improvement to existing technology. In both cases, a specific invention or end result is contemplated. Specific inventive employment applies to the class of employees who are hired or employed to "invent," including research scientists, design engineers, and other employees whose "work" involves specific inventive activity. * * *
>
> "General inventive" employment applies to the same class of employees who are subject to specific inventive employment, except that no specific invention or end result is contemplated. General research or design work usually is involved and, in many instances, the employee volunteers, or is encouraged by the employer, to pursue his or her creative instincts, even though they may diverge from assigned work. * * *
>
> "Non-inventive" employment, as the term implies, does not involve any expectation of inventive activity. Shop or manufacturing employees, as well as non-technical employees, fall into this category.

Gullette, *State Legislation Governing Ownership Rights in Inventions Under Employee Invention Agreements*, 62 J. PAT. OFF. SOC. 732, 733 (1980).[11]

The employer is generally found to own inventions of specific inventive employees. Courts have reasoned that specific inventive employees impliedly assign their inventions to their employer. The Supreme Court explained the rationale behind the rule in Solomons v. United States, 137 U.S. 342, 346, 11 S.Ct. 88, 89, 34 L.Ed. 667, 669 (1890):

> If one is employed to devise or perfect an instrument, or a means for accomplishing a prescribed result, he cannot, after successfully accomplishing the work for which he was employed, plead title thereto as against his employer. That which he has been employed and paid to accomplish becomes, when accomplished, the property of his employer. Whatever rights as an individual he may have had in and to his inventive powers, and that which they are able to accomplish, he has sold in advance to his employer.

By contrast, noninventive employees generally will be found to retain ownership of their creations, even though they made them at work, with the employer's materials, or during work hours (though the invention may be subject to a shop right in the employer, as described in note 2 below).

General inventive employees pose the difficult problems, and the results of employers' claims of an implied assignment by such employees are mixed. The court's finding may be influenced by any of a number of factors, including the nature and scope of the employment relationship, the amount of money or other resources the employer devoted to the inventive activity, how closely the employee's invention is related to the employer's business, whether the employee has assigned inventions to the employer in the past, and any other evidence of an implicit understanding between the parties about ownership of inventions. Compare Cahill v. Regan, 5 N.Y.2d 292, 184 N.Y.S.2d 348, 157 N.E.2d 505, 121 U.S.P.Q. 58 (1959) (Court found defendant employee owned the re-usable can he developed during his employment. The court reasoned that employment to design or construct or devise methods of manufacture is not the same as specific employment to invent. Moreover, while the defendant was told to develop the idea of the reusable can, which he had already conceived, he had not initially been directed to conceive of the idea.), with White's Electronics, Inc. v. Teknetics, Inc., 67 Or.App. 63, 677 P.2d 68 (1984) (Plaintiff, a manufacturer of metal detectors, hired defendant, an electrical engineer, "to invent and develop improvements in [plaintiff's] product line." Defendant conceived of an idea that would enable a metal detector automatically to provide the user with target identifying information. The court found that if the defendant made the invention while employed, he was obliged to assign it to the plaintiff, especially since he had assigned inventions to plaintiff in the past.)

In the *Structural Dynamics* case, who does the court find to be the owner of the computer program under the common-law rule—the plaintiff, or the defendants? Why? What was the impact of the nondisclosure agreement the defendants signed?

Note that the same common-law rule for determining ownership of employee-made inventions applies, regardless of whether the owner decides to rely on trade secret law or apply for a patent. While an application for patent must be made in the name of the inventor, an assignment of ownership implied by state law will vest title to the resulting patent in the employer. For further information and insights about the rule, see I R. MILGRIM, MILGRIM ON TRADE SECRETS, § 5.02[4] (1991); Van Slyke & Friedman, *Employer's Rights to Inventions and Patents of Its Officers, Directors and Employees*, 18 AIPLA Q. J. 127 (1990); Witte & Guttag, *Employee Inventions*, 71 J. PAT. & TRADEMARK OFF. SOC. 467 (1989); Baker & Brunel, *Restructuring the Judicial Evaluation of Employed Inventor's Rights*, 35 ST. LOUIS L. J. 399 (1991).

2. *Shop rights*. When an employee/inventor is found to own the trade secret she developed during her employment, the employer will obtain a shop right in the trade secret if it is related to the employer's business and the employee, in developing it, used her employer's time, facilities, personnel, materials, money or other resources. Some courts have also required that the employee have initially allowed the employer to use the trade secret without paying special compensation for the right. See, e.g., Aetna–Standard Engineering Co. v. Rowland, 343 Pa.Super. 64, 70, 493 A.2d 1375, 1378, 228 U.S.P.Q. 292, 296 (1985). A shop right is an irrevocable, nonexclusive, non-assignable right to use the trade secret, without an obligation to pay royalties. As one court described it: "This is an application of equitable principles. Since the servant uses his master's time, facilities and materials to attain a concrete result, the latter is in equity entitled to use that which embodies his own property" in his business. Cahill v. Regan, 5 N.Y.2d 292, 298, 184 N.Y.S.2d 348, 353, 157 N.E.2d 505, 509, 121 U.S.Q.P. 58, 60 (1959). The shop right rule applies to inventions in which the inventor/employee maintains trade secret protection as well as to inventions that the employee/inventor patents.

For more information on shop rights, see I R. MILGRIM, MILGRIM ON TRADE SECRETS, § 5.02[4][c] (1991); Sondrock, *Evolution and Modern Application of the Shop Right Rule*, 38 BUS. LAW. 953 (1983).

3. *Express assignment provisions*. In order to avoid the uncertainties of the common-law rule of invention ownership (and perhaps to obtain more rights in employee-made inventions than the common law would provide) many employers require employees to sign advance assignment agreements expressly assigning to the employer rights in any inventions they make during their employment. These provisions are generally enforced by the courts, as long as the inventions have some reasonable relationship to the employer's business and do not extend unduly beyond the period of the employee's employment. See, e.g., Ingersoll–Rand v. Ciavatta, 110 N.J. 609, 627, 542 A.2d 879, 888, 8 U.S.P.Q.2d 1537, 1543 (N.J.1988) (court finds employee assignment of inventions made after termination of employment enforceable if reasonable. Such an assignment is not reasonable, and thus is unenforceable if it "(1) extends beyond any apparent protection that the employer reasonably requires; (2) prevents the inventor from seeking other employment; or (3) adversely impacts on the public.") Is widespread use of broad advance assignment agreements likely to have an impact on employees' incentive to invent?

In an effort to avoid employer abuses, some states have enacted statutes to regulate employee invention assignment agreements. See, e.g., CAL. LAB. CODE §§ 2870–2872 (West Supp. 1989) (contractual provision requiring employee to assign rights to inventions is unenforceable with regard to inventions made entirely on employee's own time and with employee's own resources unless the invention relates to employer's business or results from work performed by employee for employer). See Gullette, *State Legislation Governing Ownership Rights in Inventions under Employee Invention Agreements*, 62 J. Pat. Off. Soc. 732 (1980).

4. *Reliance on contract.* In *Structural Dynamics*, the court says it is not relying on trade secret law to determine the respective rights of the parties, but on the express contractual provisions signed by the defendants. Within the context of that case, what are the implications of that decision?

Consider the following criticism of the *Structural Dynamics* opinion:

> We do not accept the analysis in *Structural Dynamics Research Corp. v. Engineering Mechanics Research Corp.*, 401 F.Supp. 1102, 1112, 1118–1119 (E.D.Mich.1975), cited by the plaintiff, in which the court held that two defendants "do not owe [the plaintiff] a duty not to use or disclose its trade secrets by reason of a relationship of confidence in employment" but were nevertheless bound by a general non-disclosure agreement. It is out of harmony with our cases and could turn a non-disclosure agreement into a non-competition agreement open ended and unenforceable as against public policy.

Dynamics Research Corp. v. Analytic Sciences Corp., 9 Mass.App.Ct. 254, 278 n. 32, 400 N.E.2d 1274, 1288 n. 32, 209 U.S.P.Q. 321, 332 n. 32 (1980). What does the court mean? In your opinion, is its criticism valid?

III. GOVERNMENT USE AND DISCLOSURE OF TRADE SECRETS

United States businesses frequently find it necessary to submit trade secret information to state and federal government agencies for regulatory purposes (for example, to obtain clearance to sell a product) or in the course of making bids for government contracts or grants. What happens to the submitter's property rights in the trade secret when this is done?

Both the federal government and the states have extensive freedom of information acts, which require their executive branch agencies to disclose "agency records" to almost anyone who requests them. For example, the federal Freedom of Information Act ("FOIA") provides:

> Each agency, upon any request for records which (A) reasonably describes such records, and (B) is made in accordance with published rules stating the time, place, fees (if any), and procedures to be followed, shall make the records promptly available to any person.

5 U.S.C.A. § 552(a)(3).[12] The purpose of the FOIA, of course, is to keep government open to public scrutiny and accountable to the electorate.

12. While we will not attempt a discussion of individual state freedom of information acts here, students should bear in mind that each state has a statute which re-

There is evidence to indicate, however, that in many cases the chief users of the FOIA are not concerned members of the public seeking to monitor government activity but businesses hoping to learn sensitive information about their competitors. See, e.g., W. CASEY, JR., J. MARTHINSEN & L. MOSS, ENTREPRENEURSHIP, PRODUCTIVITY, AND THE FREEDOM OF INFORMATION ACT, 47–86 (1983); Casey, Marthinsen & Moss, *The Economic Impact of the Freedom of Information Act*, 12 AIPLA Q. J. 76 (1984); Schorr, *How Law is Being Used To Pry Business Secrets From Uncle Sam's Files*, Wall St. J., May 9, 1977, p. 1, col. 6. Obviously, if a private business's trade secrets have become part of a government agency's records, and the agency fully discloses the records to the business' competitors, the business' property interest in the trade secrets will be lost.

Freedom of information statutes generally have specific exemptions which shelter narrowly-drawn categories of documents from disclosure, or leave disclosure of these documents to the discretion of the agencies. They typically have a specific exemption for trade secrets. For example, the federal FOIA has nine exemptions. For our present purposes, exemptions three and four are the most relevant.

Exemption four, 5 U.S.C.A. § 552(b)(4), exempts from mandatory disclosure "trade secrets and commercial or financial information obtained from a person and privileged or confidential." In construing the meaning of "trade secrets" in this context, the United States Court of Appeals for the District of Columbia rejected the broad Restatement of Torts section 757 definition as inconsistent with the language of the FOIA and its underlying policies. Public Citizen Health Research Group v. F.D.A., 704 F.2d 1280, 1288 (D.C.Cir.1983). Instead, the court defined "trade secrets" for purposes of exemption four "in its narrower common law sense, which incorporates a direct relationship between the information at issue and the productive process." *Id.* According to the court, for purposes of FOIA, a trade secret is "a secret, commercially valuable plan, formula, process, or device that is used for the making, preparing, compounding, or processing of trade commodities and that can be said to be the end product of either innovation or substantial effort." *Id.* at 1288–89. Presumably, customer lists, marketing information and practices, as well as some results of research and development, which may be protected as trade secrets under state law, would be excluded.

Exemption four also exempts "confidential commercial or financial information" from mandatory disclosure, which may encompass much of the information excluded by the D.C. Circuit's narrow definition of trade secret. However, in order for information to qualify under this part of the exemption, it must appear that disclosure is likely either to impair the government's ability to obtain necessary information in the future (e.g., have a chilling effect on other businesses' willingness to submit

quires disclosure of state agency records. For a complete listing of the state statutes, see M. JAGER, TRADE SECRETS LAW, Appendix F (1988).

such information) or to cause substantial harm to its submitter's competitive position. National Parks and Conservation Ass'n v. Morton, 498 F.2d 765, 770 (D.C.Cir.1974). Since these standards differ from the state law standards for trade secret protection, it is likely that some information protectible under state law will fail to qualify for protection from FOIA disclosure under exemption four.

Exemption three provides that information "specifically exempted from disclosure by statute" is not subject to mandatory disclosure, "provided that such statute (A) requires that the matters be withheld from the public in such a manner as to leave no discretion on the issue, or (B) establishes particular criteria for withholding or refers to particular types of matters to be withheld." 5 U.S.C.A. § 552 (b)(3). Accordingly, statues found elsewhere in the United States Code, such as section 301(j) of the Food, Drug and Cosmetic Act, which provides that trade secret information contained in new drug applications may not be disclosed to the public, may provide the foundation for exemption from FOIA mandatory disclosure.

One issue that has concerned the courts is the relationship of the Trade Secrets Act, 18 U.S.C.A. § 1905, to the FOIA. The Trade Secrets Act makes it a crime for any officer or employee of any federal agency to disclose to any extent "not authorized by law," information that "concerns or relates to the trade secrets, processes, operations, style of work, or apparatus, or to the identity, confidential statistical data, amount or source of any income, profits, losses or expenditures of any person, firm, partnership corporation or association * * *." The United States Court of Appeals for the District of Columbia has determined that the Trade Secrets Act does not satisfy the requirements for "exempting statutes" under FOIA exemption number three. CNA Financial Corp. v. Donovan, 830 F.2d 1132, 1137–43 (D.C.Cir.1987), *cert. denied* 485 U.S. 977, 108 S.Ct. 1270, 99 L.Ed.2d 481 (1988).[13]

The case law to date indicates that the scope of section 1905 is essentially the same as that of FOIA exemption four. See, e.g., Chrysler Corp. v. Brown, 441 U.S. 281, 319 n. 49, 99 S.Ct. 1705, 1726 n. 49, 60 L.Ed.2d 208, 235 n. 49 (1979).[14] In the *Chrysler* case, the Supreme Court held that the FOIA exemptions were discretionary, permitting but not requiring agencies to refrain from disclosing records falling within them. *Id.*, 441 U.S. at 294, 99 S.Ct. at 1713–14, 60 L.Ed.2d at 220. The apparent impact of section 1905 is to prohibit agencies from disclosing records falling within the perimeters of exemption four, unless there is another valid statute or substantive agency regulation which indepen-

13. But see Westinghouse Electric Corp. v. Schlesinger, 542 F.2d 1190, 1198–1203 (4th Cir.1976), *cert. denied* 431 U.S. 924, 97 S.Ct. 2199, 53 L.Ed.2d 239 (1977) (Fourth Circuit finds that section 1905 is an exemption three statute).

14. While the Supreme Court left open the possibility that material outside of exemption four might still fall within the provisions of section 1905, to date no such case has arisen. Presumably, in such a case, the FOIA itself would constitute "authorization by law," which would permit disclosure of the material under section 1905. Chrysler Corp. v. Brown, 441 U.S. at 319 n. 49, 99 S.Ct. at 1726 n. 49, 60 L.Ed.2d at 235 n. 49.

dently renders the release "authorized by law." See General Motors Corp. v. Marshall, 654 F.2d 294, 297 (4th Cir.1981).

Assume that X Company submits a valuable trade secret to a government regulatory agency, and the agency discloses it to X Company's competitors, either upon a finding that the information does not fall within the freedom of information act exemptions, or that some other independent statute authorizes the disclosure. Might the X Company have a cause of action against the government for taking private property for a public use without paying just compensation, pursuant to the fifth amendment of the U.S. Constitution (or, in the case of a state agency, the fourteenth amendment)? That issue was set before the Supreme Court in Ruckelshaus v. Monsanto Company, 467 U.S. 986, 104 S.Ct. 2862, 81 L.Ed.2d 815 (1984).

The *Monsanto* case involved the Federal Insecticide, Fungicide, and Rodenticide Act ("FIFRA"), 7 U.S.C.A. §§ 136 *et seq.* FIFRA provides that in order to obtain permission to sell a new insecticide, fungicide, herbicide, plant regulator or rodenticide, manufacturers must submit a wide array of test data to the Environmental Protection Agency ("EPA") to demonstrate the product's safety. This test data often contains or reveals the submitting company's trade secrets.

Prior to 1972, FIFRA contained no provisions concerning disclosure of the health and safety data submitted with an application, though, as a matter of practice, the Department of Agriculture (the designated regulatory agency at that time) did not publicly disclose the data. In 1972, Congress amended FIFRA by adopting the Federal Environmental Pesticide Control Act of 1972, 86 Stat. 973. Among other things, the amendments provided that the submitter of data could designate any portions of the submitted material it believed to be "trade secrets or commercial or financial information." *Id.*, § 10(a). Another section prohibited EPA (now in charge of administering FIFRA) from publicly disclosing information which, in its judgement, contained or related to "trade secrets or commercial or financial information." *Id.*, § 10(b). In 1978, Congress again amended FIFRA. Federal Pesticide Act of 1978, 92 Stat. 819. The 1978 amendments added a new subsection, § 10(d), 7 U.S.C. § 136h(d), which provided for disclosure of all health, safety, and environmental data to qualified requesters (*i.e.*, requesters who were not representatives of foreign or multinational pesticide companies), notwithstanding the prohibition against disclosure of trade secrets contained in § 10(b).

Monsanto Company, an inventor, developer, and producer of products falling under the FIFRA provisions, brought suit challenging the 1978 disclosure provisions as unconstitutional, alleging that they constituted a "taking" of private property without just compensation, in violation of the fifth amendment. The Supreme Court held that state-created trade secret rights were property interests subject to takings clause protection, and assumed for purposes of its decision that Monsanto data submitted pursuant to FIFRA contained trade secrets protected under Missouri law.

The Court held that the appropriate test for a "taking" under the circumstances of this case was whether EPA disclosure of the trade secrets would interfere with reasonable investment-backed expectations of confidentiality on Monsanto's part.

> We find that with respect to any health, safety, and environmental data that Monsanto submitted to EPA after the effective date of the 1978 FIFRA amendments—that is, on or after October 1, 1978—Monsanto could not have had a reasonable, investment-backed expectation that EPA would keep the data confidential beyond the limits prescribed in the amended statute itself. Monsanto was on notice of the manner in which EPA was authorized to use and disclose any data turned over to it by an applicant for registration.
>
> * * * If, despite the * * * data-disclosure provisions in the statute, Monsanto chose to submit the requisite data in order to receive a registration, it can hardly argue that its reasonable investment-backed expectations are disturbed when EPA acts to use or disclose the data in a manner that was authorized by law at the time of the submission.
>
> Monsanto argues that the statute's requirement that a submitter give up its property interest in the data constitutes placing an unconstitutional condition on the right to a valuable government benefit. But Monsanto has not challenged the ability of the Federal Government to regulate the marketing and use of pesticides. Nor could Monsanto successfully make such a challenge, for such restrictions are the burdens we all must bear in exchange for " 'the advantage of living and doing business in a civilized community.' " *Andrus v. Allard*, 444 U.S. 51, 67, 100 S.Ct. 318, 327, 62 L.Ed.2d 210 (1979), quoting *Pennsylvania Coal Co. v. Mahon*, 260 U.S. 393, 422, 43 S.Ct. 158, 162, 67 L.Ed. 322 (1922) (Brandeis, J., dissenting). This is particularly true in an area, such as pesticide sale and use, that has long been the source of public concern and the subject of government regulation. That Monsanto is willing to bear this burden in exchange for the ability to market pesticides in this country is evidenced by the fact that it has continued to expand its research and development and to submit data to EPA despite the enactment of the 1978 amendments to FIFRA.[11]
>
> Thus, as long as Monsanto is aware of the conditions under which the data are submitted, and the conditions are rationally related to a legitimate government interest, a voluntary submission

11. Because the market for Monsanto's pesticide products is an international one, Monsanto could decide to forgo registration in the United States and sell a pesticide only in foreign markets. Presumably, it will do so in those situations where it deems the data to be protected from disclosure more valuable than the right to sell in the United States.

of data by an applicant in exchange for the economic advantages of a registration can hardly be called a taking. * * *

Prior to the 1972 amendments, FIFRA was silent with respect to EPA's authorized use and disclosure of data submitted to it in connection with an application for registration. Another statute, the Trade Secrets Act, 18 U.S.C. § 1905, however, arguably is relevant. That Act is a general criminal statute that provides a penalty for any employee of the United States Government who discloses, in a manner not authorized by law, any trade secret information that is revealed to him during the course of his official duties. * * *

It is true that, prior to the 1972 amendments, neither FIFRA nor any other provision of law gave EPA authority to disclose data obtained from Monsanto. But the Trade Secrets Act is not a guarantee of confidentiality to submitters of data, and, absent an express promise, Monsanto had no reasonable, investment-backed expectation that its information would remain inviolate in the hands of EPA. In an industry that long has been the focus of great public concern and significant government regulation, the possibility was substantial that the Federal Government, which had thus far taken no position on disclosure of health, safety, and environmental data concerning pesticides, upon focusing on the issue, would find disclosure to be in the public interest. Thus, with respect to data submitted to EPA in connection with an application for registration prior to October 22, 1972, the Trade Secrets Act provided no basis for a reasonable investment-backed expectation that data submitted to EPA would remain confidential.

* * *

The situation may be different, however, with respect to data submitted by Monsanto to EPA during the period from October 22, 1972, through September 30, 1978. Under the statutory scheme then in effect, a submitter was given an opportunity to protect its trade secrets from disclosure by designating them as trade secrets at the time of submission. * * * [FIFRA] gave Monsanto explicit assurance that EPA was prohibited from disclosing publicly * * * any data submitted by an applicant if both the applicant and EPA determined the data to constitute trade secrets. Thus, with respect to trade secrets submitted under the statutory regime in force between the time of the adoption of the 1972 amendments and the adoption of the 1978 amendments, the Federal Government had explicitly guaranteed to Monsanto and other registration applicants an extensive measure of confidentiality and exclusive use. This explicit governmental guarantee formed the basis of a reasonable investment-backed expectation. If EPA, consistent with the authority granted it by the 1978 FIFRA amendments, were now to disclose trade-secret data * * * in a manner not authorized by the version of FIFRA in effect between 1972 and 1978, EPA's actions would

> frustrate Monsanto's reasonable investment-backed expectation with respect to its control over the use and dissemination of the data it had submitted.
>
> The right to exclude others is generally "one of the most essential sticks in the bundle of rights that are commonly characterized as property." *Kaiser Aetna*, 444 U.S., at 176, 100 S.Ct., at 391. With respect to a trade secret, the right to exclude others is central to the very definition of the property interest. Once the data that constitutes a trade secret is disclosed to others, or others are allowed to use that data, the holder of the trade secret has lost his property interest in the data. That the data retain usefulness for Monsanto even after they are disclosed—for example, as bases from which to develop new products or refine old products, as marketing and advertising tools, or as information necessary to obtain registration in foreign countries—is irrelevant to the determination of the economic impact of the EPA action on Monsanto's property right. The economic value of that property right lies in the competitive advantage over others that Monsanto enjoys by virtue of its exclusive access to the data, and disclosure or use by others of the data would destroy that competitive edge.

Id., 467 U.S. at 1006–1012, 104 S.Ct. at 2874–77, 81 L.Ed.2d at 834–38.

Notes and Questions

1. *No taking: the role of the Trade Secrets Act.* Why did the majority of the Court find that public disclosure of the pre–1972 data would not constitute a taking? Why did the Trade Secrets Act, 18 U.S.C.A. § 1905, not provide the basis for a reasonable, investment-backed expectation of confidentiality? After the *Monsanto* decision, will agency disclosure of private trade secrets contained in agency records give rise to a taking when the only applicable statutes are the FOIA and the Trade Secrets Act?

2. *Policy considerations.* Assume that Company A engages in significant testing in order to demonstrate that its new drug is safe and effective, and submits its test data, in confidence, to the appropriate government regulatory agency in order to obtain approval to put the new drug on the market. Company B later decides to market the same or a similar drug. As a matter of public policy, should Company B be permitted, over Company A's objections, to rely on Company A's data, now lodged with the agency, to obtain permission to sell the drug in competition with Company A? What are the relevant considerations?

Chapter Three

PATENTS

I. UTILITY PATENTS

A. INTRODUCTION

GRAHAM v. JOHN DEERE CO.

Supreme Court of the United States, 1966.
383 U.S. 1, 86 S.Ct. 684, 15 L.Ed.2d 545, 148 U.S.P.Q. 459.

Mr. Justice Clark delivered the opinion of the Court.

* * *

[I]t must be remembered that the federal patent power stems from a specific constitutional provision which authorizes the Congress "To promote the Progress of * * * useful Arts, by securing for limited Times to * * * Inventors the exclusive Right to their * * * Discoveries." Art. I, § 8, cl. 8. The clause is both a grant of power and a limitation. This qualified authority, unlike the power often exercised in the sixteenth and seventeenth centuries by the English Crown, is limited to the promotion of advances in the "useful arts." It was written against the backdrop of the practices—eventually curtailed by the Statute of Monopolies—of the Crown in granting monopolies to court favorites in goods or businesses which had long before been enjoyed by the public. The Congress in the exercise of the patent power may not overreach the restraints imposed by the stated constitutional purpose. Nor may it enlarge the patent monopoly without regard to the innovation, advancement or social benefit gained thereby. Moreover, Congress may not authorize the issuance of patents whose effects are to remove existent knowledge from the public domain, or to restrict free access to materials already available. Innovation, advancement, and things which add to the sum of useful knowledge are inherent requisites in a patent system which by constitutional command must "promote the Progress of * * * useful Arts." This is the *standard* expressed in the Constitution and it may not be ignored. And it is in this light that patent validity "requires reference to a standard written into the Constitution." *Great A. & P. Tea Co. v. Supermarket Equipment Corp., supra*, 340 U.S. at 154, 71 S.Ct. at 131 (concurring opinion).

Within the limits of the constitutional grant, the Congress may, of course, implement the stated purpose of the Framers by selecting the policy which in its judgment best effectuates the constitutional aim. This is but a corollary to the grant to Congress of any Article I power.

Within the scope established by the Constitution, Congress may set out conditions and tests for patentability. It is the duty of the Commissioner of Patents and of the courts in the administration of the patent system to give effect to the constitutional standard by appropriate application, in each case, of the statutory scheme of the Congress.

Congress quickly responded to the bidding of the Constitution by enacting the Patent Act of 1790 during the second session of the First Congress. It created an agency in the Department of State headed by the Secretary of State, the Secretary of the Department of War and the Attorney General, any two of whom could issue a patent for a period not exceeding 14 years to any petitioner that "hath * * * invented or discovered any useful art, manufacture, * * * or device, or any improvement therein not before known or used" if the board found that "the invention or discovery (was) sufficiently useful and important * * *." 1 Stat. 110. This group, whose members administered the patent system along with their other public duties, was known by its own designation as "Commissioners for the Promotion of Useful Arts."

Thomas Jefferson, who as Secretary of State was a member of the group, was its moving spirit and might well be called the "first administrator of our patent system." He was not only an administrator of the patent system under the 1790 Act, but was also the author of the 1793 Patent Act. In addition, Jefferson was himself an inventor of great note. His unpatented improvements on plows, to mention but one line of his inventions, won acclaim and recognition on both sides of the Atlantic. Because of his active interest and influence in the early development of the patent system, Jefferson's views on the general nature of the limited patent monopoly under the Constitution, as well as his conclusions as to conditions for patentability under the statutory scheme, are worthy of note.

Jefferson, like other Americans, had an instinctive aversion to monopolies. It was a monopoly on tea that sparked the Revolution and Jefferson certainly did not favor an equivalent form of monopoly under the new government. His abhorrence of monopoly extended initially to patents as well. From France, he wrote to Madison (July 1788) urging a Bill of Rights provision restricting monopoly, and as against the argument that limited monopoly might serve to incite "ingenuity," he argued forcefully that "the benefit even of limited monopolies is too doubtful to be opposed to that of their general suppression." V Writings of Thomas Jefferson, at 47 (Ford ed., 1895).

His views ripened, however, and in another letter to Madison (Aug. 1789) after the drafting of the Bill of Rights, Jefferson stated that he would have been pleased by an express provision in this form:

> "Art. 9. Monopolies may be allowed to persons for their own productions in literature, & their own inventions in the arts, for a term not exceeding ___ years, but for no longer term & no other purpose." *Id.*, at 113.

And he later wrote:

> "Certainly an inventor ought to be allowed a right to the benefit of his invention for some certain time. * * * Nobody wishes more than I do that ingenuity should receive a liberal encouragement." Letter to Oliver Evans (May 1807), V Writings of Thomas Jefferson, at 75–76 (Washington ed.).

Jefferson's philosophy on the nature and purpose of the patent monopoly is expressed in a letter to Isaac McPherson (Aug. 1813), a portion of which we set out in the margin.[2] He rejected a natural-rights theory in intellectual property rights and clearly recognized the social and economic rationale of the patent system. The patent monopoly was not designed to secure to the inventor his natural right in his discoveries. Rather, it was a reward, an inducement, to bring forth new knowledge. The grant of an exclusive right to an invention was the creation of society—at odds with the inherent free nature of disclosed ideas—and was not to be freely given. Only inventions and discoveries which furthered human knowledge, and were new and useful, justified the special inducement of a limited private monopoly. Jefferson did not believe in granting patents for small details, obvious improvements, or frivolous devices. His writings evidence his insistence upon a high level of patentability.

As a member of the patent board for several years, Jefferson saw clearly the difficulty in "drawing a line between the things which are worth to the public the embarrassment of an exclusive patent, and those which are not." The board on which he served sought to draw such a line and formulated several rules which are preserved in Jefferson's correspondence.[3] Despite the board's efforts, Jefferson saw "with what

2. "Stable ownership is the gift of social law, and is given late in the progress of society. It would be curious then, if an idea, the fugitive fermentation of an individual brain, could, of natural right, be claimed in exclusive and stable property. If nature has made any one thing less susceptible than all others of exclusive property, it is the action of the thinking power called an idea, which an individual may exclusively possess as long as he keeps it to himself; but the moment it is divulged, it forces itself into the possession of every one, and the receiver cannot dispossess himself of it. Its peculiar character, too, is that no one possesses the less, because every other possesses the whole of it. He who receives an idea from me, receives instruction himself without lessening mine; as he who lights his taper at mine, receives light without darkening me. That ideas should freely spread from one to another over the globe, for the moral and mutual instruction of man, and improvement of his condition, seems to have been peculiarly and benevolently designed by nature, when she made them, like fire, expansible over all space, without lessening their density in any point, and like the air in which we breathe, move, and have our physical being, incapable of confinement or exclusive appropriation. Inventions then cannot, in nature, be a subject of property. Society may give an exclusive right to the profits arising from them, as an encouragement to men to pursue ideas which may produce utility, but this may or may not be done, according to the will and convenience of the society, without claim or complaint from anybody." VI Writings of Thomas Jefferson, at 180–181 (Washington ed.).

3. "[A] machine of which we are possessed, might be applied by every man to any use of which it is susceptible." Letter to Isaac McPherson, *supra*, at 181.

"[A] change of material should not give title to a patent. As the making a ploughshare of cast rather than of wrought iron; a comb of iron instead of horn or of ivory * * *." *Ibid.*

"[A] mere change of form should give no right to a patent, as a high-quartered shoe instead of a low one; a round hat instead of a three-square; or a square bucket instead of a round one." *Id.*, at 181–182.

slow progress a system of general rules could be matured." Because of the "abundance" of cases and the fact that the investigations occupied "more time of the members of the board than they could spare from higher duties, the whole was turned over to the judiciary, to be matured into a system, under which every one might know when his actions were safe and lawful." Letter to McPherson, *supra*, at 181, 182. Apparently Congress agreed with Jefferson and the board that the courts should develop additional conditions for patentability. Although the Patent Act was amended, revised or codified some 50 times between 1790 and 1950, Congress steered clear of a statutory set of requirements other than the bare novelty and utility tests reformulated in Jefferson's draft of the 1793 Patent Act.

* * *

The difficulty of formulating conditions for patentability was heightened by the generality of the constitutional grant and the statutes implementing it, together with the underlying policy of the patent system that "the things which are worth to the public the embarrassment of an exclusive patent," as Jefferson put it, must outweigh the restrictive effect of the limited patent monopoly. The inherent problem was to develop some means of weeding out those inventions which would not be disclosed or devised but for the inducement of a patent.

* * *

Notes and Questions

1. *Patentability and the public benefit.* Thomas Jefferson's desire to provide an incentive to invent, but draw "a line between the things which are worth to the public the embarrassment of an exclusive patent, and those which are not," is reflected in our present Patent Act, 35 U.S.C.A. §§ 1–376, and in the extensive case law that construes and applies it. The Patent Act provides that in order to qualify for a utility patent, an invention must be "novel," *id.*, § 102; "non-obvious," *id.*, § 103; and "useful," *id.*, § 101.

The United States Patent and Trademark Office ("PTO"), which is a part of the Department of Commerce, initially determines whether an invention merits a patent. Inventors seeking a patent must submit a detailed application, containing specific claims which describe the innovative qualities of the invention.[1] A patent examiner, with technical training in the field of the invention, then conducts a search of the prior art, or existing knowledge in the field, and determines whether the invention meets the novelty, non-obviousness, usefulness and other Patent Act requirements. A disappointed applicant may appeal a rejection to the Board of Patent Appeals

"[A combined use of old implements.] A man has a right to use a saw, an axe, a plane separately; may he not combine their uses on the same piece of wood?" Letter to Oliver Evans, (Jan. 1814), VI Writings of Thomas Jefferson, at 298 (Washington ed.).

1. The claims are often compared to the description of real property in a deed to land, as they set forth the "metes and bounds" of the invention, and notify others of what the inventor claims as his exclusive property.

and Interferences, 35 U.S.C.A. § 134, and from there he may either appeal directly to the United States Court of Appeals for the Federal Circuit, *id.*, §§ 141, 144, or obtain de novo review of the denial in the U.S. District Court for the District of Columbia. *Id.*, § 145.

If it is determined that patentability requirements are satisfied, the PTO will issue a patent. The PTO's issuance of a patent, however, only provides a presumption that the invention is patentable. *Id.*, § 282. If the patentee attempts to enforce her monopoly in an infringement action, the defendant may challenge the validity of the patent, leading the court to undertake its own review. If the court determines that the invention fails to satisfy the provisions of the Patent Act, it will declare the patent invalid and refuse to enforce it.

To further ensure that the public benefits from the patent monopoly grant, the Patent Act requires the inventor to fully disclose his invention and the best mode of practicing it in the patent application. The PTO then publishes this information when the patent is granted. *Id.*, §§ 112–113. The publication enables the public to learn from the invention during the period of the monopoly, and apply what it learns by analogy to other endeavors. Moreover, as expressly required in the patent and copyright clause, art. I, § 8, cl. 8, the duration of the patent monopoly is limited. Utility patents have traditionally lasted only seventeen years. The Patent Act has recently been amended to provide a term that commences at the date the patent issues and endures for twenty years measured from the date of patent application filing. *Id.*, § 154. Once the patent term expires, the inventor has no further exclusive rights: the public is free to exploit the invention as it wishes, and it is assisted in doing so by the inventor's earlier disclosures.

While a patent is the most difficult form of intellectual property protection to obtain, it is also provides the strongest rights. The patent owner obtains the right to exclude others from making, using, or selling the patented invention within the United States, and, if the invention is a process, from using, selling, or importing products made by that process. *Id.*, § 154. Effective January l, 1996, patent owners will have the additional rights to exclude others from offering to sell and importing the patented invention, and when the invention is a process, from offering to sell products made by that process. Uruguay Round Agreements Act, Pub. L. No. 103–465, §§ 532–534, 108 Stat. 4809, 4983–90 (1994). It is unnecessary for the patent owner to demonstrate that an alleged infringer copied her invention, for unlike trade secret law, patent law does not permit others to create the invention independently.

2. *The Court of Appeals for the Federal Circuit.* Creation of the United States Court of Appeals for the Federal Circuit, in 1982, was a landmark in the development and administration of U.S. patent law. The U.S. district courts have exclusive jurisdiction of cases arising under the Patent Act. 28 U.S.C. § 1338. Prior to 1982, appeals from district court decisions in patent cases were taken to the regional U.S. Courts of Appeals. Appeals from PTO decisions went to the U.S. Court of Customs and Patent Appeals. Over

time, the various Courts of Appeals reached differing interpretations of the Patent Act, which led to considerable uncertainty and chronic forum shopping. See S. REP. NO. 275, 97th Cong., 1st Sess. 3–6 (1981).

The Federal Courts Improvement Act of 1982, Pub. L. No. 97–164, 96 Stat. 25, merged the Court of Customs and Patent Appeals and the U.S. Court of Claims to form the U.S. Court of Appeals for the Federal Circuit ("CAFC"). It provided that in addition to the jurisdiction exercised by the two constituent courts,[2] the new CAFC would have exclusive jurisdiction of all appeals from district courts in patent cases. 28 U.S.C. § 1295.[3] By consolidating all patent matters in one Court of Appeals, the Act alleviated the disparities between Circuits and the resulting forum shopping. In addition, concentrating patent matters in one court has provided greater expertise in the resolution of patent issues. In the ensuing years, the CAFC has tended to ease the standards for obtaining patents and strengthen their protection. Indeed, many authorities have credited the new court with dramatically increasing the value of patents. See, e.g., Sirvilla, Edgell & Hess, *The Advice of Counsel Defense to Increased Patent Damages*, 74 J. PAT. & TRADEMARK OFF. SOC. 705 (1992). For a thorough evaluation of the CAFC's work with patents, see R. HARMON, PATENTS AND THE FEDERAL CIRCUIT (3d ed. 1994). For a practitioner's perspective, see Kastriner, *The Revival of Confidence in the Patent System*, 73 J. PAT. & TRADEMARK OFF. SOC. 5 (1991).

3. *Additional resources.* There are several treatises that provide a comprehensive discussion and analysis of United States patent law and practice. Perhaps the foremost is Donald Chisum's eight-volume treatise, entitled PATENTS: A TREATISE ON THE LAW OF PATENTABILITY, VALIDITY, AND INFRINGEMENT, which is updated regularly with looseleaf supplements. Also useful are P. ROSENBERG, PATENT LAW FUNDAMENTALS (2d ed. 1988), E. LIPSCOMB, LIPSCOMB'S WALKER ON PATENTS, (3d ed. 1984 & Supp.), and J. DRATLER, INTELLECTUAL PROPERTY LAW: COMMERCIAL, CREATIVE AND INDUSTRIAL PROPERTY (1991). For excellent discussions of patent decisions in the Court of Appeals for the Federal Circuit, see R. HARMON, PATENTS AND THE FEDERAL CIRCUIT (3d ed. 1994). For an economic perspective on patent law, see J.W. SCHLICHER, PATENT LAW: LEGAL AND ECONOMIC PRINCIPLES (1992). For information about the patent laws of other nations, see J.W. BAXTER & J.P. SINNOTT, WORLD PATENT LAW AND PRACTICE (1993).

2. In addition to assuming the jurisdiction of these courts, the new CAFC adopted their precedents as its own. See South Corp. v. United States, 690 F.2d 1368, 1370, 215 U.S.P.Q. 657, 658 (C.A.F.C. 1982).

3. The CAFC's jurisdiction also includes appeals in Plant Variety Protection Act cases, and appeals from decisions of the International Trade Commission under section 337 of the Tariff Act of 1930, as well as

B. THE SUBJECT MATTER OF UTILITY PATENTS [4]

DIAMOND v. CHAKRABARTY

United States Supreme Court, 1980.
447 U.S. 303, 100 S.Ct. 2204, 65 L.Ed.2d 144.

MR. CHIEF JUSTICE BURGER delivered the opinion of the Court.

We granted certiorari to determine whether a live, human-made micro-organism is patentable subject matter under 35 U.S.C. § 101.

I

In 1972, respondent Chakrabarty, a microbiologist, filed a patent application, assigned to the General Electric Co. The application asserted 36 claims related to Chakrabarty's invention of "a bacterium from the genus *Pseudomonas* containing therein at least two stable energy-generating plasmids, each of said plasmids providing a separate hydrocarbon degradative pathway." [1] This human-made, genetically engineered bacterium is capable of breaking down multiple components of crude oil. Because of this property, which is possessed by no naturally occurring bacteria, Chakrabarty's invention is believed to have significant value for the treatment of oil spills.

Chakrabarty's patent claims were of three types: first, process claims for the method of producing the bacteria; second, claims for an inoculum comprised of a carrier material floating on water, such as straw, and the new bacteria; and third, claims to the bacteria themselves. The patent examiner allowed the claims falling into the first two categories, but rejected claims for the bacteria. His decision rested on two grounds: (1) that micro-organisms are "products of nature," and (2) that as living things they are not patentable subject matter under 35 U.S.C. § 101.

Chakrabarty appealed the rejection of these claims to the Patent Office Board of Appeals, and the Board affirmed the Examiner on the second ground. Relying on the legislative history of the 1930 Plant Patent Act, in which Congress extended patent protection to certain asexually reproduced plants, the Board concluded that § 101 was not intended to cover living things such as these laboratory created micro-organisms.

appeals from PTO trademark registration decisions. 28 U.S.C.A. § 1295.

4. Utility patents are the most prevalent form of patents, and the broadest in scope. The Patent Act also provides for plant patents and design patents. Most of this Chapter will focus on utility patents. Plant patents and design patents will be examined in Sections II and III of this Chapter, respectively.

1. Plasmids are hereditary units physically separate from the chromosomes of the cell. In prior research, Chakrabarty and an associate discovered that plasmids control the oil degradation abilities of certain bacteria. In particular, the two researchers discovered plasmids capable of degrading camphor and octane, two components of crude oil. In the work represented by the patent application at issue here, Chakrabarty discovered a process by which four different plasmids, capable of degrading four different oil components, could be transferred to and maintained stably in a single *Pseudomonas* bacterium, which itself has no capacity for degrading oil.

[The Court of Customs and Patent Appeals reversed.]

II

The Constitution grants Congress broad power to legislate to "promote the Progress of Science and useful Arts, by securing for limited Times to Authors and Inventors the exclusive Right to their respective Writings and Discoveries." Art. I, § 8, cl. 8. The patent laws promote this progress by offering inventors exclusive rights for a limited period as an incentive for their inventiveness and research efforts. The authority of Congress is exercised in the hope that "[t]he productive effort thereby fostered will have a positive effect on society through the introduction of new products and processes of manufacture into the economy, and the emanations by way of increased employment and better lives for our citizens." *Kewanee Oil Co. v. Bicron Corp.*, 416 U.S. 470, 480, 94 S.Ct. 1879, 1885–86, 40 L.Ed.2d 315 (1974).

The question before us in this case is a narrow one of statutory interpretation requiring us to construe 35 U.S.C. § 101, which provides:

> "Whoever invents or discovers any new and useful process, machine, manufacture, or composition of matter, or any new and useful improvement thereof, may obtain a patent therefor, subject to the conditions and requirements of this title."

Specifically, we must determine whether respondent's micro-organism constitutes a "manufacture" or "composition of matter" within the meaning of the statute.

III

In cases of statutory construction we begin, of course, with the language of the statute. And "unless otherwise defined, words will be interpreted as taking their ordinary, contemporary common meaning." *Perrin v. United States*, 444 U.S. 37, 42, 100 S.Ct. 311, 314, 62 L.Ed.2d 199 (1979). We have also cautioned that courts "should not read into the patent laws limitations and conditions which the legislature has not expressed." *United States v. Dubilier Condenser Corp.*, 289 U.S. 178, 199, 53 S.Ct. 554, 561, 77 L.Ed. 1114 (1933).

Guided by these canons of construction, this Court has read the term "manufacture" in § 101 in accordance with its dictionary definition to mean "the production of articles for use from raw or prepared materials by giving to these materials new forms, qualities, properties, or combinations, whether by hand-labor or by machinery." *American Fruit Growers, Inc. v. Brogdex Co.*, 283 U.S. 1, 11, 51 S.Ct. 328, 330, 75 L.Ed. 801 (1931). Similarly, "composition of matter" has been construed consistent with its common usage to include "all compositions of two or more substances and ... all composite articles, whether they be the results of chemical union, or of mechanical mixture, or whether they be gases, fluids, powders or solids." *Shell Development Co. v. Watson*, 149 F.Supp. 279, 280 (D.C.1957). In choosing such expansive terms as "manufacture" and "composition of matter," modified by the comprehensive "any," Congress plainly contemplated that the patent laws would be given wide scope.

The relevant legislative history also supports a broad construction. The Patent Act of 1793, authored by Thomas Jefferson, defined statutory subject matter as "any new and useful art, machine, manufacture, or composition of matter, or any new or useful improvement [thereof]." Act of Feb. 21, 1793, § 1, 1 Stat. 319. The Act embodied Jefferson's philosophy that "ingenuity should receive a liberal encouragement." 5 Writings of Thomas Jefferson 75–76 (Washington ed. 1871). Subsequent patent statutes in 1836, 1870, and 1874 employed this same broad language. In 1952, when the patent laws were recodified, Congress replaced the word "art" with "process," but otherwise left Jefferson's language intact. The Committee Reports accompanying the 1952 Act inform us that Congress intended statutory subject matter to "include anything under the sun that is made by man." S.Rep.No.1979, 82d Cong., 2d Sess., 5 (1952); H.R.Rep.No.1923, 82d Cong., 2d Sess., 6 (1952).

This is not to suggest that § 101 has no limits or that it embraces every discovery. The laws of nature, physical phenomena, and abstract ideas have been held not patentable. Thus, a new mineral discovered in the earth or a new plant found in the wild is not patentable subject matter. Likewise, Einstein could not patent his celebrated law that $E=mc^2$; nor could Newton have patented the law of gravity. Such discoveries are "manifestations of ... nature, free to all men and reserved exclusively to none." *Funk Bros. Seed Co. v. Kalo Inoculant Co.*, 333 U.S. 127, 130, 68 S.Ct. 440, 441, 92 L.Ed. 588 (1948).

Judged in this light, respondent's micro-organism plainly qualifies as patentable subject matter. His claim is not to a hitherto unknown natural phenomenon, but to a nonnaturally occurring manufacture or composition of matter—a product of human ingenuity "having a distinctive name, character [and] use." *Hartranft v. Wiegmann*, 121 U.S. 609, 615, 7 S.Ct. 1240, 1243, 30 L.Ed. 1012 (1887). The point is underscored dramatically by comparison of the invention here with that in *Funk*. There, the patentee had discovered that there existed in nature certain species of root-nodule bacteria which did not exert a mutually inhibitive effect on each other. He used that discovery to produce a mixed culture capable of inoculating the seeds of leguminous plants. Concluding that the patentee had discovered "only some of the handiwork of nature," the Court ruled the product nonpatentable:

> "Each of the species of root-nodule bacteria contained in the package infects the same group of leguminous plants which it always infected. No species acquires a different use. The combination of species produces no new bacteria, no change in the six species of bacteria, and no enlargement of the range of their utility. Each species has the same effect it always had. The bacteria perform in their natural way. Their use in combination does not improve in any way their natural functioning. They serve the ends nature

originally provided and act quite independently of any effort of the patentee." 333 U.S., at 131, 68 S.Ct., at 442.

Here, by contrast, the patentee has produced a new bacterium with markedly different characteristics from any found in nature and one having the potential for significant utility. His discovery is not nature's handiwork, but his own; accordingly it is patentable subject matter under § 101.

IV

Two contrary arguments are advanced, neither of which we find persuasive.

(A)

The petitioner's first argument rests on the enactment of the 1930 Plant Patent Act, which afforded patent protection to certain asexually reproduced plants, and the 1970 Plant Variety Protection Act, which authorized protection for certain sexually reproduced plants but excluded bacteria from its protection. In the petitioner's view, the passage of these Acts evidences congressional understanding that the terms "manufacture" or "composition of matter" do not include living things; if they did, the petitioner argues, neither Act would have been necessary.

We reject this argument. Prior to 1930, two factors were thought to remove plants from patent protection. The first was the belief that plants, even those artificially bred, were products of nature for purposes of the patent law. This position appears to have derived from the decision of the Patent Office in *Ex parte Latimer*, 1889 Dec.Com.Pat. 123, in which a patent claim for fiber found in the needle of the *Pinus australis* was rejected. The Commissioner reasoned that a contrary result would permit "patents [to] be obtained upon the trees of the forest and the plants of the earth, which of course would be unreasonable and impossible." *Id.*, at 126. The *Latimer* case, it seems, came to "se[t] forth the general stand taken in these matters" that plants were natural products not subject to patent protection. Thorne, Relation of Patent Law to Natural Products, 6 J. Pat.Off.Soc. 23, 24 (1923). The second obstacle to patent protection for plants was the fact that plants were thought not amenable to the "written description" requirement of the patent law. See 35 U.S.C. § 112. Because new plants may differ from old only in color or perfume, differentiation by written description was often impossible.

In enacting the Plant Patent Act, Congress addressed both of these concerns. It explained at length its belief that the work of the plant breeder "in aid of nature" was patentable invention. S.Rep.No.315, 71st Cong., 2d Sess., 6–8 (1930); H.R.Rep.No.1129, 71st Cong., 2d Sess., 7–9 (1930). And it relaxed the written description requirement in favor of "a description ... as complete as is reasonably possible." 35 U.S.C. § 162. No Committee or Member of Congress, however, expressed the broader view, now urged by the petitioner, that the terms "manufacture" or "composition of matter" exclude living things. * * * The Reports observe:

> "There is a clear and logical distinction between the discovery of a new variety of plant and of certain inanimate things, such, for example, as a new and useful natural mineral. The mineral is created wholly by nature unassisted by man.... On the other hand, a plant discovery resulting from cultivation is unique, isolated, and is not repeated by nature, nor can it be reproduced by nature unaided by man...." S.Rep.No.315, *supra*, at 6; H.R.Rep.No.1129, *supra*, at 7 (emphasis added).

Congress thus recognized that the relevant distinction was not between living and inanimate things, but between products of nature, whether living or not, and human-made inventions. Here, respondent's micro-organism is the result of human ingenuity and research. Hence, the passage of the Plant Patent Act affords the Government no support.

Nor does the passage of the 1970 Plant Variety Protection Act support the Government's position. As the Government acknowledges, sexually reproduced plants were not included under the 1930 Act because new varieties could not be reproduced true-to-type through seedlings. By 1970, however, it was generally recognized that true-to-type reproduction was possible and that plant patent protection was therefore appropriate. The 1970 Act extended that protection. There is nothing in its language or history to suggest that it was enacted because § 101 did not include living things.

In particular, we find nothing in the exclusion of bacteria from plant variety protection to support the petitioner's position. The legislative history gives no reason for this exclusion. As the Court of Customs and Patent Appeals suggested, it may simply reflect congressional agreement with the result reached by that court in deciding *In re Arzberger*, 27 C.C.P.A. (Pat.) 1315, 112 F.2d 834 (1940), which held that bacteria were not plants for the purposes of the 1930 Act. Or it may reflect the fact that prior to 1970 the Patent Office had issued patents for bacteria under § 101.[9] In any event, absent some clear indication that Congress "focused on [the] issues ... directly related to the one presently before the Court," *SEC v. Sloan*, 436 U.S. 103, 120–121, 98 S.Ct. 1702, 1713, 56 L.Ed.2d 148 (1978), there is no basis for reading into its actions an intent to modify the plain meaning of the words found in § 101.

(B)

The petitioner's second argument is that micro-organisms cannot qualify as patentable subject matter until Congress expressly authorizes such protection. His position rests on the fact that genetic technology was unforeseen when Congress enacted § 101. From this it is argued

9. In 1873, the Patent Office granted Louis Pasteur a patent on "yeast, free from organic germs of disease, as an article of manufacture." And in 1967 and 1968, immediately prior to the passage of the Plant Variety Protection Act, that Office granted two patents which, as the petitioner concedes, state claims for living micro-organisms.

that resolution of the patentability of inventions such as respondent's should be left to Congress. The legislative process, the petitioner argues, is best equipped to weigh the competing economic, social, and scientific considerations involved, and to determine whether living organisms produced by genetic engineering should receive patent protection. In support of this position, the petitioner relies on our recent holding in *Parker v. Flook*, 437 U.S. 584, 98 S.Ct. 2522, 57 L.Ed.2d 451 (1978), and the statement that the judiciary "must proceed cautiously when . . . asked to extend patent rights into areas wholly unforeseen by Congress." *Id.*, at 596, 98 S.Ct. at 2529.

It is, of course, correct that Congress, not the courts, must define the limits of patentability; but it is equally true that once Congress has spoken it is "the province and duty of the judicial department to say what the law is." *Marbury v. Madison*, 1 Cranch 137, 177, 2 L.Ed. 60 (1803). Congress has performed its constitutional role in defining patentable subject matter in § 101; we perform ours in construing the language Congress has employed. In so doing, our obligation is to take statutes as we find them, guided, if ambiguity appears, by the legislative history and statutory purpose. Here, we perceive no ambiguity. The subject-matter provisions of the patent law have been cast in broad terms to fulfill the constitutional and statutory goal of promoting "the Progress of Science and the useful Arts" with all that means for the social and economic benefits envisioned by Jefferson. Broad general language is not necessarily ambiguous when congressional objectives require broad terms.

* * *

* * * This Court frequently has observed that a statute is not to be confined to the "particular application[s] . . . contemplated by the legislators." *Barr v. United States*, 324 U.S. 83, 90, 65 S.Ct. 522, 525, 89 L.Ed. 765 (1945). This is especially true in the field of patent law. A rule that unanticipated inventions are without protection would conflict with the core concept of the patent law that anticipation undermines patentability. Mr. Justice Douglas reminded that the inventions most benefiting mankind are those that "push back the frontiers of chemistry, physics, and the like." *Great A. & P. Tea Co. v. Supermarket Corp.*, 340 U.S. 147, 154, 71 S.Ct. 127, 131, 95 L.Ed. 162 (1950) (concurring opinion). Congress employed broad general language in drafting § 101 precisely because such inventions are often unforeseeable.

To buttress his argument, the petitioner, with the support of *amicus*, points to grave risks that may be generated by research endeavors such as respondent's. The briefs present a gruesome parade of horribles. Scientists, among them Nobel laureates, are quoted suggesting that genetic research may pose a serious threat to the human race, or, at the very least, that the dangers are far too substantial to permit such research to proceed apace at this time. We are told that genetic research and related technological developments may spread pollution and disease, that it may result in a loss of genetic diversity, and that its practice may tend to depreciate the value of human life. These arguments are forcefully, even passionately, presented; they remind us that, at times, human ingenuity seems unable to control fully the forces it creates—that with Hamlet, it is sometimes better "to bear those ills we have than fly to others that we know not of."

It is argued that this Court should weigh these potential hazards in considering whether respondent's invention is patentable subject matter under § 101. We disagree. The grant or denial of patents on micro-organisms is not likely to put an end to genetic research or to its attendant risks. The large amount of research that has already occurred when no researcher had sure knowledge that patent protection would be available suggests that legislative or judicial fiat as to patentability will not deter the scientific mind from probing into the unknown any more than Canute could command the tides. Whether respondent's claims are patentable may determine whether research efforts are accelerated by the hope of reward or slowed by want of incentives, but that is all.

What is more important is that we are without competence to entertain these arguments—either to brush them aside as fantasies generated by fear of the unknown, or to act on them. The choice we are urged to make is a matter of high policy for resolution within the legislative process after the kind of investigation, examination, and study that legislative bodies can provide and courts cannot. That process involves the balancing of competing values and interests, which in our democratic system is the business of elected representatives. Whatever their validity, the contentions now pressed on us should be addressed to the political branches of the Government, the Congress and the Executive, and not to the courts.

We have emphasized in the recent past that "[o]ur individual appraisal of the wisdom or unwisdom of a particular [legislative] course ... is to be put aside in the process of interpreting a statute." *TVA v. Hill*, 437 U.S. 153, 194, 98 S.Ct. 2279, 2302, 57 L.Ed.2d 117 (1978). Our task, rather, is the narrow one of determining what Congress meant by the words it used in the statute; once that is done our powers are exhausted. Congress is free to amend § 101 so as to exclude from patent protection organisms produced by genetic engineering. Cf. 42 U.S.C. § 2181(a), exempting from patent protection inventions "useful solely in the utilization of special nuclear material or atomic energy in an atomic weapon." Or it may chose to craft a statute specifically designed for such living things. But, until Congress takes such action, this Court must construe the language of § 101 as it is. The language of that section fairly embraces respondent's invention.

* * *

MR. JUSTICE BRENNAN, with whom MR. JUSTICE WHITE, MR. JUSTICE MARSHALL, and MR. JUSTICE POWELL join, dissenting.

* * *

The patent laws attempt to reconcile this Nation's deep seated antipathy to monopolies with the need to encourage progress. Given the complexity and legislative nature of this delicate task, we must be careful to extend patent protection no further than Congress has provided. In particular, where there is an absence of legislative direction, the courts should leave to Congress the decisions whether and how far to extend the patent privilege into areas where the common understanding has been that patents are not available.[1]

In this case, however, we do not confront a complete legislative vacuum. The sweeping language of the Patent Act of 1793, as re-enacted in 1952, is not the last pronouncement Congress has made in this area. In 1930 Congress enacted the Plant Patent Act affording patent protection to developers of certain asexually reproduced plants. In 1970 Congress enacted the Plant Variety Protection Act to extend protection to certain new plant varieties capable of sexual reproduction. Thus, we are not dealing—as the Court would have it—with the routine problem of "unanticipated inventions." In these two Acts Congress has addressed the general problem of patenting animate inventions and has chosen carefully limited language granting protection to some kinds of discoveries, but specifically excluding others. These Acts strongly evidence a congressional limitation that excludes bacteria from patentability.

First, the Acts evidence Congress' understanding, at least since 1930, that § 101 does not include living organisms. If newly developed living organisms not naturally occurring had been patentable under § 101, the plants included in the scope of the 1930 and 1970 Acts could have been patented without new legislation. Those plants, like the bacteria involved in this case, were new varieties not naturally occurring. Although the Court rejects this line of argument, it does not explain why the Acts were necessary unless to correct a pre-existing situation.[4] I cannot share the Court's implicit assumption that Congress was engaged in either idle exercises or mere correction of the public record when it enacted the 1930 and 1970 Acts. And Congress certainly thought it was doing something significant. The Committee Reports contain expansive prose about the previously unavailable benefits to be derived from extending patent protection to plants. Because Congress thought it had to legislate in order to make agricultural "human-made inventions" patentable and because the legislation Congress enacted is limited, it follows that Congress never meant to make items outside the scope of the legislation patentable.

Second, the 1970 Act clearly indicates that Congress has included bacteria within the focus of its legislative concern, but not within the

1. I read the Court to admit that the popular conception, even among advocates of agricultural patents, was that living organisms were unpatentable.

4. If the 1930 Act's only purpose were to solve the technical problem of description referred to by the Court, most of the Act, and in particular its limitation to asexually reproduced plants, would have been totally unnecessary.

scope of patent protection. Congress specifically excluded bacteria from the coverage of the 1970 Act. The Court's attempts to supply explanations for this explicit exclusion ring hollow. It is true that there is no mention in the legislative history of the exclusion, but that does not give us license to invent reasons. The fact is that Congress, assuming that animate objects as to which it had not specifically legislated could not be patented, excluded bacteria from the set of patentable organisms.

* * *

Notes and Questions

1. *Plant patents and utility patents for plants.* The 1930 Plant Patent Act and the Plant Variety Protection Act, which provide patents or patent-like protection for certain plants, will be discussed in Section II, below. In 1985, following the reasoning in *Chakrabarty*, the Board of Patent Appeals and Interferences held that a corn plant, seed and tissue culture with increased free tryptophan levels were proper utility patent subject matter. The Board found it irrelevant that the plant and seed might also qualify for protection under the Plant Patent Act or the Plant Variety Protection Act. See *Ex parte* Hibberd, 227 U.S.P.Q. 443 (P.T.O. Bd. Pat. App. 1985).

2. *The aftermath of Chakrabarty.* Since the Supreme Court's decision in *Chakrabarty*, the PTO has issued a number of patents for genetically engineered microbes. In 1987, the PTO Board of Patent Appeals and Interferences, citing *Chakrabarty*, held that polyploid oysters manipulated and rendered sterile (and thus suitable for year-round consumption) were nonnaturally occurring manufactures or compositions of matter within the meaning of section 101 of the Patent Act. *Ex parte* Allen, 2 U.S.P.Q.2d 1425 (PTO Bd. Pat. App. 1987), *affirmed on other grounds* 846 F.2d 77 (C.A.F.C. 1988). Shortly thereafter, Donald Quigg, the Commissioner of Patents and Trademarks, published an interpretative rule announcing that the PTO now considered "nonnaturally occurring non-human multicellular living organisms, including animals, to be patentable subject matter within the scope of 35 U.S.C. 101." 1077 PAT. & TRADEMARK OFF. GAZETTE 24 (1987). The Commissioner elaborated,

> A claim directed to or including within its scope a human being will not be considered to be patentable subject matter under 35 U.S.C. 101. The grant of a limited, but exclusive property right in a human being is prohibited by the Constitution. Accordingly, it is suggested that any claim directed to a non-plant multicellular organism which would include a human being within its scope include the limitation "non-human" to avoid this ground of rejection.

Id. Does the Constitution prohibit the granting of patents for genetically-engineered people? If so, on what basis? See Note, *Patents on People and the U.S. Constitution: Creating Slaves or Enslaving Science?*, 16 HASTINGS CONST. L.Q. 221 (1989).

The following year, the PTO granted the first patent for a genetically engineered warm-blooded animal—a mouse developed at Harvard University which had been genetically altered to carry cancer genes in its cells and thus develop tumors quickly if exposed to even small amounts of cancer-causing chemicals. The mouse was designed to be used in testing to determine the cancer-causing potential of chemicals and was expected to be especially useful in breast cancer research. U.S. Patent # 4,736,866. Notwithstanding numerous applications for genetically engineered animals such as goats and pigs, it was four years before the PTO granted additional animal patents—again, for genetically engineered mice for use in research. *PTO Issues Three Patents for Genetically Engineered Mice*, 45 PAT., TRADEMARK & COPYRIGHT J. (BNA) 159 (1993).

Throughout the period following the decision in *Chakrabarty*, debates about the ethical, economic, environmental and political implications of patenting life forms raged both in the media and in Congress. Farmers expressed grave concerns about the economic impact of having to pay royalties whenever patented livestock were reproduced. Some scientists argued that granting patents for biotechnological inventions would drive up research costs, leading researchers to channel their efforts into immediately profitable pursuits at the cost of long-term gains, and would encourage counter-productive secrecy among researchers. Hudson, *Biotechnology Patents after the "Harvard Mouse": Did Congress Really Intend* Everything Under the Sun *to Include Shiny Eyes, Soft Fur and Pink Feet?*, 74 J. PAT. & TRADEMARK OFF. SOC. 510, 521–22 (1992). Environmentalists expressed concerns about the environmental impact of genetically engineered agricultural and medical microorganisms, which might be freely released into the atmosphere. There were also worries that genetic engineering would endanger the diversity of the natural gene pool. Numerous people posed ethical questions about the new relationship between humans and animals, and about the physical suffering that might be imposed on animals due to the incentive of patent monopolies. *Id.* at 522–524. See, e.g., *Patents and the Constitution: Transgenic Animals Hearings before the Subcomm. on Courts, Civil Liberties and the Administration of Justice of the House Comm. on the Judiciary*, 100th Cong., 1st Sess. (1987); Merges, *Intellectual Property in Higher Life Forms: The Patent System and Controversial Technologies,* 47 MD. L. REV. 1051 (1988); Dresser, *Ethical and Legal Issues in Patenting New Animal Life*, 28 JURIMETRICS J. 399 (1988); Gore, *Planning a New Biotechnology Policy*, 5 HARV. J. L. & PUB. POL'Y. 19 (1991). While numerous bills were introduced to restrict or regulate animal patents, see, e.g., H.R. 4970, 100th Cong., 2d Sess. (1988); H.R. 5598, 101st Cong., 2d Sess. (1990); S. 387, 103rd Cong., 1st Sess. (1993), Congress passed no significant legislation.

For a discussion of the possibilities of patenting new breeds of animals derived from classic methods of cross-breeding, see Clark, *Animal Invention Protection*, 16 AIPLA Q. J. 442 (1988–89); Lesser, *Animal Variety Protection: A Proposal for a U.S. Model Law 75*, J. PAT. & TRADEMARK OFF SOC. 398 (1993). For a discussion of patenting life forms abroad, see O'Connor, *Patenting Animals and Other Living Things*, 65 S. CAL. L. REV. 597, 616 (1991).

3. *Statutory exclusions from patentability.* Notwithstanding the broad coverage of section 101, 42 U.S.C.A. § 2181(a) prohibits the patenting of "any invention or discovery which is useful solely in the utilization of special nuclear material or atomic energy in an atomic weapon." Also, see section

181 *et. seq.* of the Patent Act, which limits the issuance of patents when issuance would be "detrimental to the national security."

DIAMOND v. DIEHR

United States Supreme Court, 1981.
450 U.S. 175, 101 S.Ct. 1048, 67 L.Ed.2d 155, 209 U.S.P.Q. 1.

JUSTICE REHNQUIST delivered the opinion of the Court.

We granted certiorari to determine whether a process for curing synthetic rubber which includes in several of its steps the use of a mathematical formula and a programmed digital computer is patentable subject matter under 35 U.S.C. § 101.

I

The patent application at issue was filed by the respondents on August 6, 1975. The claimed invention is a process for molding raw, uncured synthetic rubber into cured precision products. The process uses a mold for precisely shaping the uncured material under heat and pressure and then curing the synthetic rubber in the mold so that the product will retain its shape and be functionally operative after the molding is completed.

Respondents claim that their process ensures the production of molded articles which are properly cured. Achieving the perfect cure depends upon several factors including the thickness of the article to be molded, the temperature of the molding process, and the amount of time that the article is allowed to remain in the press. It is possible using well-known time, temperature, and cure relationships to calculate by means of the Arrhenius equation [2] when to open the press and remove the cured product. Nonetheless, according to the respondents, the industry has not been able to obtain uniformly accurate cures because the temperature of the molding press could not be precisely measured, thus making it difficult to do the necessary computations to determine cure time. Because the temperature *inside* the press has heretofore been viewed as an uncontrollable variable, the conventional industry practice has been to calculate the cure time as the shortest time in which all parts of the product will definitely be cured, assuming a reasonable amount of mold-opening time during loading and unloading. But the shortcoming of this practice is that operating with an uncontrollable variable inevitably led in some instances to overestimating the mold-opening time and overcuring the rubber, and in other instances to underestimating that time and undercuring the product.

Respondents characterize their contribution to the art to reside in the process of constantly measuring the actual temperature inside the mold. These temperature measurements are then automatically fed into a computer which repeatedly recalculates the cure time by use of the Arrhenius equation. When the recalculated time equals the actual time

2. The equation is named after its discoverer Svante Arrhenius and has long been used to calculate the cure time in rubber-molding presses. * * *

that has elapsed since the press was closed, the computer signals a device to open the press. According to the respondents, the continuous measuring of the temperature inside the mold cavity, the feeding of this information to a digital computer which constantly recalculates the cure time, and the signaling by the computer to open the press, are all new in the art.

The patent examiner rejected the respondents' claims on the sole ground that they were drawn to nonstatutory subject matter under 35 U.S.C. § 101.[5] He determined that those steps in respondents' claims

5. Respondents' application contained 11 different claims. Three examples are claims 1, 2, and 11 which provide:

"1. A method of operating a rubber-molding press for precision molded compounds with the aid of a digital computer, comprising:

"providing said computer with a data base for said press including at least,

"natural logarithm conversion data (ln),

"the activation energy constant (C) unique to each batch of said compound being molded, and

"a constant (x) dependent upon the geometry of the particular mold of the press,

"initiating an interval timer in said computer upon the closure of the press for monitoring the elapsed time of said closure,

"constantly determining the temperature (Z) of the mold at a location closely adjacent to the mold cavity in the press during molding,

"constantly providing the computer with the temperature (Z),

"repetitively calculating in the computer, at frequent intervals during each cure, the Arrhenius equation for reaction time during the cure, which is

"ln v = CZ + x

"where v is the total required cure time,

"repetitively comparing in the computer at said frequent intervals during the cure each said calculation of the total required cure time calculated with the Arrhenius equation and said elapsed time, and

"opening the press automatically when a said comparison indicates equivalence.

"2. The method of claim 1 including measuring the activation energy constant for the compound being molded in the press with a rheometer and automatically updating said data base within the computer in the event of changes in the compound being molded in said press as measured by said rheometer.

"* * *

"11. A method of manufacturing precision molded articles from selected synthetic rubber compounds in an openable rubber molding press having at least one heated precision mold, comprising:

"(a) heating said mold to a temperature range approximating a pre-determined rubber curing temperature,

"(b) installing prepared unmolded synthetic rubber of a known compound in a molding cavity of predetermined geometry as defined by said mold,

"(c) closing said press to mold said rubber to occupy said cavity in conformance with the contour of said mold and to cure said rubber by transfer of heat thereto from said mold,

"(d) initiating an interval timer upon the closure of said press for monitoring the elapsed time of said closure,

"(e) heating said mold during said closure to maintain the temperature thereof within said range approximating said rubber curing temperature,

"(f) constantly determining the temperature of said mold at a location closely adjacent said cavity thereof throughout closure of said press,

"(g) repetitively calculating at frequent periodic intervals throughout closure of said press the Arrhenius equation for reaction time of said rubber to determine total required cure time v as follows:

"ln v = cz + x

"wherein c is an activation energy constant determined for said rubber being molded and cured in said press, z is the temperature of said mold at the time of each calculation of said Arrhenius equation, and x is a constant which is a function of said predetermined geometry of said mold,

"(h) for each repetition of calculation of said Arrhenius equation herein comparing the resultant calculated total required cure time with the monitored elapsed time measured by said interval timer,

that are carried out by a computer under control of a stored program constituted nonstatutory subject matter under this Court's decision in *Gottschalk v. Benson*, 409 U.S. 63, 93 S.Ct. 253, 34 L.Ed.2d 273 (1972). The remaining steps—installing rubber in the press and the subsequent closing of the press—were "conventional and necessary to the process and cannot be the basis of patentability." The examiner concluded that respondents' claims defined and sought protection of a computer program for operating a rubber-molding press.

The Patent and Trademark Office Board of Appeals agreed with the examiner, but the Court of Customs and Patent Appeals reversed. The court noted that a claim drawn to subject matter otherwise statutory does not become nonstatutory because a computer is involved. The respondents' claims were not directed to a mathematical algorithm or an improved method of calculation but rather recited an improved process for molding rubber articles by solving a practical problem which had risen in the molding of rubber products.

* * *

II

* * * As in *Chakrabarty*, we must here construe 35 U.S.C. § 101 * * *.

In cases of statutory construction, we begin with the language of the statute. Unless otherwise defined, "words will be interpreted as taking their ordinary, contemporary, common meaning," *Perrin v. United States*, 444 U.S. 37, 42, 100 S.Ct. 311, 314, 62 L.Ed.2d 199 (1979), and, in dealing with the patent laws, we have more than once cautioned that "courts 'should not read into the patent laws limitations and conditions which the legislature has not expressed.'" *Diamond v. Chakrabarty*, 449 U.S. at 308, 100 S.Ct., at 2207 quoting *United States v. Dubilier Condenser Corp.*, 289 U.S. 178, 199, 53 S.Ct. 554, 561, 77 L.Ed. 1114 (1933).

The Patent Act of 1793 defined statutory subject matter as "any new and useful art, machine, manufacture or composition of matter, or any new or useful improvement [thereof]." Act of Feb. 21, 1793, ch. 11, § 1, 1 Stat. 318. Not until the patent laws were recodified in 1952 did Congress replace the word "art" with the word "process." It is that latter word which we confront today, and in order to determine its meaning we may not be unmindful of the Committee Reports accompanying the 1952 Act which inform us that Congress intended statutory subject matter to "include anything under the sun that is made by man." Although the term "process" was not added to 35 U.S.C. § 101 until 1952 a process has historically enjoyed patent protection because it was considered a form of "art" as that term was used in the 1793 Act. In defining the nature of a patentable process, the Court stated:

"(i) opening said press when a said comparison of calculated total required cure time and monitored elapsed time indicates equivalence, and

"(j) removing from said mold the resultant precision molded and cured rubber article."

> "That a process may be patentable, irrespective of the particular form of the instrumentalities used, cannot be disputed.... A process is a mode of treatment of certain materials to produce a given result. It is an act, or a series of acts, performed upon the subject-matter to be transformed and reduced to a different state or thing. If new and useful, it is just as patentable as is a piece of machinery. In the language of the patent law, it is an art. The machinery pointed out as suitable to perform the process may or may not be new or patentable; whilst the process itself may be altogether new, and produce an entirely new result. The process requires that certain things should be done with certain substances, and in a certain order; but the tools to be used in doing this may be of secondary consequence." *Cochrane v. Deener*, 94 U.S. 780, 787–788, 24 L.Ed. 139 (1877).
>
> * * *

Analyzing respondents' claims according to the above statements from our cases, we think that a physical and chemical process for molding precision synthetic rubber products falls within the § 101 categories of possibly patentable subject matter. That respondents' claims involve the transformation of an article, in this case raw, uncured synthetic rubber, into a different state or thing cannot be disputed. The respondents' claims describe in detail a step-by-step method for accomplishing such, beginning with the loading of a mold with raw, uncured rubber and ending with the eventual opening of the press at the conclusion of the cure. Industrial processes such as this are the types which have historically been eligible to receive the protection of our patent laws.

III

Our conclusion regarding respondents' claims is not altered by the fact that in several steps of the process a mathematical equation and a programmed digital computer are used. This Court has undoubtedly recognized limits to § 101 and every discovery is not embraced within the statutory terms. Excluded from such patent protection are laws of nature, natural phenomena, and abstract ideas. * * *

Our recent holdings in *Gottschalk v. Benson*, *supra*, and *Parker v. Flook*, [437 U.S. 584, 98 S.Ct. 2522, 57 L.Ed.2d 451 (1978)], both of which are computer-related, stand for no more than these long-established principles. In *Benson*, we held unpatentable claims for an algorithm used to convert binary code decimal numbers to equivalent pure binary numbers. The sole practical application of the algorithm was in connection with the programming of a general purpose digital computer. We defined "algorithm" as a "procedure for solving a given type of mathematical problem," and we concluded that such an algorithm, or mathematical formula, is like a law of nature, which cannot be the subject of a patent.

Parker v. Flook, *supra*, presented a similar situation. The claims were drawn to a method for computing an "alarm limit." An "alarm limit" is simply a number and the Court concluded that the application sought to protect a formula for computing this number. Using this formula, the updated alarm limit could be calculated if several other variables were known. The application, however, did not purport to explain how these other variables were to be determined, nor did it purport "to contain any disclosure relating to the chemical processes at work, the monitoring of process variables, or the means of setting off an alarm or adjusting an alarm system. All that it provides is a formula for computing an updated alarm limit." 437 U.S., at 586, 98 S.Ct., at 2523.

In contrast, the respondents here do not seek to patent a mathematical formula. Instead, they seek patent protection for a process of curing synthetic rubber. Their process admittedly employs a well-known mathematical equation, but they do not seek to pre-empt the use of that equation. Rather, they seek only to foreclose from others the use of that equation in conjunction with all of the other steps in their claimed process. These include installing rubber in a press, closing the mold, constantly determining the temperature of the mold, constantly recalculating the appropriate cure time through the use of the formula and a digital computer, and automatically opening the press at the proper time. Obviously, one does not need a "computer" to cure natural or synthetic rubber, but if the computer use incorporated in the process patent significantly lessens the possibility of "overcuring" or "undercuring," the process as a whole does not thereby become unpatentable subject matter.

Our earlier opinions lend support to our present conclusion that a claim drawn to subject matter otherwise statutory does not become nonstatutory simply because it uses a mathematical formula, computer program, or digital computer. In *Gottschalk v. Benson*, we noted: "It is said that the decision precludes a patent for any program servicing a computer. We do not so hold." 409 U.S., at 71, 93 S.Ct., at 257. Similarly, in *Parker v. Flook*, we stated that "a process is not unpatentable simply because it contains a law of nature or a mathematical algorithm." 437 U.S., at 590, 98 S.Ct., at 2526. It is now commonplace that an *application* of a law of nature or mathematical formula to a known structure or process may well be deserving of patent protection. As Justice Stone explained four decades ago:

> "While a scientific truth, or the mathematical expression of it, is not a patentable invention, a novel and useful structure created with the aid of knowledge of scientific truth may be." *Mackay Radio & Telegraph Co. v. Radio of America*, 306 U.S. 86, 94, 59 S.Ct. 427, 431, 83 L.Ed. 506 (1939).

We think this statement in *Mackay* takes us a long way toward the correct answer in this case. Arrhenius' equation is not patentable in isolation, but when a process for curing rubber is devised which incorporates in it a more efficient solution of the equation, that process is at the very least not barred at the threshold by § 101.

In determining the eligibility of respondents' claimed process for patent protection under § 101, their claims must be considered as a whole. It is inappropriate to dissect the claims into old and new elements and then to ignore the presence of the old elements in the analysis. This is particularly true in a process claim because a new combination of steps in a process may be patentable even though all the constituents of the combination were well known and in common use before the combination was made. The "novelty" of any element or steps in a process, or even of the process itself, is of no relevance in determining whether the subject matter of a claim falls within the § 101 categories of possibly patentable subject matter.[12]

It has been urged that novelty is an appropriate consideration under § 101. Presumably, this argument results from the language in § 101 referring to any "new and useful" process, machine, etc. Section 101, however, is a general statement of the type of subject matter that is eligible for patent protection "subject to the conditions and requirements of this title." Specific conditions for patentability follow and § 102 covers in detail the conditions relating to novelty. The question therefore of whether a particular invention is novel is "wholly apart from whether the invention falls into a category of statutory subject matter." *In re Bergy*, 596 F.2d 952, 961 (Cust. & Pat.App., 1979) (emphasis deleted). * * *

In this case, it may later be determined that the respondents' process is not deserving of patent protection because it fails to satisfy the statutory conditions of novelty under § 102 or nonobviousness under § 103. A rejection on either of these grounds does not affect the determination that respondents' claims recited subject matter which was eligible for patent protection under § 101.

IV

We have before us today only the question of whether respondents' claims fall within the § 101 categories of possibly patentable subject matter. We view respondents' claims as nothing more than a process for molding rubber products and not as an attempt to patent a mathematical formula. We recognize, of course, that when a claim recites a mathematical formula (or scientific principle or phenomenon of nature), an inquiry must be made into whether the claim is seeking patent protection for that formula in the abstract. A mathematical formula as

12. It is argued that the procedure of dissecting a claim into old and new elements is mandated by our decision in *Flook* which noted that a mathematical algorithm must be assumed to be within the "prior art." It is from this language that the petitioner premises his argument that if everything other than the algorithm is determined to be old in the art, then the claim cannot recite statutory subject matter. The fallacy in this argument is that we did not hold in *Flook* that the mathematical algorithm could not be considered at all when making the § 101 determination. To accept the analysis proffered by the petitioner would, if carried to its extreme, make all inventions unpatentable because all inventions can be reduced to underlying principles of nature which, once known, make their implementation obvious. The analysis suggested by the petitioner would also undermine our earlier decisions regarding the criteria to consider in determining the eligibility of a process for patent protection.

such is not accorded the protection of our patent laws, and this principle cannot be circumvented by attempting to limit the use of the formula to a particular technological environment. Similarly, insignificant post-solution activity will not transform an unpatentable principle into a patentable process.[14] To hold otherwise would allow a competent draftsman to evade the recognized limitations on the type of subject matter eligible for patent protection. On the other hand, when a claim containing a mathematical formula implements or applies that formula in a structure or process which, when considered as a whole, is performing a function which the patent laws were designed to protect (*e. g.*, transforming or reducing an article to a different state or thing), then the claim satisfies the requirements of § 101. Because we do not view respondents' claims as an attempt to patent a mathematical formula, but rather to be drawn to an industrial process for the molding of rubber products, we affirm the judgment of the Court of Customs and Patent Appeals.[15]

14. Arguably, the claims in *Flook* did more than present a mathematical formula. The claims also solved the calculation in order to produce a new number or "alarm limit" and then replaced the old number with the number newly produced. The claims covered all uses of the formula in processes "comprising the catalytic chemical conversion of hydrocarbons." There are numerous such processes in the petrochemical and oil refinery industries and the claims therefore covered a broad range of potential uses. The claims, however, did not cover every conceivable application of the formula. We rejected in *Flook* the argument that because all possible uses of the mathematical formula were not pre-empted, the claim should be eligible for patent protection. Our reasoning in *Flook* is in no way inconsistent with our reasoning here. A mathematical formula does not suddenly become patentable subject matter simply by having the applicant acquiesce to limiting the reach of the patent for the formula to a particular technological use. A mathematical formula in the abstract is nonstatutory subject matter regardless of whether the patent is intended to cover all uses of the formula or only limited uses. Similarly, a mathematical formula does not become patentable subject matter merely by including in the claim for the formula token postsolution activity such as the type claimed in *Flook*. We were careful to note in *Flook* that the patent application did not purport to explain how the variables used in the formula were to be selected, nor did the application contain any disclosure relating to chemical processes at work or the means of setting off an alarm or adjusting the alarm unit. All the application provided was a "formula for computing an updated alarm limit."

15. The dissent's analysis rises and falls on its characterization of respondents' claims as presenting nothing more than "an improved method of calculating the time that the mold should remain closed during the curing process." The dissent states that respondents claim only to have developed "a new method of programming a digital computer in order to calculate—promptly and repeatedly—the correct curing time in a familiar process." Respondents' claims, however, are not limited to the isolated step of "programming a digital computer." Rather, respondents' claims describe a process of curing rubber beginning with the loading of the mold and ending with the opening of the press and the production of a synthetic rubber product that has been perfectly cured—a result heretofore unknown in the art. The fact that one or more of the steps in respondents' process may not, in isolation, be novel or independently eligible for patent protection is irrelevant to the question of whether the claims as a whole recite subject matter eligible for patent protection under § 101. As we explained when discussing machine patents in *Deepsouth Packing Co. v. Laitram Corp.*, 406 U.S. 518, 92 S.Ct. 1700, 32 L.Ed.2d 273 (1972):

> "The patents were warranted not by the novelty of their elements but by the novelty of the combination they represented. Invention was recognized because Laitram's assignors combined ordinary elements in an extraordinary way—a novel union of old means was designed to achieve new ends. Thus, for both inven-

JUSTICE STEVENS, with whom JUSTICE BRENNAN, JUSTICE MARSHALL, and JUSTICE BLACKMUN join, dissenting.

The starting point in the proper adjudication of patent litigation is an understanding of what the inventor claims to have discovered. The Court's decision in this case rests on a misreading of the Diehr and Lutton patent application. Moreover, the Court has compounded its error by ignoring the critical distinction between the character of the subject matter that the inventor claims to be novel—the § 101 issue—and the question whether that subject matter is in fact novel—the § 102 issue.

* * *

II

* * *

In the first sentence of its opinion, the Court states the question presented as "whether a process for curing synthetic rubber ... is patentable subject matter." Of course, that question was effectively answered many years ago when Charles Goodyear obtained his patent on the vulcanization process. The patent application filed by Diehr and Lutton, however, teaches nothing about the chemistry of the synthetic rubber-curing process, nothing about the raw materials to be used in curing synthetic rubber, nothing about the equipment to be used in the process, and nothing about the significance or effect of any process variable such as temperature, curing time, particular compositions of material, or mold configurations. In short, Diehr and Lutton do not claim to have discovered anything new about the process for curing synthetic rubber.

As the Court reads the claims in the Diehr and Lutton patent application, the inventors' discovery is a method of constantly measuring the actual temperature inside a rubber molding press. As I read the claims, their discovery is an improved method of calculating the time that the mold should remain closed during the curing process. If the Court's reading of the claims were correct, I would agree that they disclose patentable subject matter. On the other hand, if the Court accepted my reading, I feel confident that the case would be decided differently.

There are three reasons why I cannot accept the Court's conclusion that Diehr and Lutton claim to have discovered a new method of constantly measuring the temperature inside a mold. First, there is not a word in the patent application that suggests that there is anything

tions 'the whole in some way exceed[ed] the sum of its parts.' *Great A. & P. Tea Co. v. Supermarket Equipment Corp.*, 340 U.S. 147, 152 [71 S.Ct. 127, 130, 95 L.Ed. 162] (1950)." *Id.*, at 521–522, 92 S.Ct., at 1703–1704.

In order for the dissent to reach its conclusion it is necessary for it to read out of respondents' patent application all the steps in the claimed process which it determined were not novel or "inventive." That is not the purpose of the § 101 inquiry and conflicts with the proposition recited above that a claimed invention may be entitled to patent protection even though some or all of its elements are not "novel."

unusual about the temperature-reading devices used in this process—or indeed that any particular species of temperature-reading device should be used in it. Second, since devices for constantly measuring actual temperatures—on a back porch, for example—have been familiar articles for quite some time, I find it difficult to believe that a patent application filed in 1975 was premised on the notion that a "process of constantly measuring the actual temperature" had just been discovered. Finally, the Patent and Trademark Office Board of Appeals expressly found that "the only difference between the conventional methods of operating a molding press and that claimed in [the] application rests in those steps of the claims which relate to the calculation incident to the solution of the mathematical problem or formula used to control the mold heater and the automatic opening of the press." This finding was not disturbed by the Court of Customs and Patent Appeals and is clearly correct.

A fair reading of the entire patent application, as well as the specific claims, makes it perfectly clear that what Diehr and Lutton claim to have discovered is a method of using a digital computer to determine the amount of time that a rubber molding press should remain closed during the synthetic rubber-curing process. There is no suggestion that there is anything novel in the instrumentation of the mold, in actuating a timer when the press is closed, or in automatically opening the press when the computed time expires. Nor does the application suggest that Diehr and Lutton have discovered anything about the temperatures in the mold or the amount of curing time that will produce the best cure. What they claim to have discovered, in essence, is a method of updating the original estimated curing time by repetitively recalculating that time pursuant to a well-known mathematical formula in response to variations in temperature within the mold. Their method of updating the curing time calculation is strikingly reminiscent of the method of updating alarm limits that Dale Flook sought to patent.

Parker v. Flook involved the use of a digital computer in connection with a catalytic conversion process. During the conversion process, variables such as temperature, pressure, and flow rates were constantly monitored and fed into the computer; in this case, temperature in the mold is the variable that is monitored and fed into the computer. In *Flook*, the digital computer repetitively recalculated the "alarm limit"—a number that might signal the need to terminate or modify the catalytic conversion process; in this case, the digital computer repetitively recalculates the correct curing time—a number that signals the time when the synthetic rubber molding press should open.

The essence of the claimed discovery in both cases was an algorithm that could be programmed on a digital computer. In *Flook*, the algorithm made use of multiple process variables; in this case, it makes use of only one. In *Flook*, the algorithm was expressed in a newly developed mathematical formula; in this case, the algorithm makes use of a well-known mathematical formula. Manifestly, neither of these differences can explain today's holding.[32] What I believe does explain today's holding is a misunderstanding of the applicants' claimed invention and a failure to recognize the critical difference between the "discovery" requirement in § 101 and the "novelty" requirement in § 102.

III

The Court misapplies *Parker v. Flook* because, like the Court of Customs and Patent Appeals, it fails to understand or completely disregards the distinction between the subject matter of what the inventor *claims* to have discovered—the § 101 issue—and the question whether that claimed discovery is in fact novel—the § 102 issue. If there is not even a claim that anything constituting patentable subject matter has been discovered, there is no occasion to address the novelty issue. Or, as was true in *Flook*, if the only concept that the inventor claims to have discovered is not patentable subject matter, § 101 requires that the application be rejected without reaching any issue under § 102; for it is irrelevant that unpatentable subject matter—in that case a formula for updating alarm limits—may in fact be novel.

Proper analysis, therefore, must start with an understanding of what the inventor claims to have discovered—or phrased somewhat differently—what he considers his inventive concept to be. It seems clear to me that Diehr and Lutton claim to have developed a new method of programming a digital computer in order to calculate—promptly and repeatedly—the correct curing time in a familiar process. In the § 101 analysis, we must assume that the sequence of steps in this programming method is novel, unobvious, and useful. The threshold question of whether such a method is patentable subject matter remains.

32. Indeed, the most significant distinction between the invention at issue in *Flook* and that at issue in this case lies not in the characteristics of the inventions themselves, but rather in the drafting of the claims. After noting that "[t]he Diehr claims are reminiscent of the claims in *Flook*," Blumenthal & Riter, *Statutory or Non–statutory?: An Analysis of the Patentability of Computer Related Inventions,* 62 J. PAT. OFF. SOC., 502–503 (1980), the authors of a recent article on the subject observe that the Court of Customs and Patent Appeals' analysis in this case "lends itself to an interesting exercise in claim drafting." *Id.*, at 505. To illustrate their point, the authors redrafted the Diehr and Lutton claims into the format employed in the *Flook* application:

"An improved method of calculating the cure time of a rubber molding process utilizing a digital computer comprising the steps of:

"a. inputting into said computer input values including

"1. natural logarithm conversion data ([l]n),

"2. an activation energy constant (C) unique to each batch of rubber being molded,

"3. a constant (X) dependent upon the geometry of the particular mold of the press, and

"4. continuous temperature values (Z) of the mold during molding;

"b. operating said computer for

"1. counting the elapsed cure time,

"2. calculating the cure time from the input values using the Arrhenius equation [l]n V = CZ + X, where V is the total cure time, and

"c. providing output signals from said computer when said calculated cure time is equal to said elapsed cure time." *Ibid.* The authors correctly conclude that even the lower court probably would have found that this claim was drawn to unpatentable subject matter under § 101.

If that method is regarded as an "algorithm" as that term was used in *Gottschalk v. Benson* and in *Parker v. Flook*,[38] and if no other inventive concept is disclosed in the patent application, the question must be answered in the negative. In both *Benson* and *Flook*, the parties apparently agreed that the inventor's discovery was properly regarded as an algorithm; the holding that an algorithm was a "law of nature" that could not be patented therefore determined that those discoveries were not patentable processes within the meaning of § 101.

As the Court recognizes today, *Flook* also rejected the argument that patent protection was available if the inventor did not claim a monopoly on every conceivable use of the algorithm but instead limited his claims by describing a specific postsolution activity—in that case setting off an alarm in a catalytic conversion process. In its effort to distinguish *Flook* from the instant case, the Court characterizes that postsolution activity as "insignificant," or as merely "token" activity. As a practical matter however, the postsolution activity described in the *Flook* application was no less significant than the automatic opening of the curing mold involved in this case. For setting off an alarm limit at the appropriate time is surely as important to the safe and efficient operation of a catalytic conversion process as is actuating the mold-opening device in a synthetic rubber-curing process. In both cases, the post-solution activity is a significant part of the industrial process. But in neither case should that activity have any *legal* significance because it does not constitute a part of the inventive concept that the applicants claimed to have discovered.[39]

* * *

IV

The broad question whether computer programs should be given patent protection involves policy considerations that this Court is not

38. In *Benson*, we explained the term "algorithm" in the following paragraph:

"The patent sought is on a method of programming a general-purpose digital computer to convert signals from binary-coded decimal form into pure binary form. A procedure for solving a given type of mathematical problem is known as an 'algorithm.' The procedures set forth in the present claims are of that kind; that is to say, they are a generalized formulation for programs to solve mathematical problems of converting one form of numerical representation to another. From the generic formulation, programs may be developed as specific applications." 409 U.S., at 65, 93 S.Ct., at 254.

39. In *Flook*, the Court's analysis of the postsolution activity recited in the patent application turned, not on the relative significance of that activity in the catalytic conversion process, but rather on the fact that that activity was not a part of the applicant's discovery:

"The notion that post-solution activity, no matter how conventional or obvious in itself, can transform an unpatentable principle into a patentable process exalts form over substance. A competent draftsman could attach some form of post-solution activity to almost any mathematical formula; the Pythagorean theorem would not have been patentable, or partially patentable, because a patent application contained a final step indicating that the formula, when solved, could be usefully applied to existing surveying techniques. The concept of patentable subject matter under § 101 is not 'like a nose of wax which may be turned and twisted in any direction....' *White v. Dunbar*, 119 U.S. 47, 51 [7 S.Ct. 72, 74, 30 L.Ed. 303]." 437 U.S., at 590, 98 S.Ct., at 2525–2526.

authorized to address. As the numerous briefs amicus curiae * * * demonstrate, that question is not only difficult and important, but apparently also one that may be affected by institutional bias. In each of those cases, the spokesmen for the organized patent bar have uniformly favored patentability and industry representatives have taken positions properly motivated by their economic self-interest. Notwithstanding fervent argument that patent protection is essential for the growth of the software industry, commentators have noted that "this industry is growing by leaps and bounds without it." In addition, even some commentators who believe that legal protection for computer programs is desirable have expressed doubts that the present patent system can provide the needed protection.

Within the Federal Government, patterns of decision have also emerged. Gottschalk, Dann, Parker, and Diamond were not ordinary litigants—each was serving as Commissioner of Patents and Trademarks when he opposed the availability of patent protection for a program-related invention. No doubt each may have been motivated by a concern about the ability of the Patent Office to process effectively the flood of applications that would inevitably flow from a decision that computer programs are patentable.[45] The consistent concern evidenced by the Commissioner of Patents and Trademarks and by the Board of Appeals of the Patent and Trademark Office has not been shared by the Court of Customs and Patent Appeals, which reversed the Board in *Benson*, *Johnston*, and *Flook*, and was in turn reversed by this Court in each of those cases.

* * *

Notes and Questions

1. *Abstract ideas, scientific principles, laws of nature and mathematical formulas.* As the *Diehr* opinion indicates, abstract ideas, scientific principles, laws of nature, and mathematical formulas are not patentable. Specific, physical applications of ideas, principles, laws or formulas are patented. Thus, while Sir Isaac Newton could not obtain a patent on the law of gravity, one could obtain a patent on a new machine or process which incorporates the law of gravity in its operation. What is the justification for the rule that abstract ideas, scientific principles, laws of nature and mathematical formulas are not themselves patentable? Why is the rule interpreted to preclude granting a patent for a computer program by itself? Is the interpretation justified?

2. *Novelty and the section 101 determination.* We will study Patent Act section 102, which defines the novelty requirement, later in the Chapter. Based on your reading of the majority and the dissent in *Diehr*, what is the

45. This concern influenced the President's Commission on the Patent System when it recommended against patent protection for computer programs. In its report, the President's Commission stated:

"The Patent Office now cannot examine applications for programs because of the lack of a classification technique and the requisite search files. Even if these were available, reliable searches would not be feasible or economic because of the tremendous volume of prior art being generated. * * *"

relationship between sections 101 and 102 of the Patent Act? According to the majority, what was wrong with the patent examiner's approach to determining whether the *Diehr* application set forth patentable subject matter? Could the examiner's procedure lead to the denial of a patent for subject matter that would otherwise pass muster as novel under section 102?

3. *The aftermath of the Diehr decision.* In the aftermath of the *Diehr* decision, the Court of Customs and Patent Appeals and its successor, the Court of Appeals for the Federal Circuit, have focused on refining and applying a two-step test for determining whether inventions including computer programs constitute statutory subject matter. In *In re* Walter, 618 F.2d 758, 767, 205 U.S.P.Q. 397, 407 (C.C.P.A.1980), the Court of Customs and Patent Appeals set forth the test as follows: The first step is to determine whether the patent claim recites, directly or indirectly, a mathematical algorithm. If it does, the second step is to determine whether the "mathematical algorithm is implemented in a specific manner to define structural relationships between the physical elements of the claim (in apparatus claims [5]) or to refine or limit claim steps (in process claims)." If the second step is satisfied, the claim states statutory subject matter. In *In re* Abele, 684 F.2d 902, 907, 214 U.S.P.Q. 682, 686 (C.C.P.A.1982), the court elaborated:

> *Walter* should be read as requiring no more than that the algorithm be "applied in any manner to physical elements or process steps," provided that its application is circumscribed by more than a field of use limitation or non-essential post-solution activity. Thus, if the claim would be "otherwise statutory," albeit inoperative or less useful without the algorithm, the claim likewise presents statutory subject matter when the algorithm is included.

For a more detailed discussion of the patentability of software-related inventions, see 1 D. CHISUM, PATENTS: A TREATISE ON THE LAW OF PATENTABILITY, VALIDITY AND INFRINGEMENT, § 1.03[6] (1992); Gable & Leaheey, *The Strength of Patent Protection for Computer Products: The Federal Circuit and the Patent Office Refine the Test for Determining which Computer–Related Inventions Constitute Patentable Subject Matter*, 17 RUTGERS COMPUTER & TECH. L.J. 87 (1991); Stern, *Tales from the Algorithm War:* Benson *to* Iwahashi, *It's Deja Vu All Over Again*, 18 AIPLA Q.J. 371 (1991).

For a discussion of the patentability of software-related inventions abroad, see Hoffman, Grossman, & Keane, *International Computer Software Protection*, 5 COMPUTER LAW. 1 (March, 1988).

4. *Should computer programs be patented?* As illustrated in Chapter Two, trade secret protection may be available for secret aspects of computer programs. Moreover, as you will see in Chapter Five, the Copyright Act treats computer programs as "literary works," and affords significant protection against unauthorized copying. Is patent protection needed for computer programs? See Swinson, *Copyright or Patent or Both: An Algorithmic Approach to Computer Software Protection*, 5 HARV. J.L. & TECH. 145

5. [By the editor: An apparatus claim is a claim that covers a product, machine, or structure, as opposed to a process.]

(1991); Chisum, *The Patentability of Algorithms*, 47 U. PITT. L. REV. 959, 1013 (1986); *Against Software Patents: The League for Programming Freedom*, 14 HASTINGS COMM. & ENT. L.J. 297 (1992); Higgins, *The Case for Software Patent Protection*, 14 HASTINGS COMM. & ENT. L.J. 315 (1992).

In 1992, 7,552 patent applications were filed in the "Computer Systems Class," and 2,832 patents were granted. Kunin, *Patentability of Computer Program Related Inventions in the United States Patent and Trademark Office*, 79 J. PAT. & TRADEMARK OFF. SOC. 149 (1994).

5. *Patents for new uses of old products.* Section 100 of the Patent Act provides that the term "process" "includes a new use of a known process, machine, manufacture, composition of matter or material." Thus, for example, a person who discovers that a known chemical compound has previously unknown medicinal qualities may obtain a patent on the process of treating patients with the compound, assuming that the other requirements of the Patent Act are satisfied. As the Supreme Court has explained, this type of "process" patent is particularly important to inventors in chemical research:

> The number of chemicals either known to scientists or disclosed by existing research is vast. It grows constantly, as those engaging in "pure" research publish their discoveries. The number of these chemicals that have known uses of commercial or social value, in contrast, is small. Development of new uses for existing chemicals is thus a major component of practical chemical research. It may take years of unsuccessful testing before a chemical having a desired property is identified, and it may take several years of further testing before a proper and safe method for using that chemical is developed.

Dawson Chemical Co. v. Rohm & Haas Co., 448 U.S. 176, 221–22, 100 S.Ct. 2601, 2626, 65 L.Ed.2d 696, 718, 206 U.S.P.Q. 385 (1980).

IN RE ALAPPAT

United States Court of Appeals for the Federal Circuit, 1994.
33 F.3d 1526, 31 U.S.P.Q.2d 1545 (en banc).

RICH, CIRCUIT JUDGE:

[The invention the applicant, Alappat, sought to patent was (in lay terms) an improvement in an oscilloscope comparable to making a TV have a clearer picture. Patent claim 15 was written completely in "means for" language, as provided in Patent Act § 112, ¶ 6:

> An element in a claim for a combination may be expressed as a means or step for performing a specified function without the recital of structure, material, or acts in support thereof, and such claim shall be construed to cover the corresponding structure, material, or acts described in the specification and equivalents thereof.

35 U.S.C.A. § 112. The Court of Appeals found that:]

When independent claim 15 is construed in accordance with § 112 ¶ 6, claim 15 reads as follows, the subject matter in brackets representing the structure which Alappat discloses in his specification as corresponding to the respective means language recited in the claims:

> A rasterizer [a "machine"] for converting vector list data representing sample magnitudes of an input waveform into anti-aliased pixel illumination intensity data to be displayed on a display means comprising:
>
> (a) [an arithmetic logic *circuit* configured to perform an absolute value function, or an equivalent thereof] for determining the vertical distance between the endpoints of each of the vectors in the data list;
>
> (b) [an arithmetic logic *circuit* configured to perform an absolute value function, or an equivalent thereof] for determining the elevation of a row of pixels that is spanned by the vector;
>
> (c) [a pair of *barrel shifters*, or equivalents thereof] for normalizing the vertical distance and elevation; and
>
> (d) [a *read only memory (ROM)* containing illumination intensity data, or an equivalent thereof] for outputting illumination intensity data as a predetermined function of the normalized vertical distance and elevation.

As is evident, claim 15 unquestionably recites a machine, or apparatus, made up of a combination of known electronic circuitry elements.

[The PTO rejected the claim on the basis that it was not directed to subject matter as defined in § 101. The Court of Appeals reverses.]

[C]laim 15, properly construed, claims a machine, namely, a rasterizer "for converting vector list data representing sample magnitudes of an input waveform into anti-aliased pixel illumination intensity data to be displayed on a display means," which machine is made up of, at the very least, the specific structures disclosed in Alappat's specification corresponding to the means-plus-function elements (a)-(d) recited in the claim. According to Alappat, the claimed rasterizer performs the same overall function as prior art rasterizers, but does so in a different way, which is represented by the combination of four elements claimed in means-plus-function terminology. Because claim 15 is directed to a "machine," which is one of the four categories of patentable subject matter enumerated in § 101, claim 15 appears on its face to be directed to § 101 subject matter.

This does not quite end the analysis, however, because the Board majority argues that the claimed subject matter falls within a judicially created exception to § 101 which the majority refers to as the "mathematical algorithm" exception. * * *

(A)

The plain and unambiguous meaning of § 101 is that any new and useful process, machine, manufacture, or composition of matter, or any new and useful improvement thereof, may be patented if it meets the requirements for patentability set forth in Title 35, such as those found in §§ 102, 103, and 112. The use of the expansive term "any" in § 101 represents Congress's intent not to place any restrictions on the subject matter for which a patent may be obtained beyond those specifically recited in § 101 and the other parts of Title 35. Indeed, the Supreme Court has acknowledged that Congress intended § 101 to extend to "anything under the sun that is made by man." *Diamond v. Chakrabarty*, 447 U.S. 303, 309, 100 S.Ct. 2204, 2208, 65 L.Ed.2d 144 (1980). Thus, it is improper to read into § 101 limitations as to the subject matter that may be patented where the legislative history does not indicate that Congress clearly intended such limitations. * * *

Despite the apparent sweep of § 101, the Supreme Court has held that certain categories of subject matter are not entitled to patent protection. In *Diamond v. Diehr*, 450 U.S. 175, 101 S.Ct. 1048, 67 L.Ed.2d 155 (1981), its most recent case addressing § 101, the Supreme Court explained that there are three categories of subject matter for which one may not obtain patent protection, namely "laws of nature, natural phenomena, and abstract ideas." Of relevance to this case, the Supreme Court also has held that certain mathematical subject matter is not, standing alone, entitled to patent protection. A close analysis of *Diehr*, *Flook*, and *Benson* reveals that the Supreme Court never intended to create an overly broad, fourth category of subject matter excluded from § 101. Rather, at the core of the Court's analysis in each of these cases lies an attempt by the Court to explain a rather straightforward concept, namely, that certain types of mathematical subject matter, standing alone, represent nothing more than *abstract ideas* until reduced to some type of practical application, and thus that subject matter is not, in and of itself, entitled to patent protection.

Diehr also demands that the focus in any statutory subject matter analysis be on *the claim as a whole*. Indeed, the Supreme Court stated in *Diehr*:

> [W]hen a claim containing a mathematical formula * * * implements or applies that formula * * * in a structure or process which, when considered *as a whole*, is performing a function which the patent laws were designed to protect (e.g., transforming or reducing an article to a different state or thing), then the claim satisfies the requirements of § 101.

Diehr, 450 U.S. at 192, 101 S.Ct. at 1059–60 (emphasis added).

It is thus not necessary to determine whether a claim contains, as merely a part of the whole, any mathematical subject matter which standing alone would not be entitled to patent protection. Indeed, because the dispositive inquiry is whether the claim *as a whole* is directed to statutory subject matter, it is irrelevant that a claim may contain, as part of the whole, subject matter which would not be patentable by itself. * * *

(B)

Given the foregoing, the proper inquiry in dealing with the so called mathematical subject matter exception to § 101 alleged herein is to see whether the claimed subject matter *as a whole* is a disembodied mathematical concept, whether categorized as a mathematical formula, mathematical equation, mathematical algorithm, or the like, which in essence represents nothing more than a "law of nature," "natural phenomenon," or "abstract idea." If so, *Diehr* precludes the patenting of that subject matter. That is not the case here.

Although many, or arguably even all, of the means elements recited in claim 15 represent circuitry elements that perform mathematical calculations, which is essentially true of all digital electrical circuits, the claimed invention as a whole is directed to a combination of interrelated elements which combine to form a machine for converting discrete waveform data samples into anti-aliased pixel illumination intensity data to be displayed on a display means. This is not a disembodied mathematical concept which may be characterized as an "abstract idea," but rather a specific machine to produce a useful, concrete, and tangible result.

The fact that the four claimed means elements function to transform one set of data to another through what may be viewed as a series of mathematical calculations does not alone justify a holding that the claim as a whole is directed to nonstatutory subject matter. Indeed, claim 15 as written is not "so abstract and sweeping" that it would "wholly pre-empt" the use of any apparatus employing the combination of mathematical calculations recited therein. Rather, claim 15 is limited to the use of a particularly claimed combination of elements performing the particularly claimed combination of calculations to transform, i.e., rasterize, digitized waveforms (data) into anti-aliased, pixel illumination data to produce a smooth waveform.

* * *

The reconsideration Board majority also erred in its reasoning that claim 15 is unpatentable merely because it "reads on a general purpose digital computer 'means' to perform the various steps under program control." The Board majority stated that it would "not presume that a stored program digital computer is not within the § 112 ¶ 6 range of equivalents of the structure disclosed in the specification." [26] Alappat admits that claim 15 would read on a general purpose computer programmed to carry out the claimed invention, but argues that this alone also does not justify holding claim 15 unpatentable as directed to nonstatutory subject matter. We agree. We have held that such programming creates a new machine, because a general purpose computer in effect becomes a special purpose computer once it is programmed to perform particular functions pursuant to instructions from program software.

Under the Board majority's reasoning, a programmed general purpose computer could never be viewed as patentable subject matter under

26. The disclosed ALU, ROM and shift registers are all common elements of stored program digital computers.

§ 101. This reasoning is without basis in the law. The Supreme Court has never held that a programmed computer may never be entitled to patent protection. * * * Consequently, a computer operating pursuant to software *may* represent patentable subject matter, provided, of course, that the claimed subject matter meets all of the other requirements of Title 35. In any case, a computer, like a rasterizer, is apparatus not mathematics.

* * *

ARCHER, CHIEF JUDGE, with whom NIES, CIRCUIT JUDGE, joins, * * * dissenting in part.

* * *

Alappat has arranged known circuit elements to accomplish nothing other than the solving of a particular mathematical equation represented in the mind of the reader of his patent application. Losing sight of the forest for the structure of the trees, the majority today holds that any claim reciting a precise arrangement of structure satisfies 35 U.S.C. § 101. * * *

* * *

Consider for example the discovery or creation of music, a new song. Music of course is not patentable subject matter; a composer cannot obtain exclusive patent rights for the original creation of a musical composition. But now suppose the new melody is recorded on a compact disc. In such case, the particular musical composition will define an arrangement of minute pits in the surface of the compact disc material, and therefore will define its specific structure. Alternatively suppose the music is recorded on the rolls of a player piano or a music box.

Through the expedient of putting his music on known structure, can a composer now claim as his invention the structure of a compact disc or player piano roll containing the melody he discovered and obtain a patent therefor? The answer must be no. The composer admittedly has invented or discovered nothing but music. The discovery of music does not become patentable subject matter simply because there is an arbitrary claim to some structure.

And if a claim to a compact disc or piano roll containing a newly discovered song were regarded as a "manufacture" and within § 101 simply because of the specific physical structure of the compact disc, the "practical effect" would be the granting of a patent for a discovery in music. Where the music is new, the precise structure of the disc or roll would be novel under § 102. Because the patent law cannot examine music for "nonobviousness," the Patent and Trademark Office could not make a showing of obviousness under § 103. The result would well be the award of a patent for the discovery of music. The majority's simplistic approach of looking *only* to whether the claim reads on structure and *ignoring* the claimed invention or discovery for which a patent is sought will result in the awarding of patents for discoveries well beyond the scope of the patent law.

* * *

The "rasterizer" as claimed is an arrangement of circuitry elements for converting data into other data according to a particular mathematical operation. The rasterizer begins with vector "data"—two numbers. "[I]t does not matter how they are ascertained." The two numbers, as they might to any algebra student, "represent" endpoints of a line.

The claimed "rasterizer" ends with other specific "data"—an array of numbers, as the original and reconsideration panels of the board both expressly agreed. The end-data of the "rasterizer" are a predetermined and claimed mathematic function of the two input numbers.

Alappat admits that each of the circuitry elements of the claimed "rasterizer" is old. He says they are merely "form." Thus, they are only a convenient and basic way of electrically representing the mathematical operations to be performed, that is, converting vector data into matrix or raster data. In Alappat's view, it is the new mathematic operation that is the "substance" of the claimed invention or discovery. Claim 15 as a whole thus claims old circuitry elements in an arrangement *defined by a mathematical operation*, which only performs the *very mathematical operation that defines it*. Rather than claiming the mathematics itself, which of course Alappat cannot do, Alappat claims the mathematically defined structure. But as a whole, there is no "application" apart from the mathematical operation that is asserted to be the invention or discovery. What is going on here is a charade. * * *

The subject matter of claim 15, as in *Flook*, "has no substance apart from the calculations involved. The calculations are the beginning and end of the claim[ ]." *Walter*, 618 F.2d at 769, 205 USPQ at 409. * * *

* * *

* * * Alappat is like a composer who claims his song on a compact disc, and then argues that the compact disc is equivalent to a player piano or a music box with the song on a roll or even sheet music because they all represent the same song. The composer is thus clearly asking for (and getting from the majority) a patent for the discovery of a song and a patent covering every physical manifestation of the song.

In any event, even if a programmed general purpose computer is "equivalent" to the rasterizer, it cannot be deemed to be within § 101 by simply reasoning as does the majority that it is a "new machine." * * *

[A] known circuit containing a light bulb, battery, and switch is not a new machine when the switch is opened and closed to recite a new story in Morse code, because the "invent[ion] or discover[y]" is merely a new story, which is nonstatutory subject matter. An old stereo playing a new song on a compact disc is not a new machine because the invention or discovery is merely a new song, which is nonstatutory subject matter. [A] player piano playing Chopin's scales does not become a "new machine" when it spins a roll to play Brahms' lullaby. The distinction between the piano before and after different rolls are inserted resides not in the piano's changing quality as a "machine" but only in the changing melodies being played by the one machine. The only invention by the creator of a roll that is new because of its music is the new music. Because the patent law does not examine musical compositions to determine their relation to those that have gone before, the distinction between new and old music can never qualify for patent protection.

> It is not the computer—the machine qua computer—that performs the [mathematic] function, but, rather, the [mathematic function] is attained only through "use" of the general-purpose computer. The general-purpose digital computer is itself a total and self-complete machine entity. Versatility in electronic data processing is its endowment, its reason for being, its stock in trade.

Digitronics Corp. v. New York Racing Ass'n. Inc., 187 USPQ 602, 640, 1975 WL 21112 (E.D.N.Y.1975), *aff'd on other grounds*, 553 F.2d 740, 193 USPQ 577 (2d Cir.1977). A programmed general purpose digital computer alleged to be patentable subject matter because of the program presents an independent § 101 inquiry that is not resolved simply by calling the structure a "new machine."

Finally, a claim formally to a general purpose computer running a certain program cannot be deemed to satisfy § 101 simply because the computer is a physical, tangible device. As the invalidated claims in *Flook* and *Benson* demonstrate, and consistent with my earlier discussion, a computer program for use in a physical electronic thing called a computer may nevertheless be held to be nonstatutory subject matter. It is illogical to say that although a claim to a newly discovered mathematical operation to be performed by a computer is merely a nonstatutory discovery of mathematics, a claim to any computer performing that same mathematics is a statutory invention or discovery. * * *

* * *

The majority's holding is dangerous in the following way. First, it reasons that one can obtain a patent for a discovery in mathematics as long as some structure is formally recited on the face of the claim. Under this aspect of the holding, many of the requirements for patentability other than "newness," such as nonobviousness, make no sense and cannot be meaningfully applied. Thus, mathematical patents will be easier to obtain than other patents. Moreover, the patent law will now engage in the charade wherein claims directed to a particular method of calculating numbers (for use in a computer) are unpatentable, but claims directed to a computer (performing a particular method of calculating numbers) are patentable.

Second, the majority accepts the argument that all digital electronic circuitry is statutory subject matter when it performs a mathematical operation, and it is all equivalent when the particular mathematical operation is the same. Under this aspect, the mathematical patents will create an enormous scope of technological exclusivity. The lack of meaningful examination and the breadth of exclusive rights conferred by patents for discoveries of bare mathematical operations are repugnant to Congress's careful statutory scheme for the promotion of the useful arts.

As the player piano playing new music is not the stuff of patent law, neither is the mathematics that is Alappat's "rasterizer." And the Supreme Court has in its decisions required it so. Alappat's claimed discovery is outside 35 U.S.C. § 101, and for this reason I would affirm the board's rejection. I dissent from the majority's decision on the merits to the contrary.

* * *

Notes and Questions

1. *"Software patents."* Are Judge Archer's analogies to music apt ones? Do you agree with his assessment of the implications of the majority's holding?

For a useful discussion (by a member of the PTO Board of Patent Appeals and Interferences) of the *Alappat* decision and the Federal Circuit's preceding opinions concerning the patentability of software-related inventions, see Barrett, *PTO Perspective on Recent Developments on Patent Protection for Computer Hardware and Software*, 16 HASTINGS COMM. & ENT. L.J. 1 (1994). See also Goodman, Marlette & Trzyna, *The* Alappat *Standard for Determining that Programmed Computers Are Patentable Subject Matter*, 76 J. PAT. & TRADEMARK OFF. SOC. 771 (1994).

C. STANDARDS OF PATENTABILITY

1. Section 101: Utility

BRENNER v. MANSON

United States Supreme Court, 1966.
383 U.S. 519, 86 S.Ct. 1033, 16 L.Ed.2d 69.

MR. JUSTICE FORTAS delivered the opinion of the Court.

[Manson filed an application to patent a process for making certain known steroids. The PTO rejected the application on the ground that the application failed to disclose any utility for the steroid produced by the process. The Court of Customs and Patent appeals reversed, holding that "where a claimed process produces a known product it is not necessary to show utility for the product," so long as the product "is not alleged to be detrimental to the public interest."]

II.

Our starting point is the proposition, neither disputed nor disputable, that one may patent only that which is "useful." [T]he concept of utility has maintained a central place in all of our patent legislation, beginning with the first patent law in 1790 and culminating in the present law's provision that

"Whoever invents or discovers any new and useful process, machine, manufacture, or composition of matter, or any new and useful improvement thereof, may obtain a patent therefor, subject to the conditions and requirements of this title."

As is so often the case, however, a simple, everyday word can be pregnant with ambiguity when applied to the facts of life. That this is so is demonstrated by the present conflict between the Patent Office and the CCPA over how the test is to be applied to a chemical process which yields an already known product whose utility—other than as a possible object of scientific inquiry—has not yet been evidenced. It was not long ago that agency and court seemed of one mind on the question. In *Application of Bremner*, 182 F.2d 216, 217, 37 C.C.P.A. (Pat.) 1032, 1034, the court affirmed rejection by the Patent Office of both process and product claims. It noted that "no use for the products claimed to be developed by the processes had been shown in the specification." It held that "It was never intended that a patent be granted upon a product, or a process producing a product, unless such product be useful." Nor was this new doctrine in the court.

The Patent Office has remained stead-fast in this view. The CCPA, however, has moved sharply away from *Bremner*. The trend began in *Application of Nelson*, 280 F.2d 172, 47 C.C.P.A. (Pat.) 1031. There, the court reversed the Patent Office's rejection of a claim on a process yielding chemical intermediates "useful to chemists doing research on steroids," despite the absence of evidence that any of the steroids thus ultimately produced were themselves "useful." The trend has accelerated, culminating in the present case where the court held it sufficient that a process produces the result intended and is not "detrimental to the public interest."

It is not remarkable that differences arise as to how the test of usefulness is to be applied to chemical processes. Even if we knew precisely what Congress meant in 1790 when it devised the "new and useful" phraseology and in subsequent re-enactments of the test, we should have difficulty in applying it in the context of contemporary chemistry where research is as comprehensive as man's grasp and where little or nothing is wholly beyond the pale of "utility"—if that word is given its broadest reach.

Respondent does not—at least in the first instance—rest upon the extreme proposition, advanced by the court below, that a novel chemical process is patentable so long as it yields the intended product and so long as the product is not itself "detrimental." Nor does he commit the outcome of his claim to the slightly more conventional proposition that any process is "useful" within the meaning of § 101 if it produces a compound whose potential usefulness is under investigation by serious scientific researchers, although he urges this position, too, as an alternative basis for affirming the decision of the CCPA. Rather, he begins with the much more orthodox argument that his process has a specific utility which would entitle him to a declaration of interference even under the Patent Office's reading of § 101. The claim is that the supporting affidavits filed pursuant to Rule 204(b), by reference to Ringold's 1956 article, reveal that an adjacent homologue of the steroid yielded by his process has been demonstrated to have tumor-inhibiting effects in mice, and that this discloses the requisite utility. We do not accept any of these theories as an adequate basis for overriding the determination of the Patent Office that the "utility" requirement has not been met.

Even on the assumption that the process would be patentable were respondent to show that the steroid produced had a tumor-inhibiting effect in mice, we would not overrule the Patent Office finding that respondent has not made such a showing. The Patent Office held that, despite the reference to the adjacent homologue, respondent's papers did not disclose a sufficient likelihood that the steroid yielded by his process would have similar tumor-inhibiting characteristics. Indeed, respondent himself recognized that the presumption that adjacent homologues have the same utility has been challenged in the steroid field because of "a greater known unpredictability of compounds in that field." In these circumstances and in this technical area, we would not overturn the finding of the Primary Examiner, affirmed by the Board of Appeals and not challenged by the CCPA.

The second and third points of respondent's argument present issues of much importance. Is a chemical process "useful" within the meaning of § 101 either (1) because it works—*i.e.*, produces the intended product? or (2) because the compound yielded belongs to a class of compounds now the subject of serious scientific investigation? These contentions present the basic problem for our adjudication. Since we find no specific assistance in the legislative materials underlying § 101, we are remitted to an analysis of the problem in light of the general intent of Congress, the purposes of the patent system, and the implications of a decision one way or the other.

In support of his plea that we attenuate the requirement of "utility," respondent relies upon Justice Story's well-known statement that a "useful" invention is one "which may be applied to a beneficial use in society, in contradistinction to an invention injurious to the morals, health, or good order of society, or frivolous and insignificant"—and upon the assertion that to do so would encourage inventors of new processes to publicize the event for the benefit of the entire scientific community, thus widening the search for uses and increasing the fund of scientific knowledge. Justice Story's language sheds little light on our subject. Narrowly read, it does no more than compel us to decide whether the invention in question is "frivolous and insignificant"—a query no easier of application than the one built into the statute. Read more broadly, so as to allow the patenting of any invention not positively harmful to society, it places such a special meaning on the word "useful" that we cannot accept it in the absence of evidence that Congress so intended. There are, after all, many things in this world which may not be considered "useful" but which, nevertheless are totally without a capacity for harm.

It is true, of course, that one of the purposes of the patent system is to encourage dissemination of information concerning discoveries and inventions. And it may be that inability to patent a process to some extent discourages disclosure and leads to greater secrecy than would otherwise be the case. The inventor of the process, or the corporate organization by which he is employed, has some incentive to keep the invention secret while uses for the product are searched out. However, in light of the highly developed art of drafting patent claims so that they disclose as little useful information as possible—while broadening the scope of the claim as widely as possible—the argument based upon the virtue of disclosure must be warily evaluated. Moreover, the pressure for secrecy is easily exaggerated, for if the inventor of a process cannot himself ascertain a "use" for that which his process yields, he has every incentive to make his invention known to those able to do so. Finally, how likely is disclosure of a patented process to spur research by others into the uses to which the product may be put? To the extent that the patentee has power to enforce his patent, there is little incentive for others to undertake a search for uses.

Whatever weight is attached to the value of encouraging disclosure and of inhibiting secrecy, we believe a more compelling consideration is that a process patent in the chemical field, which has not been developed and pointed to the degree of specific utility, creates a monopoly of knowledge which should be granted only if clearly commanded by the statute. Until the process claim has been reduced to production of a product shown to be useful, the metes and bounds of that monopoly are not capable of precise delineation. It may engross a vast, unknown, and perhaps unknowable area. Such a patent may confer power to block off whole areas of scientific development, without compensating benefit to the public. The basic *quid pro quo* contemplated by the Constitution and the Congress for granting a patent monopoly is the benefit derived by the public from an invention with substantial utility. Unless and until a process is refined and developed to this point—where specific benefit exists in currently available form—there is insufficient justification for permitting an applicant to engross what may prove to be a broad field.

These arguments for and against the patentability of a process which either has no known use or is useful only in the sense that it may be an object of scientific research would apply equally to the patenting of the product produced by the process. Respondent appears to concede that with respect to a product, as opposed to a process, Congress has struck the balance on the side of nonpatentability unless "utility" is shown. Indeed, the decisions of the CCPA are in accord with the view that a product may not be patented absent a showing of utility greater than any adduced in the present case. We find absolutely no warrant for the proposition that although Congress intended that no patent be granted on a chemical compound whose sole "utility" consists of its potential role as an object of use-testing, a different set of rules was meant to apply to the process which yielded the unpatentable product. That proposition seems to us little more than an attempt to evade the impact of the rules which concededly govern patentability of the product itself.

This is not to say that we mean to disparage the importance of contributions to the fund of scientific information short of the invention of something "useful," or that we are blind to the prospect that what now seems without "use" may tomorrow command the grateful attention of the public. But a patent is not a hunting license. It is not a reward for the search, but compensation for its successful conclusion. "[A] patent system must be related to the world of commerce rather than to the realm of philosophy. . . ."

* * *

MR. JUSTICE DOUGLAS dissents on the merits of the controversy for substantially the reasons stated by MR. JUSTICE HARLAN.

MR. JUSTICE HARLAN, concurring in part and dissenting in part.

* * *

Respondent has contended that a workable chemical process, which is both new and sufficiently nonobvious to satisfy the patent statute, is by its existence alone a contribution to chemistry and "useful" as the statute employs that term. Certainly this reading of "useful" in the statute is within the scope of the constitutional grant, which states only that "[t]o promote the Progress of Science and useful Arts," the exclusive right to "Writings and Discoveries" may be secured for limited times to those who produce them. Art. I, § 8. Yet the patent statute is somewhat differently worded and is on its face open both to respondent's construction and to the contrary reading given it by the Court. In the absence of legislative history on this issue, we are thrown back on policy and practice. Because I believe that the Court's policy arguments are not convincing and that past practice favors the respondent, I would reject the narrow definition of "useful" and uphold the judgment of the Court of Customs and Patent Appeals (hereafter CCPA).

The Court's opinion sets out about half a dozen reasons in support of its interpretation. Several of these arguments seem to me to have almost no force. For instance, it is suggested that "[u]ntil the process claim has been reduced to production of a product shown to be useful, the metes and bounds of that monopoly are not capable of precise delineation" and "[i]t may engross a vast, unknown, and perhaps unknowable area." I fail to see the relevance of these assertions; process claims are not disallowed because the products they produce may be of "vast" importance nor, in any event, does advance knowledge of a specific product use provide much safeguard on this score or fix "metes and bounds" precisely since a hundred more uses may be found after a patent is granted and greatly enhance its value.

The further argument that an established product use is part of "[t]he basic *quid pro quo* " for the patent or is the requisite "successful conclusion" of the inventor's search appears to beg the very question whether the process is "useful" simply because it facilitates further research into possible product uses. The same infirmity seems to inhere in the Court's argument that chemical products lacking immediate utility cannot be distinguished for present purposes from the processes which create them, that respondent appears to concede and the CCPA holds that the products are nonpatentable, and that therefore the processes are nonpatentable. Assuming that the two classes cannot be distinguished, a point not adequately considered in the briefs, and assuming further that the CCPA has firmly held such products nonpatentable, this permits us to conclude only that the CCPA is wrong either as to the products or as to the processes and affords no basis for deciding whether both or neither should be patentable absent a specific product use.

More to the point, I think, are the Court's remaining, prudential arguments against patentability: namely, that disclosure induced by allowing a patent is partly undercut by patent-application drafting techniques, that disclosure may occur without granting a patent, and that a patent will discourage others from inventing uses for the product. How far opaque drafting may lessen the public benefits resulting from the issuance of a patent is not shown by any evidence in this case but, more important, the argument operates against all patents and gives no reason for singling out the class involved here. The thought that these inventions may be more likely than most to be disclosed even if patents are not allowed may have more force; but while empirical study of the industry might reveal that chemical researchers would behave in this fashion, the abstractly logical choice for them seems to me to maintain secrecy until a product use can be discovered. As to discouraging the search by others for product uses, there is no doubt this risk exists but the price paid for any patent is that research on other uses or improvements may be hampered because the original patentee will reap much of the reward. From the standpoint of the public interest the Constitution seems to have resolved that choice in favor of patentability.

What I find most troubling about the result reached by the Court is the impact it may have on chemical research. Chemistry is a highly interrelated field and a tangible benefit for society may be the outcome of a number of different discoveries, one discovery building upon the next. To encourage one chemist or research facility to invent and disseminate new processes and products may be vital to progress, although the product or process be without "utility" as the Court defines the term, because that discovery permits someone else to take a further but perhaps less difficult step leading to a commercially useful item. In my view, our awareness in this age of the importance of achieving and publicizing basic research should lead this Court to resolve uncertainties in its favor and uphold the respondent's position in this case.

* * *

Notes and Questions

1. *The policy considerations.* If the purpose of patent law is to reach the optimal balance between promoting invention and preserving free competition, how stringent should the usefulness requirement be? Did the Court reach the correct balance? Should possible future usefulness of a chemical compound in scientific research suffice to demonstrate usefulness? What if it can presently be shown that a chemical compound has a tumor-inhibiting effect on laboratory animals, but as yet, no tests demonstrate whether the compound will inhibit tumors in humans? See Nelson v. Bowler, 626 F.2d 853, 206 U.S.P.Q. 881 (C.C.P.A.1980) (patent application for a chemical compound can satisfy the utility requirement by demonstrating a therapeutic use with animals—for example, inhibiting tumors in laboratory animals). Would granting a patent in situations such as *Brenner* serve as a roadblock to further research in the field? In your opinion, what is the likely impact of the Court's decision on public disclosure of newly discovered chemical compounds and processes for making them?

While earlier cases suggested that "immoral" inventions lacked utility, see, e.g., Meyer v. Buckley Mfg. Co., 15 F.Supp. 640 (N.D.Ill.1936) (invention found to be "at most a device for playing a game of chance" and thus lacking in utility), the trend is away from this approach to making the usefulness determination. But see Mirabel, *"Practical Utility" Is a Useless Concept*, 36 AM. U. L. REV. 811 (1987), for an argument that inquiry into the morality of an invention is the only type of "use examination" that can be supported by precedent or logic.

2. *Inoperability as lack of utility.* A patent may be denied for lack of usefulness if the invention fails to operate as claimed. For example, in Newman v. Quigg, 877 F.2d 1575, 11 U.S.P.Q.2d 1340 (C.A.F.C.), *modified* 886 F.2d 329 (C.A.F.C. 1989), *cert. denied* 495 U.S. 932, 110 S.Ct. 2173, 109 L.Ed.2d 502 (1990), the applicant claimed to have invented a device that generated more usable energy than it consumed (a "perpetual motion" machine). The P.T.O. found that such a device would violate "either the first or second law of thermodynamics," and rejected the application. In the course of district court review of the rejection, the applicant was ordered to submit a working model of the invention to the National Bureau of Standards for testing. When the National Bureau of Standards reported that tests failed to support the applicant's claims of more energy output than input, the district court held the claimed invention unpatentable for lack of usefulness. The Court of Appeals for the Federal Circuit affirmed.

See also Fregeau v. Mossinghoff, 776 F.2d 1034, 227 U.S.P.Q. 848 (C.A.F.C. 1985). In that case the applicant claimed a method for enhancing the flavor of beverages by passing them through a magnetic field. A highly skeptical patent examiner rejected the claims for lack of utility due to inoperativeness. The applicant then submitted declarations from a Professor of Food Science who had conducted taste tests, averring that the test results demonstrated that the invention worked. The examiner remained unconvinced, finding that the declaration was not "evidence of the type convincing to the scientific community." The Board of Patent Appeals and Interferences and the district court agreed with the examiner. The Federal Circuit affirmed, noting that a *prima facie* case of inoperability had been established simply by the nature of the invention, thus shifting the burden to the applicant to rebut the presumption.

For further discussion of operability, see Ederer, *On Operability as an Aspect of Patent Law*, 42 J. PAT. OFF. SOC. 398 (1960).

3. *Usefulness and pharmaceutical inventions.* If a patent applicant asserts that a chemical compound has therapeutic or pharmacological uses in humans, he must demonstrate that the compound is safe and effective for that purpose. See, e.g., Application of Novak, 306 F.2d 924, 134 U.S.P.Q. 335 (C.C.P.A.1962). The showing need not rise to the level required by the Food and Drug Administration, however. See Application of Anthony, 414 F.2d 1383, 162 U.S.P.Q. 594 (C.C.P.A.1969).

Of course, the granting of a patent for a chemical compound does not in itself authorize the patentee to sell it commercially, if sale is prohibited by health and safety laws. The new patentee may still face lengthy regulatory proceedings in agencies such as the Food and Drug Administration in order to obtain permission to market its new compound. This regulatory review may take a number of years, so that by the time the patentee obtains the necessary permission to enter the market, much of its patent term has expired. To compensate for delays caused by the pre-market regulatory process, Congress amended section 156 of the Patent Act in 1984, and again in 1988, to provide patent term extensions of up to five years for human and animal drugs, food and color additives, medical devices, and related method claims. For more information about the patent term restoration legislation, see Lourie, *Patent Term Restoration*, 66 J. PAT. OFF. SOC. 526 (1984). In addition, from time to time, Congress enacts private relief bills to extend patent terms upon a showing of "extraordinary circumstances."

2. *Section 102: Novelty*

Most nations grant patents to the first inventor to file an application, which leads to a "race to the patent office" when two or more sets of inventors are working on similar projects. The United States, in contrast, favors granting a patent to the first person to make the invention. The novelty provisions in section 102(a), (e), and (g) work together to make it very difficult for a "subsequent inventor" to obtain a patent.

Section 102(a) provides that an applicant will be denied a patent if, prior to the applicant's invention date, any of four things happened: 1) the invention was "known" in the United States; 2) the invention was "used" in the United States; 3) the invention was the subject of a patent anywhere in the world; or 4) the invention was revealed in a "printed publication" anywhere in the world.

Section 102(e) provides that even if the earlier invention was not disclosed to the public in any of the ways enumerated in subsection (a), it's existence will preclude the subsequent inventor from obtaining a patent if it was disclosed in a U.S. patent application that was pending on the subsequent inventor's invention date and was later granted. Note that pending patent applications are kept in secrecy, 35 U.S.C.A.

§ 122, so that our subsequent-inventor applicant may have had no way of knowing of the earlier invention's existence.

Section 102(g) places a final obstacle in the subsequent inventor's path to the Patent Office by providing that the earlier invention's existence will preclude a patent if the earlier invention was made in the United States and was not abandoned, suppressed or concealed.

Oak Industries, Inc. v. Zenith Electronics Corp., set forth below, explores subsections 102(a) and (g). However, given section 102's emphasis on the first to invent, it is useful first to discuss how the first inventor is identified.

The act of invention consists of two parts: the conception and the reduction to practice. An inventor conceives of the invention when he formulates a definite, complete idea of the operative invention, so that all that remains is the physical realization of it. The mental concept must be complete to the point that a person with ordinary skill in the art could then produce it out without further invention. Coleman v. Dines, 754 F.2d 353, 359, 224 U.S.P.Q. 857, 862 (C.A.F.C. 1985). The inventor may reduce the concept to practice in either of two ways. He may perform an actual reduction to practice by building a physical prototype of the invention (or in the case of a process, by actually carrying out the steps of the process) and ascertaining that it works for the intended purpose. Kimberly–Clark Corp. v. Johnson & Johnson, 745 F.2d 1437, 1445, 223 U.S.P.Q. 603, 607 (C.A.F.C. 1984). The inventor may constructively reduce the invention to practice by filing a patent application which fully discloses the invention with the PTO. Travis v. Baker, 137 F.2d 109, 111, 58 U.S.P.Q. 558, 560 (C.C.P.A.1943).

The presumption is that the first person to reduce the invention to practice is the first to invent. However, a person making a later reduction to practice may rebut that presumption by showing that he was the first to conceive of the invention and was diligent in reducing it to practice from a date prior to the conception date of the first to reduce to practice. See 3 D.S. CHISUM, PATENTS: A TREATISE ON THE LAW OF PATENTABILITY, VALIDITY, AND INFRINGEMENT § 10.03 (1991).

Griffith v. Kanamaru explores the meaning of diligence in reducing an invention to practice.

GRIFFITH v. KANAMARU

United States Court of Appeals for the Federal Circuit, 1987.
816 F.2d 624, 2 U.S.P.Q.2d 1361.

NICHOLS, SENIOR CIRCUIT JUDGE.

Owen W. Griffith (Griffith) appeals the decision of the Board of Patent Appeals and Interferences (board) that Griffith failed to establish a prima facie case that he is entitled to an award of priority against the filing date of Tsuneo Kanamaru, et al. (Kanamaru) for a patent on aminocarnitine compounds. We affirm.

Background

This patent interference case involves the application of Griffith, an Associate Professor in the Department of Biochemistry at Cornell University Medical College, for a patent on an aminocarnitine compound, useful in the treatment of diabetes, and a patent issued for the same invention to Kanamaru, an employee of Takeda Chemical Industries. The inventors assigned their rights to the inventions to the Cornell Research Foundation, Inc. (Cornell) and to Takeda Chemical Industries respectively. * * *

Griffith had established conception by June 30, 1981, and reduction to practice on January 11, 1984. Kanamaru filed for a United States patent on November 17, 1982. The board found, however, that Griffith failed to establish reasonable diligence for a *prima facie* case of prior invention * * *.

* * *

Analysis

I

* * *

Griffith must establish a *prima facie* case of reasonable diligence, as well as dates of conception and reduction to practice, to avoid summary judgment on the issue of priority. 37 C.F.R. § 1.617(a). * * * Griffith is burdened with establishing a *prima facie* case of reasonable diligence from immediately before Kanamaru's filing date of November 17, 1982, until Griffith's reduction to practice on January 11, 1984.

On appeal, Griffith presents two grounds intended to justify his inactivity on the aminocarnitine project between June 15, 1983, and September 13, 1983. The first is that, notwithstanding Cornell University's extraordinary endowment, it is reasonable, and as a policy matter desirable, for Cornell to require Griffith and other research scientists to obtain funding from outside the university. The second reason Griffith presents is that he reasonably waited for Ms. Debora Jenkins to matriculate in the Fall of 1983 to assist with the project. He had promised her she should have that task which she needed to qualify for her degree. We reject these arguments and conclude that Griffith has failed to establish grounds to excuse his inactivity prior to reduction to practice.

II

The reasonable diligence standard balances the interest in rewarding and encouraging invention with the public's interest in the earliest possible disclosure of innovation. Griffith must account for the entire period from just before Kanamaru's filing date until his reduction to practice. * * *

The board in this case was, but not properly, asked to pass judgment on the reasonableness of Cornell's policy regarding outside funding of research. The correct inquiry is rather whether it is reasonable for Cornell to require the public to wait for the innovation, given the well settled policy in favor of early disclosure. As the board notes, Chief Judge Markey has called early public disclosure the "linchpin of the patent system." *Horwath v. Lee*, 564 F.2d 948, 950, 195 USPQ 701, 703 (CCPA 1977). A review of caselaw on excuses for inactivity in reduction to practice reveals a common thread that courts may consider the reasonable everyday problems and limitations encountered by an inventor. *See, e.g., Bey v. Kollonitsch*, 806 F.2d 1024, 231 USPQ 967 (Fed.Cir. 1986) (delay in filing excused where attorney worked on a group of related applications and other applications contributed substantially to the preparation of Bey's application); *Reed v. Tornqvist*, 436 F.2d 501, 168 USPQ 462 (CCPA 1971) (concluding it is not unreasonable for inventor to delay completing a patent application until after returning from a three week vacation in Sweden, extended by illness of inventor's father); *Keizer v. Bradley*, 270 F.2d 396, 47 CCPA 709, 123 USPQ 215 (1959) (delay excused where inventor, after producing a component for a color television, delayed filing to produce an appropriate receiver for testing the component); *Courson v. O'Connor*, 227 F. 890, 894 (7th Cir.1915) ("exercise of reasonable diligence * * * does not require an inventor to devote his entire time thereto, or to abandon his ordinary means of livelihood") * * *.

Griffith argues that the admitted inactivity of three months between June 15, 1983, and September 13, 1983, which he attributes to Cornell's "reasonable" policy requiring outside funding and to Griffith's "reasonable" decision to delay until a graduate student arrived, falls within legal precedent excusing inactivity in the diligence context. We disagree. We first note that, in regard to waiting for a graduate student, Griffith does not even suggest that he faced a genuine shortage of personnel. He does not suggest that Ms. Jenkins was the *only* person capable of carrying on with the aminocarnitine experiment. We can see no application of precedent to suggest that the convenience of the timing of the semester schedule justifies a three-month delay for the purpose of reasonable diligence. Neither do we believe that this excuse, absent even a suggestion by Griffith that Jenkins was uniquely qualified to do his research, is reasonable.

Griffith's second contention that it was reasonable for Cornell to require outside funding, therefore causing a delay in order to apply for such funds, is also insufficient to excuse his inactivity. The crux of Griffith's argument is that outside funding is desirable as a form of peer review, or monitoring of the worthiness of a given project. He also suggests that, as a policy matter, universities should not be treated as businesses, which ultimately would detract from scholarly inquiry. * * *

* * *

Griffith's excuses sound more in the nature of commercial development, not accepted as an excuse for delay, than the "hardship" cases most commonly found and discussed *supra*. Delays in reduction to practice caused by an inventor's efforts to refine an invention to the most marketable and profitable form have not been accepted as sufficient excuses for inactivity. Griffith's case is analogous to that in *Seeberger v. Dodge*, 24 App.D.C. 476 (1905). In that case, the inventor was the first to conceive of an improvement in an escalator and was attempting to show diligence. The court noted:

> The testimony shows that he [Seeberger] was a man of means, and might have constructed an escalator had he undertaken to do so. Instead of this, his constant effort was to organize corporations, or to interest capital in other ways, for the purpose of engaging in the general manufacture of escalators.

Id. at 484–85.

The court held this unacceptable:

> One having the first complete conception of an invention cannot hold the field against all comers by diligent efforts, merely, to organize and procure sufficient capital to engage in the manufacture of his device or mechanism for commercial purposes. This is a different thing from diligence in actual reduction to practice.

Id. at 485.

* * *

III

The board in this case considered primarily Griffith's contention that the Cornell policy was reasonable and therefore acceptable to excuse his delay in reduction to practice. Although we agree with the board's conclusion, it is appropriate to go further and consider other circumstances as they apply to the reasonable diligence analysis of 35 U.S.C. § 102(g). The record reveals that from the relevant period of November 17, 1982 (Kanamaru's filing date), to September 13, 1983 (when Griffith renewed his efforts towards reduction to practice), Griffith interrupted and often put aside the aminocarnitine project to work on other experiments. Between June 1982 and June 1983 Griffith admits that, at the request of the chairman of his department, he was primarily engaged in an unrelated research project on mitochondrial glutathione metabolism. Griffith also put aside the aminocarnitine experiment to work on a grant proposal on an unrelated project. Griffith's statement in the record that his unrelated grant application, if granted, might "support" a future grant request directed to the aminocarnitine project does not overcome the conclusion that he preferred one project over another and was not "continuously" or "reasonably" diligent. Griffith made only minimal efforts to secure funding directly for the aminocarnitine project.

The conclusion we reach from the record is that the aminocarnitine project was second and often third priority in laboratory research as well as the solicitation of funds. We agree that Griffith failed to establish a *prima facie* case of reasonable diligence or a legally sufficient excuse for inactivity to establish priority over Kanamaru.

* * *

Notes and Questions

1. *Reasonable diligence.* Based on the *Griffith* opinion, what considerations will courts find influential in deciding whether an inventor has acted with reasonable diligence? In your view, should research universities and academic researchers be held to the same standards of diligence as commercial enterprises?

2. *Patent Interferences.* The date or priority of an invention may become an issue in two different settings. First, the defendant in a patent infringement case may raise the defense that the plaintiff's patent is invalid for lack of novelty under section 102. More frequently, however, as in *Griffith*, the question of priority is litigated before the PTO in an interference proceeding. The PTO may declare an interference between pending applications or between an issued patent and an application, when each claims substantially the same invention. The interference procedure is quite complex. For an excellent description of it, see R.L. HARMON, PATENTS AND THE FEDERAL CIRCUIT, 465–477 (2d ed., 1991).

3. *Evidence of conception and diligence.* Because the timing of an inventor's conception and subsequent efforts to reduce his invention to practice can be crucial, well-advised researchers keep elaborate laboratory notebooks in which they record their daily efforts, and have the notebooks notarized or witnessed on a regular basis. Such corroborating evidence may be essential in a priority contest. See, e.g., Knorr v. Pearson, 671 F.2d 1368, 1373, 213 U.S.P.Q. 196 (C.C.P.A.1982).

OAK INDUSTRIES, INC. v. ZENITH ELECTRONICS CORP.

United States District Court, Northern District of Illinois, 1989.
726 F.Supp. 1525, 14 U.S.P.Q.2d 1417.

MORAN, DISTRICT JUDGE.

[Plaintiffs, licensee and owner of the Mandell patent, have sued defendant Zenith for infringement, and have moved for summary judgement on Zenith's defense of patent invalidity under 35 U.S.C.A. § 102.]

* * * The Mandell patent claimed a method for eliminating direct interference on community antenna television (CATV) systems. This interference is caused by the small time difference in reception between the cable signal and the over-the-air VHF broadcast signal, and occurs when the broadcast signal is strong. Zenith produces devices called converters, which are capable of practicing the Mandell method, and sells such converters to cable operators. However, these converters also perform other functions such as expanding the number of channels that the subscriber may receive, providing subscribers with the ability to unscramble protected signals, thus allowing cable operators to scramble protected frequencies, and allowing cable operators to address and remotely control subscribers' programming.

* * *

For the purposes of this motion plaintiffs concede that Merle Davis, Brad Harrison and James MacKenzie, members of the Seattle Group, conceived a method of eliminating the direct pickup interference with a converter device which could be attached to subscribers' television sets. This work became known as the Manhattan Project. Davis constructed a single conversion device (Davis Do–All) in June 1965, which eliminated the direct pickup interference by converting and outputting CATV signals directly to channel 2 (a channel not used by the Seattle area over the air stations) while preventing interference by local over-the-air-signals. There were still some problems with the Davis Do–All method so, in July 1965, Davis retained one Dale Crowe to further develop an interference-eliminating device. During July and August, Crowe constructed and delivered a device which plaintiffs concede "was capable of performing all the steps of the Mandell method." * * *

Davis then discussed further work with a Don McGory and an Irwin Wagner of Mutual Electric Supply (a Seattle Group member). Mutual submitted plans, breadboarded some converter circuits, and issued its last report on November 22, 1965. The Seattle Group members also approached one Philip Hamlin concerning possible manufacture of interference-preventing devices.

During this time a technician in the Seattle Group, Jerry Brown, used two or three converters in 30 or 40 homes to troubleshoot possible interference problems. It is unclear if those converters were left at subscribers' homes overnight. Around August 1965 the Seattle Group also demonstrated the converters to some visitors.

For the purposes of this motion plaintiffs acknowledge that both the Davis and Crowe devices were completed prior to November 4, 1965, the date plaintiffs concede to be the conception date of the Mandell invention. The parties also agree that the Crowe converter anticipates Mandell * * *. [Thus, if the Crowe device was known or used by others in the U.S. prior to November 4, the Mandell invention is invalid under § 102(a). If the Seattle Group did not abandon, suppress or conceal the Crowe device, the Mandell invention is invalid under § 102(g). The court notes that the main issues are whether the invention was known or used, or if it was abandoned, suppressed or concealed prior to November 4, 1965.]

[The court finds that plaintiffs bear the burden of establishing infringement by a preponderance of the evidence. On the issue of invalidity, however, a patent is presumed valid and the challenging party has the burden of establishing its invalidity by clear and convincing evidence. The party claiming anticipation under § 102(g) must show by clear and convincing evidence prior invention and that the invention was not abandoned, suppressed or concealed. A party is entitled to summary judgment where there is no genuine issue as to any material fact and the moving party is entitled to judgment as a matter of law. The court resolves doubts as to whether a genuine issue of material fact exists in favor of the non-moving party and must draw all reasonable inferences in that party's favor. Since the party challenging the validity of the patent has the burden of establishing invalidity by clear and convincing evidence, the court must determine whether, based on the evidence, a reasonable jury could find that the defendant clearly and convincingly proved the patent was invalid.]

A. Continued Development

The evidence shows that in July or August 1965, after Crowe finished his work, Davis discussed further work with Don McGory and Irwin Wagner of Mutual Electronic Supply. One Carl Winge authorized Mutual to proceed with the converter development on October 12, 1965. On November 2, 1965, Winge approved plans which Mutual submitted. During this time Wagner built breadboard circuits of converters. The last written progress report was dated November 22, 1965, and Davis stated that Wagner and Mutual ended project work not later than December 1965. On September 27, 1965, Winge contacted an engineer named Lockwood to refine the Crowe device into a solid state version. Lockwood apparently accomplished nothing and was paid in March 1966, although Winge recalled that Lockwood ended his efforts sometime earlier. Also in the fall of 1965, Davis contacted Hamlin about manufacturing converters. MacKenzie also contacted Hamlin, though both men were unsure of the approximate date.

B. Use in Subscribers' Homes

Brown stated that he used converters in 30 or 40 subscribers' homes for a four- to six-month period after those units were built. Because the Crowe converters were delivered in July and August of 1965, Davis claims this shows usage past the admitted November 4 Mandell conception date.

The evidence conflicts concerning whether Brown used both the Davis and the Crowe converters, or only the Davis device. Brown was shown a photograph of the Crowe device and stated that he had probably used it in the same manner as the Davis Do–All. On the other hand, Brown stated that he could not remember being given converters that he was told were different from the Davis Do–All. MacKenzie thought Brown used some Crowe converters in subscribers' homes but wasn't really sure. MacKenzie claims that Brown left converters in subscribers' homes overnight. Brown, the technician, stated that he never left a converter at any location overnight, although his answer was somewhat equivocal. Brown did state that he used the converters in subscribers' homes as test devices to determine if interference was getting into the television set or into the cable signal itself. He would hook up a converter and see if this eliminated the interference. If the interference disappeared he knew that the cable signal was problem-free and then attempted certain adjustments.

C. Demonstration to Others

Brown stated that he demonstrated a converter for "two or three other gentlemen who were not from his company." Davis further testified that he showed converters to "visiting dignitaries from out of town," including a Charlie Clements, who was installing cable systems in

New York. Apparently Davis was referring to the testing and demonstration of the Crowe converter in August 1965. However, Davis was unsure as to whether Clements had an ownership interest in the Seattle Group companies at the time of the demonstration, although Davis was sure that Clements worked closely with the Seattle Group.

D. Failure to File Patent Application

In August 1965 Winge consulted with a patent attorney, Christensen, about the possibility of patenting one of the devices. This was the only contact between Seattle Group members and Christensen, and apparently Winge sent no documents to Christensen. According to Winge, he decided not to pursue patenting any further. Davis also stated that he, MacKenzie and Harrison, of Mutual Electric Supply, believed that the converters were not patentable. No patent application was ever filed by the Seattle Group members.

IV. Are Seattle Group Converters Prior Art?

A. Prior Invention Not Abandoned, Suppressed or Concealed—35 U.S.C. § 102(g)

Although § 102(g) is normally an issue when the PTO determines priority in an interference proceeding, an alleged infringer may use § 102(g) as a defense in an infringement action where the earlier inventor never filed a patent application. To qualify as prior art under § 102(g), a prior invention must be conceived and reduced to practice. Furthermore, the prior inventor must not have abandoned, suppressed or concealed the invention. There is no requirement under § 102(g) that the prior invention be known to the patentee or "to the art." *E.I. DuPont de Nemours & Co. v. Phillips Petroleum Co.*, 849 F.2d [1430,] 1436–37, 7 U.S.P.Q.2d [1129,] 1134–35 [(C.A.F.C.), *cert. denied*, 488 U.S. 986 109 S.Ct. 542, 102 L.Ed.2d 572 (1988)]. * * *

A court may find that an invention was abandoned, suppressed or concealed if within a reasonable time after the invention was reduced to practice the inventor took no steps to make the invention publicly known. Factors supporting a finding of abandonment, concealment or suppression include not filing a patent application, not publicly disseminating documents describing the invention, and not publicly using the invention. Most important, however, a court's conclusion of abandonment, suppression or concealment depends on the total facts of each case.

1. Abandonment

Abandonment means that the original inventor has voluntarily terminated any effort to exploit the invention. However, in order to preclude a § 102(g) defense, abandonment must occur prior to the time of the second invention. Thus Zenith must show that the Seattle Group did not abandon their invention prior to November 4, 1965.

Zenith points to evidence showing further work by Wagner and a disclosure to Hamlin, as showing continued development after November

4. Defendant also claims that one or both of the devices were used in subscribers' homes for a four-to six-month period extending past November 4. Plaintiffs, on the other hand, claim that Wagner was only refining or improving Crowe's work, and further argue that as a matter of law any use in subscribers' homes terminated prior to November 4. Finally, plaintiffs contend that the Seattle Group's deliberate decision not to file a patent—based on the erroneous belief that the devices were unpatentable—is evidence of abandonment.

Although not filing a patent application within a reasonable time after reduction to practice may negate a § 102(g) defense, it is only one factor. It appears that not filing or delaying the filing of a patent application may support a conclusion of suppression and concealment. However, it is not clear that failure to file a patent application would show abandonment. In fact, there simply is no requirement to file a patent application if a party is not seeking protection of the patent laws. Other factors shed more light on the question of abandonment.

For example, there is ample evidence to show continued development by Wagner past November 4, 1965. In spite of this plaintiffs contend that Wagner's work only refined or improved on the Crowe device and thus did not excuse their failure to file a patent application. *See Lutzker v. Plet*, 843 F.2d 1364, 1367, 6 U.S.P.Q.2d 1370, 1372 (Fed.Cir.1988).[6] We do not believe *Lutzker* is applicable to our question of abandonment for two reasons: First, *Lutzker* concerned a junior party in an interference proceeding attempting to overcome an inference of concealment or suppression (not abandonment) by claiming he was perfecting his invention during the 51–month delay in filing an application. Second, *Lutzker* 's activities were directed at commercialization and he made no changes in the construction of the apparatus during the 51–month delay. However, Wagner's work clearly differs in degree from what was done in *Lutzker*.

Wagner experimented with a different intermediate frequency than that used in the Crowe device (400 megahertz versus approximately 40 megahertz). Furthermore, Davis stated that the Crowe device needed further shielding because there were problems if the device was placed right over the television's local oscillator. Although some of Wagner's work was aimed at the channel expander function, we believe that it is reasonable to infer that Wagner's job included perfecting and improving on Crowe's work. Moreover, it is undisputed that Wagner's work continued past November 4, 1965. Lockwood was also hired to refine the Crowe converter and it is reasonable to infer that by hiring Lockwood the Seattle Group was continuing development. On the other hand, even interpreting testimony most favorable to Zenith concerning any work by Hamlin, that testimony adds little to support the claim of continuing development by Hamlin.

6. The full statement from *Lutzker* is that a delay in filing a patent application will not be excused where the improvements and refinements made are not disclosed in the final patent application. *Lutzker*, 843 F.2d at 1367, 6 U.S.P.Q.2d at 1372.

We must also consider any use in subscribers' homes as evidence of non-abandonment. Plaintiffs argue that Zenith, as a party having the burden of proof, may only rely on the least advantageous time period—in this case four months of usage. This argument, if applicable, is only relevant if the use period started in June 1965 with Davis Do–Alls, rather than July or August 1965 with Crowe converters. While Brown's testimony is not completely clear on the matter, on a motion for summary judgment we draw all inferences in favor of the non-moving party. Consequently, we believe it is reasonable to infer that Brown used Crowe converters as test devices in subscribers' homes. Since Crowe only delivered his first converters in mid-July, even four months of usage would put the use period past November 4.

Looking at this evidence as a whole, taking all inferences in Zenith's favor, we believe the jury could find, by clear and convincing evidence, that the Seattle Group did not abandon their invention prior to November 4, 1965. The development work alone clearly shows no abandonment. Brown's use of the devices for test purposes supports this conclusion, while failure to file a patent application does not really shed much light on the abandonment question.

2. Suppression and Concealment

Courts decide on whether an inventor has suppressed or concealed an invention on the facts in each individual case. A decision on whether an inventor has suppressed or concealed an invention is a conclusion of law. Thus courts look to the policy behind § 102(g)—encouraging public disclosure of inventions—to determine suppression or concealment. We also note that courts have distinguished between deliberate concealment or suppression, and an inference of concealment or suppression based on an excessive delay in filing a patent application.

Zenith puts forward two arguments to show no suppression or concealment. First, Zenith contends that the converters were publicly used in subscribers' homes through November 4, 1965. Second, defendant claims that the converters were demonstrated to persons outside of the Seattle Group organization. Plaintiffs, however, argue that Brown's use of the converters in 30 or 40 homes does not show "steps . . . taken to make the invention publicly known" because Brown tried not to explain information about the converters. Plaintiffs also argue, as above, that Brown's use did not extend past November 4, 1965. Plaintiffs also note that the Seattle Group referred to their project as the "Manhattan project" because of the need to keep the work secret. Finally, plaintiffs reiterate that the Seattle Group never filed a patent application on any of their work.

a. Deliberate Suppression or Concealment

Plaintiffs argue that by characterizing the development work as the "Manhattan project" the Seattle Group intended to suppress and conceal any invention. Zenith counters that the reason for secrecy concerned the channel expander function of the converters and not the direct pickup interference function. However, if an invention was kept secret, the reason for the secrecy is irrelevant. We believe that the Seattle Group's characterization of the development work as the "Manhattan project" is evidence of an intent to keep the work secret. However, we must look at other factors because keeping a project secret does not necessarily mean we must conclude that the work is concealed or suppressed.

Although Zenith claims that Brown's use of the converters in 30 or 40 homes defeats a claim of concealment, plaintiffs argue that Brown's actions were irrelevant because he did not make the information about the invention known to others. We believe that in order to avoid a finding of suppression or concealment, Zenith need only show that the public enjoyed the use and benefits of the Seattle converters. A non-informing public use, as opposed to a secret public use, will defeat a claim of concealment, at least where the public benefits.

We do not believe Brown's use of the converters as test devices rises to the level of public use or benefit necessary to defeat an allegation of concealment under § 102(g). The converters were not "freely accessible to the public at large," so potential competitors could not discover the invention. Brown's use is also quite different from the sale of large quantities of products to the general public, which courts have found sufficient to show non-concealment and non-suppression.

The only evidence of overnight use is from MacKenzie, and Brown contradicts that testimony. MacKenzie was not directly involved in placing the converters in homes and, consequently, we do not believe that a jury could find no suppression or concealment based on such evidence.

Zenith is on firmer ground, however, in arguing that the Seattle Group's demonstration to outsiders of the converters precludes a finding of deliberate suppression and concealment. Brown stated that he demonstrated a converter to two or three men who were not from his company. Davis also recalled showing converters to out-of-town visitors. Although plaintiffs argue that these gentlemen could have been from other Seattle Group companies, or could have been subject to secrecy obligations, on this summary judgment motion we must give Zenith the benefit of reasonable inferences. Consequently, we infer that these visitors were outside the Seattle Group and not subject to secrecy obligations. We also note that Davis identified one of the visitors as Charlie Clements from New York. Although Davis was unsure of Clements' relation to the Seattle Group companies, for this motion we must infer that Clements, too, was an outsider and under no obligation of secrecy. Taking into account the inferences we must make, we believe there is sufficient evidence in these demonstrations for a jury to conclude, by clear and convincing evidence, that the Seattle Group did not intend to suppress or conceal the inventions.

b. *Inference of Suppression and Concealment*

While we do not believe that the Seattle Group's decision not to file a patent shows deliberate concealment or suppression, we must however determine if these same actions give rise to an inference of suppression and concealment. Delay in filing a patent application can give rise to an inference of suppression or concealment. Most courts have questioned whether delay in filing was sufficient to infer suppression of concealment. Here, because no patent was filed, Zenith must rely on other actions to defeat an inference of suppression or concealment. The other actions were the demonstrations of the converters to outsiders. These demonstrations took place in the summer and fall of 1965, within months of Davis and Crowe reducing their devices to practice. Such a short delay time, we believe, clearly and convincingly demonstrates that inferring suppression or concealment is not appropriate. *See Correge v. Murphy*, 705 F.2d 1326, 1330, 217 U.S.P.Q. 753, 756 (Fed.Cir.1983) ("No authority has held that a 7–month period is per se unreasonable between reduction to practice and making the invention publicly known"). *Ransburg Corp. v. Champion Spark Plug Co.*, No. 86 C 103, slip op. at 10, 1988 WL 67566 (N.D. Ill. June 20, 1988) ("No court has held that a one-year delay ... constitutes suppression ...").

B. Seattle Group Invention Known or Used by Others Prior to November 4, 1965

Zenith also claims that the [converter was] "known or used by others" prior to the date of conception of the Mandell method. Courts construe this phrase to mean that the public must have access to the knowledge of the prior art. While there is no per se rule on the number of persons who must have knowledge of, or who used the prior invention, it appears that more than just a few persons must know or use the invention for it to be publicly known. However, where those skilled in the relevant art know of or use an invention, courts may infer the knowledge will become known to a sufficient number of people to become "public." * * * Furthermore, the court may find a public use where there is a "non-secret use of a claimed process in the usual course of producing articles for commercial purposes." *W.L. Gore & Assocs. v. Garlock, Inc.*, 721 F.2d 1540, 1549, 220 U.S.P.Q. 303, 309 (Fed.Cir.1983), *cert. denied*, 469 U.S. 851, 105 S.Ct. 172, 83 L.Ed.2d 107 (1984).

Zenith argues that there was sufficient prior use or knowledge of the [Crowe device to qualify it] as § 102(a) prior art because (1) converters were left in subscribers' homes overnight; (2) the converters were demonstrated to individuals other than those belonging to the Seattle Group; and (3) information on the converters was disclosed to Hamlin. Plaintiffs claim that none of these actions show public use or knowledge by clear and convincing evidence and reiterate that the Seattle Group called their development work the "Manhattan project" to hide the work from the public.

[In light of its findings in connection with § 102(g), the court finds that Zenith also has not shown that overnight use of the converters qualifies them as § 102(a) prior art.]

We also discussed the evidence concerning the demonstration of converters to others * * *. The testimony of Brown and Davis refers to their demonstrating the converters to several people, at least some of whom were very knowledgeable in the electronics field, as well as at least one engineer involved with cable systems. For the purposes of this motion we must infer that the persons who saw the demonstration were skilled in the relevant art.

Davis also testified in the fall of 1965 that he explained to Hamlin how to make a converter. Although Hamlin did not corroborate Davis' statements, neither did he contradict them. Plaintiffs argue that Hamlin never saw a converter prior to November 4, 1965 and, in any event, Hamlin, as a potential manufacturer, was under an obligation not to disclose confidential information.

While it is true that Davis could not recall if he showed Hamlin a converter, he stated that explaining how to make the device was sufficient to allow one to reproduce the converter. MacKenzie, however, did not know when he contacted Hamlin and it is also unclear what information MacKenzie gave him.

Overall, we believe a jury could find by clear and convincing evidence that information about the converters was publicly known prior to November 4. The testimony by Brown and Davis, together with reasonable inferences, supports this conclusion. We believe Davis' statements concerning the disclosure to Hamlin provides additional support. While we do not believe MacKenzie's discussion with Hamlin was a sufficient disclosure for the purposes of § 102(a), the overall evidence supports Zenith's position. We also are not convinced that under the circumstances of Davis' disclosure to Hamlin, Washington state law would impose on Hamlin an obligation of secrecy, because we believe it is questionable as to whether the information given to Hamlin by Davis was confidential. Finally, we reiterate that although characterizing converter development work as the "Manhattan project" is evidence of secrecy, this cannot overcome other evidence of public disclosure. Zenith need only show that a genuine issue of material fact exists to defeat plaintiffs' motion. We believe Zenith has met its burden * * *.

* * *

Notes and Questions

1. *Identity of invention.* Lack of novelty ("anticipation") under section 102 of the Patent Act entails "the presence in a single prior art disclosure of all elements of a claimed invention arranged as in that claim." Connell v. Sears, Roebuck and Co., 722 F.2d 1542, 1548, 220 U.S.P.Q. 193, 198 (C.A.F.C. 1983). Essentially, the test for anticipation is the same as that for literal infringement. If something disclosed in a single reference would have literally infringed the patent if it arose after the patent issued, then it will

anticipate if it arises before the applicant's invention. See R.L. HARMON, PATENTS AND THE FEDERAL CIRCUIT, 44–45 (2d ed. 1991).

The novelty, statutory bar, and obviousness determinations are all made with reference to the prior art—earlier patents, publications and other "disclosing" events identified in section 102. However, while the obviousness determination may be made by combining two or more prior art references, section 102 anticipation requires that the invention be revealed in a single reference—a single earlier invention, patent or publication. Additional references may only be used to interpret the single reference, or show that the single reference would have enabled a person with ordinary skill in the art to practice the invention. *Id.* at 49.

In *Zenith*, the court found that the original version of the converter, the "Davis Do–All," did not anticipate the Mandell patent, but that the improved version, the "Crowe" device, did. This was because the Davis Do–All lacked some of the steps included in the Mandell method, which were later added by Crowe. Once completed, the Crowe converter contained "all the elements of [the] claimed invention arranged as in that claim." The court found, however, that the Davis Do–All, while not anticipating the Mandell method, did render it obvious. We will investigate the obviousness determination later in the Chapter.

2. *Section 102(a).* Section 102(a) sets forth four different types of disclosure (or "prior art") that will anticipate a later invention and thus render it unpatentable.

a) The invention was known by others in this country prior to the applicant's invention. In Application of Borst, 345 F.2d 851, 145 U.S.P.Q. 554 (C.C.P.A.1965), *cert. denied* 382 U.S. 973, 86 S.Ct. 537, 15 L.Ed.2d 465 (1966), the Court of Customs and Patent Appeals set forth two requirements that must be satisfied in order to demonstrate that an invention was "known" prior to the applicant's invention, within the meaning of section 102(a). First, the invention must have been fully disclosed. Second, the invention must have been accessible to the public. *Id.*, 345 F.2d at 854, 145 U.S.P.Q. at 556.

With regard to the first requirement, prior case law had held that in order to anticipate, an earlier invention must have been "reduced to practice," either actually or constructively. Actual reduction to practice entails making a physical embodiment of the invention (or in the case of a process, carrying out the steps of the process) and ascertaining that the invention works for the intended purpose. Constructive reduction to practice entails filing a patent application for the invention. The *Borst* court reasoned that "the criterion should be whether the disclosure [was] sufficient to enable one skilled in the art to reduce the disclosed invention to practice. In other words, the disclosure must [have been such as would] give possession of the invention to the person of ordinary skill." *Id.*, 345 F.2d at 855, 145 U.S.P.Q. at 557. While actual or constructive reduction to practice would sufficiently disclose the invention, some other form of disclosure [in that case, an unpublished document] containing "a description of the invention fully commensurate with" a patent application could, too. Thus, as long as the disclosure was enabling, it "need not be of an invention reduced to practice, either actually or constructively." *Id.*

On what basis could the defendants prove that the Crowe converter was "known" in the United States prior to the Mandell invention?

b) The invention was used by others in this country prior to the applicant's invention. Prior use of an invention, by its nature, requires that the invention have been actually reduced to practice. In addition, the prior use of the invention must have been accessible to the public. Connecticut Valley Enterprises, Inc. v. United States, 348 F.2d 949, 952, 146 U.S.P.Q. 404, 406 (Ct.Cl. 1965). At least in this context, however, the "accessibility" requirement entails little more than an absence of affirmative steps to conceal. The prior user need not have taken any affirmative steps to make the invention known widely to the public or those skilled in the art. Rosaire v. Baroid Sales Division, National Lead Co., 218 F.2d 72, 74–75, 104 U.S.P.Q. 100, 101 (5th Cir.1955), *cert. denied* 349 U.S. 916, 75 S.Ct. 605, 99 L.Ed. 1249, 105 U.S.P.Q. 518 (1955). Moreover, the prior use need not have lead to public understanding of the invention. Gillman v. Stern, 114 F.2d 28, 46 U.S.P.Q. 430 (2d Cir.1940), *cert. denied* 311 U.S. 718, 61 S.Ct. 441, 85 L.Ed. 468 (1941). See generally 1 D.S. CHISUM, PATENTS: A TREATISE ON THE LAW OF PATENTABILITY, VALIDITY, AND INFRINGEMENT § 3.05[2][a]-[h] (1992).

c) The invention was patented in this or a foreign country before the applicant's invention. Patents generally become part of the prior art for purposes of anticipation on the date they become effective, provided that their contents are at least minimally accessible to the public. In order to anticipate, the patent must fully describe the later invention. See 1 D.S. CHISUM, PATENTS: A TREATISE ON THE LAW OF PATENTABILITY, VALIDITY AND INFRINGEMENT § 3.06 (1992). Why is it necessary to provide that patents will anticipate a U.S. invention—won't patents also constitute "printed publications?" Note that while U.S. patents are published and constitute "printed publications" at the time they are issued, foreign patents may not be.

d) The invention was described in a printed publication in this or a foreign country before the applicant's invention.

> The statutory phrase "printed publication" has been interpreted to give effect to ongoing advances in the technologies of data storage, retrieval, and dissemination. Because there are many ways in which a reference may be disseminated to the interested public, "public accessibility" has been called the touchstone in determining whether a reference constitutes a "printed publication" * * *. [It must appear that] the reference was sufficiently accessible, at least to the public interested in the art, so that such a one by examining the reference could make the claimed invention without further research or experimentation.

In re Hall, 781 F.2d 897, 898–99, 228 U.S.P.Q. 453, 454 (C.A.F.C. 1986). The range of references that may constitute a printed publication is quite wide: microfilm, photographs, and slides have all been found sufficient. It seems clear, however, that the information must be "fixed" or made tangible. Presumably, if a sales person at a trade show orally described a new invention to customers, this would not create a printed publication for purposes of section 102, no matter how detailed and precise the description. What if the sales person's description were videotaped and shown on a monitor for the public to view at the trade show? See Rothschild & White, *Printed Publication: What is it Now?*, 70 J. PAT. & TRADEMARK OFF. SOC. 42, 49–50 (1988). What about information stored in an electronic data base? Information sent over the Internet?

When will a tangible reference be sufficiently accessible to the public to constitute a printed publication? In *In re* Wyer, 655 F.2d 221, 210 U.S.P.Q. 790 (C.C.P.A.1981), microfilm copies of a patent application were made available upon request in the Australian Patent Office and in its five sub-offices, and means were available in these locations for visitors to make their own copies. The Court of Customs and Patent Appeals found this sufficient to constitute a printed publication. In *Hall, supra*, the Federal Circuit found that a single graduate thesis in one German university library was sufficiently accessible, since it was indexed in a special dissertations catalogue which was part of the general users' catalogue, and was freely available to students, faculty and the general public. By contrast, in *In re* Cronyn, 890 F.2d 1158, 13 U.S.P.Q.2d 1070 (C.A.F.C.1989), the Federal Circuit found that a student thesis at an American college did not constitute a printed publication. In that case, undergraduate theses were described on individual index cards, which were filed alphabetically under the authors' names and kept in a shoe box in the chemistry department library. The court noted that these theses were not sufficiently accessible to the public since they were not cataloged or indexed in a meaningful way.

In Massachusetts Institute of Technology v. AB Fortia, 774 F.2d 1104, 227 U.S.P.Q. 428 (C.A.F.C. 1985), a paper was presented orally at a conference attended by 50 to 500 persons skilled in the subject matter. A copy of the paper was provided to the head of the conference and copies were distributed on request, without any restrictions, to as many as six persons. The court found that the paper constituted a printed publication. Compare Northern Telecom, Inc. v. Datapoint Corp., 908 F.2d 931, 15 U.S.P.Q.2d 1321 (C.A.F.C.), *cert. denied* 498 U.S. 920, 111 S.Ct. 296, 112 L.Ed.2d 250 (1990), where the Federal Circuit declined to find a printed publication. In that case, four reports were distributed to approximately fifty persons or organizations involved in a complex military project. While the reports were not under security classification, some or all of the reports contained the legend "Reproduction or further dissemination is not authorized . . . not for public release." The reports were also housed in the library of a private corporation, with library access restricted to authorized persons. The court reasoned that there was no clear and convincing evidence that an interested person could have had access to the documents by the exercise of reasonable diligence.

For further discussion of the printed publication provision, see Vick, *Publish* and *Perish: The Printed Publication as a Bar to Patentability*, 18 AIPLA Q. J. 235 (1990); Rothschild & White, *supra*.

3. *Section 102(g)*. What is the policy behind permitting a later inventor to obtain a patent if the earlier inventor has abandoned, suppressed or concealed the invention? Do the terms "abandon," "suppress" and "conceal" have separate meanings in the context of section 102(g), or are the terms duplicative? What evidence does the *Zenith* court find convincing with regard to the abandonment/suppression/concealment issue?

The *Zenith* court distinguished Lutzker v. Plet, 843 F.2d 1364, 6 U.S.P.Q.2d 1370 (C.A.F.C. 1988). In *Lutzker*, the Federal Circuit affirmed a finding that the first inventor suppressed or concealed his invention, a device for making canapes. Lutzker, the first inventor, conceived of the invention as of February 1, 1976, and actually reduced it to practice by the end of March the same year. He disclosed a commercially acceptable version of the invention to the public at a July 14, 1980 housewares show, and filed a patent application on November 24, 1980. The second inventor, Plet, had filed an application several months earlier. Lutzker argued that during the 51 months between his reduction to practice and public disclosure he had been continuously active preparing molds and perfecting different shapes of the canape maker for commercial release. He had also developed a recipe book to be sold along with the canape maker and a blister card on which to package the canape maker for sale.

The court observed that an inventor's work to improve or perfect his invention may excuse a delay in filing, but when "the delay is caused by working on refinements and improvements which are not reflected in the final patent application, the delay will not be excused. Further, when the activities which cause the delay go to commercialization of the invention, the delay will not be excused." *Id.*, 843 F.2d at 1367, 6 U.S.P.Q.2d at 1372. The court noted that there was nothing in Lutzker's application disclosure regarding the production molds, the recipe book or the blister card. "Since Lutzker's activities were directed to commercialization of his invention and since none of his activities were reflected in his patent application, such activities will not excuse the delay." *Id.*, 843 F.2d at 1368, 6 U.S.P.Q.2d at 1372.

Suppose that the first inventor abandons, suppresses or conceals his invention, but later resumes activity and files a patent application. Will section 102(g) deprive him of a patent if no second inventor has appeared on the scene and filed an application? What if a second inventor files an application, but only after the first inventor has resumed? Consider Paulik v. Rizkalla, 760 F.2d 1270, 226 U.S.P.Q. 224 (C.A.F.C. 1985).

In *Paulik*, Paulik, an employee of the Monsanto Company, reduced his invention to practice in November, 1970, and again in April, 1971. Paulik immediately sent information about the invention to the Patent Department of his assignee, the Monsanto Company. While the Patent Department kept the project on active status, it assigned it a lower priority than other pending projects. Despite prodding from Paulik, the Patent Department only began work toward filing a patent application in January or February of 1975. On March 10, 1975, Rizkalla filed an application for patent for the same invention. On June 30, 1975, Monsanto's Patent Department filed its application for the Paulik invention. In the subsequent interference proceeding, Rizkalla relied on his filing date as his date of invention. The PTO Board of Patent Interferences held that Paulik's four-year delay from reduction to practice to filing was prima facie suppression or concealment, and awarded priority to Rizkalla. The Federal Circuit vacated and remanded.

The court held that Paulik was entitled to demonstrate that he (through his assignee) had renewed activity on the invention and had proceeded diligently to file his patent application from a date prior to Rizkalla's invention date. Upon making this proof, he could rely on his date of renewed activity as his date of invention for purposes of the priority determination. While Paulik's four years of inactivity would deprive him of the benefit of his original date of invention, his date of renewed activity, which predated Rizkalla's invention, would entitle him to priority and a patent. The court reasoned:

> The reason for the patent system is to encourage innovation and its fruits: new jobs and new industries, new consumer goods and trade benefits. We must keep this purpose in plain view as we consider the consequences of interpretations of the patent law such as in the Board's decision.
>
> A foreseeable consequence of the Board's ruling is to discourage inventors and their supporters from working on projects that had been "too long" set aside, because of the impossibility of relying, in a priority contest, on either their original work or their renewed work. This curious result is neither fair nor in the public interest. We do not see that the public interest is served by placing so severe a sanction on failure to file premature patent applications on immature inventions of unknown value. In reversing the Board's decision we do not hold that such inventions are necessarily entitled to the benefits of their earliest dates in a priority contest; we hold only that they are not barred from entitlement to their dates of renewed activity.

Id., 760 F.2d at 1276, 226 U.S.P.Q. at 228.

4. *The "first-to-invent" system vs. the "first-to-file" system.* The United States has always subscribed to the belief that patents should be reserved for the first, or "true," inventor. The U.S., however, stands almost alone in awarding priority to the first to invent. Almost all other nations award patents to the first inventor to file an application. See THE ADVISORY COMMISSION ON PATENT LAW REFORM, A REPORT TO THE SECRETARY OF COMMERCE 43, 67 n.2 (1992). There has been considerable debate about whether the U.S. should change to a first-to-file system. What are the advantages and disadvantages of each approach?

Proponents of a change have argued that as markets become increasingly global, a uniform, world-wide system of determining priority is essential. Complying with two systems in the course of seeking world-wide patent protection is burdensome, and the burden outweighs any advantage that the first-to-invent system might offer over a first-to-file system. Moreover, proponents have argued that the first-to-file system is more efficient: it dispenses with lengthy, costly interference procedures and provides greater predictability. A first-to-file system may also lead to earlier disclosure of inventions, which can only benefit the public. Some have observed that the United States already has a *de facto* first-to-file system, since only a small percentage of applications entail interferences, and when they do, the first applicant to file usually wins. They further note that adopting a first-to-file system will not appreciably change the practice of U.S. inventors, since many U.S. companies, which file both for domestic and foreign patents on new inventions, already plan their patent-filing strategies with the foreign first-to-file requirements in mind.

Opponents to change counter that the first-to-invent system is fairer: the first person to invent is more deserving of a patent than the first inventor to file, and the public more readily accepts a system that rewards the first inventor. Moreover, a first-to-file system gives an undue advantage to large companies over small, back-yard inventors, who may lack the financial resources to file applications early in the inventive process and win a race to the Patent Office. Opponents also argue that a first-to-file system leads to a decrease in the quality of disclosure in patent applications. The inventor may be rushed to file an application before he has perfected the invention, fully tested it, and ascertained the best mode of practicing it. He is also rushed to file before having an opportunity to explore the commercial value of the invention. The resulting decrease in quality and increase in number of applications will overburden the PTO and affect the quality of its examination process.

What do you think? For a fuller discussion of these issues, see REPORT TO THE SECRETARY OF COMMERCE, *supra*, at 43–46 (recommending that the United States change to a first-to-file system); Banner & McDonnell, *First-to-File, Mandatory Reexamination, and Mandatory "Exceptional Circumstance": Ideas for Better? Or Worse?*, 69 J. PAT. & TRADEMARK OFF. SOC. 595 (1987) (arguing against changing to a first-to-file system); Dunner, *First To File: Should Our Interference System Be Abolished?*, 68 J. PAT. & TRADEMARK OFF. SOC. 561 (1986) (arguing for a change); and Frost, *The 1967 Patent Law Debate—First–To–Invent Vs. First–To–File*, [1967] DUKE L. J. 923 (1967) (comparing the two systems and arguing that the present U.S. system is a hybrid which draws both from the first-to-file and the first-to-invent systems, giving an advantage to the first person to file while retaining important aspects of a first-to-invent system).

3. Section 102: The Statutory Bar

MOLECULON RESEARCH CORP. v. CBS, INC.

United States Court of Appeals, Federal Circuit, 1986.
793 F.2d 1261, 229 U.S.P.Q. 805, *cert. denied*
479 U.S. 1030, 107 S.Ct. 875, 93 L.Ed.2d 829 (1987).

BALDWIN, CIRCUIT JUDGE.

* * *

A puzzle enthusiast since childhood, Nichols, in the summer of 1957, conceived of a three-dimensional puzzle capable of rotational movement. He envisioned an assembly of eight cubes attached in a 2 x 2 x 2 arrangement, with each of the six faces of the composite cube distinguished by a different color and the individual cubes being capable of rotation in sets of four around one of three mutually perpendicular axes.

During the period 1957–1962, while doing graduate work in organic chemistry, Nichols constructed several paper models of his puzzle, making cubes of heavy file-card type paper and affixing small magnets to the inside of the cubes. Although these models confirmed the feasibility of Nichols' conception, they lacked durability. A few close friends, including two roommates and a colleague in the chemistry department, had occasion to see one of these paper models in Nichols' room and Nichols explained its operation to at least one of them.

In 1962, Nichols accepted employment as a research scientist at Moleculon. In 1968, Nichols constructed a working wood block prototype of his puzzle which he usually kept at home but on occasion brought into his office. In January 1969, Dr. Obermayer, the president of Moleculon, entered Nichols' office and happened to see the model sitting on his desk. Obermayer expressed immediate interest in the puzzle and Nichols explained its workings. Obermayer asked whether Nichols intended to commercialize the puzzle. When Nichols said no, Obermayer suggested that Moleculon try to do so. In March 1969, Nichols assigned all his rights in the puzzle invention to Moleculon in return for a share of any proceeds of commercialization. On March 7, 1969, Moleculon sent Parker Brothers an actual model and a description of the cube puzzle. In the next three years, Moleculon contacted between fifty and sixty toy and game manufacturers, including Ideal. Ideal responded to the effect that it did not currently have an interest in marketing the puzzle. Moleculon itself did not succeed in marketing the Nichols cube.

On March 3, 1970, Nichols filed on behalf of Moleculon a patent application covering his invention. The '201 patent issued on April 11, 1972.

[In this suit, Moleculon alleges that the well-known Rubick's Cube puzzle infringes the '201 patent.]

Opinion

1. § 102(b) on sale and public use bars

CBS argues that the subject matter of the '201 patent was in "public use" and "on sale" by Nichols, prior to the March 3, 1969 critical date (i.e., one year prior to filing of the patent application), thus rendering the patent invalid under section 102(b).

(a) Public Use

CBS labels as public use Nichols' displaying of the models to other persons (such as his colleagues at school) without any mention of secrecy. CBS ascribes only commercial purpose and intent to Obermayer's use of the wood model and argues that a conclusion of barring public use under § 102(b) is compelled. We disagree.

This is what the district court had to say:

> The essence of "public use" is the free and unrestricted giving over of an invention to a member of the public or the public in general. What I see here, by contrast, is the inventor's private use of his own invention for his own enjoyment. "Private use of one's own invention is permissible."

While it is true that Nichols explained his puzzle to a few close colleagues who inquired about it and allowed Obermayer to in fact use it, the personal relationships and other surrounding circumstances were such that Nichols at all times retained control over its use as well as over the distribution of information concerning it. He never used the puzzle or permitted it used in a place or at a time when he did not have a legitimate expectation of privacy and of confidentiality. In these respects, I consider the exposure to Obermayer in Nichols' office no different than the exposure of Nichols' close friends in his home.

Here also the relationship between the participants in the alleged uses evidences a retention of control by Nichols. None of those participants had any basis for inferring that the puzzle was being given over by Nichols for their free and unrestricted use. Holding the public use bar inapplicable in these circumstances will not remove anything from the public domain. Moreover, there is absolutely no evidence in this case of commercially motivated activity by Nichols during the relevant period. Accordingly, the underlying policy against extending the effective term of exclusivity is not offended by a finding that the Nichols invention was not in public use.

CBS correctly recognizes that the district court's conclusion on public use under § 102(b) is subject to review as a question of law while the facts underlying the conclusion on public use are subject to the clearly erroneous standard of review.

CBS urges that the decision in *Egbert v. Lippmann*, 104 U.S. 333, 26 L.Ed. 755 (1881), compels a conclusion of public use in the present case. In *Egbert*, the claimed invention was drawn to improved corset-springs, also called corset-steels. In 1855, the inventor made and presented to his lady friend a pair of corset-steels which embodied the invention. She wore the steels for a long time. The inventor made and gave her another pair three years later which she also wore a long time. On several occasions, when the corset itself wore out, the steels were removed and placed into a new corset. In 1866, an application for patent was filed. It was on those facts that the Court observed that: "If an inventor, having made his device, gives or sells it to another, to be used by the donee or vendee, without limitation or restriction, or injunction of secrecy, and it is so used, such use is public, even though the use and knowledge of the use may be confined to one person." *Id.* 104 U.S. at 336.

The district court distinguished *Egbert* because here Nichols had not given over the invention for free and unrestricted use by another person. Based on the personal relationships and surrounding circumstances, the court found that Nichols at all times retained control over the puzzle's use and the distribution of information concerning it. The court characterized Nichols' use as private and for his own enjoyment. We see neither legal error in the analysis nor clear error in the findings.

As for Obermayer's brief use of the puzzle, the court found that Nichols retained control even though he and Obermayer had not entered into any express confidentiality agreement. The court held, and we agree, that the presence or absence of such an agreement is not determinative of the public use issue. It is one factor to be considered in assessing all the evidence. There can be no question that the court looked at the totality of evidence, and evaluated that evidence in view of time, place, and circumstances.

With regard to the question of control, CBS complains that "[t]he record is devoid of any testimony from the friends, associates and fellow workers who saw Nichols' cube and to whom its operation was explained." The simple answer is that CBS had the burden at trial to prove public use with facts supported by clear and convincing evidence. We think the district court's characterization of the evidence of record is entirely apt and we see no ground for reversal. Moreover, we agree with the district court that its conclusion on public use is consistent with the policies underlying the bar.

CBS further argues in connection with public use that the district court erred when it found no evidence of commercially motivated activity by Nichols prior to the critical date.[3] Although CBS attempts to paint a picture of commercialization from the discussions between Obermayer and Nichols, we see only the brush strokes of speculation. The record lacks hard evidence. Discussion between employer and employee does not by itself convert an employee's private pursuit into commercial enterprise with the employer. CBS also makes much of a February 6, 1969 phone call by Obermayer to Parker Brothers to see if the latter was interested in receiving a submission of a puzzle idea from an outside inventor. Nothing concerning the nature or workings of Nichols' puzzle was disclosed. Obermayer simply inquired whether and how an outsider could submit a puzzle for Parker Brothers' consideration. We agree with the district court that those facts do not show commercialization. Thus this case differs from other cases where commercial activity was said to violate the policies of section 102(b).

(b) On Sale

CBS argues that the claimed invention was on sale within the meaning of 35 U.S.C. § 102(b) because Nichols orally agreed prior to the critical date (e.g., during a January 1969 conversation between Nichols and Obermayer) to assign "all his rights in the puzzle invention" to Moleculon. According to CBS, Nichols not only assigned the right to apply for a patent on the invention but also conveyed title in his single wooden model.

Although the formal written assignment occurred after the critical date, the district court held that even if there were an earlier oral agreement, an assignment or sale of the rights in the invention and potential patent rights is not a sale of "the invention" within the meaning of section 102(b). We agree. The few cases we have found on

3. In some instances, commercially motivated activities may implicate both the public use and the on sale bars.

this issue have uniformly held that such a sale of patent rights does not come within the section 102(b) bar. Such a result comports with the policies underlying the on sale bar, and with the business realities ordinarily surrounding a corporation's prosecution of patent applications for inventors.

As for CBS' contention that Nichols sold or agreed to sell the wood model of the puzzle, we quote the district court's relevant findings:

> There is no indication in the subsequent written instrument that the parties contemplated the sale or transfer to Moleculon of the single physical embodiment of the puzzle then in existence. Nor is there any other evidence in the record to that effect.

CBS has shown nothing approaching clear error concerning those findings.

Accordingly, we sustain the district court's determination that the claims are not invalid under section 102(b).

* * *

UMC ELECTRONICS CO. v. UNITED STATES

United States Court of Appeals for the Federal Circuit, 1987.
816 F.2d 647, 2 U.S.P.Q.2d 1465, *cert. denied*
484 U.S. 1025, 108 S.Ct. 748, 98 L.Ed.2d 761 (1988).

NIES, CIRCUIT JUDGE.

UMC Electronics Company brought this action, pursuant to 28 U.S.C. § 1498(a), to recover compensation for use of its patented invention by the United States. UMC is the owner of Patent No. 3,643,513, issued February 22, 1972, by assignment from the inventor Preston Weaver. The United States Claims Court upheld the validity of all claims (1–4) but dismissed the complaint on the ground of no infringement or, more accurately, no use of the patented invention by the United States. Both parties appeal. We reverse the Claims Court's holding that the patented invention was not on sale within the meaning of 35 U.S.C. § 102(b). * * *

I. BACKGROUND

The claimed invention is an aviation counting accelerometer (ACA), a device for sensing and for recording the number of times an aircraft has been subjected to predetermined levels of acceleration. The sensor component is mounted on the aircraft in a direction to measure acceleration loading and is connected electrically to the recorder component. Records produced by an ACA can indicate an aircraft's remaining useful life and show the need for structural inspection, overhaul, or rotation to less demanding service.

The patent application which became the patent in this suit ('513) was filed on August 1, 1968. Under 35 U.S.C. § 102(b) the commercial exploitation and the state of development of the invention one year before the filing of the application for the subject invention are critical to resolution of the on-sale issue.

Prior to the late 1960's when UMC first entered this field, the U.S. Navy had procured ACA's from Maxson Electronics Company and from Giannini Controls Corporation. The Navy was dissatisfied with these ACA's because they sometimes recorded data that defied common sense, failed to count accelerations, or counted accelerations that never occurred. In 1966 the Navy contacted Preston Weaver, an employee of UMC, told him of the problems with existing ACA's and informed him of the Navy's interest in buying improved devices. Weaver designed an accelerometer, model UMC–A, and in late 1966, UMC was awarded a contract to supply the Navy with approximately 1600 units.

In early 1967, UMC concluded that its model UMC–A would not meet the Navy's performance specification required by its contract. Like the Maxson and Giannini ACA's, the UMC–A accelerometer utilized, as part of its sensor, an electromechanical transducer to mechanically generate signals that indicate levels of acceleration. Like the Maxson and Giannini devices, the UMC–A device sometimes counted and sometimes did not count the same acceleration load. The problem lay in the inherent frequency of the mass-spring system in the transducer. The devices could not distinguish between acceleration due to inflight maneuvers, which determines actual stress, and acceleration from other sources, e.g., windgusts or weapons release.

To prevent UMC from losing the ACA contract, Weaver began work to improve the sensor portion of an ACA and conceived his invention which uses an analog transducer in the sensor. An analog transducer electrically generates a varying signal (in contrast to the mechanically produced signal of prior devices) which can be filtered electronically to selectively remove the effects of superimposed vibrations. The Claims Court found that in April–May of 1967 Weaver built and tested an engineering prototype of his ACA containing a commercial analog transducer, a filter, a timing circuit and a voltage sensor that measured one load level. UMC sought to modify the existing contract for ACA's to substitute an analog transducer for the electro-mechanical transducer specified in the contract, but was unsuccessful in negotiating a modification.

In late May, 1967, the Navy issued new specifications and in July, 1967, requested proposals from contractors to deliver ACA's built to the new specification. Technically, the request for proposals called separately for a certain number of sensor components of an ACA system and a certain number of recorders, the two units being compatible in combination. UMC responded to the request on July 27, 1967, the final date for making a proposal, with an offer to supply $1,668,743 worth of its improved ACA (hereinafter model UMC–B). UMC represented as part of its proposal that the sensor portion "has been constructed and tested in conjunction with voltage sensing and time controlled circuitry." In response to a Navy inquiry, on August 2, 1967, after the critical date,

UMC submitted a technical proposal which described the model UMC–B in detail and included test results and schematic drawings. On August 9, 1967, UMC gave a demonstration of its device to the Navy at the UMC facility.

In early 1968 the Navy canceled the request to which the above submission of UMC was directed, and in July 1968, it issued another. The latter request eventually led to a contract with Systron–Donner Corporation, which company has been providing the Navy with ACA's utilizing analog transducers since 1970. In June, 1980, UMC filed the instant action against the United States seeking compensation (after attempting for a number of years to obtain compensation directly from the Navy) by reason of the Navy's alleged use of its invention in the Systron–Donner ACA's. The Claims Court upheld the validity of the patent claims, which were challenged by the government on a number of grounds, but found that the Systron–Donner ACA's did not fall within the scope of the claims. Both parties appeal: UMC asking for reversal of the Claims Court's finding of no infringement; the government seeking to have the claims in suit held invalid. Since we conclude that the Claims Court erred as a matter of law in holding that the claims of the '513 patent were not invalid under section 102(b), we need discuss only that issue in detail.

II. The Claims Court Decision

The Claims Court analyzed the on-sale bar under the following three-part test set out in *In re Corcoran*, 640 F.2d 1331, 1333–34, 208 USPQ 867, 870 (CCPA 1981), taken from *Timely Prods. Corp. v. Arron*, 523 F.2d 288, 302, 187 USPQ 257, 267–68 (2d Cir.1975):

> (1) The complete invention claimed must have been embodied in or obvious in view of the thing offered for sale.... Complete readability of the claim on the thing offered is not required because whatever is published (or on sale) more than one year prior to the filing of a patent application becomes part of the prior art over which the claim must be patentable....
>
> (2) The invention must have been tested sufficiently to verify that it is operable and commercially marketable. This is simply another way of expressing the principle that an invention cannot be offered for sale until it is completed, which requires not merely its conception but its reduction to practice....
>
> (3) Finally, the sale must be primarily for profit rather than for experimental purposes....

Proceeding through the *Timely Products* requirements in reverse order, the Claims Court first noted that UMC had admitted that its offer to the Navy was for profit, not for experimentation. The court then found that the invention of the '513 patent had been reduced to practice before the critical date by Weaver's tests of the engineering prototype of the ACA in April–May, 1967, because Weaver admitted that as a result of those tests he was satisfied that his invention would serve its intended purpose. However, the court found the first requirement that the complete invention must be embodied in the thing offered for sale was not met because the engineering prototype did not include all elements of the claims. The court found that the evidence established that the inventor had not built a physical embodiment of the invention including all limitations of the claims before the critical date.

* * * Based on those findings, the court held that the invention of the '513 patent was not on sale within the meaning of section 102(b).

The court also held that the invention would not have been obvious from the prototype, which the court considered to be the thing offered for sale. This was error in the court's analysis, the *prototype* not being the thing offered for sale. The subject matter of the offer for sale is admittedly the claimed invention. The government maintains that, properly interpreted, all three *Timely Products* requirements had been met, namely, (1) there was an offer to sell model UMC–B accelerometers which embodied the invention of the claims, (2) the invention had been reduced to practice, and (3) the offer to sell was for profit, not experimentation. Thus, per the government, the Claims Court erred as a matter of law in not holding the claims barred under section 102(b). UMC counters that because the inventor never built a physical embodiment containing all elements of the claims, the Claims Court erred in finding a reduction to practice of the invention, but that the court's error was cancelled out by its separate requirement for a physical embodiment.

III

As an initial matter, UMC is correct in pointing out the inconsistency between the Claims Court's conclusion that the claimed invention was "reduced to practice" before the critical date and its separate finding that no physical embodiment of the invention existed at that time. It is not sufficient for a reduction to practice that Weaver built and tested only a part of the later-claimed model UMC–B accelerometer. Under our precedent there cannot be a reduction to practice of the invention here without a physical embodiment which includes all limitations of the claim. Because the court found and the parties do not dispute that there was no physical embodiment containing all limitations of the claimed invention before the critical date, we conclude that the Claims Court erred in holding that there had been a reduction to practice.

The clarification of that issue, however, does not resolve the precise dispute here. Per the government, UMC's substantial attempted commercial exploitation of the claimed invention contravenes the policies of the on-sale bar despite the absence of a complete embodiment and, thus, raises an on-sale bar under section 102(b). For this proposition the government relies on the decision of this court in *Barmag* [Barmer Maschinenfabrik AG v. Murata Mach., Ltd., 731 F.2d 831, 221 U.S.P.Q. 561 (Fed.Cir. 1984)]. On the other hand, UMC maintains that, as a matter of law, there is no on-sale bar unless the claimed invention had been reduced to practice before the critical date, and urges that we here reject the contrary suggestion in *Barmag*. Thus, we address first the issue whether reduction to practice of the claimed invention before the critical date is required to invoke the on-sale bar, and conclude, for reasons that follow, that reduction to practice is not always a requirement of the on-sale bar.[5] This leads to the issue whether there is an on-sale bar in this case. On the undisputed facts, we hold that the invention of the '513 patent was on sale within the meaning of section 102(b).

IV

Whether a reduction to practice is a requirement of the on-sale bar of 35 U.S.C. § 102(b) requires a review of our precedent. However, the issue has been directly addressed by this court or its predecessors in only two cases, *Barmag* and *General Electric Co. v. United States*, 654 F.2d 55, 60–61, 211 USPQ 867, 872–73 (Ct.Cl.1981) (en banc), although the issue has surfaced in others. In *General Electric Co. v. United States*, the Court of Claims, one of this court's predecessors, analyzed an on-sale bar issue by focusing on the policies underlying the bar to determine whether application of the bar would further those policies. Those policies were stated to be:

> First, there is a policy against removing inventions from the public which the public has justifiably come to believe are freely available to all as a consequence of prolonged sales activity. Next, there is a policy favoring prompt and widespread disclosure of new inventions to the public. The inventor is forced to file promptly or risk possible forfeiture of his invention [patent] rights due to prior sales. A third policy is to prevent the inventor from commercially exploiting the exclusivity of his invention substantially beyond the statutorily authorized 17–year period. The on-sale bar forces the inventor to choose between seeking patent protection promptly following sales activity or taking his chances with his competitors without the benefit of patent protection. The fourth and final identifiable policy is to give the inventor a reasonable amount of time following sales activity (set by statute as 1 year) to determine whether a patent is a worthwhile investment. This benefits the public because it tends to minimize the filing of inventions [sic] of only marginal public interest.

654 F.2d at 61, 211 USPQ at 873. On the facts of that case, the court held that the policies were violated and that there was a reduction to practice before the critical date. The latter holding obviated the need to agree or disagree with a detailed analysis of the trial judge, who had concluded that reduction to practice was not "indispensable in every case."

In *Barmag*, the court went out of its way to reserve the question whether a physical embodiment should be a requirement of the on-sale

5. The public use bar of section 102(b) implicates different considerations and nothing said here should be construed to encompass that part of the statute.

bar in all cases. Without a physical embodiment, as stated above, there can be no reduction to practice.

* * *

In *Western Marine Elecs., Inc. v. Furuno Elec. Co.*, 764 F.2d 840, 844, 226 USPQ 334, 337 (Fed.Cir.1985), the argument was made that the patented invention, a gravity stabilized sonar device used on fishing boats, had not been reduced to practice and, thus, had not been on sale before the critical date. Because the device had not been mounted on a boat, it was argued, the device had not been sufficiently tested and, thus, had not been reduced to practice. In holding the invention to be on sale, the court did not directly answer that issue, stating that the "totality of the circumstances" determined whether the device was on sale. It reiterated:

> Rigid standards are especially unsuited to the on sale provision where the policies underlying the bar, in effect, define it. * * *

[The Court discusses opinions of other courts suggesting that the requirements for a reduction to practice might be eased when the facts of a case fall within the intent of the statute, but do not technically satisfy the requirements for reduction to practice.]

Adoption of a "sufficiently" reduced-to-practice requirement is in fact an abandonment of reduction to practice as that term is used in other contexts. This court observed in *Barmag,* that our case law does not support a variegated definition of reduction to practice. At this point, we point out that "reduction to practice" is a term of art which developed in connection with interference practice to determine priority of invention between rival claimants. In that context Judge Rich has said: "There are no degrees of reduction to practice; either one has or has not occurred." *Wolter v. Belicka*, 409 F.2d 255, 262, 161 USPQ 335, 340 (CCPA 1969) (Rich, J., dissenting). It can only cause confusion in interference law, with its special technical considerations, and in operation of the on-sale bar, which is guided by entirely different policies, to adopt modifiers in connection with "reduction to practice," whatever the context.

Moreover, since reduction to practice is a term of art under this court's precedent, any specific ruling in one context on whether there is or is not a "reduction to practice" necessarily carries over into the other. For example, a holding here, like the trial court's, that there can be a reduction to practice without an embodiment containing all elements of the claim would have a major unintended impact on interference law. Conversely, by invoking reduction to practice as developed in interference law, an inventor might be able to escape the on-sale bar simply through deft claim draftsmanship.[9]

* * *

9. Weaver could have claimed "an aircraft with an accelerometer ..." instead of "an accelerometer...." In that instance, the claimed invention would not have been reduced to practice even if Weaver had built and tested the entire ACA.

In view of all of the above considerations, we conclude that reduction to practice of the claimed invention has not been and should not be made an absolute requirement of the on-sale bar.

We hasten to add, however, that we do not intend to sanction attacks on patents on the ground that the inventor or another offered for sale, before the critical date, the mere concept of the invention. Nor should inventors be forced to rush into the Patent and Trademark Office prematurely. On the other hand, we reject UMC's position that as a matter of law no on-sale bar is possible unless the claimed invention has been reduced to practice in the interference sense.

We do not reject "reduction to practice" as an important analytical tool in an on-sale analysis. A holding that there has or has not been a reduction to practice of the claimed invention before the critical date may well determine whether the claimed invention was in fact the subject of the sale or offer to sell or whether a sale was primarily for an experimental purpose. A holding that there is a reduction to practice of the claimed invention "may, of course, lighten the burden of the party asserting the bar." *General Electric*, 206 USPQ at 271. Thus, we simply say here that the on-sale bar does not necessarily turn on whether there was or was not a reduction to practice of the claimed invention. All of the circumstances surrounding the sale or offer to sell, including the stage of development of the invention and the nature of the invention, must be considered and weighed against the policies underlying section 102(b).

The above conclusion does not lend itself to formulation into a set of precise requirements such as that attempted by the *Timely Products* court. However, we point out certain critical considerations in the on-sale determination and the respective burdens of proof which have already been established in our precedent. Thus, without question, the challenger has the burden of proving that there was a definite sale or offer to sell more than one year before the application for the subject patent, and that the subject matter of the sale or offer to sell fully anticipated the claimed invention or would have rendered the claimed invention obvious by its addition to the prior art. If these facts are established, the patent owner is called upon to come forward with an explanation of the circumstances surrounding what would otherwise appear to be commercialization outside the grace period. The possibilities of such circumstances cannot possibly be enumerated. If the inventor had merely a conception or was working towards development of that conception, it can be said there is not yet any "invention" which could be placed on sale. A sale made because the purchaser was participating in experimental testing creates no on-sale bar.

V

The issue of whether an invention is on sale is a question of law. Because the Claims Court's factual findings are not disputed, and the issue may be resolved by application of the proper rule of law to those findings, we need not remand.

UMC made a definite offer to sell its later patented UMC–B accelerometer to the Navy more than one year prior to the date of the application for the patent in suit. In its bid, UMC specified a price of $404.00 for each sensor component of the ACA and $271.00 for the compatible recorder component. The total contract price was in excess of $1.6 million. This written offer which revealed use of the analog transducer in the ACA was supplied on July 27, 1967. UMC admits that the offer it made was for profit, not to conduct experiments.

UMC's activities evidence, at least *prima facie,* an attempt to commercialize the invention of the '513 patent by bidding on a large government contract more than one year prior to the filing of the underlying application and thereby to expand the grace period in contravention of the policies underlying the statute. Countering the *prima facie* case, UMC offers only the purely technical objection that no complete embodiment of the invention existed at the time of the sale. In this case, that circumstance is unavailing when we look at the realities of the development of this invention. While UMC asserts that its improved ACA required further "development," as evidenced by its seeking a waiver of the liquidated damages provision in the RFP, that fact might weigh in UMC's favor if UMC had sought by convincing evidence to prove that the primary purpose of the sale was for experimental work. However, the contract was not a research and development contract, and UMC admits that the offer it made was for profit, not to conduct experimental work.

We do not attempt here to formulate a standard for determining when something less than a complete embodiment of the invention will suffice under the on-sale bar. However, the development of the subject invention was far beyond a mere conception. Much of the invention was embodied in tangible form. The prior art devices embodied each element of the claimed invention, save one, and that portion was available and had been sufficiently tested to demonstrate to the satisfaction of the inventor that the invention as ultimately claimed would work for its intended purpose. Thus, we conclude from the unchallenged facts with respect to the commercial activities of UMC, coupled with the extent to which the invention was developed, the substantial embodiment of the invention, the testing which was sufficient to satisfy the inventor that his later claimed invention would work, and the nature of the inventor's contribution to the art, that the claimed invention was on sale within the meaning of section 102(b).

* * *

Notes and Questions

1. *"In public use or on sale."* Are you satisfied that the *Egbert* and the *Moleculon* situations can be distinguished?

Suppose that Nichols had hosted a party for 20–30 guests, during which he demonstrated the puzzle to some of the guests for the purpose of getting feedback about it. Some of the guests picked the puzzle up and inspected it, and Nichols never asked the guests to maintain the puzzle in secrecy. Same result? See Beachcombers International, Inc. v. Wildewood Creative Products, Inc., 31 F.3d 1154, 31 U.S.P.Q.2d 1653 (C.A.F.C. 1994).

Suppose that the applicant/inventor of a new process for making widgets secretly used the process to produce widgets for commercial sale more than a year prior to applying for a patent. The widgets placed on the market did not reveal the process used to make them. Should that use be deemed a "public use" that triggered the section 102(b) one-year statutory bar against the applicant/inventor? The Federal Circuit has held that it should. Kinzenbaw v. Deere and Co., 741 F.2d 383, 390, 222 U.S.P.Q. 929, 934 (C.A.F.C. 1984), *cert. denied* 470 U.S. 1004, 105 S.Ct. 1352, 84 L.Ed.2d 379 (1985). On the other hand, the Federal Circuit has held that a similar secret use by a person unrelated to the applicant does not constitute a public use for purposes of section 102(b) against the applicant. See W.L. Gore & Associates, Inc. v. Garlock, Inc., 721 F.2d 1540, 1550, 220 U.S.P.Q. 303, 310 (C.A.F.C. 1983), *cert. denied* 469 U.S. 851, 105 S.Ct. 172, 83 L.Ed.2d 107 (1984). Normally, either the applicant's or a third party's public use or sale will trigger the section 102(b) statute of limitations. Why should a distinction be made in this case?

For a discussion of the history and policies underlying section 102(b), see Carstens and Ward, *Conception and the "On Sale" Bar*, 34 WM. & MARY L. REV. 393 (1993). For more detailed analysis of the *UMC* case and its progeny, see Rooklidge, *Application of the On–Sale Bar to Activities Performed Before Reduction to Practice*, 72 J. PAT. & TRADEMARK OFF. SOC. 543 (1990); Shurn, *Through the Public Policy Looking Glass of On–Sale Bars*, 29 IDEA 199 (1989).

2. *Experimental use or sale.* As the *UMC* opinion suggests, an experimental use or sale will not trigger the section 102(b) statute of limitations, even though it may otherwise be "public" in nature. The Supreme Court made this distinction in City of Elizabeth v. American Nicholson Pavement Co., 97 U.S. (7 Otto) 126, 24 L.Ed. 1000 (1877). In that case, the inventor had tested a 75–foot stretch of his new pavement on a well-traveled toll road for six years before applying for a patent. He inspected the pavement regularly and questioned the toll-collector about the public's reaction to it. In upholding the patent, the Court noted:

> The use of an invention by the inventor himself, or by any other person under his direction, by way of experiment, and in order to bring the invention to perfection, has never been regarded as [a public] use. * * *
>
> Now, the nature of a street pavement is such that it cannot be experimented upon satisfactorily except on a highway, which is always public.
>
> [S]uch use is not a public use, within the meaning of the statute, so long as the inventor is engaged, in good faith, in testing its operation. He may see cause to alter it and improve it, or not. His experiments will reveal the fact whether any and what alterations may be necessary. If durability is one of the qualities to be attained, a long period, perhaps years, may be necessary to enable the inventor to discover whether his purpose is accomplished. * * * So long as he does not voluntarily allow

> others to make it and use it, and so long as it is not on sale for general use, he keeps the invention under his own control, and does not lose his title to a patent.

Id., 97 U.S. (7 Otto) at 134–35, 24 L.Ed. at 1004. The Court stressed that it made no difference whether, during the period of experimental use, the public incidentally derived a benefit. Nor did it matter that the experimental use revealed how the invention was constructed. The inventor was entitled to take the necessary measures to perfect his invention, and it was in the public's interest that his invention be properly tested before a patent was granted. Since the inventor was engaging in a *bona fide* effort to perfect his invention, and was not using it for profit, the delay in filing did not unfairly prolong his monopoly beyond the period intended by the law. *Id.*, 97 U.S. (7 Otto) at 135–137, 24 L.Ed. at 1004–05.

Following *Elizabeth*, the Court of Appeals for the Federal Circuit found that an orthodontist/inventor did not lose the right to patent his dental appliance by using it on three patients over a period of six years prior to applying for a patent. TP Laboratories, Inc. v. Professional Positioners, Inc., 724 F.2d 965, 220 U.S.P.Q. 577 (C.A.F.C.), *cert. denied* 469 U.S. 826, 105 S.Ct. 108, 83 L.Ed.2d 51 (1984). The court noted that disclosure of the appliance to the patients was unavoidable in order to test it, and that while the inventor had failed to obtain pledges of confidentiality from the patients, it was unlikely under the circumstances that the patients would show the appliance to others who would understand its function or want to duplicate it. "In any event, a pledge of confidentiality is indicative of the inventor's continued control which here is established inherently by the dentist-patient relationship of the parties." *Id.*, 724 F.2d at 972, 220 U.S.P.Q. at 583. The court concluded:

> A factor in favor of the patentee is that during this critical time the inventor had readily available all of the facilities of TP to commercially exploit the device. Yet, [the devices were not offered for sale to] competing orthodontists despite the fact this was one facet of the inventor's total business activity. Further, the inventor made no extra charge for fitting the three patients with the improved positioners although that in itself is not critical. The facts here indicate the inventor was testing the device, not the market. No commercial exploitation having been made to even a small degree prior to filing the patent application, the underlying policy of prohibiting an extension of the term is clearly not offended in this respect.
>
> Indeed, none of the policies which underlie the public use bar and which, in effect, define it have been shown to be violated.

Id. 724 F.2d at 972–73, 220 U.S.P.Q. at 583.

Contrast *In re* Smith, 714 F.2d 1127, 218 U.S.P.Q. 976 (C.A.F.C. 1983). In *Smith*, Airwick conducted a test of the invention (a powered carpet deodorizer) with 76 homemakers more than a year prior to its application for patent. In the first phase of the test, Airwick showed homemakers a video presentation of the product concept, and obtained their reaction to the new product. In the second stage of the test, 40 of the homemakers were given a granular version of the composition and 36 were given a powdered version. The homemakers were allowed to use the products in their own homes for about two weeks and were instructed to return any unused portion. Airwick imposed no confidentiality or other restrictions upon them, and made no attempt to control or observe the homemakers' use of the samples. After two weeks, Airwick interviewed 68 of the homemakers, asking, among other things, how the product vacuumed up, whether it deodorized, whether the homemakers had experienced any mechanical problems with their vacuum cleaners, which version the homemakers would buy, and what they would be willing to pay. As Airwick had predicted, the homemakers seemed to favor the powdered version over the granular version. There had been some problems with regard to the fragrance. After the test, Airwick continued to work on the product scent and experiment with different product formulations.

The Federal Circuit rejected arguments that Airwick's use was experimental, noting that the experimental use exception to section 102(b) "does not include market testing where the inventor is attempting to gauge consumer demand for his claimed invention. The purpose of such activities is commercial exploitation and not experimentation." *Id.*, 714 F.2d at 1135, 218 U.S.P.Q. at 983. The court observed that Airwick could have performed experiments to obtain scientific data on its invention's operation and usefulness in its own laboratories. Its use of "typical housewives" to test the product, without restriction or supervision, indicated that it was seeking information that would assist it to gear its product to maximize potential sales before placing it on the market. *Id.* The use of two versions of the product was only meant to determine which version the typical consumer would prefer, not to determine which version was technically superior. The use of the homemaker/consumers to evaluate the fragrance of the product was irrelevant because fragrance strength was not a claimed element of the invention. "It is settled law that the experimental use exception is not applicable to experiments performed with respect to unclaimed features of an invention." *Id.*, 714 F.2d at 1136, 218 U.S.P.Q. at 984. As to the continued experimentation with product formulations, the court noted that Airwick already knew that the powdery product would have better antistatic and antisoil properties than the granular type. Since it already knew the technical efficacy of these properties, further tests were not necessary and must have been planned for marketing purposes.

For further discussion of the experimental use and sale exception to the statutory bar, see West & Linck, *The Law of "Public Use" and "On Sale": Past, Present and Future*, 72 J. PAT. & TRADEMARK OFF. SOC. 114, 125–154 (1990).

3. *Section 102(c).* Though section 102(c) refers to abandonment of the invention, the case law makes it clear that the provision actually deals with abandonment of the right to a patent. Such abandonment occurs when the inventor expressly or implicitly manifests an intention to relinquish the right to a patent. See 2 D.S. CHISUM, PATENTS: A TREATISE ON THE LAW OF PATENTABILITY, VALIDITY, AND INFRINGEMENT § 6.03 (1991). Courts in early cases used a finding of abandonment to prevent inventors from waiting too long to apply for a patent. For example, in MacBeth–Evans Glass Co. v. General Electric Co., 246 Fed. 695 (6th Cir. 1917), *cert. denied* 246 U.S. 659, 38 S.Ct. 316, 62 L.Ed. 926 (1918), the inventor of a process for making glass opted to use the process as a trade

secret and did so for nearly ten years. At that point he applied for and got a patent. Upon suit to enforce the patent, the court held the patent invalid as abandoned, reasoning that the plaintiff's election of trade secrecy implied a decision to forego a patent, and thus an abandonment. In law, a finding of "abandonment" generally turns on an evaluation of the relevant party's intent. In the section 102(c) context, one must consider whether the evidence indicates that the applicant intended to relinquish a patent. In *MacBeth*, the court acknowledged that the plaintiff might *in fact* have intended to retain the option of a patent as a backup in the event that secrecy later was lost. However, such an intent contemplated "an indefinite delay in disclosure of the invention and a practical and substantial enlargement of any period of monopoly recognized by statute," contrary to a "declared and subsisting public policy." *Id.*, 246 F.2d at 700. That being the case, the court deemed it appropriate to hold that as a matter of law, the plaintiff was put to an election between a patent and trade secrecy, and that his choice to pursue trade secrecy would be treated as a decision to forego a patent.

Today, section 102(b) would provide a means of invalidating the patent in *MacBeth*, and in many other instances in which an abandonment might be found within the meaning of section 102(c). As a result, section 102(c) is rarely invoked. Can you think of an instance in which a section 102(c) abandonment might not fall under the section 102(b) statutory bar?

Note that the issue of "abandonment" under section 102(g) may turn on different considerations than it would under section 102(c). Would the *Zenith* court have found that the inventor in *MacBeth* abandoned the invention if the applicant were a subsequent inventor? See 2 D.S. CHISUM, PATENTS: A TREATISE ON THE LAW OF PATENTABILITY, VALIDITY, AND INFRINGEMENT § 6.03, at 6–126 (1991).

4. *Section 102(d).* Section 102(d) requires inventors who have filed for a patent or inventor's certificate abroad to apply promptly for a United States patent. Study the language of subsection (d) closely. When, exactly, does it apply? For an explanation of the scope of subsection (d), see *In re* Kathawala, 9 F.3d 942, 28 U.S.P.Q.2d 1785 (C.A.F.C. 1993).

4. *Section 103: Non-Obviousness*

GRAHAM v. JOHN DEERE COMPANY

United States Supreme Court, 1966.
383 U.S. 1, 86 S.Ct. 684, 15 L.Ed.2d 545, 148 U.S.P.Q. 459.

MR. JUSTICE CLARK delivered the opinion of the Court.

After a lapse of 15 years, the Court again focuses its attention on the patentability of inventions under the standard of Art. I, § 8, cl. 8, of the Constitution and under the conditions prescribed by the laws of the United States. Since our last expression on patent validity, the Congress has for the first time expressly added a third statutory dimension to the two requirements of novelty and utility that had been the sole statutory test since the Patent Act of 1793. This is the test of obviousness * * *.

The questions, involved in each of the companion cases before us, are what effect the 1952 Act had upon traditional statutory and judicial tests of patentability and what definitive tests are now required. We have concluded that the 1952 Act was intended to codify judicial precedents embracing the principle long ago announced by this Court in *Hotchkiss v. Greenwood*, 11 How. 248, 13 L.Ed. 683 (1851), and that, while the clear language of § 103 places emphasis on an inquiry into obviousness, the general level of innovation necessary to sustain patentability remains the same.

* * *

III.

The difficulty of formulating conditions for patentability was heightened by the generality of the constitutional grant and the statutes implementing it, together with the underlying policy of the patent system that "the things which are worth to the public the embarrassment of an exclusive patent," as Jefferson put it, must outweigh the restrictive effect of the limited patent monopoly. The inherent problem was to develop some means of weeding out those inventions which would not be disclosed or devised but for the inducement of a patent.

This Court formulated a general condition of patentability in 1851 in *Hotchkiss v. Greenwood*, 11 How. 248, 13 L.Ed. 683. The patent involved a mere substitution of materials—porcelain or clay for wood or metal in doorknobs—and the Court condemned it, holding:

> "[U]nless more ingenuity and skill * * * were required * * * than were possessed by an ordinary mechanic acquainted with the business, there was an absence of that degree of skill and ingenuity which constitute essential elements of every invention. In other words, the improvement is the work of the skilful mechanic, not that of the inventor." At p. 267.

Hotchkiss, by positing the condition that a patentable invention evidence more ingenuity and skill than that possessed by an ordinary mechanic acquainted with the business, merely distinguished between new and useful innovations that were capable of sustaining a patent and those that were not. The *Hotchkiss* test laid the cornerstone of the judicial evolution suggested by Jefferson and left to the courts by Congress. The language in the case, and in those which followed, gave birth to "invention" as a word of legal art signifying patentable inventions. Yet, as this Court has observed, "[t]he truth is, the word ['invention'] cannot be defined in such manner as to afford any substantial aid in determining whether a particular device involves an exercise of the inventive faculty or not." *McClain v. Ortmayer*, 141 U.S. 419, 427, 12 S.Ct. 76, 78, 35 L.Ed. 800 (1891). Its use as a label brought about a large variety of opinions as to its meaning both in the Patent Office, in the courts, and at the bar. The *Hotchkiss* formulation, however, lies not in any label, but in its functional approach to questions of patentability. In practice, *Hotchkiss* has required a comparison between the subject matter of the patent, or patent application, and the background skill of the calling. It has been from this comparison that patentability was in each case determined.

IV.

The 1952 Patent Act.

The Act sets out the conditions of patentability in three sections. An analysis of the structure of these three sections indicates that patentability is dependent upon three explicit conditions: novelty and utility as articulated and defined in § 101 and § 102, and nonobviousness, the new statutory formulation, as set out in § 103. The first two sections, which trace closely the 1874 codification, express the "new and useful" tests which have always existed in the statutory scheme and, for our purposes here, need no clarification. The pivotal section around which the present controversy centers is § 103. It provides:

> "A patent may not be obtained though the invention is not identically disclosed or described as set forth in section 102 of this title, if the differences between the subject matter sought to be patented and the prior art are such that the subject matter as a whole would have been obvious at the time the invention was made to a person having ordinary skill in the art to which said subject matter pertains. Patentability shall not be negatived by the manner in which the invention was made."

The section is cast in relatively unambiguous terms. Patentability is to depend, in addition to novelty and utility, upon the "non-obvious" nature of the "subject matter sought to be patented" to a person having ordinary skill in the pertinent art. The first sentence of this section is strongly reminiscent of the language in *Hotchkiss*. Both formulations place emphasis on the pertinent art existing at the time the invention was made and both are implicitly tied to advances in that art. The major distinction is that Congress has emphasized "nonobviousness" as the operative test of the section, rather than the less definite "invention" language of *Hotchkiss* that Congress thought had led to "a large variety" of expressions in decisions and writings. In the title itself the Congress used the phrase "Conditions for patentability; *non-obvious subject matter* " (italics added), thus focusing upon "nonobviousness" rather than "invention." The Senate and House Reports, S.Rep. No. 1979, 82d Cong., 2d Sess. (1952); H.R.Rep. No. 1923, 82d Cong., 2d Sess. (1952), U.S.Code Congressional and Administrative News 1952, p. 2394, reflect this emphasis in these terms:

> "Section 103, for the first time in our statute, provides a condition which exists in the law and has existed for more than 100 years, but only by reason of decisions of the courts. An invention which has been made, and which is new in the sense that the same thing has not been made before, may still not be patentable if the difference between the new thing and what was known before is not considered sufficiently great to warrant a patent. That has been expressed in a large variety of ways in decisions of the courts and in writings. Section 103 states this requirement in the title. It refers

to the difference between the subject matter sought to be patented and the prior art, meaning what was known before as described in section 102. If this difference is such that the subject matter as a whole would have been obvious at the time to a person skilled in the art, then the subject matter cannot be patented.

"That provision paraphrases language which has often been used in decisions of the courts, and the section is added to the statute for uniformity and definiteness. This section should have a stabilizing effect and minimize great departures which have appeared in some cases." H.R.Rep., *supra*, at 7; S.Rep., *supra*, at 6.

It is undisputed that this section was, for the first time, a statutory expression of an additional requirement for patentability, originally expressed in *Hotchkiss*. It also seems apparent that Congress intended by the last sentence of § 103 to abolish the test it believed this Court announced in the controversial phrase "flash of creative genius," used in *Cuno Engineering Corp. v. Automatic Devices Corp.*, 314 U.S. 84, 62 S.Ct. 37, 86 L.Ed. 58 (1941).[7]

* * *

We believe that [the] legislative history, as well as other sources, shows that the revision was not intended by Congress to change the general level of patentable invention. We conclude that the section was intended merely as a codification of judicial precedents embracing the *Hotchkiss* condition, with congressional directions that inquiries into the obviousness of the subject matter sought to be patented are a prerequisite to patentability.

V.

Approached in this light, the § 103 additional condition, when followed realistically, will permit a more practical test of patentability. The emphasis on non-obviousness is one of inquiry, not quality, and, as such, comports with the constitutional strictures.

While the ultimate question of patent validity is one of law, the § 103 condition, which is but one of three conditions, each of which must be satisfied, lends itself to several basic factual inquiries. Under § 103, the scope and content of the prior art are to be determined; differences between the prior art and the claims at issue are to be ascertained; and the level of ordinary skill in the pertinent art resolved. Against this background, the obviousness or nonobviousness of the subject matter is determined. Such secondary considerations as commercial success, long felt but unsolved needs, failure of others, etc., might be utilized to give

7. The sentence in which the phrase occurs reads: "[T]he new device, however useful it may be, must reveal the flash of creative genius not merely the skill of the calling." At p. 91, 62 S.Ct. at p. 41. Although some writers and lower courts found in the language connotations as to the frame of mind of the inventors, none were so intended. [T]he reference to "flash of creative genius" was but a rhetorical embellishment of language going back to 1833. Rather than establishing a more exacting standard, *Cuno* merely rhetorically restated the requirement that the subject matter sought to be patented must be beyond the skill of the calling. * * *

light to the circumstances surrounding the origin of the subject matter sought to be patented. As indicia of obviousness or nonobviousness, these inquiries may have relevancy.

This is not to say, however, that there will not be difficulties in applying the nonobviousness test. What is obvious is not a question upon which there is likely to be uniformity of thought in every given factual context. The difficulties, however, are comparable to those encountered daily by the courts in such frames of reference as negligence and scienter, and should be amenable to a case-by-case development. We believe that strict observance of the requirements laid down here will result in that uniformity and definiteness which Congress called for in the 1952 Act.

While we have focused attention on the appropriate standard to be applied by the courts, it must be remembered that the primary responsibility for sifting out unpatentable material lies in the Patent Office. To await litigation is—for all practical purposes—to debilitate the patent system. We have observed a notorious difference between the standards applied by the Patent Office and by the courts. While many reasons can be adduced to explain the discrepancy, one may well be the free rein often exercised by Examiners in their use of the concept of "invention." In this connection we note that the Patent Office is confronted with a most difficult task. Almost 100,000 applications for patents are filed each year. Of these, about 50,000 are granted and the backlog now runs well over 200,000. This is itself a compelling reason for the Commissioner to strictly adhere to the 1952 Act as interpreted here. This would, we believe, not only expedite disposition but bring about a closer concurrence between administrative and judicial precedent.

Although we conclude here that the inquiry which the Patent Office and the courts must make as to patentability must be beamed with greater intensity on the requirements of § 103, it bears repeating that we find no change in the general strictness with which the overall test is to be applied. We have been urged to find in § 103 a relaxed standard, supposedly a congressional reaction to the "increased standard" applied by this Court in its decisions over the last 20 or 30 years. The standard has remained invariable in this Court. Technology, however, has advanced—and with remarkable rapidity in the last 50 years. Moreover, the ambit of applicable art in given fields of science has widened by disciplines unheard of a half century ago. It is but an evenhanded application to require that those persons granted the benefit of a patent monopoly be charged with an awareness of these changed conditions. The same is true of the less technical, but still useful arts. He who seeks to build a better mousetrap today has a long path to tread before reaching the Patent Office.

VI.

We now turn to the application of the conditions found necessary for patentability to the cases involved here:

A. The Patent in Issue in No. 11, Graham v. John Deere Co.

This patent, No. 2,627,798 (hereinafter called the '798 patent) relates to a spring clamp which permits plow shanks to be pushed upward when they hit obstructions in the soil, and then springs the shanks back into normal position when the obstruction is passed over. The device, which we show diagrammatically in the accompanying sketches (Appendix, Fig. 1), is fixed to the plow frame as a unit. The mechanism around which the controversy centers is basically a hinge. The top half of it, known as the upper plate (marked 1 in the sketches), is a heavy metal piece clamped to the plow frame (2) and is stationary relative to the plow frame. The lower half of the hinge, known as the hinge plate (3), is connected to the rear of the upper plate by a hinge pin (4) and rotates downward with respect to it. The shank (5), which is bolted to the forward end of the hinge plate (at 6), runs beneath the plate and parallel to it for about nine inches, passes through a stirrup (7), and then continues backward for several feet curving down toward the ground. The chisel (8), which does the actual plowing, is attached to the rear end of the shank. As the plow frame is pulled forward, the chisel rips through the soil, thereby plowing it. In the normal position, the hinge plate and the shank are kept tight against the upper plate by a spring (9), which is atop the upper plate. A rod (10) runs through the center of the spring, extending down through holes in both plates and the shank. Its upper end is bolted to the top of the spring while its lower end is hooked against the underside of the shank.

When the chisel hits a rock or other obstruction in the soil, the obstruction forces the chisel and the rear portion of the shank to move upward. The shank is pivoted (at 11) against the rear of the hinge plate and pries open the hinge against the closing tendency of the spring. (See sketch labeled "Open Position," Appendix, Fig. 1.) This closing tendency is caused by the fact that, as the hinge is opened, the connecting rod is pulled downward and the spring is compressed. When the obstruction is passed over, the upward force on the chisel disappears and the spring pulls the shank and hinge plate back into their original position. The lower, rear portion of the hinge plate is constructed in the form of a stirrup (7) which brackets the shank, passing around and beneath it. The shank fits loosely into the stirrup (permitting a slight up and down play). The stirrup is designed to prevent the shank from recoiling away from the hinge plate, and thus prevents excessive strain on the shank near its bolted connection. The stirrup also girds the shank, preventing it from fishtailing from side to side.

In practical use, a number of spring-hinge-shank combinations are clamped to a plow frame, forming a set of ground-working chisels capable of withstanding the shock of rocks and other obstructions in the soil without breaking the shanks.

Background of the Patent

Chisel plows, as they are called, were developed for plowing in areas where the ground is relatively free from rocks or stones. Originally, the shanks were rigidly attached to the plow frames. When such plows were used in the rocky, glacial soils of some of the Northern States, they were found to have serious defects. As the chisels hit buried rocks, a vibratory motion was set up and tremendous forces were transmitted to the shank near its connection to the frame. The shanks would break. Graham, one of the petitioners, sought to meet that problem, and in 1950 obtained a patent, U.S. No. 2,493,811 (hereinafter '811), on a spring clamp which solved some of the difficulties. Graham and his companies manufactured and sold the '811 clamps. In 1950, Graham modified the '811 structure and filed for a patent. That patent, the one in issue, was granted in 1953. This suit against competing plow manufacturers resulted from charges by petitioners that several of respondents' devices infringed the '798 patent.

The Prior Art

Five prior patents indicating the state of the art were cited by the Patent Office in the prosecution of the '798 application. Four of these patents, 10 other United States patents and two prior-use spring-clamp arrangements not of record in the '798 file wrapper were relied upon by respondents as revealing the prior art. The District Court and the Court of Appeals found that the prior art "as a whole in one form or another contains all of the mechanical elements of the 798 Patent." One of the prior-use clamp devices not before the Patent Examiner—Glencoe—was found to have "all of the elements."

We confine our discussion to the prior patent of Graham, '811, and to the Glencoe clamp device, both among the references asserted by respondents. The Graham '811 and '798 patent devices are similar in all elements, save two: (1) the stirrup and the bolted connection of the shank to the hinge plate do not appear in '811; and (2) the position of the shank is reversed, being placed in patent '811 above the hinge plate, sandwiched between it and the upper plate. The shank is held in place by the spring rod which is hooked against the bottom of the hinge plate passing through a slot in the shank. Other differences are of no consequence to our examination. In practice the '811 patent arrangement permitted the shank to wobble or fishtail because it was not rigidly fixed to the hinge plate; moreover, as the hinge plate was below the shank, the latter caused wear on the upper plate, a member difficult to repair or replace.

Graham's '798 patent application contained 12 claims. All were rejected as not distinguished from the Graham '811 patent. The inverted position of the shank was specifically rejected as was the bolting of the shank to the hinge plate. The Patent Office examiner found these to be "matters of design well within the expected skill of the art and devoid of invention." Graham withdrew the original claims and substituted the two new ones which are substantially those in issue here. His contention was that wear was reduced in patent '798 between the shank and the heel or rear of the upper plate.[11] He also emphasized several new

11. In '811, where the shank was above the hinge plate, an upward movement of the chisel forced the shank up against the underside of the rear of the upper plate.

features, the relevant one here being that the bolt used to connect the hinge plate and shank maintained the upper face of the shank in continuing and constant contact with the underface of the hinge plate.

Graham did not urge before the Patent Office the greater "flexing" qualities of the '798 patent arrangement which he so heavily relied on in the courts. The sole element in patent '798 which petitioners argue before us is the interchanging of the shank and hinge plate and the consequences flowing from this arrangement. The contention is that this arrangement—which petitioners claim is not disclosed in the prior art—permits the shank to flex under stress for its *entire* length. As we have sketched (see sketch, "Graham '798 Patent" in Appendix, Fig. 2), when the chisel hits an obstruction the resultant force (A) pushes the rear of the shank upward and the shank pivots against the rear of the hinge plate at (C). The natural tendency is for that portion of the shank between the pivot point and the bolted connection (*i.e.*, between C and D) to bow downward and away from the hinge plate. The maximum distance (B) that the shank moves away from the plate is slight—for emphasis, greatly exaggerated in the sketches. This is so because of the strength of the shank and the short—nine inches or so—length of that portion of the shank between (C) and (D). On the contrary, in patent '811 (see sketch, "Graham '811 Patent" in Appendix, Fig. 2), the pivot point is the upper plate at point (c); and while the tendency for the shank to bow between points (c) and (d) is the same as in '798, the shank is restricted because of the underlying hinge plate and cannot flex as freely. In practical effect, the shank flexes only between points (a) and (c), and not along the entire length of the shank, as in '798. Petitioners say that this difference in flex, though small, effectively absorbs the tremendous forces of the shock of obstructions whereas prior art arrangements failed.

The Obviousness of the Differences

We cannot agree with petitioners. We assume that the prior art does not disclose such an arrangement as petitioners claim in patent '798. Still we do not believe that the argument on which petitioners' contention is bottomed supports the validity of the patent. The tendency of the shank to flex is the same in all cases. If free-flexing, as petitioners now argue, is the crucial difference above the prior art, then it appears evident that the desired result would be obtainable by not boxing the shank within the confines of the hinge. The only other effective place available in the arrangement was to attach it below the hinge plate and run it through a stirrup or bracket that would not disturb its flexing qualities. Certainly a person having ordinary skill in

The upper plate thus provided the fulcrum about which the hinge was pried open. Because of this, as well as the location of the hinge pin, the shank rubbed against the heel of the upper plate causing wear both to the plate and to the shank. By relocating the hinge pin and by placing the hinge plate between the shank and the upper plate, as in '798, the rubbing was eliminated and he wear point was changed to the hinge plate, a member more easily removed or replaced for repair.

the prior art, given the fact that the flex in the shank could be utilized more effectively if allowed to run the entire length of the shank, would immediately see that the thing to do was what Graham did, *i.e.*, invert the shank and the hinge plate.

Petitioners' argument basing validity on the free-flex theory raised for the first time on appeal is reminiscent of *Lincoln Engineering Co. of Illinois v. Stewart–Warner Corp.*, 303 U.S. 545, 58 S.Ct. 662, 82 L.Ed. 1008 (1938), where the Court called such an effort "an afterthought. No such function * * * is hinted at in the specifications of the patent. If this were so vital an element in the functioning of the apparatus, it is strange that all mention of it was omitted." At p. 550, 58 S.Ct. at p. 665. No "flexing" argument was raised in the Patent Office. Indeed, the trial judge specifically found that "flexing is not a claim of the patent in suit * * * " and would not permit interrogation as to flexing in the accused devices. Moreover, the clear testimony of petitioners' experts shows that the flexing advantages flowing from the '798 arrangement are not, in fact, a significant feature in the patent.

We find no nonobvious facets in the '798 arrangement. The wear and repair claims were sufficient to overcome the patent examiner's original conclusions as to the validity of the patent. However, some of the prior art, notably Glencoe, was not before him. There the hinge plate is below the shank but, as the courts below found, all of the elements in the '798 patent are present in the Glencoe structure. Furthermore, even though the position of the shank and hinge plate appears reversed in Glencoe, the mechanical operation is identical. The shank there pivots about the underside of the stirrup, which in Glencoe is *above* the shank. In other words, the stirrup in Glencoe serves exactly the same function as the heel of the hinge plate in '798. The mere shifting of the wear point to the heel of the '798 hinge plate from the stirrup of Glencoe—itself a part of the hinge plate—presents no operative mechanical distinctions, much less nonobvious differences.

* * *

Figure 1.—GRAHAM '798 PATENT

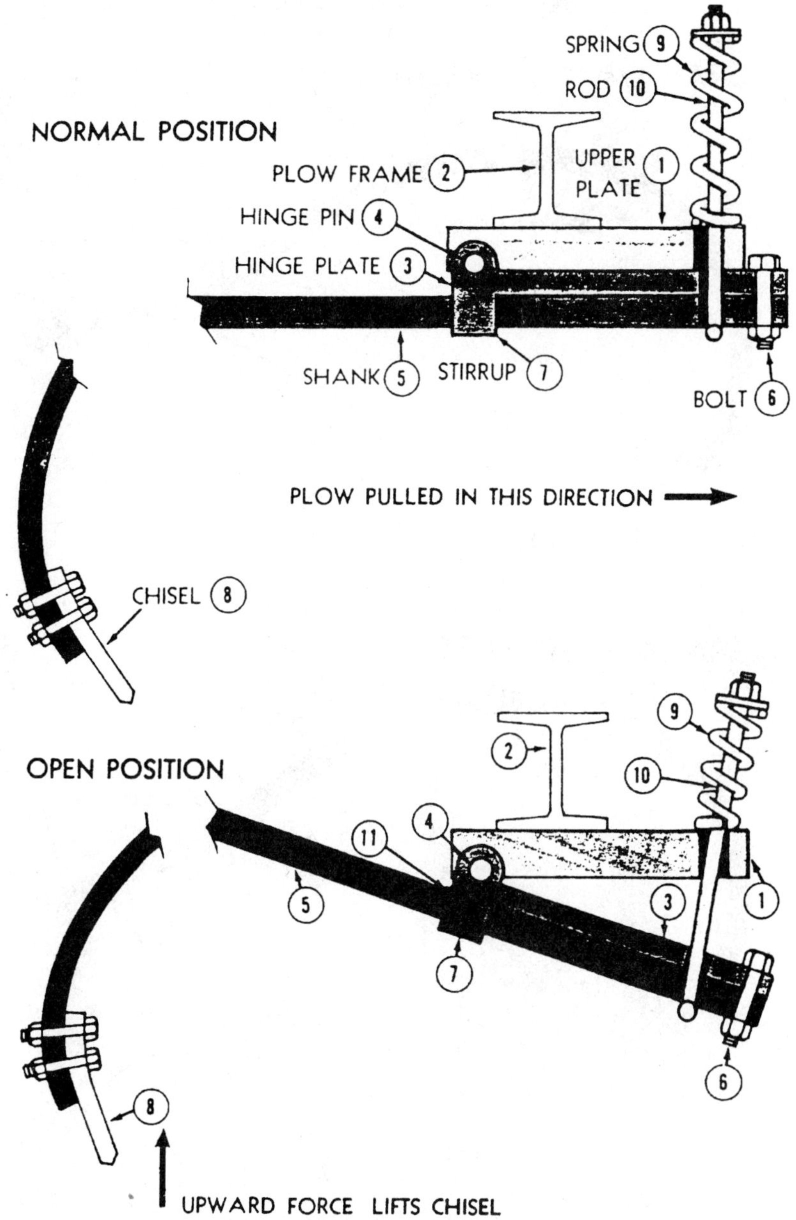

206-856 O - 66 (Face blank p. 38) No. 1

Figure 2.—FLEX COMPARISON

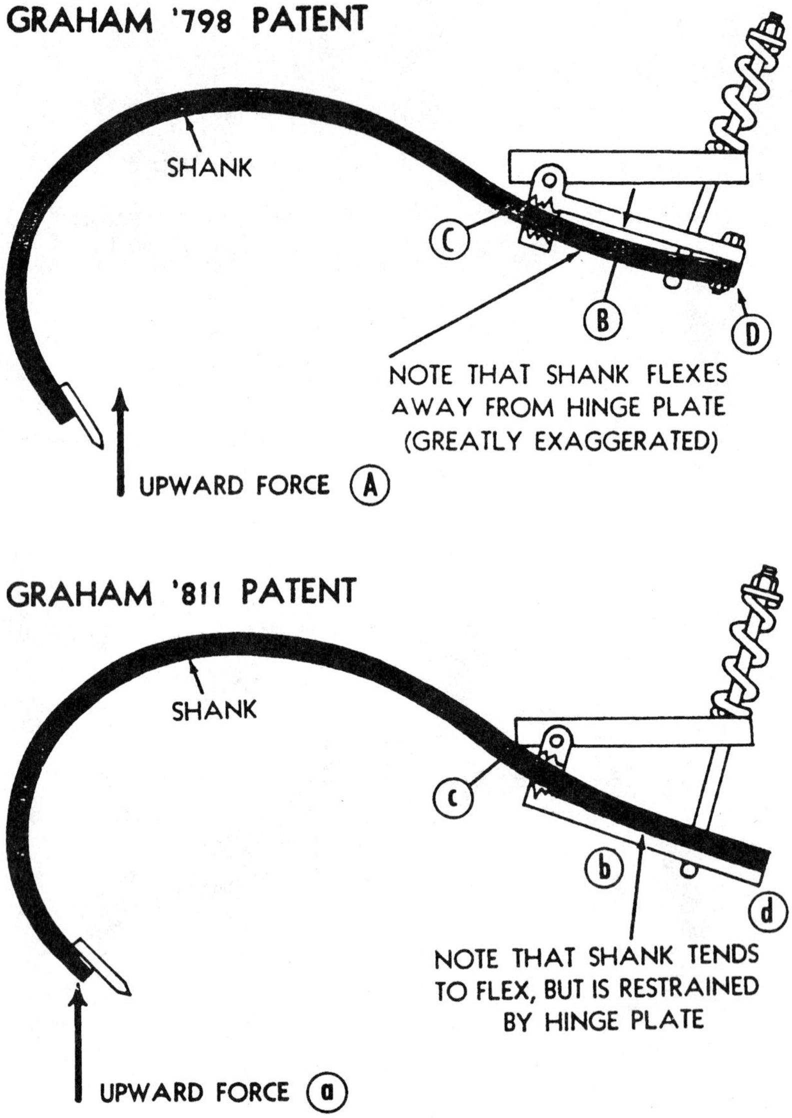

Notes and Questions

1. *The obviousness standard.* The obviousness determination distinguishes which inventions are worthy of the "public embarrassment of a monopoly" and which are not. It is the most difficult standard to satisfy, and the most difficult to administer. The *John Deere* Court states that in order to assess the obviousness of an invention under section 103, three basic factual findings must be made: 1) the scope and content of the prior art; 2) the differences between the prior art and the claims at issue; and 3) the level of ordinary skill in the pertinent art. Once these facts are

ascertained, then the question of law can be determined: would the subject matter of the patent application have been obvious at the time the invention was made to a person having ordinary skill in the art and knowledge of the pertinent prior art?

a. The scope and content of the prior art. Patent Act section 102 identifies prior art for purposes of the section 103 obviousness determination. Pursuant to section 102(a), the prior art includes printed publications and patents anywhere in the world, as well as earlier inventions known or used in the United States before the applicant's invention. In addition, pursuant to sections 102(g) and (e), the prior art encompasses inventions made in the United States prior to the applicant's and not abandoned, suppressed or concealed, and the contents of United States patent applications pending in the PTO at the time of the applicant's invention and later granted. (With regard to the latter, see the *Hazeltine* case, below.) Indeed, information which the applicant derived from another under the terms of section 102(f) may constitute "prior art" for purposes of determining the obviousness of the applicant's invention (at least if the other is not a joint inventor). See generally Chisum, *Sources of Prior Art in Patent Law*, 52 WASH. L. REV. 1 (1976). See also Stiefel, *Section 102(f) as a Basis for Section 103 Prior Art—Myth or Reality*, 61 J. PAT. OFF. SOC. 734 (1979); Walterscheid, *The Ever Evolving Meaning of Prior Art*, 64 J. PAT. OFF. SOC. 457, 571, 632 (1982); *id.*, 65 J. PAT. OFF. SOC. 3, 477 (1983). Recall that two or more pieces of prior art, or "references," may be combined to demonstrate that an invention is obvious.

Of course, for purposes of the obviousness determination, only the "pertinent" or "analogous" prior art is considered. Prior art is considered analogous if it is "from the same field of endeavor, regardless of the problem addressed," or if not in the same field as the inventor's endeavor, if it "is reasonably pertinent to the particular problem with which the inventor is involved." *In re* Clay, 966 F.2d 656, 659, 23 U.S.P.Q.2d 1058, 1060 (1992). The *Clay* case is illustrative. The applicant's invention was a process for storing refined liquid hydrocarbon product in a storage tank having a dead volume between the tank bottom and its outlet port. The process involved preparing a gelatin solution which gelled after it was placed in the tank's dead volume. A prior patent (the Hetherington patent) disclosed an apparatus for displacing dead space liquid using impervious bladders, or large bags, formed with flexible membranes. A second prior patent (the Sydansk patent) disclosed a process for reducing the permeability of hydrocarbon-bearing formations and thus improving oil production, using a gel similar to that used by Clay. The PTO had rejected the Clay application on the finding that while neither prior patent alone rendered the Clay patent obvious, the two in combination did. On appeal, the applicant argued that the Sydansk patent should not have been considered, because it was not analogous.

The Federal Circuit reasoned that the Sydansk patent could not be considered to be within Clay's field of endeavor simply because both related to the petroleum industry: Sydansk taught "the use of a gel in unconfined and irregular volumes within generally underground natural oil-bearing formations to channel flow in a desired direction," while the Clay application taught "the introduction of gel to the confined dead volume of a man-made storage tank." Clay's field of endeavor was "the storage of refined liquid hydrocarbons." The field of endeavor for the Sydansk patent was "the extraction of crude petroleum." *Id.* Nor did the court find the Sydansk patent reasonably pertinent to the problem Clay was trying to solve, so that he might have been motivated to consider it in resolving his own problem:

> Sydansk's gel treatment of underground formations functions to fill anomalies so as to improve flow profiles and sweep efficiencies of injection and production fluids through a formation, while Clay's gel functions to displace liquid product from the dead volume of a storage tank. Sydansk is concerned with plugging formation anomalies so that fluid is subsequently diverted by the gel into the formation matrix, thereby forcing bypassed oil contained in the matrix toward a production well. Sydansk is faced with the problem of recovering oil from rock, *i.e.*, from a matrix which is porous, permeable sedimentary rock of a subterranean formation where water has channeled through formation anomalies and bypassed oil present in the matrix. Such a problem is not reasonably pertinent to the particular problem with which Clay was involved—preventing loss of stored product to tank dead volume while preventing contamination of such product. Moreover, the subterranean formation of Sydansk is not structurally similar to, does not operate under the same temperature and pressure as, and does not function like Clay's storage tanks.
>
> * * *
>
> A person having ordinary skill in the art would not reasonably have expected to solve the problem of dead volume in tanks for storing refined petroleum by considering a reference dealing with plugging underground formation anomalies.

Id., 966 F.2d at 659–60, 23 U.S.P.Q.2d at 1061.

b. The differences between the prior art and the claims at issue. Section 103 provides that the claimed invention must be evaluated as a whole, taking the total mix of elements into account. See R. HARMON, PATENTS AND THE FEDERAL CIRCUIT, 93–97 (2d ed. 1991).

c. The level of ordinary skill in the pertinent art. The obviousness determination is made from the perspective of the person with ordinary skill in the art, a fictitious person who is somewhat reminiscent of the ubiquitous "reasonable person" of torts law. In order to make the obviousness evaluation from this person's perspective, one must first determine his or her level of sophistication, skill and knowledge. According to the Court of Appeals for the Federal Circuit:

> Factors that may be considered in determining level of ordinary skill in the art include: (1) the educational level of the inventor; (2) type of problems encountered in the art; (3) prior art solutions to those problems; (4) rapidity with which innovations are made; (5) sophistication of the technology; and (6) educational level of active workers in the field. Not all such factors may be present in every case, and one or more of these or other factors may predominate in a particular case. The important consideration lies in the need to adhere to the statute, i.e., to hold that an invention would or would not have been obvious, as

> a whole, when it was made, to a person of "ordinary skill in the art"—not to the judge, or to a layman, or to those skilled in remote arts, or to geniuses in the art at hand.

Environmental Designs, Ltd. v. Union Oil Co. of California, 713 F.2d 693, 696–97, 218 U.S.P.Q. 865, 868–69 (C.A.F.C. 1983). While the person from whose perspective the obviousness determination is made has only ordinary skill, that person is deemed to have knowledge of *all* the pertinent prior art. *In re* Nilssen, 851 F.2d 1401, 7 U.S.P.Q.2d 1500 (C.A.F.C. 1988).

d. The legal determination based on the findings of fact. Determining obviousness requires consideration of whether the prior art 1) would have suggested to the person of ordinary skill in the art that he should pursue the invention at issue and 2) would have revealed that he had a reasonable chance of success. *In re* Vaeck, 947 F.2d 488, 20 U.S.P.Q.2d 1438 (C.A.F.C. 1991). The determination must be made as of the time the invention was made, without the benefit of hindsight. As one practitioner/scholar has pointed out:

> [O]ne must * * * be quite vigilant, lest one commit the insidious sin of "hindsight": one may not use the teachings of the present invention as a guide to interpretation of the prior art, and of what the prior art would suggest to the hypothetical person of ordinary skill in the art, who knows the prior art but not the present invention. * * * [O]f course, the determination of what the prior art would suggest to this hypothetical person is to be made by one who *does* know the present invention, but who is expected to, in a sense, put that knowledge momentarily aside while viewing the prior art through the eyes of the person of ordinary skill, while at the same time keeping that knowledge well in mind, since he must recall clearly just *what it is* that the prior art must suggest, in order to render the invention obvious.

Harris, *Prospects for Supreme Court Review of the Federal Circuit Standards for Obviousness of Inventions Combining Old Elements*, 68 J. PAT. & TRADEMARK OFF. SOC. 66, 75 (1986).[6]

2. *The secondary considerations.* In *John Deere*, the Supreme Court provided for "secondary considerations" in the obviousness determination:

> Such secondary considerations as commercial success, long felt but unsolved needs, failure of others, etc., might be utilized to give light to the circumstances surrounding the origin of the subject matter sought to be patented. As indicia of obviousness or nonobviousness, these inquiries may have relevancy.

383 U.S. at 17–18, 86 S.Ct. at 694, 15 L.Ed.2d at 556. Why should evidence of commercial success, long felt but unsolved needs, or failure of others be relevant to the determination of obviousness?

While the Court's reference to these considerations as "secondary" suggests that they may not be essential, the Court of Appeals for the Federal Circuit has emphasized their importance. The Federal Circuit has held that evidence relating to the "secondary considerations" (or "objective factors," as the Federal Circuit prefers to call them) must *always* be considered when

6. © Robert W. Harris, 1986. Reprinted by permission of the copyright owner.

present, regardless of whether the case is otherwise a close one or not. According to the Federal Circuit, this evidence "may often be the most probative and cogent evidence in the record. It may often establish that an invention appearing to have been obvious in light of the prior art was not." Stratoflex, Inc. v. Aeroquip Corp., 713 F.2d 1530, 1538–39, 218 U.S.P.Q. 871, 879 (C.A.F.C. 1983). Moreover, the objective factors may serve "as insurance against the insidious attraction of the siren hindsight when confronted with a difficult task of evaluating the prior art" and may "reassure the decision maker." W.L. Gore & Assoc. v. Garlock, Inc., 721 F.2d 1540, 1553, 220 U.S.P.Q. 303, 313 (C.A.F.C. 1983).

Under the Federal Circuit's guidance, the Supreme Court's short list of "secondary considerations" has grown considerably to include such factors as

(1) movement of the persons skilled in the art in a different direction from that taken by the inventor, Panduit Corp. v. Dennison Manufacturing Co., 810 F.2d 1561, 1568, 1 U.S.P.Q.2d 1593, 1597 (C.A.F.C. 1987), *cert. denied* 481 U.S. 1052, 107 S.Ct. 2187, 95 L.Ed.2d 843 (1987);

(2) skepticism on the part of experts regarding the approach taken by the inventor, *In re* Dow Chemical Co., 837 F.2d 469, 473, 5 U.S.P.Q.2d 1529, 1532 (C.A.F.C. 1988);

(3) recognition and acceptance of the patent by competitors who take licenses under it to avail themselves of the merits of the invention, *Stratoflex, supra*, 713 F.2d at 1539, 218 U.S.P.Q. at 879; and

(4) the fact that the defendant copied the invention at issue, rather than alternatives in the public domain, Custom Accessories, Inc. v. Jeffrey–Allan Industries, Inc., 807 F.2d 955, 960, 1 U.S.P.Q.2d 1196, 1199 (C.A.F.C. 1986).

At the same time, the court has stressed that absence of such factors must not be taken as an indication that the invention is obvious. The Federal Circuit has ruled that such absence is a neutral factor. *Custom Accessories, supra*, 807 F.2d at 960, 1 U.S.P.Q.2d at 1199.

Of course, a nexus must be demonstrated between objective factor evidence and the issue of obviousness before the evidence can carry any weight. For example, evidence of commercial success may be relevant to prove nonobviousness because marketplace competitors can be expected to take advantage of obvious opportunities for profit. If the commercially successful invention were obvious, persons seeking profit would have made the invention earlier. Before evidence of commercial success can be deemed reliable, however, it must appear that the commercial success was due to the innovative aspects of the invention, and not to such factors as heavy advertisement and sales promotions or to features of the finished product that are not a part of the patented invention. See McClain v. Ortmayer, 141 U.S. 419, 428–29, 12 S.Ct. 76, 79, 35 L.Ed. 800, 803–04 (1891); Walker, *Objective Evidence of Nonobviousness: The Elusive Nexus Requirement*, 69 J. PAT. & TRADEMARK OFF. SOC. 175–196, 229–248 (1987).

Is it appropriate for the court to place such heavy emphasis on these objective factors? Strong arguments have been made that it is not. See, e.g., Kitch, *Graham v. John Deere Co.: New Standards for Patents*, [1966] SUP. CT. REV. 293 (arguing that relating evidence of commercial success to nonobviousness depends on a series of faulty inferences); Merges, *Commercial Success and Patent Standards: Economic Perspectives on Innovation*, 76 CAL. L. REV. 803 (1988) (arguing that by relying on the objective factors, the Federal Circuit "threatens to transform patents into rewards for such nontechnical achievements as superior distribution systems, marketing decisions, and service networks," and thus "undermine the patent system's traditional emphasis on rewarding invention"); Harris, *The Emerging Primacy of "Secondary Considerations" as Validity Ammunition: Has the Federal Circuit Gone Too Far?*, 71 J. PAT. & TRADEMARK OFF. SOC. 185 (1989) (arguing that the Federal Circuit's increased emphasis on secondary considerations will have a chilling effect upon legitimate competitors' innovative activities, due to greatly increased uncertainty regarding patent validity in situations where the prior art by itself indicates invalidity).

3. *The mental state of the inventor.* Suppose that an applicant made an invention by mistake (for example, she mistakenly added the wrong ingredient to a composition), or out of ignorance (she expected one result and got a different but useful one)? Should the mental state of the inventor make a difference for purposes of determining whether to grant a patent? Should it matter whether the applicant made the invention in a "flash of creative genius" or through long years of methodical trial and error? As the *John Deere* Court points out at footnote 7, some had construed an earlier Supreme Court opinion, Cuno Engineering Corp. v. Automatic Devices Corp., 314 U.S. 84, 62 S.Ct. 37, 86 L.Ed. 58 (1941), to suggest that the mental state of the inventor may be relevant to the issue of "invention" or "obviousness." When it enacted section 103, Congress expressly negated such an approach: "Patentability shall not be negatived by the manner in which the invention was made."

4. *Special standard for "combination patents."* In Great Atlantic & Pacific Tea Co. v. Supermarket Equipment Corp., 340 U.S. 147, 71 S.Ct. 127, 95 L.Ed. 162, 87 U.S.P.Q. 303 (1950), the Supreme Court considered the patentability of a grocery check-out counter whose individual components were all previously known, but whose particular combination of those elements was new. The Court observed that the patentee's new combination of old elements did not achieve "unusual or surprising consequences," and that the individual components failed to perform "any additional or different function in the combination" than they did out of it. As the Court put it: "Two and two have been added together, and still they only make four." The Court reasoned that the patent must be found invalid:

> Courts should scrutinize combination patent claims with a care proportioned to the difficulty and improbability of finding invention in an assembly of old elements. The function of a patent is to add to the sum of useful knowledge. Patents cannot be sustained, when on the contrary, their effect is to subtract from former resources freely available to skilled artisans. A patent for a combination which only unites old elements with no change in their respective functions, such as is presented here, obviously withdraws what already is known into the field of its monopoly and diminishes the resources available to skillful men. This patentee has added nothing to the total stock of knowledge, but has merely brought together segments of prior art and claims them in congregation as a monopoly.

340 U.S. at 152–53, 71 S.Ct. at 130, 95 L.Ed. at 167.

A quarter of a century later, in Sakraida v. Ag Pro, Inc., 425 U.S. 273, 96 S.Ct. 1532, 47 L.Ed.2d 784 (1976), the Court repeated its suggestion that new combinations of old elements must provide unusual or surprising results (a "synergistic effect") before they will be deemed nonobvious and thus patentable. Citing *Great Atlantic & Pacific Tea* with approval, the Court held the new combination of old elements at issue, a system for cleaning cow manure from barn floors, unpatentable:

> We cannot agree that the combination of these old elements to produce an abrupt release of water directly on the barn floor from storage tanks or pools can properly be characterized as synergistic, that is, "result[ing] in an effect greater than the sum of the several effects taken separately." Anderson's-Black Rock v. Pavement Co., 396 U.S. 57, 61 (1960). Rather, this patent simply arranges old elements with each performing the same function it had been known to perform, although perhaps producing a more striking result than in previous combinations. Such combinations are not patentable under standards appropriate for a combination patent.

425 U.S. at 287, 96 S.Ct. at 1537, 47 L.Ed.2d at 791.

Notwithstanding the *Great Atlantic & Pacific Tea* and *Sakraida* decisions, the Court of Appeals for the Federal Circuit has rejected any special classification or obviousness standard for "combination patents." The court explained in Stratoflex, Inc. v. Aeroquip Corp., 713 F.2d 1530, 1540, 218 U.S.P.Q. 871, 880 (C.A.F.C. 1983):

> A requirement for "synergism" or a "synergistic effect" is nowhere found in the statute, 35 U.S.C. § 103. When present, for example in a chemical case, synergism may point toward nonobviousness, but its absence has no place in evaluating the evidence on obviousness. * * *
>
> The reference to a "combination patent" is equally without support in the statute. There is no warrant for judicial classification of patents, whether into "combination" patents and some other unnamed and undefined class or otherwise. Nor is there warrant for differing treatment or consideration of patents based on a judicially devised label. Reference to "combination" patents is, moreover, meaningless. Virtually all patents are "combination patents," if by that label one intends to describe patents having claims to inventions formed of a combination of elements. It is difficult to visualize, at least in the mechanical-structural arts, a "non-combination" invention, i.e., an invention consisting of a *single* element. Such inventions, if they exist, are rare indeed.

According to the Court of Appeals for the Federal Circuit, in cases involving new combinations of known elements, obviousness depends on whether "there is something in the prior art as a whole *to suggest* the desirability, and thus the obviousness, of making the combination." Lindemann Maschinenfabrik GmbH v. American Hoist & Derrick Co., 730 F.2d 1452, 1462, 221 U.S.P.Q. 481, 488 (C.A.F.C. 1984).

For further discussion of the obviousness determination for combination patents, see Harris, *Prospects for Supreme Court Review of the Federal*

Circuit Standards for Obviousness of Inventions Combining Old Elements, 68 J. PAT. & TRADEMARK OFF. SOC. 66 (1986).

5. *Novelty vs. obviousness.* It would seem that an invention that is disqualified for lack of novelty would also be disqualified for obviousness. As the Federal Circuit has noted, anticipation is "the epitome of obviousness." Jones v. Hardy, 727 F.2d 1524, 1529, 220 U.S.P.Q. 1021, 1025 (C.A.F.C. 1984). That being the case, do we need a separate novelty provision? See R. L. HARMON, PATENTS AND THE FEDERAL CIRCUIT 43–44 (2d ed. 1991).

HAZELTINE RESEARCH, INC. v. BRENNER

United States Supreme Court, 1965.
382 U.S. 252, 86 S.Ct. 335, 15 L.Ed.2d 304.

MR. JUSTICE BLACK delivered the opinion of the Court.

The sole question presented here is whether an application for patent pending in the Patent Office at the time a second application is filed constitutes part of the "prior art" as that term is used in 35 U.S.C. § 103 (1964 ed.), which reads in part:

> "A patent may not be obtained * * * if the differences between the subject matter sought to be patented and the prior art are such that the subject matter as a whole would have been obvious at the time the invention was made to a person having ordinary skill in the art * * *."

The question arose in this way. On December 23, 1957, petitioner Robert Regis filed an application for a patent on a new and useful improvement on a microwave switch. On June 24, 1959, the Patent Examiner denied Regis' application on the ground that the invention was not one which was new or unobvious in light of the prior art and thus did not meet the standards set forth in § 103. The Examiner said that the invention was unpatentable because of the joint effect of the disclosures made by patents previously issued, one to Carlson (No. 2,491,644) and one to Wallace (No. 2,822,526). The Carlson patent had been issued on December 20, 1949, over eight years prior to Regis' application, and that patent is admittedly a part of the prior art insofar as Regis' invention is concerned. The Wallace patent, however, was pending in the Patent Office when the Regis application was filed. The Wallace application had been pending since March 24, 1954, nearly three years and nine months before Regis filed his application and the Wallace patent was issued on February 4, 1958, 43 days after Regis filed his application.[1]

After the Patent Examiner refused to issue the patent, Regis appealed to the Patent Office Board of Appeals on the ground that the Wallace patent could not be properly considered a part of the prior art because it

1. It is not disputed that Regis' alleged invention, as well as his application, was made after Wallace's application was filed. There is, therefore, no question of priority of invention before us.

had been a "co-pending patent" and its disclosures were secret and not known to the public. The Board of Appeals rejected this argument and affirmed the decision of the Patent Examiner. Regis and Hazeltine, which had an interest as assignee, then instituted the present action in the District Court pursuant to 35 U.S.C. § 145 (1964 ed.) to compel the Commissioner to issue the patent. The District Court agreed with the Patent Office that the co-pending Wallace application was a part of the prior art and directed that the complaint be dismissed. On appeal the Court of Appeals affirmed *per curiam*. We granted certiorari to decide the question of whether a co-pending application is included in the prior art, as that term is used in 35 U.S.C. § 103.

Petitioners' primary contention is that the term "prior art," as used in § 103, really means only art previously publicly known. In support of this position they refer to a statement in the legislative history which indicates that prior art means "what was known before as described in section 102." They contend that the use of the word "known" indicates that Congress intended prior art to include only inventions or discoveries which were already publicly known at the time an invention was made.

If petitioners are correct in their interpretation of "prior art," then the Wallace invention, which was not publicly known at the time the Regis application was filed, would not be prior art with regard to Regis' invention. This is true because at the time Regis filed his application the Wallace invention, although pending in the Patent Office, had never been made public and the Patent Office was forbidden by statute from disclosing to the public, except in special circumstances, anything contained in the application.[3]

The Commissioner, relying chiefly on *Alexander Milburn Co. v. Davis–Bournonville Co.*, 270 U.S. 390, 46 S.Ct. 324, 70 L.Ed. 651, contends that when a patent is issued, the disclosures contained in the patent become a part of the prior art as of the time the application was filed, not, as petitioners contend, at the time the patent is issued. In that case a patent was held invalid because, at the time it was applied for, there was already pending an application which completely and adequately described the invention. In holding that the issuance of a patent based on the first application barred the valid issuance of a patent based on the second application. Mr. Justice Holmes, speaking for the Court, said, "The delays of the patent office ought not to cut down the effect of what has been done ... [The first applicant] had taken steps that would make it public as soon as the Patent Office did its work, although, of course, amendments might be required of him before the end could be reached. We see no reason in the words or policy of the law for allowing [the second applicant] to profit by the delay ...." At p. 401, 46 S.Ct. at p. 325.

3. 35 U.S.C. § 122 (1964 ed.) states: "Applications for patents shall be kept in confidence by the Patent Office and no information concerning the same given without authority of the applicant or owner unless necessary to carry out the provisions of any Act of Congress or in such special circumstances as may be determined by the Commissioner."

In its revision of the patent laws in 1952, Congress showed its approval of the holding in *Milburn* by adopting 35 U.S.C. § 102(e) (1964 ed.) which provides that a person shall be entitled to a patent unless "(e) the invention was described in a patent granted on an application for patent by another filed in the United States before the invention thereof by the applicant for patent." Petitioners suggest, however, that the question in this case is not answered by mere reference to § 102(e), because in *Milburn*, which gave rise to that section, the co-pending applications described the same identical invention. But here the Regis invention is not precisely the same as that contained in the Wallace patent, but is only made obvious by the Wallace patent in light of the Carlson patent. We agree with the Commissioner that this distinction is without significance here. While we think petitioners' argument with regard to § 102(e) is interesting, it provides no reason to depart from the plain holding and reasoning in the *Milburn case*. The basic reasoning upon which the Court decided the *Milburn* case applies equally well here. When Wallace filed his application, he had done what he could to add his disclosures to the prior art. The rest was up to the Patent Office. Had the Patent Office acted faster, had it issued Wallace's patent two months earlier, there would have been no question here. As Justice Holmes said in *Milburn*, "The delays of the patent office ought not to cut down the effect of what has been done." P. 401, 46 S.Ct. at p. 325.

To adopt the result contended for by petitioners would create an area where patents are awarded for unpatentable advances in the art. We see no reason to read into § 103 a restricted definition of "prior art" which would lower standards of patentability to such an extent that there might exist two patents where the Congress has plainly directed that there should be only one.

Notes and Questions

1. *Secret prior art.* In the *Milburn* case, the pending application described the same invention as the later one. In *Hazeltine*, the pending application only rendered the later invention obvious. The court says this distinction "is without significance." Do you agree? From a logical standpoint, can information that is secret make the invention of another obvious? In *Milburn* and *Hazeltine*, the Court credited the PTO with delays in making the contents of the pending application available to the public. However, an applicant has considerable control over the timing of the ultimate granting and publication of her application, as well. If we are to justify the rule in *Hazeltine* on the basis of fairness to the pending applicant, should we, in each case, examine the actions of the pending applicant to ensure that she pressed her application diligently? Should we consider whether the pending applicant took advantage of other opportunities, such as professional journals and conferences, to make her invention public as soon as possible? See Leuzzi, *A Re-evaluation of the Use of 35 U.S.C. 102(e), Secret Prior Art, in Obviousness Determinations*, 29 IDEA 167 (1988–89).

What are the practical ramifications of considering disclosures in pending applications that are later granted?

2. *Statutory Invention Registrations.* Section 157 of the Patent Act authorizes the PTO to publish, without examination, a "statutory invention registration" if, among other things, the registration application satisfies the invention disclosure requirements of section 112 and waives the right to receive a patent on the invention. Statutory invention registrations are defensive in nature. They provide a means for inventors who do not seek a patent on their inventions to ensure that others cannot later patent the same invention. Though the statutory invention registration gives no exclusive rights in the disclosed invention, it has the defensive attributes of a patent: the registration is effective as prior art for purposes of sections 102 and 103.

One question that has arisen is whether the registration will be treated as a patent pursuant to section 102(e) and *Hazeltine*, so that the registration will relate back to its filing date and serve as prior art from that time forward. The legislative history of the provision suggests that it will. See 130 CONG. REC. H10,525 (Oct. 1, 1984). For a discussion of the benefits of statutory invention registrations, see Klivans, *Comment: Use of Statutory Invention Registrations*, 73 J. PAT. & TRADEMARK OFF. SOC. 731 (1991).

3. *Section 102(g) secret and in-house prior art.* Section 102(g) references are included within the prior art for purposes of section 103. E.I. du Pont de Nemours & Co. v. Phillips Petroleum Co., 849 F.2d 1430, 7 U.S.P.Q.2d 1129 (C.A.F.C.), *cert. denied* 488 U.S. 986, 109 S.Ct. 542, 102 L.Ed.2d 572 (1988). Accordingly, an earlier invention in the United States that has not been abandoned, suppressed or concealed may be used to demonstrate that an applicant's invention was obvious, even though that invention was not known or available to the public or to the applicant. In your opinion, is this a wise policy?

What is the prior art impact of work done by separate inventors in the same shop? Assume that X and Y are both employees of ABC Corporation and both have a legal obligation to assign inventions they make while on the job to ABC Corp. In 1990, X makes an invention, in which Y is not involved. In 1991, Y makes his own invention which is rendered obvious in light of X's earlier work. Assuming that X's invention has not been abandoned, suppressed or concealed, should it be considered part of the prior art for purposes of evaluating the obviousness of Y's invention? See 35 U.S.C.A. § 103, ¶ 2.

5. *Sections 102(b) and 103: The Interface*

APPLICATION OF FOSTER

United States Court of Customs and Patent Appeals, 1965.
343 F.2d 980, 145 U.S.P.Q. 166, *cert. denied*
383 U.S. 966, 86 S.Ct. 1270, 16 L.Ed.2d 307, 149 U.S.P.Q. 906 (1966).

ALMOND, JUDGE.

[The patent applicant appealed from a decision of the PTO Board of Appeals affirming the rejection of his application. At issue was the impact of an article, written by Binder and published in the magazine "Industrial and Engineering Chemistry," on the patentability of the applicant's invention. The article had appeared more than a year before the applicant had filed his application for patent. However, the applicant had introduced an affidavit demonstrating that he had made his invention before the article was published. (This is known as "swearing back"—making a sworn statement that the applicant completed the invention before the date of the prior art reference that the PTO examiner considers relevant in determining the patentability of the applicant's invention.) The court found that the Binder "reference" did not anticipate the applicant's claims—that is, the article did not fully disclose the applicant's invention. The court then turned to the remaining arguments.]

* * * Appellant argues that the affidavit establishes a date of invention prior to the publication date of the Binder reference, and that this * * * compels a finding that Binder cannot be considered in establishing obviousness of the claimed invention under 35 U.S.C. 103.

* * *

It is assumed by both parties—and it is unquestionably true—that when a reference fully discloses in every detail the subject matter of a claim, the statutory basis of a rejection on that reference is 35 U.S.C. 102(a) if the reference date is before the applicant's *date of invention*, thereby establishing want of novelty, and section 102(b) if the reference date is more than one year prior to the actual United States *filing date*, thereby establishing a so-called "statutory bar," more accurately, a one-year time-bar which results in loss of right to a patent, regardless of when the invention was made. In either of these situations, it is often said that the invention is "anticipated" by the reference and the reference is termed an "anticipation."

Proofs submitted in this case under Patent Office Rule 131 with respect to a reference not before us (because it was overcome thereby) have established that the applicant's invention date was prior to December 26, 1952. The Binder reference is the August 1954 issue of a periodical. It is seen, therefore, that it is subsequent to the date of invention but more than one year prior to the filing date, which was August 21, 1956. * * * Since the date of invention is earlier than the reference date, section 102(a) is necessarily inapplicable because the printed publication was not "before the invention thereof by the applicant" and there is statutory novelty. This leaves paragraph (b) of section 102 as the only paragraph of that section having possible relevancy.

It is appellant's position, as stated in his Reply Brief, that

> "The *only* issue on this appeal is whether the claims define subject matter which is obvious in view of the reference and hence unpatentable under 35 U.S.C. 103. * * * "

Deeming that to be the sole issue, appellant further contends that the assumed rejection under section 103 is not before the court because

* * * the Binder reference has been disposed of by the proof of an invention date prior to the date of Binder * * *.

* * *

Because of the importance of the question to the law of patents, we have deemed it desirable to reconsider * * * the result again urged on us here, as allegedly authorized by section 103, that a reference having a date more than a year prior to the filing date may be disposed of by showing an invention date prior to the reference date, contrary to the express provision in Patent Office Rule 131.[8]

Sections 101, 102 and 103, generally speaking, deal with two different matters: (1) the factors to be considered in determining whether a patentable invention has been *made*, i.e., novelty, utility, unobviousness, and the categories of patentable subject matter; and (2) "loss of right to patent" as stated in the heading of section 102, even though an otherwise patentable invention has been made. On the subject of loss of right, appellant's brief contains a helpful review of the development of the statutory law since 1793. It says:

* * *

> "Manifestly, Section 102(b) from its earliest beginnings has been and was intended to be directed toward the encouragement of *diligence* in the filing of patent applications and the protection of the public from monopolies on subject matter which had already been fully disclosed to it."

These statements are in accord with our understanding of the history and purposes of section 102(b). It presents a sort of statute of limitations, formerly two years, now one year, within which an inventor, even though he has made a patentable invention, must act on penalty of loss of his right to patent. What starts the period running is clearly the availability of the invention *to the public* through the categories of disclosure enumerated in 102(b), which include "a printed publication" anywhere describing the invention. There appears to be no dispute about the operation of this statute in "complete anticipation" situations but *the contention seems to be that 102(b) has no applicability where the invention is not completely disclosed in a single patent or publication*, that is to say where the rejection involves the addition to the disclosure of the reference of the ordinary skill of the art or the disclosure of

8. "131. *Affidavit of prior invention to overcome cited patent or publication.*

(a) When any claim of an application is rejected on reference to a domestic patent which substantially shows or describes but does not claim the rejected invention, or on reference to a foreign patent or to a printed publication, and the applicant shall make oath to facts showing a completion of the invention in this country before the filing date of the application on which the domestic patent issued, or before the date of the foreign patent, or before the date of the printed publication, then the patent or publication cited shall not bar the grant of a patent to the applicant, *unless the date of such patent or printed publication be more than one year prior to the date on which the application was filed in this country.*" [Emphasis ours.]

* * *

another reference which indicates what those of ordinary skill in the art are presumed to know, *and to have known for more than a year before the application was filed.* Upon a complete reexamination of this matter, we are convinced that the contention is contrary to the policy consideration which motivated the enactment by Congress of a statutory bar. On logic and principle we think this contention is unsound, and we also believe it is contrary to the patent law as it has actually existed since at least 1898.

First, as to principle, since the purpose of the statute has always been to require filing of the application within the prescribed period after the time the public came into possession of the invention, we cannot see that it makes any difference *how* it came into such possession, whether by a public use, a sale, a single patent or publication, or by combinations of one or more of the foregoing. In considering this principle *we assume*, of course, that by these means *the invention has become obvious* to that segment of the "public" having ordinary skill in the art. Once this has happened, the purpose of the law is to give the inventor only a year within which to file and this would seem to be liberal treatment. Whenever an applicant undertakes, under Rule 131, to swear back of a reference having an effective date more than a year before his filing date, he is automatically conceding that he made his invention more than a year before he filed. If the reference contains enough disclosure to make his invention obvious, the principle of the statute would seem to require denial of a patent to him. The same is true where a combination of two publications or patents makes the invention obvious and they both have dates more than a year before the filing date.

As to dealing with the express language of 102(b), for example, "described in a printed publication," technically, we see no reason to so read the words of the statute as to preclude the use of more than one reference; nor do we find in the context anything to show that "a printed publication" cannot include two or more printed publications. * * *

* * *

* * * It follows that where the time-bar is involved, *the actual date of invention becomes irrelevant* and that it is not in accordance with either the letter or the principle of the law, or its past interpretation over a very long period, to permit an applicant to dispose of a reference having a date more than one year prior to his filing date by proving his actual date of invention.

* * *

We wish to make it clear that this ruling is predicated on our construction of section 102(b) and has no effect on the * * * determination of obviousness under section 103 when a statutory time-bar is not involved. The existence of unobviousness under that section, as a necessary prerequisite to patentability, we reiterate, must be determined as of "the time the invention was made" without utilizing after-acquired knowledge.

The determination of unobviousness, however, relates to the determination of whether a patentable invention has been *made*. Whether there has been a *loss of right to a patent* on such invention is a distinct and separate issue, with which section 103 per se has nothing whatever to do. Its legislative history, which is well known and uncomplicated, shows that section 103 had but a single purpose which was to add to the statute a provision to take the place of the judge-made "requirement for invention." In doing that, the history also shows, the words "at the time the invention was made" were included for the sole purpose of precluding the use of hindsight in deciding whether an invention is obvious. We are sure Congress had no intent thereby to modify the law respecting *loss of right* based on the existence of a time-bar. * * *

Since we must reject Foster's contention that he can dispose entirely of Binder by showing an earlier invention date, it becomes necessary for us to consider whether there was a loss of right to a patent, i.e., whether the invention became obvious to the public at the time of the Binder publication.

* * *

Notes and Questions

1. *Section 102(b) vs. section 103.* In his dissent to the *Foster* opinion, Judge Smith wrote:

> [T]he majority decision amounts to an interpretation of section 102(b) as though it contained the following italicized words:
>
> > "A person shall be entitled to a patent unless—* * * (b) the invention was patented or described in a printed publication in this or a foreign country or in public use or on sale in this country or *unless the invention became obvious* more than one year prior to the date of the application for patent in the United States * * *."
>
> Thus, within the rationale of the majority opinion and its construction of section 102, it is no longer necessary for a patent or a publication to "describe" the invention to lay the basis for the loss of right to a patent under section 102(b). It is sufficient that a patent or a publication be found, or that some combination of the same can be put together after the applicant's date of invention and with the accuracy characteristic of perfect hindsight which make the invention "obvious" more than one year prior to the date of filing the patent application. Thus, in addition to changing the wording of section 102(b) as above suggested, the majority must also intend to rewrite section 103 so that the phrase "at the time the invention was made" now is to be limited by a proviso which reduces this time to a period of one year prior to the filing of the application.

343 F.2d at 996–97, 145 U.S.P.Q. at 180. Do you agree with Judge Smith's characterization of the majority's result? Does the *Foster* opinion change the meaning of section 103 so that obviousness is tested as of one year prior to the filing date of the application, rather than as of the date the invention was made?

6. *Section 112: Disclosure*

SPECTRA–PHYSICS, INC. v. COHERENT, INC.

United States Court of Appeals for the Federal Circuit, 1987.
827 F.2d 1524, 3 U.S.P.Q.2d 1737, *cert. denied*
484 U.S. 954, 108 S.Ct. 346, 98 L.Ed.2d 372 (1987).

RICH, CIRCUIT JUDGE.

[Coherent owns both the Hobart and the Mefferd patents. The Hobart patent is directed to an ion laser structure and the Mefferd patent is directed to a method of fabricating the Hobart ion laser structure. The Hobart laser includes a series of copper cups attached to the inside of a ceramic tube.]

[Both the Hobart and Mefferd patents stress the importance of the bond between the copper cups and the tube. Dr. Hobart initially approached the problem of how to make the critical copper to ceramic bond by experimenting with soldering. These attempts were unsuccessful. Mefferd was then brought in to solve the attachment problem. His solution was brazing. While the patent specifications disclose pulse soldering as one method of bonding, brazing is clearly the preferred method of bonding. The patents disclose "TiCuSil" as the preferred brazing material. The titanium in this compound invades and wets the ceramic so that the copper-silver braze material can hold the copper to the ceramic. In the absence of an active metal alloy component such as titanium, the ceramic must be premetalized with, for example, moly-manganese, to provide a metallic surface to which the copper-silver braze material will adhere. The TiCuSil active metal process is preferred because it requires only one step and avoids the need for premetalization.]

[Through experimentation, Mefferd developed a six-stage braze cycle for using TiCuSil to attach the copper cups to the ceramic tube. "Braze cycle" is a term of art which refers to a process defined by specific parameters of temperature, length of times at given temperatures, atmosphere, and pressure. Mefferd's six-stage cycle produced a reliable braze joint between the copper cups and the ceramic tube. Because this approach worked, Coherent continued to use TiCuSil and never investigated the moly-manganese process or further experimented with soldering. Neither the Hobart nor the Mefferd patent, however, discloses the braze cycle or any additional information on brazing copper to ceramic using TiCuSil.]

[Spectra–Physics brought a declaratory judgment action against Coherent seeking a declaration that both the Hobart and the Mefferd patents were invalid. The lower court held both patents invalid for failure to disclose the six-stage braze cycle used by Coherent to manufacture the laser, which the court deemed a lack of enabling disclosure under the first paragraph of Patent Act section 112. The court found that section 112's best mode requirement was satisfied, however, because neither Hobart nor Mefferd deliberately or accidentally concealed brazing as the best mode of attaching the copper cups to the ceramic tube.]

To constitute adequate disclosure under the first paragraph of 35 U.S.C. § 112, a patent specification must set forth both the manner and process of making and using the invention (the enablement requirement) and the best mode contemplated by the inventor of carrying out the invention (the best mode requirement). The difference between these two is explained in *In re Gay*, 309 F.2d 769, 135 USPQ 311 (CCPA 1962):

> The essence of [the enablement requirement] is that a specification shall disclose an invention in such a manner as will enable one skilled in the art to make and utilize it. *Separate and distinct* from [enablement] is [the best mode requirement], the essence of which requires the inventor to disclose the best mode *contemplated by him*, as of the time he executes the application, of carrying out his invention. Manifestly, the sole purpose of this latter requirement is to restrain inventors from applying for patents while at the same time concealing from the public preferred embodiments of their inventions which they have in fact conceived.
>
> ... The question of whether an inventor has or has not disclosed what he feels is his best mode is, however, a question separate and distinct from the question of the *sufficiency* of his disclosure to satisfy the requirements of [enablement].

Id. at 772, 135 USPQ at 315 (emphasis in original).

Thus, compliance with the best mode requirement focuses on a different matter than does compliance with the enablement requirement. Enablement looks to placing the subject matter of the claims generally in the possession of the public. If, however, the applicant develops specific instrumentalities or techniques which are recognized at the time of filing as the best way of carrying out the invention, then the best mode requirement imposes an obligation to disclose that information to the public as well.

The situation before us is one in which the patent specifications disclose more than one means for making the claimed invention, but do not adequately disclose the best means actually known to the inventors. The district court recognized that the specifications were inadequate under § 112, but incorrectly based its decision on a lack of enablement. As we explain, the problem is really one of best mode, and thus, while we disagree with the district court's views on these issues, the judgment that the patents are both invalid was correct and must be sustained.

2. Enablement

* * *

To be enabling under § 112, a patent specification must disclose sufficient information to enable those skilled in the art to make and use the claimed invention. The district court held both of the patents in suit invalid for lack of enablement based on their failure to disclose Coherent's six-stage braze cycle for brazing TiCuSil. The court found that the braze cycle was "necessary to the enjoyment of the invention [sic]."

Coherent's braze cycle, however, is applicable only to TiCuSil brazing, which is just one of the ways to make and use the claimed inventions. The Hobart patent calls for "means for attaching" the copper cups to the inside of the ceramic tube and Mefferd has essentially the same step of "permanently securing" the cups to the tube. The specifications identify as suitable attachment techniques the alternatives of TiCuSil brazing, moly-manganese brazing, and low-temperature pulse-soldering.

If an invention pertains to an art where the results are predictable, e.g., mechanical as opposed to chemical arts, a broad claim can be enabled by disclosure of a single embodiment, and is not invalid for lack of enablement simply because it reads on another embodiment of the invention which is inadequately disclosed.[5] Thus, it is sufficient here with respect to enablement that the patents disclose at least one attachment means which would enable a person of ordinary skill in the art to make and use the claimed inventions. Because the patents disclose the alternatives of moly-manganese brazing and pulse-soldering, their failure to also disclose Coherent's TiCuSil braze cycle is not fatal to enablement under § 112.

Spectra argues that the patents' references to the "moly-manganese process" is only in regard to low-temperature pulse-soldering, not brazing. We disagree. A fair reading of that paragraph as part of the general discussion of brazing, given that moly-manganese brazing was the most common method of bonding metal to ceramic, is that one skilled in the art would recognize that moly-manganese brazing was an alternative means of attachment. Spectra's Dave Wright, among others, testified that moly-manganese brazing was common in the industry and was well-known for brazing copper to ceramic.

The district court ignored the moly-manganese process, however, for the erroneous reason that it was "neither described nor advocated in the patents in suit." A patent need not teach, and preferably omits, what is well known in the art. While there is no elaboration of moly-manganese brazing in the patent specifications, the district court found that brazing was an old and well-known technique when the applications were filed.

* * *

As for the court's statement that moly-manganese was not "advocated" in the patents, this is another matter entirely. We can only surmise that the court somehow confused the enablement requirement with the best mode. Nonenablement is the failure to disclose *any* mode, and does not depend on the applicant advocating a particular embodiment or method for making the invention. In practical terms, where only an alternative embodiment is enabled, the disclosure of the best mode may

5. This is also the logical implication of having a separate best mode requirement under § 112 which contemplates that the specification can enable one to make and use the invention and still not disclose a single preferred embodiment.

be inadequate. But that is a question separate and distinct from the question whether the specification enabled one to make the invention at all.

* * *

3. Best Mode

* * *

Because the best mode provision of § 112 speaks in terms of the best mode "contemplated by the inventor," there is no objective standard by which to judge the adequacy of a best mode disclosure. Instead, only evidence of "concealment," whether accidental or intentional, is considered. The specificity of disclosure required to comply with the best mode requirement must be determined by the knowledge of facts within the possession of the inventor at the time of filing the application.

Compliance with the best mode requirement, because it depends on the applicant's state of mind, is a question of fact subject to the clearly erroneous standard of review. This assumes, however, a proper legal understanding of the best mode requirement, which we find missing from the district court's analysis. In general, we do not disagree with the facts as found by the district court. It is only the court's ultimate conclusion that the best mode requirement was satisfied that we reject.

In analyzing compliance with the best mode requirement, the district court focused only on the generic rather than the specific information known to the inventors and found that neither Mefferd nor Hobart intentionally, deliberately, or accidentally "concealed the braze technique as the best mode of attaching the heat web to the alumina tube." The patent specifications make clear, however, that the best mode contemplated by the inventors, as least as far as the critical "means for attaching" the copper cups to the ceramic tube is concerned, was more than just brazing in general—it was TiCuSil active metal brazing. Coherent acknowledges as much by its references to TiCuSil as the "preferred" brazing material and by the fact that Coherent never used anything else.

The appropriate question then is not whether the inventors disclosed TiCuSil brazing *at all*—they did—but whether TiCuSil brazing was *adequately* disclosed. Even though there may be a general reference to the best mode, the quality of the disclosure may be so poor as to effectively result in concealment.

The facts found by the district court, when placed in the proper framework, plainly demonstrate that the TiCuSil brazing technique used by Coherent was not adequately disclosed. The court stated in findings of fact under the heading "ENABLEMENT":

> 2. The use to which Coherent put the TiCuSil braze material was, and was known to be by Coherent at the time, contrary to criteria for the use of TiCuSil as contained in the literature.

and again,

> 9. The references to brazing as used in the patents and the extraneous texts (Kohl, Wesgo Brochure) relied upon by Coherent, do not describe for the benefit of one skilled in the art of laser construction the manner in which the Mefferd method is usable for the construction of the Hobart apparatus by means of [TiCuSil] brazing.

The district court also found that the inventors were aware of the problems associated with TiCuSil:

> 4. The known difficulty recognized by Hobart and Mefferd in working with TiCuSil as a braze material for the purpose to which they put it is reflected in Hobart's disclosure dated March 1, 1979 . . . that the titanium-copper-silver process is "not in high favor in the ceramic industry" and "not preferred as compared with what is called the moly-manganese technique which produces stronger and also less leak-prone seals" and essentially the same language in the May, 1979 patent disclosure signed by all of Hobart, Mefferd and Johnston.

Coherent admits that its braze cycle is not disclosed in either patent nor is it contained in the prior art. Instead, it maintains that its braze cycle is unique to its ovens, and because the performance of industrial ovens varies considerably, the actual parameters would be meaningless to someone who used a different oven. In support of its position, Coherent cites *In re Gay*, 309 F.2d at 769, 135 USPQ at 316, which states that "[n]ot every last detail is to be described, else patent specifications would turn into production specifications, which they were never meant to be." In doing so, however, Coherent was not discussing whether it had complied with the best mode requirement because the court had held in its favor on that issue; it was discussing whether it had complied with the enablement requirement on which the court had held against it.

First, it is not up to the courts to decide *how* an inventor should disclose the best mode, but *whether* he has done so adequately under the statute. Second, far from being a "production specification," Coherent did not disclose *any* details about its brazing process. It is this complete lack of detail which effectively resulted in its concealment.

Where the district court went wrong on the law while reaching the right result is starkly revealed in its conclusions of law. Under the heading of "BEST MODE" is this conclusion:

> 4. There was no concealment deliberate or otherwise by Hobart or Mefferd of the brazing process as the best mode of bonding the heating web to the alumina tube.

As we have pointed out, however, this refers to brazing in general, not the actual brazing cycle with TiCuSil and all of the parameters which Coherent found to be its best mode, admittedly not disclosed. In contrast, but under the heading "ENABLEMENT," is the key conclusion of law which supports our conclusion and the judgment, reading as follows:

> 3. The six stage braze cycle employed by Coherent, and developed by it, are [sic, is] necessary to the enjoyment of the invention taught by the patents in suit by a person skilled in the art of laser construction, and are [sic] not *sufficiently disclosed* by the patents in suit. [Original emphasis.]

For reasons above explained, Coherent's failure to disclose its "six stage braze cycle" fully supports the defense of non-compliance with the best mode requirement of the first paragraph of § 112 although the inventions as broadly claimed could be practiced without knowledge of it, which means that the patent specifications are enabling. The trial court evidently had a grasp on the essential facts but somehow got them into the wrong legal pigeonholes. With the aid of lawyers, this is not difficult to do.

Spectra's claim in this declaratory judgment complaint that the two patents in suit are invalid must therefore be sustained on the ground that they fail to disclose the best mode contemplated by the inventors for practicing their respective inventions.

* * *

Notes and Questions

1. *The quid pro quo.* Section 112 sets forth terms of the "bargain" struck between the inventor and the public when a patent is granted. In return for the privilege of a monopoly in the invention, the inventor must fully disclose the invention and the method of making and using it, so that the public may benefit from the new knowledge it represents during the patent term, and others can readily make, use and sell the invention when the patent expires. Full disclosure is the consideration the inventor pays for the patent. Failure to make that payment renders the patent invalid.

Section 112 imposes three separate requirements with regard to disclosure. First, the disclosure must include one or more claims which clearly and distinctly describe the subject matter which the applicant regards to be his invention and give the public adequate notice of what is to be protected. This requirement is sometimes called the "claiming" or "description" requirement. Second, the disclosure must fully, clearly, and concisely describe how to make or practice the invention, sufficient to enable a person with ordinary skill in the art to make and use the invention without undue experimentation. This is sometimes called the "enablement requirement." Third, the disclosure must set forth the "best mode" that the inventor knows for carrying out the invention at the time he files the application.

The claims constitute the official definition of the invention to be patented. A claim is sometimes equated to the "metes and bounds" description of land in a deed to real estate. Like the metes and bounds description, the claim clearly identifies the scope, or perimeter of the private property that is the subject of the patent grant. Novelty and nonobviousness are judged by the claims, and when a patent is granted, infringement is determined by reference to the claims.

The enabling and best mode disclosures take place in the specification, which precedes the claims. As one authority has put it, "[t]he specification describes: the claims define." J.T. McCARTHY, McCARTHY'S DESK ENCYCLOPEDIA OF INTELLECTUAL PROPERTY, 313 (1991). Nonetheless, when there is doubt about the meaning of a claim, the specification may be used to interpret it.

For a discussion of the Federal Circuit case law construing and applying the various disclosure requirements of section 112, see Irving, Kaminski, Boyd, and Helmberger–Jones, *The Significant Federal Circuit Cases Interpreting Section 112*, 41 AM. U. L. REV. 621 (1992).

2. *Enablement.* Section 112 requires the patent applicant to describe the manner of making and using the invention sufficiently to enable a person skilled in the art to which it pertains to make and use the invention without undue experimentation. What are the implications of designating persons skilled in the art as the applicant's audience, as opposed to persons generally? In *Spectra-Physics*, the Hobart patent claim recited "means for attaching" the copper cups to the inside of the ceramic tube as an element of the invention. What are the implications of this language for a person seeking to determine the scope of the patent monopoly? What, if any, implications did the applicant's use of this language have with regard to the enablement requirement?

Does enabling a person with ordinary skill to make and use the invention include enabling her to mass produce the invention? Should it? See Christianson v. Colt Industries Operating Corp., 822 F.2d 1544, 1562–63, 3 U.S.P.Q.2d 1241, 1255 (C.A.F.C. 1987), *vacated on jurisdictional gds. and remanded for transfer to 7th Cir.* 486 U.S. 800, 108 S.Ct. 2166, 100 L.Ed.2d 811 (1988).

In the case of inventions involving living materials, such as microorganisms or genetically engineered cells, it may be impossible to enable persons skilled in the art to make or use the invention with just a written description. In such cases, an alternative form of enablement is available. The patent applicant may deposit the living materials in a recognized depository which complies with the United States' treaty obligations under the Budapest Treaty on the International Recognition of the Deposit of Microorganisms for the Purposes of Patent Procedure.[7] The depository will then make samples of the material available to those wishing to learn more about the invention. For a discussion of the procedures for making deposits, see U.S. PATENT AND TRADEMARK OFFICE, MANUAL OF PATENT EXAMINING PROCEDURE, § 608.01 (1992). For further discussion of the disclosure problems biotechnology inventors face, see *In re* Wands, 858 F.2d 731, 8 U.S.P.Q.2d 1400 (C.A.F.C. 1988); Hall & Chwang, *Deposit Requirements for Biological Materials*, 14 HOUS. J. INT'L L. 565 (1992).

3. *The best mode.* What purpose does the "best mode" requirement serve? How does the purpose differ from that of the "enablement" requirement? In *Spectra-Physics*, the patentees disclosed TiCuSil brazing in their

7. Budapest Treaty on the International Recognition of the Deposit of Microorganisms for the Purposes of Patent Procedure, April 28, 1977, 32 U.S.T. 1241, T.I.A.S. 9768.

application, but the court found that they did not do so adequately. What more was required? Why?

The Federal Circuit provided further elaboration on the best mode requirement in Chemcast Corp. v. Arco Industries Corp., 913 F.2d 923, 926–28, 16 U.S.P.Q. 1033, 1035–36 (C.A.F.C. 1990):

> The best mode inquiry focuses on the inventor's state of mind as of the time he filed his application—a subjective, factual question. But this focus is not exclusive. Our statements that "there is no objective standard by which to judge the adequacy of a best mode disclosure," and that "only evidence of concealment (accidental or intentional) is to be considered," * * * assumed that both the level of skill in the art and the scope of the claimed invention were additional, objective metes and bounds of a best mode disclosure.
>
> Of necessity, the disclosure required by section 112 is directed to those skilled in the art. * * * Therefore, one must consider the level of skill in the relevant art in determining whether a specification discloses the best mode. We have consistently recognized that whether a best mode disclosure is adequate, that is, whether the inventor concealed a better mode of practicing his invention than he disclosed, is a function of not only what the inventor knew but also how one skilled in the art would have understood his disclosure. *See, e.g.*, * * * *W.L. Gore*, 721 F.2d [at] 1556, 220 USPQ [at] 315 (no best mode violation where inventor did not disclose the only mode of calculating stretch rate that he used, because that "mode would have been employed by those of ordinary skill in the art at the time the application was filed. As indicated, Dr. Gore's disclosure must be examined for § 112 compliance in light of knowledge extant in the art on his application filing date.") * * *. Thus, the level of skill in the art is a relevant and necessary consideration in assessing the adequacy of a best mode disclosure.
>
> The other objective limitation on the extent of the disclosure required to comply with the best mode requirement is, of course, the scope of the claimed invention. "It is concealment of the best mode of practicing the *claimed invention* that section 112 ¶ 1 is designed to prohibit." *Randomex*, 849 F.2d at 588, 7 USPQ2d at 1053. Thus, in *Randomex*, the inventor's deliberate concealment of his cleaning fluid formula did not violate the best mode requirement because his "invention neither added nor claimed to add anything to the prior art respecting cleaning fluid." 849 F.2d at 590, 7 USPQ2d at 1054. * * * Finally, in *DeGeorge* we reversed a finding that an inventor's nondisclosure of unclaimed circuitry with which his claimed circuitry interfaced violated the best mode requirement: "Because the properly construed claim does not include a word processor, failure to meet the best mode requirement here should not arise from an absence of information on the word processor." 768 F.2d at 1325, 226 USPQ at 763.
>
> In short, a proper best mode analysis has two components. The first is whether, at the time the inventor filed his patent application, he knew of a mode of practicing his claimed invention that he considered to be better than any other. This part of the inquiry is wholly subjective, and resolves whether the inventor must disclose any facts in addition to

those sufficient for enablement. If the inventor in fact contemplated such a preferred mode, the second part of the analysis compares what he knew with what he disclosed—is the disclosure adequate to enable one skilled in the art to practice the best mode or, in other words, has the inventor "concealed" his preferred mode from the "public"? Assessing the *adequacy* of the disclosure, as opposed to its *necessity*, is largely an objective inquiry that depends upon the scope of the claimed invention and the level of skill in the art.

For an exhaustive discussion of the Federal Circuit's application and development of the best mode requirement, see Strobos, *The Best Mode Inquiry: Resolution of Legal Issues by the Court of Appeals for the Federal Circuit*, 75 J. PAT. & TRADEMARK OFF. SOC. 260 (1993).

4. *The duty of candor.* While the Patent and Trademark Office has a large patent and technical library which PTO examiners use to identify prior art relevant to the novelty and obviousness of an invention, the library cannot supply examiners with all the information relevant to patentability. For example, it may be difficult or impossible for a patent examiner to learn of such things as public use or sale of an applicant's patented invention more than a year prior to the application, or lesser-known printed publications in foreign nations. To ensure that as much relevant information reaches the patent examiner as possible, the PTO's Rule 56 provides as follows:

> (a) * * * Each individual associated with the filing and prosecution of a patent application has a duty of candor and good faith in dealing with the Office, which includes a duty to disclose to the Office all information known to that individual to be material to patentability as defined in this section. The duty to disclose information exists with respect to each pending claim until the claim is cancelled or withdrawn from consideration, or the application becomes abandoned. [N]o patent will be granted on an application in connection with which fraud on the Office was practiced or attempted or the duty of disclosure was violated through bad faith or intentional misconduct. * * *
>
> * * *
>
> (b) Under this section, information is material to patentability when it is not cumulative to information already of record or being made of record in the application, and
>
> (1) It establishes, by itself or in combination with other information, a prima facie case of unpatentability of a claim; or
>
> (2) It refutes, or is inconsistent with, a position the applicant takes in:
>
> (i) Opposing an argument of unpatentability relied on by the Office, or
>
> (ii) Asserting an argument of patentability.
>
> A prima facie case of unpatentability is established when the information compels a conclusion that a claim is unpatentable under the preponderance of evidence burden-of-proof standard, giving each term in the claim its broadest reasonable construction consistent with the specification, and before any consideration is given to evidence which may be

submitted in an attempt to establish a contrary conclusion of patentability.

(c) Individuals associated with the filing or prosecution of a patent application within the meaning of this section are:

(1) Each inventor named in the application;

(2) Each attorney or agent who prepares or prosecutes the application; and

(3) Every other person who is substantively involved in the preparation or prosecution of the application and who is associated with the inventor, with the assignee or with anyone to whom there is an obligation to assign the application.

(d) Individuals other than the attorney, agent or inventor may comply with this section by disclosing information to the attorney, agent, or inventor.

37 C.F.R. § 1.56 (1992). For a more detailed exploration of the Rule 56 duty of candor and its implications, see the articles in 20 AIPLA Q.J. 131–230 (1992).

Related to Rule 56 is the court-developed doctrine of inequitable conduct. Under this doctrine, in a manner similar to the doctrine of unclean hands, courts have refused to enforce patents when it is shown that the patentee acted inequitably in the course of procuring her patent. More specifically, courts may refuse to enforce an otherwise valid patent upon a showing that the patentee knowingly failed to disclose information material to the patentability of her invention during the patent application procedure, with the intent to mislead the PTO. FMC Corp. v. Manitowoc Co., 835 F.2d 1411, 1415, 1417 n.14, 5 U.S.P.Q.2d 1112, 1116 n.14 (C.A.F.C. 1987). For an argument that the standards courts apply to determine whether inequitable conduct has occurred may differ from the standards of Rule 56, due to recent amendment of Rule 56's definition of materiality, see Moy, *The Effect of New Rule 56 on the Law of Inequitable Conduct*, 74 J. PAT. & TRADEMARK OFF. SOC. 257 (1992).

7. *Inventorship*

The Patent Act makes it clear that it is the actual inventor who is entitled to apply for a patent. See, e.g., § 101 ("whoever invents or discovers any new and useful process, machine, manufacture, or composition of matter ... may obtain a patent"); § 102(f) ("A person shall be entitled to a patent unless ... he did not himself invent the subject matter sought to be patented"); § 111 ("Application for patent shall be made, or authorized to be made, by the inventor"); § 115 ("The applicant shall make oath that he believes himself to be the original and first inventor...."). The application must be pursued in the actual inventor's name even when she has assigned all rights in the invention to another, such as her employer.[8] The only exceptions to this rule are set

8. The general rules regarding the ownership of an invention made by an employee during the course of employment are discussed in Chapter 2, Section II, *supra*. For example, if the employee/inventor was hired to do the research that lead to the inven-

forth in sections 117 (legal representatives of a deceased or incapacitated inventor may apply in his place) and 118 (persons with a sufficient proprietary interest in the patent may apply in the place of an inventor who refuses to execute an application or cannot be found or reached after diligent effort).

When an invention is made by two or more persons jointly, they must apply for a patent jointly. 35 U.S.C. § 116. When will persons qualify as joint inventors? First, each person claiming to be a joint inventor must have contributed to the final concept of the invention. Mueller Brass Co. v. Reading Industries, 352 F.Supp. 1357, 176 U.S.P.Q. 361 (E.D.Pa.1972). In addition, the purported joint inventors must have collaborated with one another. Kimberly–Clark Corp. v. Procter & Gamble Distributing Co., Inc., 973 F.2d 911, 23 U.S.P.Q.2d 1921 (C.A.F.C. 1992), is illustrative.

In 1979 and 1982, Buell, a Procter & Gamble employee, made a disposable diaper with inner flaps to control leakage. In 1982, Enloe, a Kimberly–Clark employee, conceived of a disposable diaper with inner flaps. Enloe's work lead to the issuance of a patent to Kimberly–Clark. In 1985, Lawson, a Proctor & Gamble employee, conceived of a disposable diaper which used inner flaps. Lawson worked alone on the invention, unaware of Buell's earlier work. (At the time, Buell was likewise unaware of Lawson.) Procter & Gamble, as Lawson's assignee, filed a patent application naming Lawson as the sole inventor and later obtained a patent.

The issue of priority arose in subsequent litigation between Procter & Gamble and Kimberly–Clark. Procter & Gamble asserted that the Lawson patent had priority over the Kimberly–Clark patent, on the grounds that Buell and Lawson were joint inventors, and that Buell's work marked the actual date of conception for the Procter & Gamble diaper. Pursuant to 35 U.S.C. § 256, Procter & Gamble asked the court to order that the omission of Buell as an inventor in the Lawson patent be corrected. The district court found that Buell and Lawson were not joint inventors, and the Court of Appeals for the Federal Circuit affirmed.

The Federal Circuit found that Congress, in amending section 116 in 1984, intended to codify the principles set forth in Monsanto Co. v. Kamp, 269 F.Supp. 818, 824, 154 U.S.P.Q. 259, 262 (D.D.C.1967). The *Monsanto* opinion had stated:

> A joint invention is the product of *collaboration* of the inventive endeavors of two or more persons *working toward the same end* and

tion, the common law may imply an assignment of ownership by the employee to the employer. Even if the common law would designate the employee as the owner of the invention, the employee may have signed an express agreement assigning to the employer in advance the rights in any inventions he makes while employed. When the employee has assigned ownership of the invention to the employer, the patent application nonetheless must be made in the name of the employee/inventor, even though the employer handles the application and the patent is issued to the employer as the assignee of the inventor of record. 35 U.S.C. § 152.

> producing an invention by their *aggregate* efforts. To constitute a joint invention, it is necessary that each of the inventors work on the same subject matter and make some contribution to the inventive thought and to the final result. Each needs to perform but a part of the task if an invention emerges from all of the steps taken together. It is not necessary that the entire inventive concept should occur to each of the joint inventors, or that the two should physically work on the project together. One may take a step at one time, the other an approach at different times. One may do more of the experimental work while the other makes suggestions from time to time. The fact that each of the inventors plays a different role and that the contribution of one may not be as great as that of another does not detract from the fact that the invention is joint if each makes some original contribution, though partial, to the final solution of the problem.

Monsanto, 269 F.Supp. at 824, 154 U.S.P.Q. at 262.

In finding that the Procter & Gamble employees, Buell and Lawson, were not joint inventors, the Federal Circuit explained:

> What is clear is that the statutory word "jointly" is not mere surplusage. For persons to be joint inventors under Section 116, there must be some element of joint behavior, such as collaboration or working under common direction, one inventor seeing a relevant report and building upon it or hearing another's suggestion at a meeting. Here there was nothing of that nature. Individuals cannot be joint inventors if they are completely ignorant of what each other has done until years after their individual independent efforts. They cannot be totally independent of each other and be joint inventors.

973 F.2d at 916–17, 23 U.S.P.Q.2d at 1926. For further discussions of the legal definition of joint invention, see Fasse, *The Muddy Metaphysics of Joint Inventorship: Cleaning Up After the 1984 Amendments to 35 U.S.C. § 116*, 5 HARV. J. L. & TECH. 153 (1992).

Especially in large research and development departments, where a number of persons may be involved in the inventive process, it may be difficult to determine exactly who qualifies as a joint inventor and include all such persons in the patent application. While failure to name the inventor or inventors correctly may result in invalidation of the patent, 35 U.S.C.A. § 102(f), errors can be corrected if they were made without deceptive intent. Section 116 provides for correcting errors in pending applications. Section 256 provides for corrections in issued patents.

8. *International Considerations*

Comparative Considerations

Many similarities exist among the patent laws of the various nations. For example, almost every country requires that inventions be novel, non-obvious and useful in order to qualify for a patent, though the requirement may differ in nomenclature, scope and detail from its counterpart in United States law. Perhaps the most important *difference* between the U.S. and other nations' patent laws is the United States' emphasis on granting a patent to the first person to invent, rather than the first inventor to file an application. See Section I C 2, *supra*. Another important difference is that most other nations lack a "grace period" comparable to Patent Act section 102(b): in many countries, virtually any introduction of the invention to the public via commercial activity or publication, either domestically or abroad, prior to the filing date will disqualify the invention. This poses a trap for unwary United States inventors—while taking advantage of the U.S. grace period, they may disqualify themselves for patents in much of the rest of the world.

Some countries decline to consider "secret prior art" such as that involved in the *Hazeltine* case, for purposes of the novelty and/or obviousness determinations. See Section I C 4, *supra*. In addition, many countries do not require an applicant to disclose the "best mode" of carrying out her invention, as the U.S. does in Patent Act section 112. In these countries, the applicant need only adequately disclose one mode of carrying out the invention. A U.S. applicant may thus find it expedient to draft a different specification for its U.S. and foreign applications. From another perspective, the United States' best mode requirement may pose a pitfall to unwary foreign applicants.

Countries have also offered different terms of patent protection. Another important difference concerns the scope of patentable subject matter. While the United States offers patent protection for a very wide range of inventions, many developing nations, in particular, deny patents for inventions such as agricultural chemicals, drugs, or other matter in which a monopoly (and the ability to charge monopoly prices) is deemed contrary to the national interest. This has lead to considerable dissatisfaction on the part of U.S. drug and chemical industries, who must compete with duplications of their own innovative inventions abroad.

Multinational Filings

Needless to say, this patent law diversity is not conducive to obtaining international patent protection for a new invention. A company wishing to launch a global marketing campaign for an invention must apply for a patent in each country in which it plans to do business. Understanding and satisfying the substantive and procedural variations in each nation's patent laws can be difficult and expensive. A number of attempts have been made to ease this process.

1. *The Paris Convention.* The Paris Convention for the Protection of Industrial Property, July 14, 1967, 21 U.S.T. 1629, 982 U.N.T.S. 369, was a first step. A multinational treaty with over 100 members (including the U.S.), the Paris Convention is founded on national treatment: it obligates each member to provide as great patent protection to the nationals of other member nations as it provides to its own nationals.

While this gets the foreign applicant's foot in the door, it does not guarantee a high level of substantive patent protection: the Paris Convention prohibits discrimination, but imposes relatively few standards regarding the scope or extent of substantive protection that member nations must provide. Nor does the Paris Convention attempt to standardize member nations' patent application procedure.

Even though it does relatively little to harmonize national patent laws, the Paris Convention makes multinational filings easier through its foreign filing priority provision. Article 4 of the Paris Convention provides, in essence, that a person who files an application for patent in any member country can claim his filing date in that country in subsequent filings in other member countries during the next twelve months. So, for example, if X Company files a patent application in member country #1 on January 1, 1995, all of the patent applications that it files in other member countries during the next twelve months will have an effective filing date in those countries of January 1, 1995.

The usefulness of this provision is made clear in article 4(B):

> [A]ny subsequent filing in any of the other countries of the Union before the expiration of the [twelve-month] period * * * shall not be invalidated by reason of any acts accomplished in the interval, in particular, another filing, the publication or exploitation of the invention * * *.

Recall that most foreign countries grant patents to the first inventor to file, rather than to the first person to invent, and lack the one-year "grace period" afforded to inventors under section 102(b) of the U.S. Patent Act. Assume that X files in country #1 on January 1, 1995. Y makes the same invention and files for a patent in country #2 in August, 1995. Z publishes a paper disclosing the invention in October, 1995. X then files for a patent in country #2 in December, 1995. In the absence of Paris Convention article 4, both Y and Z's actions are likely to disqualify X from obtaining a patent in country #2, because they occurred prior to his filing date. However, because of article 4, country #2 will treat X's application as though it were filed on January 1, his filing date in country #1. X will be saved from the consequences of the intervening actions of Y and Z.

Article 4 thus gives an inventor some "breathing space." As long as it files an application in one member country (which may be its own country), the inventor can take up to twelve months to test the marketability of the invention, and make the necessary preparations for foreign filings, without fear of losing its patent opportunities abroad in the interim. The substance of article 4 is implemented in section 119 of the United States Patent Act.[9]

9. The United States does not treat an article 4 foreign filing date as the U.S. filing date in all circumstances. Suppose, for example, that a printed publication discloses X's invention (or renders it obvious) in May, 1994. X files for a patent in member country #1 in July, 1994. X then files for a patent in the U.S. in June, 1995. Will his foreign priority date of June, 1994 protect him against the running of section 102(b)?

2. *The Patent Cooperation Treaty.* The Patent Cooperation Treaty ("PCT"), June 19, 1970, 28 U.S.T. 7645, 1037 U.N.T.S. 213, was an important second step in aiding the procurement of international patent protection. The PCT simplifies international patent filings by providing a centralized means of filing, searching and examining patent applications for a number of countries simultaneously. Administered by the International Bureau of the World Intellectual Property Organization ("WIPO"),[10] the PCT now has over 70 members, including the U.S. and most other developed nations.

The PCT entitles nationals or residents of member nations to file "international applications" for patents. They may do this by simply filing a standardized international application with their home patent office, which designates all the other PCT member nations in which the applicant wishes to file. The applicant generally files in its own language and pays a fee in its own nation's currency. The receiving office checks to see that the application is in proper form and, if it is, assigns an international filing date, which will be either the date of a qualifying earlier filing under the Paris Convention or the date of the international filing itself. The effect of this is the same as if a patent application had been filed with the national patent office of each designated member nation on that date. The application is then forwarded (if necessary) to an international searching authority, which conducts an international search of the relevant prior art. The United States' PTO is one of the international searching authorities. The search authority examines published patent documents and technical literature, and produces an international search report.

This search report gives the applicant a good sense of how likely it is to obtain a patent. The applicant then has the opportunity to amend its claims in order to avoid the prior art that has been found, or withdraw its application altogether, if it finds proceeding impractical in light of the search results. If the application is not withdrawn, it is published 18

Consider the explicit wording of section 119 of the Patent Act:

> [N]o patent shall be granted on any application for patent for an invention which had been patented or described in a printed publication in any country more than one year before the date of the *actual filing of the application in this country*, or which had been in public use or on sale in this country more than one year prior to such filing.

(emphasis added). Moreover, in *In re* Hilmer, 359 F.2d 859, 149 U.S.P.Q. 480 (C.C.P.A.1966), the Court of Customs and Patent Appeals held that, for purposes of section 102(e), the filing date of a U.S. patent is the actual date in which the application was filed in the U.S., rather than the foreign priority date. Thus, once a U.S. patent is granted, it only "relates back" to become part of the prior art against third parties as of its U.S. filing date. What are the implications of this holding?

For further reading on these and related subjects, see Chisum, *Foreign Activity: Its Effect on Patentability Under United States Law*, 11 IIC 26 (1980); Murashige, *The* Hilmer *Doctrine, Self–Collision, Novelty and the Definition of Prior Art*, 26 J. MARSHALL L. REV. 549 (1993).

10. The World Intellectual Property Organization is a specialized agency of the United Nations, whose objective is to promote the protection of intellectual property throughout the world. It administers the Paris Convention and the PCT, as well as a number of other intellectual property treaties.

months after the international filing date. By the end of the twentieth month, the application must be sent to the patent office of each of the designated nations in which a patent is sought. This begins the "national stage" of the process.

At this point, the applicant must send national fees to each national office and supply a translation of the application whenever required. It may need to hire local counsel to prosecute the patent in each national patent office. Each nation proceeds to apply its own law to determine whether a patent will be granted.

If the applicant chooses, directly after the international search and before the application is sent to the national patent offices, it can request an international preliminary examination. The purpose of this examination is to produce a nonbinding opinion about the novelty, inventiveness and industrial applicability of the invention.[11] While the preliminary examination is not binding on the national offices, it is generally highly regarded and thus is persuasive. When the preliminary examination is requested, this adds an additional ten months before the application must be sent to the designated national patent offices, initiating the "national stage."

Even though the PCT procedure does not avoid the cost and difficulty of prosecuting the application before each of the individual national patent offices, it nonetheless has proved popular, and is widely perceived as offering important advantages to patent applicants. One of the most important perceived advantages is the period of time that it provides between the initial application and the point at which national fees and translations are due and appearances must be made before the individual national offices. This permits applicants to reserve their patent priority while testing the commercial viability of their inventions. If the commercial prospects are not promising, they may discontinue prosecution prior to the national stage, avoiding the considerable cost and effort that the national stage entails.

Another advantage, of course, is that the applications can all be prepared in the same format. Applications meeting the form and content requirements of the PCT must be accepted in all member nations, though the nations may impose different requirements for direct applications. There may also be a savings of attorney time, as amendments to the claims can be made during the centralized international phase, avoiding duplicative actions in the various national offices.

The PCT is implemented in sections 351–76 of the United States' Patent Act. For more information about the Patent Cooperation Treaty and its advantages, see WORLD INTELLECTUAL PROPERTY ORGANIZATION, PCT APPLICANT'S GUIDE (1991); *Streamlined Procedures Under the Patent Cooperation Treaty (PCT)*, 73 J. PAT. & TRADEMARK OFF. SOC. 799 (1991); Cartiglia, *The Patent Cooperation Treaty:*

11. Novelty, inventiveness and industrial applicability are the international criteria for patentability. They are conceptually similar to the U.S. requirements of novelty, nonobviousness and usefulness.

A Rational Approach to International Patent Filing, 73 J. PAT. & TRADEMARK OFF. SOC. 261 (1994).[12]

3. Other Efforts. As international marketing of goods and services has become increasingly common, many nations have sought additional ways to "harmonize" the patent laws of the world. A series of meetings were held in the late 1980's and early 1990's under the auspices of the World Intellectual Property Organization, to attempt to draft a harmonization treaty that would be acceptable to a wide range of participants. See Moy, *The History of the Patent Harmonization Treaty: Economic Self-Interest as an Influence*, 26 J. MARSHALL L. REV. 457 (1993); Fiorito, *The "Basic Proposal" for Harmonization of U.S. and Worldwide Patent Laws Submitted by WIPO*, 73 J. PAT. & TRADEMARK OFF. SOC. 83 (1991). On another front, efforts were made to introduce harmonizing provisions into the GATT Uruguay Round negotiations. These latter efforts met with some success, primarily harmonizing the patent term and the substantive rights and remedies adherents must afford to patentees.

The GATT Uruguay Round Agreement on Trade Related Aspects of Intellectual Property Rights, Including Trade in Counterfeited Goods ("TRIPs"), provides that the term of patent protection must not end "before the expiration of a period of twenty years counted from the filing date." *Id.*, Article 33. In accepting the Uruguay Round, the United States was required to implement this term, in place of a patent term of 17 years following the grant of the patent, which it traditionally had provided. Uruguay Round Agreements Act, Pub. L. No. 103–465 § 532, 108 Stat. 4809, 4983–88 (1994).[13]

TRIPs Article 28 mandates that member countries provide patentees the right to prevent third parties from "making, using, offering for sale, selling or importing" their patented products. Process patents must convey the right to prevent third parties from using the process and from using, offering for sale, selling, or importing products obtained directly by the process. This provision also necessitated amendments to the United States Patent Act. Uruguay Round Agreements Act, *supra,* §§ 532, 533.[14]

12. Another international patent agreement to which the U.S. adheres, the Strasbourg Agreement Concerning the International Patent Classification, March 24, 1971, 26 U.S.T. 1793, T.I.A.S. 8140, eases the international prior art search by imposing an international classification system for patented subject matter.

13. Uruguay Round Agreements Act section 532 specifies that United States patent protection begins on the date the patent is issued and ends 20 years from the date on which the application for patent was filed *in the United States*. The term is not to be measured by reference to an earlier Paris Convention foreign filing priority date. Should the foreign filing of a PCT application that designates the United States trigger the 20-year term? See 35 U.S.C.A. § 363.

14. For further discussion of the rights afforded U.S. patentees, see Section I E 1, *infra.*

The TRIPs agreement also places important limitations on members' ability to impose compulsory licenses and patent forfeiture. With regard to patentable subject matter, Article 27 provides that "patents shall be available for any inventions, whether products or processes, in all fields of technology, provided that they are new, involve an inventive step and are capable of industrial application." This broad state-

TRIPs Article 27 provides that "patent rights shall be available and patent rights enjoyable without discrimination as to the place of invention." This provision required amendment of section 104 of the United States Patent Act—a very important change. To better envision the issue, suppose that A invents and files an application for patent in Paris Convention member country #1 on January 1, 1994. B makes the same invention in the U.S. in July, 1994 and files for a patent in September, 1994. A then files for a U.S. patent in November, 1994. A has priority because he is treated as having filed in the U.S. on January 1 (prior to B's invention and filing) pursuant to Patent Act section 119.

Suppose, in contrast, the following facts: A conceives and reduces to practice in member country #1 in January, 1994. B conceives and reduces to practice the same invention in the U.S. in March, 1994. A files for a patent in member country #1 in June, 1994. B files for a patent in the U.S. in July. A then files for a patent in the U.S. in August, 1994. Who has priority? A has the earlier filing date (June) by virtue of Patent Act section 119. However, B can "swear back" to show that his actual date of invention was March, prior to A's filing date. Can A then swear back to show an invention date in member country #1 that precedes B's? Prior to amendments of Patent Act section 104 necessitated by U.S. adherence to the North American Free Trade Agreement ("NAFTA") and TRIPs, A could only rely on her effective date of application, or the date on which she "introduced" the invention into the United States, as her date of invention. See 3 D.S. CHISUM, PATENTS: A TREATISE ON THE LAW OF PATENTABILITY, VALIDITY, AND INFRINGEMENT § 10.03[3][c] (1991). Section 104 provided that "[i]n proceedings in the Patent and Trademark Office and in the courts, an applicant for a patent, or a patentee, may not establish a date of invention by reference to knowledge or use thereof, or other activity with respect thereto, in a foreign country, except as provided [in section 119]." This discrimination against foreign inventors had long rankled the United States' trading partners.

Review the amended version of section 104. When the United States joined the NAFTA, it was required to amend section 104 to except evidence of earlier invention in other NAFTA member countries. Pub. L. No. 103–182, § 331, 107 Stat. 2057, 2113–14 (1994). Adherence to the Uruguay Round required amendment to add another, larger exception, permitting evidence of earlier invention in any other World Trade Organization member country. Uruguay Round Agreements Act, Pub. L. No. 103–465 § 531, 108 Stat. 4809, 4982–83 (1994).[15]

ment is diluted by the further provision that members may exclude (1) inventions whose commercial exploitation threatens "*ordre public* or morality, including to protect human, animal or plant life or health or to avoid serious prejudice to the environment;" (2) "diagnostic, therapeutic and surgical methods for the treatment of humans or animals;" and (3) "plants and animals other than microorganisms, and essentially biological processes for the production of plants or animals other than nonbiological and microbiological processes." *Id.*

15. The Uruguay Round amendment of section 104 is effective for patent applications filed on or after January 1, 1996. Applicants and patentees may not establish a date of invention that is earlier than

What, if any, effect is the amendment of section 104 likely to have on the United States' continued adherence to a first-to-invent system?

D. THE PATENT APPLICATION PROCESS

Patent applications are "one of the most difficult legal instruments to draw with accuracy." Sperry v. Florida, 373 U.S. 379, 383, 83 S.Ct. 1322, 1325, 10 L.Ed.2d 428, 431 (1963). The drafter must understand the technology underlying the invention, be able to describe the invention accurately, in a manner that satisfies the requirements of Patent Act section 112, and draft the patent claims in a manner that obtains for her client the broadest possible scope of patent protection. The patent attorney must also master the procedural rules that govern representation of clients before the PTO. The process of filing a patent application and pursuing it to its conclusion is called "patent prosecution."

Examples of patent claims were provided in some of the prior case opinions. Copies of patents are available for examination in libraries throughout the country that have been designated as PTO Depository Libraries. WESTLAW and other computerized legal research data bases provide the full text of more recent patents. Techniques of patent drafting are beyond the scope of a survey course in Intellectual Property. There are, however, several useful authorities that address this subject. See, e.g., S.A. BECKER, PATENT APPLICATIONS HANDBOOK (1993); R.C. FARBER, LANDIS ON MECHANICS OF PATENT CLAIM DRAFTING (3d ed. 1990).

Following is a general overview of patent prosecution and related procedures, which has been excerpted from a PTO publication. For more detailed information, see the Patent Act, the applicable regulations, 37 C.F.R. § 1.1, *et. seq.*, and volumes 2, 3 and 4 of D.S. CHISUM, PATENTS: A TREATISE ON THE LAW OF PATENTABILITY, VALIDITY AND INFRINGEMENT (1991).

GENERAL INFORMATION CONCERNING PATENTS

U.S. Department of Commerce.
Patent and Trademark Office.
Revised May 1992.

* * *

Application for Patent

An application for a patent is made to the Commissioner of Patents and Trademarks and includes:

(1) A written document which comprises a specification (description and claims), and an oath or declaration;

(2) A drawing in those cases in which a drawing is necessary; and;

January 1, 1996 by reference to knowledge, use or other activity in another World Trade Organization member country. Uruguay Round Agreements Act, Pub. L. No. 103–465 § 531, 108 Stat. 4809, 4982–83 (1994).

(3) The filing fee. * * *

All applications are numbered in serial order, and the applicant is informed of the serial number and filing date of the application by a filing receipt. The filing date of the application is the date on which the names of the inventors, a specification (including claims) and any required drawings are received in the patent and Trademark Office; or the date on which the last part completing the application is received in the case of a previously incomplete or defective application.

* * *

Models are not required in most patent applications since the description of the invention in the specification and the drawings must be sufficiently full and complete and capable of being understood to disclose the invention without the aid of a model. A model will not be admitted unless specifically requested by the examiner.

A working model, or other physical exhibit, may be required by the Office if deemed necessary. This is not done very often. A working model may be requested in the case of applications for patent for alleged perpetual motion devices.

When the invention relates to a composition of matter, the applicant may be required to furnish specimens of the composition, or of its ingredients or intermediates, for inspection or experiment. If the invention is a microbiological invention, a deposit of the micro-organism involved is required.

Examination of Applications and Proceedings in the Patent and Trademark Office

Applications filed in the Patent and Trademark Office and accepted as complete applications are assigned for examination to the respective examining groups having charge of the areas of technology related to the invention. In the examining group, applications are taken up for examination by the examiner to whom they have been assigned in the order in which they have been filed in accordance with examining procedures established by the Commissioner.

[Applications may be advanced out of turn in limited circumstances.]

The examination of the application consists of a study of the application for compliance with the legal requirements and a search through United States patents, prior foreign patent documents which are available in the Patent and Trademark Office, and available literature, to see if the claimed invention is new and unobvious. A decision is reached by the examiner in the light of the study and the result of the search.

Office Action

The applicant is notified in writing of the examiner's decision by an "action" which is normally mailed to the attorney or agent. The reasons for any adverse action or any objection or requirement are stated in the action and such information or references are given as may be useful in aiding the applicant to judge the propriety of continuing the prosecution of his application.

* * * It is not uncommon for some or all of the claims to be rejected on the first action by the examiner; relatively few applications are allowed as filed.

Applicant's Response

The applicant must request reconsideration in writing, and must distinctly and specifically point out the supposed errors in the examiner's action. The applicant must respond to every ground of objection and rejection in the prior Office action. * * *

In amending an application in response to a rejection, the applicant must clearly point out why he/she thinks the amended claims are patentable in view of the state of the art disclosed by the prior references cited or the objections made. He/she must also show how the claims as amended avoid such references or objections.

After response by applicant the application will be reconsidered, and the applicant will be notified if claims are rejected, or objections or requirements made, in the same manner as after the first examination. The second Office action usually will be made final.

Final Rejection

On the second or later consideration, the rejection or other action may be made final. The applicant's response is then limited to appeal in the case of rejection of any claim and further amendment is restricted. * * * Response to a final rejection or action must include cancellation of, or appeal from the rejection of, each claim so rejected and, if any claim stands allowed, compliance with any requirement or objection as to form.

* * *

As a result of the examination by the Office, patents are granted in the case of about two out of every three applications for patents which are filed.

* * *

Appeal to the Board of Patent Appeals and Interferences and to the Courts

If the examiner persists in the rejection of any of the claims in an application, or if the rejection has been made final, the applicant may appeal to the Board of Patent Appeals and Interferences in the Patent and Trademark Office. The Board of Patent Appeals and Interferences consists of the Commissioner of Patents and Trademarks, the Deputy Commissioner, the Assistant Commissioners, and the examiners-in-chief, but normally each appeal is heard by only three members. An appeal fee is required and the applicant must file a brief to support his/her position. An oral hearing will be held if requested upon payment of the specified fee.

As an alternative to appeal, in situations where an applicant desires consideration of different claims or further evidence, a new continuation application is often filed. The new application requires a filing fee and should submit the claims and evidence for which consideration is desired. If it is filed before expiration of the period for appeal and specific reference is made therein to the earlier application, applicant will be entitled to the earlier filing date for subject matter common to both applications.

If the decision of the Board of Patent Appeals and Interferences is still adverse to the applicant, an appeal may be taken to the Court of Appeals for the Federal Circuit or a civil action may be filed against the Commissioner in the United States District Court for the District of Columbia. The Court of Appeals for the Federal Circuit will review the record made in the Office and may affirm or reverse the Office's action. In a civil action, the applicant may present testimony in the court, and the court will make a decision.

Interferences

Occasionally two or more applications are filed by different inventors claiming substantially the same patentable invention. The patent can only be granted to one of them, and a proceeding known as an "interference" is instituted by the Office to determine who is the first inventor and entitled to the patent. About 1 percent of the applications filed become involved in an interference proceeding. Interference proceedings may also be instituted between an application and a patent already issued, provided the patent has not been issued for more than one year prior to the filing of the conflicting application, and provided that the conflicting application is not barred from being patentable for some other reason.

Each party to such a proceeding must submit evidence of facts proving when the invention was made. * * * The priority question is determined by a board of three Examiners-in-Chief on the evidence submitted. From the decision of the Board of Patent Appeals and Interferences, the losing party may appeal to the Court of Appeals for the Federal Circuit or file a civil action against the winning party in the appropriate United States district court.

* * *

Allowance and Issue of Patent

If, on examination of the application, or at a later stage during the reconsideration of the application, the patent application is found to be allowable, a notice of allowance will be sent to the applicant, or to applicant's attorney or agent, and a fee for issuing the patent is due within three months from the date of the notice.

* * *

When the issue fee is paid, the patent issues as soon as possible after the date of payment, dependent upon the volume of printing on hand. The patent grant then is delivered or mailed on the day of its grant, or as soon thereafter as possible, to the inventor's attorney or agent if there is one of record, otherwise directly to the inventor. On the date of the grant, the patent file becomes open to the public. Printed copies of the specification and drawing are available on the same date.

* * *

The term of a patent is 17 years. A maintenance fee is due 3½, 7½, and 11½ years after the original grant for all patents issuing from the applications filed on and after December 12, 1980. The maintenance fee must be paid at the stipulated times to maintain the patent in force. * * *

Correction of Patents

Once the patent is granted, it is outside the jurisdiction of the Patent and Trademark Office except in a few respects.

The Office may issue * * * a certificate correcting a clerical error it has made in the patent when the printed patent does not correspond to the record in the Office. These are mostly corrections of typographical errors made in printing.

* * *

The patentee may disclaim one or more claims of this patent by filing in the Office a disclaimer as provided by the statute.

When the patent is defective in certain respects, the law provides that the patentee may apply for a reissue patent. This is a patent granted to replace the original and is granted only for the balance of the unexpired term. However, the nature of the changes that can be made by means of the reissue are rather limited; new matter cannot be added.

Any person may file a request for reexamination of a patent, along with the required fee, on the basis of prior art consisting of patents or printed publications. At the conclusion of the reexamination proceedings, a certificate setting forth the results of the reexamination proceeding is issued.

Assignments and Licenses

A patent is personal property and may be sold to others or mortgaged; it may be bequeathed by a will, and it may pass to the heirs of [a] deceased patentee. The patent law provides for the transfer or sale of a patent, or of an application for patent, by an instrument in writing. Such an instrument is referred to as an assignment and may transfer the entire interest in the patent. * * *

The statute also provides for the assignment of a part interest, that is, a half interest, a fourth interest, etc., in a patent. There may also be a grant which conveys the same character of interest as an assignment but only for a particularly specified part of the United States.

* * *

The Office records assignments, grants and similar instruments sent to it for recording, and the recording serves as notice. If an assignment, grant or conveyance of a patent or an interest in a patent (or an application for patent) is not recorded in the Office within three months from its date, it is void against a subsequent purchaser for a valuable consideration without notice, unless it is recorded prior to the subsequent purchase. * * *

Notes and Questions

1. *The Patent Bar.* Any lawyer who is qualified to practice in the federal courts may represent clients in patent litigation. However, the PTO regulates who may represent clients in patent prosecutions. Both lawyers and non-lawyers are eligible. To qualify, among other things, one must have a college degree in engineering or physical science or its equivalent and must pass a written examination on the substance and procedure of patent law. Persons registered to practice before the PTO who are not lawyers are known as patent agents. Those who are lawyers are called patent attorneys. The specific requirements for PTO registration as a patent attorney are set forth at 37 C.F.R. §§ 10.5–10.8.

2. *Reexamination.* There is little opportunity for interested third parties who oppose the granting of a patent to influence the PTO's initial granting or non-granting decision. Generally they must wait and challenge the validity of the patent once it is issued. This may be done as a defense against a patent infringement claim or in a declaratory judgment action, if standing requirements are satisfied. For those wishing to avoid the burden of such litigation, a third approach is possible pursuant to the reexamination provisions set forth in sections 302–307 of the Patent Act.

Section 302 provides that any person at any time may request that the validity of an issued patent claim be reexamined in light of newly discovered prior art patents or printed publications. If the Commissioner of Patents determines that the request raises a substantial question of patentability that was not considered in the course of the patent application, he must issue an order for reexamination to resolve the question.

At this point the patent owner may file a statement addressing the relevance of the newly discovered prior art. She may propose amendments or new claims to distinguish the invention as claimed from the prior art (though she may not thus enlarge the scope of a disputed claim). The person requesting the reexamination may reply. Upon termination of the reexamination and any appeals, the Commissioner will issue and publish a certificate canceling any claims determined to be unpatentable, confirming any claims determined to be patentable, and incorporating in the patent any proposed amended or new claims that have been determined to be patentable.

How useful an alternative does this procedure provide to third parties wishing to challenge an issued patent? It has been suggested that the *ex parte* nature of the reexamination procedure, which limits the third party's opportunity to argue his position, discourages use of reexamination requests as an alternative to court challenges. See, e.g., ADVISORY COMMISSION ON PATENT LAW REFORM, A REPORT TO THE SECRETARY OF COMMERCE, 117–123 (1992); Lowin, *Comment: Reexamination "Catch 22"*, 14 AIPLA Q. J. 218 (1986).

The Commissioner may initiate a reexamination at his own initiative. Note also that the patentee may herself request a reexamination. Why might a patentee wish to do so? For a thorough discussion of the patent reexamination procedure, see Pickett, *The Patent Reexamination Procedure—A Complete Guide through the Statutes, the Rules and the Caselaw*, 75 J. PAT. & TRADEMARK OFF. SOC. 297 (1993).

Corrections to an issued patent may also be made through the patent reissue procedure, which is set forth at sections 251–252 of the Patent Act. We will examine these provisions more closely in connection with the *Graver Tank* case, *infra*.

3. *The Patent Term.* Review the language of Patent Act section 154, as recently amended by the Uruguay Round Agreements Act, Pub. L. No. 103–465, § 532, 108 Stat. 4809, 4983–88 (1994). The United States had for many years granted a term of 17 years for utility patents, commencing at the time the patent issued. After the amendments, the new basic term commences on the date on which the patent issues and ends 20 years from the patentee's earliest United States filing date. United States' acceptance of the Uruguay Round TRIPs provisions necessitated the change. In his testimony in support of the Uruguay Round Agreements Act, Bruce Lehman, the Commissioner of Patents and Trademarks, explained and further justified the new measure:

> [One] complaint I have received involves the so-called "submarine patent." A submarine patent is one where the applicant makes use of procedural devices, such as continuation applications and appeals, to extend the processing time of the patent application. In one case, a patent issued 36 years after the first application was filed. Under current law, the term of protection does not start until the application is issued as a patent. Thus, the applicant waits until the market is mature before his patent term starts, instead of having the term start reasonably close to the time the invention is conceived and reduced to practice. As the Patent and Trademark Office (PTO) does not disclose information about pending patent applications, competitors are often surprised when these patents surface many years after the competitors have invested in technology that they assumed was in the public domain. This practice discourages innovation and investment, rather than encouraging them.
>
> By counting the term from the filing date of the original application, as proposed in this bill, and not the issue date of the patent based on the last continuing application, we will provide the incentive for the prompt processing * * * and it will no longer be possible to use the patent system to create submarine patents.
>
> Some users of the patent system are concerned that delays caused by the Office and delays that are inherent in some of the complex

procedures that are necessary might, in effect, reduce the actual time between a patent's issuance and its expiration. By September 30, 1994, the Office-wide average time to dispose of a patent application will be approximately 19.6 months. The pendency period for biotechnology applications will be 20.5 months after the application is filed and for computer-related applications, 26.5 months. Thus, most applicants will receive a longer period of patent protection under a 20–year from filing approach than under the current system—even in the technologies with the longest current pendency. Furthermore, measuring the term from the filing date will encourage applicants to prosecute their applications more swiftly than they do now; thus, they can have it within their power to effectively increase the term of protection beyond that predicted using existing data.

To ensure equitable treatment, [the bill provides] for restoration of the term in instances where issuance of the patent was delayed due to national security concerns, to interference proceedings, and to successful appeals of PTO decisions. We believe that this scheme reasonably compensates for delays not within the control of the applicant, but does not permit applicants to use the patent system to delay the issuance of the patent unnecessarily.

* * *

The Paris Convention for the Protection of Industrial Property requires that the terms of protection of patents for the same invention granted by different countries should generally be independent of one another. This precludes the United States from measuring the term of protection from the filing date of a foreign filed application, even though the benefit of that foreign filing date is subsequently claimed in an application to the same invention filed in the United States. To give U.S. inventors a similar opportunity of having an initial application filing which does not serve as the basis from which the term of protection is measured, the implementing bills provide for a provisional application filing in the United States.

Section 111 of the patent law is amended to provide for a provisional application which must be followed within 12 months by an application for the same invention. The provisional application will not require claims and will have a filing fee of only $150, which may be paid after the filing of the application. The provisional application will become abandoned after 12 months. The later filed application is able to claim the benefit of the filing date of the provisional application. The term of protection for the patent that results from the application runs from the filing date of the application, even though the application has the benefit of the filing date of the provisional application. The benefit of the filing date of the provisional application may also be claimed when filing applications for the same invention abroad.

General Agreement on Tariffs and Trade (GATT) Intellectual Property Provisions: Joint Hearing before the Subcomm. on Intellectual Property and Judicial Administration of the House Comm. on the Judiciary, and the Subcomm. on Patents, Copyrights and Trademarks of the Senate Comm. on the Judiciary, 103d Cong., 2d Sess. 114–16, 128–29, (1994) (statement of

Bruce A. Lehman, Commissioner of Patents and Trademarks). See also 35 U.S.C.A. §§ 111, 119(e).

The new term is effective for patents granted on applications filed after June 8, 1995. Under a transition provision, patents in existence on June 8, 1995 or granted on applications filed prior to that date will endure for the longer of 17 years from issuance or 20 years from application date. See 35 U.S.C.A. § 154(c).

E. THE PATENTEE'S RIGHTS

1. The Right to Exclude Others From Directly Infringing the Patent

DEEPSOUTH PACKING CO., INC. v. LAITRAM CORP.

Supreme Court of the United States, 1972.
406 U.S. 518, 92 S.Ct. 1700, 32 L.Ed.2d 273, 173 U.S.P.Q. 769.

MR. JUSTICE WHITE delivered the opinion of the Court.

* * * Petitioner and respondent both hold patents on machines that devein shrimp more cheaply and efficiently than competing machinery or hand labor can do the job. Extensive litigation below has established that respondent, the Laitram Corp., has the superior claim and that the distribution and use of petitioner Deepsouth's machinery in this country should be enjoined to prevent infringement of Laitram's patents. We granted certiorari to consider a related question: Is Deepsouth, barred from the American market by Laitram's patents, also foreclosed by the patent laws from exporting its deveiners, in less than fully assembled form, for use abroad?

I

A rudimentary understanding of the patents in dispute is a prerequisite to comprehending the legal issue presented. The District Court determined that the Laitram Corp. held two valid patents for machinery used in the process of deveining shrimp. One, granted in 1954, accorded Laitram rights over a "slitter" which exposed the veins of shrimp by using water pressure and gravity to force the shrimp down an inclined through studded with razor blades. As the shrimp descend through the trough their backs are slit by the blades or other knife-like objects arranged in a zig-zag pattern. The second patent, granted in 1958, covers a "tumbler," "a device to mechanically remove substantially all veins from shrimp whose backs have previously been slit," by the machines described in the 1954 patent. This invention uses streams of water to carry slit shrimp into and then out of a revolving drum fabricated from commercial sheet metal. As shrimp pass through the drum the hooked "lips" of the punched metal, "projecting at an acute angle from the supporting member and having a smooth rounded free edge for engaging beneath the vein of a shrimp and for wedging the vein between the lip and the supporting member," engage the veins and remove them.

Both the slitter and the tumbler are combination patents; that is,

> [n]one of the parts referred to are new, and none are claimed as new; nor is any portion of the combination less than the whole claimed as new, or stated to produce any given result. The end in view is proposed to be accomplished by the union of all, arranged and combined together in the manner described. And this combination, composed of all the parts mentioned in the specification, and arranged with reference to each other, and to other parts of the (machine) in the manner therein described, is stated to be the improvement and is the thing patented. *Prouty v. Ruggles*, 16 Pet. 336, 341, 10 L.Ed. 985 (1842).

The slitter's elements as recited in Laitram's patent claim were: an inclined trough, a "knife" (actually, knives) positioned in the trough, and a means (water sprayed from jets) to move the shrimp down the trough. The tumbler's elements include a "lip," a "support member," and a "means" (water thrust from jets). As is usual in combination patents, none of the elements in either of these patents were themselves patentable at the time of the patent, nor are they now. The means in both inventions, moving water, was and is, of course, commonplace. (It is not suggested that Deepsouth infringed Laitram's patents by its use of water jets.) The cutting instruments and inclined troughs used in slitters were and are commodities available for general use. The structure of the lip and support member in the tumbler were hardly novel: Laitram concedes that the inventors merely adapted punched metal sheets ordered from a commercial catalog in order to perfect their invention. The patents were warranted not by the novelty of their elements but by the novelty of the combination they represented. Invention was recognized because Laitram's assignors combined ordinary elements in an extraordinary way—a novel union of old means was designed to achieve new ends. * * *

II

The lower court's decision that Laitram held valid combination patents entitled the corporation to the privileges bestowed by 35 U.S.C. § 154, the keystone provision of the patent code. "[F]or the term of seventeen years" from the date of the patent, Laitram had "the right to exclude others from making, using, or selling the invention throughout the United States...." The § 154 right in turn provides the basis for affording the patentee an injunction against direct, induced, and contributory infringement, 35 U.S.C. § 283, or an award of damages when such infringement has already occurred, 35 U.S.C. § 284. Infringement is defined by 35 U.S.C. § 271 in terms that follow those of § 154:

> "(a) Except as otherwise provided in this title, whoever without authority makes, uses or sells any patented invention, within the United States during the term of the patent therefor, [directly] infringes the patent.
>
> "(b) Whoever actively induces infringement of a patent shall be liable as an infringer.

"(c) Whoever sells a component of a patented machine, manufacture, combination or composition, or a material or apparatus for use in practicing a patented process, constituting a material part of the invention, knowing the same to be especially made or especially adapted for use in an infringement of such patent, and not a staple article or commodity of commerce suitable for substantial noninfringing use, shall be liable as a contributory infringer."

As a result of these provisions the judgment of Laitram's patent superiority forecloses Deepsouth and its customers from any future use (other than a use approved by Laitram or occurring after the Laitram patent has expired) of its deveiners "throughout the United States." The patent provisions taken in conjunction with the judgment below also entitle Laitram to the injunction it has received prohibiting Deepsouth from continuing to "make" or, once made, to "sell" deveiners "throughout the United States." Further, Laitram may recover damages for any past unauthorized use, sale, or making "throughout the United States." This much is not disputed.

But Deepsouth argues that it is not liable for every type of past sale and that a portion of its future business is salvageable. Section 154 and related provisions obviously are intended to grant a patentee a monopoly only over the United States market; they are not intended to grant a patentee the bonus of a favored position as a flagship company free of American competition in international commerce. Deepsouth, itself barred from using its deveining machines, or from inducing others to use them "throughout the United States," barred also from making and selling the machines in the United States, seeks to make the parts of deveining machines, to sell them to foreign buyers, and to have the buyers assemble the parts and use the machines abroad.[5] Accordingly, Deepsouth seeks judicial approval, expressed through a modification or interpretation of the injunction against it, for continuing its practice of shipping deveining equipment to foreign customers in three separate boxes, each containing only parts of the 1¾–ton machines, yet the whole assemblable in less than one hour. The company contends that by this means both the "making" and the "use" of the machines occur abroad and Laitram's lawful monopoly over the making and use of the machines throughout the United States is not infringed.

Laitram counters that this course of conduct is based upon a hypertechnical reading of the patent code that, if tolerated, will deprive it of its right to the fruits of the inventive genius of its assignors. * * * Deepsouth in all respects save final assembly of the parts "makes" the invention. It does so with the intent of having the foreign user effect

5. Deepsouth is entirely straightforward in indicating that its course of conduct is motivated by a desire to avoid patent infringement. Its president wrote a Brazilian customer: "We are handicapped by a decision against us in the United States. This was a very technical decision and we can manufacture the entire machine without any complication in the United States, with the exception that there are two parts that must not be assembled in the United States, but assembled after the machine arrives in Brazil."

the combination without Laitram's permission. Deepsouth sells these components as though they were the machines themselves; the act of assembly is regarded, indeed advertised, as of no importance.

* * * The District Court held that its injunction should not be read as prohibiting export of the elements of a combination patent even when those elements could and predictably would be combined to form the whole.

> "It may be urged that ... [this] result is not logical ... But it is founded on twin notions that underlie the patent laws. One is that a combination patent protects only the combination. The other is that monopolies—even those conferred by patents—are not viewed with favor. These are logic enough."

The Court of Appeals for the Fifth Circuit reversed, thus departing from the established rules of the Second, Third, and Seventh Circuits. In the Fifth Circuit panel's opinion, those courts that previously considered the question "worked themselves into ... a conceptual box" by adopting "an artificial, technical construction" of the patent laws, a construction, moreover, which in the opinion of the panel, "[subverted] the Constitutional scheme of promoting 'the Progress of Science and useful Arts' by allowing an intrusion on a patentee's rights."

III

We disagree with the Court of Appeals for the Fifth Circuit. Under the common law the inventor had no right to exclude others from making and using his invention. If Laitram has a right to suppress Deepsouth's export trade it must be derived from its patent grant, and thus from the patent statute. We find that 35 U.S.C. § 271, the provision of the patent laws on which Laitram relies, does not support its claim.

Certainly if Deepsouth's conduct were intended to lead to use of patented deveiners inside the United States its production and sales activity would be subject to injunction as an induced or contributory infringement. But it is established that there can be no contributory infringement without the fact or intention of a direct infringement. "In a word, if there is no [direct] infringement of a patent there can be no contributory infringer." *Mercoid Corp. v. Mid–Continent Co.*, 320 U.S. 661, 677, 64 S.Ct. 268, 276, 88 L.Ed. 376 (1944) (Frankfurter, J., dissenting on other grounds). * * *

The statute makes it clear that it is not an infringement to make or use a patented product outside of the United States. 35 U.S.C. § 271. Thus, in order to secure the injunction it seeks, Laitram must show a § 271(a) direct infringement by Deepsouth in the United States, that is, that Deepsouth "makes," "uses," or "sells" the patented product within the bounds of this country.

Laitram does not suggest that Deepsouth "uses" the machines. Its argument that Deepsouth sells the machines—based primarily on Deepsouth's sales rhetoric and related indicia such as price[9]—cannot carry the day unless it can be shown that Deepsouth is selling the "patented invention." The sales question thus resolves itself into the question of manufacture: did Deepsouth "make" (and then sell) something cognizable under the patent law as the patented invention, or did it "make" (and then sell) something that fell short of infringement?

The Court of Appeals, believing that the word "makes" should be accorded "a construction in keeping with the ordinary meaning of that term," held against Deepsouth on the theory that "makes" "means what it ordinarily connotes—the substantial manufacture of the constituent parts of the machine." Passing the question of whether this definition more closely corresponds to the ordinary meaning of the term than that offered by Judge Swan in *Andrea* 35 years earlier (something is made when it reaches the state of final "operable" assembly), we find the Fifth Circuit's definition unacceptable because it collides head on with a line of decisions so firmly embedded in our patent law as to be unassailable absent a congressional recasting of the statute.

We cannot endorse the view that the "substantial manufacture of the constituent parts of [a] machine" constitutes direct infringement when we have so often held that a combination patent protects only against the operable assembly of the whole and not the manufacture of its parts. "For as we pointed out in *Mercoid v. Mid-Continent Investment Co.*, 320 U.S. 661, 676, 64 S.Ct. 268, 276, a patent on a combination is a patent on the assembled or functioning whole, not on the separate parts." *Mercoid Corp. v. Minneapolis-Honeywell Regulator Co.*, 320 U.S. 680, 684, 64 S.Ct. 278, 280 (1944). See also *Leeds & Catlin Co. v. Victor Talking Machine Co.*, 213 U.S. 301, 29 S.Ct. 495, 53 L.Ed. 805:

> "A combination is a union of elements, which may be partly old and partly new, or wholly old or wholly new. But whether new or old, the combination is a means—an invention—distinct from them." *Id.*, at 318, 29 S.Ct., at 500.

* * * In sum,

> "[i]f anything is settled in the patent law, it is that the combination patent covers only the totality of the elements in the claim and that no element, separately viewed, is within the grant." *Aro Mfg. Co. v. Convertible Top Replacement Co.*, 365 U.S. 336, 344, 81 S.Ct. 599, 604, 5 L.Ed.2d 592 (1961).

It was this basic tenet of the patent system that led Judge Swan to hold in the leading case, *Radio Corp. of America v. Andrea*, 79 F.2d 626 (CA2 1935), that unassembled export of the elements of an invention did not infringe the patent.

"[The] relationship is the essence of the patent.

9. Deepsouth sold the less than completely assembled machine for the same price as it had sold fully assembled machines. Its advertisements, correspondence, and invoices frequently referred to a "machine," rather than to a kit or unassembled parts.

> "... No wrong is done the patentee until the combination is formed. His monopoly does not cover the manufacture or sale of separate elements capable of being, but never actually, associated to form the invention. Only when such association is made is there a direct infringement of his monopoly, and not even then if it is done outside the territory for which the monopoly was granted." *Id.*, at 628.
>
> * * *

We reaffirm this conclusion today.

IV

It is said that this conclusion is derived from too narrow and technical an interpretation of the statute, and that this Court should focus on the constitutional mandate

> "[t]o promote the Progress of Science and useful Arts, by securing for limited Times to Authors and Inventors the exclusive Right to their respective Writings and Discoveries ...," Art. I, § 8,

and construe the statute in a manner that would, allegedly, better reflect the policy of the Framers.

We cannot accept this argument. The direction of Art. I is that *Congress* shall have the power to promote the progress of science and the useful arts. When, as here, the Constitution is permissive, the sign of how far Congress has chosen to go can come only from Congress. We are here construing the provisions of a statute passed in 1952. The prevailing law in this and other courts as to what is necessary to show a patentable invention when a combination of old elements is claimed was clearly evident from the cases when the Act was passed; and at that time *Andrea*, representing a specific application of the law of infringement with respect to the export of elements of a combination patent, was 17 years old. When Congress drafted § 271, it gave no indication that it desired to change either the law of combination patents as relevant here or the ruling of *Andrea*. Nor has it on any more recent occasion indicated that it wanted the patent privilege to run farther than it was understood to run for 35 years prior to the action of the Court of Appeals for the Fifth Circuit.

Moreover, we must consider petitioner's claim in light of this Nation's historical antipathy to monopoly and of repeated congressional efforts to preserve and foster competition. As this Court recently said without dissent:

> "[I]n rewarding useful invention, the 'rights and welfare of the community must be fairly dealt with and effectually guarded.' *Kendall v. Winsor*, 21 How. 322, 329, 16 L.Ed. 165 (1859). To that end the prerequisites to obtaining a patent are strictly observed, and when the patent has issued the limitations on its exercise are equally strictly enforced." *Sears, Roebuck & Co. v. Stiffel Co.*, 376 U.S. 225, 230, 84 S.Ct. 784, 788, 11 L.Ed.2d 661 (1964).

It follows that we should not expand patent rights by overruling or modifying our prior cases construing the patent statutes, unless the argument for expansion of privilege is based on more than mere inference from ambiguous statutory language. We would require a clear and certain signal from Congress before approving the position of a litigant who, as respondent here, argues that the beachhead of privilege is wider, and the area of public use narrower, than courts had previously thought. No such signal legitimizes respondent's position in this litigation.

In conclusion, we note that what is at stake here is the right of American companies to compete with an American patent holder in foreign markets. Our patent system makes no claim to extraterritorial effect; "these acts of Congress do not, and were not intended to, operate beyond the limits of the United States," *Brown v. Duchesne*, 19 How., at 195, 15 L.Ed. 595 (1856), and we correspondingly reject the claims of others to such control over our markets. To the degree that the inventor needs protection in markets other than those of this country, the wording of 35 U.S.C. §§ 154 and 271 reveals a congressional intent to have him seek it abroad through patents secured in countries where his goods are being used. Respondent holds foreign patents; it does not adequately explain why it does not avail itself of them.

V

In sum: the case and statutory law resolves this case against the respondent. When so many courts have so often held what appears so evident—a combination patent can be infringed only by combination—we are not prepared to break the mold and begin anew. And were the matter not so resolved, we would still insist on a clear congressional indication of intent to extend the patent privilege before we could recognize the monopoly here claimed. Such an indication is lacking. * * *

MR. JUSTICE BLACKMUN, with whom the CHIEF JUSTICE, MR. JUSTICE POWELL, AND MR. JUSTICE REHNQUIST join, dissenting.

* * *

* * * I do not see how one can escape the conclusion that the Deepsouth machine was *made* in the United States, within the meaning of the protective language of §§ 154 and 271(a). The situation, perhaps, would be different were parts, or even only one vital part, manufactured abroad. Here everything was accomplished in this country except putting the pieces together as directed (an operation that, as Deepsouth represented to its Brazilian prospect, would take "less than one hour"), all much as the fond father does with his little daughter's doll house on Christmas Eve. To say that such assembly, accomplished abroad, is not the prohibited combination and that it avoids the restrictions of our patent law, is a bit too much for me. The Court has opened the way to deny the holder of the United States combination patent the benefits of his invention with respect to sales to foreign purchasers.

* * *

By a process of only the most rigid construction, the Court, by its decision today, fulfills what Judge Clark, in his able opinion for the Fifth Circuit, distressingly forecast:

> "To hold otherwise [as the Court does today] would subvert the Constitutional scheme of promoting 'the Progress of Science and useful Arts, by securing for limited Times to Authors and Inventors the exclusive Right to their respective Writings and Discoveries.' U.S. Const., art. I § 8 Cl. 8. It would allow an infringer to set up shop next door to a patent-protected inventor whose product enjoys a substantial foreign market and deprive him of this valuable business. If this Constitutional protection is to be fully effectuated, it must extend to an infringer who manufactures in the United States and then captures the foreign markets from the patentee. The Constitutional mandate cannot be limited to just manufacturing and selling within the United States. The infringer would then be allowed to reap the fruits of the American economy—technology, labor, materials, etc.—but would not be subject to the responsibilities of the American patent laws. We cannot permit an infringer to enjoy these benefits and then be allowed to strip away a portion of the patentee's protection."

I share the Fifth Circuit's concern and I therefore dissent.

PAPER CONVERTING MACHINE CO. v. MAGNA-GRAPHICS CORP.

United States Court of Appeals, Federal Circuit, 1984.
745 F.2d 11, 223 U.S.P.Q. 591.

NICHOLS, SENIOR CIRCUIT JUDGE.

[This appeal is from a judgment of the United States District Court awarding plaintiff Paper Converting damages for patent infringement.]

I

Although the technology involved here is complex, the end product is one familiar to most Americans. The patented invention relates to a machine used to manufacture rolls of densely wound ("hard-wound") industrial toilet tissue and paper toweling. The machine, commonly known as an automatic rewinder, unwinds a paper web continuously under high tension at speeds up to 2,000 feet per minute from a large-diameter paper roll—known as the parent roll or bedroll—and simultaneously rewinds it onto paperboard cores to form individual consumer products.

Before the advent of automatic rewinders, toilet tissue and paper towel producers used "stop-start" rewinders. With these machines, the entire rewinding operation had to cease after a retail-sized "log" was finished so that a worker could place a new mandrel (the shaft for carrying the paperboard core) in the path of the paper web. In an effort to increase production, automatic rewinders were introduced in the early 1950's. These machines automatically moved a new mandrel into the path of the paper web while the machine was still winding the paper web onto another mandrel, and could operate at a steady pace at speeds up to about 1,200 feet per minute.

In 1962, Nystrand, Bradley, and Spencer invented the first successful "sequential" automatic rewinder, a machine which not only overcame previous speed limitations, but also could handle two-ply tissue. This rewinder simultaneously cut the paper web and impaled it on pins against the parent roll. Then, after a new mandrel was automatically moved into place, a "pusher" would move the paper web away from the parent roll and against a glue-covered paperboard core to begin winding a new paper log.

On April 20, 1965, United States Patent No. 3,179,348 (the '348 patent) issued, giving to Paper Converting (to whom rights in the invention had been assigned) patent protection for machines incorporating the sequential rewinding approach. On September 1, 1972, Paper Converting applied to have the claims of the '348 patent narrowed by reissue, and on March 4, 1975, United States Patent No. Re. 28,353 (the '353 patent) issued on this application. The '353 patent, like the original '348 patent on which it is based, received an expiration date of April 20, 1982. Claim 1 of the '353 patent defines the improvement in the web-winding apparatus as an improvement comprising:

> (C) means for transversely severing said web to provide a free leading edge on said web for approaching a mandrel on which said web is to be wound in said path, and
>
> (D) pin means extensibly mounted on said roll for maintaining a web portion spaced from said edge in contact with said roll, and pusher means extensibly mounted on said roll to urge said maintained web portion against an adjacent mandrel.

Paper Converting achieved widespread commercial success with its patented automatic rewinder. Although there are not many domestic producers of toilet tissue and paper toweling, Paper Converting has sold more than 500 machines embodying the invention.

In 1979, Paper Converting brought the present action against Magna–Graphics for infringement of the '353 patent. After a trial concerning only issues of liability, the district court held the '353 patent valid and found it willfully infringed. * * *

[The district court found that Magna–Graphics had made two sales of infringing rewinders and associated equipment: one to the Fort Howard Paper Company (Fort Howard) under circumstances to be described, and one to the Scott Paper Company (Scott).]

III

A.

Magna–Graphics * * * argues that it should bear no liability whatsoever for its manufacture, sale, or delivery of the Fort Howard rewinder because that machine was never *completed* during the life of the '353 patent. We disagree.

In early 1980 Fort Howard became interested in purchasing a new high-speed rewinder line. Both Paper Converting and Magna–Graphics offered bids. Because Magna–Graphics offered to provide an entire rewinder line for about 10 percent less than did Paper Converting, it won the contract. Delivery would have been before the '353 patent expired. Magna–Graphics began to build the contracted for machinery, but before it completed the rewinder, on February 26, 1981, the federal district court in Wisconsin determined that a similar Magna–Graphics' rewinder built for and sold to Scott infringed the '353 patent. The court enjoined Magna–Graphics from any future infringing activity.

Because at the time of the federal injunction the rewinder intended for Fort Howard was only 80 percent complete, Magna–Graphics sought a legal way to fulfill its contract with Fort Howard rather than abandon its machine. First, Magna–Graphics tried to change the construction of the rewinder so as to avoid infringement. It submitted to Paper Converting's counsel three drawings illustrating three proposed changes, and asked for an opinion as to whether the changes would avoid infringement. Paper Converting's counsel replied, however, that until a fully built and operating machine could be viewed, no opinion could be given. Magna–Graphics, believing such a course of action unfeasible because of the large risks in designing, engineering, and building a machine without knowing whether it would be considered an infringement, instead negotiated with Fort Howard to delay the final assembly and delivery of an otherwise infringing rewinder until after the '353 patent expired in April 1982.

Magna–Graphics thereafter continued to construct the Fort Howard machine, all the while staying in close consultation with its counsel. After finishing substantially all of the machine, Magna–Graphics tested it to ensure that its moving parts would function as intended at a rate of 1,600 feet of paper per minute. Although Magna–Graphics normally *fully* tested machines at its plant before shipment, to avoid infringement in this instance, Magna–Graphics ran its tests in two stages over a period of several weeks in July and August of 1981.

To understand Magna–Graphics' testing procedure, it is necessary to understand the automatic transfer operation of the patented machine. First, from within a 72–inch long "cutoff" roll, a 72–inch blade ejects to sever the continuous web of paper which is wound around the bedroll. Then, pins attached to the bedroll hold the severed edge of the web while pushers, also attached to the bedroll, transfer the edge of the web towards the mandrel (the roll on which the paperboard core is mounted).

In the first stage of its test, Magna–Graphics checked the bedroll to determine whether the pushers actuated properly. It installed on the bedroll two pusher pads instead of the thirty pads normally used in an operating machine. It greased the pads and operated the bedroll to determine whether the pads, when unlatched, would contact the core on the mandrel. (Magna-Graphics greased the pads so as to provide a visual indication that they had touched the core.) During this stage of tests, no cutoff blades or pins were installed.

In the second stage of the test, Magna–Graphics checked the cutoff roll to determine whether the cutting blade actuated as intended. It tested the knife actuating mechanism by installing into the cutoff roll a short 4–inch section of cutter blade rather than the 72–inch blade normally used. After taping a 4–inch wide piece of paper to the outer surface of the cutoff roll, Magna–Graphics operated the cutoff roll to determine whether the latch mechanism would eject the blade to cut the paper. During *this* phase of the testing, no pins or pusher pads were installed. At no time during the tests were the pins, pushers, and blade installed and operated together.

To further its scheme to avoid patent infringement, Magna–Graphics negotiated special shipment and assembly details with Fort Howard. Under the advice of counsel, Fort Howard and Magna–Graphics agreed that the rewinder's cutoff and transfer mechanism would not be finally assembled until April 22, 1982, two days after the expiration of the '353 patent. With this agreement in hand, Magna–Graphics shipped the basic rewinder machine to Fort Howard on September 17, 1981, and separately shipped the cutoff roll and bedroll on October 23, 1981. The rewinder machine was not assembled or installed at the Fort Howard plant until April 26, 1982.

B

With this case we are once again confronted with a situation which tests the temporal limits of the American patent grant. *See Roche Products, Inc. v. Bolar Pharmaceutical Co.*, 733 F.2d 858, 221 USPQ 937 (Fed.Cir.1984). We must decide here the extent to which a competitor of a patentee can *manufacture* and test during the life of a patent a machine intended solely for post-patent use. Magna–Graphics asserts that no law prohibits it from soliciting orders for, *substantially* manufacturing, testing, or even delivering machinery which, if *completely* assembled during the patent term, would infringe. We notice, but Magna–Graphics adds that it is totally irrelevant, that Paper Converting has lost, during the term of its patent, a contract for the patented machine which it would have received but for the competitor's acts.

Clearly, any federal right which Paper Converting has to suppress Magna–Graphics' patent-term activities, or to receive damages for those activities, must be derived from its patent grant, and thus from the patent statutes. "Care should be taken not to extend by judicial construction the rights and privileges which it was the purpose of Congress to bestow." *Bauer v. O'Donnell*, 229 U.S. 1, 10, 33 S.Ct. 616, 617, 57 L.Ed. 1041 (1913). * * *

The disjunctive language of the patent grant gives a patentee the "right to exclude others from making, using or selling" a patented invention during the 17 years of the patent's existence. 35 U.S.C. § 154. *See also* 35 U.S.C. § 271. Congress has never deemed it necessary to define any of this triad of excludable activities, however, leaving instead the meaning of "make," "use," and "sell" for judicial interpretation. Nevertheless, by the terms of the patent grant, *no* activity other than the unauthorized making, using, or selling of the claimed invention can constitute direct infringement of a patent, *no matter* how great the adverse impact of that activity on the economic value of a patent. * * *

Here, the dispositive issue is whether Magna–Graphics engaged in the making, use, or sale of something which the law recognizes as embodying an invention protected by a patent. Magna–Graphics relies on *Deepsouth Packing Co. v. Laitram Corp.*, 406 U.S. 518, 92 S.Ct. 1700, 32 L.Ed.2d 273, 173 USPQ 769 (1972). That case dealt with a "combination patent" covering machinery for shrimp deveining. The only active issue was whether certain export sales were properly prohibited in the district court's injunction and whether damages should include compensation for past infringement by these exports. The infringer had put in effect a practice of selling the machines disassembled for export, but with the subassemblies so far advanced, and with such instructions, that the foreign consignee could put them together on receipt in operable condition with an hour's work. The Supreme Court's five to four holding that these exports did not infringe was interwoven of three strands of thought: (1) that the patent laws must be construed strictly because they create a "monopoly" in the patentee; (2) that a "combination patent" is not infringed until its elements are brought together into an "operable assembly;" and (3) that an attempt to enforce the patent against a machine assembled abroad was an attempt to give it extraterritorial application and to invade improperly the sovereignty of the country where the final assembly and the intended use occurred.

Magna–Graphics' effort to apply *Deepsouth* as precedential runs into the obvious difficulty that the element of extraterritoriality is absent here, yet it obviously was of paramount importance to the *Deepsouth* Court. We must be cautious in extending five to four decisions by analogy. The analysis of *where* infringement occurs is applicable, Magna–Graphics says, to determining *when* an infringement occurs, whether before or after a patent expires. We have not found any case that has so held, and are not cited to any. It does not at all necessarily follow, for the *Deepsouth* analysis is made to avert a result, extraterritoriality, that would not occur whatever analysis was made in the instant case.

Although in *Deepsouth* the Court at times used broad language in reaching its decision, it is clear that *Deepsouth* was intended to be narrowly construed as applicable only to the issue of the extraterritorial effect of the American patent law. The Court so implied not only in *Deepsouth* ("[A]t stake here is the right of American companies to compete with an American patent holder *in foreign markets. Our patent system makes no claim to extraterritorial effect,* * * *" 406 U.S. at 531, 92 S.Ct. at 1708, 173 USPQ at 774 (emphasis added)), but in a subsequent decision as well ("The question under consideration [in *Deepsouth*] was whether a patent is infringed when unpatented elements are assembled into the combination *outside the United States.*" *Dawson*

Chemical Co. v. Rohm & Haas Co., 448 U.S. 176, 216, 100 S.Ct. 2601, 2623, 65 L.Ed.2d 696, 206 USPQ 385, 405 (1980) (emphasis added)). * * *

While there is thus a horror of giving extraterritorial effect to United States patent protection, there is no corresponding horror of a valid United States patent giving economic benefits not cut off entirely on patent expiration. Thus, we hold that the expansive language used in *Deepsouth* is not controlling in the present case. The facts in *Deepsouth* are *not* the facts here. Because no other precedent controls our decision here, however, we nevertheless look to *Deepsouth* and elsewhere for guidance on the issue of whether what Magna-Graphics did is an infringement of the '353 patent.

* * *

* * * It does seem as if the concept of an "operable assembly" put forward by Justice White in his majority opinion is probably something short of a full and complete assembly; thus, if the infringer makes an "operable assembly" of the components of the patented invention, sufficient for testing, it need not be the same thing as the complete and entire invention. The other thing is, if the infringer has tested his embodiment of the invention sufficiently to satisfy him, this may be a "use," because as held in *Roche Products, Inc.*, "use" includes use for the purpose of testing. * * *

* * *

It is undisputed that Magna–Graphics intended to finesse Paper Converting out of the sale of a machine on which Paper Converting held a valid patent during the life of that patent. Given the amount of testing performed here, coupled with the sale and delivery during the patent-term of a "completed" machine (completed by being ready for assembly and with no useful noninfringing purpose), we are not persuaded that the district court committed clear error in finding that the Magna–Graphics' machine infringed the '353 patent.

To reach a contrary result would emasculate the congressional intent to prevent the making of a patented item during the patent's full term of 17 years. If without fear of liability a competitor can assemble a patented item past the point of testing, the last year of the patent becomes worthless whenever it deals with a long lead-time article. Nothing would prohibit the unscrupulous competitor from aggressively marketing its own product and constructing it to all but the final screws and bolts, as Magna–Graphics did here. We rejected any reduction to the patent-term in *Roche*; we cannot allow the inconsistency in the patent law which would exist if we permitted it here. Magna–Graphics built and tested a patented machine, albeit in a less than preferred fashion. Because an "operable assembly" of components was tested, this case is distinguishable from *Interdent Corp. v. United States*, 531 F.2d 547, 552 (Ct.Cl.1976) (omission of a claimed element from the patented combination avoids infringement). Where, as here, significant, unpatented assemblies of elements are tested during the patent term, enabling the infringer to deliver the patented combination in parts to the buyer, without testing the entire combination together as was the infringer's usual practice, testing the assemblies can be held to be in essence testing the patented combination and, hence, infringement.

That the machine was not operated in its optimum mode is inconsequential: imperfect practice of an invention does not avoid infringement. We affirm the district court's finding that "[d]uring the testing of the Fort Howard machine in July and August 1981, Magna–Graphics completed an operable assembly of the infringing rewinder."

* * *

NIES, CIRCUIT JUDGE, dissenting-in-part.

I dissent from the majority's holding that Magna–Graphics' activities in connection with the Fort Howard machine constitute direct infringement of any claim of Paper Converting's patent. The majority's conclusion necessitates giving a meaning to "patented invention" contrary to the definition set forth by the Supreme Court in *Deepsouth Packing Co. v. Laitram Corp.*

* * *

The majority holds that *incomplete assembly* of the patented invention is making, *testing of subassemblies* is using, and a *sale of an unassembled* machine is selling the *patented invention* within the meaning of the above section. The majority reasons that a contrary result would emasculate the congressional intent to prevent the making of a patented item during the patent's full term of 17 years. It could be said with equal validity that, given the lead time necessary to make the invention here, the majority effectively extends the patentee's right of exclusivity beyond the statutory 17 years.

I do not see in *Deepsouth* that the Supreme Court's only concern was the extraterritorial operation of our patent laws. The activities of Deepsouth under attack were all performed in the United States and were found not to result in direct or contributory infringement of the patent. That the activities of final assembly occurred abroad merely precluded a holding that Deepsouth's activities constituted contributory infringement. Contributory infringement cannot arise without a direct infringement. The situation in *Deepsouth* is exactly comparable to the one at hand. That the activities of final assembly occurred after the patent expired precludes holding Magna–Graphics to be a contributory infringer, there being no direct infringement by another to which the charge can be appended.

Thus, we are back to the dispositive direct infringement issue in *Deepsouth*, which is the same as the issue here. What is the meaning of "patented invention" in 35 U.S.C. § 271(a)? The alleged infringer, in each case, made and sold something, but was it the "patented invention"?

* * *

Nothing in Justice White's opinion in *Deepsouth* indicates that the concept of an operable assembly is "probably something short of a full and complete assembly," as the majority states. The Court had before it the Fifth Circuit opinion which had analyzed just such less-than-full-assembly situations. Repeatedly, the Court emphasized that the "patented invention" means that *all* of its claimed elements must be united.

Thus, if the *claimed* invention comprises the elements A, B, C and D, it is only the *combination* in its entirety that is protected. The making of the lesser combination A, B and D falls short of direct infringement, even though the missing element C is also supplied by the alleged infringer.

* * *

It is not surprising that Magna–Graphics' counsel read *Deepsouth* as permitting the course of conduct condemned here. The majority opinion is no less than a reversal of *Deepsouth*. Regardless of the reasonableness of the alternative interpretation of § 271(a) given by the majority, we are bound by the Supreme Court's decision. No greater prerogative to modify it accrues to us from a 5–4 vote than from a unanimous decision. Change must be left to Congress, or the Court itself. In *Deepsouth* the extension of patent protection which had been urged was viewed as a matter for a legislative directive * * *.

* * * We cannot assume that the present Court would find reason to depart from Deepsouth in the face of congressional inaction over the twelve years since the decision was handed down.[3]

Indeed, the *Deepsouth* decision is not without redeeming virtue. This is one of the few areas of patent law where a bright line can be, and has been, drawn. That consideration in itself has merit. A competitor should be able to look to the patent claims and know whether his activity infringes or not. Here, the majority provides no guidance to industry or the district courts. One cannot tell from the opinion whether testing and sales activity must also accompany substantial assembly, as it appears to hold, or whether simply substantially making the device preparatory to selling after the patent expires would be sufficient. Given the disjunctive language of the statute, no basis appears for "summing up" partial making with the testing of partial assemblies and with sales made by the alleged infringer. Those activities do not, in some nebulous way, supply the missing physical elements of the "patented invention."

* * *

3. Legislative efforts to overrule *Deepsouth* have been extensive. However, the thrust of proposed legislation has not been directed to changing the meaning of "patented invention." For example, pending H.R. 4526, 98th Congress, 1st Session, provides in relevant part:

> (f) Whoever without authority supplies or causes to be supplied in the United States the material components of a patented invention, where such components are uncombined in whole or in part, intending that such components will be combined outside of the United States, and knowing that if such components were combined within the United States the combination would be an infringement of the patent, shall be liable as an infringer.

Notes and Questions

1. *The right to exclude.* Section 154 of the Patent Act, as amended, states the rights afforded by patent in the negative: The patentee has the right to "*exclude others* from making, using, offering for sale or selling the invention throughout the United States or importing the invention into the United States." If the invention is a process, the patentee has the right to "*exclude others* from using, offering for sale or selling throughout the United States, or importing into the United States, products made by that process." (Emphasis added.) Note that a patent does not convey any affirmative rights to the patentee to make, use, sell, offer to sell or import the invention herself. Why not? Under what sorts of circumstances might a patentee be precluded from exploiting her own patented invention?

Likewise, the grant of a patent does not compel the patentee to make, use, sell or import the invention, or license others to do so. Some nations subject patentees who fail to "work" their patents (exploit their inventions) domestically to compulsory licenses, which are issued to third parties wishing to exploit the invention, or provide that the "non-working" patentee forfeits the patent. The United States does not. Should it?

2. *Direct Infringement (§ 271(a)).* Patent Act section 271(a), as amended, provides that "whoever without authority makes, uses, offers to sell, or sells any patented invention within the United States, or imports into the United States any patented invention during the term of the patent therefor, infringes the patent." Note that any one of the enumerated acts will be sufficient to support liability. So, for example, a person who uses the invention without authority will be liable, even though she neither made nor sold it. See, e.g., Roche Products, Inc. v. Bolar Pharmaceutical Co., 733 F.2d 858, 221 U.S.P.Q. 937 (C.A.F.C.1984), *cert. denied* 469 U.S. 856, 105 S.Ct. 183, 83 L.Ed.2d 117, 225 U.S.P.Q. 792 (1984). Indeed, since no intent or knowledge is required for direct infringement liability, the unknowing purchaser of an unauthorized patented product who subsequently uses the product may be liable. Likewise, a "middle person" who merely purchases and resells an infringing product will be liable, even though he never used it, and may not have known that it infringed.

How does the Court in *Deepsouth* define "making?" How does it define "selling?" How does the Court's definition of "sale" compare with the Federal Circuit's definition of "sale" for purposes of section 102(b) in the *U.M.C.* case, *supra*? Should the existence of a "sale" be determined through use of the same criteria in both contexts? What constitutes "use?" Would a sales demonstration? How about a simple testing of an infringing article, to ensure that it works? Would display of an infringing article suffice?

Do you agree with the majority in *Magna-Graphics* that the Supreme Court intended its *Deepsouth* definitions of "making" and "selling" to be "narrowly construed as applicable only to the issue of the extraterritorial effect of the American patent law?" If you are not so sure, can you find a way to distinguish the two cases on their facts, so that the *Magna-Graphics* result is still justified? Under the *Magna-Graphics* decision, what exactly does it take to "make" a patented apparatus?

The Uruguay Round Agreements Act endowed United States patentees with two additional rights that they did not have when *Deepsouth* and

Magna-Graphics were decided: the right to exclude others from offering to sell and the right to exclude others from importing the patented invention. Uruguay Round Agreements Act, Pub. L. No. 103–465, §§ 532, 533, 108 Stat. 4809, 4983–90 (1994). These rights are effective January 1, 1996. As a practical matter, how much do they add? If the *Deepsouth* patentee's rights had included the right to exclude offers to sell, would the Supreme Court have reached a different result? How might a right to exclude offers to sell have figured into the Federal Circuit's legal analysis in *Magna-Graphics*? See the definition of "offer to sell" in 35 U.S.C.A. § 271(i).

3. *The geographic and temporal scope of a patent.* As *Deepsouth* points out, a U.S. patent is only effective to prevent infringing acts *in* the United States, *during* the prescribed patent term. In *Magna-Graphics*, the majority expressed concern that a ruling in favor of the defendant would effectively deprive the patentee of the benefit of the last year of its patent term. What lead the majority to that conclusion? In her dissent, Judge Nies argues that the majority may effectively have extended the patentee's right of exclusivity beyond the statutory patent term. What leads her to that conclusion? Do you agree?

Assume that A owns a patent for a process, and B begins to market a machine that carries out the patented process. Construction of the machine begins upon completion of a sales contract, and usually takes five years to build. A's patent will expire in four years. Under *Magna-Graphics*, is there an infringement? See Joy Technologies Inc. v. Flakt Inc., 6 F.3d 770, 28 U.S.P.Q.2d 1378 (C.A.F.C. 1993).

As we have seen in prior cases, the law generally looks unfavorably on a patentee's attempts to extend her monopoly beyond the intended patent term. Licenses to exploit a patented invention that attempt to impose royalty obligations beyond the expiration of the patent are deemed unenforceable as a matter of public policy. Brulotte v. Thys Co., 379 U.S. 29, 85 S.Ct. 176, 13 L.Ed.2d 99 (1964).

Patent protection commences when the patent issues. There can be no infringement liability for acts occurring before that time. Because a patent gives no retroactive rights, the legend "patent pending," often found on articles of commerce, has no legal significance. It only notifies the public that the invention *may* later be the subject of monopoly rights, if the PTO acts positively on the application. State Industries, Inc. v. A.O. Smith Corp., 751 F.2d 1226, 1236, 224 U.S.P.Q. 418, 425 (C.A.F.C. 1985). The public is free to exploit the invention until the day the patent issues.

Some countries provide a limited measure of protection for inventions prior to the time that the patent issues. One model is to publish patent applications 18 months after they are filed, and give the applicant limited rights against persons who exploit the invention between the date of publication and the date the patent issues. There has been some support in the United States for adopting such a measure, as a means of harmonizing our laws with other nations'. See, e.g., THE ADVISORY COMMISSION ON PATENT LAW REFORM, A REPORT TO THE SECRETARY OF COMMERCE, 61–63 (1992); Blommer, *Washington Letter*, AIPLA BULL. 455–461 (April–May–June, 1992). Why should rights against pre-issuance infringement be limited? How should they be limited?

4. *Combination patents.* The Supreme Court, in *Deepsouth*, stresses that the plaintiff's patent is a "combination patent." Does the Court suggest how broad the category of "combination patents" is? As noted *supra*, the Court of Appeals for the Federal Circuit has expressed skepticism about any "combination patent" categorization and has tended to avoid it. Stratoflex, Inc. v. Aeroquip Corp., 713 F.2d 1530, 218 U.S.P.Q. 871 (C.A.F.C. 1983).

5. *Section 271(f).* The result in the *Deepsouth* case was unpopular with many U.S. industries, and lead to lobbying for Congress to eliminate the perceived loophole *Deepsouth* created in U.S. patent protection. After several attempts, in 1984, Congress amended the Patent Act to add the provisions set forth in section 271(f). Patent Law Act of 1984, Pub. L. No. 98–622, § 101, 98 Stat. 3383.

Subsection (f)(1) makes it an infringement to supply all or a substantial portion of the components of a patented invention from the U.S. in a manner that actively induces combination of the components outside the U.S., if the extraterritorial combination would infringe if it occurred domestically. Under subsection 271(f)(2), it is an infringement to supply even a single component of a patented invention from the U.S. if (1) the component is especially made or adapted for use in the patented invention and is not a staple article or commercial commodity that is suitable for substantial noninfringing uses, (2) the supplier knows that the component is so made or adapted, and (3) the supplier intends that the component be combined abroad in the patented invention in a manner that would infringe if it occurred in the U.S.

This clearly puts a stop to the practice at issue in *Deepsouth*, and addresses the dissents' concern that the *Deepsouth* decision allowed the infringer to reap the fruits of the American economy—its technology, labor, materials, etc.—but avoid responsibility for the American patent laws. Enactment of subsection (f) also suggests that there is not as great a "horror" of extraterritorial protection as the *Magna-Graphics* court supposed.

What, if any, impact does subsection (f) have on the precedential value of the *Deepsouth* opinion? On the reasoning in *Magna-Graphics*?

6. *Section 271(g).* Congress addressed another perceived loophole in the Process Patent Amendments Act of 1988, Omnibus Trade and Competitiveness Act of 1988, Pub.L. No. 100–418, §§ 9001–9007, 102 Stat. 1563. In this case, businesses were using U.S. patented processes abroad (where use would not infringe) to manufacture products which they then imported into the United States to sell in competition with the U.S. process patent holder. The products themselves were not patented, so that the U.S. process patentee had little redress.[16] This practice deprived the U.S. process patent holder of much of the economic benefit of its patent monopoly.

The Process Patent Amendments Act added subsection (g) to Patent Act section 271. Subsection (g), as later amended by the Uruguay Round Agreements Act, makes it an infringement to import into the U.S. or to sell,

16. The Tariff Act, section 337, provided the opportunity to petition the International Trade Commission to bar such products from entering the country, in some circumstances. 19 U.S.C.A. § 1337.

offer to sell or use within the U.S. a product made by a U.S. patented process. To avoid infringement claims regarding products that are only remotely derived from a patented process, subsection (g) provides that a "product which is made by a patented process will * * * not be considered to be so made after—(1) it is materially changed by subsequent processes; or (2) it becomes a trivial and nonessential component of another product." For a two-step approach to making this determination, see the Senate Report, S. REP. NO. 100–83, 100th Cong., 1st Sess. 50 (1987).

During the legislative process, some parties expressed concern about the potential difficulty of avoiding liability under the new section 271(g), due to the difficulty of discovering that products were made by patented processes. To address this concern and avoid inequitable results, the Process Patents Amendments Act channeled infringement claims toward persons practicing the patented process and those controlling them, and persons having prior knowledge of infringement. It limited remedies against unknowing, innocent infringers, permitting such persons to sell or use inventory that they accumulated prior to notice that the inventory infringes. See 35 U.S.C.A. § 287(b). The Act also provides that a remedy against noncommercial users or retail sellers of products made by infringing processes will only be available if no adequate remedy is available against importers or other users or sellers. *Id.*, § 271(g).

Patentees may face considerable difficulty proving that their process was used to create the accused product, especially when the manufacturer is not subject to discovery under the Federal Rules of Civil Procedure. In recognition of this difficulty, the Process Patents Amendments Act provided for a presumption. If the court finds that a "substantial likelihood exists that the product was made by the patented process" and that "the plaintiff has made a reasonable effort to determine the process actually used," the product will be presumed to have been made with the patented process. The burden will shift to the defendant to prove that it was not. 35 U.S.C.A. § 295.

Assume that a U.S. patent claims cells that have been genetically altered to produce a human hormone, but does not specifically claim a process of using the altered cell to produce the hormone, or the hormone itself.[17] A foreign company uses the claimed altered cells to produce the hormone abroad, and imports the hormone into the U.S. to sell in competition with the U.S. patentee. Will section 271(g) provide relief to the patentee? See Amgen Inc. v. U.S. International Trade Commission, 902 F.2d 1532, 14 U.S.P.Q.2d 1734 (Fed.Cir.1990).[18]

17. In *In re* Durden, 763 F.2d 1406, 226 U.S.P.Q. 359 (C.A.F.C. 1985), the Court of Appeals for the Federal Circuit held that a novel, nonobvious starting material (such as a genetically engineered cell) does not in itself render an otherwise obvious chemical process patentable. This ruling has lead to considerable dissatisfaction among persons in the biotechnology industry, who argue that the application of a known process to a novel invention constitutes innovation in biotechnology, and that such innovations should be protected by process patents. See *Bill Seeks Stronger Protection Against Foreign Infringement of Biotech Patents*, 39 PAT. TRADEMARK & COPYRIGHT J. 262 (BNA) (Jan. 8, 1990); *Senate Judiciary Committee Clears Three Intellectual Property Bills*, 45 PAT. TRADEMARK & COPYRIGHT J. 453 (BNA) (Ap. 1, 1993).

18. Congress has introduced and considered a number of bills to address the biotechnology industry's concerns about the *Durden* decision and the inability to prevent import of products made by unpatented processes using patented starting materials. For example, S. 298, introduced Feb-

For a thorough discussion of the products of patented process provisions, see J. DRATLER, INTELLECTUAL PROPERTY LAW: COMMERCIAL, CREATIVE, AND INDUSTRIAL PROPERTY, 3–1—3–42 (1991); Katsh, *New Trade Legislation Dramatically Enhances the Rights of Process Patent Owners*, 1 J. PROPRIETARY RTS. 3 (1988); Wojick, *The Perilous Process of Protecting Process Patents from Infringing Importations*, 14 LOY. L.A. INT'L & COMP. L.J. 207 (1992).

7. *Section 271(e).* Assume that X has a patent for a drug. Y, a generic drug manufacturer, wishes to enter the market with a generic version of the drug as soon as X's patent expires. A drug cannot be marketed without F.D.A. approval, and in order to obtain the necessary F.D.A. approval, Y must perform tests and submit data to demonstrate the drugs's safety and efficacy.

Y would like to perform the necessary tests during the final months of X's patent so that it can file for F.D.A. approval as soon as X's patent expires. Is Y free to use the patented drug to perform its tests during the final months of X's patent, or must it wait until the patent expires?

In Roche Products, Inc. v. Bolar Pharmaceutical Co., 733 F.2d 858, 221 U.S.P.Q. 937 (C.A.F.C.1984), *cert. denied* 469 U.S. 856, 105 S.Ct. 183, 83 L.Ed.2d 117 (1984), the Court of Appeals for the Federal Circuit held that performing the tests during the patent term would infringe X's patent. Given the significant time necessary to perform the tests, and the fact that no competitor could compete with X until it had performed the tests and obtained the necessary agency approval, the practical effect of this finding was to give X a considerable *de facto* extension of its patent term.

Congress enacted section 271(e) in response to the *Roche* decision. Subsection (e)(1), as amended, provides that the unauthorized manufacture, use, offer for sale, sale or importation of specified types of inventions is not infringement if done "solely for uses reasonably related to the development and submission of information under a Federal law which regulates the manufacture, use, or sale of drugs or veterinary biological products." Subsection (e)(2) provides a narrow exception to (e)(1). For an informative discussion of the rationale underlying subsection (e), see the Supreme Court's opinion in Eli Lilly & Co. v. Medtronic, Inc., 496 U.S. 661, 110 S.Ct. 2683, 110 L.Ed.2d 605 (1990).

DANA CORP. v. AMERICAN PRECISION CO.

United States District Court, N. D. Illinois, 1985.
618 F.Supp. 288, *aff'd*, 827 F.2d 755,
3 U.S.P.Q.2d 1852 (C.A.F.C. 1987).

ruary 23, 1993, would have amended Patent Act § 103 to effectively repeal *Durden*—providing that biotechnological processes using novel and nonobvious starting materials may not be rejected for obviousness. § 298 would also have amended section 271 to make in an infringement to import a product made by using biotechnological material covered by a U.S. patent.

For criticisms of this and similar proposed bills, see *Amending Title 35, United States Code, With Respect to Patents on Certain Processes, 1993: Hearing on H.R. 760 Before the Subcomm. on Intellectual Property and Judicial Administration of the House of Representatives, Comm. on the Judiciary*, 103d Congress, 1st Sess. (1993) (statement of William L. LaFuze, President, American Intellectual Property Law Assn.), reprinted in [April–May–June] AIPLA BULL. 429 (1993).

HOLDERMAN, DISTRICT JUDGE.

Plaintiff Dana Corporation ("Dana") brought this action against defendants Century Clutch and Brake Supply, Inc. and Century Parts, Inc. (collectively "Century"), American Precision Company (division of Avnet) and American Precision Company, Inc. ("APC"), and Illinois Auto Truck Co., Inc. ("IAT") for patent infringement and unfair competition.

PROCEDURAL BACKGROUND

[Dana's complaint claims infringement of four patents: 1) a "Spring Loaded Clutch," (" '788 Patent"); 2) a "Self–Adjusting Clutch," (" '286 Patent"); 3) a "Clutch with Friction Reducing Lever Assembly," (" '836 Patent"); and 4) a "Coaxial Spring Damper Drive," (" '855 Patent"). Dana alleges that APC infringed the '788, '286, and '836 patents and IAT and Century infringed all the patents.]

Although the nature of the defendants' allegedly infringing conduct is not specified in the amended complaint, it is now clear from the briefs of the parties that Century is accused of direct infringement by "reconstructing" Dana clutches and Coaxial Spring Driven Discs when it rebuilds them using one or more non-Dana "key" new parts. Dana has identified these "key" parts as follows:

Patent	Description of Part
788	Pressure Springs Release Sleeve Retainer Flywheel Cover Spring Pivot
286	Adjusting Ring Release Sleeve Retainer Self–Adjusting Assembly
836	Adjusting Ring K/e Levers
855	C/A Assemblies Inner Cover Hubs

IAT and APC are accused of contributory infringement by selling these "key" parts to Century and other rebuilders for use in the allegedly impermissible reconstruction of clutches. IAT is also charged with directly infringing the Coaxial Spring Driven Disc patent.

* * *

Summary judgment is a drastic remedy which should be granted only when it is clear that the requirements of Rule 56, Fed.R.Civ.P., have been met. All allegations and inferences are to be construed in the light most favorable to the non-moving party. * * * Based upon the undisputed material facts, it is clear that defendants are entitled to judgment as a matter of law.

BACKGROUND FACTS

Since its founding in 1946, Century has been in the business of rebuilding clutches. There are essentially two types of clutch rebuilders. "R & R" or custom rebuilders disassemble a worn clutch, locate defective parts and replace them with new or salvaged parts, clean the useable parts, and then reassemble the clutch using as many of its original parts as are still serviceable. A "production" rebuilder acquires a number of worn clutches, called cores, primarily as trade-ins for rebuilt clutches, disassembles the cores, cleans and sorts individual parts, salvaging those that can be reused and placing them in bins. Then, using a production line set-up, a number of clutches will be reassembled from as many salvaged parts as possible (although no care is taken to ensure that the parts from core "A" are all used to reassemble rebuilt core "A"). To the extent there are insufficient used parts, new replacements are included in the assembly.

Century is a production rebuilder. APC and IAT have supplied Century with new parts, including those identified by Dana as "key" parts, for use in the rebuilding process. Century does not have records sufficient to show how many new or key parts have been used in any particular rebuilt clutch, but it is undisputed that Century uses as few new parts as possible in its rebuilding process.

DISCUSSION

It is important at the outset to determine exactly which conduct Dana alleges to constitute patent infringement. [According to Dana,] "R & R" rebuilding or "one-at-a-time repair of Angle Spring clutches, even with non-Dana parts, is not infringement." And rebuilding "without the use of any new parts (or using only unimportant new parts)" is also not challenged. Rather, Dana poses the issue as follows:

> The question in this case is whether rebuilding worn out Angle Spring clutches employing new [one or more] *key parts* [of non-Dana origin]—parts that are intimately connected with the *essential gist* of the patented inventions—amounts to infringing reconstruction.

Based upon a review of the case law on reconstruction, this Court concludes the answer to the above question is a resounding "No".

The leading case on the repair/reconstruction distinction is *Aro Manufacturing Company v. Convertible Top Replacement Co.*, 365 U.S. 336, 81 S.Ct. 599, 5 L.Ed.2d 592 (1961) (*"Aro I"*). *Aro I* was a contributory infringement action seeking damages and an injunction based upon the manufacture and sale of fabric replacements for convertible roofs on automobiles. The convertible roof was subject to a combination patent. The Court first found that no patent was claimed as to the fabric or its shape; that "the fabric is no more than an unpatented element of the combination which was claimed as the invention." 81 S.Ct. at 601. Thus, "the principal and we think the determinative question presented here is whether the owner of a combination patent, comprised entirely of unpatented elements, has a patent monopoly on the manufacture, sale or use of the several unpatented components of the patented combination." *Id.* But as the Court had held in *Mercoid Corp. v. MidContinent Co.*, 320 U.S. 661, 64 S.Ct. 268, 88 L.Ed. 376 (1944):

> The patent is for a combination only. Since none of the separate elements of the combination is claimed as the invention none of them when dealt with separately is protected by the patent monopoly.

64 S.Ct. 272. *See, also, Mercoid Corp. v. Minneapolis–Honeywell Regulator Co.*, 320 U.S. 680, 64 S.Ct. 278, 88 L.Ed. 396 (1944), in which the Court explained:

> The fact that an unpatented part of a combination patent may distinguish the invention does not draw to it the privileges of a patent. That may be done only in the manner provided by law. However worthy it may be, however essential to the patent, an unpatented part of a combination patent is no more entitled to monopolistic protection than any other unpatented device.

64 S.Ct. at 280.

Based on its holdings in the *Mercoid* cases, the *Aro I* Court concluded that the manufacture and sale of the replacement fabric was not itself a direct infringement under 35 U.S.C. § 271(a).

Aro was also charged with contributory infringement under 35 U.S.C. § 271(c) based upon the activities of Aro's customers. Since there can be no finding of contributory infringement under § 271(c) without a finding of direct infringement by customers of the alleged contributory infringer, the question thus became whether purchasers of the replacement fabric directly infringed the subject patent by "reconstructing" the article or merely engaged in "permissible repair." The Supreme Court found that the applicable test was stated in *Wilson v. Simpson*, 9 How. 109, 50 U.S. 109, 13 L.Ed. 66 (1850) as interpreted by *United States v. Aluminum Company of America*, 148 F.2d 416 (2d Cir.1945), which stated "the [patent] monopolist cannot prevent those to whom he sells from . . . reconditioning articles worn by use unless they in fact make a new article." 148 F.2d at 425, quoted at 81 S.Ct. at 603.

The Court of Appeals had adopted an erroneous test in *Aro I* by focusing upon the relative importance of the fabric to the patented combination and the fact that although the life span of the fabric top was expectably shorter than the other components, the fabric top was not "an element that would expectedly wear out in a very short period of use." 270 F.2d 200, at 205, quoted 81 S.Ct. at 603. According to the Court of Appeals, only "minor" repairs were permissible and replacement of the fabric top was a "major reconstruction." *Id.* The patent holders in *Aro I* defended the erroneous Circuit Court test arguing:

> [T]hat when an element of a patented machine or combination is relatively durable—even though not so durable as the entire patented device which the owner purchased—relatively expensive, relative-

> ly difficult to replace, and is an "essential" or "distinguishing" part of the patent combination, any replacement of that element when it wears out or is otherwise spent, constitutes infringing "reconstruction" and, therefore, a new license must be obtained from, and another royalty paid to, the patentee for that privilege.

81 S.Ct. at 603.

The Court disagreed with this statement of the repair/reconstruction test:

> *[t]he basic fallacy in respondent's position is that it requires ascribing to one element of the patent combination the status of the patented invention in itself* ... *there is no legally recognizable or protected "essential" element "gist" or "heart" of the invention in a combination patent.*

81 S.Ct. at 604 (emphasis added).

Noting that the owner of a patented article has an implied license "to preserve its fitness for use so far as it may be affected by wear or breakage," the Court held that the maintenance of the "use of the whole" of the patented combination through the replacement of a spent unpatented element does not constitute reconstruction.

> [Reconstruction] is limited to such a true reconstruction of the entity as to in fact make a new article, after the entity viewed as a whole has become spent. In order to call the monopoly, conferred by the patent grant into operation for the second time it must indeed be a second creation of the patented entity ... [m]ere replacement of individual patented parts, one at a time, whether of the same part repeatedly or a different part successively, is no more than the legal right of the owner to repair his property.

81 S.Ct. at 604.

* * *

Aro I and its progeny thus clearly "eschewed the suggestion that the legal distinction between 'reconstruction' and 'repair' should be affected by whether the element of the combination that has been replaced is an 'essential' or 'distinguishing' part of the invention." *Dawson Chemical Co. v. Rohm and Haas Co.*, 448 U.S. 176, 217, 100 S.Ct. 2601, 2623, 65 L.Ed.2d 696 (1980). Dana's claim that the use of even *one* new "key" part of non-Dana origin in production rebuilding constitutes reconstruction is therefore clearly without merit.

The question remains, however, how much is too much? Dana has identified four key parts for the 788 patent, three key parts for the 286 and 855 patents, and two key parts for the 836 patent. If Century utilizes, for example, all four "key" parts for the 286 patent, can it be said that it has "recreated a new article" in violation of the patent laws?

The case law suggests not.

In *Wilbur-Ellis Co. v. Kuther*, 377 U.S. 422, 84 S.Ct. 1561, 12 L.Ed.2d 419 (1964), petitioner was a second-hand purchaser of machines (on which respondent held a patent) which were originally designed to pack fish into "1–pound" cans, 3 inches in diameter and $4^{11}/_{16}$ inches high. When the machines were purchased by Wilbur–Ellis, they were corroded, rusted and inoperable. After cleaning, sandblasting the machines and resizing 6 of the 35 elements that made up the patented combination, the machines could operate to pack fish into "5–ounce" cans, $2^{1}/_{8}$ inches in diameter and $3^{1}/_{2}$ inches long. Both the trial court and the Ninth Circuit found impermissible reconstruction under *Aro I*, holding that the defendant's activities were "a true reconstruction of the entity as to in fact make a new article." 314 F.2d 71, at 73.

The Supreme Court reversed, summarily dismissing the claim that impermissible reconstruction was involved:

> These four machines were not spent; they had years of usefulness remaining though they needed cleaning and repair. Had they been renovated and put to use on the 1–pound cans, there could have been no question but that they were "repaired", not "reconstructed".

377 U.S. at 424, 84 S.Ct. at 1563.

Since the sale of the machines was absolute with no limitation as to the size of the cans to be processed and since the size of the can to be used in the machine was not within the patent claims, the resizing of the machine was permissible repair.

The Seventh Circuit in *TSC Industries, Inc. v. International Harvester Company*, 406 F.2d 53 (7th Cir.1968) has also indicated that substantial rebuilding of a non-spent patented item may be undertaken without engaging in reconstruction. In *TSC Industries*, plaintiff brought a declaratory judgment action seeking a declaration that its conduct did not constitute impermissible reconstruction. Defendant held a patent on a "doffer," the heart of a mechanized cotton picking machine. The "doffer" was a rotating element consisting of a metal carrier plate that had spaced rubber coated fingers that removed the cotton from the picking spindles. The Seventh Circuit's description of the defendants' rebuilding activities is similar, to a certain decree, with the challenged activity here:

> Plaintiff does not take the worn doffer to be repaired and thereafter return it to the original owner. Plaintiff purchases worn out '930 doffer assemblies for a nominal sum. After reclaiming the plate from the doffer assembly, plaintiff carries out additional steps which are identical with those performed by the defendant and which have been hereinbefore described. Plaintiff claims that what it has done is a "rerubbering" process and that it is a permissible repair and therefore, not an infringement. After accumulating a substantial number of defendant's worn and spent doffers, plaintiff follows the practice of initiating its "rerubbering" program. Plaintiff destroys what is left of the patented doffer combination by removing the molded rubber lugs and the wafer-like web including the resilient lug sustaining portions of the web, spanning the space between the

> fingers of the carrier plate. It is possible to reuse the metal plate a number of times.

Id. at 55. The trial court found that plaintiff had destroyed the patented doffer and then reconstructed a new one. The Seventh Circuit reversed, holding that the challenged conduct constituted permissible repair.

This Court therefore concludes that even if Century replaced *all* of the so-called "key" parts with new non-Dana parts, no "second creation" of the patented combination would occur. Accordingly, Century does not engage in reconstruction simply by using new key parts in rebuilding, and APC and IAT are not contributory infringers for selling such parts to Century or other rebuilders.

But Dana has one more argument. Dana argues that because in the production rebuilding process it is unlikely "that any two parts in a Century rebuilt Angle Spring clutch originated from the same clutch," the rebuilt core loses its "identity" and is therefore "created" anew.

This Court cannot agree. Dana's argument, in essence, is that Century's production line *method* of rebuilding can transform repair into reconstruction. Such a claim appears precluded by the Seventh Circuit's decision in *TSC Industries, supra.* The rebuilding process there, while not precisely a "production line," would seem similar enough to suggest a similar result here.

This conclusion is buttressed by the Court of Claims' decision in *General Electric Co. v. United States*, 572 F.2d 745, 215 Ct.Cl. 636 (1978). In *General Electric*, G.E. held patents on certain naval gun mounts which the navy repaired pursuant to its Ordinance Replacement Program. The Replacement Program's stated goal was to provide ships with "new or completely rebuilt" guns. 572 F.2d at 770. Under the Replacement Program, gun mounts with a history of frequent repair were sent to Louisville, Kentucky, where they were disassembled to their "smallest readily separable part." 572 F.2d at 780. The parts from various mounts were treated as fungible and two out of five mounts were scrapped and cannibalized for parts. Some parts, particularly wiring, were replaced without regard to wear. Finally, the result of the Replacement Program was to increase performance "beyond original specification" in many instances. Relying in part on *Monroe Auto Equipment Co. v. Precision Rebuilders, Inc.*, 229 F.Supp. 347 (D.Kan.1964) (a case relied upon here by plaintiff), the trial court found that the Navy had engaged in impermissible reconstruction. The Appellate Court reversed:

> In these circumstances it seems to us that the user of the combination (the Navy) was not creating a "new article" in the sense of *Aro I*, even though the gun mounts were disassembled in order to be overhauled, and even though, in some or most or all instances, the reassembled elements were not returned to the same gun mount or the same ship .... The assembly-line method adopted at Louisville was simply a speedier, less expensive, more efficient, and more effective means of refurbishing the gun mounts than if they had been disassembled and renovated gun mount by

> individual gun mount, and then returned to the same ship—and the end-result as precisely the same. Disassembly and renovation by individual gun mount would surely not be enough to show reconstruction—or *Wilbur-Ellis* could not have been decided as it was—but it would have been a much more burdensome, time-consuming, and costly procedure. Achieving precisely the same result by a more practical, economical and convenient process is surely not required by patent law in order to avoid imposition of further liability. The substance of what was done to the mounts would be the same by either method, the difference being simply that the procedure followed by the Navy at Louisville was easier, quicker and less expensive.

Id. at 784, 786. While it is true that the Navy utilized primarily GE parts for its reconditioning, the Court of Claims strongly suggested that the source of "one or two" elements would not alter its analysis. Assuming *arguendo* that replacement of all the "key" parts were accomplished with non-Dana parts, production line rebuilding would still not constitute reconstruction because as stated in *General Electric*:

> Achieving precisely the same result by a more practical, economical and convenient process is surely not required by patent law in order to avoid imposition of further liability.

CONCLUSION

The Court accordingly concludes that, as a matter of law, Century's production line rebuilding process utilizing one or more "key" parts of non-Dana origin does not constitute impermissible reconstruction. Century is therefore entitled to summary judgment on this claim. There being no direct infringement, there can be contributory infringement, and APC and IAT are therefore also entitled to summary judgment on this claim.

Notes and Questions

1. *The doctrine of first sale.* In *Dana*, the patentee sold its patented clutches to an original buyer. Assume that the original buyer then sold the clutch to an intermediate buyer, and that the intermediate buyer resold the clutch to Century. Under section 154 of the Patent Act, the patentee had the right to exclude others from selling the patented invention. Why wouldn't the original buyer's sale to the intermediate buyer, and the intermediate buyer's resale to Century themselves constitute infringements of the patent?

The doctrine of first sale (also known as the doctrine of exhaustion) provides that once the patentee releases a patented product into the stream of commerce by selling or authorizing it to be sold to another, he exhausts his legal right to control that product. The exhaustion principle is often characterized as a license, implied by operation of law when the patentee makes or authorizes sale to the first buyer. The implied license permits the buyer and others deriving title from him to use and resell the product at will. See, e.g., Aro Manufacturing Co. v. Convertible Top Replacement Co.,

377 U.S. 476, 84 S.Ct. 1526, 12 L.Ed.2d 457, 141 U.S.P.Q. 681 (1964). Why impose this limitation on the patentee's power? Does the doctrine of first sale properly balance the respective interests of the patentee, the buyer, and the public?

Note that the first sale must have been authorized by the patentee before the doctrine of first sale applies. If the first sale was not authorized, each subsequent use and resale of the patented article will constitute a separate infringement of the patent. *Id.*

Assume that a United States patentee sells a large quantity of its patented products to X Company, which then exports the products to Brazil. Y Company buys the products in Brazil and imports them back to the United States. Will Y company be in violation of the patentee's new right of importation under 35 U.S.C.A. § 271(a)? Would it make any difference if the patentee itself originally made and sold the goods in Brazil?

2. *Repair vs. reconstruction.* As the *Dana* decision makes clear, the right to use, granted by implied license at the first sale, encompasses the right to repair. Only when "repair" amounts to "reconstruction" is there an unauthorized "making," or second creation of the patented invention, which exceeds the scope of the implied license and constitutes infringement. At what point does permissible repair become impermissible reconstruction?

Does the rule regarding the dividing line, announced by the majority in *Aro I*, properly accommodate the respective interests of the patentee, the owner of the patented product, and the public? See Aro Manufacturing Co. v. Convertible Top Replacement Co., 365 U.S. 336, 362, 81 S.Ct. 599, 613, 5 L.Ed.2d 592, 608, 128 U.S.P.Q. 354 (1961), where Justice Brennan, concurring in the result, argued that the majority's standard for determining what constitutes "reconstruction" is too narrow. According to Justice Brennan, the determination should be based on consideration of a number of factors, including "the life of the part replaced in relation to the useful life of the whole combination, the importance of the replaced element to the inventive concept, the cost of the component relative to the cost of the combination, the common sense understanding and intention of the patent owner and the buyer of the combination as to its perishable components, whether the purchased component replaces a worn-out part or is brought for some other purpose, and other pertinent factors."

How does one tell when the article "viewed as a whole has become spent?" In its appeal to the Court of Appeals for the Federal Circuit, Dana Corporation, the patentee, offered two theories. First, Dana argued that an article becomes spent if the owner voluntarily disassembles it in a manner that destroys its original identity, as was the case in the production-line method used by Century. The court rejected this argument, noting that the practical impact would be to impose liability for doing more efficiently what could otherwise legally be done. Second, Dana argued that whether the patented product is spent should turn on the owner's economic evaluation of the product: "a patented product should be deemed 'spent' when a user, making an objective economic decision, would replace the product rather than repair it, because it has no value to the owner except as scrap." 827 F.2d 755, 760, 3 U.S.P.Q.2d 1852, 1856 (C.A.F.C. 1987). While finding this approach "interesting," the court rejected it, finding it too uncertain: "In the present case, for example, truck owners desiring to keep their trucks on the road would desire a quick replacement of their inoperative clutch with an existing rebuilt clutch. That decision rests little, if at all, on the owner's objective view of the defective clutch's condition." *Id.* How, then, should the "spentness" determination be made? See FMC Corp. v. Up–Right Inc., 21 F.3d 1073, 30 U.S.P.Q.2d 1361 (C.A.F.C. 1994) (court rejects argument that successive repairs to one machine may, over time, cumulatively amount to an infringing reconstruction). For further discussion of the repair/reconstruct question, see Farley, *Infringement Questions Stemming From the Repair or Reconstruction of Patented Combinations*, 68 J. PAT. & TRADEMARK OFF. SOC. 149 (1986).

What if the owner replaces parts that are not worn out? Should that constitute reconstruction? See Everpure, Inc. v. Cuno, Inc., 875 F.2d 300, 10 U.S.P.Q.2d 1855 (C.A.F.C.1989), *cert. denied* 493 U.S. 853, 110 S.Ct. 154, 107 L.Ed.2d 112 (1989).

Would it be possible for a patentee, as a condition of sale, to place an express restriction on the extent to which a buyer could use or repair the patented article, thus overriding the "implied license" imposed by the doctrine of first sale? Courts traditionally have hesitated to recognize or enforce patentee-imposed resale price restrictions and tying agreements (e.g., agreements authorizing use of the patented product or process only in connection with another product sold by the patentee), due to their antitrust implications. In Mallinckrodt Inc. v. Medipart Inc., 976 F.2d 700, 24 U.S.P.Q.2d 1173 (C.A.F.C. 1992), however, the Federal Circuit held that a patentee's express provision restricting purchasers to a single use of its patented medical device and prohibiting reconditioning or reuse could be enforced through a suit for patent infringement, if it passed muster under the antitrust law's rule of reason. For a discussion of the implications of the *Mallinckrodt* decision, see Kobak, *Contracting Around Exhaustion: Some Thoughts About the CAFC's* Mallinckrodt *Decision*, 75 J. PAT. & TRADEMARK OFF. SOC. 550 (1993).

3. *Experimental use.* Notwithstanding the all-encompassing language of sections 154 and 271(a), a minor exception to infringement liability has been recognized for purely experimental uses. The exception had its origin in Justice Story's opinion in Whittemore v. Cutter, 29 F.Cas. 1120, 1121 (C.C.Mass.1813), in which Justice Story noted: "[I]t could never have been the intention of the legislature to punish a man, who constructed [a patented] machine merely for philosophical experiments, or for the purpose of ascertaining the sufficiency of the machine to produce its described effects." Justice Story elaborated on this exception to liability in Sawin v. Guild, 21 Fed.Cas. 554, 555 (C.C.Mass.1813): "[T]he making of a patented machine to be an offense * * * must be the making with an intent to use for profit, and not for the mere purpose of philosophical experiments, or to ascertain the verity and exactness of the specification * * *." By 1861, the law was "well-settled that an experiment with a patented article for the sole purpose of gratifying a philosophical taste, or curiosity, or for mere amusement is not an infringement of the rights of the patentee." Poppenhusen v. Falke, 19 Fed.Cas. 1048, 1049 (C.C.S.D.N.Y. 1861).

This "experimental use" exception has rarely been applied, and remains very narrow. For example, in *Roche Products, Inc. v. Bolar Pharmaceutical Co., Inc.*, discussed in note 7 of the prior section, the defendant generic drug company argued that the experimental use doctrine sheltered its use of plaintiff's patented drug in tests to demonstrate safety and efficacy and thus obtain F.D.A. approval to market a generic equivalent. The Court of Appeals for the Federal Circuit disagreed:

> Despite Bolar's argument that its tests are "true scientific inquiries" to which a literal interpretation of the experimental use exception logically should extend, we hold the experimental use exception to be truly narrow, and we will not expand it under the present circumstances. * * *
>
> * * *
>
> Bolar's intended "experimental" use is solely for business reasons and not for amusement, to satisfy idle curiosity, or for strictly philosophical inquiry. * * * Bolar may intend to perform "experiments," but unlicensed experiments conducted with a view to the adaption of the patented invention to the experimenter's business is a violation of the rights of the patentee to exclude others from using his patented invention. It is obvious here that it is a misnomer to call the intended use *de minimis*. It is no trifle in its economic effect on the parties even if the quantity used is small. It is no dilettante affair such as Justice Story envisioned. We cannot construe the experimental use rule so broadly as to allow a violation of the patent laws in the guise of "scientific inquiry," when that inquiry has definite, cognizable, and not insubstantial commercial purposes.

Id., 733 F.2d at 863, 221 U.S.P.Q. at 940–941.

Recently, several commentators have advocated reevaluating the experimental use exception, and enlarging its role to better balance the incentive function of patents against researchers' legitimate need for access to others' inventions. See, e.g., Eisenberg, *Patents and the Progress of Science: Exclusive Rights and Experimental Use*, 56 U. CHI. L. REV. 1017 (1989); Bruzzone, *The Research Exemption: A Proposal*, 21 AIPLA Q. J. 52 (1993); Feit, *Biotechnology Research and the Experimental Use Exception to Patent Infringement*, 71 J. PAT. & TRADEMARK OFF. SOC. 819 (1989).

2. *The Right to Exclude Others From Assisting Third Parties to Infringe*

HEWLETT–PACKARD CO. v. BAUSCH & LOMB INC.

United States Court of Appeals for the Federal Circuit, 1990.
909 F.2d 1464, 15 U.S.P.Q.2d 1525.

RICH, CIRCUIT JUDGE.

* * *

Section 271(b) provides that "Whoever actively induces infringement of a patent shall be liable as an infringer." At the outset, we feel that it is necessary to make clear the distinction, often confused, between active inducement of infringement under § 271(b) and contributory infringement under § 271(c). Prior to the enactment of the Patent Act of 1952, there was no statute which defined what constituted infringement. However, infringement was judicially divided into two categories: "direct infringement," which was the unauthorized making, using or selling of the patented invention, and "contributory infringement," which was any other activity where, although not technically making, using or selling, the defendant displayed sufficient culpability to be held liable as an infringer. Such liability was under a theory of joint tortfeasance, wherein one who intentionally caused, or aided and abetted, the commission of a tort by another was jointly and severally liable with the primary tortfeasor.

The most common pre–1952 contributory infringement cases dealt with the situation where a seller would sell a component which was not itself technically covered by the claims of a product or process patent but which had no other use except with the claimed product or process. In such cases, although a plaintiff was required to show intent to cause infringement in order to establish contributory infringement, many courts held that such intent could be presumed because the component had no substantial non-infringing use.

The legislative history of the Patent Act of 1952 indicates that no substantive change in the scope of what constituted "contributory infringement" was intended by the enactment of § 271. However, the single concept of "contributory infringement" was divided between §§ 271(b) and 271(c) into "active inducement" (a type of direct infringement) and "contributory infringement," respectively. Section 271(c) codified the prohibition against the common type of contributory infringement referred to above, and made clear that only proof of a defendant's knowledge, not intent, that his activity cause infringement was necessary to establish contributory infringement.[4] Section 271(b) codified the prohibition against all other types of activity which, prior to 1952, had constituted "contributory infringement."

That, however, leaves open the question of what level of knowledge or intent is required to find active inducement under § 271(b). On its face, § 271(b) is much broader than § 271(c) and certainly does not speak of any intent requirement to prove active inducement. However, in view of the very definition of "active inducement" in pre–1952 case law and the fact that § 271(b) was intended as merely a codification of pre–1952 law, we are of the opinion that proof of actual intent to cause the acts which constitute the infringement is a necessary prerequisite to finding active inducement. * * *

* * *

4. Although not clear on the face of the statute, subsequent case law held that § 271(c) required not only knowledge that the component was especially made or adapted for a particular use but also knowledge of the patent which proscribed that use.

Notes and Questions

1. *Contributory infringement.* Notwithstanding the Supreme Court's admonition, in *Deepsouth* and *Aro I*, that the separate components of a patented combination are not protected by the patent monopoly, section 271(c) extends the patentee's property rights to unpatented components of her invention in some circumstances. If the sale, offer for sale or importation of an unpatented component leads to direct infringement by purchasers, the component has no substantial noninfringing use, and the other prerequisites of subsection (c) are satisfied, then the patentee may prohibit the sale, offer for sale or importation of the component, and/or recover damages. In some cases, subsection (c) may enable the patentee to completely control the U.S. market for the unpatented component.

The *Aro* case was itself a claim for contributory infringement pursuant to subsection (c). Recall that the "combination" patent at issue claimed a top for convertible automobiles. General Motors and Ford both included structures embodying the patented top as original equipment in their 1952–54 convertible models. GM was licensed to use the top, but Ford was not. Thus, Ford's manufacture and sale of its automobiles infringed the patent. The defendant Aro, which also was unlicensed, manufactured and sold fabric components specially tailored to replace the fabric in the Ford and G.M. convertible tops when the original fabric wore out. The patentee sued Aro for contributory infringement.

In its first ("*Aro I*") opinion, the Supreme Court dealt only with the G.M. cars. The court reasoned that Aro could only be liable for contributory infringement in selling the replacement fabric for the G.M. models if its purchasers used the fabric to directly infringe the patent. It found that there was no direct infringement because the purchasers' replacement of the worn fabric constituted permissible "repair," rather than reconstruction. Aro Manufacturing Co. v. Convertible Top Replacement Co., Inc., 365 U.S. 336, 81 S.Ct. 599, 5 L.Ed.2d 592, 128 U.S.P.Q. 354 (1961).

The Supreme Court addressed Aro's sales of fabric for the Ford convertible models in a later opinion. Aro Manufacturing Co. v. Convertible Top Replacement Co., Inc., 377 U.S. 476, 84 S.Ct. 1526, 12 L.Ed.2d 457, 141 U.S.P.Q. 681 (1964) ("*Aro II*"). In that opinion the majority reasoned that since Ford's tops were unauthorized, subsequent purchasers had no implied license to use them and infringed the patent when they did so. The fact that replacing the fabric constituted "repair" rather than "reconstruction" was irrelevant: "Where use infringes, repair does also, for it perpetuates the infringing use." *Id.*, 377 U.S. at 484, 84 S.Ct. at 1531, 12 L.Ed.2d at 467. Thus, the legality of the purchasers' repair ultimately depended upon whether the original sale of the tops they repaired was authorized (licensed) by the patentee. Having established direct infringement on the part of the purchasers of Ford convertibles, the majority turned to the claim of contributory infringement against Aro:

> The language of [section 271(c)] fits perfectly Aro's activity of selling "a component of a patented * * * combination * * *, constituting a material part of the invention, * * * especially made or especially adapted for use in an infringement of such patent and not a staple article or commodity of commerce suitable for substantial noninfringing use."

> Indeed, this is the almost unique case in which the component was hardly suitable for *any* noninfringing use.

Id., 377 U.S. at 487–88, 84 S.Ct. at 1533, 12 L.Ed.2d at 469. The Court noted that the fabric replacements in question not only were specially designed for the Ford convertibles but would not fit the top-structures of any other cars. The majority then turned to the requirement that the defendant know that the component it is selling is "especially made or especially adapted for use in an infringement" of the patent:

> Was Aro "knowing" within the statutory meaning because—as it admits, and as the lower courts found—it knew that its replacement fabrics were especially designed for use in the 1952–54 Ford convertible tops and were not suitable for other use? Or does the statute require a further showing that Aro knew that the tops were patented, and knew also that Ford was not licensed under the patent so that any fabric replacement by a Ford car owner constituted infringement?
>
> On this question a majority of the Court is of the view that § 271(c) does require a showing that the alleged contributory infringer knew that the combination for which his component was especially designed was both patented and infringing. With respect to many of the replacement-fabric sales involved in this case, Aro clearly had such knowledge. For by letter dated January 2, 1954, [the patentee] informed Aro that it held the * * * patent; that it had granted a license to General Motors but to no one else; and that "It is obvious, from the foregoing and from an inspection of the convertible automobile sold by the Ford Motor Company, that anyone selling ready-made replacement fabrics for these automobiles would be guilty of contributory infringement of said patents." Thus the Court's interpretation of the knowledge requirement affords Aro no defense with respect to replacement-fabric sales made after January 2, 1954. * * * With respect to any sales that were made before that date, however, Aro cannot be held liable in the absence of a showing that at the time it had already acquired the requisite knowledge that the Ford car tops were patented and infringing.

Id., 377 U.S. at 488–91, 84 S.Ct. at 1533–34, 12 L.Ed.2d at 469–71.

Why does the patentee need a cause of action for contributory infringement, given that it already has a cause of action against the direct infringer? In light of the careful attempt to balance the conflicting goals of incentive to invent and free competition, does it make sense to extend the patentee's rights beyond the patented invention itself to its components?

2. *Active inducement to infringe.* Under section 271(b), a person who actively, intentionally solicits or assists another to infringe, with knowledge that infringement is likely to occur, will be liable if the other does in fact directly infringe the patent as a result. See 4 D.S. CHISUM, PATENTS: A TREATISE ON THE LAW OF PATENTABILITY, VALIDITY AND INFRINGEMENT § 17.04 (1991). What kinds of acts might constitute active inducement? Is there any overlap between subsections (b) and (c), so that a defendant's conduct might simultaneously violate both? See generally Miller, *Some Views on the Law of Patent Infringement by Inducement*, 53 J.

PAT. OFF. SOC. 86 (1971). Why is the active inducement cause of action needed, given that there will always be a direct infringement, as well?

A cause of action for active inducement to infringe may provide a means of reaching corporate officers and directors (normally protected against liability for corporate acts) who have caused their corporation directly to infringe. A recent example of an unsuccessful attempt to avoid the corporate shield against officer/director liability occurred in Manville Sales Corp. v. Paramount Systems, Inc., 917 F.2d 544, 16 U.S.P.Q.2d 1587 (C.A.F.C. 1990). In *Manville*, Paramount's corporate secretary obtained a copy of a drawing of Manville's patented device that had been submitted to the Florida Department of Transportation, and sent it to Paramount's president. The president gave the drawing to a designer for use in designing Paramount's device. The resulting device was found to infringe the Manville patent. The question before the Court of Appeals for the Federal Circuit was whether the Paramount secretary and president could be held liable along with Paramount, either under section 271(a) or (b). With regard to the section 271(a) claim, the court observed:

> [T]here must be evidence to justify piercing the corporate veil. * * * Often a party asking a court to disregard the corporate existence will attempt to show that the corporation was merely the alter ego of its officers. * * * More generally, a court may exert its equitable powers and disregard the corporate entity if it decides that piercing the veil will prevent fraud, illegality, injustice, a contravention of public policy, or prevent the corporation from shielding someone from criminal liability. The court, however, must "start from the general rule that the corporate entity should be recognized and upheld, unless specific, unusual circumstances call for an exception." [citation omitted.]

Id., 917 F.2d at 552; 16 U.S.P.Q.2d at 1593. The court noted that while the facts supported the conclusion that the officers had knowledge of their acts, and the acts assisted the corporation to infringe, the district court had abused its discretion in piercing the veil. The officers' acts were within the scope of their employment. Moreover, the district court had found that the officers were not the alter egos of the corporation, that Paramount and its officers did not know of the patent prior to the suit, and that they had only continued to infringe after the suit was filed on the good faith belief, based on the advice of counsel, that there was no infringement. Nor was there any evidence that the officers were attempting to avoid liability through use of the corporate form. *Id.*, 917 F.2d at 552–3, 16 U.S.P.Q.2d at 1593.

With regard to the section 271(b) active inducement claim, the court observed:

> Under [subsection (b)], corporate officers who actively assist with their corporation's infringement may be personally liable for inducing infringement regardless of whether the circumstances are such that a court should disregard the corporate entity and pierce the corporate veil. * * * The alleged infringer must be shown, however, to have knowingly induced infringement. * * * It must be established that the defendant possessed specific intent to encourage another's infringement and not merely that the defendant had knowledge of the acts alleged to constitute inducement. The plaintiff has the burden of showing that the

> alleged infringer's actions induced infringing acts and that he knew or should have known his actions would induce actual infringements.

Id., 917 F.2d at 553, 16 U.S.P.Q.2d at 1594. In this case, the court stressed that the officers were not aware of Manville's patent until suit was filed and that Paramount's subsequent infringing acts continued upon the officers' good faith belief, based on advice of counsel, that Paramount's product did not infringe. There was insufficient evidence that the officers had the requisite specific intent. *Id.* For a different result, see Orthokinetics, Inc. v. Safety Travel Chairs, Inc., 806 F.2d 1565, 1 U.S.P.Q.2d 1081 (C.A.F.C. 1986).

Could there, in addition to the section 271(a), (b) and (c) causes of action, be a cause of action for conspiracy to infringe a patent? The Court of Appeals for the Federal Circuit has held that there cannot. See Ernster v. Ralston Purina Co., 757 F.Supp. 1030, 18 U.S.P.Q.2d 1724 (E.D.Mo.1991), *reversed in part, vacated in part* 980 F.2d 743, 27 U.S.P.Q.2d 1692 (C.A.F.C. 1992), *cert. denied* ___ U.S. ___ 113 S.Ct. 1848, 123 L.Ed.2d 472 (1993).

F. CLAIM INTERPRETATION

In order to determine whether a defendant has infringed the patented invention, it must be determined exactly what the invention is, through interpretation of the patent claims.

> The scope of every patent is limited to the invention described in the claims contained in it, read in the light of the specification. These so mark where the progress claimed by the patent begins and where it ends that they have been aptly likened to the description in a deed, which sets the bounds to the grant which it contains.

Motion Picture Patents Co. v. Universal Film Manufacturing Co., 243 U.S. 502, 510, 37 S.Ct. 416, 418, 61 L.Ed. 871, 876 (1917). The defendant's product or process must be compared to the patent claims, not to the defendant's commercial embodiment of the invention. To infringe, the defendant's product or process must fall within the bounds of at least one claim, either literally or through the doctrine of equivalents.

GRAVER TANK & MFG. CO. v. LINDE AIR PRODUCTS CO.

United States Supreme Court, 1950.
339 U.S. 605, 70 S.Ct. 854, 94 L.Ed. 1097, 85 U.S.P.Q. 328.

MR. JUSTICE JACKSON delivered the opinion of the Court.

Linde Air Products Co., owner of the Jones patent for an electric welding process and for fluxes to be used therewith, brought an action for infringement against Lincoln and the two Graver companies. The trial court held four flux claims valid and infringed and certain other flux claims and all process claims invalid. The Court of Appeals affirmed findings of validity and infringement as to the four flux claims but reversed the trial court and held valid the process claims and the remaining contested flux claims. We granted certiorari and reversed the judgment of the Court of Appeals insofar as it reversed that of the trial court, and reinstated the District Court decree. Rehearing was granted, limited to the question of infringement of the four valid flux claims and to the applicability of the doctrine of equivalents to findings of fact in this case.

At the outset it should be noted that the single issue before us is whether the trial court's holding that the four flux claims have been infringed will be sustained. * * *

In determining whether an accused device or composition infringes a valid patent, resort must be had in the first instance to the words of the claim. If accused matter falls clearly within the claim, infringement is made out and that is the end of it.

But courts have also recognized that to permit imitation of a patented invention which does not copy every literal detail would be to convert the protection of the patent grant into a hollow and useless thing. Such a limitation would leave room for—indeed encourage—the unscrupulous copyist to make unimportant and insubstantial changes and substitutions in the patent which, though adding nothing, would be enough to take the copied matter outside the claim, and hence outside the reach of law. One who seeks to pirate an invention, like one who seeks to pirate a copyrighted book or play, may be expected to introduce minor variations to conceal and shelter the piracy. Outright and forthright duplication is a dull and very rare type of infringement. To prohibit no other would place the inventor at the mercy of verbalism and would be subordinating substance to form. It would deprive him of the benefit of his invention and would foster concealment rather than disclosure of inventions, which is one of the primary purposes of the patent system.

The doctrine of equivalents evolved in response to this experience. The essence of the doctrine is that one may not practice a fraud on a patent. Originating almost a century ago in the case of *Winans v. Denmead*, 15 How. 330, 14 L.Ed. 717, it has been consistently applied by this Court and the lower federal courts, and continues today ready and available for utilization when the proper circumstances for its application arise. "To temper unsparing logic and prevent an infringer from stealing the benefit of the invention" a patentee may invoke this doctrine to proceed against the producer of a device "if it performs substantially the same function in substantially the same way to obtain the same result." *Sanitary Refrigerator Co. v. Winters*, 280 U.S. 30, 42, 50 S.Ct. 9, 13, 74 L.Ed. 147. The theory on which it is founded is that "if two devices do the same work in substantially the same way, and accomplish substantially the same result, they are the same, even though they differ in name, form or shape." *Union Paper–Bag Machine Co. v. Murphy*, 97 U.S. 120, 125, 24 L.Ed. 935. The doctrine operates not only in favor of the patentee of a pioneer or primary invention, but also for the patentee of a secondary invention consisting of a combination of old ingredients which produce new and useful results, *Imhaeuser v. Buerk*, 101 U.S. 647, 655, 25 L.Ed. 945, although the area of equivalence may vary under the circumstances. The wholesome realism of this doctrine is not always applied in favor of a patentee but is sometimes used against him. Thus, where a device is so far changed in principle from a patented article that it performs the same or a similar function in a substantially different way, but nevertheless falls within the literal words of the claim, the doctrine of equivalents may be used to restrict the claim and defeat the patentee's action for infringement. In its early development, the doctrine was usually applied in cases involving devices where there was equivalence in mechanical components. Subsequently, however, the same principles were also applied to compositions, where there was equivalence between chemical ingredients. Today the doctrine is applied to mechanical or chemical equivalents in compositions or devices.

What constitutes equivalency must be determined against the context of the patent, the prior art, and the particular circumstances of the case. Equivalence, in the patent law, is not the prisoner of a formula and is not an absolute to be considered in a vacuum. It does not require complete identity for every purpose and in every respect. In determining equivalents, things equal to the same thing may not be equal to each other and, by the same token, things for most purposes different may sometimes be equivalents. Consideration must be given to the purpose for which an ingredient is used in a patent, the qualities it has when combined with the other ingredients, and the function which it is intended to perform. An important factor is whether persons reasonably skilled in the art would have known of the interchangeability of an ingredient not contained in the patent with one that was.

A finding of equivalence is a determination of fact. Proof can be made in any form: through testimony of experts or others versed in the technology; by documents, including texts and treatises; and, of course, by the disclosures of the prior art. Like any other issue of fact, final determination requires a balancing of credibility, persuasiveness and weight of evidence. It is to be decided by the trial court and that court's decision, under general principles of appellate review, should not be disturbed unless clearly erroneous. Particularly is this so in a field where so much depends upon familiarity with specific scientific problems and principles not usually contained in the general storehouse of knowledge and experience.

In the case before us, we have two electric welding compositions or fluxes: the patented composition, Unionmelt Grade 20, and the accused composition, Lincolnweld 660. The patent under which Unionmelt is made claims essentially a combination of alkaline earth metal silicate and calcium fluoride; Unionmelt actually contains, however, silicates of calcium and magnesium, two alkaline earth metal silicates. Lincolnweld's composition is similar to Unionmelt's, except that it substitutes silicates of calcium and manganese—the latter not an alkaline earth metal—for silicates of calcium and magnesium. In all other respects, the two compositions are alike. The mechanical methods in which these compositions are employed are similar. They are identical in operation and produce the same kind and quality of weld.

The question which thus emerges is whether the substitution of the manganese which is not an alkaline earth metal for the magnesium which is, under the circumstances of this case, and in view of the technology and the prior art, is a change of such substance as to make the doctrine of equivalents inapplicable; or conversely, whether under the circumstances the change was so insubstantial that the trial court's invocation of the doctrine of equivalents was justified.

Without attempting to be all-inclusive, we note the following evidence in the record: Chemists familiar with the two fluxes testified that manganese and magnesium were similar in many of their reactions. There is testimony by a metallurgist that alkaline earth metals are often found in manganese ores in their natural state and that they serve the same purpose in the fluxes; and a chemist testified that "in the sense of the patent" manganese could be included as an alkaline earth metal. Much of this testimony was corroborated by reference to recognized texts on inorganic chemistry. Particularly important, in addition, were the disclosures of the prior art, also contained in the record. The Miller patent, No. 1,754,566, which preceded the patent in suit, taught the use of manganese silicate in welding fluxes. Manganese was similarly disclosed in the Armor patent, No. 1,467,825, which also described a welding composition. And the record contains no evidence of any kind to show that Lincolnweld was developed as the result of independent research or experiments.

It is not for this Court to even essay an independent evaluation of this evidence. This is the function of the trial court. And, as we have heretofore observed, "To no type of case is this * * * more appropriately applicable than to the one before us, where the evidence is largely the testimony of experts as to which a trial court may be enlightened by scientific demonstrations. This trial occupied some three weeks, during which, as the record shows, the trial judge visited laboratories with counsel and experts to observe actual demonstrations of welding as taught by the patent and of the welding accused of infringing it, and of various stages of the prior art. He viewed motion pictures of various welding operations and tests and heard many experts and other witnesses."

The trial judge found on the evidence before him that the Lincolnweld flux and the composition of the patent in suit are substantially identical in operation and in result. He found also that Lincolnweld is in all respects equivalent to Unionmelt for welding purposes. And he concluded that "for all practical purposes, manganese silicate can be efficiently and effectively substituted for calcium and magnesium silicates as the major constituent of the welding composition." These conclusions are adequately supported by the record; certainly they are not clearly erroneous.

It is difficult to conceive of a case more appropriate for application of the doctrine of equivalents. The disclosures of the prior art made clear that manganese silicate was a useful ingredient in welding compositions. Specialists familiar with the problems of welding compositions understood that manganese was equivalent to and could be substituted for magnesium in the composition of the patented flux and their observations were confirmed by the literature of chemistry. Without some explanation or indication that Lincolnweld was developed by independent research, the trial court could properly infer that the accused flux is the result of imitation rather than experimentation or invention. Though infringement was not literal, the changes which avoid literal infringement are colorable only. We conclude that the trial court's judgment of infringement respecting the four flux claims was proper, and we adhere to our prior decision on this aspect of the case.

MR. JUSTICE BLACK, with whom MR. JUSTICE DOUGLAS concurs, dissenting.

I heartily agree with the Court that "fraud" is bad, "piracy" is evil, and "stealing" is reprehensible. But in this case, where petitioners are not charged with any such malevolence, these lofty principles do not justify the Court's sterilization of Acts of Congress and prior decisions, none of which are even mentioned in today's opinion.

The only patent claims involved here describe respondent's product as a flux "containing a major proportion of alkaline earth metal silicate." The trial court found that petitioners used a flux "composed principally of manganese silicate." Finding also that "manganese is not an alkaline earth metal," the trial court admitted that petitioners' flux did not "literally infringe" respondent's patent. Nevertheless it invoked the judicial "doctrine of equivalents" to broaden the claim for "alkaline earth metals" so as to embrace "manganese." On the ground that "the fact that manganese is a proper substitute * * * is fully disclosed in the specification" of respondent's patent, it concluded that "no determination need be made whether it is a known chemical fact *outside* the teachings of the patent that manganese is an equivalent * * *." Since today's affirmance unquestioningly follows the findings of the trial court, this Court necessarily relies on what the specifications revealed. In so doing, it violates a direct mandate of Congress without even discussing that mandate.

R.S. § 4888, as amended, 35 U.S.C.A. § 33, provides that an applicant "shall particularly point out and distinctly claim the part, improvement, or combination which he claims as his invention or discovery." We have held in this very case that this statute precludes invoking the specifications to alter a claim free from ambiguous language, since "it is the claim which measures the grant to the patentee." *Graver Mfg. Co. v. Linde Co.*, 336 U.S. 271, 277, 69 S.Ct. 535, 538, 93 L.Ed. 672. What is not specifically claimed is dedicated to the public. For the function of claims under R.S. § 4888, as we have frequently reiterated, is to exclude from the patent monopoly field all that is not specifically claimed, whatever may appear in the specifications. Today the Court tacitly rejects those cases. It departs from the underlying principle which, as the Court pointed out in *White v. Dunbar*, 119 U.S. 47, 51, 7 S.Ct. 72, 74, 30 L.Ed. 303, forbids treating a patent claim "like a nose of wax, which may be turned and twisted in any direction, by merely referring to the specification, so as to make it include something more than, or something different from, what its words express. * * * The claim is a statutory requirement, prescribed for the very purpose of making the patentee define precisely what his invention is; and it is unjust to the public, as well as an evasion of the law, to construe it in a manner different from the plain import of its terms." Giving this patentee the benefit of a grant that it did not precisely claim is no less "unjust to the public" and no less an evasion of R.S. § 4888 merely because done in the name of the "doctrine of equivalents."

In seeking to justify its emasculation of R.S. § 4888 by parading potential hardships which literal enforcement might conceivably impose on patentees who had for some reason failed to claim complete protection for their discoveries, the Court fails even to mention the program for alleviation of such hardships which Congress itself has provided. 35 U.S.C. § 64, 35 U.S.C.A. § 64, authorizes reissue of patents where a patent is "wholly or partly inoperative" due to certain errors arising from "inadvertence, accident, or mistake" of the patentee. And while the section does not expressly permit a patentee to expand his claim, this Court has reluctantly interpreted it to justify doing so. That interpretation, however, was accompanied by a warning that "Reissues for the enlargement of claims should be the exception and not the rule." *Miller v. Brass Co.*, 104 U.S. 350, 355, 26 L.Ed. 783. And Congress was careful to hedge the privilege of reissue by exacting conditions. It also entrusted the Patent Office, not the courts, with initial authority to determine whether expansion of a claim was justified, and barred suits for retroactive infringement based on such expansion. Like the Court's opinion, this congressional plan adequately protects patentees from "fraud," "piracy," and "stealing." Unlike the Court's opinion, it also protects business men from retroactive infringement suits and judicial expansion of a monopoly sphere beyond that which a patent expressly authorizes. The plan is just, fair, and reasonable. In effect it is nullified by this decision undercutting what the Court has heretofore recognized as wise safeguards. One need not be a prophet to suggest that today's rhapsody on the virtue of the "doctrine of equivalents" will, in direct contravention of the *Miller* case *supra*, make enlargement of patent claims the "rule" rather than the "exception."

Whatever the merits of the "doctrine of equivalents" where differences between the claims of a patent and the allegedly infringing product are *de minimis*, colorable only, and without substance, that doctrine should have no application to the facts of this case. For the differences between respondent's welding substance and petitioner's claimed flux were not nearly so slight. The claims relied upon here did not involve any mechanical structure or process where invention lay in the construction or method rather than in the materials used. Rather they were based wholly on using particular materials for a particular purpose. Respondent's assignors experimented with several metallic silicates, including that of manganese. According to the specifications (if these are to be considered) they concluded that while several were "more or less efficacious in our process, we prefer to use silicates of the alkaline earth metals." Several of their claims which this Court found too broad to be valid encompassed manganese silicate; the only claims found valid did not. Yet today the Court disregards that crucial deficiency, holding those claims infringed by a composition of which 88.49% by weight is manganese silicate.

In view of the intense study and experimentation of respondent's assignors with manganese silicate, it would be frivolous to contend that failure specifically to include that substance in a precise claim was unintentional. Nor does respondent attempt to give that or any other explanation for its omission. But the similar use of manganese in prior expired patents, referred to in the Court's opinion, raises far more than a suspicion that its elimination from the valid claims stemmed from fear that its inclusion by name might result in denial or subsequent invalidation of respondent's patent.

Under these circumstances I think petitioner had a right to act on the belief that this Court would follow the plain mandates of Congress that a patent's precise claims mark its monopoly boundaries, and that expansion of those claims to include manganese could be obtained only in a statutory reissue proceeding. The Court's ruling today sets the stage for more patent "fraud" and "piracy" against business than could be expected from faithful observance of the congressionally enacted plan to protect business against judicial expansion of precise patent claims. Hereafter a manufacturer cannot rely on what the language of a patent claims. He must be able, at the peril of heavy infringement damages, to forecast how far a court relatively unversed in a particular technological field will expand the claim's language after considering the testimony of technical experts in that field. To burden business enterprise on the assumption that men possess such a prescience bodes ill for the kind of competitive economy that is our professed goal.

The way specific problems are approached naturally has much to do with the decisions reached. A host of prior cases, to some of which I have referred, have treated the 17–year monopoly authorized by valid patents as a narrow exception to our competitive enterprise system. For that reason, they have emphasized the importance of leaving business men free to utilize all knowledge not preempted by the precise language of a patent claim. *E.g., Sontag Stores Co. v. Nut Co.*, 310 U.S. 281, 60 S.Ct. 961, 84 L.Ed. 1204, and cases there cited. In the *Sontag* case Mr. Justice McReynolds, speaking for a unanimous Court, said in part: "In the case under consideration the patentee might have included in the application for the original patent, claims broad enough to embrace petitioner's accused machine, but did not."

This "gave the public to understand" that whatever was not claimed "did not come within his patent and might rightfully be made by anyone." 310 U.S. at page 293, 60 S.Ct. at page 966, 967, 84 L.Ed. 1204.

The Court's contrary approach today causes it to retreat from this sound principle. The damages retroactively assessed against petitioner for what was authorized until today are but the initial installment on the cost of that retreat.

MR. JUSTICE DOUGLAS, dissenting.

The Court applies the doctrine of equivalents in a way which subverts the constitutional and statutory scheme for the grant and use of patents.

The claims of the patent are limited to a flux "containing a major proportion of alkaline earth metal silicate." Manganese silicate, the flux which is held to infringe, is not an alkaline earth metal silicate. It was disclosed in the application and then excluded from the claims. It therefore became public property. It was, to be sure, mentioned in the specifications. But the measure of the grant is to be found in the claims, not in the specifications. The specifications can be used to limit but never to expand the claim.

The Court now allows the doctrine of equivalents to erase those time-honored rules. Moreover, a doctrine which is said to protect against practicing "a fraud on a patent" is used to extend a patent to a composition which could not be patented. For manganese silicate had been covered by prior patents, now expired. Thus we end with a strange anomaly: a monopoly is obtained on an unpatented and unpatentable article.

Notes and Questions

1. *Literal infringement.* As the Court notes, the first step in resolving an infringement claim is to determine whether the accused product or process falls within the express language of a claim. Claims are comprised of a series of "limitations" (also called "elements") which in combination define the boundaries of the invention. To get a sense of this you should study some of the claims set forth in the case opinions in this Chapter. (See, e.g., footnote 5 of the *Diamond v. Diehr* case, *supra*, p. 108.) In order to literally infringe, a defendant's process or product must have every limitation, or element, of the claim. The fact that the defendant's product or process has additional elements will not necessarily avoid infringement.

While the language of the claim determines the scope of the invention, extrinsic material may be used in interpreting the claim. The specification, in particular, may serve as a dictionary to define the terms used in the claim. Other claims in the same patent and expert testimony may also be helpful. However, while these materials may be used to interpret the claim, they may not be used to add a limitation to the claim. See, e.g., E.I. du Pont de Nemours & Co. v. Phillips Petroleum Co., 849 F.2d 1430, 1433, 7 U.S.P.Q.2d 1129, 1131 (C.A.F.C.1988), *cert. denied* 488 U.S. 986, 109 S.Ct. 542, 102 L.Ed.2d 572 (1988).

2. *The doctrine of equivalents.* The doctrine of equivalents applies not just to compounds like the patented flux in *Graver*, but to all categories of inventions. Bear in mind that the question of equivalency is determined as of the date of infringement, so that the defendant's matter may be found equivalent, even if it was not known to be at the time the invention was made or the patent was issued. Marsh–McBirney, Inc. v. Montedoro–Whitney Corp., 882 F.2d 498, 504, 11 U.S.P.Q.2d 1794, 1798 (C.A.F.C.1989), *vacated* 498 U.S. 1061, 111 S.Ct. 775, 112 L.Ed.2d 838 (1991).

The Court states that the doctrine of equivalents applies if the invention "performs substantially the same function in substantially the same way to obtain the same result." What kinds of evidence are relevant to make this determination?

The equivalency test has not proven easy to apply, and the Court of Appeals for the Federal Circuit has struggled to refine it, with questionable success. While the *Graver* opinion refers to the equivalency of the patented invention and the accused process or device as a whole, the Federal Circuit has held, *en banc*, that equivalence must be established on an element-by-element basis:

> It is * * * well settled that each element of a claim is material and essential, and that in order for a court to find infringement, the plaintiff must show the presence of every element or its substantial equivalent in the accused device. To be a "substantial equivalent," the element substituted in the accused device for the element set forth in the claim must not be such as would substantially change the way in which the function of the claimed invention is performed.

Pennwalt Corp. v. Durand–Wayland, Inc., 833 F.2d 931, 935, 4 U.S.P.Q.2d 1737, 1741 (C.A.F.C. 1987), *cert. denied*, 485 U.S. 961, 108 S.Ct. 1226, 99 L.Ed.2d 426 (1988). This analysis is known as the "all-elements" rule.

In Corning Glass Works v. Sumitomo Electric U.S.A., 868 F.2d 1251, 1259, 9 U.S.P.Q.2d 1962, 1968 (C.A.F.C. 1989), a panel of the court lamented the "confusion sometimes encountered because of misunderstanding or misleading uses of the term 'element' in discussing claims." The court clarified:

> "Element" may be used to mean a single limitation, but it has also been used to mean a series of limitations which taken together, make up a component of the claimed invention. In the All Elements rule, "element" is used in the sense of a *limitation* of a claim.

The panel then elaborated that

> [a]n equivalent must be found for every limitation of the claim somewhere in an accused device, but not necessarily in a corresponding component, although that is generally the case.

Id. Thus, there need not be a one-to-one correspondence of components.

In Malta v. Schulmerich Carillons, Inc., 952 F.2d 1320, 1325–26, 21 U.S.P.Q.2d 1161, 1165 (C.A.F.C. 1991), *cert. denied* ___ U.S. ___, 112 S.Ct. 2942, 119 L.Ed.2d 566 (1992), another Federal Circuit panel clarified that the *Graver* tripartite function/way/result test need not be satisfied in order to find *limitations* equivalent:

> In order to prove infringement under the doctrine of equivalents, a patentee must show that the accused device performs substantially the same function in substantially the same way to achieve substantially the same result as the claimed device. The "substantially the same way" prong of this test may be met if an equivalent of a recited limitation has been substituted in the accused device. * * *
>
> * * * This court has never adopted the three prong approach to determining equivalency of a *limitation* * * *. *Pennwalt* did not set forth a test as to *how* one proves that an element in an accused device is the "substantial equivalent" of a claim limitation * * *. Thus, while comparison of function/way/result is an acceptable way of showing that structure in an accused device is the "substantial equivalent" of a claim limitation, it is not the only way to do so. * * * How equivalency to a required limitation is met necessarily varies from case to case. * * *

Thus, the court declined to provide a specific, generally applicable formula for determining equivalency to a claim limitation.

A number of articles have criticized the Federal Circuit's efforts. See, e.g., Adelman & Francione, *The Doctrine Equivalents in Patent Law: Questions that* Pennwalt *Did Not Answer*, 137 U. PA. L. REV. 673, 678–79 (1989) ("Unfortunately, *Pennwalt* did very little to resolve the ambiguities created by the doctrine [of equivalents]. In many respects, the choice of an element-by-element or entirety approach has little consequence for a fact-finder seeking guidance in answering the real question at issue: What is an 'equivalent?' * * * To compound the uncertainty, the Federal Circuit in *Pennwalt* indicated that it is prepared to allow the jury to decide in virtually every case whether the doctrine of equivalents applied."); Klein, *Establishing Infringement under the Doctrine of Equivalents after Malta*, 75 J. PAT. & TRADEMARK OFF. SOC. 5, 19 (1993) ("a great deal of ambiguity remains concerning the establishment of infringement under the doctrine of equivalents. By adopting vague standards and then refusing to apply them uniformly, the Federal Circuit has done little to clarify this issue."); Larson, *Balancing the Competing Policies Underlying the Doctrine of Equivalents in Patent Law*, 21 AIPLA Q.J. 1, 6–8 (1993) ("The doctrine of equivalents requires judges and juries with no technical training to determine whether parts of complex technology are equivalent to complex patent claims. The *Graver* formulation provides little or no guidance for such a determination. If the function of the device, the way in which the function is performed, and the result achieved are defined broadly, an accused product technically remote from the claimed subject matter can be characterized as equivalent. If the function, way, and result are defined narrowly, an accused product technically proximate to the claimed subject matter can be characterized as nonequivalent. * * * *Pennwalt* has resulted in little or no clarification of the doctrine of equivalents.")

What alternative approaches might the Federal Circuit take to accomplish the purposes set forth in *Graver*? Is the doctrine of equivalents really necessary? See Adelman & Francione, *supra*, at 715–728.

3. *Prior art.* The *Graver* Court makes a number of references to the prior art. Why is the prior art relevant to the question of infringement?

Apart from the uses the Court discusses, prior art in the relevant field of the invention may be important in two ways.

First, the range of equivalents the court will accord an invention depends upon the importance or "pioneer status" of the invention in its particular field. As the Supreme Court has explained:

> [T]he court first looks into the art to find what the real merit of the alleged discovery or invention is and whether it has advanced the art substantially. If it has done so, then the court is liberal in its construction of the patent to secure to the inventor the reward he deserves. If what he has done works only a slight step forward and that which he says is a discovery is on the border line between mere mechanical change and real invention, then his patent, if sustained, will be given a narrow scope and infringement will be found only in approximate copies of the new device. It is this differing attitude of the courts toward genuine discoveries and slight improvements that reconciles the sometimes apparently conflicting [breadth of equivalents accepted from one case to the next].

Eibel Process Co. v. Minnesota & Ontario Paper Co., 261 U.S. 45, 63, 43 S.Ct. 322, 328, 67 L.Ed. 523, 532 (1923). For an in-depth exploration of the economic impact of decisions concerning patent scope, see Merges & Nelson, *On the Complex Economics of Patent Scope*, 90 COLUM. L. REV. 839 (1990).

Second, the relevant prior art directly limits application of the doctrine of equivalents, for the doctrine of equivalents may never be used to give a patentee rights in the prior art. The patentee may not obtain through the doctrine of equivalents a scope of patent coverage that he could not have obtained directly from the PTO through literal claims. Wilson Sporting Goods Co. v. David Geoffrey & Associates, 904 F.2d 677, 14 U.S.P.Q.2d 1942 (C.A.F.C.1990), *cert. denied* 498 U.S. 992, 111 S.Ct. 537, 112 L.Ed.2d 547 (1990). In *Wilson*, the Federal Circuit stated a test for determining the impact of the prior art in applying the doctrine of equivalents:

> Whether prior art restricts the range of equivalents of what is literally claimed can be a difficult question to answer. To simplify analysis and bring the issue onto familiar turf, it may be helpful to conceptualize the limitation on the scope of equivalents by visualizing a *hypothetical* patent claim, sufficient in scope to *literally* cover the accused product. The pertinent question then becomes whether that hypothetical claim could have been allowed by the PTO over the prior art. If not, then it would be improper to permit the patentee to obtain that coverage in an infringement suit under the doctrine of equivalents. If the hypothetical claim could have been allowed, then *prior art* is not a bar to infringement under the doctrine of equivalents.

Id., 904 F.2d at 684–85, 14 U.S.P.Q.2d at 1498. For an interesting discussion of the *Wilson* and related cases, see Wexler, *Patent Law: Bridling the Doctrine of Equivalents—Preclusion by Prior Art*, [1991] ANN. SURV. AM. L. 571.

4. *Policy concerns.* What policy concerns underlie the dissenting justices' objections to the majority's application of the doctrine of equivalents in *Graver*? Justice Black discusses at some length the "reissue" procedure,

formally found at 35 U.S.C.A. § 64, now codified at 35 U.S.C.A. §§ 251–252. Review the provisions of sections 251 and 252.

Why does Justice Black consider the reissue procedure to be relevant? Why does he consider its use preferable to the majority's use of the doctrine of equivalents in *Graver*? What are the relative advantages and disadvantages of the two approaches to curing error from the standpoint of the patentee? From the public's standpoint?

5. *The reverse doctrine of equivalents.* In *Graver*, the majority notes that "where a device is so far changed in principle from a patented article that it performs the same or a similar function in a substantially different way, but nevertheless falls within the literal words of the claim, the doctrine of equivalents may be used to restrict the claim and defeat the patentee's action for infringement." This is known as the "reverse doctrine of equivalents." Situations justifying its application arise only rarely. For an example of its application, see SRI Int'l v. Matsushita Elec. Corp. 775 F.2d 1107, 227 U.S.P.Q. 577 (C.A.F.C. 1985) (en banc).

6. *Prosecution history estoppel.* "Prosecution history estoppel" is the term that the Federal Circuit prefers for a doctrine that was previously known as "file wrapper estoppel." The earlier name referred to the folder, or "file wrapper," that the PTO used to hold a patent application and the various documents generated in the course of prosecuting the application, including amendments, office actions, and correspondence between the examiner and the applicant or her attorney. The doctrine limits application of the doctrine of equivalents by binding the patentee to the amendments and representations she made limiting the breadth of patent coverage during the course of prosecution. If the patentee expressly relinquished breadth of coverage during prosecution in order to convince the PTO to grant a patent, she is estopped from recovering it in infringement litigation through application of the doctrine of equivalents. The court's decision in Mannesmann Demag Corp. v. Engineered Metal Products Co., Inc., 793 F.2d 1279, 230 U.S.P.Q. 45 (C.A.F.C. 1986), is illustrative.

The *Mannesmann* patent involved a vessel for a metal smelting furnace that included at least one cooling pipe coil to circulate water to protect the vessel from the corrosive action of hot slag. The claim at issue provided:

> 1. A vessel for a metal smelting furnace having a smelting zone including a heat-resistant interior wall, and cooling means for protecting the interior of said vessel, characterized by
>
> (a) at least a portion of the interior wall of said vessel above the smelting zone consisting of at least one cooling pipe coil;
>
> (b) said coil including fluid passage-forming sections;
>
> (c) said cooling pipe coil being exposed to the center of the vessel; and
>
> (d) neighboring sections of said coil *being arranged in a contacting relation.*

Id., 793 F.2d at 1281, 230 U.S.P.Q. at 46 (emphasis added). With regard to clause (d), the prosecution history indicated that the patentee's assignor had originally employed the term "closely adjacent" to describe the spacing between pipe sections. The examiner had objected to "closely adjacent" both on the ground that it was indefinite and on the ground that it failed to distinguish the invention from prior references. In response, the assignor substituted the words "in a contacting relation."

In the defendant's cooling pipe coil, the pipe sections were separated from neighboring pipe sections by a bar of about ⅝ inch diameter, which was welded to one side of a pipe section and separated from the neighboring section by a tolerance of 1/16 to 1/32 inch. In interpreting the claim language for purposes of determining whether literal infringement had occurred, the district court properly took the prosecution history into account and interpreted clause (d) to require that the pipe sections actually touch. Since defendant's did not, the Federal Circuit affirmed the district court's finding that there was no literal infringement.

The Federal Circuit also upheld the district court's finding of no infringement under the doctrine of equivalents, agreeing that the insertion of "in a contacting relation" into clause (d) barred the patentee's recourse to the doctrine of equivalents to cover the defendant's coils:

> The doctrine of prosecution history estoppel is "an equitable tool for determining the permissible scope of patent claims" as against a specific structure accused of infringement. This doctrine bars a patentee from construing its claims in a way that would resurrect subject matter previously surrendered during prosecution of the patent application, and thus prevents a patentee from enforcing its claims against otherwise legally equivalent structures if those structures were excluded by claim limitations added in order to avoid prior art.
>
> Amendment of claims during patent prosecution does not necessarily bar all benefit of the doctrine of equivalents. * * * Depending on the nature and purpose of an amendment, it may have a limiting effect within a spectrum ranging from great to small to zero. * * *
>
> Mannesmann thus argues that it is entitled to some range of equivalents, while accepting that it is not entitled to the original scope of its unamended claims. Mannesmann argues that in amending its claims to meet the examiner's rejections under 35 U.S.C. §§ 103 and 112, it relinquished no more than was necessary to distinguish the references. Mannesmann argues that it is entitled to the benefit of its inventive concept, plainly distinguished from the prior art, and that the claims retain a scope of equivalency that is more than sufficient to encompass the [defendant's] structure.
>
> Determination of the scope of an estoppel deriving from actions taken before the Patent and Trademark Office requires review of not only the nature of such actions, but the reasons therefor * * *. In cases where a patentee's amendments were not required in response to an examiner's rejection or critical to the allowance of the claims, no estoppel has been found. Similarly, estoppel is not necessarily created by an amendment designed only to remove a § 112 indefiniteness rejection.
>
> [Mannesmann's assignor's] application was rejected under 35 U.S.C. § 103 based on a patent to Hennenberger et al. (U.S. Patent No.

> 3,034,776, issued May 15, 1962) in view of certain patents to Moore and Wamser. These references were discussed in detail by the district court, principally in connection with validity, but are plainly pertinent to the court's interpretation of the claims. In changing "closely adjacent" to "in a contacting relation" and thereby obtaining allowance of the claims, [patentee's assignor] wrote that the claim "has now been amended to clearly recite the significant, novel and non-obvious features of the invention disclosed in the subject application ... wherein neighboring sections of the coil are arranged in a contacting relation".
>
> On the basis of this amendment the district court held that estoppel lies, even if the [defendant's] structure were equivalent to that of the claims. The district court found that Mannesmann was attempting "to reclaim the very thing it surrendered by way of amendment", and that Mannesmann was estopped to recover the "closely adjacent" scope it had relinquished. The district court held that limiting amendments made in response to rejections under 35 U.S.C. § 103 must be "strictly construed" * * *.
>
> The district court did not hold that Mannesmann is deprived of all equivalents to the invention as claimed in the '060 patent, and precedent does not so require. However, the enlarged claim interpretation that Mannesmann seeks to apply to the [defendant's] structure falls squarely within the claim scope that Mannesmann relinquished to overcome the cited references. There is little distance between "closely adjacent" and "in a contacting relation", and on these facts we discern no error in the district court's application of prosecution history estoppel to hold that [the patentee's] claims are not infringed.

Id., 793 F.2d at 1284–85, 230 U.S.P.Q. at 48–49.

Why should the reason for amendment matter? What, exactly, is the purpose of the doctrine of prosecution history estoppel? How does it differ from the common-law doctrine of equitable estoppel, applied in more general contexts?

How does one determine exactly what subject matter the patentee relinquished during the course of prosecution? According to the Court of Appeals for the Federal Circuit, the legal standard is "an objective one, measured from the vantage point of what a competitor was reasonably entitled to conclude, from the prosecution history, that the applicant gave up to procure issuance of the patent." Hoganas AB v. Dresser Industries, Inc., 9 F.3d 948, 952, 28 U.S.P.Q.2d 1936, 1939 (C.A.F.C. 1993). As the court explained:

> Ordinarily, the test for determining the meaning of a claim term is from the vantage point of one skilled in the art. This test would seem equally appropriate for determining what subject matter was relinquished in the context of prosecution history estoppel. Our precedent dealing with this specific question recites that the test is measured from the vantage point of a reasonable competitor. We do not see these formulations as necessarily inconsistent—the point is the knowledge of one reasonably skilled in the art who views the question from the perspective of a competitor in the marketplace.

Id., 9 F.3d at 952 n.15, 28 U.S.P.Q.2d at 1939 n.15.

The doctrine of prosecution history estoppel may apply even in the absence of an amendment to the claim the patentee is seeking to enforce. See, e.g., Builders Concrete, Inc. v. Bremerton Concrete Products Co., 757 F.2d 255, 225 U.S.P.Q. 240 (C.A.F.C. 1985) (amendment of a different claim may provide grounds for estoppel); Jonsson v. The Stanley Works, 903 F.2d 812, 14 U.S.P.Q.2d 1863 (C.A.F.C. 1990) (remarks made to the examiner to distinguish his invention from prior art may serve as grounds for estoppel). For a discussion of the history and development of the doctrine of prosecution history estoppel, see Hantman, *Prosecution History Estoppel*, 73 J. PAT. & TRADEMARK OFF. SOC. 121, 235 (1991).

G. DEFENSES AND REMEDIES

1. *Remedies*

STATE INDUSTRIES, INC. v. MOR–FLO INDUSTRIES, INC.

United States Court of Appeals for the Federal Circuit, 1989.
883 F.2d 1573, 12 U.S.P.Q.2d 1026, *cert. denied*
493 U.S. 1022, 110 S.Ct. 725, 107 L.Ed.2d 744 (1990).

MAYER, CIRCUIT JUDGE.

Mor–Flo Industries, Inc. and its subsidiary, American Appliance Manufacturing Corporation (Mor–Flo), infringed State Industries, Inc's. (State) Patent No. 4,447,377, covering a method of insulating water heaters with foam. After the damages trial, the district court awarded State lost profits on approximately 40% of Mor–Flo's infringing sales and a royalty of 3% on the remaining 60%. It concluded that Mor–Flo's infringement was not willful and denied enhanced damages and attorney's fees. We affirm the judgment insofar as it awards lost profits and a 3% royalty, but vacate and remand for a redetermination of the judgment that the infringement was not willful.

BACKGROUND

The '377 patent claims a method of insulating the tank of a water heater by using polyurethane foam. The method includes wrapping the tank with a plastic sheet shaped as an envelope, installing a surrounding jacket and cover, pouring foam through an opening in the cover into the envelope, and then plugging the opening. The method contains the liquid foam while it rises and prevents it from invading areas, such as the electrical components and combustion chamber, which must be kept free of foam. State also has another patent, U.S. Patent No. 4,527,543, not contested here, that claims water heaters using the '377 envelope construction.

Mor–Flo's method found to be infringing used a cylindrical piece of plastic that was pulled over the top of the tank with fiberglass positioned around the combustion chamber at the bottom of the tank. The "sleeve" was taped below the top of the fiberglass. A jacket was then installed over the tank and sleeve, a top was installed, and foam was shot into the sleeve through an opening in the top.

In the liability trial, Mor–Flo maintained that the sleeve was not an "envelope" or " 'wrapped' around the tank" as required by the '377 patent. The sleeve, however, was identical to an embodiment shown in the patent (partial envelope), and was merely secured differently at the bottom of the tank. The illustrated embodiment also revealed a pull-over structure similar to Mor–Flo's sleeve. The district court found that it was especially damaging to Mor–Flo that it did not conceive of its "strikingly similar" sleeve method until after purchasing and disassembling a State foam-insulated water heater. Therefore, the court held that Mor–Flo's method literally infringed the '377. The district court alternatively held that it infringed the patent under the doctrine of equivalents.

The water heater industry is intensely competitive and marked by small profit margins. The invention is pertinent to all water heaters, but the infringement at issue here is restricted to residential gas water heaters, in particular those deemed "energy efficient" by the American Society of Heating, Refrigeration and Air Conditioning Engineers. Foam provides greater insulating capacity than the other alternative, fiberglass; therefore, foam-insulated heaters have cost advantages in terms of material, packaging and freight. The greater insulating capacity enables foam-insulated heaters to meet the energy code requirements imposed by many states by using less space than fiberglass-insulated heaters. The density of foam also strengthens the outer jacket of the water heater and makes it more resistant to denting.

In deciding the damages question, the district court faced three issues: lost profits, reasonable royalty and willful infringement. Infringement occurred between May 8, 1984, when the patent issued, and June 9, 1986, when Mor–Flo switched to the noninfringing method of fiberglass foam stops, which eliminates need for the envelope taught by the patent in suit yet keeps foam from invading the combustion chamber. State produced evidence of lost sales, and took the position that it should recover lost profits for its market share of Mor–Flo's infringing sales and a reasonable royalty for the remainder. It also asked increased damages for willful infringement and attorney fees.

The district court agreed with State in the award of lost profits for part of its damages and a royalty for the rest. The court found there was a growing demand for foam-insulated water heaters, the '377 patent was the first method developed to meet this demand, and there were no other methods available during the pertinent period that were either noninfringing or acceptable as substitutes. Specifically, the court found "that, during the period of infringement, all but one of State's competitors in the United States sold foam insulated water heaters made using State's patented method, or one of a strikingly similar configuration, and/or Denton Patent No. 4,527,543 * * *."

A.O. Smith Corporation, the only clearly noninfringing competitor used the less preferable fiberglass insulation. Hoyt also sold only fiberglass-insulated heaters until 1985 when it added a foam-insulated heater to its inventory. The court found that fiberglass was not an acceptable substitute for foam because of foam's advantages in reducing the size of water heaters, increasing resistance to denting, and meeting governmental energy standards.

The court also found that State was capable of producing during the relevant period, and had sales and distribution capacity to ship and sell, sufficient foam-insulated water heaters to exploit its market share of Mor–Flo's sales. Finding that State has approximately 40% of the gas water heater market nationwide, the court awarded State the profits it lost on 40% of the sales of 754,181 infringing Mor–Flo water heaters.

For the remaining 60% of Mor–Flo's sales, State asked for a royalty of 8 to 10%. Mor–Flo presented no evidence of what it would have paid for a license, but argued that in no event should the royalty rate be above its net profit margin which, for the seventeen months preceding the date infringement began, was 2.1%. The district court awarded a royalty of 3% on the remaining 60% of infringing sales. Finally, the court concluded the infringement was not willful because Mor–Flo relied in good faith on advice of outside counsel that its process was not infringing. Mor–Flo appeals both the award of actual damages and the reasonableness of the royalty. State cross-appeals the reasonableness of the royalty and the court's failure to hold Mor–Flo's infringement willful and to award increased damages and attorney's fees.

DISCUSSION

Deciding how much to award as damages is not an exact science, and the methodology of assessing and computing damages is committed to the sound discretion of the district court. A challenger must show that "the district court abused its discretion by basing its award on clearly erroneous factual findings, legal error, or a manifest error of judgment." *DataScope Corp. v. SMEC, Inc.*, 879 F.2d 820, 823–24, 11 USPQ2d 1321, 1323 (Fed.Cir.1989) (quoting *Nickson Indus. v. Rol Mfg. Co.*, 847 F.2d 795, 798, 6 USPQ2d 1878, 1879 (Fed.Cir.1988)).

The measure of damages is an amount which will compensate the patent owner for the pecuniary loss sustained because of the infringement. But the floor for a damage award is no less than a reasonable royalty, and the award may be split between lost profits as actual damages to the extent they are proven and a reasonable royalty for the remainder.

A.

To get lost profits as actual damages, the patent owner must demonstrate that there was a reasonable probability that, but for the infringement, it would have made the infringer's sales. But "[t]he patent holder does not need to negate *all* possibilities that a purchaser might have bought a different product or might have foregone the purchase altogether." *Paper Converting Mach. Co. v. Magna–Graphics Corp.*, 745 F.2d 11, 21, 223 USPQ 591, 598 (Fed.Cir.1984).

A standard way of proving lost profits, first announced in *Panduit Corp. v. Stahlin Bros. Fibre Works*, 575 F.2d 1152, 1156, 197 USPQ 726, 730 (6th Cir.1978), is for the patent owner to prove: "(1) demand for the patented product, (2) absence of acceptable noninfringing substitutes, (3) his manufacturing and marketing capability to exploit the demand, and (4) the amount of the profit he would have made." The district court relied heavily on this test and we have accepted it as a nonexclusive standard for determining lost profits. With only slight modification we think it fits here and confirms the district court's judgment.

Absence of Substitutes and Market Share

This is the first time we have considered whether lost profits can be based on market share. * * *

We start with the presumption that the judgment of the district court is correct, of course, and that the only limit on its discretion in selecting a remedy is that it be adequate to compensate for the damages suffered as a result of the infringement. Any doubt about the correctness of the award is resolved against the infringer.

Frequently, the patent owner and infringer are the only suppliers in the market, and the owner is seeking to recover profits lost through every sale made by the infringer. In the two-supplier market, it is reasonable to assume, provided the patent owner has the manufacturing and marketing capabilities, that it would have made the infringer's sales. In these instances, the *Panduit* test is usually straightforward and dispositive.

Here we have multiple competitors and the patent owner contends that all the competitors infringed or sold a far less preferable alternative—fiberglass. The district court made the absence of acceptable substitutes, *Panduit* item (2), a neutral factor by crediting all the other competitors with their market shares as State requested. If the court is correct in its finding that the other competitors were likely infringers of one or the other of State's patents, State would have been entitled to their shares of the market on top of its own, and a correspondingly greater share of Mor–Flo's sales. If it is wrong in whole or in part, State would have been entitled to its current share or to a lesser increase in share. We need not decide which it is because it would make no difference to the outcome. State would get at least what it asked for, because as discussed further below the district court found, and we agree, that State's share of the market was proven.

But Mor–Flo should not complain because if anything it received a windfall from this approach. To the extent infringing competitors got credit for sales that should have gone to State, the share of the market against which Mor–Flo's damages might be assessed is reduced. So we think that in these circumstances the presence or absence of acceptable noninfringing alternatives does not matter. The question then becomes whether an established market share combined with the other *Panduit* factors is sufficient to show State's loss to a reasonable probability.

Demand

At the infringement phase of this case, the district court said, "Both sides admit that there was a great need to develop foam insulated heaters in the late 1970's. The patented method solved the[ ]problems [of foam leakage and invasion], and was apparently the first to do so in the water heater industry." In a 1979 internal memo, Mor–Flo's own vice president of engineering stated: "With reference to heaters with foam insulation, it was felt that the word foam has a magic sound to it at this time, and even if a fiberglass were available that would be equal to foam, a foam insulated heater would be required."

After the introduction of foam insulation, State's annual sales jumped from less than two hundred thousand to more than four hundred thousand heaters between 1984 and 1986, and accounted for 1,275,525 sales for a net revenue of $155.2 million. Sales of foam heaters by Mor–Flo amounting to more than $83.9 million in total revenue are further evidence of demand. Mor–Flo used the foam insulation feature to "sell up" its entire line of heaters in its trade brochures. Three of the other four competitors used foam insulation. At the damages trial, Mor–Flo presented no evidence on what, if any, unique value any other components of its water heater added.

In describing the demand for State's method, the district court said, "Although there was no demand by customers or consumers of residential gas water heaters that heaters be foamed in accordance with any particular method, during the period of infringement of State's patent, there was no acceptable non-infringing method of satisfactorily foaming gas water heaters in the market place." In effect then, the demand went to the method.

* * *

Manufacturing and Marketing

The finding that State has a 40% national market share is unassailable, and Mor–Flo does not seriously contend otherwise, or that State did not have the capacity to produce enough heaters to satisfy at least 40% of Mor–Flo's sales. * * *

* * * We accordingly agree with the court that it is probable, at least, that State could have met the demand.

Amount of Profit

The district court awarded State its incremental profit on foam-insulated gas water heaters reflecting the percentage of sales revenue State lost because of Mor–Flo's infringement that would have been its profit. This approach is well established and appropriate for determining damages for patent infringement. There is some testimony that fixed costs might have varied slightly, but the district court did not abuse its discretion in concluding that any increase in fixed costs was minimal and that award of incremental profits was appropriate. No greater precision is required.

The court based the award on the profit margin of the heater as a unit in accord with the entire market value rule, which permits recovery of damages based on the value of the entire apparatus containing several features, where the patent related feature is the basis for customer demand. In the face of the district court's finding to the contrary, Mor–Flo now argues that foam insulation was not the basis for consumer demand and several unidentified nonpatented components were key. But it did not identify or present evidence of the value of these nonpatented components. In any event, no components can be used separately, except as spare and repair parts for which State does not claim damages. *See Kori Corp. v. Wilco Marsh Buggies & Draglines, Inc.*, 761 F.2d 649, 656, 225 USPQ 985, 989 (Fed.Cir.1985) (the entire market rule is properly applied when the nonpatented devices cannot be sold without the patented feature). There is no merit to this argument and we leave undisturbed the district court's adoption of the entire market rule.

In our view, the foregoing discussion compels the conclusion that the district court acted well within its discretion when it awarded damages for Mor–Flo's infringing activity based on State's share of the market. The court had the obligation to decide the case, and to decide it on the evidence and theories the parties proposed. * * * [O]n the record actually made, there was sufficient evidence for the court to find facts and draw inferences that support its damage award.

B.

The only direct evidence on what a reasonable royalty would have been is testimony of State's president that he would have asked for 8 to 10% of Mor–Flo's infringing sales, and its expert's declaration that a reasonable royalty would have been 8% of net infringing sales. Mor–Flo's actual net profit margin was 2.1% for the seventeen months preceding issuance of the patent, and Mor–Flo argues that it should pay a royalty no higher than that. Indeed, it says the rate should be minimal—before the district court it urged an effective rate of .163%.

The determination of a reasonable royalty, however, is based not on the infringer's profit margin, but on what a willing licensor and licensee would bargain for at hypothetical negotiations on the date infringement started. There is no rule that a royalty be no higher than the infringer's net profit margin. State's was a proven process upon which Mor–Flo had already built an established, successful line of heaters, and which it had expanded upon since its introduction in 1981. The value of foam to Mor–Flo was obvious: it never considered fiberglass as an alternative and risked infringement with foam insulation.

The value of collateral sales could also be factored into the royalty rate. Foam insulation was used to promote Mor–Flo's entire line of heaters. And it was not inappropriate for the district court to consider gross profits. Mor–Flo's gross profit during the preceding seventeen months was 19.6% with a net incremental profit of 17.48%. Finally, during the period of infringement, Mor–Flo's net profits varied from 5.9% to 7.3%. In light of all this, it seems to us the district court could very well conclude that a royalty of 3% of Mor–Flo's net sales is reasonable.

Mor–Flo repeats the argument that there were other methods available—the Rheem patented plastic foam belt, the "top-off" method, and the fiberglass foam stop. As discussed earlier, State has not shown that the "top-off" method or fiberglass foam stop were available during the period of infringement. The district court may have overlooked that the Rheem patented plastic foam belt might have provided an alternative way to foam insulate heaters, but Mor–Flo presented no evidence that it could have licensed the Rheem foam belt, and at what cost. Again, the district court could only decide the case on the evidence before it, and we see no objection to its decision not to allow Mor–Flo to rely on the availability of third party patents to mitigate damages.

Turning to State's cross-appeal, the district court found that the water heater industry was intensely competitive with small profit margins and fiberglass was a lesser alternative that manufacturers, however reluctantly, would opt for if the licensing fee for foam was too high. State argues that fiberglass was simply not an alternative, but it is undisputed that fiberglass-insulated heaters were and are sold in direct competition with foam-insulated ones. So, notwithstanding State's asserted hope to license the method in the 8 to 10% range, it was well within the district court's province to conclude it would not have succeeded, that potential licensees would have stayed with lesser alternatives promising some profit, rather than risk losing money by signing on at that high a rate. The award of a 3% royalty may be too low for State and too high for Mor–Flo, but the district court did not abuse its discretion in reaching it.

C.

Willful infringement is a question of fact reviewed under the clearly erroneous standard. To establish willful infringement, a plaintiff must prove by clear and convincing evidence that the defendant acted with no reasonable basis for believing it had the right to do so. There are no "hard and fast *per se* rules," and the finding is based on the totality of the circumstances.

In its finding of nonwillfulness, the district court stated:

> Under the totality of the circumstances in this case, Mor–Flo/American should have known that their method of foaming gas residential water heaters infringed State's patent. Nevertheless, the Court finds that the evidence is insufficient to establish clearly and convincingly that Mor–Flo/American actually knew that their method infringed State's patent. Apparently, Mor–Flo/American did rely on advice of counsel. The advice was erroneous, but there is no evidence that Mor–Flo/American knew that the advice was erroneous. Thus, Mor–Flo/American's infringement was not willful and the Court will not award punitive damages in this case.

The standard for proving willfulness, however, is "whether, under all the circumstances, a reasonable person would prudently conduct himself with any confidence that a court might hold the patent invalid or not infringed." *Ryco, Inc. v. Ag–Bag Corp.*, 857 F.2d 1418, 1428, 8 USPQ2d 1323, 1331 (Fed.Cir.1988). Actual knowledge is not required. Therefore, the court's finding that Mor–Flo should have known of the infringement is inconsistent with its finding of nonwillfulness. But the district court also found that Mor–Flo relied in good faith on the erroneous advice of counsel that their method was not infringing. On the other hand, it said that Mor–Flo "purposely patterned its foaming method upon State's;" copying is evidence of willful infringement.

In view of the unresolved conflicting evidence, we vacate the judgment insofar as it denies increased damages under 35 U.S.C. § 284, and remand to the district court to reconsider whether a finding of willful infringement and enhanced damages is justified. Because this could also affect its conclusion on attorney's fees, we do not reach them.

* * *

Notes and Questions

1. *Monetary Relief.* Section 284 of the Patent Act provides that upon finding for the claimant, "the court shall award the claimant damages adequate to compensate for the infringement, but in no event less than a reasonable royalty for the use made of the invention by the infringer, together with interest and costs." Regardless of whether the damages are found by a jury or the court, the court "may increase the damages up to three times the amount found or assessed." Section 285 adds that the court may, "in exceptional cases," award reasonable attorney fees to the prevailing party.

a) Compensatory damages. Compensatory damages usually take the form of lost profits or a reasonable royalty. Both measures are illustrated in the *State Industries* case.

(1) Lost profits. According to the *State Industries* opinion, what is the proper standard for proving lost profits? Can you explain why each of the four factors set forth in *Panduit* is relevant to satisfying that standard? Did State Industries ask for too little under this measure? How would you have advised it to approach the lost profits measure?

The Federal Circuit approved the district court's use of the "incremental profit" or "incremental income" approach to computing lost profits. What does this entail? The Federal Circuit has explained:

> The approach recognizes that it does not cost as much to produce unit N + 1 if the first N (or fewer) units produced already have paid the fixed costs. Thus fixed costs—those costs which do not vary with increases in production, such as management salaries, property taxes, and insurance—are excluded when determining profits.

Paper Converting Machine Co. v. Magna–Graphics Corp., 745 F.2d 11, 22, 223 U.S.P.Q. 591, 599 (C.A.F.C. 1984).

The *State Industries* court also approved the district court's application of the "entire market value" rule. The *Magna-Graphics* court elaborated on this provision, as well:

> The "entire market value rule" allows for the recovery of damages based on the value of an entire apparatus containing several features, even though only one feature is patented. * * * [U]nder the entire market value rule:
>
> > [I]t is not the physical joinder or separation of the contested items that determines their inclusion in or exclusion from the compensation base, so much as their financial and marketing dependence on the patented item under standard marketing procedures for the goods in question.

Magna-Graphics, 745 F.2d at 23–24, 223 U.S.P.Q. at 599–600 (quoting Leesona Corp. v. United States, 599 F.2d 958, 974, 202 U.S.P.Q. 424, 439 (Ct.Cl. 1981)). The *Magna-Graphics* court noted that while the unpatented components encompassed by the entire market value rule usually are part of a single machine, physically separate components, such as auxiliary equipment used with the patented invention, can qualify under the rule, even though the patentee could not prevent manufacture or sale of them. The court stressed that the deciding factor is

> whether "[n]ormally the patentee (or its licensee) can anticipate sale of such unpatented components as well as of the patented" ones. If in all reasonable probability the patent owner would have made the sales which the infringer has made, what the patent owner in reasonable probability would have netted from the sales denied to him is the measure of his loss, and the infringer is liable for that.

Id. (quoting Tektronix, Inc. v. United States, 552 F.2d 343, 351, 193 U.S.P.Q. 385, 393 (Ct.Cl.1977)).

(2) A reasonable royalty. Section 284 states that the damage award shall not be "less than a reasonable royalty." The Federal Circuit has stressed that

> the purpose of this alternative is not to provide a simple accounting method, but to set a floor below which the courts are not authorized to go. * * * [an award based on a reasonable royalty] is suited to circumstances where there is an established royalty or licensing program, or if the patentee is not itself in the business, or if profits are too speculative to estimate.

Del Mar Avionics, Inc. v. Quinton Instrument Co., 836 F.2d 1320, 1326, 1328, 5 U.S.P.Q.2d 1255, 1260 (C.A.F.C. 1987). The fact of infringement itself establishes injury, because the patentee's right to exclude has been violated. Thus, the patentee may recover damages based on a reasonable royalty even if it can show no actual pecuniary loss at all. If the patentee can demonstrate lost profits that exceed the reasonable royalty rate, however, that will be the preferred measure, since the mission of the court is ensure that the patentee is fully compensated.

According to the *State Industries* court, what is the proper standard for determining a reasonable royalty? What kinds of evidence are likely to be relevant to this determination? See Georgia–Pacific v. U.S. Plywood Corp.,

318 F.Supp. 1116, 166 U.S.P.Q. 235 (S.D.N.Y.1970), *modified* 446 F.2d 295, 170 U.S.P.Q. 369 (2d Cir.1971), *cert. denied* 404 U.S. 870, 92 S.Ct. 105, 30 L.Ed.2d 114, 171 U.S.P.Q. 322 (1971).

(3) Prejudgment interest. In General Motors Corp. v. Devex Corp., 461 U.S. 648, 103 S.Ct. 2058, 76 L.Ed.2d 211, 217 U.S.P.Q. 1185 (1983), the Supreme Court stressed the importance of prejudgment interest awards, explaining:

> Under the pre–1946 statute, the owner of a patent could recover both his own damages and the infringer's profits. A patent owner's ability to recover the infringer's profits reflected the notion that he should be able to force the infringer to disgorge the fruits of the infringement even if it caused him no injury. In 1946 Congress excluded consideration of the infringer's gain by eliminating the recovery of his profits, the determination of which had often required protracted litigation. At the same time, Congress sought to ensure that the patent owner would in fact receive full compensation for "any damages" he suffered as a result of the infringement. Accordingly, Congress expressly provided in § 284 that the court "shall award the claimant damages *adequate to compensate* for the infringement." (Emphasis added.)
>
> The standard governing the award of prejudgment interest under § 284 should be consistent with Congress' overriding purpose of affording patent owners complete compensation. In light of that purpose, we conclude that prejudgment interest should ordinarily be awarded. In the typical case an award of prejudgment interest is necessary to ensure that the patent owner is placed in as good a position as he would have been in had the infringer entered into a reasonable royalty agreement. An award of interest from the time that the royalty payments would have been received merely serves to make the patent owner whole, since his damages consist not only of the value of the royalty payments but also of the foregone use of the money between the time of infringement and the date of the judgment.

Id., 461 U.S. at 654–56, 103 S.Ct. at 2062–63, 76 L.Ed.2d at 217–18.

Prejudgment interest may prove to be a very significant item in the patentee's recovery. In the protracted *Devex* litigation, for example, the lower court determined that the patentee was entitled to a reasonable royalty of $8,813,945.50 for the defendant's infringement. It awarded prejudgment interest of $11,022,854.97.

The courts have some discretion in setting the interest rate, and often award compound interest at a market rate. See, e.g., Lam, Inc. v. Johns–Manville Corp., 718 F.2d 1056, 219 U.S.P.Q. 670 (C.A.F.C. 1983).

A number of recent articles explore the Federal Circuit's approach to measuring damages. See, e.g., Janicke, *Contemporary Issues in Patent Damages*, 42 AM. U. L. REV. 691 (1993); Pincus, *The Computation of Damages in Patent Infringement Actions*, 5 HARV. J. L. & TECH. 95 (1991); Filardi, *The Adequacy of Compensation for Patent Infringement—An Analysis of Monetary Relief under 35 U.S.C. § 284*, 3 FORDHAM ENT. MEDIA & INTELL. PROP. L. F. 56 (1992).

b. Enhanced damages and attorney fees. Section 284 provides that the court may increase the actual damages up to three times. According to the *State Industries* court, what is the appropriate standard for determining whether such enhanced damages are warranted? What sort of evidence is relevant? What is the purpose underlying the enhanced damages provision? For a thorough exploration of the "advice of counsel" defense, see Sirilla, Edgell, & Hess, *The Advice of Counsel Defense to Increased Patent Damages*, 74 J. PAT. & TRADEMARK OFF. SOC. 705 (1992).

Section 285 permits the court, in its discretion, to award attorney fees to the prevailing party "in exceptional cases." An exceptional case may be found when the losing defendant's infringement was willful, or when either losing party has acted in bad faith—for example, when the losing party (plaintiff or defendant) pursued or conducted the infringement litigation in bad faith. See generally 5 D.S. CHISUM, PATENTS: A TREATISE ON THE LAW OF PATENTABILITY, VALIDITY AND INFRINGEMENT §§ 20.03 [4][b] & [c] (1991).

Does patent law overemphasize considerations of the morality of parties' conduct? See Chisum, *Patent Law and the Presumption of Moral Regularity: A Critical Review of Recent Federal Circuit Decisions on Inequitable Conduct and Willful Infringement*, 69 J. PAT. & TRADEMARK OFF. SOC. 27 (1987).

Review Patent Act section 287(a), which provides for marking goods with notice of patent. Failure to properly mark patented articles may result in denial of damages for infringements occurring before the defendant received actual notice of the infringement.

2. *Injunctive Relief.* Courts routinely grant permanent injunctions against further infringement in the final resolution of patent infringement suits. Historically, however, courts have been far more hesitant to grant requests for preliminary injunctions to prevent alleged infringement during the course of the litigation. A preliminary injunction's potential impact on competition is considerable: an injunction against making, using, offering to sell, selling or importing a product during the course of protracted patent litigation could permanently injure the defendant's competitive position. If the defendant ultimately is acquitted, it may never regain its market share, notwithstanding the plaintiff's posting of a bond to reimburse it for losses incurred as a result of the injunction. The only realistic alternative may be to settle on disadvantageous terms, which also may be injurious to competition.

In Smith Int'l, Inc. v. Hughes Tool Co., 718 F.2d 1573, 1578–79, 219 U.S.P.Q. 686, 690–91 (C.A.F.C.1983), *cert. denied* 464 U.S. 996, 104 S.Ct. 493, 78 L.Ed.2d 687 (1983), the newly created Court of Appeals for the Federal Circuit described the state of the law concerning preliminary injunctions in patent cases as it existed at that time:

> The standard for granting such relief has been characterized as "unusually stringent." * * * The usual requirement of a showing of probability of success on the merits before a preliminary injunction will issue has historically been even stronger in a patent case. Besides having to prove title to the patent, it has been stated as a general proposition that the movant must show that the patent is beyond question valid and

> infringed. In order to meet the burden of showing validity, the movant has sometimes been required to show either that his patent has previously been adjudicated valid, that there has been public acquiescence to its validity, or that there is conclusive direct technical evidence proving its validity. However, other courts have employed a less stringent standard of proof on the issue of validity. The basis for the more severe rule appears to be both a distrust of and unfamiliarity with patent issues and a belief that the ex parte examination by the Patent and Trademark Office is inherently unreliable.
>
> As with preliminary injunctions in other types of cases, the movant is also required to demonstrate in a patent case that he will suffer immediate irreparable harm if the injunction is not granted. Some courts refuse to find irreparable injury where the alleged infringer is solvent and money will adequately compensate the injury. However, at least one court is of the opinion that where the showing on patent validity is very strong, invasion of the inventor's right to exclude granted by the patent laws should be sufficient irreparable harm without a showing that the infringer is financially irresponsible.
>
> Finally, where relevant, the court should take into account both the possibility of harm to other interested persons from the grant or denial of the injunction, and the public interest. In reaching its decision, the district court must consider the above factors and balance all of the elements. No one element will necessarily be dispositive of the case.

In *Smith*, the court adopted the rule that a clear showing of validity and infringement would permit the court to presume irreparable injury. Two years later, in Atlas Powder Co. v. Ireco Chemicals, 773 F.2d 1230, 1233, 227 U.S.P.Q. 289, 292 (C.A.F.C.1985), the Federal Circuit rejected an argument that validity and infringement must be demonstrated "beyond question:"

> [Defendant] is arguing for a rule, said to be followed by various other circuits, that [the patentee] must prove validity and infringement "beyond question," in order to meet its burden of proof on irreparable harm.
>
> The burden upon the movant should be no different in a patent case than for other kinds of intellectual property, where, generally, only a "clear showing" is required. Requiring a "final adjudication," "full trial," or proof "beyond question" would support the issuance of a permanent injunction and nothing would remain to establish the liability of the accused infringer. That is not the situation before us. We are dealing with a provisional remedy which provides equitable *preliminary* relief. Thus, when a patentee "clearly shows" that his patent is valid and infringed, a court may, after a balance of all of the competing equities, preliminarily enjoin another from violating the rights secured by the patent.

What competing equities should be balanced, and how? The court's finding in *Atlas* provides some insights. In that case the accused infringer argued that a preliminary injunction would cause it, as well as the mining industry it served, irreparable injury. The allegedly infringing products accounted for 66% of its total sales. It would have to lay off approximately

200 employees as a result of the injunction, though the patent at issue would expire within a year. The Federal Circuit was unimpressed:

> Balancing the equities is within the discretion of the district court. It found, on the basis of Atlas's strong showing of validity and infringement, that the injury to Ireco was not sufficient to outweigh the injury to Atlas's patent rights. We are unpersuaded that the district court abused its discretion in this respect.
>
> The fact that the patent has only one year to run is not a factor in favor of Ireco in the balance of equities. Patent rights do not peter out as the end of the patent term, usually 17 years, is approached.

Id., 773 F.2d at 1234, 227 U.S.P.Q. at 293. Under what kinds of circumstances might a defendant be able to demonstrate that the balance of equities tips in its favor? See 5 D.S. CHISUM, PATENTS: A TREATISE ON THE LAW OF PATENTABILITY, VALIDITY AND INFRINGEMENT § 20.04[1] (1991).

What about the public interest factor? In Hybritech Inc. v. Abbott Laboratories, 849 F.2d 1446, 1458, 7 U.S.P.Q.2d 1191, 1201 (C.A.F.C. 1988), the court noted that "the focus of the district court's public interest analysis should be whether there exists some critical public interest that would be injured by the grant of preliminary relief." In that case, the court upheld the district court's decision to exclude Abbott's allegedly infringing cancer test kits and hepatitis kits from the preliminary injunction order due to the public interest in having those products readily available. It also upheld the district court's decision to preliminarily enjoin sale of Abbott's other allegedly infringing medical products. In the case of these products, Abbot argued that 1) the diagnostic community relied upon the products; 2) forcing the public to switch vendors would be expensive and time consuming; and 3) supply shortages to the public might result because the patentee allegedly had experienced substantial difficulties in filling orders quickly. After considering these arguments, the district court found that, as to these products, the public interest in enforcing valid patents outweighed the public interest considerations that Abbott invoked.

2. *Defenses*

NOTE: PATENT MISUSE

Concerns about the anticompetitive effects of patents underlie and shape patent law throughout, but perhaps most directly through the doctrine of patent misuse. "Patent misuse" may occur when a patentee uses her patent as leverage to obtain more market power than Congress intended to convey through the grant of a patent. Using a patent in a manner that violates the antitrust laws constitutes misuse, but the patent misuse doctrine has not been expressly restricted to antitrust violations.

Perhaps the most common form of patent misuse has been the "tying" arrangement: conditioning a license to make, use or sell the patented invention upon the licensee's purchase of an unpatented product from the patentee, or taking another license under a separate patent. Courts have reasoned that in imposing such "packaging" arrangements, the patentee unfairly uses the market power conferred by the patent to gain an advantage in sales of things falling outside the scope of the patent claims.

The doctrine of patent misuse gives an accused patent infringer a defense that is similar to the "unclean hands" doctrine traditionally applied in courts of equity. If the defendant convinces the court that the plaintiff has engaged in patent misuse, the court will simply refuse to enforce the otherwise valid and infringed patent until the misuse stops and the market effects of the misuse have been dissipated. It is not necessary for the defendant to demonstrate that he himself has been damaged by the alleged misuse. See generally 5 D.S. CHISUM, PATENTS: A TREATISE ON THE LAW OF PATENTABILITY, VALIDITY AND INFRINGEMENT § 19.04 (1991).

In many respects, the concepts of patent misuse and contributory infringement rest on antithetical underpinnings, and it is useful to consider the development of both doctrines together, in order to understand the scope of the misuse doctrine today. The Supreme Court provided a thorough review of the development of the patent misuse and contributory infringement doctrines in Dawson Chemical Co. v. Rohm & Haas Co., 448 U.S. 176, 100 S.Ct. 2601, 65 L.Ed.2d 696, 206 U.S.P.Q. 385 (1980).

The courts developed the doctrine of contributory infringement first, and expanded it to the point that it permitted considerable anticompetitive behavior on the part of patentees. For example, a patentee might sell its patented mimeograph machine with a license provision that restricted purchasers/licensees to use of the machine with supplies, including "staple articles" such as ink, purchased from the patentee. If the licensee later used the machine with ink purchased from someone other than the patentee, the patentee could sue the licensee for direct infringement and sue the seller of the ink for contributory infringement, as well, if the requisite knowledge could be demonstrated. See Henry v. A.B. Dick Co., 224 U.S. 1, 32 S.Ct. 364, 56 L.Ed. 645 (1912). This enabled patentees to exert considerable control in markets for unpatented, common-place goods. The prospect of contributory infringement claims against sellers of products related to the patented invention, and the market opportunities this prospect provided, fueled such tying arrangements.

In reaction to growing concerns about their anticompetitive effect, courts developed the patent misuse doctrine. To do so, they turned to the rule that the scope of a patent monopoly must be limited to the invention described in the patent claims. The Supreme Court ruled, in Motion Picture Patents Co. v. Universal Film Mfg. Co., 243 U.S. 502, 37 S.Ct. 416, 61 L.Ed. 871 (1917), that a patentee could not license use of its patented film feeder for use in projection of motion pictures on the condition that the licensee only show films leased from designated sources, since the films were outside the scope of the patent claims. The Court reasoned that enforcement of such a condition would impermissibly extend the scope of the monopoly beyond that intended by Congress.

Since such license conditions were unenforceable, licensees using the patented feeder with films leased from other sources would not be liable for direct infringement. In the absence of direct infringement, those leasing films to the licensees in violation of the condition could not be liable for contributory infringement.

In Mercoid Corp. v. Mid–Continent Investment Co., 320 U.S. 661, 64 S.Ct. 268, 88 L.Ed. 376 (1944), and Mercoid Corp. v. Minneapolis–Honeywell Regulator Co., 320 U.S. 680, 64 S.Ct. 278, 88 L.Ed. 396 (1944), the Court extended the rule set forth in *Motion Picture Patents* to prevent license conditions requiring licensees to purchase nonstaple articles, created and useful only in connection with the patented invention, from the patentee. The Court reasoned, "[h]owever worthy it may be, however essential to the patent, an unpatented part of a combination patent is no more entitled to monopolistic protection than any other unpatented device." *Mercoid v. Minneapolis–Honeywell*, 320 U.S. at 684, 64 S.Ct. at 280, 88 L.Ed. at 399. Thus, virtually any type of tying arrangement was prohibited. Needless to say, this cut back considerably on the contributory infringement cause of action.

At that point, at the urging of the patent bar, Congress stepped in and essentially restored the status quo as it existed prior to the *Mercoid* decisions. The relevant statutory provision is 35 U.S.C.A. § 271(d), which, prior to its amendment in 1988, provided:

> No patent owner otherwise entitled to relief for infringement or contributory infringement of a patent shall be denied relief or deemed guilty of misuse or illegal extension of the patent right by reason of his having done one or more of the following: (1) derived revenue from acts which if performed by another without his consent would constitute contributory infringement of the patent; (2) licensed or authorized another to perform acts which if performed without his consent would constitute contributory infringement of the patent; (3) sought to enforce his patent rights against infringement or contributory infringement.

In section 271(c) Congress confined the cause of action for contributory infringement to sale of *nonstaple* articles having no substantial, noninfringing use. Thus, the patentee's rights turned upon the character of a "tied" good as staple or nonstaple.

Dawson Chemical Co. v. Rohm & Haas Co., 448 U.S. 176, 100 S.Ct. 2601, 65 L.Ed.2d 696, 206 U.S.P.Q. 385 (1980), involved the defendants' sale of propanil, an unpatentable chemical compound. Though propanil had long been known, no use had been found for it until the patentee discovered and patented a method of applying propanil to growing rice crops to kill weeds. The patentee marketed propanil in containers with printed directions for applying it by the patented method. This constituted an implied license permitting farmers who purchased the patentee's propanil to use the method. The patentee did not license persons purchasing propanil from other sources to use the method, however, and refused to license other manufacturers to sell propanil.

The defendants sold propanil to farmers, knowing that the farmers would infringe the patent by applying it through the patented method. The patentee sued them, claiming both inducement and contributory infringement. The defendants admitted that propanil was a "nonstaple" within the meaning of section 271(c), but asserted that the patentee engaged in patent misuse by tying licenses to use the patented method to purchase of the propanil it offered for sale. By limiting licenses to those purchasing from it, the patentee monopolized the market for propanil, which was an unpatented article.

The Court focused on the contributory infringement cause of action, and undertook to construe section 271(d). Characterizing section 271(c) and (d) as a compromise between the competing policies underlying contributory infringement and patent misuse, the *Dawson* Court found that these provisions

> effectively confer upon the patentee, as a lawful adjunct of his patent rights, a limited power to exclude others from competition in nonstaple goods. A patentee may sell a nonstaple article himself while enjoining others from marketing that same good without his authorization. By doing so, he is able to eliminate competitors and thereby to control the market for that product. Moreover, his power to demand royalties from others for the privilege of selling the nonstaple item itself implies that the patentee may control the market for the nonstaple good; otherwise, his "right" to sell licenses for the marketing of the nonstaple good would be meaningless, since no one would be willing to pay him for a superfluous authorization.
>
> Rohm & Haas' conduct is not dissimilar in either nature or effect from the conduct that is thus clearly embraced within § 271(d). It sells propanil; it authorizes others to use propanil; and it sues contributory infringers. These are all protected activities. Rohm & Haas does *not* license others to sell propanil, but nothing on the face of the statute requires it to do so. To be sure, the sum effect of Rohm & Haas' actions is to suppress competition in the market for an unpatented commodity. But as we have observed, in this its conduct is no different from that which the statute expressly protects.

Id., 448 U.S. at 201–02, 100 S.Ct. at 2616, 65 L.Ed.2d at 715–16.

In 1988, Congress amended section 271(d) to list two more activities that would not constitute patent misuse:

> No patent owner otherwise entitled to relief for infringement or contributory infringement of a patent shall be denied relief or deemed guilty of misuse or illegal extension of the patent right by reason of his having done one or more of the following * * * (4) refused to license or use any rights to the patent; or (5) conditioned the license of any rights to the patent or the sale of the patented product on the acquisition of a license to rights in another patent or purchase of a separate product, unless, in view of the circumstances,

> the patent owner has market power in the relevant market for the patent or patented product on which the license or sale is conditioned.

35 U.S.C.A. § 271(d).

Notes and Questions

1. *The misuse doctrine.* What is the justification for permitting the kind of tying arrangement involved in *Dawson*, and the contributory infringement claim? In your view, did Congress, in enacting sections 271(c) and (d), reach the right balance between the potentially conflicting policies underlying the contributory infringement and patent misuse doctrines? For a provocative evaluation of the rule in *Dawson*, see Oddi, *Contributory Infringement/Patent Misuse: Metaphysics and Metamorphosis*, 44 U. PITT. L. REV. 73 (1982).

What is the relationship between the misuse doctrine and antitrust law? Should misuse extend to actions not violating the antitrust laws? Does it, after the 1988 amendments? See Merges, *Reflections on Current Legislation Affecting Patent Misuse*, 70 J. PAT. & TRADEMARK OFF. SOC. 793 (1988); Webb & Locke, *Intellectual Property Misuse: Recent Developments in the Misuse Doctrine*, 72 J. PAT. & TRADEMARK OFF. SOC. 399 (1990).

What is the impact of the 1988 amendments? Why might Congress have deemed them necessary? See Statement of Bernard R. Pravel, reprinted in S. REP. NO. 492, 100th Cong., 2d Sess. 13–14 (1988):

> Very often, the creators and owners of advances in technology in the form of intellectual property are not able to fully develop its commercial applications. In these cases, the most effective, and often the only, method of bringing this technology to the market place is for its owner to license it to another with the ability to do so. However, despite the practical benefits of licensing to the industrial innovation process, courts have sometimes found intellectual property licensing practices to be unlawful without fully considering the effect of the practices on competition.

Do the amendments go far enough? See Kobak, *The New Patent Misuse Law*, 71 J. PAT. & TRADEMARK OFF. SOC. 859 (1989).

2. *Inequitable conduct.* The inequitable conduct defense, sometimes called "fraud on the Patent Office," is closely related to the patent misuse defense and the defense of unclean hands. It holds, essentially, that if the patentee intentionally misrepresented or withheld material information about the patentability of the invention from the PTO in the course of prosecution, the patent will not be enforceable. The Court of Appeals for the Federal Circuit has explained:

> "Inequitable conduct" is not, or should not be, a magic incantation to be asserted against every patentee. Nor is that allegation established upon a mere showing that art or information having some degree of materiality was not disclosed. To be guilty of inequitable conduct, one must have intended to act inequitably. Thus, one who alleges a "failure to disclose" form of inequitable conduct must offer clear and convincing proof of: (1) prior art or information that is material; (2) knowledge

> chargeable to applicant of that prior art or information and of its materiality; and (3) failure of the applicant to disclose the art or information resulting from an intent to mislead the PTO.

FMC Corp. v. Manitowoc Co., Inc. 835 F.2d 1411, 1415, 5 U.S.P.Q.2d 1112, 1115 (C.A.F.C. 1987). For an detailed evaluation of the development of the inequitable conduct doctrine, see Goldman, *Evolution of the Inequitable Conduct Defense in Patent Litigation*, 7 HARV. J. L. & TECH. 37 (1993).

3. *Patent invalidity.* Patent invalidity is frequently raised as a defense to an infringement action. In recognition of the PTO's expertise, the Patent Act provides that a patent will be presumed valid. 35 U.S.C.A. § 282. Thus, the challenger bears the burden of proving, with clear and convincing evidence, that the provisions of the Patent Act governing patentability have not been satisfied. See Atlas Powder Co. v. E.I. du Pont De Nemours & Co., 750 F.2d 1569, 1573, 224 U.S.P.Q. 409, 411 (C.A.F.C. 1984).

Assume that X enters into a license agreement with a patentee, in which the patentee grants X permission to use the patented invention, in return for X's promise to pay royalties. X later stops paying royalties, but continues to use the invention, in violation of the agreement. As a matter of public policy, should X, in a subsequent suit for infringement, be estopped from challenging the validity of the patent by virtue of his agreement to the license? See Lear, Inc. v. Adkins, 395 U.S. 653, 89 S.Ct. 1902, 23 L.Ed.2d 610 (1969) (no licensee estoppel in patent cases). See also, Dreyfuss, *Dethroning* Lear*: Licensee Estoppel and the Incentive to Innovate*, 72 VA. L. REV. 677 (1986); McCarthy, *"Unmussling" the Patent Licensee: Chaos in the Wake of Lear v. Adkins*, 45 GEO. WASH. L. REV. 429 (1977). What if A obtains a patent for his invention, and then assigns the patent to B for valuable consideration. Later, A wishes to exploit the patented invention, and challenges the validity of the patent. Should A be estopped? See Diamond Scientific Co. v. Ambico, Inc. 848 F.2d 1220, 6 U.S.P.Q.2d 2028 (C.A.F.C.1988), *cert. dismissed* 487 U.S. 1265, 109 S.Ct. 28, 101 L.Ed.2d 978 (1988) (estoppel is appropriate).

Assume that a patentee sues Y for infringement, and in that action, Y prevails in his defense that the patent is invalid. The patentee then brings suit against Z for infringement. As a matter of policy, should the patentee be permitted to relitigate the issue of patent validity in this new suit, or should it be estopped from asserting patent validity? See Blonder–Tongue Laboratories, Inc. v. University of Illinois Foundation, 402 U.S. 313, 91 S.Ct. 1434, 28 L.Ed.2d 788, 169 U.S.P.Q. 513 (1971).

H. CONCLUDING CONSIDERATIONS

AN ECONOMIC REVIEW OF THE PATENT SYSTEM

Fritz Machlup.
Study No. 15, Subcommittee on Patents, Trademarks and Copyrights
of the Committee on the Judiciary, U.S. Senate
85th Cong., 2d Sess., 21, 44–45, 50–54, 79–80 (1958).

* * *

The four best-known positions on which advocates of patent protection for inventors have rested their case may be characterized as the "natural-law" thesis, the "reward-by-monopoly" thesis, the "monopoly-profit-incentive" thesis, and the "exchange-for-secrets" thesis.

The "natural-law" thesis assumes that man has a natural property right in his own ideas. Appropriation of his ideas by others, that is, their unauthorized use, must be condemned as stealing. Society is morally obligated to recognize and protect his property right. Property is, in essence, exclusive. Hence, enforcement of exclusivity in the use of a patented invention is the only appropriate way for society to recognize this property right.

The "reward-by-monopoly" thesis assumes that justice requires that a man receive reward for his services in proportion to their usefulness to society, and that, where needed, society must intervene to secure him such reward. Inventors render useful services, and the most appropriate way to secure them commensurate rewards is by means of temporary monopolies in the form of exclusive patent rights in their inventions.

The "monopoly-profit-incentive" thesis assumes that industrial progress is desirable, that inventions and their industrial exploitation are necessary for such progress, but that inventions and/or their exploitation will not be obtained in sufficient measure if inventors and capitalists can hope only for such profits as the competitive exploitation of all technical knowledge will permit. To make it worthwhile for inventors and their capitalist backers to make their efforts and risk their money, society must intervene to increase their profit expectations. The simplest, cheapest, and most effective way for society to hold out these incentives is to grant temporary monopolies in the form of exclusive patent rights in inventions.

The "exchange-for-secrets" thesis presumes a bargain between inventor and society, the former surrendering the possession of secret knowledge in exchange for the protection of a temporary exclusivity in its industrial use. The presupposition again is that industrial progress at a sustained rate is desirable but cannot be obtained if inventors and innovating entrepreneurs keep inventions secret; in this case, the new technology may only much later become available for general use; indeed, technological secrets may die with their inventors and forever be lost to society. Hence, it is in the interest of society to bargain with the inventor and make him disclose his secret for the use of future generations. This can best be done by offering him exclusive patent rights in return for public disclosure of the invention.

* * *

Patents, by giving their owners exclusive rights to the commercial exploitation of inventions, secure to these owners profits (so-called "quasi-rents") which are ultimately collected from consumers as part of the price paid for goods and services. The consumers pay; the patent owners receive. Are the consumers—the non-patent-owning people—worse off for it?

"No, they are not," says one group of economists. Patents are granted on inventions which would not have been made in the absence of a patent system; the inventions make it possible to produce more or better products than could have been produced without them; hence, whatever the consumers pay to the patent owners is only a part of the increase in real income that is engendered by the patent-induced inventions.

"Wrong," says another group of economists. Many of the inventions for which patents are granted would also be made and put to use without any patent system. The consumers could have the fruits of this technical progress without paying any toll charges. Even if *some* inventions are made and used thanks only to the incentives afforded by the patent system, consumers must pay for *all* patented inventions and, hence, lose by the bargain. Moreover, if patents result in monopolistic restrictions which hold down production and hinder the most efficient utilization of resources, it is possible that total real income is less than what it would be without the patent system. Of course, there is impressive technical progress and a substantial growth of national income under the patent system, yet perhaps less so than there would be without patents.

This is but one of the fundamental conflicts in the economics of the patent system. There is another, which is quite independent of any profits collected by the patent owners and of any monopolistic restrictions imposed on production. This second basic problem relates to the overall allocation of productive resources in a developing economy, and to the question whether at any one time the allocation to industrial research and development is deficient, excessive, or just right.

* * *

Not only is research in general competitive with other economic activities, but research on particular problems and in particular fields is competitive with research on other problems and in other fields. This needs to be mentioned chiefly because in recent years another concept of "competitive research" has received increased attention: different firms and different research teams competing with one another in finding solutions to the same research problem in the same field.

Competition among rival firms which takes the form of a race between their research teams—a race, ultimately, to the patent office—may have various objectives: *(a)* To be the first to find a patentable solution to a problem posed by the needs and preferences of the customers—a better product—or by the technological needs and hopes of the producers—better machines, tools, processes; *(b)* after a competitor has found such a solution and has obtained exclusive patent rights in its exploitation, to find an alternative solution to the same problem in order to be able to compete with him in the same market—in other words, to "invent around" the competitor's patent; and *(c)* after having found and patented the first solution, to find and patent all possible alternative solutions, even inferior ones, in order to "block" competitors' efforts to "invent around" the first patent.

These forms of "competitive research" were described and discussed by antipatent economists during the patent controversy of the 19th century. Concerning the first form, there was much complaint that other inventors who discovered practically simultaneously "the same utility," but were not the first in the race to the patent office, had to forego their "natural privilege of labor" and were barred from using their own inventions. The fact that there was competition in making new inventions was found to be healthy. But that he who lost the race to the patent office should be barred from using his own invention, and should have to search for a substitute invention, was found to be absurd.

What may appear absurd to a disinterested observer, or unjust and unfair to one who lost the right to use the fruit of his own labor and investment, must to an economist appear as sheer economic waste. Of course, one may regard this as an incidental expense of an otherwise beneficial institution, an unfortunate byproduct, an item of social cost, which, perhaps, is unavoidable and must be tolerated in view of the social advantages of the system as a whole. However, from merely defending the need of "invention around a patent" as a minor item of waste, the discussion has recently proceeded to eulogize it as one of the advantages of the system, indeed as one of its "justifications."

The advantage is seen in the additional "encouragement" to research. If the competitors were given licenses under the patent of the firm that won the race, they would have to pay royalties but would not be compelled to "invent around" it. Exclusivity, however, forces some of them to search for a "substitute invention." But why should this be regarded as an advantage? The idea is probably that, if industrial research is desirable, more research is more desirable, and that it does not matter what kind of knowledge the research effort is supposed to yield. From an economic point of view, research is costly since it absorbs particularly scarce resources which could produce other valuable things. The production of the knowledge of how to do in a somewhat different way what we have already learned to do in a satisfactory way would hardly be given highest priority in a rational allocation of resources.

This same, or a still lower, evaluation must be accorded to the third form of "competitive research"—inventive effort for the purpose of obtaining patents on all possible alternatives of an existing patented invention just in order to "block" a rival from "inventing around" that patent. In this case inventive talent is wasted on a project which, even (or especially) if it succeeds exactly in achieving its objective, cannot possibly be as valuable as would be other tasks to which the talent might be assigned. When thousands of potential inventions are waiting to be made—inventions which might be of great benefit to society—how can one seriously justify the assignment of a research force to search for inventions that are not intended for use at all—but merely for satisfying a dog-in-a-manger ambition?

There is, however, another "justification" for this kind of "competitive research": it can be summarized in the colorful word "serendipity." This means "the faculty of making happy and unexpected discoveries by accident." The idea is that the research teams engaged in "inventing around patents," or in inventing to obtain patents to "block" other people's efforts to "invent around patents," might by sheer accident hit upon something really useful. In other words, the work of these research forces is justified by the possibility or probability that they might find something which they did not set out to find.

There is no doubt that these happy accidents occur again and again. But can one reasonably let an effort to produce something without social value take the credit for accidental byproducts that happen to be useful? Can one reasonably assert that research not oriented toward important objectives is more likely to yield useful results than are research efforts that are so oriented? Is it easier to find the important by seeking the unimportant?

There is good historical evidence for the truth in the old saying that "necessity is the mother of invention." The continental blockade in the Napoleonic War led to the development of beet sugar; the blockade in World War I led to the process of obtaining nitrogen from air; the U-boat blockade in World War II led to the invention of atabrine as a substitute for quinine; etc, etc. Does it follow that it would be a good idea to institute more blockades? Perhaps the necessity of seeking substitutes would help us find many fine things; "serendipity" might yield splendid results.

[T]here is a scarcity of imaginative scientists and there is no scarcity of unsolved problems. The use of scarce research resources for seeking alternative solutions to satisfactorily solved problems can hardly be justified under the circumstances—no matter how well serendipity works.

* * *

A slight inconsistency can be discovered with regard to the bargain theory—that patent protection is exchanged for the disclosure of secrets. The theory asserts that great benefits are obtained for society by securing the general availability, after 17 years or so, of now secret information; actual patenting practice, however, implies that others may be ready any minute to put the same information to work. Is the conviction that valuable technical information might remain secret for years, if not forever, fully consistent with the attorney's advice to his clients that they rush to the Patent Office lest someone else with the same idea beat them to it? If several inventors actually come up with the same idea, is it likely to be one that anybody could have kept secret? And is not society likely to lose, then, by restricting the use of such an idea for several years?

* * *

An old fallacy relates to the "adequacy" of the "reward" to the inventor. The assertion has been made, and is still being repeated, that the "rewards" which inventors or their assignees earn through profits from exclusive use of the patented inventions are in proportion to the "social usefulness" of these inventions. There is no reason why this should be so, and in fact no such proportionality, or approximate proportionality, can possibly be shown. It is well known that several inventions which have later proved to be of immense usefulness to society were somewhat "ahead of their time" when they were made and patented, and have earned nothing for their creators. It is firmly established that patents on some trivial gadgets have earned millions for their owners while patents on technically highly significant processes have been financially unrewarding. In general, the profits made from the commercial exploitation of a patent depend in part on the degree of restriction on the output produced under the patent. It is more than probable that the socially most important inventions, say, of drugs or vaccines for the cure or prevention of cancer, would not be allowed to be exploited with the same monopolistic restrictions that are freely tolerated in the exploitation of patents on hair curlers, bottle caps, or television screens.

* * *

* * * The literature abounds with discussions of the "economic consequences" of the patent system, purporting to present definitive judgments, without even stating the assumptions on which the arguments are based, let alone submitting supporting evidence for the actual realization of these assumptions. No economist, on the basis of present knowledge, could possibly state with certainty that the patent system, as it now operates, confers a net benefit or a net loss upon society. The best he can do is to state assumptions and make guesses about the extent to which reality corresponds to these assumptions.

If one does not know whether a system "as a whole" (in contrast to certain features of it) is good or bad, the safest "policy conclusion" is to "muddle through"—either with it, if one has long lived with it, or without it, if one has lived without it. If we did not have a patent system, it would be irresponsible, on the basis of our present knowledge of its economic consequences, to recommend instituting one. But since we have had a patent system for a long time, it would be irresponsible, on the basis of our present knowledge, to recommend abolishing it. * * *

* * *

THE PATENT SYSTEM AND COMPETITIVE POLICY [19]

Donald F. Turner.
44 N.Y.U. L. REV. 450, 452–58 (1969).

* * *

No one knows what the magnitude of underinvestment in the production of knowledge would be in the absence of special rewards, because it is fairly certain that a large amount of invention and innovation would take place in any event. Much research, as in universities and similar institutions, is relatively unaffected by the profit motive. Moreover, both economic analysis and empirical study indicate that a good deal of the research and other inventive and innovative activities of business enterprises would go on without special rewards of any kind. In many situations, this is a matter of competitive necessity; he who lags in invention and innovation will find himself driven from the market. Even without benefit of statutory protection, the inventor and innovator will often, if not usually, benefit from a headstart, full imitation lagging well behind. And in many of our imperfectly competitive markets, price competition may simply not be vigorous enough to prevent the inventor or innovator from recovering his developmental costs.

* * *

There is no doubt that the patent system, by giving a monopoly to the holder of a patentable invention and thus increasing the realizable reward for successful inventive activity, produces a substantial amount of invention and innovation that would not otherwise take place. There is also little doubt that the patent system evokes disclosure of some new knowledge that would otherwise remain secret, or at least remain secret for a longer period of time. The magnitude of the latter benefit may not be in fact very great: it has been contended that patents are often granted without full disclosure of all that must be known to make effective use of the invention; and it is also contended that in many areas patents are sought only for inventions that cannot be kept concealed anyway. But the patent system must make some net contribution to disclosure for the simple reason that it could hardly cause anyone to conceal what he would disclose if the patent system did not exist.

Offsetting these benefits, however, are several significant costs. The first is the cost of having a patent system: the cost of administering it, the cost of patent litigation, and the cost of trying to figure out whether one has a patentable invention and whether one's activity infringes the patents of others. The second cost, and a substantial one, is underutilization of all the new patentable knowledge what would have been produced without a patent system. Generally speaking, the marginal cost of using new knowledge, once produced, is zero. Ideally, therefore, it should be freely available without cost to anyone for whom it has any positive value at all. By its very nature, of course, the patent

19. Reprinted by permission. © New York University Law Review, 1969.

monopoly restricts the use of new knowledge well below the social ideal, because even if its use is made generally available by licensing, it comes only at a price. Third, the patent system has contributed to the creation and perpetuation of monopoly power of dimensions and duration well beyond that intrinsic to the patents themselves. Fourth, the patent system often leads competitors of patent holders to invest resources in duplicating research, *i.e.*, to find noninfringing ways of obtaining the same or nearly the same result. * * * Fifth, the patent system has at times induced the use of research resources solely for the purpose of producing blocking patents. Sixth, the patent system has adverse effects on inventive activity in two respects. It tends to inhibit research in areas heavily hedged in by existing patents; the existence of large numbers of patents in a particular field reduces the likelihood of coming up with noninfringing results that can be profited from—in short, it reduces the probable rewards from inventive activity in that area. In addition, existing patents tend to increase the cost of solving any given research problem by shutting off those avenues of solution that would entail infringement.

Finally, the patent system would appear to worsen, rather than improve, the allocation of research resources as between applied research on the one hand and basic research on the other. As we have noted, unless there are special inducements, underinvestment in basic research is likely to be much more substantial than underinvestment in the production of new knowledge generally. Given the standards of invention incorporated in typical patent statutes, basic research would appear to be much less likely than applied research to produce what the law will call "invention." Thus, the patent system will tend to divert research resources away from basic research. This effect would not be a clear loss if the patent system so increased the total resources devoted to research that the resources spent on basic research, though relatively less, were absolutely greater. But even if this were so, the patent system obviously is not the ideal system for incentives in that it does not allocate research resources in the most beneficial way.

Can these adverse effects of the patent system, as we have known it, be reduced or eliminated by appropriate statutory revisions? I see no way of eliminating the loss caused by underutilization of new patentable knowledge that would have been produced without patent protection, for there is simply no feasible way of determining precisely or even crudely what those cases are. The underutilization cost could be reduced by requiring compulsory licensing at reasonable royalties, but could by no means be eliminated, for any positive royalty excludes uses of less value than the royalty price.

Compulsory licensing would also reduce, though not eliminate, the contribution of the patent system to monopoly power, to wasteful duplicating research, to the devotion of resources to obtaining blocking patents, and to the inhibitions on research imposed by patents in being. But compulsory licensing of course raises problems of its own. Arguably, it might so reduce the potential rewards of patents as to materially affect the patent incentive to inventive activity. Related to that problem, but involving more, compulsory licensing requires a determination of what is a "reasonable" royalty, a question for which there is simply no happy answer.

* * *

Finally, I see no practical way within the patent system itself for eliminating the probable bias against basic research. The solution would have to lie in some revision of the definition of patentable invention. But surely it would be intolerable to give a patent on most of the fundamental ideas that arise from basic research.

I believe this last consideration also demonstrates how unpersuasive the moral defense of the patent system is. Even if we assume that in an ideal world society should pay each creator of a new idea its full economic value, the impossibility of devising any workable scheme for doing so leaves no moral ground for paying some but not others—particularly when it is the fundamental discovery (and such important innovations in business methods as the assembly line, the self-service supermarket, and computerization) that typically must go substantially underrewarded.

But a moment's reflection leads us to question the proposition that were it possible, society should feel a moral obligation to compel all who use an idea to pay monetary tribute to its creator. On this point, I can do no better than to quote Professor Rahl:

> In most of the important fields of human activity it is not usually considered wrong to imitate valuable things, ideas and methods. The more acceptable to society the thing is, the more others are encouraged to imitate it. Education is founded upon this premise, as is progress in science, art, literature, music, and government.
>
> * * *
>
> We have but to look around us to see that our "dynamic" economy is one which thrives upon and requires rapid imitation of innovated trade values.
>
> * * *
>
> * * * [W]e cannot have a general rule against copying of published trade values and at the same time have an effective system of competition. Although competition has many definitions and descriptions, it is clear to all that it cannot exist without the availability of reasonably close alternatives for the satisfaction of economic wants.
>
> * * *
>
> It is not freedom of competition which requires apology. It is

interference with freedom which must always be explained.[5]

Therefore, the case for the patent system, if a case there be, must be an economic one, and, as we have seen, a clear case cannot be made. But neither can one make a convincing case against it. * * *

Notes and Questions

1. *Patent theory.* In your view, what, if any, place should the "natural-law" thesis, described by Professor Machlup, have in the patent law? Does it in fact have a meaningful impact on U.S. patent law? Does our existing patent law reflect the "reward-by-monopoly" thesis, which rewards invention in proportion to its usefulness to society? With regard to the "monopoly-profit-incentive" thesis, do we actually need patents to provide incentives to invent and make inventions available to the public?

Some economists have suggested that in some, or even many cases, a patent may not be needed to ensure that the inventor is able to recoup his investment in research and development and turn a profit. The inventor has the advantage of lead time, which permits him to enter the market in advance of competitors and recoup much of his investment during the time that competitors are gearing up to enter. Moreover, by being the first in the market, he may be able to establish long-lasting commercial relationships which will continue to give him an advantage after his competitors have produced rival products. What is your opinion of this "head start" theory? Is the head start likely to provide the inventor with enough opportunity in enough cases to make patents unnecessary? See Machlup, *supra*, at 23, 38–39. Would your evaluation of the lead time argument vary, depending upon the subject area of the invention?

If, as Professor Turner suggests, our patent system has a detrimental effect on the allocation of research resources between applied and basic research, should we amend the patent laws to provide more patents for the results of basic research?

On balance, does the patent system tend to increase or decrease the risk of investing in research and development?

If you believe that a "reward" or incentive system is needed, but are dissatisfied with our existing patent system, what alternative approaches are available? In his study, Professor Machlup mentions several:

> Proposals for systems of prizes and bonuses to inventors, as alternatives to patents, are almost as old as the patent system. In the United States, in the 1787 discussions of the powers to be reserved for Federal legislation, Madison proposed a premium system instead of a patent system. In 1834, Russia established a commission to determine awards for inventors in lieu of exclusive privileges. And similar proposals were debated almost everywhere during the 19th century * * *.

Id., at 15. How might such a "prize" system be structured? In your view, would it be preferable to the patent system?

5. Rahl, The Right to "Appropriate" Trade Values, 23 Ohio St. L.J. 56, 70–72 (1962). * * *

Another approach is government financing—subsidies for research in areas deemed to be in the public interest but which private firms might find unprofitable in the absence of government funding. *Id.* at 16–17. The government already provides substantial research subsidies as a back-up to the patent system. Is this effective? Should even greater reliance be placed on government subsidies? What other alternatives might there be to the patent system?

The Machlup study provides an excellent survey of the literature concerning the economic effects of patents. For a more recent evaluation, see Kitch, *The Nature and Function of the Patent System*, 20 J. L. & ECON. 265 (1977); Merges, *Uncertainty and the Standard of Patentability*, 7 HIGH TECH. L.J. 1 (1993). For an interesting evaluation of the effect of patents on the traditions of open communication and free flow of information and on the traditional reward structure in the scientific community, see Eisenberg, *Proprietary Rights and the Norms of Science in Biotechnology Research*, 97 YALE L. J. 177 (1987).

2. *Patents vs. trade secrets.* As we have seen, both trade secret and patent law extend property rights to inventions, though the level and nature of the protection each offers differs significantly. In many instances, the inventor may not have a meaningful choice between the two. For example, the invention may not be sufficiently novel or nonobvious to qualify for a patent but may nonetheless be sufficiently secret and valuable to qualify for trade secret protection. Conversely, an invention may qualify for a patent but not be capable of maintenance as a trade secret because it is easily ascertained through examination of the product the owner places on the market.

On the other hand, inventors sometimes have a meaningful choice between a patent and maintaining the invention as a trade secret. Of course, the inventor cannot avail herself of both avenues of protection simultaneously for the same invention, since publication of the patent at the time it is granted will destroy any trade secret status the invention might otherwise have enjoyed.

Assuming that both options were available for a specific invention, would you ever advise a client to choose trade secret protection over a patent? If so, under what circumstances, and why? What are the disadvantages of trade secret protection as compared to a patent? Are there significant cost considerations? Are there public relations considerations? See generally 1 R. MILGRIM, TRADE SECRETS § 2.03 (1991).

Inventors may hedge their bets somewhat by applying for a patent, but maintaining the invention as a trade secret during the prosecution process. The PTO retains applications in secrecy. 35 U.S.C.A. § 122. Thus, if a patent ultimately is denied, trade secrecy is still an option. Indeed, since an application can be abandoned at any point prior to issuance of a patent, the inventor may decide to apply for a patent and test his ability to use the invention as a trade secret during the pendency of the application. If, down the line, the prospects of retaining secrecy look good, the inventor may simply abandon the application.

Of course, if the inventor is applying for patents abroad as well as in the United States, he must bear in mind that issuance of the patent or publication of the application abroad may lead to destruction of trade secrecy status in the U.S. Indeed, most countries publish patent applications after a stated period of time—frequently 18 months from the priority filing date. Congress has considered the possibility of adopting such a practice in the United States, as well. Pre-issuance publication would curtail the inventor's option to retain the invention as a trade secret when the PTO ultimately denies a patent, and would limit an inventor's options to maintain a pending application as a back-up to maintenance of a trade secret. See Fiorito, *The WIPO "Basic Proposal" for Harmonization of Patent Laws Viewed from the U.S. Practitioner's Point of View*, 19 AIPLA Q. J. 24, 42 (1991).

While an inventor cannot simultaneously enjoy both trade secret and patent protection on the same invention, bear in mind that both forms of protection may be available to give rights in separate aspects of the same overall invention/commercialization process. See, e.g., Tabor v. Hoffman, 118 N.Y. 30, 23 N.E. 12 (1889); Christianson v. Colt Industries Operating Corp., 822 F.2d 1544, 3 U.S.P.Q.2d 1241 (C.A.F.C. 1987), *vacated on jurisdictional grounds & remanded for transfer* 486 U.S. 800, 108 S.Ct. 2166, 100 L.Ed.2d 811, 7 U.S.P.Q.2d 1109 (1988). While Patent Act section 112 requires full disclosure of the invention and the best mode of practicing it, much of the know-how that goes into mass production or other commercial exploitation of the invention need not be disclosed, and may be retained as a trade secret.

II. PLANT PATENTS

YODER BROTHERS, INC. v. CALIFORNIA–FLORIDA PLANT CORP.

United States Court of Appeals, Fifth Circuit, 1976.
537 F.2d 1347, 193 U.S.P.Q. 264, *cert. denied*
429 U.S. 1094, 97 S.Ct. 1108, 51 L.Ed.2d 540, 200 U.S.P.Q. 128 (1977).

GOLDBERG, CIRCUIT JUDGE:

In this clash between two giants of the chrysanthemum business, we confront a myriad of antitrust and plant patent issues. Yoder Brothers (Yoder), plaintiff in the district court, sued, alleging infringement of twenty-one chrysanthemum plant patents by California–Florida Plant Corp. (CFPC) and California–Florida Plant Corp. of Florida (CFPCF) (sometimes referred to collectively as Cal–Florida). CFPC and CFPCF denied the infringement and filed antitrust counterclaims under sections 1 and 2 of the Sherman Act. As to seven of the chrysanthemum plant patents, the lower court directed verdicts for Yoder that the patents were valid and infringed and awarded treble damages. * * *

Because many of the issues in this case turn on the particular nature of the ornamental plant industry and the specific characteristics of chrysanthemums, we shall describe the background facts in some detail before discussing the many complex legal issues presented on this appeal. * * *

I. General Background

A. *The Chrysanthemum Industry*

Chrysanthemums, in their natural state, blossom only during the fall. This is because they are photoperiodic in nature, meaning that their growth is affected by the relative lengths of lightness and darkness in the day. When the days are long, the chrysanthemum plant remains in a vegetative state. As the nights become longer, the initiation process of the chrysanthemum bud begins. Thus, in early August, when the nights achieve a duration of nine and one-half continuous dark hours, the chrysanthemum plant in its natural state will begin the process of developing a flower. During the fall and early winter months, the mature flower appears.

Yoder began doing business in the 1930's as a simple greenhouse operator, specializing in tomatoes. Soon thereafter, because the fall tomato crop was less profitable than the spring crop, it decided to replace the fall crop with chrysanthemums. In 1939 or 1940, Yoder employees began research into out-of-season flowering of chrysanthemums. By applying black cloth shades over the chrysanthemums when dark hours were needed and applying artificial light when light hours were needed, it became possible to flower chrysanthemums on a year-round basis. Yet this breakthrough was not without its problems. For example, the use of black cloth shades resulted in an abnormally high temperature build-up around the plants, which in turn retarded bud initiation. Similarly, when the finishing temperatures were too warm, the chrysanthemums would not hold their color. In an effort to adjust for these conditions and to improve the quality of the chrysanthemum generally, Yoder initiated a breeding program in the early 1940's. One of the most important goals of the breeding program was the development of new varieties for consumers.

* * *

Chrysanthemums have been subject to intensive breeding efforts over the past thirty years; each individual specimen is a genetically unique complex organism. Several definitions of the term "variety" of chrysanthemum were offered at trial. Mr. Duffett, Yoder's head breeder, defined a variety as a group of individual plants which, on the basis of observation by skilled floriculturists and according to reasonable commercial tolerances, display identical characteristics under similar environments. Cal–Florida defined variety in its complaint as "a subspecies or class of chrysanthemums distinguishable from other subspecies or classes of chrysanthemums by distinct characteristics, such as color, hue, shape and size of petal or blossom or any of them."

New varieties of chrysanthemums are developed in two major ways: by sexual reproduction and by mutagenic techniques. Sexual reproduction, the result of self or cross pollination, produces a genetically unique seedling, the characteristics of which are impossible to predict. Mutagenic techniques simply accelerate the natural rate of mutation in the chrysanthemum plant itself. A mutation was defined by Mr. Duffett as "a change in the number of chromosomes or a change in the chromosome position or a specific change in the genes within those chromosomes." Technically, only those mutations that first express themselves as bud variations are properly called "sports"; however, the word is used loosely in the industry as a general synonym for mutation, and we will so use it. Two types of sports can appear: spontaneous sports and radiation sports. The cells of all living things occasionally mutate, and spontaneous sports are simply the result of that process. Radiation sports, on the other hand, are induced artificially, through exposure to such things as gamma radiation from radioactive cobalt and X-rays. These techniques do nothing that could not occur in nature apart from speeding up the natural mutation process. Although most of the mutations induced by radiation are not commercially usable plants, a skilled breeder will select for further development those that display such desirable characteristics as fast response time, temperature tolerance, durability, size, and vigor.

After a breeder has successfully isolated a new variety, the only way he can preserve his creation is by means of asexual reproduction. In the case of chrysanthemums, the most common technique of asexual reproduction is the taking of cuttings from a stock plant. Cuttings, as defined in the Cal–Florida complaint, are "sections or parts of chrysanthemum plants which may be grown into mature plants for sale as cut flowers and/or potted plants or from which additional cuttings may be harvested." According to Yoder's suggested definition, cuttings are simply immature chrysanthemum plants. Since a cutting is genetically identical to the parent plant, it will develop into a plant whose characteristics match the parent's exactly, so long as the same environmental conditions obtain. A central fact of life in the chrysanthemum industry is the ease with which cuttings can be taken from parent plants: from one chrysanthemum, it is theoretically possible to develop an infinitely large stock, by taking cuttings, maturing some into flowered plants, taking more cuttings, and so on.

Over the years since Yoder first entered the chrysanthemum business, the industry has become internally specialized. At the first functional level are the breeders, who create new varieties of chrysanthemums. Breeding is an expensive, complex procedure. The breeder must possess the skill and discrimination to spot potential new varieties and recognize whether they possess desirable traits; facilities for elaborate testing and development must be available. Because chrysanthemums mutate rapidly, a breeder must always be on the lookout for new changes.

At the next level in the industry are the propagator-distributors. The propagator-distributors build up mother stock from sources such as breeders, retail florists, or their existing flowers, and reproduce cuttings from that mother stock. In a sense they are simply mass producers of cuttings. They do not develop cuttings to the mature flower stage (except for purposes of their own testing). Next are the growers, who develop cuttings purchased from propagator-distributors into mature plants either for cut flowers or potted plants. Combining the function of propagator-distributors and growers are the self-propagators. Cal–Florida defined a "self-propagator" as "a person who either buys or establishes stock and takes cuttings for the sole purpose of producing cut flowers and/or potted plants for resale or own use." In other words, the self-propagators are vertically integrated into one step. Finally, the growers (or self-propagators) sell their products to retail florists, who in turn sell to ultimate consumers.

B. *The Parties*

During the times relevant to this litigation, Yoder operated on two levels in the business: as a substantial (if not the largest) breeder of new varieties of chrysanthemums, and as a large propagator-distributor. * * *

CFPC * * * was a propagator-distributor. CFPCF, a wholly owned subsidiary of CFPC, was also a propagator-distributor. * * *

* * *

IV. Plant Patents

A. *Introduction*

* * * [T]he only issues before this Court concern the seven patents that the district court ruled valid and infringed as a matter of law: Red Torch, Gold Marble, Morocco, Promenade, Southern Gold, Mountain Snow, and Mountain Sun. After considerable thought, we have decided that the district court correctly ruled that Cal–Florida failed to rebut the statutory presumption of validity with sufficient relevant evidence. * * *

B. *Constitutional and Statutory Background*

* * *

* * * In its present form, the principal statute allowing patents on plants reads:

> Whoever invents or discovers and asexually reproduces any distinct and new variety of plant, including cultivated sports, mutants, hybrids, and newly found seedlings, other than an tuberpropagated plant or a plant found in an uncultivated state, may obtain a patent therefor, subject to the conditions and requirements of this title.
>
> The provision of this title relating to patents for inventions shall apply to patents for plants, except as otherwise provided.

35 U.S.C. § 161. Since section 161 makes the general patent law

applicable to plant patents except as otherwise provided,[32] we take as our starting point the general requisites for patentability, and then apply them as well as we can to plants.

Normally, the three requirements for patentability are novelty, utility, and obviousness. For plant patents, the requirement of distinctness replaces that of utility, and the additional requirement of asexual reproduction is introduced.

The concept of novelty refers to novelty of conception, rather than novelty of use; no single prior art structure can exist in which all of the elements serve substantially the same function. In *Beckman Instruments, Inc. v. Chemtronics, Inc.*, 5 Cir., 439 F.2d 1369, 1375, cert. denied, 1970, 400 U.S. 956, 91 S.Ct. 353–54, 27 L.Ed.2d 264, this Court said:

> [S]ection 102, which pertains to novelty, requires that the patentee be the original inventor of the object claimed in his patent, and also that the invention not have been known or used by others before his discovery of it.... Furthermore the prior art is to be considered as covering all uses to which it could have been put.

As applied to plants, the Patent Office Board of Appeals held that a "new" plant had to be one that literally had not existed before, rather than one that had existed in nature but was newly found, such as an exotic plant from a remote part of the earth.[34] In *Application of Greer*, Ct.Cust. & Pat.App.1973, 484 F.2d 488, the court indicated that the Board believed that novelty was to be determined by a detailed comparison with other known varieties.

The legislative history of the Plant Patent Act is of considerable assistance in defining "distinctness." The Senate Report said:

> [I]n order for the new variety to be distinct it must have characteristics clearly distinguishable from those of existing varieties and it is immaterial whether in the judgment of the Patent Office the new characteristics are inferior or superior to those of existing varieties. Experience has shown the absurdity of many views held as to the value of new varieties at the time of their creation.
>
> The characteristics that may distinguish a new variety would include, among others, those of habit; immunity from disease; or soil conditions; color of flower, leaf, fruit or stems; flavor; productivity, including ever-bearing qualities in case of fruits; storage qualities; perfume; form; and ease of asexual reproduction. With-

32. The only express provision modifying the applicability of the invention patent statutes for plant patents is contained in 35 U.S.C. § 162, which says that no plant patent will be invalidated for noncompliance with § 112 (description) if the description is as complete as is reasonably possible. No description issue is before us.

34. In order for a plant to have "existed" before in nature, we think that it must have been capable of reproducing itself. Thus, we have concluded that the mere fact that a sport of a plant had appeared in the past would not be sufficient to preclude the patentability of the plant on novelty grounds, since each sport is a one-time phenomenon absent human intervention. See in this connection the discussion on validity, at IV.C., *infra*.

> in any one of the above or other classes of characteristics the differences which would suffice to make the variety a distinct variety, will necessarily be differences of degree.

S.Rep. 315, 71st Cong., 2d Sess. (1930). A definition of "distinctness" as the aggregate of the plant's distinguishing characteristics seems to us a sensible and workable one.

The third requirement, nonobviousness, is the hardest to apply to plants, though we are bound to do so to the best of our ability. The traditional three part test for obviousness, as set out in *John Deere, supra*, inquires as to (1) the scope and content of the prior art, (2) the differences between the prior art and the claims at issue, and (3) the level of ordinary skill in the prior art. Secondary characteristics such as commercial success, long felt but unsolved needs, and failure of others can be used to illuminate the circumstances surrounding the subject matter sought to be patented.

The Supreme Court has viewed the obviousness requirement of section 103 as Congress' articulation of the constitutional standard of invention. *Dann v. Johnston*, 425 U.S. 219, 225, 96 S.Ct. 1393, 1397, 47 L.Ed.2d 692, 698 (1976). In *Dann*, the Court commented that

> [a]s a judicial test, "invention"—i.e., "an exercise of the inventive faculty," . . .—has long been regarded as an absolute prerequisite to patentability.

425 U.S. at 225, 96 S.Ct. at 1397, 47 L.Ed.2d at 697–98. An "invention" is characterized by a degree of skill and ingenuity greater than that possessed by an ordinary mechanic acquainted with the business. The obviousness requirement appears to presume that if the gap between the prior art and the claimed improvement is small, then an ordinary mechanic skilled in the art would have been able to create the improvement, thus leading to the conclusion that the improvement was obvious and a patentable invention not present. Section 103 requires the determination of obviousness *vel non* to be made with reference to the time the invention was made. Obviousness, like the general question of patent validity, is ultimately a question of law, though factual inquiries are often necessary to its resolution.

Rephrasing the *John Deere* tests for the plant world, we might ask about (1) the characteristics of prior plants of the same general type, both patented and nonpatented, and (2) the differences between the prior plants and the claims at issue. We see no meaningful way to apply the third criterion to plants—*i.e.*, the level of ordinary skill in the prior art. Criteria one and two are reminiscent of the "distinctness" requirement already in the Plant Patent Act. Thus, if we are to give obviousness an independent meaning, it must refer to something other than observable characteristics.

We think that the most promising approach toward the obviousness requirement for plant patents is reference to the underlying constitutional standard that it codifies—namely, invention.

The general thrust of the "invention" requirement is to ensure that minor improvements will not be granted the protection of a seventeen year monopoly by the state. In the case of plants, to develop or discover a new variety that retains the desirable qualities of the parent stock and adds significant improvements, and to preserve the new specimen by asexually reproducing it constitutes no small feat.

This Court's case dealing with the patent on the chemical compound commonly known as the drug "Darvon," *Eli Lilly & Co. v. Generix Drug Sales, Inc.*, 5 Cir.1972, 460 F.2d 1096, provides some insight into the problem of how to apply the "invention" requirement to a new and esoteric subject matter. The court first noted that

> [a]nalogical reasoning is necessarily restricted in many chemical patent cases because of the necessity for physiological experimentation before any use can be determined.
>
> In fact, such lack of predictability of useful result from the making of even the slightest variation in the atomic structure or spatial arrangement of a complex molecule ... deprives the instant claims of obviousness and anticipation of most of their vitality....

460 F.2d at 1101. The court resolved the apparent dilemma by looking to the therapeutic value of the new drug instead of to its chemical composition:

> [R]eason compels us to agree that novelty, usefulness and non-obviousness inhere in the true discovery that a chemical compound exhibits a new needed medicinal capability, even though it be closely related in structure to a known or patented drug.

460 F.2d at 1103.

The same kind of shift in focus would lead us to a more productive inquiry for plant patents. If the plant is a source of food, the ultimate question might be its nutritive content or its prolificacy. A medicinal plant might be judged by its increased or changed therapeutic value. Similarly, an ornamental plant would be judged by its increased beauty and desirability in relation to the other plants of its type, its usefulness in the industry, and how much of an improvement it represents over prior ornamental plants, taking all of its characteristics together.

Before reaching the issues on appeal, we make a final comment about the requirement of asexual reproduction.[36] It has been described as the "very essence" of the patent. Asexual reproduction is literally the only way that a breeder can be sure he has reproduced a plant identical in every respect to the parent. It is quite possible that infringement of a plant patent would occur only if stock obtained from one of the patented plants is used, given the extreme unlikelihood that any other plant could actually infringe. If the alleged infringer could somehow prove that he had developed the plant in question independently, then he would not be

36. Lest the reader fear that Congress neglected to make adequate provision for reproduction of the sexual type, we hasten to note that the Plant Variety Protection statute, 7 U.S.C. §§ 2321–2583, applies only to sexually reproducing plants.

liable in damages or subject to an injunction for infringement.[37] This example illustrates the extreme extent to which asexual reproduction is the heart of the present plant patent system: the whole key to the "invention" of a new plant is the discovery of new traits *plus* the foresight and appreciation to take the step of asexual reproduction.

C. *Yoder's Plant Patents—Validity*

During the trial, Cal–Florida offered as evidence certain documents showing that growers had found mutations on the Mandalay variety that were the same as the patented variety Glowing Mandalay—*i.e.*, evidence that the sport Glowing Mandalay had recurred. Although Glowing Mandalay is no longer in the case, Cal–Florida later proffered similar evidence with respect to Gold Marble, Promenade, and Red Torch, which are three of the patents whose validity is challenged on appeal. Gold Marble, Promenade, and Red Torch are all sport patents, meaning that they first appeared as a sport of another plant, in contrast to seedling patents, which develop from seeds. Of the remaining four challenged patents, two were sport patents and two were seedling patents. Cal–Florida never proffered any sport recurrence evidence as to the other two sport patents, Mountain Sun and Southern Gold, nor did it offer any specific evidence attacking the seedling patents, Morocco and Mountain Snow. Since we find that the district court's ruling on the sport recurrence evidence did not preclude Cal–Florida from introducing other types of evidence to attack the validity of the patents, and since no sport recurrence evidence was introduced as to Mountain Sun and Southern Gold, we find no warrant on appeal to disturb the ruling that Mountain Sun, Southern Gold, Morocco, and Mountain Snow were valid and infringed. Plant patents, like others, enjoy a statutory presumption of validity that was not rebutted as to those four.

At the time the court rejected the sport return evidence for Glowing Mandalay, it made a ruling designed to apply to the rest of the trial with respect to that kind of evidence. That ruling is the focus of Cal–Florida's cross appeal on the plant patent validity point. Because of its importance, we set out the pertinent parts in some detail here:

> [I]t seems clear that it was the Congressional intent that a person who discovered an asexually reproduced variety of a new and distinct plant was entitled to a patent.
>
> It was not contemplated, apparently, that he invent, in the term that is used, or in the significance of that term, as we understand it, traditional concept of inventing a machine....
>
> In any event, the issue presented here is a rather narrow one and it has some practical overtones.
>
> I am frank to confess that I think Mr. Foster's [Yoder's counsel's] presentation here ... is very persuasive. In all probability, this will be, or may be, the ultimate result of this trial. It may not

37. Whether he might also be entitled to a patent on his plant is more problematic, although we would not want to rule out the possibility.

> be, after we have listened to the testimony, of course, of Mr. Boone's [Cal–Florida's counsel's] other witnesses who are coming in to testify on the genetics of this thing, but on this one narrow limited issue, it would seem that the plaintiffs [Yoder] were entitled to prevail. Therefore, the objection to the introduction of the various letters and documents from ... the growers and plant propagators around the country, which were forwarded to Yoder Brothers over the years, is sustained.

Cal–Florida construes the above-quoted ruling as an all-encompassing holding that the constitutional standard of invention does not apply to plant patents. It further claims that since the ruling was admittedly intended to apply to the entire trial, it was precluded from offering evidence on the issues of newness, distinctness, and obviousness by the court's action. In fact, it never even tried to introduce the expected expert genetics testimony, although it did make a formal offer of more sport return evidence at a later time in the trial.

Yoder disputes the breadth of the ruling and its effect on any other evidence Cal–Florida might have offered, and notes that the court's actual ruling on the issues of newness and distinctness did not come until some two weeks later. With regard to the ruling on the admissibility of the evidence, Yoder argues that the documents would not have shown lack of distinctness, since the fact that a sport with particular traits recurs says nothing about what those traits are and how they differ from other plants. Furthermore, Yoder argues that the documents would not have shown obviousness, because if sport recurrence were evidence of obviousness, then almost no mutations would be patentable, and that would be contrary to Congress' intent.

We do not construe the district court's evidentiary ruling as anything more than that; in our opinion, it simply held that the sport recurrence evidence was not relevant to any of the patent validity issues. We therefore confine our remarks accordingly.

The only possible probative value of the sport recurrence evidence would be to show that a sport of that particular size, shape, color, or other trait is predictable from a given variety of parent plant. Thus, we must first determine whether Congress intended predictability to negate the possibility of "invention." Next, if Congress considered that factor irrelevant, we must decide if the Constitution is offended by permitting patents on the kinds of sports that recur.[39]

39. In this discussion, we are concerned only with the "invention" or obviousness issue. As we have defined novelty, *supra*, the recurrence of a sport of a particular color would be irrelevant. Similarly, sport recurrence says nothing about the new plant's particular characteristics. The testimony at the trial amply established that Yoder's patented chrysanthemums were distinct to those skilled in the field—*i.e.*, those in the breeding business. We note that there is a distinction between looking to the opinion of persons in the industry to prove a feature of patentability and relying on commercial success to prove nonobviousness. Yoder's arguments relied on the former kind of evidence.

Both the language of the statute and its legislative history persuade us that Congress did not intend to exclude the kind of mutation that might recur from the Act's protection. Instead, both Senate Report 315, 71st Cong., 2d Sess. (1930), on the original bill, and Senate Report 1937, 83d Cong., 2d Sess. (1954), on the 1954 amendment, speak generally about sports and mutations. The 1954 amendment was added to clarify Congress' intention that seedlings should be patentable, but in the process of describing the bill, the report states:

> The enactment of this legislation will remove any doubt that the legislative intent of the Congress clearly means that sports, mutants, hybrids, and seedlings, discovered by persons engaged in agriculture or horticulture, should be patentable . . .

S.Rep. 1937, *supra.*

Although we are willing to assume for purposes of this argument that some mutations may appear that would have been genetically impossible before—*i.e.*, that a fundamental change in the biochemical structure of the chromosome may take place—by far the majority of mutations and sports of chrysanthemums are predictable to some extent for those skilled in the field. For example, the testimony at trial indicated that a yellow sport could be expected from a white chrysanthemum. Indeed, part of the skill required of a chrysanthemum breeder is to know what to look for and to take steps immediately to preserve it by asexual reproduction if the desired trait appears. Given that fact, we think that the purpose of the Plant Patent Act would be frustrated by a requirement that only those rare, never-before-seen, if not genetically impossible sports or mutations would be patentable. That purpose was "to afford agriculture, so far as practicable, the same opportunity to participate in the benefits of the patent system as has been given industry, and thus assist in placing agriculture on a basis of economic equality with industry." S.Rep. 315, *supra.* To make it significantly more difficult to obtain a plant patent than another type of patent would frustrate that purpose.

We therefore find that Congress did not intend to exclude the kind of sport that recurs frequently from the Plant Patent Act. That being the case, the district court correctly ruled that the evidence proffered by Cal–Florida was irrelevant, as a matter of statutory law.

The only way that the Constitution would be offended by permitting patents on recurring sports would be if such leniency indicated that no "invention" was present. We do not think that sport recurrence would negate invention, however. An infinite number of a certain sized sport could appear on a plant, but until someone recognized its uniqueness and difference and found that the traits could be preserved by asexual reproduction in commercial quantities, no patentable plant would exist. An objective judgment of the value of the sport's new and different characteristics—*i.e.*, nutritive value, ornamental value, hardiness, longevity, etc.—would not depend in any way on whether a similar sport had appeared in the past, or whether that particular sport was predictable. We therefore find no reason to disturb our approval of the district court's evidentiary ruling based on the constitutional standard of invention. As that standard applies to plant patents, the proffered evidence was irrelevant.

Viewing the evidence offered on the patent validity question as a whole, we find that Cal–Florida failed to rebut the statutory presumption of validity as to Gold Marble, Promenade, and Red Torch, as well as the other four discussed above. Thus, the lower court's finding of validity must be affirmed on this record.

D. Patent Infringement

On cross appeal, Cal–Florida asserts that the absence of flowering plants grown from the cuttings it had admittedly taken from Yoder's patented plants was fatal to Yoder's infringement counts. This is because the patent claim in each instance describes a mature flowering plant, and it is Cal-Florida's position that only another mature flowering plant could directly infringe. Yoder retorts that the Plant Patent Act provides that

> [i]n the case of a plant patent the grant shall be of the right to exclude others from asexually reproducing the plant or selling or using the plant so reproduced.

35 U.S.C. § 163. The district court ruled that the act of asexual reproduction was complete at the time the cutting was taken. Finally, the pretrial stipulations established that Cal–Florida had taken plant material, or cuttings, from Yoder's patented plants.

We agree with Yoder that it was not necessary to prove that the cuttings actually matured into flowered plants to show infringement. Under such a rule, it would be virtually impossible for a propagator-distributor directly to infringe a patent, despite the vital role he plays in dissemination of plant material. Furthermore, we think section 163 is plain in its statement that a patentee may exclude others from asexually reproducing, selling or using the plant. The negative inference to be drawn from this is that commission of one of those acts would constitute infringement. We therefore affirm the finding of infringement.

* * *

Notes and Questions

1. *Plant patents.* The Plant Patent Act was passed in 1930, long after utility patents had been established in the United States. It was later codified in the Patent Act of 1952 at sections 161–64. Section 161 provides that utility patent provisions should apply to plant patents, except as otherwise provided. As the Fifth Circuit's opinion indicates, adapting provisions created and construed with new and useful machines, compositions of matter, manufactures and processes in mind to plants raises some conceptual problems. How does the court adapt the nonobviousness requirement of section 103 to the plant patent context? What about the novelty requirement? Why shouldn't the evidence that the same patented sports had

appeared prior to Yoder's discovery and application be relevant to the Court's novelty and nonobviousness determinations? Indeed, could one argue that the evidence that sports recur naturally, with no help from humans, indicates that there was no "invention" on Yoder's part?

What does the "distinctiveness" requirement, set forth in section 161, entail?

Once a plant patent is granted, what conduct will infringe it? What if the patented plant has seeds, and A takes the seeds, plants them without permission, and grows a new plant? Will A be liable for infringement? See 35 U.S.C.A. § 163. What if, after the patent is granted, the patented sport recurs naturally, B discovers it and asexually reproduces it? Will B be liable for infringement? Compare the Fifth Circuit's view, at footnote 37 of *Yoder*, with Pan–American Plant Co. v. Matsui, 433 F.Supp. 693, 694 n.2, 198 U.S.P.Q. 462, 463 n.2 (N.D.Cal.1977) (stating, in *dictum*, "the [Plant Patent] Act bars the asexual reproduction and sale of any plant which is the same variety (i.e., has the same essential characteristics) as the patented plant, whether or not the infringing plant was originally cloned from the patented plant."). Does the language of section 163 provide an answer? Which view is more consistent with the law of utility patents? Which view makes more sense in the context of plant patents? As it happens, the plant patent provisions have generated relatively few court opinions to clarify their scope and application.

What problems might an applicant for a plant patent have in satisfying the enabling disclosure provisions of section 112? The perceived problems in making enabling disclosure had been an important obstacle to patenting plants prior to passage of the Plant Patent Act. Congress directly addressed the issue in section 162: "no plant patent shall be declared invalid for noncompliance with section 112 of this title if the description is as complete as is reasonably possible." The disclosure and claiming for plant patents is done primarily through color drawings. See 37 C.F.R. § 1.165.

Section 162 does not, however, directly address a related problem: what sort of "printed publication" will trigger the one-year statutory bar of section 102(b)? The Court of Customs and Patent Appeals addressed the "printed publication" question in *Application of* LeGrice, 301 F.2d 929, 133 U.S.P.Q. 365 (C.C.P.A.1962). In *LeGrice*, the patent applicant's roses had been depicted and described in English publications more than a year before he filed his United States patent application. The publications included color pictures and descriptions such as the following:

> Glowing dark scarlet with dusky velvety sheen. Single blooms carried in large trusses. Size when open 3–in. in diameter. Very fragrant. Vigorous. Foliage dark green and abundant. Bedding. Trail Ground Certificate, 1945. Prune 34.

Id., 301 F.2d at 931, 133 U.S.P.Q. at 368. The court held that the provisions of section 102(b) were fully applicable, and that they should be interpreted in the same manner for plant patents as for utility patents. Utility patent opinions specified that the printed publication must be sufficiently full, clear and exact to enable a person skilled in the relevant art to make or practice the invention. The English publications did not enable anyone to "make" the applicant's rose. The applicant's roses were the result of cross-pollenization, but even identification of the parent plants would not be sufficiently enabling, since "the principles of heredity and plant genetics introduce such variables that no two seeds from the parent cross can be expected to produce identical plants." *Id.*, 301 F.2d at 938, 133 U.S.P.Q. at 373. Thus, the statutory bar had not been triggered.

The court rejected the examiner's and Board of Appeals' argument that its finding essentially rendered the section 102(b) printed publication provision inapplicable to plants:

> [I]t requires that the facts of each case be carefully considered to determine whether the description in the printed publication in question *does in fact* place the invention in the possession of the public. * * * While the present knowledge of plant genetics may mean as a practical matter, that the descriptions in such general publications as are here involved cannot be relied upon as a statutory bar under section 102(b), we must be mindful of the scientific efforts which are daily adding to the store of knowledge in the fields of plant heredity and plant eugenics which one skilled in this art will be presumed to possess.

Id., 301 F.2d at 939, 133 U.S.P.Q. at 374.

2. *The Plant Variety Protection Act.* Congress excluded sexually reproduced plants (plants reproduced from seeds, rather than through cloning) from the Plant Patent Act because in 1930, it was not believed that new varieties could be reproduced true-to-type through seeds. By 1970, however, it was generally recognized that true-to-type reproduction was in fact possible. This lead Congress to enact the Plant Variety Protection Act ("PVPA") to extend patent-like protection to new sexually reproduced varieties of plants. The PVPA, which is codified at 7 U.S.C.A. §§ 2321–2582, protects new varieties through certificates of plant variety protection, issued by the Department of Agriculture.

As recently amended by the Plant Variety Protection Act Amendments of 1994, Pub. L. No. 103–349, 108 Stat. 3136, the PVPA extends protection to sexually reproduced and tuberpropagated plant varieties other than fungi and bacteria. 7 U.S.C.A. § 2402. To qualify, the new variety must be new, distinct, uniform, and stable. *Id.*. The latter two conditions underscore the need to ensure that the variety reproduces itself true-to-type. Congress declined to include a nonobviousness requirement. There are, however, statutory bar provisions reminiscent of Patent Act section 102(b). 7 U.S.C.A. § 2402.

A certificate of plant variety protection enables the owner to exclude others from selling the variety, offering the variety for sale, reproducing it, importing it, exporting it, or using it in producing (as opposed to developing) a hybrid or different variety. *Id.*, § 2483. The term of protection, previously 18 years, is now 20 years (and in the case of trees and vines, 25 years) from the date of issuance. (The new term measure applies to certificates granted on applications filed after April 4, 1995). Pub. L. No. 103–349 §§ 7, 15, 108 Stat. 3140, 3145. There are opportunities for protection prior to issuance of the certificate, as well. *Id.*, §§ 2541, 2567.

There are some exceptions to liability. Most notably, a "research exemption" permits "use and reproduction of a protected variety for plant breeding or other bona fide research." *Id.*, § 2544. Farmers may save seed descended from seed originally acquired under the certificate owner's authority, and use it to produce new crops. The 1994 amendments deleted a controversial "farmers exemption," which permitted farmers to sell saved seed in some circumstances for reproductive purposes. Pub. L. No. 103–349, § 10, 108 Stat. 3140, 3142. This exception will continue to apply, however, in the case of certificates in existence or granted on applications pending on April 4, 1995, the amendments' effective date. *Id.*, § 14, 108 Stat. at 3144.

3. *Utility patents for plants.* After the Supreme Court determined, in *Diamond v. Chakrabarty*, that the scope of utility patents extends to living matter, it became evident that new plant matter could qualify for utility patent protection even if it also qualified for a plant patent or a certificate of plant variety protection. The PTO's Board of Patent Appeals and Interferences confirmed this in *Ex parte* Hibberd, 227 U.S.P.Q.2d 443 (PTO Bd. Pat. App. 1985), when it found that plants, plant seeds, and plant tissue cultures constituted patentable subject matter under section 101 of the Patent Act. How will an applicant satisfy the section 112 enablement requirements? Which form of patent protection would the developer of a new plant variety be likely to prefer?

4. *The International Convention for the Protection of New Varieties of Plants.* The United States is a member of the International Convention for the Protection of New Varieties of Plants, Dec. 2, 1961, *last revised,* 1991, 33 U.S.T. 2703, T.I.A.S. No. 10,199. The Convention, which is administered by the Union for the Protection of New Varieties of Plants ("UPOV"), in Geneva, provides for national treatment and a filing right of priority, as well as a number of substantive common rules. Among other things, it specifies a minimum number of genera and species that must be protected, standards for protectibility, a minimum term of protection, and minimum rights that must be offered. It provides, however, that member nations may design their protection either in the form of a special title, such as a plant variety protection certificate, or a patent.

III. DESIGN PATENTS

A. THE LAW OF DESIGN PATENTS

Congress created design patents in 1842. The present design provisions can be found at sections 171–173 of the Patent Act. Section 171 authorizes patents for "any new, original and ornamental design for an article of manufacture," and specifies that the provisions relating "to patents for inventions shall apply to patents for designs, except as otherwise provided." 35 U.S.C.A. § 171. Pursuant to this directive, courts have imposed the "novelty" and "nonobviousness" standards developed in connection with utility patents to judge the patentability of designs. "Ornamentality" replaces "usefulness" as the third standard of design patentability.

According to the Supreme Court:

> The acts of Congress which authorize the grant of patents for designs were plainly intended to give encouragement to the decora-

> tive arts. They contemplate not so much utility as appearance * * *. [T]he thing invented or produced, for which a patent is given, is that which gives a peculiar or distinctive appearance to the manufacture, or article to which it may be applied, or to which it gives form. The law manifestly contemplates that giving certain new and original appearances to a manufactured article may enhance its salable value, may enlarge the demand for it, and may be a meritorious service to the public. It therefore proposes to secure for a limited time to the ingenious producer of those appearances the advantages flowing from them.

Gorham v. White, 81 U.S. (14 Wall.) 511, 524–25, 20 L.Ed. 731, 736 (1871).

BLACK & DECKER INC. v. PITTWAY CORP.

United States District Court for the Northern District of Illinois, 1986.
636 F.Supp. 1193, 231 U.S.P.Q. 252.

SHADUR, DISTRICT JUDGE.

[Black & Decker ("B & D") sued Pittway Corp. for design patent infringement. Pittway now moves for summary judgment.]

In early 1980 B & D decided to design a rechargeable flashlight, assigning that project to B & D employee Donald McCloskey ("McCloskey"). B & D wanted the flashlight design to resemble its Dustbuster cordless vacuum cleaner system, and McCloskey in fact used Dustbuster as a "reference" in developing a flashlight design.

* * * On January 31, 1984 U.S. Design Patent 272,476 ("Design Patent 476") issued to B & D, covering "[t]he ornamental design for a flashlight or similar article, as shown and described". B & D's "Spotliter" rechargeable flashlight embodies that design. B & D claims Pittway's "Ready–Lite" rechargeable flashlight infringes Design Patent 476.

PITTWAY'S CONTENTIONS

Pittway advances three contentions in support of its summary judgment motion:

> 1. Design Patent 476 is invalid under 35 U.S.C. § 102 because the prior art anticipated B & D's flashlight design.
>
> 2. Design Patent 476 is invalid under 35 U.S.C. § 103 because the prior art rendered the flashlight design obvious.
>
> 3. Pittway's Ready–Lite flashlight does not infringe B & D's Design Patent 476.

In accordance with the "better practice" identified by the Court of Appeals for the Federal Circuit in *Medtronic, Inc. v. Cardiac Pacemakers, Inc.*, 721 F.2d 1563, 1582–83 (Fed.Cir.1983), this opinion will address each of those arguments, though either would be dispositive here.

ANTICIPATION

Anticipation doctrine has essentially been codified in Section 102 [of the Patent Act]. *Continental Oil Co. v. Cole*, 634 F.2d 188, 195 (5th Cir.), *cert. denied*, 454 U.S. 830, 102 S.Ct. 124, 70 L.Ed.2d 106 (1981) states the general rule:

> [U]nless all of the same elements or their equivalents are found in substantially the same situation where they do substantially the same work in the same way, there is no anticipation.

By definition anticipation exists only where a *single prior art reference* contains each element of a patent claim.

Pittway Mem. 5 relies on an internal B & D patent memorandum to identify six distinct features of Design Patent 476 (for convenience in comparison, the following numbering will be retained throughout this opinion in referring to these features):

1. a square head;
2. an asymmetric placement of the handle;
3. a sloping interconnection between the handle and the head;
4. an angularity of profile;
5. a handle with flattened sides; and
6. a reflector axis parallel to the axis of the handle.

Pittway has pointed out two relevant prior art references:

1. a flash attachment called the Mecablitz Model No. 107 ("Metz 107"); and
2. B & D's own Dustbuster design.

Pittway says each of those devices contains every claimed element of Design Patent 476.[3]

Clark Equipment Co. v. Keller, 570 F.2d 778, 799 (8th Cir.), *cert. denied*, 439 U.S. 825, 99 S.Ct. 96, 58 L.Ed.2d 118 (1978), states the "ordinary observer" test for determining Section 102 anticipation:

> The novelty of a design patent ... is tested by determining the impact of the design upon an ordinary observer. A design patent is novel when the "average observer takes the new design for a different, and not a modified already existing design." ... This is

3. Pittway initially claimed U.S. Design Patent 205,679 ("Design Patent 679") also anticipated Design Patent 476. But Pittway Mem. 20 admits Design Patent 679 lacks three features of Design Patent 476:

1. a square head;

5. a handle with flattened sides; and

6. a reflector axis parallel to the axis of the handle.

In an effort to close that gap, Pittway Mem. 19 urged another prior art reference (U.S. Design Patent 204,904) ("Design Patent 904") contained those three features. Pittway then said the "combination" formed by adding Design Patent 679's features to Design Patent 904's elements collectively anticipated B & D's Design Patent 476. But as noted in the text of this opinion, anticipation (as contrasted with obviousness) exists only where a single prior art reference contains each element of a patent claim. * * *

the prevailing and now well-settled test for the novelty of a design patent.

That standard is readily applicable to evaluate the similarity of Design Patent 476 to the prior art references identified by Pittway.

1. Metz 107

Metz 107 was manufactured as a flash attachment by the Metz Company of Fuerth, West Germany. It was sold in the United States at least as early as 1961. Side-by-side drawings of the designs embodied in Design Patent 476 and Metz 107 facilitate their comparison (attached as Appendix 1 to this opinion).

That visual comparison reveals Metz 107 clearly has five of B & D's self-identified six features of Design Patent 476:

1. a large square head;
2. an asymmetric placement of the handle;
3. a sloping interconnection between the handle and the head;
4. an angularity of profile; and
5. a handle with flattened sides.

Only two arguable differences between Metz 107 and Design Patent 476 require separate consideration:

1. Metz 107 is a camera flash attachment and not a flashlight.
2. Unlike the Spotliter, Metz 107's reflector axis is not parallel to the axis of the handle (B & D's claimed sixth feature).

Neither defeats Pittway's anticipation claim.

First, a mere difference in Metz 107's function does not negate Pittway's claim that the Metz 107 design anticipates Design Patent 476. As *In re Glavas*, 230 F.2d 447, 450 (C.C.P.A.1956) put it:

> * * *
>
> [T]he use to which an article is to be put has no bearing on its patentability as a design and that if the prior art discloses any article of substantially the same appearance as that of an applicant, it is immaterial what the use of such article is.... Accordingly, so far as anticipation by a single prior art disclosure is concerned, there can be no question as to nonanalogous art in design cases.

See also *Revlon, Inc. v. Carson Products Co.*, 602 F.Supp. 1071, 1083 (S.D.N.Y.1985) ("Unlike the doctrine of obviousness ..., anticipation does not require that the prior references be analogous or even relevant arts to the invention"). Even were that not the rule, Metz 107 and the Spotliter perform a similar function (providing artificial light) in any event. Without question the Metz 107 design constitutes relevant prior art to Design Patent 476.

As for the only other difference between Metz 107 and Spotliter (that of reflector axis orientation), Pittway says that represents a purely functional consideration and hence cannot support the validity of Design

Patent 476. *Kwik-Site Corp. v. Clear View Manufacturing Co.*, 758 F.2d 167, 171 (6th Cir.1985) states the general principle on which Pittway relies:

> A design patent may be issued for "any new, original and *ornamental* design for an article of manufacture." 35 U.S.C. § 171 (emphasis added). In order to be valid, a design patent "must disclose a design that is new, original and ornamental, unanticipated and inventive in character, and beyond the skill of the ordinary designer or draftsman.... *A design patent cannot be obtained to protect a mechanical function or cover an article whose configuration affects its utility alone*". *Spaulding v. Guardian Light Co.*, 267 F.2d 111, 112 (7th Cir.1959) (emphasis added).

Here Pittway argues the difference in reflector axis orientation stems not from aesthetic considerations but solely from the different functions of a camera flash attachment and a hand-held flashlight. In support of that position Pittway points to McCloskey Dep. 92:

> Q. I'm not really focusing on the particular angle of the handle. What I'm saying is that you'd want the beam directed from the front of the unit as opposed to some of the other designs, earlier designs we saw, referring to exhibit 2, as opposed to coming out of what would be the bottom of the head or the top of the head, is that correct?
>
> A. Yes, that's correct.
>
> Q. That was a functional consideration that dictated that, am I correct?
>
> A. Yes, you are.

Because the direction of the light serves a purpose dictated only by the function of the product, that feature cannot serve to distinguish Design Patent 476 from Metz 107.

In summary, Metz 107 fully anticipates Design Patent 476. Though that alone would be dispositive here, it is worth examining Pittway's other prior art reference.

2. B & D's Dustbuster

Pittway also says B & D's own Dustbuster anticipates each element of Design Patent 476 (depictions of both are attached as Appendix 2 to this opinion). But a visual comparison reveals Design Patent 476 and Dustbuster share only two of B & D's stated six features of Design Patent 476:

2. an asymmetric placement of the handle; and
4. an angularity of profile.

Dustbuster clearly lacks:

1. a large square head;
3. a sloping interconnection between the handle and the head;

5. a handle with flattened sides; and

6. a reflector axis parallel to the handle.

In short, Dustbuster's design simply does not sufficiently resemble Design Patent 476 to anticipate it.

Though Pittway thus misses the mark as to Dustbuster, it is correct in contending Metz 107 fully anticipates Design Patent 476. * * *

OBVIOUSNESS

Pittway also seeks summary judgment on the ground Design Patent 476 is invalid as "obvious" under Section 103 [of the Patent Act]:

> A patent may not be obtained though the invention is not identically disclosed or described as set forth in section 102 of this title, if the differences between the subject matter sought to be patented and the prior art are such that the subject matter as a whole would have been obvious at the time the invention was made to a person having ordinary skill in the art to which said subject matter pertains.

That reference to "a person having ordinary skill in the art," in the field of design patents, has been taken to mean "the designer of ordinary capability who designs articles of the type presented in the application." *In re Nalbandian*, 661 F.2d 1214, 1216 (C.C.P.A.1981).

Of course the holding Design Patent 476 was fully anticipated by Metz 107 carries with it a fortiori a holding of obviousness under Section 103. *In re Fracalossi*, 681 F.2d 792, 794 (C.C.P.A.1982) put that "obvious" conclusion in these terms:

> Though the composition might have been obvious, though not anticipated, it cannot have been anticipated and not have been obvious. Thus evidence establishing lack of all novelty in the claimed invention necessarily evidences obviousness. * * *

Even were Metz 107 not fully anticipatory (and hence the "epitome of obviousness"), Pittway's submissions support an independent finding of obviousness. That defense (unlike anticipation) does not require every element of the claimed patent to appear in a single reference. Here Pittway has identified several references besides Metz 107 that, in combination, reveal each distinct feature of Design Patent 476:

1. U.S. Design Patents 226,022 and 226,219 reveal a square head.

2. U.S. Design Patent 230,068 includes an asymmetric placement of the handle.

3. U.S. Design Patents 226,022 and 208,940 show a sloping interconnection between the handle and the head.

4. U.S. Design Patents 226,022, 209,163 and 226,219 all demonstrate an angularity of profile.

5. U.S. Design Patent 226,022 contains a handle with flattened sides.

> 6. Each of the prior references cited by Pittway includes a reflector axis parallel to the axis of the handle.

Thus the relevant prior art would clearly suggest Design Patent 476.

That approach of course poses some peril. Especially in the field of design patents, an undue splintering of the whole into too many small parts could well result in the nonpatentability of almost any design as "obvious." But more to the point, such a two-patent combination as has been rejected in n. 3 for anticipation purposes states a powerful case for the obviousness and hence invalidity of Design Patent 476.

B & D tries to resist the obviousness result by pointing to the commercial success of its Spotliter as raising a factual issue on that score. That argument stems from the seminal expression in *Graham v. John Deere Co.*, 383 U.S. 1, 17–18, 86 S.Ct. 684, 693–94, 15 L.Ed.2d 545 (1966):

> Under § 103, the scope and content of the prior art are to be determined; differences between the prior art and the claims at issue are to be ascertained; and the level of ordinary skill in the pertinent art resolved. Against this background, the obviousness or nonobviousness of the subject matter is determined. Such secondary considerations as commercial success, long felt but unsolved needs, failure of others, etc., might be utilized to give light to the circumstances surrounding the origin of the subject matter sought to be patented. As indicia of obviousness or nonobviousness, these inquiries may have relevancy.

To support its commercial-success claim, B & D relies on Aff. ¶¶ 3–4 of its Product Manager of Lighting Products, Carol Dores:

> 3. I have examined business records of Black & Decker (U.S.) Inc. pertaining to sales of SPOTLITER rechargeable lights which incorporate the design of the McCloskey et al. patent.
>
> 4. The said records indicate that, since product introduction, sales have been in excess of three million units, producing revenues in excess of sixty million dollars ($60,000,000.00).

But whatever that statement says about commercial success, it wholly fails to establish a link between that success and the distinct features of Design Patent 476. That omission is fatal, for *Simmons Fastener Corp. v. Illinois Tool Works, Inc.*, 739 F.2d 1573, 1575 (Fed.Cir.1984), *cert. denied*, ___ U.S. ___, 105 S.Ct. 2138, 85 L.Ed.2d 496 (1985) teaches:

> A nexus between the merits of the claimed invention and the evidence of secondary considerations is required in order for the evidence to be given substantial weight in an obviousness decision.

Dores' affidavit thus creates no material fact issue as to nonobviousness based on commercial success.

* * *

In summary, B & D has failed to "set forth specific facts" controverting Pittway's submissions. Pittway has also established the obviousness of Design Patent 476 as a matter of law.

Infringement

Litton Systems, Inc. v. Whirlpool Corp., 728 F.2d 1423, 1444 (Fed. Cir.1984) summarizes the legal standard of infringement in design patent cases:

> More than one hundred years ago, the Supreme Court established a test for determining infringement of a design patent which, to this day, remains valid. *Gorham Co. v. White*, 81 U.S. (14 Wall.) 511, 20 L.Ed. 731 (1871). This test requires that "if, in the eye of an ordinary observer, giving such attention as a purchaser usually gives, two designs are substantially the same, if the resemblance is such as to deceive such an observer, inducing him to purchase one supposing it to be the other, the first one patented is infringed by the other." *Id.* at 528, 20 L.Ed. 731.
>
> For a design patent to be infringed, however, no matter how similar two items look, "the accused device must appropriate the novelty in the patented device which distinguishes it from the prior art." *Sears, Roebuck & Co. v. Talge*, 140 F.2d 395, 396 (8th Cir.1944). That is, even though the court compares two items through the eyes of the ordinary observer, it must nevertheless, to find infringement, attribute their similarity to the novelty which distinguishes the patented device from the prior art.

Pittway argues its Ready–Lite does not transgress that standard and therefore does not infringe Design Patent 476.

1. Gorham's "Eye" Test

Pittway Mem. 29–30 first urges McCloskey Dep. 220–30 concedes twelve differences exist between Ready–Lite and Spotliter:

> (1) the "canted" or downward sloping joining of the head-to-handle in the RL30, which is not present in the Spotliter, the latter having a handle parallel to the reflector axis;
>
> (2) the head of the Spotliter is much larger in proportion to its handle than is the RL30, the head of the RL30 being substantially smaller than the Spotliter's;
>
> (3) a thicker, rounder handle on the RL30;
>
> (4) the different angle of the head (10 to 15 degrees of difference) when both the RL30 and the Spotliter are either resting on a horizontal surface or hand-held;
>
> (5) the shoulder of the Spotliter angles back toward the handle, whereas the shoulder on the RL30 angles toward the front;
>
> (6) the "on-off" switches are substantially different in size and shape, with the RL30's being about twice as long;

(7) the housings of the two units are different—the RL30 using a single molded part, whereas the Spotliter is a two-piece construction with visible screw openings and a visible mating line;

(8) the top of the RL30 handle is flat whereas the Spotliter's is rounded;

(9) the back of the RL30 handle is more slanted and does not have the retaining lip of the Spotliter;

(10) the RL30 does not have the Spotliter's adjustable wire bale, for angling the beam of light, or a finger recess in the housing to enable the bale to be gripped;

(11) the LED indicators are on opposite sides of the two units; and

(12) the RL30 bezel (front-most portion of the head) is square and of a uniform wall thickness, whereas the bezel of the Spotliter is sculptured and tapers toward the round lens opening.

D. Ex. 11 (attached as Appendix 3 to this opinion), a side-by-side photograph of Ready–Lite and Spotliter, facilitates an evaluation of those claimed differences, which have been confirmed by this Court's own physical inspection of Ready–Lite and Spotliter (in a literal application of the *Gorham* "eye of an ordinary observer" standard).

Perhaps no individual distinction would by itself justify a conclusion of noninfringement. However, the combination of those differences in Ready–Lite's design creates a distinct impression of an overall difference in appearance. In that respect, *Black & Decker, Inc. v. North American Phillips Corp.*, 632 F.Supp. 185, 190–191, 228 U.S.P.Q. 659, 661 (D.Conn.1986) (rejecting an infringement claim as to Dustbuster) might well have been written for this case:

> Plaintiffs also argue that comparison of the individual elements of the respective machines is impermissible. While the *Gorham* "eye" test anticipates that the court will make a judgment based on an overall impression of the products in issue and not compare individual components of a product[,] the court cannot avoid a consideration of the constituent elements of the machines, if only to use these elements as a point of reference for making a general comparison. Moreover, when the elemental differences are numerous and substantial, their combined effect causes the product in overall appearance to be distinct and different. The Court notes the differences between the constituent parts of the opposing designs not as determinative by themselves, but as part of the process of evaluating the overall appearances of the product. The Court would "have been deficient if it had not so specified the underlying reasons for its appraisal." *Tappan Co. v. General Motors Corp.*, 380 F.2d 888, 891, 154 USPQ 561, 563 (6th Cir.1967).
>
> * * *

Here B & D does not dispute the design differences identified by Pittway. Instead B & D says a factual issue as to infringement is created by its evidentiary submissions:

1. a survey purporting to demonstrate that Ready–Lite and Spotliter appear confusingly similar to an ordinary observer; and

2. two affidavits from B & D's Customer Service Manager Walter Biedermann purporting to establish actual instances of consumer confusion between Ready–Lite and Spotliter.

Like the rest of B & D's contentions, this one fails.

First, B & D's survey information does not surmount even the low threshold of Fed.R.Evid. 401's relevance definition. B & D's survey "expert" first showed a number of people a printed advertisement displaying a variety of household products, including only one flashlight—B & D's Spotliter. Then the advertisement was removed from view, and the interviewees were asked to recall several of the products advertised. Those who remembered seeing a flashlight were then taken into a room with various household products on display, including only one flashlight—this time Pittway's Ready–Lite. At that point the respondents were asked which products on display they had earlier seen in the advertisement. According to B & D, 88% of those people incorrectly identified Pittway's Ready–Lite as the B & D Spotliter they had actually seen in the advertisement.

Just to describe that procedure shows how nonprobative it is of a confusing resemblance between Ready–Lite and Spotliter. It strongly resembles a card trick in which the magician forces on his subject the card he wants selected. * * *

As for B & D's second type of evidentiary submission—the Biedermann affidavits—each refers to some customer correspondence received in connection with B & D's rebate policy, but in each instance actually relating to one of Pittway's products (and not B & D's), and then states Biedermann's own conclusions as to the significance of that correspondence. Neither affidavit suffices to create the necessary factual issue to block summary judgment.

[The court finds that the affidavits are hearsay, depending on out-of-court statements to establish the truth of the matters asserted.]

There is more. Even were confusion between the products properly established (as it has not been), there is nothing at all to suggest the confusion stemmed from the patent-distinctive (that is, the allegedly "novel" or invented) part of B & D's design. That independently deprives the affidavits of any probative force, and it logically leads to the final phase of this opinion.

2. *"Point of Novelty" Test*

This Court's conclusion that Ready–Lite and Spotliter do not share the same overall design compels a finding of noninfringement under *Gorham's* "eye" test. But the second paragraph previously quoted from

Litton, 728 F.2d at 1444, also identifies a second and independent "point of novelty" standard for determining design patent noninfringement. That doctrine, under which the court must "attribute the [ ]similarity [between the two designs] to the novelty which distinguishes the patented device from the prior art," is of course simply an application of the general (and tautological) concept that only *invention* is entitled to patent-law protection. Except for such part of a design as is truly novel (and hence patentable), anyone is absolutely free to copy it, jot and tittle.

During discovery Pittway served an interrogatory on B & D designed to pinpoint the novel features of Design Patent 476. When B & D initially refused to answer that interrogatory, Magistrate James Balog ordered it to do so. B & D then identified just two features of Spotliter as novel:

> 1. a square-shaped head with a round lens and reflector blended into a single rearwardly-extending stick handle; and
>
> 2. a switch on top of the handle.

But Pittway's Ready–Lite incorporates neither of those features as stated:

> 1. In contrast to Spotliter's round lens, Ready–Lite incorporates a square lens. * * *
>
> 2. Spotliter's switch in fact appears on top of the flashlight's large square head. Ready–Lite's switch, as B & D asserts, is located on the handle itself. Hence Ready–Lite does not incorporate Spotliter's assertedly novel switch placement.

Thus B & D fails the "point of novelty" test as well.[13]

In sum on the infringement issue:

> 1. Pittway's Ready–Lite does not look sufficiently similar to B & D's Spotliter so as to confuse an ordinary observer.
>
> 2. Moreover and independently, Pittway's Ready–Lite has not appropriated the asserted novelty of Spotliter. For each of those separate reasons, Pittway has not infringed Design Patent 476.

Conclusion

There is no genuine issue of material fact, and Pittway is entitled to a judgment as a matter of law, on B & D's Complaint. Design Patent 476 is neither valid nor infringed by Pittway's Ready–Lite. * * *

13. In fairness, B & D was brought to the point of identifying "points of novelty" kicking and screaming. Its basic position has been that everything in Design Patent 476 is novel in its totality. And it must be recognized *Litton* approached the "point of novelty" inquiry (728 F.2d at 1444) after the court had already narrowed the scope of the design patent in that case in the course of holding it valid. This opinion, which addresses noninfringement as an alternative defense (and must for that purpose also assume the patent's validity arguendo, though this Court has ruled otherwise on the merits) cannot indulge the *Litton* luxury of limiting the patent claim. * * * In any event, candor here compels the acknowledgement that if B & D could have avoided being pinned down to identify the specific features it claimed as "novel," the Spotliter might perhaps have survived the "point of novelty" test—but it could not pass the "eye" test in any event. That latter failure would remain just as fatal to B & D.

APPENDIX 1

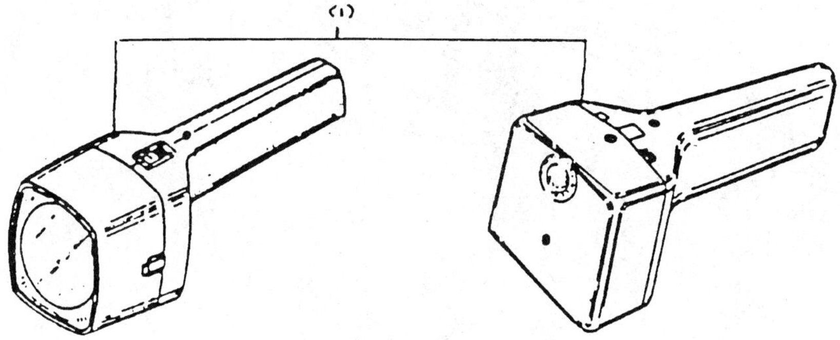

[Figure 1--'476 patent] [Metz 107 device]

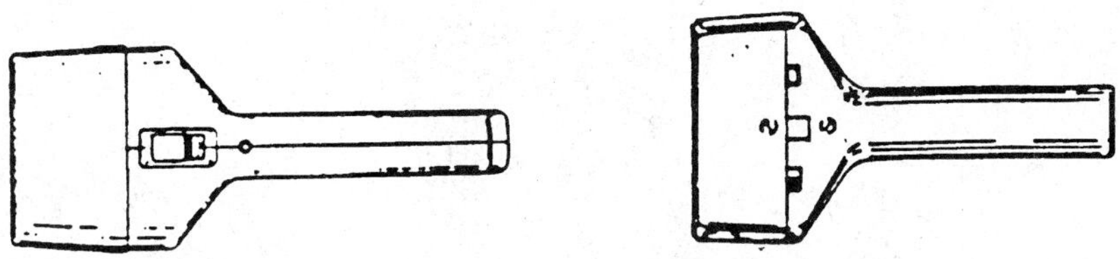

[Figure 2--'476 patent] [Metz 107 device]

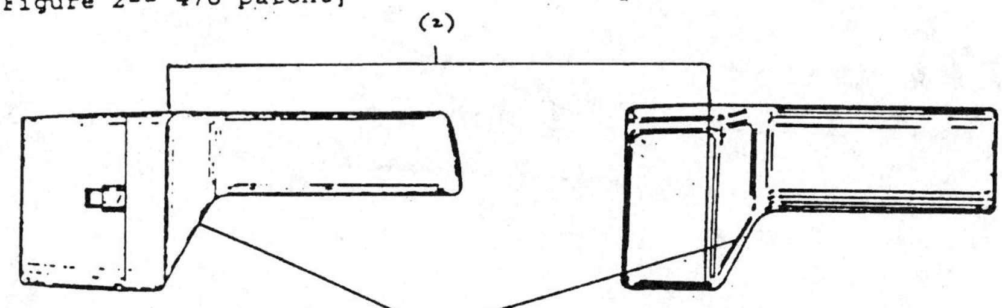

[Figure 3--'476 patent] [Metz 107 device]

(3)

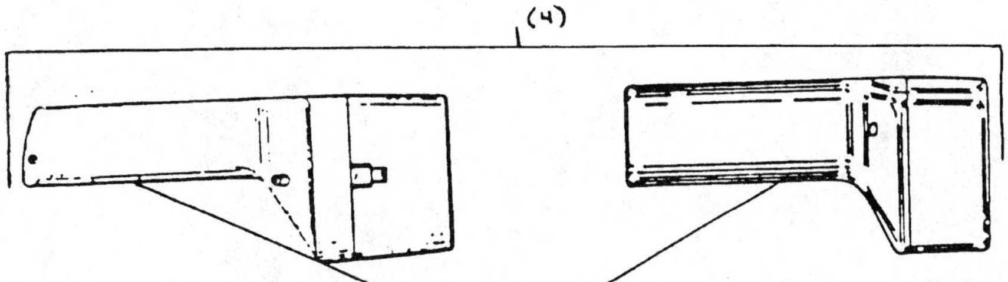

[Figure 4--'476 patent] [Metz 107 device]

(5)

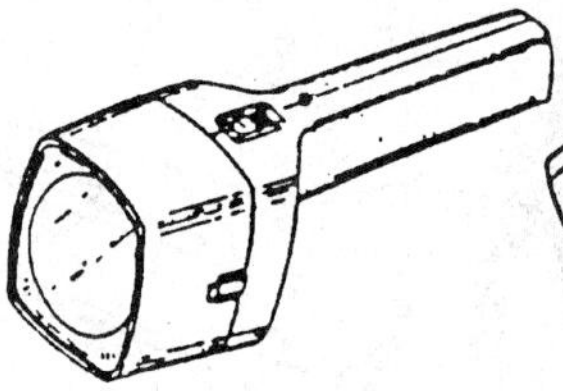

DESIGN PATENT 476

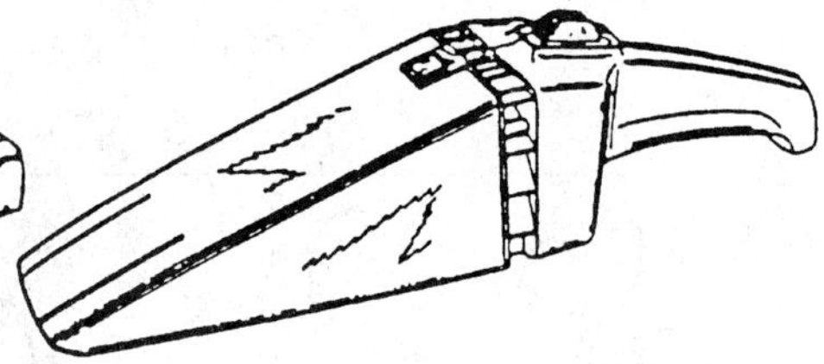

DUSTBUSTER

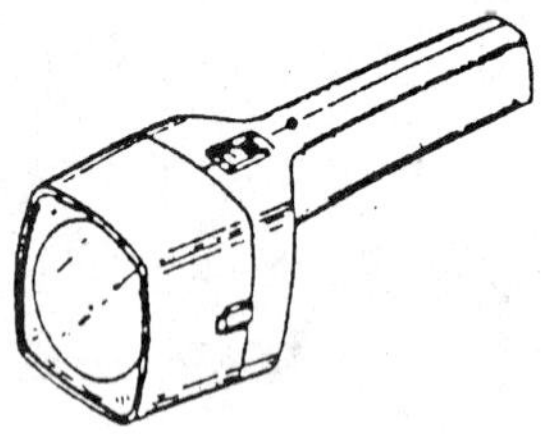

DESIGN PATENT 476

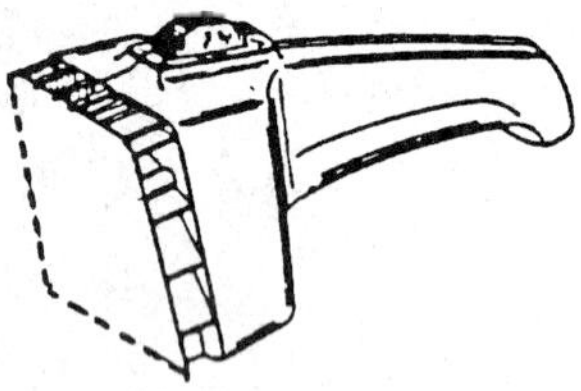

DUSTBUSTER
(snout removed to facilitate comparison)

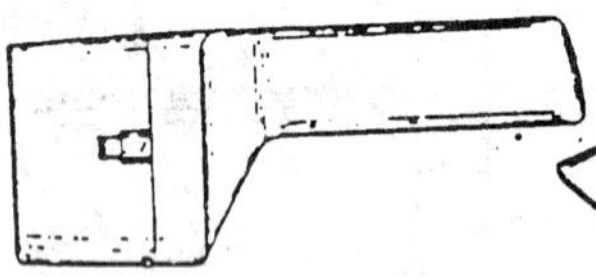

DESIGN PATENT 476

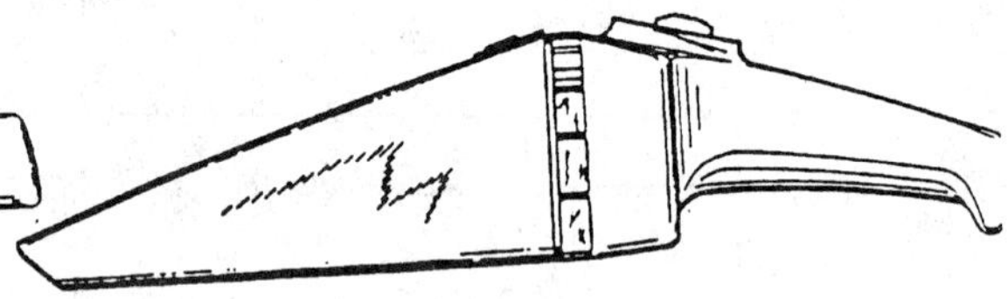

DUSTBUSTER

APPENDIX 3

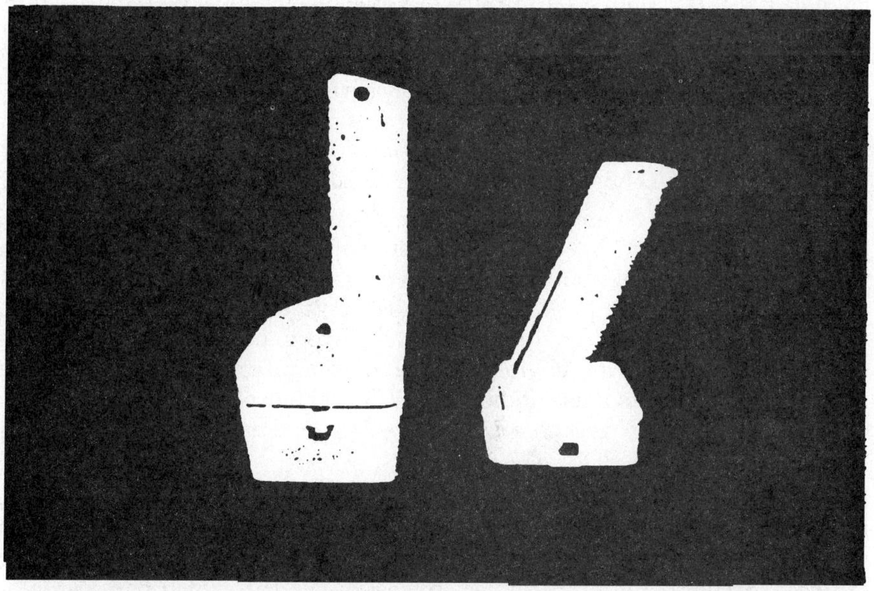

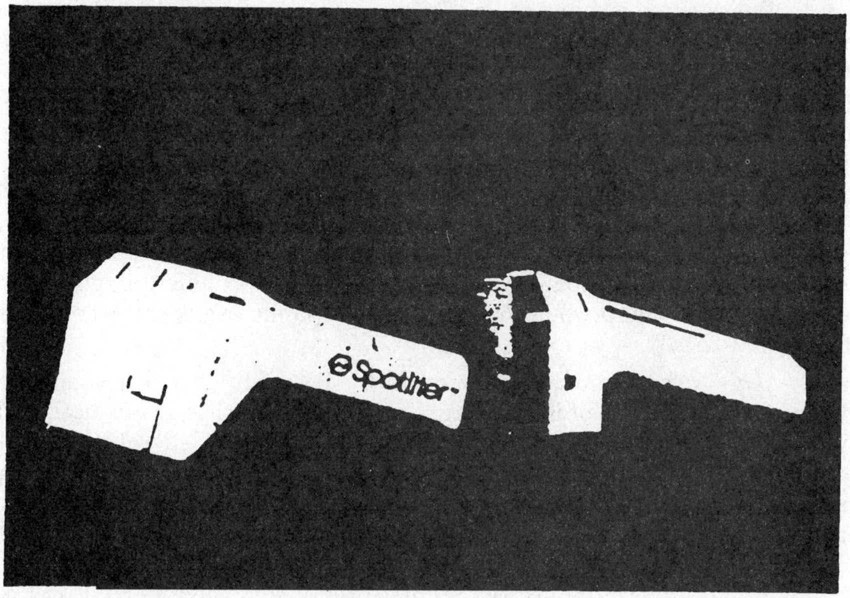

Notes and Questions

1. *Design patents.* A design patent is not concerned with how an article of manufacture was made or how it works. It is only concerned with how it looks. The protected design may consist of surface ornamentation, the article's configuration, or a combination of both. Given the purpose of

design patents, however, only those design aspects open to human view are eligible for protection. The Court of Appeals for the Federal Circuit has held that an article's design is eligible for protection if, at some point in the life of the article, its appearance is a matter of concern. Thus, for example, if the appearance of an article of manufacture, such as a vitamin tablet or a casket, is designed to attract purchasers, it is patentable even though the appearance will be hidden when the article is put to its intended use. *In re* Webb, 916 F.2d 1553, 1558, 16 U.S.P.Q.2d 1433, 1436 (C.A.F.C. 1990).

What qualifies as an "article of manufacture" for purposes of the design patent provisions? The term has been defined very broadly: "anything made 'by the hands of man' from raw materials, whether literally by hand or by machinery or by art." *In re* Hruby, 373 F.2d 997, 1000–01, 153 U.S.P.Q. 61, 65 (C.C.P.A.1967) (holding that the pattern of water generated by a water fountain was an eligible article of manufacture). Lawn mowers, fabrics, dishes are obvious candidates. What about ornamental plants? See Trzyna, *Are Plants Protectible Under the Design Patent Act?*, 69 J. PAT. & TRADEMARK OFF. SOC. 487 (1987).

Do the novelty and nonobviousness standards of patentability, developed in connection with utility patents, seem an appropriate vehicle for judging the protectibility of an ornamental design? The fit is not always clear. For example, design patents are subject to section 102(b), which bars patents on applications filed more than a year after public use or sale of the "invention." But is there a conceivable design patent corollary to the "experimental use" exception to the section 102(b) statutory bar? Compare *In re* Mann, 861 F.2d 1581, 1582, 8 U.S.P.Q.2d 2030, 2031 (C.A.F.C. 1988) ("[w]e see no way in which an ornamental design for an article of manufacture can be subject to the 'experimental use' exception applicable in the case of functioning machines, manufactures, or processes. Obtaining the reactions of people to a design—whether or not they like it—is not 'experimentation' in that sense.") with Tone Brothers Inc. v. Sysco Corp., 28 F.3d 1192, 1200, 31 U.S.P.Q.2d 1321, 1326 (C.A.F.C. 1994) ("experimentation directed to functional features of a product also containing an ornamental design may negate what otherwise would be considered a public use within the meaning of section 102(b)").

2. *The "ornamentality" requirement.* To qualify for a design patent, the design of an article of manufacture must be primarily ornamental, rather than functional. As the Court of Appeals for the Federal Circuit has explained, "[w]hen function dictates a design, protection would not promote the decorative arts, a purpose of the design patent statute." Avia Group International, Inc. v. L.A. Gear California, Inc., 853 F.2d 1557, 1563, 7 U.S.P.Q.2d 1548, 1553 (C.A.F.C. 1988). Moreover, protection of functional designs would undermine utility patents. See Lee v. Dayton–Hudson Corp., Matrix International, Inc., 838 F.2d 1186, 1188, 5 U.S.P.Q.2d 1625, 1627 (C.A.F.C. 1988). In *Lee*, the patented article was a massage device consisting of an elongated handle with two opposing balls at one end. The patentee argued that the scope of design patent extended to the configuration of the device, and thus that any massage device with that general configuration infringed the patent. The court rejected the argument, limiting the scope of the patent to the surface ornamentation of the device, on the grounds that the configuration was dictated primarily by functional considerations. The

court observed that "by obtaining a design patent, not a utility patent, Mr. Lee limited his patent protection to the ornamental design of the article. * * * Design patents do not and cannot include claims to the structural or functional aspects of the article * * *."

The *Avia* case, *supra*, involved two design patents—one claiming an ornamental design for an athletic shoe outer sole (the '420 patent), and the other claiming an ornamental design for an athletic shoe upper (the '301 patent). In finding the designs ornamental and the patents valid, the Court of Appeals for the Federal Circuit explained:

> There is no dispute that shoes are functional and that certain features of the shoe designs in issue perform functions. However, a distinction exists between the functionality of an article or features thereof and the functionality of the particular design of such article or features thereof that perform a function. Were that not true, it would not be possible to obtain a design patent on a utilitarian article of manufacture. * * *

Id., 853 F.2d at 1563, 7 U.S.P.Q.2d at 1553. With regard to the ornamentality of the athletic shoe upper, covered by the '301 patent, the defendant had argued that many aspects or features of the upper performed a function. The Court found this essentially irrelevant. The Court of Appeals quoted with approval the district court's findings on this issue:

> "If the functional aspect or purpose could be accomplished in many other ways [than are] involved in this very design, that fact is enough to destroy the claim that this design is primarily functional. There are many things in the ['301] patent on the upper which are clearly ornamental and nonfunctional such as the location of perforations and how they are arranged, and the stitching and how it's arranged, and the coloration of elements between black and white colors. The overall aesthetics of the various components and the way they are combined are quite important and are not functional. They are purely aesthetic * * *."
>
> *Pensa, Inc.* v. *L.A. Gear California*, 4 U.S.P.Q.2d 1016, 1019 (C.D.Cal. 1987).

Avia, 853 F.2d at 1563, 7 U.S.P.Q.2d at 1553. The Court of Appeals likewise found the soles ornamental, again quoting and approving the district court's findings:

> "[E]very function which [defendant] says is achieved by one of the component aspects of the sole in this case could be and has been achieved by different components. And that is a very persuasive rationale for the holding that the design overall is not primarily functional. Moreover, there is no function which even defendant assigns to the swirl effect around the pivot point, which swirl effect is a very important aspect of the design. [T]his is a unique and pleasing design and [its patentability] is not offset or destroyed by the fact that the utility patent is utilized and incorporated in this aesthetically pleasing design. Plaintiff has given us evidence of other shoes that incorporate the utility patent and its concavity—others of its own shoes—but with a totally different design, and has thus established that the utility patent does not make the design patent invalid in this case."

Pensa, Inc., 4 U.S.P.Q.2d at 1019–20.

Avia, 853 F.2d at 1563, 7 U.S.P.Q.2d at 1553. Based on the *Lee* and *Avia* opinions, how might you articulate a general test for ornamentality? Of what relevance might the existence of a utility patent on the article of manufacture be? Should the aesthetic merits of the design be relevant? See generally 1 D.S. CHISUM, PATENTS: A TREATISE ON THE LAW OF PATENTABILITY, VALIDITY AND INFRINGEMENT § 1.04[2][c] and [d] (1991).

3. *Infringement.* How does the two-part test applied in *Black & Decker* compare to the infringement determination in utility patent cases? See Chavez, *The Standard for Determining Infringement of a Design Patent*, 73 J. PAT. & TRADEMARK OFF. SOC. 843 (1991).

4. *The relationship of design patents to utility patents.* Although most of the provisions concerning utility patents are applicable to design patents, there are a few important differences, in addition to those mentioned in Note 2. To begin, the term of design patents is 14 years, commencing on the date of issuance. Design patent applicants enjoy a shorter foreign filing priority period, and do not have the benefit of the new provisional application procedure, made available for utility and plant patents under the Uruguay Round Agreements Act. See 35 U.S.C.A. § 172. On the other hand, unlike utility and plant patentees, design patentees may recover certain infringing defendants' profits, as well as actual damages, as long as there is no double recovery. 35 U.S.C.A. § 289.

Another important difference lies in the application and claims. While utility patent applications entail detailed written descriptions, the design patent application contains a single claim for the ornamental design "as shown" in the accompanying drawings. 37 C.F.R. § 1.153. Thus, in the case of designs, the drawings define the scope of the patent monopoly.[20] What impact is this difference likely to have on courts' determination of the patentability and infringement issues?

Courts have been careful to ensure that the functions of utility and design patents remain distinct. As demonstrated in the *Lee* case, *supra*, a design patent may not be granted or construed to give rights in utilitarian aspects of an article of manufacture. As the *Avia* opinion suggests, it is possible to obtain both a design patent and a utility patent to protect different aspects of the same article of manufacture.

5. *Resources.* Donald Chisum's treatise on patents, volume 1, section 1.04, provides an excellent overview of the law of design patents. Other useful sources include Brown, *Design Protection: An Overview*, 34 U.C.L.A. L. REV. 1341 (1987); Fryer, *Industrial Design Protection in the United States of America—Present Situation and Plans for Revision*, 70 J. PAT. & TRADEMARK OFF. SOC. 820 (1988); Saidman & Mondry, *Sneakers, Design Patents and Summary Judgments: Opening a New Era in the Protection of Consumer Product Designs*, 71 J. PAT. & TRADEMARK OFF. SOC. 524 (1989).

20. Due to the nature of the subject matter and the claim, the best mode requirement is not applicable. See Racing Strollers, Inc. v. TRI Industries, Inc., 878 F.2d 1418, 11 U.S.P.Q.2d 1300 (C.A.F.C. 1989).

B. PERCEIVED DEFICIENCIES IN THE PROTECTION OF INDUSTRIAL DESIGNS

DESIGNERS WANT MORE PROTECTION FROM IMITATORS

Linda Lehrer
Wall Street Journal.[21]
October 2, 1985, at 35.

A few years ago Hillenbrand Industries Inc. introduced a line of side-pleated soft luggage under the American Tourister name. In just a few months, six other companies were marketing copycat versions.

Hillenbrand found, however, that it could do little to control such imitators. For though original works of art are protected by copyright and inventions by patent, the design of a functional object is fair game for imitators.

Design patents exist but are difficult to obtain and even harder to uphold in court. Only half the patents filed are granted, says William Thompson, a patent counsel for Caterpillar Tractor Co. And of those granted, about three out of four are held invalid by the courts, he adds.

In this vacuum, the copycat market has flourished. A recent International Trade Commission report estimates that American Business loses nearly $8 billion and 131,000 jobs annually to counterfeiting, a term that also applies to pirated products bearing phony trademarks, like fake Gucci handbags.

Discourages Innovation

"Industrial-design counterfeiting never goes away," laments Thomas Lowy, head of the lighting-design firm Koch & Lowy. Mr. Lowy says that patent attorneys have advised him not to waste time and money applying for design patents that in the end don't afford protection. But he contends, "Without design protection there is no innovation. That's why, at this point, the U.S. can't compete with foreign design."

Gary Newtson, chief patent counsel for Chrysler Corp., concedes that his company wasn't concerned with design protection 20 years ago. "We weren't being hurt by off-shore copyists at that time," he explains. Today, however, the American automotive industry is beset by a steady stream of copycat parts for Chryslers, Fords and other U.S. cars.

As soon as a new model rolls off the assembly line, "copyists in Taiwan pick out the most crash-prone (and thereby most frequently replaced) parts to duplicate," Mr. Newtson says. For example, fenders made in Taiwan from inferior materials are sold in the U.S. as parts for Crysler cars. Not only do these fenders rob Chrysler of customers for its own parts, Mr. Newtson complains, but when they quickly rust and

21. Reprinted by permission of The Wall Street Journal, © 1985 Dow Jones & Company, Inc. All rights reserved worldwide.

deteriorate, it sullies the image of the entire car. "We lose good-will," he says. "We could lose a car customer as well as a fender customer."

The cumbersome quest for a design patent—typically a two-year process—is all but useless for fashion products with short life spans. That was true for American Tourister, which was finally granted a patent last February, nearly three years after it applied. That date, says company attorney Brian Leitten, "coincided almost exactly with the end of the life cycle of the product." And patents don't provide retroactive protection, he notes.

THWARTING COUNTERFEITS

Kazuna Tanaka, a principal of Tanaka Kapec Design Group in South Norwalk, Conn., says that all an imitator need do is "change a small feature and the court will say it's not the same design." Thus, he adds, designers often try to create pieces and intricate features that are costly to copy.

Or, they try Adam Tihany's ploy. "I knock myself off before someone else does," the New York architect and product designer says. If a product lends itself to both a limited and a commercial market, Mr. Tihany says, he designs a small line of signed and numbered handmade pieces as well as a popular, less expensive line.

* * * Designers argue that the U.S. lags other countries in protecting design. [Proposed U.S. legislation, supported by some companies] would no longer require a product to meet the so-called standard of unobviousness, which now demands that an object be new by a sufficient margin from things already in existence. "It's a subjective test not really geared to design," says Mr. Thompson of Caterpillar Tractor, noting that designers often create products to resemble something else.

That was certainly the case with Model & Instrument Works Inc. The Seattle company developed a prosthetic foot with a cosmetic surface that simulates musculature, veins and skin. But the firm, says designer David Moeller, was denied a patent because the foot, of course, resembled something already existing. Says a rueful Mr. Moeller, "God designed it first."

Notes and Questions

1. *Criticism of Design Patents.* Mr. Thompson, quoted above, expands upon his criticisms of the design patent in Thompson, *Product Protection Under Current and Proposed Design Laws*, 19 U. BALT. L. REV. 271 (1989–90), concluding: "The design patent is a waste of natural resources and a fraud on the public." *Id.* at 273. For other criticisms, see Fryer, *supra*, and *In re* Nalbandian, 661 F.2d 1214, 1218, 211 U.S.P.Q. 782, 786–87 (C.A.F.C. 1981) (Judge Rich concurring).

Another practitioner, who handled the successful infringement claim in the *Avia* case, discussed in the prior section, has challenged many of Mr. Thompson's arguments. Saidman, *Design Patents—the Whipping Boy Bites Back*, 73 J. PAT. & TRADEMARK OFF. SOC. 859 (1991). Among other things, Mr. Saidman argues that statistical surveys demonstrating high rates of design patent failures (such as the one cited by Mr. Thompson in the article above) are "flawed in that they were done too early, before the beneficial effect of the Federal Circuit had time to trickle down to design patents." *Id.* at 865. He conducted his own survey of the design patent decisions reported between January 1, 1986 and December 31, 1990, "by which time the effect of the Federal Circuit's admittedly pro-patent stance had a chance to be felt," and reported much more favorable results:

> To begin with, preliminary injunctions, a very potent weapon for design patent owners, were granted in over 2 out of every 3 cases! * * * [I]n fully 70% of the cases, the owners of design patents were able to satisfy a judge, long before a full trial on the merits, that they had a likelihood of success of proving that their design patent was valid and infringed. To say that this is a great statistic for design patent owners is a gross understatement. It is reason enough to obtain design patents.
>
> In 21 cases where the issue of validity was decided, the design patents were held invalid in only 1 out of 3 instances! * * * Furthermore, in only 14% of the cases was the design patent found invalid for having been obvious. This should greatly diminish the concern expressed by several earlier commentators that for some reason the obviousness requirement for design patents is unworkable or causes many invalidity problems. * * *
>
> The only area where the results of the statistical survey were even slightly discouraging was in the issue of infringement. In those cases where infringement was decided, either after a full trial or a motion for summary judgment, only 41% of the design patents were held infringed. This seemingly low number may be understood first by noting that the issue of infringement is highly dependent on the vastly different facts of any particular case. Also, one would expect a result of about 50% in closely contested litigation, so 41% doesn't seem too far off. Finally, and I believe this to be the major culprit, patent attorneys who "dabble" in design patent prosecution tend to do more harm than good. That is, most design patents are held not infringed for the reason that too little care was put into the preparation of the design patent application. In case after case, I have seen evidence of where the design patent drawings, which are critical in that they define the scope of protection for the design patent, illustrate the product in too much detail. In other words, the design patent claim is far too narrow. It is a relatively easy matter for an infringer to change certain aspects of the design shown in the patentee's drawing in its attempt to avoid infringement. Those who prepare design patent applications need to be more mindful of what the important design elements of the product are, and need to craft the design patent drawings to cover them, and not cover extraneous, immaterial design aspects that an infringer doesn't want to copy anyway.
>
> * * *
>
> Overall, the statistics on preliminary injunctions and design patent validity and infringement demonstrate that design patents are an effective tool for protecting designs in the U.S. marketplace.

Id. at 865–869.[22]

2. *Protection of designs in other countries.* Many countries have chosen to protect industrial designs through means other than patent law. For discussions of approaches to design protection in other countries, see Reichman, *Design Protection After the Copyright Act of 1976: A Comparative View of the Emerging Interim Models*, 66 J. COPYRIGHT SOC. 267 (1984); Fryer, *International Review of Pending U.S. Design Legislation: Is it on the Right Track?*, 73 J. PAT. & TRADEMARK OFF. SOC. 905 (1991); Henning–Bodewig & Ruijsenaars, *Alternative Protection for Product Designs: A Comparative View on German and Benelux Law*, 83 TRADEMARK REP. 439 (1993).

22. Reprinted by permission. © Perry J. Saidman, 1991.

Chapter Four

IDEA LAW

I. INTRODUCTION

The patent and trade secret laws often fail to extend rights in ideas [1] such as marketing schemes, new product suggestions, or underlying themes for radio or television programs. The question of legal rights in such ideas frequently arises when a person discloses her idea to someone in a position to implement it, and the disclosee proceeds to use it without the discloser's permission and without paying her for it. For example, an employee discloses an idea for a time-saving cargo-loading device to her employer, who builds and uses the device but refuses to compensate the employee for the idea; or an applicant for an insurance sales position in the course of an interview discloses a system for selling insurance, the insurance company implements the system, but refuses to hire the applicant-discloser.

Members of the public inundate the entertainment industry and manufacturers with unsolicited suggestions for new programs or products. While some of the suggestions may prove useful, many of the suggestions are old and redundant. Most recipients treat unsolicited suggestions with caution. An example illustrates the potential problem. In 1954 the National Broadcasting Corporation (NBC), which received thirty to forty thousand program suggestions each year, began broadcasting "Home," a "service-type" program like a magazine-of-the-air. On the basis of advance publicity, before the first program was aired, six different individuals made claims for compensation, alleging that the program would be based on the idea they had submitted to NBC. Following the first broadcast, three more persons made the same claim. None of these nine claimants' submissions dated back to 1929, the time at which, according to NBC's records, it had first begun to receive unsolicited suggestions for such a program. When the program went off the air in 1957, two lawsuits were still pending, and one claimant was still trying to enjoin the series. Olsson, *Dreams for Sale*, 23 L. & CONTEMP. PROBS. 34, 55 (1958).

Assuming that a plaintiff can prove that the defendant did use her idea without permission, should she have a property right in the idea that entitles her to compensation? What are the policy implications? As in other areas of intellectual property, courts must consider not only

1. The term "undeveloped idea" is often used in this context, but the term may be misleading. As will be discussed *infra*, the doctrines developed to accommodate plaintiffs in this setting generally only protect ideas that are "concrete," and many courts have defined "concrete" as meaning "developed."

the need for incentives to create, but also the danger that provision of property rights may retard the overall progress of the arts and marketplace competition. As Justice Traynor has noted:

> [C]reativeness thrives on freedom; men find new implications in old ideas when they range with open minds through open fields. They would indeed be stifled in their efforts to create forms worth protecting, if in the common through which they ranged they were diverted from their course by one enclosure after another.

Stanley v. Columbia Broadcasting System, Inc., 35 Cal.2d 653, 673, 221 P.2d 73, 84–85, 86 U.S.P.Q. 520, 528 (1950) (Traynor, J., dissenting). Assuming that property rights are to be recognized, the timing may be an important consideration, too. If rights are given too early in the development of an idea, there may be less incentive for the originator to turn the idea into a finished work. On the other hand, the person who conceives of the idea may not be in a position to execute it. What rule of law will best facilitate cooperation between creators and executors, who may not be members of the same company?

Though traditional intellectual property doctrines often withheld a remedy for the idea submitter in circumstances such as those described above, shortly after the turn of the century, courts began to compile, somewhat haphazardly, a loose body of state common law to resolve such claims. Over time, courts and commentators began to categorize the accumulated "idea law" case opinions into several "theories" through which a plaintiff/idea submitter could recover the value of his idea or of his service in providing the idea to the defendant. These theories of idea law are widely recognized today.

First, if the plaintiff can prove that the defendant made an explicit promise to pay for the idea, or can demonstrate an implied agreement to pay under the particular facts of the case, the courts will invoke traditional doctrines of contract law to enforce the promise as either an express or implied-in-fact contract. Due to the kinds of concerns expressed by Justice Traynor, however, many jurisdictions have manipulated traditional contract law to add a requirement that the idea be "novel" and "concrete" before the express or implied contract to pay will be enforced.

Courts have also relied on a quasi-contract, or unjust enrichment, theory, which permits recovery when denial of payment will result in an injustice. Another theory finds a right to payment for an idea if the parties were in a confidential relationship in which the plaintiff reposed trust and confidence in the defendant's good faith. Again, in most quasi-contract and confidential relationship contexts the courts have superimposed a requirement that the idea at issue be novel and concrete. Finally, a number of courts and commentators have at least paid lip service to the existence of a "property theory" for recovery for ideas, which appears to recognize property rights in an idea that is novel and concrete, even in the absence of a contract, unjust enrichment or a confidential relationship.

As you read the following cases, consider whether the courts have reached the proper accommodation of the conflicting public and private interests.

II. THE THEORIES OF RECOVERY

SMITH v. RECRION CORP.

Supreme Court of Nevada, 1975.
91 Nev. 666, 541 P.2d 663, 191 U.S.P.Q. 397.

ZENOFF, JUSTICE:

Gilbert C. Smith, while employed as a keno writer by the Stardust Hotel in Las Vegas, conceived that a recreational vehicle park constructed and operated as a part of the luxury hotel would be a profitable idea. After developing a brochure somewhat detailing his idea, he arranged for and had a meeting with Allan Sachs, General Manager of the Stardust, later to become President. The hotel was owned and operated by Recrion Corporation through its subsidiary Karat, Inc.

After presenting the idea to Sachs, Smith indicated that he desired to be compensated in the form of an unspecified amount of money or by participation in the venture in an executive capacity. Sachs expressed no interest in the proposal except to suggest that Smith contact him at a later date. Smith's subsequent attempts to meet with Sachs were unsuccessful and culminated in a note from Sachs' secretary stating simply that Mr. Sachs was not interested.

Two years later, the Stardust opened a recreational vehicle park known as "Camperland" adjacent to the hotel. The project had been initiated and carried forward by the Stardust Director of Public Relations, Dick Odessky.

After the opening of Camperland, asserting that the hotel had implemented his idea, Smith made several demands for compensation; all of which were refused. Finally, Smith requested a letter from Sachs acknowledging that the Camperland idea was his. The letter was never forthcoming. Smith sued for money damages, claiming he was entitled to compensation upon alternate theories of express contract, implied contract, contract implied in law (quasi contract), common law copyright and fraud. Smith appeals from the summary judgment granted in favor of respondents.

Although some of the facts set forth above are not uncontroverted, they have been construed in a manner most favorable to the appellant as required on an appeal from a summary judgment.

1. The terms of an express contract are stated in words while those of an implied contract are manifested by conduct. Both types of contracts are founded upon an ascertainable agreement. Here, there is no evidence that the parties expressly contracted for the purchase and sale

of Smith's idea. Smith only alleged that he expected compensation, not that he was promised compensation.

In order to prevail on the theory of a contract implied in fact, the court would necessarily have to determine that both parties intended to contract, and that promises were exchanged; the crucial promise being that of Sachs to compensate Smith. There is no evidence of conduct on the part of Sachs suggesting an intention to enter into a contract with Smith, nor any evidence from which it would be inferred that he promised to compensate Smith.

There being no evidence of contractual intent or the exchange of mutual promises, express or implied, there was no genuine issue of fact.

Prior to the time Smith and Sachs first met to discuss Smith's idea, Sachs had no knowledge of the purpose of the meeting. Smith's idea was entirely unsolicited and he voluntarily disclosed his idea before the subject of compensation had been discussed. Even if Sachs subsequently promised Smith compensation, the promise would be unenforceable for the reason that it would have been unsupported by consideration. Past consideration is the legal equivalent to no consideration. An abstract idea cannot be protected by an express or implied contract unless the contract was made before the disclosure of the idea.

2. Neither statutory nor common law copyright protects against the borrowing of ideas as distinguished from the expression of such ideas. Generally, abstract ideas will not be protected without a showing of "concreteness" and "novelty." Concreteness pertains to the developmental stage of the idea, i.e., the idea must be sufficiently developed as to constitute a protectible interest. An idea in order to meet the test of concreteness must be ready for immediate use without any additional embellishment. Novelty pertains to originality and, in some jurisdictions, the innovative character of the idea. The purpose of the test is to insure that the idea merits protection: That it is "tangible" and would not exist but for the independent efforts of the author.

Smith's idea does not meet the test of concreteness. His brochure was hardly capable of "immediate use without any additional embellishment." The most that can be said is that respondents may have gleaned the raw idea of a recreational vehicle part from Smith. However, to develop that idea to the point where it was ripe for implementation required extensive investigation, research and planning.

3. An idea must also meet the test of concreteness and novelty before its author is entitled to quasi contractual recovery. Smith is denied compensation on the theory of quasi contract for this reason and for the reason that the idea was entirely unsolicited. One who officiously confers a benefit on another is not entitled to compensation therefor.

[The court also rejected the fraud argument.]

Summary judgment was appropriate. Affirmed.

MURRAY v. NATIONAL BROADCASTING COMPANY, INC.

United States Court of Appeals, Second Circuit, 1988.
844 F.2d 988, 6 U.S.P.Q.2d 1618, *cert. denied*
488 U.S. 955, 109 S.Ct. 391, 102 L.Ed.2d 380 (1988).

ALTIMARI, CIRCUIT JUDGE:

It was almost a generation ago that a young comedian named Bill Cosby became the first black entertainer to star in a dramatic network television series. That program, *I Spy*, earned Cosby national recognition as an actor, including three Emmy Awards (1966, 1967 and 1968) for best performance in a dramatic series, and critical acclaim for the portrayal of a character without regard to the actor's race. Although keenly aware of the significance of his achievement in breaking the color line on network television, Cosby set his sights then on "accomplish[ing] something more significant for the Negro on TV." [1] In an interview in 1965, he envisioned a different approach to the situation comedy genre made popular by *The Dick Van Dyke Show*. The *Daily News* described Cosby's "dream" series as not

> unlike other situation comedies. There'll be the usual humorous exchanges between husband and wife.... Warmth and domestic cheerfulness will pervade the entire program.
>
> Everything on the screen will be familiar to TV viewers. But this series will be radically different. Everyone in it will be a Negro.
>
> * * *
>
> ... "I'm interested in proving there's no difference between people," [explained Cosby]. "My series would take place in a middle-income Negro neighborhood. People who really don't know Negroes would find on this show that they're just like everyone else."

Nearly twenty years later, on September 20, 1984, Cosby's dream for a "color- blind" family series materialized with the premier of *The Cosby Show*—a situation comedy about a family known as the Huxtables. Bill Cosby stars in the leading role as Heathcliff ("Cliff") Huxtable together with his TV wife Clair and their five children.

Plaintiff-appellant Hwesu Murray, an employee of defendant-appellee ("NBC"), claims in the instant case that in 1980, four years prior to the premier of *The Cosby Show* on NBC's television network, he proposed to NBC a "new" idea for a half-hour situation comedy starring Bill Cosby. In a written proposal submitted to NBC, Murray described his series called "Father's Day" as "wholesome ... entertainment"

1. Lardine, *Looking to the Future: Bill Cosby Has Dreams of an All–Negro TV Series*, New York Daily News, Sept. 19, 1965, Sunday Magazine, at 6.

> which will focus upon the family life of a Black American family.... The leading character will be the father, ... a devoted family man and a compassionate, proud, authority figure....
>
> * * *
>
> ... The program may well resemble "Father Knows Best" and "The Dick Van Dyke Show." It will be radically different from "The Jeffersons," "Good Times," "Different Strokes," and "That's My Mama." The father will not be a buffoon, a supermasculine menial, or a phantom.... The program will show how a Black father can respond with love ..., and will present ... a closely-knit family....

On this appeal from an order of the United States District Court for the Southern District of New York (Cedarbaum, J.) granting defendants-appellees' motion for summary judgment, we are asked to determine whether, under New York law, plaintiff has a legally protectible interest in his idea which he maintains was used by NBC in developing *The Cosby Show*. Because we agree with the district court's conclusion that, under New York law, lack of novelty in an idea precludes plaintiff from maintaining a cause of action to prevent its unauthorized use, we affirm the district court's order granting summary judgment and dismissing the complaint.

BACKGROUND

Plaintiff Hwesu S. Murray has been employed in the television industry for the past ten years. Murray holds a Bachelor of Arts degree in English and graduate degrees in broadcast journalism and law. In 1979, defendant-appellee NBC hired Murray as a Unit Manager and financial analyst in its sports division. A year later, plaintiff contacted an NBC official outside of NBC Sports about some "extracurricular" ideas he had for future television programs, and the official apparently instructed him to submit his proposals in writing. Soon thereafter, in June 1980, plaintiff submitted five written proposals, one of which was entitled "Father's Day." Murray allegedly informed NBC that if it were interested in any of the proposals, he expected to be named executive producer and to receive appropriate credit and compensation as the creator of the eventual program. Plaintiff also allegedly told NBC that his ideas were being submitted in confidence.

Murray's proposal for "Father's Day" is the subject matter of this action. The NBC official who originally had requested it encouraged Murray to "flesh out" his proposal and submit it to Josh Kane, then an NBC vice-president and a top official with NBC Entertainment, the division of NBC responsible for network television programming. Plaintiff thereupon submitted to Kane an expanded proposal for "Father's Day." In a two-page memorandum dated November 1, 1980, Murray first suggested that Bill Cosby play the part of the father. At that time, plaintiff also made several other casting suggestions, including roles for a working spouse and five children, and again indicated that the proposed series would "combine humor with serious situations in a manner similar to that of the old *Dick Van Dyke Show* " but "with a Black perspective." Murray's expanded proposal concluded with the observation that, "[l]ike *Roots*, the show will attempt to depict life in a [closely-knit] Black family, with the addition of a contemporary, urban setting."

NBC apparently decided not to pursue Murray's proposal. On November 21, 1980, Kane returned the "Father's Day" submission to plaintiff and informed him that "we are not interested in pursuing [its] development at this time."

Four years later, in the fall of 1984, *The Cosby Show* premiered on NBC. *The Cosby Show* is a half-hour weekly situation comedy series about everyday life in an upper middle-class black family in New York City. The father, played by Bill Cosby, is a physician, and the mother is a lawyer. In its first season, *The Cosby Show* soared to the top of the Nielsen ratings and has become one of the most popular programs in television history. The show is highly regarded by critics and is also a huge commercial success.

Less than a month after viewing the premier, plaintiff wrote to NBC to advise it that *The Cosby Show* had been derived from his idea for "Father's Day." In January 1985, NBC responded through its Law Department, stating its position that " 'Father's Day' played absolutely no role in the development of 'The Cosby Show' ... [since m]uch of the substance and style of 'The Cosby Show' is an outgrowth of the humor and style developed by Bill Cosby throughout his career." NBC further maintained that *The Cosby Show* was developed and produced by The Carsey–Werner Company ("Carsey–Werner"), an independent production company and the executive producers of the series.

In his complaint, plaintiff claimed that *The Cosby Show's* portrayal of a strong black family in a nonstereotypical manner is the essence of "Father's Day," and "[i]t is that portrayal of Black middle-class life that originated with plaintiff." Murray also alleged that Josh Kane showed plaintiff's "Father's Day" proposal to his superiors at NBC, including defendant-appellee Brandon Tartikoff, President of NBC Entertainment. Tartikoff, together with Cosby and Carsey–Werner, have been credited with the creation and development of *The Cosby Show*. Plaintiff maintains that NBC and Tartikoff deliberately deceived plaintiff into believing that NBC had no interest in "Father's Day" and then proceeded to develop and eventually produce plaintiff's idea as *The Cosby Show*.

Plaintiff's complaint stated a number of causes of action arising out of defendants' alleged appropriation of his idea. Among those relevant to this appeal are plaintiff's claims of race discrimination under 42 U.S.C. §§ 1981 and 1982, false designation of origin under the Lanham Act, 15 U.S.C. § 1125, and various state law claims, including misappropriation, conversion, breach of implied contract, unjust enrichment and fraud. Plaintiff sought, *inter alia*, damages and declaratory and injunctive relief as the "sole owner of all rights in and to the idea, proposal and property [known as] 'Father's Day.' "

In a decision dated July 15, 1987, the district court considered whether plaintiff's idea was "property" that could be subject to legal protection. Since the parties agreed that New York law applied to plaintiff's claims, the district court proceeded to analyze defendants' motion for summary judgment in light of the New York Court of Appeals decision in *Downey v. General Foods Corp.*, 31 N.Y.2d 56, 334 N.Y.S.2d 874, 286 N.E.2d 257 (1972). In *Downey*, the New York court established the general proposition that "[l]ack of novelty in an idea is fatal to *any* cause of action for its unlawful use." 334 N.Y.S.2d at 877, 286 N.E.2d at 259 (quoting *Bram v. Dannon Milk Prods., Inc.*, 33 A.D.2d 1010, 307 N.Y.S.2d 571, 571 (1st Dep't 1970)) (emphasis added). The district court, therefore, determined that the "sole issue" before it was the novelty of plaintiff's "Father's Day" proposal, and accordingly assumed, for purposes of defendants' motion, that defendants in fact used plaintiff's idea in the development of *The Cosby Show*.

In focusing on the novelty of plaintiff's proposal, the district court determined that Murray's idea was not subject to legal protection from unauthorized use because "Father's Day" merely combined two ideas which had been circulating in the industry for a number of years—namely, the family situation comedy, which was a standard formula, and the casting of black actors in non-stereotypical roles. The district court found that, to the extent "Father's Day," in Murray's words, "may well resemble 'Father Knows Best' and 'The Dick Van Dyke Show,' " it could not be considered novel. In addition, the portrayal of a black family in nonstereotypical roles, according to the court, precluded a finding of novelty because 1) the television networks already had cast some black actors, including Bill Cosby himself, e.g., *I Spy* (1965–68), *The Bill Cosby Show* (1969–71), and *Fat Albert and the Cosby Kids* (1972–79), in such roles, and 2) the idea of combining the family situation comedy theme with an all-black cast already had been suggested publicly by Bill Cosby some twenty years before the creation of *The Cosby Show*. The district court also determined that Murray's casting of Bill Cosby in the lead role in "Father's Day" was no mere coincidence. Rather, it was "further evidence that Cosby is connected—even in plaintiff's mind—with the concept that plaintiff seeks to monopolize."

In view of the foregoing, the district court granted defendants' motion for summary judgment and dismissed the various claims presented in the complaint, concluding that the lack of novelty in plaintiff's proposal was fatal to any cause of action for unauthorized use of that idea.

Discussion

I.

Our review of the instant appeal is limited to deciding whether the district court properly concluded that there was "no genuine issue as to any material fact" entitling defendants to "judgment as a matter of law." Fed.R.Civ.P. 56(c). Summary judgment is appropriate when, after drawing all reasonable inferences in favor of the party against whom summary judgment is sought, no reasonable trier of fact could find in favor of the non-moving party.

As the district court recognized, the dispositive issue in this case is whether plaintiff's idea is entitled to legal protection. Plaintiff points to "unique"—"even revolutionary"—aspects of his "Father's Day" proposal that he claims demonstrate "genuine novelty and invention," which preclude the entry of summary judgment against him. Specifically, plaintiff contends that his idea suggesting the nonstereotypical portrayal of black Americans on television is legally protectible because it represents a real breakthrough. As he stated in his affidavit in opposition to defendants' motion,

> [w]hen I created "Father's Day", I had in mind ... a show that ... would portray a Black family as it had never been shown before on television.... I also ... desire[d] to produce a show with strong and positive role models for the Black community, and to make a statement regarding the love and integrity of the Black family to the world. I think every Black person in this country knows there has been a need for this, and that never before on television had there been a portrayal of a Black family as I created it for "Father's Day."

Murray claims that the novelty of his idea subsequently was confirmed by the media and the viewing public which instantly recognized the "unique" and "revolutionary" portrayal of a black family on *The Cosby Show*.

We certainly do not dispute the fact that the portrayal of a nonstereotypical black family on television was indeed a breakthrough. Nevertheless, that breakthrough represents the achievement of what many black Americans, including Bill Cosby and plaintiff himself, have recognized for many years—namely, the need for a more positive, fair and realistic portrayal of blacks on television. While NBC's decision to broadcast *The Cosby Show* unquestionably was innovative in the sense that an intact, nonstereotypical black family had never been portrayed on television before, the mere fact that such a decision had not been made before does not necessarily mean that the idea for the program is itself novel.

Consequently, we do not agree with appellant's contention that the nonstereotypical portrayal of a black middle-class family in a situation comedy is novel because

> [t]o argue otherwise would be the equivalent of arguing that since there had always been baseball, and blacks in baseball, there was nothing new about Jackie Robinson playing in the major leagues—or that since there had always been schools in Little Rock, Arkansas, and blacks in schools, there was nothing new about integrating schools in Little Rock.

As appellees persuasively point out in response to this analogy, Murray has "confuse[d] the 'idea' with its execution.... Indeed, the idea of integration ... had been discussed for decades prior to the actual events taking place." Similarly, we believe, as a matter of law, that plaintiff's idea embodied in his "Father's Day" proposal was not novel because it merely represented an "adaptation of existing knowledge" and of "known ingredients" and therefore lacked "genuine novelty and invention." *Educational Sales Programs, Inc. v. Dreyfus Corp.*, 65 Misc.2d 412, 317 N.Y.S.2d 840, 844 (Sup.Ct.N.Y.Cty.1970).

We recognize of course that even novel and original ideas to a greater or lesser extent combine elements that are themselves not novel. Originality does not exist in a vacuum. Nevertheless, where, as here, an idea consists in essence of nothing more than a variation on a basic theme—in this case, the family situation comedy—novelty cannot be found to exist. The addition to this basic theme of the portrayal of blacks in nonstereotypical roles does not alter our conclusion, especially in view of the fact that Bill Cosby previously had expressed a desire to do a situation comedy about a black family and that, as the district court found, Cosby's entire career has been a reflection of the positive portrayal of blacks and the black family on television.

Appellant would have us believe that by interpreting New York law as we do, we are in effect condoning the theft of ideas. On the contrary, ideas that reflect "genuine novelty and invention" are fully protected against unauthorized use. But those ideas that are not novel "are in the public domain and may freely be used by anyone with impunity." *Ed Graham Productions, Inc. v. National Broadcasting Co.*, 75 Misc.2d 334, 347 N.Y.S.2d 766, 769 (Sup.Ct.N.Y.Cty.1973). Since such non-novel ideas are not protectible as property, they cannot be stolen.

In assessing whether an idea is in the public domain, the central issue is the uniqueness of the creation. Murray insists that there is at least a question of fact as to the novelty of "Father's Day" because *The Cosby Show* is indisputably unique. In support of this contention, plaintiff points to the fact that NBC contracted with Carsey–Werner for the right of NBC to broadcast *The Cosby Show*. The contract apparently was executed by the parties before there had been any written development of the proposed series. The "program idea" for *The Cosby Show*, however, was described in the contract as "unique, intellectual property." According to plaintiff, the inescapable conclusion is that the idea—whether it be "Father's Day" or *The Cosby Show*—could not possibly have been in the public domain if NBC expressly contracted to purchase it from Carsey–Werner.

We disagree. The Carsey–Werner contract contemplates a fully-produced television series. The contract refers to, *inter alia*, the program format, titles, set designs, theme music, stories, scripts, and art work as well as to the "program idea." Taken together, these elements no doubt would be considered original and therefore protectible as property. On the other hand, we think it equally apparent that the mere idea for a situation comedy about a nonstereotypical black family—whether that idea is in the hands of Murray, Carsey–Werner, NBC, or anyone else—is not novel and thus may be used with impunity.

Finally, as an alternative attack on the propriety of the district court's order granting summary judgment, plaintiff posits that even if his idea was not novel as a matter of law, summary judgment still was inappropriate because his proposal was solicited by defendants and submitted to them in confidence. In this regard, Murray relies on *Cole v. Phillips H. Lord, Inc.*, 262 A.D. 116, 28 N.Y.S.2d 404 (1st Dep't 1941). Murray contends that *Cole* stands for the proposition that when an idea is protected by an agreement or a confidential relationship, a cause of action arises for unauthorized use of that idea irrespective of the novelty of the subject matter of the contract. Plaintiff's reliance on *Cole* is misplaced in light of subsequent cases, particularly the New York Court of Appeals decision in *Downey v. General Foods Corp.*, 31 N.Y.2d 56, 334 N.Y.S.2d 874, 286 N.E.2d 257 (1972). See also *Ferber v. Sterndent Corp.*, 51 N.Y.2d 782, 433 N.Y.S.2d 85, 86, 412 N.E.2d 1311 (1980) ("[a]bsent a showing of novelty, plaintiff's action to recover damages for illegal use of 'confidentially disclosed ideas' must fail as a matter of law"); *Educational Sales Programs*, 317 N.Y.S.2d at 844 ("[o]ne cannot be forever barred from using a worthwhile but unoriginal idea merely because it was once asked to be treated in confidence").

Consequently, we find that New York law requires that an idea be original or novel in order for it to be protected as property. Since, as has already been shown, plaintiff's proposal for "Father's Day" was lacking in novelty and originality, we conclude that the district court correctly granted defendants' motion for summary judgment.

II.

* * *

"[W]hen one submits an idea to another, no promise to pay for its use may be implied, and no asserted agreement enforced, if the elements of novelty and originality are absent...." *Downey*, 334 N.Y.S.2d at 877, 286 N.E.2d at 259. As the district court recognized, non-novel ideas do not constitute property. As a result, there can be no cause of action for unauthorized use of Murray's proposal since it was not unlawful for defendants to use a non-novel idea. We conclude therefore that the district court properly dismissed plaintiff's state law claims for breach of implied contract, misappropriation, conversion, and unjust enrichment.

Similarly, plaintiff's fraud claim also fails since, as the district court recognized, plaintiff "cannot be defrauded of property that he does not own." * * *

[The Court also affirmed dismissal of the plaintiff's civil rights and false designation of origin claims.]

GEORGE C. PRATT, CIRCUIT JUDGE, dissenting:

Today this court holds that the idea underlying what may well be the most successful situation comedy in television history was, in 1980, so unoriginal and so entrenched in the public domain that, as a matter of law, it did not constitute intellectual property protected under New York law. Because I am convinced that the novelty issue in this case presents a factual question subject to further discovery and ultimate scrutiny by a trier of fact, I respectfully dissent.

At least for purposes of this appeal, it is given that Murray presented NBC with an idea for a television series; that, after showing interest in Murray's initial idea, NBC then asked him to submit a more detailed proposal; and that NBC then actually used his proposal in developing *The Cosby Show*, but at the same time refused to provide any compensation to Murray. The only question on appeal is whether there is evidence to indicate that Murray's idea possessed the novelty and originality required under New York law. * * *

I agree with the majority that there is some evidence that Murray's idea was not novel. But clearly, there is also evidence indicating novelty. Initially, there is the admission by NBC, in its agreement with Carsey–Werner, that the television series is "unique, intellectual property." [Judge Pratt argues that, contrary to the majority's interpretation, the agreement can be interpreted to provide that the underlying idea itself, rather than the "fully-produced television series," was "unique intellectual property."]

Nor is the agreement the only piece of evidence indicating an issue of fact as to novelty. In 1985, NBC admitted that Murray had "rights" in his idea, but determined it had no interest in acquiring those rights. At trial, both Cosby and Tartikoff stated that they believed The Cosby Show to be novel and unique. NBC admitted that the reason it normally returned rejected submissions, as it did in Murray's case, was that the "material belong[ed] to the submitter." In short, there is substantial evidence, both within and independent of the Carsey–Werner development agreement, which directly conflicts with the majority's holding that, as a matter of law, Murray's idea was not novel.

The fact that the basic idea had been expressed by Cosby some fifteen years before Murray submitted his proposal to NBC does not erase these factual issues. To say, as a matter of law, that an idea is not novel because it already exists in general form, would be to deny governmental protection to any idea previously mentioned anywhere, at anytime, by anyone. I do not believe New York law defines "novelty" so strictly, especially in the area of mass communications, an area long recognized by state courts as "a specialized field having customs and usages of its own" where "a property right exists" in "a combination of ideas evolved into a program." *Cole v. Phillip H. Lord, Inc.*, 262 A.D. 116, 121, 28 N.Y.S.2d 404, 409 (1st Dep't 1941). Indeed, in a market the very existence of which depends on the generation and development of ideas, it may be impossible to formulate a concept that has not previously been expressed by someone, somewhere.

Novelty, by its very definition, is highly subjective. As fashion, advertising, and television and radio production can attest, what is novel today may not have been novel 15 years ago, and what is commonplace today may well be novel 15 years hence. In this instance, where Cosby expressed the concept almost a decade and a half before Murray submitted his proposal, where it was Murray's idea that NBC actually used, where there is no evidence indicating NBC knew anything of the program idea until Murray submitted it, compare *Downey v. General Foods Corp.*, 31 N.Y.2d 56, 60, 334 N.Y.S.2d 874, 877–78, 286 N.E.2d 257 (1972) (no novelty because defendant had "envisaged" and "utilized" plaintiff's idea for "years before the plaintiff submitted it") with *Werlin v. Readers Digest Ass'n Inc.*, 528 F.Supp. 451, 466 (S.D.N.Y.1981) (even though plaintiff's idea was in public domain, no evidence that defendant knew about or would have discovered the idea except through plaintiff's proposal; hence, the "idea was novel" as far as defendant was concerned), and where substantial conflicting evidence exists as to the "novelty" of the idea under New York law, there seems to be at least a triable issue.

The majority's decision prematurely denies Murray a fair opportunity to establish his right to participate in the enormous wealth generated by *The Cosby Show*. Accordingly, I would reverse the district court judgment and remand the case for further consideration.

Notes and Questions

1. *Novelty.* What, according to the *Murray* court, does it take to satisfy the novelty requirement? Why does the *Murray* majority find that the plaintiff's idea lacked novelty? Are the dissent's arguments convincing? If the plaintiff's idea had been more detailed than it was, would the majority have been more inclined to find it novel? If so, why?

What is the court's purpose in applying a novelty requirement at all? Courts have differed in their definition of "novelty." Some have suggested that an idea will be novel if it is original to the plaintiff, see, e.g., Stevens v. Continental Can Co., 308 F.2d 100, 104, 135 U.S.P.Q. 111, 115 (6th Cir. 1962), *cert. denied* 374 U.S. 810, 83 S.Ct.1702, 10 L.Ed.2d 1034 (1963), while others have stated that the idea must be innovative in character. See, e.g., Lueddecke v. Chevrolet Motor Co., 70 F.2d 345, 348 (8th Cir.1934) (novelty requirement means that idea must be "nonobvious"). Others have suggested that the idea must be both original to the plaintiff *and* innovative in character. See, e.g. Downey v. General Foods Corp., 31 N.Y.2d 56, 286 N.E.2d 257, 334 N.Y.S.2d 874, 175 U.S.P.Q. 374 (1972). Which of these definitions most effectively fulfills the purposes of the novelty requirement? See Barrett, *The "Law of Ideas" Reconsidered*, 71 J. PAT. & TRADEMARK OFF. SOC. 691, 710–12 (1989).

2. *Concreteness.* What, according to the *Smith* court, does it take to satisfy the concreteness requirement? Why did the plaintiff's idea fail to qualify? What is the purpose underlying imposition of the concreteness requirement? Was the purpose satisfied? Would it have been satisfied with a lower standard?

"Concreteness" has proven even more uncertain than "novelty" in its definition. Essentially, the cases can be divided into two general approaches. In the first approach, courts appear to require that the idea be reduced to some tangible form. Some opinions have stated that the idea must be in writing. See. e.g., Bailey v. Haberle–Congress Brewing Co., 193

Misc. 723, 85 N.Y.S.2d 51 (1948). Other opinions have stated that the idea must be incorporated into a tangible product. See, e.g., Tutelman v. Stokowski, 44 U.S.P.Q. 47, 48 (Pa.C.P. 1939).

The second approach to "concreteness" suggests that the idea must be fully developed—completed, fleshed-out in detail and ready to use. See, e.g., Hamilton Bank v. Belt, 210 F.2d 706, 708–9, 99 U.S.P.Q. 388, 390 (D.C.Cir. 1953). This view has been particularly prevalent in connection with claims involving television and radio program ideas. When the idea has been developed into a detailed format, a plan for an entire series with descriptions of the characters' personalities, methods of portrayals, sample plots, and such, courts have found the ideas sufficiently concrete to merit protection. In *Hamilton Bank, supra,* the Court of Appeals for the District of Columbia found the plaintiff's plan for a weekly radio program featuring talent from local high schools sufficiently concrete to justify relief:

> We think * * * that in the field of radio broadcasting concreteness may lie between the boundaries of mere generality on the one hand and, on the other, a full script containing the words to be uttered and delineating the action to be portrayed. Where the plan is for a series of broadcasts the contents of which depend upon selection of talent at different times, a detailed program cannot be presented at the preliminary stages of negotiation. This should not in and of itself deprive the originator of a property right in his plan. * * * As we have seen, in addition to the utilization of student talent selected for each broadcast from a different high school, the show was to be presented and recorded as a student assembly, retaining the atmosphere of a school by referring to the show as a class, to the acts as assignments and to the action as recitations. There was to be a rendition of several pieces by the school glee club, a minimum of conversation and introductions, a brief acknowledgment of sponsorship at the beginning and end of the broadcast, and no provision for commercial "spots." And a very important element in the plan was the cooperation and participation of the school authorities through the use of school buildings and facilities and the assistance of faculty members. These details, when added to the basic general idea which, alone, would be too abstract, give sufficient concreteness.

Id., 210 F.2d at 709, 99 U.S.P.Q. at 390.

Given the purposes of the concreteness requirement, how would you evaluate each approach? See Barrett, *supra*, at 712–16.

3. *The express contract theory of recovery.* The *Murray* court suggests that an express agreement to pay for an idea will not be enforced if the idea lacks novelty. The Connecticut Supreme Court imposed this rule in Masline v. New York, New Haven & Hartford Railroad Co., 95 Conn. 702, 112 A. 639 (1921). In *Masline*, the plaintiff, a brakeman and baggage master on the defendant's railroad, told the defendant that he had "information of value" that, if used by the defendant, would enable it to earn at least $100,000 a year without any expense. Plaintiff said he would furnish this information if the defendant would agree to give him five percent of the receipts gained from use. The defendant, through one of its vice presidents and another officer, agreed. Plaintiff then disclosed his idea, which was to sell advertis-

ing space in or on the railroad's stations, depots, rights of way, cars and fences. The defendant had not sold advertising before but immediately began to do so, earning a large amount of money. It refused to pay anything to plaintiff. When plaintiff sued to enforce the agreement, the court denied relief, stating:

> An idea may undoubtedly be protected by contract * * *. But it must be the plaintiff's idea. Upon communication to the defendant it at once did appear that the idea was not original with the plaintiff, but was a matter of common knowledge, well known to the world at large. He had thought of nothing new, and had therefore no property right to protect which would make his idea a basis of consideration for anything.

Id., 95 Conn. at 710–11, 112 A. at 641–42. An appreciable number of other jurisdictions have followed the *Masline* court's lead, and have also imposed a concreteness requirement on contracts to pay for ideas. Is the *Masline* reasoning consistent with the traditional rules of contract law regarding consideration?

Another approach which leads to the same result as *Masline* implies a condition into the express contract to pay that the idea must be novel and concrete. See, e.g., Soule v. Bon Ami Co., 201 A.D. 794, 796, 195 N.Y.S. 574, 576 (1922), *affirmed* 235 N.Y. 609, 139 N.E. 754 (1923). Why should the law *assume* that this was the parties' intent, when neither expressly so provided?

Is there any policy justification for refusing to enforce contractual agreements to pay for non-novel, non-concrete ideas? See Justice Traynor's famous dissent in Stanley v. Columbia Broadcasting System, Inc., 35 Cal.2d 653, 674, 221 P.2d 73, 84, 86 U.S.P.Q. 520, 528 (1950). Some jurisdictions have declined to apply the novelty and concreteness restrictions when express agreements to pay are proven. See, e.g., Donahue v. Ziv Television Programs, Inc. 245 Cal.App.2d 593, 54 Cal.Rptr. 130, 151 U.S.P.Q. 657 (1966).

4. *The implied contract theory.* What kinds of factors might be relevant to determine whether parties made an implied agreement to pay for an unsolicited idea upon use? A solicited idea? What role should industry custom play in the analysis? See Whitfield v. Lear, 751 F.2d 90, 224 U.S.P.Q. 540 (2d Cir.1984).

Putting aside the questions of novelty and concreteness, could the plaintiff in *Murray* have proven an implied contract to pay, based on the facts given? Could the plaintiff in *Smith*?

Companies receiving numerous unsolicited idea submissions have implemented practices, on the advice of their lawyers, that make it very difficult for submitters to demonstrate either an express or an implied contract to pay. Some companies simply return such submissions unopened. Another approach is to designate an employee to open all mail and send a standard release form to unsolicited idea submitters, notifying them that their ideas will not be forwarded to the appropriate department for consideration unless the sender signs and returns the release. The release, of course, expressly disclaims or limits contractual obligation on the company's part. A third approach is to review the idea, but require a signed release from the submitter before proceeding with it. Submitters often have little choice but to sign the releases, since it is very much a buyer's market. See Hawkins & Udell, *Corporate Caution and Unsolicited New Product Ideas: A Survey of Corporate Waiver Requirements*, 58 J. PAT. OFF. SOC. 375 (1976). See M. EPSTEIN, MODERN INTELLECTUAL PROPERTY LAW, 288–288.8 (1992 Supp.).

5. *The quasi-contract theory.* Quasi-contracts, or "contracts implied at law," are not based on the apparent intentions of the parties. They are obligations created by law for reasons of justice and equity. Did the defendant receive a benefit from the plaintiff under circumstances that as a matter of fairness obligate the defendant to pay? If so, the court may find an obligation, implied by law, to pay. See Weitzenkorn v. Lesser, 40 Cal.2d 778, 794, 256 P.2d 947, 959, 97 U.S.P.Q. 545, 553 (1953).

Putting aside questions of novelty and concreteness, why did the plaintiff in *Smith* fail to state a claim in quasi-contract? Could the plaintiff in *Murray* have done so?

One case in which the court did permit recovery on a quasi-contract basis is Matarese v. Moore–McCormack Lines, 158 F.2d 631, 71 U.S.P.Q. 311 (2d Cir.1946). In that case plaintiff, an immigrant of little education who worked as a part-time stevedore on the defendant's pier, informed defendant's agent in charge of the pier that he had something which would facilitate cargo loading, save the defendant money and prevent accidents. The agent agreed to visit plaintiff's home, where plaintiff demonstrated models of the devices he had invented. The agent promised the plaintiff one-third of what the defendant would save by use of the devices and offered plaintiff the job of supervising construction of the devices for the defendant, which plaintiff accepted. Defendant built and used a number of the devices, but refused to pay the plaintiff as promised and ultimately fired him. The plaintiff later obtained two patents on his devices. Plaintiff's claim of an express contract to pay for use of the devices failed because the agent lacked authority to bind the defendant company. The court nonetheless granted the plaintiff's prayer for recovery upon the theory of unjust enrichment:

> Courts have justly been assiduous in defeating attempts to delve into the pockets of business firms through spurious claims attempts made by telephoning or writing vague general ideas to business corporations and then seizing upon some later general similarity between their products and the notions propounded as a basis for damages. * * * Such schemes are quite different from the situation * * * at bar. Here the relationship between the parties before and after the disclosure, the seeking of disclosure by [the agent], [the agent's] promise of compensation, the specific character, novelty, and patentability of plaintiff's invention, the subsequent use made of it by defendants, and the lack of compensation given the plaintiff—all indicate that the application of the principle of unjust enrichment is required.

Id., 158 F.2d at 634, 71 U.S.P.Q. at 313–14.

Again, the courts generally require that the plaintiff's idea be novel and concrete before permitting recovery under a quasi-contract theory. They have reasoned that abstract or non-novel ideas cannot be the property of any individual, that they may be freely borrowed. When a defendant takes such an idea he is not unjustly enriched, because what he took was common property. The plaintiff had no right of exclusive ownership in it. See, e.g., Stanley v. Columbia Broadcasting System, Inc., 35 Cal.2d 653, 675, 221 P.2d 73, 86, 86 U.S.P.Q. 520, 529 (1950) (Traynor, J., dissenting). Does this reasoning beg the question? Suppose that the plaintiff performed a valuable service for the defendant by bringing the idea to the defendant's attention, even though the idea was not novel or concrete. Should that be relevant? Should it matter whether the plaintiff was an amateur "idea person" or a professional, such as an advertising executive, a financial advisor, or a lawyer, giving advice within the field of his or her professional expertise?

6. *The confidential relationship theory.* Cases under this heading are sometimes treated as implied contract cases, since confidential relationships often are founded on implied agreements to retain information in confidence. Subsequent unauthorized disclosure or use can be viewed as a breach of contract. Confidential relationships are also found, however, when the parties have a preexisting relationship, one placing trust in the other to act in good faith. Thus, for example, family relationships, agency relationships, lawyer and client relationships may all give rise to a duty of confidentiality, without the need to find a specific implied agreement. See Davies v. Krasna, 245 Cal.App.2d 535, 548, 54 Cal.Rptr. 37, 45, 151 U.S.P.Q. 591, 596 (1966). For this reason, some authorities recognize breach of confidential relationship as a separate theory of recovery based in tort. If the person placing trust in the other reveals an idea to the other in the course of the confidential relationship, then the other has a duty to refrain from using or disclosing it, and may be liable if he does so without permission. Again, however, most courts will require that the idea be novel and concrete before they will grant relief.

Note that the tort or contractual character of an idea claim may affect the applicable statute of limitations, as well as the available remedies. See 3 M. NIMMER & D. NIMMER, NIMMER ON COPYRIGHT § 16.06 (1994).

7. *The property theory.* Though courts and commentators routinely list the "property theory" as one of the accepted theories of recovery for ideas, there have been few, if any, attempts to fully define or explore its perimeters or its implications. The property theory appears to provide that a person with a novel, concrete idea has property rights in it that are enforceable against the world. Anyone who copies the idea without the owner's authorization will be liable, as in an action for conversion. The idea owner's property rights in the idea might last until death or after, passing to successors in interest. What are the implications of this? Is the property theory compatible with established intellectual property law policy?

While courts frequently refer to a "property theory" for recovery, it is not clear that a court has *ever* actually relied on this theory to provide relief to a claimant. See Barrett, *The "Law of Ideas" Reconsidered*, *supra*, at 698–709. The cases in which courts arguably *may* have relied on a kind of property theory involve claims for radio and television show formats. For example, in Fink v. Goodson–Todman Enterprises, Ltd., 9 Cal.App.3d 996, 88 Cal.Rptr. 679, 169 U.S.P.Q. 106 (1970), the plaintiff had submitted, at the defendant's request, a "presentation" explaining the central theme and nature of a proposed television series, along with character sketches of the main characters and summaries of several individual program plots. Five years later, defendant broadcast a series with a similar theme but different setting.[2] The California Court of Appeal held that common-law copyright could afford relief to a person in plaintiff's position if the allegedly copied ideas were sufficiently novel and concrete. The court acknowledged that it was extending the copyright doctrine into an "uncertain middle ground" by finding rights in format *ideas*, rather than in the expression of ideas. *Id.*, 9 Cal.App.3d at 1016, 88 Cal.Rptr. at 695, 169 U.S.P.Q. at 116. See also Szczesny v. W.G.N. Continental Broadcasting, 20 Ill.App.3d 607, 315 N.E.2d 263, 183 U.S.P.Q. 427 (1974); John W. Shaw Advertising, Inc. v. Ford Motor Co., 112 F.Supp. 121, 98 U.S.P.Q. 186 (N.D.Ill.1953).

Extending common-law copyright protection to ideas is conceptually similar to adopting the "property theory" for rights in ideas: copying is precluded in either case, regardless of the lack of a contractual or confidential relationship between the parties or a specific showing of unjust enrichment.

As we will discuss in the following Chapter on Copyrights, copyright protection traditionally has been limited to a person's particular method of expressing ideas, giving no rights in the ideas themselves. However, the *selection and arrangement* of a number of ideas into one story or fictitious plot may constitute copyrightable "expression," even though the individual ideas are not copyrightable by themselves. As the court acknowledged in the *Fink* case, television or radio formats generally are a highly developed, complex combination of a number of ideas, in which the line between what constitutes idea and what constitutes expression can be very vague. Thus, opinions finding a right to protection in a format under a "common-law copyright" theory could be understood not as finding a new right to protection of ideas *per se*, but rather as finding that the selection and arrangement of ideas in the format context constitutes expression, which is protectible under traditional copyright doctrine.

It is not surprising that courts would come the closest to recognizing a pure "property theory" in ideas in television and radio format cases, since an especially great need has been felt for legal protection in that context. See, e.g., Comment, *Television Formats, the Search for Protection,* 58 CAL. L. REV. 1169 (1970); Note, *Beyond the Realm of Copyright: Is there Legal Sanctuary for the Merchant of Ideas?*, 41 BROOK. L. REV. 284 (1974). Many jurisdictions, however, expressly reject the notion of property rights for ideas, in the absence of a contractual or confidential relationship, unjust enrichment, trade secret status, or a patent. See, e.g., Vantage Point, Inc. v. Parker Bros., Inc., 529 F.Supp. 1204, 213 U.S.P.Q. 782 (E.D.N.Y.1981), *affirmed* 697 F.2d 301 (2d Cir.1982). Moreover, to the extent that state law does provide copyright-like protection in ideas, that right may be preempted by federal law. See Chapter 9, *infra*.

8. *The relationship of idea law and trade secret law.* Is the body of "idea law" identified in this Chapter needed? Why aren't trade secret and

2. Plaintiff's series, "The Coward," centered around a World War II lieutenant who surrendered his company to the enemy and was thereafter shunned as a coward. He later became a policeman who regularly performed feats of bravery to prove his courage. Defendant's series, "Branded," involved a calvary officer who was "branded" as a coward in a battle with Indians and later became a wandering cowhand who routinely performed feats of bravery to prove his courage.

routine contract law sufficient to redress idea submission claims? Could idea claims brought on a quasi-contract or confidential relationship theory be resolved satisfactorily under trade secret law?

9. *Resources.* The following additional sources provide useful information about the law of ideas: R. MILGRIM, TRADE SECRETS § 8.03 (1991); M. NIMMER & D. NIMMER, NIMMER ON COPYRIGHT §§ 16.01–08 (1994); P. GOLDSTEIN, COPYRIGHT PRINCIPLES, LAW AND PRACTICE §§ 15.7–9 (1989); M. EPSTEIN, MODERN INTELLECTUAL PROPERTY LAW Ch. 7 (1989 & Supp.).

*

Part Three

RIGHTS IN ORIGINAL FORMS OF EXPRESSION

Chapter Five

COPYRIGHT

I. INTRODUCTION

REPORT OF THE REGISTER OF COPYRIGHTS ON THE GENERAL REVISION OF THE U.S. COPYRIGHT LAW, 3–6 (1961)

* * *

B. The Nature of Copyright

1. *In General*

In essence, copyright is the right of an author to control the reproduction of his intellectual creation. As long as he keeps his work in his sole possession, the author's absolute control is a physical fact. When he discloses the work to others, however, he makes it possible for them to reproduce it. Copyright is a legal device to give him the right to control its reproduction after it has been disclosed.

Copyright does not preclude others from using the ideas or information revealed by the author's work. It pertains to the literary, musical, graphic, or artistic form in which the author expresses intellectual concepts. It enables him to prevent others from reproducing his individual expression without his consent. But anyone is free to create his own expression of the same concepts, or to make practical use of them, as long as he does not copy the author's form of expression.

2. *Copyright as Property*

Copyright is generally regarded as a form of property, but it is property of a unique kind. It is intangible and incorporeal. The thing to which the property right attaches—the author's intellectual work—is incapable of possession except as it is embodied in a tangible article such as a manuscript, book, record, or film. The tangible articles containing the work may be in the possession of many persons other than the copyright owner, and they may use the work for their own enjoyment, but copyright restrains them from reproducing the work without the owner's consent.

Justice Holmes, in his famous concurring opinion in White–Smith Music Publishing Co. v. Apollo Co. (209 U.S. 1 (1908)), gave a classic definition of the special characteristics of copyright as property:

> The notion of property starts, I suppose, from confirmed possession of a tangible object and consists in the right to exclude others from interference with the more or less free doing with it as one

wills. But in copyright property has reached a more abstract expression. The right to exclude is not directed to an object in possession or owned, but is now in vacuo, so to speak. It restrains the spontaneity of men where, but for it, there would be nothing of any kind to hinder their doing as they saw fit. It is a prohibition of conduct remote from the persons or tangibles of the party having the right. It may be infringed a thousand miles from the owner and without his ever becoming aware of the wrong.

3. *Copyright as a Personal Right*

a. Generally

Some commentators, particularly in European countries, have characterized copyright as a personal right of the author, or as a combination of personal and property rights. It is true that an author's intellectual creation has the stamp of his personality and is identified with him. But insofar as his rights can be assigned to other persons and survive after this death, they are a unique kind of personal rights.

b. Moral rights

On the theory of personal right, some countries have included in their copyright laws special provisions for "moral rights" of authors. These provisions are intended to protect the author against certain acts injurious to his personal identity or reputation. They give the author the following rights:

- To have his name appear on copies of his work;
- To prevent the attribution to him of another person's work;
- To prevent the reproduction of his work in a distorted or degrading form.

These moral rights are regarded as not assignable, but the author may sometimes agree to waive them in particular cases. In some countries the moral rights survive the author's death and may be enforced by his heirs or representatives.

In the United States the moral rights of authors have never been treated as aspects of copyright. But authors have been given much the same protection of personal rights under general principles of the common law such as those relating to implied contracts, unfair competition, misrepresentation, and defamation. * * *

4. *Copyright as a Monopoly*

Copyright has sometimes been said to be a monopoly. This is true in the sense that the copyright owner is given exclusive control over the market for his work. And if his control were unlimited, it could become an undue restraint on the dissemination of the work.

On the other hand, any one work will ordinarily be competing in the market with many others. And copyright, by preventing mere duplication, tends to encourage the independent creation of competitive works.

The real danger of monopoly might arise when many works of the same kind are pooled and controlled together.

C. The Purposes of Copyright

1. *Constitutional Basis of the Copyright Law*

The copyright law of the United States must be founded on the provision of the Constitution (art. I, sec. 8) which empowers Congress—

> * * * To Promote the Progress of Science and useful Arts, by securing for limited Times to Authors and Inventors the exclusive Right to their respective Writings and Discoveries.

As reflected in the Constitution, the ultimate purpose of copyright legislation is to foster the growth of learning and culture for the public welfare, and the grant of exclusive rights to authors for a limited time is a means to that end. A fuller statement of these principles was contained in the legislative report (H. Rep. No. 2222, 60th Cong., 2d Sess.) on the Copyright Act of 1909:

> The enactment of copyright legislation by Congress under the terms of the Constitution is not based upon any natural right that the author has in his writings, for the Supreme Court has held that such rights as he has are purely statutory rights, but upon the ground that the welfare of the public will be served and the progress of science and useful arts will be promoted by securing to authors for limited periods the exclusive rights to their writings. The Constitution does not establish copyrights, but provides that Congress shall have the power to grant such rights if it thinks best. Not primarily for the benefit of the author, but primarily for the benefit of the public, such rights are given. Not that any particular class of citizens, however worthy, may benefit, but because the policy is believed to be for the benefit of the great body of people, in that it will stimulate writing and invention to give some bonus to authors and inventors.
>
> In enacting the copyright law Congress must consider * * * two questions: First, how much will the legislation stimulate the producer and so benefit the public, and second, how much will the monopoly granted be detrimental to the public? The granting of such exclusive rights, under the proper terms and conditions, confers a benefit upon the public that outweighs the evils of the temporary monopoly.

2. *The Rights of Authors and the Public Interest*

a. In general

Although the primary purpose of the copyright law is to foster the creation and dissemination of intellectual works for the public welfare, it also has an important secondary purpose: To give authors the reward due them for their contribution to society.

These two purposes are closely related. Many authors could not devote themselves to creative work without the prospect of remuneration. By giving authors a means of securing the economic reward afforded by the market, copyright stimulates their creation and dissemination of intellectual works. Similarly, copyright protection enables publishers and other distributors to invest their resources in bringing those works to the public.

b. Limitations on authors' rights

Within reasonable limits, the interests of authors coincide with those of the public. Both will usually benefit from the widest possible dissemination of the author's works. But it is often cumbersome for would-be users to seek out the copyright owner and get his permission. There are many situations in which copyright restrictions would inhibit dissemination, with little or no benefit to the author. And the interests of authors must yield to the public welfare where they conflict.

Accordingly, the U.S. copyright law has imposed certain limitations and conditions on copyright protection:

- The rights of the copyright owner do not extend to certain uses of the work. * * *
- The term of copyright is limited, as required by the Constitution. * * *
- A notice of copyright in published works has been required. * * * The large mass of published material for which the authors do not wish copyright is thus left free of restrictions.
- The registration of copyrights and the recordation of transfers of ownership have been required. * * * The public thus is given the means of determining the status and ownership of copyright claims.

c. The author's reward

While some limitations and conditions on copyright are essential in the public interest, they should not be so burdensome and strict as to deprive authors of their just reward. Authors wishing copyright protection should be able to secure it readily and simply. And their rights should be broad enough to give them a fair share of the revenue to be derived from the market for their works.

D. SUMMARY

Copyright is a legal device to give authors the exclusive right to exploit the market for their works. It has certain features of property rights, personal rights, and monopolies, but it differs from each of these. The legal principles usually applicable to property, personal rights, or monopolies are not always appropriate for copyright.

The primary purpose of copyright is to stimulate the creation and dissemination of intellectual works, thus advancing "the progress of science and useful arts." The grant of exclusive rights to authors is a means of achieving this end, and of compensating authors for their labors and their contributions to society.

Within limits, the author's interests coincide with those of the public. Where they conflict, the public interest must prevail. The ultimate task of the copyright law is to strike a fair balance between the author's right to control the dissemination of this works and the public interest in fostering their widest dissemination.

Notes and Questions

1. *United States copyright legislation.* The first United States copyright statute was enacted in 1790. Heavily influenced by the English Statute of Anne, 8 Anne C.19, 1710, this first Copyright Act granted protection to maps, charts and books for a term of fourteen years that could be renewed once. Copyright Act of May 31, 1790, 1 Stat. 124. Over time, Congress extended the duration of federal copyright and brought additional subject matter under its protection, including prints (1802); musical compositions (1831); dramatic compositions (1856); photographs (1865); and works of fine art (1870). The landmark Copyright Act of 1909, which remained in effect for 68 years, extended protection to "all the writings of an author," 17 U.S.C.A. § 4 (1909 Act), though this language ultimately was construed not to encompass all the expression that Congress was constitutionally empowered to protect. The Copyright Act of 1909 provided for a term of 28 years, commencing upon publication, which could be renewed once for a total of 56 years. *Id.*, § 24.

The REPORT OF THE REGISTRAR OF COPYRIGHTS, excerpted above, was prepared in anticipation of the revisions ultimately enacted as the Copyright Act of 1976, which became effective on January 1, 1978, and governs today. 17 U.S.C.A. § 101 *et. seq.* Years of study and negotiation went into the formulation of the 1976 Act, and it represented a significant departure from the prior law. Among other things, the 1976 Act terminated the dual system of copyright that had existed under the 1909 Act, in which state common-law copyright protected unpublished works, and federal statutory copyright became available upon publication of the work with proper notice of the author's copyright claim. The Act unified the law by extending federal copyright protection to both published and unpublished works, commencing on the date the work is first "fixed" in tangible form. The 1976 Act expressly preempted state copyright protection for all works so fixed. 17 U.S.C.A. § 301. In addition, the Act replaced the former system of renewable terms with a single term consisting, for most works, of the life of the author plus 50 years. *Id.*, § 302.

2. *The Berne Convention.* In October, 1988, after a century of hesitation and debate, the United States ratified the Berne Convention for the Protection of Literary and Artistic Works,[1] a venerable multinational copyright treaty to which approximately 100 nations already adhered. In contrast to the Paris Convention for the Protection of Industrial Property (discussed in Chapter 3, *supra*) and the Universal Copyright Convention (a

1. The Berne Convention for the Protection of Literary and Artistic Works, Sept. 9, 1886, *as last revised* at Paris July 24, 1971, Treaty Doc. 99–27, 828 U.N.T.S. 221. The Berne Convention, like the Paris Convention for the Protection of Industrial Property, is administered by the World Intellectual Property Organization, which is part of the United Nations.

multinational copyright treaty to which the U.S had adhered in 1952) [2], the Berne Convention imposes strong substantive standards upon its members.

The Berne Convention is founded on the principle of national treatment: each member nation must provide essentially the same copyright protection to other members' authors as it does to its domestic authors.[3] However, the Berne Convention imposes a number of minimum standards for the copyright protection each member must provide to foreign authors. Among other things, the Berne Convention prescribes a minimum term of protection, specifies subject matter that must be protected, and specifies the rights that must be provided in connection with that subject matter. The Berne Convention has strong foundations in the civil law "natural right" approach to copyright. In contrast to the highly pragmatic view of copyright set forth in the REPORT OF THE REGISTER OF COPYRIGHTS, the natural right approach views copyright as protecting an author's inherent, natural right to reap the fruits of his own creation and to control and protect the integrity of his work as a natural extension of his personality.

In order to comply with the provisions of the Berne Convention, the United States was compelled to revise its law in several important respects. Most notably, by virtue of the natural rights influence, the Berne Convention prohibits the conditioning of copyright protection on compliance with formalities such as notice or registration. The U.S. was obliged, in its implementing legislation, to relinquish its long tradition of requiring authors to provide notice of copyright on all published copies of their work, and to revise its registration and renewal requirements. Indeed, in subsequent legislation, the United States restored copyright in foreign works which had been forfeited for failure of foreign authors to comply with the strict U.S. notice and renewal provisions. Compliance with the Berne also led the United States to introduce a limited version of "moral rights," which the Register describes in the REPORT, into U.S. copyright law for the first time, and to expand copyright protection for architectural works.

Some argue that Congress has failed to bring the United States fully into compliance with the Berne Convention's requirements. Would it be possible for a U.S. copyright infringement plaintiff to base her claim directly upon the Berne Convention provisions? In the Berne Convention Implementation Act of 1988, Pub. L. No. 100–568, 102 Stat. 2853, Congress expressly declared that the Berne Convention is not self-executing. Thus, its terms are not incorporated directly into domestic law, and litigants may not rely on it as an independent basis for infringement relief. For an

2. The Universal Copyright Convention, September 6, 1952, 6 U.S.T. 2731, 216 U.N.T.S. 132 ("UCC"), is administered by the United Nations Educational, Scientific and Cultural Organization (UNESCO). Newer and substantively weaker than the Berne Convention, the Universal Copyright Convention was created in part to permit the United States to join a multinational copyright treaty: at the time, the United States was unwilling to revise its copyright laws to comply with the requirements of the Berne Convention. The United States still depends upon the UCC, with its national treatment provisions and more minimal substantive standards, to govern its copyright relations with nations that have adhered to the UCC but not to the Berne Convention or to the GATT TRIPs Agreement, which incorporates most of the Berne Convention provisions.

3. For a complete listing of circumstances under which a foreign author is entitled to U.S. copyright protection, see section 104 of the Copyright Act of 1976. 17 U.S.C.A. § 104.

argument that the Berne Convention might in fact be self-executing, see I M.B. NIMMER & D. NIMMER, NIMMER ON COPYRIGHT, § 1.12 (1994).

For an excellent discussion of international copyright relations and treaties from an American perspective, see Leaffer, *International Copyright from an American Perspective*, 43 ARK. L. REV. 373 (1990); II P. GOLDSTEIN, COPYRIGHT PRINCIPLES, LAW AND PRACTICE, §§ 16.0–9 (1989). For a detailed explanation of how the Berne Convention works, see P. GELLER, INTERNATIONAL COPYRIGHT LAW AND PRACTICE (1988 & Supp.); S. RICKETSON, THE BERNE CONVENTION FOR THE PROTECTION OF LITERARY AND ARTISTIC WORKS: 1886–1986 (1987); WORLD INTELLECTUAL PROPERTY ORGANIZATION, GUIDE TO THE BERNE CONVENTION FOR THE PROTECTION OF LITERARY AND ARTISTIC WORKS (1978).

3. *The nature of copyright.* As you will see in the following sections, the standards for copyright—originality and fixation—are much lower than those for obtaining a patent. Moreover, in contrast to patents, federal copyright arises automatically, as a matter of law, as soon as a qualifying work of authorship is fixed in a tangible medium of expression (e.g., a manuscript, canvas, or audiotape). It is unnecessary to apply for a copyright, and registration of an existing copyright with the Copyright Office, when necessary, is relatively simple, entailing little substantive examination. The term of protection is significantly longer for copyrights than for patents, as well.

On the other hand, the level of protection afforded by copyright is much lower than that afforded by a patent. Copyright only prohibits copying: independent creation does not infringe. Moreover, the Copyright Act contains numerous exceptions to infringement liability, permitting the public to make specified unauthorized uses of the copyrighted work. Perhaps most importantly, as the REPORT OF THE REGISTER OF COPYRIGHTS notes, copyright only prevents others from copying the author's particular method of expressing ideas or facts: it gives no rights in the ideas or facts themselves.

Thus, in providing property rights in an individual's expression, Congress has struck a unique balance. Making copyright easier to obtain can be justified because there are usually numerous ways to express a concept: providing rights in one of those ways takes less from society than granting rights in the concept itself. Moreover, protection of all expression satisfying a minimal originality standard avoids censorship and encourages the creation of a more diverse, robust array of expression, to the ultimate enrichment of society.

At the same time, Congress clearly recognized the need to limit the scope of copyright protection. It is essential to retain in the public domain those basic building blocks—ideas, facts, generic forms of expression—needed for future authorship. Indeed, in order to avoid stagnation, there must be some leeway for new authorship to draw upon preexisting forms of expression. As one commentator has observed, it is inappropriate to base copyright law

> on the charming notion that authors create something from nothing, that works owe their origin to the authors who produce them. * * *

> The process of authorship * * * is more equivocal than that romantic model admits. To say that every new work is in some sense based on the works that preceded it is such a truism that it has long been a cliche, invoked but not examined. But the very act of authorship in *any* medium is more akin to translation and recombination than it is to creating Aphrodite from the foam of the sea. Composers recombine sounds they have heard before; playwrights base their characters on bits and pieces drawn from real human beings and other playwrights' characters; novelists draw their plots from lives and other plots within their experience; software writers use the logic they find in other software; lawyers transform old arguments to fit new facts; cinematographers, actors, choreographers, architects, and sculptors all engage in the process of adapting, transforming, and recombining what is already "out there" in some other form. This is not parasitism: it is the essence of authorship. And, in the absence of a vigorous public domain, much of it would be illegal.

Litman, *The Public Domain*, 39 EMORY L. J. 965, 965–66 (1990).[4] As you proceed through this Chapter, you should evaluate how Congress has balanced the interest of providing an incentive to create against the interest in maintaining the widest possible public access and a viable public domain from which future authors may draw. Has Congress struck the optimal balance?

4. *First amendment considerations.* By prohibiting the unauthorized use of copyrighted expression, the copyright laws undoubtedly abridge the freedoms of speech and press, to some extent. Can they be applied consistently with the first amendment?

The first amendment has not been construed in an absolute, literal sense to prohibit all laws abridging speech. In evaluating the constitutionality of laws under the first amendment, the Supreme Court has tended to weigh the interest advanced by the law in question against the interest in free speech and press, and to evaluate the extent of the law's interference with first amendment interests. See, e.g., Zacchini v. Scripps–Howard Broadcasting Co., 433 U.S. 562, 97 S.Ct. 2849, 53 L.Ed.2d 965 (1977). Copyright is limited in ways that minimize its intrusion on the exercise of free speech and press.

First, as noted above, copyright does not prohibit others from copying, discussing or making other uses of an author's ideas. It merely prohibits unauthorized use of his particular mode of expressing the ideas, when those ideas may be expressed in a number of different ways. Second, the fair use defense, codified at 17 U.S.C.A. § 107, and other more specific exceptions to liability, give the public some leeway to use an author's expression when such use promotes first amendment interests. Finally, limitations on the duration of copyright undertake to ensure that the author's protection does not extend beyond what is needed to provide the necessary incentive to create and accomplish the legitimate purposes of copyright law.

These limitations on the copyright law, combined with the weight of the interest the copyright laws advance (indeed the interest—providing an

4. © Jessica Litman, 1990. Reprinted by permission.

incentive to authors to express and disseminate their ideas—is highly consistent with first amendment interests), have convinced most commentators that the law's intrusion on free speech withstands first amendment scrutiny in most, if not all cases. See, e.g., Nimmer, *Does Copyright Abridge the First Amendment Guarantees of Free Speech and Press?*, 17 U.C.L.A. L. REV. 1180 (1970); Denicola, *Copyright and Free Speech: Constitutional Limitations on the Protection of Expression*, 67 CAL. L REV. 283 (1979); Goldstein, *Copyright and the First Amendment*, 70 COLUM. L. REV. 983 (1970).

5. *Additional resources.* There are several excellent multi-volume treatises on Copyright: M.B. NIMMER & D. NIMMER, NIMMER ON COPYRIGHT (1994); P. GOLDSTEIN, COPYRIGHT PRINCIPLES, LAW AND PRACTICE (1989); and W.F. PATRY, COPYRIGHT LAW AND PRACTICE (1994). Useful one-volume treatises include M. LEAFFER, UNDERSTANDING COPYRIGHT LAW (1989); and N. BOORSTYN, COPYRIGHT LAW (1981 & Supp.). For a discussion of the history and development of the copyright law, see L.R. PATTERSON & S.W. LINDBERG, THE NATURE OF COPYRIGHT: A LAW OF USERS' RIGHTS (1991). For an examination of the unusual legislative history of the Copyright Act of 1976 and its implications, see Litman, *Copyright, Compromise, and Legislative History*, 72 CORNELL L. REV. 857 (1987). For an economic evaluation of copyright law, see Landes & Posner, *An Economic Analysis of Copyright*, 18 J. LEGAL STUD. 325 (1989). The Journal of the Copyright Society, published bi-monthly, contains numerous relevant articles.

II. THE SUBJECT MATTER OF COPYRIGHT

§ 102. Subject Matter of Copyright: In General

(a) Copyright protection subsists, in accordance with this title, in original works of authorship fixed in any tangible medium of expression, now known or later developed, from which they can be perceived, reproduced, or otherwise communicated, either directly or with the aid of a machine or device. Works of authorship include the following categories:

(1) literary works;

(2) musical works, including any accompanying words;

(3) dramatic works, including any accompanying music;

(4) pantomimes and choreographic works;

(5) pictorial, graphic, and sculptural works;

(6) motion pictures and other audiovisual works;

(7) sound recordings; and

(8) architectural works.

(b) In no case does copyright protection for an original work of authorship extend to any idea, procedure, process, system, method of operation, concept, principle, or discovery, regardless of the form in which it is described, explained, illustrated, or embodied in such work.

17 U.S.C.A. § 102.

Section 102 of the Copyright Act provides protection for "original works of authorship." The Copyright Act of 1909 had provided protection for "all the writings of an author," tracking the Constitutional language, empowering Congress to secure to authors exclusive rights in their "writings." U.S. CONST. art. I, § 8, cl. 8. The House Report accompanying the bill that was to become the Copyright Act of 1976 explained the change in language:

> In using the phrase "original works of authorship," rather than "all the writings of an author" * * *, the committee's purpose is to avoid exhausting the constitutional power of Congress to legislate in this field, and to eliminate the uncertainties arising from the latter phrase. Since the present statutory language is substantially the same as the empowering language of the Constitution, a recurring question has been whether the statutory and the constitutional provisions are coextensive. If so, the courts would be faced with the alternative of holding copyrightable something that Congress clearly did not intend to protect, or of holding constitutionally incapable of copyright something that Congress might one day want to protect. To avoid these equally undesirable results, the courts have indicated that "all the writings of an author" under the [1909] statute is narrower in scope than the "writings" of "authors" referred to in the Constitution. The bill avoids this dilemma by using a different phrase—"original works of authorship"—in characterizing the general subject matter of statutory copyright protection.
>
> The history of copyright law has been one of gradual expansion in the types of works accorded protection, and the subject matter affected by this expansion has fallen into two general categories. In the first, scientific discoveries and technological developments have made possible new forms of creative expression that never existed before. In some of these cases the new expressive forms—electronic music, filmstrips, and computer programs, for example—could be regarded as an extension of copyrightable subject matter Congress had already intended to protect, and were thus considered copyrightable from the outset without the need of new legislation. In other cases, such as photographs, sound recordings, and motion pictures, statutory enactment was deemed necessary to give them full recognition as copyrightable works.
>
> Authors are continually finding new ways of expressing themselves, but it is impossible to foresee the forms that these new expressive methods will take. The bill does not intend either to freeze the scope of copyrightable subject matter at the present stage of communications technology or to allow unlimited expansion into areas completely outside the present congressional intent. Section 102 implies neither that that subject matter is unlimited nor that

new forms of expression within that general area of subject matter would necessarily be unprotected.

The historic expansion of copyright has also applied to forms of expression which, although in existence for generations or centuries, have only gradually come to be recognized as creative and worthy of protection. The first copyright statute in this country, enacted in 1790, designated only "maps, charts, and books"; major forms of expression such as music, drama, and works of art achieved specific statutory recognition only in later enactments. Although the coverage of the present statute is very broad, and would be broadened further by the explicit recognition of all forms of choreography, there are unquestionably other areas of existing subject matter that this bill does not propose to protect but that future Congresses may want to.

H.R. REP. NO. 1476, 94th Cong., 2d Sess. 51–52 (1976).

Section 102(a) requires that works of authorship be: 1) "fixed in any tangible medium of expression" and 2) "original" in order to qualify for federal copyright. This Section of the Chapter will examine the fixation and originality requirements, and then focus on the prohibition, in section 102(b), of copyright protection for ideas and facts. While it is unnecessary to examine in depth each of the eight categories of subject matter set forth in section 102(a), the rest of the Section will address some particular "problem" areas that merit special consideration.

A. THE FIXATION REQUIREMENT

§ 101. Definitions

* * *

A work is "fixed" in a tangible medium of expression when its embodiment in a copy or phonorecord, by or under the authority of the author, is sufficiently permanent or stable to permit it to be perceived, reproduced, or otherwise communicated for a period of more than transitory duration. A work consisting of sounds, images, or both, that are being transmitted, is "fixed" for purposes of this title if a fixation of the work is being made simultaneously with its transmission.

17 U.S.C.A. § 101.

HOUSE REPORT ON COPYRIGHT ACT OF 1976

H.R. Rep. No. 1476, 94th Cong., 2d Sess. 52–53 (1976).

FIXATION IN TANGIBLE FORM

As a basic condition of copyright protection, the bill perpetuates the existing requirement that work be fixed in a "tangible medium of expression," and adds that this medium may be one "now known or later developed," and that the fixation is sufficient if the work "can be perceived, reproduced, or otherwise communicated, either directly or with the aid of a machine or device." This broad language is intended to avoid the artificial and largely unjustifiable distinctions, derived from cases such as White–Smith Publishing Co. v. Apollo Co., 209 U.S. 1 (1908), under which statutory copyrightability in certain cases has been made to depend upon the form or medium in which the work is fixed. Under the bill it makes no difference what the form, manner, or medium of fixation may be—whether it is in words, numbers, notes, sounds, pictures, or any other graphic or symbolic indicia, whether embodied in a physical object in written, printed, photographic, sculptural, punched, magnetic, or any other stable form, and whether it is capable of perception directly or by means of any machine or device "now known or later developed."

Under the bill, the concept of fixation is important since it not only determines whether the provisions of the statute apply to a work, but it also represents the dividing line between common law and statutory protection. As will be noted in more detail in connection with section 301, an unfixed work of authorship, such as an improvisation or an unrecorded choreographic work, performance, or broadcast, would continue to be subject to protection under State common law or statute, but would not be eligible for Federal statutory protection under section 102.

The bill seeks to resolve, through the definition of "fixation" in section 101, the status of live broadcasts—sports, news coverage, live performances of music, etc.—that are reaching the public in unfixed form but that are simultaneously being recorded. When a football game is being covered by four television cameras, with a director guiding the activities of the four cameramen and choosing which of their electronic images are sent out to the public and in what order, there is little doubt that what the cameramen and the director are doing constitutes "authorship." The further question to be considered is whether there has been a fixation. If the images and sounds to be broadcast are first recorded (on a video tape, film, etc.) and then transmitted, the recorded work would be considered a "motion picture" subject to statutory protection against unauthorized reproduction or retransmission of the broadcast. If the program content is transmitted live to the public while being recorded at the same time, the case would be treated the same; the copyright owner would not be forced to rely on common law rather than statutory rights in proceeding against an infringing user of the live broadcast.

Thus, assuming it is copyrightable—as a "motion picture" or "sound recording," for example—the content of a live transmission should be regarded as fixed and should be accorded statutory protection if it is being recorded simultaneously with its transmission. On the other hand, the definition of "fixation" would exclude from the concept purely evanescent or transient reproductions such as those projected briefly on a screen, shown electronically on a television or other cathode ray tube, or captured momentarily in the "memory" of a computer.

Under the first sentence of the definition of "fixed" in section 101, a work would be considered "fixed in a tangible medium of expression" if there has been an authorized embodiment in a copy or phonorecord and if that embodiment "is sufficiently permanent or stable" to permit the work "to be perceived, reproduced, or otherwise communicated for a period of more than transitory duration." * * *

Under this definition "copies" and "phonorecords" together will comprise all of the material objects in which copyrightable works are capable of being fixed. The definitions of these terms in section 101, together with their usage in section 102 and throughout the bill, reflect a fundamental distinction between the "original work" which is the product of "authorship" and the multitude of material objects in which it can be embodied. Thus, in the sense of the bill, a "book" is not a work of authorship, but is a particular kind of "copy." Instead, the author may write a "literary work," which in turn can be embodied in a wide range of "copies" and "phonorecords," including books, periodicals, computer punch cards, microfilm, tape recordings, and so forth. It is possible to have an "original work of authorship" without having a "copy" or "phonorecord" embodying it, and it is also possible to have a "copy" or "phonorecord" embodying something that does not qualify as an "original work of authorship." Two essential elements—original work and tangible object—must merge through fixation in order to produce subject matter copyrightable under the statute.

Notes and Questions

1. *"Works of authorship" vs. "copies" and "phonorecords."* As the House Report suggests, copyright law provides rights in works of authorship, which are intangible creations of the mind. Though the existence of a tangible embodiment is a prerequisite to copyright protection, the copyright interest in the work of authorship is separate and distinct from the ownership interest in the tangible manuscript, canvas, or audio tape that embodies it. As Copyright Act section 202 explains:

> Ownership of a copyright, or of any of the exclusive rights under a copyright, is distinct from ownership of any material object in which the work is embodied. Transfer of ownership of any material object, including the copy or phonorecord in which the work is first fixed, does not of itself convey any rights in the copyrighted work embodied in the object; nor, in the absence of an agreement, does transfer of ownership of a copyright or of any exclusive rights under a copyright convey property rights in any material object.

17 U.S.C.A. § 202. Copyright Act section 204(a) provides that a transfer of copyright (other than by operation of law) is not valid unless in writing and signed by the owner. Sections 202 and 204(a) superseded an earlier state common-law doctrine which presumed that authors or artists transferred their common-law copyright when they sold their manuscript or work of art, unless they specifically reserved the copyright. See H.R. REP. NO. 1476, 94th Cong., 2d Sess. 124 (1976).

Assume that artist makes a painting and sells the canvas to X. X obtains personal property rights in the canvas and may prevent others (including artist) from taking or using it without permission. He may also transfer the canvas to another. However, artist's retention of copyright in the intangible work of authorship (the painting), imposes some limits on what X can do with the physical embodiment of it. For example, since artist, as the owner of copyright, has the exclusive right to reproduce, adapt and publicly distribute the painting, he can create and sell posters depicting the painting. Notwithstanding his ownership of the canvas, X will be liable to artist for infringement if he does the same. In addition, since artist owns the exclusive right to display the painting, he can also prevent X from making certain public displays of the canvas. Under the Visual Artists Rights Act of 1990, enacted to comply with the Berne Convention's moral rights provisions, artist may prevent X from using the canvas in a manner that intentionally distorts, mutilates or modifies the painting, if doing so is prejudicial to artist's honor or reputation. See 17 U.S.C.A. § 106A.

Note that works of authorship may be embodied in copies or phonorecords. Review the definitions of these terms in section 101 of the Copyright Act. What is the difference between a copy and a phonorecord?

2. *Fixation.* Suppose that, in the course of giving a live performance, a dance group improvises, producing a new work of choreography. At that point, would there be federal copyright in the new work? Suppose that a member of the audience, unknown to the dance group, makes a simultaneous video recording of the performance. Would that constitute a fixation sufficient to qualify the new work for federal copyright?

Assume, instead, that a member of the dance group keeps a video recorder nearby on the stage, and records the new work of choreography as it is created. Members of the audience make unauthorized recordings at the same time. Would the group have a cause of action for federal copyright infringement against them? If your answer is no, why should the dance group's claim be viewed differently from the claim of the producer of a live football game broadcast that is being recorded simultaneously with the broadcast?

For that matter, why have a fixation requirement at all? Is it constitutionally mandated? See 1 M.B. NIMMER & D. NIMMER, NIMMER ON COPYRIGHT, § 1.08[C][2] (1994).

3. *Interactive computer systems.* Are interactive computer programs and their visual displays "fixed" for purposes of copyright protection? Consider, for example, a video game which responds to the specific input of the individual playing the game. The game provides a different set of responses and displays from one game to the next. On what basis might one argue that such works are not fixed? What is the best argument that they are? Courts have generally found interactive computer systems sufficiently fixed to qualify for copyright. See, e.g., Williams Electronics, Inc. v. Arctic International, Inc., 685 F.2d 870, 215 U.S.P.Q. 405 (3d Cir.1982).

4. *State protection for unfixed works.* Though the Copyright Act of 1976 preempts state copyright protection for fixed works (see Chapter 9, *infra*), the states remain free to provide rights in unfixed works, such as oral statements and improvised, unrecorded pantomimes. While some states

have explicitly asserted an intention to provide such protection, see, e.g., CAL. CIV. CODE § 980(a)(1) (West Supp. 1994), there is little case law to define the extent of the protection. As a matter of policy, should unfixed works be protected, and if so, how broad should state protection for unfixed works be? Do you foresee any problems in enforcing such rights? See Hemingway v. Random House, Inc., 23 N.Y.2d 341, 244 N.E.2d 250, 296 N.Y.S.2d 771, 160 U.S.P.Q. 561 (1968).

B. THE ORIGINALITY REQUIREMENT

BURROW-GILES LITHOGRAPHIC CO. v. SARONY

United States Supreme Court, 1884.
111 U.S. 53, 4 S.Ct. 279, 28 L.Ed. 349.

MR. JUSTICE MILLER delivered the opinion of the Court.

* * *

The suit was commenced by an action at law in which Sarony was plaintiff and the lithographic company was defendant, the plaintiff charging the defendant with violating his copyright in regard to a photograph, the title of which is "Oscar Wilde, No. 18." A jury being waived, the court made a finding of facts on which a judgment in favor of the plaintiff was rendered. * * *

* * *

Other findings leave no doubt that plaintiff had taken all the steps required by the act of Congress to obtain copyright of this photograph, and section 4952 names photographs, among other things, for which the author, inventor, or designer may obtain copyright, which is to secure him the sole privilege of reprinting, publishing, copying, and vending the same. That defendant is liable, under that section and section 4965, there can be no question if those sections are valid as they relate to photographs.

[The issue is whether Congress has the Constitutional power to protect photographs and negatives by copyright.]

The Constitutional question is not free from difficulty.

The eighth section of the first article of the Constitution is the great repository of the powers of Congress, and by the eight clause of that section Congress is authorized:

> "to promote the progress of science and useful arts, by securing, for limited times to authors and inventors the exclusive right to their respective writings and discoveries."

The argument here is that a photograph is not a writing nor the production of an author. * * *

It is insisted, in argument, that a photograph being a reproduction, on paper, of the exact features of some natural object, or of some person, is not a writing of which the producer is the author.

Section 4952 of the Revised Statutes places photographs in the same class as things which may be copyrighted with "books, maps, charts, dramatic or musical compositions, engravings, cuts, prints, paintings, drawings, statues, statuary, and models or designs intended to be perfected as works of the fine arts." * * *

* * *

Unless * * * photographs can be distinguished in the classification of this point from the maps, charts, designs, engravings, etchings, cuts, and other prints, it is difficult to see why Congress cannot make them the subject of copyright as well as the others.

These statutes certainly answer the objection that books only, or writing, in the limited sense of a book and its author, are within the Constitutional provision. Both these words are susceptible of a more enlarged definition than this. An author in that sense is "he to whom anything owes its origin; originator; maker; one who completes a work of science or literature." Worcester. So, also, no one would now claim that the word "writing" in this clause of the Constitution, though the only word used as to subjects in regard to which authors are to be secured, is limited to the actual script of the author, and excludes books and all other printed matter. By writings in that clause is meant the literary productions of those authors, and Congress very properly has declared these to include all forms of writing, printing, engravings, etchings, &c., by which the ideas in the mind of the author are given visible expression. The only reason why photographs were not included in the extended list in the Act of 1802 is, probably, that they did not exist, as photography, as an art, was then unknown, and the scientific principle on which it rests, and the chemicals and machinery by which it is operated, have all been discovered long since that statute was enacted.

* * *

We entertain no doubt that the Constitution is broad enough to cover an act authorizing copyright of photographs, so far as they are representatives of original intellectual conceptions of the author.

But it is said that an engraving, a painting, a print, does embody the intellectual conception of its author, in which there is novelty, invention, originality, and therefore comes within the purpose of the Constitution in securing its exclusive use or sale to its author, while a photograph is the mere mechanical reproduction of the physical features or outlines of some object, animate or inanimate, and involves no originality of thought or any novelty in the intellectual operation connected with its visible reproduction in shape of a picture. * * *

This may be true in regard to the ordinary production of a photograph, and that in such case a copyright is no protection. On the question as thus stated we decide nothing.

* * *

The third finding of facts says, in regard to the photograph in question, that it is a "useful, new, harmonious, characteristic, and graceful picture, and that plaintiff made the same . . . entirely from his own original mental conception, to which he gave visible form by posing the said Oscar Wilde in front of the camera, selecting and arranging the costume, draperies, and other various accessories in said photograph, arranging the subject so as to present graceful outlines, arranging and disposing the light and shade, suggesting and evoking the desired expression, and from such disposition, arrangement, or representation, made entirely by plaintiff, he produced the picture in suit."

These findings, we think, show this photograph to be an original work of art, the product of plaintiff's intellectual invention, of which plaintiff is the author, and of a class of inventions for which the Constitution intended that Congress should secure to him the exclusive right to use, publish, and sell, as it has done by section 4952 of the Revised Statutes.

* * *

Photograph of Oscar Wilde by Napoleon Sarony at issue in Burrow -Giles Lithograhic Co. v. Sarony. Reproduced from the collections of the Library of Congress.

Notes and Questions

1. *The originality standard.* How does the *Sarony* Court define "originality?" What, exactly, is original in the photograph of Oscar Wilde?

Would all photographs be likely to qualify? For example, instead of a studio photograph, suppose the plaintiff had taken a photograph of a public building and the surrounding city street scene? Would the requisite originality exist? See Pagano v. Chas. Beseler Co., 234 Fed. 963 (S.D.N.Y.1916). What about a standard driver's license photo?

Should it matter that the purported "author" intended to make a realistic representation of an existing object? Consider the Supreme Court's remarks in Bleistein v. Donaldson Lithographing Co., 188 U.S. 239, 249–50, 23 S.Ct. 298, 300, 47 L.Ed. 460, 462 (1903), involving chromolithographs advertising a circus, which featured a likeness of the circus owner and of circus performers in action:

> Even if [the depictions were] drawn from the life, that fact would not deprive them of protection. The opposite proposition would mean that a portrait by Velasquez or Whistler was common property because others might try their hand on the same face. Others are free to copy the original. They are not free to copy the copy. The copy is the personal reaction of an individual upon nature. Personality always contains something unique. It expresses its singularity even in handwriting, and a very modest grade of art has in it something irreducible, which is one man's alone. That something he may copyright unless there is a restriction in the words of the Act.

In *Bleistein*, the Court also addressed the relevance of the artistic merit of a work to its "originality" and copyrightability:

> It would be a dangerous undertaking for persons trained only to the law to constitute themselves final judges of the worth of pictorial illustrations, outside of the narrowest and most obvious limits. At the one extreme, some works of genius would be sure to miss appreciation. Their very novelty would make them repulsive until the public had learned the new language in which their author spoke. It may be more than doubted, for instance, whether the etchings of Goya or the paintings of Manet would have been sure of protection when seen for the first time. At the other end, copyright would be denied to pictures which appealed to a public less educated than the judge. Yet if they command the interest of any public, they have a commercial value,—it would be bold to say that they have not an aesthetic and educational value,—and the taste of any public is not to be treated with contempt. * * *

Id., 188 U.S. at 251–52, 23 S.Ct. at 300, 47 L.Ed. at 462. Does the public benefit from affording copyright to advertising materials, and other works of questionable artistic stature? If so, how? Is the benefit sufficient to justify the impediment to free access and competition?

How would you compare the "originality" standard for copyrights with the "novelty" and "nonobviousness" standards for patents? Consider Judge Learned Hand's comments in Sheldon v. Metro–Goldwyn Pictures Corp., 81 F.2d 49, 53–54 (2d Cir.1936), *affirmed* 309 U.S. 390, 60 S.Ct. 681, 84 L.Ed. 825 (1940), in which the plaintiff claimed copyright infringement of its play:

> We are to remember that it makes no difference how far the play was anticipated by works in the public demesne which the plaintiffs did not use. The defendants appear not to recognize this, for they have

filled the record with earlier instances of the same dramatic incidents and devices, as though, like a patent, a copyrighted work must be not only original, but new. That is not however the law, as is obvious in the case of maps or compendia, where later works will necessarily be anticipated. * * * Borrowed the work must indeed not be, for a plagiarist is not himself pro tanto an "author;" but if by some magic a man who had never known it were to compose anew Keats' Ode on a Grecian Urn, he would be an "author," and, if he copyrighted it, others might not copy that poem, though they might of course copy Keats'. But though a copyright is for this reason less vulnerable than a patent, the owner's protection is more limited, for just as he is no less an "author" because others have preceded him, so another who follows him, is not a tort-feasor unless he pirates his work.

FEIST PUBLICATIONS, INC. v. RURAL TELEPHONE SERVICE CO., INC.

United States Supreme Court, 1991.
499 U.S. 340, 111 S.Ct. 1282, 113 L.Ed.2d 358.

JUSTICE O'CONNOR delivered the opinion of the Court.

This case requires us to clarify the extent of copyright protection available to telephone directory white pages.

I

Rural Telephone Service Company is a certified public utility that provides telephone service to several communities in northwest Kansas. It is subject to a state regulation that requires all telephone companies operating in Kansas to issue annually an updated telephone directory. Accordingly, as a condition of its monopoly franchise, Rural publishes a typical telephone directory, consisting of white pages and yellow pages. The white pages list in alphabetical order the names of Rural's subscribers, together with their towns and telephone numbers. The yellow pages list Rural's business subscribers alphabetically by category and feature classified advertisements of various sizes. Rural distributes its directory free of charge to its subscribers, but earns revenue by selling yellow pages advertisements.

Feist Publications, Inc., is a publishing company that specializes in area-wide telephone directories. Unlike a typical directory, which covers only a particular calling area, Feist's area-wide directories cover a much larger geographical range, reducing the need to call directory assistance or consult multiple directories. The Feist directory that is the subject of this litigation covers 11 different telephone service areas in 15 counties and contains 46,878 white pages listings—compared to Rural's approximately 7,700 listings. Like Rural's directory, Feist's is distributed free of charge and includes both white pages and yellow pages. Feist and Rural compete vigorously for yellow pages advertising.

As the sole provider of telephone service in its service area, Rural obtains subscriber information quite easily. Persons desiring telephone service must apply to Rural and provide their names and addresses; Rural then assigns them a telephone number. Feist is not a telephone company, let alone one with monopoly status, and therefore lacks independent access to any subscriber information. To obtain white pages listings for its area-wide directory, Feist approached each of the 11 telephone companies operating in northwest Kansas and offered to pay for the right to use its white pages listings.

Of the 11 telephone companies, only Rural refused to license its listings to Feist. Rural's refusal created a problem for Feist, as omitting these listings would have left a gaping hole in its area-wide directory, rendering it less attractive to potential yellow pages advertisers. * * *

Unable to license Rural's white pages listings, Feist used them without Rural's consent. Feist began by removing several thousand listings that fell outside the geographic range of its area-wide directory, then hired personnel to investigate the 4,935 that remained. These employees verified the data reported by Rural and sought to obtain additional information. As a result, a typical Feist listing includes the individual's street address; most of Rural's listings do not. Notwithstanding these additions, however, 1,309 of the 46,878 listings in Feist's 1983 directory were identical to listings in Rural's 1982–1983 white pages. Four of these were fictitious listings that Rural had inserted into its directory to detect copying.

Rural sued for copyright infringement in the District Court for the District of Kansas taking the position that Feist, in compiling its own directory, could not use the information contained in Rural's white pages. Rural asserted that Feist's employees were obliged to travel door-to-door or conduct a telephone survey to discover the same information for themselves. Feist responded that such efforts were economically impractical and, in any event, unnecessary because the information copied was beyond the scope of copyright protection. The District Court granted summary judgment to Rural, explaining that "[c]ourts have consistently held that telephone directories are copyrightable" and citing a string of lower court decisions. In an unpublished opinion, the Court of Appeals for the Tenth Circuit affirmed "for substantially the reasons given by the district court." We granted certiorari, to determine whether the copyright in Rural's directory protects the names, towns, and telephone numbers copied by Feist.

II

A

This case concerns the interaction of two well-established propositions. The first is that facts are not copyrightable; the other, that compilations of facts generally are. Each of these propositions possesses an impeccable pedigree. That there can be no valid copyright in facts is universally understood. The most fundamental axiom of copyright law is that "[n]o author may copyright his ideas or the facts he narrates." *Harper & Row, Publishers, Inc. v. Nation Enterprises*, 471 U.S. 539, 556,

105 S.Ct. 2218, 2228, 85 L.Ed.2d 588 (1985). Rural wisely concedes this point, noting in its brief that "[f]acts and discoveries, of course, are not themselves subject to copyright protection." At the same time, however, it is beyond dispute that compilations of facts are within the subject matter of copyright. Compilations were expressly mentioned in the Copyright Act of 1909, and again in the Copyright Act of 1976.

There is an undeniable tension between these two propositions. Many compilations consist of nothing but raw data—*i.e.*, wholly factual information not accompanied by any original written expression. On what basis may one claim a copyright in such a work? Common sense tells us that 100 uncopyrightable facts do not magically change their status when gathered together in one place. Yet copyright law seems to contemplate that compilations that consist exclusively of facts are potentially within its scope.

The key to resolving the tension lies in understanding why facts are not copyrightable. The *sine qua non* of copyright is originality. To qualify for copyright protection, a work must be original to the author. Original, as the term is used in copyright, means only that the work was independently created by the author (as opposed to copied from other works), and that it possesses at least some minimal degree of creativity. To be sure, the requisite level of creativity is extremely low; even a slight amount will suffice. The vast majority of works make the grade quite easily, as they possess some creative spark, "no matter how crude, humble or obvious" it might be. M. Nimmer & D. Nimmer, Copyright § 1.08[C] [1] (1990). Originality does not signify novelty; a work may be original even though it closely resembles other works so long as the similarity is fortuitous, not the result of copying. To illustrate, assume that two poets, each ignorant of the other, compose identical poems. Neither work is novel, yet both are original and, hence, copyrightable.

Originality is a constitutional requirement. The source of Congress' power to enact copyright laws is Article I, § 8, cl. 8, of the Constitution, which authorizes Congress to "secur[e] for limited Times to Authors ... the exclusive Right to their respective Writings." In two decisions from the late 19th Century—*The Trade–Mark Cases*, 100 U.S. 82, 25 L.Ed. 550 (1879); and *Burrow-Giles Lithographic Co. v. Sarony*, 111 U.S. 53, 4 S.Ct. 279, 28 L.Ed. 349 (1884)—this Court defined the crucial terms "authors" and "writings." In so doing, the Court made it unmistakably clear that these terms presuppose a degree of originality.

* * *

The originality requirement articulated in *The Trade–Mark Cases* and *Burrow-Giles* remains the touchstone of copyright protection today. It is the very "premise of copyright law." *Miller v. Universal City Studios, Inc.*, 650 F.2d 1365, 1368 (CA5 1981). Leading scholars agree on this point. As one pair of commentators succinctly puts it: "The originality requirement is *constitutionally mandated* for all works." Patterson & Joyce, Monopolizing the Law: The Scope of Copyright

Protection for Law Reports and Statutory Compilations, 36 UCLA L.Rev. 719, 763, n. 155 (1989). * * *

It is this bedrock principle of copyright that mandates the law's seemingly disparate treatment of facts and factual compilations. "No one may claim originality as to facts." Nimmer, § 2.11[A], p. 2–157. This is because facts do not owe their origin to an act of authorship. The distinction is one between creation and discovery: the first person to find and report a particular fact has not created the fact; he or she has merely discovered its existence. To borrow from *Burrow-Giles*, one who discovers a fact is not its "maker" or "originator." 111 U.S., at 58, 4 S.Ct., at 281. "The discoverer merely finds and records." Nimmer § 2.03[E]. Census-takers, for example, do not "create" the population figures that emerge from their efforts; in a sense, they copy these figures from the world around them. Census data therefore do not trigger copyright because these data are not "original" in the constitutional sense. The same is true of all facts—scientific, historical, biographical, and news of the day. "[T]hey may not be copyrighted and are part of the public domain available to every person." *Miller*, *supra*, at 1369.

Factual compilations, on the other hand, may possess the requisite originality. The compilation author typically chooses which facts to include, in what order to place them, and how to arrange the collected data so that they may be used effectively by readers. These choices as to selection and arrangement, so long as they are made independently by the compiler and entail a minimal degree of creativity, are sufficiently original that Congress may protect such compilations through the copyright laws. Thus, even a directory that contains absolutely no protectible written expression, only facts, meets the constitutional minimum for copyright protection if it features an original selection or arrangement.

This protection is subject to an important limitation. The mere fact that a work is copyrighted does not mean that every element of the work may be protected. Originality remains the *sine qua non*; accordingly, copyright protection may extend only to those components of a work that are original to the author. Thus, if the compilation author clothes facts with an original collocation of words, he or she may be able to claim a copyright in this written expression. Others may copy the underlying facts from the publication, but not the precise words used to present them. In *Harper & Row*, for example, we explained that President Ford could not prevent others from copying bare historical facts from his autobiography, but that he could prevent others from copying his "subjective descriptions and portraits of public figures." Id., 471 U.S. at 563, 105 S.Ct., at 2232. Where the compilation author adds no written expression but rather lets the facts speak for themselves, the expressive element is more elusive. The only conceivable expression is the manner in which the compiler has selected and arranged the facts. Thus, if the selection and arrangement are original, these elements of the work are eligible for copyright protection. No matter how original the format, however, the facts themselves do not become original through association.

This inevitably means that the copyright in a factual compilation is thin. Notwithstanding a valid copyright, a subsequent compiler remains free to use the facts contained in another's publication to aid in preparing a competing work, so long as the competing work does not feature the same selection and arrangement. As one commentator explains it: "[N]o matter how much original authorship the work displays, the facts and ideas it exposes are free for the taking.... [T]he very same facts and ideas may be divorced from the context imposed by the author, and restated or reshuffled by second comers, even if the author was the first to discover the facts or to propose the ideas." Ginsburg, Creation and Commercial Value: Copyright Protection of Works of Information, 90 Colum. L. Rev. 1865, 1868 (1990).

It may seem unfair that much of the fruit of the compiler's labor may be used by others without compensation. As Justice Brennan has correctly observed, however, this is not "some unforeseen byproduct of a statutory scheme." *Harper & Row*, 471 U.S., at 589, 105 S.Ct., at 2245 (dissenting opinion). It is, rather, "the essence of copyright," *ibid.*, and a constitutional requirement. The primary objective of copyright is not to reward the labor of authors, but "[t]o promote the Progress of Science and useful Arts." Art. I, § 8, cl. 8. To this end, copyright assures authors the right to their original expression, but encourages others to build freely upon the ideas and information conveyed by a work. This principle, known as the idea/expression or fact/expression dichotomy, applies to all works of authorship. As applied to a factual compilation, assuming the absence of original written expression, only the compiler's selection and arrangement may be protected; the raw facts may be copied at will. This result is neither unfair nor unfortunate. It is the means by which copyright advances the progress of science and art.

This Court has long recognized that the fact/expression dichotomy limits severely the scope of protection in fact-based works. More than a century ago, the Court observed: "The very object of publishing a book on science or the useful arts is to communicate to the world the useful knowledge which it contains. But this object would be frustrated if the knowledge could not be used without incurring the guilt of piracy of the book." *Baker v. Selden*, 101 U.S. 99, 103, 25 L.Ed. 841 (1880). * * *

This, then, resolves the doctrinal tension: Copyright treats facts and factual compilations in a wholly consistent manner. Facts, whether alone or as part of a compilation, are not original and therefore may not be copyrighted. A factual compilation is eligible for copyright if it features an original selection or arrangement of facts, but the copyright is limited to the particular selection or arrangement. In no event may copyright extend to the facts themselves.

B

As we have explained, originality is a constitutionally mandated prerequisite for copyright protection. The Court's decisions announcing this rule predate the Copyright Act of 1909, but ambiguous language in the 1909 Act caused some lower courts temporarily to lose sight of this requirement.

* * *

[These ambiguities] led some courts to infer erroneously that directories and the like were copyrightable *per se*, "without any further or precise showing of original—personal—authorship." Ginsburg 1895.

Making matters worse, these courts developed a new theory to justify the protection of factual compilations. Known alternatively as "sweat of the brow" or "industrious collection," the underlying notion was that copyright was a reward for the hard work that went into compiling facts. The classic formulation of the doctrine appeared in *Jeweler's Circular Publishing Co.*, 281 F., at 88:

> "The right to copyright a book upon which one has expended labor in its preparation does not depend upon whether the materials which he has collected consist or not of matters which are publici juris, or whether such materials show literary skill *or originality*, either in thought or in language, or anything more than industrious collection. The man who goes through the streets of a town and puts down the names of each of the inhabitants, with their occupations and their street number, acquires material of which he is the author" (emphasis added).

The "sweat of the brow" doctrine had numerous flaws, the most glaring being that it extended copyright protection in a compilation beyond selection and arrangement—the compiler's original contributions—to the facts themselves. Under the doctrine, the only defense to infringement was independent creation. A subsequent compiler was "not entitled to take one word of information previously published," but rather had to "independently wor[k] out the matter for himself, so as to arrive at the same result from the same common sources of information." *Id.*, at 88–89. "Sweat of the brow" courts thereby eschewed the most fundamental axiom of copyright law—that no one may copyright facts or ideas. * * *

* * *

Without a doubt, the "sweat of the brow" doctrine flouted basic copyright principles. Throughout history, copyright law has "recognize[d] a greater need to disseminate factual works than works of fiction or fantasy." *Harper & Row*, 471 U.S., at 563, 105 S.Ct., at 2232. But "sweat of the brow" courts took a contrary view; they handed out proprietary interests in facts and declared that authors are absolutely precluded from saving time and effort by relying upon the facts contained in prior works. In truth, "[i]t is just such wasted effort that the proscription against the copyright of ideas and facts . . . [is] designed to prevent." *Rosemont Enterprises, Inc. v. Random House, Inc.*, 366 F.2d 303, 310 (CA2 1966), cert. denied, 385 U.S. 1009, 87 S.Ct. 714, 17 L.Ed.2d 546 (1967). "Protection for the fruits of such research . . . may in certain circumstances be available under a theory of unfair competition. But to accord copyright protection on this basis alone distorts basic copyright principles in that it creates a monopoly in public domain materials without the necessary justification of protecting and encouraging the creation of 'writings' by 'authors.' " Nimmer § 3.04, p. 3–23.

C

"Sweat of the brow" decisions did not escape the attention of the Copyright Office. When Congress decided to overhaul the copyright statute and asked the Copyright Office to study existing problems, the Copyright Office promptly recommended that Congress clear up the confusion in the lower courts as to the basic standards of copyrightability. * * *

Congress took the Register's advice. In enacting the Copyright Act of 1976, Congress dropped the reference to "all the writings of an author" and replaced it with the phrase "original works of authorship." 17 U.S.C. § 102(a). In making explicit the originality requirement, Congress announced that it was merely clarifying existing law: "The two fundamental criteria of copyright protection [are] originality and fixation in tangible form.... The phrase 'original works of authorship,' which is purposely left undefined, is intended to incorporate without change *the standard of originality established by the courts under the present [1909] copyright statute.*" H.R.Rep. No. 94–1476, p. 51 (1976) (emphasis added). * * *

To ensure that the mistakes of the "sweat of the brow" courts would not be repeated, Congress took additional measures. * * * The 1976 Act [section 102(b)] identifies specifically those elements of a work for which copyright is not available: "In no case does copyright protection for an original work of authorship extend to any idea, procedure, process, system, method of operation, concept, principle, or discovery, regardless of the form in which it is described, explained, illustrated, or embodied in such work." § 102(b) is universally understood to prohibit any copyright in facts. * * *

* * *

The definition of "compilation" is found in § 101 of the 1976 Act. It defines a "compilation" in the copyright sense as "a work formed by the collection and assembly of preexisting materials or of data *that* are selected, coordinated, or arranged *in such a way that* the resulting work as a whole constitutes an original work of authorship" (emphasis added).

The purpose of the statutory definition is to emphasize that collections of facts are not copyrightable *per se*. It conveys this message through its tripartite structure, as emphasized above by the italics. The statute identifies three distinct elements and requires each to be met for a work to qualify as a copyrightable compilation: (1) the collection and assembly of pre-existing material, facts, or data; (2) the selection, coordination, or arrangement of those materials; and (3) the creation, by virtue of the particular selection, coordination, or arrangement, of an "original" work of authorship. * * *

* * *

As discussed earlier, however, the originality requirement is not particularly stringent. A compiler may settle upon a selection or arrangement that others have used; novelty is not required. Originality requires only that the author make the selection or arrangement independently (*i.e.*, without copying that selection or arrangement from another work), and that it display some minimal level of creativity. Presumably, the vast majority of compilations will pass this test, but not all will. There remains a narrow category of works in which the creative spark is utterly lacking or so trivial as to be virtually nonexistent. * * *

Even if a work qualifies as a copyrightable compilation, it receives only limited protection. This is the point of § 103 of the Act. Section 103 explains that "[t]he subject matter of copyright ... includes compilations," § 103(a), but that copyright protects only the author's original contributions—not the facts or information conveyed:

> "The copyright in a compilation ... extends only to the material contributed by the author of such work, as distinguished from the preexisting material employed in the work, and does not imply any exclusive right in the preexisting material." § 103(b).

As § 103 makes clear, copyright is not a tool by which a compilation author may keep others from using the facts or data he or she has collected. * * * [T]he facts contained in existing works may be freely copied because copyright protects only the elements that owe their origin to the compiler—the selection, coordination, and arrangement of facts.

In summary, the 1976 revisions to the Copyright Act leave no doubt that originality, not "sweat of the brow," is the touchstone of copyright protection in directories and other fact-based works. * * *

III

There is no doubt that Feist took from the white pages of Rural's directory a substantial amount of factual information. At a minimum, Feist copied the names, towns, and telephone numbers of 1,309 of Rural's subscribers. Not all copying, however, is copyright infringement. To establish infringement, two elements must be proven: (1) ownership of a valid copyright, and (2) copying of constituent elements of the work that are original. The first element is not at issue here; Feist appears to concede that Rural's directory, considered as a whole, is subject to a valid copyright because it contains some foreword text, as well as original material in its yellow pages advertisements.

The question is whether Rural has proved the second element. In other words, did Feist, by taking 1,309 names, towns, and telephone numbers from Rural's white pages, copy anything that was "original" to Rural? Certainly, the raw data does not satisfy the originality requirement. Rural may have been the first to discover and report the names, towns, and telephone numbers of its subscribers, but this data does not

" 'ow[e] its origin' " to Rural. *Burrow-Giles*, 111 U.S., at 58, 4 S.Ct., at 281. Rather, these bits of information are uncopyrightable facts; they existed before Rural reported them and would have continued to exist if Rural had never published a telephone directory. * * *

* * *

The question that remains is whether Rural selected, coordinated, or arranged these uncopyrightable facts in an original way. As mentioned, originality is not a stringent standard; it does not require that facts be presented in an innovative or surprising way. It is equally true, however, that the selection and arrangement of facts cannot be so mechanical or routine as to require no creativity whatsoever. The standard of originality is low, but it does exist. As this Court has explained, the Constitution mandates some minimal degree of creativity, and an author who claims infringement must prove "the existence of ... intellectual production, of thought, and conception." *Burrow-Giles, supra*, 111 U.S., at 59–60, 4 S.Ct., at 281–282.

The selection, coordination, and arrangement of Rural's white pages do not satisfy the minimum constitutional standards for copyright protection. As mentioned at the outset, Rural's white pages are entirely typical. Persons desiring telephone service in Rural's service area fill out an application and Rural issues them a telephone number. In preparing its white pages, Rural simply takes the data provided by its subscribers and lists it alphabetically by surname. The end product is a garden-variety white pages directory, devoid of even the slightest trace of creativity.

Rural's selection of listings could not be more obvious: it publishes the most basic information—name, town, and telephone number—about each person who applies to it for telephone service. This is "selection" of a sort, but it lacks the modicum of creativity necessary to transform mere selection into copyrightable expression. Rural expended sufficient effort to make the white pages directory useful, but insufficient creativity to make it original.

We note in passing that the selection featured in Rural's white pages may also fail the originality requirement for another reason. Feist points out that Rural did not truly "select" to publish the names and telephone numbers of its subscribers; rather, it was required to do so by the Kansas Corporation Commission as part of its monopoly franchise. Accordingly, one could plausibly conclude that this selection was dictated by state law, not by Rural.

Nor can Rural claim originality in its coordination and arrangement of facts. The white pages do nothing more than list Rural's subscribers in alphabetical order. This arrangement may, technically speaking, owe its origin to Rural; no one disputes that Rural undertook the task of alphabetizing the names itself. But there is nothing remotely creative about arranging names alphabetically in a white pages directory. It is an age-old practice, firmly rooted in tradition and so commonplace that it has come to be expected as a matter of course. It is not only unoriginal, it is practically inevitable. This time-honored tradition does not possess the minimal creative spark required by the Copyright Act and the Constitution.

We conclude that the names, towns, and telephone numbers copied by Feist were not original to Rural and therefore were not protected by the copyright in Rural's combined white and yellow pages directory. As a constitutional matter, copyright protects only those constituent elements of a work that possess more than a *de minimis* quantum of creativity. Rural's white pages, limited to basic subscriber information and arranged alphabetically, fall short of the mark. As a statutory matter, 17 U.S.C. § 101 does not afford protection from copying to a collection of facts that are selected, coordinated, and arranged in a way that utterly lacks originality. Given that some works must fail, we cannot imagine a more likely candidate. Indeed, were we to hold that Rural's white pages pass muster, it is hard to believe that any collection of facts could fail.

Because Rural's white pages lack the requisite originality, Feist's use of the listings cannot constitute infringement. This decision should not be construed as demeaning Rural's efforts in compiling its directory, but rather as making clear that copyright rewards originality, not effort. As this Court noted more than a century ago, " 'great praise may be due to the plaintiffs for their industry and enterprise in publishing this paper, yet the law does not contemplate their being rewarded in this way.' " *Baker v. Selden*, 101 U.S., at 105. * * *

Notes and Questions

1. *Creativity.* As the *Feist* opinion makes clear, modern formulations of the originality requirement tend to break the requirement into two parts: first, the work must be the author's independent creation, and second, the work must demonstrate a minimal, threshold level of creativity. Why impose a creativity requirement? Based on the *Feist* opinion, how would you describe the level of creativity that must be demonstrated? Why was the creativity requirement not satisfied in the *Feist* case? See Abrams, *Originality and Creativity in Copyright Law*, 55 L. & CONTEMP. PROBS. 3, 14–20 (1992); Ginsburg, *No "Sweat"? Copyright and Other Protection of Works of Information after* Feist v. Rural Telephone, 92 COLUM. L. REV. 339, 343–48 (1992); Gorman, *The* Feist *Case: Reflections on a Pathbreaking Copyright Decision*, 18 RUTGERS COMPUTER & TECH. L. J. 731 (1992). Can you think of any practical way that telephone white pages listings might be made sufficiently creative to obtain copyright protection? Are there any aspects of a typical telephone book that are likely to satisfy the creativity requirement? If so, which aspects?

Compilations of facts often have been found sufficiently original to merit copyright. For example, in Eckes v. Card Prices Update, 736 F.2d 859, 222 U.S.P.Q. 762 (2d Cir.1984), the court found the plaintiff's "selection, creativity and judgement in choosing" 5,000 "premium" baseball cards from among 18,000 sufficient to merit copyright protection. In Kregos v. Associated Press, 937 F.2d 700, 19 U.S.P.Q.2d 1161 (2d Cir.1991), the claimant's selection of nine categories of statistics for use in predicting a baseball pitcher's performance sufficed. The court noted, "there are at least scores of available statistics about pitching performance available to be calculated from the underlying data and therefore thousands of combinations of data that a selector can choose to include in a pitching form." Moreover, there were no prior pitching forms which combined the same set of statistics to suggest that the plaintiff's selection was "entirely typical," "garden-variety," or "obvious." *Id.*, 937 F.2d at 704–05, 19 U.S.P.Q.2d at 1164.

In West Publishing Co. v. Mead Data Central, Inc., 799 F.2d 1219, 230 U.S.P.Q. 801 (8th Cir.1986), *cert. denied* 479 U.S. 1070, 107 S.Ct. 962, 93 L.Ed.2d 1010 (1987), the court held that West's selection and arrangement of opinions in its case reporters qualified for copyright:

> West publishes opinions not from just one court, but from every state and all the federal courts in the United States. As it collects these opinions, West separates the decisions of state courts from federal-court decisions. West further divides the federal opinions and the state opinions and then assigns them to the appropriate West reporter series. State court decisions are divided by geographic region and assigned to West's corresponding regional reporter. Federal decisions are first divided by the level of the court they come from into district court decisions, court of appeals decisions, and Supreme Court decisions; Court of Claims and military court decisions are also separated out. Before being assigned to a reporter, district court decisions are subdivided according to subject matter into bankruptcy decisions, federal rules decisions, and decisions on other topics. After an opinion is assigned to a reporter, it is assigned to a volume of the reporter and then arranged within the volume. Federal court of appeals decisions, for example, are arranged according to circuit within each volume of West's *Federal Reporter, Second Series*, though there may be more than one group of each circuit's opinions in each volume.
>
> We conclude, as did the District Court, that the arrangement West produces through this process is the result of considerable labor, talent, and judgment. * * * [T]o meet intellectual-creation requirements a work need only be the product of a modicum of intellectual labor; West's case arrangements easily meet this standard. Further, since there is no allegation that West copies its case arrangements from some other source, the requirement of originality poses no obstacle to copyrighting the arrangements.

Id., 799 F.2d at 1226–27, 230 U.S.P.Q. at 805.

Automated data bases constitute compilations which may qualify for copyright, subject to the same rules that courts have developed for hard-copy compilations. Are the creators of automated data bases likely to face any greater problems in obtaining copyrights and reaping their benefits than hard-copy compilers? See J. DRATLER, INTELLECTUAL PROPERTY LAW: COMMERCIAL, CREATIVE, AND INDUSTRIAL PROPERTY § 5.02[2][c]-[e] (1991); Note, *Copyright and Computer Databases: Is Traditional Compilation Law Adequate?*, 65 TEX. L. REV. 993 (1987).

2. *Protection for facts.* Are you satisfied with the Court's explanation of why facts can never be considered "original" to an author? Can one be

said to "create" a fact by causing it to occur? If so, could the telephone company be deemed to "create" the telephone numbers at issue by accepting customer orders and assigning specific numbers to individual customers? What if the telephone company undertook to develop "easy-to-remember" telephone numbers, which it then assigned to customers? See generally Gordon, *Reality as Artifact: From* Feist *to Fair Use*, 55 L. & CONTEMP. PROBS. 93 (1992).

From whose viewpoint should the status of something as "fact" be determined? The author's? The court's? The "typical" member of the public's? Might the selection of viewpoint make a difference in the outcome of the determination? Are facts strictly objective discoveries, or may they also consist of a person's subjective interpretation of events or other facts? If the latter, should this make a difference for purposes of copyright protection? See Bilder, *The Shrinking Back: The Law of Biography*, 43 STAN. L. REV. 299 (1991).

Assume that X Company publishes a used car valuation book which sets forth X Company's projections of the values of "average" versions of most of the used cars sold in a particular geographic region for the next six weeks. These predicted values are set forth separately for each automobile make, model number, body style, and engine type. The book also provides predicted value adjustments for various options and for mileage in 5,000 mile increments. The valuation figures given in the book are not historical market prices, quotations, or averages; nor are they derived by mathematical formulas from available statistics. They represent X Company's editors' predictions, based on a wide variety of informational sources and their professional judgment, of expected values for "average" vehicles for the upcoming six weeks in the particular geographic region.

Are the valuations themselves facts or protectable expression? See CCC Information Services, Inc. v. Maclean Hunter Market Reports, Inc., 44 F.3d 61, 33 U.S.P.Q.2d 1183 (2d Cir.1994).

Apart from the originality issue, are there other justifications for refusing to afford copyright protection for facts?

Of what relevance is the certainty that the defendant will get a "free ride" at the plaintiff's expense if permitted to copy the facts the plaintiff has gone to the effort and expense of gathering? From a public policy standpoint, should the plaintiff's investment and effort be protected against such free riding? Given the *Feist* decision, could Congress amend the copyright laws to provide such protection? Is there any other constitutional provision that would empower Congress to provide such protection? Could the states provide effective protection? See Ginsburg, *No "Sweat"?*, *supra*, 92 COLUM. L. REV. 338; Litman, *After* Feist, 17 U. DAYTON L. REV. 607 (1992); Chapter 7, Sec. V, *infra*.

For a variety of views and insights concerning the implications of the *Feist* decision for data bases, see *Copyright Symposium: Copyright Protection for Computer Databases, CD–Roms and Factual Compilations*, 17 U. DAYTON L. REV. 323–629, 731–1018 (1992).

3. *Words, short phrases, titles, labels and other "minimal" works.* Courts and the Copyright Office generally refuse to recognize copyright in

"[w]ords and short phrases such as names, titles, and slogans; familiar symbols or designs; mere variations of typographic ornamentation, lettering or coloring; [and] mere listings of ingredients or contents * * *." 37 C.F.R. § 202.1(a) (1993). There are two justifications for this rule. First, such minimal works are viewed as insufficiently original to merit copyright. See, e.g., Laskowitz v. Marie Designer, Inc., 119 F.Supp. 541, 551, 100 U.S.P.Q. 367, 373 (S.D.Cal.1954) ("I do not think that phrases such as 'This is Nature's most restful posture' or phrases emphasizing 'the relaxing' qualities of the chair, which are so purely descriptive of the product, comply even with the slight requirement of originality in the law of copyright * * *"). In addition, it is often reasoned that granting rights in words or short phrases, in particular, may interfere with others' ability to express the underlying idea. We will examine this latter issue at greater depth in the following Section.

Courts occasionally deviate from the general rule in the case of short phrases or slogans. See, e.g., Universal City Studios, Inc. v. Kamar Industries, Inc., 217 U.S.P.Q. 1162, 1166 (S.D.Tex.1982) (recognizing copyright in "I love you E.T." and "E.T. Phone Home"). But they have steadfastly refused to recognize copyright in titles. Apart from the questionable originality of titles comprised simply of individual words or short phrases, titles "serve mainly to identify and describe the work itself." 1 P. GOLDSTEIN, COPYRIGHT PRINCIPLES, LAW AND PRACTICE § 2.7.3 (1989). Authors wishing to prevent others' use of their titles must seek redress under the trademark and unfair competition laws, which will be explored in Chapters 6 and 7, *infra*.

Product labels that do more than list ingredients or contents sometimes raise originality issues. Would you find the following material, printed on the label of a hair care product, sufficiently original to merit protection?

> Hair stays wet-looking as long as you like. Brushes out to full-bodied dry look. WET 4 is one step-four choice (finishing) in Sebastian's four step program for a healthy scalp and head of hair. WET is not oily, won't flake and keeps hair wet-looking for hours, allowing you to sculpture, contour, wave or curl. It stays looking wet until it's brushed out. When brushed, hair looks and feels thicker, extra full. Try brushing partly, leaving some parts wet for a different look.

See Sebastian International, Inc. v. Consumer Contacts (PTY) Ltd., 664 F.Supp. 909, 913, 3 U.S.P.Q.2d 1401, 1404 (D.N.J.1987), *vacated* 847 F.2d 1093, 7 U.S.P.Q.2d 1077 (3d Cir.1988).

C. PROTECTION OF EXPRESSION vs. IDEA

BAKER v. SELDEN

United States Supreme Court, 1879.
101 U.S. (11 Otto) 99, 25 L.Ed. 841.

MR. JUSTICE BRADLEY delivered the opinion of the court.

Charles Selden, the testator of the complainant in this case, in the year 1859 took the requisite steps for obtaining the copyright of a book, entitled "Selden's Condensed Ledger, or Book-keeping Simplified," the object of which was to exhibit and explain a peculiar system of book-keeping. In 1860 and 1861, he took the copyright of several other books, containing additions to and improvements upon the said system. The bill of complaint was filed against the defendant, Baker, for an alleged infringement of these copyrights. * * *

* * *

The book or series of books of which the complainant claims the copyright consists of an introductory essay explaining the system of book-keeping referred to, to which are annexed certain forms or banks, consisting of ruled lines, and headings, illustrating the system and showing how it is to be used and carried out in practice. This system effects the same results as book-keeping by double entry; but, by a peculiar arrangement of columns and headings, presents the entire operation, of a day, a week, or a month, on a single page, or on two pages facing each other, in an account-book. The defendant uses a similar plan so far as results are concerned; but makes a different arrangement of the columns, and uses different headings. If the complainant's testator had the exclusive right to the use of the system explained in his book, it would be difficult to contend that the defendant does not infringe it, notwithstanding the difference in his form of arrangement; but if it be assumed that the system is open to public use, it seems to be equally difficult to contend that the books made and sold by the defendant are a violation of the copyright of the complainant's book considered merely as a book explanatory of the system. Where the truths of a science or the methods of an art are the common property of the whole world, any author has the right to express the one, or explain and use the other, in his own way. As an author, Selden explained the system in a particular way. It may be conceded that Baker makes and uses account-books arranged on substantially the same system; but the proof fails to show that he has violated the copyright of Selden's book, regarding the latter merely as an explanatory work; or that he has infringed Selden's right in any way, unless the latter became entitled to an exclusive right in the system.

The evidence of the complainant is principally directed to the object of showing that Baker uses the same system as that which is explained and illustrated in Selden's books. It becomes important, therefore, to determine whether, in obtaining the copyright of his books, he secured the exclusive right to the use of the system or method of book-keeping which the said books are intended to illustrate and explain. It is contended that he has secured such exclusive right, because no one can use the system without using substantially the same ruled lines and headings which he was appended to his books in illustration of it. In other words, it is contended that the ruled lines and headings, given to illustrate the system, are a part of the book, and, as such, are secured by the copyright; and that no one can make or use similar ruled lines and headings, or ruled lines and headings made and arranged on substantially the same system, without violating the copyright. And this is really the question to be decided in this case. Stated in another form, the question is, whether the exclusive property in a system of book-keeping can be claimed, under the law of copyright, by means of a book in which that system is explained? The complainant's bill, and the case made under it, are based on the hypothesis that it can be.

* * *

There is no doubt that a work on the subject of book-keeping, though only explanatory of well-known systems, may be the subject of a copyright; but, then, it is claimed only as a book. Such a book may be explanatory either of old systems, or of an entirely new system; and, considered as a book, as the work of an author, conveying information on the subject of book-keeping, and containing detailed explanations of the art, it may be a very valuable acquisition to the practical knowledge of the community. But there is a clear distinction between the book, as such, and the art which it is intended to illustrate. The mere statement of the proposition is so evident, that it requires hardly any argument to support it. The same distinction may be predicated of every other art as well as that of book-keeping. A treatise on the composition and use of medicines, be they old or new; on the construction and use of ploughs, or watches, or churns; or on the mixture and application of colors for painting or dyeing; or on the mode of drawing lines to produce the effect of perspective,—would be the subject of copyright; but no one would contend that the copyright of the treatise would give the exclusive right to the art or manufacture described therein. The copyright of the book, if not pirated from other works, would be valid without regard to the novelty, or want of novelty, of its subject-matter. The novelty of the art or thing described or explained has nothing to do with the validity of the copyright. To give to the author of the book an exclusive property in the art described therein, when no examination of its novelty has ever been officially made, would be a surprise and a fraud upon the public. That is the province of letters-patent, not of copyright. The claim to an invention or discovery of an art or manufacture must be subjected to the examination of the Patent Office before an exclusive right therein can be obtained; and it can only be secured by a patent from the government.

* * *

The copyright of a book on perspective, no matter how many drawings and illustrations it may contain, gives no exclusive right to the modes of drawing described, though they may never have been known or used before. By publishing the book, without getting a patent for the art, the latter is given to the public. The fact that the art described in the book by illustrations of lines and figures which are reproduced in practice in the application of the art, makes no difference. Those illustrations are the mere language employed by the author to convey his ideas more clearly. Had he used words of description instead of diagrams (which merely stand in the place of words), there could not be the slightest doubt that others, applying the art to practical use, might lawfully draw the lines and diagrams which were in the author's mind, and which he thus described by words in his book.

The copyright of a work on mathematical science cannot give to the author an exclusive right to the methods of operation which he propounds, or to the diagrams which he employs to explain them, so as to prevent an engineer from using them whenever occasion requires. The very object of publishing a book on science or the useful arts is to communicate to the world the useful knowledge which it contains. But this object would be frustrated if the knowledge could not be used without incurring the guilt of piracy of the book. And where the art it teaches cannot be used without employing the methods and diagrams used to illustrate the book, or such as are similar to them, such methods and diagrams are to be considered as necessary incidents to the art, and given therewith to the public; not given for the purpose of publication in other works explanatory of the art, but for the purpose of practical application.

Of course, these observations are not intended to apply to ornamental designs, or pictorial illustrations addressed to the taste. Of these it may be said, that their form is their essence, and their object, the production of pleasure in their contemplation. This is their final end. They are as much the product of genius and the result of composition, as are the lines of the poet or the historian's period. On the other hand, the teachings of science and the rules and methods of useful art have their final end in application and use; and this application and use are what the public derive from the publication of a book which teaches them. But as embodied and taught in a literary composition or book, their essence consists only in their statement. This alone is what is secured by the copyright. The use by another of the same methods of statement, whether in words or illustrations, in a book published for teaching the art, would undoubtedly be an infringement of the copyright.

Recurring to the case before us, we observe that Charles Selden, by his books, explained and described a peculiar system of book-keeping, and illustrated his method by means of ruled lines and blank columns, with proper headings on a page, or on successive pages. Now, whilst no one has a right to print or publish his book, or any material part thereof, as a book intended to convey instruction in the art, any person may practice and use the art itself which he has described and illustrated therein. The use of the art is a totally different thing from a publication of the book explaining it. The copyright of a book on book-keeping cannot secure the exclusive right to make, sell, and use account-books prepared upon the plan set forth in such book. Whether the art might or might not have been patented, is a question which is not before us. It was not patented, and is open and free to the use of the public. And, of course, in using the art, the ruled lines and headings of accounts must necessarily be used as incident to it.

The plausibility of the claim put forward by the complainant in this case arises from a confusion of ideas produced by the peculiar nature of the art described in the books which have been made the subject of copyright. In describing the art, the illustrations and diagrams employed happen to correspond more closely than usual with the actual work performed by the operator who uses the art. Those illustrations and diagrams consist of ruled lines and headings of accounts; and it is similar ruled lines and headings of accounts which, in the application of the art, the book-keeper makes with his pen, or the stationer with his press; whilst in most other cases the diagrams and illustrations can only be represented in concrete forms of wood, metal, stone, or some other physical embodiment. But the principle is the same in all. The description of the art in a book, though entitled to the benefit of copyright, lays no foundation for an exclusive claim to the art itself. The object of the one is explanation; the object of the other is use. The former may be secured by copyright. The latter can only be secured, if it can be secured at all, by letters-patent.

* * *

The conclusion to which we have come is, that blank account-books are not the subject of copyright; and that the mere copyright of Selden's book did not confer upon him the exclusive right to make and use account-books, ruled and arranged as designated by him and described and illustrated in said book.

* * *

Notes and Questions

1. *The* Baker *opinion.* How would you characterize the Supreme Court's holding in *Baker*? Which (if any) of the following accurately describes the Court's reasoning?

1) The Court found that the accounting forms did not constitute copyrightable expression because they lacked originality or creativity;

2) the Court found that the forms were not copyrightable expression, but rather were utilitarian objects outside the protection of the copyright laws;

3) the Court found that regardless of whether the forms constituted copyrightable expression, the defendant did not copy that expression—he only copied the underlying idea or accounting system, which was not protected by copyright;

4) the Court assumed that the forms constituted copyrightable expression, and that the defendant copied that expression, but found that the copying did not infringe because it was done for the purpose of using the accounting system, rather than for purposes of explaining the accounting system;

5) the Court found that, regardless of whether forms are copyrightable as a general matter, no copyright in the forms could be enforced in this case because the forms constituted the only means by which the underlying idea or accounting system could be implemented or expressed. Enforcing the copyright would give the plaintiff a *de facto* monopoly in the accounting system.

What are the implications of each interpretation? If alternative 5) is accurate, was there in fact only one way to implement or express the accounting system? Are there likely to be many instances in which there is only one way to implement or express an idea?

2. *The "blank form" rule.* The Copyright Office has adopted the following rule:

> The following are examples of works not subject to copyright and applications for registration of such works cannot be entertained:
>
> * * *
>
> (c) Blank forms, such as time cards, graph paper, account books, diaries, bank checks, scorecards, address books, report forms, order forms and the like, which are designed for recording information and do not in themselves convey information. * * *

37 C.F.R. § 202.1(c) (1993). The rule, which parallels modern case law, is frequently attributed to the *Baker* decision. What in *Baker* compels or supports such a rule? Is there any alternative basis for the rule?

In implementing this rule, how does one determine whether a form conveys or merely records information? Presumably, a form which contains lengthy, complex instructions for its use and completion conveys information. See, e.g., Edwin K. Williams & Co. v. Edwin K. Williams, 542 F.2d 1053, 191 U.S.P.Q. 563 (9th Cir.1976), *cert. denied* 433 U.S. 908, 97 S.Ct. 2973, 53 L.Ed.2d 1092 (1977) (account books with several pages of instructions on the use of the forms and advice on the successful management of a service station conveyed information and were therefore copyrightable). Assume that a form provides no significant instructions. Might the manner in which information is solicited in itself convey information? For example, might the questions asked convey information about what is deemed relevant or important? If so, should that finding be sufficient to take the form out of the rule against copyrightability of blank forms? Compare Bibbero Systems, Inc. v. Colwell Systems, Inc., 893 F.2d 1104, 13 U.S.P.Q.2d 1634 (1990), with Kregos v. Associated Press, 937 F.2d 700, 19 U.S.P.Q.2d 1161 (2d Cir.1991).

MORRISSEY v. THE PROCTER & GAMBLE CO.

United States Court of Appeals for the First Circuit, 1967.
379 F.2d 675, 154 U.S.P.Q. 193.

ALDRICH, CHIEF JUDGE.

This is an appeal from a summary judgment for the defendant. The plaintiff, Morrissey, is the copyright owner of a set of rules for a sales promotional contest of the "sweepstakes" type involving the social security numbers of the participants. Plaintiff alleges that the defendant, Procter & Gamble Company, infringed, by copying, almost precisely, Rule 1. In its motion for summary judgment, based upon affidavits and depositions, defendant denies that plaintiff's Rule 1 is copyrightable material * * *. The district court held for the defendant * * *.

* * *

[W]e recite plaintiff's Rule 1, and defendant's Rule 1, the italicizing in the latter being ours to note the defendant's variations or changes.

> "1. Entrants should print name, address and social security number on a boxtop, or a plain paper. Entries must be accompanied by * * * boxtop or by plain paper on which the name * * * is copied from any source. Official rules are explained on * * * packages or leaflets obtained from dealer. If you do not have a social security number you may use the name and number of any member of your immediate family living with you. Only the person named on the entry will be deemed an entrant and may qualify for prize.
>
> "Use the correct social security number belonging to the person named on entry * * * wrong number will be disqualified."

(Plaintiff's Rule)

> "1. Entrants should print name, address and Social Security number on a Tide boxtop, or *on* [a] plain paper. Entries must be accompanied by Tide boxtop *(any size)* or by plain paper on which the name 'Tide' is copied from any source. Official rules are *available* on Tide Sweepstakes packages, or *on* leaflets *at* Tide dealers, *or you can send a stamped, self-addressed envelope to:* Tide 'Shopping Fling' Sweepstakes, P.O. Box 4459, Chicago 77, Illinois.
>
> "If you do not have a Social Security number, you may use the name and number of any member of your immediate family living with you. Only the person named on the entry will be deemed an entrant and may qualify for a prize.
>
> "Use the correct Social Security number, belonging to the person named on *the* entry—wrong numbers will be disqualified."

(Defendant's Rule)

The district court * * * took the position that since the substance of the contest was not copyrightable, which is unquestionably correct, Baker v. Selden, 1879, 101 U.S. 99, 25 L.Ed. 841, and the substance was relatively simple, it must follow that plaintiff's rule sprung directly from the substance and "contains no original creative authorship." 262 F.Supp. at 738. This does not follow. Copyright attaches to form of expression, and defendant's own proof, introduced to deluge the court on the issue of access, itself established that there was more than one way of expressing even this simple substance. Nor, in view of the almost precise similarity of the two rules, could defendant successfully invoke the principle of a stringent standard for showing infringement which some courts apply when the subject matter involved admits of little variation in form of expression.

Nonetheless, we must hold for the defendant. When the uncopyrightable subject matter is very narrow, so that "the topic necessarily requires," Sampson & Murdock Co. v. Seaver–Radford Co., 1 Cir., 1905, 140 F. 539, 541, if not only one form of expression, at best only a limited number, to permit copyrighting would mean that a party or parties, by copyrighting a mere handful of forms, could exhaust all possibilities of future use of the substance. In such circumstances it does not seem accurate to say that any particular form of expression comes from the subject matter. However, it is necessary to say that the subject matter would be appropriated by permitting the copyrighting of its expression. We cannot recognize copyright as a game of chess in which the public can be checkmated.

Upon examination the matters embraced in Rule 1 are so straightforward and simple that we find this limiting principle to be applicable. Furthermore, its operation need not await an attempt to copyright all possible forms. It cannot be only the last form of expression which is to be condemned, as completing defendant's exclusion from the substance. Rather, in these circumstances, we hold that copyright does not extend to the subject matter at all, and plaintiff cannot complain even if his particular expression was deliberately adopted.

Notes and Questions

1. *The merger doctrine.* A direct outgrowth of the idea/expression dichotomy, the merger doctrine tells us that when there is only one or a limited number of ways to express an idea, the expression "merges" with the idea and becomes unprotectible. The issue of merger arises most frequently in cases such as *Morrissey*, involving highly functional, straightforward utilitarian works.

In determining the range of alternatives, should one count all conceivable means of expressing the idea? In Matthew Bender & Co., Inc. v. Kluwer Law Book Publishers, Inc., 672 F.Supp. 107, 5 U.S.P.Q.2d 1363 (S.D.N.Y. 1987), the plaintiff published a work documenting the range of personal injury recoveries. The plaintiff organized its illustrative cases according to the body part injured and arranged the body-part categories alphabetically. Within each body-part category plaintiff subdivided the cases according to type and amount of recovery, and by jurisdiction. For each reported case the plaintiff provided information in six categories: "Amount;" "Case;" "Plaintiff;" "Event;" "Injury;" and "Relevant Data."

In an infringement suit against a defendant who used a similar organization and format, the court found the plaintiff's organization and format uncopyrightable on the basis of the merger and the blank form doctrines. With regard to the merger issue, the court observed:

> In this case, the "idea" embodied in Bender's work is to provide attorneys working on a medical malpractice case with a useful guide, in chart form, outlining the results achieved in prior similar cases. The expression of this "idea," it seems, can be achieved in a variety of ways by organizing the charts differently. * * *
>
> While in theory there are numerous ways to place this information in chart form, from a practical point of view the number of ways to organize this information in a useful and accessible manner is limited. It would make little sense, for example, to arrange the information by listing all of the cases alphabetically or chronologically, or by organizing the cases according to the names of the attorneys listed alphabetically. These arrangements, while possible, would be of little value to a practitioner seeking relevant information.

672 F.Supp. at 110, 5 U.S.P.Q.2d at 1365.

How many practical, effective ways are there to express the idea underlying the sweepstakes rule in *Morrissey*? Would your answer depend upon the range of variations that would infringe the copyright on the plaintiff's rule? Clearly, if loose paraphrasing infringes, there will be fewer alternative methods of expressing the idea than if only close, nearly verbatim copying infringes, and a defendant's use of words or phrases commonly used in connection with the concept at issue is overlooked. Some courts, in situations like *Morrissey*, prefer to find a "thin copyright," rather than a merger. While a merger may deny the plaintiff copyright protection altogether, finding an enforceable, but thin copyright entitles the plaintiff to protection against close copying only—permitting closer versions than might be permitted under other circumstances. For example, in Continental Casualty Co. v. Beardsley, 253 F.2d 702, 117 U.S.P.Q. 1 (2d Cir.1958), *cert. denied* 358 U.S. 816, 79 S.Ct. 25, 3 L.Ed.2d 58 (1958), the court recognized copyright in Beardsley's forms and insurance instruments, but cautioned that it would be strict in finding infringement:

> [I]n the fields of insurance and commerce the use of specific language in forms and documents may be so essential to accomplish a desired result and so integrated with the use of a legal or commercial conception that the proper standard of infringement is one which will protect as far as possible the copyrighted language and yet allow free use of the thought beneath the language.

Id., 253 F.2d at 706, 117 U.S.P.Q. at 4. Does the thin copyright approach make better sense than finding a merger, when there are a limited number of ways to express the idea?

If the court in *Morrissey* had taken the thin copyright approach, would the outcome have differed? If so would this have been a good result?

Might the *Morrissey* court have found plaintiff's Rule 1 insufficiently original to merit copyright protection, as an alternative ground for refusing relief? Might some short phrases and product labels, deemed uncopyrightable because insufficiently original, alternatively be denied copyright by virtue of the merger rule?

2. *Applying the idea/expression dichotomy to non-utilitarian works.* The *Baker* Court stressed that the forms there in issue were utilitarian, rather than "ornamental designs, or pictorial illustrations addressed to the taste." Does this suggest that the concern about granting a *de facto* monopoly in the idea underlying a work is inapplicable in cases involving nonutilitarian works? Consider the following case.

HERBERT ROSENTHAL JEWELRY CORP. v. KALPAKIAN

United States Court of Appeals for the Ninth Circuit, 1971.
446 F.2d 738, 170 U.S.P.Q. 557.

BROWNING, CIRCUIT JUDGE:

Plaintiff and defendants are engaged in the design, manufacture, and sale of fine jewelry.

Plaintiff charged defendants with infringing plaintiff's copyright registration of a pin in the shape of a bee formed of gold encrusted with jewels. * * *

Plaintiff contends that its copyright registration of a jeweled bee entitles it to protection from the manufacture and sale by others of any object that to the ordinary observer is substantially similar in appearance. The breadth of this claim is evident. For example, while a photograph of the copyrighted bee pin attached to the complaint depicts a bee with nineteen small white jewels on its back, plaintiff argues that its copyright is infringed by defendants' entire line of a score or more jeweled bees in three sizes decorated with from nine to thirty jewels of various sizes, kinds, and colors.

Although plaintiff's counsel asserted that the originality of plaintiff's bee pin lay in a particular arrangement of jewels on the top of the pin, the elements of this arrangement were never identified. Defendants' witnesses testified that the "arrangement" was simply a function of the size and form of the bee pin and the size of the jewels used. Plaintiff's counsel, repeatedly pressed by the district judge, was unable to suggest how jewels might be placed on the back of a pin in the shape of a bee without infringing plaintiff's copyright. He eventually conceded, "not being a jeweler, I can't conceive of how he might rearrange the design so it is dissimilar."

If plaintiff's understanding of its rights were correct, its copyright would effectively prevent others from engaging in the business of manufacturing and selling jeweled bees. We think plaintiff confuses the balance Congress struck between protection and competition under the Patent Act and the Copyright Act.

The owner of a patent is granted the exclusive right to exploit for a period of seventeen years (a maximum of fourteen years for design patents) the conception that is the subject matter of the patent. The grant of this monopoly, however, is carefully circumscribed by substantive and procedural protections. To be patentable the subject matter must be new and useful, and represent a nonobvious advance * * *. A patent is granted only after an independent administrative inquiry and determination that these substantive standards have been met. This determination is subject to both administrative and court review.

Copyright registration, on the other hand, confers no right at all to the conception reflected in the registered subject matter. "Unlike a patent, a copyright gives no exclusive right to the art disclosed; protection is given only to the expression of the idea—not the idea itself." Mazer v. Stein, 347 U.S. 201, 217, 74 S.Ct. 460, 470, 98 L.Ed. 630 (1954). Accordingly, the prerequisites for copyright registration are minimal. The work offered for registration need only be the product of the registrant. * * * [R]egistration is accomplished simply by filing a claim and depositing copies of the work with the Register of Copyrights. There is no administrative investigation or determination of the validity of the claim. A certificate is refused only if the object falls outside the broad category of matter subject to copyright registration. * * *

Obviously a copyright must not be treated as equivalent to a patent lest long continuing private monopolies be conferred over areas of gainful activity without first satisfying the substantive and procedural prerequisites to the grant of such privileges.

* * *

* * * A copyright, we have seen, bars use of the particular "expression" of an idea in a copyrighted work but does not bar use of the "idea" itself. Others are free to utilize the "idea" so long as they do not plagiarize its "expression." As the court said in Trifari, Krussman & Fishel, Inc. v. B. Steinberg–Kaslo Co., 144 F.Supp. 577, 580 (S.D.N.Y. 1956), where the copyrighted work was a jeweled pin representing a hansom cab, "though an alleged infringer gets the idea of a hansom cab pin from a copyrighted article there can be no infringement unless the article itself has been copied. The idea of a hansom cab cannot be copyrighted. Nevertheless plaintiff's expression of that idea, as embodied in its pin, can be copyrighted." * * *

The critical distinction between "idea" and "expression" is difficult to draw. As Judge Hand candidly wrote, "Obviously, no principle can be stated as to when an imitator has gone beyond copying the 'idea,' and has borrowed its 'expression.'" Peter Pan Fabrics, Inc. v. Martin Weiner Corp., 274 F.2d 487, 489 (2d Cir.1960). At least in close cases, one may suspect, the classification the court selects may simply state the result reached rather than the reason for it. In our view, the difference is really one of degree as Judge Hand suggested in his striking "abstraction" formulation in Nichols v. Universal Pictures Corp., 45 F.2d 119, 121 (2d Cir.1930). The guiding consideration in drawing the line is the preservation of the balance between competition and protection reflected in the patent and copyright laws.

What is basically at stake is the extent of the copyright owner's monopoly—from how large an area of activity did Congress intend to allow the copyright owner to exclude others? We think the production of jeweled bee pins is a larger private preserve than Congress intended to be set aside in the public market without a patent. A jeweled bee pin is therefore an "idea" that defendants were free to copy. Plaintiff seems to agree, for it disavows any claim that defendants cannot manufacture and sell jeweled bee pins and concedes that only plaintiff's particular design or "expression" of the jeweled bee pin "idea" is protected under its copyright. The difficulty, as we have noted, is that on this record the "idea" and its "expression" appear to be indistinguishable. There is no greater similarity between the pins of plaintiff and defendants than is inevitable from the use of jewel-encrusted bee forms in both.

When the "idea" and its "expression" are thus inseparable, copying the "expression" will not be barred, since protecting the "expression" in such circumstances would confer a monopoly of the "idea" upon the copyright owner free of the conditions and limitations imposed by the patent law. Baker v. Selden, 101 U.S. 99, 103, 25 L.Ed. 841 (1879).

Notes and Questions

1. *Distinguishing idea from expression.* What method does the *Kalpakian* court suggest for identifying the idea underlying a work? Once identified, how is the idea to be distinguished from the author's protectible expression of the idea? How easy will the *Kalpakian* court's approach be to apply?

Distinguishing a work's "idea" from its "expression" has proven to be the most difficult aspect of copyright law. The *Kalpakian* court refers to Judge Learned Hand's famous "abstractions" formulation for distinguishing idea from expression, set forth in Nichols v. Universal Pictures Corp., 45 F.2d 119 (2d Cir.1930), *cert. denied* 282 U.S. 902, 51 S.Ct. 216, 75 L.Ed. 795 (1931). In *Nichols*, the plaintiff claimed that the defendant's motion picture, "The Cohens and the Kellys," infringed the copyright in her play, "Abie's Irish Rose." Both works involved a secret marriage of the children of Jewish and Irish Catholic fathers, a quarrel between the fathers, the birth of grandchildren, and an ultimate reconciliation of the fathers. In other respects, the works differed significantly.

In "Abie's Irish Rose," the prosperous Jewish father, a New York widower, was obsessed with the notion that his only son should marry an orthodox Jewess. The Irish Catholic father, a California widower, was equally obsessed with the notion that his daughter should marry within her faith. The son and daughter secretly married, and a series of scenes ensued in which the children tried to deceive the fathers about their respective religious backgrounds. The fathers ultimately learned the truth, and after trying unsuccessfully to dissolve the marriage, disowned their children. The children subsequently had twins (a boy and a girl), and each father learned that a child had been born. Yearning to see his grandchild, each father went to the children's house, and discovered the other there. Upon meeting, the fathers argued about the gender of what each believed to be a single grandchild. Ultimately learning that there were two grandchildren, and that each had been named for one of their grandparents, the fathers were reconciled with their children and with one another.

"The Cohens and the Kelleys" involved full families, rather than just widowed fathers, who were neighbors in a poor New York neighborhood. Neither the Jewish nor the Irish Catholic family was particularly religious. Rather, the families had a more general kind of on-going personal feud. After the Jewish daughter and the Irish son secretly married, the Jewish father was informed that he had inherited a large sum of money from a great aunt, moved his family to a luxurious home, and began to live in vulgar opulence. When the Irish son sought to visit the Jewish daughter at the new home, the Jewish father chased him away, decrying such a lowly alliance, and then abused the Irish father over the telephone. In so doing, the Jewish father became so upset that he was forced to go to Florida to recuperate. When he returned he learned of the marriage between his daughter and the Irish boy and that the pair had borne a child. An altercation ensued between the Irish and the Jewish fathers, and the Jewish father disowned his daughter. The daughter and her baby went to live with the Irish family. The Jewish father then learned that a mistake had been made: the Irish father, rather than he, had inherited from the great aunt. Rejecting opportunities fraudulently to conceal the fact, the Jewish father went to the Irish father to admit this, and the two were reconciled, with the Irish father offering to share the wealth with the Jew. The grandchild had little, if anything to do with the reconciliation. Rather, the reconciliation was due to the Jew's honesty and the Irishman's generosity.

The problem before the *Nichols* court was to determine whether the defendant had taken copyrightable expression from "Abie's Irish Rose," or only the idea underlying the play. Only the unauthorized taking of copyrighted expression would constitute infringement. The court thus set out to differentiate the idea underlying the plaintiff's play from the plaintiff's expression of the idea.

Writing for the court, Judge Hand noted that "copyrightable expression" was not limited to the literal words that the plaintiff used. The defendant might infringe if it took an "abstract" of the plaintiff's work as a whole. The problem lay in determining whether the "abstract" consisted only of the idea underlying the plaintiff's work or incorporated "expression" as well:

> Upon any work, and especially upon a play, a great number of patterns of increasing generality will fit equally well, as more and more of the incident is left out. The last may perhaps be no more than the most general statement of what the play is about, and at times might consist only of its title; but there is a point in this series of abstractions where they are no longer protected, since otherwise the playwright could prevent the use of his "ideas," to which, apart from their expression, his property is never extended. Nobody has ever been able to fix that boundary, and nobody ever can. In some cases the question has been treated as though it were analogous to lifting a portion out of the copyrighted work; but the analogy is not a good one, because, though the skeleton is a part of the body, it pervades and supports the whole. In such cases we are rather concerned with the line between expression and what is expressed. As respects plays, the controversy chiefly centers upon the characters and sequence of incident, these being the substance.
>
> We did not in Dymow v. Bolton, 11 F.2d 690, hold that a plagiarist was never liable for stealing a plot * * *. We found the plot of the second play was too different to infringe, because the most detailed pattern, common to both, eliminated so much from each that its content went into the public domain; and for this reason we said, "this mere subsection of a plot was not susceptible of copyright." But we do not doubt that two plays may correspond in plot closely enough for infringement. How far that correspondence must go is another matter. * * *
>
> In the two plays at bar we think both as to incident and character, the defendant took no more—assuming that it took anything at all—than the law allowed. The stories are quite different. One is of a religious zealot who insists upon his child's marrying no one outside his faith; opposed by another who is in this respect just like him, and is his

> foil. Their difference in race is merely an obbligato to the main theme, religion. They sink their differences through grandparental pride and affection. In the other, zealotry is wholly absent; religion does not even appear. It is true that the parents are hostile to each other in part because they differ in race; but the marriage of their son to a Jew does not apparently offend the Irish family at all, and it exacerbates the existing animosity of the Jew, principally because he has become rich, when he learns it. They are reconciled through the honesty of the Jew and the generosity of the Irishman; the grandchild has nothing whatever to do with it. The only matter common to the two is a quarrel between a Jewish and an Irish father, the marriage of their children, the birth of grandchildren and a reconciliation.
>
> If the defendant took so much from the plaintiff, it may well have been because her amazing success seemed to prove that this was a subject of enduring popularity. * * * Though the plaintiff discovered the vein, she could not keep it to herself; so defined, the theme was too generalized an abstraction from what she wrote. It was only a part of her "ideas."

45 F.2d at 121–22.

Judge Hand indicated that taking a portion of a plaintiff's plot could constitute copyright infringement, even in the absence of taking the plaintiff's literal language: what aspects of the plot constitute copyrightable expression?

2. *Copyright in characters.* One issue that has perplexed courts and commentators alike is the extent to which fictitious characters created in literary, dramatic, audiovisual, or other works are copyrightable in themselves, outside of the context in which they were created. Characters such as Sherlock Holmes, Nancy Drew or Captain James T. Kirk have great commercial value. May the owner of the copyright in the original "Star Trek" television series prevent, via copyright law, others from building their own unique stories around Captain Kirk, if they take no other protectible elements from the series?

The name of the character, by itself, is unlikely to be protectible under copyright law (though trademark or unfair competition protection may be available). With regard to the author's delineation of the character, the basic issue is whether the character, by itself, constitutes merely an idea or protectible expression. Judge Hand addressed the issue in the *Nichols* case, discussed above:

> [W]e do not doubt that two plays may correspond in plot closely enough for infringement. * * * Nor need we hold that the same may not be true as to the characters, quite independently of the "plot" proper, though, as far as we know, such a case has never arisen. If Twelfth Night were copyrighted, it is quite possible that a second comer might so closely imitate Sir Toby Belch or Malvolio as to infringe, but it would not be enough that for one of his characters he cast a riotous knight who kept wassail to the discomfort of the household, or a vain and foppish steward who became amorous of his mistress. These would be no more than Shakespeare's "ideas" in the play, as little capable of monopoly as Einstein's Doctrine of Relativity, or Darwin's theory of the Origin of the

> Species. It follows that the less developed the characters, the less they can be copyrighted; that is the penalty an author must bear for marking them too indistinctly.

Nichols, 45 F.2d at 121. How much development is necessary? Professor Goldstein, in his treatise, has suggested the following rule of thumb: "A literary character can be said to have a distinctive personality, and thus to be protectible, when it has been delineated to the point at which its behavior is relatively predictable so that, when placed in a new plot situation, it will react in ways that are at once distinctive and unsurprising." P. GOLDSTEIN, COPYRIGHT PRINCIPLES, LAW AND PRACTICE § 2.7.2 at 128 (1989).

The rule in *Nichols* has not been universally followed. Warner Brothers, Inc. v. Columbia Broadcasting System, 216 F.2d 945, 104 U.S.P.Q. 103 (9th Cir.1954), *cert. denied* 348 U.S. 971, 75 S.Ct. 532, 99 L.Ed. 756, 105 U.S.P.Q. 518 (1955), involved Dashiell Hammett's mystery, *The Maltese Falcon*, and its hero, Sam Spade. The issue was whether Hammett would infringe copyright in *The Maltese Falcon* (now claimed by another) if he wrote a new story featuring Sam Spade as the detective. The Ninth Circuit found that the copyright in *The Maltese Falcon* gave no exclusive rights in the character, suggesting that characters *per se* are not protected unless they "constitute the story being told."

> It is conceivable that the character really constitutes the story being told, but if the character is only the chessman in the game of telling the story he is not within the area of the protection afforded by the copyright. * * * [E]ven if the Owners assigned their complete rights in the copyright to the *Falcon*, such assignment did not prevent the author from using the characters used therein, in other stories. The characters were vehicles for the story told, and the vehicles did not go with the sale of the story.

Id., 216 F.2d at 950, 104 U.S.P.Q. at 107. This standard will rarely be satisfied. It has not been widely adopted, however, and the Ninth Circuit has subsequently limited its application. See Walt Disney Productions v. Air Pirates, 581 F.2d 751, 199 U.S.P.Q. 769 (9th Cir.1978), *cert. denied* 439 U.S. 1132, 99 S.Ct. 1054, 59 L.Ed.2d 94 (1979).

The characters at issue in both *Nichols* and *Warner* were strictly literary characters. Characters possessing a visual, as well as a conceptual or literary aspect, such as cartoon characters, may be more readily protected because of their more concrete delineation. See, e.g., *Walt Disney*, *supra* (Mickey Mouse, Donald Duck, Goofy, and other characters protected).

For a more detailed discussion of copyright in characters, see Nevins, *Copyright + Character = Catastrophe*, 39 J. COPYRIGHT SOC. 303 (1992). For discussion of trademark and unfair competition protection for characters, see Chapter 7, § III, *infra*.

3. *Scenes a faire.* Judge Hand's abstractions test in *Nichols*, *supra*, suggests that copyrightable "expression" may be found in an author's choice of specific details—scenes, characters, settings, incidents, etc.—for use in telling his story. Use of some such details, however, is excluded from protection under the "*scenes a faire*" doctrine:

> *Scenes a faire* refers to "incidents, characters or settings which are as a practical matter indispensable, or at least standard, in the treatment of a given topic." * * * Such stock literary devices are not protectible by copyright.

Atari v. North American Philips Consumer Electronics, 672 F.2d 607, 616, 214 U.S.P.Q. 33, 41 (7th Cir.1982), *cert. denied* 459 U.S. 880, 103 S.Ct. 176, 74 L.Ed.2d 145 (1982).

For example, in Walker v. Time Life Films, Inc., 784 F.2d 44, 228 U.S.P.Q. 505 (2d Cir.1986), *cert. denied* 476 U.S. 1159, 106 S.Ct. 2278, 90 L.Ed.2d 721 (1986), the Second Circuit found that

> [e]lements such as drunks, prostitutes, vermin and derelict cars would appear in any realistic work about the work of policemen in the South Bronx. These similarities therefore are unprotectible as "*scenes a faire,*" that is, scenes that necessarily result from the choice of a setting or situation.

Id., 784 F.2d at 50, 228 U.S.P.Q. at 509.

Likewise, when the plaintiff's story concerned the crash of the German dirigible Hindenburg in 1937, the court found that scenes of revelry in a German beer hall, use of the greeting "Heil Hitler," and the passionate singing of the German national anthem were unprotectible *scenes a faire*: their presence in the defendant's story on the same topic did not assist the plaintiff's infringement claim. The court reasoned that it would be "virtually impossible to write" about that period in German history without employing such " 'stock' or standard literary devices." Hoehling v. Universal City Studios, Inc., 618 F.2d 972, 979, 205 U.S.P.Q. 681, 685 (2d Cir.1980), *cert. denied* 449 U.S. 841, 101 S.Ct. 121, 66 L.Ed.2d 49 (1980). See also *Atari, supra* (court finds that standard "maze-chase game" devices in the "PAC–MAN" video game, including the maze, scoring table, and tunnel exits, are unprotectible under the *scenes a faire* doctrine).

Stock or standard devices falling under the *scenes a faire* doctrine can be said to merge with the underlying idea, because they are needed by all in order to express the idea. Also, because they are a form of cliche, or generic expression, they may be characterized as lacking originality.

For further discussion of the *scenes a faire* doctrine, see Kurtz, *Copyright: The Scenes A Faire Doctrine*, 41 FLA. L. REV. 79 (1989).

D. SPECIAL PROBLEM AREAS

The following subsections examine the challenges courts have faced in applying the principles discussed in the prior sections to particular types of copyrightable subject matter.

1. *Derivative Works*

§ 101. Definitions

* * *

A "derivative work" is a work based upon one or more preexisting works, such as a translation, musical arrangement, dramatization, fictionalization, motion picture version, sound recording, art reproduction, abridgment, condensation, or any other form in which a work may be recast, transformed, or adapted. A work consisting of editorial revisions, annotations, elaborations, or other modifications which, as a whole, represent an original work of authorship, is a "derivative work."

* * *

17 U.S.C.A. § 101.

GRACEN v. THE BRADFORD EXCHANGE

United States Court of Appeals for the Seventh Circuit, 1983.
698 F.2d 300, 217 U.S.P.Q. 1294.

POSNER, CIRCUIT JUDGE.

This appeal brings up to us questions of some novelty, at least in this circuit, regarding * * * the required originality for copyrighting a derivative work.

In 1939 MGM produced and copyrighted the movie "The Wizard of Oz." The central character in the movie, Dorothy, was played by Judy Garland. The copyright was renewed by MGM in 1966 and is conceded, at least for purposes of this case, to be valid and in effect today. In 1976 MGM licensed Bradford Exchange to use characters and scenes from the movie in a series of collectors' plates. Bradford invited several artists to submit paintings of Dorothy as played by Judy Garland, with the understanding that the artist who submitted the best painting would be offered a contract for the entire series. Bradford supplied each artist with photographs from the movie and with instructions for the painting that included the following: "We do want *your* interpretation of these images, but your interpretation must evoke all the warm feeling the people have for the film and its actors. So, *your* Judy/Dorothy must be very recognizable as everybody's Judy/Dorothy."

Jorie Gracen, an employee in Bradford's order-processing department, was permitted to join the competition. From photographs and her recollections of the movie (which she had seen several times) she made a painting of Dorothy as played by Judy Garland; Figure 1 at the end of this opinion is a reproduction of a photograph of Miss Gracen's painting (an inadequate one, because the original is in color). Bradford exhibited it along with the other contestants' paintings in a shopping center. The passersby liked Miss Gracen's the best, and Bradford pronounced her the winner of the competition and offered her a contract to do the series, as well as paying her, as apparently it paid each of the other contestants, $200. But she did not like the contract terms and refused to sign, and Bradford turned to another artist, James Auckland, who had not been one of the original contestants. He signed a contract to do the series and Bradford gave him Miss Gracen's painting to help him in doing his painting of Dorothy. * * *

[Gracen registered copyright in her painting and filed suit against M.G.M., Bradford, Auckland, and the manufacturer of the plates, alleging that Auckland's painting of Dorothy was a "piratical copy" of her painting. The District Court granted summary judgment against Gracen, primarily on the ground that her painting was not sufficiently original to merit copyright protection. The Court of Appeals discusses the extent of Gracen's implied license to make the painting, questioning whether it authorized her to obtain copyright, and then turns to the issue of whether her painting is sufficiently original to merit copyright protection.]

Miss Gracen does not claim that she painted the 16–year-old Judy Garland who appeared in "The Wizard of Oz" in 1939 from life or from photographs taken from the movie, or that her painting is not of Judy Garland but is an imaginative conception of the character Dorothy. The painting was based on the movie, both as independently recollected by Miss Gracen and as frozen in the still photographs that Bradford supplied her. As with any painting there was an admixture of the painter's creativity—how much we shall consider later—but that it is a painting of Judy Garland as she appears in photographs from the movie (such as the photograph reproduced at the end of this opinion as Figure 2), and is therefore a derivative work, is beyond question. * * *

* * *

Miss Gracen reminds us that judges can make fools of themselves pronouncing on aesthetic matters. But artistic originality is not the same thing as the legal concept of originality in the Copyright Act. Artistic originality indeed might inhere in a detail, a nuance, a shading too small to be apprehended by a judge. A contemporary school of art known as "Super Realism" attempts with some success to make paintings that are indistinguishable to the eye from color photographs. These paintings command high prices; buyers must find something original in them. Much Northern European painting of the Renaissance is meticulously representational, and therefore in a sense—but not an aesthetic sense—less "original" than Cubism or Abstract Expressionism. A portrait is not unoriginal for being a good likeness.

But especially as applied to derivative works, the concept of originality in copyright law has as one would expect a legal rather than aesthetic function—to prevent overlapping claims. Suppose Artist A produces a reproduction of the Mona Lisa, a painting in the public domain, which differs slightly from the original. B also makes a reproduction of the Mona Lisa. A, who has copyrighted his derivative work, sues B for infringement. B's defense is that he was copying the original, not A's reproduction. But if the difference between the original and A's reproduction is slight, the difference between A's and B's reproductions will also be slight, so that if B had access to A's reproductions the trier of fact will be hard-pressed to decide whether B was copying A or copying the Mona Lisa itself. * * *

* * * A comparison of Figures 1 and 2 reveals perceptible differences. A painting (except, perhaps, one by a member of the Super Realist school mentioned earlier) is never identical to the subject paint-

ed, whether the subject is a photograph, a still life, a landscape, or a model, because most painters cannot and do not want to achieve a photographic likeness of their subject. Nevertheless, if the differences between Miss Gracen's painting of Dorothy and the photograph of Judy Garland as Dorothy were sufficient to make the painting original in the eyes of the law, then a painting by an Auckland also striving, as per his commission, to produce something "very recognizable as everybody's Judy/Dorothy" would look like the Gracen painting, to which he had access; and it would be difficult for the trier of fact to decide whether Auckland had copied her painting or the original movie stills. True, the background in Miss Gracen's painting differs from that in Figure 2, but it is drawn from the movie set. We do not consider a picture created by superimposing one copyrighted photographic image on another to be "original"—always bearing in mind that the purpose of the term in copyright law is not to guide aesthetic judgments but to assure a sufficiently gross difference between the underlying and the derivative work to avoid entangling subsequent artists depicting the underlying work in copyright problems.

We are speaking, however, only of the requirement of originality in derivative works. If a painter paints from life, no court is going to hold that his painting is not copyrightable because it is an exact photographic likeness. If that were the rule photographs could not be copyrighted—the photographs of Judy Garland in "The Wizard of Oz," for example—but of course they can be. The requirement of originality is significant chiefly in connection with derivative works, where if interpreted too liberally it would paradoxically inhibit rather than promote the creation of such works by giving the first creator a considerable power to interfere with the creation of subsequent derivative works from the same underlying work.

Justice Holmes' famous opinion in *Bleistein v. Donaldson Lithographing Co.*, 188 U.S. 239, 23 S.Ct. 298, 47 L.Ed. 460 (1903), heavily relied on by Miss Gracen, is thus not in point. The issue was whether lithographs of a circus were copyrightable under a statute (no longer in force) that confined copyright to works "connected with the fine arts." Holmes' opinion is a warning against using aesthetic criteria to answer the question. If Miss Gracen had painted Judy Garland from life, her painting would be copyrightable even if we thought it *kitsch*; but a derivative work must be substantially different from the underlying work to be copyrightable. This is the test of *L. Batlin & Son, Inc. v. Snyder*, 536 F.2d 486, 491 (2d Cir.1976), a decision of the Second Circuit—the nation's premier copyright court—sitting en banc. Earlier Second Circuit cases discussed in *Batlin* that suggest a more liberal test must be considered superseded.

We agree with the district court that under the test of *Batlin* Miss Gracen's painting, whatever its artistic merit, is not an original derivative work within the meaning of the Copyright Act. Admittedly this is a harder case than *Durham Industries, Inc. v. Tomy Corp.*, 630 F.2d 905 (2d Cir.1980), heavily relied on by the defendants. The underlying works in that case were Mickey Mouse and other Walt Disney cartoon characters, and the derivative works were plastic reproductions of them. Since the cartoon characters are extremely simple drawings, the reproductions were exact, differing only in the medium. The plastic Mickey and its cartoon original look more alike than Judy Garland's Dorothy and Miss Gracen's painting. But we do not think the difference is enough to allow her to copyright her painting even if, as we very much doubt, she was authorized by Bradford to do so.

The judgment dismissing the complaint is therefore affirmed. * * *

Figure 1

Figure 2

Notes and Questions

1. *A higher originality standard?* Did the *Gracen* court intentionally embrace a higher standard of originality for derivative works than for works not based on preexisting works? If so, what is its justification for doing so? Is there authority for such a distinction in the Constitution or Copyright Act? Are the difficulties of proving (or disproving) copying likely to be greater in the case of derivative works than in the case of works "taken from life," such as photographs or "super realist" paintings? To the extent that

such problems of proof exist, can they be handled through rules allocating the burden of proving copying?

Judge Posner argues that liberal interpretation of the originality requirement will inhibit rather than promote the creation of adaptations, because it will enable the first adaptor to interfere with subsequent adaptations of the same underlying work. Could it not be argued that interpreting the originality requirement too strictly will also inhibit the creation of adaptations?

Based on the court's opinion, would a less skillful rendition of Judy Garland/Dorothy, which failed to capture the essence of the movie, have been more likely to qualify for copyright protection? If so, does that make sense?

2. *The* Batlin *Case.* The *Gracen* court refers with approval to the Second Circuit's opinion in L. Batlin & Son, Inc. v. Snyder, 536 F.2d 486, 189 U.S.P.Q. 753 (2d Cir.1976), *cert. denied* 429 U.S. 857, 97 S.Ct. 156, 50 L.Ed.2d 135 (1976). In *Batlin*, the issue was whether Snyder's plastic version of a public domain cast-iron bank was sufficiently original to support a copyright. The court described the preexisting cast-iron bank as follows:

> * * * Uncle Sam, dressed in his usual stove pipe hat, blue full dress coat, starred vest and red and white striped trousers, and leaning on his umbrella, stands on a four-or-five-inch wide base, on which sits his carpetbag. A coin may be placed in Uncle Sam's extended hand. When a lever is pressed, the arm lowers, and the coin falls into the bag, while Uncle Sam's whiskers move up and down. The base has an embossed American eagle on it with the words "Uncle Sam" on streamers above it, as well as the word "Bank" on each side.

Id., 536 F.2d at 488, 189 U.S.P.Q. at 754.

Snyder wanted his version of the bank to be made of plastic and to be shorter than the cast-iron bank "in order to fit into the required price range and quality and quantity of material to be used." He thus shortened the figure of Uncle Sam from eleven to nine inches, and shortened and narrowed the base. In addition, he changed the shape of the carpetbag and placed the umbrella, which stood apart from Uncle Sam in the original, against Uncle Sam's leg "so as not to have a problem with a loose umbrella or a separate molding process." *Id.* Snyder also had the eagle on the base of his bank hold leaves in its talons, rather than arrows, because "the arrows did not reproduce well in plastic on a smaller size." *Id.*

The district court found insufficient originality in Snyder's bank to support a derivative work copyright. It dismissed changes such as the shape of the satchel and the leaves in the eagle's talons as trivial and/or dictated primarily by functional considerations. The court then rejected the change in medium and size as evidence of originality. The Court of Appeals affirmed, explaining:

> According to Professor Nimmer, * * * "the mere reproduction of a work of art in a different medium should not constitute the required originality for the reason that no one can claim to have independently evolved any particular medium." Professor Nimmer refers to *Doran v. Sunset House Distributing Corp.*, 197 F.Supp. 940 (S.D.Cal.1961), *aff'd,*

> 304 F.2d 251 (9th Cir.1962), as suggesting "the ludicrous result that the first person to execute a public domain work of art in a different medium thereafter obtains a monopoly on such work in such medium, at least as to those persons aware of the first such effort." 1 M. Nimmer, The Law of Copyright, § 20.2, at 94 (1975). We do not follow the *Doran* case. We do follow the school of cases in this circuit and elsewhere supporting the proposition that to support a copyright there must be at least some substantial variation, not merely a trivial variation such as might occur in the translation to a different medium.
>
> Nor can the requirement of originality be satisfied simply by the demonstration of "physical skill" or "special training" which, to be sure, Judge Metzner found was required for the production of the plastic molds that furnished the basis for appellants' plastic bank. A considerably higher degree of skill is required, true artistic skill, to make the reproduction copyrightable.

Id., 536 F.2d at 491, 189 U.S.P.Q. at 757.

Snyder had relied on the opinion in Alfred Bell & Co. v. Catalda Fine Arts, Inc., 191 F.2d 99, 90 U.S.P.Q. 153 (2d Cir.1951), in which the court found a reproduction in a different medium sufficiently original to support a copyright. In *Alfred Bell*, the plaintiff had made mezzotint engravings of masterpiece oil paintings, endeavoring to make as faithful a copy of the oil paintings as possible. Apart from the medium, the only variations from the original paintings were unintentional, attributable to the engraver's inability to make perfect copies. The *Alfred Bell* court found that the departures from the paintings were "distinguishable variations" capable of supporting a copyright, and that their inadvertent nature was irrelevant: "A copyist's bad eyesight or defective musculature, or a shock caused by a clap of thunder, may yield sufficiently distinguishable variations. * * * Having hit upon such a variation unintentionally, the 'author' may adopt it as his and copyright it." *Alfred Bell, supra*, 191 F.2d at 104–05, 90 U.S.P.Q. at 158–59.

The *Batlin* court found the *Alfred Bell* decision distinguishable because

> * * * the mezzotint engraver's art there concerned required "great labor and talent" to effectuate the "management of light and shade ... produced by different lines and dots ...." * * * Here on the basis of appellants' own expert's testimony it took [Snyder's designer] "[a]bout a day and a half, two days work" to produce the plastic mold sculpture from the metal Uncle Sam bank. If there be a point in the copyright law pertaining to reproductions at which sheer artistic skill and effort can act as a substitute for the requirement of substantial variation, it was not reached here.

Batlin, supra, at 491, 189 U.S.P.Q. at 757.

Should a change in medium or size *ever* suffice to support a derivative work copyright? Should the purpose (or lack of purpose) of a variation be relevant in determining whether the variation renders the derivative work original?

The court in *Batlin* suggested that the transfer of medium in that case demonstrated merely "physical" skill, as opposed to "artistic" skill. It implied that the exercise of artistic skill might render a change of medium original, but the exercise of physical skill could not. What is the difference between physical skill and artistic skill in this context? Are courts well equipped to determine the difference? As a matter of policy, should the difference dictate the availability of copyright protection for a work?

What, if any, impact might the Supreme Court's more recent opinion in *Feist Publications, Inc. v. Rural Telephone Service Co., Inc.* have on the reasoning in *Batlin* or *Alfred Bell*?

2. *Compilations*

§ 101. Definitions

* * *

A "collective work" is a work, such as a periodical issue, anthology, or encyclopedia, in which a number of contributions, constituting separate and independent works in themselves, are assembled into a collective whole.

A "compilation" is a work formed by the collection and assembling of preexisting materials or of data that are selected, coordinated, or arranged in such a way that the resulting work as a whole constitutes an original work of authorship. The term "compilation" includes collective works.

* * *

17 U.S.C.A. § 101.

ROULO v. RUSS BERRIE & CO., INC.

United States Court of Appeals for the Seventh Circuit, 1989.
886 F.2d 931, 12 U.S.P.Q.2d 1423, *cert. denied*
493 U.S. 1075, 110 S.Ct. 1124, 107 L.Ed.2d 1030 (1990).

CUMMINGS, CIRCUIT JUDGE.

Defendant, Russ Berrie & Co., Inc. (Berrie), appeals from a judgment entered on a jury verdict of $4.3 million in favor of plaintiff, Georgia Lee Miller Roulo (Roulo), for infringement of her copyright and trade-dress rights in a greeting card line known as "Feeling Sensitive" (FS) cards. * * *

* * *

Since Berrie's challenges on appeal inextricably involve the visual appearance of the two greeting card lines, and indeed a display of each was presented to the jury for a side-by-side comparison, a detailed description of each is necessary and black and white reproductions of the cards are appended to this opinion. Roulo's FS cards are beige, single-face (no fold) cards containing sentimental verses and frequently using ellipses written in Roulo's handwriting with brown ink. An example of a verse reads: "I want to shout and tell the world how much I love you ... but instead I'll just ... whisper." Flanking the message on the left and right borders are a series of four stripes, two silver foil stripes enveloping one brown and one colored stripe in the middle. * * *

The TY cards are designed for occasions similar to the FS line, employing like, although not identical, sentimental verses. The TY cards are identically sized and priced, single-face cards on cream paper with cursive written messages in brown ink. The cards combine two stripes of color on the left side and one colored stripe on the right side, none of which are in foil. A colored foil butterfly is superimposed on the left stripes. * * *

* * *

To demonstrate an infringement of Roulo's copyright, Roulo must establish: (1) that she owns the copyright in question; (2) that Berrie had access to the copyrighted work; and (3) that there was substantial similarity between the two works. Defendant concedes the existence of the second element of the test but challenges the sufficiency of the evidence on the scope of Roulo's copyright and the jury's finding of substantial similarity between the two card lines. * * *

* * *

* * * Berrie insists that the jury was allowed to consider elements of similarity unprotected by copyright laws, such as the size of the cards, the color of the paper, ink, and border designs, the general concept of stripes, the ellipses and the single-side format. While it is true that these elements are not individually capable of protection, just as individual words do not deserve copyright protection, it is the unique combination of these common elements which form the copyrighted material. * * * Defendant fails to acknowledge that its TY cards not only used the same unprotectible elements as the FS cards, but also used them in a format nearly identical to that used by the FS cards. It cannot be disputed that Berrie could have produced a non-infringing card with colored stripes, but Berrie used similar stripes flanking the verse on both the left and right side from top to bottom just as the FS cards did. The color of paper is unprotected, yet the TY cards are printed on a nearly identical beige paper. The use of cursive writing is also a common element as well as the brown ink used, yet TY cards, out of the entire range of colors and handwritings available, chose brown ink and a similar cursive writing. The minute differences which Berrie painstakingly incorporated to prevent a mirror image copy of FS cards are insignificant in light of the nearly identical composition and appearance used in both card lines. Berrie's contention that there is no support in law for the proposition that a compilation of common elements is subject to copyright protection is ridiculous. "[C]ards, considered as a whole, represent a tangible expression of an idea.... Greeting cards are protected under 17 U.S.C. § 5(a) or (k) as a book (citations omitted). They are the embodiment of humor, praise, regret or some other message in a pictorial and literary arrangement." *Roth Greeting Cards v. United Card Co.*, 429 F.2d 1106, 1110 (9th Cir.1970). Of course Roulo could not copyright the use of beige paper for greeting cards. Her copyright is in the artistic combination of all the common elements in the previously described design. There was ample evidence for the jury

to find substantial similarity and the jury was properly instructed as to which elements were subject to copyright protection.

* * *

Appendix

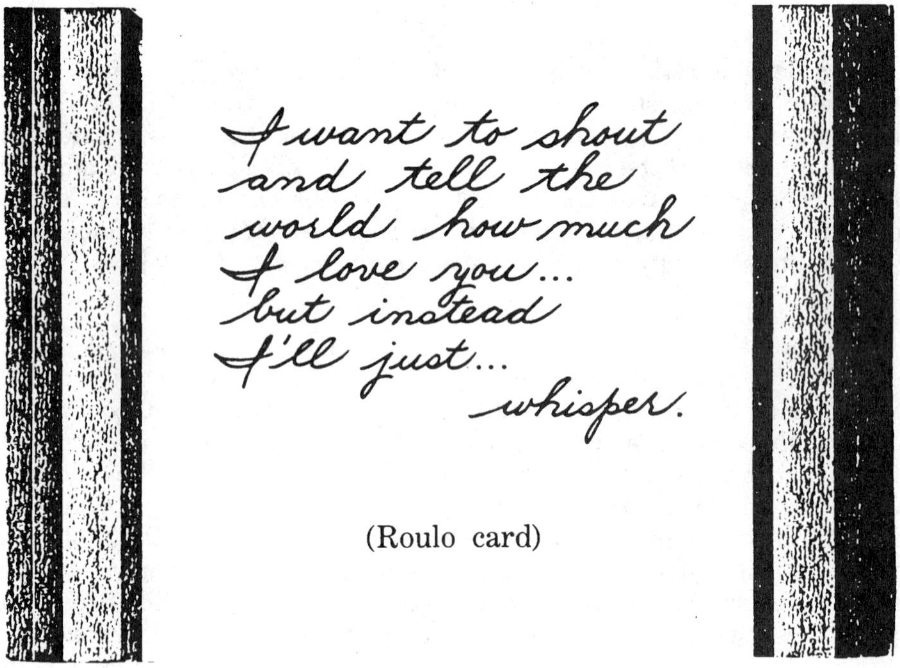

(Roulo card)

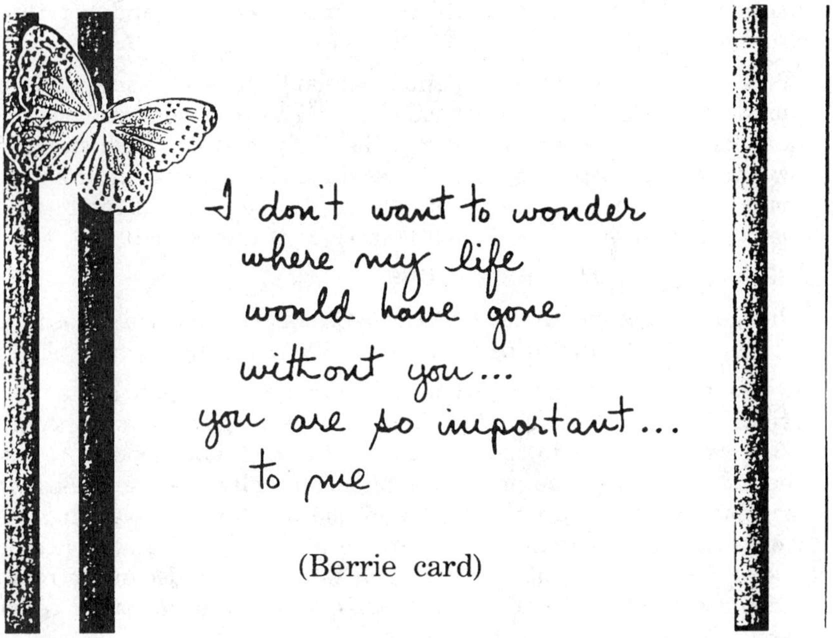

(Berrie card)

Notes and Questions

1. *Originality in compilations.* Like the derivative work copyright, the compilation copyright protects only the original authorship that the compilation author has contributed—usually his selection, coordination and arrangement of preexisting elements. 17 U.S.C.A. § 103. Data bases, such as the telephone directory in *Feist Publications v. Rural Telephone Service, supra*, are the quintessential compilations. However, as Professor Nimmer has observed, virtually any work falling within the section 102 subject matter categories may be regarded as a compilation, "in that it inevitably is based in whole or in part upon pre-existing materials or data which are not in themselves capable of copyright. If nothing else, every work consists of 'the collecting and assembling of pre-existing' ideas." 1 M.B. NIMMER & D. NIMMER, NIMMER ON COPYRIGHT, § 3.02 (1988).

When courts rely on such selection, coordination and arrangement to satisfy the originality requirement in nonfactual, nonutilitarian works such as greeting cards, the protected element is sometimes called the "total concept and feel" of the work. See Roth Greeting Cards v. United Card Co., 429 F.2d 1106, 1110, 166 U.S.P.Q. 291, 294 (9th Cir.1970).

2. *Maps.* For the most part, map making consists of collecting and synthesizing preexisting information from prior maps and other public domain sources. Therefore, many map makers seeking copyright must rely on their selection, coordination and arrangement of uncopyrightable elements in their map to demonstrate originality.

In Amsterdam v. Triangle Publications, Inc., 189 F.2d 104, 89 U.S.P.Q. 468 (3d Cir.1951), the Court of Appeals for the Third Circuit denied copyright for a map providing a new combination of information because the information had been obtained from the public domain and not through direct observation:

> [T]he presentation of information available to everybody, such as is found on maps, is protected only when the publisher of the map in question obtains originally some of that information by the sweat of his own brow. Almost anybody could combine the information from several maps onto one map, but not everybody can go out and get that information originally and then transcribe it into a map.

Id., 189 F.2d at 106, 89 U.S.P.Q. at 469.

The Court of Appeals for the Ninth Circuit rejected this reasoning in United States v. Hamilton, 583 F.2d 448, 200 U.S.P.Q. 14 (9th Cir.1978):

> *Amsterdam* [suggests] that we should insist upon a standard of originality that is more demanding in cases respecting maps than with other works subject to copyright. * * * *Amsterdam* appears to rest on the judgment that the only facet of cartography that can result in an original product, the only feature of the art worth protecting, results from direct observation. However, we are unable to find a persuasive reason for adopting this premise, and we therefore decline to rule that maps present considerations that are distinct from all other copyright cases. * * *
>
> * * * When a work displays a significant element of compilation, that element is protectible even though the individual components of the work may not be, for originality may be found in taking the commonplace and making it into a new combination or arrangement.

Id., 583 F.2d at 450–52, 200 U.S.P.Q. at 16–17.

What, if any, impact might the Supreme Court's decision in the *Feist* case, *supra*, have on copyrights for maps? See Mason v. Montgomery Data, Inc., 967 F.2d 135, 23 U.S.P.Q.2d 1676 (5th Cir.1992); Wolf, *Is There Any Copyright Protection for Maps After Feist?*, 39 J. COPYRIGHT SOC. 224 (1992).

Is the merger doctrine likely to pose problems for map makers? See Kern River Gas Transmission v. Coastal Corp., 899 F.2d 1458, 14 U.S.P.Q.2d 1898 (5th Cir.1990), *cert. denied* 498 U.S. 952, 111 S.Ct. 374, 112 L.Ed.2d 336 (1990).

3. *Factual Narratives*

HOEHLING v. UNIVERSAL CITY STUDIOS, INC.

United States Court of Appeals for the Second Circuit, 1980.
618 F.2d 972, 205 U.S.P.Q. 681, *cert. denied*
449 U.S. 841, 101 S.Ct. 121, 66 L.Ed.2d 49 (1980).

IRVING R. KAUFMAN, CHIEF JUDGE:

A grant of copyright in a published work secures for its author a limited monopoly over the expression it contains. The copyright provides a financial incentive to those who would add to the corpus of existing knowledge by creating original works. Nevertheless, the protection afforded the copyright holder has never extended to history, be it documented fact or explanatory hypothesis. The rationale for this doctrine is that the cause of knowledge is best served when history is the common property of all, and each generation remains free to draw upon the discoveries and insights of the past. Accordingly, the scope of copyright in historical accounts is narrow indeed, embracing no more than the author's original expression of particular facts and theories already in the public domain. As the case before us illustrates, absent wholesale usurpation of another's expression, claims of copyright infringement where works of history are at issue are rarely successful.

I.

This litigation arises from three separate accounts of the triumphant introduction, last voyage, and tragic destruction of the Hindenburg, the colossal dirigible constructed in Germany during Hitler's reign. The zeppelin, the last and most sophisticated in a fleet of luxury airships, which punctually floated its wealthy passengers from the Third Reich to the United States, exploded into flames and disintegrated in 35 seconds as it hovered above the Lakehurst, New Jersey Naval Air Station at 7:25 p.m. on May 6, 1937. Thirty-six passengers and crew were killed but, fortunately, 52 persons survived. Official investigations conducted by both American and German authorities could ascertain no definitive cause of the disaster, but both suggested the plausibility of static electricity or St. Elmo's Fire, which could have ignited the highly explosive hydrogen that filled the airship. Throughout, the investigators refused to rule out the possibility of sabotage.

The destruction of the Hindenburg marked the concluding chapter in the chronicle of airship passenger service, for after the tragedy at Lakehurst, the Nazi regime permanently grounded the Graf Zeppelin I and discontinued its plan to construct an even larger dirigible, the Graf Zeppelin II.

The final pages of the airship's story marked the beginning of a series of journalistic, historical, and literary accounts devoted to the Hindenburg and its fate. Indeed, weeks of testimony by a plethora of witnesses before the official investigative panels provided fertile source material for would-be authors. Moreover, both the American and German Commissions issued official reports, detailing all that was then known of the tragedy. A number of newspaper and magazine articles had been written about the Hindenburg in 1936, its first year of trans-Atlantic service, and they, of course, multiplied many fold after the crash. In addition, two passengers—Margaret Mather and Gertrud Adelt—published separate and detailed accounts of the voyage. C. E. Rosendahl, commander of the Lakehurst Naval Air Station and a pioneer in airship travel himself, wrote a book titled *What About the Airship?*, in which he endorsed the theory that the Hindenburg was the victim of sabotage. In 1957, Nelson Gidding, who would return to the subject of the Hindenburg some 20 years later, wrote an unpublished "treatment" for a motion picture based on the deliberate destruction of the airship. In that year as well, John Toland published *Ships in the Sky* which, in its seventeenth chapter, chronicled the last flight of the Hindenburg. In 1962, Dale Titler released *Wings of Mystery*, in which he too devoted a chapter to the Hindenburg.

Appellant A. A. Hoehling published *Who Destroyed the Hindenburg?*, a full-length book based on his exhaustive research in 1962. Mr. Hoehling studied the investigative reports, consulted previously published articles and books, and conducted interviews with survivors of the crash as well as others who possessed information about the Hindenburg. His book is presented as a factual account, written in an objective, reportorial style.

The first half recounts the final crossing of the Hindenburg, from Sunday, May 2, when it left Frankfurt, to Thursday, May 6, when it exploded at Lakehurst. Hoehling describes the airship, its role as an instrument of propaganda in Nazi Germany, its passengers and crew, the danger of hydrogen, and the ominous threats received by German officials, warning that the Hindenburg would be destroyed. The second portion, headed *The Quest*, sets forth the progress of the official investigations, followed by an account of Hoehling's own research. In the final chapter, spanning eleven pages, Hoehling suggests that all proffered explanations of the explosion, save deliberate destruction, are unconvincing. He concludes that the most likely saboteur is one Eric Spehl, a "rigger" on the Hindenburg crew who was killed at Lakehurst.

According to Hoehling, Spehl had motive, expertise, and opportunity to plant an explosive device, constructed of dry-cell batteries and a flashbulb, in "Gas Cell 4," the location of the initial explosion. An amateur photographer with access to flashbulbs, Spehl could have destroyed the Hindenburg to please his ladyfriend, a suspected communist dedicated to exploding the myth of Nazi invincibility.

Ten years later appellee Michael MacDonald Mooney published his book, *The Hindenburg*. Mooney's endeavor might be characterized as more literary than historical in its attempt to weave a number of symbolic themes through the actual events surrounding the tragedy. His dominant theme contrasts the natural beauty of the month of May, when the disaster occurred, with the cold, deliberate progress of "technology." The May theme is expressed not simply by the season, but also by the character of Spehl, portrayed as a sensitive artisan with needle and thread. The Hindenburg, in contrast, is the symbol of technology, as are its German creators and the Reich itself. The destruction is depicted as the ultimate triumph of nature over technology, as Spehl plants the bomb that ignites the hydrogen. Developing this theme from the outset, Mooney begins with an extended review of man's efforts to defy nature through flight, focusing on the evolution of the zeppelin. This story culminates in the construction of the Hindenburg, and the Nazis' claims of its indestructibility. Mooney then traces the fateful voyage, advising the reader almost immediately of Spehl's scheme. The book concludes with the airship's explosion.

Mooney acknowledges, in this case, that he consulted Hoehling's book, and that he relied on it for some details. He asserts that he first discovered the "Spehl-as-saboteur" theory when he read Titler's *Wings of Mystery*. Indeed, Titler concludes that Spehl was the saboteur, for essentially the reasons stated by Hoehling. Mooney also claims to have studied the complete National Archives and New York Times files concerning the Hindenburg, as well as all previously published material. Moreover, he traveled to Germany, visited Spehl's birthplace, and conducted a number of interviews with survivors.

After Mooney prepared an outline of his anticipated book, his publisher succeeded in negotiations to sell the motion picture rights to appellee Universal City Studios. Universal * * * called upon Nelson Gidding to write a final screenplay. Gidding, it will be recalled, had engaged in preliminary work on a film about the Hindenburg almost twenty years earlier.

The Gidding screenplay follows what is known in the motion picture industry as a "Grand Hotel" formula, developing a number of fictional characters and subplots involving them. This formula has become standard fare in so-called "disaster" movies, which have enjoyed a certain popularity in recent years. In the film, which was released in late 1975, a rigger named "Boerth," who has an anti-Nazi ladyfriend, plans to destroy the airship in an effort to embarrass the Reich. Nazi officials, vaguely aware of sabotage threats, station a Luftwaffe intelligence officer on the zeppelin, loosely resembling a Colonel Erdmann who was aboard the Hindenburg. This character is portrayed as a likable fellow who soon discovers that Boerth is the saboteur. Boerth, however, convinces him that the Hindenburg should be destroyed and the two join forces, planning the explosion for several hours after the landing at Lakehurst, when no people would be on board. In Gidding's version, the airship is delayed by a storm, frantic efforts to defuse the bomb fail, and the Hindenburg is destroyed. The film's subplots involve other possible suspects, including a fictional countess who has had her estate expropriated by the Reich, two fictional confidence men wanted by New York City police, and an advertising executive rushing to close a business deal in America.

Upon learning of Universal's plans to release the film, Hoehling instituted this action against Universal for copyright infringement [and he later added Mooney as a defendant].

II.

It is undisputed that Hoehling has a valid copyright in his book. To prove infringement, however, he must demonstrate that defendants "copied" his work and that they "improperly appropriated" his "expression." Ordinarily, wrongful appropriation is shown by proving a "substantial similarity" of *copyrightable* expression. * * * [Ruling on the party's motions for summary judgement,] Judge Metzner assumed both copying and substantial similarity, but concluded that all similarities pertained to various categories of non-copyrightable material. Accordingly, he granted appellees' motion for summary judgment. We affirm the judgment of the district court.

A

Hoehling's principal claim is that both Mooney and Universal copied the essential plot of his book *i. e.*, Eric Spehl, influenced by his girlfriend, sabotaged the Hindenburg by placing a crude bomb in Gas Cell 4. * * *

[Appellees] argue that Hoehling's plot is an "idea," and ideas are not copyrightable as a matter of law.

Hoehling, however, correctly rejoins that while ideas themselves are not subject to copyright, his "expression" of *his* idea is copyrightable. He relies on Learned Hand's opinion in *Sheldon v. Metro–Goldwyn Pictures Corp.*, 81 F.2d 49, 54, (2d Cir.), *cert. denied*, 298 U.S. 669, 56 S.Ct. 835, 80 L.Ed. 1392 (1936), holding that *Letty Lynton* infringed *Dishonored Lady* by copying its story of a woman who poisons her lover, and Augustus Hand's analysis in *Detective Comics, Inc. v. Bruns Publications, Inc.*, 111 F.2d 432 (2d Cir.1940), concluding that the exploits of "Wonderman" infringed the copyright held by the creators of "Superman," the original indestructible man. Moreover, Hoehling asserts that, in both these cases, the line between "ideas" and "expression" is drawn, in the first instance, by the fact finder. *Sheldon* and *Detective Comics*, however, dealt with works of fiction, where the distinction between an idea and its expression is especially elusive. But, where, as here, the idea at issue is an interpretation of an historical event, our cases hold that such interpretations are not copyrightable as a matter of law. In *Rosemont Enterprises, Inc. v. Random House, Inc.*, 366 F.2d 303 (2d Cir.1966), *cert. denied*, 385 U.S. 1009, 87 S.Ct. 714, 17 L.Ed.2d 546 (1967), we held that the defendant's biography of Howard Hughes did not infringe an earlier biography of the reclusive alleged billionaire. Although the plots of the two works were necessarily similar, there could be no infringement because of the "public benefit in encouraging the development of historical and biographical works and their public distribution." *Id.* at 307. To avoid a chilling effect on authors who contemplate tackling an historical issue or event, broad latitude must be granted to subsequent authors who make use of historical subject matter, including theories or plots. Learned Hand counseled in *Myers v. Mail & Express Co.*, 36 C.O.Bull. 478, 479 (S.D.N.Y.1919), "[t]here cannot be any such thing as copyright in the order of presentation of the facts, nor, indeed, in their selection." [5]

In the instant case, the hypothesis that Eric Spehl destroyed the Hindenburg is based entirely on the interpretation of historical facts,

5. This circuit has permitted extensive reliance on prior works of history. See, e. g., *Gardner v. Nizer*, 391 F.Supp. 940 (S.D.N.Y.1975) (the story of the Rosenberg trial not copyrightable). The commentators are in accord with this view. See, e. g. 1 Nimmer on Copyright § 2.11(A) (1979); Chafee, *Reflections on the Law of Copyright*: I, 45 Colum.L.Rev. 503, 511 (1945).

including Spehl's life, his girlfriend's anti-Nazi connections, the explosion's origin in Gas Cell 4, Spehl's duty station, discovery of a dry-cell battery among the wreckage, and rumors about Spehl's involvement dating from a 1938 Gestapo investigation. Such an historical interpretation, whether or not it originated with Mr. Hoehling, is not protected by his copyright and can be freely used by subsequent authors.

B

The same reasoning governs Hoehling's claim that a number of specific facts, ascertained through his personal research, were copied by appellees. The cases in this circuit, however, make clear that factual information is in the public domain. Each appellee had the right to "avail himself of the facts contained" in Hoehling's book and to "use such information, whether correct or incorrect, in his own literary work." *Greenbie v. Noble*, 151 F.Supp. 45, 67 (S.D.N.Y.1957). * * * In *Rosemont Enterprises, Inc., supra*, 366 F.2d at 310, we refused to "subscribe to the view that an author is absolutely precluded from saving time and effort by referring to and relying upon prior published material.... It is just such wasted effort that the proscription against the copyright of ideas and facts ... are designed to prevent."

C

The remainder of Hoehling's claimed similarities relate to random duplications of phrases and sequences of events. For example, all three works contain a scene in a German beer hall, in which the airship's crew engages in revelry prior to the voyage. Other claimed similarities concern common German greetings of the period, such as "Heil Hitler," or songs, such as the German National anthem. These elements, however, are merely *scenes a faire*, that is, "incidents, characters or settings which are as a practical matter indispensable, or at least standard, in the treatment of a given topic." *Alexander v. Haley*, 460 F.Supp. 40, 45 (S.D.N.Y.1978). Because it is virtually impossible to write about a particular historical era or fictional theme without employing certain "stock" or standard literary devices, we have held that *scenes a faire* are not copyrightable as a matter of law.

D

All of Hoehling's allegations of copying, therefore, encompass material that is non-copyrightable as a matter of law, rendering summary judgment entirely appropriate. We are aware, however, that in distinguishing between themes, facts, and *scenes a faire* on the one hand, and copyrightable expression on the other, courts may lose sight of the forest for the trees. By factoring out similarities based on non-copyrightable elements, a court runs the risk of overlooking wholesale usurpation of a prior author's expression. A verbatim reproduction of another work, of course, even in the realm of nonfiction, is actionable as copyright infringement. Thus, in granting or reviewing a grant of summary judgment for defendants, courts should assure themselves that the works before them are not virtually identical. In this case, it is clear that all three authors relate the story of the Hindenburg differently.

In works devoted to historical subjects, it is our view that a second author may make significant use of prior work, so long as he does not bodily appropriate the expression of another. This principle is justified by the fundamental policy undergirding the copyright laws—the encouragement of contributions to recorded knowledge. The "financial reward guaranteed to the copyright holder is but an incident of this general objective, rather than an end in itself." *Berlin v. E. C. Publications, Inc.*, 329 F.2d 541, 543–44 (2d Cir.), *cert. denied*, 379 U.S. 822, 85 S.Ct. 46, 13 L.Ed.2d 33 (1964). Knowledge is expanded as well by granting new authors of historical works a relatively free hand to build upon the work of their predecessors.

* * *

Notes and Questions

1. *The scope of copyright in factual narratives.* The implications of the *Hoehling* opinion extend beyond historical works to other factual narratives, such as biographies and news stories. Why does the court find that an author's hypotheses or interpretations of fact are not subject to protection? On what basis might one argue that they should be? See Ginsburg, *Sabotaging and Reconstructing History: A Comment on the Scope of Copyright Protection in Works of History after* Hoehling v. Universal City Studios, 72 J. COPYRIGHT SOC. 647, 657–60 (1982).

Did the *Hoehling* court find that the factual narrative author's selection and arrangement of facts can *never* constitute copyrightable expression? In Arica Institute, Inc. v. Palmer, 970 F.2d 1067, 23 U.S.P.Q.2d 1593 (2d Cir.1992), a case involving alleged infringement of psychological and emotional self-help materials, the Second Circuit clarified its position on this issue:

> An original *expression* of facts is copyrightable, even where the facts themselves are not. Thus, a sufficiently creative sequence will merit copyright protection. Our decision in *Hoehling v. Universal City Studios, Inc.*, in which we quoted Judge Learned Hand's statement that "[t]here cannot be any such thing as copyright in the order of presentation of the facts, nor, indeed, in their selection," is not to the contrary. Both *Hoehling* and the case it quotes, *Myers v. Mail & Express Co.*, 36 C.O.Bull. 478, 479 (S.D.N.Y.1919), dealt with historical works containing chronological narrations of events. Since "the narration of history must proceed chronologically," *id.*, this ordering is inevitable and thus is devoid of creativity. In such circumstances sequence is non-copyrightable, but it need not be so in all cases. * * * [A]n original selection and arrangement of facts is copyrightable even where the facts themselves are not.

Arica, 970 F.2d at 1075–76, 23 U.S.P.Q.2d at 1599.

Can others effectively copy an author's hypothesis or interpretation of events without also copying the way the author selected and arranged facts in the course of stating or defending the hypothesis or interpretation? If not, then might a significant portion of the author's selection and arrangement be deprived of protection through application of the merger doctrine? For an interesting discussion of this issue, see Ginsburg, *supra*, at 669–71.

4. *Computer Programs*

Courts have encountered a number of conceptual dilemmas in the course of applying copyright protection to computer programs. Part of the difficulty arises from the early relegation of programs to the "literary works" category of copyrightable subject matter. Rules and concepts developed for more traditional literary works—such as books, poetry and letters—have often proven a poor fit for highly utilitarian, technical computer programs. In addition, the ever-perplexing task of distinguishing a work's ideas from its expression appears particularly difficult in the case of software.

The Copyright Office began registering computer programs as literary works in the mid–1960s, though the status and scope of the copyright protection remained uncertain. In enacting the Copyright Act of 1976, Congress found the issues surrounding copyright protection for programs insufficiently developed for definitive legislative resolution. Accordingly, in section 117 of the Act, Congress preserved the legal status quo, such as it was, until the recently appointed Commission on New Technological Uses of Copyrighted Works ("CONTU") could study the issue and make specific recommendations. Acting on the Commission's subsequent report, in 1980 Congress amended the Copyright Act to define "computer programs" in section 101 of the Act, and to set forth limitations on the software copyright in section 117. Pub. L. No. 96–517 § 10, 94 Stat. 3028, 3028.

As amended, section 101 provides: "A 'computer program' is a set of statements or instructions to be used directly or indirectly in a computer in order to bring about a certain result." Congress had already indicated in the '76 Act legislative history that computer programs should be treated as "literary works." H.R. REP. NO. 1476, 94th Cong., 2d Sess. 54 (1976). The original '76 Act definition of "literary works" was sufficiently broad to encompass computer programs:

> "Literary works" are works, other than audiovisual works, expressed in words, numbers, or other verbal or numerical symbols or indicia, regardless of the nature of the material objects, such as books, periodicals, manuscripts, phonorecords, film, tapes, disks, or cards, in which they are embodied.

17 U.S.C.A. § 101.

The initial infringement suits involved claims that defendants had copied or closely paraphrased the plaintiffs' program code. Computer programmers write programs in "source code," using computer languages such as BASIC or FORTRAN, which consist of words, numbers and symbols which trained humans can read. Once the program is written, the source code is compiled, or translated, into object code—a binary language consisting of ones and zeros which indicate an open or closed switch. The object code communicates directly with the computer hardware—a machine. Humans generally cannot read the program in that form. Programs sold to users on disks or chips are in object code form, ready to be used in computers. Programmers generally do not release the source code version of their programs to the public.

One of the first legal issues to arise was whether copyright protection extended only to the source code version of the program, or to the object code, as well. Defendants argued that "a copyrightable work must be intelligible to human beings and must be intended as a medium of communication to human beings." Williams Electronics, Inc. v. Arctic International, Inc., 685 F.2d 870, 876–77, 215 U.S.P.Q. 405, 410 (3d Cir.1982). Courts rejected this argument as contrary to the literal language of the section 101 definitions of "computer program" and "literary works," as well as to the language of section 102(a), which specifies that copyrightable works may be "perceived, reproduced, or otherwise communicated, either directly or with the aid of a machine or device." See Apple Computer, Inc. v. Franklin Computer Corp., 714 F.2d 1240, 1248–49, 219 U.S.P.Q. 113, 120–21 (3d Cir.1983), *cert. dismissed* 464 U.S. 1033, 104 S.Ct. 690, 79 L.Ed.2d 158 (1984).

Courts also considered and rejected arguments that programs embedded on a silicon chip (a "read only memory" or "ROM"), as opposed to magnetic disks or tapes, could not be protected. For example, in the *Apple* case, *supra*, the defendants argued that chips—which are incorporated into the circuitry of the computer—are machine parts, not writings. The Third Circuit responded that programs on chips "should no more be considered machine parts than videotapes should be considered parts of projectors or phonorecords parts of sound reproduction equipment." *Id.*, 714 F.2d at 1249, 1251, 219 U.S.P.Q. at 121, 122. Likewise, courts rejected attempts to distinguish between application programs (which perform a specific task for the user, such as word processing) and operating system programs (which manage the internal operations of the computer and have no direct interaction with the user) for purposes of copyright protection. *Id.*, 714 F.2d at 1251, 219 U.S.P.Q. at 122.

Later cases raised the issue of whether there could be "non-literal" infringement of computer programs—that is, liability for copying internal structural elements of a program, rather than the code. It was well established that nonliteral, structural elements of a novel, such as the selection and arrangement of plot elements, were protected subject matter. Would protection extend by analogy to the structure or organization of a computer program?

The U.S. Court of Appeals for the Third Circuit was the first appellate court to review this issue, in Whelan Associates, Inc. v. Jaslow Dental Laboratory, Inc., 797 F.2d 1222, 230 U.S.P.Q. 481 (3d Cir.1986), *cert. denied* 479 U.S. 1031, 107 S.Ct. 877, 93 L.Ed.2d 831 (1987). The program at issue in *Whelan* was a custom computer program written to assist in the business operations of a dental laboratory—processing orders, maintaining inventory, dealing with accounts receivable, etc.

The defendants, who were accused of copying structural aspects of this program, but no literal code, argued that the structure constituted the idea of the program, rather than expression, and thus was not copyrightable subject matter. The Third Circuit thus had to distinguish the program's idea from its expression.

The court found that the Supreme Court's opinion in Baker v. Selden

> suggests a way to distinguish idea from expression. Just as Baker v. Selden focused on the end sought to be achieved by Selden's book, the line between idea and expression may be drawn with reference to the end sought to be achieved by the work in question. In other words, *the purpose or function of a utilitarian work would be the work's idea, and everything that is not necessary to the purpose or function would be part of the expression of the idea.* * * * Where there are various means of achieving the desired purpose, then the particular means chosen is not necessary to the purpose; hence, there is expression, not idea.

Whelan, 797 F.2d at 1236, 230 U.S.P.Q. at 490. Turning to the case before it, the court noted:

> it is clear that the purpose of the utilitarian Dentalab program was to aid in the business operations of a dental laboratory. It is equally clear that the structure of the program was not essential to that task: there are other programs on the market * * * that perform the same functions but have different structures and designs.

Id., 797 F.2d at 1238, 230 U.S.P.Q. at 492. Thus, the structure of the plaintiff's program was protected subject matter under the plaintiff's copyright. In a footnote, the court elaborated:

> We do not mean to imply that the idea or purpose behind every utilitarian or functional work will be precisely what it accomplishes, and that structure and organization will therefore always be part of the expression of such works. The idea or purpose behind a utilitarian work may be to accomplish a certain function *in a certain way, see, e.g., Baker v. Selden*, 101 U.S. at 100 (referring to Selden's book as explaining "a peculiar system of book-keeping"), and the structure or function of a program might be essential to that task. There is no suggestion in the record, however, that the purpose of the Dentalab program was anything so refined; it was simply to run a dental laboratory in an efficient way.

Whelan, 797 F.2d at 1238 n.34, 230 U.S.P.Q. at 492 n.34.

The court found additional support in its observation that the majority of the expense and difficulty in creating computer programs is attributable to developing the structure and logic of the program, not to the writing of code. The court noted that the rule it proposed, which allowed copyright protection beyond the literal computer code, "would provide the proper incentive for programmers by protecting their most valuable efforts, while not giving them a stranglehold over the development of new computer devices that accomplish the same end." *Id.*, at 1237, 230 U.S.P.Q. at 491.

The court rejected arguments that "progress in the area of computer technology is achieved by means of 'stepping-stones,' a process that 'requires plagiarizing in some manner the underlying copyrighted work.'" The court declared itself unconvinced that progress in computer technology differed from progress in other fields, or that protection of a program's organization and structure would retard progress in the field.

The court found further support for its approach in section 103 of the Copyright Act, which it interpreted as manifesting Congress' intent to extend copyright protection to an author's original sequencing and ordering of uncopyrightable elements. *Id.*, at 1239–40, 230 U.S.P.Q. at 493.

COMPUTER ASSOCIATES INTERNATIONAL, INC. v. ALTAI, INC.

United States Court of Appeals for the Second Circuit, 1992.
982 F.2d 693.

WALKER, CIRCUIT JUDGE:

* * *

Among other things, this case deals with the challenging question of whether and to what extent the "non-literal" aspects of a computer program, that is, those aspects that are not reduced to written code, are protected by copyright. While a few other courts have already grappled with this issue, this case is one of first impression in this circuit. As we shall discuss, we find the results reached by other courts to be less than satisfactory. Drawing upon long-standing doctrines of copyright law, we take an approach that we think better addresses the practical difficulties embedded in these types of cases. In so doing, we have kept in mind the necessary balance between creative incentive and industrial competition.

* * *

COMPUTER PROGRAM DESIGN

Certain elementary facts concerning the nature of computer programs are vital to the following discussion. The Copyright Act defines a computer program as "a set of statements or instructions to be used directly or indirectly in a computer in order to bring about a certain result." 17 U.S.C. § 101. In writing these directions, the programmer works "from the general to the specific." *Whelan Assocs., Inc. v. Jaslow Dental Lab., Inc.*, 797 F.2d 1222, 1229 (3d Cir.1986), *cert. denied*, 479 U.S. 1031, 107 S.Ct. 877, 93 L.Ed.2d 831 (1987).

The first step in this procedure is to identify a program's ultimate function or purpose. An example of such an ultimate purpose might be the creation and maintenance of a business ledger. Once this goal has been achieved, a programmer breaks down or "decomposes" the program's ultimate function into "simpler constituent problems or 'subtasks,'" Englund, Note, *Idea, Process, or Protected Expression?: Determining the Scope of Copyright Protection of the Structure of Computer Programs*, 88 MICH.L.REV. 866, 870 (1990), which are also known as subroutines or modules. In the context of a business ledger program, a module or subroutine might be responsible for the task of updating a list of outstanding accounts receivable. Sometimes, depending upon the complexity of its task, a subroutine may be broken down further into sub-subroutines.

Having sufficiently decomposed the program's ultimate function into its component elements, a programmer will then arrange the subroutines or modules into what are known as organizational or flow charts. Flow charts map the interactions between modules that achieve the program's end goal.

In order to accomplish these intra-program interactions, a programmer must carefully design each module's parameter list. A parameter list, according to the expert appointed and fully credited by the district court, Dr. Randall Davis, is "the information sent to and received from a subroutine." The term "parameter list" refers to the form in which information is passed between modules (e.g. for accounts receivable, the designated time frame and particular customer identifying number) and the information's actual content (e.g. 8/91–7/92; customer No. 3). With respect to form, interacting modules must share similar parameter lists so that they are capable of exchanging information.

"The functions of the modules in a program together with each module's relationships to other modules constitute the 'structure' of the program." Englund, at 871. Additionally, the term structure may include the category of modules referred to as "macros." A macro is a single instruction that initiates a sequence of operations or module interactions within the program. Very often the user will accompany a macro with an instruction from the parameter list to refine the instruction (e.g. current total of accounts receivable (macro), but limited to those for 8/91 to 7/92 from customer No. 3 (parameters)).

In fashioning the structure, a programmer will normally attempt to maximize the program's speed, efficiency, as well as simplicity for user operation, while taking into consideration certain externalities such as the memory constraints of the computer upon which the program will be run. "This stage of program design often requires the most time and investment." Kretschmer, Note, *Copyright Protection For Software Architecture: Just Say No!*, 1988 COLUM.BUS.L.REV. 823, 826 (1988).

Once each necessary module has been identified, designed, and its relationship to the other modules has been laid out conceptually, the resulting program structure must be embodied in a written language that the computer can read. This process is called "coding," and requires two steps. First, the programmer must transpose the program's structural blue-print into a source code. This step has been described as "comparable to the novelist fleshing out the broad outline of his plot by crafting from words and sentences the paragraphs that convey the ideas." Kretschmer, at 826. The source code may be written in any one of several computer languages, such as COBAL, FORTRAN, BASIC, EDL, etc., depending upon the type of computer for which the program is intended. Once the source code has been completed, the second step is to translate or "compile" it into object code. Object code is the binary language comprised of zeros and ones through which the computer directly receives its instructions.

After the coding is finished, the programmer will run the program on the computer in order to find and correct any logical and syntactical errors. This is known as "debugging" and, once done, the program is complete.

Facts

[Both Computer Associates ("CA") and Altai are in the computer software industry—designing, developing and marketing various types of computer programs. This litigation concerns one of CA's marketed programs entitled CA–SCHEDULER. CA–SCHEDULER is a job scheduling program designed for IBM mainframe computers. CA–SCHEDULER contains a sub-program entitled ADAPTER, also developed by CA.]

[An "operating system" is a program that manages the resources of the computer, allocating those resources to other programs as needed. Generally, a computer program written to run with one operating system will not, without modification, run with another operating system. ADAPTER is an "operating system compatibility component," or translator, which enables a program written to be compatible with one operating system to run under another operating system. ADAPTER translates the language of the program into the particular language that the computer's operating system can understand.]

[Starting in 1982, Altai began marketing its own job scheduling program entitled ZEKE. In 1983, Williams, then an employee of Altai and now its President, recruited Arney, a computer programmer with CA, to assist Altai in designing a version of ZEKE to run with another operating system. Though Williams did not know it, Arney was intimately familiar with various aspects of ADAPTER. When Arney left CA to work for Altai in January, 1984, he took with him copies of the source code for two versions of ADAPTER. Once at Altai, Arney persuaded Williams that the best way to make the needed modifications was to introduce a "common system interface" component into ZEKE. He did not tell Williams that his idea stemmed from his familiarity with ADAPTER. They decided to name this new component-program OSCAR.]

[Arney went to work creating OSCAR at Altai's offices using the ADAPTER source code. The district court accepted Williams' testimony that no one at Altai, with the exception of Arney, affirmatively knew that Arney had the ADAPTER code, or that he was using it to create OSCAR. Arney copied approximately 30% of OSCAR's code from CA's ADAPTER program.]

[The first generation of OSCAR programs was known as OSCAR 3.4. In 1988, CA first learned that Altai may have appropriated parts of ADAPTER, and brought this copyright action against Altai. Only at this point did Altai learn that Arney had copied much of the OSCAR code from ADAPTER. Upon obtaining advice of counsel, Williams initiated a rewrite of OSCAR. The project's goal was to save as much of OSCAR 3.4 as legitimately could be used, and to excise those portions which had been copied from ADAPTER. Arney was entirely excluded from the process. Eight new programmers were assigned to rewrite the appropriate code. The resulting program was entitled OSCAR 3.5. From that point on, Altai shipped only OSCAR 3.5 to its new customers. Altai also shipped OSCAR 3.5 as a "free upgrade" to all customers that had previously purchased OSCAR 3.4.]

[In the infringement suit, the court found that Altai's OSCAR 3.4 program infringed CA's copyrighted ADAPTER program, but that the OSCAR 3.5 program was not substantially similar to plaintiff's program, and thus did not infringe. The issue before the court on appeal is whether OSCAR 3.5 infringes ADAPTER.]

I. Copyright Infringement

* * *

As a general matter, and to varying degrees, copyright protection extends beyond a literary work's strictly textual form to its non-literal components. As we have said, "[i]t is of course essential to any protection of literary property ... that the right cannot be limited literally to the text, else a plagiarist would escape by immaterial variations." *Nichols v. Universal Pictures Co.*, 45 F.2d 119, 121 (2d Cir.1930) (L. Hand, J.), *cert. denied*, 282 U.S. 902, 51 S.Ct. 216, 75 L.Ed. 795 (1931). Thus, where "the fundamental essence or structure of one work is duplicated in another," 3 Melville B. Nimmer & David Nimmer, Nimmer on Copyright § 13.03[A][1], at 13–24, courts have found copyright infringement. This black letter proposition is the springboard for our discussion.

A. Copyright Protection for the Non-literal Elements of Computer Programs

* * *

In this case, the hotly contested issues surround OSCAR 3.5. As recounted above, OSCAR 3.5 is the product of Altai's carefully orchestrated rewrite of OSCAR 3.4. After the purge, none of the ADAPTER source code remained in the 3.5 version; thus, Altai made sure that the literal elements of its revamped OSCAR program were no longer substantially similar to the literal elements of CA's ADAPTER.

* * *

CA argues that, despite Altai's rewrite of the OSCAR code, the resulting program remained substantially similar to the *structure* of its ADAPTER program. As discussed above, a program's structure includes its non-literal components such as general flow charts as well as the more specific organization of inter-modular relationships, parameter lists, and macros. In addition to these aspects, CA contends that OSCAR 3.5 is also substantially similar to ADAPTER with respect to the list of services that both ADAPTER and OSCAR obtain from their respective operating systems. We must decide whether and to what extent these elements of computer programs are protected by copyright law.

The statutory terrain in this area has been well explored. The Copyright Act affords protection to "original works of authorship fixed in any tangible medium of expression. . . ." 17 U.S.C. § 102(a). This broad category of protected "works" includes "literary works," id. at § 102(a)(1) * * *. [T]he legislative history leaves no doubt that Congress intended [computer programs] to be considered literary works.

The syllogism that follows from the foregoing premises is a powerful one: if the non-literal structures of literary works are protected by copyright; and if computer programs are literary works, as we are told by the legislature; then the non-literal structures of computer programs are protected by copyright. We have no reservation in joining the company of those courts that have already ascribed to this logic. However, that conclusion does not end our analysis. We must determine the scope of copyright protection that extends to a computer program's non-literal structure.

* * *

1) Idea vs. Expression Dichotomy

It is a fundamental principle of copyright law that a copyright does not protect an idea, but only the expression of the idea. This axiom of common law has been incorporated into the governing statute. Section 102(b) of the Act provides:

> In no case does copyright protection for an original work of authorship extend to any idea, procedure, process, system, method of operation, concept, principle, or discovery, regardless of the form in which it is described, explained, illustrated, or embodied in such work.

* * *

Drawing the line between idea and expression is a tricky business. Judge Learned Hand noted that "[n]obody has ever been able to fix that boundary, and nobody ever can." *Nichols*, 45 F.2d at 121. * * *

The essentially utilitarian nature of a computer program further complicates the task of distilling its idea from its expression. In order to describe both computational processes and abstract ideas, its content "combines creative and technical expression." See Spivack, Comment, *Does Form Follow Function? The Idea/Expression Dichotomy In Copyright Protection of Computer Software*, 35 U.C.L.A. L. REV. 723, 755 (1988). The variations of expression found in purely creative compositions, as opposed to those contained in utilitarian works, are not directed towards practical application. For example, a narration of Humpty Dumpty's demise, which would clearly be a creative composition, does not serve the same ends as, say, a recipe for scrambled eggs—which is a more process oriented text. Thus, compared to aesthetic works, computer programs hover even more closely to the elusive boundary line described in § 102(b).

The doctrinal starting point in analyses of utilitarian works, is the seminal case of *Baker v. Selden*, 101 U.S. 99, 25 L.Ed. 841 (1879). * * *

[From the reasoning in *Baker*,] we conclude that those elements of a computer program that are necessarily incidental to its function are * * * unprotectible.

While *Baker v. Selden* provides a sound analytical foundation, it offers scant guidance on how to separate idea or process from expression, and moreover, on how to further distinguish protectible expression from that expression which "must necessarily be used as incident to" the work's underlying concept. In the context of computer programs, the Third Circuit's noted decision in *Whelan* has, thus far, been the most thoughtful attempt to accomplish these ends.

[In separating idea and expression, the *Whelan*] court settled upon the following conceptual approach:

> [T]he line between idea and expression may be drawn with reference to the end sought to be achieved by the work in question. In other words, *the purpose or function of a utilitarian work would be the work's idea, and everything that is not necessary to that purpose or function would be part of the expression of the idea*.... Where there are various means of achieving the desired purpose, then the particular means chosen is not necessary to the purpose; hence, there is expression, not idea.

797 F.2d at 1236. The "idea" of the program at issue in *Whelan* was identified by the court as simply "the efficient management of a dental laboratory." *Id.* at n. 28.

So far, in the courts, the *Whelan* rule has received a mixed reception. * * *

Whelan has fared even more poorly in the academic community, where its standard for distinguishing idea from expression has been widely criticized for being conceptually overbroad. The leading commentator in the field has stated that "[t]he crucial flaw in [*Whelan*'s] reasoning is that it assumes that only one 'idea,' in copyright law terms, underlies any computer program, and that once a separable idea can be identified, everything else must be expression." 3 Nimmer § 13.03[F], at 13–62.34. This criticism focuses not upon the program's ultimate purpose but upon the reality of its structural design. As we have already noted, a computer program's ultimate function or purpose is the composite result of interacting subroutines. Since each subroutine is itself a program, and thus, may be said to have its own "idea," *Whelan* 's general formulation that a program's overall purpose equates with the program's idea is descriptively inadequate.

Accordingly, we think that Judge Pratt wisely declined to follow *Whelan*. In addition to noting the weakness in the *Whelan* definition of "program-idea," mentioned above, Judge Pratt found that *Whelan* 's synonymous use of the terms "structure, sequence, and organization," demonstrated a flawed understanding of a computer program's method of operation. * * * Rightly, the district court found *Whelan* 's rationale suspect because it is so closely tied to what can now be seen—with the passage of time—as the opinion's somewhat outdated appreciation of computer science.

2) Substantial Similarity Test for Computer Program Structure: Abstraction–Filtration–Comparison

We think that *Whelan* 's approach to separating idea from expression in computer programs relies too heavily on metaphysical distinctions and does not place enough emphasis on practical considerations. * * * As the cases that we shall discuss demonstrate, a satisfactory answer to this problem cannot be reached by resorting, *a priori*, to philosophical first principals.

As discussed herein, we think that district courts would be well-advised to undertake a three-step procedure, based on the abstractions test utilized by the district court, in order to determine whether the non-literal elements of two or more computer programs are substantially similar. This approach breaks no new ground; rather, it draws on such familiar copyright doctrines as merger, *scenes a faire*, and public domain. In taking this approach, however, we are cognizant that computer technology is a dynamic field which can quickly outpace judicial decision-making. Thus, in cases where the technology in question does not allow for a literal application of the procedure we outline below, our opinion should not be read to foreclose the district courts of our circuit from utilizing a modified version. In ascertaining substantial similarity under this approach, a court would first break down the allegedly infringed program into its constituent structural parts. Then, by examining each of these parts for such things as incorporated ideas, expression that is necessarily incidental to those ideas, and elements that are taken from the public domain, a court would then be able to sift out all non-protectible material. Left with a kernel, or possible kernels, of creative expression after following this process of elimination, the court's last step would be to compare this material with the structure of an allegedly infringing program. The result of this comparison will determine whether the protectible elements of the programs at issue are substantially similar so as to warrant a finding of infringement. It will be helpful to elaborate a bit further.

Step One: Abstraction

As the district court appreciated, the theoretic framework for analyzing substantial similarity expounded by Learned Hand in the *Nichols* case is helpful in the present context. In *Nichols*, we enunciated what has now become known as the "abstractions" test for separating idea from expression:

> Upon any work ... a great number of patterns of increasing generality will fit equally well, as more and more of the incident is left out. The last may perhaps be no more than the most general statement of what the [work] is about, and at times might consist only of its title; but there is a point in this series of abstractions where they are no longer protected, since otherwise the [author] could prevent the use of his "ideas," to which, apart from their expression, his property is never extended.

Nichols, 45 F.2d at 121.

While the abstractions test was originally applied in relation to literary works such as novels and plays, it is adaptable to computer programs. In contrast to the *Whelan* approach, the abstractions test "implicitly recognizes that any given work may consist of a mixture of numerous ideas and expressions." 3 Nimmer § 13.03[F], at 13–62.34–63.

As applied to computer programs, the abstractions test will comprise the first step in the examination for substantial similarity. Initially, in a manner that resembles reverse engineering on a theoretical plane, a court should dissect the allegedly copied program's structure and isolate each level of abstraction contained within it. This process begins with the code and ends with an articulation of the program's ultimate function. Along the way, it is necessary essentially to retrace and map each of the designer's steps—in the opposite order in which they were taken during the program's creation.

As an anatomical guide to this procedure, the following description is helpful:

> At the lowest level of abstraction, a computer program may be thought of in its entirety as a set of individual instructions organized into a hierarchy of modules. At a higher level of abstraction, the instructions in the lowest-level modules may be replaced conceptually by the functions of those modules. At progressively higher levels of abstraction, the functions of higher-level modules conceptually replace the implementations of those modules in terms of lower-level modules and instructions, until finally, one is left with nothing but the ultimate function of the program.... A program has structure at every level of abstraction at which it is viewed. At low levels of abstraction, a program's structure may be quite complex; at the highest level it is trivial.

Englund, at 897–98.

Step Two: Filtration

Once the program's abstraction levels have been discovered, the substantial similarity inquiry moves from the conceptual to the concrete.

Professor Nimmer suggests, and we endorse, a "successive filtering method" for separating protectible expression from non-protectible material. This process entails examining the structural components at each level of abstraction to determine whether their particular inclusion at that level was "idea" or was dictated by considerations of efficiency, so as to be necessarily incidental to that idea; required by factors external to the program itself; or taken from the public domain and hence is nonprotectible expression. The structure of any given program may reflect some, all, or none of these considerations. Each case requires its own fact specific investigation.

Strictly speaking, this filtration serves "the purpose of defining the scope of plaintiff's copyright." *Brown Bag Software v. Symantec Corp.*, 960 F.2d 1465, 1475 (9th Cir.) (endorsing "analytic dissection" of computer programs in order to isolate protectible expression), *cert. denied*, ___ U.S. ___, 113 S.Ct. 198, 121 L.Ed.2d 141 (1992). By applying well developed doctrines of copyright law, it may ultimately leave behind a "core of protectible material." 3 Nimmer § 13.03[F][5], at 13–72. Further explication of this second step may be helpful.

(a) *Elements Dictated by Efficiency*

The portion of *Baker v. Selden*, discussed earlier, which denies copyright protection to expression necessarily incidental to the idea being expressed, appears to be the cornerstone for what has developed into the doctrine of merger. The doctrine's underlying principle is that "[w]hen there is essentially only one way to express an idea, the idea and its expression are inseparable and copyright is no bar to copying that expression." *Concrete Machinery Co. v. Classic Lawn Ornaments, Inc.*, 843 F.2d 600, 606 (1st Cir.1988). Under these circumstances, the expression is said to have "merged" with the idea itself. In order not to confer a monopoly of the idea upon the copyright owner, such expression should not be protected.

* * *

[W]hen one considers the fact that programmers generally strive to create programs "that meet the user's needs in the most efficient manner," the applicability of the merger doctrine to computer programs becomes compelling. In the context of computer program design, the concept of efficiency is akin to deriving the most concise logical proof or formulating the most succinct mathematical computation. Thus, the more efficient a set of modules are, the more closely they approximate the idea or process embodied in that particular aspect of the program's structure.

While, hypothetically, there might be a myriad of ways in which a programmer may effectuate certain functions within a program,—i.e., express the idea embodied in a given subroutine—efficiency concerns may so narrow the practical range of choice as to make only one or two forms of expression workable options. Of course, not all program structure is informed by efficiency concerns. It follows that in order to determine whether the merger doctrine precludes copyright protection to an aspect of a program's structure that is so oriented, a court must inquire "whether the use of *this particular set* of modules is necessary efficiently to implement that part of the program's process" being implemented. Englund, at 902. If the answer is yes, then the expression represented by the programmer's choice of a specific module or group of modules has merged with their underlying idea and is unprotected.

* * *

(b) *Elements Dictated By External Factors*

We have stated that where "it is virtually impossible to write about a particular historical era or fictional theme without employing certain 'stock' or standard literary devices," such expression is not copyrightable. *Hoehling v. Universal City Studios, Inc.*, 618 F.2d 972, 979 (2d Cir.), *cert. denied*, 449 U.S. 841, 101 S.Ct. 121, 66 L.Ed.2d 49 (1980). For example, the *Hoehling* case was an infringement suit stemming from several works on the Hindenburg disaster. There we concluded that similarities in representations of German beer halls, scenes depicting German greetings such as "Heil Hitler," or the singing of certain German songs would not lead to a finding of infringement because they were " 'indispensable, or at least standard, in the treatment of' " life in Nazi Germany. This is known as the *scenes a faire* doctrine, and like "merger," it has its analogous application to computer programs.

Professor Nimmer points out that "in many instances it is virtually impossible to write a program to perform particular functions in a specific computing environment without employing standard techniques." 3 Nimmer § 13.03[F][3], at 13–65. This is a result of the fact that a programmer's freedom of design choice is often circumscribed by extrinsic considerations such as (1) the mechanical specifications of the computer on which a particular program is intended to run; (2) compatibility requirements of other programs with which a program is designed to operate in conjunction; (3) computer manufacturers' design standards; (4) demands of the industry being serviced; and (5) widely accepted programming practices within the computer industry.

Courts have already considered some of these factors in denying copyright protection to various elements of computer programs. In the *Plains Cotton* case, the Fifth Circuit refused to reverse the district court's denial of a preliminary injunction against an alleged program infringer because, in part, "many of the similarities between the ... programs [were] dictated by the externalities of the cotton market." 807 F.2d at 1262.

In *Manufacturers Technologies*, the district court noted that the program's method of screen navigation "is influenced by the type of hardware that the software is designed to be used on." 706 F.Supp. at 995. Because, in part, "the functioning of the hardware package impact[ed] and constrain[ed] the type of navigational tools used in plaintiff's screen displays," the court denied copyright protection to that aspect of the program.

* * *

Building upon this existing case law, we conclude that a court must also examine the structural content of an allegedly infringed program for elements that might have been dictated by external factors.

(c) *Elements Taken From the Public Domain*

Closely related to the non-protectibility of *scenes a faire*, is material found in the public domain. Such material is free for the taking and cannot be appropriated by a single author even though it is included in a copyrighted work. We see no reason to make an exception to this rule for elements of a computer program that have entered the public domain by virtue of freely accessible program exchanges and the like. See *Brown Bag Software*, 960 F.2d at 1473 (affirming the district court's finding that " '[p]laintiffs may not claim copyright protection of an ... expression that is, if not standard, then commonplace in the computer software industry.' "). Thus, a court must also filter out this material from the allegedly infringed program before it makes the final inquiry in its substantial similarity analysis.

Step Three: Comparison

The third and final step of the test for substantial similarity that we believe appropriate for non-literal program components entails a comparison. Once a court has sifted out all elements of the allegedly infringed program which are "ideas" or are dictated by efficiency or external factors, or taken from the public domain, there may remain a core of protectible expression. In terms of a work's copyright value, this is the golden nugget. At this point, the court's substantial similarity inquiry focuses on whether the defendant copied any aspect of this protected expression, as well as an assessment of the copied portion's relative importance with respect to the plaintiff's overall program.

3) Policy Considerations

We are satisfied that the three step approach we have just outlined not only comports with, but advances the constitutional policies underlying the Copyright Act. Since any method that tries to distinguish idea from expression ultimately impacts on the scope of copyright protection afforded to a particular type of work, "the line [it draws] must be a pragmatic one, which also keeps in consideration 'the preservation of the balance between competition and protection....' " *Apple Computer*, 714 F.2d at 1253.

CA and some *amici* argue against the type of approach that we have set forth on the grounds that it will be a disincentive for future computer program research and development. At bottom, they claim that if programmers are not guaranteed broad copyright protection for their work, they will not invest the extensive time, energy and funds required to design and improve program structures. While they have a point, their argument cannot carry the day. The interest of the copyright law is not in simply conferring a monopoly on industrious persons, but in advancing the public welfare through rewarding artistic creativity, in a manner that permits the free use and development of non-protectible ideas and processes.

In this respect, our conclusion is informed by Justice Stewart's concise discussion of the principles that correctly govern the adaptation of the copyright law to new circumstances. In *Twentieth Century Music Corp. v. Aiken*, he wrote:

> The limited scope of the copyright holder's statutory monopoly, like the limited copyright duration required by the Constitution, reflects a balance of competing claims upon the public interest: Creative work is to be encouraged and rewarded, but private motivation must ultimately serve the cause of promoting broad public availability of literature, music, and the other arts.
>
> The immediate effect of our copyright law is to secure a fair return for an "author's" creative labor. But the ultimate aim is, by this incentive, to stimulate artistic creativity for the general public good.... When technological change has rendered its literal terms ambiguous, the Copyright Act must be construed in light of this basic purpose.

422 U.S. 151, 156, 95 S.Ct. 2040, 2043–44, 45 L.Ed.2d 84 (1975).

Recently, the Supreme Court has emphatically reiterated that "[t]he primary objective of copyright is not to reward the *labor* of authors...." *Feist Publications, Inc. v. Rural Tel. Serv. Co.*, — U.S. —, —, 111 S.Ct. 1282, 1290, 113 L.Ed.2d 358 (1991) (emphasis added). While the *Feist* decision deals primarily with the copyrightability of purely factual compilations, its underlying tenets apply to much of the work involved in computer programming. *Feist* put to rest the "sweat of the brow" doctrine in copyright law. The rationale of that doctrine "was that copyright was a reward for the hard work that went into compiling facts." *Id.* at —, 111 S.Ct. at 1291. The Court flatly rejected this justification for extending copyright protection, noting that it "eschewed the most fundamental axiom of copyright law—that no one may copyright facts or ideas." *Id.*

Feist teaches that substantial effort alone cannot confer copyright status on an otherwise uncopyrightable work. As we have discussed, despite the fact that significant labor and expense often goes into computer program flow-charting and debugging, that process does not always result in inherently protectible expression. Thus, *Feist* implicitly undercuts the *Whelan* rationale, "which allow[ed] copyright protection beyond the literal computer code ... [in order to] provide the proper incentive for programmers by protecting their most valuable efforts...." *Whelan*, 797 F.2d at 1237. We note that *Whelan* was decided prior to *Feist* when the "sweat of the brow" doctrine still had vitality. In view of the Supreme Court's recent holding, however, we must reject the legal basis of CA's disincentive argument.

Furthermore, we are unpersuaded that the test we approve today will lead to the dire consequences for the computer program industry that plaintiff and some *amici* predict. To the contrary, serious students of the industry have been highly critical of the sweeping scope of copyright protection engendered by the *Whelan* rule, in that it "enables first comers to 'lock up' basic programming techniques as implemented in programs to perform particular tasks." Menell, *An Analysis of the Scope of Copyright Protection for Application Programs*, 41 STAN. L.REV. 1045, 1087 (1989).

To be frank, the exact contours of copyright protection for non-literal program structure are not completely clear. We trust that as future cases are decided, those limits will become better defined. Indeed, it may well be that the Copyright Act serves as a relatively weak barrier against public access to the theoretical interstices behind a program's source and object codes. This results from the hybrid nature of a computer program, which, while it is literary expression, is also a highly functional, utilitarian component in the larger process of computing.

Generally, we think that copyright registration—with its indiscriminating availability—is not ideally suited to deal with the highly dynamic technology of computer science. Thus far, many of the decisions in this area reflect the courts' attempt to fit the proverbial square peg in a round hole. The district court and at least one commentator have suggested that patent registration, with its exacting up-front novelty and non-obviousness requirements, might be the more appropriate rubric of protection for intellectual property of this kind. In any event, now that more than 12 years have passed since CONTU issued its final report, the resolution of this specific issue could benefit from further legislative investigation—perhaps a CONTU II.

In the meantime, Congress has made clear that computer programs are literary works entitled to copyright protection. Of course, we shall abide by these instructions, but in so doing we must not impair the overall integrity of copyright law. While incentive based arguments in favor of broad copyright protection are perhaps attractive from a pure policy perspective, ultimately, they have a corrosive effect on certain fundamental tenets of copyright doctrine. If the test we have outlined results in narrowing the scope of protection, as we expect it will, that result flows from applying, in accordance with Congressional intent, long-standing principles of copyright law to computer programs. Of course, our decision is also informed by our concern that these fundamental principles remain undistorted.

[The Court of Appeals reviewed the decision of the District Court, which had found no substantial similarity of copyrighted expression, and held that it was not clearly erroneous.]

CONCLUSION

In adopting the above three step analysis for substantial similarity between the non-literal elements of computer programs, we seek to insure two things: (1) that programmers may receive appropriate copyright protection for innovative utilitarian works containing expression; and (2) that non-protectible technical expression remains in the public domain for others to use freely as building blocks in their own work. At first blush, it may seem counter-intuitive that someone who has benefitted to some degree from illicitly obtained material can emerge from an infringement suit relatively unscathed. However, so long as the appropriated material consists of non-protectible expression, "[t]his result is neither unfair nor unfortunate. It is the means by which copyright advances the progress of science and art." *Feist*, — U.S. at —, 111 S.Ct. at 1290.

* * *

Notes and Questions

1. *Copyright in a program's structure.* After the abstraction and filtration steps are applied to the plaintiff's program, how much copyrightable expression is likely to be left to compare with the defendant's program? Does the *Altai* approach take account of the synergy generated by the programmer's selection and arrangement of uncopyrightable elements? If so, at what point in the analysis? Should it?

As the Second Circuit noted, many critics have characterized the *Whelan* approach as too broad. See, e.g., I P. GOLDSTEIN, COPYRIGHT PRINCIPLES, LAW AND PRACTICE 210 (1989) ("Applying *Whelan's* approach to the play, *Romeo and Juliet*, would lead to the totally unprecedented conclusion that the play's only unprotectible element is the idea of a play about two star-crossed lovers, and that all of its other elements, such as theme, basic character types and individual words, are protectible"). Does the *Altai* approach strike the right balance? Compare Butler, *Pragmatism in Software Copyright: Computer Associates v. Altai*, 6 HARV. J. L & TECH. 183 (1992), with Comment, *The Copyrightability of Nonliteral Elements of Computer Programs*, 94 COLUM. L. REV. 242 (1994).

In discussing its "filtration" step, the *Altai* court specifies that elements necessary to achieve compatibility with a specific computer or with other programs should be deemed unprotectible. What are the policy implications of permitting such elements to be copied? See Teter, *Merger and the Machines: An Analysis of the Pro–Compatibility Trend in Computer Software Copyright Cases*, 45 STAN. L. REV. 1061 (1993).

Should the programming languages used to write software themselves be the subject of copyright? Why or why not? See Stern, *Copyright in Computer Programming Languages*, 17 RUTGERS COMPUTER & TECH. L.J. 321 (1991); Tache, *Copyrightability of Computer Languages: Natural Expansion of Copyright Law or Destruction of the Copyright/Patent Distinction?*, 72 J. PAT. & TRADEMARK OFF. SOC. 564 (1990).

2. *Alternative methods of protecting computer programs.* You have now examined three different approaches to creating and protecting proprie-

tary interests in computer programs: trade secret protection, patents, and copyright. From a strategic standpoint, what are the relative advantages and disadvantages of each? See FINAL REPORT OF THE NATIONAL COMMISSION ON NEW TECHNOLOGICAL USES OF COPYRIGHTED WORKS, 16–19 (1978). Is there any objection to businesses pursuing more than one of these forms of protection simultaneously?

As the *Altai* court notes, the National Commission on New Technological Uses of Copyrighted Works ("CONTU") reviewed the various approaches to protecting computer programs and recommended that Congress retain copyright protection. The CONTU Report found that programs fit well into existing copyright doctrine, and that copyright afforded some advantages over existing alternatives. FINAL REPORT, *supra*, at 9–26. The *Altai* court questions the continuing validity of the CONTU findings and suggests further legislative investigation. There has been significant criticism of copyright as a vehicle for software protection. What is it about the nature of computer programs that leads the *Altai* court to characterize use of copyright as a "square peg in a round hole"? In your opinion, what, if any, practical or policy problems arise from applying copyright law to computer programs? Are the problems sufficiently great to justify a change? Compare Miller, *Copyright Protection for Computer Programs, Databases, and Computer–Generated Works: Is Anything New Since CONTU?*, 106 HARV. L. REV. 977 (1993), with Samuelson, *CONTU Revisited: The Case Against Copyright Protection for Computer Programs in Machine–Readable Form*, [1984] DUKE L.J. 663.

Assuming that changes are needed, would amendments to the existing copyright law be sufficient to remedy the problems? If so, what kind of amendments would be advantageous? In May, 1992, the Congressional Office of Technology Assessment ("OTA") issued a lengthy report in which it reviewed the present state of software protection in the United States and the criticisms that have been directed toward copyright protection. Though the report made no definitive recommendations, it identified several alternatives that Congress might wish to explore:

1. Expanding the Copyright Act section 102 language on the "subject matter of copyright" explicitly to include or to exclude computer languages, algorithms, design specifications, user and other interfaces, and/or other aspects of software;

2. Creating a special category for computer programs in the Copyright Act, rather than treating them as literary works;

3. Maintaining software in the literary works category, but limiting protection in that category to the code, excluding the program's operational behavior and interfaces. Consider protecting the behavior and interfaces in a complementary *sui generis* regime;

4. Removing computer programs entirely from the scope of copyright protection, and protecting them instead "under a *sui generis* framework, including protection for the program code, as well as other elements of program functionality and design."

OFFICE OF TECHNOLOGY ASSESSMENT, FINDING A BALANCE: COMPUTER SOFTWARE, INTELLECTUAL PROPERTY AND THE

CHALLENGE OF TECHNOLOGICAL CHANGE, 30–32 (1992). Which of these approaches makes the most sense to you?

A recent survey of U.S. software development companies found that 78% of the surveyed companies believed that software should have its own unique type of legal protection. Samuels & Cao, *Survey of the Opinion of Software Development Companies Concerning Intellectual Property Protection*, 32 IDEA 343, 349 (1992). What form should such *sui generis* protection take? For suggestions, see, e.g., Samuelson, Davis, Kapor & Reichman, *A Manifesto Concerning the Legal Protection of Computer Programs,* 94 COLUM. L. REV. 2308 (1994); Menell, *Tailoring Legal Protection for Computer Software*, 39 STAN. L. REV. 1329 (1987). Compare Raskind, *The Uncertain Case for Special Legislation Protecting Computer Software*, 47 U. PITT. L. REV. 1131 (1986).

Where do other countries stand on these issues? The United States was one of the first countries expressly to recognize computer programs as copyrightable subject matter. It continues to be at the forefront in resolving issues such as those raised in *Altai.* Most other countries to study alternative forms of protection for software have followed the U.S. lead, designating copyright as an appropriate vehicle for protection. In the course of doing this, however, many countries have engaged in the same kinds of debate about the "fit" of copyright to software, and the relative merits of a *sui generis* approach to protection. For example, Japan strongly considered opting for a *sui generis* approach, though it ultimately acquiesced to pressure to conform to the rest of the world and provide copyright. For an intriguing description of the Japanese debate on this issue, see Karjala, *Lessons from the Computer Software Protection Debate in Japan*, [1984] ARIZ. ST. L.J. 53.

Although the Berne Convention does not expressly refer to computer programs in its description of protected works, the language of article 2 is sufficiently broad to encompass them. The GATT Uruguay Round Agreement on Trade–Related Aspects of Intellectual Property Rights provides, at Part II, Section I, Article 10, that GATT members must protect computer programs "as literary works under the Berne Convention."

Given the international move to copyright for computer programs, and the need for uniformity in order to facilitate international trade, advocates of a change to *sui generis* protection in the U.S. have a stiff, up-hill climb, indeed.

3. *Protection for a program's user interface.* In a portion of the *Altai* decision not reprinted above, the Second Circuit specified that its decision should not control infringement actions regarding "categorically distinct works," such as a program's screen display. The court explained that screen displays "represent products of computer programs, rather than the programs themselves, and fall under the copyright rubric of audiovisual works." *Altai*, 982 F.2d at 703.[5] Copyright protection for a program's screen display

5. For purposes of copyright registration, the program, its screen display and other aspects of the program's user interface are considered one single work. See Registration Decision: Registration and De-

and other aspects of a program's "user interface," [6] such as the correspondence between particular commands and keys on the keyboard, has also provided courts with conceptual difficulties. The screen display itself is relatively familiar territory, though issues of merger, blank forms and originality may frequently arise. How should one analyze the assignment of particular keys to particular commands? See Derwin, *It Is Time to Put "Look and Feel" Out To Pasture*, 15 HASTINGS COMM. & ENT. L.J. 605 (1993). How about the use of a joy stick, a dial, or a power glove?

In Lotus Development Corp. v. Borland International, Inc., 49 F.3d 807, 34 U.S.P.Q.2d 1014 (1st Cir.1995), the Court of Appeals for the First Circuit undertook to determine whether the menu command hierarchy of the Lotus 1-2-3 Spreadsheet program constituted copyrightable subject matter. The Lotus 1-2-3 program enables users to perform accounting functions electronically on a computer. Users manipulate and control the program via a series of menu commands, such as "Copy," "Print," and "Quit." Users choose commands either by highlighting them on the screen or by typing their first letter. In all, Lotus 1-2-3 has 469 commands arranged into more than 50 menus and submenus. The defendant, Borland, incorporated a virtually identical copy of the 1-2-3 menu tree into its programs, in order to make its programs compatible with 1-2-3, and enable spreadsheet users who were already familiar with 1-2-3 to switch to the Borland programs without having to learn new commands or rewrite their Lotus macros. Borland did not copy any of Lotus' underlying computer code. It copied only the words and structure of Lotus' menu command hierachy.

In determining whether Borland had taken copyrightable subject matter, the First Circuit immediately distinguished *Altai*:

> In the instant appeal, we are not confronted with alleged nonliteral copying of computer code. Rather, we are faced with Borland's deliberate, literal copying of the Lotus menu command hierarchy. Thus, we must determine not whether nonliteral copying occurred in some amorphous sense, but rather whether the literal copying of the Lotus menu command hierarchy constitutes copyright infringement.
>
> While the *Altai* test may provide a useful framework for assessing the alleged nonliteral copying of computer code, we find it to be of little help in assessing whether the literal copying of a menu command hierarchy constitutes copyright infringement. In fact, we think that the *Altai* test in this context may actually be misleading because, in instructing courts to abstract the various levels, it seems to encourage them to find a base level that includes copyrightable subject matter that, if literally copied, would make the copier liable for copyright infringement. While that base (or literal) level would not be at issue in a nonliteral-copying case like *Altai*, it is precisely

posit of Computer Screen Displays, 53 Fed. Reg. 21,817 (1988).

6. The term "user interface" generally refers to the visual and aural elements through which a computer program communicates with its user.

> what is at issue in this appeal. We think that abstracting menu command hierarchies down to their individual word and menu levels and then filtering idea from expression at that stage, as [the *Altai* test requires], obscures the more fundamental question of whether a menu command hierarchy can be copyrighted at all. The initial inquiry should not be whether individual components of a menu command hierarchy are expressive, but rather whether the menu command hierarchy as a whole can be copyrighted.

Lotus, 49 F.3d at 814–15, 34 U.S.P.Q.2d at 1020–21.

The First Circuit found that the menu command hierarchy constituted a "method of operation," which could not be protected under the terms of Copyright Act section 102.

> We think that "method of operation," as that term is used in § 102(b), refers to the means by which a person operates something, whether it be a car, a food processor, or a computer. Thus a text describing how to operate something would not extend copyright protection to the method of operation itself; other people would be free to employ that method and to describe it in their own words. Similarly, if a new method of operation is used rather than described, other people would still be free to employ or describe that method.
>
> We hold that the Lotus menu command hierarchy is an uncopyrightable "method of operation." The Lotus menu command hierarchy provides the means by which users control and operate Lotus 1-2-3. If users wish to copy material, for example, they use the "Copy" command. If users wish to print material, they use the "Print" command. Users must use the command terms to tell the computer what to do. Without the menu command hierarchy, users would not be able to access and control, or indeed make use of, Lotus 1-2-3's functional capabilities.
>
> The Lotus menu command hierarchy does not merely explain and present Lotus 1-2-3's functional capabilities to the user; it also serves as the method by which the program is operated and controlled. The Lotus menu command hierarchy is different from the Lotus long prompts, for the long prompts are not necessary to the operation of the program; users could operate Lotus 1-2-3 even if there were no long prompts. The Lotus menu command hierarchy is also different from the Lotus screen displays, for users need not "use" any expressive aspects of the screen displays in order to operate Lotus 1-2-3; because the way the screens look has little bearing on how users control the program, the screen displays are not part of Lotus 1-2-3's "method of operation." The Lotus menu command hierarchy is also different from the underlying computer code, because while code is necessary for the program to work, its precise formulation is not. In other words, to offer the same capabilities as Lotus 1-2-3, Borland did not have to copy Lotus's underlying code (and indeed it did not); to allow users to operate its programs in substantially the same way, however, Borland had to

copy the Lotus menu command hierarchy. Thus the Lotus 1-2-3 code is not an uncopyrightable "method of operation."

The district court held that the Lotus menu command hierarchy, with its specific choice and arrangement of command terms, constituted an "expression" of the "idea" of operating a computer program with commands arranged hierarchically into menus and submenus. Under the district court's reasoning, Lotus's decision to employ hierarchically arranged command terms to operate its program could not foreclose its competitors from also employing hierarchically arranged command terms to operate their programs, but it did foreclose them from employing the specific command terms and arrangement that Lotus had used. In effect, the district court limited Lotus 1-2-3's "method of operation" to an abstraction.

Accepting the district court's finding that the Lotus developers made some expressive choices in choosing and arranging the Lotus command terms, we nonetheless hold that that expression is not copyrightable because it is part of Lotus 1-2-3's "method of operation." We do not think that "methods of operation" are limited to abstractions; rather, they are the means by which a user operates something. If specific words are essential to operating something, then they are part of a "method of operation" and, as such, are unprotectable. This is so whether they must be highlighted, typed in, or even spoken, as computer programs no doubt will soon be controlled by spoken words.

The fact that Lotus developers could have designed the Lotus menu command hierarchy differently is immaterial to the question of whether it is a "method of operation." In other words, our initial inquiry is not whether the Lotus menu command hierarchy incorporates any expression. Rather, our initial inquiry is whether the Lotus menu command hierarchy is a "method of operation." Concluding, as we do, that users operate Lotus 1-2-3 by using the Lotus menu command hierarchy, and that the entire Lotus menu command hierarchy is essential to operating Lotus 1-2-3, we do not inquire further whether that method of operation could have been designed differently. The "expressive" choices of what to name the command terms and how to arrange them do not magically change the uncopyrightable menu command hierarchy into copyrightable subject matter.

* * *

In many ways, the Lotus menu command hierarchy is like the buttons used to control, say, a video cassette recorder ("VCR"). A VCR is a machine that enables one to watch and record video tapes. Users operate VCRs by pressing a series of buttons that are typically labeled "Record, Play, Reverse, Fast Forward, Pause, Stop/Eject." That the buttons are arranged and labeled does not make them a "literary work," nor does it make them an "expression" of the abstract "method of operating" a VCR via a set of labeled buttons. Instead, the buttons are themselves the "method of operating" the VCR.

> When a Lotus 1-2-3 user choose a command, either by highlighting it on the screen or by typing its first letter, he or she effectively pushes a button. Highlighting the "Print" command on the screen, or typing the letter "P," is analogous to pressing a VCR button labeled "Play."
>
> Just as one could not operate a buttonless VCR, it would be impossible to operate Lotus 1-2-3 without employing its menu command hierarchy. Thus the Lotus command terms are not equivalent to the labels on the VCR's buttons, but are instead equivalent to the buttons themselves. Unlike the labels on a VCR's buttons, which merely make operating a VCR easier by indicating the buttons' functions, the Lotus menu commands are essential to operating Lotus 1-2-3. Without the menu commands, there would be no way to "push" the Lotus buttons, as one could push unlabeled VCR buttons. While Lotus could probably have designed a user interface for which the command terms were mere labels, it did not do so here. Lotus 1-2-3 depends for its operation on use of the precise command terms that make up the Lotus menu command hierarchy.

Lotus, 49 F.3d at 815–17, 34 U.S.P.Q.2d at 1021–22.

Do you agree with the Court's analogy? As a matter of public policy, does the outcome of *Lotus* make sense? See generally Stern, *Legal Protection of Screen Displays and Other User Interfaces for Computers: A Problem in Balancing Incentives of Creation Against Need for Free Access to the Utilitarian,* 14 COLUM-VLA J.L. & ARTS 283 (1990).

Note: The Semiconductor Chip Protection Act

Congress has enacted a *sui generis* scheme of protection in the case of one newly-emerging technology, which was deemed insufficiently protected by existing intellectual property laws. The Semiconductor Chip Protection Act of 1984 ("SCPA"), 17 U.S.C.A. §§ 901–914, draws elements from both the Copyright and Patent Acts in an attempt to custom-tailor rights in the intricate design lay-outs of semiconductor chips.

Chips consist of a collection of transistors laid out in a single integrated structure to perform an electronic function, such as processing, memory, or logic. They are used in a wide array of electronic products. Creation of chips entails extensive investment of engineering talent, time and money. The process begins with the creation of drawings setting forth the chip's electronic circuitry design. The drawings are then used to produce stencils, called "masks." The masks are used in connection with a chemical process to produce the various layers of the chip.

As the semiconductor chip industry grew, so did a sense that the industry needed protection from pirating. Copyright law did not appear to be a good "fit" for chip lay-outs. While the technical drawings, like other types of blueprints, could be protected under the "pictorial, graphic or sculptural works" category of copyrightable subject matter, the chips and masks themselves could not. They are "useful articles," as defined in section 101 of the Copyright Act of 1976, whose design generally is not physically or conceptually separable from their utilitarian function. See Section II D 5, *infra*. Moreover, though the technical drawings are protected, existing copyright doctrine does not view the creation of a finished object portrayed in technical drawings as an infringement of the drawings. *Id.*

Patent law provides relatively little protection because few chips can satisfy the rigorous "non-obviousness" requirement for patentable inventions. Design patents are unlikely to be available because the circuitry designs are not "ornamental" within the meaning of section 171 of the Patent Act, and are generally not open to human view during use. Trade secret law provides little protection because chip lay-outs are readily discoverable through reverse engineering.

Congress initially considered amending the Copyright Act to provide the semiconductor industry with the protection it desired. A bill was introduced to add the following sentence to the section 101 definition of "pictorial, graphic and sculptural works":

> Such pictorial, graphic, and sculptural works shall also include the photographic masks used to imprint patterns on integrated circuit chips and include the imprinted patterns themselves even though they are used in connection with the manufacture of, or incorporated in a useful article.

H.R. 1007, 96th Cong., 1st Sess. (1979). A number of objections were raised to this approach, including concerns that protection of useful articles was inconsistent with fundamental premises of copyright law, and concerns that the provision would prohibit use of reverse engineering to discover new techniques. Ultimately, in 1984, Congress settled on legislation creating *sui generis* protection. See Kastenmeier & Remington, *The Semiconductor Chip Protection Act of 1984: A Swamp or Firm Ground?*, 70 MINN. L. REV. 417 (1985). The United States was the first country to enact specific legislation to protect chip designs.

As enacted, the SCPA protects "original" mask works that are "fixed" in chips. The Act defines "fixation" for this purpose much as the Copyright Act does. 17 U.S.C.A. § 901(a)(3). To be "original," the mask work must be an independent creation, and it must not consist of designs that are staple, commonplace or familiar in the semiconductor industry, or obvious variations of such designs. *Id.*, § 902(b). Protection commences when the work is registered with the Copyright Office or is first commercially exploited anywhere in the world, and lasts for ten years. *Id.*, § 904. The SCPA gives no rights in the ideas, systems or methods underlying or embodied in the mask work—only in the creator's particular means of expressing or implementing them. *Id.*, § 902(c).

Mask work owners are granted the exclusive rights 1) to reproduce the mask work by optical, electronic or any other means; 2) to import or distribute chips embodying the protected mask work; and 3) to induce or knowingly cause another person to do the acts described in 1) and 2). *Id.*, § 905. However, the SCPA imposes several important limitations on the mask work owner's rights. For example, there is an innocent purchaser defense. *Id.*, § 907. In addition, the SCPA permits reverse engineering by expressly providing that others may copy a protected mask work if their purpose is solely to teach, analyze or evaluate it. Concepts or techniques learned from analyzing or evaluating the chip can be incorporated in reverse engineers' own original chips. *Id.*, § 906(a).

The SCPA requires that mask works be registered with the Copyright Office within two years of commercial exploitation anywhere in the world.

Id., § 908(a). The registration procedure is much closer to copyright registration than to the extensive, substantive patent examination.

The ten years following enactment of the SCPA produced only one reported infringement case. Why so little litigation under the Act? At least a couple of explanations have been advanced. First, the Act addressed itself to the technology existing in the late 1970's and early 1980's, under which it was relatively easy and inexpensive to copy and manufacture another company's chip. Subsequent advances in technology have rendered piracy less feasible and cost-effective. Second, through its broad exemption for reverse engineering and use of the product of reverse engineering, the SCPA excluded much chip copying from its coverage. See Rauch, *The Realities of Our Times: The Semiconductor Chip Protection Act of 1984 and the Evolution of the Semiconductor Industry*, 75 J. PAT. & TRADEMARK OFF. SOC. 93 (1993); Kasch, *The Semiconductor Chip Protection Act: Past, Present, and Future*, 7 HIGH TECH. L.J. 71 (1992).

Since the U.S. adopted the SCPA, a number of other developed countries have enacted similar forms of *sui generis* protection for semiconductor chips and mask works. The GATT Uruguay Round TRIPs provisions, Part II, Sec. 6, require all adhering countries to provide protection for the "layout designs of integrated circuits" either pursuant to a *sui generis* law or as part of their copyright, patent, or other existing intellectual property laws.

5. Pictorial, Graphic and Sculptural Works—Copyright in Useful Articles

§ 101. Definitions

* * *

"Pictorial, graphic, and sculptural works" include two-dimensional and three-dimensional works of fine, graphic, and applied art, photographs, prints and art reproductions, maps, globes, charts, diagrams, models, and technical drawings, including architectural plans. Such works shall include works of artistic craftsmanship insofar as their form but not their mechanical or utilitarian aspects are concerned; the design of a useful article, as defined in this section, shall be considered a pictorial, graphic, or sculptural work only if, and only to the extent that, each such design incorporates pictorial, graphic, or sculptural features that can be identified separately from, and are capable of existing independently of, the utilitarian aspects of the article.

* * *

A "useful article" is an article having an intrinsic utilitarian function that is not merely to portray the appearance of the article or to convey information. An article that is normally a part of a useful article is considered a "useful article."

* * *

17 U.S.C.A. § 101.

HOUSE REPORT ON THE COPYRIGHT ACT OF 1976

H.R. Rep. No. 1476, 94th Cong., 2d Sess. 47, 54–55 (1976).

[T]he definition of "pictorial, graphic, and sculptural works" carries with it no implied criterion of artistic taste, aesthetic value, or intrinsic quality. The term is intended to comprise not only "works of art" in the traditional sense but also works of graphic art and illustration, art reproductions, plans and drawings, photographs and reproductions of them, maps, charts, globes, and other cartographic works, works of these kinds intended for use in advertising and commerce, and works of "applied art." * * *

In accordance with the Supreme Court's decision in Mazer v. Stein, 347 U.S. 201 (1954), works of "applied art" encompass all original pictorial, graphic, and sculptural works that are intended to be or have been embodied in useful articles, regardless of factors such as mass production, commercial exploitation, and the potential availability of design patent protection. * * *

The Committee has added language to the definition of "pictorial, graphic, and sculptural works" in an effort to make clearer the distinction between works of applied art protectible under the bill and industrial designs not subject to copyright protection. The declaration that "pictorial, graphic, and sculptural works" include "works of artistic craftsmanship insofar as their form but not their mechanical or utilitarian aspects are concerned" is classic language: it is drawn from Copyright Office regulations promulgated in the 1940's and expressly endorsed by the Supreme Court in the Mazer case.

The second part of the amendment states that "the design of a useful article ... shall be considered a pictorial, graphic, or sculptural work only if, and only to the extent that, such design incorporates pictorial, graphic, or sculptural features that can be identified separately from, and are capable of existing independently of, the utilitarian aspects of the article." * * *

In adopting this amendatory language, the Committee is seeking to draw as clear a line as possible between copyrightable works of applied art and uncopyrighted works of industrial design. A two-dimensional painting, drawing, or graphic work is still capable of being identified as such when it is printed on or applied to utilitarian articles such as textile fabrics, wallpaper, containers, and the like. The same is true when a statue or carving is used to embellish an industrial product or, as in the Mazer case, is incorporated into a product without losing its ability to exist independently as a work of art. On the other hand, although the shape of an industrial product may be aesthetically satisfying and valuable, the Committee's intention is not to offer it copyright protection under the bill. Unless the shape of an automobile, airplane, ladies' dress, food processor, television set, or any other industrial product contains some element that, physically or conceptually, can be identified as separable from the utilitarian aspects of that article, the design would not be copyrighted under the bill. The test of separability and independence from "the utilitarian aspects of the article" does not depend upon the nature of the design—that is, even if the appearance of an article is determined by aesthetic (as opposed to functional) considerations, only elements, if any, which can be identified separately from the useful article as such are copyrightable. And, even if the three-dimensional design contains some such element (for example, a carving on the back of a chair or a floral relief design on silver flatware), copyright protection would extend only to that element, and would not cover the over-all configuration of the utilitarian article as such.

BRANDIR INTERNATIONAL, INC. v. CASCADE PACIFIC LUMBER CO.

United States Court of Appeals for the Second Circuit, 1987.
834 F.2d 1142, 5 U.S.P.Q.2d 1089.

OAKES, CIRCUIT JUDGE:

In passing the Copyright Act of 1976 Congress attempted to distinguish between protectible "works of applied art" and "industrial designs not subject to copyright protection." The courts, however, have had difficulty framing tests by which the fine line establishing what is and what is not copyrightable can be drawn. Once again we are called upon to draw such a line, this time in a case involving the "RIBBON Rack," a bicycle rack made of bent tubing that is said to have originated from a wire sculpture. (A photograph of the rack is contained in the appendix to this opinion.) [The Register of Copyright denied copyrightability. The district court granted summary judgement to the defendant, Cascade Pacific, with regard to the copyright claim.]

* * *

As courts and commentators have come to realize, * * * the line Congress attempted to draw between copyrightable art and noncopyrightable design "was neither clear nor new." Denicola, *Applied Art and Industrial Design: A Suggested Approach to Copyright in Useful Articles*, 67 Minn.L.Rev. 707, 720 (1983). One aspect of the distinction that has drawn considerable attention is the reference in the House Report to "physically *or conceptually*" (emphasis added) separable elements. The District of Columbia Circuit in *Esquire, Inc. v. Ringer*, 591 F.2d 796, 803–04 (D.C.Cir.1978) (holding outdoor lighting fixtures ineligible for copyright), *cert. denied*, 440 U.S. 908, 99 S.Ct. 1217, 59 L.Ed.2d 456 (1979), called this an "isolated reference" and gave it no significance. * * * [I]n *Kieselstein-Cord v. Accessories by Pearl, Inc.*, 632 F.2d 989, 993 (2d Cir.1980), this court accepted the idea that copyrightability can adhere in the "conceptual" separation of an artistic element. Indeed, the court went on to find such conceptual separation in reference to ornate belt buckles that could be and were worn separately as jewelry. * * *

In *Carol Barnhart Inc. v. Economy Cover Corp.*, 773 F.2d 411 (2d Cir.1985), a divided panel of this circuit affirmed a district court grant of summary judgment of noncopyrightability of four life-sized, anatomically correct human torso forms. *Carol Barnhart* distinguished *Kieselstein-Cord*, but it surely did not overrule it. The distinction made was that the ornamented surfaces of the *Kieselstein-Cord* belt buckles "were not in any respect required by their utilitarian functions," but the features claimed to be aesthetic or artistic in the *Carol Barnhart* forms were "inextricably intertwined with the utilitarian feature, the display of clothes." 773 F.2d at 419. As Judge Newman's dissent made clear, the *Carol Barnhart* majority did not dispute "that 'conceptual separability' is distinct from 'physical separability' and, when present, entitles the creator of a useful article to a copyright on its design." 773 F.2d at 420.

"Conceptual separability" is thus alive and well, at least in this circuit. The problem, however, is determining exactly what it is and how it is to be applied. Judge Newman's illuminating discussion in dissent in *Carol Barnhart*, *see* 773 F.2d at 419–24, proposed a test that aesthetic features are conceptually separable if "the article ... stimulate[s] in the mind of the beholder a concept that is separate from the concept evoked by its utilitarian function." *Id.* at 422. This approach has received favorable endorsement by at least one commentator, W. Patry, *Latman's The Copyright Law* 43–45 (6th ed. 1986), who calls Judge Newman's test the "temporal displacement" test. It is to be distinguished from other possible ways in which conceptual separability can be tested, including whether the primary use is as a utilitarian article as opposed to an artistic work, whether the aesthetic aspects of the work can be said to be "primary," and whether the article is marketable as art, none of which is very satisfactory. But Judge Newman's test was rejected outright by the majority as "a standard so ethereal as to amount to a 'nontest' that would be extremely difficult, if not impossible, to administer or apply." 773 F.2d at 419 n. 5.

Perhaps the differences between the majority and the dissent in *Carol Barnhart* might have been resolved had they had before them the Denicola article on *Applied Art and Industrial Design: A Suggested Approach to Copyright in Useful Articles, supra*. There, Professor Denicola points out that although the Copyright Act of 1976 was an effort " 'to draw as clear a line as possible,' " in truth "there is no line, but merely a spectrum of forms and shapes responsive in varying degrees to utilitarian concerns." 67 Minn.L.Rev. at 741. Denicola argues that "the statutory directive requires a distinction between works of industrial design and works whose origins lie outside the design process, despite the utilitarian environment in which they appear." He views the statutory limitation of copyrightability as "an attempt to identify elements whose form and appearance reflect the unconstrained perspective of the artist," such features not being the product of industrial design. *Id.* at 742. "Copyrightability, therefore, should turn on the relationship between the proffered work and the process of industrial design." *Id.* at 741. He suggests that "the dominant characteristic of industrial design is the influence of nonaesthetic, utilitarian concerns" and hence concludes that copyrightability "ultimately should depend on the extent to which the work reflects artistic expression uninhibited by functional considerations."[2] *Id.* To state the Denicola test in the language of conceptual separability, if design elements reflect a merger of aesthetic and functional considerations, the artistic aspects of a work cannot be said to be conceptually separable from the utilitarian elements. Conversely, where design elements can be identified as reflecting the designer's artistic judgment exercised independently of functional influences, conceptual separability exists.

We believe that Professor Denicola's approach provides the best test for conceptual separability and, accordingly, adopt it here for several reasons. First, the approach is consistent with the holdings of our previous cases. * * * Second, the test's emphasis on the influence of utilitarian concerns in the design process may help, as Denicola notes, to "alleviate the de facto discrimination against nonrepresentational art that has regrettably accompanied much of the current analysis." *Id.* at 745. Finally, and perhaps most importantly, we think Denicola's test will not be too difficult to administer in practice. The work itself will continue to give "mute testimony" of its origins. In addition, the parties will be required to present evidence relating to the design process and the nature of the work, with the trier of fact making the determination whether the aesthetic design elements are significantly influenced by functional considerations.

Turning now to the facts of this case, we note first that Brandir contends, and its chief owner David Levine testified, that the original design of the RIBBON Rack stemmed from wire sculptures that Levine had created, each formed from one continuous undulating piece of wire. These sculptures were, he said, created and displayed in his home as a means of personal expression, but apparently were never sold or displayed elsewhere. He also created a wire sculpture in the shape of a bicycle and states that he did not give any thought to the utilitarian application of any of his sculptures until he accidentally juxtaposed the bicycle sculpture with one of the self-standing wire sculptures. It was not until November 1978 that Levine seriously began pursuing the utilitarian application of his sculptures, when a friend, G. Duff Bailey, a bicycle buff and author of numerous articles about urban cycling, was at Levine's home and informed him that the sculptures would make excellent bicycle racks, permitting bicycles to be parked under the overloops as well as on top of the underloops. Following this meeting, Levine met several times with Bailey and others, completing the designs for the RIBBON Rack by the use of a vacuum cleaner hose, and submitting his

2. Professor Denicola rejects the exclusion of all works created with some utilitarian application in view, for that would not only overturn *Mazer v. Stein*, 347 U.S. 201, 74 S.Ct. 460, 98 L.Ed. 630 (1954), on which much of the legislation is based, but also "a host of other eminently sensible decisions, in favor of an intractable factual inquiry of questionable relevance." 67 Minn.L.Rev. at 741. He adds that "[a]ny such categorical approach would also undermine the legislative determination to preserve an artist's ability to exploit utilitarian markets." *Id.* (citing 17 U.S.C. § 113(a) (1976)).

drawings to a fabricator complete with dimensions. The Brandir RIBBON Rack began being nationally advertised and promoted for sale in September 1979.

In November 1982 Levine discovered that another company, Cascade Pacific Lumber Co., was selling a similar product. [Levine attempted to register the RIBBON Rack, but the] Copyright Office refused registration by letter, stating that the RIBBON Rack did not contain any element that was "capable of independent existence as a copyrightable pictorial, graphic or sculptural work apart from the shape of the useful article." * * *

* * * The RIBBON Rack has been featured in *Popular Science, Art and Architecture*, and *Design 384* magazines, and it won an Industrial Designers Society of America design award in the spring of 1980. In the spring of 1984 the RIBBON Rack was selected from 200 designs to be included among 77 of the designs exhibited at the Katonah Gallery in an exhibition entitled "The Product of Design: An Exploration of the Industrial Design Process," an exhibition that was written up in the *New York Times*.

Sales of the RIBBON Rack from September 1979 through January 1985 were in excess of $1,367,000. * * *

Applying Professor Denicola's test to the RIBBON Rack, we find that the rack is not copyrightable. It seems clear that the form of the rack is influenced in significant measure by utilitarian concerns and thus any aesthetic elements cannot be said to be conceptually separable from the utilitarian elements. This is true even though the sculptures which inspired the RIBBON Rack may well have been—the issue of originality aside—copyrightable.

Brandir argues correctly that a copyrighted work of art does not lose its protected status merely because it subsequently is put to a functional use. The Supreme Court so held in *Mazer v. Stein*, 347 U.S. 201, 74 S.Ct. 460, 98 L.Ed. 630 (1954), and Congress specifically intended to accept and codify *Mazer* in section 101 of the Copyright Act of 1976. The district court thus erred in ruling that, whatever the RIBBON Rack's origins, Brandir's commercialization of the rack disposed of the issue of its copyrightability.

Had Brandir merely adopted one of the existing sculptures as a bicycle rack, neither the application to a utilitarian end nor commercialization of that use would have caused the object to forfeit its copyrighted status. Comparison of the RIBBON Rack with the earlier sculptures, however, reveals that while the rack may have been derived in part from one of more "works of art," it is in its final form essentially a product of industrial design. In creating the RIBBON Rack, the designer has clearly adapted the original aesthetic elements to accommodate and further a utilitarian purpose. These altered design features of the RIBBON Rack, including the spacesaving, open design achieved by widening the upper loops to permit parking under as well as over the rack's curves, the straightened vertical elements that allow in- and above-ground installation of the rack, the ability to fit all types of bicycles and mopeds, and the heavy-gauged tubular construction of rustproof galvanized steel, are all features that combine to make for a safe, secure, and maintenance-free system of parking bicycles and mopeds. Its undulating shape is said in *Progressive Architecture*, January 1982, to permit double the storage of conventional bicycle racks. Moreover, the rack is manufactured from 2⅜-inch standard steam pipe that is bent into form, the six-inch radius of the bends evidently resulting from bending the pipe according to a standard formula that yields bends having a radius equal to three times the nominal internal diameter of the pipe.

Brandir argues that its RIBBON Rack can and should be characterized as a sculptural work of art within the minimalist art movement. Minimalist sculpture's most outstanding feature is said to be its clarity and simplicity, in that it often takes the form of geometric shapes, lines, and forms that are pure and free of ornamentation and void of association. As Brandir's expert put it, "The meaning is to be found in, within, around and outside the work of art, allowing the artistic sensation to be experienced as well as intellectualized." People who use Foley Square in New York City see in the form of minimalist art the "Tilted Arc," which is on the plaza at 26 Federal Plaza. Numerous museums have had exhibitions of such art, and the school of minimalist art has many admirers.

It is unnecessary to determine whether to the art world the RIBBON Rack properly would be considered an example of minimalist sculpture. The result under the copyright statute is not changed. Using the test we have adopted, it is not enough that, to paraphrase Judge Newman, the rack may stimulate in the mind of the reasonable observer a concept separate from the bicycle rack concept. While the RIBBON Rack may be worthy of admiration for its aesthetic qualities alone, it remains nonetheless the product of industrial design. Form and function are inextricably intertwined in the rack, its ultimate design being as much the result of utilitarian pressures as aesthetic choices. Indeed, the visually pleasing proportions and symmetricality of the rack represent design changes made in response to functional concerns. Judging from the awards the rack has received, it would seem in fact that Brandir has achieved with the RIBBON Rack the highest goal of modern industrial design, that is, the harmonious fusion of function and aesthetics. Thus there remains no artistic element of the RIBBON Rack that can be identified as separate and "capable of existing independently, of, the utilitarian aspects of the article." Accordingly, we must affirm on the copyright claim.

* * *

Appendix

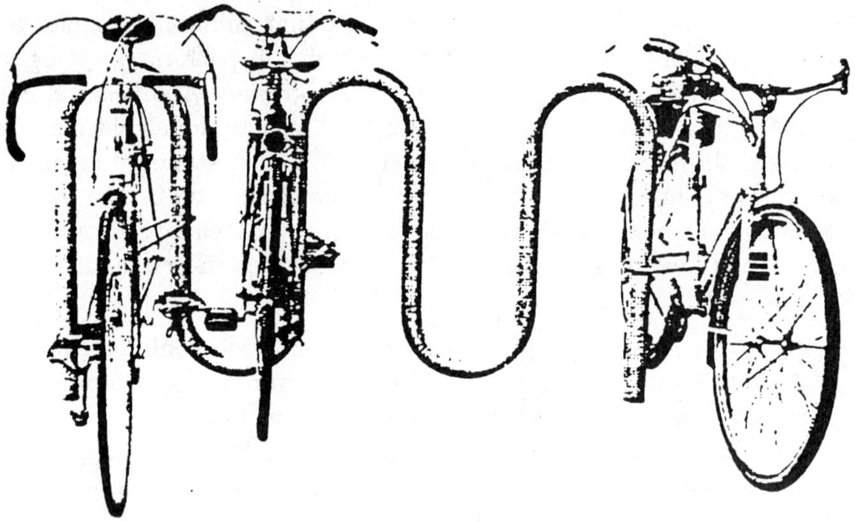

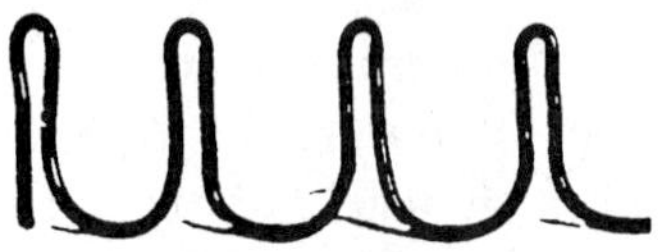

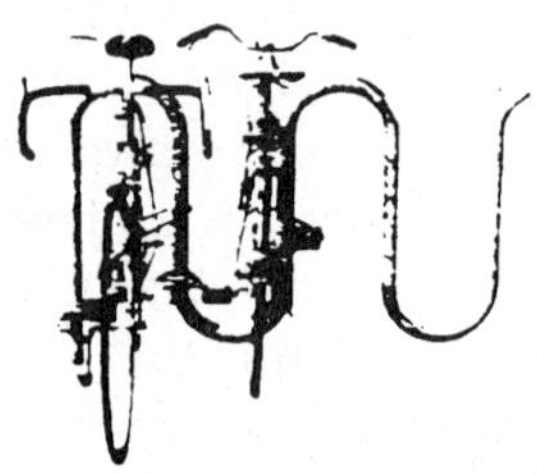

WINTER, CIRCUIT JUDGE, concurring in part and dissenting in part:

* * * I respectfully dissent from the majority's discussion and disposition of the copyright claim.

My colleagues, applying an adaptation of Professor Denicola's test, hold that the aesthetic elements of the design of a useful article are not conceptually separable from its utilitarian aspects if "[f]orm and function are inextricably intertwined" in the article, and "its ultimate design [is] as much the result of utilitarian pressures as aesthetic choices." Applying that test to the instant matter, they observe that the dispositive fact is that "in creating the Ribbon Rack, [Levine] has clearly adapted the *original* aesthetic elements to accommodate and further a utilitarian purpose." (emphasis added). The grounds of my disagreement are that: (1) my colleagues' adaptation of Professor Denicola's test diminishes the statutory concept of "conceptual separability" to the vanishing point; and (2) their focus on the process or sequence followed by the particular designer makes copyright protection depend upon largely fortuitous circumstances concerning the creation of the design in issue.

* * *

[T]he relevant question is whether the design of a useful article, however intertwined with the article's utilitarian aspects, causes an ordinary reasonable observer to perceive an aesthetic concept not related to the article's use. The answer to this question is clear in the instant case because any reasonable observer would easily view the Ribbon Rack as an ornamental sculpture.[2] Indeed, there is evidence of actual confusion over whether it is strictly ornamental in the refusal of a building manager to accept delivery until assured by the buyer that the Ribbon Rack was in fact a bicycle rack. Moreover, Brandir has received a request to use the Ribbon Rack as environmental sculpture, and has offered testimony of art experts who claim that the Ribbon Rack may be valued solely for its artistic features. As one of those experts observed: "If one were to place a Ribbon Rack on an island without access, or in a park and surround the work with a barrier, ... its status as a work of art would be beyond dispute."

My colleagues also allow too much to turn upon the process or sequence of design followed by the designer of the Ribbon Rack. They thus suggest that copyright protection would have been accorded "had Brandir merely adopted ... as a bicycle rack" an enlarged version of one of David Levine's original sculptures rather than one that had wider upper loops and straightened vertical elements. I cannot agree that copyright protection for the Ribbon Rack turns on whether Levine serendipitously chose the final design of the Ribbon Rack during his initial sculptural musings or whether the original design had to be slightly modified to accommodate bicycles. Copyright protection, which is intended to generate incentives for designers by according property rights in their creations, should not turn on purely fortuitous events. For that reason, the Copyright Act expressly states that the legal test is

2. The reasonable observer may be forgiven, however, if he or she does not recognize the Ribbon Rack as an example of minimalist art.

how the final article is perceived, not how it was developed through various stages. It thus states in pertinent part:

> the design of a useful article ... shall be considered a ... sculptural work only if, and only to the extent that, such design incorporates ... *sculptural features that can be identified separately from, and are capable of existing independently of, the utilitarian aspects of the article.*

17 U.S.C. § 101 (1982) (emphasis added). * * *

Notes and Questions

1. *The "separability" issue.* In discussing the best means of distinguishing the artistic features of a design from its utilitarian aspects, it is useful to consider why Congress desired to make such a distinction in the first place. What was Congress' purpose? What are the practical social implications of construing the separability requirement liberally to permit copyright protection for a wide array of useful article designs?

As the *Brandir* opinion indicates, the Second Circuit has interpreted the House Report to permit copyright upon a showing of *either* physical *or* conceptual separability. There has been relatively little debate about the meaning of physical separability. Courts have found a pictorial, graphic, or sculptural feature of a useful article "physically separable" if it can be physically separated from the article and stand alone as a work of art in the traditional sense. I P. GOLDSTEIN, COPYRIGHT PRINCIPLES, LAW AND PRACTICE, § 2.5.3 at 106 (1989). Mazer v. Stein, *supra*, the Supreme Court decision that established the applicability of copyright to works of applied art, provides a good example of physical separability. The works in that case were sculptures of dancers used as the base of table lamps, one of which is illustrated below. If the statue were physically detached from the table lamp electrical wiring and shade apparatus, it would stand alone as a sculptural work. In *Mazer*, the Supreme Court found that such a statue did not lose its copyrightable status simply because its creator intended to and did embed it in a useful article and mass produce it.

Conceptual separability, which was at issue in *Brandir*, has proven more difficult. One case in which the Second Circuit *did* find conceptual separability was Kieselstein–Cord v. Accessories by Pearl, Inc., 632 F.2d 989, 208 U.S.P.Q. 1 (2d Cir.1980). The useful articles at issue in that case were belt buckles ornamented with a sculpted metal surface, as depicted below:

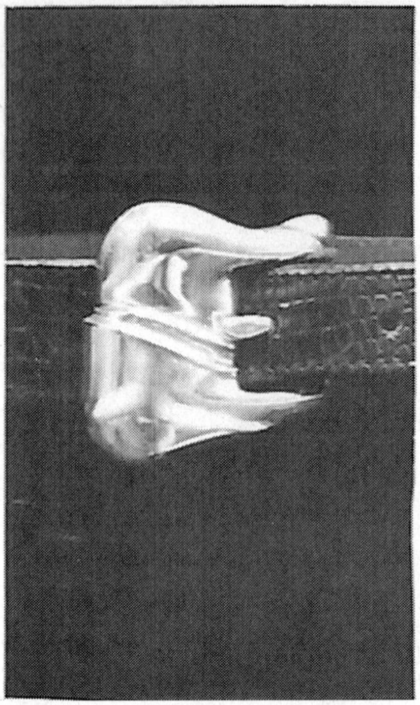

Winchester

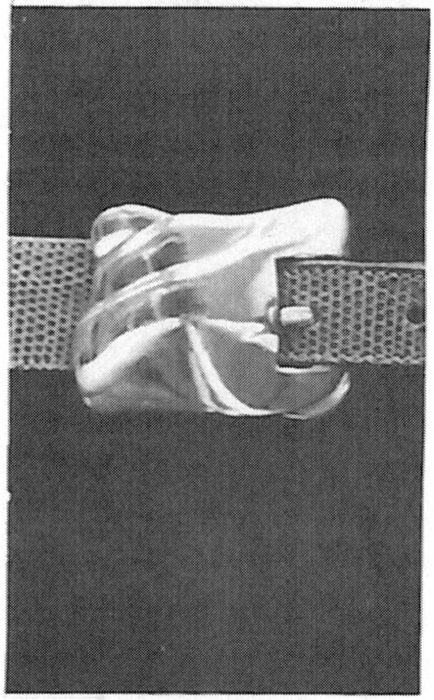

Vaquero

These buckles, made of precious metals, were sold at jewelry and high-fashion stores, and had been accepted by the Metropolitan Museum of Art for its permanent collection. There was evidence that at least one of the buckles had been worn as ornamentation around the neck, rather than around the waist. In finding that the buckles were protected by copyright, the court stated that "the primary ornamental aspect of the * * * buckles is conceptually separable from their subsidiary utilitarian function." *Id.*, 632 F.2d at 993, 208 U.S.P.Q. at 5. Did the court mean to suggest that conceptual separability should depend on whether the aesthetically pleasing aspect of the article is primary and the utilitarian function subsidiary? Unfortunately, the court did not elaborate. In subsequent opinions, panels of the Second Circuit have revisited the case of the belt buckles, and offered other justifications for the finding that their sculpted ornamental metal surfaces were "conceptually separable." For example, in Carol Barnhart Inc. v. Economy Cover Corp., 773 F.2d 411, 419, 228 U.S.P.Q. 385, 390 (2d Cir.1985), the court explained that

> the ornamented surfaces of the buckles were not in any respect required by their utilitarian functions; the artistic and aesthetic features could thus be conceived of as having been added to, or superimposed upon, an otherwise utilitarian article. The unique artistic design was wholly unnecessary to performance of the utilitarian function.

In *Brandir*, the court noted that in *Kieselstein-Cord*, "the artistic aspects of the belt buckles reflected purely aesthetic choices, independent of the buckles' function." 834 F.2d at 1145, 5 U.S.P.Q.2d at 1092.

In your opinion, which is the better approach to determining conceptual separability—the approach advocated by the *Brandir* majority, or that advocated by the *Brandir* dissent? Why? Which approach more effectively promotes Congress' underlying purpose in restricting copyright to elements that are physically or conceptually separable from the utilitarian aspects of the useful article? Which approach is easier to apply, or more likely to lead to consistent and fair results?

The majority states that its approach to determining conceptual separability may help "to alleviate the *de facto* discrimination against nonrepresentational art that has regrettably accompanied much of the current analysis." Do you agree?

What is your evaluation of the following approach, advocated by the late Professor Melvile Nimmer: "conceptual separability exists where there is any substantial likelihood that even if the article had no utilitarian use it would still be marketable to some significant segment of the community simply because of its aesthetic qualities." 1 M.B. NIMMER & D. NIMMER, NIMMER ON COPYRIGHT § 2.08[B], 2–96.1 (1985). See *Carol Barnhart*, *supra*, 773 F.2d at 421, 228 U.S.P.Q. at 393 (Newman, J., dissenting).

If you find none of the proposed tests ideal, can you suggest a better one?

2. *Useful articles.* Before reaching the separability issue one must, of course, find that the pictorial, graphic or sculptural work is part of the design of a "useful article." A "useful article" is one "having an intrinsic utilitarian function that is not merely to portray the appearance of the article or to convey information." 17 U.S.C.A. § 101.

Is a toy plane a "useful article?" It could be argued that toys are an important aspect of childhood, and even necessary as stimuli to proper emotional and intellectual development. The district court in Gay Toys, Inc. v. Buddy L Corp., 522 F.Supp. 622, 216 U.S.P.Q. 766 (E.D.Mich.1981), *vacated* 703 F.2d 970, 218 U.S.P.Q. 13 (6th Cir.1983), accepted such an argument, noting that a toy airplane "permits a child to dream and to let his or her imagination soar." *Id.* at 625. On appeal, the U.S. Court of Appeals for the Sixth Circuit proved more difficult to persuade:

> [A] toy airplane is merely a model which portrays a real airplane. * * * The intention of Congress was to exclude from copyright protection industrial products such as automobiles, food processors, and television sets. The function of toys is much more similar to that of works of art than it is to the "intrinsic utilitarian function" of industrial products.
>
> Indeed, under the district court's reasoning, virtually any "pictorial, graphic, and sculptural work" would not be copyrightable as a useful article. A painting of Lindbergh's Spirit of St. Louis invites the viewer "to dream and to let his or her imagination soar," and would not be copyrightable under the district court's approach. But the statute clearly intends to extend copyright protection to paintings. The district

> court would have the "useful article" exception swallow the general rule, and its rationale is incorrect.

703 F.2d 970, 973, 218 U.S.P.Q. 13, 15 (6th Cir.1983).

Much to the regret of high-fashion designers, items of clothing are considered to be useful articles, and thus are subject to the separability analysis. Should the same be true of halloween costumes? Could it not be argued that the function of a "Ladybug" costume is merely to portray the appearance of an insect, and thus is exempted from the useful article category? See Copyright Office, Registrability of Costume Designs, 56 Fed. Reg. 56,530 (Nov. 5, 1991) (Fanciful costumes will be treated as useful articles because they serve the dual purpose of clothing the body and portraying the appearance of something. However, masks will not be treated as useful articles, since they have no inherent utility other than their appearance.).

How would you categorize an article, created by a fashion designer and artist, which resembles a two-piece women's swimsuit but is made of clear vinyl filled with colored crushed rocks? Is it an item of clothing, and thus a useful article, or a soft sculpture? The U.S. Court of Appeals for the Ninth Circuit found the article's status to be a disputed issue of material fact and identified several types of evidence that might be relevant to making a proper determination: 1) expert testimony about the usefulness of the article (e.g., could it actually be used as a swimsuit?); 2) evidence of the creator's intent in designing the article; 3) testimony concerning the custom and usage within the art world and the clothing trade; and 4) evidence of the marketability of the work as a work of art. Poe v. Missing Persons, 745 F.2d 1238, 1243, 223 U.S.P.Q. 1297 (9th Cir.1984).

3. *Alternative forms of protection.* Copyright is not the only form of protection available for designs of useful articles. Indeed, in *Brandir*, the plaintiff claimed trademark rights in the configuration of its RIBBON Rack pursuant to section 43(a) of the Lanham Act, 15 U.S.C.A. § 1125(a), and New York unfair competition law, and the court remanded for further findings of fact on these claims. Trademark and unfair competition law may protect surface ornamentation and the configuration of an article if these features are "nonfunctional" and sufficiently distinctive to indicate the commercial source of the article to consumers. Trademark and unfair competition law will be discussed in Chapters 6 and 7, *infra*.

In addition, Brandir might have pursued a design patent for his bike rack. As a practical matter, how would you compare the respective standards for obtaining a design patent and copyright protection? How about the respective levels of protection that each provides? Assuming that either would apply, would one be preferable? Would it be possible to obtain and enforce both a design patent and copyright in the same design? The Court of Customs and Patent Appeals, in *In re* Yardley, 493 F.2d 1389, 181 U.S.P.Q. 331 (C.C.P.A.1974), held that a design patent could be issued for a design that had already been registered for copyright. During the following 21 years, the Copyright Office refused to register a copyright claim in pictorial, graphic, or sculptural works for which a design patent had been issued. It abandoned this practice effective April 24, 1995. 37 C.F.R. § 202.10.

Notwithstanding the number of alternative routes to proprietary rights in design features of useful articles, many commercial designers believe that their work receives insufficient protection against the creation and sale of less expensive "knock-offs." Commercial designers have, for many years, lobbied Congress to enact *sui generis* legislation to provide broad-based, readily obtainable protection for the designs of useful articles, unfettered by considerations of physical or conceptual separability or the demanding nonobviousness standard of design patents.

Bills to create this protection have been introduced in Congress repeatedly over the past several decades, but none has ever been enacted. For a brief history of the attempts to enact design legislation, see *The Industrial Innovation and Technology Act, 1987: Hearings on S. 791 Before the Subcomm. on Patents, Copyrights and Trademarks of the Senate Comm. on the Judiciary*, 100th Cong., 1st Sess. 223 (1987) (statement of Ralph Oman, Register of Copyrights).

While the bills introduced in recent years vary in their particulars, H.R. 1790, 102nd Cong., 2nd Sess. (1991), the "Design Innovation and Technology Act of 1991," is representative. Version 4 of H.R. 1790 provided protection for "original" designs of useful articles. A design would be deemed "original" if it was

> the result of the designer's creative endeavor that provides a distinguishable variation over prior work pertaining to similar articles which is more than merely trivial and has not been copied from another source.

Id., § 1001. Section 1002 provided:

> Protection under this chapter shall not be available for a design that is—
>
> (1) not original;
>
> (2) staple or commonplace, such as a standard geometric figure, familiar symbol, emblem, or motif, or other shape, pattern, or configuration which has become standard, common, prevalent, or ordinary;
>
> (3) different from a design excluded by paragraph (2) only in insignificant details or in elements which are variants commonly used in the relevant trades;
>
> (4) dictated solely by a utilitarian function of the article that embodies it;
>
> (5) embodied in a useful article that was made public by the designer or owner in the United States or a foreign country more than 1 year before the date of the application for registration under this chapter;
>
> (6) composed of three-dimensional features of shape and surface with respect to men's, women's, and children's apparel, including undergarments and outerwear;
>
> (7) a semiconductor chip product which is protected under chapter 9 of this title;

(8) an idea, procedure, process, system, method of operation, concept, principle, or discovery, regardless of the form in which it is described, explained, illustrated, or embodied in such design; or

(9) for motor vehicle glass, including windshields and side and rear vision glass.

With respect to articles which are normally part of a larger useful article * * * that portion of the article shape dictated by the mechanical interface, perimeter, or envelope restrictions necessary to permit the physical and functional substitution of an article shall be considered to be a design for which protection under this chapter is not available under paragraph (4).

While the bill required that designs be registered with the Register of Copyrights, *id.*, § 1010, the Register's review of the application would be relatively cursory, consisting only of a determination of "whether or not the application relates to a design which on its face appears to be subject to protection." *Id.*, § 1013. Protection would commence upon the earlier of the date the registration was published or the date the design was first made public. *Id.*, § 1004. H.R. 1790 provided the owner of a qualifying design the exclusive right to "make, have made, or import, for sale or for use in trade, any useful article embodying that design" and to "sell or distribute for sale or for use in trade any useful article embodying that design." *Id.*, § 1008. The term of protection would be ten years. *Id.*, § 1005.

How does H.R. 1790 differ from existing design patent protection? From copyright protection? What does it borrow from each? What is your evaluation of the scope of the bill? Is it well adapted to the need? Do you see any potential problems? For thoughtful evaluations of recently proposed *sui generis* design protection bills, see Reichman, *Design Protection and the Legislative Agenda*, 55 L & CONTEMP. PROBS. 281 (1992); Brown, *Design Protection: An Overview*, 34 U.C.L.A. L. REV. 1341, 1395–1403 (1987).

Notwithstanding considerable support, H.R. 1790, like its many predecessors, failed to be enacted. *Should* such legislation be enacted? There have been numerous arguments made both for and against extending protection to designs failing to qualify for design patent or copyright protection.

Consumer groups have been among the strongest adversaries of the proposed legislation, arguing that the bill would raise prices for virtually all consumer products, including many that are not truly innovative. Automobile insurers have also fought the bill, arguing that by protecting automobile replacement parts, the bill would raise the price of automobile repairs (and presumably, automobile insurance). The Insurance Institute for Highway Safety, a research organization supported by insurance companies, cited an example: In 1984, Chrysler Corporation charged $180 for the left fender of a four-door Plymouth Reliant. In 1985, after an imitation part became available, it dropped the price to $87. At the same time the price for a left-quarter panel, for which no imitation part existed, increased. Edmund L. Andrews, *Patents: A New and Disputed Push to Ease Design Protection*, N.Y. TIMES, Aug. 4, 1989, § 1 at 31. Note that the drafters of H.R. 1790 included some provisions to address these concerns. Are the provisions sufficient?

Other opponents of the proposed legislation argue that existing laws are adequate to provide the necessary design protection: through all the years of lobbying for enhanced design protection, the American market has been highly creative and productive, demonstrating that no further legislation-based incentive is needed. They have also argued that the ability to copy design ideas is essential to free competition. Because the number of design choices for many functional products is highly limited, a few companies could tie up all the practical design alternatives, leading to greater concentration of monopoly power. See *Hearings on S. 791*, (statement of Ralph Oman), *supra*, at 232–35.

6. *Architectural Works*

While many countries fully protect works of architecture through copyright, the United States has a history of hesitation, particularly with regard to architectural works as embodied in three-dimensional buildings. Because the Berne Convention, Article 2, mandates full copyright protection, Congress enacted the Architectural Works Copyright Protection Act ("AWCPA"), Pub. L. No. 101–650, 104 Stat. 5133, in 1990 to bring the United States into compliance. The AWCPA only applies prospectively, however, to architectural works created on or after the enactment date and to works that were "unconstructed and embodied in unpublished plans or drawings" on the enactment date. *Id.* at § 706. Existing architectural works falling outside the scope of the Act will continue to be governed by the earlier law.

The Law Prior to the AWCPA

Architectural plans, or blueprints, have long been protected as pictorial, graphic and sculptural works. See I M.B. NIMMER & D. NIMMER, NIMMER ON COPYRIGHT § 2.08[D] (1994). But copyright law has provided significantly less protection for architectural works embodied in buildings, rather than plans. This is because buildings are deemed to be useful articles. Though pictorial, graphic or sculptural aspects of buildings may be protected, they are subject to the "physical or conceptual separability" test discussed in the last Section. Thus, most aspects of building design, which integrate form and function, have enjoyed no protection. While a defendant will be liable for making an unauthorized copy of blueprints embodying an architectural work, absent the AWCPA, she is unlikely to be liable if she copies the architectural work by simply viewing the finished building in which the work is embodied.

What if the defendant lawfully obtained authorized copies of blueprints and used them to create an unauthorized building? One could argue that this would constitute the making of an unauthorized copy of the protected plans, since copying is prohibited in any medium. See NIMMER, *supra*, at 2–122. Nonetheless, the making of an unauthorized building from copyrighted architectural plans has been deemed not to infringe the copyright in the plans. See I P. GOLDSTEIN, COPYRIGHT PRINCIPLES, LAW AND PRACTICE § 2.5.3 at 114 (1989).

The building is a useful article. By analogy to the reasoning in *Baker v. Selden*, courts have found that copyright in technical plans can give no rights in the useful article they depict. See, NIMMER, *supra* at 2–123; H.R. REP. NO. 94–1476, 94th Cong., 2d Sess. 105 (1976).

The Architectural Works Copyright Protection Act of 1990

Among other things, the AWCPA amended section 102(a) of the Copyright Act to add "architectural works" as a new category of copyrightable subject matter. See 17 U.S.C.A. § 102(a)(8). It amended section 101 to define the new category as follows:

> An "architectural work" is the design of a building as embodied in any tangible medium of expression, including a building, architectural plans, or drawings. The work includes the overall form as well as the arrangement and composition of spaces and elements in the design, but does not include individual standard features.

17 U.S.C.A. § 101.

COPYRIGHT AMENDMENTS ACT OF 1990

H.R. Rep. No. 101–735, 101st Cong., 2d Sess. 18–21 (1990).

Section 202.—Definitions

* * * The definition [of an "architectural work"] has two components. First, it states what is protected. Second, it specifies the material objects in which the architectural work may be embodied. The protected work is the design of a building. The term "design" includes the overall form as well as the arrangement and composition of spaces and elements in the design. The phrase "arrangement and composition of spaces and elements" recognizes that: (1) creativity in architecture frequently takes the form of a selection, coordination, or arrangement of unprotectible elements into an original, protectible whole; (2) an architect may incorporate new, protectible design elements into otherwise standard, unprotectible building features; and (3) interior architecture may be protected.

Consistent with other provisions of the Copyright Act and Copyright Office regulations, the definition makes clear that protection does not extend to individual standard features, such as common windows, doors, and other staple building components. A grant of exclusive rights in such features would impede, rather than promote, the progress of architectural innovation. The provision is not, however, intended to exclude from the copyright in the architectural work any individual features that reflect the architect's creativity. * * *

Section 203.—Subject Matter of Copyright

This provision amends section 102, title 17, United States Code, to create a new category of protected subject matter: "architectural works." By creating a new category of protectible subject matter in new section 102(a)(8), and, therefore, by deliberately not encompassing architectural works as pictorial, graphic, or sculptural works in existing section 102(a)(5), the copyrightability of architectural works shall not be evaluated under the separability test applicable to pictorial, graphic, or sculptural works embodied in useful articles. There is considerable scholarly and judicial disagreement over how to apply the separability test, and the principal reason for not treating architectural works as pictorial, graphic, or sculptural works is to avoid entangling architectural works in this disagreement.

The Committee does not suggest, though, that in evaluating the copyrightability or scope of protection for architectural works, the Copyright Office or the courts should ignore functionality. A two-step analysis is envisioned. First, an architectural work should be examined to determine whether there are original design elements present, including overall shape and interior architecture. If such design elements are present, a second step is reached to examine whether the design elements are functionally required. If the design elements are not functionally required, the work is protectible without regard to physical or conceptual separability. As a consequence, contrary to the Committee's report accompanying the 1976 Copyright Act with respect to industrial products, the aesthetically pleasing overall shape of an architectural work could be protected under this bill.

The proper scope of protection for architectural works is distinct from registrability. Functional considerations may, for example, determine only particular design elements. Protection would be denied for the functionally determined elements, but would be available for the nonfunctionally determined elements. Under such circumstances, the Copyright Office should issue a certificate of registration, letting the courts determine the scope of protection. In each case, the courts must be free to decide the issue upon the facts presented, free of the separability conundrum presented by the useful articles doctrine applicable for pictorial, graphic, and sculptural works. Evidence that there is more than one method of obtaining a given functional result may be considered in evaluating registrability or the scope of protection.

The proposed legislation incorporates the general standards of originality applicable for all other copyrightable subject matter. This standard "does not include requirements of novelty, ingenuity, or [a]esthetic merit." Subjective determinations of artistic or aesthetic merit are inappropriate and contrary to fundamental principles of copyright law. * * *

Notes and Questions

1. *Protection for "architectural works."* What in the *Baker v. Selden* opinion suggests that the owner of copyrighted blue prints may not prevent others from using the blue prints to create the depicted building?

How would you articulate the changes to existing law wrought by the AWCPA? The legislative history of the AWCPA makes it clear that the courts should avoid applying copyright to functional features of architectural works. What is your evaluation of the method the House Report suggests for doing this? How would you compare that method to the "separability" inquiry used in the case of pictorial, graphic, and sculptural works in useful articles?

Should architectural works be the subject of copyright? Are they writings? Is there a policy justification for granting greater copyright protection to building designs than to other useful designs, such as the design of an automobile or a fine piece of furniture?

For additional information about the AWCPA, see Winick, *Copyright Protection for Architecture after the Architectural Works Copyright Protection Act of 1990*, 41 DUKE L.J. 1598 (1992).

7. *Sound Recordings*

HOUSE REPORT ON COPYRIGHT ACT OF 1976

H.R. Rep. No. 1476, 94th Cong., 2d Sess. 55–56 (1976).

Enactment of Public Law 92–140 in 1971 marked the first recognition in American copyright law of sound recordings as copyrightable works. As defined in section 101, copyrightable "sound recordings" are original works of authorship comprising an aggregate of musical, spoken, or other sounds that have been fixed in tangible form. The copyrightable work comprises the aggregation of sounds and not the tangible medium of fixation. Thus, "sound recordings" as copyrightable subject matter are distinguished from "phonorecords," the latter being physical objects in which sounds are fixed. They are also distinguished from any copyrighted literary, dramatic, or musical works that may be reproduced on a "phonorecord."

As a class of subject matter, sound recordings are clearly within the scope of the "writings of an author" capable of protection under the Constitution, and the extension of limited statutory protection to them was too long delayed. * * *

The copyrightable elements in a sound recording will usually, though not always, involve "authorship" both on the part of the performers whose performance is captured and on the part of the record producer responsible for setting up the recording session, capturing and electronically processing the sounds, and compiling and editing them to make the final sound recording. There may, however, be cases where the record producer's contribution is so minimal that the performance is the only copyrightable element in the work, and there may be cases (for example, recordings of birdcalls, sounds of racing cars, *et cetera*) where only the record producer's contribution is copyrightable.

Sound tracks of motion pictures, long a nebulous area in American copyright law, are specifically included in the definition of "motion pictures," and excluded in the definition of "sound recordings." * * *

Notes and Questions

1. *Sound recordings.* As the House Report suggests, sound recordings were only recently granted the status of copyrightable subject matter. Only

those sound recordings "fixed" on or after February 15, 1972, are eligible for copyright protection, though sound recordings fixed prior to that time may be protected under state law. 17 U.S.C.A. § 301(c).

The sound recording copyright is separate from any copyright that might exist in the musical, literary or dramatic work that is recorded. The sound recording copyright protects the particular performance of the underlying work that is fixed in the phonorecord, and protects only against misappropriation of the actual recorded sounds. As we will explore more fully later, the rights afforded the owner of a sound recording copyright are narrower than those afforded owners of copyright in other subject matter.

8. Government Works

HOUSE REPORT ON COPYRIGHT ACT OF 1976

H.R. Rep. No. 1476, 94th Cong., 2d Sess. 58–60 (1976).

The general prohibition against copyright in section 105 applies to "any work of the United States Government," which is defined in section 101 as "a work prepared by an officer or employee of the United States Government as part of that person's official duties." Under this definition a Government official or employee would not be prevented from securing copyright in a work written at that person's own volition and outside his or her duties, even though the subject matter involves the Government work or professional field of the official or employee. Although the wording of the definition of "work of the United States Government" differs somewhat from that of the definition of "work made for hire," the concepts are intended to be construed in the same way.

A more difficult and far-reaching problem is whether the definition should be broadened to prohibit copyright in works prepared under U.S. Government contract or grant. As the bill is written, the Government agency concerned could determine in each case whether to allow an independent contractor or grantee to secure copyright in works prepared in whole or in part with the use of Government funds. The argument that has been made against allowing copyright in this situation is that the public should not be required to pay a "double subsidy," and that it is inconsistent to prohibit copyright in works by Government employees while permitting private copyrights in a growing body of works created by persons who are paid with Government funds. Those arguing in favor of potential copyright protection have stressed the importance of copyright as an incentive to creation and dissemination in this situation, and the basically different policy considerations applicable to works written by Government employees and those applicable to works prepared by private organizations with the use of Federal funds.

The bill deliberately avoids making any sort of outright, unqualified prohibition against copyright in works prepared under Government contract or grant. There may well be cases where it would be in the public interest to deny copyright in the writings generated by Government research contracts and the like; it can be assumed that, where a Government agency commissions a work for its own use merely as an alternative to having one of its own employees prepare the work, the right to secure a private copyright would be withheld. However, there are almost certainly many other cases where the denial of copyright protection would be unfair or would hamper the production and publication of important works. Where, under the particular circumstances, Congress or the agency involved finds that the need to have a work freely available outweighs the need of the private author to secure copyright, the problem can be dealt with by specific legislation, agency regulations, or contractual restrictions.

The prohibition on copyright protection for United States Government works is not intended to have any effect on protection of these works abroad. Works of the governments of most other countries are copyrighted. There are no valid policy reasons for denying such protection to United States Government works in foreign countries, or for precluding the Government from making licenses for the use of its works abroad.

The effect of section 105 is intended to place all works of the United States Government, published or unpublished, in the public domain. This means that the individual Government official or employee who wrote the work could not secure copyright in it or restrain its dissemination by the Government or anyone else, but it also means that, as far as the copyright law is concerned, the Government could not restrain the employee or official from disseminating the work if he or she chooses to do so. The use of the term "work of the United States Government" does not mean that a work falling within the definition of that term is the property of the U.S. Government.

Notes and Questions

1. *Copyright in government works.* What purposes might Congress have had in prohibiting copyright in federal government works? Do the reasons vary depending on the type of work it is? Do the same reasons exist for prohibiting copyright in state and local government works?

Section 105 does not address the copyrightability of state and local government works. Nonetheless, while some state and local government works can be and are copyrighted, it is generally accepted that statutes, ordinances, and state judicial opinions are in the public domain. See I P. GOLDSTEIN, COPYRIGHT PRINCIPLES, LAW AND PRACTICE, § 2.52 (1989). This uncopyrightable subcategory of state and local government works is sometimes called "official legal documents." *Id.* Do you see what distinguishes them from other government-produced works? Does the distinction explain why "official legal documents" are deemed uncopyrightable?

Assume that a state legislature enacted model code provisions drafted and promulgated by a private organization. Should the private organization retain copyright in the provisions? See Building Officials & Code Administrators v. Code Technology, Inc., 628 F.2d 730, 734, 207 U.S.P.Q. 81, 83 (1st Cir.1980). In *Building Officials*, the court rejected arguments that private authorship of laws in itself rendered the laws copyrightable. According to the court, "the public owns the law not just because it usually pays the salaries of those who draft legislation" but also because "[t]he citizens are the authors of the law, and therefore its owners, regardless of who actually drafts the provisions." "[T]he law derives its authority from the consent of the public, expressed through the democratic process."

The court also expressed concern that enforcement of copyright might undermine "the very important and practical policy that citizens must have free access to the laws which govern them. This policy is, at bottom, based on the concept of due process."

> Due process requires people to have notice of what the law requires of them so that they may obey it and avoid its sanctions. So long as the law is generally available for the public to examine, then everyone may be considered to have constructive notice of it; any failure to gain actual notice results from simple lack of diligence. But if access to the law is limited, then the people will or may be unable to learn of its requirements and may be thereby deprived of the notice to which due process entitles them. [T]he holder of a copyright has the right to refuse to publish the copyrighted material at all and may prevent anyone else from doing so, thereby preventing any public access to the material. We cannot see how this aspect of copyright protection can be squared with the right of the public to know the law to which it is subject.

Id., 628 F.2d at 734–35, 207 U.S.P.Q. at 85.

For additional discussion of these issues, see 1 M.B. NIMMER & D. NIMMER, NIMMER ON COPYRIGHT § 5.06 (1994); Nodiff, *Copyrightability of Works of the Federal and State Governments Under the 1976 Act*, 29 ST. LOUIS L.J. 91 (1982).

III. THE EXCLUSIVE RIGHTS OF COPYRIGHT AND THEIR INFRINGEMENT

A. INTRODUCTION

§ 106. Exclusive rights in copyrighted works

Subject to sections 107 through 120, the owner of copyright under this title has the exclusive rights to do and to authorize any of the following:

(1) to reproduce the copyrighted work in copies or phonorecords;

(2) to prepare derivative works based upon the copyrighted work;

(3) to distribute copies or phonorecords of the copyrighted work to the public by sale or other transfer of ownership, or by rental, lease or lending;

(4) in the case of literary, musical, dramatic, and choreographic works, pantomimes, and motion pictures and other audiovisual works, to perform the copyrighted work publicly; and

(5) in the case of literary, musical, dramatic, and choreographic works, pantomimes, and pictorial, graphic, or sculptural works, including the individual images of a motion picture or other audiovisual work, to display the copyrighted work publicly.

17 U.S.C.A. § 106.

HOUSE REPORT ON COPYRIGHT ACT OF 1976

H.R. Rep. No. 1476, 94th Cong., 2d Sess. 61 (1976).

The five fundamental rights that the bill gives to copyright owners—the exclusive rights of reproduction, adaptation, publication, performance, and display—are stated generally in section 106. These exclusive rights, which comprise the so-called "bundle of rights" that is a copyright, are cumulative and may overlap in some cases. Each of the five enumerated rights may be subdivided indefinitely and, as discussed below in connection with section 201, each subdivision of an exclusive right may be owned and enforced separately.

The approach of the bill is to set forth the copyright owner's exclusive rights in broad terms in section 106, and then to provide various limitations, qualifications, or exemptions in the * * * sections that follow. Thus, everything in section 106 is made "subject to sections 107 through [120]," and must be read in conjunction with those provisions.

The exclusive rights accorded to a copyright owner under section 106 are "to do and to authorize" any of the activities specified in the five numbered clauses. Use of the phrase "to authorize" is intended to avoid any questions as to the liability of contributory infringers. For example, a person who lawfully acquires an authorized copy of a motion picture would be an infringer if he or she engages in the business of renting it to others for purposes of unauthorized public performance.

The five exclusive rights set forth in section 106 are sometimes referred to as the copyright owner's "economic rights," since they are geared toward protecting the owner's opportunities to exploit the work economically. As discussed previously, United States copyright law traditionally recognized only economic rights. Berne Convention Article 6*bis,* however, requires its members to provide the "moral rights" of attribution and integrity to authors, as well. Moral rights protect the author's personal interests in reputation and self-expression. In 1990, Congress enacted the Visual Artists Rights Act, Pub. L. No. 101–650, 104 Stat. 5128, which amended the Copyright Act of 1976 to extend these moral rights to authors of a very limited class of works. See 17 U.S.C.A. §§ 101, 106A.

In this Section we will examine the nature and scope of each of the economic and moral rights and how it may be infringed. We will also examine some of the statutory exceptions to the exclusive rights, as set forth in sections 108 through 120 of the Copyright Act. The Copyright Act strikes a balance between the interest in immediate, unlimited public access to works and the interest in providing an incentive to create by granting property rights in authors' creations. The need for this balance informed Congress' selection and definition of the rights to be afforded to copyright owners. The exceptions set forth in sections 108 through 120 represent Congress' attempts to further "fine tune" the balance by singling out and authorizing particular types of public use of copyrighted works that promote the public's interest but do not unduly interfere with the copyright owner's incentive.

At the heart of any infringement action is the allegation that the work the defendant reproduced, adapted, or publicly distributed, performed or displayed was the "copyrighted work" as that concept is employed in section 106. The work the defendant made or used must be, or be derived or "copied" from the plaintiff's copyrighted work of authorship, and must be "substantially similar" in its expression. Thus, before examining the section 106 and 106A exclusive rights and their exceptions, we will review the methods by which the courts determine whether a defendant's work meets the "copied" and "substantially similar" criteria.

B. INFRINGEMENT OF THE COPYRIGHTED WORK

ARNSTEIN v. PORTER

United States Court of Appeals for the Second Circuit, 1946.
154 F.2d 464, 68 U.S.P.Q. 288.

[The plaintiff charged the defendant, Cole Porter, with infringing copyrights in several of his musical compositions.] Plaintiff took the deposition of defendant, and defendant, the deposition of plaintiff. Defendant then moved for an order striking out plaintiff's jury demand, and for summary judgment. Attached to defendant's motion papers were the depositions, phonograph records of piano renditions of the plaintiff's compositions and defendant's alleged infringing compositions, and the court records of five previous copyright infringement suits brought by plaintiff in the court below against other persons, in which judgments had been entered, after trials, against plaintiff. Defendant also moved for dismissal of the action on the ground of "vexatiousness."

Plaintiff alleged that defendant's "Begin the Beguine" is a plagiarism from plaintiff's "The Lord Is My Shepherd" and "A Mother's Prayer." Plaintiff testified, on deposition, that "The Lord Is My Shepherd" had been published and about 2,000 copies sold, that "A Mother's Prayer" had been published, over a million copies having been sold. In his depositions, he gave no direct evidence that defendant saw or heard these compositions. He also alleged that defendant's "My Heart Belongs to Daddy" had been plagiarized from plaintiff's "A Mother's Prayer."

Plaintiff also alleged that defendant's "I Love You" is a plagiarism from plaintiff's composition "La Priere," stating in his deposition that the latter composition had been sold. He gave no direct proof that plaintiff knew of this composition.

He also alleged that defendant's song "Night and Day" is a plagiarism of plaintiff's song "I Love You Madly," which he testified had not been published but had once been publicly performed over the radio, copies having been sent to divers radio stations but none to defendant; a copy of this song, plaintiff testified, had been stolen from his room. He also alleged that "I Love You Madly" was in part plagiarized from "La Priere." He further alleged that defendant's "You'd Be So Nice To Come Home To" is plagiarized from plaintiff's "Sadness Overwhelms My Soul." He testified that this song had never been published or publicly performed but that copies had been sent to a movie producer and to several publishers. He also alleged that defendant's "Don't Fence Me In" is a plagiarism of plaintiff's song "A Modern Messiah" which has not been published or publicly performed; in his deposition he said that about a hundred copies had been sent to divers radio stations and band leaders but that he sent no copy to defendant. Plaintiff said that defendant "had stooges right along to follow me, watch me, and live in the same apartment with me," and that plaintiff's room had been ransacked on several occasions. Asked how he knew that defendant had anything to do with any of these "burglaries," plaintiff said, "I don't know that he had to do with it, but I only know that he could have." He also said "* * * many of my compositions had been published. No one had to break in to steal them. They were sung publicly."

Defendant in his deposition categorically denied that he had ever seen or heard any of plaintiff's compositions or had had any acquaintance with any persons said to have stolen any of them.

The prayer of plaintiff's original complaint asked "at least one million dollars out of the millions the defendant has earned and is earning out of all the plagiarism." In his amended complaint the prayer is "for judgment against the defendant in the sum of $1,000,000 as damages sustained by the plagiarism of all the compositions named in the complaint." Plaintiff, not a lawyer, appeared pro se below and on this appeal.

FRANK, CIRCUIT JUDGE.

* * *

The principal question on this appeal is whether the lower court, under Rule 56, properly deprived plaintiff of a trial of his copyright infringement action. * * * [I]t is important to avoid confusing two separate elements essential to a plaintiff's case in such a suit: (a) that defendant copied from plaintiff's copyrighted work and (b) that the copying (assuming it to be proved) went so far as to constitute improper appropriation.

As to the first—copying—the evidence may consist (a) of defendant's admission that he copied or (b) of circumstantial evidence—usually evidence of access—from which the trier of the facts may reasonably infer copying. Of course, if there are no similarities, no amount of evidence of access will suffice to prove copying. If there is evidence of access and similarities exist, then the trier of the facts must determine whether the similarities are sufficient to prove copying. On this issue, analysis ("dissection") is relevant, and the testimony of experts may be received to aid the trier of the facts. If evidence of access is absent, the similarities must be so striking as to preclude the possibility that plaintiff and defendant independently arrived at the same result.

If copying is established, then only does there arise the second issue, that of illicit copying (unlawful appropriation). On that issue (as noted more in detail below) the test is the response of the ordinary lay hearer; accordingly, on that issue, "dissection" and expert testimony are irrelevant.

In some cases, the similarities between the plaintiff's and defendant's work are so extensive and striking as, without more, both to justify an inference of copying and to prove improper appropriation. But such double-purpose evidence is not required; that is, if copying is otherwise shown, proof of improper appropriation need not consist of similarities which, standing alone, would support an inference of copying.

Each of these two issues—copying and improper appropriation—is an issue of fact. If there is a trial, the conclusions on those issues of the trier of the facts—of the judge if he sat without a jury, or of the jury if there was a jury trial—bind this court on appeal, provided the evidence supports those findings, regardless of whether we would ourselves have reached the same conclusions. But a case could occur in which the similarities were so striking that we would reverse a finding of no access, despite weak evidence of access (or no evidence thereof other than the similarities); and similarly as to a finding of no illicit appropriation.

We turn first to the issue of copying. After listening to the compositions as played in the phonograph recordings submitted by defendant, we find similarities; but we hold that unquestionably, standing alone, they do not compel the conclusion, or permit the inference, that defendant copied. The similarities, however, are sufficient so that, if there is enough evidence of access to permit the case to go to the jury, the jury may properly infer that the similarities did not result from coincidence.

Summary judgment was, then, proper if indubitably defendant did not have access to plaintiff's compositions. Plainly that presents an issue of fact. On that issue, the district judge, who heard no oral testimony, had before him the depositions of plaintiff and defendant. The judge characterized plaintiff's story as "fantastic"; and, in the light of the references in his opinion to defendant's deposition, the judge obviously accepted defendant's denial of access and copying. Although part of plaintiff's testimony on deposition (as to "stooges" and the like) does seem "fantastic," yet plaintiff's credibility, even as to those improbabilities, should be left to the jury. If evidence is "of a kind that greatly taxes the credulity of the judge, he can say so, or, if he totally disbelieves it, he may announce that fact, leaving the jury free to believe it or not." * * *

But even if we were to disregard the improbable aspects of plaintiff's story, there remain parts by no means "fantastic." On the record now before us, more than a million copies of one of his compositions were sold; copies of others were sold in smaller quantities or distributed to radio stations or band leaders or publishers, or the pieces were publicly performed. If, after hearing both parties testify, the jury disbelieves defendant's denials, it can, from such facts, reasonably infer access. It follows that, as credibility is unavoidably involved, a genuine issue of material fact presents itself. With credibility a vital factor, plaintiff is entitled to a trial where the jury can observe the witnesses while testifying. Plaintiff must not be deprived of the invaluable privilege of cross-examining the defendant—the "crucial test of credibility"—in the presence of the jury. Plaintiff, or a lawyer on his behalf, on such examination may elicit damaging admissions from defendant; more important, plaintiff may persuade the jury, observing defendant's manner when testifying, that defendant is unworthy of belief.

* * *

With all that in mind, we cannot now say—as we think we must say to sustain a summary judgment—that at the close of a trial the judge could properly direct a verdict.

* * *

Assuming that adequate proof is made of copying, that is not enough; for there can be "permissible copying," copying which is not illicit. Whether (if he copied) defendant unlawfully appropriated presents, too, an issue of fact. The proper criterion on that issue is not an analytic or other comparison of the respective musical compositions as they appear on paper or in the judgment of trained musicians.[19] The plaintiff's legally protected interest is not, as such, his reputation as a musician but his interest in the potential financial returns from his compositions which derive from the lay public's approbation of his efforts. The question, therefore, is whether defendant took from plaintiff's works so much of what is pleasing to the ears of lay listeners, who comprise the audience for whom such popular music is composed, that defendant wrongfully appropriated something which belongs to the plaintiff.

Surely, then, we have an issue of fact which a jury is peculiarly fitted to determine.[22] Indeed, even if there were to be a trial before a

19. Where plaintiff relies on similarities to prove copying (as distinguished from improper appropriation) paper comparisons and the opinions of experts may aid the court.

22. It would, accordingly, be proper to exclude tone-deaf persons from the jury.

judge, it would be desirable (although not necessary) for him to summon an advisory jury on this question.

We should not be taken as saying that a plagiarism case can never arise in which absence of similarities is so patent that a summary judgment for defendant would be correct. Thus suppose that Ravel's "Bolero" or Shostakovitch's "Fifth Symphony" were alleged to infringe "When Irish Eyes Are Smiling." But this is not such a case. For, after listening to the playing of the respective compositions, we are, at this time, unable to conclude that the likenesses are so trifling that, on the issue of misappropriation, a trial judge could legitimately direct a verdict for defendant.

At the trial, plaintiff may play, or cause to be played, the pieces in such manner that they may seem to a jury to be inexcusably alike, in terms of the way in which lay listeners of such music would be likely to react. The plaintiff may call witnesses whose testimony may aid the jury in reaching its conclusion as to the responses of such audiences. Expert testimony of musicians may also be received, but it will in no way be controlling on the issue of illicit copying, and should be utilized only to assist in determining the reactions of lay auditors. The impression made on the refined ears of musical experts or their views as to the musical excellence of plaintiff's or defendant's works are utterly immaterial on the issue of misappropriation; for the views of such persons are caviar to the general—and plaintiff's and defendant's compositions are not caviar.

* * *

Clark, Circuit Judge (dissenting).

* * *

[A]fter repeated hearings of the records, I could not find therein what my brothers found. The only thing definitely mentioned seemed to be the repetitive use of the note e in certain places by both plaintiff and defendant, surely too simple and ordinary a device of composition to be significant. In our former musical plagiarism cases we have, naturally, relied on what seemed the total sound effect; but we have also analyzed the music enough to make sure of an intelligible and intellectual decision. Thus in Arnstein v. Edward B. Marks Music Corp., 2 Cir., 82 F.2d 275, 277, Judge L. Hand made quite an extended comparison of the songs, concluding, inter alia: "* * * the seven notes available do not admit of so many agreeable permutations that we need be amazed at the re-appearance of old themes, even though the identity extend through a sequence of twelve notes." See also the discussion in Marks v. Leo Feist, Inc., 2 Cir., 290 F. 959, and Darrell v. Joe Morris Music Co., 2 Cir., 113 F.2d 80, where the use of six similar bars and of an eight-note sequence frequently repeated were respectively held not to constitute infringement, and Wilkie v. Santly Bros., 2 Cir., 91 F.2d 978, affirming D.C.S.D.N.Y., 13 F.Supp. 136, certiorari denied Santly Bros. v. Wilkie, 302 U.S. 735, 58 S.Ct. 120, 82 L.Ed. 568, where use of eight bars with other similarities amounting to over three-quarters of the significant parts was held infringement.[1] It is true that in Arnstein v. Broadcast Music, Inc., 2 Cir., 137 F.2d 410, 412, we considered "dissection" or "technical analysis" not the proper approach to support a finding of plagiarism, and said that it must be "more ingenuous, more like that of a spectator, who would rely upon the complex of his impressions." But in its context that seems to me clearly sound and in accord with what I have in mind. Thus one may look to the total impression to repulse the charge of plagiarism where a minute "dissection" might dredge up some points of similarity. Hence one cannot use a purely theoretical disquisition to supply a tonal resemblance which does not otherwise exist. Certainly, however, that does not suggest or compel the converse—that one must keep his brain in torpor for fear that otherwise it would make clear differences which do exist. Music is a matter of the intellect as well as the emotions; that is why eminent musical scholars insist upon the employment of the intellectual faculties for a just appreciation of music.

Consequently I do not think we should abolish the use of the intellect here even if we could. When, however, we start with an examination of the written and printed material supplied by the plaintiff in his complaint and exhibits, we find at once that he does not and cannot claim extensive copying, measure by measure, of his compositions. He therefore has resorted to a comparative analysis—the "dissection" found unpersuasive in the earlier cases—to support his claim of plagiarism of small detached portions here and there, the musical fillers between the better known parts of the melody. And plaintiff's compositions, as pointed out in the cases cited above, are of the simple and trite character where small repetitive sequences are not hard to discover. It is as though we found Shakespeare a plagiarist on the basis of his use of articles, pronouns, prepositions, and adjectives also used by others. The surprising thing, however, is to note the small amount of even this type of reproduction which plaintiff by dint of extreme dissection has been able to find.

Though it is most instructive, it will serve no good purpose for me to restate here this showing as to each of the pieces in issue. As an example of the rest, we may take plaintiff's first cause of action. This involves his "A Modern Messiah" with defendant's "Don't Fence Me In." The first is written in 6/8 time, the second in common or 4/4 time; and there is only one place where there is a common sequence of as many as five consecutive notes, and these without the same values. Thus it goes. The usual claim seems to be rested upon a sequence of

1. * * * I find nowhere any suggestion of two steps in adjudication of this issue, one of finding copying which may be approached with musical intelligence and assistance of experts, and another that of illicit copying which must be approached with complete ignorance; nor do I see how rationally there can be any such difference, even if a jury—the now chosen instrument of musical detection—could be expected to separate those issues and the evidence accordingly. If there is actual copying, it is actionable, and there are no degrees; what we are dealing with is the claim of similarities sufficient to justify the inference of copying. This is a single deduction to be made intelligently, not two with the dominating one to be made blindly.

three, of four, or of five—never more than five—identical notes, usually of different rhythmical values. Nowhere is there anything approaching the twelve-note sequence of the Marks case, supra. * * *

In the light of these utmost claims of the plaintiff, I do not see a legal basis for the claim of plagiarism. So far as I have been able to discover, no earlier case approaches the holding that a simple and trite sequence of this type, even if copying may seem indicated, constitutes proof either of access or of plagiarism. * * *

Notes and Questions

1. *Copying.* The issue of "similarity" arises in both parts of the *Arnstein* two-step test for infringement. First, evidence of similarities between the parties' works, coupled with evidence of access, will support a finding that the defendant copied from the plaintiff. In this context, similarities in both the copyrightable and uncopyrightable aspects of the works may be relevant. The level of similarity that the plaintiff must demonstrate may vary, depending upon the strength of the evidence of access.

Once copying has been demonstrated, the "improper appropriation" step entails deciding whether the defendant has taken too much of the plaintiff's copyrightable expression. Ultimately, the issue is whether the audience for whom the works were intended "would perceive substantial similarities between the defendant's work and the plaintiff's protected expression." II P. GOLDSTEIN, COPYRIGHT PRINCIPLES, LAW AND PRACTICE, § 7.3 at 22 (1989). The term, "substantial similarity" is often used with reference to both the step one and step two "similarity" inquiries, and is sometimes used as a synonym for the overall "copying/improper appropriation" determination, as well. Do not permit the interchangeable use of the "substantial similarity" term confuse you. Note that the "similarity" inquiry in step one is not the same as in step two, and does not entail the same standard. See Latman, *"Probative Similarity" As Proof of Copying: Toward Dispelling Some Myths in Copyright Infringement*, 90 COLUM. L. REV. 1187 (1990).

The *Arnstein* court suggests that "striking" similarities between the plaintiff's and defendant's works could support a finding of copying even absent evidence of access. In such cases, copying is the only reasonable explanation for the similarities, given their nature and extent. In Selle v. Gibb, 741 F.2d 896, 901, 223 U.S.P.Q. 195, 196 (7th Cir.1984), the Court of Appeals for the Seventh Circuit took a narrower view:

> Striking similarity is just one piece of circumstantial evidence tending to show access and must not be considered in isolation; it must be considered together with other types of circumstantial evidence relating to access. * * * [T]here must be at least some other evidence which would establish a reasonable possibility that the complaining work was *available* to the alleged infringer.

Notwithstanding the Seventh Circuit's view, the Court of Appeals for the Second Circuit has adhered to its language in *Arnstein*:

> In this Circuit, the test for proof of access in cases of striking similarity is less rigorous. * * *
>
> Appellants contend that undue reliance on striking similarity to show access precludes protection for the author who independently creates a similar work. However, the jury is only permitted to infer access from striking similarity; it need not do so. Though striking similarity alone can raise an inference of copying, that inference must be reasonable in light of all the evidence. A plaintiff has not proved striking similarity sufficient to sustain a finding of copying if the evidence as a whole does not preclude any reasonable possibility of independent creation.

Gaste v. Kaiserman, 863 F.2d 1061, 1067–68, 9 U.S.P.Q.2d 1300, 1306 (2d Cir.1988).

Note that intent is irrelevant to the issue of copying. Actionable copying may be entirely innocent, or subconscious, as was the case in Bright Tunes Music Corp. v. Harrisongs Music, Ltd., 420 F.Supp. 177 (S.D.N.Y. 1976), *affirmed sub nom.* ABKCO Music, Inc. v. Harrisongs Music, Ltd., 722 F.2d 988, 221 U.S.P.Q. 490 (2d Cir.1983). In *Bright Tunes*, the court found that former Beatle George Harrison's song, "My Sweet Lord," infringed the plaintiff's "He's So Fine," which had been made popular by The Chiffons. The Chiffons' recording had been a hit in both the United States and England, so that Harrison was highly likely to have heard it. The court fully credited Harrison's testimony that he did not deliberately copy:

> What happened? I conclude that the composer, in seeking musical materials to clothe his thoughts, was working with various possibilities. As he tried this possibility and that, there came to the surface of his mind a particular combination that pleased him as being one he felt would be appealing to a prospective listener; in other words, that this combination of sounds would work. Why? Because his subconscious knew it already had worked in a song his conscious mind did not remember. * * * [I]t is clear that My Sweet Lord is the very same song as He's So Fine with different words, and Harrison had access to He's So Fine. This is, under the law, infringement of copyright, and is no less so even though subconsciously accomplished.

Id., 420 F.Supp. at 180–81.

Assuming that a plaintiff has provided sufficient evidence of access and similarity to give rise to an inference of copying, how might the defendant rebut that inference?

2. *Improper appropriation/substantial similarity.* The *Arnstein* majority advises that the second step of the infringement test, "improper appropriation," should be determined from the standpoint of the "lay listeners, who comprise the audience" for whom the work was created. This standard, sometimes called the "ordinary observer" or "audience" test, is widely accepted. In Dawson v. Hinshaw Music Inc., 905 F.2d 731, 15 U.S.P.Q.2d 1132 (4th Cir.1990), *cert. denied* 498 U.S. 981, 111 S.Ct. 511, 112 L.Ed.2d 523 (1990), the Court of Appeals for the Fourth Circuit elaborated on the standard:

> Although *Arnstein* established a sound foundation for the appeal to audience reaction, its reference to "lay listeners" may have fostered the development of a rule that has come to be stated too broadly. Under the facts before it, with a popular composition at issue, the *Arnstein* court appropriately perceived "lay listeners" and the works' "audience" to be the same. However, under *Arnstein's* sound logic, the lay listeners are relevant only because they comprise the relevant audience. Although *Arnstein* does not address the question directly, we read the case's logic to require that where the intended audience is significantly more specialized than the pool of lay listeners, the reaction of the intended audience would be the relevant inquiry. In light of the copyright law's purpose of protecting a creator's market, we think it sensible to embrace *Arnstein's* command that the ultimate comparison of the works at issue be oriented towards the works' intended audience.
>
> * * *
>
> We suspect that courts have been slow to recognize explicitly the need for refining the ordinary observer test in such a way that it would adopt the perspective of the intended audience because, in most fact scenarios, the general lay public fairly represents the works' intended audience. * * * Fortunately, the advent of computer programming infringement actions has forced courts to recognize that sometimes the non-interested or uninformed lay observer simply lacks the necessary expertise to determine similarities or differences between products. * * * [T]he judgment should be informed by people who are familiar with the media at issue.
>
> * * *
>
> Under the foregoing logic, we state the law to be as follows. When conducting the second prong of the substantial similarity inquiry, a district court must consider the nature of the intended audience of the plaintiff's work. If, as will most often be the case, the lay public fairly represents the intended audience, the court should apply the lay observer formulation of the ordinary observer test. However, if the intended audience is more narrow in that it possesses specialized expertise, relevant to the purchasing decision, that lay people would lack, the court's inquiry should focus on whether a member of the intended audience would find the two works to be substantially similar. Such an inquiry may include, and no doubt in many cases will require, admission of testimony from members of the intended audience or, possibly, from those who possess expertise with reference to the tastes and perceptions of the intended audience.

Id., 905 F.2d at 734–36, 15 U.S.P.Q.2d at 1134–36. Under similar reasoning, courts have held that infringement of works intended for children should be judged by the "impact of the respective works upon the minds and imaginations of young people." Sid & Marty Krofft Television Products, Inc. v. McDonald's Corp., 562 F.2d 1157, 1166, 196 U.S.P.Q. 97, 104 (9th Cir.1977).

What conclusion must the appropriate audience be likely to reach in order to justify a finding of infringement? Why not permit expert testimony and dissection in the course of the "improper appropriation" inquiry, as the *Arnstein* dissent would seem to advocate?

Copyright infringement can only be found upon substantial similarity of copied *expression*. Defendants are perfectly free to copy elements of a plaintiff's work that belong to the public domain. Yet the audience test seems geared to gauge the intended audience's general impression of the parties' respective works. Dissection or analysis of the works is prohibited. What assurance is there that the finder of fact will base its finding on similarity of expression, disregarding similarities in such things as ideas, *scenes a faire,* facts, preexisting material, and other uncopyrightable elements of the parties' works?

In order to avoid giving the plaintiff rights in uncopyrightable subject matter, should the fact-finder be instructed to remove the uncopyrightable elements and compare only what remains? Would such an approach adequately protect all of the plaintiff's copyrightable expression? See Apple Computer, Inc., v. Microsoft Corp., 779 F.Supp. 133, 20 U.S.P.Q.2d 1236, (N.D.Cal.1991), *affirmed*, 35 F.3d 1435, 32 U.S.P.Q.2d 1086 (9th Cir.1994). Do either the majority or the dissent in *Arnstein* take these concerns into account or provide a satisfying solution? Consider the Ninth Circuit's approach in the *Shaw* opinion, set forth below. Does it provide any guidance?

SHAW v. LINDHEIM

United States Court of Appeals for the Ninth Circuit, 1990.
919 F.2d 1353.

ALARCON, CIRCUIT JUDGE:

Lou Shaw and Eastbourne Productions, Inc. (Shaw) appeal from a grant of summary judgment in favor of Richard Lindheim, Michael Sloan, and three entertainment corporations (defendants). On appeal, Shaw argues that the district court erred in finding that, as a matter of law, there was no substantial similarity between his script entitled "The Equalizer" and defendants' pilot script for their "Equalizer" television series. Because a reasonable trier of fact could have found that the two works are substantially similar, Shaw argues, the district court erred in dismissing his copyright and Lanham Act claims on summary judgment. We reverse and remand.

STATEMENT OF THE CASE

Lou Shaw is a well-known writer and producer in the entertainment industry in Los Angeles. At one time during the 1976–1977 television season, there were eight network television programs on the air that Shaw had created, written for, or produced.[1] In February 1978, Shaw entered into an option contract with Richard Lindheim, an executive in the Dramatic Programming Division of NBC Television, that granted NBC the option to develop "The Equalizer," a pilot script created by Shaw, into a television series. Shaw delivered the script to Lindheim on

1. These series were "Quincy," "Nancy Drew," "McCloud," "Columbo," "Switch," "Maude," "Six Million Dollar Man," and "Barnaby Jones." Shaw has also been a writer for such television mainstays as "Mission: Impossible," "Ironside," "Love American Style," and "The Munsters."

July 27, 1978. Lindheim read Shaw's script. Because NBC declined to produce it, all rights in the script reverted back to Shaw.

Lindheim left NBC in 1979 and began work for Universal Television. In 1981, Lindheim wrote a television series treatment entitled "The Equalizer." Lindheim admits that he copied the title of his treatment from Shaw's script. In 1982, defendant Michael Sloan expanded Lindheim's treatment, and the revised version became the pilot script for defendants' Equalizer series, which was broadcast on CBS beginning in 1985.

On November 19, 1987, Shaw filed an action for copyright infringement and unfair competition, alleging that defendants' pilot script and series were substantially similar to the script he had submitted. On August 8, 1988, defendants moved for summary judgment. On October 28, 1988, the district court found that there was no substantial similarity between the two works as a matter of law and granted summary judgment on Shaw's copyright and Lanham Act claims. Shaw timely appeals.

Standard of Review

We review a grant of summary judgment de novo: *Narell v. Freeman*, 872 F.2d 907, 909 (9th Cir.1989). "Although summary judgment is not highly favored on questions of substantial similarity in copyright cases, summary judgment is appropriate if the court can conclude, after viewing the evidence and drawing inferences in a manner most favorable to the non-moving party, that no reasonable juror could find substantial similarity of ideas and expression." *Id.* at 909–10. * * *

Discussion

Copyright law protects an author's expression; facts and ideas within a work are not protected. To establish a successful copyright infringement claim, Shaw must show that he owns the copyright and that defendant copied protected elements of the work. Because, in most cases, direct evidence of copying is not available, a plaintiff may establish copying by showing that the infringer had access to the work and that the two works are substantially similar. The defendants conceded Shaw's ownership of the original Equalizer script and their access to the script for purposes of the summary judgment motion. As a result, the only issue before the district court on the copyright claim was whether defendants' version of the Equalizer is substantially similar to Shaw's original script.

Any test for substantial similarity is necessarily imprecise:

> "Upon any work, and especially upon a play, a great number of patterns of increasing generality will fit equally well, as more and more of the incident is left out. The last may perhaps be no more than the most general statement of what the play is about and at times might consist of only its title; but there is a point in this series of abstractions where they are no longer protected, since

> otherwise the playwright could prevent the use of his 'ideas,' to which, apart from their expression, his property is never extended."

Sid & Marty Krofft Television Prods. Inc. v. McDonald's Corp., 562 F.2d 1157, 1163 (9th Cir.1977) (quoting *Nichols v. Universal Pictures Corp.*, 45 F.2d 119, 121 (2d Cir.1930), *cert. denied*, 282 U.S. 902, 51 S.Ct. 216, 75 L.Ed. 795 (1931)). It is thus impossible to articulate a definitive demarcation that measures when the similarity between works involves copying of protected expression; decisions must inevitably be ad hoc.

A. *The Krofft Framework*

The Ninth Circuit employs a two-part test for determining whether one work is substantially similar to another. Established in *Sid & Marty Krofft Television Prods. Inc. v. McDonald's Corp.*, 562 F.2d 1157, 1164 (9th Cir.1977), the test permits a finding of infringement only if a plaintiff proves *both* substantial similarity of general ideas under the "extrinsic test" and substantial similarity of the protectible expression of those ideas under the "intrinsic test."

1. *Scope of the Krofft Tests*

Krofft defined the extrinsic test as a "test for similarity of ideas" under which "analytic dissection and expert testimony are appropriate." 562 F.2d at 1164. The intrinsic test, according to *Krofft*, should measure "substantial similarity in expressions ... depending on the response of the ordinary reasonable person.... [I]t does not depend on the type of external criteria and analysis which marks the extrinsic test." *Id.* In decisions under the intrinsic test, "analytic dissection and expert testimony are not appropriate." *Id.*

Relying on this language, panels applying *Krofft* to literary works have included a lengthy list of concrete elements under the extrinsic test. Whereas *Krofft* listed "the type of artwork involved, the materials used, the subject matter, and the setting for the subject" as criteria for consideration under the extrinsic test, *id.*, a series of opinions beginning with the district court opinion in *Jason v. Fonda*, 526 F.Supp. 774 (C.D.Cal.1981), *aff'd and incorporated by reference*, 698 F.2d 966 (9th Cir.1982), have listed "plot, themes, dialogue, mood, setting, pace, and sequence" as extrinsic test criteria. *See also Narell*, 872 F.2d at 912 (adding "characters" to the list and transforming "sequence" into "sequence of events").

Now that it includes virtually every element that may be considered concrete in a literary work, the extrinsic test as applied to books, scripts, plays, and motion pictures can no longer be seen as a test for mere similarity of ideas. Because the criteria incorporated into the extrinsic test encompass all objective manifestations of creativity, the two tests are more sensibly described as objective and subjective analyses of *expression*, having strayed from *Krofft* 's division between expression and ideas. Indeed, a judicial determination under the intrinsic test is now virtually devoid of analysis, for the intrinsic test has become a mere subjective judgment as to whether two literary works are or are not similar.

2. *The District Court's Application of Krofft*

An example of how the absence of legal analysis may frustrate appellate review of the intrinsic test is the district court's order in this matter. The district court found, after extensive analysis, that reasonable minds might conclude that plaintiffs' and defendants' works were substantially similar as to the objective characteristics of theme, plot, sequence of events, characters, dialogue, setting, mood, and pace. Nevertheless, the court made a subjective determination under the intrinsic test that no reasonable juror could determine that the works had a substantially similar total concept and feel. * * *

The district court's decision to grant summary judgment solely on a subjective assessment under *Krofft* 's intrinsic test conflicts with the prescriptions of *Krofft*. In *Krofft*, this court stated that the outcome of the extrinsic test "may often be decided as a matter of law." 562 F.2d at 1164. In contrast, "[i]f there is substantial similarity in ideas, then *the trier of fact* must decide [under the intrinsic test] whether there is substantial similarity in the expressions of the ideas so as to constitute infringement." *Id.* (emphasis added); *see also id.* at 1166 ("[T]he intrinsic test for expression is uniquely suited for determination by the *trier of fact.*" (emphasis added)). * * *

3. *Krofft and the Summary Judgment Standard*

* * *

We must determine in this matter whether a party that demonstrates a triable issue of fact under the extrinsic test has made a sufficient showing of substantial similarity to defeat a summary judgment motion. As noted above, the extrinsic test focuses on "specific similarities between the plot, theme, dialogue, mood, setting, pace, characters, and sequence of events... 'the actual concrete elements that make up the total sequence of events and the relationships between the major characters.'" *Narell*, 872 F.2d at 912 (quoting *Berkic*, 761 F.2d at 1293). These are the measurable, objective elements that constitute a literary work's expression. Because these elements are embodied in the extrinsic test, we hold that it is improper for a court to find, as the district court did, that there is no substantial similarity as a matter of law after a writer has satisfied the extrinsic test. To conclude otherwise would allow a court to base a grant of summary judgment on a purely subjective determination of similarity. This result would conflict with the Court's instruction in *Anderson*, that "at the summary judgment stage, the judge's function is not [herself] to weigh the evidence and determine the truth of the matter but to determine whether there is a genuine issue for trial." 477 U.S. at 249, 106 S.Ct. at 2510.

The rule we announce today—that satisfaction of the extrinsic test creates a triable issue of fact in a copyright action involving a literary work—is in harmony with our prior decisions. Although various panels of this circuit have affirmed grants of summary judgment on the issue of substantial similarity between books, scripts, films, or plays, none of these decisions have rested on application of the intrinsic test alone. * * *

Defendants point to *Aliotti v. R. Dakin & Co.*, 831 F.2d 898, 901–02 (9th Cir.1987), and *Data East USA, Inc. v. Epyx, Inc.*, 862 F.2d 204 (9th Cir.1988), as cases in which we have indicated that it is proper for a court to engage in a subjective assessment of substantial similarity in ruling on a motion for summary judgment. In *Aliotti*, we affirmed a grant of summary judgment based upon our conclusion that the stuffed dinosaur toys produced by the defendant were not substantially similar to the plaintiff's product under a "total concept and feel" standard. 831 F.2d at 902. Similarly, in *Data East* we concluded that "a discerning 17.5 year-old boy could not regard [two karate video games] as substantially similar." 862 F.2d at 209–10.

Both *Aliotti* and *Data East* relied on the principle that "[n]o substantial similarity of expression will be found when 'the idea and its expression are . . . inseparable,' given that 'protecting the expression in such circumstances would confer a monopoly of the *idea* upon the copyright owner.'" *Data East*, 862 F.2d at 208 (quoting *Aliotti*, 831 F.2d at 901 (quoting *Herbert Rosenthal Jewelry Corp. v. Kalpakian*, 446 F.2d 738, 742 (9th Cir.1971))) (emphasis in *Data East*). Thus, both cases should be read as involving a union of idea and expression. Where idea and expression are unified, extending copyright protection to the objective elements of expression would grant the copyright holder a monopoly over the ideas expressed in the works, in violation of 17 U.S.C. § 102(b). *See Morrissey v. Procter & Gamble Co.*, 379 F.2d 675, 678–79 (1st Cir.1967) (where the topic permits only a limited amount of expression, "the subject matter would be appropriated by permitting the copyrighting of its expression").

By creating a discrete set of standards for determining the objective similarity of literary works, the law of this circuit has implicitly recognized the distinction between situations in which idea and expression merge in representational objects and those in which the idea is distinct from the written expression of a concept by a poet, a playwright, or a writer. A high degree of similarity is "inevitable from the use of [the] jewel-encrusted bee forms" at issue in *Kalpakian*, 446 F.2d at 742, or the stuffed dinosaur forms at issue in *Aliotti*, or the karate video games in *Data East*. As a result, the scope of the copyright protection afforded such works is necessarily narrow. In contrast, there is an infinite variety of novel or creative expression available to the author of a book, script, play, or motion picture based on a preexisting idea.

Given the variety of possible expression and the objective criteria available under the extrinsic test to analyze a literary work's expression, as distinct from the ideas embodied in it, the intrinsic test cannot be the sole basis for a grant of summary judgment. Once a court has established that a triable question of objective similarity of expression exists, by analysis of each element of the extrinsic test, its inquiry should proceed no further. What remains is a subjective assessment of the "concept and feel" of two works of literature—a task no more suitable for a judge than for a jury. This subjective assessment is not a legal conclusion; rather it involves the audience in an interactive process with the author of the work in question, and calls on us "to transfer from our inward nature a human interest and a semblance of truth sufficient to procure for these shadows of imagination that willing suspension of disbelief for the moment, which constitutes poetic faith." S.T. Coleridge, *Biographia Literaria*, ch. 14, *reprinted in 5 English Literature: The Romantic Period* (A. Reed ed. 1929). This interactive assessment is by nature an individualized one that will provoke a varied response in each juror, for what "makes the unskillful laugh, cannot but make the judicious grieve." W. Shakespeare, *Hamlet*, Act III, scene ii, 11. 27–28. It is not the district court's role, in ruling on a motion for a summary judgment, to limit the interpretive judgment of each work to that produced by its own experience.

A determination that a bee fashioned by a jeweler, or a stuffed animal produced by a toymaker, embodies an idea—the form of a natural creature—that cannot be separated from its expression, primarily involves the observer's physical senses. Where idea and expression merge, a court is well-suited to make the required determination of similarity on a motion for summary judgment. A comparison of literary works, on the other hand, generally requires the reader or viewer to engage in a two-step process. The first step involves the objective comparison of concrete similarities; the second employs the subjective process of comprehension, reasoning, and understanding. The imagery presented in a literary work may also engage the imagination of the audience and evoke an emotional response. Because each of us differs, to some degree, in our capability to reason, imagine, and react emotionally, subjective comparisons of literary works that are objectively similar in their expression of ideas must be left to the trier of fact.

For these reasons, a showing of substantial similarity with reference to the eight objective components of expression in the extrinsic test applied to literary works creates a genuine issue for trial. If a district court concludes, after analyzing the objective criteria under the extrinsic test, that reasonable minds might differ as to whether there is substantial similarity between the protected expression of ideas in two literary works, and the record supports the district court's conclusion, there is a triable issue of fact that precludes summary judgment. This rule is necessary because our expansion of the extrinsic test as applied to literary works has incorporated all objective elements of expression, leaving a mere subjective assessment of similarity for the intrinsic test. Because such an assessment may not properly be made as a matter of law, it is for the trier of fact to determine whether the intrinsic test is satisfied. Accordingly, our decision in this matter turns on whether Shaw has raised a triable issue of fact under *Krofft* 's extrinsic test.

B. *The Extrinsic Test*

1. *Role of Access*

Although access was not an issue before the district court for purposes of the defendants' summary judgment motion, we must consider defendants' access to Shaw's script in determining substantial similarity. The holding in *Krofft* itself rested in part on a finding that the defendants' "degree of access justifies a lower standard of proof to show substantial similarity." 562 F.2d at 1172. As we stated in *Krofft*:

> No amount of proof of access will suffice to show copying if there are no similarities. This is not to say, however, that where clear and convincing evidence of access is presented, the quantum of proof required to show substantial similarity may not be lower than when access is shown merely by a preponderance of the evidence. * * *

Because no subsequent decision has disturbed the access rule established in *Krofft*, we believe that it is the law of this circuit. Thus, defendants' admission that they had access to Shaw's script is a factor to be considered in favor of Shaw.

2. *Effect of Identical Title on Substantial Similarity*

The fact that the two works have identical titles also weighs in Shaw's favor. In *Arnstein v. Porter*, 154 F.2d 464 (2d Cir.1946), the Second Circuit held that "[a] title cannot be copyrighted." *Id.* at 474. This is true in the sense that titles, in and of themselves, cannot claim statutory copyright. Nevertheless, "[i]f the copying of a title is not an act of copyright infringement, it may ... have copyright significance as one factor in establishing whether the substance of plaintiff's work (not the title) has been copied." 1 M. Nimmer, *Nimmer on Copyright*, § 2.16, at 2–188 (1989). * * * Thus, we acknowledge and consider defendants' admitted copying of Shaw's title in determining whether there is substantial similarity of protected expression between the two works.

3. *The Extrinsic Test Applied*

As noted earlier, a court applying the extrinsic test must compare "the individual features of the works to find specific similarities between the plot, theme, dialogue, mood, setting, pace, characters, and sequence of events." *Narell*, 872 F.2d at 912. "The test focuses not on basic plot ideas, which are not protected by copyright, but on 'the actual concrete elements that make up the total sequence of events and the relationships between the major characters.'" *Narell*, 872 F.2d at 912 (quoting *Berkic*, 761 F.2d at 1293). Our study of the two scripts at issue reveals the following objective similarities in protected expression under the extrinsic test:

a) Theme

As the district court noted, the theme of both works revolves around the character of the Equalizer—"a man who will equalize the odds, a lone man working outside the system." This, in itself, is but an unprotectible idea—the same could be said of literary characters from Aladdin to Zorro. Yet the similarity in theme extends beyond this basic idea—the Equalizer in each script solicits clients requiring assistance that conventional law enforcement cannot offer, and each lead character describes his role as to "equalize" or "shake up" the odds. Defendants point to differences in their pilot, contending that their Equalizer is motivated by his dissatisfaction with prior covert government employment and his desire to renew his relationship with his estranged wife and son. These themes, although different, are secondary and do little to erode the similarity between the central themes embodied in the titles of the two works. " 'No plagiarist can excuse the wrong by showing how much of his work he did not pirate.' " *Nimmer on Copyright* § 13.03[B][1][a], at 13–48 to 13–49 (quoting *Sheldon v. Metro-Goldwyn Pictures Corp.*, 81 F.2d 49 (2d Cir.), *cert. denied*, 298 U.S. 669, 56 S.Ct. 835, 80 L.Ed. 1392 (1936)). The similarity in themes in the two works before the court extends to elements of protectible expression.

b) Plot/Sequence of Events

Shaw provides a list of "26 strikingly similar events" that he claims appear in both works in substantially the same sequence. Examination of this list after a reading of both scripts, however, reveals that it is, for the most part, a compilation of "random similarities scattered throughout the works" that this court discounted in *Litchfield*. Shaw's list misrepresents the order and similarity of many of these events, and relies heavily on "scenes a faire"—that is, scenes that flow naturally from a basic plot premise. Indeed, defendants provide a list of similarities between "The Wizard of Oz" and "Star Wars" that is virtually as compelling as Shaw's.

Shaw's overexuberance, however, does not change the fact that many of the events in the two works are substantially similar. Both works involve a criminal organization that blackmails a candidate for public office. Both organizations attempt to kill a prospective Equalizer client, who has discovered their operation, by means of an oncoming truck. In both scripts, henchmen for the criminal organization interrupt the Equalizer's initial meeting with the client, chase and shoot at the Equalizer and the client, and are foiled as the Equalizer saves the client. In both scripts, the uninvited Equalizer appears at a party in a tuxedo. In both, the Equalizer confronts the candidate/blackmail victim after a campaign speech. After thwarting the leader of the criminal conspiracy, the Equalizer rushes to save a female client from danger. The Equalizer's actions in both scripts result in the candidate/blackmail victim's withdrawal from the political race.

Even if none of these plot elements is remarkably unusual in and of itself, the fact that both scripts contain all of these similar events gives rise to a triable question of substantial similarity of protected expression. As the district court noted, "the respective plots parallel each other.... [T]he plots in both scripts share a common sequence and rhythm."

"Where plot is ... properly defined as 'the "sequence of events" by which the author expresses his "theme" or "idea," ' it constitutes a pattern which is sufficiently concrete so as to warrant a finding of substantial similarity if it is common to both plaintiff's and defendant's works." *Nimmer on Copyright* § 1303[A], at 13–31 (quoting *Shipman v. RKO Radio Pictures, Inc.*, 100 F.2d 533, 537 (2d Cir.1938)).

c) Mood, Setting and Pace

Both works are fast-paced, have ominous and cynical moods that are lightened by the Equalizer's victory, and are set in large cities. These similarities are common to any action adventure series, however, and do not weigh heavily in our decision.

d) Characters and Dialogue

As the district court noted, both the dialogue and the characters in the respective works share some striking similarities. A particularly glaring example of similar personal traits is revealed by a comparison of the principal characters in both works. As the district court found, both scripts have "similar lead characters.... Both leads are well dressed, wealthy and have expensive tastes. The most striking similarity is their self-assuredness, and unshakable faith in the satisfactory outcome of any difficult situation." Although James Bond may have the Equalizers' demeanor and the Ghostbusters may have their penchant for unpopular assignments, the totality of the similarities between the two characters goes beyond the necessities of the "Equalizer" theme and belies any claim of literary accident. We find that defendants' copying of the Equalizer character and other characters extends to elements of protected expression. Because the similarities between the principals in each script and among the other common characters point to copying of more than a general theme or plot idea, they support the district court's finding that Shaw raised a triable issue of fact regarding substantial similarity under the extrinsic test.

4. *Conclusion*

We conclude that Shaw has satisfied the extrinsic test for literary works and thus has presented a triable issue of fact regarding substantial similarity of protected expression. "Even if a copied portion be relatively small in proportion to the entire work, if qualitatively important, the finder of fact may properly find substantial similarity." *Baxter*, 812 F.2d at 425. A reasonable trier of fact could find that the similarity between Shaw's script and defendants' pilot is not so general as to be beyond the protections of copyright law. Because Shaw has produced a triable issue of fact under the extrinsic test, we reverse the district court's grant of summary judgment on Shaw's copyright claim.

* * *

Notes and Questions

1. *The Ninth Circuit's extrinsic/intrinsic test.* Does the Ninth Circuit's test for improper appropriation differ substantively from the *Arnstein* ap-

proach? If so, how would you articulate the differences? Which approach is preferable?

As the *Shaw* opinion explains, the Ninth Circuit first stated it's extrinsic/intrinsic approach to determining infringement in Sid & Marty Krofft Television Productions, Inc. v. McDonald's Corp., 562 F.2d 1157, 196 U.S.P.Q. 97 (9th Cir.1977). As originally framed in *Krofft*, the extrinsic test was a "test for similarity of ideas," while the intrinsic test measured "substantial similarity in expressions * * * depending on the response of the ordinary reasonable person." What did division of the infringement inquiry in this fashion accomplish?

Over the years, in cases involving infringement of *literary works*, panels of the Ninth Circuit added a lengthy list of concrete elements to be considered under the extrinsic test, including plot, themes, dialogue, mood, setting, pace, characters, and sequence of events. This leads the court in *Shaw* to conclude that "the extrinsic test as applied to books, scripts, plays, and motion pictures can no longer be seen as a test for mere similarity of ideas. Because the criteria incorporated into the extrinsic test encompass all objective manifestations of creativity, the two tests are more sensibly described as objective and subjective analyses of expression, having strayed from *Krofft's* division between expression and ideas." What are the implications of this change? Has the basic purpose of the extrinsic test changed? If so, has this change in purpose affected the scope of the intrinsic test in the case of literary works, as well? If so, how?

Under the *Krofft* extrinsic/intrinsic approach, a plaintiff must satisfy both the extrinsic and the intrinsic tests in order to prevail. In *Shaw*, the court held that by satisfying the extrinsic test, the plaintiff had demonstrated a triable issue of fact. It was error for the trial court to grant summary judgement against the plaintiff based on its analysis of the intrinsic test. The court found its ruling consistent with its opinion in *Aliotti v. R. Dakin & Co.*, 831 F.2d 898, 4 U.S.P.Q.2d 1869 (9th Cir.1987).

In *Aliotti*, the allegedly infringed works were six toy stuffed dinosaurs. After seeing the plaintiff's dinosaurs, the defendant brought out its own line of stuffed dinosaurs, choosing the same six species as the plaintiff had chosen. Plaintiff's dinosaurs had exaggerated facial and other anatomical features, and large, sleepy eyes. The dinosaurs were constructed of a suede-like material and had raised, distinctive stitching. The defendant's dinosaurs had more accurate, realistic features, and reflected less personality. They were constructed from a plush material, and had hidden stitching. The district court properly found that the extrinsic test was satisfied because the parties' dinosaurs reflected similar ideas—stuffed dinosaur toys. It nonetheless granted summary judgment against the plaintiff on the ground that the plaintiff could not satisfy the intrinsic test. The Court of Appeals affirmed:

> The inquiry into similarity of expression is modified by a line of cases recognized by *Krofft* but never satisfactorily integrated into the two-part *Krofft* framework. No substantial similarity of expression will be found when "the idea and its expression are * * * inseparable," given that "protecting the expression in such circumstances would

confer a monopoly in the idea upon the copyright owner." *Herbert Rosenthal Jewelry Corp. v. Kalpakian*, 446 F.2d 738, 742 (9th Cir.1971).

Because these cases involve elements of expression, they properly may be assimilated within the analytical framework of the intrinsic test. To the extent that it is necessary to determine whether similarities result from unprotectible expression, it is appropriate under *Krofft's* intrinsic test to perform analytic dissection of similarities. Although even unprotectible material should be considered when determining if there is substantial similarity of expression, no substantial similarity may be found under the intrinsic test where analytic dissection demonstrates that all similarities in expression arise from the use of common ideas.

No copyright protection may be afforded to the idea of producing stuffed dinosaur toys or to elements of expression that necessarily follow from the idea of such dolls. Appellants therefore may place no reliance upon any similarity in expression resulting from either the physiognomy of dinosaurs or from the nature of stuffed animals. * * *

Thus, the intrinsic test is not satisfied merely because the Ding–A–Saurs and the Prehistoric Pets share similar postures and body designs. Substantial similarity of expression cannot be established by the fact that both lines of dinosaurs are gentle and cuddly, given that stuffed animals are intended for children and are usually designed to be soft and nonthreatening. Although the eye style and stitching of the Ding–A–Saurs are not dictated by the idea of stuffed dinosaur dolls and thus constitute protectible expression, Dakin's Prehistoric Pets do not incorporate these elements of expression.

Under the intrinsic test, we may find substantial similarity of expression only if a reasonable observer would infer that [defendant's] dolls capture the "total concept and feel" of [plaintiff's] designs. Because children are the intended market for the dolls, we must filter the intrinsic inquiry through the perception of children. Upon *de novo* review, we find that summary judgment was appropriate because there exists no substantial similarity of protectible expression.

Aliotti, 831 F.2d at 901–902, 4 U.S.P.Q.2d at 1871–72.

How does the court in *Shaw* reconcile its ruling with *Aliotti*? Do you find its reasoning convincing?

How should the Ninth Circuit apply its extrinsic/intrinsic test to computer programs? See Brown Bag Software v. Symantec Corp., 960 F.2d 1465, 22 U.S.P.Q.2d 1429 (9th Cir.1992), *cert. denied* ___ U.S. ___, 113 S.Ct. 198, 121 L.Ed.2d 141 (1992). Is a two-part test, patterned either after *Arnstein* or *Krofft*, appropriate for assessing infringement of computer programs? Some courts have expressed a preference for a single inquiry about substantial similarity, in which expert testimony is admissible, in copyright litigation involving computer programs. See, e.g., Whelan Associates v. Jaslow Dental Laboratory, 797 F.2d 1222, 1232–33, 230 U.S.P.Q. 481, 488 (3d Cir.1986), *cert. denied* 479 U.S. 1031, 107 S.Ct. 877, 93 L.Ed.2d 831 (1987).

2. *Literal vs. non-literal similarity.* In *Shaw*, the plaintiff alleged "non-literal" similarity. That is, apart from the title, the defendant did not take the actual language that the plaintiff employed in his script. Rather, the defendant took non-literal elements of expression—the plaintiff's particular selection and arrangement of plot devices, characters, etc. Copyright infringement liability may be based either on literal or non-literal similarity, or on a combination of both.

Suppose that the defendant had engaged only in literally copying or closely paraphrasing fragments of the plaintiff's script. How much must he have taken in order to infringe? In determining substantial similarity, courts examine both the quantity of literal expression taken and the quality, or importance, of the copied portion. Thus, for example, in Harper & Row Publishers, Inc. v. Nation Enterprises, 471 U.S. 539, 105 S.Ct. 2218, 85 L.Ed.2d 588, 225 U.S.P.Q. 1073 (1985), the defendant was held liable for the verbatim copying of 300–400 words from President Ford's 200,000–word memoirs. The court noted that the 300–400 words that the defendant took were essentially "the heart of the book," because they constituted President Ford's explanation of why he pardoned President Nixon. See also Roy Export Co. Establishment v. Columbia Broadcasting System, Inc., 503 F.Supp. 1137, 208 U.S.P.Q. 580 (S.D.N.Y.1980), *affirmed* 672 F.2d 1095, 215 U.S.P.Q. 289 (2d.Cir.1982), *cert. denied* 459 U.S. 826, 103 S.Ct. 60, 74 L.Ed.2d 63 (1982) (taking 55 seconds out of a one-hour and 29–minute film may be sufficient to infringe).

What, if any, relevance should be assigned to the dissimilarities between the party's works? See generally 3 M.B. NIMMER & D. NIMMER, NIMMER ON COPYRIGHT § 13.03[A] & [B] (1994).

C. SECTION 106(1): THE RIGHT TO REPRODUCE THE COPYRIGHTED WORK IN COPIES OR PHONORECORDS

HOUSE REPORT ON COPYRIGHT ACT OF 1976

H.R. Rep. No. 1476, 94th Cong., 2d Sess. 61–62 (1976).

Read together with the relevant definitions in section 101, the right "to reproduce the copyrighted work in copies or phonorecords" means the right to produce a material object in which the work is duplicated, transcribed, imitated, or simulated in a fixed form from which it can be "perceived, reproduced, or otherwise communicated, either directly or with the aid of a machine or device." As under the present law, a copyrighted work would be infringed by reproducing it in whole or in any substantial part, and by duplicating it exactly or by imitation or simulation. Wide departures or variations from the copyrighted works would still be an infringement as long as the author's "expression" rather than merely the author's "ideas" are taken. An exception to this general principle, applicable to the reproduction of copyrighted sound recordings, is specified in section 114.

"Reproduction" under clause (1) of section 106 is to be distinguished from "display" under clause (5). For a work to be "reproduced," its fixation in tangible form must be "sufficiently permanent or stable to permit it to be perceived, reproduced, or otherwise communicated for a period of more than transitory duration." Thus, the showing of images on a screen or tube would not be a violation of clause (1), although it might come within the scope of clause (5).

Notes and Questions

1. *The exclusive right to reproduce the work.* The reproduction right is the most fundamental of the economic rights, and is applicable to all categories of copyrightable subject matter. It is important, however, to note the "material object" limitation: copying that produces no material copy or phonorecord, such as unauthorized performance of a work, does not infringe the section 106(1) reproduction right, though it may infringe one of the other exclusive rights.

Each of the section 106 rights is independent. Thus, a defendant may violate the right of reproduction even though he never sells or otherwise transfers the unauthorized copy he makes, and never makes the copy available to the public through display or performance. Likewise, a single act may violate more than one of the section 106 rights. For example, in the *Shaw* case, the defendant might be found to have violated both the right of reproduction and the right of adaptation, § 106(2), if the portions he took from the plaintiff's script were sufficient to render the works substantially similar. After all, he not only reproduced the plaintiff's expression but also combined it with his own to form a new version.

2. *The reproduction right in sound recordings.* Congress only recognized sound recordings as copyrightable subject matter in the early 1970s, and when it did, it extended a narrower range of rights than it had extended to owners of copyright in other categories of subject matter. Review Copyright Act section 114 carefully. Based on your reading thus far, how would you compare the scope of the right to reproduce sound recordings to the scope of the right to reproduce other types of copyrighted subject matter? What explains or justifies such differential treatment?

Under the terms of section 114, will the mechanical recapture of sounds from a copyrighted sound recording, in itself, constitute infringement of the right of reproduction, or must the plaintiff also demonstrate substantial similarity pursuant to the audience test? In United States v. Taxe, 540 F.2d 961, 192 U.S.P.Q. 204 (9th Cir.1976), *cert. denied* 429 U.S. 1040, 97 S.Ct.737, 50 L.Ed.2d 751 (1977), the defendants faced criminal copyright infringement charges pursuant to the predecessor of section 114, the Sound Recording Amendment of 1971, Pub. L. No. 92–140, 85 Stat. 391. The defendants had mechanically reproduced copyrighted sound recordings in their entirety, but had altered them by changing the speed, deleting certain frequencies or tones, and introducing reverberations, echoes, and additional synthesized sounds, then sold them to the public. In its jury instructions, the district court had suggested that the prosecutor must prove that the defendants had recaptured sounds from the copyrighted recordings, but that he need not prove substantial similarity. The Court of Appeals for the Ninth Circuit disapproved the instruction: "We believe the instruction went beyond the law insofar as it purported to characterize any and all re-recordings as infringements." *Id.*, 540 F.2d at 965, 192 U.S.P.Q. at 206.

Do modern digital sampling techniques, now used extensively in the recording industry, infringe sampled sound recordings? See Grand Upright Music Ltd. v. Warner Brothers Records, Inc., 780 F.Supp. 182, 22 U.S.P.Q.2d 1556 (S.D.N.Y.1991) (Rap artist Biz Markie held liable for using digital sample of ten seconds of music from Ramond "Gilbert" O'Sullivan's "Alone Again (Naturally)," repeating the sample in the background throughout his own recording).

3. *Home audiotaping.* Music and sound recording copyright owners have long been concerned that home audiotaping for private enjoyment will displace retail sales of sound recordings. The advent of digital audiotape, which permits serial copying without loss of sound quality, greatly increased their concerns. In an attempt to prevent losses, the copyright owners argued that makers and distributors of digital tape recording equipment would be liable for contributory copyright infringement if they placed their goods on the market, for by selling the equipment, these businesses would assist home tapers' inevitable direct infringement of copyrighted musical works and sound recordings.

After extensive negotiations, copyright owners and the makers and distributors of the new digital audiotaping technology reached a compromise, which Congress ultimately enacted as the Audio Home Recording Act of 1992, Pub. L. No. 102–563, 106 Stat. 4237. The Act has three main aspects. First, it prohibits contributory infringement claims against manufacturers, importers and distributors of digital *and* analog recording devices and tapes, and prohibits direct infringement claims against consumers of these devices who use them to make "noncommercial" digital or analog musical recordings. 17 U.S.C.A. § 1008. Second, persons manufacturing or importing and distributing digital audio tape recorders and blank tapes must pay royalties, one-third of which will be distributed to composers and publishers of music, the remainder to be distributed to sound recording producers and performers. 17 U.S.C.A. § 1004–1007. Finally, manufacturers, importers and distributors of digital audiotaping machines must include "serial copy management systems" on all their machines, to prevent the machines from recording copies from copies. 17 U.S.C.A. § 1002.

For an analysis of the Audio Home Recording Act, see McKuin, *Home Audio Taping of Copyrighted Works and the Audio Home Recording Act of 1992: A Critical Analysis*, 16 HASTINGS COMM. & ENT. L.J. 311 (1994).

4. *Exceptions to the right to reproduce computer programs.* Review the provisions of Copyright Act section 117. In enacting the present section 117, Congress adopted almost verbatim the statutory language recommended in the CONTU Final Report. FINAL REPORT OF THE COMMISSION ON NEW TECHNOLOGICAL USES OF COPYRIGHTED WORKS 12 (1979). Thus, the Final Report is frequently consulted in the course of construing section 117. The Final Report justified the provision as follows:

> Because the placement of a work into a computer is the preparation of a copy, the law should provide that persons in rightful possession of copies of programs be able to use them freely without fear of exposure to copyright liability. Obviously, creators, lessors, licensors, and vendors

> of copies of programs intend that they be used by their customers, so that rightful users would but rarely need a legal shield against potential copyright problems. It is easy to imagine, however, a situation in which the copyright owner might desire, for good reason or none at all, to force a lawful owner or possessor of a copy to stop using a particular program. One who rightfully possesses a copy of a program, therefore, should be provided with a legal right to copy it to that extent which will permit its use by that possessor. This would include the right to load it into a computer and to prepare archival copies of it to guard against destruction or damage by mechanical or electrical failure. But this permission would not extend to other copies of the program. Thus, one could not, for example, make archival copies of a program and later sell some while retaining some for use. * * *

Id. at 13.

Courts have encountered several important issues in construing and applying section 117. For example, how strictly should courts construe the exemption's limitation to copying "as an essential step" in the use of the program in conjunction with a machine? Taken to extremes, the "essential step" language could be construed to limit the section 117 exemption to the loading of the program into random access memory, through use of the floppy disk on which it was sold. Loading the program into a computer's hard disk drive would not be exempted, since this more permanent type of copy arguably is not "essential" to the use of the program in a computer. See Kreiss, *Section 117 of the Copyright Act*, [1991] B.Y.U. L. REV. 1496, 1424–26. One court has construed the "essential step" language to exclude a computer manufacturer's practice of copying programs from disks it purchased onto semiconductor chips, which it inserted into its computers. According to the court, "essential" means "indispensable and necessary," not merely "convenient." The court reasoned that the "essential step" requirement limits the section 117 exemption to copies that are "no more permanent than is reasonably necessary." Apple Computer, Inc. v. Formula International, Inc., 594 F.Supp. 617, 224 U.S.P.Q. 560 (C.D.Cal.1984).

Compare Vault Corp. v. Quaid Software Ltd., 847 F.2d 255, 7 U.S.P.Q.2d 1281 (5th Cir.1988). In that case, the plaintiff produced and sold disks containing an anticopying program to prevent users from duplicating other programs on the disk in a useable form. The defendant produced and sold a program designed to "unlock" the plaintiff's anticopying program. In the course of creating its "unlocking" program, the defendant inserted plaintiff's anticopying program into its computer memory in order to study it. The Fifth Circuit found that this reproduction was permitted under section 117 as an essential step in using the program. The court rejected plaintiff's argument that section 117 only permitted loading a program into a computer for the purpose *its creator* intended, in this case preventing the copying of other programs on the disk. *Id.* at 261.

Note that section 117 exempts the "owner of a computer program" from liability, rather than the "rightful possessor," as recommended by the CONTU Final Report. What are the implications of this change in language?

5. *Other exceptions to the reproduction right.* Sections 108 through 120 of the Copyright Act contain a number of additional exceptions to the exclusive right of reproduction. Some, like sections 114 and 117, specifically address a particular category of copyrightable subject matter. Section 113, for example, sets forth exceptions to the pictorial, graphic, and sculptural works category. Among other things, it permits owners of useful articles embodying pictorial, graphic and sculptural works to make, distribute and display drawings and photographs of the useful articles to advertise their sale. Section 120 relates specifically to architectural works. Among other things, it permits the making, distributing and public display of photographs and other pictorial representations of protected buildings located in public places. Congress concluded that such "reproductions" serve an "important public purpose" and "do not interfere with the normal exploitation of architectural works." H.R. REP. NO. 735, 101st Cong., 2d Sess. 22 (1990).

Other exceptions focus on the particular use being made of a protected work, or the identity of the user. For example, section 108 permits libraries and archives to reproduce and distribute protected works for their own non-commercial purposes or for their patrons, as long as specific guidelines are followed. Section 112 gives broadcasters who are otherwise entitled to transmit performances or displays of copyrighted works limited rights to record their transmissions.

6. *Compulsory licenses.* Unlike other United States intellectual property doctrines, the Copyright Act expressly provides for compulsory licenses in several situations. For example, section 115 provides a compulsory license to produce and distribute sound recordings of non-dramatic musical works. This license is sometimes called the "mechanical license." Once the owner of copyright in a nondramatic musical work has authorized the making and public distribution of a sound recording of the work, others may freely make and distribute their own independent sound recordings of the work, as long as they follow the procedure set out in the statute and pay the prescribed royalty fee to the copyright owner.

Why did Congress deem it necessary to create a compulsory license to make sound recordings of musical works? The Court of Appeals for the District of Columbia has explained:

> The phonorecord compulsory licensing system dates back to 1909, when Congress first extended a composer's copyright protection to include the right to control manufacture of "parts of instruments serving to reproduce mechanically the musical work." * * * Industry representatives expressed a fear that this protection ran the risk of "establishing a great music monopoly" because the Aeolian Company, a manufacturer of player piano rolls, was acquiring exclusive contract rights from composers and publishers. * * * The music industry has undergone major transformations in the intervening years, but record producers have continued to argue that a danger of monopolization and discriminatory practices exists, and Congress has concluded that a compulsory licensing system is still warranted.
>
> Although the availability of the compulsory license under the 1909 Act has been very important to the structure of the recording industry, the statutory procedures for invoking the license have rarely been used.

> * * * The usual effect of the system is to make the statutory royalty rate a ceiling on the price copyright owners can charge for use of their songs under negotiated contracts: if the owner demands a higher price in voluntary negotiations, the manufacturer can turn to the statutory scheme, but if the owner is willing to accept less than the statutory rate, he is free to do so. * * * Today, the vast majority of contracts for use of copyrighted musical works involve voluntary payment at precisely the statutory rate. * * *

Record Industry Association of America v. Copyright Royalty Tribunal, 662 F.2d 1, 3–4, 212 U.S.P.Q. 69, 72 (D.C.Cir.1981).

Are compulsory licenses justified? Are there disadvantages to having them? Other United States intellectual property doctrines, including the Patent Act, do not expressly provide for compulsory licenses. Is there something about the subject matter of copyright that makes compulsory licenses more necessary or desirable than, for example, the subject matter of patents or trademarks?

D. SECTION 106(2): THE EXCLUSIVE RIGHT TO PREPARE DERIVATIVE WORKS BASED UPON THE COPYRIGHTED WORK

HOUSE REPORT ON COPYRIGHT ACT OF 1976

H.R. Rep. No. 1476, 94th Cong., 2d Sess. 62 (1976).

The exclusive right to prepare derivative works, specified separately in clause (2) of section 106, overlaps the exclusive right of reproduction to some extent. It is broader than that right, however, in the sense that reproduction requires fixation in copies or phonorecords, whereas the preparation of a derivative work, such as a ballet, pantomime, or improvised performance, may be an infringement even though nothing is ever fixed in tangible form.

To be an infringement the "derivative work" must be "based upon the copyrighted work," and the definition in section 101 refers to "a translation, musical arrangement, dramatization, fictionalization, motion picture version, sound recording, art reproduction, abridgment, condensation, or any other form in which a work may be recast, transformed, or adapted." Thus, to constitute a violation of section 106(2), the infringing work must incorporate a portion of the copyrighted work in some form; for example, a detailed commentary on a work or a programmatic musical composition inspired by a novel would not normally constitute infringements under this clause.

MIRAGE EDITIONS, INC. v. ALBUQUERQUE A.R.T. CO.

United States Court of Appeals for the Ninth Circuit, 1988.
856 F.2d 1341, 8 U.S.P.Q.2d 1171, *cert. denied*
489 U.S. 1018, 109 S.Ct. 1135, 103 L.Ed.2d 196 (1989).

BRUNETTI, CIRCUIT JUDGE:

[Plaintiffs/Appellees Dumas and Mirage own copyrights to Nagel art works. They licensed Van Der Marck Editions, Inc. to publish a commemorative book entitled *NAGEL: The Art of Patrick Nagel,* which includes prints of some of Nagel's works. Defendant/Appellant's primary business is 1) purchasing artwork prints or books including good quality artwork page prints therein; 2) gluing each individual print or page print onto a rectangular sheet of black plastic material exposing a narrow black margin around the print; 3) gluing the black sheet with print onto a major surface of a rectangular white ceramic tile; 4) applying a transparent plastic film over the print, black sheet and ceramic tile surface; and 5) offering the tile with artwork mounted thereon for sale in the retail market. Defendant acquired the Nagel book and performed this process with some of the prints. The plaintiffs sued, alleging copyright infringement, and the district court granted summary judgement in their favor.]

Appellant contends that there has been no copyright infringement because its tiles are not derivative works * * *.

The Copyright Act of 1976, 17 U.S.C. § 101 defines a derivative work as:

> [A] work based upon one or more preexisting works such as a translation, musical arrangement, dramatization, fictionalization, motion picture version, sound recording, art reproduction, abridgment, condensation or *any other form in which a work may be recast, transformed, or adapted.* * * * (emphasis added).
>
> * * *

What appellant has clearly done here is to make another version of Nagel's art works, and that amounts to preparation of a derivative work. By borrowing and mounting the preexisting, copyrighted individual art images without the consent of the copyright proprietors—Mirage and Dumas as to the art works and Van Der Marck as to the book—appellant has prepared a derivative work and infringed the subject copyrights.

Appellant's contention that * * * it has not engaged in "art reproduction" and therefore its tiles are not derivative works is not fully dispositive of this issue. Appellant has ignored the disjunctive phrase "or any other form in which a work may be recast, transformed or adapted." The legislative history of the Copyright Act of 1976 indicates that Congress intended that for a violation of the right to prepare derivative works to occur "the infringing work must incorporate a portion of the copyrighted work in *some form*." 1976 U.S.Code Cong. & Admin.News 5659, 5675. (emphasis added). The language "recast, transformed or adapted" seems to encompass other alternatives besides simple art reproduction. By removing the individual images from the book and placing them on the tiles, perhaps the appellant has not accomplished reproduction. We conclude, though, that appellant has certainly recast or transformed the individual images by incorporating them into its tile-preparing process.

* * *

LEWIS GALOOB TOYS, INC. v. NINTENDO OF AMERICA, INC.

United States Court of Appeals for the Ninth Circuit, 1992.
964 F.2d 965, 22 U.S.P.Q.2d 1857, *cert. denied*
___ U.S. ___, 113 S.Ct. 1582, 123 L.Ed.2d 149 (1993).

FARRIS, CIRCUIT JUDGE:

[Nintendo appeals the district court's decision that Lewis Galoob Toys' Game Genie does not violate any of Nintendo's copyrights.]

The Nintendo Entertainment System is a home video game system marketed by Nintendo. To use the system, the player inserts a cartridge containing a video game that Nintendo produces or licenses others to produce. By pressing buttons and manipulating a control pad, the player controls one of the game's characters and progresses through the game. The games are protected as audiovisual works under 17 U.S.C. § 102(a)(6).

The Game Genie is a device manufactured by Galoob that allows the player to alter up to three features of a Nintendo game. For example, the Game Genie can increase the number of lives of the player's character, increase the speed at which the character moves, and allow the character to float above obstacles. The player controls the changes made by the Game Genie by entering codes provided by the Game Genie Programming Manual and Code Book. The player also can experiment with variations of these codes.

The Game Genie functions by blocking the value for a single data byte sent by the game cartridge to the central processing unit in the Nintendo Entertainment System and replacing it with a new value. If that value controls the character's strength, for example, then the character can be made invincible by increasing the value sufficiently. The Game Genie is inserted between a game cartridge and the Nintendo Entertainment System. The Game Genie does not alter the data that is stored in the game cartridge. Its effects are temporary.

DISCUSSION

The Copyright Act of 1976 confers upon copyright holders the exclusive right to prepare and authorize others to prepare derivative works based on their copyrighted works. *See* 17 U.S.C. § 106(2). Nintendo argues that the district court erred in concluding that the audiovisual displays created by the Game Genie are not derivative works. * * *

A derivative work must incorporate a protected work in some concrete or permanent "form." The Copyright Act defines a derivative work as follows:

> A "derivative work" is a work based upon one or more preexisting works, such as a translation, musical arrangement, dramatization, fictionalization, motion picture version, sound recording, art reproduction, abridgment, condensation, *or any other form in which a work may be recast, transformed, or adapted.* A work consisting of editorial revisions, annotations, elaborations, or other modifications which, as a whole, represent an original work of authorship, is a "derivative work."

17 U.S.C. § 101 (emphasis added). The examples of derivative works provided by the Act all physically incorporate the underlying work or works. The Act's legislative history similarly indicates that "the infringing work must incorporate a portion of the copyrighted work in some form." 1976 U.S.Code Cong. & Admin.News 5659, 5675.

Our analysis is not controlled by the Copyright Act's definition of "fixed." The Act defines copies as "material objects, other than phonorecords, in which a work is *fixed* by any method." 17 U.S.C. § 101 (emphasis added). The Act's definition of "derivative work," in contrast, lacks any such reference to fixation. Further, we have held in a copyright infringement action that "[i]t makes no difference that the derivation may not satisfy certain requirements for statutory copyright registration itself." *Lone Ranger Television v. Program Radio Corp.*, 740 F.2d 718, 722 (9th Cir.1984). A derivative work must be fixed to be *protected* under the Act, see 17 U.S.C. § 102(a), but not to *infringe.* * * *

The district court's finding that no independent work is created is supported by the record. The Game Genie merely enhances the audiovisual displays (or underlying data bytes) that originate in Nintendo game cartridges. The altered displays do not incorporate a portion of a copyrighted work in some concrete or permanent *form.* Nintendo argues that the Game Genie's displays are as fixed in the hardware and software used to create them as Nintendo's original displays. Nintendo's argument ignores the fact that the Game Genie cannot produce an audiovisual display; the underlying display must be produced by a Nintendo Entertainment System and game cartridge. Even if we were to rely on the Copyright Act's definition of "fixed," we would similarly conclude that the resulting display is not "embodied," *see* 17 U.S.C. § 101, in the Game Genie. It cannot be a derivative work.

Mirage Editions is illustrative. Albuquerque A.R.T. transferred artworks from a commemorative book to individual ceramic tiles. We held that "[b]y borrowing and mounting the preexisting, copyrighted individual art images without the consent of the copyright proprietors

... [Albuquerque A.R.T.] has prepared a derivative work and infringed the subject copyrights." The ceramic tiles *physically* incorporated the copyrighted works in a form that could be sold. Perhaps more importantly, sales of the tiles supplanted purchasers' demand for the underlying works. Our holding in *Mirage Editions* would have been much different if Albuquerque A.R.T. had distributed lenses that merely enabled users to view several artworks simultaneously.

Nintendo asserted at oral argument that the existence of a $150 million market for the Game Genie indicates that its audiovisual display must be fixed. We understand Nintendo's argument; consumers clearly would not purchase the Game Genie if its display was not "sufficiently permanent or stable to permit it to be perceived ... for a period of more than transitory duration." 17 U.S.C. § 101. But, Nintendo's reliance on the Act's definition of "fixed" is misplaced. Nintendo's argument also proves too much; the existence of a market does not, and cannot, determine conclusively whether a work is an infringing derivative work. For example, although there is a market for kaleidoscopes, it does not necessarily follow that kaleidoscopes create unlawful derivative works when pointed at protected artwork. The same can be said of countless other products that enhance, but do not replace, copyrighted works.

Nintendo also argues that our analysis should focus exclusively on the audiovisual displays created by the Game Genie, *i.e.*, that we should compare the altered displays to Nintendo's original displays. Nintendo emphasizes that " '[a]udiovisual works' are works that consist of a series of related images ... *regardless of the nature of the material objects ... in which the works are embodied*." 17 U.S.C. § 101 (emphasis added). The Copyright Act's definition of "audiovisual works" is inapposite; the *only* question before us is whether the audiovisual displays created by the Game Genie are "derivative works." The Act does not similarly provide that a work can be a derivative work regardless of the nature of the material objects in which the work is embodied. A derivative work must incorporate a protected work in some concrete or permanent form. We cannot ignore the actual source of the Game Genie's display.

Nintendo relies heavily on *Midway Mfg. Co. v. Arctic Int'l, Inc.*, 704 F.2d 1009 (7th Cir.), *cert. denied*, 464 U.S. 823, 104 S.Ct. 90, 78 L.Ed.2d 98 (1983). *Midway* can be distinguished. The defendant in *Midway*, Arctic International, marketed a computer chip that could be inserted in Galaxian video games to speed up the rate of play. The Seventh Circuit held that the speeded-up version of Galaxian was a derivative work. Arctic's chip substantially copied and *replaced* the chip that was originally distributed by Midway. Purchasers of Arctic's chip also benefited economically by offering the altered game for use by the general public. The Game Genie does not physically incorporate a portion of a copyrighted work, nor does it supplant demand for a component of that work. The court in *Midway* acknowledged that the Copyright Act's definition of "derivative work" "must be stretched to accommodate speeded-up video games." *Id.* at 1014. Stretching that definition further would chill innovation and fail to protect "society's competing interest in the free flow of ideas, information, and commerce." *Sony Corp. of America v. Universal Studios, Inc.*, 464 U.S. 417, 429, 104 S.Ct. 774, 782, 78 L.Ed.2d 574 (1984).

In holding that the audiovisual displays created by the Game Genie are not derivative works, we recognize that technology often advances by improvement rather than replacement. Some time ago, for example, computer companies began marketing spell-checkers that operate within existing word processors by signalling the writer when a word is misspelled. These applications, as well as countless others, could not be produced and marketed if courts were to conclude that the word processor and spell-checker combination is a derivative work based on the word processor alone. The Game Genie is useless by itself, it can only enhance, and cannot duplicate or recast, a Nintendo game's output. It does not contain or produce a Nintendo game's output in some concrete or permanent form, nor does it supplant demand for Nintendo game cartridges. Such innovations rarely will constitute infringing derivative works under the Copyright Act.

* * *

Notes and Questions

1. *The adaptation right.* The right to make derivative works is often called the right to adapt the copyrighted work. In most cases, the same acts that constitute an unauthorized adaptation will also infringe the exclusive right to reproduce the work. A defendant who, without authorization, makes a motion picture based on a novel, creates three-dimensional dolls based on popular two-dimensional cartoon characters, or translates a biography from English to French clearly is making a derivative work. But she is also reproducing the original work in copies. Regardless of which of these two rights a plaintiff alleges to be infringed, the plaintiff must prove that the defendant's work was copied from his own copyrighted work and is substantially similar to it in expression. See, e.g., Horgan v. Macmillan, Inc., 789 F.2d 157, 229 U.S.P.Q. 684 (2d Cir.1986).

Thus, the adaptation right generally is duplicative and cumulative. Only when the defendant's adaptation fails to create a tangible copy of the copyrighted work will the plaintiff be unable to rely on the reproduction right.[7] This might occur when the defendant physically alters an existing, authorized copy of the original work, as in *Mirage*. As the House Report suggests, it might also occur if the defendant created a performance which borrowed from the plaintiff's copyrighted work. The dancing of an improvised ballet based on a copyrighted work of choreography presumably would constitute the making of a derivative work, but unless the defendant fixed the improvised dance in tangible form—for example, by notation or filming—it would not infringe the right of reproduction. Of course, if the dance occurred in a public place or was performed for the public, it would also infringe the plaintiff's exclusive right of public performance.

7. Of course, a plaintiff may allege infringement of the adaptation right when it has licensed the defendant to reproduce the work, but not to alter it.

If you had represented the defendant in *Mirage*, what arguments would you have made to convince the court that your client's actions fell short of an infringing adaptation?

In the *Galoob* case, Nintendo alleged that consumers, who used the Game Genie with Nintendo games, directly infringed its adaptation rights in the games. In naming Galoob Toys as its defendant, Nintendo relied on a contributory infringement theory. We will examine the contributory infringement cause of action later.

If Nintendo had authorized Galoob Toys' actions, could either consumers or Galoob have obtained a derivative work copyright? Should it matter? Is the Court's opinion in *Galoob* consistent with Congress' intent, as evidenced in the House Report excerpt quoted at the beginning of this Subsection? What would the implications be in finding that the right of adaptation was infringed in *Galoob*?

For an interesting discussion of the issues raised in *Mirage* and *Galoob*, see Stern, *Framing Prints, Giving the Mona Lisa a Moustache, Speeding Up Video Games, and Marketing Add-on Software: A Comment on the* Mirage *Case*, 37 PAT. TRADEMARK & COPYRIGHT J. (BNA) 305 (1989).

2. *Exceptions to the exclusive right to adapt computer programs.* To what extent does the *Galoob* opinion permit companies to market add-on or enhancement programs that modify or improve the performance of others' successful programs? See Stern, *supra*, at 310–13. If the legality of their acts is uncertain, is section 117 likely to provide any additional shelter? Section 117 provides that the owner of a copy of a computer program may make or authorize an adaptation of the program if the "adaptation is created as an essential step in the utilization of the computer program in conjunction with a machine and * * * is used in no other manner." With regard to this language, the CONTU Report stated:

> Because of a lack of complete standardization among programming languages and hardware in the computer industry, one who rightfully acquires a copy of a program frequently cannot use it without adapting it to that limited extent which will allow its use in the possessor's computer. The copyright law, which grants to copyright proprietors the exclusive right to prepare translations, transformations, and adaptations of their work, should no more prevent such use than it should prevent rightful possessors from loading programs into their computers. Thus, a right to make those changes necessary to enable the use for which it was both sold and purchased should be provided. The conversion of a program from one higher-level language to another to facilitate use would fall within this right, as would the right to add features to the program that were not present at the time of rightful acquisition. These rights would necessarily be more private in nature than the right to load a program by copying it and could only be exercised so long as they did not harm the interests of the copyright proprietor. * * * The adaptor could not vend the adapted program, under the proposed revision of the new law, nor could it be sold as the original without the author's permission. * * *

FINAL REPORT OF THE COMMISSION ON NEW TECHNOLOGICAL USES OF COPYRIGHTED WORKS 13 (1979). In Foresight Resources

Corp. v. Pfortmiller, 719 F.Supp. 1006, 13 U.S.P.Q.2d 1721 (D.Kan.1989), the defendant altered a copy of the plaintiff's copyrighted program, at the request of the copy's lawful owner, by adding five files of his own creation. The owner used the enhanced program in its own business, and made no attempt to market it to others. In denying the plaintiff's motion for a preliminary injunction, the court reasoned that construing section 117 to shelter the defendant from liability would serve two important goals:

> On the one hand, allowing sophisticated software users to enhance copies of copyrighted programs they have purchased eliminates the need to choose between either buying the latest version of a program or possibly infringing the program's owner's copyright. At the same time, allowing such enhancements to be used only in-house preserves the market for improvements made by the copyright holder.

Id., 719 F.Supp. at 1010, 13 U.S.P.Q.2d at 1723–1724. For further discussion of the scope of the section 117 exemption, see Conley & Brown, *Revisiting § 117 of the Copyright Act: An Economic Approach*, 7 COMPUTER LAW. 1 (Nov. 1990). As a matter of policy, should program owners be entitled to prevent sales of unauthorized program enhancements?

3. *Exceptions to the right to adapt architectural works.* An exception to the right to adapt architectural works can be found in section 120(b):

> Notwithstanding the provisions of section 106(2), the owners of a building embodying an architectural work may, without the consent of the author or copyright owner of the architectural work, make or authorize the making of alterations to such building, and destroy or authorize the destruction of such building.

17 U.S.C.A. § 120(b). What justifies permitting unauthorized alterations of architectural works when such alterations would not be permitted in the case of other categories of copyrightable works? Should it matter what the building owner's purposes are in making the alterations?

E. SECTION 106(3): THE EXCLUSIVE RIGHT TO DISTRIBUTE COPIES OR PHONORECORDS OF THE COPYRIGHTED WORK TO THE PUBLIC BY SALE OR OTHER TRANSFER OF OWNERSHIP, OR BY RENTAL, LEASE, OR LENDING

The right to distribute copies or phonorecords to the public includes the right of first publication. Like the adaptation right, the right of public distribution overlaps the right of reproduction in many cases. For example, a defendant who makes and distributes unauthorized copies of a work to the public will be liable under either right. A defendant may infringe the right of public distribution by itself, however. Assume that A writes a song and B, with A's permission, makes a sound recording in which he performs the song. X makes unauthorized tapes of B's sound recording and sells them to a middle person, who sells them to Y Company. Y Company then sells the tapes to the public through its retail record stores. Regardless of whether Y Company knew that the tapes were bootlegged, it would be liable for infringing both A's and B's exclusive rights to distribute their respective works to the public. In such situations, A and B may sue X (for infringing the rights of reproduction and distribution), and the middle person and Y Company (who both are direct infringers of A's and B's rights of distribution). For a thoughtful overview of the distribution right, see Kernochan, The *Distribution Right in the United States of America: Review and Reflections*, 42 VAND. L. REV. 1407 (1989).

The right of public distribution is limited by the doctrine of first sale, which is codified in section 109(a) of the Copyright Act: "Notwithstanding the provisions of section 106(3), the owner of a particular copy or phonorecord lawfully made under this title, or any person authorized by such owner, is entitled, without the authority of the copyright owner, to sell or otherwise dispose of the possession of that copy or phonorecord." The doctrine of first sale, in turn, is subject to exceptions which permit the copyright owner to exert some control over copies or phonorecords even after transferring or authorizing their transfer to the public. We turn to the doctrine of first sale and its exceptions below.

1. The Doctrine of First Sale

HOUSE REPORT ON COPYRIGHT ACT OF 1976

H.R. Rep. No. 1476, 94th Cong., 2d Sess. 79 (1976).

Section 109(a) restates and confirms the principle that, where the copyright owner has transferred ownership of a particular copy or phonorecord of a work, the person to whom the copy or phonorecord is transferred is entitled to dispose of it by sale, rental, or any other means. Under this principle, which has been established by the court decisions and section 27 of the present law, the copyright owner's exclusive right of public distribution would have no effect upon anyone who owns "a particular copy or phonorecord lawfully made under this title" and who wishes to transfer it to someone else or to destroy it.

Thus, for example, the outright sale of an authorized copy of a book frees it from any copyright control over its resale price or other conditions of its future disposition. A library that has acquired ownership of a copy is entitled to lend it under any conditions it chooses to impose. This does not mean that conditions on future dispositions of copies of phonorecords, imposed by a contract between their buyer and seller, would be unenforceable between the parties as a breach of contract, but it does mean that they could not be enforced by an action for infringement of copyright. Under section 202 however, the owner of the physical copy or phonorecord cannot reproduce or perform the copyrighted work publicly without the copyright owner's consent.

To come within the scope of section 109(a), a copy or phonorecord must have been "lawfully made under this title," though not necessarily with the copyright owner's authorization. For example, any resale of any illegally "pirated" phonorecord would be an infringement, but the disposition of a phonorecord legally made under the compulsory licensing provisions of section 115 would not.

Notes and Questions

1. *The doctrine of first sale.* The copyright doctrine of first sale is similar in many respects to the doctrine of first sale, or doctrine of exhaustion, applied in patent law. As you will see, trademark law employs its own counterpart. Are the justifications for the doctrine the same in copyright as in patent law?

2. *Record and software rentals.* In response to concerns voiced by the recording and software industries, Congress amended the Copyright Act in 1984, and again in 1990, to carve out narrow exceptions to the first sale doctrine.

The Record Rental Amendments Act of 1984, Pub. L. No. 98–450, 98 Stat. 1727, codified at 17 U.S.C.A. § 109(b), prevents owners of phonorecords of musical sound recordings from renting the phonorecords to the public for commercial advantage without the permission of both the sound recording and the underlying musical work copyright owners. This amendment responded to the advent of commercial record rental establishments which offered records, tapes and compact disks for short-term rental, and often sold blank tapes, as well. These businesses made it extremely easy for renters to engage in home taping to save the price of purchasing recordings. As the House Report noted, "[o]ne such establishment advertised, 'Never, ever buy another record.'" H.R. REP. NO. 987, 98th Cong., 2d Sess. 2 (1984). In the absence of the amendment, of course, the first sale doctrine would permit the owner of an authorized phonorecord of a sound recording to rent it to others. Under the amendment, such rental without the permission of the affected copyright owners constitutes copyright infringement in violation of section 106(3).

The Computer Software Rental Amendments Act of 1990, Pub. L. No. 101–650, 104 Stat. 5134, amended section 109(b) to extend a similar prohibition against commercial rentals of computer programs. The House Report explained:

> Congress has now been presented with similar evidence [of commercial rentals] by the computer software industry. Indeed, in some respects, the evidence is even more compelling in the case of software. The price disparity between the sale and rental prices is greater than the case with phonorecords: software selling for $495 has been rented for $35. And, unlike phonorecords, which are an entertainment product, software is typically a utilitarian product. Short term rental of software is, under most circumstances, inconsistent with the purposes for which software is intended. Rental of software will, most likely, encourage unauthorized copying, deprive copyright owners of a return on investment, and thereby discourage creation of new products.

H.R. REP. NO. 735, 101st Cong., 2d Sess. 8 (1990).

Section 109(b) expressly permits not-for-profit lending of records and software by non-profit libraries and educational institutions. It also specifies that its prohibitions against rental do not apply to "a computer program which is embodied in a machine or product and which cannot be copied during the ordinary operation or use of the machine or product." 17 U.S.C.A. § 109(b)(1)(B)(i). As the House Report explained: "[t]his provision recognizes that many consumer products contain computer programs, including automobiles, calculators, and microwave ovens. Computer programs are typically embodied in electronic circuitry embedded in these products, and cannot be copied by consumers during the ordinary operation or use of the product." H.R. REP. NO. 735, *supra*, at 15.

Review the provisions of section 109(b). In your opinion, how much assistance are they likely to give the affected copyright owners against unauthorized home copying? Should the provisions be extended to other subject matter? For example, should unauthorized rentals of video tapes of motion pictures be prohibited? Should non-profit public lending, such as that by public libraries, be prohibited or subjected to a compulsory royalty payment? See Seemann, *A Look at the Public Lending Right*, 30 A.S.C.A.P. COPYRIGHT L. SYMPOSIUM 71 (1983).

For a review of the events leading up to the record and software rental amendments and assessments of their provisions, see Horowitz, *The Record Rental Amendment of 1984: A Case Study in the Effort to Adapt Copyright Law to New Technology*, 12 COLUM.-VLA J.L. & ARTS 31 (1987).

3. *The Droit de Suite.* In a report issued in 1992, the Copyright Office discussed the *droit de suite*, which originated in Europe:

> [T]he *droit de suite*—the right of an artist to collect a part of the price paid when a work is resold—is based on the premise that visual artists are entitled to participate in an increase in the value of their works in ways that are not otherwise adequately addressed by copyright law.
>
> The copyright law's rights of reproduction and distribution are better suited to exploitation of literary or musical works. A visual artist's expression is usually embodied in an end product, sold to a single purchaser. The artist's current work and reputation continue to affect the value of that earlier work. Many European countries, in the event of resale, allow artists to benefit from any increase in value of their works.
>
> In 1920, France became the first country to recognize the *droit de suite*. Today, some 36 countries have the resale royalty, and several other countries are considering legislation to enact it. Roughly half of the countries that now purport to have *droit de suite*, however, lack implementing legislation. The level of commitment and the characteristics of the national laws vary widely.
>
> * * * The Berne Convention for the Protection of Literary and Artistic Property contains statements of principle in favor of the *droit de suite*. * * *
>
> Whether the *droit de suite* will make the transition from an idealistic notion to an international norm depends both on commitment to *droit de suite* and creation of practical means to implement the goal of allowing artists to share in the profit of their work once it has left their hands.
>
> Those countries that have most successfully implemented the *droit de suite* share certain characteristics. In France, Germany, and Belgium, for instance, the royalty is collected on the total resale price of the

work. Measuring the royalty by the resale price departs from the rationale allowing artists to participate in an *increase* in value, but is considered simpler and more practical. * * *

Auctions are the minimum field of application in all countries which have adopted the *droit de suite*, because auctions sales are easiest to monitor. Including dealer sales increases the administrative challenge and the risk of noncompliance. * * * Although the *droit de suite* is inalienable and non-waivable, in almost all effective systems it may be transferred for purposes of collection through an artists' collecting agency.

* * *

[T]here have been efforts to realize this European concept in the United States since as early as 1940. In the early 1960's, proposals were made to incorporate *droit de suite* into state or federal law in the United States. To date, only California's efforts have resulted in law. * * *

The State of California passed a resale royalty law in 1976. The law mandates a five percent royalty of the resale price to the artist when a work is resold in California or resold anywhere by a California resident. Several artists report significant financial gain under the law. However, the law is widely criticized as underused and underenforced, and a 1986 survey of California artists and dealers was inconclusive. Some commentators claim that the law places California's art market at a competitive disadvantage, but others say that it has had no effect on the California market.

* * * Any state resale royalty scheme may be preempted under section 301 of the 1976 Act because it inhibits the section 106 distribution right as modified by the section 109 "first sale" doctrine (which allows the owner of a lawfully-made copy, including an original, to dispose of that copy as he or she pleases). Given potential problems of preemption, enforcement, and multiple application, any *droit de suite* that is enacted in the United States should be at the federal level.

* * *

U.S. COPYRIGHT OFFICE, *DROIT DE SUITE*: THE ARTIST'S RESALE ROYALTY, i-iv (1992).

In your opinion, are visual artists disadvantaged vis-a-vis other authors under the Copyright Act? If so, are resale royalties as described in the Copyright Office Report the best way to level the playing field? If not, what alternatives might Congress consider? After further discussion, the Copyright Office concluded that it was "not persuaded that sufficient economic and copyright policy justification exists to establish *droit de suite* in the United States." What copyright policies are likely to be implicated in the *droit de suite* debate?

In 1992, the JOURNAL OF THE COPYRIGHT SOCIETY OF THE U.S.A. published a series of useful articles discussing the pros and cons and the practical implications of U.S. enactment of *droit de suite*. See 40 J. COPYRIGHT SOC. 241–323 (1992).

2. *The Importation Right*

Section 602 of the Copyright Act prohibits importing, "without the authority of the owner of copyright under this title," copies or phonorecords of a work that have been acquired outside the United States. 17 U.S.C.A. § 602. Unless one of the specified exceptions applies, such unauthorized importation is actionable as an infringement of the exclusive right to distribute under section 106(3). *Id.*

Since importation is to be deemed a violation of the copyright owner's exclusive right to distribute the work to the public, the question arises whether the doctrine of first sale is applicable. Under its own terms the doctrine would not apply when pirated copies or phonorecords are imported. By definition, pirated copies and phonorecords are not "lawfully made under this title." See H.R. REP. NO. 1476, 94th Cong., 2d Sess. 169–70 (1976). Many imports are not pirated, however, but are "gray market goods." Gray market goods constitute legitimate copies and phonorecords whose manufacture and first sale was authorized by the copyright owner. The copyright owner intended, however, that the copies or phonorecords would be distributed in foreign markets and remain outside of the United States. Others purchase the copies abroad and import them into the United States without the copyright owner's permission. The "gray marketeers" sell the imported copies and phonorecords in the United States in competition with the copyright owner. Indeed, since they are able to purchase them abroad for less than their U.S. sales price, they may resell their copies at a lower price than the U.S. copyright owner charges.

Congress clearly intended that section 602 would apply to at least some gray market goods. According to the House Report, section 602

> deals with two separate situations: importation of "piratical" articles (that is, copies or phonorecords made without any authorization of the copyright owner), and unauthorized importation of copies or phonorecords that were lawfully made. The general approach of section 602 is to make unauthorized importation an act of infringement in both cases * * *.

H. REP. NO. 1476, *supra,* at 169. The courts have been left to wrestle with the question of when, if ever, the doctrine of first sale applies to shield gray marketeers from liability. The issue has been presented in two scenarios.

In the first scenario, the U.S. copyright owner authorized or licensed a foreign company to manufacture and sell copies or phonorecords of the work abroad. Third parties purchased the copies and imported them into the United States without the copyright owner's permission. In such a setting, several courts have found the doctrine of first sale inapplicable. In Columbia Broadcasting System, Inc. v. Scorpio Music Distributors, Inc. 569 F.Supp. 47, 222 U.S.P.Q. 975 (E.D.Pa.1983), *affirmed* 738 F.2d 421 (3d Cir.1984), the court responded to the defendant's argument that it was shielded from liability under the first sale doctrine because the phonorecords at issue had already been the subject of an authorized sale and had entered the stream of commerce prior to importation:

> Defendant's contentions would be more persuasive were it not for the phrase—lawfully made under this title—in § 109(a). I conclude that the section grants first sale protection to the third party buyer of copies which have been legally manufactured and sold within the United States and not to purchasers of imports such as are involved here. The protection afforded by the United States Code does not extend beyond the borders of this country unless the Code expressly states. * * *
>
> Construing § 109(a) as superseding the prohibition on importation set forth in the more recently enacted § 602 would render § 602 virtually meaningless. * * * The copyright owner would be unable to exercise control over copies of the work which entered the American market in competition with copies lawfully manufactured and distributed under this title. This court cannot construe the statute so as to alter the intent of Congress, which has set restrictions on the importation of phonorecords in order that rights of United States copyright owners can be preserved.

Id., 569 F.Supp. at 49–50, 222 U.S.P.Q. at 977. The United States Court of Appeals for the Ninth Circuit has subsequently approved and adopted the reasoning in *Scorpio*. BMG Music v. Perez, 952 F.2d 318, 21 U.S.P.Q.2d 1315 (9th Cir.1991), *cert. denied* ___ U.S. ___, 112 S.Ct. 2997, 120 L.Ed.2d. 873 (1992) ("The words 'lawfully made under this title' in § 109(a) grant first sale protection only to copies legally made and sold in the United States.")

In the second scenario, the copyright owner manufactured copies or phonorecords in the United States and exported them for distribution in foreign markets. Third parties purchased them abroad and imported them back into the United States without the copyright owner's authorization. In such a case, the Court of Appeals for the Third Circuit found the doctrine of first sale applicable against the plaintiff/copyright owner:

> The first sale rule is statutory, but finds its origins in the common law aversion to limiting the alienation of personal property.
>
> There is, however, an economic reason for the rule as well. * * * "[T]he ultimate question under the 'first sale' doctrine is whether or not there has been such a disposition of the copyrighted article that it may fairly be said that the copyright proprietor has received his reward for its use."
>
> At first glance, section 602(a)—the importation clause—appears to clash with the first sale doctrine. We conclude, nonetheless, that the two provisions were intended to function interdependently and may be read in harmony with each other.
>
> * * *
>
> The interrelationship between sections 602(a) and 109(a) may be interpreted in two possible ways, although neither is conclusively

> supported by the statutory language or legislative history. The first, and most sweeping, construction declares that in addition to the distribution rights conferred by section 106(3), section 602(a) grants copyright owners yet another distinct right—one that frees them from the first sale right of section 109(a), which otherwise limits section 106(3), and allows them to prevent the unauthorized importation of copyrighted copies. The district court adopted that view in this case.
>
> The second interpretation reconciles sections 106(3) and 602(a) by reasoning that the importation prohibition does not enlarge the distribution rights, but serves only as a specific example of those rights subject still to the first sale limitation. This analysis poses a problem in the case of unauthorized imports of copies made abroad pursuant to a license restricting sales to a particular country. Although the domestic copyright holder undoubtedly would prefer to block such importation, the statutory language does not expressly authorize such control.

Sebastian International, Inc. v. Consumer Contacts (PYT) Ltd, 847 F.2d 1093, 1096–97, 7 U.S.P.Q.2d 1077, 1080 (3d Cir.1988) (quoting Burk & Van Heusen, Inc. v. Arrow Drug, Inc. 233 F.Supp. 881, 884, 143 U.S.P.Q. 17 (E.D.Pa.1964)). The court noted the *Scorpio* opinion and distinguished it on its facts. Though it declined to pass on the *Scorpio* interpretation of section 109(a), the court confessed "some uneasiness with this construction of "lawfully made." The court then turned to the facts before it:

> [Plaintiff] produced and sold the same copies which it now seeks to control.
>
> Under the first sale doctrine, when plaintiff made and then sold its copies, it relinquished all further rights "to sell or otherwise dispose of possession of that copy." Unquestionably that includes any right to claim infringement of the section 106(3) distributive rights for copies made and sold in the United States. With respect to future distribution of those copies in this country, clearly the copyright owner already has received its reward through the purchase price.
>
> Nothing in the wording of section 109(a), its history or philosophy, suggests that the owner of copies who sells them abroad does not receive a "reward for his work." Nor does the language of section 602(a) intimate that a copyright owner who elects to sell copies abroad should receive a "more adequate award" than those who sell domestically. That result would occur if the holder were to receive not only the purchase price, but a right to limit importation as well.
>
> Consequently, we agree with the district court that the place of sale is not the critical factor in determining whether section 602(a) governs. We differ, however, with the district court's finding of infringement because, in our view, a first sale by the copyright

> owner extinguishes any right later to control importation of those copies.
>
> Section 602(a) does not purport to create a right in addition to those conferred by section 106(3), but states that unauthorized importation is an infringement of "the exclusive [section 106(3)] right to distribute copies." Because that exclusive right is specifically limited by the first sale provisions of § 109(a), it necessarily follows that once transfer of ownership has cancelled the distribution right to a copy, the right does not survive so as to be infringed by importation.[3] * * *

Id., 847 F.2d at 1098–99, 7 U.S.P.Q.2d at 1081–82.

Notes and Questions

1. *Importations and the first sale doctrine.* When U.S. copyright owners sell their copies abroad or license foreign companies to manufacture and sell them, they frequently negotiate for contractual provisions which prohibit the foreign purchaser/licensee from reselling the copies in the United States. If the purchaser/licensee participates in importing the goods back into the U.S., the copyright owner will have a cause of action for breach of contract. In some cases, however, the copyright owner's purchaser/licensee sells the copies in compliance with the contract. Gray marketeers purchase the copies from intermediate owners and then import them. Since the gray marketeers are not in privity with the copyright owner, contract law provides no redress.

Are you satisfied with the *Scorpio* court's interpretation of the words "lawfully made under this title" in section 109? Note that the first sale doctrine clearly applies to copies and phonorecords that are domestically manufactured and sold by the copyright owner's domestic licensees. Under *Scorpio*, application of the doctrine of first sale turns not on whether the copyright owner or its licensee manufactures the copies and makes the first sale but on where that person is when he does so. It would seem to follow that unauthorized importation would infringe even if the *U.S. copyright owner himself* manufactured and sold the goods abroad.

In *Sebastian*, the Third Circuit stressed that applicability of the doctrine of first sale turns on whether "it may fairly be said that the copyright proprietor has received his reward" in connection with the copy or phonorecord sold. The court noted that when the copyright owner itself makes the first sale, it receives its reward and the doctrine of first sale applies. To hold otherwise would give the copyright owner double compensation. Copyright owners who license others to manufacture copies of their works generally receive a negotiated royalty payment for each copy made and sold. Since the doctrine of first sale applies to works manufactured and sold domestically by licensees, it might be assumed that this royalty payment is deemed a sufficient reward to the copyright owner. Why should that not also be the case when the copies are manufactured and sold abroad by a licensee?

3. This situation differs from that in which a licensee manufactures the copy. In that instance, the copyright holder does not own the tangible copy.

Could it be argued that applicability of the first sale doctrine should turn on the copyright owner's opportunity to profit from the first sale, rather than on the place of manufacture and sale or on who actually made the sale? Could the words "lawfully made under this title" in section 109(a) be construed consistently with this theory? Could this theory be squared with section 602 and its legislative history?

U.S. intellectual property owners often sell their goods at a higher price in the United States than the price they or their licensees charge in less affluent nations. Gray marketeers take advantage of this price differential when they buy abroad and resell the goods in the United States. They often can resell their imported copies in the U.S. for a lower price than the U.S. intellectual property owner charges its U.S. customers and still turn a profit. A rule that the doctrine of first sale is inapplicable to imported copies rids the U.S. copyright owner of this competition, furthering its ability to engage in price discrimination against U.S. consumers. Is this appropriate as a matter of policy? In Parfums Givenchy, Inc. v. C & C Beauty Sales, Inc., 832 F.Supp. 1378, 1390–91, 29 U.S.P.Q.2d 1026, 1035 (C.D.Cal.1993), the court gave a resounding "yes."

For a discussion of how trademark law treats gray market goods, see Chapter 6, § VI D 1., *infra*.

F. SECTION 106(4): THE RIGHT TO PERFORM THE COPYRIGHTED WORK PUBLICLY

HOUSE REPORT ON COPYRIGHT ACT OF 1976

H.R. Rep. No. 1476, 94th Cong., 2d Sess. 62–65 (1976).

Under the definitions of "perform," "display," "publicly," and "transmit" in section 101, the concepts of public performance and public display cover not only the initial rendition or showing, but also any further act by which that rendition or showing is transmitted or communicated to the public. Thus, for example: a singer is performing when he or she sings a song; a broadcasting network is performing when it transmits his or her performance (whether simultaneously or from records); a local broadcaster is performing when it transmits the network broadcast; a cable television system is performing when it retransmits the broadcast to its subscribers; and any individual is performing whenever he or she plays a phonorecord embodying the performance or communicates the performance by turning on a receiving set. Although any act by which the initial performance or display is transmitted, repeated, or made to recur would itself be a "performance" or "display" under the bill, it would not be actionable as an infringement unless it were done "publicly," as defined in section 101. Certain other performances and displays, in addition to those that are "private," are exempted or given qualified copyright control under sections 107 through 118.

To "perform" a work, under the definition in section 101, includes reading a literary work aloud, singing or playing music, dancing a ballet or other choreographic work, and acting out a dramatic work or pantomime. A performance may be accomplished "either directly or by means of any device or process," including all kinds of equipment for reproducing or amplifying sounds or visual images, any sort of transmitting apparatus, any type of electronic retrieval system, and any other techniques and systems not yet in use or even invented.

* * *

Under clause (1) of the definition of "publicly" in section 101, a performance or display is "public" if it takes place "at a place open to the public or at any place where a substantial number of persons outside of a normal circle of a family and its social acquaintances is gathered." One of the principal purposes of the definition was to make clear that, contrary to the decision in Metro–Goldwyn–Mayer Distributing Corp. v. Wyatt, 21 C.O.Bull. 203 (D.Md.1932), performances in "semipublic" places such as clubs, lodges, factories, summer camps, and schools are "public performances" subject to copyright control. The term "a family" in this context would include an individual living alone, so that a gathering confined to the individual's social acquaintances would normally be regarded as private. Routine meetings of businesses and governmental personnel would be excluded because they do not represent the gathering of a "substantial number of persons."

Clause (2) of the definition of "publicly" in section 101 makes clear that the concepts of public performance and public display include not only performances and displays that occur initially in a public place, but also acts that transmit or otherwise communicate a performance or display of the work to the public by means of any device or process. The definition of "transmit"—to communicate a performance or display "by any device or process whereby images or sound are received beyond the place from which they are sent"—is broad enough to include all conceivable forms and combinations of wires and wireless communications media, including but by no means limited to radio and television broadcasting as we know them. Each and every method by which the images or sounds comprising a performance or display are picked up and conveyed is a "transmission," and if the transmission reaches the public in any form, the case comes within the scope of clauses (4) or (5) of section 106.

Under the bill, as under the present law, a performance made available by transmission to the public at large is "public" even though the recipients are not gathered in a single place, and even if there is no proof that any of the potential recipients was operating his receiving apparatus at the time of the transmission. The same principles apply whenever the potential recipients of the transmission represent a limited segment of the public, such as the occupants of hotel rooms or the subscribers of a cable television service. Clause (2) of the definition of "publicly" is applicable "whether the members of the public capable of receiving the performance or display receive it in the same place or in separate places and at the same time or at different times."

COLUMBIA PICTURES INDUSTRIES, INC. v. AVECO, INC.

United States Court of Appeals for the Third Circuit, 1986.
800 F.2d 59, 230 U.S.P.Q. 869.

STAPLETON, CIRCUIT JUDGE.

Plaintiffs, appellees in this action, are producers of motion pictures ("Producers") and bring this copyright infringement action against the defendant, Aveco, Inc. Producers claim that Aveco's business, which includes renting video cassettes of motion pictures in conjunction with rooms in which they may be viewed, violates their exclusive rights under the Copyright Act of 1976. * * *

* * * The district court found that Aveco had infringed on Producers' exclusive rights to publicly perform and authorize public performances of their copyrighted works and so granted their motion for partial summary judgment. * * *

I

Among their other operations, Producers distribute video cassette copies of motion pictures in which they own registered copyrights. They do so knowing that many retail purchasers of these video cassettes, including Aveco, rent them to others for profit. Aveco also makes available private rooms of various sizes in which its customers may view the video cassettes that they have chosen from Aveco's offerings. For example, at one location, Lock Haven, Aveco has thirty viewing rooms, each containing seating, a video cassette player, and television monitor. Aveco charges a rental fee for the viewing room that is separate from the charge for the video cassette rental.

Customers of Aveco may (1) rent a room and also rent a video cassette for viewing in that room, (2) rent a room and bring a video cassette obtained elsewhere to play in the room, or (3) rent a video cassette for out-of-store viewing.

Aveco has placed its video cassette players inside the individual viewing rooms and, subject to a time limitation, allows the customer complete control over the playing of the video cassettes. Customers operate the video cassette players in each viewing room and Aveco's employees assist only upon request. Each video cassette may be viewed only from inside the viewing room, and is not transmitted beyond the particular room in which it is being played. Aveco asserts that it rents its viewing rooms to individual customers who may be joined in the room only by members of their families and social acquaintances. Furthermore, Aveco's stated practice is not to permit unrelated groups of customers to share a viewing room while a video cassette is being played. For purposes of this appeal we assume the veracity of these assertions.

II

* * * Producers do not, in the present litigation, allege infringement of their exclusive rights "to do and to authorize [the distribution of]

copies or phonorecords of the copyrighted work to the public by sale or other transfer of ownership, or by rental, lease, or lending." Thus, Aveco's rental of video cassettes for at-home viewing is not challenged.

Producers' claim in this litigation is based on the alleged infringement of their "exclusive right ... to perform the copyrighted work publicly" and to "authorize" such performances. Producers assert that Aveco, by renting its viewing rooms to the public for the purpose of watching Producers' video cassettes, is authorizing the public performance of copyrighted motion pictures.

Our analysis begins with the language of the Act. We first observe that there is no question that "performances" of copyrighted materials take place at Aveco's stores. "To perform" a work is defined in the Act as, "in the case of a motion picture or other audiovisual work, to show its images in any sequence or to make the sounds accompanying it audible." As the House Report notes, this definition means that an individual is performing a work whenever he does anything by which the work is transmitted, repeated, or made to recur.

Producers do not argue that Aveco itself performs the video cassettes. They acknowledge that under the Act Aveco's *customers* are the ones performing the works, for it is they who actually place the video cassette in the video cassette player and operate the controls. * * * However, if there is a public performance, Aveco may still be responsible as an infringer even though it does not actually operate the video cassette players. In granting copyright owners the exclusive rights to "authorize" public performances, Congress intended "to avoid any questions as to the liability of contributory infringers. For example, a person who lawfully acquires an authorized copy of a motion picture would be an infringer if he or she engages in the business of renting it to others for purposes of an unauthorized public performance." H.R.Rep. No. 1476, 94th Cong., 2d Sess. 61, *reprinted in* 1976 U.S.Code Cong. & Ad.News at 5674. In our opinion, this rationale applies equally to the person who knowingly makes available other requisites of a public performance. Accordingly, we agree with the district court that Aveco, by enabling its customers to perform the video cassettes in the viewing rooms, authorizes the performances.

The performances of Producers' motion pictures at Aveco's stores infringe their copyrights, however, only if they are "public." The copyright owners' rights do not extend to control over private performances.

* * *

We recently parsed this definition in *Columbia Pictures Industries v. Redd Horne*, 749 F.2d 154 (3d Cir.1984), a case similar to the one at bar. The principal factual distinction is that in Redd Horne's operation, known as Maxwell's Video Showcase, Ltd. ("Maxwell's"), the video cassette players were located in the stores' central areas, not in each individual screening room. Maxwell's customers would select a video cassette from Maxwell's stock and rent a room which they entered to watch the motion picture on a television monitor. A Maxwell's employee would play the video cassette for the customers in one of the centrally-located video cassette players and transmit the performance to the monitor located in the room. Thus, unlike Aveco's customers, Maxwell's clientele had no control over the video cassette players.

The *Redd Horne* court began its analysis with the observation that the two components of clause (1) of the definition of a public performance are disjunctive. "The first category is self-evident; it is 'a place open to the public.' The second category, commonly referred to as a semi-public place, is determined by the size and composition of the audience." 749 F.2d at 159.

The court then concluded that the performances were occurring at a place open to the public, which it found to be the entire store, including the viewing rooms.

> Any member of the public can view a motion picture by paying the appropriate fee. The services provided by Maxwell's are essentially the same as a movie theatre, with the additional feature of privacy. The relevant "place" within the meaning of Section 101 is each of Maxwell's two stores, not each individual booth within each store. Simply because the cassettes can be viewed in private does not mitigate the essential fact that Maxwell's is unquestionably open to the public.

749 F.2d at 159.

The *Redd Horne* court reached this conclusion despite the fact that when a customer watched a movie at Maxwell's, the viewing room was closed to other members of the public. Nevertheless, Aveco asserts that factual differences between Maxwell's stores and its own require a different result in this case.

Aveco first observes that when Maxwell's employees "performed" the video cassettes, they did so in a central location, the store's main area. This lobby was undeniably "open to the public." Aveco suggests that, in *Redd Horne*, the location of the customers in the private rooms was simply irrelevant, for the *performers* were in a public place, the lobby. In the case at bar, Aveco continues, its employees do not perform anything, the customers do. Unlike Maxwell's employees located in the public lobby, Aveco's customers are in private screening rooms. Aveco argues that while these viewing rooms are available to anyone for rent, they are private during each rental period, and therefore, not "open to the public." The performance—the playing of the video cassette—thus occurs not in the public lobby, but in the private viewing rooms.

We disagree. The necessary implication of Aveco's analysis is that *Redd Horne* would have been decided differently had Maxwell's located its video cassette players in a locked closet in the back of the stores. We do not read *Redd Horne* to adopt such an analysis. The Copyright Act speaks of performances at a place open to the public. It does not require that the public place be actually crowded with people. A telephone booth, a taxi cab, and even a pay toilet are commonly regarded as "open to the public," even though they are usually occupied only by one party at a time. Our opinion in *Redd Horne* turned not on the precise whereabouts of the video cassette players, but on the nature of Maxwell's stores. Maxwell's, like Aveco, was willing to make a viewing room and video cassette available to any member of the public with the inclination to avail himself of this service. It is this availability that made Maxwell's stores public places, not the coincidence that the video cassette players were situated in the lobby. Because we find *Redd Horne* indistinguishable from the case at bar, we find that Aveco's operations constituted an authorization of public performances of Producers' copyrighted works.

Aveco's reliance on the first sale doctrine is likewise misplaced. The first sale doctrine, codified at 17 U.S.C. § 109(a), prevents the copyright owner from controlling future transfers of a particular copy of a copyrighted work after he has transferred its "material ownership" to another. When a copyright owner parts with title to a particular copy of his copyrighted work, he thereby divests himself of his exclusive right to vend that particular copy. Accordingly, under the first sale doctrine, Producers cannot claim that Aveco's rentals or sales of lawfully acquired video cassettes infringe on their exclusive rights to vend those cassettes.

* * *

* * * The rights protected by copyright are divisible and the waiver of one does not necessarily waive any of the others. In particular, the transfer of ownership in a particular copy of a work does not affect Producers' Section 106(4) exclusive rights to do and to authorize public performances. It therefore cannot protect one who is infringing Producers' Section 106(4) rights by the public performance of the copyrighted work.

* * *

Notes and Questions

1. *The public performance right.* Under the facts in the *Redd Horne* case, is there an alternative theory on which a finding of "public performance" could be based?

Assume that a hotel rents videodiscs of motion pictures to its guests for a fee of $5 to $7.50. Guests check out videodiscs at the hotel lobby and play them in their rooms, which are all equipped with a large screen projection television and a videodisc player. In light of the *Redd Horne* and *Aveco* decisions, should the hotel be liable to motion picture copyright holders for infringement of their exclusive right of public performance? See Columbia Pictures Industries, Inc. v. Professional Real Estate Investors, Inc., 866 F.2d 278, 9 U.S.P.Q.2d 1653 (9th Cir.1989).

What if the hotel has a system for electronic delivery of videotaped motion pictures to individual guest rooms? The guest operates the system from her room by remote control. After the television is turned on, the screen lists a menu of available motion pictures. The guest selects one by entering the appropriate code on the remote control. The hotel maintains a bank of video cassette players ("VCPs") in a hotel equipment room. These VCPs are connected to the guest rooms by wiring. Whenever a guest requests a movie, a computer program dedicates the particular VCP containing the tape of the requested motion picture to the appropriate room and starts the video. The video can only be viewed in the room occupied by the guest who selected it. Should this arrangement infringe the right of public performance in the movies? See On Command Video Corp. v. Columbia Pictures Industries, 777 F.Supp. 787, 21 U.S.P.Q.2d 1545 (N.D.Cal.1991).

2. *Sound recordings.* By its terms, section 106(4) extends the right of public performance to "literary, musical, dramatic, and choreographic works, pantomimes, and motion pictures and other audiovisual works." Pictorial, graphic and sculptural works and architectural works are excluded. This exclusion is easy to understand, since such works generally are not performed. Pictorial, graphic and sculptural works, at least, are adequately protected by the exclusive right of public display.

Note, however, that section 106(4) also withholds the performance right in the case of sound recordings. The exclusion is reiterated in section 114(a). Radio stations, night clubs and others who publicly perform sound recordings must pay royalties to the owners of copyright in the musical works that they perform by means of sound recordings. They do not, however, owe any legal obligation to the owners of copyright in the sound recordings themselves.

The question of performance rights for sound recordings has generated several Congressional hearings and considerable lobbying by interested parties. In hearings leading to enactment of the Copyright Act of 1976, the House Committee on the Judiciary considered at length proposals to establish a limited performance right in sound recordings. It concluded, however, that the problem required further study. H.R. REP. NO. 1476, 94th Cong., 2d Sess. 106 (1976). The Committee added section 114(d) to the Act, directing the Register of Copyrights to conduct a comprehensive study of the issue and make recommendations. The Copyright Office submitted its report in 1978, recommending enactment of a bill creating performance rights for sound recordings, subject to a compulsory license provision to facilitate public performances by commercial exploiters such as radio broadcasters and cable companies. The proposed bill provided that royalties from public performances would be divided between the sound recording copyright owners and persons participating as performers on the recording. See *Performance Rights in Sound Recordings: Hearings Before the Subcomm. on Courts, Civil Liberties, and the Administration of Justice of the House Committee on the Judiciary*, 95th Cong., 2d Sess. 111–138 (1978). Congress has declined to enact such a bill.

What accounts for the opposition to creating a performance right for sound recordings? See Bard & Kurlantzick, *A Public Performance Right in Recordings: How to Alter the Copyright System Without Improving It*, 43 GEO. WASH. L. REV. 152 (1974); *Performance Rights in Sound Recordings: Hearings Before the Subcomm. on Courts, Civil Liberties, and the Administration of Justice, supra.* What justifications exist for allocating royalties to performers who do not own copyright in the recording embodying their performance?

Many developed nations provide a performance right for sound recordings, either through copyright or "neighboring rights." For more information about the ways that other countries provide performance rights for sound recordings, see Johoram, *The Nature of Neighboring Rights of Performing Artists, Phonogram Producers and Broadcasting Organizations*, 15 COLUM.-VLA J.L. & ARTS 75 (1990); Note, *Toward Better Protection of Performers in the United States: A Comparative Look at Performers' Rights in the United States, Under the Rome Convention and in France*, 28 COLUM. J. TRANSNAT'L L. 775 (1990).

3. *Rights in performances, as such.* Many nations provide rights to performers in their performances, frequently through the vehicle of "neighboring rights"—a body of law who's name reflects its close relationship to copyright. Among other things, neighboring rights may permit performers to prevent unauthorized fixation and/or broadcasting of their live performances.

In the United States, copyright law protects fixed works of authorship, such as sound recordings and audio-visual works, that incorporate a live performance. However, a live performance, as such, does not qualify as copyrightable subject matter. In implementing the GATT Uruguay Round TRIPs Agreement, Congress enacted a form of "neighboring rights" in live musical performances. Uruguay Round Agreements Act, Pub. L. No. 103–465, § 512, 108 Stat. 4809, 4974 (1994), adds a new section 1101 to the Copyright Act, prohibiting transmission of the sounds and/or images of live musical performances to the public without the performers' authorization. It also prohibits the unauthorized fixation of the sounds and/or images of live musical performances, and reproduction, distribution, offers to distribute, and "trafficking" of such unauthorized fixations. Persons engaging in these prohibited acts are subject to civil copyright infringement remedies, to the same extent as copyright infringers. Uruguay Round Agreements Act section 513 amends the criminal code to provide criminal penalties, as well. See 18 U.S.C.A. § 2319A. These new federal "anti-bootlegging" remedies are intended to supplement, rather than supersede, existing state remedies, such as a state right of publicity or unfair competition claim. They have been justified not only as necessary to bring the U.S. into compliance with TRIPs Article 14, but also to provide a uniform, nation-wide cause of action. See, e.g., S. REP. NO. 412, 103d Cong., 2d Sess. 225 (1994).

Note that these new provisions give rights to performers in their performance, and are independent of any copyright in the musical works being performed, which may be simultaneously infringed by the prohibited transmission, reproduction or distribution of the live performance.

4. *Performing rights societies.* Copyrighted musical works are publicly performed in numerous ways every day—in live concerts, through radio and television broadcasts and background music services, in night clubs—throughout the country. Individual musical work copyright owners cannot hope to negotiate separate licenses for every such performance of their works. Nor can they effectively police the marketplace to ensure that performers are obtaining licenses. By the same token, it is inefficient for

large-scale performers, like radio broadcasters, to negotiate individual licenses for each work they publicly perform.

To manage the licensing of public performances and effectively enforce musical work copyrights, interested parties formed performing rights societies, such as the American Society of Composers, Authors and Publishers (ASCAP) and Broadcast Music, Inc. (BMI). Today, most domestic musical work copyright owners are represented by one or the other of these two societies. Each represented copyright owner grants a non-exclusive right to the society to license non-dramatic public performance of his works. By representing large numbers of copyright owners, the societies can issue "blanket licenses" authorizing performance of all the works of a particular type in the society's huge repertoire for a stated period of time. In addition to licensing performances, the societies collect royalties and distribute them among the copyright owners they represent. ASCAP and BMI also send their representatives into the marketplace to monitor compliance with the copyright laws and bring suits on behalf of owners to enforce public performance rights against infringement. For a more detailed description of performing rights society operations and some of the antitrust issues that have surrounded them, see Broadcast Music, Inc. v. Columbia Broadcasting System, Inc., 441 U.S. 1, 99 S.Ct. 1551, 60 L.Ed.2d 1 (1979); Buffalo Broadcasting Co., Inc. v. American Society of Composers, Authors and Publishers, 744 F.2d 917 (1984), *cert. denied*, 469 U.S. 1211, 105 S.Ct. 1181, 84 L.Ed.2d 329 (1985).

5. *Exceptions to the exclusive right of public performance.* Because many of the statutory exceptions to the public performance right apply to the display right, as well, these exceptions will be considered in the following section on the right of public display.

G. SECTION 106(5): THE RIGHT TO DISPLAY THE COPYRIGHTED WORK PUBLICLY

HOUSE REPORT ON COPYRIGHT ACT OF 1976

H.R. Rep. No. 1476, 94th Cong., 2d Sess. 63–64 (1976).

Clause (5) of section 106 represents the first explicit statutory recognition in American copyright law of an exclusive right to show a copyrighted work, or an image of it, to the public. The existence or extent of this right under the present statute is uncertain and subject to challenge. The bill would give the owners of copyright in "literary, musical, dramatic, and choreographic works, pantomimes, and pictorial, graphic, or sculptural works," including the individual images of a motion picture or other audiovisual work, the exclusive right "to display the copyrighted work publicly."

* * *

The corresponding definition of "display" covers any showing of a "copy" of the work, "either directly or by means of a film, slide, television image, or any other device or process." Since "copies" are defined as including the material object "in which the work is first fixed," the right of public display applies to original works of art as well as to reproductions of them. With respect to motion pictures and other audiovisual works, it is a "display" (rather than a "performance") to show their "individual images nonsequentially." In addition to the direct showing of a copy of a work, "display" would include the projection of an image on a screen or other surface by any method, the transmission of an image by electronic or other means, and the showing of an image on a cathode ray tube, or similar viewing apparatus connected with any sort of information storage and retrieval system.

Notes and Questions

1. *The right of public display.* The right of public display extends to all copyrightable subject matter except sound recordings and architectural works. Like performances, unauthorized displays must be "public" to infringe. The definition of "public" in section 101 applies equally to displays and performances.

How economically important is the newly recognized right of public display likely to be to copyright owners?

2. *Exceptions to the right of public display.* Section 109(c) provides that "[n]otwithstanding the provisions of section 106(5), the owner of a particular copy lawfully made under this title, or any person authorized by such owner, is entitled, without the authority of the copyright owner, to display that copy publicly, either directly or by the projection of no more than one image at a time, to viewers present at the place where the copy is located." According to the House Report, this exception "adopts the general principle that the lawful owner of a copy of a work should be able to put his copy on public display without the consent of the copyright owner."

> The exclusive right of public display granted by section 106(5) would not apply where the owner of a copy wishes to show it directly to the public, as in a gallery or display case, or indirectly, as through an opaque projector. Where the copy itself is intended for projection, as in the case of a photographic slide, negative, or transparency, the public projection of a single image would be permitted as long as the viewers are "present at the place where the copy is located."
>
> On the other hand, section 109[(c)] takes account of the potentialities of the new communications media, notably television, cable and optical transmission devices, and information storage and retrieval devices, for replacing printed copies with visual images. First of all, the public display of an image of a copyrighted work would not be exempted from copyright control if the copy from which the image was derived were outside the presence of the viewers. In other words, the display of a visual image of a copyrighted work would be an infringement if the image were transmitted by any method (by closed or open circuit television, for example, or by a computer system) from one place to members of the public located elsewhere.
>
> Moreover, the exemption would extend only to public displays that are made "either directly or by the projection of no more than one image at a time." Thus, even where the copy and the viewers are located at

> the same place, the simultaneous projection of multiple images of the work would not be exempted. For example, where each person in a lecture hall is supplied with a separate viewing apparatus, the copyright owner's permission would generally be required in order to project an image of a work on each individual screen at the same time.
>
> The committee's intention is to preserve the traditional privilege of the owner of a copy to display it directly, but to place reasonable restrictions on the ability to display it indirectly in such a way that the copyright owner's market for reproduction and distribution of copies would be affected.

H.R. REP. NO. 1476, 94th Cong., 2d Sess. 79–80 (1976).

3. *Exceptions to the rights of public performance and display.*

(a) The non-profit exemptions. Review Copyright Act section 110, and consider the following problems.

In the course of his basic humanities class, a community college professor has class members perform the first act of a Sam Shepard play. The performance takes place on the stage of the large lecture auditorium where the class regularly meets. There are 250 students enrolled in the class, and most of them are present for the class in which the performance takes place. Directly before the students take the stage, the professor shows the class a photograph of the set used in the original Broadway production of the play. The photograph is in a book that the professor checked out of the library. To enable the whole class to see it, he places the page containing the photograph on an opaque projector. After the performance, the class discusses various dramatic elements of the Shepard play's first act. Assuming that the Shepard play and the photograph are copyrighted, do these activities fall under any of the section 110 exceptions to infringement liability?

Assume that the humanities class described above is videotaped and broadcast over the community college television station as part of the college's "College of the Air" program. Through this program, members of the general community can sign up for a course, view the class presentations on their television sets at home, send in the written assignments by mail and receive college credit. The broadcast videotape of the class includes both the performance and the display of the photograph of the set. Does this fall into any of the section 110 exceptions?

Assume that the students who perform the first act of the Shepard play enjoy it so much that they decide to present the same performance on the campus commons during lunch time. They take along the opaque projector, project the photograph of the Broadway set on a screen, and tell the audience to imagine that they are performing on the depicted set. A number of students and college staff sit and eat their lunch on the commons while watching the performance. No admission is charged. Are any of the exceptions applicable?

Assume that one of the student actors convinces the others to make the same performance and display at her church's regular Sunday night "Young Adults Group" gathering at the church. The group shares a covered dish supper and then goes to the church sanctuary to view the performance and display. Do any of the section 110 exceptions apply?

Assume that a college marching band, lead by the faculty member who normally conducts the band, assembles in a park on a sunny afternoon. The band plays songs written by the Beatles, Roy Orbison, and other relatively recent popular composers for an hour. After a recess, they play a series of tunes from the rock-opera "Tommy." The band displays a sign stating that its performance is for the benefit of AIDS patients, and during the course of the performance band members pass around a bucket for donations from the passers-by who stop to listen. After the performance, the band turns all the donations over to a local charitable organization that assists AIDS patients. Will the band's performance fall under any of the section 110 exceptions?

What if a local television reporter and film crew tape the band's performance of one of the Beatles' songs, and their station broadcasts the tape on the evening news. Will the television station's actions be exempted from liability under any of the section 110 exceptions?

One of the regular employees at a restaurant plays popular dinner music on the piano for the enjoyment of diners between 8:00 and 10:00 each evening. The restaurant makes no special charge for the entertainment. Will this be excepted?

(b) The section 110(5) public reception exception. The 1976 Act House Report discussed section 110(5) at some length:

> [Section 110(5)] applies to performances and displays of all types of works, and its purpose is to exempt from copyright liability anyone who merely turns on, in a public place, an ordinary radio or television receiving apparatus of a kind commonly sold to members of the public for private use.
>
> The basic rationale of this clause is that the secondary use of the transmission by turning on an ordinary receiver in public is so remote and minimal that no further liability should be imposed. * * *
>
> [The Report discusses the fact situation in Twentieth Century Music Corp. v. Aiken, 422 U.S. 151, 95 S.Ct. 2040, 45 L.Ed.2d 84, 186 U.S.P.Q. 65 (1975): the defendant, owner and operator of a fast-service food shop in downtown Pittsburgh, played a radio with outlets to four speakers in the ceiling in his shop during the business day.]
>
> Under the particular fact situation in the *Aiken* case, assuming a small commercial establishment and the use of a home receiver with four ordinary loudspeakers grouped within a relatively narrow circumference from the set, it is intended that the performances would be exempt under clause (5). However, the Committee considers this fact situation to represent the outer limit of that exemption, and believes that the line should be drawn at that point. Thus, the clause would exempt small commercial establishments whose proprietors merely bring onto their premises standard radio or television equipment and turn it on for their customers' enjoyment, but it would impose liability where the proprietor has a commercial "sound system" installed or converts a standard home receiving apparatus (by augmenting it with sophisticated or extensive amplification equipment) into the equivalent

> of a commercial sound system. Factors to consider in particular cases would include the size, physical arrangement, and noise level of the areas within the establishment where the transmissions are made audible or visible, and the extent to which the receiving apparatus is altered or augmented for the purpose of improving the aural or visual quality of the performance for individual members of the public using those areas.

H.R. REP. NO. 1476, 94th Cong., 2d Sess. 86–87 (1976). The Conference Report added that a small commercial establishment of the type involved in Aiken "which merely augmented a home-type receiver and which was not of sufficient size to justify, as a practical matter, a subscription to a commercial background music service," would be exempt. H.R. REP. NO. 1733, 94th Cong., 2d Sess. 75 (1976).

Given this legislative history, would you find section 110(5) applicable under the following facts?

Defendant owns and operates a total of 749 retail stores located throughout the United States. Seven hundred and nineteen of the stores, operating under the name "Claire's Boutique," range in size from 458 to 2,000 square feet, with an average size of 861 square feet. The other 30 stores, operating under the name Arcadia, have an average size of 2,022 square feet. During fiscal year 1990, defendant earned a net income of $13,402,000. Defendant purchases and supplies to each of its retail stores the following equipment: a 5–watt Radio Shack stereo receiver, two Realistic Minimus 7 speakers, an indoor antenna, and speaker wire. In the three-and-a-half-year period from 1987 to July 1990, Defendant purchased at least 527 receivers, 1,240 speakers, FM antennas, and speaker wire at a total cost of $108,112.42. The stores use the equipment to receive and play radio broadcasts during regular business hours. The receivers are ordinarily kept in a small storage room at the back of the store. Wires from the receiver run to speakers, one of which is located an average of 5–15 feet from the receiver, the other of which is located an average of 20–35 feet from the receiver. Speakers and wires are hidden by a decorative dropped ceiling. See Broadcast Music, Inc. v. Claire's Boutiques, Inc., 949 F.2d 1482, 21 U.S.P.Q.2d 1181 (7th Cir.1991), *cert. denied* 504 U.S. 911, 112 S.Ct. 1942, 118 L.Ed.2d 547 (1992).

Assume that a small, "mom and pop" convenience store keeps a small, inexpensive stereo receiver/tape deck and two small speakers on the back counter of the shop. Its proprietors play tapes of popular music, purchased at a nearby record shop, for workers and customers during regular business hours. Will section 110(5) apply? See generally Shipley, *Copyright Law and Your Neighborhood Bar and Grill: Recent Developments in Performances and the Section 110(5) Exception*, 29 ARIZ. L. REV. 475 (1987).

4. *Other Exceptions and Compulsory License Provisions.* As the House Report notes, public performance and display include not only the initial rendition or showing of a work, but also "any further act by which that rendition or showing is transmitted or communicated to the public." Accordingly, the Copyright Act includes several provisions addressing the retransmission of broadcast signals. Section 111 creates a complex compulsory licensing system that permits cable systems to pick up broadcasting signals and retransmit them to their subscribers. In addition, section 111

permits hotels, apartment houses, and similar establishments to relay broadcast signals to the private rooms or apartments of guests or residents, and exempts from liability "passive carriers," such as AT&T, which merely provide the wires or cables for retransmissions by others. Section 119 provides a compulsory license for satellite retransmissions.

Section 118 provides compulsory licenses to assist public broadcasting stations in transmitting certain public performances and displays of copyrighted works.

H. MORAL RIGHTS AND SECTION 106A

GILLIAM v. AMERICAN BROADCASTING COMPANIES, INC.

United States Court of Appeals for the Second Circuit, 1976.
538 F.2d 14, 192 U.S.P.Q. 1.

LUMBARD, CIRCUIT JUDGE:

Plaintiffs, a group of British writers and performers known as "Monty Python," appeal from a denial by Judge Lasker in the Southern District of a preliminary injunction to restrain the American Broadcasting Company (ABC) from broadcasting edited versions of three separate programs originally written and performed by Monty Python for broadcast by the British Broadcasting Corporation (BBC). We agree with Judge Lasker that the appellants have demonstrated that the excising done for ABC impairs the integrity of the original work. We further find that the countervailing injuries that Judge Lasker found might have accrued to ABC as a result of an injunction at a prior date no longer exist. We therefore direct the issuance of a preliminary injunction by the district court.

Since its formation in 1969, the Monty Python group has gained popularity primarily through its thirty-minute television programs created for BBC as part of a comedy series entitled "Monty Python's Flying Circus." In accordance with an agreement between Monty Python and BBC, the group writes and delivers to BBC scripts for use in the television series. This scriptwriters' agreement recites in great detail the procedure to be followed when any alterations are to be made in the script prior to recording of the program. The essence of this section of the agreement is that, while BBC retains final authority to make changes, appellants or their representatives exercise optimum control over the scripts consistent with BBC's authority and only minor changes may be made without prior consultation with the writers. Nothing in the scriptwriters' agreement entitles BBC to alter a program once it has been recorded. The agreement further provides that, subject to the terms therein, the group retains all rights in the script.

Under the agreement, BBC may license the transmission of recordings of the television programs in any overseas territory. The series has been broadcast in this country primarily on non-commercial public broadcasting television stations, although several of the programs have been broadcast on commercial stations in Texas and Nevada. In each instance, the thirty-minute programs have been broadcast as originally recorded and broadcast in England in their entirety and without commercial interruption.

In October 1973, Time–Life Films acquired the right to distribute in the United States certain BBC television programs, including the Monty Python series. Time–Life was permitted to edit the programs only "for insertion of commercials, applicable censorship or governmental ... rules and regulations, and National Association of Broadcasters and time segment requirements." No similar clause was included in the scriptwriters' agreement between appellants and BBC. Prior to this time, ABC had sought to acquire the right to broadcast excerpts from various Monty Python programs in the spring of 1975, but the group rejected the proposal for such a disjointed format. Thereafter, in July 1975, ABC agreed with Time–Life to broadcast two ninety-minute specials each comprising three thirty-minute Monty Python programs that had not previously been shown in this country.

* * *

ABC broadcast the first of the specials on October 3, 1975. Appellants did not see a tape of the program until late November and were allegedly "appalled" at the discontinuity and "mutilation" that had resulted from the editing done by Time–Life for ABC. Twenty-four minutes of the original 90 minutes of recording had been omitted. Some of the editing had been done in order to make time for commercials; other material had been edited, according to ABC, because the original programs contained offensive or obscene matter.

In early December, Monty Python learned that ABC planned to broadcast the second special on December 26, 1975. The parties began negotiations concerning editing of that program and a delay of the broadcast until Monty Python could view it. These negotiations were futile, however, and on December 15 the group filed this action to enjoin the broadcast and for damages. Following an evidentiary hearing, Judge Lasker found that "the plaintiffs have established an impairment of the integrity of their work" which "caused the film or program ... to lose its iconoclastic verve." According to Judge Lasker, "the damage that has been caused to the plaintiffs is irreparable by its nature." Nevertheless, the judge denied the motion for the preliminary injunction on the grounds that it was unclear who owned the copyright in the programs produced by BBC from the scripts written by Monty Python; that there was a question of whether Time–Life and BBC were indispensable parties to the litigation; that ABC would suffer significant financial loss if it were enjoined a week before the scheduled broadcast; and that Monty Python had displayed a "somewhat disturbing casualness" in their pursuance of the matter.

* * *

I

In determining the availability of injunctive relief at this early stage of the proceedings, Judge Lasker properly considered the harm that would inure to the plaintiffs if the injunction were denied, the harm that defendant would suffer if the injunction were granted, and the likelihood that plaintiffs would ultimately succeed on the merits. We direct the issuance of a preliminary injunction because we find that all these factors weigh in favor of appellants.

There is nothing clearly erroneous in Judge Lasker's conclusion that any injury suffered by appellants as a result of the broadcast of edited versions of their programs was irreparable by its nature. ABC presented the appellants with their first opportunity for broadcast to a nationwide network audience in this country. If ABC adversely misrepresented the quality of Monty Python's work, it is likely that many members of the audience, many of whom, by defendant's admission, were previously unfamiliar with appellants, would not become loyal followers of Monty Python productions. The subsequent injury to appellants' theatrical reputation would imperil their ability to attract the large audience necessary to the success of their venture. Such an injury to professional reputation cannot be measured in monetary terms or recompensed by other relief.

In contrast to the harm that Monty Python would suffer by a denial of the preliminary injunction, Judge Lasker found that ABC's relationship with its affiliates would be impaired by a grant of an injunction within a week of the scheduled December 26 broadcast. The court also found that ABC and its affiliates had advertised the program and had included it in listings of forthcoming television programs that were distributed to the public. Thus a last minute cancellation of the December 26 program, Judge Lasker concluded, would injure defendant financially and in its reputation with the public and its advertisers.

However valid these considerations may have been when the issue before the court was whether a preliminary injunction should immediately precede the broadcast, any injury to ABC is presently more speculative. * * *

We then reach the question whether there is a likelihood that appellants will succeed on the merits. In concluding that there is a likelihood of infringement here, we rely especially on the fact that the editing was substantial, i.e., approximately 27 per cent of the original program was omitted, and the editing contravened contractual provisions that limited the right to edit Monty Python material. It should be emphasized that our discussion of these matters refers only to such facts as have been developed upon the hearing for a preliminary injunction. Modified or contrary findings may become appropriate after a plenary trial.

Judge Lasker denied the preliminary injunction in part because he was unsure of the ownership of the copyright in the recorded program. Appellants first contend that the question of ownership is irrelevant because the recorded program was merely a derivative work taken from the script in which they hold the uncontested copyright. Thus, even if BBC owned the copyright in the recorded program, its use of that work would be limited by the license granted to BBC by Monty Python for use of the underlying script. We agree.

* * *

Since the copyright in the underlying script survives intact despite the incorporation of that work into a derivative work, one who uses the script, even with the permission of the proprietor of the derivative work, may infringe the underlying copyright.

If the proprietor of the derivative work is licensed by the proprietor of the copyright in the underlying work to vend or distribute the derivative work to third parties, those parties will, of course, suffer no liability for their use of the underlying work consistent with the license to the proprietor of the derivative work. Obviously, it was just this type of arrangement that was contemplated in this instance. The scriptwriters' agreement between Monty Python and BBC specifically permitted the latter to license the transmission of the recordings made by BBC to distributors such as Time–Life for broadcast in overseas territories.

One who obtains permission to use a copyrighted script in the production of a derivative work, however, may not exceed the specific purpose for which permission was granted. Most of the decisions that have reached this conclusion have dealt with the improper extension of the underlying work into media or time, i.e., duration of the license, not covered by the grant of permission to the derivative work proprietor.[4] Appellants herein do not claim that the broadcast by ABC violated media or time restrictions contained in the license of the script to BBC. Rather, they claim that revisions in the script, and ultimately in the program, could be made only after consultation with Monty Python, and that ABC's broadcast of a program edited after recording and without consultation with Monty Python exceeded the scope of any license that BBC was entitled to grant.

The rationale for finding infringement when a licensee exceeds time or media restrictions on his license—the need to allow the proprietor of the underlying copyright to control the method in which his work is presented to the public—applies equally to the situation in which a licensee makes an unauthorized use of the underlying work by publishing it in a truncated version. Whether intended to allow greater economic exploitation of the work, as in the media and time cases, or to ensure that the copyright proprietor retains a veto power over revisions desired for the derivative work, the ability of the copyright holder to

4. Thus, a leading commentator on the subject concludes:

> If the copyright owner of an underlying work limits his consent for its use in a derivative work to a given medium (e.g. opera), the copyright owner of the derivative work may not exploit such derivative work in a different medium (e.g. motion pictures) to the extent the derivative work incorporates protectible material from the underlying work.

1 M. Nimmer, Copyright § 45.3.

control his work remains paramount in our copyright law. We find, therefore, that unauthorized editing of the underlying work, if proven, would constitute an infringement of the copyright in that work similar to any other use of a work that exceeded the license granted by the proprietor of the copyright.

If the broadcast of an edited version of the Monty Python program infringed the group's copyright in the script, ABC may obtain no solace from the fact that editing was permitted in the agreements between BBC and Time–Life or Time–Life and ABC. BBC was not entitled to make unilateral changes in the script and was not specifically empowered to alter the recordings once made; Monty Python, moreover, had reserved to itself any rights not granted to BBC. Since a grantor may not convey greater rights than it owns, BBC's permission to allow Time–Life, and hence ABC, to edit appears to have been a nullity.

* * *

Our resolution of these technical arguments serves to reinforce our initial inclination that the copyright law should be used to recognize the important role of the artist in our society and the need to encourage production and dissemination of artistic works by providing adequate legal protection for one who submits his work to the public. We therefore conclude that there is a substantial likelihood that, after a full trial, appellants will succeed in proving infringement of their copyright by ABC's broadcast of edited versions of Monty Python programs. In reaching this conclusion, however, we need not accept appellants' assertion that any editing whatsoever would constitute infringement. Courts have recognized that licensees are entitled to some small degree of latitude in arranging the licensed work for presentation to the public in a manner consistent with the licensee's style or standards. That privilege, however, does not extend to the degree of editing that occurred here especially in light of contractual provisions that limited the right to edit Monty Python material.

II

It also seems likely that appellants will succeed on the theory that, regardless of the right ABC had to broadcast an edited program, the cuts made constituted an actionable mutilation of Monty Python's work. This cause of action, which seeks redress for deformation of an artist's work, finds its roots in the continental concept of droit moral, or moral right, which may generally be summarized as including the right of the artist to have his work attributed to him in the form in which he created it.

American copyright law, as presently written, does not recognize moral rights or provide a cause of action for their violation, since the law seeks to vindicate the economic, rather than the personal, rights of authors. Nevertheless, the economic incentive for artistic and intellectual creation that serves as the foundation for American copyright law cannot be reconciled with the inability of artists to obtain relief for mutilation or misrepresentation of their work to the public on which the artists are financially dependent. Thus courts have long granted relief for misrepresentation of an artist's work by relying on theories outside the statutory law of copyright, such as contract law or the tort of unfair competition. Although such decisions are clothed in terms of proprietary right in one's creation, they also properly vindicate the author's personal right to prevent the presentation of his work to the public in a distorted form.

* * *

* * * We find that the truncated version at times omitted the climax of the skits to which appellants' rare brand of humor was leading and at other times deleted essential elements in the schematic development of a story line.[12] We therefore agree with Judge Lasker's conclusion that the edited version broadcast by ABC impaired the integrity of appellants' work and represented to the public as the product of appellants what was actually a mere caricature of their talents. * * *

Notes and Questions

1. *Moral rights.* The *Gilliam* court recognizes that the plaintiffs essentially were seeking to vindicate moral rights through the vehicle of the economic right of adaptation. American copyright law, pragmaticly seeking to benefit the general public, has focused exclusively on granting authors economic rights as an incentive to create. In contrast, many countries' copyright laws recognize and protect an author's personal, as well as economic, interests in his work. The personal rights, referred to generally as "*droit moral*," or "moral rights," protect the author's interest in his professional honor and reputation, self-expression and privacy.

The right of integrity enables the author to prevent mutilation or distortion of his work which may injure his professional reputation. The right of attribution, or right of paternity, protects the author's right to be acknowledged as the author of the work, to avoid having the work misattributed to others, and to avoid having the works of others misattributed to him. As one scholar has explained: "The notion is that the work of art is an expression of the artist's personality. Distortion, dismemberment or misrepresentation of the work mistreats an expression of the artist's personality, affects his artistic identity, personality, and honor, and thus impairs a legally protected personality interest." Merryman, *The Refrigerator of Bernard Buffet*, 27 HASTINGS L.J. 1023, 1027 (1976).[8]

12. A single example will illustrate the extent of distortion engendered by the editing. In one skit, an upper class English family is engaged in a discussion of the tonal quality of certain words as "woody" or "tinny." The father soon begins to suggest certain words with sexual connotations as either "woody" or "tinny," whereupon the mother fetches a bucket of water and pours it over his head. The skit continues from this point. The ABC edit eliminates this middle sequence so that the father is comfortably dressed at one moment and, in the next moment, is shown in a soaked condition without any explanation for the change in his appearance.

8. Some countries recognize two additional moral rights. First, the right of disclosure, or divulgation, recognizes the author's right to control when, whether, and under what circumstances the work will be published or disclosed to the public. United States copyright law protects this interest through the economic rights of distribution to the public, reproduction, public performance, and public display, as long as the author refrains from conveying the copy-

Is the injury the *Gilliam* court finds to Monty Python economic or personal in nature?

The Berne Convention, Article 6bis, provides:

> (1) Independently of the author's economic rights, and even after the transfer of the said rights, the author shall have the right to claim authorship of the work, and to object to any distortion, mutilation or other modification of, or other derogatory action in relation to, the said work, which would be prejudicial to his honor or reputation.
>
> * * *

This requirement was an important factor in the United States' long hesitation to join the Berne Union. Why might there be opposition to bringing the United States into compliance?

When Congress ultimately ratified the Berne Convention, it determined that in combination, existing federal and state law doctrines were sufficient to satisfy the United States' Article 6bis obligations, so that no further legislation would be needed:

> [T]here is a composite of laws in this country that provides the kind of protection envisioned by Article 6bis. Federal laws include 17 U.S.C. § 106, relating to derivative works; 17 U.S.C. § 115(a)(2), relating to distortions of musical works used under the compulsory license respecting sound recordings; 17 U.S.C. § 203, relating to termination of transfers and licenses and section 43(a) of the Lanham Act, relating to false designations of origin and false descriptions. State and local laws include those relating to publicity, contractual violations, fraud and misrepresentation, unfair competition, defamation, and invasion of privacy. In addition, eight states have recently enacted specific statutes protecting the rights of integrity and paternity in certain works of art. Finally, some courts have recognized the equivalent of such rights.

Berne Convention Implementation Act of 1988, H.R. REP. NO. 609, 100th Cong., 2d Sess. 33–34 (1988).

How, exactly, did the *Gilliam* court find that the ABC specials infringed the Monty Python copyright? Will the economic right of adaptation generally be available to vindicate an author's moral rights? As a back-up, the *Gilliam* court found that the plaintiffs stated a cause of action under section 43(a) of the Lanham Act, 15 U.S.C.A. § 1125(a). For a discussion of how section 43(a) has been used to vindicate moral rights, see Chapter 7, § III, *infra*. For a discussion of common-law protection for moral rights, see Damich, *The Right of Personality: A Common–Law Basis for the Protection of the Moral Rights of Authors*, 23 GA. L. REV. 1 (1988). For a comparison of moral rights in other countries, see Merryman, *supra*.

State statutory moral rights provisions, mentioned in the House Report, tend to be limited to works of fine art. They vary somewhat in their approach. For example, the California statute, CAL. CIV. CODE § 987

right. The right of withdrawal recognizes an author's right to withdraw a work after it has already been published (upon payment of an indemnity to the owner) or to modify it. This right has no parallel in United States copyright law, and little parallel in any United States law. See generally P. GOLDSTEIN, COPYRIGHT PRINCIPLES, LAW AND PRACTICE § 15.23–15.24.4 (1989).

(West Supp. 1993), declares that "the physical alteration or destruction of fine art, which is an expression of the artist's personality, is detrimental to the artist's reputation," and that there is "a public interest in preserving the integrity of cultural and artistic creations." *Id.*, § 987(a). It prohibits persons other than the artist from intentionally committing or authorizing "any physical defacement, mutilation, alteration, or destruction of a work of fine art." *Id.*, § 987(c). The New York statute, N.Y. ART & CULT. AFF. LAW § 14.03 (McKinney Supp. 1994), on the other hand, prohibits knowing, unauthorized publication or public display of a mutilated work of fine art if the publication or display expressly or impliedly indicates that the work is that of the artist and is reasonably likely to damage the artist's reputation. *Id.*, § 14.03(1). It also grants the artist the right to claim authorship, or, "for just and valid reason," to disclaim authorship of a work. *Id.*, § 14.03(2).

Because Congress has subsequently enacted a narrow moral rights provision for fine arts, discussed below, causes of action under these state moral rights statutes may be preempted. See 17 U.S.C.A. § 301(f) and Chapter 9 § II, *infra*. For a practical assessment of litigation under the state statutes, see Karlen, *Moral Rights and Real Life Artists*, 15 HASTINGS COMM. & ENT. L.J. 929 (1993).

2. *The Visual Artists Rights Act of 1990.* Even though Congress concluded that the United States complied with the requirements of Berne Convention Article 6bis, it continued to consider the issue of moral rights and, just two years after implementing the Berne Convention, enacted the Visual Artists Rights Act of 1990, Pub. L. No. 101–650, 104 Stat. 5128–5133 ("VARA"), which is codified in sections 101 (definition of "a work of visual art") and 106A of the Copyright Act. VARA constituted the first express recognition of moral rights in United States copyright law. Congress justified its decision in the accompanying House Report:

> "The theory of moral rights is that they result in a climate of artistic worth and honor that encourages the author in the arduous act of creation." Artist's rights are consistent with the purpose behind the copyright laws and the Constitutional provision they implement: "To promote the Progress of Science and useful Arts." * * *
>
> > * * * These rights :
> >
> > promote * * * the interests of artists and public alike. [T]hey benefit artists by assuring their rights to recognition for the works they have created and by protecting the works themselves against destruction or mutilation. These safeguards may enhance the creative environment in which artists labor. Equally important, these safeguards enhance our cultural heritage. The attribution right not only affords basic fairness to artists, it promotes the public interest by increasing available information concerning artworks and their provenance, and by helping ensure that information is accurate. The integrity right helps preserve artworks intact for all of us to enjoy.

H.R. REP. NO. 514, 101st Cong., 2d Sess. 5, 14 (1990) (quoting, in order, *The Visual Artists Rights Act of 1989: Hearings on H.R. 2690 Before the Subcommittee on Courts, Intellectual Property, and the Administration of*

Justice of the House Committee on the Judiciary, 101st Cong., 1st Sess. (Statement of the Honorable Ralph Oman) (1989); U.S. CONST. art. I, § 8, cl. 8; *Hearings on H.R. 2690, supra,* (statement of Prof. Jane C. Ginsburg).

Study the section 101 definition of "works of visual art" and section 106A of the Copyright Act. Why should VARA's protection be restricted to original and limited edition copies? What is the relationship between the artist's inalienable right of integrity and the copyright owner's right to make derivative works? Are they likely to conflict?

How might an artist establish prejudice to his honor or reputation, as required in sections 106A(a)(2) and (3)(A), or that his work is of recognized stature, as required in 106A(a)(3)(B)? The district court in Carter v. Helmsley–Spear, Inc., 861 F.Supp. 303, 33 U.S.P.Q.2d 1225 (S.D.N.Y.1994), undertook to provide the first judicial answers to these questions.

The court first considered whether "intentional distortion, mutilation, or modification" of the plaintiffs' work would be "prejudicial to plaintiffs' honor or reputation." It found that the drafters of VARA intended courts to apply the ordinary dictionary meanings of "prejudice," "honor" and "reputation." The question was whether "alteration would cause injury to plaintiffs' good name, public esteem, or reputation in the artistic community." *Id.*, 861 F.Supp. at 323, 33 U.S.P.Q.2d at 1236. The court rejected the testimony of the defendants' expert witness that "alteration of the work would not adversely impact plaintiffs' reputation because, in his opinion, the artists have no reputation." *Id.*, 861 F.Supp. at 324, 33 U.S.P.Q.2d at 1237. The court observed that the artist need not have a reputation independent of the particular work of art at issue—Congress intended to protect less-known or appreciated artists, as well as famous ones. Thus, the court found, the appropriate framework is to focus on the professional honor or reputation of the plaintiff "as embodied in the work that is protected." *Id.* Does this transform the issue into whether the defendant's intentional distortion, mutilation, or modification of the protected work prejudices the work's reputation?

The court then turned to the issue of whether the work at issue was one of "recognized stature." The court observed:

> The phrase "recognized stature" is not defined in VARA. In light of the preservative goal of this Section, however, the recognized stature requirement is best viewed as a gate-keeping mechanism—protection is afforded only to those works that art experts, the art community, or society in general views as possessing stature. A plaintiff need not demonstrate that his or her art work is equal in stature to that created by artists such as Picasso, Chagall, or Giacometti. As one commentator has noted, "The advantages of the 'of recognized stature' qualification include barring nuisance law suits, such as [a law suit over] the destruction of a five-year-old's fingerpainting by her class mate...." Damich, The Visual Artists Rights Act of 1990: Toward a Federal System of Moral Rights Protection for Visual Art, 39 Cath.U.L.Rev. 945, 954 (1990). Nor must the trier of fact personally find the art to be aesthetically pleasing; indeed, courts have persistently shunned the role of art critic.

> The recognized stature requirement must be interpreted in such manner as to maintain the preservative purpose of 17 U.S.C. § 106(a)(3)(B) and in light of this Section's plain meaning. Thus, for a work of visual art to be protected under this Section, a plaintiff must make a two-tiered showing: (1) that the visual art in question has "stature," i.e. is viewed as meritorious, and (2) that this stature is "recognized" by art experts, other members of the artistic community, or by some cross-section of society. In making this showing, plaintiffs generally, but not inevitably, will need to call expert witnesses to testify before the trier of fact. * * *

Id., 861 F.Supp. at 324–25, 33 U.S.P.Q.2d at 1237–38.

Suppose that the owner of an original metal sculpture allows it to rust through lack of proper maintenance. Would this violate the artist's right of integrity in the work? What if a shopping mall which owned an original sculpture of geese in flight tied red ribbons around the geese's necks during the Christmas shopping season? Would that be a violation? Why or why not? See H.R. REP. NO. 514, *supra*, at 17–18; Gorman, *Visual Artists Rights Act of 1990*, 38 J. COPYRIGHT SOC. 233, 235–36 (1991).

Suppose that a church commissioned an artist to create a mural on the back wall of the church sanctuary in 1993. The reaction of the congregation to the finished product was mixed. Some members thought it was merely ugly and lacking in artistic merit. Others found it generally offensive, and the rest found it sacrilegious. They would all like to remove it from their sanctuary wall. Will VARA permit it? See 17 U.S.C.A. § 113(d).

How much impact on visual artists' rights is VARA likely ultimately to have? For a full assessment of VARA, see Gorman, *supra*. For comparisons of VARA and state fine arts statutes, see American Association of Law Schools Art Law Section Symposium, *California Art Legislation Goes Federal*, 15 HASTINGS COMM. & ENT. L.J 893–987 (1993).

3. *Problem.* Assume that in 1995, A, a fine-art photographer, took a photograph of an elderly woman gazing at children in an urban park. Due to A's method of capturing the sunlight, her composition and her use of special filters, the photograph had a highly artistic, spiritual quality. A titled the photograph "Time Passes," and created three copies, which she signed and numbered and displayed for sale in galleries.

The following year, A sold the negative of "Time Passes" and the copyright in the photograph to B, a publisher who wished to include the photograph in a high quality "coffee table" book of photographs of urban scenes. Due to a mix-up, when the book was published it identified Z as the photographer of "Time Passes."

B later sold the negative and copyright to C, a manufacturer of knick-knacks. C used the negative to produce ash trays. "Time Passes" was laminated onto the bottom of each ash tray, where users would stub out their cigarette butts. Because of the lamination process and the cheap materials C used, the colors were very different than the colors in the negative.

Meanwhile, the gallery sold one of A's copies of "Time Passes" to X. X died, and his heir, D, inherited the copy of "Time Passes." D, a multimedia artist, cut the elderly woman's face out of the copy and combined it with cuttings from other photographs and materials to make his own work.

Have there been any violations of section 106A?

4. *What's next?* Should Congress consider extending moral rights to other types of works? If so, which types?

Film directors have argued forcefully that moral rights should be extended to motion pictures. Their concerns arise from practices such as "colorization," (a process by which black and white film prints are transferred to videotape and electronically encoded with color), "panning and scanning" (a process by which theatrical motion pictures are altered to fit the television screen), "lexiconning" (electronic time compression of motion pictures to fit into television broadcast time slots), and "letterboxing" (a technique which reduces the size of the image in order to retain the original theatrical motion picture composition on the television screen, thus leaving black bands across the top and bottom of the screen). These practices, they have argued, are an unacceptable interference with the artistic integrity of the original films, and should be regulated through the granting of moral rights to a motion picture's director and principal screen writer. See REGISTER OF COPYRIGHTS, REPORT ON TECHNOLOGICAL ALTERATIONS TO MOTION PICTURES AND OTHER AUDIOVISUAL WORKS: IMPLICATIONS FOR CREATORS, COPYRIGHT OWNERS, AND CONSUMERS (1989) (*reprinted at* 10 LOY. ENT. L.J. 1 (1990)).

While Congress has held hearings on the issue and entertained bills, it has declined thus far to amend the Copyright Act to extend moral rights to motion pictures. See H.R. REP. NO. 514, *supra*, at 10. What concerns might Congress have in extending moral rights as the directors have requested? See *id.*; Beyer, *Internationalism, Art, and the Suppression of Innovation: Film Colorization and the Philosophy of Moral Rights*, 82 N.W. U. L. REV. 1011 (1988). Would enacting this legislation alleviate the problems identified in the prior paragraph?

I. INDIRECT INFRINGEMENT

Though the Copyright Act of 1976 does not expressly prescribe liability for the direct infringement of others, it is well accepted that such liability exists. Section 106 grants copyright owners not only the exclusive right to exploit their works themselves, but also to authorize others to do so. The House Report states: "Use of the phrase 'to authorize' is intended to avoid any questions as to the liability of contributory infringers. For example, a person who lawfully acquires an authorized copy of a motion picture would be an infringer if he or she engages in the business of renting it to others for purposes of unauthorized public performance." H.R. REP. NO. 1476, 94th Cong., 2d Sess. 61 (1976).

There are two distinct doctrines under which a party can be held liable for the direct copyright infringement of others. They are identified as "vicarious liability" and "contributory liability." Any defendant found to have infringed under one of these doctrines will be jointly and severally liable with the direct infringer. Like direct copyright infringement, both indirect infringement doctrines draw conceptually from the law of torts. Needless to say, under either doctrine, there must have been a direct infringement by a third party before a defendant can be held liable.

1. *Vicarious Liability*

The Court of Appeals for the Second Circuit set forth the elements of vicarious liability in Shapiro, Bernstein & Co. v. H. L. Green Co., 316 F.2d 304, 137 U.S.P.Q. 275 (2d Cir.1963). In *Green*, the defendant, Green Company licensed Jalen to operate a phonograph record department in its department stores, as a concessionaire. Green and Jalen's licensing agreement provided that Jalen and its employees would "abide by, observe and obey all rules and regulations promulgated from time to time by H.L. Green Company, Inc." Green reserved the right in its "unreviewable discretion" to discharge employees believed to be conducting themselves improperly, and Jalen agreed to save Green harmless from any claims arising from Jalen's conduct of the record concession. The parties agreed that Jalen would pay Green ten (or in some cases twelve) percent of Jalen's gross receipts from the sale of records as its license fee for the concession. *Id.*, 316 F.2d at 308, 137 U.S.P.Q. at 278.

During the course of the parties' relationship, Jalen ordered, purchased and paid for the records it sold. Jalen employees made all the record sales, and were controlled and supervised by Jalen. Completely unknown to Green, Jalen manufactured infringing records and sold them in the Green stores. Notwithstanding the fact that Green did not know of the infringement or actively participate in it, the court found it vicariously liable for Jalen's infringement:

> When the right and ability to supervise coalesce with an obvious and direct financial interest in the exploitation of copyrighted materials—even in the absence of actual knowledge that the copyright monopoly is being impaired—the purposes of copyright law may be best effectuated by the imposition of liability upon the beneficiary of that exploitation.
>
> The two lines of precedent most nearly relevant to the case before us are those which deal, on the one hand, with the landlord leasing his property at a fixed rental to a tenant who engages in copyright infringing conduct on the leased premises and, on the other hand, the proprietor or manager of a dance hall or music hall leasing his premises to or hiring a dance band, which brings in customers and profits to the proprietor by performing copyrighted music but without complying with the terms of the Copyright Act. If the landlord lets his premises without knowledge of the impending infringement by his tenant, exercises no supervision over him, charges a fixed rental and receives no other benefit from the infringement, and contributes in no way to it, it has been held that the landlord is not liable for his tenant's wrongdoing. But, the cases are legion which hold the dance hall proprietor liable for the

> infringement of copyright resulting from the performance of a musical composition by a band or orchestra whose activities provide the proprietor with a source of customers and enhanced income. He is liable whether the bandleader is considered, as a technical matter, an employee or an independent contractor, and whether or not the proprietor has knowledge of the compositions to be played or any control over their selection.
>
> We believe that the principle which can be extracted from the dance hall cases is a sound one and, under the facts of the case before us, is here applicable. * * * Green's relationship to its infringing licensee, as well as its strong concern for the financial success of the phonograph record concession, renders it liable for the unauthorized sales of the "bootleg" records.

Id., 316 F.2d at 307–08, 137 U.S.P.Q. at 277–78.

Notes and Questions

1. *Vicarious liability.* The vicarious liability doctrine is based on principles similar to those underlying the tort doctrine of *respondeat superior*, but, as the *Green* case demonstrates, it requires no strict employment relationship. What leads the *Green* court to suggest that the landlord does not stand to benefit from its tenant's copyright infringement? How does the landlord's position differ from that of the dance hall operator? With regard to the defendant's ability to control the infringer's activities, should the mere legal right to control the infringer suffice for liability, or should courts require a showing that the defendant has the practical ability to do so?

A number of case opinions have found officers and directors of closely held corporations vicariously liable for their corporation's direct copyright infringement, when it is demonstrated that they had the ability to control the corporation's actions and stood to gain financially by virtue of possible salary bonuses, increased dividends or increased share value. In some cases, courts have found such vicarious liability even when the officer did not herself participate in the infringement, or know of it. See, e.g., Mallven Music v. 2001 VIP of Lexington, Inc., 230 U.S.P.Q. 543 (E.D.Ky.1986). Does this give copyright plaintiffs an advantage over plaintiffs seeking to hold officers and directors personally liable for other types of corporate wrongs, such as corporate breaches of contract or personal injuries? If so, does that make sense?

2. *Contributory Infringement Liability*

To be liable for contributory infringement, the defendant must know of the infringing activity and induce, cause or materially contribute to it. See Gershwin Publishing Corp. v. Columbia Artists Management, Inc., 443 F.2d 1159, 170 U.S.P.Q. 182 (2d Cir.1971). Given these elements, contributory infringement may be found in a wide array of settings.

A defendant might materially assist the direct infringer by selling him the means through which the infringement is accomplished, knowing that the infringing activity will occur. However, the Supreme Court has imposed an additional prerequisite to liability when the defendant's only involvement is to sell materials or equipment used in the direct infringement. In Sony Corp. v. Universal City Studios, Inc., 464 U.S. 417, 104 S.Ct. 774, 78 L.Ed.2d 574 (1984), owners of copyright in broadcast television programs sued the defendant, Sony, alleging that Sony sold video tape recorders which made it possible for purchasers (generally, members of the public) to make unauthorized copies of their programs. The plaintiffs made no attempt to sue the individual members of the public who made the allegedly infringing copies. Rather, they sought to cut off their means of infringing by enjoining further sale of the video recorders. They also sought damages and an equitable accounting of Sony's profits. In denying relief, the Court explained:

> If vicarious liability is to be imposed on Sony in this case, it must rest on the fact that it has sold equipment with constructive knowledge of the fact that its customers may use that equipment to make unauthorized copies of copyrighted material. There is no precedent in the law of copyright for the imposition of vicarious liability on such a theory. The closest analogy is provided by the patent law cases to which it is appropriate to refer because of the historic kinship between patent law and copyright law.
>
> In the Patent Act both the concept of infringement and the concept of contributory infringement are expressly defined by statute. The prohibition against contributory infringement is confined to the knowing sale of a component especially made for use in connection with a particular patent. There is no suggestion in the statute that one patentee may object to the sale of a product that might be used in connection with other patents. Moreover, the Act expressly provides that the sale of a "staple article or commodity of commerce suitable for substantial noninfringing use" is not contributory infringement. 35 U.S.C. § 271(c).
>
> When a charge of contributory infringement is predicated entirely on the sale of an article of commerce that is used by the purchaser to infringe a patent, the public interest in access to that article of commerce is necessarily implicated. A finding of contributory infringement does not, of course, remove the article from the market altogether; it does, however, give the patentee effective control over the sale of that item. Indeed, a finding of contributory infringement is normally the functional equivalent of holding that the disputed article is within the monopoly granted to the patentee.
>
> For that reason, in contributory infringement cases arising under the patent laws the Court has always recognized the critical importance of not allowing the patentee to extend his monopoly beyond the limits of his specific grant. * * *
>
> We recognize there are substantial differences between the patent and copyright laws. But in both areas the contributory infringement doctrine is grounded on the recognition that adequate protection of a monopoly may require the courts to look beyond actual duplication of a device or publication to the products or

> activities that make such duplication possible. The staple article of commerce doctrine must strike a balance between a copyright holder's legitimate demand for effective—not merely symbolic—protection of the statutory monopoly, and the rights of others freely to engage in substantially unrelated areas of commerce. Accordingly, the sale of copying equipment, like the sale of other articles of commerce, does not constitute contributory infringement if the product is widely used for legitimate, unobjectionable purposes. Indeed, it need merely be capable of substantial noninfringing uses.

Id., 464 U.S. at 439–42, 104 S.Ct. at 787–89, 78 L.Ed.2d at 591–592. In the case before it, the Court found that many purchasers used the video recorders merely to "time-shift"—record a program they could not view as it was being televised in order to watch it at a later time. Some copyright owners did not object to taping for this purpose, and even when the taping was unauthorized, the Court found that it constituted a "fair use," and thus did not infringe the copyrights in the time-shifted programs. Thus, a substantial noninfringing use existed for the video recorders, and Sony could not be held liable for contributory copyright infringement, even though some purchasers might use the video recorders to infringe plaintiffs' copyrights.

Notes and Questions

1. *Contributory infringement liability.* Was it appropriate for the Court to transfer the limitation Congress placed on contributory patent infringement to the context of contributory copyright infringement? See 1 P. GOLDSTEIN, COPYRIGHT PRINCIPLES, LAW AND PRACTICE § 6.2.2 (1989). Is there a better, more equitable way to accommodate the conflicting interests in cases such as *Sony*? See generally Oddi, *Contributory Copyright Infringement: The Tort and Technological Tensions*, 64 NOTRE DAME L. REV. 47 (1989).

IV. FAIR USE

HARPER & ROW, PUBLISHERS, INC. v. NATION ENTERPRISES

United States Supreme Court, 1985.
471 U.S. 539, 105 S.Ct. 2218, 85 L.Ed.2d 588.

JUSTICE O'CONNOR delivered the opinion of the Court.

This case requires us to consider to what extent the "fair use" provision of the Copyright Revision Act of 1976, (hereinafter the Copyright Act) 17 U.S.C. § 107, sanctions the unauthorized use of quotations from a public figure's unpublished manuscript. * * *

I

In February 1977, shortly after leaving the White House, former President Gerald R. Ford contracted with petitioners Harper & Row and Reader's Digest, to publish his as yet unwritten memoirs. The memoirs were to contain "significant hitherto unpublished material" concerning the Watergate crisis, Mr. Ford's pardon of former President Nixon and "Mr. Ford's reflections on this period of history, and the morality and personalities involved." In addition to the right to publish the Ford memoirs in book form, the agreement gave petitioners the exclusive right to license prepublication excerpts, known in the trade as "first serial rights." Two years later, as the memoirs were nearing completion, petitioners negotiated a prepublication licensing agreement with Time, a weekly news magazine. Time agreed to pay $25,000, $12,500 in advance and an additional $12,500 at publication, in exchange for the right to excerpt 7,500 words from Mr. Ford's account of the Nixon pardon. The issue featuring the excerpts was timed to appear approximately one week before shipment of the full length book version to bookstores. Exclusivity was an important consideration; Harper & Row instituted procedures designed to maintain the confidentiality of the manuscript, and Time retained the right to renegotiate the second payment should the material appear in print prior to its release of the excerpts.

Two to three weeks before the Time article's scheduled release, an unidentified person secretly brought a copy of the Ford manuscript to Victor Navasky, editor of The Nation, a political commentary magazine. Mr. Navasky knew that his possession of the manuscript was not authorized and that the manuscript must be returned quickly to his "source" to avoid discovery. He hastily put together what he believed was "a real hot news story" composed of quotes, paraphrases, and facts drawn exclusively from the manuscript. Mr. Navasky attempted no independent commentary, research or criticism, in part because of the need for speed if he was to "make news" by "publish[ing] in advance of publication of the Ford book." The 2,250–word article * * * appeared on April 3, 1979. As a result of The Nation's article, Time canceled its piece and refused to pay the remaining $12,500.

[The Petitioners brought suit, alleging copyright infringement. The district court found The Nation liable for infringement and rejected its argument that its article constituted a fair use. The Court of Appeals for the Second Circuit reversed.] The Court of Appeals was especially influenced by the "politically significant" nature of the subject matter and its conviction that it is not "the purpose of the Copyright Act to impede that harvest of knowledge so necessary to a democratic state" or "chill the activities of the press by forbidding a circumscribed use of copyrighted words."

II

We agree with the Court of Appeals that copyright is intended to increase and not to impede the harvest of knowledge. But we believe the Second Circuit gave insufficient deference to the scheme established by the Copyright Act for fostering the original works that provide the seed and substance of this harvest. * * * As we noted last Term: "[This] limited grant is a means by which an important public purpose may be achieved. It is intended to motivate the creative activity of authors and inventors by the provision of a special reward, and to allow the public access to the products of their genius after the limited period of exclusive control has expired." *Sony Corp. of America v. Universal City Studios, Inc.*, 464 U.S. 417, 429, 104 S.Ct. 774, 782, 78 L.Ed.2d 574 (1984). "The monopoly created by copyright thus rewards the individual author in order to benefit the public." *Id.*, at 477, 104 S.Ct., at 807 (dissenting opinion). This principle applies equally to works of fiction and nonfiction. The book at issue here, for example, was two years in the making, and began with a contract giving the author's copyright to the publishers in exchange for their services in producing and marketing the work. In preparing the book, Mr. Ford drafted essays and word portraits of public figures and participated in hundreds of taped interviews that were later distilled to chronicle his personal viewpoint. It is evident that the monopoly granted by copyright actively served its intended purpose of inducing the creation of new material of potential historical value.

* * *

[T]here is no dispute that the unpublished manuscript of "A Time to Heal," as a whole, was protected by § 106 from unauthorized reproduction. Nor do respondents dispute that verbatim copying of excerpts of the manuscript's original form of expression would constitute infringement unless excused as fair use. * * *

* * * The Nation has admitted to lifting verbatim quotes of the author's original language totaling between 300 and 400 words and constituting some 13% of The Nation article. In using generous verbatim excerpts of Mr. Ford's unpublished manuscript to lend authenticity to its account of the forthcoming memoirs, The Nation effectively arrogated to itself the right of first publication, an important marketable subsidiary right. For the reasons set forth below, we find that this use of the copyrighted manuscript, even stripped to the verbatim quotes conceded by The Nation to be copyrightable expression, was not a fair use within the meaning of the Copyright Act.

III

A

Fair use was traditionally defined as "a privilege in others than the owner of the copyright to use the copyrighted material in a reasonable manner without his consent." H. Ball, Law of Copyright and Literary Property 260 (1944) (hereinafter Ball). The statutory formulation of the defense of fair use in the Copyright Act reflects the intent of Congress to codify the common-law doctrine. Section 107 requires a case-by-case determination whether a particular use is fair, and the statute notes four nonexclusive factors to be considered. This approach was "intended to restate the [pre-existing] judicial doctrine of fair use, not to change, narrow, or enlarge it in any way." H.R.Rep. No. 94–1476, p. 66 (1976) (hereinafter House Report), U.S.Code Cong. & Admin.News 1976, pp. 5659, 5680.

"[T]he author's consent to a reasonable use of his copyrighted works ha[d] always been implied by the courts as a necessary incident of the constitutional policy of promoting the progress of science and the useful arts, since a prohibition of such use would inhibit subsequent writers from attempting to improve upon prior works and thus . . . frustrate the very ends sought to be attained." Ball 260. * * *

As early as 1841, Justice Story gave judicial recognition to the doctrine in a case that concerned the letters of another former President, George Washington.

> "[A] reviewer may fairly cite largely from the original work, if his design be really and truly to use the passages for the purposes of fair and reasonable criticism. On the other hand, it is as clear, that if he thus cites the most important parts of the work, with a view, not to criticize, but to supersede the use of the original work, and substitute the review for it, such a use will be deemed in law a piracy." *Folsom v. Marsh*, 9 F.Cas. 342, 344–345 (No. 4,901) (CC Mass.)

As Justice Story's hypothetical illustrates, the fair use doctrine has always precluded a use that "supersede[s] the use of the original." *Ibid.*

Perhaps because the fair use doctrine was predicated on the author's implied consent to "reasonable and customary" use when he released his work for public consumption, fair use traditionally was not recognized as a defense to charges of copying from an author's as yet unpublished works. Under common-law copyright, "the property of the author . . . in his intellectual creation [was] absolute until he voluntarily part[ed] with the same." *American Tobacco Co. v. Werckmeister*, 207 U.S. 284, 299, 28 S.Ct. 72, 77, 52 L.Ed. 208 (1907). This absolute rule, however, was tempered in practice by the equitable nature of the fair use doctrine. In a given case, factors such as implied consent through *de facto* publication on performance or dissemination of a work may tip the balance of equities in favor of prepublication use. * * * But it has never been seriously disputed that "the fact that the plaintiff's work is unpublished . . . is a factor tending to negate the defense of fair use." 3 M. Nimmer, Copyright § 13.05, at 13–62, n.2 (1984). Publication of an author's expression before he has authorized its dissemination seriously infringes the author's right to decide when and whether it will be made public, a factor not present in fair use of published works. Respondents contend, however, that Congress, in including first publication among the rights enumerated in § 106, which are expressly subject to fair use under § 107, intended that fair use would apply *in pari materia* to published and unpublished works. The Copyright Act does not support this proposition.

The Copyright Act represents the culmination of a major legislative reexamination of copyright doctrine. Among its other innovations, it eliminated publication "as a dividing line between common law and statutory protection,'' House Report, at 129 U.S.Code Cong. & Admin.News 1976, p. 5745, extending statutory protection to all works from the time of their creation. It also recognized for the first time a distinct statutory right of first publication, which had previously been an element of the common-law protections afforded unpublished works. The Report of the House Committee on the Judiciary confirms that ''Clause (3) of section 106, establishes the exclusive right of publications.... Under this provision the copyright owner would have the right to control the first public distribution of an authorized copy ... of his work.'' *Id.*, at 62 U.S.Code Cong. & Admin.News 1976, p. 5675.

Though the right of first publication, like the other rights enumerated in § 106, is expressly made subject to the fair use provision of § 107, fair use analysis must always be tailored to the individual case. The nature of the interest at stake is highly relevant to whether a given use is fair. From the beginning, those entrusted with the task of revision recognized the ''overbalancing reasons to preserve the common law protection of undisseminated works until the author or his successor chooses to disclose them.'' Copyright Law Revision, Report of the Register of Copyrights on the General Revision of the U.S. Copyright Law, 87th Cong., 1st Sess., 41 (Comm. Print 1961). The right of first publication implicates a threshold decision by the author whether and in what form to release his work. First publication is inherently different from other § 106 rights in that only one person can be the first publisher; as the contract with Time illustrates, the commercial value of the right lies primarily in exclusivity. Because the potential damage to the author from judicially enforced ''sharing'' of the first publication right with unauthorized users of his manuscript is substantial, the balance of equities in evaluating such a claim of fair use inevitably shifts.

* * *

* * * We conclude that the unpublished nature of a work is ''[a] key, though not necessarily determinative, factor'' tending to negate a defense of fair use. S. Rep. No. 94–473, 64 (1975).

We also find unpersuasive respondents' argument that fair use may be made of a soon-to-be-published manuscript on the ground that the author has demonstrated he has no interest in nonpublication. This argument assumes that the unpublished nature of copyrighted material is only relevant to letters or other confidential writings not intended for dissemination. It is true that common-law copyright was often enlisted in the service of personal privacy. In its commercial guise, however, an author's right to choose when he will publish is no less deserving of protection. The period encompassing the work's initiation, its preparation, and its grooming for public dissemination is a crucial one for any literary endeavor. The Copyright Act, which accords the copyright owner the ''right to control the first public distribution'' of his work, House Report, at 62, echos the common law's concern that the author or copyright owner retain control throughout this critical stage. The obvious benefit to author and public alike of assuring authors the leisure to develop their ideas free from fear of expropriation outweighs any short-term "news value" to be gained from premature publication of the author's expression. * * * The author's control of first public distribution implicates not only his personal interest in creative control but his property interest in exploitation of prepublication rights, which are valuable in themselves and serve as a valuable adjunct to publicity and marketing. * * * Under ordinary circumstances, the author's right to control the first public appearance of his undisseminated expression will outweigh a claim of fair use.

B

Respondents, however, contend that First Amendment values require a different rule under the circumstances of this case. The thrust of the decision below is that "[t]he scope of [fair use] is undoubtedly wider when the information conveyed relates to matters of high public concern." *Consumers Union of the United States, Inc. v. General Signal Corp.*, 724 F.2d 1044, 1050 (CA2 1983), cert. denied, 469 U.S. 823, 104 S.Ct. 2655, 81 L.Ed.2d 362 (1984). Respondents advance the substantial public import of the subject matter of the Ford memoirs as grounds for excusing a use that would ordinarily not pass muster as a fair use—the piracy of verbatim quotations for the purpose of "scooping" the authorized first serialization. Respondents explain their copying of Mr. Ford's expression as essential to reporting the news story it claims the book itself represents. In respondents' view, not only the facts contained in Mr. Ford's memoirs, but "the precise manner in which [he] expressed himself [were] as newsworthy as what he had to say." Respondents argue that the public's interest in learning this news as fast as possible outweighs the right of the author to control its first publication.

The Second Circuit noted, correctly, that copyright's idea/expression dichotomy "strike[s] a definitional balance between the First Amendment and the Copyright Act by permitting free communication of facts while still protecting an author's expression." No author may copyright his ideas or the facts he narrates. As this Court long ago observed: "[T]he news element—the information respecting current events contained in the literary production—is not the creation of the writer, but is a report of matters that ordinarily are *publici juris*; it is the history of the day." *International News Service v. Associated Press*, 248 U.S. 215, 234, 39 S.Ct. 68, 71, 63 L.Ed. 211 (1918). But copyright assures those who write and publish factual narratives such as "A Time to Heal" that they may at least enjoy the right to market the original expression contained therein as just compensation for their investment.

Respondents' theory, however, would expand fair use to effectively destroy any expectation of copyright protection in the work of a public figure. Absent such protection, there would be little incentive to create or profit in financing such memoirs, and the public would be denied an important source of significant historical information. The promise of copyright would be an empty one if it could be avoided merely by dubbing the infringement a fair use "news report" of the book.

Nor do respondents assert any actual necessity for circumventing the copyright scheme with respect to the types of works and users at issue here. Where an author and publisher have invested extensive resources in creating an original work and are poised to release it to the public, no legitimate aim is served by pre-empting the right of first publication. The fact that the words the author has chosen to clothe his narrative may of themselves be "newsworthy" is not an independent justification for unauthorized copying of the author's expression prior to publication. To paraphrase another recent Second Circuit decision:

> "[Respondent] possessed an unfettered right to use any factual information revealed in [the memoirs] for the purpose of enlightening its audience, but it can claim no need to 'bodily appropriate' [Mr. Ford's] 'expression' of that information by utilizing portions of the actual [manuscript]. The public interest in the free flow of information is assured by the law's refusal to recognize a valid copyright in facts. The fair use doctrine is not a license for corporate theft, empowering a court to ignore a copyright whenever it determines the underlying work contains material of possible public importance." *Iowa State University Research Foundation, Inc. v. American Broadcasting Cos., Inc.*, 621 F.2d 57, 61 (CA2 1980).

In our haste to disseminate news, it should not be forgotten that the Framers intended copyright itself to be the engine of free expression. By establishing a marketable right to the use of one's expression, copyright supplies the economic incentive to create and disseminate ideas. * * *

It is fundamentally at odds with the scheme of copyright to accord lesser rights in those works that are of greatest importance to the public. Such a notion ignores the major premise of copyright and injures author and public alike. * * * And as one commentator has noted: "If every volume that was in the public interest could be pirated away by a competing publisher, ... the public [soon] would have nothing worth reading." Sobel, Copyright and the First Amendment: A Gathering Storm?, 19 ASCAP Copyright Law Symposium 43, 78 (1971).

Moreover, freedom of thought and expression "includes both the right to speak freely and the right to refrain from speaking at all." *Wooley v. Maynard*, 430 U.S. 705, 714, 97 S.Ct. 1428, 1435, 51 L.Ed.2d 752 (1977) (Burger, C.J.). We do not suggest this right not to speak would sanction abuse of the copyright owner's monopoly as an instrument to suppress facts. But in the words of New York's Chief Judge Fuld:

> "The essential thrust of the First Amendment is to prohibit improper restraints on the *voluntary* public expression of ideas; it shields the man who wants to speak or publish when others wish him to be quiet. There is necessarily, and within suitably defined areas, a concomitant freedom not to speak publicly, one which serves the same ultimate end as freedom of speech in its affirmative aspect."

Estate of Hemingway v. Random House, Inc., 23 N.Y.2d 341, 348, 296 N.Y.S.2d 771, 776, 244 N.E.2d 250, 255 (1968).

Courts and commentators have recognized that copyright, and the right of first publication in particular, serve this countervailing First Amendment value.

In view of the First Amendment protections already embodied in the Copyright Act's distinction between copyrightable expression and uncopyrightable facts and ideas, and the latitude for scholarship and comment traditionally afforded by fair use, we see no warrant for expanding the doctrine of fair use to create what amounts to a public figure exception to copyright. Whether verbatim copying from a public figure's manuscript in a given case is or is not fair must be judged according to the traditional equities of fair use.

IV

[W]hether The Nation article constitutes fair use under § 107 must be reviewed in light of the principles discussed above. The factors enumerated in the section are not meant to be exclusive: "[S]ince the doctrine is an equitable rule of reason, no generally applicable definition is possible, and each case raising the question must be decided on its own facts." House Report, at 65, U.S.Code Cong. & Admin.News 1976, p. 5678. The four factors identified by Congress as especially relevant in determining whether the use was fair are: (1) the purpose and character of the use; (2) the nature of the copyrighted work; (3) the substantiality of the portion used in relation to the copyrighted work as a whole; (4) the effect on the potential market for or value of the copyrighted work. We address each one separately.

Purpose of the Use. The Second Circuit correctly identified news reporting as the general purpose of The Nation's use. News reporting is one of the examples enumerated in § 107 to "give some idea of the sort of activities the courts might regard as fair use under the circumstances." Senate Report, at 61. This listing was not intended to be exhaustive, or to single out any particular use as presumptively a "fair" use. The drafters resisted pressures from special interest groups to create presumptive categories of fair use, but structured the provision as an affirmative defense requiring a case-by-case analysis. * * * The fact that an article arguably is "news" and therefore a productive use is simply one factor in a fair use analysis.

* * * The Nation has every right to seek to be the first to publish information. But The Nation went beyond simply reporting uncopyrightable information and actively sought to exploit the headline value of its infringement, making a "news event" out of its unauthorized first publication of a noted figure's copyrighted expression.

The fact that a publication was commercial as opposed to nonprofit is a separate factor that tends to weigh against a finding of fair use. "[E]very commercial use of copyrighted material is presumptively an unfair exploitation of the monopoly privilege that belongs to the owner of the copyright." *Sony Corp. of America v. Universal City Studios, Inc.*, 464 U.S., at 451, 104 S.Ct., at 793. In arguing that the purpose of news reporting is not purely commercial, The Nation misses the point entirely. The crux of the profit/nonprofit distinction is not whether the sole motive of the use is monetary gain but whether the user stands to profit from exploitation of the copyrighted material without paying the customary price.

In evaluating character and purpose we cannot ignore The Nation's stated purpose of scooping the forthcoming hardcover and Time abstracts. The Nation's use had not merely the incidental effect but the *intended purpose* of supplanting the copyright holder's commercially valuable right of first publication. * * * Also relevant to the "character" of the use is "the propriety of the defendant's conduct." 3 Nimmer § 13.05[A], at 13–72. "Fair use presupposes 'good faith' and 'fair dealing.'" *Time Inc. v. Bernard Geis Associates*, 293 F.Supp. 130, 146 (SDNY 1968), quoting Schulman, Fair Use and the Revision of the Copyright Act, 53 Iowa L.Rev. 832 (1968). The trial court found that The Nation knowingly exploited a purloined manuscript. Unlike the typical claim of fair use, The Nation cannot offer up even the fiction of consent as justification. Like its competitor newsweekly, it was free to bid for the right of abstracting excerpts from "A Time to Heal." Fair use "distinguishes between 'a true scholar and a chiseler who infringes a work for personal profit.'" *Wainwright Securities Inc. v. Wall Street Transcript Corp.*, 558 F.2d, at 94, quoting from Hearings on Bills for the General Revision of the Copyright Law before the House Committee on the Judiciary, 89th Cong., 1st Sess., ser. 8, pt. 3, p. 1706 (1966) (statement of John Schulman).

Nature of the Copyrighted Work. Second, the Act directs attention to the nature of the copyrighted work. "A Time to Heal" may be characterized as an unpublished historical narrative or autobiography. The law generally recognizes a greater need to disseminate factual works than works of fiction or fantasy.

> "[E]ven within the field of fact works, there are gradations as to the relative proportion of fact and fancy. One may move from sparsely embellished maps and directories to elegantly written biography. The extent to which one must permit expressive language to be copied, in order to assure dissemination of the underlying facts, will thus vary from case to case." Gorman, Fact or Fancy? The Implications for Copyright, 29 J. Copyright Soc. 560, 563 (1982).

Some of the briefer quotes from the memoirs are arguably necessary adequately to convey the facts; for example, Mr. Ford's characterization of the White House tapes as the "smoking gun" is perhaps so integral to the idea expressed as to be inseparable from it. But The Nation did not stop at isolated phrases and instead excerpted subjective descriptions and portraits of public figures whose power lies in the author's individualized expression. Such use, focusing on the most expressive elements of the work, exceeds that necessary to disseminate the facts.

The fact that a work is unpublished is a critical element of its "nature." 3 Nimmer § 13.05[A]. Our prior discussion establishes that the scope of fair use is narrower with respect to unpublished works. While even substantial quotations might qualify as fair use in a review of a published work or a news account of a speech that had been delivered to the public or disseminated to the press, the author's right to control the first public appearance of his expression weighs against such use of the work before its release. The right of first publication encompasses not only the choice whether to publish at all, but also the choices of when, where, and in what form first to publish a work.

In the case of Mr. Ford's manuscript, the copyright holders' interest in confidentiality is irrefutable; the copyright holders had entered into a contractual undertaking to "keep the manuscript confidential" and required that all those to whom the manuscript was shown also "sign an agreement to keep the manuscript confidential." While the copyright holders' contract with Time required Time to submit its proposed article seven days before publication, The Nation's clandestine publication afforded no such opportunity for creative or quality control. It was hastily patched together and contained "a number of inaccuracies." A use that so clearly infringes the copyright holder's interests in confidentiality and creative control is difficult to characterize as "fair."

Amount and Substantiality of the Portion Used. Next, the Act directs us to examine the amount and substantiality of the portion used in relation to the copyrighted work as a whole. In absolute terms, the words actually quoted were an insubstantial portion of "A Time to Heal." The District Court, however, found that "[T]he Nation took what was essentially the heart of the book." We believe the Court of Appeals erred in overruling the District Judge's evaluation of the qualitative nature of the taking. A Time editor described the chapters on the pardon as "the most interesting and moving parts of the entire manuscript." The portions actually quoted were selected by Mr. Navasky as among the most powerful passages in those chapters. He testified that he used verbatim excerpts because simply reciting the information could not adequately convey the "absolute certainty with which [Ford] expressed himself," or show that "this comes from President Ford," or carry the "definitive quality" of the original. In short, he quoted these passages precisely because they qualitatively embodied Ford's distinctive expression.

As the statutory language indicates, a taking may not be excused merely because it is insubstantial with respect to the *infringing* work. As Judge Learned Hand cogently remarked, "no plagiarist can excuse the wrong by showing how much of his work he did not pirate." *Sheldon v. Metro–Goldwyn Pictures Corp.*, 81 F.2d 49, 56 (CA2), cert. denied, 298 U.S. 669, 56 S.Ct. 835, 80 L.Ed. 1392 (1936). Conversely, the fact that a substantial portion of the infringing work was copied verbatim is evidence of the qualitative value of the copied material, both to the originator and to the plagiarist who seeks to profit from marketing someone else's copyrighted expression.

Stripped to the verbatim quotes, the direct takings from the unpublished manuscript constitute at least 13% of the infringing article. The Nation article is structured around the quoted excerpts which serve as its dramatic focal points. In view of the expressive value of the excerpts and their key role in the infringing work, we cannot agree with the Second Circuit that the "magazine took a meager, indeed an infinitesimal amount of Ford's original language."

Effect on the Market. Finally, the Act focuses on "the effect of the use upon the potential market for or value of the copyrighted work." This last factor is undoubtedly the single most important element of fair use.[9] "Fair use, when properly applied, is limited to copying by others which does not materially impair the marketability of the work which is copied." 1 Nimmer § 1.10[D], at 1–87. The trial court found not merely a potential but an actual effect on the market. Time's cancellation of its projected serialization and its refusal to pay the $12,500 were the direct effect of the infringement. The Court of Appeals rejected this factfinding as clearly erroneous, noting that the record did not establish a causal relation between Time's nonperformance and respondents' unauthorized publication of Mr. Ford's *expression* as opposed to the facts taken from the memoirs. We disagree. Rarely will a case of copyright infringement present such clear-cut evidence of actual damage. * * *

More important, to negate fair use one need only show that if the challenged use "should become widespread, it would adversely affect the *potential* market for the copyrighted work." *Sony Corp. of America v. Universal City Studios, Inc.*, 464 U.S., at 451, 104 S.Ct., at 793 (emphasis added). This inquiry must take account not only of harm to the original but also of harm to the market for derivative works. * * *

It is undisputed that the factual material in the balance of The Nation's article, besides the verbatim quotes at issue here, was drawn exclusively from the chapters on the pardon. The excerpts were employed as featured episodes in a story about the Nixon pardon—precisely the use petitioners had licensed to Time. The borrowing of these verbatim quotes from the unpublished manuscript lent The Nation's piece a special air of authenticity—as Navasky expressed it, the reader would know it was Ford speaking and not The Nation. Thus it directly competed for a share of the market for prepublication excerpts. The Senate Report states:

> "With certain special exceptions . . . a use that supplants any part of the normal market for a copyrighted work would ordinarily be considered an infringement." Senate Report, at 65.

Placed in a broader perspective, a fair use doctrine that permits extensive prepublication quotations from an unreleased manuscript without

9. Economists who have addressed the issue believe the fair use exception should come into play only in those situations in which the market fails or the price the copyright holder would ask is near zero. As the facts here demonstrate, there is a fully functioning market that encourages the creation and dissemination of memoirs of public figures. In the economists' view, permitting "fair use" to displace normal copyright channels disrupts the copyright market without a commensurate public benefit.

the copyright owner's consent poses substantial potential for damage to the marketability of first serialization rights in general. "Isolated instances of minor infringements, when multiplied many times, become in the aggregate a major inroad on copyright that must be prevented." *Ibid.*

V

The Court of Appeals erred in concluding that The Nation's use of the copyrighted material was excused by the public's interest in the subject matter. It erred, as well, in overlooking the unpublished nature of the work and the resulting impact on the potential market for first serial rights of permitting unauthorized prepublication excerpts under the rubric of fair use. Finally, in finding the taking "infinitesimal," the Court of Appeals accorded too little weight to the qualitative importance of the quoted passages of original expression. In sum, the traditional doctrine of fair use, as embodied in the Copyright Act, does not sanction the use made by The Nation of these copyrighted materials. Any copyright infringer may claim to benefit the public by increasing public access to the copyrighted work. But Congress has not designed, and we see no warrant for judicially imposing, a "compulsory license" permitting unfettered access to the unpublished copyrighted expression of public figures.

The Nation conceded that its verbatim copying of some 300 words of direct quotation from the Ford manuscript would constitute an infringement unless excused as a fair use. Because we find that The Nation's use of these verbatim excerpts from the unpublished manuscript was not a fair use, the judgment of the Court of Appeals is reversed, and the case is remanded for further proceedings consistent with this opinion.

Notes and Questions

1. *The fair use defense.* Because the Court found The Nation's verbatim quotes enough to infringe the plaintiffs' copyright by themselves, it was unnecessary to determine whether The Nation took protectible non-literal expression from the Ford manuscript, as well. A full copy of The Nation article can be found in the Appendix to the Court's opinion.

Fair use is an affirmative defense. It does not become relevant until the plaintiff has made a *prima facie* case of infringement. At that point, the defendant must bear the burden of establishing that his use is privileged under the fair use doctrine. What is the purpose of the fair use defense? In cases in which copyright owners generally would not be expected to object to the defendant's use, the fair use defense may alleviate unnecessary transaction costs entailed in obtaining a license. The purpose of the fair use doctrine is considerably greater than that, however. Judge Pierre Leval has described the purpose of the defense as follows:

> Notwithstanding the need for monopoly protection of intellectual creators to stimulate creativity and authorship, excessively broad protection would stifle, rather than advance, the objective.

> First, all intellectual creative activity is in part derivative. There is no such thing as a wholly original thought or invention. Each advance stands on building blocks fashioned by prior thinkers. Second, important areas of intellectual activity are explicitly referential. Philosophy, criticism, history, and even the natural sciences require continuous reexamination of yesterday's theses.
>
> Monopoly protection of intellectual property that impeded referential analysis and the development of new ideas out of old would strangle the creative process. Three judicially created copyright doctrines have addressed this problem: first, the rule that the copyright does not protect *ideas*, but only the manner of expression; second, the rule that *facts* are not within the copyright protection, notwithstanding the labor expended by the original author in uncovering them; and finally, the fair use doctrine, which protects secondary creativity as a legitimate concern of the copyright. * * *
>
> Fair use should not be considered a bizarre, occasionally tolerated departure from the grand conception of the copyright monopoly. To the contrary, it is a necessary part of the overall design. Although no simple definition of fair use can be fashioned, and inevitably disagreement will arise over individual applications, recognition of the function of fair use as integral to copyright's objectives leads to a coherent and useful set of principles. Briefly stated, the use must be of a character that serves the copyright objective of stimulating productive thought and public instruction without excessively diminishing the incentives for creativity. One must assess each of the issues that arise in considering a fair use defense in light of the governing purpose of copyright law.

Leval, *Toward a Fair Use Standard*, 103 HARV. L. REV. 1105, 1109–1110 (1990).[9]

What is the relationship of the fair use defense to the statutory exemptions to copyright infringement, found in Copyright Act sections 108–120?

2. *The four factors.* The *Harper & Row* opinion considered each of the four factors specified in section 107. Does either the statute or the Court's opinion indicate how these factors are to be weighted in deciding whether a defendant's use was fair? Was the Court influenced by any additional factors apart from the four listed in section 107?

a. Factor One: the purpose and character of the use. How does this factor relate to the purpose of the fair use doctrine, as described by Judge Leval in the prior note?

The preamble to section 107 provides several examples of potentially proper "purposes" for using copyrighted material: "criticism, comment, news reporting, teaching (including multiple copies for classroom use), scholarship, or research." The statutory language suggests that Congress did not intend for this list to be exclusive. Is Congress' selection of the particular examples set forth in the preamble useful in evaluating whether other purposes are proper? If so, how? The *Harper & Row* majority refers to "productive" uses of copyrighted material. What is a productive use?

9. © Pierre N. Leval, 1990. Reprinted by permission of the copyright owner.

Section 107's preamble expressly refers to "teaching (including multiple copies for classroom use)," and factor one directs courts to consider whether a use was made for "nonprofit educational purposes." The permissibility of reproduction for educational purposes, and particularly photocopying for classroom use, generated considerable debate in the course of drafting and enacting section 107. The House Committee ultimately concluded that "a specific exemption freeing certain reproductions of copyrighted works for educational and scholarly purposes from copyright control is not justified." H.R. REP. NO. 1476, 94th Cong., 2d Sess. 66 (1976). Nonetheless, the Committee acknowledged that there was a "need for greater certainty and protection for teachers." *Id.* at 67. At the Committee's urging, representatives of the interested parties—educators, authors, and publishers—met independently to discuss permissible educational uses of copyrighted material. They ultimately drafted an "Agreement on Guidelines for Classroom Copying in Not–For–Profit Educational Institutions," which set forth guidelines for "fair use" reproduction of books and periodicals for classroom use. Among other things, the guidelines look to the "brevity," "spontaneity," and the cumulative effect of the copying. The Committee incorporated the Agreement into the House Report. See *id.* at 67–70.[10] While incorporation into the House Report does not give the guidelines the status of law, it undoubtedly will be persuasive to courts, thus providing a form of safe harbor for teachers who confine their copying to that approved by the guidelines.[11] Since the guidelines only purport to set forth minimum standards for fair use, reproduction beyond that approved in the guidelines should not be automatically disqualified from a finding of fair use. For an application of the guidelines, see Marcus v. Rowley, 695 F.2d 1171, 217 U.S.P.Q. 691 (9th Cir.1983). For a more general discussion of the copyright implications of new reproduction technology in university research and teaching, see Ginsburg, *Reproduction of Protected Works for University Research or Teaching*, 39 J. COPYRIGHT SOC. 181 (1992).

Why was The Nation's news reporting deemed "commercial" in nature? Does the *Harper & Row* majority's emphasis on the commercial nature of The Nation's article undercut Congress' intent in listing news reporting as an example of fair use in the preamble? See *Harper & Row*, 471 U.S. at 592, 105 S.Ct. at 2247, 85 L.Ed.2d at 627 (Justice Brennan, dissenting). Why should a defendant's commercial purpose, as defined by the Court, weigh against a finding of fair use?

b. Factor two: the nature of the copyrighted work. Apart from the published or unpublished status of the plaintiff's work, why is the *type* of the plaintiff's work relevant to the fair use inquiry?

In *Harper & Row*, the Court placed considerable importance on the fact that the plaintiff's work was not yet published. Does the opinion create a presumption against a finding of fair use when the plaintiff's work is unpublished? Should it matter whether the plaintiff intended eventually to

10. The Committee also incorporated negotiated "Guidelines for Educational Uses of Music." *Id.* at 70–772.

11. The Committee stated: "The Committee believes the guidelines are a reasonable interpretation of the minimum standards of fair use. Teachers will know that copying within the guidelines is fair use. Thus, the guidelines serve the purpose of fulfilling the need for greater certainty and protection for teachers." *Id.*, at 72.

publish the work? See Leval, *Toward a Fair Use Standard*, 103 HARV. L. REV. 1105, 1116–22 (1990).

The Court of Appeals for the Second Circuit interpreted *Harper & Row* to provide that "unpublished letters normally enjoy insulation from fair use copying" and "complete protection." Salinger v. Random House, Inc., 811 F.2d 90, 95, 97, 1 U.S.P.Q.2d 1673, 1676, 1677 (2d Cir.1987), *cert. denied* 484 U.S. 890, 108 S.Ct. 213, 98 L.Ed.2d 177 (1987). In accordance with this interpretation, the court enjoined publication of a biography of J.D. Salinger which incorporated quotes and paraphrases from Salinger's letters which, while "unpublished," were available to scholars in libraries. The Second Circuit appeared to reinforce this interpretation two years later in New Era Publications International v. Henry Holt & Co., 873 F.2d 576, 10 U.S.P.Q.2d 1561 (2d Cir.1989), *cert. denied* 493 U.S. 1094, 110 S.Ct. 1168, 107 L.Ed.2d 1071 (1990). Historians, biographers and other authors who rely on unpublished letters and other documents in their work responded very strongly to these opinions, fearing that they signaled a general denial of the fair use defense for use of unpublished works. They argued that the absence of a fair use defense would make it difficult or impossible for them to write effectively, to the ultimate detriment of the public. They also argued that the Second Circuit's trend would permit copyright to be used as a tool for censorship and suppression. See Conley, *Fair Use, Fair Game*, LEGAL TIMES, June 17, 1991, at 45. Judge Leval stated the concern as follows:

> A ban on fair use of unpublished documents establishes a new despotic potentate in the politics of intellectual life—the "widow censor." A historian who wishes to quote personal papers of deceased public figures now must satisfy heirs and executors for fifty years after the subject's death. When writers ask permission, the answer will be, "show me what you write. Then we'll talk about permission." If the manuscript does not exude pure admiration, permission will be denied.

Leval, *Toward a Fair Use Standard*, *supra*, at 1118.[12]

In response to the controversy, Congress considered legislation to clarify the status of unpublished expression for purposes of fair use. Notwithstanding evidence that the Second Circuit was rethinking its view on the issue, and opposition by the software industry,[13] Congress amended section 107 by adding the following language: "The fact that a work is unpublished shall not itself bar a finding of fair use if such finding is made upon consideration of all of the above factors." Pub.L. No. 102–492, 106 Stat. 3145 (1992). What are the implications of this amendment? For further discussion of these events, see Miller, *Fair Use, Biographers, and Unpublished Works: Life After H.R. 4412*, 40 J. COPYRIGHT SOC. 349 (1993); Litman, *Copyright and Information Policy*, 55 L. & CONTEMP. PROB. 185 (1992).

c. Factor three: the amount and substantiality of the portion used in relation to the copyrighted work as a whole. Given that the defendant took

12. © Pierre N. Leval, 1990. Reprinted by permission of the copyright owner.

13. The software industry was concerned that legislation approving limited access to unpublished works might weaken protection for their unpublished source code and assist competitors in decompiling their programs. See Perry, *What Publishers Call Quoting, Computer Firms Call Piracy as Industries Face Off on Capitol Hill*, WALL ST. J., Ap. 23, 1991, at A20.

enough to infringe, what does further assessment of the amount taken add to the fair use analysis?

In *Harper & Row*, the Court found that the 300–400 words the defendant took from the plaintiff's 200,000–word manuscript constituted a substantial portion of the manuscript for purposes of factor 3. Could the taking of the plaintiff's entire work ever be found to constitute a fair use? See Sony Corp. of America v. Universal City Studios, Inc., 464 U.S. 417, 442, 104 S.Ct. 774, 789, 78 L.Ed.2d 574, 592, 220 U.S.P.Q. 665 (1984) (fair use found even though members of the public taped entire television programs for purposes of time shifting.).

Courts have sometimes considered the amount and substantiality of the portion the defendant used in relation to the *defendant's* work as a whole, though section 107 does not specifically list that as a factor. Why might it be relevant?

d. *Factor four: the effect of the use upon the potential market for or value of the copyrighted work.* In *Harper & Row*, the Supreme Court stated that this factor was the "single most important element of fair use." Why should this be so?

Is this factor relevant in the case of works, such as private letters, which the plaintiff has no intention to publish? In the *Salinger* case, *supra*, the Second Circuit held that it was:

> [T]he need to assess the effect on the market for Salinger's letters is not lessened by the fact that their author has disavowed any intention to publish them during his lifetime. First, the proper inquiry concerns the "potential market" for the copyrighted work. Second, Salinger has the right to change his mind. He is entitled to protect his *opportunity* to sell his letters, an opportunity estimated by his literary agent to have a current value in excess of $500,000.

Id., 811 F.2d at 98, 1 U.S.P.Q.2d at 1678.

Suppose that the defendant published a scathingly negative review of the plaintiff's novel, which impermissibly quoted from the novel and thus infringed. In response to the defendant's fair use defense, plaintiff demonstrates that the defendant's sarcastically critical review brought the novel into public contempt, decreasing readership and sales. Should this evidence be deemed relevant to the factor four inquiry?

How much market interference should be necessary to place factor four in the plaintiff's favor? See Leval, *supra*, at 1124–25.

For a deeper analysis of the fair use defense and its four factors, see, e.g., Dratler, *Distilling the Witches' Brew of Fair Use in Copyright Law*, 43 U. MIAMI L. REV. 233 (1988); Fisher, *Reconstructing the Fair Use Doctrine*, 101 HARV. L. REV. 1659 (1988); Gordon, *Fair Use as Market Failure: A Structural and Economic Analysis of the* Betamax *Case and its Predecessors*, 82 COLUM. L. REV. 1600 (1982).

3. *Parody.* The Supreme Court first addressed application of the fair use defense to parody in Campbell v. Acuff–Rose Music, Inc., ___ U.S. ___, 114 S.Ct. 1164, 127 L.Ed.2d 500, 29 U.S.P.Q.2d 1961 (1994). In *Campbell*, Campbell, a member of the popular rap music group 2 Live Crew, wrote a

song entitled "Pretty Woman," which he described as intended, "through comical lyrics, to satirize" the song "Oh, Pretty Woman," made popular by Roy Orbison. The words of the 2 Live Crew song copied the original's first line, but then degenerated into a play on words, substituting shocking lyrics, derisively demonstrating the blandness of the Orbison original. In addition to the first line of lyrics, Campbell copied the characteristic opening bass riff (or musical phrase) of the Orbison original and repeated it throughout. 2 Live Crew sent a recording of Campbell's song to Acuff–Rose, the owner of copyright in the Orbison song, and attempted to obtain a license. Acuff–Rose refused. 2 Live Crew then released recordings of Campbell's song for sale to the public.

When Acuff–Rose sued for infringement, 2 Live Crew asserted the fair use defense. The district court granted summary judgment to 2 Live Crew, and the Court of Appeals for the Sixth Circuit reversed. When the case reached the Supreme Court, the Court undertook a factor-by-factor analysis, as it did in *Harper & Row*.

With regard to the "purpose and character of the use," the Court first stressed that a productive, or "transformative" use is favored:

> The central purpose of this investigation is to see, in Justice Story's words, whether the new work merely "supersede[s] the objects" of the original creation, or instead adds something new, with a further purpose or different character, altering the first with new expression, meaning, or message; it asks, in other words, whether and to what extent the new work is "transformative." Although such transformative use is not absolutely necessary for a finding of fair use, the goal of copyright, to promote science and the arts, is generally furthered by the creation of transformative works. Such works thus lie at the heart of the fair use doctrine's guarantee of breathing space within the confines of copyright, and the more transformative the new work, the less will be the significance of other factors, like commercialism, that may weigh against a finding of fair use.

Id., ___ U.S. at ___, 114 S.Ct. at 1171, 127 L.Ed.2d at 515–16. The Court found that parody had "an obvious claim to transformative value." The Court emphasized that parodies generally imitate the work or style of another author for comic effect or ridicule. "Like less ostensibly humorous forms of criticism, [parody] can provide social benefit, by shedding light on an earlier work, and, in the process, creating a new one." *Id.*

The Court stressed, however, that a defendant's parody should be aimed at the plaintiff's work, at least in part, in order to justify copying it. A parody of an existing work "needs to mimic [the] original to make its point, and so has some claim to use the creation of its victim's (or victims') imagination." "If, on the contrary, the commentary has no critical bearing on the substance or style of the original composition, which the alleged infringer merely uses to get attention or to avoid the drudgery in working up something fresh, the claim to fairness in borrowing from another's work diminishes accordingly (if it does not vanish), and other factors, like the extent of its commerciality, loom larger." *Id.*, ___ U.S. at ___, 114 S.Ct. at 1172, 127 L.Ed.2d at 516.

While the Court of Appeals had questioned whether the Campbell song was a parody of the Orbison original, the Supreme Court found that it "reasonably could be perceived as commenting on the original or criticizing it, to some degree." *Id.*

In its first factor inquiry, the Court of Appeals had relied on the Supreme Court's statement in Sony Corp. of America v. Universal City Studios, Inc., 464 U.S. 417, 104 S.Ct. 774, 78 L.Ed.2d 574, 220 U.S.P.Q. 665 (1984), that "every commercial use of copyrighted material is presumptively unfair," and had given "virtually dispositive effect" to the commercial nature of 2 Live Crew's use of the Orbison song. The Supreme Court found this to be error.

> The language of the statute makes clear that the commercial or nonprofit educational purpose of a work is only one element of the first factor inquiry into its purpose and character. * * * As we explained in *Harper & Row*, Congress resisted attempts to narrow the ambit of this traditional inquiry by adopting categories of presumptively fair use, and it urged courts to preserve the breadth of their traditionally ample view of the universe of relevant evidence. * * * If, indeed, commerciality carried presumptive force against a finding of fairness, the presumption would swallow nearly all of the illustrative uses listed in the preamble paragraph of § 107, including news reporting, comment, criticism, teaching, scholarship, and research, since these activities "are generally conducted for profit in this country."

Id. ___ U.S. at ___, 114 S.Ct. at 1174, 127 L.Ed.2d at 518–19.

In discussing the third factor, "the amount and substantiality of the portion used in relation to the copyrighted work as a whole," the Court emphasized the interrelationship of all the factors. According to the Court, the third factor asks whether the amount of the defendant's taking is "reasonable in relation to the purpose of the copying."

> Here, attention turns to the persuasiveness of a parodist's justification for the particular copying done, and the inquiry will harken back to the first of the statutory factors, for, as in prior cases, we recognize that the extent of permissible copying varies with the purpose and character of the use. The facts bearing on this factor will also tend to address the fourth, by revealing the degree to which the parody may serve as a market substitute for the original or potentially licensed derivatives.

Id., ___ U.S. at ___, 114 S.Ct. at 1175, 127 L.Ed.2d at 520.

In finding that the third factor weighed against the defendants, the Court of Appeals had emphasized the extent of the defendants' verbatim copying and the quality of the material copied, opining that the defendants had taken "the heart of the original" and made it "the heart of a new work." The Supreme Court disagreed with the Court of Appeals' method of applying these considerations to parody:

> Parody presents a difficult case. Parody's humor, or in any event its comment, necessarily springs from recognizable allusion to its object through distorted imitation. Its art lies in the tension between a known original and its parodic twin. When parody takes aim at a particular original work, the parody must be able to "conjure up" at least enough

> of that original to make the object of its critical wit recognizable. What makes for this recognition is quotation of the original's most distinctive or memorable features, which the parodist can be sure the audience will know. Once enough has been taken to assure identification, how much more is reasonable will depend, say, on the extent to which the song's overriding purpose and character is to parody the original or, in contrast, the likelihood that the parody may serve as a market substitute for the original. But using some characteristic features cannot be avoided.
>
> * * * [I]f quotation of the opening riff and the first line [of the Orbison original] may be said to go to the "heart" of the original, the heart is also what most readily conjures up the song for parody, and it is the heart at which parody takes aim. Copying does not become excessive in relation to parodic purpose merely because the portion taken was the original's heart. If 2 Live Crew had copied a significantly less memorable part of the original, it is difficult to see how its parodic character would have come through.
>
> This is not, of course, to say that anyone who calls himself a parodist can skim the cream and get away scot free. In parody, as in news reporting, context is everything, and the question of fairness asks what else the parodist did besides go to the heart of the original. It is significant that 2 Live Crew not only copied the bass riff and repeated, but also produced otherwise distinctive sounds, interposing "scraper" noise, overlaying the music with solos in different keys, and altering the drum beat. This is not a case, then, where "a substantial portion" of the parody itself is composed of a "verbatim" copying of the original. It is not, that is, a case where the parody is so insubstantial, as compared to the copying, that the third factor must be resolved as a matter of law against the parodists.
>
> Suffice it to say here that, as to the lyrics, we think the Court of Appeals correctly suggested that "no more was taken than necessary," but just for that reason, we fail to see how the copying can be excessive in relation to its parodic purpose, even if the portion taken is the original's "heart." As to the music, we express no opinion whether repetition of the bass riff is excessive copying, and we remand to permit evaluation of the amount taken, in light of the song's parodic purpose and character, its transformative elements, and considerations of the potential for market substitution * * * .

Id., ___ U.S. at ___, 114 S.Ct. at 1176–77, 127 L.Ed.2d at 521–22.

In turning to the fourth and final factor, the effect of the use upon the potential market for the copyrighted work, the Court again found fault with the Court of Appeals' analysis.

> In assessing the likelihood of significant market harm, the Court of Appeals quoted from language in *Sony* that "[i]f the intended use is for commercial gain, that likelihood may be presumed. But if it is for a noncommercial purpose, the likelihood must be demonstrated." The court reasoned that because "the use of the copyrighted work is wholly commercial, * * * we presume a likelihood of future harm to Acuff–Rose exists." In so doing, the court resolved the fourth factor against 2 Live

> Crew, just as it had the first, by applying a presumption about the effect of commercial use, a presumption which as applied here we hold to be error.
>
> No "presumption" or inference of market harm that might find support in *Sony* is applicable to a case involving something beyond mere duplication for commercial purposes. *Sony's* discussion of a presumption contrasts a context of verbatim copying of the original in its entirety for commercial purposes, with the non-commercial context of *Sony* itself (home copying of television programming). In the former circumstances, what *Sony* said simply makes common sense: when a commercial use amounts to mere duplication of the entirety of an original, it * * * serves as a market replacement for it, making it likely that cognizable market harm to the original will occur. But when, on the contrary, the second use is transformative, market substitution is at least less certain, and market harm may not be so readily inferred. Indeed, as to parody pure and simple, it is more likely that the new work will not affect the market for the original in a way cognizable under this factor, that is, by acting as a substitute for it * * *. This is so because the parody and the original usually serve different market functions.
>
> We do not, of course, suggest that a parody may not harm the market at all, but when a lethal parody, like a scathing theater review, kills demand for the original, it does not produce a harm cognizable under the Copyright Act. Because "parody may quite legitimately aim at garroting the original, destroying it commercially as well as artistically," B. Kaplan, *An Unhurried View of Copyright* 69 (1967), the role of the courts is to distinguish between "[b]iting criticism [that merely] suppresses demand [and] copyright infringement, [which] merely usurps it." *Fisher v. Dees*, 794 F.2d, at 438.

Id., ___ U.S. at ___, 114 S.Ct. at 1177–78, 127 L.Ed.2d at 523–24.

The Court stressed the importance of evaluating the effect of the defendant's copying not only on the market for the original work, but also on the potential market for adaptations of the original. The Court rejected the notion that the defendant's use had undermined the potential market for parodies of the plaintiff's work:

> The market for potential derivative uses includes only those that creators of original works would in general develop or license others to develop. [T]he unlikelihood that creators of imaginative works will license critical reviews or lampoons of their own productions removes such uses from the very notion of a potential licensing market. * * * Thus, to the extent that the opinion below may be read to have considered harm to the market for parodies of "Oh, Pretty Woman," the court erred.
>
> In explaining why the law recognizes no derivative market for critical works, including parody, we have, of course, been speaking of the later work as if it had nothing but a critical aspect * * *. But the later work may have a more complex character, with effects not only in the arena of criticism but also in protectible markets for derivative works, too. In that sort of case, the law looks beyond the criticism to the other elements of the work, as it does here. 2 Live Crew's song comprises not

> only parody but also rap music, and the derivative market for rap music is a proper focus of enquiry. Evidence of substantial harm to it would weigh against a finding of fair use, because the licensing of derivatives is an important economic incentive to the creation of originals. * * *

Id., ___ U.S. at ___, 114 S.Ct. at 1178, 127 L.Ed.2d at 524. The Court remanded for further findings on the extent to which the defendant's song interfered with a market for a non-parody, rap version of "Oh, Pretty Woman."

A copy of the lyrics of the Orbison and the Campbell songs can be found in an Appendix to the Court's opinion. Does it appear that the *Campbell* court afforded a wider fair use privilege for parody than exists for other types of uses, such as that in *Harper & Row*? Would a wider fair use privilege be justified?

Justice Kennedy, in his concurring opinion, expressed concern that

> [a]lmost any revamped modern version of a familiar composition can be construed as a "comment on the naivete of the original," because of the difference in style and because it will be amusing to hear how the old tune sounds in the new genre. Just the thought of a rap version of Beethoven's Fifth Symphony or "Achy, Breacky Heart" is bound to make people smile. If we allow any weak transformation to qualify as parody, however, we weaken the protection of copyright. * * *
>
> * * * As future courts apply our fair use analysis, they must take care to ensure that not just any commercial take-off is rationalized *post hoc* as a parody.

Id., ___ U.S. at ___, 114 S.Ct. at 1181–82, 127 L.Ed.2d at 528–29. Does the Court's test for parody (whether "a parodic character may reasonably be perceived"), coupled with its instructions for applying the four factors in the case of parody, adequately alleviate this concern?

Is the fact that 2 Live Crew sought and was denied a license relevant to the fair use inquiry? If so, how?

For an economic analysis of fair use for parody, see Yen, *When Authors Won't Sell: Parody, Fair Use, and Efficiency in Copyright Law*, 62 U. COLO. L. REV. 79 (1991); Posner, *When is Parody Fair Use?*, 21 J. LEGAL STUD. 67 (1992).

4. *Reverse engineering.* Suppose that the plaintiff manufactures and sells a video entertainment console and video game cartridges designed to play in the console. The defendant develops and sells video game cartridges that are compatible with several computer systems. While the plaintiff licenses some independent companies to develop and sell video games that are compatible with plaintiff's console, it has not licensed the defendant to do so.

In an effort to render its video games compatible with the plaintiff's console, defendant "reverse engineers" several of plaintiff's different video game programs in order to discover the requirements for compatibility with the console. This entails transforming the machine-readable object code of commercially available copies of plaintiff's games into human-readable source code through a process called "disassembly" or "decompilation." Playing the games in one of plaintiff's commercially available consoles, defendant wires a decompiler into the console circuitry and generates printouts of the resulting source code. Defendant studies and annotates the printouts in order to identify areas of commonality among the video games it has decompiled. Defendant then loads the disassembled code back into a computer and experiments to discover the interface specifications for the console by modifying the programs and studying the results.

At the end of the process, defendant creates a development manual that incorporates the information it discovered about the requirements for a game to be compatible with the plaintiff's console. The manual contains only functional descriptions of the interface requirements and none of plaintiff's code. Defendant then creates its own games for the console. At this stage it does not copy any of plaintiff's programs, relying only on the information concerning interface specifications for the console contained in the manual. None of the code in defendant's programs is derived from plaintiff's programs, except for the interface specifications.

The plaintiff sues defendant for infringement, claiming that defendant's intermediate copying of its games during the process of reverse engineering to learn the console interface specifications violates its copyrights. Should the defendant's copying be privileged under the fair use defense? Why or why not? See Sega Enterprises v. Accolade, Inc., 977 F.2d 1510, 24 U.S.P.Q.2d 1561 (9th Cir.1992). For discussions of this issue and of the *Sega* decision and its implications, see McManis, *Intellectual Property Protection and Reverse Engineering of Computer Programs in the United States and the European Community*, 8 HIGH TECH. L.J. 25 (1993); Soma, Winfield and Friesen, *Software Interoperability and Reverse Engineering*, 20 RUTGERS COMPUTER & TECH. L.J. 189 (1994). For a more general commentary on fair use for computer programs, see Samuelson, *Fair Use for Computer Programs and Other Copyrightable works in Digital Form: The Implications of* Sony, Galoob *and* Sega, 1 J. INTELL. PROP. L. 49 (1993).

V. OWNERSHIP OF COPYRIGHT

Copyright initially vests in the "author" of a work. 17 U.S.C.A. § 201. Generally, the "author" is the person who conceives of the copyrightable expression and fixes or causes it to be fixed in tangible form. Andrien v. Southern Ocean County Chamber of Commerce, 927 F.2d 132, 18 U.S.P.Q.2d 1041 (3d Cir.1991). When a work is "made for hire," however, the employer or commissioning party, who finances creation of the work and takes the economic risk of it, is deemed the "author," rather than the employee or commissioned party who actually conceives and fixes the work. 17 U.S.C.A. § 201(b).

The following Subsection A will discuss when a work is one "for hire," so that the employer or commissioning party is deemed the "author." Subsection B will address the difficulties that arise in determining when a claimant will qualify as a "joint author" of a work, and thus a co-owner of the copyright in it. Subsection C will discuss the divisibility and transfer of copyright ownership.

A. WORKS MADE FOR HIRE

§ 101. Definitions

* * *

A "work made for hire" is—

(1) a work prepared by an employee within the scope of his or her employment; or

(2) a work specially ordered or commissioned for use as a contribution to a collective work, as a part of a motion picture or other audiovisual work, as a translation, as a supplementary work, as a compilation, as an instructional text, as a test, as answer material for a test, or as an atlas, if the parties expressly agree in a written instrument signed by them that the work shall be considered a work made for hire. * * *

* * *

17 U.S.C.A. § 101.

M.G.B. HOMES, INC. v. AMERON HOMES, INC.

United States Court of Appeals for the Eleventh Circuit, 1990.
903 F.2d 1486, 15 U.S.P.Q.2d 1282.

JOHN R. BROWN, SENIOR CIRCUIT JUDGE:

* * *

MGB and Ameron are competing home builders in the town of Sebastian, Florida. The principals of both MGB and Ameron, Ballough and Brognano respectively, were once shareholders and controllers of Ameron. In this action, MGB claims that Ameron copied one of its floor plans—for an "Islander II" home * * *. The plan appeared on an advertising flyer prepared by Unlimited Drafting Services, Inc. (Unlimited), along with an artist's rendition of the outside of the home and some text about the home. [While the actual architectural plans for the "Islander II" were never registered with the Copyright Office, the advertising flyer was.]

Ameron had access to the advertising flyers for the "Islander II" which were available in the model home for prospective customers. Ameron constructed a home for the Sterns which has a floor plan substantially similar to the "Islander II." The differences are insignificant. The Sterns' floor plan was copied from the advertising flyer for the "Islander II" home.

* * *

The primary question raised by this appeal is whether MGB is an "owner" of the copyright in the advertising flyer. * * *

In its copyright application, MGB identified itself as a "work-for-hire" author of the advertising flyer depicting the "Islander II" floor plan. Ameron asserted, as a complete defense to the infringement claim against it, that MGB is not a valid copyright owner under this doctrine.

First, we hold that Ameron does have the right to assert this defense. It is not unheard of, as MGB asserts, for the "work-for-hire" issue to arise "as a defensive tactic adopted by a third-party infringer to dispute the validity of the plaintiff's copyright." *Easter Seal Society for Crippled Children and Adults of Louisiana, Inc. v. Playboy Enterprises*, 815 F.2d 323, 333 (5th Cir.1987), *cert. denied*, 485 U.S. 981, 108 S.Ct. 1280, 99 L.Ed.2d 491 (1988). As that court pointed out, and we adopt, this defense gives the putative infringer, rather than the creator of the work, the benefits of finding a work was not a "work-for-hire." *Id.*

Under the Copyright Act of 1909, the "work-for-hire" doctrine created a rebuttable presumption of authorship in the employer. *See Murray v. Gelderman*, 566 F.2d 1307, 1309 (5th Cir.1978). The crucial factor in applying this presumption was "whether the work was created at the employer's insistence and expense, or, in other words, whether the motivating factor in producing the work was the employer who induced its creation." *Id.* at 1310. The trial court apparently relied on this formulation. We hold that *Murray* is no longer valid precedent because (i) it was overruled by the amendments to the Copyright Act in 1976 and (ii) its rationale was rejected by *Community for Creative Non–Violence v. Reid*, 490 U.S.——, 109 S.Ct. 2166, 104 L.Ed.2d 811 (1989) [*CCNV*], which defined the "work for hire" doctrine under the 1976 Act.

* * *

> To determine whether a work is for hire under the Act, a court first should ascertain, using principles of general common law of agency, whether the work was prepared by an employee or an independent contractor. After making this determination, the court can apply the appropriate subsection of § 101.

CCNV, 490 U.S. at——, 109 S.Ct. at 2178, 104 L.Ed.2d at 831. According to the Supreme Court, under the general law of agency, we look to the hiring party's right to control the way in which the product—here the architectural plans and house drawings that made up the advertising flyer—is made in order to determine if the hired party is an employee or an independent contractor. Some of the factors relevant to this determination are:

> the skill required; the source of the instrumentalities and tools; the location of the work; the duration of the relationship between the parties; whether the hiring party has the right to assign additional projects to the hired party; the extent of the hired party's discretion over when and how long to work; the method of payment; the hired party's role in hiring and paying assistants; whether the work is part of the regular business of the hiring party; whether the hiring party is in business; the provision of employee benefits; and the tax treatment of the hired party.

490 U.S. at ___, 109 S.Ct. at 2178–79, 104 L.Ed.2d at 831–32.[15]

The facts giving rise to the *CCNV* case were as follows. The organization, CCNV, hired a sculptor, Reid, to make a statue called "Third World America." CCNV conceived the idea. It decided there would be two adults and one child in it. It determined these people would be black; they would be portrayed as contemporary homeless people; the figures would be lifesized; they would be positioned over a steam grate in a pedestal (made by CCNV) rigged to send steam over them; and certain materials would be used. Dozens of CCNV members assisted Reid during the creative process and coordinated their work with his. CCNV members took Reid out to observe homeless families and pointed out to him common features which were incorporated into the sculpture. CCNV decided on the caption that would be included on the pedestal of the sculpture. In light of these facts, the Supreme Court found that although "CCNV members directed enough of Reid's work to ensure that he produced a sculpture that met their specifications.... the extent of control the hiring party exercises over the details of the product is not dispositive. Indeed, all the other circumstances weigh heavily against finding an employment relationship." 490 U.S. at ___, 109 S.Ct. at 2179, 104 L.Ed.2d at 832. Thus the Supreme Court held that Reid was not an employee of CCNV, but an independent contractor. CCNV could not show that the terms of § 101(2) were satisfied, thus it could not be a statutory author under the "work-for-hire" provision.

Our case is much the same. Although Ballough exercised control and direction over the finished product that Unlimited Drafting Services produced, all the other circumstances militate against finding the drawings were done as a work for hire. Unlimited provided skilled drafting services. It provided its own office space, tools and supplies. Unlimited was retained for a comparatively short period of time—a few weeks. MGB did not have the ability to assign new projects to Unlimited during that time (other than by entering a new contract). Unlimited was free to determine the days and hours on which its employees worked.

15. According to the Restatement (2d) of Agency, in determining whether one acting for another is a servant or an independent contractor, the following matters of fact, among others, are considered:

(a) the extent of control which, by the agreement, the master may exercise over the details of the work;

(b) whether or not the one employed is engaged in a distinct occupation or business;

(c) the kind of occupation, with reference to whether, in the locality, the work is usually done under the direction of the employer or by a specialist without supervision;

(d) the skill required in the particular occupation;

(e) whether the employer or the workman supplies the instrumentalities, tools, and the place of work for the person doing the work;

(f) the length of time for which the person is employed;

(g) the method of payment, whether by the time or by the job;

(h) whether or not the work is a part of the regular business of the employer;

(i) whether or not the parties believe they are creating the relation of master and servant; and

(j) whether the principal is or is not in business.

Restatement (Second) of Agency § 220(2) (1958).

Unlimited had total discretion in hiring and firing its own employees without interference by MGB. Unlimited paid its own taxes and withholding for its employees. Drafting was not a part of the regular business of MGB which always used an outside drafting firm. In short, Unlimited was an independent contractor, not an employee.

Once this decision has been made, under the mandate of *CCNV* we look to the language of § 101(2) to determine if the advertising flyer was a work for hire. The language of the statute was not complied with in two regards: (i) architectural drafting does not fall within the nine enumerated categories of activities which may be done by independent contractors "for hire" and (ii) there is no evidence that MGB and Unlimited had a contract stating that the drawings would be considered a work for hire. We therefore conclude that MGB was not the author of the house drawings under the "work-for-hire" doctrine.

* * *

Notes and Questions

1. *Works for hire.* Designation as a work for hire has significance for several reasons in addition to determining the initial owner of the copyright. For example, the Visual Artists Rights Act provides no moral rights in works of visual art that are made for hire. 17 U.S.C.A. § 101. Moreover, designation as a work for hire affects the duration of the copyright, *id.*, § 302(c); it determines who has the right to renew copyright in some cases, *id.*, § 304(a); and it determines whether authors or their successors will enjoy the right to terminate transfers of rights, *id.*, §§ 203, 304(c).

The *M.G.B.* court discusses *C.C.N.V. v. Reid*, and repeats the factors the Supreme Court named as relevant in determining whether the creator of a work is an employee or an independent contractor. Can you explain why each of these factors may be relevant? In Aymes v. Bonelli, 980 F.2d 857, 25 U.S.P.Q.2d 1181 (2d Cir.1992), the Court of Appeals for the Second Circuit reversed a district court which had given each of the factors equal weight and simply counted the number of factors favoring each claimant to determine who should win.

> [T]he *Reid* test can be easily misapplied, since it consists merely of a list of possible considerations that may or may not be relevant in a given case. *Reid* established that no one factor was dispositive, but gave no direction concerning how the factors were to be weighed. It does not necessarily follow that because no one factor is dispositive all factors are equally important, or indeed that all factors will have relevance in every case. The factors should not merely be tallied but should be weighted according to their significance in the case.
>
> For example, the factors relating to the authority to hire assistants will not normally be relevant if the very nature of the work requires the hired party to work alone. In such a case, that factor should be accorded no weight in applying the *Reid* test. * * *
>
> [T]here are some factors that will be significant in virtually every situation. These include: (1) the hiring party's right to control the manner and means of creation; (2) the skill required; (3) the provision

> of employee benefits; (4) the tax treatment of the hired party; and (5) whether the hiring party has the right to assign additional projects to the hired party. These factors will almost always be relevant and should be given more weight in the analysis, because they will usually be highly probative of the true nature of the employment relationship.

Id., 980 F.2d at 861, 25 U.S.P.Q.2d at 1184.

The *M.G.B.* court points out that the present Copyright Act's work-for-hire provisions differ from those that existed under the 1909 Act. The 1909 Act work-for-hire provisions applied broadly, encompassing not only works created by salaried employees in the scope of their employment but also numerous works created by independent contractors. In the latter case, the law created a rebuttable presumption of work-for-hire status and copyright in a customer if the independent contractor produced the work at the customer's instance and expense and the customer retained the right to supervise and control the work's production. This standard is still applicable in determining the work-for-hire status of works created before January 1, 1978, the effective date of the Copyright Act of 1976. Serious due process issues would arise if the new '76 Act standard were applied retroactively to alter the ownership of works created before the Act became effective. See Roth v. Pritikin, 710 F.2d 934, 219 U.S.P.Q. 204 (2d Cir.1983), *cert. denied* 464 U.S. 961, 104 S.Ct. 394, 78 L.Ed.2d 337 (1983). For a fuller discussion of the earlier standard, see Easter Seal Society for Crippled Children and Adults of Louisiana, Inc. v. Playboy Enterprises, 815 F.2d 323, 2 U.S.P.Q.2d 1585 (5th Cir.1987), *cert. denied* 485 U.S. 981, 108 S.Ct. 1280, 99 L.Ed.2d 491 (1988).

B. JOINT WORKS

ERICKSON v. TRINITY THEATRE, INC.

United States Court of Appeals for the Seventh Circuit, 1994.
13 F.3d 1061, 29 U.S.P.Q.2d 1347.

RIPPLE, CIRCUIT JUDGE.

The plaintiff Karen Erickson brought this action seeking a preliminary and permanent injunction to prevent the defendant Trinity Theatre d/b/a/ Trinity Square Ensemble ("Trinity") from performing three plays * * *. [T]he district court enjoined Trinity * * *. Trinity now appeals. We now affirm.

I. BACKGROUND

Ms. Erickson was one of the founders of a theatre company in Evanston, Illinois, that ultimately became known as Trinity Theatre. Between 1981 and January 1991, Ms. Erickson served Trinity in various capacities: as playwright, artistic director, actress, play director, business manager, and member of the board of directors. This suit revolves around Ms. Erickson's role as playwright.

At issue here are the rights to three plays: *Much Ado About Shakespeare ("Much Ado"); The Theatre Time Machine ("Time Machine"); and Prairie Voices: Tales from Illinois ("Prairie Voices").*

Much Ado is a compilation of scenes and sonnets from William Shakespeare and other writers of his time. Ms. Erickson revised this work from an earlier script entitled *Sounds and Sweet Aires.* Michael Osborne, a Trinity actor, testified that Ms. Erickson compiled *Much Ado* in 1988 and that many decisions about what was to be included were made during rehearsals. Osborne identified two portions of the copyrighted script that resulted from his suggestions: a passage to *Macbeth* and the introduction to the play. The editing of the text, Osborne continued, was accomplished largely by consensus; however, when a consensus could not be had, Ms. Erickson made the final decisions. Osborne further testified that he understood at the time that the play was being created for Trinity and not for Ms. Erickson. Ms. Erickson does not dispute the process described by Osborne, but characterizes it differently. She perceived the process only as actors making suggestions for her script.

Time Machine is a play of five scenes based on a public domain Native American folk tale. Each scene depicts dramatic styles from different historical periods. * * * [Ms. Erickson] described the development of the play as beginning in 1977 when she was in school. At that time, she wrote the Greek-style drama scene. Later, while teaching high school drama, she wrote the second scene based on *commedia dell'arte.* She also began work on the melodrama and improvisational scenes of the play at that time. Ms. Erickson started producing the play independently of Trinity in 1984 with two other actors, Paddy Lynn and Will Clinger. Ms. Erickson claimed that she worked to develop the scenes alone; however, the evidence shows that the actors were involved in the development of the melodrama and improvisational scenes. The improvisational process, as described by Ms. Lynn, is a form of theatre in which there is no script. Rather, actors work with an idea and a loose structure to create a play. Ms. Lynn described the development of the improvisational scene in *Time Machine* as a collaborative effort. However, she conceded that Ms. Erickson took all of the notes from rehearsals and compiled them into the script; furthermore, nothing was included in the script without Ms. Erickson's approval. Initially, Ms. Erickson attributed the script to both herself and to Ms. Lynn. Ms. Lynn also received royalties for performances of the play. Ms. Erickson denied that she ever intended to include Ms. Lynn as joint author. She conceded that Ms. Lynn was credited on publicity materials as an author but denied that she approved such credit. The later change in attribution, Ms. Erickson claims, merely corrected the initial error.

In 1990, Ms. Erickson developed *Prairie Voices*, a play based on tales from Illinois history. She had the idea to develop the play as a Trinity production. Her original intent was to launch a collaborative effort in which each of the actors would contribute a story to the play. However, none of the actors initiated writing a script and the play, as it resulted, was based entirely on tales provided by Ms. Erickson. As with *Time Machine*, Ms. Erickson worked with the actors in the improvisational format. Although testifying that she alone wrote the play, Ms. Erickson admitted that the actors provided ideas for the dialogue. Another actor, Ruth Ann Weyna, testified that the writing of the play was a creative process involving a number of actors. However, she conceded that Ms. Erickson controlled what eventually was put in the script.

In 1987, Trinity began paying Ms. Erickson royalties for its performances of her plays. On July 5, 1988, Ms. Erickson entered into a two-year licensing agreement with Trinity that designated her as a "playwright" entitling her to royalties for performances of two of her plays, *Much Ado* and *Time Machine*. Trinity stipulated that it also paid Erickson royalties for its performances of *Prairie Voices*, although that play was not expressly covered by the licensing agreement. Trinity continued to pay Ms. Erickson royalties after the expiration of the licensing agreement. Trinity discontinued making royalty payments on November 15, 1990.

* * *

Ms. Erickson left Trinity Theatre in January 1991. Shortly thereafter, she applied for and was issued copyright registration for *Much Ado* and *Prairie Voices*. * * * She had previously obtained a copyright certificate for *Time Machine* on September 12, 1988. On January 21, 1991, Ms. Erickson's attorneys wrote Trinity a letter demanding that the theatre discontinue performing the plaintiff's plays. Trinity refused to comply with the request.

[Ms. Erickson filed a complaint against Trinity Theatre, members of Trinity's management, and individual Trinity actors seeking relief for copyright infringement, and moved for a preliminary injunction. Defendants alleged that several of Trinity's members were joint authors of the plays, and that they had authorized Trinity to perform the plays.]

II. Analysis

A. *Standard of Review*

* * *

The central issue in this appeal is whether Ms. Erickson is likely to succeed on the merits of her case. Whether Ms. Erickson will succeed depends greatly on whether Trinity can establish that the works at issue were joint works within the meaning of the Copyright Act of 1976. Statutory interpretation is a question of law and therefore we review the district court's determination of this issue de novo.

B. *Joint Work*

* * * In a joint work, the joint authors hold undivided interests in a work, despite any differences in each author's contribution. 17 U.S.C. § 201. Each author as co-owner has the right to use or to license the use of the work, subject to an accounting to the other co-owners for any profits. Thus, even a person whose contribution is relatively minor, if accorded joint authorship status, enjoys a significant benefit.

In determining whether any of the works at issue in this case may be classified as a "joint work," our starting point must be the language of the statute. Section 101 of the Copyright Act defines a "joint work" as

> a work prepared by two or more authors with the intention that their contributions be merged into inseparable or interdependent parts of a unitary whole.

1.

Neither the Act nor its legislative history defines "inseparable" or "interdependent." The legislative history states that examples of inseparable parts are the joint contributions of two authors to a single novel or the contributions of two painters to a single work; an example of interdependent parts are the lyrics and music for a song. Apart from these examples, the reports do little to clarify the criteria for determining joint authorship. Indeed, they increase the ambiguity. The committee reports state:

> [A] work is "joint" if the authors collaborated with each other, *or* if *each* of the authors prepared his or her contribution with the knowledge and *intention* that it would be merged with the contributions of other authors as "inseparable or interdependent parts of a unitary whole." The touchstone here is *the intention, at the time the writing is done,* that the parts be absorbed or combined into an integrated unit....

House Report at 120; Senate Report at 103, U.S.Code Cong. & Admin.News 1976, pp. 5736 (emphasis added). The statute clearly requires a focus on the intention to collaborate. However, the disjunctive first sentence in the legislative reports, set out directly above, seemingly contradicts that statutory language by focusing on collaboration and not mentioning intent to create a joint work.

This ambiguity presents analytical problems in cases such as this one, in which the parties have collaborated in some sense but dispute whether there was a mutual intent to create a joint work. In resolving this ambiguity, we believe that it is important to note, at the outset, that the statute itself requires that there be an intent to create a joint work. Therefore, reliance on collaboration alone, as Trinity suggests, would be incompatible with the clear statutory mandate. * * * [W]e believe that the statutory language clearly requires that each author intend that their respective contributions be merged into a unitary whole. Focusing solely upon the fact of contemporaneous input by several parties does not satisfy the statutory requirement that the parties intend to merge their contributions into a unified work. In addition, the "collaboration alone" standard would frustrate the goal of the Act "[t]o promote the Progress of Science and the useful Arts." U.S. CONST. art. I, § 8, cl. 8. Seldom would an author subject his work to pre-registration peer review if this were the applicable test. Those seeking copyrights would not seek further refinement that colleagues may offer if they risked losing their sole authorship. Thus, we cannot accept Trinity's proposed "collaboration alone" test as compatible with the language and purpose of the Act.

2.

Even if two or more persons collaborate with the intent to create a unitary work, the product will be considered a "joint work" only if the collaborators can be considered "authors." Courts have applied two tests to evaluate the contributions of authors claiming joint authorship status: Professor Nimmer's de minimis test and Professor Goldstein's copyrightable subject matter ("copyrightability") test. The de minimis and copyrightability tests differ in one fundamental respect. The de minimis test requires that only the combined product of joint efforts must be copyrightable. By contrast, Professor Goldstein's copyrightability test requires that each author's contribution be copyrightable. We evaluate each of these tests in turn.

In undertaking this task, we focus on how well the test promotes the primary objective of the Act. This objective is not to reward an author for her labors, but "[t]o promote the Progress of Science and useful Arts." This objective is accomplished by "assur[ing] authors the right to their original expression," but also by "encourag[ing] others to build freely upon the ideas and information conveyed by a work." *Feist Publications*, 499 U.S. at 349–50, 111 S.Ct. at 1290. * * *

In addition to promoting the Act's primary objective, we must consider how well the test will further goals of administrative and judicial efficiency. In this inquiry, we must adopt a standard that is sufficiently clear to enable parties to predict whether their contributions to a work will receive copyright protection. A standard satisfying these aims will allow contributors to avoid post-contribution disputes concerning authorship, and to protect themselves by contract if it appears that they would not enjoy protections of the Act itself.

a. Professor Nimmer's de minimis standard

Professor Nimmer, the late scholar on copyright, took the position that all that should be required to achieve joint author status is more than a de minimis contribution by each author. "De minimis" requires that "more than a word or line must be added by one who claims to be a joint author." 1 *Nimmer on Copyright* § 6.07, at 6–21. Professor Nimmer distinguishes his de minimis standard from the standard for copyrightability. As an example, Professor Nimmer asserts that if two authors collaborate, with one contributing only uncopyrightable plot ideas and another incorporating those ideas into a completed literary expression, the two authors should be regarded as joint authors of the resulting work.

This position has not found support in the courts. The lack of support in all likelihood stems from one of several weaknesses in Professor Nimmer's approach. First, Professor Nimmer's test is not consistent with one of the Act's premises: ideas and concepts standing alone should not receive protection. Because the creative process necessarily involves the development of existing concepts into new forms, any restriction on the free exchange of ideas stifles creativity to some extent. Restrictions on an author's use of existing ideas in a work, such as the threat that accepting suggestions from another party might jeopardize the author's sole entitlement to a copyright, would hinder creativity. Second, contribution of an idea is an exceedingly ambiguous concept. Professor Nimmer provides little guidance to courts or parties regarding when a contribution rises to the level of joint authorship except to state that the contribution must be "more than a word or a line."

* * *

b. Professor Goldstein's copyrightability test

The copyrightable subject matter test was formulated by Professor Paul Goldstein and has been adopted, in some form, by a majority of courts that have considered the issue. According to Professor Goldstein, "[a] collaborative contribution will not produce a joint work, and a contributor will not obtain a co-ownership interest, unless the contribution represents original expression that could stand on its own as the subject matter of copyright." Paul Goldstein, *Copyright: Principles, Law, and Practice* § 4.2.1.2, at 379 (1989). Furthermore, the parties must have intended to be joint authors at the time the work was created. Professor Goldstein and the courts adopting his test justify this position by noting that § 101's and § 302(b)'s use of the word "authors" suggests that each collaborator's contribution must be a copyrightable "work of authorship" within the meaning of § 102(a).

We agree that the language of the Act supports the adoption of a copyrightability requirement. Section 101 of the Act defines a "joint work" as a "work prepared by two or more *authors* " (emphasis added). To qualify as an author, one must supply more than mere direction or ideas. An author is "the party who actually creates the work, that is, the person who translates an idea into a fixed, tangible expression entitled to copyright protection." *Community for Creative Non–Violence v. Reid*, 490 U.S. 730, 737, 109 S.Ct. 2166, 2171, 104 L.Ed.2d 811 (1989). * * *

The copyrightable subject matter test does not suffer from the same infirmities as Professor Nimmer's de minimis test. The copyrightability test advances creativity in science and art by allowing for the unhindered exchange of ideas, and protects authorship rights in a consistent and predictable manner. It excludes contributions such as ideas which are not protected under the Copyright Act. This test also enables parties to predict whether their contributions to a work will entitle them to copyright protection as a joint author. Compared to the uncertain exercise of divining whether a contribution is more than de minimis, reliance on the copyrightability of an author's proposed contribution yields relatively certain answers. The copyrightability standard allows contributors to avoid post-contribution disputes concerning authorship, and to protect themselves by contract if it appears that they would not enjoy the benefits accorded to authors of joint works under the Act.

We agree with the *Childress* court's observation that the copyrightability test "strikes an appropriate balance in the domains of both copyright and contract law." *Childress v. Taylor*, 945 F.2d 500, 507 (2d

Cir.1991). Section 201(b) of the Act allows any person to contract with another to create a work and endow the employer with authorship status under the Act. A contributor of uncopyrightable ideas may also protect her rights to compensation under the Act by contract. Section 201(d) of the Act provides in part that any of the exclusive ownership rights comprised in a copyright may be transferred from the person who satisfied the requirements for obtaining the copyright to one who contracts for such rights. Thus, anyone who contributes to the creation of a work, either as patron, employer, or contributor of ideas, has the opportunity to share in the profits produced by the work through an appropriate contractual arrangement.

C. *Application*

We now address Trinity's claims of joint authorship under the copyrightability test. As stated above, Trinity must clear two hurdles in order to establish that the plays at issue are joint works. First, it must show the parties intended to be joint authors at the time the work was created. Second, Trinity must show that its contributions to the works were independently copyrightable.

It is clear that, with regard to at least two works, *Much Ado* and *Prairie Voices*, Trinity cannot clear the first hurdle. *Much Ado* is based on a work that Ms. Erickson had largely completed before Trinity actors improvised based on Ms. Erickson's creation. The fact that one actor, Michael Osborne, suggested that Ms. Erickson include a passage from *Macbeth* and an introduction to the play does not make him a joint author. He conceded that whether his contributions were included and where they went into the compilation were entirely Ms. Erickson's decisions. Furthermore, neither Ms. Erickson nor Trinity considered any of the actors to be co-authors with her in *Much Ado*, as is evidenced by the licensing agreement. Similarly with *Prairie Voices*, Ms. Erickson provided the stories on which the play was based, and she decided which of the actors' suggestions were incorporated into the script. The actors did not consider themselves to be joint authors with Ms. Erickson, and there is no evidence that Ms. Erickson considered the actors as co-authors of the script. Because Trinity cannot establish the requisite intent for *Much Ado* or *Prairie Voices*, the actors cannot be considered joint authors for the purposes of copyright protection.

Time Machine, as both the magistrate judge and the district court noted, is more problematic. Paddy Lynn testified that at least two scenes from *Time Machine* were developed through a collaborative process. Ms. Lynn considered the created dialogue to be hers as well as Ms. Erickson's. Furthermore, there is evidence that Ms. Erickson, too, intended at the time to create a joint work because she initially attributed the script to both Ms. Lynn and herself. Consequently, Trinity has produced some evidence that there was the requisite intent for joint authorship with regard to *Time Machine*. * * *

In order for the plays to be joint works under the Act, Trinity also must show that actors' contributions to Ms. Erickson's work could have been independently copyrighted. Trinity cannot establish this requirement for any of the above works. The actors, on the whole, could not identify specific contributions that they had made to Ms. Erickson's works. Even when Michael Osborne was able to do so, the contributions that he identified were not independently copyrightable. Ideas, refinements, and suggestions, standing alone, are not the subjects of copyrights. Consequently, Trinity cannot establish the two necessary elements of the copyrightability test and its claims must fail.

Trinity cannot establish joint authorship to the plays at issue. As a result, Trinity cannot overcome the presumption in favor of the validity of Ms. Erickson's copyrights. Consequently, Ms. Erickson is very likely to succeed on the merits of her claims for copyright infringement.

* * *

Notes and Questions

1. *Joint works.* Both the statutory definition of joint works and the House Report stress the mutual intent of the parties to contribute to a joint work. What kinds of evidence might be useful to demonstrate the existence of such an intent? On what basis does the court find that the parties in *Erickson* lacked the intent to contribute to a joint work in "Much Ado" and "Prairie Voices?"

Why shouldn't the contribution of creative ideas entitle one to ownership rights in the resulting work, even if she contributed no "expression" as such?

Assume that the court found that the *Erickson* plays constituted joint works. Apart from relieving the defendants from liability to the plaintiff, what would the practical implications be?

For a thorough discussion of the law of joint authorship, see Brophy, *Joint Authorship Under the Copyright Law*, 16 HASTINGS COMM. & ENT. L.J. 451 (1994).

2. *Joint works, derivative works, collective works.* How would you articulate the difference between joint works, derivative works and contributions to collective works?

In Shapiro, Bernstein & Co. v. Jerry Vogel Music Co., 221 F.2d 569, 105 U.S.P.Q. 178 (2d Cir.1955), *modified* 223 F.2d 252, 105 U.S.P.Q. 460 (2d Cir.1955) (the "12th Street Rag" case), X composed an instrumental piece for solo piano, intending it to be complete as it was. Two years later he assigned his copyright in the piece to Y and two years after that, Y had Z write lyrics to accompany the instrumental. The Court of Appeals for the Second Circuit held that the resulting song, comprised of music and lyrics, constituted a joint work, even though X had not intended to contribute to a unified whole at the time he created the music. The court found it sufficient that Y, the subsequent copyright holder, had later formed that intent.

This result was much criticized and Congress explicitly rejected it in enacting the Copyright Act of 1976. The '76 Act defines a joint work as one "*prepared* by two or more authors *with the intention* that their contributions be merged into inseparable or interdependent parts of a unitary whole." 17

U.S.C.A. § 101 (emphasis added). The House Report specifies that the touchstone "is the intention, *at the time the writing is done*, that the parts be absorbed or combined into an integrated unit." H.R. REP. NO. 1476, 94th Cong., 2d Sess. 120 (1976) (emphasis added). Why should the Second Circuit's acceptance of an intent formed after creation be considered problematic?

Suppose that X and Y collaborate to write a scholarly paper which qualifies as a joint work. X later revises the paper unilaterally, and Y, without X's authorization, reproduces the revised paper. Is Y liable to X for copyright infringement? See Weissmann v. Freeman, 868 F.2d 1313, 10 U.S.P.Q.2d 1014 (2d Cir.1989), *cert. denied* 493 U.S. 883, 110 S.Ct. 219, 107 L.Ed.2d 172 (1989).

C. DIVISIBILITY AND TRANSFER OF OWNERSHIP

Copyright Act section 201(d) provides the first explicit statutory recognition of copyright divisibility. As the House Report explained:

> This provision, which has long been sought by authors and their representatives, and which has attracted wide support from other groups, means that any of the exclusive rights that go to make up a copyright, including those enumerated in section 106 and any subdivision of them, can be transferred and owned separately. The definition of "transfer of copyright ownership" in section 101 makes clear that the principle of divisibility applies whether or not the transfer is "limited in time or place of effect," and another definition in the same section provides that the term "copyright owner," with respect to any one exclusive right, refers to the owner of that particular right. The last sentence of section 201(d)(2) adds that the owner, with respect to the particular exclusive right he or she owns, is entitled "to all of the protection and remedies accorded to the copyright owner by this title." It is thus clear, for example, that a local broadcasting station holding an exclusive license to transmit a particular work within a particular geographic area and for a particular period of time, could sue, in its own name as copyright owner, someone who infringed that particular exclusive right.

H.R. REP. NO. 1476, 94th Cong., 2d Sess. 123 (1976).

Copyright Act section 204(a) provides that the transfer of any ownership right (that is, any exclusive, as opposed to non-exclusive right), other than by operation of law, must be made by means of a writing signed by the transferor or his agent. Congress made doubly sure, in section 202, that there would be no implied transfers of copyright ownership: "Transfer of ownership of any material object, including the copy or phonorecord in which the work is first fixed, does not of itself convey any rights in the copyrighted work embodied in the object * * *." 17 U.S.C.A. § 202. As the House Report explained:

> As a result of the interaction of this section and the provisions of section 201(a) and 301, the bill would change a common law doctrine exemplified by the decision in *Pushman v. New York*

> *Graphic Society, Inc.*, 287 N.Y. 302, 39 N.E.2d 249 (1942). Under that doctrine, authors or artists are generally presumed to transfer common law literary property rights when they sell their manuscript or work of art, unless those rights are specifically reserved. This presumption would be reversed under the bill, since a specific written conveyance of rights would be required in order for sale of any material object to carry with it a transfer of copyright.

H.R. REP. NO. 1476, *supra,* at 124. Bear in mind that the 1976 Act's ownership provisions do not apply retroactively. The ramifications of a transaction are judged under the law in effect when the transaction occurred. Thus, for example, if the creator of an unpublished oil painting sold the canvas on which the painting was fixed, without an express reservation of copyright, prior to January 1, 1978 (the effective date of the 1976 Act) in a state that followed the *Pushman* doctrine, then it is likely that the buyer obtained the artist's common-law copyright. The buyer or his successors would continue to own the copyright, which, under the 1976 Act, was subsequently transformed into a federal copyright. See Section VII, *infra.*

For more information about the transfer of copyright interests, and the Copyright Act's provisions regarding the recording of transfers with the Copyright Office, see 3 M.B. NIMMER & D. NIMMER, NIMMER ON COPYRIGHT, Ch. 10 (1994).

VI. COPYRIGHT FORMALITIES: NOTICE, REGISTRATION AND DEPOSIT

A. NOTICE OF COPYRIGHT

Contrary to the practice in most other developed nations, the United States has emphasized the placement of copyright notice on published copies of works. From 1802 until 1989, United States copyright law provided that all authorized published copies of works *must* bear notice, in a specified form, as a condition of copyright protection. Publication of copies lacking such notice would result in forfeiture of copyright in the work.

Nations following civil law traditions view copyright as a natural right in an author flowing from the act of authorship. The notion of imposing conditions on its enjoyment, such as notice or registration, is inconsistent with that view. Influenced by civil law traditions, the Berne Convention for the Protection of Literary and Artistic Works, Article 5(2), specifically directs that the enjoyment and exercise of copyright in member nations "shall not be subject to any formality."

In the United States, where copyright is viewed primarily as a statutory privilege afforded to authors in order to promote the general public welfare, conditions to enjoyment of copyright, such as notice, are consistent whenever they appear to promote the general welfare. Congress justified the notice requirement on essentially two grounds. First, it informs the public whether a particular work is copyrighted and assists those seeking to use it by identifying the copyright owner and the date of first publication (which may be important in determining whether the copyright is still in effect). Second, "it has the effect of placing in the public domain a substantial body of published material that no one is interested in copyrighting." H.R. REP. NO. 1476, 94th Cong., 2d Sess. 143 (1976).

The study of United States copyright notice provisions must be divided into three "epochs:" (1) the Copyright Act of 1909; (2) January 1, 1978 to March 1, 1989; and (3) March 1, 1989 through the present.

The Copyright Act of 1909. Prior to enactment of the Copyright Act of 1976, a dual system of copyright protection existed in the United States. State common-law copyright protected unpublished works. When the work was published, common-law protection ceased and federal statutory copyright protection commenced *if* all the authorized published copies of the work bore notice of copyright in the statutorily prescribed form and location. See 17 U.S.C.A. §§ 10, 19–21 (1909 Act).[14] In the absence of proper notice, the work fell into the public domain.

The 1909 Act's notice provisions were highly technical, and unintentional omissions or errors in the notice often lead to forfeiture of copyright. While section 21 of the Act provided some reprieve in the case of omissions "by accident or mistake," this provision was construed and applied very narrowly. Omissions due to negligence or mistake of law were not excused. Generally, the only excused omissions of notice were those attributable to mechanical accidents, such as damage to printing equipment, when only a relatively small number of copies were involved. See 1 P. GOLDSTEIN, COPYRIGHT PRINCIPLES, LAW AND PRACTICE § 3.7.2 (1989).

January 1, 1978 to March 1, 1989. When Congress enacted the Copyright Act of 1976, it provided that federal copyright would commence upon a work's creation, rather than upon publication, and preempted state protection for copyrightable subject matter fixed in tangible form. 17 U.S.C.A. §§ 301, 302. While relaxing some of the 1909 Act's technical rules regarding the form, position, and content of notice, the 1976 Act still required that authorized published copies and phonorecords of the work bear proper copyright notice. *Id.*, §§ 401–402. Failure to comply with the notice requirements would still result in loss of the copyright, though Congress tempered the impact of this consequence through broader "saving" provisions, set forth in sections 405–406. The House Report explained:

> One of the strongest arguments for revision of the present statute has been the need to avoid the arbitrary and unjust forfeitures now resulting from unintentional or relatively unimportant omissions or errors in the copyright notice. It has been contended that the

14. Section 12 of the 1909 Act permitted common-law copyright owners to obtain federal copyright protection for unpublished works. This provision, however, was not widely used.

> disadvantages of the notice requirement out-weigh its values and that it should therefore be eliminated or substantially liberalized.
>
> The fundamental principle underlying the notice provisions of the bill is that the copyright notice has real values which should be preserved, and that this should be done by inducing use of notice without causing outright forfeiture for errors or omissions. Subject to certain safeguards for innocent infringers, protection would not be lost by the complete omission of copyright notice from large numbers of copies or from a whole edition, if registration for the work is made before or within 5 years after publication. Errors in the name or date in the notice could be corrected without forfeiture of copyright.

H.R. REP. NO. 1476, 94th Cong., 2d Sess. 143–44 (1976).

March 1, 1989 through the present. When the United States finally joined the Berne Convention, it had to relinquish its notice requirement in order to comply with the Berne provision that copyright "not be subject to any formality." The Berne Convention Implementation Act, Pub.L. No. 100–568, 102 Stat. 2853 (1988), amended the 1976 Act notice provisions to make compliance voluntary rather than mandatory for copies and phonorecords distributed to the public after March 1, 1989, the effective date of the Implementation Act. See 17 U.S.C.A. §§ 401(a), 402(a). In order to encourage voluntary compliance with the notice provisions, the Act further provided:

> If a notice of copyright in the form and position specified by this section appears on the published copy or copies to which a defendant in a copyright infringement suit had access, then no weight shall be given to such a defendant's interposition of a defense based on innocent infringement in mitigation of actual or statutory damages, except as provided in the last sentence of section 504(c)(2).

17 U.S.C.A. § 401(d) (as amended). See also *id.*, § 402(d) (same provision, except "copy or copies" is replaced by "phonorecord or phonorecords").

Neither the 1976 Copyright Act's notice provisions nor the Berne Convention Implementation Act amendments apply retroactively. Thus, when it appears that copies or phonorecords were publicly distributed without proper notice, the consequences must be judged by the law in effect at the time of the distribution. If the publication occurred prior to January 1, 1978 (the effective date of the Copyright Act of 1976), then the copyright is likely to be forfeited unless the narrow provisions of section 21 of the 1909 Act apply. If the distribution occurred between January 1, 1978 and March 1, 1989, sections 405 and 406 will be available to save the work from forfeiture of copyright, if the copyright owner falls within the terms of those statutory provisions. The Berne Convention Implementation Act does not resurrect copyrights lost for lack of proper notice prior to its effective date. If the copyright was forfeited under the law applicable at the time of the distribution, then it remains invalid and unenforceable, unless it falls within the provisions of Copyright Act section 104A, which restores copyright in certain foreign works. See note 4, *infra*. If the distribution was made after the effective date of the Berne Convention Implementation Act (March 1, 1989), then there will be no forfeiture of copyright. However, the copyright owner may be deprived of remedies for infringement that would otherwise be available.

Notes and Questions

1. *Publication.* "Publication" is an important concept in copyright law. Under the 1909 Act, publication marked the end of common-law copyright protection and (if proper notice was given) the beginning of federal statutory copyright. Publication without proper notice resulted in complete loss of copyright protection. Even though the 1976 Act dispensed with publication as the starting point for copyright, and the Berne Convention Implementation Act did away with mandatory notice on published copies and phonorecords, publication remains important for a number of other purposes. Among other things, the date of publication must be given as a part of proper (voluntary) notice, and is used in measuring the duration of copyright in works for hire, anonymous and pseudonymous works. Publication is also relevant with regard to deposit and registration requirements, and in determining the applicability of the fair use defense and some of the statutory exceptions to copyright infringement.

The Copyright Act of 1909. The 1909 Act left definition of "publication" to the courts. In their hands the issue became highly complex. One thing, however, was clear: the fact that a work had been made public, or commercially exploited, did not necessarily mean that it had been "published."

There was general agreement that publication entailed physically distributing tangible copies of the work to members of the public. However, the circumstances under which such a distribution would constitute a publication varied. Faced with the desire to avoid finding forfeiture of copyright in compelling cases, the courts began to distinguish between "divestive" and "investive" publications. If the issue was whether a distribution divested the owner of copyright protection, the courts required a greater distribution than if the issue was whether the distribution invested the owner with federal statutory copyright. As Judge Frank explained:

> [C]ourts apply different tests of publication depending on whether plaintiff is claiming protection because he did not publish and hence has a common law claim of infringement—in which case the distribution must be quite large to constitute "publication"—or whether he is claiming under the copyright statute—in which case the requirements for publication are quite narrow.

American Visuals Corp. v. Holland, 239 F.2d 740, 744, 111 U.S.P.Q. 288, 290 (2d Cir.1956).

In the course of finding that not every public distribution of copies constituted "publication," courts developed the concept of "limited publication," which, as a legal matter, did not constitute publication at all. As one court described it, a limited publication is a distribution of copies "to a definitely selected group and for a limited purpose, and without the right of diffusion, reproduction, distribution or sale * * *." White v. Kimmell, 193 F.2d 744, 746–47, 92 U.S.P.Q. 400, 401 (9th Cir.1952), *cert. denied* 343 U.S. 957, 72 S.Ct. 1052, 96 L.Ed. 1357 (1952). The limited purpose could be express or implied. Burke v. National Broadcasting Co., 598 F.2d 688, 692, 202 U.S.P.Q. 531, 543 (1st Cir.1979), *cert. denied* 444 U.S. 869, 100 S.Ct. 144, 62 L.Ed.2d 93, 203 U.S.P.Q. 640 (1979).

A good discussion of limited publication can be found in Academy of Motion Picture Arts and Sciences v. Creative House Promotions, Inc., 944 F.2d 1446, 19 U.S.P.Q.2d 1491 (9th Cir., 1991). In that case, the court found that the Academy's coveted "Oscar" statuette had not been subject to a general (divestive) publication prior to 1941, when it obtained federal statutory copyright. Citing the rule set forth in the *White* case, *supra*, the court noted that the plaintiff had certainly limited its distribution of copies of the Oscar to a "selected group": "The Academy distributes the coveted Oscar to performers and members of the motion picture industry selected for outstanding achievement." *Id.*, 944 F.2d at 1453, 19 U.S.P.Q.2d at 1491. The Academy had never sold or distributed the award to the general public. The court then found that the Academy's purpose in distributing the Oscar—to honor distinguished recipients and to promote the film industry—was limited. In so finding, the court stressed that at most, any commercial benefit the Academy received in distributing the statuettes was indirect, and indirect commercial benefit was not sufficient to undermine a claim of limited purpose. *Id.* Finally, the court found an implied restriction on recipients' right to further distribute the Oscars: each Oscar was personalized with the name of the individual winner, reflecting the Academy's expectation that the trophy would belong to the recipient alone. Moreover, the Academy had never given permission or otherwise suggested that it was permissible for recipients to sell or distribute the Oscars to the general public, and none had. Since the Academy's distributions qualified as a "limited publication," it was not divested of its common-law copyright, and was protected by copyright today. Compare *American Visuals*, *supra* (unsupervised distribution of approximately two hundred copies of a book at a convention of persons potentially interested in using it held to be an investive publication).

Since public performance of a work generally entails no distribution of tangible copies of the work to the public, it did not constitute a "publication" for purposes of the 1909 Act. Similarly, a public display did not constitute a publication, though there is some authority that it would when photographs of the work were freely permitted to be taken and published. See Letter Edged in Black Press, Inc. v. Public Building Commission of Chicago, 320 F.Supp. 1303, 168 U.S.P.Q. 559 (N.D.Ill.1970).

King v. Mister Maestro, Inc., 224 F.Supp. 101, 140 U.S.P.Q. 366 (S.D.N.Y.1963), is a famous example of how far the courts were willing to go in some cases to avoid a forfeiture of copyright. The case involved Martin Luther King's "I Have A Dream" speech. Dr. King distributed copies of his speech to numerous members of the press in advance, to assist their reporting. He delivered the speech orally to an audience of thousands, certainly realizing that members of the audience were recording or transcribing it, and that radio and television stations were broadcasting it throughout the nation. Dr. King's public performance of the speech did not constitute a publication, and the court found that his distribution of copies to the press constituted a limited publication, notwithstanding that the reporters undoubtedly would, through their reporting, reproduce and distribute the speech to the general public.

The Copyright Act of 1976. Section 101 of the 1976 Act provides:

> "Publication" is the distribution of copies or phonorecords of a work to the public by sale or other transfer of ownership, or by rental, lease, or lending. The offering to distribute copies or phonorecords to a group of persons for purposes of further distribution, public performance, or public display, constitutes publication. A public performance or display of a work does not of itself constitute publication.

17 U.S.C.A. § 101. Does this statutory definition change or clarify the pre-1976 Act law, as described above? If so, how?

2. *The mechanics of notice.* Review the provisions of 1976 Act sections 401 through 404.

Sections 401 and 402, as amended by the Berne Convention Implementation Act, are essentially the same as the original 1976 Act notice provisions, except that they are now permissive, rather than mandatory, and provide (at subsections (d)) that use of notice may avoid an innocent infringer defense. Do the section 401 and 402 notice provisions apply to all copyrightable works, or are some omitted?

Why have separate symbols (©, ℗) to indicate copyright in "copies" and "phonorecords?" See H.R. REP. NO. 1476, 94th Cong., 2d Sess. 145 (1976).

How useful is the required notice information—the symbol of copyright, name of copyright owner, year of publication—to someone seeking to determine the status of the copyright or seek a license to use the work? Note that under the Copyright Act of 1976, the duration of copyright in most works other than works made for hire is measured by the life of the author plus fifty years. Under the 1909 Copyright Act, the duration of copyright depended on whether a proper renewal was made, though renewal was not indicated in the notice. See Section VII, *infra.* Was mandating provision of this information worth the numerous inadvertent forfeitures of copyright to which it led, or the delay in the United States' joining the Berne Convention?

What concerns are sections 403 and 404 meant to alleviate?

For a detailed analysis of the notice provisions under both the 1909 and 1976 Copyright Acts, see 2 M.B. NIMMER & D. NIMMER, NIMMER ON COPYRIGHT, §§ 7.02–7.15 (1994).

3. *The Berne Convention Implementation Act amendments.* Lawyers appear to be advising their clients to continue applying notice to the copies and phonorecords of works they distribute to the public. Are the "innocent infringer" incentives the Berne Convention Implementation Act provided in sections 401(d) and 402(d) a sufficient reason to do so? See Arden, *The Questionable Utility of Copyright Notice: Statutory and Nonlegal Incentives in the Post–Berne Era*, 24 LOY. L. REV. 259 (1993), for arguments that in most cases in which notice is omitted, these provisions will have no impact on the recovery of damages. Are there other reasons why copyright owners

might wish to continue giving notice? Compare Arden, *supra*, with 1 P. GOLDSTEIN, *supra*, at § 3.5.1, pp. 265–66.

4. *Foreign Copyright Restoration.* Review the complex provisions of Copyright Act section 104A, as amended by section 514 of the Uruguay Round Agreements Act. The Senate Report on the Uruguay Round Agreements Act explained:

> The legislation includes language to restore copyright protection to certain foreign works from countries that are members of the Berne Convention or WTO [World Trade Organization] that have fallen into the public domain for reasons other than the normal expiration of their term of protection.
>
> The [Uruguay Round TRIPs] Agreement requires WTO countries to comply with Article 18 of the Berne Convention. While the United States declared its compliance with the Berne Convention in 1989, it never addressed or enacted legislation to implement Article 18 of the Convention. Article 18 requires that the terms of the Convention apply to all works that have fallen into the public domain by reasons other than the expiration of its term of protection. (Examples include failure to file a timely renewal application and failure to affix a copyright notice.)
>
> The bill would automatically restore copyright protection for qualifying works of authors from Berne or WTO countries one year after the WTO comes into being. In order for the restored copyright to be enforced against a "reliance party," it is necessary for the author or copyright owner (rightholder) of the foreign work to either file a "notice of intent" with the Copyright Office during the 24 months after the effective date of the Uruguay Round Agreement or provide actual notice (for the life of the copyright term) directly by notifying the reliance party. Reliance parties then have one year from publication of the constructive notice or receipt of the actual notice to continue to use or sell off copies of the work that have been restored to a foreign author or rightholder. Reproduction of the work during this period is not permitted. After this period, reliance parties are subject to remedies for infringement, except in certain cases.
>
> Section 104A(d)(3) provides additional protection to a reliance party who used a restored foreign work to create a derivative work because a one year sell off period might have been an inadequate period to recoup the investment. In the case of a derivative work that was created based upon a foreign work that was in the public domain but has been restored, the reliance party may continue to sell the derivative work in exchange for providing reasonable compensation to the owner of the restored copyright. In the event that an agreement cannot be reached regarding compensation a district court may determine reasonable compensation, based upon the contribution made by the reliance party as well as the author of the underlying restored work. The court is to take into consideration any damage to the market for the restored work.

S. REP. NO. 412, 103d Cong., 2d Sess. 225–26 (1994). Copyright is restored effective January 1, 1996 [15] for eligible works whose source country adhered to the Berne Convention or the World Trade Organization on that date. Copyright in works from countries who later adhere to the Berne or WTO, or which are extended protection by Presidential proclamation will be restored on the date of adherence or proclamation. 17 U.S.C.A. § 104A(h)(2)(A), as amended, Uruguay Round Agreements Act, Pub. L. No. 103–465 § 514, 108 Stat. 4809, 4976 (1994). The restored copyright lasts for the remainder of the term that the work would have enjoyed in the United States had it not entered the public domain. See 17 U.S.C.A. § 104A(a)(1)(B), as amended.

The amended section 104A provides copyright in works from eligible countries if the works fell into the U.S. public domain because

1) the copyright owner failed to comply with U.S. copyright formalities, such as notice or renewal;

2) they constituted sound recordings fixed prior to February 15, 1972 (and thus did not constitute copyrightable subject matter under U.S. copyright law); or

3) their source country did not have copyright relations with the U.S. at the time they were published.

Thus, section 104A does more than just "restore" lost copyrights—it provides copyright in foreign works that never before enjoyed copyright in the United States. See 17 U.S.C.A. § 104A(h)(6), as amended.

The restored copyright is enforceable immediately against infringers who are not "reliance parties." See *id.*, § 104A(d)(1). However, as the Senate Report explains, notice of intent to enforce the restored copyright must be given before reliance parties will be liable. Who qualifies as a reliance party? See *id.*, § 104A(h)(4). Do the elaborate notice requirements imposed by section 104A, as amended, condition enjoyment and exercise of copyright on compliance with formalities, in violation of the Berne Convention Article 5(2)? See *General Agreement on Tariffs and Trade (GATT) Intellectual Property Provisions: Joint Hearing before the Subcomm. on Intellectual Property and Judicial Administration of the House Comm. on the Judiciary, and the Subcomm. on Patents, Copyrights and Trademarks of the Senate Comm. on the Judiciary,* 103d Cong., 2d Sess. 187–232 (statements of Prof. Shira Perlmutter and Prof. Irwin Karp). Does restoring foreign copyrights constitute an unconstitutional "taking" of private property without just compensation, in violation of reliance parties' fifth amendment rights? See *id.*, at 145–62, 173–232 (statements of Christopher Schroeder, Counsellor to the Assistant Attorney General, Prof. Eugene Volokh, Prof. Shira Perlmutter, & Prof. Irwin Karp).

Note that section 104A does not restore domestic copyrights that were lost due to failure to comply with notice, renewal or other formalities. Nor does it provide copyright for domestic sound recordings fixed prior to February 15, 1972. However, U.S. copyright owners will benefit by recipro-

15. The Copyright Office and the United States Trade Representative have taken the position that January 1, 1996, is the date of foreign copyright restoration under the amended section 104A. This position is consistent with the Senate Report, excerpted above, and the language of TRIPs Article 65. However, a creditable argument can be made that section 104A(h)(2)(A), in combination with Uruguay Round Agreements Act § 101(b) and (d), specifies a restoration date of January 1, 1995.

cal restoration of copyright for their works in other Berne and World Trade Organization countries.

B. DEPOSIT AND REGISTRATION

The Deposit Requirement

Within three months of publishing a work in the United States, "the owner of copyright or of the exclusive right of publication" in the work must deposit two copies or phonorecords of the "best edition" of the work with the Copyright Office. 17 U.S.C.A. § 407. Failure to comply may be penalized by fine, but does not lead to forfeiture of copyright. The copies or phonorecords are for the use of the Library of Congress, for the express purpose of section 407 is to enrich the Library of Congress' collection. Given this end, the Register of Copyrights has flexibility to adjust the deposit requirement for various categories of works to conform with the Library's needs and housing capabilities. In addition, the Register may adjust the deposit requirements to avoid causing undue practical or financial hardship to copyright owners. See 17 U.S.C.A. § 407(c); H.R. REP. NO. 1476, 94th Cong., 2d Sess. 151 (1976). The exemptions to deposit set forth by the Register can be found at 37 C.F.R. §§ 202.20–21.

Congress reviewed the mandatory deposit provisions in the course of enacting the Berne Convention Implementation Act. It determined to maintain the requirement, notwithstanding suggestions that it would subjugate "enjoyment and exercise of copyright" to compliance with formalities, in violation of the Berne Convention. The House Report explained:

> Since 1865 the Library of Congress has been the permanent beneficiary of copyright deposits, the copyright system therefore being one of the primary sources of acquisitions for the Library. Some of the collections were built almost exclusively through copyright deposits. * * *
>
> Since noncompliance with the mandatory deposit requirement does not result in forfeiture of any copyright protection, mandatory deposit is compatible with Berne.

H.R. REP. NO. 609, 100th Cong., 2d Sess. 44 (1988).

The Registration Requirement

The Copyright Act's registration provisions are meant to create a comprehensive record of copyright claims throughout the country. The Copyright Office keeps extensive files of registration documents, as well as records of transfers of ownership and other matters relevant to copyright ownership. The public is free to go to the Copyright Office to search these records to determine the status of works in which they are interested, or avail themselves of the search service which the Copyright Office offers for a modest fee.

Copyright arises automatically upon fixation of a qualifying work, and is not conditioned on registration. However, the 1976 Act makes registration (or an unsuccessful attempt to register) a prerequisite to suit for infringement. See 17 U.S.C.A. §§ 408(a), 411(a). Once the copyright is registered, the owner may sue for events that occurred prior to the registration. See H.R. REP. NO. 1476, 94th Cong., 2d Sess. 157 (1976).

While a copyright owner is permitted to register at any time during the copyright term (and may never register, if she never seeks to enforce the copyright), Congress designed sections 408 through 412 to encourage owners to register and register early. Section 410(c) provides:

> In any judicial proceedings the certificate of a registration made before or within five years after first publication of the work shall constitute prima facie evidence of the validity of the copyright and of the facts stated in the certificate. The evidentiary weight to be accorded the certificate of a registration made thereafter shall be within the discretion of the court.

17 U.S.C.A. § 410(c). The House Report commented:

> It is true that, unlike a patent claim, a claim to copyright is not examined for basic validity before a certificate is issued. On the other hand, endowing a copyright claimant who has obtained a certificate with a rebuttable presumption of the validity of the copyright does not deprive the defendant in an infringement suit of any rights; it merely orders the burdens of proof. The plaintiff should not ordinarily be forced in the first instance to provide all of the multitude of facts that underline the validity of the copyright unless the defendant, by effectively challenging them, shifts the burden of doing so to the plaintiff.

H.R. REP. NO. 1476, *supra,* at 157.

Section 412 also encourages early registration by prohibiting award of statutory damages and attorney's fees to copyright owner/plaintiffs who failed to register their works before the infringement at suit began (in the case of unpublished works) or within three months after first publication. 17 U.S.C.A. § 412. Copyright owners failing to file within the section 412 time frame are not denied the "ordinary" remedies of injunctive relief, actual damages and applicable profits. H.R. REP. NO. 1476, *supra*, at 158.

Copyright registration is relatively simple and inexpensive. The registration process consists of completing a printed form and sending it, the applicable fee, and a copy of the work for deposit to the Copyright Office. 17 U.S.C.A. §§ 408, 409. If a copyright owner is required to make a deposit under section 407, that deposit may serve for purposes of registration, as well, if he sends the application and fee along with the section 407 deposit. *Id.*, § 408(b). Pursuant to section 410(a), the Copyright Office will issue a certificate of registration if "the material deposited constitutes copyrightable subject matter and * * * the other legal and formal requirements * * * have been met." As suggested by the House Report excerpt above, the Copyright Office reviews the application for obvious errors, but does not attempt to verify the facts set forth in it, or search the prior art.

Arguably, the 1976 Act made the formality of registration a prerequisite to enjoyment and exercise of copyright, contrary to Berne Convention requirements. Reluctant to give up its record-keeping system, Congress adopted a compromise position, taking advantage of its latitude under the Berne Convention to restrict copyrights for domestic works in ways that copyrights on works originating in other member nations may not be restricted. The Berne Convention Implementation Act amended section 411 to delete the registration requirement for works whose country of origin is another Berne Convention country, while retaining it for works whose country of origin is the United States. See 17 U.S.C.A. § 411(a) (as amended). As a general matter, a work's country of origin is the United States if it was first published in the United States (or simultaneously published in the United States and another country) or, in the case of unpublished works, was created entirely by United States authors. See 17 U.S.C.A. § 101 (describing when a Berne Convention work's "country of origin" is the United States). Congress retained the section 410 and 412 incentives for early registration for foreign works, in the hopes that foreign copyright owners would continue to register voluntarily.

Subsequent to the Berne Convention Implementation Act, bills have been introduced to eliminate the pre-suit registration requirement for all works, and eliminate the registration requirement for statutory damages and attorney's fees. See, e.g., S. 373, 103d Cong., 1st Sess. (1993).

Apart from the registration process, the Copyright Act provides a system for recording transfers of copyright interests, in order to give notice to subsequent purchasers and establish priority of ownership. See 17 U.S.C.A. § 205. Prior to the Berne Convention Implementation Act, the 1976 Act required transferees to record their interests as a prerequisite to instituting an infringement action. That requirement no longer exists with regard to causes of action arising after March 1, 1989. Pub. L. No. 100–568, § 5(1), 102 Stat. 2853, 2857 (1988).

VII. DURATION OF COPYRIGHT

HOUSE REPORT ON COPYRIGHT ACT OF 1976

H.R. Rep. No. 1476, 94th Cong., 2d Sess. 133–36 (1976).

The debate over how long a copyright should last is as old as the oldest copyright statute and will doubtless continue as long as there is a copyright law. With certain exceptions, there appears to be strong support for the principle, as embodied in the bill, of a copyright term consisting of the life of the author and 50 years after his death. * * *

Under the present law statutory copyright protection begins on the date of publication (or on the date of registration in unpublished form) and continues for 28 years from that date; it may be renewed for a second 28 years, making a total potential term of 56 years in all cases.[1] The principal elements of this system—a definite number of years, computed from either publication or registration, with a renewal feature—have been a part of the U.S. copyright law since the first statute in 1790. The arguments for changing this system to one based on the life of the author can be summarized as follows:

1. The present 56–year term is not long enough to insure an author and his dependents the fair economic benefits from his works. Life expectancy has increased substantially, and more and more authors are seeing their works fall into the public domain during their lifetimes, forcing later works to compete with their own early works in which copyright has expired.

2. The tremendous growth in communications media has substantially lengthened the commercial life of a great many works. A short term is particularly discriminatory against serious works of music, literature, and art, whose value may not be recognized until after many years.

3. Although limitations on the term of copyright are obviously necessary, too short a term harms the author without giving any substantial benefit to the public. The public frequently pays the same for works in the public domain as it does for copyrighted works, and the only result is a commercial windfall to certain users at the author's expense. In some cases the lack of copyright protection actually restrains dissemination of the work, since publishers and other users cannot risk investing in the work unless assured of exclusive rights.

4. A system based on the life of the author would go a long way toward clearing up the confusion and uncertainty involved in the vague concept of "publication," and would provide a much simpler, clearer method for computing the term. The death of the author is a definite, determinable event, and it would be the only date that a potential user would have to worry about. All of a particular author's works, including successive revisions of them, would fall into the public domain at the same time, thus avoiding the present problems of determining a multitude of publication dates and of distinguishing "old" and "new" matter in later editions. The bill answers the problems of determining when relatively obscure authors died, by establishing a registry of death dates and a system of presumptions.

5. One of the worst features of the present copyright law is the provision for renewal of copyright. A substantial burden and ex-

1. Under Public Laws 87–668, 89–142, 90–141, 90–416, 91–147, 91–555, 92–170, 92–566, and 93–573, copyrights that were subsisting in their renewal term on Sept. 19, 1962, and that were scheduled to expire before Dec. 31, 1976, have been extended to that later date, in anticipation that general revision legislation extending their terms still further will be enacted by then.

pense, this unclear and highly technical requirement results in incalculable amounts of unproductive work. In a number of cases it is the cause of inadvertent and unjust loss of copyright. Under a life-plus–50 system the renewal device would be inappropriate and unnecessary.

6. Under the preemption provisions of section 301 and the single Federal system they would establish, authors will be giving up perpetual, unlimited exclusive common law rights in their unpublished works, including works that have been widely disseminated by means other than publication. A statutory term of life-plus–50 years is no more than a fair recompense for the loss of these perpetual rights.

7. A very large majority of the world's countries have adopted a copyright term of the life of the author and 50 years after the author's death. Since American authors are frequently protected longer in foreign countries than in the United States, the disparity in the duration of copyright has provoked considerable resentment and some proposals for retaliatory legislation. Copyrighted works move across national borders faster and more easily than virtually any other economic commodity, and with the techniques now in common use this movement has in many cases become instantaneous and effortless. The need to conform the duration of U.S. copyright to that prevalent throughout the rest of the world is increasingly pressing in order to provide certainty and simplicity in international business dealings. Even more important, a change in the basis of our copyright term would place the United States in the forefront of the international copyright community. Without this change, the possibility of future United States adherence to the Berne Copyright Union would evaporate, but with it would come a great and immediate improvement in our copyright relations. All of these benefits would accrue directly to American and foreign authors alike.

* * *

A point that has concerned some educational groups arose from the possibility that, since a large majority (now about 85 percent) of all copyrighted works are not renewed, a life-plus–50 year term would tie up a substantial body of material that is probably of no commercial interest but that would be more readily available for scholarly use if free of copyright restrictions. A statistical study of renewal registrations made by the Copyright Office in 1966 supports the generalization that most material which is considered to be of continuing or potential commercial value is renewed. Of the remainder, a certain proportion is of practically no value to anyone, but there are a large number of unrenewed works that have scholarly value to historians, archivists, and specialists in a variety of fields. This consideration lay behind the proposals for retaining the renewal device or for limiting the term for unpublished or unregistered works.

It is true that today's ephemera represent tomorrow's social history, and that works of scholarly value, which are now falling into the public domain after 28 years, would be protected much longer under the bill. Balanced against this are the burdens and expenses of renewals, the near impossibility of distinguishing between types of works in fixing a statutory term, and the extremely strong case in favor of a life-plus–50 system. Moreover, it is important to realize that the bill would not restrain scholars from using any work as source material or from making "fair use" of it * * *. The advantages of a basic term of copyright enduring for the life of the author and for 50 years after the author's death outweigh any possible disadvantages.

Notes and Questions

1. *The duration of copyright.* The Constitution empowers Congress to "promote the Progress of Science and useful Arts, by securing *for limited times* to Authors and Inventors the exclusive Right to their respective Writings and Discoveries." U.S. CONST. art. I, § 8, cl. 8 (emphasis added). Federal copyright may not be perpetual. It should last for the period best calculated to "promote the Progress of Science and useful Arts"—presumably, long enough to provide a sufficient incentive to authors, but no longer, so that works move into the public domain, accessible to all, as quickly as possible. How long is that?

The House Report recites arguments that Congress found persuasive in abandoning the renewable 28 year term (potentially giving 56 years of copyright protection) and adopting a term measured by the life of the author plus 50 years (estimated to give an average of about 75 years protection). Which arguments do you find most persuasive? Are you convinced by the argument that the public may pay the same for works in the public domain as it does for copyrighted works?

Are there any convincing arguments *against* moving to the longer term? What are the costs? Consider Lord Macaulay's famous argument against a long posthumous copyright monopoly:

> [T]he evil effects of the monopoly are proportioned to the length of its duration. But the good effects for the sake of which we bear with the evil effects are by no means proportioned to the length of its duration. A monopoly of sixty years produces twice as much evil as a monopoly of thirty years, and thrice as much evil as a monopoly of twenty years. But it is by no means the fact that a posthumous monopoly of sixty years gives to an author thrice as much pleasure and thrice as strong a motive as a posthumous monopoly of twenty years. On the contrary, the difference is so small as to be hardly perceptible. We all know how faintly we are affected by the prospect of very distant advantages, even when they are advantages which we may reasonably hope that we shall ourselves enjoy. But an advantage that is to be enjoyed more than half a century after we are dead, by somebody, we know not by whom, perhaps by somebody unborn, by somebody utterly unconnected with us, is really no motive at all to action.... Considered as a boon to [authors, long posthumous duration of the copyright monopoly] is a mere nullity; but, considered as an impost on the public,

it is no nullity, but a very serious and pernicious reality. I will take an example. Dr. Johnson died fifty-six years ago. If the law [prolonged the copyright for sixty years after the author's death], somebody would now have the monopoly of Dr. Johnson's works. Who that somebody would be is impossible to say; but we may venture to guess. I guess, then, that it would have been some bookseller, who was the assign of another bookseller, who was the grandson of a third bookseller, who had bought the copyright from Black Frank, the Doctor's servant and residuary legatee, in 1785 or 1786. Now, would the knowledge that this copyright would exist in 1841 have been a source of gratification to Johnson? Would it have stimulated his exertions? Would it have once drawn him out of his bed before noon? Would it have once cheered him under a fit of the spleen? Would it have induced him to give us one more allegory, one more life of a poet, one more imitation of Juvenal? I firmly believe not. I firmly believe that a hundred years ago, when he was writing our debates for the Gentleman's Magazine, he would very much rather have had twopence to buy a plate of shin of beef at a cook's shop underground. Considered as a reward to him, the difference between a twenty years' term and a sixty years' term of posthumous copyright would have been nothing or next to nothing. But is the difference nothing to us? I can buy Rassselas for sixpence; I might have had to give five shillings for it. I can buy the Dictionary, the entire genuine Dictionary, for two guineas, perhaps for less; I might have had to give five or six guineas for it. Do I grudge this to a man like Dr. Johnson? Not at all. Show me that the prospect of this boon roused him to any vigorous effort, or sustained his spirits under depressing circumstances, and I am quite willing to pay the price of such an object, heavy as that price is. But what I do complain of is that my circumstances are to be worse, and Johnson's none the better; that I am to give five pounds for what to him was not worth a farthing.

8 Macaulay, Works (Trevelyan ed. 1879) 199–201, reprinted in Chaffee, *Reflections on the Law of Copyright: II*, 45 COLUM. L. REV. 719, 719–20 (1945). In your opinion, how much is the posthumous duration of copyright likely to affect an author's incentive to create? How much is it likely to affect the amount that a publisher is willing to pay the author for the copyright? See Chaffee, *supra*, at 720–21. Assuming that posthumous copyright protection would be an incentive to authors wishing to provide for a surviving spouse and children, is there justification for recognizing such a copyright if no such surviving spouse or children exist at the author's death?

European countries, whose copyright laws are based on a natural rights philosophy, have moved to a copyright term of life of the author plus 70 years. Should the United States follow suit? See Karjala, *Comment of U.S. Law Professors on the Copyright Office Term of Protection Study*, 12 EUR. INTELL. PROP. REV. 531 (1994). Is the first amendment a consideration?

Should copyright for product labels, business forms and computer programs be protected for the same length of time as works of fine art and classical music? If not, would it be feasible to provide different terms of copyright protection for different types of works?

For excellent discussions regarding the proper length of copyright, see Cohen, *Duration*, 24 U.C.L.A. L. REV. 1180 (1977); Ricketson, *The Copyright Term*, 23 INT'L REV. INDUS. PROP. & COPYRIGHT L. 753 (1992).

Review sections 302 through 305 of the Copyright Act of 1976. Why have a separate measure for the term of works for hire, anonymous and pseudonymous works? ("Anonymous" and "pseudonymous" works, for purposes of the Copyright Act, are defined in section 101 of the Act.)

Note that in addition to adopting a "life plus 50" term for works created after the effective date of the 1976 Act, Congress extended the second (renewal) term of federal copyrights already in existence on the effective date from 28 to 47 years. In what way does this benefit the public? Congress also converted common-law copyrights existing on the effective date to federal copyrights. Even works that had enjoyed common-law copyright protection for more than fifty years after the author's death received federal copyright to endure through the year 2002. Why should Congress do this?

2. *Calculating duration.* Carefully review sections 302–305 again, and consider the following questions:

a) A. Allen writes a poem on April 3, 1990, and publishes it with proper notice on April 8, 1994. She dies on August 4, 2009. When will copyright in the poem expire? What if Allen never publishes the poem?

b) B. Brown writes a letter on June 1, 1948. He never publishes it, and dies on August 10, 2003. When will copyright in the letter expire?

c) C. Chin composes a song on June 1, 1911. She never publishes it, and dies on October 17, 1917. When will copyright in the song expire?

d) Donald and Delores Doe collaborate to write a novel, which is completed on April 4, 1982. They publish the novel with proper notice of copyright in 1984. Donald dies on September 8, 1993. Delores dies December 10, 2020. When will copyright in the novel expire?

e) E. Edwards takes a photograph in his capacity as staff photographer for the local newspaper in 1962. The newspaper publishes the photograph with proper notice of copyright in 1968. Edwards dies in 1988. When will copyright in the photograph expire?

f) F. Fernandez creates artwork for an advertising brochure in her capacity as a staff artist of the X advertising firm in 1979. X firm publishes the artwork in a brochure with proper copyright notice in 1987. Fernandez dies in 2018. When will copyright in the artwork expire?

g) G. Grosskoff writes a play in 1932, publishes it in 1934 with proper copyright notice, and properly renews the copyright in 1962. He dies in 1971. When does the copyright in the play expire?

h) H. Horowitz writes a short story in 1918 and publishes it with proper copyright notice in 1919. He properly renews copyright in 1947. When will copyright in the short story expire?

i) I. Insbrook writes a biography of George Washington in 1956 and publishes it with proper notice in 1957. He dies in 1981. When will copyright in the biography expire?

j) J. Jones creates an oil painting on February 14, 1993. She sells the painting in 1994, and assigns all her rights in the copyright in 1998. She dies in 2019. When do her moral rights in the painting expire? See 17 U.S.C.A. § 106A(d).

k) Assume that an author writes the first chapter of a novel in 1982. He writes four more chapters in 1983. He then puts the novel aside for several years to work on another project. In 1989, he writes the remainder of the first draft of the novel. In 1991, he completes revisions and sends the manuscript to publishers. In 1992 a publisher accepts the manuscript and edits it. The finished novel is published with notice in 1994. When does copyright commence? See 17 U.S.C.A. § 101 (definition of "created").

l) Assume that X wrote a play and published it, with proper copyright notice, in 1923. He properly renewed copyright in the play in 1951. In 1938, X licensed Y to produce a motion picture based on the play. The motion picture received federal copyright in 1940. Because Y failed properly to renew copyright in the motion picture, it fell into the public domain in 1968. What, if any, rights should X have against Z if, in 1970, Z wishes to reproduce and sell copies of the motion picture? See Russell v. Price, 612 F.2d 1123, 205 U.S.P.Q. 206 (9th Cir.1979), *cert. denied* 446 U.S. 952, 100 S.Ct. 2919, 64 L.Ed.2d 809 (1980).

3. *Renewal of copyright.* The 1909 Copyright Act provided for a 28–year copyright term which could, if a proper filing was made, be renewed for a second 28–year term, to give a total of 56 years of protection. Failure to make a proper filing for renewal placed the work in the public domain at the end of the first 28–year term.[16] In enacting the 1976 Act, Congress retained the renewable term configuration for federal copyrights already in existence on the effective date of the new Act (January 1, 1978). The only important change Congress made with regard to the term of existing copyrights was to add 19 years to the second ("renewal") term. Case law construing the 1909 Act renewal provisions remains relevant not only to interpret the effect of acts occurring before the effective date of the 1976 Act, but also to interpret the 1976 Act renewal provisions for federal copyrights existing on January 1, 1978.

Copyright Act section 304, like its predecessor in the 1909 Act, specifies that in most cases the *author (or the author's statutory successors)*, rather than the person owning the copyright at the end of the first term, has the right to renew the copyright and enjoy the renewal term. Upon proper renewal during the last year of the first term, the author (or his statutory successors) takes a whole new term, rather than a continuance of the old term. The renewal term operates much like a future estate in land: when it vests in possession, the recipient takes the copyright free of any assignments or licenses made in the first copyright term. See RINGER, RENEWAL OF COPYRIGHT, COPYRIGHT REVISION STUDY NO. 31 (1960), reprinted in COPYRIGHT REVISION: STUDIES PREPARED FOR THE SUBCOMM. ON PATENTS, TRADEMARKS, AND COPYRIGHTS OF THE COMM. ON THE JUDICIARY, 86th Cong., 2d Sess., 105, 124 (Comm. Print 1961).

16. As discussed *supra*, qualifying foreign copyrights forfeited for failure to renew are restored under the provisions of Uruguay Round Agreements Act section 514. 17 U.S.C.A. § 104A.

Congress created this renewal term in the author or her successors in order to give authors and their families a second opportunity to market the copyright. Works often are incapable of accurate monetary valuation before they are exploited and public reaction to them can be gaged. Unknown authors, in particular, may be in a poor bargaining position when first seeking to sell rights in a work. The renewal procedure gives the author, or if the author is dead, her family, an opportunity to renegotiate earlier assignments and licenses once the real value of the work has been ascertained, and obtain the benefit of any increase over the initial estimated value. See *id.* at 125; Fred Fisher Music Co. v. M. Witmark & Sons, 318 U.S. 643, 63 S.Ct. 773, 87 L.Ed. 1055 (1943).

Just as the renewal term operates like a future estate, the expectancy of the right to renew and take the renewal term is like a contingent future interest in the succession of persons specified in section 304(a)(1)(C). The author is entitled to renew the copyright and enjoy the renewal term if he is still living when the renewal right vests. If the author is not living, the author's widow, widower, and/or children (as defined in section 101) are entitled to take the renewal term. If there are no surviving spouse or children, the author's executor is entitled to take on behalf of the author's legatees.[17] In the absence of a will, the interest vests directly in the author's next of kin, as determined by the intestacy laws of the author's domicile.[18]

In *Fred Fisher Music*, *supra*, the Supreme Court held that the author (and, by implication, the author's statutory successors) may convey her expectancy of renewal, if she clearly indicates her intention to do so. Thus, for example, if a publisher requires an author to assign both her present and renewal term, and the author's written assignment makes it clear that she intends to assign her rights in the renewal term, the assignment will be honored. If the author is alive when the renewal term is to vest, the publisher/assignee may make the renewal in the author's name, and retain

17. Note that the Copyright Act gives the renewal term to surviving spouse and children if they exist, regardless of what the author has provided in his will. See Saroyan v. William Saroyan Foundation, 675 F.Supp. 843, 5 U.S.P.Q.2d 1532 (S.D.N.Y. 1987), *affirmed*, 862 F.2d 304 (2d Cir.1988) (author's express attempt to leave all his copyrights to charity would not defeat his estranged children's renewal rights under section 304). Only if there are no surviving spouse or children can the author direct who the recipient will be.

When the renewal right vests in the author's executor, the executor claims the renewal as the legatees' personal representative, rather than as representative of the estate, so that the author's creditors are unable to reach the renewal term. See Ringer, *supra*, at 152–6. Why should Congress wish to favor the legatees at the expense of the author's creditors?

18. Section 304(a)(1)(B) specifies four categories of works in which the copyright proprietor (the person owning the copyright at the end of the first term), *rather than the author or her successors*, has the right to renew:

1) any posthumous work (A "posthumous work" has been defined as a work for which no assignment or contract for exploitation has been made during the author's life. Bartok v. Boosey & Hawkes, Inc., 523 F.2d 941, 187 U.S.P.Q. 529 (2d Cir.1975));

2) "any periodical, cyclopedic, or other composite work upon which the copyright was originally secured by the proprietor thereof;"

3) works "copyrighted by a corporate body (otherwise than as assignee or licensee of the individual author);" and

4) works copyrighted by an employer for whom the work was made for hire.

What justification exists for exempting each of these categories of works from the general rule? When is a work likely to fall into the third category but not the fourth? See generally Ringer, *supra*, at 127–49.

the rights to the work during the second term. If, on the other hand, the author is deceased at vesting time, the publisher/assignee will take nothing. The author could not assign more than she had—a contingent future interest who's contingency has not been satisfied. The surviving spouse and children will receive the renewal interest, and if they do not exist, the executor or next of kin will take. See Miller Music Corp. v. Charles N. Daniels, Inc., 362 U.S. 373, 80 S.Ct. 792, 4 L.Ed.2d 804, 125 U.S.P.Q. 147 (1960). Does permitting assignment of the renewal right make sense in light of Congress' purpose to benefit the author and her family?

Prior to the Copyright Amendments Act of 1992, Pub.L. No. 102–307, 106 Stat. 264, renewal term claimants were required to file an application for renewal with the Copyright Office during the 28th year of the first copyright term. Failure to do so cast the work into the public domain when the first term ended. Through ignorance or inattentiveness, many qualified claimants lost their right to a renewal term. Apart from leading to unintended forfeitures, the renewal filing requirement arguably was inconsistent with the Berne Convention's prohibition of formalities as a precondition to copyright. In 1992, Congress amended section 304 to dispense with the filing requirement and provide for automatic renewal of all remaining first-term copyrights (those secured after January 1, 1964). See Pub. L. No. 102–307, 106 Stat. 264.

The amendment nonetheless seeks to encourage voluntary filings for renewal. Among other things, the amended section 304 provides that registration through a proper application to renew will "constitute prima facie evidence as to the validity of the copyright during its renewal and extended term and of the facts stated in the certificate." Moreover, if a person who is entitled to renew (or his renewal right assignee) registers the renewal term by filing a voluntary application to renew, the renewal interest will vest in that person as of the date of application (*during* the 28th year of the first term). If the renewal is automatic, the interest will vest in the person entitled to renew at the end of the 28th year. *Id.*, § 304 (a)(2)(B). Thus, for example, assume that the author assigned his renewal rights to X. X files and renews at the beginning of the 28th year of the first term, while the author is still alive. The author dies a month later, prior to the end of the first term. X will take the renewal term. If X had relied on automatic renewal, he would have lost the term to the author's surviving spouse and children.

Assume that A writes a story prior to January 1, 1978, and obtains federal copyright. While the copyright is in its first term, A grants to B the exclusive right to make and commercially exploit a movie based on the story. B does so. A dies. At the end of the first term of copyright in the story, A's widow successfully renews and obtains the renewal term. Is B free to reproduce, publicly distribute, perform and display the movie during the second term? See Stewart v. Abend, 495 U.S. 207, 110 S.Ct. 1750, 109 L.Ed.2d 184 (1990); 17 U.S.C.A. § 304(a)(4); Nimmer, *Refracting the Window's Light:* Stewart v. Abend *in Myth and in Fact*, 39 J. COPYRIGHT SOC'Y 18 (1991).

A. TERMINATION OF TRANSFERS.

Review the complex provisions of 1976 Act sections 203 and 304(c). According to the House Report, provisions of this sort are needed "because of the unequal bargaining position of authors, resulting in part from the impossibility of determining a work's value until it has been exploited." H.R. REP. NO. 1476, 94th Cong., 2d Sess. 124 (1976). Section 203, which applies to all *inter vivos* licenses and assignments of copyright executed by a work's author after 1977, serves much the same purpose as the old renewal provisions did: it permits the author or his designated successors to participate in the work's appreciation in value by terminating the author's earlier licenses and assignments and reselling rights in the work. The House Report explained:

> Instead of being automatic, as is theoretically the case under the present renewal provision, the termination of a transfer or license under section 203 would require the serving of an advance notice within specified time limits and under specified conditions. However, although affirmative action is needed to effect a termination, the right to take this action cannot be waived in advance or contracted away. * * *
>
> The right of termination would be confined to inter vivos transfers or licenses executed by the author, and would not apply to transfers by the author's successors in interest or to the author's own bequests. The scope of the right would extend not only to any "transfer of copyright ownership," as defined in section 101, but also to nonexclusive licenses. The right of termination would not apply to "works made for hire" * * *.
>
> * * * With respect to the ultimate effective date, section 203(a)(3) provides, as a general rule, that a grant may be terminated during the 5 years following the expiration of a period of 35 years from the execution of the grant. As an exception to this basic 35–year rule, the bill also provides that "if the grant covers the right of publication of the work, the period begins at the end of 35 years from the date of publication of the work under the grant or at the end of 40 years from the date of execution of the grant, whichever term ends earlier." This alternative method of computation is intended to cover cases where years elapse between the signing of a publication contract and the eventual publication of the work.
>
> The effective date of termination, which must be stated in the advance notice, is required to fall within the 5 years following the end of the applicable 35–or 40–year period, but the advance notice itself must be served earlier. Under section 203(a)(4)(A), the notice must be served "not less than two or more than ten years" before the effective date stated in it.
>
> * * *
>
> Section 203(b) makes clear that, unless effectively terminated within the applicable 5–year period, all rights covered by an existing

> grant will continue unchanged, and that rights under other Federal, State, or foreign laws are unaffected. * * *

H.R. REP. NO. 1476, 94th Cong., 2d Sess. 124–27 (1976). In your opinion, is section 203 likely to be more successful than the old renewal regime?

Section 304 permits authors and their statutorily designated successors to terminate pre–1978 transfers of rights in the renewal term in order to recapture and enjoy the bonus 19 years added to the renewal term by the 1976 Act. According to the House Report:

> Subsection (c) of section 304 is a close but not exact counterpart of section 203. In the case of either a first-term or renewal copyright already subsisting when the new statute becomes effective, any grant of the rights covering the renewal copyright in the work, executed before the effective date [of the 1976 Act], may be terminated under conditions and limitations similar to those provided in section 203. Except for transfers and licenses covering renewal copyrights already extended under Public Laws 87–668, 89–142, 90–141, 90–416, 91–147, 91–555, 92–170, 92–566, and 93–573, which would become subject to termination immediately upon the coming into effect of the revised law, the 5–year period during which termination could be made effective would start 56 years after copyright was originally secured.
>
> The bill distinguishes between the persons who can terminate a grant under 203 and those entitled to terminate a grant covering an extended term under section 304. Instead of being limited to transfers and licensees executed by the author, the right of termination under section 304(c) also extends to grants executed by those beneficiaries of the author who can claim renewal under the present law: his or her widow or widower, children, executors, or next of kin. * * *

Id., at 140. Instead of imposing the section 304(c) termination procedure, why not just provide that the additional 19 years added to the renewal term automatically vests in the author or her designated successors?

Assume that an author grants X the right to make and exploit a derivative work (e.g., a motion picture) based on the copyrighted work, and later terminates the grant pursuant to section 203 or 304(c). May X continue to exploit the derivative work? See 17 U.S.C.A. §§ 203(b)(1), 304(c)(6)(a); Abrams, *Who's Sorry Now? Termination Rights and the Derivative Works Exception*, 62 U. DET. L. REV. 181 (1985).

For a thorough examination of the termination provisions and discussion of how they may influence the drafting of assignment and licensing agreements, see Stein, *Termination of Transfers and Licenses under the New Copyright Act: Thorny Problems for the Copyright Bar*, 24 U.C.L.A. L. REV. 1141 (1977).

VIII. REMEDIES

ABESHOUSE v. ULTRAGRAPHICS, INC.

United States Court of Appeals for the Second Circuit, 1985.
754 F.2d 467.

FEINBERG, CHIEF JUDGE:

* * *

In September 1981, Tevin and Matthew Abeshouse obtained a copyright for a large poster entitled "The Cube Solution," which described in great detail the solution to the popular puzzle known as "Rubik's Cube." Shortly before, Tevin Abeshouse, acting for Amity Products, Ltd.—the partnership under whose name he and his brother Matthew did business—entered into an exclusive distribution agreement with Ultragraphics, which was represented by its president, Richard Calio. The agreement took effect immediately and ran until December 31, 1981; under it, Ultragraphics became the exclusive North American distributor of "The Cube Solution" poster, which would be supplied by Amity at the rate of $0.90 per poster for the first 10,000 posters and $0.75 per poster thereafter.

This arrangement, however, soon broke down. In early October, apparently fearing that Amity would be unable to provide Ultragraphics with enough posters to meet customer demand, Calio placed an order with D & M, a printer, for 20,000 posters. Although these posters were slightly modified, they were substantially based on "The Cube Solution" poster. Calio also ordered two "separations" (negatives), to be used in the production of the poster overseas. It appears that D & M delivered 21,500 posters to Ultragraphics and that the latter distributed them at a wholesale price of $2.00 per poster until it had exhausted its supply. D & M also provided the two separations to Ultragraphics, which shipped them to two English publishing companies; for these separations, Ultragraphics received $2,500 credited to its account. At the expiration of the agreement with Ultragraphics, the Abeshouses entered into an agreement licensing Ideal Toy Co. to produce and sell their poster.

In September 1982, plaintiffs Abeshouses brought suit against Ultragraphics, Calio and D & M for copyright infringement, unfair competition, breach of contract and unjust enrichment. * * * On the copyright infringement claim, the jury found Ultragraphics and D & M jointly and severally liable for $55,368 and $2,441.53 respectively. * * * The district court awarded attorney's fees pursuant to 17 U.S.C. § 505 against Ultragraphics but refused to do so against D & M. These appeals and the cross-appeal followed.

II. THE APPEAL OF ULTRAGRAPHICS

The Copyright Act of 1976 entitles a copyright owner to choose between statutory damages, as defined in 17 U.S.C. § 504(c), or "the actual damages suffered by him or her as a result of the infringement, and any profits of the infringer that are attributable to the infringement and are not taken into account in computing the actual damages," 17 U.S.C. § 504(b). In this respect, the 1976 Act clearly departs from the previous copyright statute, under which a copyright holder could receive a cumulative award of his own damages, including profits the owner would have earned on lost sales, and the infringer's actual profits, regardless of the latter's relationship to the holder's damages. The House Report that preceded the 1976 Act reasoned:

> Damages are awarded to compensate the copyright owner for losses from the infringement, and profits are awarded to prevent the infringer from unfairly benefiting from a wrongful act. Where the defendant's profits are nothing more than a measure of the damages suffered by the copyright owner, it would be inappropriate to award damages and profits cumulatively, since in effect they amount to the same thing. However, in cases where the copyright owner has suffered damages not reflected in the infringer's profits, or where there have been profits attributable to the copyrighted work but not used as a measure of damages, subsection (b) authorizes the award of both.

H.R. REP. NO. 1476, 94th Cong., 2d Sess. 161, reprinted in 1976 U.S. Code Cong. & Ad. News 5659, 5777.

In reviewing an award made under § 504(b), we must therefore ensure that it was not based upon undue speculation, and that it does not entail the double-counting of profits and damages expressly barred by that provision. Ultragraphics argues that the jury engaged in both undue speculation and improper double-counting in finding it liable for $55,368.

With regard to the profits component of § 504(b), we believe that the jury had before it a sufficient basis from which to calculate Ultragraphics' profits from sales of the modified "Cube Solution" posters produced by D & M. While Calio testified that he had ordered 20,000 of these posters, Robert Davidson, the president of D & M, recalled having actually delivered 21,500; the jury was entitled to use the larger number in computing Ultragraphics' profits. Since Calio testified that Ultragraphics had distributed all of the "Cube Solution" posters in its inventory, and the evidence suggested that the wholesale price for these posters was $2.00 per poster, the jury could fairly calculate Ultragraphics' gross revenues from the infringing posters to be $43,000. Once a copyright owner has shown evidence of an infringer's gross revenues, § 504(b) places upon the infringer the burden of proving his deductible expenses.[2] Ultragraphics met that burden here by presenting evidence that its printing costs were $7,932. The jury thus could have found that

2. The relevant portion of § 504(b) states:

> In establishing the infringer's profits, the copyright owner is required to present proof only of the infringer's gross revenue, and the infringer is required to prove his or her deductible expenses and the elements of profit attributable to factors other than the copyrighted work.

Ultragraphics' profits on infringing posters distributed domestically were $35,068. Adding to this sum the $2,500 in credit that Ultragraphics received for the separations it sold to the English publishers, but deducting the $300 that Ultragraphics paid D & M for these separations, the jury was entitled to fix Ultragraphics' profits from infringement at $37,268.

Since the jury found Ultragraphics liable for $18,100 beyond this amount, we may assume that the additional amount represents the jury's assessment of the actual damages suffered by appellees. Appellees argue that the jury's award of $55,368 against Ultragraphics represents actual damages, in the form of compensation for profits appellees would have earned by selling 20,000 of their own posters directly to the public for between $4.50 and $5.50. However, during the period in which Ultragraphics sold most of the infringing posters, appellees were bound by the agreement making Ultragraphics the exclusive distributor of "The Cube Solution" poster in North America. Furthermore, upon the expiration of this agreement, appellees granted Ideal Toy Co. a two-year license to produce and market the poster. Appellees failed to present any evidence that under these two agreements they would have been allowed to make direct sales themselves or that, even if permitted, they would have been equipped to do so. Similarly, appellees failed to offer any evidence suggesting they might actually have done business in foreign markets.

Appellees also contend that the jury awarded them actual damages, by compensating them for "damage to the reputation of the posters resulting from the inferior quality of the infringing posters" and for damage to their ability to sell their posters in the future caused by the absence of a copyright notice on the infringing posters. However, appellees did not offer any proof that the terms of their two-year exclusive license to Ideal Toy had been affected by Ultragraphics' conduct; nor did appellees make any effort to assess the marketability of their copyright during any time following that sale. These claims were thus too speculative to support any award of actual damages.

The only actual damages for which appellees did adduce sufficient evidence were for the profits they would have earned on sales to their distributor, Ultragraphics, had Ultragraphics not sought out an alternative source of supply for "The Cube Solution" posters. If appellees, rather than D & M, had supplied Ultragraphics with 21,500 posters pursuant to the exclusive distribution agreement, appellees would have received $0.75 per poster. Out of this sum, they would have had to pay printing costs that the jury could have found to be as low as $0.22 per poster, leaving appellees with damages in the form of lost profits of $11,395. In charging Ultragraphics with these damages, the jury would not have been engaging in the double-counting forbidden by § 504(b), even though the jury also awarded to appellees Ultragraphics' profits of $37,268. Double-counting may occur when an infringing seller has to disgorge profits on sales that a copyright holder might have made and for which he may therefore claim damages in the form of lost profits.[3] But here, appellees could not have sold their posters domestically to anyone but their exclusive distributor, Ultragraphics, at $0.75 apiece. Ultragraphics sold to wholesalers at $2.00 per poster. Appellees could not properly have made the latter sales and therefore cannot claim any lost profits on them. Thus, requiring Ultragraphics to disgorge to appellees its profits on those sales contains no element of double-counting, even though appellees are also recovering damages of $11,395.

In the absence of any consideration of joint and several liability, appellees thus appear to have been entitled to an award of only $48,663 against Ultragraphics. This figure represents the total of Ultragraphics' profits of $37,268 and appellees' damages of $11,395. Since appellees were awarded $55,368 by the jury, a remittitur would therefore seem appropriate. The precise amount of any remittitur, however, cannot be determined without an examination of the extent to which Ultragraphics shares joint liability with D & M.

III. The Appeal of D & M and the Joint and Several Liability of Both Appellants

The jury found D & M liable for $2,441.53, an amount D & M concedes to be the profits it gained producing the infringing posters for Ultragraphics. The essence of D & M's appeal is that the jury should not have found D & M and Ultragraphics jointly and severally liable both for this sum and for the $55,368 charged to Ultragraphics. For reasons indicated below, this argument is correct.

Section 504(b) was designed to serve the dual purposes of compensating a copyright owner for his actual losses and preventing infringers from unfairly benefiting from their wrongful acts. The section appears to require no departure from the rule prevailing under the predecessor provision that a co-infringer ordinarily may be held jointly liable only for the actual damages suffered by a plaintiff copyright holder, not for the illegal profits of his fellow infringers. Exceptions to this general rule may be appropriate only where the infringement was not innocent or where the defendants "engaged in a partnership, joint venture, or similar enterprise." 3 M. Nimmer, *Nimmer on Copyright* § 12.04[C][3], at 12–50 to–51 (1984).

In this case, the jury was not instructed on either of these limited exceptions. Moreover, it is clear that the evidence would not have supported a finding that Ultragraphics and D & M were joint venturers. D & M was simply an independent contractor that, after receiving payment for printing the infringing poster at Ultragraphics' request, retained no further interest in Ultragraphics' marketing activities. We have already determined, see part II, supra, that if the jury's award is to stand, $37,268 of the total must be considered profits attributable to Ultragraphics. This amount could not properly be chargeable to D & M.

3. Double-counting would occur in this case, for example, if appellees were to recover both the profits D & M made on its sales to Ultragraphics and the profits appellees lost because Ultragraphics sought out D & M as an alternative supplier.

In sum, while we find that the jury might fairly have found appellants jointly liable for appellees' actual damages, we conclude that the verdict exposing D & M to joint liability for the entire award against Ultragraphics was excessive as a matter of law. For similar reasons, the jury verdict that Ultragraphics is jointly liable for the $2,441.53 in profits earned by D & M cannot stand.

This does not necessarily leave D & M liable merely for the $2,441.53 in profits gained by it from the infringement. As we have already held, one component of the sum that Ultragraphics would owe after remittitur would be appellees' actual damages of $11,395, representing the profits that appellees would have made but for the infringement. For these, under the jury's verdict, D & M must be held jointly liable. However, because of § 504(b)'s bar against double counting, this $11,395 award of damages to appellees must be in lieu of, rather than in addition to, the $2,441.53 verdict against D & M since, as noted above in note 3, appellees lost these profits on the same sales as those on which D & M gained its wrongful profit of $2,441.53. But appellees are certainly entitled to the larger of the two figures. While D & M is thus to be jointly liable for the actual damages of appellees, we do not believe that the purposes of the Copyright Act would be served if, in the event appellees seek to recover this entire amount from Ultragraphics, D & M were permitted to escape with no obligation to disgorge its illegal profits of $2,441.53. Consequently, we hold that D & M must be solely liable for at least $2,441.53 of the $11,395 charged against it and Ultragraphics jointly. In essence, the portion of D & M's liability for which it is jointly liable with Ultragraphics is thus reduced to $8,953.47.

We therefore hold that unless appellees agree to remit $46,414.53 of the $55,368 damages with which D & M has been jointly charged, thus leaving a joint liability for D & M of $8,953.47, a new trial on the question of the joint award against D & M must be held. D & M remains solely liable for $2,441.53.

* * *

Finally, we find that the district court did not abuse the discretion given to it by 17 U.S.C. § 505 when it refused to award attorney's fees against D & M. The court reasoned that D & M had acted at the direction of Ultragraphics, had made only a small profit from the infringement and had diligently pursued settlement. We cannot say that the court should not have been swayed by these considerations.

* * *

RSO RECORDS, INC. v. PERI

United States District Court, Southern District of New York, 1984.
596 F.Supp. 849, 225 U.S.P.Q. 407.

HAIGHT, DISTRICT JUDGE:

This is a civil action for willful copyright infringement. Plaintiffs are the producers, manufacturers, and distributors of some thirty-five copyrighted sound recordings which they claim have been infringed by the defendants. The corporate defendants are Creative Disc, Inc. ("Creative"), which manufactured and packaged phonograph records, and Dynasty Graphics, Inc. ("Dynasty"), which prepared photographic materials used in the printing of labels and paper packaging for phonograph records and prerecorded cassette and eight-track tapes. * * * The individual defendants have all been involved in the manufacture of sound recordings. Defendants Joseph Peri ("Joe Peri") and Carl Feuerstein have admitted being officers and shareholders in Dynasty, and the evidence demonstrates that both were also in control of operations at Creative. Salvatore "Sam" Peri ("Sam Peri") worked in a cassette and eight-track tape duplicating facility called Delmonico Audio Sounds, Inc. ("Delmonico"), which was housed in the same building as Creative. Plaintiffs accuse defendants of copying plaintiffs' copyrighted sound recordings and the packaging of those recordings—in essence, of record counterfeiting. They have requested damages, attorney's fees, and destruction of various tools of reproduction seized from the corporate defendants' places of business. The action was tried to the Court sitting without a jury over the course of seven trial days. This opinion constitutes the Court's findings of fact and conclusions of law pursuant to Rule 52(a), Fed.R.Civ.P.

[The court finds that the defendants engaged in two varieties of infringement. First, they produced counterfeit copies of the plaintiffs' copyrighted sound recordings. Counterfeit records and tapes are exact copies of sound recordings made without the permission of the copyright holder. Second, the defendants contributed to the production of counterfeit records and tapes by producing materials essential to printing packaging for the counterfeits. In order to make successful counterfeits, the packaging materials ("graphics")—labels and jackets for records, labels and cardboard boxes for tapes—must look exactly like those of the original. This is done by photographing a legitimate copy of the graphics of a sound recording and producing "color separations"—a series of four negative or positive photographs, each in a different color, of the same set of graphics. These four photographs are used to reproduce four-color printed copies of the original graphics. The court finds that the defendants produced separations for their own use and also produced and sold them to other record producers, both legitimate and counterfeit.]

[In the course of a criminal investigation, the FBI had found on the Creative and Dynasty premises copies of color separations for the graphics of twenty-seven sound recordings copyrighted by the plaintiffs. There was also direct evidence that the defendants had manufactured copies of three of the plaintiffs' copyrighted sound recordings—"Breezin' " by George Benson (records), "Bat Out of Hell" by Meatloaf (records), and "Saturday Night Fever" (tapes). The plaintiffs had copies of production records seized by the FBI from Creative, as well as some copies of counterfeit phonorecords seized on the premises. The defendants refused to answer virtually all questions and refused to produce documents at their depositions, invoking their fifth amendment right to avoid self-incrimination. They also declined to testify at trial. They did, however, present witnesses who established that a significant amount of Creative's output was produced for legitimate record production companies.]

[While the corporate defendants made the infringing color separations and counterfeit copies, the court found that the individual defendants all either personally participated or were vicariously liable for at least some of the companies' infringements. The court also found that the defendants' infringement was willful.]

[The plaintiffs were unable to quantify their actual damages because the defendants refused to turn over any further production records, aid in the interpretation of the records which had already been seized, or provide information about how the color separations were to be used. The court found the available evidence only sufficient to establish a sum of damages and profits totalling $42,239.85—$29,964 for "Breezin'," $5,875.00 for "Bat Out of Hell," $4,700.00 for "Saturday Night Fever," and $2,700.00 for the twenty-seven color separations. The court noted that the actual profits and damages were likely much higher.]

B. Statutory Damages

Statutory damages are the other option. Section 504(c)(2) permits an award of statutory damages of up to $50,000 per infringed work [16] when, as in this case, the infringement was willful. The statute leaves the exact amount of the award to the discretion of the Court, to be set "as the court deems just." 17 U.S.C. § 504(c)(1). The case law on statutory damages is still in its formative stages. Undoubtedly assessed statutory damages should bear some relation to actual damages suffered. Because statutory damages are often used in cases where actual damages cannot be precisely calculated, however, they cannot be expected to correspond exactly. Further, courts have also recognized that Congress's provision for a greater award in cases of willful infringement indicates that statutory damages may in such cases exceed the amount of documented damages. By taking on a partially punitive character, such awards serve the Copyrights Act's twofold purpose of compensation and deterrence. For example, after finding actual damages of $5,000, Judge Duffy in *Lauratex Textile Corp. v. Allton Knitting Mills Inc.*, 519 F.Supp. 730, 733 (S.D.N.Y.1981) awarded $40,000 in statutory damages because of defendant's willful and repeated infringements. * * * An additional factor must be considered in setting statutory damages in this action.

16. The language of § 504(c)(1) makes it clear that plaintiffs may not recover multiple statutory awards where they have copyrighted both graphics for a recording and the recording itself. Nor can they recover separate statutory damages for record and tape infringement. Each "work" is entitled to only one award of damages. House Report No. 94–1476, at 162, quoted in 1976 U.S.Code Cong. & Admin.News 565, 577. Inasmuch as graphics simply complement the recording and have no separate economic value, whatever their artist value, they must be considered part of the musical "work" for purposes of the copyright statute. A separate award for their infringement is not permitted. Similarly, tape and phonograph record are simply two media for presenting the same "work," precluding separate awards.

Any information which may be available on the exact amount of profits or damages is entirely in the hands of the defendants. They are the only ones capable of interpreting their own production records and specifying how the infringing color separations were used. They have chosen to remain silent. Plaintiffs should not be penalized thereby.

The one incident of infringement on which partial information on damages is available demonstrates that defendants made a minimum of $30,000 in illicit profits. It is likely that the other infringed phonograph record, "Bat Out of Hell," and the infringed tape, "Saturday Night Fever," were produced in quantities similar to "Breezin'," since all were very popular recordings. Defendants, in any event, have not shown "Breezin' "to have been exceptional. The probable size of the damages combined with the large-scale and willful infringing activity of defendants thus makes appropriate an award of maximum statutory damages of $50,000 for each infringement. Plaintiffs will recover a total of $150,000 for these three infringements.

For similar reasons, I reach the same conclusion as to the color separation infringements. Joe Peri admitted selling color separations to Jerry Pettus, regarded as the most active counterfeiter in the nation. Another Dynasty customer was Murry Kaplan, who was also under investigation by the FBI for counterfeiting. Thus, it is clear that Dynasty provided color separations not only for their own counterfeiting operations but those of others. In this manner Dynasty likely contributed to the making of thousands of counterfeit records and tapes. Again, the information which would indicate the scope of this activity is wholly in defendants' hands, and they have not disclosed it. Because it is likely that Dynasty's color separations each contributed to the counterfeiting of thousands of records and tapes, thus depriving plaintiffs of thousands of sales and was undertaken in a wholly willful manner, the maximum statutory award is again appropriate. Statutory damages of $50,000 are awarded for each of the [27 works for which color separations were produced] except "Saturday Night Fever," which was already the subject of a maximum award. See footnote 16, *supra*.

If plaintiffs elect statutory damages, the total award will be $1,450,000. * * *

* * *

I will require plaintiffs to file a notice of election stating which type of damages they prefer. If they elect actual damages and profits, final judgment for $42,239.85 plus costs and attorney's fees will be entered. If plaintiffs elect statutory damages, final judgment of $1,450,000, plus costs and attorney's fees will be entered. * * *

Notes and Questions

1. *Actual damages and profits.* Since proving actual damages can be difficult, plaintiffs frequently focus on recovering the defendant's profits, instead. Under section 504(b), a plaintiff must only prove an infringer's gross revenues. The defendant/infringer must prove his costs in generating

the revenues in order to deduct them from the award. If the profits are not totally attributable to the infringement, the defendant bears the burden of proving what portion of the profit is attributable to other factors, and thus not subject to recovery. For example, assume that the defendant makes a movie that borrows impermissibly from the plot of plaintiff's novel. The defendant adds its own creative elements to the plot, hires popular stars to play the leading rolls, and promotes the movie heavily through advertising. It is unlikely that all of the defendant's profit from the movie is attributable to its infringement of the plaintiff's novel. How might the defendant prove the amount of profit that is attributable to the other factors mentioned above? See generally Sheldon v. Metro–Goldwyn Pictures Corp., 309 U.S. 390, 60 S.Ct. 681, 80 L.Ed. 825 (1940) (Court credits expert testimony, and, giving plaintiff the "benefit of every doubt," finds that twenty percent of the defendant's net profit was attributable to the infringement.).

Suppose that the floor show at defendant's Las Vegas gambling casino infringed the plaintiff's work. How should the profits attributable to the infringement be calculated? Should plaintiff be able to recover a portion of the defendant's overall hotel and gambling revenues on the theory that the infringing floor show brought more guests and gamblers to the casino? See Frank Music Corp. v. Metro–Goldwyn–Mayer, Inc., 772 F.2d 505, 516–17, 227 U.S.P.Q. 687, 694–95 (9th Cir.1985) (indirect profits from the hotel and gaming operations, as well as direct profits from the show itself, are recoverable).

Should plaintiffs be able to collect prejudgment interest on damage awards? The Copyright Act makes no express provision. The Circuit Courts have disagreed. Compare Kleier Advertising Inc. v. Premier Pontiac Inc., 921 F.2d 1036, 1041–2, 17 U.S.P.Q.2d 1200, 1203–04 (10th Cir.1990) ("it would be 'anomalous' to hold that a plaintiff would be entitled to recover profits flowing from infringement but not revenue generated by the *use* of the profits"), with Robert R. Jones Associates v. Nino Homes, 858 F.2d 274, 282, 8 U.S.P.Q.2d 1224, 1231 (6th Cir.1988) (The damages granted were sufficient to serve the purposes of promoting innovation and deterring unauthorized exploitation of others' creative expression. A grant of prejudgment interest was thus unnecessary.).

2. *Statutory damages.* Recall that the statutory damages option is only available to those copyright owners who registered their copyright before the defendant's infringement commenced or, in the case of published works, within three months of first publication. 17 U.S.C.A. § 412. In order to heighten the allure of statutory damages as an incentive to register, in 1988, Congress raised the monetary limits. Pub.L. No. 100–568, § 10(b), 102 Stat. 2860. For causes of action arising after March 1, 1989, Copyright Act section 504(c), as amended, provides for awards ranging from $500 to $20,000. The ceiling is $100,000 in the case of wilful infringement. "Wilful" infringement occurs when the defendant knows that his actions constitute infringement, though a showing that the defendant should have known or acted with reckless disregard has been found to suffice. See Fitzgerald Publishing Co., Inc. v. Baylor Publishing Co., 807 F.2d 1110, 1115, 1 U.S.P.Q.2d 1261, 1265 (2d Cir.1986).

Section 504(c)(2) also provides that "[i]n a case where the infringer sustains the burden of proving, and the court finds, that such infringer was not aware and had no reason to believe that his or her acts constituted an infringement of copyright, the court in its discretion may reduce the award of statutory damages to a sum of not less than $200." As an incentive for copyright owners to continue providing notice of copyright, the Berne Convention Implementation Act amended Copyright Act sections 401 and 402 to deny an innocent infringer defense when notice was properly given on the published copy or phonorecord to which the defendant had access. How effective is this incentive likely to be?

In *RSO Records*, the court found that the plaintiffs were only entitled to one $50,000 award in connection with the "Saturday Night Fever" infringement, even though the defendants infringed both the sound recording and the copyrighted graphics accompanying the recording. Why should the plaintiffs not be entitled to two awards? Review the language of section 504(c).

Assume that the defendants made unauthorized reproductions of "Saturday Night Fever" on three different occasions during a period of three years. Would plaintiffs be entitled to three separate awards?

Assume a plaintiff owned the exclusive right to reproduce the sound recordings, but another party, X, owned the exclusive right to distribute the sound recordings to the public. The defendants infringed both rights. Would plaintiff and X each be entitled to recover a separate award of statutory damages?

Assume that the plaintiff published a book of photographs it had taken of emerging seedlings of various plants. Defendants, in the business of selling seeds, reproduced 122 of the photographs without the plaintiff's authorization and featured them on their seed packages. Under section 504(c), would the plaintiff be entitled to 122 awards of damages or only one? See Stokes Seeds Ltd. v. Geo. W. Park Seed Co., Inc., 783 F.Supp. 104, 108–09, 21 U.S.P.Q.2d 1934, 1936–37 (W.D.N.Y.1991) (only one award could be made). See generally H.R. REP. NO. 1476, *supra*, at 162.

3. *Injunctions.* Section 502 of the Copyright Act authorizes both preliminary and permanent injunctive relief in copyright actions.

The Court of Appeals for the Second Circuit will grant a preliminary injunction if the moving party establishes possible irreparable harm and either 1) a likelihood of success on the merits or 2) sufficiently serious questions going to the merits to make them a fair ground for litigation, and a balance of hardship "tipping decidedly" toward the moving party. See Hasbro Bradley, Inc. v. Sparkle Toys, Inc., 780 F.2d 189, 192, 228 U.S.P.Q. 423, 424 (2d Cir.1985). The Court of Appeals for the Ninth Circuit requires that a moving party show "either (1) a likelihood of success on the merits and the possibility of irreparable injury, or (2) the existence of serious questions going to the merits and the balance of hardships tipping in its favor." Apple Computer, Inc. v. Formula Intl. Inc., 725 F.2d 521, 523, 221 U.S.P.Q. 762, 763–64 (9th Cir.1984). In both and other circuits, irreparable injury will generally be presumed when the moving party makes out a prima facie case for infringement. See *Hasbro Bradley*, *supra*, 780 F.2d at 192, 228

U.S.P.Q. at 424; *Apple Computer*, *supra*, 725 F.2d at 525, 221 U.S.P.Q. at 765.

While courts grant permanent injunctions freely when infringement is found, they do not grant them automatically. It must appear that the defendant is likely to infringe again in the future. Courts have found evidence of previous acts of infringement and wilful infringement sufficient to satisfy this requirement. Doubts on this issue tend to be resolved in favor of granting injunctive relief. See generally 2 P. GOLDSTEIN, COPYRIGHT PRINCIPLES, LAW AND PRACTICE § 11.2.1 (1989).

4. *Costs and attorney's fees.* Section 505 authorizes courts to award costs by or against any party, and "a reasonable attorney's fee to the prevailing party." The "prevailing party" may be either the plaintiff or the defendant, though section 412 conditions fee awards on copyright claimants' timely registration. Unlike its Patent Act counterpart, section 505 does not reserve fee awards for exceptional cases.

Several Circuit Courts of Appeals imposed a dual standard for fee awards, in which prevailing plaintiffs were awarded attorney's fees as a matter of course, while prevailing defendants were required to show that the original suit was frivolous or brought in bad faith. See Fogerty v. Fantasy, Inc., ___ U.S. ___, 114 S.Ct. 1023, 127 L.Ed.2d 455 (1994). They justified this distinction on policy grounds: a more generous standard for plaintiffs would encourage the bringing of meritorious infringement claims. In *Fogerty*, *supra*, the Supreme Court rejected this dual standard, adopting instead an "evenhanded" approach. The Court specifically discredited the policy justification that had been given for the dual standard:

> We think the argument is flawed because it expresses a one-sided view of the purposes of the Copyright Act. While it is true that *one* of the goals of the Copyright is to discourage infringement, it is by no means the *only* goal of that Act. In the first place, it is by no means always the case that the plaintiff in an infringement action is the only holder of a copyright; often times, defendants hold copyrights too * * *.
>
> More importantly, the policies served by the Copyright Act are more complex, more measured, than simply maximizing the number of meritorious suits for copyright infringement. * * * We have often recognized the monopoly privileges that Congress has authorized, while "intended to motivate the creative activity of authors and inventors by the provision of a special reward," are limited in nature and ultimately must serve the public good. For example, in *Twentieth Century Music Corp. v. Aiken*, 422 U.S. 151, 156, 95 S.Ct. 2040, 2043, 45 L.Ed.2d 84 (1975), we discussed the policies underlying the 1909 Copyright Act as follows:
>
>> The limited scope of the copyright holder's statutory monopoly . . . reflects a balance of competing claims upon the public interest; creative work is to be encouraged and rewarded, but private motivation must ultimately serve the cause of promoting broad public availability of literature, music, and the other arts.
>
> * * *

> Because copyright law ultimately serves the purpose of enriching the general public through access to creative works, it is peculiarly important that the boundaries of copyright be demarcated as clearly as possible. To that end, defendants who seek to advance a variety of meritorious copyright defenses should be encouraged to litigate them to the same extent that plaintiffs are encouraged to litigate meritorious claims of infringement. * * * Thus a successful defense of a copyright infringement action may further the policies of the Copyright Act every bit as much as a successful prosecution of an infringement claim by the holder of a copyright.

Id., ___ U.S. at ___, 114 S.Ct. at 1029–30, 127 L.Ed.2d at 465–66.

The Court likewise rejected arguments that section 505 was intended to adopt the "British Rule" that both prevailing plaintiffs and defendants should be awarded attorney's fees as a matter of course, absent exceptional circumstances. The Court stressed that there was no precise rule or formula for making the fee determination. Rather, courts should exercise equitable discretion in each case, in light of all the circumstances. *Id.*, ___ U.S. at ___, 114 S.Ct. at 1033, 127 L.Ed.2d at 470.

5. *Criminal sanctions.* The Copyright Act also provides for criminal sanctions against persons who infringe "a copyright willfully and for purposes of commercial advantage or private financial gain." 17 U.S.C.A. § 506.

Part Four

RIGHTS IN CONSUMER GOOD WILL AND RELATED TRADE VALUES

Chapter Six

TRADEMARK LAW

I. INTRODUCTION

TRADE–MARKS—REGISTRATION AND PROTECTION

S. Rep. No. 1333, 79th Cong., 2d Sess., 1–17 (1946).

BASIC PURPOSES OF TRADE–MARK LEGISLATION

The purpose underlying any trade-mark statute is twofold. One is to protect the public so it may be confident that, in purchasing a product bearing a particular trade-mark which it favorably knows, it will get the product which it asks for and wants to get. Secondly, where the owner of a trade-mark has spent energy, time, and money in presenting to the public the product, he is protected in his investment from its misappropriation by pirates and cheats. This is the well-established rule of law protecting both the public and the trade-mark owner. It is succinctly stated by Mr. Justice Frankfurter in Mishawaka Rubber and Woolen Company v. S.S. Kresge Company, decided on May 4, 1942: "The protection of trade-marks is the law's recognition of the psychological function of symbols."

Your committee believes the proposed bill accomplishes these two broad basic principles.

TRADE–MARKS DEFEAT MONOPOLY BY STIMULATING COMPETITION

This bill, as any other proper legislation on trade-marks, has as its object the protection of trade-marks, securing to the owner the good will of his business and protecting the public against spurious and falsely marked goods. The matter has been approached with the view of protecting trade-marks and making infringement and piracy unprofitable. This can be done without any misgivings and without the fear of fostering hateful monopolies, for no monopoly is involved in trade-mark protection.

Trade-marks are not monopolistic grants like patents and copyrights. In Prestonettes v. Coty (264 U.S. 359), Mr. Justice Holmes said:

> It [a trade-mark] does not confer a right to prohibit the use of the word or words. It is not a copyright. * * * A trade-mark only gives the right to prohibit the use of it so far as to protect the owner's good will against the sale of another's product as his.

In United Drug Co. v. Rectanus (284 U.S. 90, 97–98), Mr. Justice Pitney said:

> The owner of a trade-mark may not, like the proprietor of a patented invention, make a negative and merely prohibitive use of it as a monopoly. * * * In truth, a trade-mark confers no monopoly whatever in a proper sense.

There is no essential difference between trade-mark infringement and what is loosely called unfair competition. Unfair competition is the genus of which trade-mark infringement is one of the species; "the law of trade-marks is but a part of the broader law of unfair competition" (United Drug Co. v. Rectanus, 248 U.S. 90, 97). All trade-mark cases are cases of unfair competition and involve the same legal wrong. As Mr. Justice Pitney observed in Hanover Star Milling Co. v. Metcalf (240 U.S. 403, 412):

> The essence of the wrong consists in the sale of the goods of one manufacturer or vendor for those of another. * * *
>
> This essential element is the same in trade-mark cases as in cases of unfair competition unaccompanied with trade-mark infringement.

The protection accorded trade-marks is merely protection against swindling.

As Mr. Justice Holmes observed in Dupont v. Masland (244 U.S. 100, 102):

> The word "property" as applied to trade-marks * * * is an unanalyzed expression of certain secondary consequences of the primary fact that the law makes some rudimentary requirements of good faith.

Trade-marks, indeed, are the essence of competition, because they make possible a choice between competing articles by enabling the buyer to distinguish one from the other. Trade-marks encourage the maintenance of quality by securing to the producer the benefit of the good reputation which excellence creates. To protect trade-marks, therefore, is to protect the public from deceit, to foster fair competition, and to secure to the business community the advantages of reputation and good will by preventing their diversion from those who have created them to those who have not. This is the end to which this bill is directed.

Notes and Questions

1. *The purposes of trademark law.* The bill the Senate Committee on Patents recommended in its Committee Report ultimately was enacted as the Trademark Act of 1946, better known as the Lanham Act. The Lanham Act, which replaced the much weaker Trademark Act of 1905, is codified at 15 U.S.C.A. §§ 1051–1127.

A trademark, when affixed to a product, is an important piece of information: it identifies the "origin" or "source" of the product. This is not to say that it *literally* notifies the consumer of the producer's identity—the trademark may differ from the name of the company that owns and uses it on its products. Rather, it notifies the consumer that the product comes from the *same* source (whatever that source may be [1]) as other products of a similar type bearing the same mark. Since the consumer assumes that products from the same source will have similar characteristics, he is able to relate whatever experience he has had with other products bearing the mark to the present product. If the source provided a satisfying product in the past, or the consumer has heard good things from others who have tried it, he will be moved to buy. If the contrary is true, the consumer will avoid repeating the bad experience. The mark enables the consumer to make meaningful choices in the marketplace, and thereby enables producers to compete effectively for his business. This process only works, however, as long as the consumer can safely assume that products bearing the same mark in fact come from the same source. The purpose of trademark law is essentially to ensure that this assumption can be made. By providing that assurance, trademark law protects both the business that owns the trademark and the consumer.

How is the business benefited? As the Committee Report states, trademark law "secur[es] to the owner the good will of his business." Assume that Acme Company places a new product—for example, a soda—on the market, under the trademark "whatacola." Acme invests considerable money and effort in promoting the soda to the public through advertising and marketing, and maintains high standards of quality in its production and packaging process. Over the years, consumers become familiar with the whatacola mark and associate it with a high quality soda. Many consumers develop brand loyalty, repeatedly choosing the whatacola drink over competing brands. This reputation and expectation of repeat patronage is known as "good will." Good will is intangible, but it can be extremely valuable, and it is directly tied to the product trademark.[2] If a competitor takes the mark, it also takes the good will.

Assume that Beta Company puts its own soda on the market, with the same or a confusingly similar trademark (for example, "watcola"). Consumers who mean to purchase whatacola are confused and buy Beta's product by mistake. Beta gets a free ride on Acme's investment and reputation, and more importantly, Acme's good will is injured in two respects. First, it has lost sales that it otherwise would have made. Second, it has lost the opportunity to control the quality of the product being sold as its own. If Beta's drink is of inferior quality, and consumers believe (mistakenly) that it

1. In this context, we use the term "source" broadly, to include not only manufacturers of goods, but also others, such as distributors, retailers, or endorsers of the goods, who may apply their own mark.

2. For example, see *Coca-Cola: Things Better Go Better*, THE ECONOMIST, May 10, 1986, at 98:

> Wall Street now values the [Coca-Cola] company at $14 billion—$7 billion more than the value of the company's assets (machinery, buildings, etc.). That, roughly, is what the trademark is worth.

Julius R. Lunsford, Jr., a lawyer for the Coca-Cola Company, has stated:

> The production plants and inventories of The Coca-Cola Company could go up in flames overnight. Yet, on the following morning there is not a bank in Atlanta, New York, or anywhere else, that would not lend this Company the funds necessary for rebuilding, accepting as security only the inherent good will in its trademarks "Coca-Cola" and "Coke."

Drescher, *The Transformation and Evolution of Trademarks—From Signals to Symbols to Myth*, 82 TRADEMARK REP. 301, 301-2 (1992).

came from Acme, Acme's reputation will be injured. Consumers may refuse to buy from Acme in the future. In preventing Beta from using a confusingly similar mark, the trademark law protects Acme's good will, and by protecting the good will, it encourages Acme and other businesses to invest in the development and promotion of other new products.

Trademark law gives businesses a cause of action to prevent trademark infringement in order to protect their good will. But in the course of doing that, the law indirectly protects consumers, as well. How, exactly, are consumers protected? Assume that Beta's cola was exactly the same as Acme's, but Beta sold it at half the price. Acme loyalists who mistakenly bought Beta's drink would be better off, financially, but the law would still permit Acme to enjoin the infringement. In Eastern Wine Corp. v. Winslow–Warren, Ltd., 137 F.2d 955, 57 U.S.P.Q. 433 (2d Cir.1943), *cert. denied* 320 U.S. 758, 64 S.Ct. 65, 88 L.Ed. 452 (1943), the Court of Appeals for the Second Circuit acknowledged this fact, and explained:

> [There] is an assumed social interest in safeguarding consumers from being deceived even if the deception may be to their financial benefit. There appears to be a related judicial policy of protecting snobbism; as this court recently put it, "People like to get what they think they are getting, and courts have steadfastly refused in this class of cases to demand justification for their preferences. * * * If the buyers wish to be snobs, the law will protect them in their snobbery." Benton Announcements, Inc. v. Federal Trade Commission, 130 F.2d 255. In other words, "the public is entitled to get what it chooses, though the choice may be dictated by caprice or by fashion or perhaps by ignorance." Federal Trade Commission v. Algoma Lumber Co., 291 U.S. 67, 54 S.Ct. 320, 78 L.Ed. 655.

Id., 137 F.2d at 958, 57 U.S.P.Q. at 436.

2. *The relationship between federal trademark law and the law of unfair competition.* The Committee comments that "the law of trade-marks is but a part of the broader law of unfair competition," which developed at common law. "Unfair competition" is an umbrella term that encompasses several related legal doctrines, all aimed at prohibiting improper conduct in the marketplace. Trademark infringement is only one of the doctrines in this family. In enacting the Lanham Act, Congress built upon existing common-law trademark doctrine, but enhanced it, primarily by providing a system for registering marks on the Lanham Act's "Principal Register." Registration, in turn, provides a number of benefits, such as rights in a broader geographic area than would be available at common law, legal presumptions of trademark validity, and the opportunity to obtain the assistance of the Customs Service in prohibiting importation of infringing products.

It is important to note that enactment of the Lanham Act did not preempt the common-law cause of action for unfair competition, even when the claim specifically alleges trademark infringement. Nor did it inhibit the states from enacting their own statutory trademark registration systems, as most have. Thus, a qualifying trademark owner may sue infringers pursuant to the Lanham Act provisions, or may pursue a state law cause of action for the same conduct. Congress anticipated that trademark owners might wish to allege both a Lanham Act claim and a state cause of action for unfair competition in the same suit, and expressly provided for pendant jurisdiction in the federal district courts to hear unfair competition claims brought with related federal trademark infringement claims. 28 U.S.C.A. § 1338(b). As we will see, many trademark owners prefer to bring Lanham Act claims whenever possible because, among other reasons, Lanham Act remedies tend to be more generous than those available at state law.

This Chapter focuses on the Lanham Act provisions for registering trademarks on the Principal Register and the legal rights of registrants. In the course of this, you will learn about the underlying common law of trademarks, as well. The following Chapter will examine other unfair competition doctrines that exist in state law and under Lanham Act section 43(a).

Congress relied on its commerce clause powers to enact the Lanham Act. U.S. CONST. art. I, § 8, cl. 3. Thus, only those marks used "in interstate commerce" are eligible to receive the benefits of its protection. The United States Patent and Trademark Office ("PTO") administers the Lanham Act's registration system. PTO decisions regarding trademark registrations may be appealed directly to the Court of Appeals for the Federal Circuit, 28 U.S.C.A. § 1295(a)(4)(B), but unlike appeals from patent infringement cases, appeals from trademark infringement cases brought in the district courts are taken to the regional United States Circuit Courts of Appeals.

3. *The place of trademarks in the competitive scheme.* In stating that "no monopoly is involved in trade-mark protection," the Committee stresses the limited nature of the rights afforded by trademark law, as compared to the patent and copyright laws. Rather than giving the trademark owner an exclusive right to use the word, symbol or device at issue, trademark law gives only the limited right to prohibit commercial use by others *when that use is likely to cause consumer confusion about the source of goods or services.* The right is narrowly drawn to avoid potential first amendment issues, and ensure that other merchants' ability to communicate useful information about their products and to adopt useful product features is not undermined. Thus, as in other areas of intellectual property law, the trademark law attempts to reach the optimal balance between potentially competing interests. See Hanover Star Milling Co. v. Metcalf, 240 U.S. 403, 413–14, 36 S.Ct. 357, 360, 60 L.Ed. 713, 718 (1915). It is frequently asserted that providing limited property rights in marks ultimately enhances competition, to the public's benefit:

> The public benefits afforded by competitive markets cannot be fully realized unless prospective consumers can differentiate the products of competing sellers. In the absence of effective trademark protection, individual sellers gain little from improvements in product quality or service since they cannot easily recapture the benefits of a favorable consumer response. The protection of trademarks encourages investment in quality and service by securing to the trademark owner the benefits of a favorable reputation in the market.

RESTATEMENT (THIRD) OF UNFAIR COMPETITION § 9, comment c (Tentative Draft No. 2, 1990).

4. *Additional resources.* J.T. McCarthy's McCARTHY ON TRADEMARKS AND UNFAIR COMPETITION (3d ed., 1992) is an excellent 3–volume resource on trademarks and related unfair competition doctrines. Other valuable reference works include J. GILSON, TRADEMARK PROTECTION AND PRACTICE (1991), and L. ALTMAN, R. CALLMANN, THE LAW OF UNFAIR COMPETITION, TRADEMARKS, AND MONOPOLIES (4th ed. 1981 & Supp.). For information abut state statutory trademark provisions, see UNITED STATES TRADEMARK ASSOCIATION, STATE TRADEMARK AND UNFAIR COMPETITION LAW (1989). For information about foreign trademark laws and practice, see E. HORWITZ, WORLD TRADEMARK LAW AND PRACTICE (1993). For the historical origins of trademark law, see F. SCHECTER, THE HISTORICAL FOUNDATIONS OF THE LAW RELATING TO TRADE–MARKS (1925); Diamond, *The Historical Development of Trademarks*, 65 TRADEMARK REP. 265 (1975).

II. TYPES OF MARKS

A. TRADEMARKS

§ 1127. (§ 45) Construction and Definitions; Intent of Chapter

* * *

The term "trademark" includes any word, name, symbol, or device, or any combination thereof—

(1) used by a person, or

(2) which a person has a bona fide intention to use in commerce and applies to register on the principal register established by this chapter,

to identify and distinguish his or her goods, including a unique product, from those manufactured or sold by others and to indicate the source of the goods, even if that source is unknown.

* * *

15 U.S.C.A. § 1127.

As the Lanham Act definition indicates, the term "trademark" refers to marks used to identify or distinguish the user's *goods* from those of other manufacturers or sellers. The Lanham Act recognizes and protects three other types of marks, in addition to trademarks: service marks, certification marks, and collective marks. The following three Subsections will explore the elements that distinguish service, certification, and collective marks from trademarks. Since most of the legal rules and concepts to be covered in this Chapter apply equally to all four types of marks, following this Section we will refer to all four types collectively as "marks" or "trademarks." Unless otherwise stated, you should assume that the legal rules and concepts being discussed apply equally to all four varieties of marks.

In order to avoid confusion, it is helpful to note some recent changes in terminology. As it originated at common law, the term "trademark" referred to a narrower range of words, symbols and devices than it does today. Originally, the term only applied to words, symbols or devices that were "inherently distinctive"—generally, words, symbols or devices that were arbitrary or fanciful in relation to the good being identified or distinguished.[3] (The mark "tango," when used to distinguish or identify ball bearings, is *arbitrary* because it does not describe the product or any of its characteristics. The mark "ked–4" for ball bearings is *fanciful*, because it has no meaning at all, apart from its meaning as a trademark.) The term "trade names" was used to refer to marks that were not "inherently distinctive," but had become distinctive through use. Trade names included such things as descriptive words (e.g. "durable" for ball bearings), personal names, and simple designs. Though not "inherently distinctive," such words, symbols or devices became distinctive, and thus worthy of protection, when they were used long and frequently enough for people to come to regard them as indications of origin.

Over the years, the significance of the distinction declined. When it enacted the Lanham Act, Congress rejected the traditional distinction by defining the term "trademark" to encompass *all* distinctive marks used to identify or distinguish goods, regardless of whether they would have been considered "trademarks" or "trade names" at earlier common law. It designated the term "trade name" to refer to the name of a business or company. 15 U.S.C.A. § 1127. Today, both federal and state law tend to use the more modern definitions adopted in the Lanham Act.

While the Lanham Act provides for registration of trademarks, service marks, certification marks and collective marks, trade names, as presently defined, may not be registered as such. The law of unfair competition, however, does provide trademark-like protection for trade names, as we will see in the next Chapter.

B. SERVICE MARKS

§ 1127. (§ 45) Construction and Definitions; Intent of Chapter

* * *

The term "service mark" means any word, name, symbol, or device, or any combination thereof—

(1) used by a person, or

(2) which a person has a bona fide intention to use in commerce and applies to register on the principal register established by this chapter,

to identify and distinguish the services of one person, including a unique service, from the services of others and to indicate the source of the services, even if that source is unknown. Titles, character names, and other distinctive features of radio or television programs may be regis-

3. The term "technical trademark" was sometimes used in this context, as well.

tered as service marks notwithstanding that they, or the programs, may advertise the goods of the sponsor.

* * *

15 U.S.C.A. § 1127.

IN RE DR. PEPPER COMPANY

United States Court of Appeals for the Federal Circuit, 1987.
836 F.2d 508, 5 U.S.P.Q.2d 1207.

NIES, CIRCUIT JUDGE.

Dr. Pepper Company appeals from the decision of the Patent and Trademark Office Trademark Trial and Appeal Board, 1 USPQ2d 1421 (TTAB 1986), affirming the examining attorney's refusal to register the mark PEPPER MAN as a service mark on the ground that applicant's asserted service of sponsoring and operating a particular contest to promote its soft drinks was not a service within the contemplation of sections 3 and 45 of the Trademark Act of 1946, 15 U.S.C. §§ 1053 and 1127 (1982 & Supp. III 1985). We affirm.

I

Appellant filed an application, Serial No. 477,600, seeking registration of PEPPER MAN which it asserts is its "service mark for sponsorship and operation of contest services." To promote its DR. PEPPER soft drinks, appellant conducts a promotional contest in which cash prizes are awarded to households found to have on hand certain specified quantities of unopened cans or bottles of DR. PEPPER soft drinks, or certain coupons called "I'M A PEPPER" cards, which can be obtained free of charge from Dr. Pepper or its bottlers. Appellant displays the name PEPPER MAN on promotional pieces for the contest.

The examining attorney refused registration, and the board affirmed, on the ground that applicant was not rendering a service within the contemplation of the Act. The crux of the board's reasoning is that

> where, as here, an activity claimed to be a service is incidental to the sale of goods, the activity cannot be separately recognizable as a service unless it is shown that the activity constitutes something clearly different from, or over and above, any activity normally involved in promoting the sale of such goods. The running of a contest to advertise and promote the sale of one's goods is not a service over and above, or materially different from, what would normally be expected from one engaged in the sale of goods.

1 USPQ2d at 1422 (citations omitted).

II

The sole issue raised on appeal is whether conducting a contest to promote the sale of one's own goods is a "service" within the meaning of sections 3 and 45 of the Trademark Act of 1946, 15 U.S.C. §§ 1053, 1127 (1982). Appellant maintains that sponsorship and operation of a promotional contest is a "service" to the public because some of them will receive the benefit of cash prizes. Thus, it maintains that the name it uses in promoting the contest is registrable as its service mark.

While this court and its predecessor have stated that "services" is a term of "broad scope" under the Lanham Act, some business activities which may be described in terms of a "service" to the public do not constitute a service within the intendment of the Act. Appellant does not challenge that general proposition, but urges that contest activities to promote one's products should not be placed in that category, particularly when denominated by a name different from the trademark for the product.

The Act itself provides no definition of a "service" and the legislative history gives no guidance beyond the general principle that, for the first time, marks of businesses engaged in rendering services, such as laundries, were made registrable. Further refinement was left to the administrative agency, now the Patent and Trademark Office, and to the courts.

Through a series of decisions it has become a settled principle that the rendering of a service which is normally "expected or routine" in connection with the sale of one's own goods is not a registrable service whether denominated by the same or a different name from the trademark for its product. This interpretation is a refinement of the basic principle that the service for which registration is sought must be rendered *to others*. Merely advertising one's own goods, while, in a sense, an "informational" or in some instances an "entertainment" service to others, was early held not to be a "service" within the purview of sections 3 and 45.

The interpretation that a company's promotional activities are not services to others under the Act was subsequently endorsed in judicial decisions of our predecessor, the Court of Customs and Patent Appeals. *In re Radio Corp. of Am.*, 205 F.2d 180, 182, 98 USPQ 157, 158 (CCPA 1953) (supplying radio stations with packaged radio programs of records is mere advertising of record company, not a "service" to consumers). *See also In re Orion Research Inc.*, 523 F.2d 1398, 1400, 187 USPQ 485, 487 (CCPA 1975) (*Orion I*) (the repair or replacement of one's own merchandise or "guaranteeing" same held not a registrable "service" because it is normally expected by purchasers from the purveyor of goods). Thus, our precedent has drawn the line in connection with promotional activities that those which are "ordinary or routine" are not registrable services, despite some extra benefit to the public beyond the existence of the goods themselves. The public does not, per our precedent, perceive such activity as a service to the public but as mere sales activity by and for the benefit of the offerer of the goods.

In several decisions the board has specifically addressed the registrability of the name for a contest promoting the goods of the company conducting the contest. In *In re Johnson Publishing Co.*, 130 USPQ 185 (TTAB 1961), the board held that the publisher of a magazine which offered prizes to readers who submitted at least one paid subscription and solved a puzzle was not providing a registrable service. * * * While the interpretations of the statute by the board are not binding on this court, under general principles of administrative law, deference should be given by a court to the interpretation by the agency charged with its administration. * * * We conclude that the board reasonably has treated promotional contests as "routine" sales activity for a producer's goods.

* * *

Appellant argues that the exclusion of services ordinarily or routinely rendered in connection with the sale of goods will preclude registration of marks for a vast array of activities currently recognized as services under the Act, such as those provided by retail department stores, mail order companies, and gasoline stations. Contrary to appellant's view, this consequence does not follow. Appellant leaves out the key element which is that the activities being questioned here relate to promotion of *its own goods*. Department stores and gasoline stations are service businesses and provide precisely the types of services intended to be brought under the Act. Indeed, advertising agency services as well as the service of conducting contests *for others* are within the Act. A parallel nonregistrability situation with a service business would be a refusal to register an asserted service of offering "free" glassware to customers who have made a certain level of purchases at a gasoline station, the service of providing "free" bags for purchasers at a grocery store, or a lottery contest by a new shopping mall. Registration of the marks identifying the services of service businesses is not endangered by continuing to apply the principle that services which are ordinary or routine in the sale of goods (or services), such as promotional activities for one's own business, are not services within the meaning of the Act. As stated by Professor McCarthy:

> The point is that a manufacturer or merchant cannot proliferate registrations by obtaining a trademark registration along with a whole raft of service mark registrations covering each and every "service" which every other competitor also provides as an adjunct to the sale of goods.... * * *

1 J. McCarthy, *Trademarks and Unfair Competition* § 19.30, at 940 (2d ed. 1984) (footnotes omitted). Such proliferation of registrations by devising ways to describe a sale-of-goods situation as a service has been held not to be within the intendment of the Act. We adhere to that precedent.

Alternatively, appellant seeks to elevate its promotional contest to a service under the Act on the ground that its contest is different from a routine advertising contest in that persons who have not purchased its goods may be contacted. However, it admits that only persons who have full containers for its soft drink or have obtained promotional coupons can win. We see nothing which takes this contest out of the ordinary advertising contest.

* * *

Notes and Questions

1. *Service marks.* Section 3 of the Lanham Act, 15 U.S.C.A. § 1053, specifies that service marks shall be registrable in the same manner and with the same effect as trademarks.

What is the difference between a service mark and a trade name? Why should a service mark be registerable when a trade name is not?

Why should the PTO and the courts reject service mark registrations for "services" entailing the sale or promotion of the applicant's goods? Should it matter whether the same mark is already registered as a trademark for the goods being sold or promoted? Why might a business want to register a service mark that is identical to a trademark it has already registered? What are the practical implications of a denial of registration?

How does one determine whether a particular "service" is "ordinarily or routinely rendered in connection with the sale of goods?" For example, could a retail store register a mark for the service of selling its own warranties for the goods it sells, to supplement the manufacturer's warranty? See *In re* Sun Valley Waterbeds, Inc., 7 U.S.P.Q.2d 1825 (T.T.A.B. 1988).

Assume that a manufacturer and seller of women's sports clothing registers "wheathervane" as a trademark for the clothing. It later begins to conduct professional women's golf tournaments under the "wheathervane" mark, and seeks to register it for the service of conducting golf tournaments. The applicant notifies retailers of its clothing that they can use the tournament publicity as a means of promoting sale of the clothing: "Schedule tie-in ads now. * * * Plan to cash in on this event that means big volume for your store." Should the applicant be granted a service mark registration? See *Ex Parte* Handmacher–Vogel, Inc., 98 U.S.P.Q. 413 (Pat. Comm'r 1953).

Should a corporation be able to register a service mark for the service of offering a stock reinvestment plan to its shareholders? See *In re* Canadian Pacific Ltd., 754 F.2d 992, 224 U.S.P.Q. 971 (C.A.F.C. 1985).

C. CERTIFICATION MARKS

§ 1127. (§ 45) Construction and Definitions; Intent of Chapter

* * *

The term "certification mark" means any word, name, symbol, or device, or any combination thereof—

(1) used by a person other than its owner, or

(2) which its owner has a bona fide intention to permit a person other than the owner to use in commerce and files an application to register on the principal register established by this chapter,

to certify regional or other origin, material, mode of manufacture, quality, accuracy, or other characteristics of such person's goods or services or that the work or labor on the goods or services was performed by members of a union or other organization.

* * *

15 U.S.C.A. § 1127.

§ 1064. (§ 14) Cancellation of Registration

A petition to cancel a registration of a mark [may be filed] by any person who believes that he is or will be damaged by the registration * * *

> (5) At any time in the case of a certification mark on the ground that the registrant (A) does not control, or is not able legitimately to exercise control over, the use of such mark, or (B) engages in the production or marketing of any goods or services to which the certification mark is applied, or (C) permits the use of the certification mark for purposes other than to certify, or (D) discriminately refuses to certify or to continue to certify the goods or services of any person who maintains the standards or conditions which such mark certifies * * *.

15 U.S.C.A. § 1064.

MIDWEST PLASTIC FABRICATORS, INC. v. UNDERWRITERS LABORATORIES, INC.

United States Court of Appeals for the Federal Circuit, 1990.
906 F.2d 1568, 15 U.S.P.Q.2d 1359.

MICHEL, CIRCUIT JUDGE.

Midwest Plastic Fabricators, Inc. (Midwest) appeals the decision of the United States Patent and Trademark Office, Trademark Trial and Appeal Board (Board), denying Midwest's petition to cancel two certification mark registrations issued to Underwriters Laboratories Inc. (UL). Because the Board's findings that UL did not misuse and did control use of its certification marks are not clearly erroneous, we affirm.

BACKGROUND

UL, a corporation that promulgates and certifies compliance with safety standards for thousands of consumer and other products, is the owner and federal registrant of the two certification marks at issue in this appeal. Each registration states, in part, that the certification is used by persons authorized by UL to certify that representative samplings of the goods conform to the safety standards or requirements established by UL. A manufacturer that wishes to use the UL marks on its products to indicate compliance with UL safety standards must first submit samples to UL for testing and evaluation. Once those samples are determined to comply with UL standards, the products become eligible for listing with UL. Usually the manufacturer will enter into a listing and follow-up service agreement with UL. [The Board found as follows:]

> This agreement provides, inter alia, that the manufacturer order UL marks through [UL] from an authorized printer; that no UL mark shall be used on products not in compliance with [UL's] requirements; that the manufacturer agrees that it will ensure that the products bearing the UL mark are in compliance with [UL's] requirements; that a testing and inspection program will be maintained by the manufacturer to assure continued compliance ...; that access to [UL's] inspectors shall be allowed together with providing adequate facilities for the conducting of product testing and that any tests which indicate noncompliance with [UL's] requirements shall result in the manufacturer's being required to either correct the problem or remove the UL mark from the noncomplying products.
>
> [The] follow-up service agreement provides for a periodic inspection program whereby [UL's] inspectors will visit factories and plants in which listed products are produced. If an inspector finds a variation from [UL's] requirements, a variation notice is issued ... [and] a manufacturer cannot ship products which are encompassed by the variation notice until the problem is resolved. The record shows that inspectors have discretion to allow products to be shipped with minor variations that do not affect the safety of the product. Inspectors are also authorized to remove the UL mark in appropriate situations.
>
> [UL] exercises authority over use of the UL certification marks as described above by employing some 500 inspectors who work out of over 200 inspection centers throughout the United States. In 1987, [UL's] inspectors conducted approximately 438,000 inspections in approximately 38,900 factories and over 9 billion UL labels were issued covering approximately 12,500 different products.

Midwest is a manufacturer and seller of polyvinyl chloride (PVC) fittings and elbows for use with PVC conduit which encases electrical wiring. The company entered into a listing and follow-up service agreement with UL which provides, in part, that Midwest "agrees that his use of the Listing Mark constitutes *his declaration* that the products are Listed by [UL] and have been made in compliance with the requirements of [UL]."

Midwest now seeks reversal of the Board's denial of its petition to cancel UL's registrations on the same two bases it presented to the Board. First, Midwest alleged that UL permits use of the certification marks for purposes other than certification, in violation of 15 U.S.C. § 1064(e)(3) (1982). According to Midwest, UL's president testified that application of UL's mark represents not UL's, but merely the manufacturer's declaration that the products meet UL standards. Midwest argued that the failure of UL itself to certify that the products carrying the UL mark meet UL standards demonstrates that UL permits use of the marks for purposes other than certification.

As the second basis for cancellation, Midwest charged UL fails to control the use of its marks. Specifically, Midwest alleged: (1) certain PVC elbows carrying the UL marks failed impact tests performed by its expert, Professor Charles E. Rogers, of Case Western Reserve University; and (2) certain conduit pipe manufactured by a competitor of Midwest, National Pipe Company (National), carried counterfeit UL marks. If UL fails to control its marks, the registrations are subject to cancellation under 15 U.S.C. § 1064(e)(1) (1982). * * *

Opinion

I. Use of the Marks for Purposes Other Than to Certify

* * *

A certification mark registration may be cancelled if the mark is not used exclusively as a certification mark. 15 U.S.C. § 1064(e)(3). For example, if a certification mark's owner also allowed the mark to be used as a trademark, there would be a basis for cancellation of the registration. * * *

Midwest argues that UL's registrations must be cancelled because the UL certification marks are not UL's own declarations to consumers that the marked products comply with UL standards, but instead are the manufacturer's declarations. Midwest asserts the failure of UL itself to make that declaration is evidence that UL "permits the use of the certification mark for purposes other than to certify" and therefore the registrations must be cancelled.

There is an important difference, however, between the mark's use and the user. That others test products and apply UL's certification marks simply is not probative that the marks are used for other than certification. Certainly, on this record, there is no evidence that these certification marks are used, by anyone, as trademarks or service marks. Instead, Midwest merely complains about who applies the mark to the product. Midwest in effect argues that third party application of a certification mark constitutes per se misuse—use for a purpose other than certification. But Midwest offers no authority to support such a proposition.

The statute, however, plainly does not require that, as the registrant, UL itself must test the products and declare to the public that items carrying UL marks meet UL standards. It merely authorizes cancellation of a registration if the registrant allows use of the mark for purposes other than certification. In addition, the general practice, in accord with the statute, allows for a third party to apply the certification mark. See U.S. Patent & Trademark Office, *Trademark Manual of Examining Procedures* § 1306.01, at 1300–14 (1986) (The certification mark is "applied by other persons, to *their* goods or services, with *authorization* from the owner of the mark.") (emphasis added in part).

Thus, both registrations at issue here include a provision that the certification marks may be used by "persons authorized by [UL]" to indicate that "representative samplings" of the products conform to safety standards established by UL. The registrations clearly state what the marks do and do not represent to the public. The registrations certainly do not require UL to represent that UL itself tests the items.

UL agrees that UL marks, when applied by Midwest to Midwest's products, are Midwest's declaration of compliance with UL standards. The Board concluded that UL's use of the UL mark as a *manufacturer's* declaration that the marked product complies with UL standards is "a reasonable one designed to reflect the realities of the limitations involved in inspecting and certifying a large number of different products. We do not find that such a statement in any way constitutes a ground for cancelling the certification marks. . . ." We cannot disagree.

* * *

II. Failure To Control Use of the Marks

Midwest also asserts UL does not control the use of the UL marks as required under 15 U.S.C. § 1064(e)(1), and cancellation is thus necessary. Section 1064(e)(1) provides for cancellation if the certification mark registrant "does not control, or is not able legitimately to exercise control over, the use of such mark."

The purpose of requiring a certification mark registrant to control use of its mark is * * * to protect the public from being misled. [A] certification mark registration sets forth specific representations about the manufacture and characteristics of the goods to which the mark is applied.

As the purpose of the control requirement is to protect the public, the requirement places an affirmative obligation on the certification mark owner to monitor the activities of those who use the mark. * * *

To obtain cancellation of the UL certification mark registrations, Midwest has the burden to demonstrate by a preponderance of the evidence that UL failed to exercise control over use of its marks. The statute, however, does not define "control" or otherwise indicate the degree of control that it requires. Clearly, the statutory requirement cannot mean absolute control, because it would be impracticable, if not impossible, to satisfy. The Board stated: "The specific degree of control necessary in determining whether or not a certification mark should be cancelled depends, of course, on the particular facts presented in each case." While interpretation of the statutory term "control" is a question of law which we review de novo, the Board explicated a rule of reasonableness which, because reasonableness cannot be gauged by some abstract standard, will vary depending on the particular facts. The "control" requirement of the statute means the mark owner must take reasonable steps, under all the circumstances of the case, to prevent the public from being misled.

This standard for demonstrating that a registrant has exercised control over the use of its marks is entirely consistent with the precedent of this court, which speaks in terms of "adequate control," as well as "sufficient control." * * * We believe the words "adequate" and "sufficient" used in our prior opinions are, in effect, shorthand expressions to denote a flexible standard of reasonableness based on the totality of the facts and circumstances.

We have construed the statutory requirement of "control" to mean reasonable control, i.e., such control as is practicable under all the circumstances of the case. Although interpreting the generalized meaning of the statute is a question of law, applying our construction of the statutory term "control" to the facts of a particular case is not. Both determining the facts of a particular case concerning control and the sufficiency of the control measures the registrant took to protect the public are questions of fact subject to the clearly erroneous standard of review.

The Board found that UL has "a vast network of inspectors making hundreds of thousands of inspections of thousands of different products across the country" and that UL conducts comprehensive follow-up programs to ensure compliance with UL standards. The Board also stated that UL demonstrated "considerable diligence in controlling the use of its marks; that while [the] inspection and follow-up procedures are not 100% accurate or foolproof, we know of no such requirement. . . ."

Midwest relies upon two types of evidence to challenge the Board finding on control. First, it relies on the results of impact tests performed on certain conduit and elbows carrying the UL mark. The Board found the tests were not "shown to be reliable and [are] entitled to very little, if any, probative value." We cannot overturn that finding as clearly erroneous because Midwest's testing of PVC conduit and elbows did not account for the age of the elbows tested or their exposure to sunlight, although it is undisputed that age and sunlight make PVC conduit brittle. Also, impact tests were performed on PVC elbows and Midwest concedes "that the [UL] standards for elbows do not require impact tests." The Board, therefore, appropriately discounted the impact tests.

The second type of evidence Midwest employs to demonstrate UL's failure to control use of its marks is the proven use of counterfeit UL marks on certain conduit manufactured by National, a competitor. The Board concluded that this limited counterfeiting problem was not sufficient to cancel UL's registrations and that UL exercised control over subsequent use of its marks by this company, based on findings about UL's responsiveness and the stringency of its corrective action. It included inspections being done solely by UL personnel and inspection of not just a "representative sampling," all that is required by the registrations, but of 100% of the conduit. These findings have not been shown to be clearly erroneous.

Because Midwest has not shown that the findings supporting the reasonableness of UL's control are clearly erroneous, we must sustain the Board's determination that UL's control avoids cancellation of its registrations in these proceedings.

* * *

Notes and Questions

1. *Certification marks.* Lanham Act section 4, 15 U.S.C.A. § 1054, provides that certification marks, including indications of regional origin, shall be registrable in the same manner and with the same effect as trademarks.

Why did Congress impose the strict requirements set forth in section 14 for certification marks? 15 U.S.C.A. § 1064. In your opinion, does the *Midwest* court's interpretation and application of the requirements adequately fulfill Congress' purpose in imposing them? More specifically, why did Congress provide that the owner of a certification mark could not use it as a trademark or service mark for its own goods or services? What if the owner's goods or services are completely different from the type of goods or services that the mark certifies? Should the certification mark still be disqualified? Why or why not? See *In re* Florida Citrus Commission, 160 U.S.P.Q. 495 (T.T.A.B. 1968).

D. COLLECTIVE MARKS

§ 1127. (§ 45) Construction and Definitions; Intent of Chapter

* * *

The term "collective mark" means a trademark or service mark—

(1) used by the members of a cooperative, an association, or other collective group or organization, or

(2) which such cooperative, association, or other collective group or organization has a bona fide intention to use in commerce and applies to register on the principal register established by this chapter, and includes marks indicating membership in a union, an association, or other organization.

* * *

15 U.S.C.A. § 1127.

ALOE CREME LABORATORIES, INC. v. AMERICAN SOCIETY FOR AESTHETIC PLASTIC SURGERY, INC.

Patent and Trademark Office Trademark Trial and Appeal Board, 1976.
192 U.S.P.Q. 170.

RICE, MEMBER.

* * *

A "collective mark" is defined as a trademark or service mark used by the members of a cooperative, an association or other collective group or organization, and includes marks used to indicate membership in a union, an association or other organization. There are two basic types of collective marks. A *collective trademark or collective service mark* is a mark adopted by a "collective" (i.e., an association, union, cooperative, fraternal organization, or other organized collective group) for use only by its members, who in turn use the mark to identify their goods or services and distinguish them from those of nonmembers. The "collective" itself neither sells goods nor performs services under a collective trademark or collective service mark, but the collective may advertise or otherwise promote the goods or services sold or rendered by its members under the mark. A *collective membership mark* is a mark adopted for the purpose of indicating membership in an organized collective group, such as a union, an association, or other organization. Neither the collective nor its members uses the collective membership mark to identify and distinguish goods or services; rather, the sole function of such a mark is to indicate that the person displaying the mark is a member of the organized collective group. For example, if the collective group is a fraternal organization, members may display the mark by wearing pins or rings upon which the mark appears, by carrying membership cards bearing the mark, etc. Of course, a collective group may itself be engaged in the marketing of its own goods or services under a particular mark, in which case the mark is not a collective mark but is rather a trademark for the collective's goods or service mark for the collective's services.

* * *

Notes and Questions

1. *Distinguishing collective trademarks and service marks.* The Trademark Trial and Appeal Board identified two types of collective marks: collective membership marks and collective trademarks and service marks. How do they differ?

How do collective trademarks and service marks differ from regular trademarks and service marks? Might one company own and register a trademark or service mark, and license other companies to use it in connection with their own goods or services? See 15 U.S.C.A. §§ 1055, 1127 (definition of "related company"). If so, what is the practical difference between this arrangement and a collective trademark or service mark?

How do collective trademarks and service marks differ from certification marks? For example, compare the following two situations. 1) A citrus producers' organization in Florida adopts the mark "Florida Fresh" as a certification mark, and permits Florida citrus producers to apply the mark to certify that their citrus comes from Florida. 2) A citrus producers' organization in Florida adopts the mark "Florida Fresh" as a collective trademark, which each member of the organization uses to identify the citrus it produces and sells. Since the mark distinguishes the members' citrus from that of non-members, it functions as a collective trademark. Assuming that only Florida citrus growers are eligible to join the organization, doesn't the mark also certify, at least indirectly, that the citrus bearing it comes from

Florida? See Breitenfeld, *Collective Marks—Should They Be Abolished?*, 47 TRADEMARK REP. 1, 3 (1957); Opticians Assn. of America v. Independent Opticians of America, 920 F.2d 187, 193 n. 8, 17 U.S.P.Q.2d 1117, 1121, n. 8 (3d Cir.1990) ("it is entirely possible for a collective trademark to legitimately function as a certification mark, or vice versa"); Professional Golfers Assn. of America v. Bankers Life & Casualty Co., 514 F.2d 665, 668, 186 U.S.P.Q. 447, 449 (1975) ("a collective service mark such as 'PGA' serves * * * to guarantee the quality of service provided by members").

In "overlap" cases in which membership in an organization also indicates compliance with the organization's standards for members' goods or services, what are the practical ramifications of registering the mark as a collective trademark or service mark rather than as a certification mark? Will registering a collective mark permit the registrant to enjoy the benefits of a certification mark while avoiding compliance with the requirements imposed by Lanham Act section 14? 15 U.S.C.A. § 1064. Does the language of section 4 fully answer the question? See 15 U.S.C.A. § 1054.

III. THE USE REQUIREMENT

BLUE BELL, INC. v. FARAH MANUFACTURING CO., INC.

United States Court of Appeals for the Fifth Circuit, 1975.
508 F.2d 1260, 185 U.S.P.Q. 1.

GEWIN, CIRCUIT JUDGE:

In the spring and summer of 1973 two prominent manufacturers of men's clothing created identical trademarks for goods substantially identical in appearance. Though the record offers no indication of bad faith in the design and adoption of the labels, both Farah Manufacturing Company (Farah) and Blue Bell, Inc. (Blue Bell) devised the mark "Time Out" for new lines of men's slacks and shirts. Both parties market their goods on a national scale, so they agree that joint utilization of the same trademark would confuse the buying public. Thus, the only question presented for our review is which party established prior use of the mark in trade. A response to that seemingly innocuous inquiry, however, requires us to define the chameleonic term "use" as it has developed in trademark law.

After a full development of the facts in the district court both parties moved for summary judgment. The motion of Farah was granted and that of Blue Bell denied. It is not claimed that summary judgment procedure was inappropriate; the controversy presented relates to the application of the proper legal principles to undisputed facts. A permanent injunction was granted in favor of Farah but no damages were awarded, and Blue Bell was allowed to fill all orders for garments bearing the Time Out label received by it as of the close of business on December 5, 1973. For the reasons hereinafter stated we affirm.

Farah conceived of the Time Out mark on May 16, after screening several possible titles for its new stretch menswear. Two days later the firm adopted an hourglass logo and authorized an extensive advertising campaign bearing the new insignia. Farah presented its fall line of clothing, including Time Out slacks, to sales personnel on June 5. In the meantime, patent counsel had given clearance for use of the mark after scrutiny of current federal registrations then on file. One of Farah's top executives demonstrated samples of the Time Out garments to large customers in Washington, D.C. and New York, though labels were not attached to the slacks at that time. Tags containing the new design were completed June 27. With favorable evaluations of marketing potential from all sides, Farah sent one pair of slacks bearing the Time Out mark to each of its twelve regional sales managers on July 3. Sales personnel paid for the pants, and the garments became their property in case of loss.

Following the July 3 shipment, regional managers showed the goods to customers the following week. Farah received several orders and production began. Further shipments of sample garments were mailed to the rest of the sales force on July 11 and 14. Merchandising efforts were fully operative by the end of the month. The first shipments to customers, however, occurred in September.

Blue Bell, on the other hand, was concerned with creating an entire new division of men's clothing, as an avenue to reaching the "upstairs" market. Though initially to be housed at the Hicks–Ponder plant in El Paso, the new division would eventually enjoy separate headquarters. On June 18 Blue Bell management arrived at the name Time Out to identify both its new division and its new line of men's sportswear. Like Farah, it received clearance for use of the mark from counsel. Like Farah, it inaugurated an advertising campaign. Unlike Farah, however, Blue Bell did not ship a dozen marked articles of the new line to its sales personnel. Instead, Blue Bell authorized the manufacture of several hundred labels bearing the words Time Out and its logo shaped like a referee's hands forming a T. When the labels were completed on June 29, the head of the embryonic division flew them to El Paso. He instructed shipping personnel to affix the new Time Out labels to slacks that already bore the 'Mr. Hicks' trademark. The new tags, of varying sizes and colors, were randomly attached to the left hip pocket button of slacks and the left hip pocket of jeans. Thus, although no change occurred in the design or manufacture of the pants, on July 5 several hundred pair left El Paso with two tags.

Blue Bell made intermittent shipments of the doubly-labeled slacks thereafter, though the out-of-state customers who received the goods had ordered clothing of the Mr. Hicks variety. Production of the new Time Out merchandise began in the latter part of August, and Blue Bell held a sales meeting to present its fall designs from September 4–6. Sales personnel solicited numerous orders, though shipments of the garments were not scheduled until October.

By the end of October Farah had received orders for 204,403 items of Time Out sportswear, representing a retail sales value of over

$2,750,000. Blue Bell had received orders for 154,200 garments valued at over $900,000. Both parties had commenced extensive advertising campaigns for their respective Time Out sportswear.

Soon after discovering the similarity of their marks, Blue Bell sued Farah for common law trademark infringement and unfair competition, seeking to enjoin use of the Time Out trademark on men's clothing. Farah counter-claimed for similar injunctive relief. The district court found that Farah's July 3 shipment and sale constituted a valid use in trade, while Blue Bell's July 5 shipment was a mere "token" use insufficient at law to create trademark rights. While we affirm the result reached by the trial court as to Farah's priority of use, the legal grounds upon which we base our decision are somewhat different from those undergirding the district court's judgment.

Federal jurisdiction is predicated upon diversity of citizenship, since neither party has registered the mark pursuant to the Lanham Act. Given the operative facts surrounding manufacture and shipment from El Paso, the parties agree the Texas law of trademarks controls. In 1967 the state legislature enacted a Trademark Statute.[5] Section 16.02 of the Act explains that a mark is "used" when it is affixed to the goods and "the goods are sold, displayed for sale, or otherwise publicly distributed." Thus the question whether Blue Bell or Farah established priority of trademark use depends upon interpretation of the cited provision. Unfortunately, there are no Texas cases construing 16.02. This court must therefore determine what principles the highest state court would utilize in deciding such a question. In view of the statute's stated purpose to preserve common law rights, we conclude the Texas Supreme Court would apply the statutory provision in light of general principles of trademark law.

A trademark is a symbol (word, name, device or combination thereof) adopted and used by a merchant to identify his goods and distinguish them from articles produced by others. Ownership of a mark requires a combination of both appropriation and use in trade. Thus, neither conception of the mark, nor advertising alone establishes trademark rights at common law. Rather, ownership of a trademark accrues when goods bearing the mark are placed on the market.

The exclusive right to a trademark belongs to one who first uses it in connection with specified goods. Such use need not have gained wide public recognition, and even a single use in trade may sustain trademark rights if followed by continuous commercial utilization.

The initial question presented for review is whether Farah's sale and shipment of slacks to twelve regional managers constitutes a valid first use of the Time Out mark. Blue Bell claims the July 3 sale was merely an internal transaction insufficiently public to secure trademark ownership. After consideration of pertinent authorities, we agree.

5. Vernon's Tex. Code Ann., Bus. & Comm. 16.01–16.28 (1968).

Secret, undisclosed internal shipments are generally inadequate to support the denomination "use." Trademark claims based upon shipments from a producer's plant to its sales office, and vice versa, have often been disallowed. Though none of the cited cases dealt with sales to intra-corporate personnel, we perceive that fact to be a distinction without a difference. The sales were not made to customers, but served as an accounting device to charge the salesmen with their cost in case of loss. The fact that some sales managers actively solicited accounts bolsters the good faith of Farah's intended use, but does not meet our essential objection: that the "sales" were not made to the public.

The primary, perhaps singular purpose of a trademark is to provide a means for the consumer to separate or distinguish one manufacturer's goods from those of another. Personnel within a corporation can identify an item by style number or other unique code. A trademark aids the public in selecting particular goods. As stated by the First Circuit:

> But to hold that a sale or sales are the *sine qua non* of a use sufficient to amount to an appropriation would be to read an unwarranted limitation into the statute, for so construed registration would have to be denied to any manufacturer who adopted a mark to distinguish or identify his product, and perhaps applied it thereon for years, if he should in practice lease his goods rather than sell them, as many manufacturers of machinery do. It seems to us that although evidence of sales is highly persuasive, the question of use adequate to establish appropriation remains one to be decided on the facts of each case, and that evidence showing, first, adoption, and, second, *use in a way sufficiently public to identify or distinguish the marked goods in an appropriate segment of the public mind as those of the adopter of the mark*, is competent to establish ownership. . . .

New England Duplicating Co. v. Mendes, 190 F.2d 415, 418 (1st Cir. 1951). Similarly, the Trademark Trial and Appeal Board has reasoned:

> To acquire trademark rights there has to be an "open" use, that is to say, a use has to be made to the relevant class of purchasers or prospective purchasers since a trademark is intended to identify goods and distinguish those goods from those manufactured or sold by others. There was no such "open" use—rather the use can be said to be an "internal" use, which cannot give rise to trademark rights.

Sterling Drug, Inc. v. Knoll A. G. Chemische Fabriken, *supra* at 631.

Farah nonetheless contends that a recent decision of the Board so undermines all prior cases relating to internal use that they should be ignored. In Standard Pressed Steel Co. v. Midwest Chrome Process Co., 183 U.S.P.Q. 758 (TTAB 1974) the agency held that internal shipment of marked goods from a producer's manufacturing plant to its sales office constitutes a valid 'use in commerce' for registration purposes.

An axiom of trademark law has been that the right to register a mark is conditioned upon its actual use in trade. Theoretically, then, common law use in trade should precede the use in commerce upon which Lanham Act registration is predicated. Arguably, since only a trademark owner can apply for registration, any activity adequate to create registrable rights must perforce also create trademark rights. A close examination of the Board's decision, however, dispels so mechanical a view. The tribunal took meticulous care to point out that its conclusion related solely to registration use rather than ownership use.

> It has been recognized and especially so in the last few years that, in view of the expenditures involved in introducing a new product on the market generally and the attendant risk involved therein prior to the screening process involved in resorting to the federal registration system and in the absence of an "intent to use" statute, a token sale or a single shipment in commerce *may be sufficient to support an application to register a trademark* in the Patent Office notwithstanding that the evidence may not show what disposition was made of the product so shipped. That is, the fact that a sale or a shipment of goods bearing a trademark was *designed primarily to lay a foundation for the filing of an application for registration* does not, per se, invalidate any such application or subsequent registration issued thereon. * * * Inasmuch as it is our belief that a most liberal policy should be followed in a situation of this kind [*in which dispute as to priority of use and ownership of a mark is not involved*], applicant's initial shipment of fasteners, although an intra-company transaction in that it was to a company sales representative, was a bona fide shipment. . . .

Standard Pressed Steel Co. v. Midwest Chrome Process Co., *supra* at 764–65.

Priority of use and ownership of the Time Out mark are the only issues before this court. The language fashioned by the Board clearly indicates a desire to leave the common law of trademark ownership intact. The decision may demonstrate a reversal of the presumption that ownership rights precede registration rights, but it does not affect our analysis of common law use in trade. Farah had undertaken substantial preliminary steps toward marketing the Time Out garments, but it did not establish ownership of the mark by means of the July 3 shipment to its sales managers. The gist of trademark rights is actual use in trade. Though technically a "sale", the July 3 shipment was not "publicly distributed" within the purview of the Texas statute.

Blue Bell's July 5 shipment similarly failed to satisfy the prerequisites of a bona fide use in trade. Elementary tenets of trademark law require that labels or designs be affixed to the merchandise actually intended to bear the mark in commercial transactions. Furthermore, courts have recognized that the usefulness of a mark derives not only from its capacity to identify a certain manufacturer, but also from its ability to differentiate between different classes of goods produced by a single manufacturer. Here customers had ordered slacks of the Mr. Hicks species, and Mr. Hicks was the fanciful mark distinguishing these slacks from all others. Blue Bell intended to use the Time Out mark on an entirely new line of men's sportswear, unique in style and cut, though none of the garments had yet been produced. While goods may be identified by more than one trademark, the use of each mark must be bona fide. Mere adoption of a mark without bona fide use, in an attempt to reserve it for the future, will not create trademark rights. In the instant case Blue Bell's attachment of a secondary label to an older line of goods manifests a bad faith attempt to reserve a mark. We cannot countenance such activities as a valid use in trade. Blue Bell therefore did not acquire trademark rights by virtue of its July 5 shipment.

We thus hold that neither Farah's July 3 shipment nor Blue Bell's July 5 shipment sufficed to create rights in the Time Out mark. Based on a desire to secure ownership of the mark and superiority over a competitor, both claims of alleged use were chronologically premature. Essentially, they took a time out to litigate their differences too early in the game. The question thus becomes whether we should continue to stop the clock for a remand or make a final call from the appellate bench. While a remand to the district court for further factual development would not be improper in these circumstances, we believe the interests of judicial economy and the parties' desire to terminate the litigation demand that we decide, if possible, which manufacturer first used the mark in trade.

Careful examination of the record discloses that Farah shipped its first order of Time Out clothing to customers in September of 1973. Blue Bell, approximately one month behind its competitor at other relevant stages of development, did not mail its Time Out garments until at least October. Though sales to customers are not the *sine qua non* of trademark use, they are determinative in the instant case. These sales constituted the first point at which the public had a chance to associate Time Out with a particular line of sportswear. Therefore, Farah established priority of trademark use; it is entitled to a decree permanently enjoining Blue Bell from utilization of the Time Out trademark on men's garments.

* * *

Notes and Questions

1. *Use in trade.* As the *Farah* opinion indicates, ownership of a mark at common law, and the right to register a mark on the Lanham Act Principal Register, both depend upon a claimant's use of the mark in trade. As we will see in the next Section, 1988 amendments to the Lanham Act made it possible for the first time to *apply* to register a mark based only on a bona fide intent to use the mark in the future. Nonetheless, the registration will not be *granted* until the requisite use is made. Thus, even after the amendments, "use" continues to be the foundation of U.S. trademark protection.

The *Farah* court, in discussing the Trademark Trial and Appeal Board's *Standard Pressed Steel* decision, suggests that "use" for purposes of federal registration might be more readily found than "use" for purposes of determining priority and ownership. What is the Board's explanation for such a dual standard? When Congress implemented the "intent to use" application procedure, referred to above, it also expressly rejected a "token use" standard for registration, amending section 45 to provide: "The term 'use in commerce' means the bona fide use of a mark in the ordinary course of trade, and not made merely to reserve a right in a mark." Trademark Law Revision Act of 1988, Pub. L. No. 100–667, 102 Stat. 3935.

What is the rationale for conditioning ownership rights and registration of marks on use in trade? Why not provide that the first business to register a mark becomes its owner, regardless of use?

On the use issue generally, see Sacoff, *The Trademark Use Requirement in Trademark Registration, Opposition and Cancellation Proceedings*, 76 TRADEMARK REP. 99 (1986).

2. *Priority.* As the *Farah* opinion illustrates, when two or more parties claim the same inherently distinctive mark, or two that are confusingly similar, the first to use the mark in trade has superior rights. Thus, the law of trademarks and unfair competition adopt the "first in time, first in right" philosophy that exists in other areas of law. When the issue of "first use" is a close one, however, more than strictly chronological considerations may come into play. Consider the Second Circuit's opinion in Manhattan Industries, Inc. v. Sweater Bee by Banff, Ltd., 627 F.2d 628, 207 U.S.P.Q. 89 (2d Cir.1980). In that case, competitors were trying to snatch up the valuable "Kimberly" trademark directly after it was formally abandoned by its owner. Essentially, each began shipping products bearing the Kimberly mark within a day of the other. Given this closeness in time, the court refused to recognize that the first shipper had gained the right to completely prohibit the other from using the mark—especially since the second shipper had expended considerable amounts on the mark in good faith:

> We have previously stated that "the concept of priority in the law of trademarks is applied 'not in its calendar sense' but on the basis of 'the equities involved.'" Chandon Champagne Corp. v. San Marino Wine Corp., 335 F.2d 531, 534 (2d Cir.1964). Given the evenly balanced equities in this case, it would be inequitable to allow only the appellees to use the "Kimberly" mark.

Id., 627 F.2d at 630, 207 U.S.P.Q. at 91. Refusing to enjoin either party's use of the mark, the court found that each party must differentiate its label from that of the other and from the original "Kimberly" mark, in order to avoid consumer confusion. Is this a satisfactory solution?

While the first to use an *inherently distinctive* mark in trade has priority over others (as long as she uses it continuously thereafter), a different rule exists for marks that are not inherently distinctive. As we have already noted, some marks which are not inherently distinctive may become distinctive, and thus qualify for trademark protection, through extensive use. For example, the mark "durable" for ball bearings is not inherently distinctive because it describes the product. While "durable" may not have trademark significance to the public at first, extensive use of the mark on the packaging and in advertisements may eventually cause the relevant public to recognize the word "durable" as an indication of origin of the ball bearings, rather than just a description. In trademark parlance, this is known as "acquisition of secondary meaning"—as a result of extensive trademark use, the word "durable" now has both its original descriptive meaning and a trademark meaning. The first user to acquire secondary meaning in a mark that is not inherently distinctive has priority over other users. See J.T. McCARTHY, McCARTHY ON TRADEMARKS AND UNFAIR COMPETITION § 16.12 (3d ed. 1992).

3. *Affixation.* "Using a mark in trade" entails using the mark in a manner that notifies prospective purchasers that it is an indication of origin. First, the mark, as used, must stand out, creating a separate commercial impression apart from other aspects of the label or packaging.

Second, the mark must be "affixed." Under earlier common law, this meant that the mark must be physically attached to the product or its packaging. More recent case law has relaxed this requirement somewhat. See RESTATEMENT (THIRD) OF UNFAIR COMPETITION § 18, comment d (Tentative Draft No. 2, 1990). Lanham Act section 45, 15 U.S.C.A. § 1127, provides that a mark will be deemed to be in use with regard to goods when:

> it is placed in any manner on the goods or their containers or the displays associated therewith or on the tags or labels affixed thereto, or if the nature of the goods makes such placement impracticable, then on documents associated with the goods or their sale * * *.

Obviously a mark cannot be physically attached to a service, so the Lanham Act finds affixation in the case of service marks when the mark is "used or displayed in the sale or advertising of services * * *." *Id.* A collective membership mark must be "publicly used to indicate the fact of membership through its appearance on membership certificates, pins, plaques, letterhead, or other materials signifying that the user is a member of the collective group." RESTATEMENT (THIRD) OF UNFAIR COMPETITION § 18, comment d (Tentative Draft No. 2, 1990).

4. *Use in commerce.* Because Congress relied upon its commerce clause power to enact the Lanham Act, a mark must be "used in commerce" in order to qualify for registration. The Lanham Act specifies that the mark must be affixed to goods sold or transported in commerce. In the case of service marks, the services must have been rendered in commerce. 15 U.S.C.A. § 1127. Section 45 defines "commerce" as "all commerce which may lawfully be regulated by Congress." 15 U.S.C.A. § 1127. The interstate commerce requirement is generally easy to meet.

In *In re* Gastown, 326 F.2d 780, 140 U.S.P.Q. 216 (C.C.P.A.1964), the Court of Customs and Patent Appeals found that though the registration applicant's service stations were all located in one state, its services qualified because they "affected" interstate commerce: the stations, some of which were located on federal highways, serviced interstate travelers, who themselves were engaged in interstate commerce. The stations also extended credit to out-of-state customers and billed them in their respective domiciliary states.

More recently, in Larry Harmon Pictures Corp. v. The Williams Restaurant Corp., 929 F.2d 662, 18 U.S.P.Q.2d 1292 (C.A.F.C.1991), *cert. denied* 502 U.S. 823, 112 S.Ct. 85, 116 L.Ed.2d 58 (1991), Bozo the Clown opposed the registration of "Bozo's" as the service mark of a single-location Tennessee restaurant, claiming that the restaurant's services were not rendered in interstate commerce. The findings of fact revealed that the restaurant was about an hour's drive from Memphis, "a major commercial center for the Mid–South region." The Memphis metropolitan statistical area comprised not only a portion of Tennessee, but also portions of Mississippi and Arkansas. The restaurant had been at least mentioned in publications originating in Memphis; New York City; Washington, D.C.; Dallas; Gila Bend, Arizona; and Palm Beach, Florida. Some interstate travelers patronized the restaurant, though the number of such travelers was in dispute. (The restaurant owner estimated that 15% of its business consisted of out-of-state customers.) In finding that the commerce requirement was satisfied, the Court of Appeals for the Federal Circuit specifically rejected arguments that single-location restaurants should not be permitted to register service marks unless they are located on an interstate highway, at least 50 percent of their meals are served to interstate travelers, or they regularly advertise in out-of-state media. *Id.*, 929 F.2d at 666, 18 U.S.P.Q.2d at 1295.

The PTO traditionally has viewed sale or transportation of goods in commerce as entailing sale or transportation of goods across state lines. The Court of Customs and Patent Appeals, however, has found that strictly intrastate sale of goods sufficed when the goods had been imported from another country. *In re* Application of Silenus Wines, Inc., 557 F.2d 806, 194 U.S.P.Q. 261 (C.C.P.A.1977). What if an Ohio applicant made only intrastate sales of goods made in Ohio? Would it make a difference if some of the purchasers were interstate travelers? See J.T. McCARTHY, McCARTHY ON TRADEMARKS AND UNFAIR COMPETITION §§ 19.37[4], 19.38 (3d ed. 1992).

IV. REGISTRATION PROCEDURE

A. APPLICATIONS BASED ON USE AND INTENT TO USE IN COMMERCE

Section 1 of the Lanham Act, 15 U.S.C.A. § 1051, sets forth two alternative procedures for registering marks on the Principal Register: 1) the original method of registration, based on use of the mark in commerce ("use applications"); and 2) the method enacted in 1988, based on a bona fide intent to use the mark in commerce ("intent-to-use applications").

Under either method, the applicant must send a written application to the Patent and Trademark Office which includes a drawing of the mark and the filing fee. Use applicants must also send information about their use of the mark in commerce, along with specimens (for example, actual labels or photographs of products bearing the mark) demonstrating their use of the mark with the claimed goods or services. Intent-to-use applicants need only assert a bona fide, good faith intention to use the mark in commerce in connection with the specified goods or services. The PTO staff reviews the application to ensure that it meets the minimum requirements, and if it does, assigns a filing date.

Subsequently, a PTO examining attorney reviews the application and determines whether the mark may be registered. (Factors that may render the mark unregistrable are set forth in Lanham Act section 2, 15 U.S.C.A. § 1052, and will be discussed later.) If the examining attorney has objections to the mark, he will notify the applicant, who may then respond to the objections and make corrections. 15 U.S.C.A. § 1062. If the applicant's response does not overcome the examining attorney's objections, the examining attorney will issue a final refusal, and the applicant may appeal his decision to the Trademark Trial and Appeal Board. 15 U.S.C.A. § 1070.

If the examining attorney has no objections, or the applicant overcomes them, the examining attorney will approve the mark for publication in the PTO's OFFICIAL GAZETTE. 15 U.S.C.A. § 1062. Interested persons who oppose registration of the published mark have thirty days from the date of publication to file an opposition. 15 U.S.C.A. § 1063. Oppositions may be based on any of the grounds for refusing registration set forth in Lanham Act section 2, and are heard in a proceeding before the Trademark Trial and Appeal Board. 15 U.S.C.A. § 1067.

If no opposition is filed, the next step in the process will depend on whether the applicant has filed a use application or an intent-to-use application. If the former, the PTO will register the mark and issue a registration certificate. Notice of the registration will be published in the OFFICIAL GAZETTE. See 15 U.S.C.A. § 1063(b)(1). The certificate of registration is

> prima facie evidence of the validity of the registered mark and of the registration of the mark, of the registrant's ownership of the mark, and of the registrant's exclusive right to use the registered mark in commerce on or in connection with the goods or services specified in the certificate.

15 U.S.C.A. § 1057(b). Thus, registration creates a rebuttable presumption of mark validity, which assists the registrant in the event of litigation.

If the application was based on a bona fide intent to use the mark in the future, the PTO will issue a Notice of Allowance. 15 U.S.C.A. § 1063(b)(2). The applicant then has six months to either 1) use the mark in commerce and file a verified statement affirming that use has been made, along with specimens of the use; or 2) request a six-month extension of time. This first extension is granted as a matter of course. Additional six-month extensions may be granted upon a showing of good cause, for up to an additional 24 months. 15 U.S.C.A. § 1051(d). Assuming that the applicant ultimately files a timely and acceptable statement of use, the PTO will then issue a registration certificate, as described above, and publish notice of the registration. *Id.*

The Lanham Act seeks to ensure that only marks actually in use are and remain registered. Accordingly, during the sixth year of registration, the registrant must file an affidavit verifying that the mark is still being used in commerce in connection with the goods or services set forth in the registration, or showing that nonuse is due to special circumstances that excuse it. The PTO will cancel the mark at the end of the sixth year if this filing is not made. 15 U.S.C.A. § 1058. Assuming that the affidavit is filed, the registration is good for ten years, *id.*, and can be renewed for periods of ten years for as long as the mark remains in use. 15 U.S.C.A. § 1059.

Applicants for registration, parties to opposition proceedings, parties who have been denied renewal of registrations, and others who are dissatisfied with the Commissioner's or the Trademark Trial and Appeal Board's disposition of their claims may seek judicial review. Lanham Act section 21, 15 U.S.C.A. § 1071, provides two alternative routes. Under subsection (a), a direct appeal may be taken to the United States Court of Appeals for the Federal Circuit, which will review the disputed PTO decision on the record before the PTO. Under subsection (b), a party may seek de novo review in a United States District Court. Appeals from the district court are taken to the appropriate regional Circuit Court of Appeals.

For more detailed information about the registration process, see J.T. McCARTHY, McCARTHY ON TRADEMARKS AND UNFAIR COMPETITION, ch. 19 (1992); J.E. HAWES, TRADEMARK REGISTRATION PRACTICE (1988); P.H. SMITH, INTENT–TO–USE TRADEMARK PRACTICE (1992). For more information concerning judicial review of PTO decisions, see McCARTHY, *supra*, ch. 21; Lefkowitz & Rice, *Adversary Proceedings Before the Trademark Trial and Appeal Board*, 75 TRADEMARK REP. 323, 400 (1985).

Notes and Questions

1. *Advantages of intent-to-use applications.* Congress amended the Lanham Act to provide the intent-to-use route to registration in 1988, after considerable public debate. Why was this avenue to registration deemed necessary? Consider the following:

> The Lanham Act's preapplication use requirement * * * creates unnecessary legal uncertainty for a U.S. business planning to introduce products or services into the marketplace. It simply has no assurance after selecting and adopting a mark, and possibly making a sizeable investment in packaging, advertising and marketing, it will not learn that its use of the mark infringes the rights of another acquired through earlier use. In an age of national, if not global, marketing, this has a chilling effect on business investment. This effect is not merely theoretical, but is real. And it can be costly: Marketing a new product domestically often exceeds $30 million for a large company and can consume the life-savings of an individual or small entrepreneur.
>
> Partially in recognition of the difficulties companies face in launching new products and services, and the sizable investments that may be

> at stake, regardless of a company's or individual's resources, the courts have sanctioned the practice of "token use." Token use is a contrived and commercially transparent practice—nothing more than a legal fiction. At the same time, token use is essential under current law because it recognizes present day marketing costs and realities; it reduces some of the legal and economic risks associated with entering the marketplace; and it nominally achieves the threshold "use" required to apply for federal registration and the creation of trademark rights in advance of commercial use.
>
> Unfortunately, token use is not available to all businesses and industries. For example, it is virtually impossible to make token use of a trademark on a large or expensive product such as an airplane. The same is true for service industries (that is, hotels, restaurants, and banks) prior to opening for business. Similarly, it is difficult for small business and individuals to avail themselves of token use because they frequently lack the resources or the knowledge to engage in the practice.
>
> Token use is also troublesome for another reason. It allows companies to obtain registration based on minimal use. Often these companies change their marketing plans and subsequently do not make commercial use. The result is that the trademark register is clogged with unused marks, making the clearance of new marks more difficult and discouraging others from adopting and using marks which should otherwise be available.

TRADEMARK LAW REVISION ACT OF 1988, S. REP. NO. 515, 100th Cong., 2d Sess. 5–6 (1988).

Given that registration is not granted, even on intent-to-use applications, until the mark is used in trade and commerce, how does the intent-to-use application assist businesses who wish to "reserve a mark" for future use? Section 7(c) provides:

> Contingent on the registration of a mark on the principal register provided by this chapter, the filing of the application to register such mark shall constitute constructive use of the mark, conferring a right of priority, nationwide in effect, on or in connection with the goods or services specified in the registration against any other person except for a person whose mark has not been abandoned and who, prior to such filing—
>
> (1) has used the mark;
>
> (2) has filed an application to register the mark which is pending or has resulted in registration of the mark; or
>
> (3) has filed a foreign application to register the mark on the basis of which he or she has acquired a right of priority, and timely files an application under section 1126(d) of this title to register the mark which is pending or has resulted in registration of the mark.

15 U.S.C.A. § 1057(c).

This provision is tempered somewhat by the fact that the Lanham Act, as amended, provides the intent-to-use applicant with no judicial remedy for infringement prior to her actual use of the mark. See Fila Sport S.p.A. v.

Diadora America, Inc., 141 F.R.D. 74, 21 U.S.P.Q.2d 1063 (N.D.Ill.1991). Should an interim remedy be provided?

2. *Rights by use vs. rights by registration.* Even after enactment of the intent-to-use application, the Lanham Act, like American common law, is firmly committed to the notion that rights in trademarks arise from adoption and use, not from the mere act of registration. In this respect, United States law differs from that of a number of nations, who impose no use requirement on persons seeking to register marks, and provide that the act of registration in itself confers ownership rights in marks. Which system is preferable—one based on use, such as the United States', or a "race to the trademark office" system, which bases rights on being the first to register? See Messerli, *Registration of a Trademark Under Section 44 of the Lanham Act and the Requirement of Actual Use*, 77 TRADEMARK REP. 103 (1987).

3. *Other registration-related proceedings before the TTAB* There are four *inter partes* proceedings which are adjudicated before the Trademark Trial and Appeal Board in the Patent and Trademark Office. The "opposition" proceeding is discussed above. A "concurrent use" proceeding arises when an applicant for registration, rather than claiming an exclusive right to a mark, claims a right that is concurrent with another user's right. The circumstances in which this might occur will be explored more fully in later sections, but include situations in which two parties obtained the right to use the same or similar marks in different parts of the country under the common law, before either registered or applied to register. Lanham Act section 2(d) authorizes issuance of a concurrent registration in such situations if it appears that "confusion, mistake, or deception is not likely to result from the continued use by more than one person." In order to ensure that confusion does not occur, the PTO, in issuing the concurrent registration, may impose "conditions or limitations" regarding the mode or place of use of the mark. 15 U.S.C.A. § 1052(d).

The third *inter partes* proceeding before the TTAB determines petitions to cancel existing registrations. "[A]ny person who believes that he is or will be damaged by the registration of a mark on the principal register" may file a petition to cancel the registration. *Id.*, § 1064. During the first five years of registration, a mark can be canceled on any of the grounds for refusing registration in the first place. See *id.*, § 1052. The grounds for cancellation are reduced thereafter. *Id.*, § 1064. See Section VI G, *infra*.

The final *inter partes* proceeding is the "interference." Lanham act section 16 provides that "[u]pon petition showing extraordinary circumstances," the Commissioner may declare an interference between an application and a previously registered mark or between two applications, when the marks involved are so similar "as to be likely * * * to cause confusion or mistake or to deceive." Since an interference usually involves a determination of priority, and this can also be done through an opposition or cancellation proceeding, "extraordinary circumstances" rarely are found to justify declaring an interference.

For more information about the *inter partes* proceedings, and procedure before the TTAB, see J.T. McCARTHY, McCARTHY ON TRADEMARKS AND UNFAIR COMPETITION ch. 20 (1992); HAWES, TRADEMARK REGISTRATION PRACTICE (1987); Lefkowitz & Rice, *Adversary Proceed-*

ings Before the Trademark Trial and Appeal Board, 75 TRADEMARK REP. 323 (1985).

4. *The supplemental register.* The PTO maintains a second trademark register, known as the "supplemental register." Section 23 of the Lanham Act, as codified, provides that "[a]ll marks *capable* of distinguishing applicant's goods or services and not registrable on the principal register * * * which are in lawful use in commerce by the owner thereof * * * may be registered on the supplemental register"[4] 15 U.S.C.A. § 1091(a) (emphasis added). As a general matter, this means that persons using words, symbols and devices that are not inherently distinctive and have not become distinctive through use and the acquisition of secondary meaning may register them on the supplemental register.

The intent-to-use registration procedure is not available to register marks on the supplemental register, *id.*, § 1094, and the registration procedure based on use is abbreviated. *Id.*, § 1092. Most of the advantages flowing from registration on the principal register are unavailable. See *id.*, § 1094. What, then, is the purpose of the supplemental register?

The primary purpose is to assist United States businesses to obtain registration of their marks abroad, in countries that condition registration of foreign marks on the mark's registration in the applicant's home country. Registration on the supplemental register also gives registrants access to the federal courts for infringement claims, assuming that their marks have become distinctive enough to support a claim of ownership rights. Such jurisdiction would be available in any event for infringement of unregistered marks under Lanham Act section 43(a). 15 U.S.C.A. § 1125(a).

Registration on the supplemental register does not preclude later registration on the principal register, once the mark has become sufficiently distinctive through use.

B. APPLICATIONS PURSUANT TO INTERNATIONAL TREATY PROVISIONS

The Paris Convention for the Protection of Industrial Property regulates international trademark, as well as patent, protection. Under its provisions, each of the over 100 member nations agrees to the principle of national treatment. That is, each undertakes to register and protect the trademarks of other members' nationals on essentially the same basis that it registers and protects its own. Each also agrees to afford certain minimal trademark rights.[5] Paris Convention for the Protection of Industrial Property, March 20, 1883, as most recently revised at Stockholm on July 14, 1967, 21 U.S.T. 1629, 828 U.N.T.S. 107. In addition to national treatment, the Paris Convention, article 4, provides a six-month filing priority period. This permits nationals of

4. Marks declared unregistrable under Lanham Act section 2(a)-(d) and, in some cases, under section 2(e)(3), are excluded from the supplemental register. 15 U.S.C.A. § 1091(a).

5. For example, Paris Convention article 5 C provides that countries mandating use of registered marks may only cancel marks for nonuse after a reasonable time, and only if the nonuse is unjustified. Article 7 provides: "The nature of the goods to which a trademark is to be applied shall in no case form an obstacle to the registration of the mark."

member nations who apply to register a mark in one member nation to obtain the benefit of that first filing date for applications filed in other member countries during the next six months. This benefit can be substantial, since most nations recognize rights in the first person to file or register, rather than the first person to use a mark. Foreign applicants filing in the United States benefit, as well, since the earlier foreign filing date will become the applicant's constructive use date in the United States under 15 U.S.C.A. § 1057(c), once U.S. registration is granted. This will give the foreign applicant priority over U.S. applicants who make their first use or file an intent-to-use application at any time after the foreign priority filing date. The Lanham Act implements the Paris Convention priority filing date provisions in section 44, 15 U.S.C.A. § 1126(d).

Since the United States adheres to the Paris Convention, nationals of other member countries may, under national treatment principles, choose to register their marks on the Lanham Act principal register on the same basis as U.S. nationals—that is, by complying with the use or intent-to-use registration provisions described in the prior section. In the alternative, by virtue of article 6*quinquies* of the Paris Convention, these foreign applicants may choose simply to rely on the fact that their marks have been registered in their countries of origin.[6] Article 6*quinquies* sets forth what is known as the *telle quelle* principle: registration in one's country of origin in itself entitles one to registration in other Paris Convention members, unless one of the exceptions enumerated in article 6*quinquies* applies.[7] Since most member nations register marks without any showing that they have been used in trade or commerce, this means that the United States must register foreign marks that have never been used—in the United States, or anywhere at all—even though it would not register unused marks on a domestic application. Lanham Act section 44(e), 15 U.S.C.A. § 1126(e), which implements the United States' *telle quelle* obligations, provides:

> A mark duly registered in the country of origin of the foreign applicant may be registered on the principal register if eligible, otherwise on the supplemental register * * *. The application

6. Article 6*quinquies* A(2) defines the "country of origin" as

> the country of the Union where the applicant has a real and effective industrial or commercial establishment, or, if he has no such establishment within the Union, the country of the Union where he has his domicile, or, if he has no domicile within the Union but is a national of a country of the Union, the country of which he is a national.

Given this definition, it is possible for an applicant to have more than one country of origin.

7. Marks are excepted when 1) "they are of such a nature as to infringe rights acquired by third parties in the country where protection is claimed;" 2) "they are devoid of any distinctive character, or consist exclusively of signs or indications which may serve, in trade, to designate the kind, quality, quantity, intended purpose, value, place of origin, of the goods, or the time of production, or have become customary in the current language or in the bona fide and established practices of the trade of the country where protection is claimed;" or 3) "they are contrary to morality or to public order and, in particular, of such a nature as to deceive the public." Paris Convention, *supra*, article 6*quinquies* B.

therefor shall be accompanied by a certification or a certified copy of the registration in the country of origin of the applicant. The application must state the applicant's bona fide intention to use the mark in commerce, but use in commerce shall not be required prior to registration.

For a full analysis of the Lanham Act's foreign filing provisions, see J.T. McCARTHY, McCARTHY ON TRADEMARKS AND UNFAIR COMPETITION ch. 29 (1992).

Notes and Questions

1. *The unequal playing field.* The U.S. system of imposing preapplication use requirements on U.S. applicants, but no use requirements on foreign *telle quelle* applicants, was criticized as unfair. The perceived unfairness was a key factor in Congress' decision in 1988 to enact the intent-to-use application process. The Senate Report stated:

> Today, the United States is the only developed country that requires use of a mark before an application for registration may be filed. Other countries, whose trademark laws are based on the common-law concept that rights in a mark are acquired by use, decided long ago that it is not in the interests of the business community to force business people to use a mark before its protection could be assured. In 1938, the United Kingdom converted to an intent-to-use system, and Canada converted in 1954.
>
> This disparity between U.S. law and that of most other countries results in foreign applicants having an advantage over U.S. applicants in obtaining trademark registration rights. * * *
>
> While it is impossible to measure the extent to which Americans are disadvantaged by the current system, the frequency with which foreign nationals avail themselves of the preference given them in Section 44 is noteworthy. As of March 1, 1988, approximately 7 percent, roughly 48,200, of the active applications and registrations in the U.S. Patent and Trademark Office claimed the benefits of Section 44. In addition, since 1983, the PTO has issued more than 17,700 Section 44 registrations to foreigners.

S. REP. NO. 515, 100th Cong., 2d Sess. 5 (1988). As another means of evening the playing field, Congress amended section 44(e), 15 U.S.C.A. § 1126(e), to provide that foreign applicants must state a bona fide intention to use the mark in commerce in their registration applications. How much of an advantage do foreign applicants now have over domestic applicants?

2. *Trademark registration filing treaties.* The United States has not joined a multinational trademark registration filing treaty, though such treaties exist.[8] While membership in such a treaty would provide welcome

8. The United States has ratified the Nice Agreement Concerning the International Classification of Goods and Services to which Trademarks are Applied, June 15, 1957, 23 U.S.T. 1336, 550 U.N.T.S. 45. While the Nice Agreement is a classification treaty, it does simplify the process of registering trademarks in a number of nations. Many nations, including the United States, require that registration applicants designate the class in which their goods or services fall, for administrative purposes.

simplification to U.S. businesses filing trademark registration applications in a number of countries, the benefit to U.S. business has been deemed outweighed by the detriment to the U.S. registration system. One concern is that U.S. adherence to a filing treaty would make it even easier for foreign applicants to register unused marks, thus flooding the principal register with such registrations. This, in turn, would make the process of searching and adopting new marks more difficult for U.S. businesses. Congress' enactment of the intent-to-use application procedure, and recent attempts of other nations to accommodate U.S. concerns, however, may pave the way toward eventual United States adherence to a multinational filing treaty. For an excellent discussion of these and related issues, see Schechter, *Facilitating Trademark Registration Abroad: The Implications of U.S. Ratification of the Madrid Protocol*, 25 GEO. WASH. J. INT'L L. & ECON. 419 (1991). See also Zelnick, *The Madrid Protocol—Some Reflections*, 82 TRADEMARK REP. 651 (1992).

3. *Protecting and exploiting U.S. trademarks abroad.* For an interesting discussion of the problems that confront U.S. businesses seeking to obtain, exploit and protect trademarks abroad, see Ball, *Attitudes of Developing Countries to Trademarks*, 74 TRADEMARK REP. 160 (1984); Mark I. Feldman, *Trademark Hazards Are Varied*, NAT. L. J., June 17, 1991, at 17; Damon Darlin, *Where Trademarks Are Up for Grabs*, WALL ST. J., Dec. 5, 1989, at B1.

V. QUALIFICATIONS FOR REGISTRATION

A. THE COMPOSITION OF MARKS

IN RE OWENS-CORNING FIBERGLAS

United States Court of Appeals for the Federal Circuit, 1985.
774 F.2d 1116, 1119–20, 227 U.S.P.Q. 417, 418–19.

* * *

Section 45 of the [Lanham] Act defines "trademark" to include "any word, name, symbol, or device or any combination thereof adopted and used by a manufacturer or merchant to identify his goods and distinguish them from those manufactured or sold by others." This was a departure from the past, as prior statutes only permitted registration of "technical" common law trademarks.

The preamble of section 2 of the Lanham Act states that "[n]o trademark * * * shall be refused registration on the principal register on account of its nature," unless one or more specific exceptions to registrability set forth in that section apply. * * *

When the classifications of goods and services differ from one country to the next, applicants may experience difficulty and expense in determining the proper classes to designate in each country. By setting up a uniform classification system, the Nice Agreement makes it easier to make multiple registration applications in the more than 60 nations that adhere to its system. For more information about the Nice Agreement classification system, see Marshall, *Classification of Services Under the International (Nice) Agreement*, 82 TRADEMARK REP. 94 (1992).

Under the Lanham Act trademark registration became available to many types of previously excluded indicia. Change was gradual and evolutionary, as the Patent and Trademark Office and the courts were presented with new concepts. Registration has been granted, for example, for containers; product configurations; and packaging, even if subject to design patent protection; for tabs having a particular location on a garment; slogans; sounds; ornamental labels; and goods which take the form of the mark itself. The jurisprudence under the Lanham Act developed in accordance with the statutory principle that if a mark is capable of being or becoming distinctive of applicant's goods in commerce, then it is capable of serving as a trademark.

* * * [F]or all marks, compliance with the legal requirements for registration depends on the particular mark and its circumstances of use.

* * *

IN RE CLARKE

Trademark Trial and Appeal Board, 1990.
17 U.S.P.Q.2d 1238.

SIMMS, MEMBER.

Applicant, Celia Clarke, doing business as Clarke's OSEWEZ, has appealed from the final refusal of the Trademark Examining Attorney to register applicant's asserted mark for "sewing thread and embroidery yarn." Applicant has described her mark in the "drawing" filed with her application as follows: "The mark is a high impact, fresh, floral fragrance reminiscent of Plumeria blossoms."

The Examining Attorney has refused registration on the ground that applicant's asserted mark does not function as a trademark because it does not identify or distinguish applicant's goods from those of others. In the initial refusal, the Examining Attorney observed that applicant's fragrance mark is analogous to other forms of product ornamentation in that it is not the type of matter which consumers would tend to perceive as an indication of origin. * * *

In support of her attempt to register this fragrance mark, counsel for applicant submitted a declaration of applicant attesting to the fact that, to the best of her knowledge, no other company has ever offered any scented embroidery yarn or thread; that she has placed advertisements stressing the fact that her company is the source of sweet-scented embroidery products, known in the trade as Russian embroidery or punch embroidery; and that due to the success of her products, applicant is now a major source of yarn and thread and supplies dealers and distributors throughout the United States. Applicant also states that her company has received a great number of favorable and positive responses to her unique product and that, to the best of her knowledge, customers, dealers and distributors throughout the embroidery field recognize applicant as the source of scented embroidery yarn and thread. While maintaining that her fragrance is registrable as a mark because it is inherently distinctive of yarns and threads, no other manufacturer having sold such goods, applicant nevertheless argues that she has presented sufficient evidence of recognition of her asserted mark. Applicant concludes, brief, 13:

> Others are free to adopt any other scent for their yarns and threads, including floral scents such as that of a lily of the valley, a carnation or a rose to give but three examples. Surely people have come [to] distinguish these floral scents from one another, just as they can distinguish the color pink (for fiberglass insulation) from other warm colors such as red, orange, and yellow. Just as the registration of the color pink for fiberglass insulation has been held to not present a significant obstacle for competitors wishing to produce fiberglass insulation, so does the applicant's particular fragrance not present a significant obstacle to competitors wishing to offer scented yarns.

Applicant has made of record a complete sealed kit containing scented yarn and thread for making a scented skunk.

Expressing unawareness of any precedent dealing with the registrability of an arbitrary, nonfunctional scent, the Examining Attorney states that the most closely analogous determinations appear to be those dealing with colors as trademarks.[2] The Examining Attorney concedes that there is no inherent bar to the registrability of an arbitrary, nonfunctional scent or fragrance and that this record discloses that the scent applicant has added to her product is not a natural or inherent feature of the goods and does not provide any utilitarian advantage. The Examining Attorney adds that, presumably, if applicant's scent does function to indicate origin, potential consumers may readily be able to distinguish among the vast array of scents in identifying competing sources of goods.

In support of his argument that applicant's fragrance mark is not of a character usually recognized by potential consumers as an indication of origin, he requests the Board to take judicial notice of the fact that there are pleasant, arbitrary and nonfunctional scents in a wide variety of products, including cosmetics and cleaning products, which have the sole purpose of making the use of those products more pleasant or attractive. Therefore, while applicant is the only source of scented yarn and thread, the Examining Attorney argues that potential consumers are unlikely to regard scent in any product as an indication of exclusive origin in view of their conditioning in the consumer product marketplace. The rarity of usage of fragrance as a feature of applicant's goods weighs against registration, according to the Examining Attorney. Rather, it is much more likely that consumers will regard the scent as a pleasant feature of the goods.

While the Examining Attorney concedes that the asserted fragrance may be registrable upon a convincing showing of trademark function, he

2. An even closer analogy might be drawn to sound marks used and registered for services. Cases involving unique packaging also seem relevant.

maintains that applicant has not specifically promoted the *particular* scent as an indication of origin. Applicant's advertising makes reference to "Clarke's Distinctive Sof–Scented Yarns," but no reference is made to a specific fragrance. Nor does the advertising make any attempt, according to the Examining Attorney, to draw attention to the scent as an indicator of origin.

Upon careful review of this record, we believe that applicant has demonstrated that the scented fragrance does function as a trademark for her thread and embroidery yarn. Under the circumstances of this case, we see no reason why a fragrance is not capable of serving as a trademark to identify and distinguish a certain type of product. It is clear from the record that applicant is the only person who has marketed yarns and threads with a fragrance.[4] That is to say, fragrance is not an inherent attribute or natural characteristic of applicant's goods but is rather a feature supplied by applicant. Moreover, applicant has emphasized this characteristic of her goods in advertising, promoting the scented feature of her goods. Applicant has demonstrated that customers, dealers and distributors of her scented yarns and threads have come to recognize applicant as the source of these goods. In view of the unique nature of applicant's product, we do not believe that the failure of applicant to indicate in her promotional materials the specific scent or fragrance of her yarn (admittedly difficult to describe except in the manner that applicant has done so) is significant. In her advertisements and at craft fairs, applicant has promoted her products as having a scented nature. We believe that applicant has presented a prima facie case of distinctiveness of her fragrance mark. Compare In re Star Pharmaceuticals, Inc., 225 USPQ 209 (TTAB 1985) (where applicant failed to demonstrate that the features (colors) sought to be registered had been promoted as a source indicator).

Decision: The refusal of registration is reversed.[6]

Notes and Questions

1. *Trademark rights in scents.* Did the TTAB find (1) that consumers were likely to consider scent to be an indication that the yarn came from the applicant, or (2) that consumers were likely to consider the particular scent—"a floral fragrance reminiscent of Plumeria blossoms"—to be an indication that the yarn came from the applicant? What difference does it make? Why did the TTAB find it relevant that the applicant was the only purveyor of scented yarns? What are the practical implications of recognizing trademark rights in scents? Do you foresee any problems? If so, do the same kinds of problems exist for trademarks in sounds?

4. It should be noted that we are not here talking about the registrability of scents or fragrances of products which are noted for those features, such as perfumes, colognes or scented household products. Nor is this a case involving the question of descriptiveness of a term which identifies a particular fragrance of a product. * * *

6. The description of applicant's mark noted above will appear on the certificate of registration as applicant's mark. Although advances are continually being made in Office operations and practices, the era of "scratch and sniff" registrations is not yet upon us.

For interesting discussions of the ramifications of registering scents as trademarks, see Hawes, *Fragrances as Trademarks*, 79 TRADEMARK REP. 134 (1989); Elias, *Do Scents Signify Source?—An Argument against Trademark Protection for Fragrances*, 82 TRADEMARK REP. 475 (1992).

2. *A separate commercial impression.* A number of different marks can be used to identify one product or service, even on the same label or package:

> The salient question is whether the designation in question, as used, will be recognized in and of itself as an indication of origin for this particular product. That is, does this component or designation create a commercial impression separate and apart from the other material appearing on the label?

Procter & Gamble Co. v. Keystone Automotive Warehouse, Inc., 191 U.S.P.Q. 468, 174 (T.T.A.B. 1976). In Chun King Corp. v. Genii Plant Line, Inc., 403 F.2d 274, 159 U.S.P.Q. 649 (C.C.P.A.1968), the Court of Customs and Patent Appeals considered whether Genii had used the mark "Living Earth" in such a manner that consumers would regard it as a trademark for its potting soil. Genii's package design featured the word "Genii" in large red letters appearing above the head of a genii with smoke emanating from a lamp. The words "Living Earth" appeared across the top of the package in smaller but prominent letters. The court rejected Chun King's argument that the display of "Living Earth" jointly with "GENII" and in much smaller print negated its status as a trademark:

> "No authority has been cited, and none has been found to the effect that a trademark use requires a display of a design of any particular size or prominence. The important question is not how readily the mark will be noticed but whether, when it is noticed it will be understood as indicating origin of the goods." And considering that "LIVING EARTH" is wholly arbitrary and has always been a separate and distinct, albeit subservient, feature of petitioner's containers, it is our opinion that it would be regarded as a trademark by purchasers of petitioner's goods.

Id., 403 F.2d at 276, 159 U.S.P.Q. at 651 (quoting *In re* The Singer Manufacturing Co., 255 F.2d 939, 118 U.S.P.Q. 310 (1958)).

Can ornamental designs on products or their packaging be registered as trademarks? It depends on whether consumers are likely to perceive the design as an indication of origin or merely as decoration. If the former, the fact that the design is also ornamental will not preclude registration. For example, in Application of Swift & Co., 223 F.2d 950, 106 U.S.P.Q. 286 (1955), the applicant sought to register two bands of red with white polka dots, which it used on the label of a can of cleanser:

The examiner had determined that this banding was merely background ornamentation, and thus could not function as a mark. The Court of Customs and Patent Appeals disagreed:

> Since the line distinguishing between mere ornamentation and ornamentation which is merely an incidental quality of a trade-mark is not always clearly ascertainable, the application of legal principles to fit one situation or the other requires proper reflection upon the impression likely to govern the ordinary purchaser in the market place. For that reason, the merits of each case of the character here presented must be individually and accordingly adjudged.
>
> In its brief on appeal, appellant refers to the fact that a great deal of purchasing in retail outlets is of a casual nature (particularly in self-

service types of stores) and, with regard thereto, it makes this observation:

> "* * * Here the purchasers often engage in 'impulse' buying. If their attention is caught by an item for which they have a need or have been induced to believe they have a need, as for example by advertising, they will pick up the item on this impulse even though the item was not one for which they entered the store to buy.
>
> "In order for this to happen, however, it is imperative that their attention be focused on the item sufficiently for the 'impulse' to occur. The focusing process often takes place at a time when the individual is too distant from the object to read any wording thereon. If the individual sees the item at a distance and is able to identify it by some symbol or device on the object that stands out at such a distance where the wording cannot, that symbol or device becomes the means by which the object is identified and the factor by which the impulse to purchase it is induced or occasioned.
>
> "This identification at a distance can be one or a combination of two kinds of identification. In the first place, it can be an identification of the nature of the product. Naturally the trademark function of indicating origin does not become a part of this identification of the product. However, in addition to the identification of the product, the symbols or devices may be such as to distinguish the product of a particular manufacturer from similar products of other manufacturers and thus serve as an indication of origin. When this is possible, and that was the intention in the adoption, that symbol or device clearly responds to the definition of a 'trade mark'. It is not important that the purchaser think to himself 'is this symbol or device a trade mark'. The significant question is was the symbol or device put on this object to enable the purchaser to pick it out and distinguish it from the goods of others, and is the purchaser able to so identify the object by means of this symbol or device."

Id., 223 F.2d at 954, 106 U.S.P.Q. at 288–89.

The court concluded:

> It is axiomatic, of course, that a trade-mark must be distinctive in order to accomplish its function of indicating the producer of the article to which it is applied, and, with particular regard to symbols and devices, should be displayed with such prominence as will enable easy recognition. * * * We think a definite and lasting impression will be created by use of the design in association with appellant's product whereby the average consumer will regard it as an unmistakable, certain, and primary means of identification pointing distinctly to the commercial origin of such product. The fact that the design may incidentally add to the attractiveness of appellant's label, and hence impart a certain distinctive appearance thereto, does not, in our opinion, vitiate its primary significance.

Id., 223 F.2d at 955, 106 U.S.P.Q. at 289.

Slogans can be effective trademarks, too. Who can doubt that "it's the real thing" and "hair color so natural only her hairdresser knows for sure" indicate the origin of the goods with which they are used? What special problems might one encounter in demonstrating that a slogan will be perceived as indicating origin? See Helget, *Slogans—Protectible Marketing Tools?*, 74 J. PAT. & TRADEMARK OFF. SOC. 551 (1992).

3. *Trademark rights in color alone.* While courts have recognized trademark rights in color combined with a design, (as in *Swift*), they traditionally have declined to recognize trademark rights in color by itself. The Court of Appeals for the Third Circuit explained the reason in the course of denying rights in the familiar red and white Campbell's Soup labels:

> What the plaintiffs are really asking for * * * is a right to the exclusive use of labels which are half red and half white for food products. If they may thus monopolize red in all of its shades the next manufacturer may monopolize orange in all its shades and the next yellow in the same way. Obviously, the list of colors will soon run out. * * * "To allow [all the colors] to be appropriated as distinguishing marks would foster monopoly by foreclosing the use by others of any tasty dress."

Campbell Soup Co. v. Armour & Co., 175 F.2d 795, 798, 81 U.S.P.Q. 430, 432–33 (3d Cir.1949) *cert. denied* 338 U.S. 847, 70 S.Ct. 88, 94 L.Ed. 518 (1949). The court apparently felt that a half-red and half-white label was too minimal a design to bring the case into the "color as an element of a design" exception.

In the *Owens-Corning Fiberglas* case, quoted at the beginning of this Section, the Court of Appeals for the Federal Circuit broke with this tradition, declining to state a general rule against registration of colors as marks, stressing that each case should be judged on its particular facts. In that case, the court found that the color pink could be registered as a trademark for the applicant's fibrous glass residential insulation. The court noted that the color was arbitrarily chosen and served no utilitarian purpose in connection with the product. While color by itself is not inherently distinctive, the applicant in that case had demonstrated secondary meaning (that is, that the public had come to associate color as an indication of origin) due to the applicant's nationwide "pink panther" advertising, which emphasized the color of the product.

During the following decade, the Court of Appeals for the Eighth Circuit aligned itself with the Federal Circuit's view, while the Seventh and Ninth Circuits refused to recognize "color alone" as a mark. The Supreme Court undertook to resolve this division of the Circuits in Qualitex Co. v. Jacobson Products Co., Inc., ___ U.S. ___, 115 S.Ct. 1300, ___ L.Ed.2d ___, 34 U.S.P.Q.2d 1161 (1995). In that case, Qualitex Co. registered the green-gold color of the pads it made and sold for dry cleaning presses, and brought an infringement suit against Jacobson, who was selling pads of a similar color. The district court found infringement, but the Court of Appeals for the Ninth Circuit set aside the judgment. It found that the Lanham Act does not permit registration of "color alone" as a trademark. The Supreme Court reversed:

> Both the language of the Act and the basic underlying principles of trademark law would seem to include color within the universe of things that can qualify as a trademark. The language of the Lanham Act describes that universe in the broadest of terms. It says that trademarks "includ[e] any word, name, symbol, or device, or any combination thereof." § 1127. Since human beings might use as a "symbol" or "device" almost anything at all that is capable of carrying meaning, this language, read literally, is not restrictive. The courts and the Patent and Trademark Office have authorized for use as a mark a particular shape (of a Coca-Cola bottle), a particular sound (of NBC's three chimes), and even a particular scent (of plumeria blossoms on sewing thread). If a shape, a sound, and a fragrance can act as symbols why, one might ask, can a color not do the same?
>
> A color is also capable of satisfying the more important part of the statutory definition of a trademark, which requires that a person "us[e]" or "inten[d] to use" the mark "to identify and distinguish his or her goods, including a unique product, from those manufactured or sold by others and to indicate the source of the goods, even if that source is unknown." 15 U.S.C. § 1127. True, a product's color is unlike "fanciful," "arbitrary," or "suggestive" words or designs, which almost automatically tell a customer that they refer to a brand. The imaginary word "Suntost," or the words "Suntost Marmalade," on a jar of orange jam immediately would signal a brand or a product "source"; the jam's orange color does not do so. But, over time, customers may come to treat a particular color on a product or its packaging (say, a color that in context seems unusual, such as pink on a firm's insulating material or red on the head of a large industrial bolt) as signifying a brand. And, if so, that color would have come to identify and distinguish the goods—i.e. to "indicate" their "source"—much in the way that descriptive words on a product (say, "Trim" on nail clippers * * *) can come to indicate a product's origin. In this circumstance, trademark law says that the word (e.g., "Trim"), although not inherently distinctive, has developed "secondary meaning." * * * Again, one might ask, if trademark law permits a descriptive word with secondary meaning to act as a mark, why would it not permit a color, under similar circumstances, to do the same?
>
> We cannot find in the basic objectives of trademark law any obvious theoretical objection to the use of color alone as a trademark, where that color has attained "secondary meaning" and therefore identifies and distinguishes a particular brand (and thus indicates its "source"). In principle, trademark law, by preventing others from copying a source-identifying mark, "reduce[s] the customer's costs of shopping and making purchasing decisions," 1 J. McCarthy, McCarthy on Trademarks and Unfair Competition

§ 2.01[2], pp. 2–3 (3d ed. 1994), for it quickly and easily assures a potential customer that this item—the item with this mark—is made by the same producer as other similarly marked items that he or she liked (or disliked) in the past. At the same time, the law helps assure a producer that it (and not an imitating competitor) will reap the financial, reputation-related rewards associated with a desirable product. The law thereby "encourage[s] the production of quality products," and simultaneously discourages those who hope to sell inferior products by capitalizing on a consumer's inability quickly to evaluate the quality of an item offered for sale. It is the source-distinguishing ability of a mark—not its ontological status as color, shape, fragrance, word, or sign—that permits it to serve these basic purposes. And, for that reason, it is difficult to find, in basic trademark objectives, a reason to disqualify absolutely the use of a color as a mark.

Id., ___ U.S. at ___, 115 S.Ct. at 1302–04, 34 U.S.P.Q.2d at ___.

Jacobson argued that due to differences in lighting and individual perceptions of color, competitors and courts will suffer from "shade confusion" in attempting to determine when use of a similar color on a similar product infringes. The Supreme Court rejected the argument.

> We do not believe * * * that color, in this respect, is special. Courts traditionally decide quite difficult questions about whether two words or phrases or symbols are sufficiently similar, in context, to confuse buyers. They have had to compare, for example, such words as "Bonamine" and "Dramamine" (motion-sickness remedies); "Huggies" and "Dougies" (diapers); "Cheracol" and "Syrocol" (cough syrup); "Cyclone" and "Tornado" (wire fences) * * *. Legal standards exist to guide courts in making such comparisons. * * * We do not see why courts could not apply those standards to a color, replicating, if necessary, lighting conditions under which a colored product is normally sold. Indeed, courts already have done so in cases where a trademark consists of a color plus a design * * *.

Id., ___ U.S. at ___, 115 S.Ct. at 1305, 34 U.S.P.Q.2d at ___. Jacobson also raised a "color depletion" argument:

> [I]n the context of a particular product, only some colors are usable. By the time one discards colors that, say, for reasons of customer appeal, are not usable, and adds the shades that competitors cannot use lest they risk infringing a similar, registered shade, then one is left with only a handful of possible colors. [T]o permit one, or a few, producers to use colors as trademarks will "deplete" the supply of usable colors to the point where a competitor's inability to find a suitable color will put that competitor at a significant disadvantage.

Id., ___ U.S. at ___, 115 S.Ct. at 1305–06, 34 U.S.P.Q.2d at ___. In rejecting the argument, the Court noted that generally there will be enough colors for all competitors in a given market to use. In cases in which a color scarcity does arise, the trademark "functionality doctrine" will intervene to prevent one or a small number of competitors from monopolizing all the available colors:

> The functionality doctrine * * * forbids the use of a product's feature as a trademark where doing so will put a competitor at a significant disadvantage because the feature is "essential to the use or purpose of the article" or "affects [its] cost or quality." * * * [W]e note that lower courts have permitted competitors to copy the green color of farm machinery (because customers wanted their farm equipment to match) and have barred the use of black as a trademark on outboard boat motors (because black has the special functional attributes of decreasing the apparent size of the motor and ensuring compatibility with many different boat colors). * * *
>
> The upshot is that, where a color serves a significant nontrademark function * * * courts will examine whether its use as a mark would permit one competitor (or a group) to interfere with legitimate (nontrademark-related) competition through actual or potential exclusive use of an important product ingredient. [This] should prevent the anticompetitive consequences of Jacobson's hypothetical "color depletion" argument, when, and if, the circumstances of a particular case threaten "color depletion."

Id., ___ U.S. at ___, 115 S.Ct. at 1306, 34 U.S.P.Q.2d at ___.

For further discussion of the functionality doctrine, see Section V C, *infra*.

B. DISTINCTIVENESS

ABERCROMBIE & FITCH CO. v. HUNTING WORLD, INC.

United States Court of Appeals for the Second Circuit, 1976.
537 F.2d 4, 189 U.S.P.Q. 759, 769.

FRIENDLY, CIRCUIT JUDGE:

* * *

The cases, and in some instances the Lanham Act, identify four different categories of terms with respect to trademark protection. Arrayed in an ascending order which roughly reflects their eligibility to trademark status and the degree of protection accorded, these classes are (1) generic, (2) descriptive, (3) suggestive, and (4) arbitrary or fanciful. The lines of demarcation, however, are not always bright. Moreover, the difficulties are compounded because a term that is in one category for a particular product may be in quite a different one for another,[6] because a term may shift from one category to another in light of differences in usage through time,[7] because a term may have one meaning to one group

6. To take a familiar example "Ivory" would be generic when used to describe a product made from the tusks of elephants but arbitrary as applied to soap.

7. See, e. g., Haughton Elevator Co. v. Seeberger, 85 U.S.P.Q. 80 (1950), in which

of users and a different one to others, and because the same term may be put to different uses with respect to a single product. * * *

A generic term is one that refers, or has come to be understood as referring, to the genus of which the particular product is a species. At common law neither those terms which were generic nor those which were merely descriptive could become valid trademarks * * *. The same was true under the Trademark Act of 1905, except for marks which had been the subject of exclusive use for ten years prior to its enactment, 33 Stat. 726.[10] While * * * the Lanham Act makes an important exception with respect to those merely descriptive terms which have acquired secondary meaning, see § 2(f), 15 U.S.C. § 1052(f), it offers no such exception for generic marks. The Act provides for the cancellation of a registered mark if at any time it [becomes generic] § 14(c). This means that even proof of secondary meaning, by virtue of which some "merely descriptive" marks may be registered, cannot transform a generic term into a subject for trademark. As explained in *J. Kohnstam, Ltd. v. Louis Marx and Company*, 280 F.2d 437, 440, 47 CCPA 1080 (1960), no matter how much money and effort the user of a generic term has poured into promoting the sale of its merchandise and what success it has achieved in securing public identification, it cannot deprive competing manufacturers of the product of the right to call an article by its name. * * * The pervasiveness of the principle is illustrated by a series of well known cases holding that when a suggestive or fanciful term has become generic as a result of a manufacturer's own advertising efforts, trademark protection will be denied save for those markets where the term still has not become generic and a secondary meaning has been shown to continue. A term may thus be generic in one market and descriptive or suggestive or fanciful in another.

The term which is descriptive but not generic[11] stands on a better basis. Although § 2(e) of the Lanham Act, 15 U.S.C. § 1052, forbids the registration of a mark which, when applied to the goods of the applicant, is "merely descriptive," § 2(f) removes a considerable part of the sting by providing that "except as expressly excluded in paragraphs (a)-(d) of this section, nothing in this chapter shall prevent the registration of a

the coined word "Escalator", originally fanciful, or at the very least suggestive, was held to have become generic.

10. Some protection to descriptive marks which had acquired a secondary meaning was given by the law of unfair competition. The Trademark Act of 1920 permitted registration of certain descriptive marks which had acquired secondary meaning.

11. A commentator has illuminated the distinction with an example of the "Deep Bowl Spoon":

> "Deep Bowl" identifies a significant characteristic of the article. It is "merely descriptive" of the goods, because it informs one that they are deep in the bowl portion.... It is not, however, "the common descriptive name" of the article [since] the implement is not a deep bowl, it is a spoon.... "Spoon" is not merely descriptive of the article—it identifies the article—[and therefore] the term is generic.

Fletcher, *Actual Confusion as to Incontestability of Descriptive Marks*, 64 Trademark Rep. 252, 260 (1974). On the other hand, "Deep Bowl" would be generic as to a deep bowl.

mark used by the applicant which has become distinctive of the applicant's goods in commerce" and that the Commissioner may accept, as prima facie evidence that the mark has become distinctive, proof of substantially exclusive and continuous use of the mark applied to the applicant's goods for five years preceding the application. * * * In the [case of generic terms] any claim to an exclusive right must be denied since this in effect would confer a monopoly not only of the mark but of the product by rendering a competitor unable effectively to name what it was endeavoring to sell. In the [case of descriptive terms] the law strikes the balance, with respect to registration, between the hardships to a competitor in hampering the use of an appropriate word and those to the owner who, having invested money and energy to endow a word with the good will adhering to his enterprise, would be deprived of the fruits of his efforts.

The category of "suggestive" marks was spawned by the felt need to accord protection to marks that were neither exactly descriptive on the one hand nor truly fanciful on the other—a need that was particularly acute because of the bar in the Trademark Act of 1905, 33 Stat. 724, 726, (with an exceedingly limited exception noted above) on the registration of merely descriptive marks regardless of proof of secondary meaning. Having created the category the courts have had great difficulty in defining it. Judge Learned Hand made the not very helpful statement:

> It is quite impossible to get any rule out of the cases beyond this: That the validity of the mark ends where suggestion ends and description begins.

Franklin Knitting Mills, Inc. v. Fashionit Sweater Mills, Inc., 297 F. 247, 248 (2 Cir.1923), aff'd per curiam, 4 F.2d 1018 (2 Cir.1925)—a statement amply confirmed by comparing the list of terms held suggestive with those held merely descriptive in 3 Callmann, Unfair Competition, Trademarks and Monopolies § 71.2 (3d ed.). Another court has observed, somewhat more usefully, that:

> A term is suggestive if it requires imagination, thought and perception to reach a conclusion as to the nature of goods. A term is descriptive if it forthwith conveys an immediate idea of the ingredients, qualities or characteristics of the goods.

Stix Products, Inc. v. United Merchants & Manufacturers Inc., 295 F.Supp. 479, 488 (S.D.N.Y.1968)—a formulation deriving from General Shoe Corp. v. Rosen, 111 F.2d 95, 98 (4 Cir.1940). Also useful is the approach taken by this court in *Aluminum Fabricating Co. of Pittsburgh v. Season–All Window Corp.*, 259 F.2d 314 (2 Cir.1958), that the reason for restricting the protection accorded descriptive terms, namely the undesirability of preventing an entrant from using a descriptive term for his product, is much less forceful when the trademark is a suggestive word since, as Judge Lumbard wrote, 259 F.2d at 317:

> The English language has a wealth of synonyms and related words with which to describe the qualities which manufacturers may wish to claim for their products and the ingenuity of the public

> relations profession supplies new words and slogans as they are needed.

If a term is suggestive, it is entitled to registration without proof of secondary meaning. Moreover, as held in the *Season-All* case, the decision of the Patent Office to register a mark without requiring proof of secondary meaning affords a rebuttable presumption that the mark is suggestive or arbitrary or fanciful rather than merely descriptive.

It need hardly be added that fanciful or arbitrary terms [12] enjoy all the rights accorded to suggestive terms as marks without the need of debating whether the term is "merely descriptive" and with ease of establishing infringement.

* * *

Notes and Questions

1. *The distinctiveness requirement.* In order to qualify as a mark, a word, symbol or device must be distinctive. That is, it must serve the purpose of a trademark by indicating the origin of the product or service to consumers, distinguishing the origin from that of other goods or services. As the *Abercrombie & Fitch* opinion indicates, arbitrary words (such as "Ivory" for soap or "tea rose" for flour) and made-up or fanciful words (such as "Kodak" for camera film and equipment and "Exxon" for gasoline) are viewed as "inherently distinctive." It can be assumed that consumers seeing or hearing such words used in the sale of products or services will understand them to be indications of origin. What other purpose could they serve?

Such an assumption cannot be made in the case of words that describe characteristics of the good or service (such as "World Book" for encyclopedias, "Beef & Brew" for restaurant services, or "Easyload" for tape recorders). Thus, descriptive words are not inherently distinctive. They are merely *capable* of becoming distinctive if, through exposure through use on labels and in advertising, consumers come to regard them as indications of origin. If a descriptive word has not become distinctive, then it is unlikely that use of the word by other competitors will lead to consumer confusion about the source of goods or services, or loss of good will. Moreover, there are good reasons not to recognize exclusive rights in descriptive words in one business enterprise too readily: other competitors may legitimately need to use such words to describe their own products or services. As Judge Posner has stated:

> it is no purpose of trademark protection to allow a firm to prevent its competitors from informing consumers about the attributes of the competitors' brands. * * * To allow a firm to use as a trademark a generic word, or a descriptive word still understood by the consuming

12. As terms of art, the distinctions between suggestive terms and fanciful or arbitrary terms may seem needlessly artificial. Of course, a common word may be used in a fanciful sense; indeed one might say that only a common word can be so used, since a coined word cannot first be put to a bizarre use. Nevertheless, the term "fanciful", as a classifying concept, is usually applied to words invented solely for their use as trademarks. When the same legal consequences attach to a common word, i. e., when it is applied in an unfamiliar way, the use is called "arbitrary."

public to describe, would make it difficult for competitors to market their own brands of the same product.

Blau Plumbing, Inc. v. S.O.S. Fix–It, Inc., 781 F.2d 604, 609, 228 U.S.P.Q. 519, 521 (7th Cir.1986). Accordingly, modern common law permits descriptive words to be protected, and the Lanham Act permits them to be registered, *if* the user is able to demonstrate that consumers do, in fact, recognize the word as an indication of origin. In such cases, the descriptive word has acquired "secondary meaning." Only then will limiting competitors' use of a descriptive word be justified by concerns about consumer confusion and protection of good will.

Suggestive words (such as "Coppertone" for suntan cream, or "Roach Motel" for insect traps), like arbitrary and fanciful words, are considered inherently distinctive, and can be protected and registered without the necessity of demonstrating secondary meaning. How does one determine whether a word is descriptive or suggestive? Is the *Abercrombie* discussion helpful? The court refers to policy considerations which justify protecting and registering suggestive marks without a showing of secondary meaning. Do those policy considerations suggest an additional test for determining which classification is appropriate in a given case?

We will examine two of the categories identified by Judge Friendly—generic marks and descriptive marks—in greater detail in the following two Subsections.

2. *Categorization of design and other nonverbal marks.* The four *Abercrombie* mark classifications are best suited for word marks. While some nonverbal marks, such as drawings of a product or of persons using it, may readily be classified as "descriptive," or "suggestive," many nonverbal marks, such as abstract designs and product or packaging shapes, cannot readily be characterized by those terms. In such cases, as a practical matter the four categories can be collapsed into two: marks that are inherently distinctive and marks that are merely capable of becoming distinctive through acquisition of secondary meaning. Marks in the first category can be protected or registered without any demonstration of secondary meaning. How is the distinctiveness determination made?

In Wiley v. American Greetings Corp., 762 F.2d 139, 226 U.S.P.Q. 101 (1st Cir.1985), the plaintiff manufactured and sold stuffed teddy bears, each of which had a red heart shape permanently affixed to its left breast. The defendants began using a similar heart on their teddy bears, and plaintiff brought a common-law suit for trademark infringement. The U.S. Court of Appeals for the First Circuit upheld summary judgement for the defendants, finding that the heart was not inherently distinctive as a matter of law, and that the plaintiff had not demonstrated secondary meaning. The court explained:

> Whether a design is "inherently distinctive," *i.e.*, whether it is arbitrary or merely descriptive, is ordinarily a question of fact that is decided by reference to the following factors:
>
> > Whether [the design] was a "common basic shape or design," whether it was unique or unusual in a particular field, whether it was a mere refinement of a commonly-adopted and well-known

> form of ornamentation for a particular class of goods viewed by the public as dress or ornamentation for the goods, or whether it was capable of creating a commercial impression distinct from the accompanying words.
>
> Seabrook Foods, Inc. v. Bar–Well Foods, Ltd., 568 F.2d 1342, 1344 (C.C.P.A.1977). Evaluating the record here in the light most favorable to Wiley, however, leads us to conclude that no genuine issue exists for the trier of fact, since we see no proper basis on which a trier could determine that Wiley's heart is commensurate with the above standards.
>
> Wiley's red heart is a "common" basic shape, similar to a geometrical design. It is hornbook law that "[o]rdinary geometric shapes such as circles, ovals, squares, etc., even when not used as background for other marks, are regarded as non-distinctive and protectible only upon proof of secondary meaning." *McCarthy, Trademarks and Unfair Competition*, § 7:12, at 172. A plain heart shape, like an "[o]rdinary geometric shape," carries no distinctive message of origin to the consumer, and could not carry such a message (absent establishment of a secondary meaning) given the heart shape's widespread use as decoration for any number of products put out by many different companies.
>
> Using a red heart as ornamentation for stuffed animals is also far from unique or unusual. The record contains pictures of, and references to, an abundance of plush animals, including many teddy bears, that sport heart designs on their chests or other parts of their anatomy. * * *
>
> The fact that Wiley's alleged mark is a red heart, *permanently* affixed to the *left* breast of a *teddy bear* does not, as she claims, serve to distinguish her use of the design from others' uses of hearts on other stuffed animals. These characteristics, even if they in combination could be deemed unique, are "mere refinement[s] of a commonly-adopted and well-known form of ornamentation for a particular class of goods viewed by the public as dress or ornamentation for a particular class of goods." *Seabrook Foods*, 568 F.2d at 1344.

Id., 762 F.2d at 141–42, 226 U.S.P.Q. at 103. See RESTATEMENT (THIRD) OF UNFAIR COMPETITION § 13, comment c (Tentative Draft No. 2, 1990) ("unless the design or symbol is striking, unusual, or otherwise likely to differentiate the products of a specific producer, the designation is not inherently distinctive").

In contrast to the red heart in *Wiley*, the red and white polka-dot bands on Swift cleanser, depicted in the prior Section, were held inherently distinctive. See also *In re* Esso Standard Oil Co., 305 F.2d 495, 134 U.S.P.Q. 402 (C.C.P.A.1962) (red, white and blue "Esso" label held inherently distinctive); Sicilia Di R. Biebow & Co. v. Cox, 732 F.2d 417 (5th Cir.1984) (tear-shape-on-a-pedestal design for bottle may be inherently distinctive).

How would you categorize "Mr. Peanut," the peanut with stick arms and legs, a top hat, spats, cane and monocle, used as a mark for Planters' nuts?

3. *Secondary meaning.* The classic definition of secondary meaning comes from G. & C. Merriam Co. v. Saalfield, 198 Fed. 369, 373 (6th Cir.1912):

> a word or phrase originally, and in that sense primarily, incapable of exclusive appropriation with reference to an article on the market, because geographically or otherwise descriptive, might nevertheless have been used so long and so exclusively by one producer with reference to his article that, in that trade and to that branch of the purchasing public, the word or phrase had come to mean that the article was his product; in other words, had come to be, to them, his trademark. So it was said that the word had come to have a secondary meaning, although this phrase, "secondary meaning," seems not happily chosen, because, in the limited field, this new meaning is primary rather than secondary: that is to say, it is, in that field, the natural meaning.

As an example, the common descriptive word "standard" has secondary meaning in the oil business, indicating to consumers that oil or gasoline comes from a particular oil company. Standard Oil Co. v. Michie, 34 F.2d 802, 2 U.S.P.Q. 232 (E.D.Mo.1929). Obviously in the context of non-verbal marks the "secondary meaning" and "primary meaning" rhetoric is not relevant. In such cases, "secondary meaning" simply means that consumers have come to regard the device or symbol as an indication of origin.

How does an applicant for registration of a mark that is not inherently distinctive prove the existence of secondary meaning? One frequent method is a consumer survey, which undertakes to ascertain consumers' perception of the particular word, symbol or device. In order to be accepted and accorded weight as evidence, however, the survey must be scientifically formulated and conducted. See, e.g., Brooks Shoe Manufacturing Co. v. Suave Shoe Corp., 716 F.2d 854, 221 U.S.P.Q. 536 (11th Cir.1983); Palladino, *Surveying Secondary Meaning*, 84 TRADEMARK REP. 155 (1994); Evans & Gunn, *Trademark Surveys*, 79 TRADEMARK REP. 1 (1989). Consumers may be called as witnesses to testify about their understanding. In addition, a wide array of circumstantial evidence may be useful. For example, evidence that the claimant has used the word, symbol or device as a mark exclusively and extensively for a substantial period of time is circumstantial evidence that consumers have been sufficiently exposed to it to understand its trademark significance. Evidence of extensive advertising which features the mark is effective for the same reason. Courts have also regarded evidence that an infringement defendant deliberately copied the mark as circumstantial evidence of secondary meaning. See, e.g., Ideal Toy Corp. v. Plawner Toy Manufacturing Corp., 685 F.2d 78, 216 U.S.P.Q. 102 (3d Cir.1982). As the *Abercrombie* court notes, the Lanham Act permits (but does not require) the PTO to accept as prima facie evidence of secondary meaning "proof of substantially exclusive and continuous use" by the applicant in commerce "for the five years before the date on which the claim of distinctiveness is made." 15 U.S.C.A. § 1052(f). The degree of proof of secondary meaning that will be required may vary according to the perceived "strength" of the mark. For example, the PTO or a court may require stronger evidence of secondary meaning in the case of a highly descriptive term than in the case of a term which is descriptive, but only slightly so.

How many consumers must understand the word, symbol or device's trademark significance? Many courts have stated that a "substantial segment" or a "substantial number" of the pool of prospective purchasers of the good or service will suffice. See, e.g., Centaur Communications, Ltd. v. A/S/M Communications, Inc., 830 F.2d 1217, 1222, 4 U.S.P.Q.2d 1541, 1545 (2d Cir.1987). This requirement appears frequently to be satisfied with less than fifty percent. *In re* Owens–Corning Fiberglas Corp., 774 F.2d 1116, 1127, 227 U.S.P.Q. 417, 424 (C.A.F.C. 1985); RESTATEMENT (THIRD) OF UNFAIR COMPETITION § 13, comment e (Tentative Draft No. 2, 1990).

1. Generic Terms

THE MURPHY DOOR BED CO., INC. v. INTERIOR SLEEP SYSTEMS, INC.

Unites States Court of Appeals for the Second Circuit, 1989.
874 F.2d 95, 10 U.S.P.Q.2d 1748.

MINER, CIRCUIT JUDGE:

Defendants-appellants appeal from a judgment entered in the United States District Court for the Eastern District of New York (Mishler, J.), awarding plaintiff, the Murphy Door Bed Company ("Murphy" or "Murphy Co."), * * * damages for breach of contract [and] trademark infringement and unfair competition. The judgment includes a permanent injunction enjoining all defendants from use of the Murphy name.

* * *

We hold that "Murphy bed" is a generic term, having been appropriated by the public to designate generally a type of bed. Consequently, defendants could not have infringed on plaintiff's trademark, alleged to be Murphy bed, and the district court erred in finding trademark infringement. * * *

BACKGROUND

At the turn of this century, William Lawrence Murphy invented and manufactured a bed that when not in use could be concealed in a wall closet. By using a counter-balancing mechanism, the bed could be lowered from or raised to a closet in a wall to which the bed is hinged. In 1918, the United States Patent Office granted Mr. Murphy a patent for a "pivot bed," which was substantially similar to the wall bed. Mr. Murphy incorporated in New York in 1925 as the Murphy Door Bed Company and began to sell the wall bed under the name of "Murphy bed." Since its inception, the Murphy Co. has used the words Murphy and Murphy bed as its trademark for concealed beds. Other manufacturers of wall beds generally describe their products as "wall beds," "concealed beds," "disappearing beds," "authentic adjustable hydraulic beds" and the like, but rarely as Murphy beds. In fact, at least twice, when independent companies marketed their products as Murphy beds, Murphy complained to them and, as a result, the companies refrained from further deliberate use of the term Murphy bed.

On March 23, 1981, and again on November 16, 1982, the Patent and Trademark Office ("PTO") denied the Murphy Co.'s application to register the Murphy bed trademark. The PTO examining attorney explained that the words "Murphy bed" had become generic and that the phrase Murphy bed was "merely descriptive of a characteristic of the goods." In August 1984, the Trademark Trial and Appeal Board ("TTAB") affirmed the denial of registration. The TTAB noted that "Murphy bed has for a long period of time been used by a substantial segment of the public as a generic term for a bed which folds into a wall or a closet."

In December 1981, Frank Zarcone, on behalf of ISS and himself, entered into a distributorship agreement with the Murphy Co. and became the exclusive distributor of the Murphy bed in the four Florida counties of Broward, Dade, Palm Beach and Monroe. The agreement, in the form of a letter signed by both Murphy and Zarcone, provided in part that:

> 4) ... Interior Sleep Systems will pay for material purchased within 30 days of date of Murphy's invoice....
>
> 5) — Whenever the Murphy name is used, it must be in capital letters and identified by the word trademark or TM adjacent to Murphy. Cabinets or other material not furnished by Murphy will not be promoted or sold as Murphy products.
>
> * * *
>
> 8) — Upon termination of this agreement Interior Sleep Systems, Inc. agrees to discontinue the use of the name "Murphy bed".

After learning of the TTAB's 1984 decision denying Murphy's application for trademark registration, Zarcone formed MBCA Ga. in December 1985, and MBCA Fl. in February 1986. In addition, Zarcone obtained a telephone listing in New York City under the name "Murphy Bed Company."

On March 20, 1986, Magnolia Builders ("Magnolia") of Pensacola, Florida ordered 109 Murphy beds, Model SL $^{60}/_{80}$, from MBCA Fl. Zarcone previously had filled similar Magnolia orders with beds of the Murphy Co. To fill this order, however, Zarcone delivered beds designated as Murphy bed Model SL 60/80 but that were, in fact, manufactured by one of his companies.

Thereafter, Zarcone ordered from the Murphy Co. forty-eight Murphy beds, which were delivered with an invoice on May 21, 1986. [Zarcone did not pay for these beds in accordance with his distributorship agreement. Murphy then notified Zarcone that it was cancelling the distributorship agreement and] that in keeping with paragraph 8 of the agreement, Zarcone was within "ten (10) days from receipt of this letter to remove the name 'Murphy Bed' from all signs, vehicles, billboards, and all advertising." * * * Zarcone continued to advertise regularly in south Florida using the Murphy name, including describing his product as "Murphy Bed Co. of America, Inc.—Original Wall–Bed Systems" and "The New Murphy Beds ... Original Wall Bed Systems."

Murphy initiated this action on December 19, 1986, seeking compensation, punitive damages, and injunctive relief based on claims of: (i) trademark infringement, (ii) unfair competition and (iii) breach of contract. * * *

A bench trial was held and in a decision and order dated May 13, 1988, the district court found for the Murphy Co. on all counts. 687 F.Supp. 754, 756 (E.D.N.Y.1988). First, the court ruled that the name Murphy was not generic because a "secondary meaning" had been attributed to it by the general public, and that the common law of trademark therefore protected the Murphy Co. Thus, the court held that the burden was on the defendants to show abandonment of the Murphy trademark—i.e. that the trademark had lost its significance. The court then found that defendants did not sustain their burden. * * *

Discussion

1. *Trade-mark Infringement*

The district court found that Murphy had shown that the term Murphy bed had secondary meaning—i.e. that the term symbolized a particular business, product or company—and thus was protectible. As a result, the court assigned to defendants the burden of proving that the term somehow had been transformed into a generic phrase. The defendants did not sustain their burden, in the view of the court. Defendants now claim that the court improperly placed the burden of proof upon them, arguing that, instead, Murphy should have been required to prove that the trademark was not generic.

A term or phrase is generic when it is commonly used to depict a genus or type of product, rather than a particular product. See *Abercromie & Fitch Co. v. Hunting World, Inc.*, 537 F.2d 4, 9 (2d Cir.1976). When a term is generic, "trademark protection will be denied save for those markets where the term still has not become generic and a secondary meaning has been shown to continue." *Id.* at 10. We have held that "the burden is on plaintiff to prove that its mark is a valid trademark ... [and] that its unregistered mark is not generic." *Reese Publishing Co. v. Hampton Int'l Communications, Inc.*, 620 F.2d 7, 11 (2d Cir.1980).

As the Murphy mark is unregistered, *Reese* suggests that the district court erred in shifting the burden of proof to the defendants. However, the words at issue in *Reese*, "Video Buyer's Guide," were of common use before the product developer applied them to his product, whereas here, the term Murphy bed was created for its purpose by the manufacturer and only thereafter was it adopted by the public as a matter of common use. * * * It was this genericness of an "invented" term that Learned Hand addressed when determining whether "aspirin," a coined word, had been so adopted by the lay public as to become generic. *See Bayer*

Co. v. United Drug Co., 272 F. 505, 509 (S.D.N.Y.1921); *see also King–Seeley Thermos Co. v. Aladdin Indus., Inc.*, 321 F.2d 577, 579 (2d Cir.1963) (wide-spread use of the word "thermos," despite having been invented by plaintiff for description of vacuum bottle, created genericness); *DuPont Cellophane Co. v. Waxed Products Co.*, 85 F.2d 75, 81 (2d Cir.) (expropriation by public of word "cellophane" created genericness), *cert. denied*, 299 U.S. 601, 57 S.Ct. 194, 81 L.Ed. 443 (1936). We find this distinction important and hold that where the public is said to have expropriated a term established by a product developer, the burden is on the defendant to prove genericness. Thus, critical to a trial court's allocation of proof burdens is a determination of whether the term at issue is claimed to be generic by reason of common usage or by reason of expropriation. This presumption of nongenericness of a product name in the case of apparent public expropriation is justified by the commercial protection a developer of innovations deserves.

The Murphy Co. was the first to employ the word Murphy to describe a bed that could be folded into a wall closet. It is claimed that over time the public adopted, or, rather, expropriated, the term Murphy bed as a synonym for any bed that folds into a closet. Accordingly, the district court was correct in placing the burden of proof of genericness upon the defendants. We find, however, that Zarcone did indeed establish the genericness of the term Murphy bed.

The following factors combined lead us to conclude that Zarcone showed at trial that today the term Murphy bed, in the eyes of "a substantial majority of the public," *King-Seeley*, 321 F.2d at 579, refers to a species of bed that can fold into a wall enclosure. First, the decision of the PTO, and certainly the TTAB, is to be accorded great weight. The district court explicitly rejected the decisions of the PTO and TTAB finding genericness, despite acknowledging their persuasive force. Second, the term Murphy bed is included in many dictionaries as a standard description of a wall-bed. *See, e.g.*, Webster's Third New International Dictionary 1489 (1981). While dictionary definitions are not conclusive proof of a mark's generic nature, they are influential because they reflect the general public's perception of a mark's meaning and implication. Third, Zarcone introduced as evidence numerous examples of newspaper and magazine use of the phrase Murphy bed to describe generally a type of bed. Again, such evidence is not proof positive, but it is a strong indication of the general public's perception that Murphy bed connotes something other than a bed manufactured by the Murphy Co.

In finding a lack of genericness, the district court was influenced by Murphy's efforts at policing its mark. The court noted with approval instances where Murphy complained to those who had used the term Murphy bed to describe beds not necessarily produced by Murphy. However, when, as here, the mark has "entered the public domain beyond recall," policing is of no consequence to a resolution of whether a mark is generic. *King-Seeley*, 321 F.2d at 579.[2]

2. Indeed, the only evidence that even arguably supports the view that the mark was not generic is the circumstance that other manufacturers did not use the term

Because we find that the evidence presented at trial demonstrated the genericness of the term Murphy bed, the claim for trademark infringement must fail. Neither statutory law, namely the Lanham Act, nor common law supports a claim for trademark infringement when the mark in question is generic. * * *

Notes and Questions

1. *Loss of a valuable trademark.* What is the rationale underlying the rule that there can be no trademark rights in generic terms? Is it valid? See Teply, *Trademarked Generic Words*, 89 YALE L.J. 1323 (1980). What is the test for determining whether a mark has become generic? Would consumer surveys be an effective way to prove or disprove genericness? See Simonson, *An Empirical Investigation of the Meaning and Measurement of "Genericness"*, 84 TRADEMARK REP. 199 (1994); Folsom & Teply, *Surveying "Genericness" in Trademark Litigation,* 78 TRADEMARK REP. 1 (1988); Swann & Paladino, *Surveying "Genericness": A Critique of Folsom and Teply*, 78 TRADEMARK REP. 179 (1988); Oddi, *Assessing "Genericness": Another View*, 78 TRADEMARK REP. 560 (1988).

In determining whether a trademark has become the generic name of a product or service, should it matter whether the product or service already has one or more generic names? In light of the test discussed in *Murphy*, what is the likely status of the mark "Xerox" for photocopiers, and "Kleenex" for facial tissues? What can a business do to avoid losing a valuable trademark by virtue of public appropriation? See 2 J.T. McCARTHY, McCARTHY ON TRADEMARKS AND UNFAIR COMPETITION § 12.09 (1992). Is there any cause of action by which a trademark owner can enjoin generic uses of its mark, for example, in the media or in dictionaries? Compare Lucasfilm Ltd. v. High Frontier, 622 F.Supp. 931, 227 U.S.P.Q. 967 (D.D.C.1985) (owner of service mark "Star Wars" cannot enjoin public interest groups from using the term "star wars" in advertisements to describe the Reagan Administration's Strategic Defense Initiative); with Selchow & Righter Co. v. McGraw–Hill Book Co., 580 F.2d 25, 198 U.S.P.Q. 577 (2d Cir.1978) (owner of "Scrabble" trademark is entitled to preliminary injunction against unauthorized publication of dictionary entitled "The Complete Scrabble Dictionary." Irreparable harm is demonstrated by fact that publication might render the "Scrabble" trademark generic.) Should there be? See Dreyfuss, *Expressive Genericity: Trademarks as Language In the Pepsi Generation,* 65 NOTRE DAME L. REV. 397 (1990).

2. *The Lanham Act.* If the plaintiff's "Murphy Bed" mark had been registered on the Lanham Act principal register, allocation of the burden of proof would have been clear. One of the advantages of registration is that registration constitutes "prima facie evidence of the validity of the registered mark and of the registration of the mark." 15 U.S.C.A. § 1057(b). This would have placed the burden of proof on the defendant to rebut the presumption of validity.

Murphy bed to describe their beds. However, that fact is not sufficient to support a conclusion that the mark is not generic, especially since Murphy's action in policing the mark might well have deterred other manufacturers from using the term Murphy bed in describing their products.

Section 2 of the Lanham Act, 15 U.S.C.A. § 1052, sets forth the grounds on which registration of marks can be refused. There is no express reference to generic terms. Is there any language in section 2 that can be interpreted as authorizing rejection of an application to register a mark on the ground that it is generic?

Lanham Act section 14(3), 15 U.S.C.A. § 1064(3), provides that a petition to cancel a registration may be filed at any time "if the registered mark becomes the generic name for the goods or services, or a portion thereof, for which it is registered." It further provides:

> A registered mark shall not be deemed to be the generic name of goods or services solely because such mark is also used as a name of or to identify a unique product or service. The primary significance of the registered mark to the relevant public rather than purchaser motivation shall be the test for determining whether the registered mark has become the generic name of goods or services on or in connection with which it has been used.

What does this mean? See 2 J.T. McCARTHY, McCARTHY ON TRADEMARKS AND UNFAIR COMPETITION § 12.02[3][b] (1992).

3. *Residual trademark significance.* In some cases, public appropriation of a once-arbitrary or fanciful mark may not be complete. For example, while 75% of the relevant public understands the term to be the name of the product, the remaining 25% may still view the term as an indication that the product (which may have other generic names) comes from one particular source. Since the primary significance is generic, the term must be adjudged generic, 15 U.S.C.A. § 1064(3), and competitors must be allowed to use it. What, if anything, can be done to prevent confusion of the remaining 25% of the public that still accords the term trademark significance? See King–Seeley Thermos Co. v. Aladdin Industries, Inc., 321 F.2d 577, 138 U.S.P.Q. 349 (2d Cir.1963).

4. *Determining the relevant "genus."* A generic term is generally defined as the name of a class or "genus" of products or services. See Park 'N Fly, Inc. v. Dollar Park & Fly, Inc., 469 U.S. 189, 194, 105 S.Ct. 658, 661, 83 L.Ed.2d 582, 587, 224 U.S.P.Q. 327 (1985) (a generic term is one that refers to the genus, while each producer's particular product is a species within the genus.) As a first step in determining whether a term is the common name of a genus, therefore, the relevant class or "genus" must be defined. In *Murphy*, the Second Circuit defined the relevant genus as "concealed" or "wall" beds. The issue was not controversial in that case, and often is not.

One case in which genus definition was quite controversial is A.J. Canfield Co. v. Honickman, 808 F.2d 291, 1 U.S.P.Q.2d 1364 (3d Cir.1986). In that case, the court had to decide, in the course of reviewing the denial of the plaintiff's motion for a preliminary injunction, whether the term "chocolate fudge" was generic for the plaintiff's diet soda. The court found that the issue hinged on whether the relevant product genus was chocolate soda (in which case the composite "chocolate fudge soda" might be deemed descriptive or even suggestive of chocolate soda) or chocolate fudge soda. This in turn depended on whether "fudge" denoted a separate flavor or flavor variation of chocolate. After considerable discussion, the court determined:

> [W]hen a producer introduces a product that differs from an established product class in a significant, functional characteristic, and uses the common descriptive term of that characteristic as its name, that new product becomes its own genus, and the term denoting the genus becomes generic if there is no commonly used alternative that effectively communicates the same functional information.

Id., 808 F.2d at 293, 1 U.S.P.Q.2d at 1365. Applying this test to the case at hand, the court noted that plaintiff itself had emphasized in its advertising the difference between soda tasting like chocolate fudge and mere chocolate soda, chocolate fudge sodas having "a particular full and rich chocolate flavor." Thus, a soda tasting like chocolate fudge did differ from chocolate soda with respect to a significant, functional characteristic, and constituted a separate product genus. The term "fudge" denoted that different characteristic. Since the court knew of no commonly used alternative to communicate the flavor variation, it determined that the name "chocolate fudge" must be viewed as the generic name of this new genus of soda. Giving plaintiff exclusive rights in the term would make it difficult, if not impossible, for a competing producer to convey to the public that its product shared this functional flavor characteristic. This, in turn, would effectively give the plaintiff an undeserved monopoly in the functional product characteristic itself.

HENRI'S FOOD PRODUCTS CO., INC. v. TASTY SNACKS, INC.

United States Court of Appeals for the Seventh Circuit, 1987.
817 F.2d 1303, 2 U.S.P.Q.2d 1856.

CUDAHY, CIRCUIT JUDGE.

Henri's Food Products Co., Inc. ("Henri's"), the owner of a federal registration for the trademark TAS–TEE for use on salad dressings, sued Tasty Snacks, Inc. ("Tasty Snacks") for trademark infringement through the use of the term "tasty" as a trademark for salad dressing. * * * The district court granted summary judgment in favor of Tasty Snacks on the ground that the word "tasty" was a generic term for salad dressing and therefore could not be a protectible trademark. We reverse.

I.

Henri's is a Wisconsin corporation located in Milwaukee, Wisconsin, that manufactures salad dressing which is sold throughout Wisconsin and elsewhere in the United States. One of Henri's products is a salad dressing made with celery seed and onion and sold under the claimed trademark TAS–TEE. Henri's has sold more than 10 million dollars worth of TAS–TEE brand salad dressing since 1947. In 1960, Henri's was refused registration by the United States Patent Office for TAS–TEE as a trademark for use on salad dressings. The mark was considered "so highly descriptive that it does not function as a trademark to distinguish applicant's goods in interstate commerce." In 1982, however, Henri's filed a second application for trademark registration, and the Patent Office granted registration for the word TAS–TEE alone.

In 1984, Tasty Snacks, an Illinois corporation, started selling salad dressings and mayonnaise under the designation "tasty," including "Tasty" mayonnaise, "Tasty" Russian dressing, "Tasty" Italian dressing and "Tasty" salad dressing with vinegar, egg yolks and oil. Tasty Snacks placed the registered trademark symbol ® next to the word "tasty" on the label of some of its dressing products.

In December 1984, Henri's began a lawsuit against Tasty Snacks seeking to enjoin Tasty Snacks from using the term "tasty" as a trademark for salad dressing and asking for damages. Henri's complaint alleges that the use of the trademark "tasty" on salad dressings by Tasty Snacks is likely to result in confusion by potential purchasers of salad dressing who may believe that salad dressing bearing the "tasty" trademark came from the same source as dressing bearing Henri's TAS–TEE trademark. * * * Henri's contends that Tasty Snacks' dressings were sold in direct competition with Henri's TAS–TEE brand with intent to deceive and unfairly compete and to trade on the goodwill of Henri's TAS–TEE trademark. * * *

II.

The district court found that the word "tasty" (and its phonetic equivalent TAS–TEE) was generic with respect to salad dressing and therefore was incapable of winning protection as a trademark either under federal law, common law or under the Illinois Deceptive Trade Practices Act. We agree with the district court that if "tasty" were generic, it could not be accorded trademark protection. We do not, however, agree that "tasty" is generic.

Trademarks run the gamut from the fanciful or arbitrary (which are fully protected), to the suggestive, to the "merely descriptive" (which require for protection a showing of secondary meaning). On the other hand, a generic name—the common name of a class of things or a "common descriptive name"—is irretrievably in the public domain, and the preservation of competition precludes its protection. Here, the district court relied on *Miller Brewing Co. v. G. Heileman Brewing Co.*, 561 F.2d 75 (7th Cir.1977), *cert. denied*, 434 U.S. 1025, 98 S.Ct. 751, 54 L.Ed.2d 772 (1978), in concluding that "tasty" was generic. In *Miller Brewing Co.*, this court stated that "[a] generic or common descriptive term is one which is commonly used as the name or description of a kind of goods. It cannot become a trademark under any circumstances." *Id.* at 79. This court also held:

> The word "light," including its phonetic equivalent "lite" . . . [is] a generic or common descriptive term as applied to beer, [and] could not be exclusively appropriated by Miller as a trademark, "despite whatever promotional effort [Miller] may have expended to exploit it."

Id. at 81 (quoting *Henry Heide, Inc. v. George Ziegler Co.*, 354 F.2d 574, 576 (7th Cir.1965)). The district court in the case before us observed that " '[l]ight' or 'lite' is a common descriptive word such as 'rose' wine, 'blended' whiskey, and 'white' bread." The district court went on to conclude:

> The term "tasty" is even more generic or commonly descriptive than "light" in light beer. A light beer is only one of a kind of beers that a manufacturer can sell; whereas, a manufacturer would not want to sell a dressing that is not tasty. It would certainly be a sad day (and a more bland one) if a food or beverage company could corner the market on words such as "tasty," "savory," "flavorful," or "delicious."

The district court also rejected Henri's argument that a generic word must be a commonly used *name* of a product, and that since the word "tasty" is an adjective, it cannot be generic. The district court stated that the mere fact that a word is an adjective does not prevent it from being a generic or common descriptive word.

The district court found that the *Miller Brewing Co.* court had held that "beer" was the name of the product, and that "light" described the qualities of that product. That is, "light" described a certain quality of that type of beer as less filling with reduced calories. In like vein, the district court thought that "salad dressing" is the name of the product and "tasty" describes the qualities of the product:

> "Tasty" describes the salad dressing as savory or appetizing. The Seventh Circuit has reasoned that if "light beer" is a generic name, then "light" is a generic word when used as part of that name. So also, if "tasty dressing" is a generic name, then "tasty" is a generic word when used as part of that name.

July 31, 1986 Order at 259.

We do not agree that "tasty" is a generic term or a "common descriptive name" or, for that matter, is comparable to "light" or "lite" in "light beer." The holding in *Miller Brewing Co.* is that an adjective can be a generic term when that word is part of a common descriptive name of a kind of goods.[1] In order to be generic, however (as the word

1. Some authors have criticized this circuit for allegedly expanding the category of generic terms to include certain descriptive adjectives, *which in connection with a noun* have been held to be "common descriptive terms" and unregistrable. See 1 J. Gilson, *Trademark Protection and Practice* § 2.02, at 20–23 (Supp. June 1986). Gilson is critical of the *Miller Brewing Co.* decision for viewing "lite" ("light") as incapable of acquiring a secondary meaning even though that word itself is descriptive. To achieve this result, the court construed "lite" as generic since it was part of the combination, "lite beer"—itself viewed as a generic name. Gilson raises a related objection to *Technical Publishing Co. v. Lebhar–Friedman, Inc.*, 729 F.2d 1136 (7th Cir.1984), which suggests that the magazine title "Software News" is generic and unprotectible irrespective of secondary meaning. *See also National Conference of Bar Examiners v. Multistate Legal Studies, Inc.*, 692 F.2d 478 (7th Cir.1982), *cert. denied*, 464 U.S. 814, 104 S.Ct. 69, 78 L.Ed.2d 83 (1983) ("multistate bar examination" held to be unprotectible). Gilson opines that the broadening of the generic/common descriptive category is perhaps misguidedly intended to implement a pro-competitive policy.

implies), the word in question must serve to denominate a type, a kind, a genus or a subcategory of goods.

It is important to observe the distinction between "*common* descriptive" (or generic) terms and "*merely* descriptive" terms:

> The provisions of the Lanham Act ... distinguish a mark that is "the common descriptive *name* of an article or substance" from a mark that is "merely descriptive." §§ 2(e), 14(c), 15 U.S.C. §§ 1052(e), 1064(c). Marks that constitute a common descriptive *name* are referred to as generic. A generic term is one that refers to the *genus* of which the particular product is a species. Generic terms are not registerable.... A "merely descriptive" mark, in contrast, describes the *qualities or characteristics* of a good or service, and this type of mark may be registered only if the registrant shows that it has acquired secondary meaning, *i.e.*, it "has become distinctive of the applicant's goods in commerce." §§ 2(e), (f), 15 U.S.C. §§ 1052(e), (f).

Park 'n Fly, Inc. v. Dollar Park and Fly, Inc., 469 U.S. 189, 193–94, 105 S.Ct. 658, 661–62, 83 L.Ed.2d 582 (1985) (citation omitted) (emphasis added). In many circumstances, the difference between a common descriptive name and a merely descriptive mark is not easily visible to the naked eye.

Here, however, unlike "light beer," "tasty salad dressing" is not a kind, sort, genus or subcategory of salad dressing. Rather, "tasty" is "merely descriptive" and describes a quality found in many genuses of salad dressing. It is not an adjective which in any way serves to classify the noun to which it is attached. This kind of "merely descriptive" word can, at least in theory, convey a secondary meaning. "Merely descriptive" terms convey a quality or characteristic of the product. The term "tasty" describes the quality of the salad dressing. There really can be no suggestion that "tasty dressing" is a kind or type or subcategory of dressing such as, for example, French dressing.

* * *

There is no question that the word "tasty" as applied to salad dressing is *highly* descriptive. There appears to be absolutely nothing suggestive or arbitrary about the use of the adjective in this connection. There is some feeling that words may be so highly descriptive that they ought to be incapable of being removed from the public domain even if they are not in the traditional sense generic. Despite the occasional surfacing of this sentiment, however, it is not the law. The Trademark Trial and Appeal Board (the "TTAB") has recently held, for example, that "law & business" for business law seminar services is so "highly descriptive" that it is incapable of serving as a mark and is unregistrable on the Supplemental Register. *In re Harcourt Brace Jovanovich, Inc.*, 222 USPQ (BNA) 820 (TTAB 1984) (citing other TTAB cases). The

Court of Appeals for the Federal Circuit has, however, apparently disapproved of the idea that a term may be so "highly descriptive" that it is incapable of ever becoming a trademark.

Thus far, at least, only generic terms are viewed as being incapable of gaining protection by acquiring secondary meaning, including, of course, terms that can be reasonably construed as generic names, such as "light" in connection with beer. We recognize that the law has traditionally treated the interest of the public in preserving generic names for general use as so important as to preclude trademark protection. Nonetheless, we do not believe it appropriate at this time to expand further the "generic" concept by extending it to "tasty" as used with salad dressing. Even if Henri's were able to establish secondary meaning for such a highly descriptive adjective, competitors would not be precluded from using it in a purely descriptive manner or in its primary sense.

Notes and Questions

1. *Trademark rights in highly descriptive words.* Should merchants be prohibited from obtaining rights in highly descriptive words, like "tasty," regardless of the existence of secondary meaning?

2. *Misspellings, abbreviations and foreign-language equivalents.* As the *Henri's* court points out, merchants cannot avoid a finding of genericness by simply misspelling the word at issue, as long as the public can still recognize the generic meaning. Likewise, an abbreviation of a generic term is generic, if it still conveys the original generic connotation. For example, in National Conference of Bar Examiners v. Multistate Legal Studies, Inc., 692 F.2d 478, 216 U.S.P.Q. 279 (7th Cir.1982), *cert. denied* 464 U.S. 814, 104 S.Ct. 69, 78 L.Ed.2d 83 (1983), the court found both the term "Multistate Bar Examination" and its abbreviation, "MBE" to be generic, and available for use by a business that prepared students to take the exam.

Under the doctrine of foreign equivalents, foreign words are treated as generic when, if translated, they would be the generic name of the product or service they identify. On this basis, for example, the TTAB has refused to register the French words "le sorbet" as a mark for fruit ice, *In re* Le Sorbet, Inc., 228 U.S.P.Q. 27 (T.T.A.B. 1985). In Weiss Noodle Co. v. Golden Cracknel & Specialty Co., 290 F.2d 845, 129 U.S.P.Q. 411 (1961), the Court of Customs and Patent Appeals found the term "Ha–Lush-ka" to be a hyphenated, phonetically spelled version of the Hungarian word "haluska," which means egg noodles. For that reason, it was generic and could not be registered as a trademark for egg noodle products. What is the justification for this rule?

The fact that a generic term is incorporated into a composite mark does not preclude registration or common-law protection of the composite mark, as long as the combination of elements is itself distinctive. Recognition of rights in the composite mark, however, gives no rights in the generic term by itself. Thus, the mark "Coca Cola" is an enforceable mark, though the

Coca Cola Company has no right to prevent others from using the word "cola" in their own composite marks. Likewise, the user of a distinctive decorative design that incorporates a generic term may prevent use of the term only as it is incorporated into the design.

2. *Descriptive marks and Lanham Act section 2(e)*

§ 1052. (§ 2) Trademarks Registrable on Principal Register

No trademark by which the goods of the applicant may be distinguished from the goods of others shall be refused registration on the principal register on account of its nature unless it—

* * *

(e) Consists of a mark which, (1) when used on or in connection with the goods of the applicant is merely descriptive or deceptively misdescriptive of them, or (2) when used on or in connection with the goods of the applicant is primarily geographically descriptive of them, except as indications of regional origin may be registrable under section 4, (3) when used on or in connection with the goods of the applicant is primarily geographically deceptively misdescriptive of them, or (4) is primarily merely a surname.

(f) Except as expressly excluded in paragraphs (a),(b),(c),(d) and (e)(3) of this section, nothing in this chapter shall prevent the registration of a mark used by the applicant which has become distinctive of the applicant's goods in commerce. The Commissioner may accept as prima facie evidence that the mark has become distinctive, as used on or in connection with the applicant's goods in commerce, proof of substantially exclusive and continuous use thereof as a mark by the applicant in commerce for the five years before the date on which the claim of distinctiveness is made. Nothing in this section shall prevent the registration of a mark which, when used on or in connection with the goods of the applicant, is primarily geographically deceptively misdescriptive of them, and which became distinctive of the applicant's goods in commerce before December 8, 1993.

15 U.S.C.A. § 1052.

The language of section 2's preamble itself can be understood to prevent registration of nondistinctive marks. Nonetheless, Lanham Act sections 2(e) and (f), read together, specifically provide that the enumerated categories of marks, which traditionally have been viewed as nondistinctive at common law, cannot be registered without a demonstration of secondary meaning (or, in the language of subsection (f), a demonstration that the mark "has become distinctive.") A review of these categories is useful.

a. *Marks That Are Merely Descriptive or Deceptively Misdescriptive*

20TH CENTURY WEAR, INC. v. SANMARK–STARDUST INC.

United States Court of Appeals for the Second Circuit, 1984
747 F.2d 81, 224 U.S.P.Q. 98, *cert. denied*
470 U.S. 1052, 105 S.Ct. 1755, 84 L.Ed.2d 818 (1985).

* * *

As one of the leading commentators reminds us, a term can be descriptive in two ways. It can literally describe the product, or it can describe the purpose or utility of the product. Under the first branch, "if qualities, ingredients, effects or other features of the product are indicated naturally and in ordinary language, so that the consumer understands its significance without any exercise of the imagination, the words are descriptive" * * *. Under the second branch, Callmann distinguishes among three subcategories of marks that describe the product's purpose or utility: (1) marks describing the problem or condition that the trademarked product is designed to remedy or otherwise deal with; (2) marks that describe the use to which the product or service is put; and (3) marks that describe the effect that the product or service is supposed to produce after it is used. * * * 3 R. Callmann, The Law of Unfair Competition, Trademarks and Monopolies § 18.05 (L. Altman 4th ed. 1983).

* * *

Notes and Questions

1. *The overall commercial impression.* To judge whether a mark is descriptive, one must consider the overall commercial impression the mark would make on the average prospective purchaser. When the mark contains more than one element (that is, when the mark is a "composite mark"), then one must evaluate the impression made by the mark as a whole, resisting the urge to break it into its constituent elements. It is not unusual to find that combining two or more descriptive elements results in a mark that is more than the sum of its elements and is inherently distinctive. See, e.g., Minnesota Mining and Manufacturing Co. v. Johnson & Johnson, 454 F.2d 1179, 172 U.S.P.Q. 491 (C.C.P.A.1972) ("skinvisible" not merely descriptive of transparent medical tape). Moreover, combining descriptive elements with distinctive elements generally makes the mark as a whole nondescriptive. See, e.g., *In re* Clutter Control Inc., 231 U.S.P.Q. 588 (T.T.A.B. 1986) (descriptive words "Construct–A–Closet" combined with tube-like rendition of a double "C" for shelf components held not merely descriptive). Since rights in composite marks are in the mark as a whole, competitors need not be deprived of the individual descriptive components.

When a mark has two possible connotations, one descriptive and the other not, it is less likely to be deemed descriptive. For example, the phrase "sugar and spice" for bakery products not only describes ingredients of the products but also invokes the nursery rhyme, "sugar and spice and everything nice." In Application of Colonial Stores, Inc., 394 F.2d 549, 157 U.S.P.Q. 382 (C.C.P.A.1968), the court found this phrase not merely descriptive, because of its "reminiscent, suggestive, or associative connotation" with a non-descriptive idea.

As discussed in connection with generic terms, for purposes of classifying a mark, foreign words are translated into English and then judged for descriptiveness or genericness. Recognized abbreviations are treated as though they were the abbreviated words. Misspelled words are treated as though properly spelled, as long as the phonetic identity between the misspelled word and the descriptive word remains. For example, the mark "C-thru" has been treated as the equivalent of the descriptive term "see-through." C–Thru Ruler Co., v. Needleman, 190 U.S.P.Q. 93 (E.D.Pa.1976).

How would you classify the following marks?

— "Supreme" as a mark for wine (Supreme Wine Co. v. American Distilling Co., 310 F.2d 888, 135 U.S.P.Q. 481 (2d Cir.1962))

— "Bufferin" for buffered aspirin (Wise v. Bristol–Myers Co., 107 F.Supp. 800, 94 U.S.P.Q. 327 (S.D.N.Y. 1952))

— "Season–All" for aluminum storm windows (Aluminum Fabricating Co. v. Season–All Window Corp. 259 F.2d 314, 119 U.S.P.Q. 61 (2d Cir.1958))

— "Volkswagen" for cars (Volkswagenwerk Aktiengesellschaft v. Church, 256 F.Supp. 626, 150 U.S.P.Q. 338 (S.D.Cal.1966), *affirmed* 411 F.2d 350, 161 U.S.P.Q. 769 (9th Cir.1969))

— "Escape from the Ordinary" for unusual clothing (Norm Thompson Outfitters, Inc. v. General Motors Corp., 448 F.2d 1293, 171 U.S.P.Q. 328 (9th Cir.1971))

— "Hula Hoop" for toy plastic hoops (In re WHAM–O Mfg. Co., 134 U.S.P.Q. 447 (T.T.A.B. 1962))

— "Kwix–Tart" for electric storage batteries (Andrew J. McPartland, Inc. v. Montgomery Ward & Co., 164 F.2d 603, 76 U.S.P.Q. 97 (1947), *cert. denied* 333 U.S. 875, 68 S.Ct. 904, 92 L.Ed. 1151 (1948))

— "Rocktober" for October rock music broadcast (Metromedia, Inc. v. American Broadcasting Cos., Inc., 210 U.S.P.Q. 21 (S.D.N.Y.1980))

— "V–8" for juice made from eight kinds of vegetables (Standard Brands, Inc. v. Smidler, 151 F.2d 34, 66 U.S.P.Q. 337 (2d Cir.1945))

2. *Deceptively misdescriptive marks.* When will a mark be "deceptively misdescriptive?" How does a deceptively misdescriptive mark differ from a deceptive mark, for which registration is prohibited under Lanham Act section 2(a), 15 U.S.C.A. § 1052(a)? Why require secondary meaning to register deceptively misdescriptive marks? Why recognize or register them at all? Consider, by way of analogy, the following case.

b. Marks That Are Primarily Geographically Descriptive or Deceptively Misdescriptive

IN RE NANTUCKET, INC.

United States Court of Customs and Patent Appeals, 1982.
677 F.2d 95, 213 U.S.P.Q. 889.

MARKEY, CHIEF JUDGE.

Nantucket, Inc. (Nantucket) appeals from a decision of the Trademark Trial and Appeal Board (board) affirming a refusal to register the mark NANTUCKET for men's shirts on the ground that it is "primarily geographically deceptively misdescriptive." We reverse.

BACKGROUND

On March 13, 1978, Nantucket, based in North Carolina, filed application serial number 162,716 for registration of NANTUCKET for men's shirts on the principal register * * *.

Refusal to register was based on § 2(e)(2) of the Lanham Act, 15 U.S.C. § 1052(e)(2) * * *.

The examiner, citing a dictionary definition of "Nantucket" as an island in the Atlantic Ocean south of Massachusetts, concluded that the mark NANTUCKET was either primarily geographically descriptive or primarily geographically deceptively misdescriptive, depending upon whether Nantucket's shirts did or did not come from Nantucket Island.

Nantucket informed the PTO that its shirts "do not originate from Nantucket Island," and insisted that the mark would not be understood by purchasers as representing that the shirts were produced there because the island has no market place significance vis-a-vis men's shirts. Nantucket further asserted that the phrase "when applied to the goods of the applicant," indicates a congressional intent that "descriptiveness" not be determined in a vacuum, but only in connection with the nature of an applicant's goods. As applied to shirts, it was argued, NANTUCKET is arbitrary and nondescriptive, because there is no association in the public mind of men's shirts with Nantucket Island.

The examiner's final refusal was based on the view that, because the shirts did not come from Nantucket Island, NANTUCKET is "primarily geographically deceptively misdescriptive."

* * *

In affirming the refusal to register here, the board referred to *In re Amerise*, 160 USPQ 687 (TTAB 1969) and *Charles S. Loeb Pipes*, as setting criteria for determining registrability of geographic terms. In its opinion in this case, the board set forth a test based on those criteria:

> (a) whether the term conveys to consumers primarily or immediately a geographical connotation, i.e., whether it conveys a readily recognizable geographical significance to the average consumer (if not, the mark is registrable); (b) if so, whether the applicant's goods

> or services do in fact come from the place so named (if they do, the term is primarily geographically descriptive; if they do not, it is primarily geographically deceptively misdescriptive); and (c) if the term conveys primarily a geographical connotation and the goods or services of the applicant do not come from the place so named, whether the use of the term is calculated, by plan, design, or implication, to deceive the public as to the geographical origin of the goods bearing the mark (if so, the mark is deceptive and falls within the absolute prohibition of Section 2(a)).[1]

* * * Regarding § 2(e)(2), the board said:

> [A]ny term which, when applied to the goods or services of the applicant, conveys to consumers primarily or immediately a geographical connotation is precluded from registration under Section 2(e)(2) notwithstanding the fact that the area or place named is not "noted for" goods or services of that type * * *.

The board concluded that the "term 'NANTUCKET' has a readily recognizable geographic meaning, and ... no alternative non-geographic significance ... and hence falls within the proscription of Section 2(e)(2)."

OPINION

The Board's Test

The board correctly notes that its test for registrability of geographic terms is "easy to administer" and "*minimizes* subjective determinations by eliminating any need to make unnecessary inquiry into the nebulous question of whether the public associates particular goods with a particular geographical area in applying Section 2(e)(2)." (Emphasis in original.) Ease-of-administration considerations aside, the board's approach does raise the question of whether public association of goods with an area must be considered in applying § 2(e)(2). That question is one of first impression in this court. We answer in the affirmative.

The board's test rests mechanistically on the one question of whether the mark is recognizable, at least to some large segment of the public, as the name of a geographical area. NANTUCKET is such. That ends the board's test. Once it is found that the mark is the name of a known place, i.e., that it has "a readily recognizable geographic meaning," the next question, whether applicant's goods do or do not come from that place, becomes irrelevant under the board's test, for if they do, the mark is "primarily geographically descriptive"; if they don't, the mark is "primarily geographically deceptively misdescriptive." Either way, the result is the same, for the mark must be denied registration on the principal register unless resort can be had to § 2(f).

1. Section 2(a) of the Lanham Act, 15 U.S.C. § 1052(a) provides in pertinent part: "No trademark ... shall be refused registration ... unless it— (a) consists of or comprises immoral, deceptive, or scandalous matter...."

The Statute

One flaw in the board's test resides in its factoring out the nature of applicant's goods, in contravention of § 2(e)(2)'s requirement that the mark be evaluated "when applied to the goods of the applicant," and that registration be denied only when the mark is geographically descriptive or deceptively misdescriptive "of them" (the goods).

Another flaw in the board's test lies in its failure to give appropriate weight to the presence of "deceptively" in § 2(e)(2). If the goods do not originate in the geographic area denoted by the mark, the mark might in a vacuum be characterized as geographically misdescriptive, but the statutory characterization required for denial of registration is "geographically *deceptively* misdescriptive." (Emphasis supplied.) Before that statutory characterization may be properly applied, there must be a reasonable basis for believing that purchasers are likely to be deceived.[5]

Thus, the board's test does not track the statute. Moreover, in rendering functionless the phrase "when applied to the goods of the applicant" and the word "deceptively," the test violates a cardinal rule of statutory construction, i.e., that a legislature is presumed to have used no superfluous words. * * *

Public Association

Geographic terms are merely a specific kind of potential trademark, subject to characterization as having a particular kind of descriptiveness or misdescriptiveness. Registration of marks that would be perceived by potential purchasers as describing or deceptively misdescribing the goods themselves may be denied under § 2(e)(1). Registration of marks that would be perceived by potential purchasers as describing or deceptively misdescribing the geographic origin of the goods may be denied under § 2(e)(2). In either case, the mark must be judged on the basis of its role in the marketplace.

As the courts have made plain, geographically deceptive misdescriptiveness cannot be determined without considering whether the public associates the goods with the place which the mark names. If the goods do not come from the place named, and the public makes no goods-place association, the public is not deceived and the mark is accordingly not geographically deceptively misdescriptive.

In *World Carpets, Inc. v. Dick Littrell's New World Carpets*, 438 F.2d 482, 486, 168 USPQ 609, 612–13 (CA 5 1971), the court said: "[T]he wording of the statute makes it plain that not all terms which are geographically suggestive are unregistrable.... Indeed, the statutory language declares nonregistrable only those words which are 'primarily geographically descriptive.' The word 'primarily' should not be overlooked, for it is not the intent of the federal statute to refuse registration

5. Reasonable persons are unlikely to believe that bananas labeled ALASKA originated or were grown in Alaska. On the other hand, reasonable persons are quite likely to believe that salmon labeled ALASKA originated in the waters of that state. * * *

of a mark where the geographic meaning is minor, obscure, remote, or *unconnected with the goods*." (Emphasis added.) Thus, if there be no connection of the geographical meaning of the mark with the goods in the public mind, that is, if the mark is arbitrary when applied to the goods, registration should not be refused under § 2(e)(2).

In *National Lead Co. v. Wolfe*, 223 F.2d 195, 199, 105 USPQ 462, 465 (CA 9), *cert. denied*, 350 U.S. 883, 76 S.Ct. 135, 100 L.Ed. 778, 107 USPQ 362 (1955), the court held that neither DUTCH, nor DUTCH BOY, as applied to paint, was used "otherwise than in a fictitious, arbitrary and fanciful manner," and noted that "there is no likelihood that the use of the name 'Dutch' or 'Dutch Boy' in connection with the appellant's goods would be understood by purchasers as representing that the goods or their constituent materials were produced or processed in Holland or that they are of the same distinctive kind or quality as those produced, processed or used in that place."

* * *

The Present Case

Section 2(e)(2) provides that registration shall not be refused unless the mark is primarily geographically deceptively misdescriptive of the goods. The only indication of record that NANTUCKET is primarily a geographical term resides in dictionary listings referring to Nantucket Island as a summer resort and former whaling center. There is no evidence of record to support a holding that the mark NANTUCKET as applied to men's shirts is "deceptively misdescriptive." There is no indication that the purchasing public would expect men's shirts to have their origin in Nantucket when seen in the market place with NANTUCKET on them. Hence buyers are not likely to be deceived, and registration cannot be refused on the ground that the mark is "primarily geographically deceptively misdescriptive."

Accordingly, the decision of the board is *reversed*.

NIES, JUDGE, concurring.

I join the court's holding that there must be an indication that "the purchasing public would expect men's shirts to have their origin in Nantucket when seen in the marketplace with NANTUCKET on them." Moreover, I agree that on the present record the board's decision holding that NANTUCKET for men's shirts is "primarily geographically deceptively misdescriptive" must be reversed. I choose to concur, however, because I reach the same conclusion from a different direction, and because the court leaves open what the PTO must show to make a prima facie case under § 2(e)(2) with respect to this application.

Appellant had urged that the court adopt the rule that a goods/place association can be established under § 2(e)(2) only if the place identified by the geographic name claimed as a mark was "noted for" the goods, like IDAHO for potatoes or PARIS for perfume. The standard of registrability enunciated by the court has not been restricted to such a stringent test. To have done so would have created as rigid a rule in favor of registration as the board had used to deny registration. If a geographic name were arbitrary in the absence of a reputation for the goods, any trader who is the *first* to use any geographic name for particular goods would, thereby, appropriate it to his exclusive use. Moreover, the rationale advanced by appellant is not limited to geographic names of places where the likelihood of future commercial exploitation by others is small but would be equally applicable if the claimed mark for shirts were CHICAGO. The answer to the basic question of public association of goods with a place, i.e., geographic descriptiveness, cannot be decided on this simplistic basis.

My reasons for rejection of appellant's position, which are based on concepts from the common law, more than on statutory construction, are set out herein.

Applicable Common Law Concepts

Protection and registration of geographic names as marks embodies concepts comparable to those applicable to surnames as well as to terms which are descriptive of the nature or quality of goods or services. A geographic name might appropriately be viewed as a hybrid in this respect. Courts do not readily recognize trademark rights in such names or terms because of the legitimate interests of other merchants in truthfully being able to use them in connection with their own wares or services.

In determining whether a geographic term is registrable under the Lanham Act and upon what conditions, the first question is whether the name is primarily of geographic significance but, contrary to the board's view, that does not end the matter.

A geographic term may be used in a manner which is (1) inherently distinctive, which includes arbitrary and suggestive usage, (2) generic, (3) descriptive, (4) deceptively misdescriptive, or, (5) deceptive. Different consequences flow from the finding of what is the appropriate category or categories for the mark, which to some extent overlap. In any event, such a determination can only be made by consideration of the specific goods on which the name or term is used. In every case the issue which must be resolved is: What meaning, if any, does the term convey to the public with respect to the goods on which the name is used?

In resolving the question of registrability of geographic names, the development of the law with respect to protection of such terms provides guidance. Basic to consideration of the registrability and protectibility of any geographic term as a trademark is the routine commercial practice of merchants, whether they are growers, manufacturers, distributors, or local retailers, in placing the name of their location on their goods or using the name in their trade names. Because the public would be aware of common trade practice, the common law originally deemed all use of geographic names wholly *informational* and unprotectible. It was believed such names could not function and, in any event, should not be recognized as the identification of a single source. Thus, we must start with the concept that a geographic name of a place of business is a descriptive term when used on the goods of that business. There is a public goods/place association, in effect, presumed.

However, as with other terms which are descriptive when first used, it came to be recognized that through substantially exclusive and extensive use, a merchant might develop a protectible goodwill in such a geographically descriptive name upon proof that the name ceased being informational to the public and came to indicate a source of goods. Thus, if a manufacturer located in Chicago were to display the name CHICAGO on his shirts, for example, it has been the law for over a century that he could prevent another's subsequent use only if he could establish "secondary meaning" in the term. Until secondary meaning has been developed in a descriptive term, the public cannot be confused that the term indicates source in a particular user and others are free to make comparable use of the term. While a merchant in Chicago will not be deprived of his right to use the name in a non-trademark display if another acquires trademark rights in CHICAGO, he does become limited in the choice of marks for related goods or services and must operate, thereafter, under the constraints of avoiding likelihood of confusion with CHICAGO per se for shirts. It is, thus, to his advantage to have the term remain in the public domain and he can take appropriate steps to keep it there by using the name himself.

Statutory Application of the Common Law

These concepts, which balance the interests of different persons, are embodied in § 2(e)(2) of the Lanham Act, which provides that a term which is primarily geographically descriptive is initially unregistrable; and § 2(f), which allows registration on a showing of distinctiveness.

Since the mark CHICAGO is, thus, unregistrable even to a Chicago manufacturer who is the first to use that name for shirts without a showing of distinctiveness, one cannot accept, as urged by appellant, that the law recognizes better rights, ipso facto, in a company not located there which happens to be the first to use that name for shirts. It is simply illogical to say that CHICAGO is descriptive of shirts if the manufacturer is located in Chicago, but arbitrary, if he is not located there. The public is not aware of the actual locations of most businesses. The public is aware of trade practice and makes, or is presumed likely to make, a goods/place association in either instance. Nor is it any less objectionable to a Chicago merchant if the term is used by a non-local rather than another local merchant.

* * * A geographic name is not unprotectible or unregistrable because it can be labelled a geographic name, but because it tells the public something about the product or the producer about which his competitor also has a right to inform the public. Thus, the names of places devoid of commercial activity are arbitrary usage.

In this category are names of places such as ANTARCTICA, MOUNT EVEREST, or GALAPAGOS, at least when used for ordinary commercial products, such as beer and shoes. Names such as SUN,

WORLD, GLOBE, MARS, or MILKY WAY are also arbitrary, not informational; competitors do not need to use the terms to compete effectively. If the pertinent issue is kept in mind, the question of geographic descriptiveness or its corollary, deceptive misdescriptiveness, can more easily be resolved.

* * *

The rejection of the "noted for" test as the sole basis for the rejection under § 2(e)(2), of course, does not determine whether NANTUCKET on shirts is or is not registrable. The question remains: Are purchasers likely to believe NANTUCKET is descriptive in that it identifies the location of the source of the shirts?

* * * In my view, it is incumbent on the PTO to put forth evidence that other businesses have or are likely to have legitimate interests in use of the geographic name claimed by the applicant. * * *

Notes and Questions

1. *Primarily geographically descriptive.* The *Nantucket* court was discussing Lanham Act section 2(e) as it existed before being amended by the North American Free Trade Agreement ("NAFTA") Implementation Act, Pub. L. No. 103–182, 107 Stat. 2057 (1993). Prior to the amendment, subsection (e)(2) prohibited the registration of either "primarily geographically descriptive or deceptively misdescriptive" marks. Subsection (f) then provided that both types of marks could be registered upon a showing that the mark had "become distinctive of the applicant's goods in commerce." The amended subsections (e) and (f) now differentiate primarily geographically descriptive and primarily geographically deceptively misdescriptive marks and provide that with regard to the latter, only those marks that became distinctive of the applicant's goods prior to the North American Free Trade Agreement Implementation Act enactment date (December 8, 1993) may be registered.

The amendment was necessitated by Article 1712 of NAFTA:

> Each party shall * * * refuse to register, or invalidate the registration of, a trademark containing or consisting of a geographical indication with respect to goods that do not originate in the indicated territory, region or locality, if use of the indication in the trademark for the goods is of such a nature as to mislead the public as to the geographic origin of the good.

What is the purpose of conditioning rights in geographically descriptive marks on a showing of secondary meaning? Does the *Nantucket* court's decision efficiently further that purpose?

In rejecting an application for registration, the PTO must make a prima facie showing that the mark fails to qualify for registration under one of the provisions of Lanham Act section 2. According to the *Nantucket* decision, in the case of rejections on the ground that the mark is primarily geographically descriptive or misdescriptive, the PTO must make a prima facie showing that the public understands the mark to indicate the geographic origin of the goods. What evidence might be available for this purpose, and what would be deemed sufficient to shift the burden of proof to the applicant?

In *In re* Loew's Theatres, Inc., 769 F.2d 764, 226 U.S.P.Q. 865 (C.A.F.C. 1985), Judge Nies, now writing for the majority on the Court of Appeals for the Federal Circuit, addressed this issue. In *Loew's*, the applicant sought to register "Durango" as a mark for chewing tobacco. The PTO rejected the application on the ground that the mark was primarily geographically deceptively misdescriptive of the goods (since they did not come from Durango), and no showing of secondary meaning had been made. In support of the rejection, the examiner cited references indicating that Durango was a populous state and city in Mexico and that tobacco was an important crop of the Durango, Mexico area. Based on this evidence, he found that it would be reasonable for the purchasing public to expect chewing tobacco bearing the name Durango to have its origin in that area. The Court of Appeals found the evidence that tobacco was a crop of Durango a sufficient prima facie showing of a public goods/place association:

> While the [*Nantucket* decision] requires a goods/place association to support a refusal to register under § 2(e)(2), it does not follow that such association embraces only instances where the place is well-known or noted for the goods * * *. Rather, our precedent continues to hold that to establish a "primarily geographically deceptively misdescriptive" bar, the PTO must show only a reasonable basis for concluding that the public is likely to believe the mark identifies the place from which the goods originate and that the goods do not come from there. * * *
>
> [The applicant] attacks the sufficiency of the evidence of record on several grounds:
>
> 1. The Gazetteer relied upon by the PTO shows that Durango is also the name of towns in Colorado and in Spain. Therefore, per appellant, Durango would not be associated with Mexico's tobacco region of that name.
>
> 2. The PTO produced no evidence that the public would actually make the asserted association.
>
> Contrary to LTI's position, we conclude that the PTO made a prima facie showing of a goods/place association between tobacco and the geographic name Durango. Durango (Mexico) is not an obscure place name to the Mexican population of this country nor to reasonably informed non-Mexicans. The cited Gazetteer shows tobacco to be one in a short list of principal crops of the region. No more can be expected from the PTO in the way of proof. The PTO does not have means to conduct a marketing survey as LTI would require. The practicalities of the limited resources available to the PTO are routinely taken into account in reviewing its administrative action. * * * We affirm that a prima facie case can be established by the type of evidence of record here where the question concerns the registrability of a geographic name.
>
> Finally, it does not detract from the prima facie case made by the PTO that there are a few other uses of Durango as a geographic name, such as Durango, Colorado. The PTO's burden is simply to establish that there is a reasonable predicate for its conclusion that the public

> would be likely to make the particular goods/place association on which it relies. That there is more than one place bearing the name or that one place is better known than another is not dispositive. The issue is not the fame or exclusivity of the place name, but the likelihood that a particular place will be associated with particular goods. Thus, the mark DURANGO for skis might also be barred (without proof of secondary meaning) if it were shown that Durango, Colorado, is a ski resort.

Id., 769 F.2d at 767–69, 226 U.S.P.Q. at 867–68.

2. *Marks certifying regional origin.* What are the implications of the reference in Lanham Act section 2(e)(2) to "indications of regional origin * * * registrable under section 4?" See Community of Roquefort v. William Faehndrich, Inc., 303 F.2d 494, 133 U.S.P.Q. 633 (2d Cir.1962).

c. *Marks That Are Primarily Merely a Surname*

EX PARTE RIVERA WATCH CORPORATION

Commissioner of Patents, 1955.
106 U.S.P.Q. 145.

LEADS, ASSISTANT COMMISSIONER.

Application has been filed to register "Rivera," displayed in a stylized script with a paraph extending from the initial "R" beneath the rest of the word, for watches. Use is claimed since June 18, 1952. Registration has been denied on the ground that "Rivera" is primarily merely a surname, and applicant has appealed.

Applicant admits that "Rivera" is, in fact, a surname, but contends that it is not primarily merely a surname within the meaning of the statute, particularly since it is a Spanish word meaning a small stream or rivulet.

The examiner's position is stated as follows:

> * * * [S]urname meaning of a word is its primary meaning, and the alternative meaning of the word can only be given weight insofar as it is sufficiently well known to replace the surname significance in the public mind. The examiner does not believe that the Spanish meaning of the word "Rivera" accomplishes that purpose.
>
> It is believed that the public would readily recognize the word as a surname, whereas it could not be expected to be aware of a somewhat obscure foreign language meaning. As a result, the primary significance of the word is a surname.
>
> The primary meaning of a word is its principal or ordinary one, that is, the meaning which is most prominent and most likely to be recognized readily.
>
> When a word is regarded to be primarily a surname, the granting of exclusive use to one person is prohibited by the Trademark Act of 1946, for such exclusive use would interfere with the

rights of the bearers of the surname, regardless of the number of persons bearing the name, and regardless of the manner in which the name may happen to be displayed.

The decisions interpreting the phrase "primarily merely a surname" are not altogether consistent, nor do they establish clear guide lines for future determinations.

In Ex parte Dallioux, 83 USPQ 262 (Comer., 1949), "Andre Dallioux" was held not to be primarily merely a surname and therefore registrable, since it comprises the entire name of an individual in which the surname was not unduly emphasized.

In Ex parte Kimberly–Clark, 83 USPQ 437 (Comer., 1949), "Kimberly–Clark" was held to be unregistrable, since it is a combination of two surnames, and it is clearly apparent that each is primarily merely a surname.

In Ex parte Reeves Brothers, Inc., 84 USPQ 19 (Comer., 1949), "Reeves" was held to be unregistrable, since it is primarily merely a surname. It was stated that "The fact that other meanings may exist does not necessarily indicate that a word would ordinarily have other than its primary meaning, and the fact that lexicographers or others might recognize a possible unusual meaning is not controlling. * * * The situation here presented is not similar to that of [a] surname, the meaning of which would not immediately be clear, even as applied to particular products. The meaning naturally attributed to it by the public would, in my opinion, be that of a surname, and as used in this application, it is clearly a surname and would be recognized as such."

In Ex parte Goodall–Sanford, Inc., 88 USPQ 26 (Comer., 1950), "Cellini" was held to be unregistrable on the ground that it is primarily merely a surname.

In Ex parte The Wayne Pump Company, 88 USPQ 437, 440 (Comer., 1951), "Wayne" was held to be unregistrable on the ground that it is primarily merely a surname, even though it is also a geographical name, as well as a name having historical significance. Applicant's argument that "Wayne" is a rare or uncommon surname was disposed of by the following statement: "Aside from the fact that 'Wayne' is not considered a rare or uncommon surname, nothing is found in the language of the statute or elsewhere making a distinction between rare surnames and common surnames. A rare and uncommon surname used as a surname and nothing else may be even more primarily merely a surname than others."

In Ex parte Stylofede Corporation, 92 USPQ 388 (Comer., 1952), "Windsor" was held not to be primarily merely a surname, but primarily a geographical name.

In Sears, Roebuck & Co. v. Watson, 96 USPQ 360 (C.A. D.C., March 12, 1953), "J C Higgins" was held to be unregistrable (affirming the decisions of the District Court and the Commissioner) on the ground that "Higgins" without the initials is primarily merely a surname and the initials are not sufficient to prevent the mark from consisting of "primarily merely a surname." The court referred to the conclusion reached in the Andre Dallioux case, apparently with approval.

In Ex parte I. Lewis Cigar Mfg. Co., 98 USPQ 265, 266, 267 (C.C.P.A., June 24, 1953), "S. Seidenberg & Co's." was held to be unregistrable on the ground that it is primarily merely a surname. The court said: "It seems to us that 'Seidenberg' is clearly a surname which can have no other meaning or significance than that of a surname. Nor do we believe that the addition of the single initial is sufficient to remove it from that category. Further, the addition of the expression ' & Co's.', whether it be in the abbreviated and possessive form present here, or in the usual form, cannot be held to distinguish or relate to anything except the surname 'Seidenberg'." The court in referring to the decision of the Commissioner in the "Dallioux" and "Higgins" cases, stated:

> "It seems to us that the Patent Office, in the difficult task of fairly interpreting the involved section, has adopted an inconsistent standard in its consideration of the two marks cited above. It would appear that had the reasoning employed in the Higgins case; namely, that 'Higgins' constituted the dominant part of the mark, been consistently employed, then that reasoning, when applied to 'Andre Dallioux', would necessarily have resulted in its rejection because 'Dallioux' is, in our opinion, the dominant part of that mark.
>
> "Conversely, it seems to us that the initials in the Higgins mark should have received equal consideration to that given 'Andre' in the Dallioux mark. We strongly doubt that Congress intended such a decisive distinction to be made between initials and given names in determining whether a mark is primarily merely a surname."

In Schnefel Bros. Corp. v. Crosston, 102 USPQ 442, 443 (Comer., 1954), where the mark "Crosston" was involved it was observed by way of footnote:

> "The application was originally filed for registration on the Principal Register, but registration was refused on the ground that the mark was 'deemed to be primarily merely a surname.' Although it does appear to be the surname of the applicant, it is extremely doubtful, in my opinion, that when used as a trademark it would be recognized by the purchasing public as a surname. Under such circumstances, I entertain considerable doubt that it is 'primarily merely a surname' within the meaning of Section 2(e) of the statute."

It is apparent from the foregoing that the interpretations leave much to be desired in establishing a pattern to be followed in administering the statutory provision. As a result, some marks are refused registration if they happen to be the name of the applicant or the person executing the papers for the applicant, whereas registration would issue if the mark did not appear to be the name of any person connected with the applicant. Such a position is untenable. If a mark is primarily merely a surname in one circumstance it is so in all circumstances, and vice versa.

The legislative history of the statute, including the testimony of the witnesses before the Congressional Committees, is just about as confused as the decisional law. * * *

Since neither the legislative history of the statute nor the decisions interpreting it provide a standard for administration, it seems highly desirable to attempt a reconciliation of the somewhat diverse views and establish a test which can be consistently applied.

The terms "primary" and "secondary" have well understood meanings in trademark law. In construing "primarily" in Section 2(e) of the statute, we should, it seems to me, draw on that meaning. A trademark is a trademark only if it is used in trade. When it is used in trade it must have some impact upon the purchasing public, and it is that impact or impression which should be evaluated in determining whether or not the primary significance of a word when applied to a product is a surname significance. If it is, *and it is only that*, then it is primarily merely a surname. "Reeves," "Higgins" and "Wayne" are thus primarily merely surnames. If the mark has well known meanings as a word in the language and the purchasing public, upon seeing it on the goods, may not attribute surname significance to it, it is not primarily merely a surname. "King," "Cotton," and "Boatman" fall in this category.

There are some names which by their very nature have only a surname significance even though they are rare surnames. "Seidenberg," if rare, would be in this class. And there are others which have no meaning-well known or otherwise-and are in fact surnames which do not, when applied to goods as trademarks, create the impression of being surnames.

It seems to me that the test to be applied in the administration of this provision in the Act is not the rarity of the name, nor whether it is the applicant's name, nor whether it appears in one or more telephone directories, nor whether it is coupled with a baptismal name or initials. The test should be: What is its primary significance to the purchasing public? Application of this test would have resulted in the same conclusions as were reached in the "Andre Dallioux" case, the "Reeves" case, the "Wayne" case, the "Windsor" case, the "Higgins" case, and the "Seidenberg" case. It might have resulted in different conclusions in the "Kimberly–Clark" case and the "Cellini" case.

Applying the test to the mark sought here to be registered, it is not believed that the average member of the purchasing public would, upon seeing "Rivera" used as a trademark on watches, be likely to think of its being a surname—even though it does not appear to have any meaning as a word in the language. The decision of the Examiner of Trademarks is reversed.

It is observed that the examiner exceeded his authority in holding that "When a word is regarded to be primarily merely a surname, the granting of exclusive use to one person is prohibited by the Trademark Act of 1946, for such exclusive use would interfere with the rights of the bearers of the surname * * *."[11] The Patent Office does not "grant exclusive use", but merely recognizes, within the boundaries delineated by statute, rights which have been acquired as a result of use.

Notes and Questions

1. *Primarily merely a surname.* In *Application of* Kahan & Weisz Jewelry Mfg. Corp., 508 F.2d 831, 184 U.S.P.Q. 421 (C.C.P.A.1975), the Court of Customs and Patent Appeals expressly adopted Assistant Commissioner Leads' approach to the surname issue. Is Commissioner Leads' standard for determining whether a mark is "primarily merely a surname" a manageable one? How would you evaluate the following marks:

— "Schaub–Lorenz" (*Application of* Standard Elecktrik Lorenz Aktiengesellschaft, 371 F.2d 870, 152 U.S.P.Q. 563 (C.C.P.A.1967))

— "Mr. King" (RESTATEMENT (THIRD) OF UNFAIR COMPETITION § 14, comment e (Tentative Draft No. 2, 1990))

— "Hutchinson Technology" (*In re* Hutchinson Technology Inc., 852 F.2d 552, 7 U.S.P.Q.2d 1490 (C.A.F.C. 1988))

— "Da Vinci" (Lucien Piccard Watch Co. v. Since 1868 Crescent Corp., 314 F.Supp. 329, 165 U.S.P.Q. 459 (S.D.N.Y.1970))

See generally Fowler, *When Are Surnames Registrable?,* 70 TRADEMARK REP. 66 (1980).

What kinds of evidence must the PTO provide to make a prima facie showing that a mark is primarily merely a surname? Compare *Kahan & Weisz, supra* (evidence of six listings of "Ducharme" in the Manhattan telephone directory, by itself, is insufficient) with *Application of* Harris–Intertype Corp., 518 F.2d 629, 186 U.S.P.Q. 238 (C.C.P.A.1975) (demonstration of 1100 listings of Harris in the Cleveland telephone directory and 800 listings in the Washington D.C. directory held sufficient to make a prima facie case. Applicant's evidence of use of "Harris" in Harris Teachers College; Harris Lake; Harris Place; Harris Street; Harris Avenue; harris hawk; harris's sparrow, harris's woodpecker; harris-buck and various towns and cities whose names included the word "Harris" was either "somewhat obscure" or represented "the normal naming of a place or other item after an individual."). See also *In re* Pohang Iron & Steel Co., 230 U.S.P.Q. 79 (T.T.A.B. 1986) (Evidence of eleven telephone listings of "Posten" and twelve media references to persons named "Posten" found in Nexis computer search held sufficient to make prima facie case.)

11. At one time in our commercial history trademarks were marks which indicated personal origin of goods; and it was during that period that the case law developed the maxim that every man has the right to use his own name in his own business. In the more complex commercial society of today, however, marks seldom indicate personal origin. The courts have recognized this fact and have frequently circumscribed the right of a person to use his own name in his own business when the natural result of such use is likely to lead to confusion or deception of the public. Congress also recognized it in enacting the Trademark Act of 1946 by limiting the defense of use of one's own name in his own business to use otherwise than as a trademark. (Sec. 33[a] of the Act) * * *.

2. *The reasons underlying the rule.* Two considerations have been cited to justify conditioning rights in personal names on a showing of secondary meaning. First, it can be argued that personal name marks, like the other marks covered under subsection (e), are descriptive of goods or services, so that consumers may not regard them as indicating origin. See, e.g., 2 J.T. McCARTHY, McCARTHY ON TRADEMARKS AND UNFAIR COMPETITION § 13.02[3] (3d ed. 1992) ("[A]ssuming that many persons have the name SMITH, the use of the name as a mark on goods will not, in the early stages of marketing, serve a trademark function. The name SMITH will merely describe to the public that someone named SMITH has something to do with the product.").

Second, there is a traditional interest in permitting individuals to use their own names in connection with their business. Courts have reasoned that this interest should be accommodated as fully as possible: no user should be able to exclude others from using a personal name unless he has secondary meaning, which makes exclusive rights necessary in order to avoid consumer confusion and appropriation of good will. As the Court of Appeals for the District of Columbia Circuit has explained:

> A seller's right to use his family name might have carried the day against a risk of buyer confusion in an era when the role of personal and localized reputation gave the right a more exalted status. In *Burgess v. Burgess*, 3 De G.M. & G. 896, 903–04, 43 Eng.Rep. 351, 354 (1853), the plaintiff's son had followed him into the trade of making anchovy paste; Lord Justice Bruce said: "All the Queen's subjects have a right, if they will, to manufacture and sell pickles and sauces, and not the less that their fathers have done so before them. All the Queen's subjects have a right to sell these articles in their own names, and not the less so that they bear the same name as their fathers." * * * But even quite old decisions have enjoined a second comer's use of his name where necessary to prevent confusion. The commentators, moreover, have been scornful of protecting the second comer's right to use his name at the expense of customer confusion, anathematizing it as the "sacred rights" theory. True, even recent decisions have invoked the right to use one's name, at least as an interest against which the senior user's are balanced. But its weight has decidedly diminished. The courts are now consistent in imposing tighter restrictions on the second comer in the face of possible confusion * * *; any residual protection of the second comer's use of his own name seems amply explained by the more general principle that an equitable remedy should be no broader than necessary to correct the wrong. * * *
>
> This trend in the law unsurprisingly reflects trends in the marketplace. In a world of primarily local trade, the goodwill of an anchovy paste seller may well have depended on his individual reputation within the community. Indeed, one elderly decision tells us that an entrepreneur's failure to use his family name once risked "the reproach of doing business under false colors." *Hat Corp.*, 4 F.Supp. at 623. By contrast, the court went on, "[i]n an age when by corporate activity, mass production, and national distribution, the truly personal element has been so largely squeezed out of business, there is naturally less legitimate pecuniary value in a family name." *Id.* That was in 1933 and the

> point is more obvious today. Other than understandable pride and sense of identity, the modern businessman loses nothing by losing the name. A junior user's right to use his name thus must yield to the extent its exercise causes confusion with the senior user's mark.

Basile, S.p.A. v. Basile, 899 F.2d 35, 39, 14 U.S.P.Q.2d 1240, 242–43 (D.C.Cir.1990).

In addition to justifying a requirement of secondary meaning, the interest in using one's name also influences the formulation of relief in trademark infringement cases. The Second Circuit's opinion in Taylor Wine Co. v. Bully Hill Vineyards, Inc., 569 F.2d 731, 196 U.S.P.Q. 593 (2d Cir.1978), is illustrative. In that case the well established plaintiff, founded in 1880 and the owner of thirteen federally registered "Taylor" trademarks for wine, sued Bully Hill Vineyards, owned by Walter S. Taylor, claiming that the defendant's use of the mark "Walter S. Taylor" for a new line of wines infringed its registered marks. In addition to featuring the name "Walter S. Taylor" in large letters, the defendant's labels also featured the words "original", "Owner of the Taylor Family Estate" and "Bully Hill." The Court of Appeals had no doubt that the defendant's use infringed the plaintiff's trademarks, and that it should be enjoined. The issue was how broad the injunction should be.

Noting the traditional respect for an individual's use of his name in business, the court recited what it regarded as the "guiding principle" in trademark surname cases: "Once an individual's name has acquired a secondary meaning in the marketplace, a later competitor who seeks to use the same or similar name must take 'reasonable precautions to prevent * * * mistake.'" *Id.*, 569 F.2d at 734, 196 U.S.P.Q. at 595. (quoting L.E. Waterman Co. v. Modern Pen Co., 235 U.S. 88, 94, 35 S.Ct. 91, 92, 59 L.Ed. 142, 146 (1914)). The court elaborated that

> the fact that an alleged infringer has previously sold his business with its goodwill to the plaintiff makes a sweeping injunction more tolerable. So, too, if an individual enters a particular line of trade for no apparent reason other than to use a conveniently confusing surname to his advantage, the injunction is unlikely to be unlimited.
>
> If, however, the second comer owns the company himself and evinces a genuine interest in establishing an enterprise in which his own skill or knowledge can be made known to the public, that argues in favor of allowing him to use his own name in some restricted fashion. * * *
>
> Speaking generally, when the defendant demonstrates a genuine desire to build a business under his own name, courts have been reluctant to proscribe all surname use whatever even though the defendant's conduct has been less than exemplary. * * * [T]he courts have given qualified relief which reflects "a judicious balancing of the countervailing interests of protecting an individual's use of his own name and the avoiding of confusion."

Id., 569 F.2d at 735–36, 196 U.S.P.Q. at 595 (quoting Friend v. H.A. Friend & Co., 416 F.2d 526, 534, 163 U.S.P.Q. 159 (9th Cir.1969), *cert. denied* 397 U.S. 914, 90 S.Ct. 916, 25 L.Ed.2d 94, 164 U.S.P.Q. 481 (1970)). The court ultimately concluded that the defendant could not use the "Taylor" name as a trademark, as such, but that it could show Walter S. Taylor's personal connection with Bully Hill. It could use Walter S. Taylor's signature on a Bully Hill label or advertisement, but only with appropriate disclaimer that he was not connected with, or a successor to, the Taylor Wine Company. It must also be restrained from using such words as "original" or "Owner of the Taylor Family Estate." *Id.*, 569 F.2d at 736, 196 U.S.P.Q. at 597.

C. NONFUNCTIONALITY

IN RE MORTON–NORWICH PRODUCTS, INC.

United States Court of Customs and Patent Appeals, 1982.
671 F.2d 1332, 213 U.S.P.Q. 9.

RICH, JUDGE.

This appeal is from the ex parte decision of the United States Patent and Trademark Office (PTO) Trademark Trial and Appeal Board (board) sustaining the examiner's refusal to register appellant's container configuration on the principal register. We reverse the holding on "functionality" and remand for a determination of distinctiveness.

BACKGROUND

Appellant's application seeks to register the following container configuration as a trademark for spray starch, soil and stain removers, spray cleaners for household use, liquid household cleaners and general grease removers, and insecticides:

Appellant owns U.S. Design Patent 238,655, issued Feb. 3, 1976, on the above configuration, and U.S. Patent 3,749,290, issued July 31, 1973, directed to the mechanism in the spray top.

The above-named goods constitute a family of products which appellant sells under the word-marks FANTASTIK, GLASS PLUS, SPRAY 'N WASH, GREASE RELIEF, WOOD PLUS, and MIRAKILL. Each of these items is marketed in a container of the same configuration but appellant varies the color of the body of the container according to the product. Appellant manufactures its own containers and stated in its application that:

> Since such first use (March 31, 1974) the applicant has enjoyed substantially exclusive and continuous use of the trademark (i.e., the

container) which has become distinctive of the applicant's goods in commerce.

[The examiner rejected the application on the grounds that the configuration was not distinctive and was functional. The TTAB upheld the examiner's decision, noting]:

> After a careful review of the evidence in the case before us, we cannot escape the conclusion that the container for applicant's products, *the configuration* of which it seeks to register, *is dictated primarily by functional (utilitarian) considerations*, and is therefore unregistrable despite any de facto secondary meaning which applicant's survey and other evidence of record might indicate. * * *

[Emphasis added by the court.]

* * *

OPINION

* * * The question is not new and in various forms we have been over the ground before: is the design sought to be registered "functional"? * * * We turn first to a consideration of the development of the law on "functionality."

A trademark is defined as "any word, name, symbol, or device or any combination thereof adopted and used by a manufacturer or merchant to *identify his goods* and distinguish them from those manufactured or sold by others" (emphasis ours). 15 U.S.C. § 1127 (1976). Thus, it was long the rule that a trademark must be something other than, and separate from, the merchandise to which it is applied.

Aside from the trademark/product "separateness" rationale for not recognizing the bare design of an article or its container as a trademark, it was theorized that all such designs would soon be appropriated, leaving nothing for use by would-be competitors. One court, for example, feared that "The forms and materials of packages to contain articles of merchandise * * * would be rapidly taken up and appropriated by dealers, until some one, bolder than the others, might go to the very root of things, and claim for his goods the primitive brown paper and tow string, as a peculiar property." *Harrington v. Libby*, 11 F.Cas. 605, 606 (C.C.S.D.N.Y.1877).

This limitation of permissible trademark subject matter later gave way to assertions that one or more features of a product or package design could legally function as a trademark. It was eventually held that the entire design of an article (or its container) could, without other means of identification, function to identify the source of the article and be protected as a trademark.

That protection was limited, however, to those designs of articles and containers, or features thereof, which were "nonfunctional." This requirement of "nonfunctionality" is not mandated by statute, but "is deduced entirely from court decisions." *In re Mogen David Wine Corp.*, 51 CCPA 1260, 1269, 328 F.2d 925, 932, 140 USPQ 575, 581 (1964)

(Rich, J., concurring). It has as its genesis the judicial theory that there exists a fundamental right to compete through imitation of a competitor's product, which right can only be *temporarily* denied by the patent or copyright laws:

> If one manufacturer should make an advance in effectiveness of operation, or in simplicity of form, or in utility of color; and if that advance did not entitle him to a monopoly by means of a machine or process or a product or a design patent; and if by means of unfair trade suits he could shut out other manufacturers who plainly intended to share in the benefits of unpatented utilities * * * he would be given gratuitously a monopoly more effective than that of the unobtainable patent in the ratio of eternity to seventeen years. [*Pope Automatic Merchandising Co. v. McCrum–Howell Co.*, 191 F. 979, 981–82 (7th Cir.1911).]

An exception to the right to copy exists, however, where the product or package design under consideration is "nonfunctional" and serves to identify its manufacturer or seller, and the exception exists even though the design is *not* temporarily protectible through acquisition of patent or copyright. Thus, when a design is "nonfunctional," the right to compete through imitation gives way, presumably upon balance of that right with the originator's right to prevent others from infringing upon an established symbol of trade identification.

This preliminary discussion leads to the heart of the matter—how do we define the concept of "functionality," and what role does the above balancing of interests play in that definitional process?

I. Functionality Defined

Many courts speak of the protectibility as trademarks of product and package configurations in terms of whether a particular design is "functional" or "nonfunctional." Without proper definition, however, such a distinction is useless for determining whether such design is registrable or protectible as a trademark, for the label "functional" has dual significance. It has been used, on the one hand, in lay fashion to indicate "the normal or characteristic action of anything," and, on the other hand, it has been used to denote a legal conclusion. * * *

Accordingly, it has been noted that one of the "distinct questions" involved in "functionality" reasoning is, "In what way is (the) subject matter functional or utilitarian, factually or legally?" *In re Honeywell, Inc.*, 497 F.2d 1344, 1350, 181 USPQ 821, 826 (CCPA 1974) (Rich, J., concurring). This definitional division * * * leads to the resolution that if the designation "functional" is to be utilized to denote the *legal* consequence, we must speak in terms of de facto functionality and de jure functionality, the former being the use of "functional" in the lay sense, indicating that although the design of a product, a container, or a feature of either is directed to performance of a function, it *may* be legally recognized as an indication of source. De jure functionality, of course, would be used to indicate the opposite—such a design may not be protected as a trademark.

This is only the beginning, however, for further definition is required to explain *how* a determination of whether a design is de jure functional is to be approached. * * *

* * * In *American-Marietta Co. v. Krigsman*, 275 F.2d 287, 289, 124 USPQ 320, 322 (2d Cir.1960), the court stated that "those features of the original goods that are not in any way essential to their use" may be termed "nonfunctional." But what does this statement mean? In the case at bar, for example, we cannot say that it means that the subject *design* is "functional" merely because a hollow body, a handhold, and a pump sprayer are "essential to its use." What this phrase must mean is not that the generic *parts* of the article or package are essential, but * * * that the particular *design* of the whole assembly of those parts must be essential. * * *

In *Luminous Unit Co. v. Williamson*, 241 F. 265 (N.D.Ill.1917), the court noted that "the owner of a fixture, machine, or device, patented or unpatented, who has obtained a trade in it, may simply exclude others from taking away that trade when they deceive the purchasing public as to the origin of the goods sold by them." *Id.* at 268. The court went on to state an exception to this rule, which is the public right to copy those "Necessary elements of mechanical construction, essential to the practical operation of a device, and which cannot be changed without either lessening the efficiency or materially increasing expense." *Id.* at 269. The court in *Diamond Match Co. v. Saginaw Match Co.*, 142 F. 727, 729 (6th Cir.1906), was of the same opinion. In response to a claim that the defendant was engaging in unfair competition by marketing matches with composite heads in two colors, the court, noting that the match was not protected by patent, stated that he who has a right to make a tipped match "has a right to put on it a head of two colors, so as to distinguish the tip on which the match should be struck, from the head itself. The two colors, therefore, serve not only a useful purpose but an essential function, for the very essence of the tipped match is the tip itself, which must be marked out by a color of its own." Another court framed the issue this way: Is the subject matter "made in the form it must be made if it is to accomplish its purpose"? *Marvel Co. v. Tullar Co.*, 125 F. 829, 830 (S.D.N.Y.1903).

Thus, it is clear that courts in the past have considered the public policy involved in this area of the law as, not the *right* to slavishly copy articles which are not protected by patent or copyright, but the *need* to copy those articles, which is more properly termed the right to compete *effectively*. Even the earliest cases, which discussed protectibility in terms of exhaustion of possible packaging forms, recognized that the real issue was whether "the effect would be to gradually throttle trade." *Harrington v. Libby*, supra at 606.

More recent cases also discuss "functionality" in light of competition. * * *

Given, then, that we must strike a balance between the "right to copy" and the right to protect one's method of trade identification, what weights do we set upon each side of the scale? That is, given that "functionality" is a question of fact, what facts do we look to in determining whether the "consuming public has an interest in making use of [one's design], superior to [one's] interest in being [its] sole vendor"? *Vaughan Novelty Mfg. Co. v. G. G. Greene Mfg. Corp.*, 202 F.2d 172, 176, 96 USPQ 277, 280 (3d Cir.), *cert. denied*, 346 U.S. 820, 74 S.Ct. 34, 98 L.Ed. 346, 99 USPQ 491 (1953).

II. Determining "Functionality"

A. In General

Keeping in mind, as shown by the foregoing review, that "functionality" is determined in light of "utility," which is determined in light of "superiority of design," and rests upon the foundation "essential to effective competition," there exist a number of factors, both positive and negative, which aid in that determination.

Previous opinions of this court have discussed what evidence is useful to demonstrate that a particular design is "superior." In *In re Shenango Ceramics, Inc.*, 53 CCPA 1268, 1273, 362 F.2d 287, 291, 150 USPQ 115, 119 (1966), the court noted that the existence of an expired utility patent which disclosed the *utilitarian advantage of the design* sought to be registered as a trademark was *evidence* that it was "functional." It may also be significant that the originator of the design touts its utilitarian advantages through advertising.

Since the effect upon competition "is really the crux of the matter," it is, of course, significant that there are other alternatives available. * * *

It is also significant that a particular design results from a comparatively simple or cheap method of manufacturing the article. In *Schwinn Bicycle Co. v. Murray Ohio Mfg. Co.*, 339 F.Supp. 973, 980, 172 USPQ 14, 19 (M.D.Tenn.1971), *aff'd*, 470 F.2d 975, 176 USPQ 161 (6th Cir. 1972), the court stated its reason for refusing to recognize the plaintiff's bicycle rim surface design as a trademark:

> The evidence is uncontradicted that the various manufacturers of bicycle rims in the United States consider it commercially necessary to mask, hide or camouflage the roughened and charred appearance resulting from welding the tubular rim sections together. The evidence represented indicates that the only other process used by bicycle rim manufacturers in the United States is the more complex and more expensive process of grinding and polishing.

B. The Case at Bar

1. The evidence of functionality

We come now to the task of applying to the facts of this case the distilled essence of the body of law on "functionality" above discussed. The question is whether appellant's plastic spray bottle is de jure functional; is it the best or one of a few superior designs available? We hold, on the basis of the evidence before the board, that it is not.

* * * Of course, the spray bottle is highly useful and performs its intended functions in an admirable way, but that is not enough to render the *design* of the spray bottle—which is all that matters here—functional.

As the examiner appreciated, the spray bottle consists of two major parts, a bottle and a trigger-operated, spray-producing pump mechanism which also serves as a closure. We shall call the latter the spray top. In the first place, a molded plastic bottle can have an infinite variety of forms or designs and still *function* to hold liquid. No one form is *necessary* or appears to be "superior." Many bottles have necks, to be grasped for pouring or holding, and the necks likewise can be in a variety of forms. The PTO has not produced one iota of evidence to show that the shape of appellant's bottle was *required* to be as it is for any de facto functional reason, which might lead to an affirmative determination of de jure functionality. The evidence, consisting of competitor's molded plastic bottles for similar products, demonstrates that the same functions can be performed by a variety of other shapes with no sacrifice of any functional advantage. There is no necessity to copy appellant's trade dress to enjoy any of the functions of a spray-top container.

As to the appearance of the spray top, the evidence of record shows that it too can take a number of diverse forms, all of which are equally suitable as housings for the pump and spray mechanisms. Appellant acquired a patent on the pump mechanism (No. 3,749,290) the drawings of which show it embodied in a structure which bears not the slightest resemblance to the appearance of appellant's spray top. The pictures of the competition's spray bottles further illustrate that no particular housing *design* is necessary to have a pump-type sprayer. Appellant's spray top, seen from the side, is rhomboidal, roughly speaking, a design which bears no relation to the shape of the pump mechanism housed within it and is an arbitrary decoration-no more de jure functional than is the grille of an automobile with respect to its under-the-hood power plant. The evidence shows that even the shapes of pump triggers can and do vary while performing the same function.

What is sought to be registered, however, is no single design feature or component but the overall composite design comprising both bottle and spray top. While that design must be *accommodated* to the functions performed, we see no evidence that it was *dictated* by them and resulted in a functionally or economically superior design of such a container.

Applying the legal principles discussed above, we do not see that allowing appellant to exclude others (upon proof of distinctiveness) from using this trade dress will hinder competition or impinge upon the rights of others to compete effectively in the sale of the goods named in the application, even to the extent of marketing them in *functionally* identical spray containers. The fact is that many others are doing so. Competitors have apparently had no need to simulate appellant's trade dress, in whole or in part, in order to enjoy all of the *functional* aspects of a spray top container. Upon expiration of any patent protection appellant may now be enjoying on its spray and pump mechanism, competitors may even copy and enjoy all of its functions without copying the external appearance of appellant's spray top.[3]

If the functions of appellant's bottle can be performed equally well by containers of innumerable designs and, thus, no one is injured in competition, why did the board state that appellant's *design* is functional and for that reason not registrable?

2. The relationship between "functionality" and distinctiveness

One who seeks to register (or protect) a product or container configuration as a trademark must demonstrate that its design is "non-functional," as discussed above, and that the design functions as an indication of source, whether inherently so, because of its distinctive nature, or through acquisition of secondary meaning. These two requirements must, however, be kept separate from one another.

The issues of distinctiveness and functionality may have been somewhat intermixed by the board. The design in issue appears to us to be relatively simple and plain, and the board, although not ruling upon appellant's contention that its design has acquired secondary meaning, discussed only distinctiveness before reaching its conclusion that the design was "functional." The unexpressed (and perhaps unconscious) thought may have been that if something is not inherently distinctive (appellant admits that its design is not), perhaps even austere, then, since it does not at a particular time function as a legally recognized indication of source, it probably never will. And since it is so plain that one may believe it is not and never will be a trademark, it will be perceived-not that the design is not inherently distinctive-but that it is "functional," without analysis of why it is believed to be "functional." The sole criterion seems to have been that the design is ordinary.

While it is certainly arguable that lack of distinctiveness may, where appropriate, permit an inference that a design was created primarily with an eye toward the utility of the article, that fact is by no means conclusive as to the "functionality" of the design of that article. Whether in fact the design is "functional" requires closer and more careful scrutiny. We cannot say that there exists an inverse proportional relationship in all cases between distinctiveness of design and functionality (de facto or de jure).

[The court remands for a determination of distinctiveness.]

Notes and Questions

1. *Utilitarian functionality.* The issue of functionality arises primarily when a business asserts trademark rights in product packaging or in features of the product itself. Functionality questions are rarely raised in

3. It is interesting to note that appellant also owns design patent 238,655 for the design in issue, which, at least presumptively, indicates that the design is *not de jure* functional.

connection with word marks, though the prohibition of rights in generic terms serves a somewhat similar purpose in the case of word marks. Note that the Lanham Act itself makes no direct reference to nonfunctionality as a condition of registration. The rule that functional features cannot serve as marks developed in the common law of unfair competition, and has been incorporated through case decisions into the rules for federal registration.

Why should businesses be prohibited from relying on trademark law to gain exclusive rights in functional features, especially when the public has come to view the feature as an indication of origin? In *Morton-Norwich*, the court distinguishes between "de facto functionality" and "de jure functionality." This terminology has been widely adopted in the case law. What, exactly, is the distinction between the two types of functionality? Why is the distinction made?

Of what relevance is the fact that an applicant seeking to register product features has a utility patent in the product? A design patent? Assuming that the applicant already has a design patent (or qualifies for one or has had one in the past) that covers the features the applicant seeks to protect as a trademark, what justification is there for providing trademark protection? Does recognizing trademark rights undercut Congress's purpose in limiting design patent protection to 14 years? Suppose that the applicant claims copyright in the design features described in the application. Should that be relevant?

The *Morton-Norwich* case deals with what is sometimes referred to as "utilitarian functionality." What if the purpose of the product or container feature at issue was purely ornamental or aesthetic? Could it be deemed "functional?" The following case wrestles with the controversial "aesthetic functionality" doctrine.

WALLACE INTERNATIONAL SILVERSMITHS, INC. v. GODINGER SILVER ART CO., INC.

United States Court of Appeals for the Second Circuit, 1990.
916 F.2d 76, 16 U.S.P.Q.2d 1555, *cert. denied*
499 U.S. 976, 111 S.Ct. 1622, 113 L.Ed.2d 720 (1991).

WINTER, CIRCUIT JUDGE:

Wallace International Silversmiths ("Wallace") appeals from Judge Haight's denial of its motion for a preliminary injunction under Section 43(a) of the Lanham Act, 15 U.S.C. § 1125(a) (1988), prohibiting Godinger Silver Art Co., Inc. ("Godinger") from marketing a line of silverware with ornamentation that is substantially similar to Wallace's GRANDE BAROQUE line. Judge Haight held that the GRANDE BAROQUE design is "a functional feature of 'Baroque' style silverware" and thus not subject to protection as a trademark. We affirm.

BACKGROUND

Wallace, a Delaware corporation, has sold sterling silver products for over one hundred years. Its GRANDE BAROQUE pattern was introduced in 1941 and is still one of the best-selling silverware lines in America. Made of fine sterling silver, a complete place setting costs several thousand dollars. Total sales of GRANDE BAROQUE silverware have exceeded fifty million dollars. The GRANDE BAROQUE pattern is fairly described as "ornate, massive and flowery [with] indented, flowery roots and scrolls and curls along the side of the shaft, and flower arrangements along the front of the shaft." Wallace owns a trademark registration for the GRANDE BAROQUE name as applied to sterling silver flatware and hollowware. The GRANDE BAROQUE design is not patented, but on December 11, 1989, Wallace filed an application for trademark registration for the GRANDE BAROQUE pattern. This application is still pending.

Godinger, a New York corporation, is a manufacturer of silver-plated products. The company has recently begun to market a line of baroque-style silver-plated serving pieces. The suggested retail price of the set of four serving pieces is approximately twenty dollars. Godinger advertised its new line under the name 20TH CENTURY BAROQUE * * * Like Wallace's silverware, Godinger's pattern contains typical baroque elements including an indented root, scrolls, curls, and flowers. The arrangement of these elements approximates Wallace's design in many ways, although their dimensions are noticeably different. The most obvious difference between the two designs is that the Godinger pattern extends further down the handle than the Wallace pattern does. The Wallace pattern also tapers from the top of the handle to the stem while the Godinger pattern appears bulkier overall and maintains its bulk throughout the decorated portion of the handle. Although the record does not disclose the exact circumstances under which Godinger's serving pieces were created, Godinger admits that its designers were "certainly inspired by and aware of [the Wallace] design when [they] created [the 20TH CENTURY BAROQUE] design."

[Wallace sought a relief against Godinger's alleged infringement relying on, among other things, Lanham Act section 43(a), 15 U.S.C.A. § 1125(a), which provides a cause of action for infringement of unregistered marks. For purposes of the court's functionality discussion, the fact that Wallace's alleged design mark was unregistered is irrelevant. The district court denied Wallace's motion for a preliminary injunction, concluding that the GRANDE BAROQUE design was a "functional" feature of baroque-style silverware. In so holding, the court stated:]

> In the case at bar, the "Baroque" curls and flowers are not "arbitrary embellishments" adopted to identify plaintiff's product. Instead, all the "Baroque" style silverware use essentially the same scrolls and flowers as a way to compete in the free market. The "Baroque" style is a line of silverware which many manufacturers produce. Just like the patterns on the chinaware in *Pagliero* [*v. Wallace China Co.*, 198 F.2d 339 (9th Cir.1952)], the "Grande Baroque" design is a functional feature of "Baroque" style silverware. Wallace may well have developed secondary meaning in the market of "Baroque"- styled silverware.

> * * * However, that does not mean that plaintiff's design is subject to protection. The "Baroque" curls, roots and flowers are not "mere indicia of source." Instead, they are requirements to compete in the silverware market. This is a classic example of the proposition that "to imitate is to compete." *Pagliero, supra*, at 344. The designs are aesthetically functional. * * *

DISCUSSION

* * * Although the paradigmatic trademark is a distinctive name, the "trade dress" of a product may also serve as a trademark. A product's trade dress ordinarily consists of its packaging. However, the design given a product by its manufacturer also may serve to distinguish it from the products of other manufacturers and hence be protectible trade dress. *See, e.g., Stormy Clime Ltd. v. Progroup, Inc.*, 809 F.2d 971, 974 (2d Cir.1987) ("The trade dress of a product 'involves the total image of a product and may include features such as size, shape, color or color combinations, texture, [or] graphics.' ") (quoting *John H. Harland Co. v. Clarke Checks, Inc.*, 711 F.2d 966, 980 (11th Cir.1983)).

In order to maintain an action for trade dress infringement under Section 43(a) of the Lanham Act, the plaintiff must show that its trade dress has acquired secondary meaning—that is, the trade dress identifies the source of the product—and that there is a likelihood of confusion between the original trade dress and the trade dress of the allegedly infringing product. Even if the plaintiff establishes these elements, the defendant may still avoid liability on a variety of grounds, including the so-called functionality doctrine. Our present view of that doctrine is derived from the Supreme Court's dictum in *Inwood Laboratories* [*v. Ives Laboratories*], stating that "[i]n general terms, a product feature is functional if it is essential to the use or purpose of the article or if it affects the cost or quality of the article." 456 U.S. [844,] 850 n. 10, 102 S.Ct. [2182,] 2187 n. 10 (1982). Our most recent elaboration of the doctrine was in *Stormy Clime*, where Judge Newman stated:

> the functionality inquiry ... should [focus] on whether bestowing trade dress protection upon [a particular] arrangement of features " 'will hinder competition or impinge upon the rights of others to compete effectively in the sale of goods.' " *Sicilia di R. Biebow & Co. v. Cox*, 732 F.2d 417, 429 (5th Cir.1984) (quoting *In re Morton–Norwich Products, Inc.*, 671 F.2d 1332, 1342 (Cust. & Pat.App. 1982)).

Id. at 976–77. *Stormy Clime* outlined the factors to be considered in determining functionality as follows:

> the degree of functionality of the similar features, the degree of similarity between non-functional (ornamental) features of the competing products, and the feasibility of alternative arrangements of functional features that would not impair the utility of the product. These factors should be considered along a continuum. On one end, unique arrangements of purely functional features constitute a functional design. On the other end, distinctive and arbitrary

> arrangements of predominantly ornamental features that do not hinder potential competitors from entering the same market with differently dressed versions of the product are non-functional and hence eligible for trade dress protection. In between, the case for protection weakens the more clearly the arrangement of allegedly distinctive features serves the purpose of the product....

Id. at 977 (citations omitted).

Turning to the instant case, Judge Haight found that the similarities between the Godinger and Wallace designs involved elements common to all baroque-style designs used in the silverware market. He noted that many manufacturers compete in that market with such designs and found that "[t]he 'Baroque' curls, roots and flowers are not 'mere indicia of source.' Instead, they are requirements to compete in the silverware market." Judge Haight concluded that "the 'Grande Baroque' design is a functional feature of 'Baroque' style silverware," relying on *Pagliero v. Wallace China Co.*, 198 F.2d 339 (9th Cir.1952).

Although we agree with Judge Haight's decision, we do not endorse his reliance upon *Pagliero*. That decision allowed a competitor to sell exact copies of china bearing a particular pattern without finding that comparably attractive patterns were not available to the competitor. It based its holding solely on the ground that the particular pattern was an important ingredient in the commercial success of the china. We rejected *Pagliero* in *LeSportsac*, and reiterate that rejection here. Under *Pagliero*, the commercial success of an aesthetic feature automatically destroys all of the originator's trademark interest in it, notwithstanding the feature's secondary meaning and the lack of any evidence that competitors cannot develop non-infringing, attractive patterns. By allowing the copying of an exact design without any evidence of market foreclosure, the *Pagliero* test discourages both originators and later competitors from developing pleasing designs.

Our rejection of *Pagliero*, however, does not call for reversal. Quite unlike *Pagliero*, Judge Haight found in the instant matter that there is a substantial market for baroque silverware and that effective competition in that market requires "use [of] essentially the same scrolls and flowers" as are found on Wallace's silverware. Based on the record at the hearing, that finding is not clearly erroneous and satisfies the requirement of *Stormy Clime* that a design feature not be given trade dress protection where use of that feature is necessary for effective competition.

Stormy Clime is arguably distinguishable, however, because it involved a design that had both aesthetic and utilitarian features. If read narrowly, *Stormy Clime* might be limited to cases in which trademark protection of a design would foreclose competitors from incorporating utilitarian features necessary to compete in the market for the particular product. In the instant case, the features at issue are strictly ornamental because they neither affect the use of the silverware nor contribute to its efficient manufacture. The question, therefore, is whether the doctrine of functionality applies to features of a product that are purely ornamental but that are essential to effective competition.

Our only hesitation in holding that the functionality doctrine applies is based on nomenclature. "Functionality" seems to us to imply only utilitarian considerations and, as a legal doctrine, to be intended only to prevent competitors from obtaining trademark protection for design features that are necessary to the use or efficient production of the product. *See Keene* [*Co. v. Paraflex Industries, Inc.*, 653 F.2d 822, 825 (3d Cir.1981)] ("inquiry should focus on the extent to which the design feature is related to the utilitarian function of the product or feature"). Even when the doctrine is referred to as "aesthetic" functionality, it still seems an apt description only of pleasing designs of utilitarian features. Nevertheless, there is no lack of language in caselaw endorsing use of the defense of aesthetic functionality where trademark protection for purely ornamental features would exclude competitors from a market. * * * Indeed, the "continuum" in Judge Newman's *Stormy Clime* opinion carefully limited the "distinctive and arbitrary arrangements of predominantly ornamental features" entitled to trademark protection to only those features "that do not hinder competitors from entering the same market." *Id.* at 977.

We put aside our quibble over doctrinal nomenclature, however, because we are confident that whatever secondary meaning Wallace's baroque silverware pattern may have acquired, Wallace may not exclude competitors from using those baroque design elements necessary to compete in the market for baroque silverware. It is a first principle of trademark law that an owner may not use the mark as a means of excluding competitors from a substantial market. Where a mark becomes the generic term to describe an article, for example, trademark protection ceases. Where granting trademark protection to the use of certain colors would tend to exclude competitors, such protection is also limited. Finally, as discussed *supra*, design features of products that are necessary to the product's utility may be copied by competitors under the functionality doctrine.

In the instant matter, Wallace seeks trademark protection, not for a precise expression of a decorative style, but for basic elements of a style that is part of the public domain. As found by the district court, these elements are important to competition in the silverware market. We perceive no distinction between a claim to exclude all others from use on silverware of basic elements of a decorative style and claims to generic names, basic colors or designs important to a product's utility. In each case, trademark protection is sought, not just to protect an owner of a mark in informing the public of the source of its products, but also to exclude competitors from producing similar products. We therefore abandon our quibble with the aesthetic functionality doctrine's nomenclature and adopt the Draft Restatement's view that, where an ornamental feature is claimed as a trademark and trademark protection would significantly hinder competition by limiting the range of adequate alternative designs, the aesthetic functionality doctrine denies such protection. *See* Third Restatement of the Law, Unfair Competition (Preliminary Draft No. 3), Ch. 3, § 17(c) at 213–14. This rule avoids the overbreadth of *Pagliero* by requiring a finding of foreclosure of alternatives [2] while still ensuring that trademark protection does not exclude competitors from substantial markets.[3]

Of course, if Wallace were able to show secondary meaning in a precise expression of baroque style, competitors might be excluded from using an identical or virtually identical design. In such a case, numerous alternative baroque designs would still be available to competitors. Although the Godinger design at issue here was found by Judge Haight to be "substantially similar," it is not identical or virtually identical, and the similarity involves design elements necessary to compete in the market for baroque silverware. Because according trademark protection to those elements would significantly hinder competitors by limiting the range of adequate alternative designs, we agree with Judge Haight's denial of a preliminary injunction.

Notes and Questions

1. *Aesthetic functionality.* In *Wallace*, the Court of Appeals for the Second Circuit, like most other Circuits, expressly rejected the test for functionality set forth by the Ninth Circuit in *Pagliero.* Indeed, the Ninth Circuit itself has since retreated from that test. First Brands Corp. v. Fred Meyer, Inc., 809 F.2d 1378 n.3, 1 U.S.P.Q.2d 1779, 1781 n.3 (9th Cir.1987). In *Pagliero*, the court held:

> If the particular feature is an important ingredient in the commercial success of the product, the interest in free competition permits its imitation in the absence of a patent or copyright. On the other hand, where the feature * * * is a mere arbitrary embellishment, a form of

2. The Draft Restatement's Illustrations expressly reject *Pagliero*. Illustration 6 reads as follows:

> A manufactures china. Among the products marketed by *A* is a set of china bearing a particular "overall" pattern covering the entire upper surface of each dish. Evidence indicates that aesthetic factors play an important role in the purchase of china, that *A's* design is attractive to a significant number of consumers, and that the number of alternative patterns is virtually unlimited. In the absence of evidence indicating that similarly attractive "overall" patterns are unavailable to competing manufacturers, *A's* pattern design is not functional under the rule stated in this Section.

3. Draft Restatement Illustrations 7 and 8 reflect this aspect of the rule. They read as follows:

> 7. The facts being otherwise as stated in Illustration 6, *A's* design consists solely of a thin gold band placed around the rim of each dish. Evidence indicates that a significant number of consumers prefer china decorated with only a gold rim band. Because the number of alternative designs available to satisfy the aesthetic desires of these prospective purchasers is extremely limited, the rim design is functional under the rule stated in this Section.
>
> 8. A is the first seller to market candy intended for Valentine's Day in heart-shaped boxes. Evidence indicates that the shape of the box is an important factor in the appeal of the product to a significant number of consumers. Because there are no alternative designs capable of satisfying the aesthetic desires of these prospective purchasers, the design of the box is functional under the rule stated in this Section.

> dress for the goods primarily adopted for purposes of identification and individuality, and hence, unrelated to basic consumer demands in connection with the product, imitation may be forbidden where the requisite showing of secondary meaning is made.

Pagliero v. Wallace China Co., 198 F.2d 339, 343, 95 U.S.P.Q. 45, 48 (9th Cir.1952). Applying this test, the court found the decorative floral border around Wallace's dinner plates to be functional, since "the attractiveness and eye-appeal of the design" were what sold the plates. The availability of alternative designs was irrelevant. *Id.*, 198 F.2d at 344, 95 U.S.P.Q. at 49. Why should this test be objectionable?

What rule does the Second Circuit adopt? Does it strike a better balance between potentially conflicting interests than the rule in *Pagliero*? Is the Second Circuit's test a manageable one? Should there be an aesthetic functionality doctrine at all? For forceful arguments against the doctrine of aesthetic functionality, see, e.g., 1 J.T. McCARTHY, McCARTHY ON TRADEMARKS AND UNFAIR COMPETITION § 7.26[5] (3d ed. 1992). Some Circuits have expressly rejected an aesthetic functionality doctrine, as such. For example, in Sicilia Di R. Biebow & Co. v. Cox, 732 F.2d 417, 429 (5th Cir.1984), the Court of Appeals for the Fifth Circuit limited functionality to utilitarian aspects of product or packaging: "a design or feature must be superior or optimal in terms of engineering, economy of manufacture, or accommodation of utilitarian function or performance." Could a decorative feature, such as the floral design on a plate, ever be deemed functional under this test?

In Brunswick Corp. v. Spinit Reel Co., 832 F.2d 513, 519, 4 U.S.P.Q.2d 1497, 1501 (10th Cir.1987), the Tenth Circuit rejected the *Pagliero* test, but explicitly adopted a test which would encompass both "utilitarian" and "aesthetic" or "ornamental" features:

> [W]e adopt a test whose focus is the effect on competition. * * * Under our test, the claim may still be made that without a particular identifying design or feature a second-comer may be less effectively able to compete. If that feature must be slavishly copied in order to have an equally functional product, then the feature is not entitled to protection. But if the feature enables the second-comer simply to market his product more effectively, it is entitled to protection. * * *
>
> This interpretation does not limit functional features to those essential to a product's operation. Because a function of certain products is aesthetic appeal, a feature intrinsic to the aesthetic appeal of those products may not be entitled to trademark protection. * * * Although the determination of functional in this setting may be difficult, the decision should nevertheless rest on whether alternative appealing designs or presentations of a product can be developed.

Compare the Third Circuit's approach in American Greetings Corp. v. Dan–Dee Imports, Inc., 807 F.2d 1136, 1 U.S.P.Q.2d 1001 (3d Cir.1986). In *Dan-Dee*, American Greetings marketed "Care Bears," pastel plush teddy bears with pictorial designs on their white stomachs, known as "tummy graphics." For example, the "Funshine Bear" had a smiling sun on his tummy, which conveyed the message, "Fun and Laughter;" the "Grumpy Bear" had a rain cloud on his tummy, which conveyed the message "It's OK to be out of sorts;" the "Bedtime Bear" had a crescent moon and star, meant to convey the message "Sweet Dreams," etc. The defendant sought to market its own teddy bears with tummy graphics. The issue was whether, in denying a preliminary injunction against the defendant, the district court had erred in concluding that the tummy graphics were unprotectible functional features. The Court of Appeals found that it had not erred:

> The district court correctly applied the standard of functionality * * *:
>
> > [T]he essence of the question is whether a particular feature of a product or service is substantially related to its value as a product or service, i.e., if the feature is part of the "function" served, or whether the primary value of a particular feature is the identification of the provider.
>
> [United States Golf Assn. v. St. Andrews Systems, 749 F.2d 1028, 1033 (3d Cir.1984).] As the district court recognized, where the feature is substantially related to the product's value as a product or service, it cannot be protected "because [its] usefulness in identifying the source of the product or service is outweighed by the social interest in competition and improvements, which are advanced by giving competitors free access to" that feature. 749 F.2d at 1033.
>
> As the district court also noted, a feature is not functional merely because it makes the product more attractive to consumers. In *Keene Corp.*, we rejected the concept of aesthetic functionality as interpreted by the Court of Appeals for the Ninth Circuit which suggests the contrary. Rather, we insisted that a feature have a significant relation to the utilitarian function of the product before it could be declared functional. 653 F.2d at 825.
>
> Finally, the district court opinion reflects the other relevant principles established in *Keene Corp.* In that case, we also rejected "a standard inquiring whether the specific design features of the product '[are] competitively essential'." 653 F.2d at 827. "[M]erely because there are other shapes and designs 'which defendant could use and still produce a workable' product, the design used is not thereby non-functional." Id. (quoting *Vaughan Novelty Mfg. Co. v. G.G. Greene Mfg. Corp.*, 202 F.2d 172, 175–76 n. 10 (3d Cir.), *cert. denied,* 346 U.S. 820, 74 S.Ct. 34, 98 L.Ed. 346 (1953)). Because "the policy predicate for the entire functionality doctrine stems from the public interest in enhancing competition," however, a court may also consider " 'whether prohibition of imitation by others will deprive the others of something which will substantially hinder them in competition'." *Keene Corp.,* 653 F.2d at 827 (quoting *Restatement of Torts* § 742 comment a (1938)).
>
> Applying these legal principles to the record before it, the district court concluded that "tummy graphics" are functional. In essence, the district judge found that tummy graphics do not merely make Care Bears more appealing to the eye; they contribute to the effectiveness and performance of Care Bears as plush toy teddy bears. Specifically, the court noted that tummy graphics serve "the purpose of communicating the particular personality of each of the Care Bear characters, and ... convey an emotional message through such personality." In addi-

tion, the court found that "the particular symbols chosen by plaintiffs for the tummy graphics are functional: they are common figures and are typically associated with the messages attributed to them by plaintiffs." Finally, because Dan–Dee has a right to utilize these functional features "in the best possible way," the court found the placement of the graphics on the bears' stomachs against a white background to be a part of the functional feature it referred to as tummy graphics.

These findings have support in the record. * * * Here, as the district court emphasized, American and CPG stressed the utilitarian aspects of tummy graphics in their promotional materials. * * *

The professed function of the Care Bears products is "to help children and adults express their feelings and share them with others" and the role of the tummy "graphics ... to convey the message of simple, human feelings—cheer, happiness, love and tenderness." Given plaintiffs' own appraisal of the utility of tummy graphics, it was not clearly erroneous for the district court to conclude that they contributed to the function performed by plaintiffs' teddy bears.

Id., 807 F.2d at 1142–43, 1 U.S.P.Q.2d at 1006.

What is your assessment of the Third Circuit's approach? The Tenth Circuit's? How does each compare with the Federal Circuit's rule, established in *Morton-Norwich*?

For a detailed review of the development and application of the functionality doctrine, see Oddi, *The Functions of "Functionality" in Trademark Law*, 76 TRADEMARK REP. 308 (1986).

2. *Functionality of color and scent.* Could color, by itself, ever be deemed functional? If so, under what kinds of circumstances? See Qualitex Co. v. Jacobson Products Co., Inc., ___ U.S. ___, 115 S.Ct. 1300, ___ L.Ed.2d ___, 34 U.S.P.Q.2d 1161 (1995); Inwood Laboratories, Inc. v. Ives Laboratories, Inc., 456 U.S. 844, 853, 102 S.Ct. 2182, 2188, 72 L.Ed.2d 606, 615, 214 U.S.P.Q. 1 (1982).

Is there any argument that the scent registered as a trademark for embroidery yarn in *In re* Clarke, *supra*, was functional? What about the scent of a perfume?

3. *Alternative means for protecting product designs.* We have now reviewed three intellectual property doctrines—copyright, design patents, and trademark/unfair competition law—which may afford property rights in product designs. How does each approach compare with regard to eligibility for protection, strength of protection, and efficiency? From a designer's standpoint, is one approach preferable to the others? Do the three alternatives, in combination, provide sufficient protection for industrial designs, or is a new, *sui generis* approach to protection needed, as many advocates have argued?

Is trademark law an appropriate way to protect industrial designs? Compare Dratler, *Trademark Protection for Industrial Designs*, [1988] U. ILL. L. REV. 887, with Pegram, *Trademark Protection of Product and Container Configurations*, 81 TRADEMARK REP. 1, 23–29 (1991).

As we will see in Chapter 9, a line of Supreme Court decisions, beginning with Sears, Roebuck & Co. v. Stiffel Co., 376 U.S. 225, 84 S.Ct. 784, 11 L.Ed.2d 661, 140 U.S.P.Q. 524 (1964), and Compco Corp. v. Day–Brite Lighting, Inc., 376 U.S. 234, 84 S.Ct. 779, 11 L.Ed.2d 669, 140 U.S.P.Q. 528 (1964), cast considerable doubt upon the use of *state* trademark and unfair competition laws to prevent the copying of product features, suggesting that they may be preempted pursuant to the supremacy clause of the United States Constitution. These decisions, however, do not prevent the use of *federal* trademark and unfair competition laws to afford rights in distinctive, non-functional aspects of a product's design. For a discussion of how the *Sears/Compco* line of cases has affected trademark protection for industrial designs, see Dratler, *supra*, at 916.

D. DECEPTIVENESS: LANHAM ACT SECTION 2(A)

§ 1052. (§ 2) Trademarks Registrable on Principal Register

No trademark by which the goods of the applicant may be distinguished from the goods of others shall be refused registration on the principal register on account of its nature unless it—

> (a) Consists of or comprises immoral, deceptive, or scandalous matter; or matter which may disparage or falsely suggest a connection with persons, living or dead, institutions, beliefs, or national symbols, or bring them into contempt, or disrepute; or a geographical indication which, when used on or in connection with wines or spirits, identifies a place other than the origin of the goods and is first used on or in connection with wines or spirits by the applicant on or after January 1, 1996.

15 U.S.C.A. § 1052(a).

IN RE HOUSE OF WINDSOR, INC.

Trademark Trial and Appeal Board, 1983.
221 U.S.P.Q. 53.

SAMS, MEMBER.

House of Windsor, Incorporated has appealed from the Trademark Examining Attorney's final refusal to register "BAHIA" as a trademark for cigars. The Examining Attorney refused registration, under Section 2(a) of the Trademark Act, on the ground that, as applied to cigars, "BAHIA" is deceptive.

* * * [T]he Examining Attorney's position on appeal may be simply stated as follows: (i) the mark "BAHIA" has geographical significance as the name of a province of Brazil; (ii) the geographical significance of "BAHIA" is its primary significance; (iii) the Bahia province of Brazil is noted for tobacco production and the making of cigars; (iv) applicant's goods are cigars; (v) the mark "BAHIA", when applied to applicant's cigars, would lead purchasers to believe applicant's cigars originate in Bahia and/or are made from tobacco from Bahia; and (vi) the mark is deceptive, because applicant's goods have no connection whatever with Bahia. * * *

Both the Examining Attorney and applicant have made of record evidence relating to the term "BAHIA." This evidence indicates that (i) Bahia is the name given to Brazilian tobaccos grown in the Bay of Salvador, (ii) tobacco is a principal product of Bahia province Brazil, (iii) as of 1954, Bahia produced one half of all Brazilian tobacco, (iv) as of 1967, Brazil ranked fifth in the world in production of tobacco, (v) as of 1967, tobacco ranked thirteenth in crop value in Brazil, (vi) as of 1967, the Brazilian states of Bahia and Rio Grande Do Sul produced approximately half of Brazil's tobacco, (vii) Brazilian tobacco tradesmen estimated the 1972 Bahia cigar leaf crop at 240,000 bales, (viii) in 1977, tobacco crops in Bahia were very disappointing, (ix) by 1977, Bahia was selling its tobacco principally to France, Portugal, Spain and North Africa, although it was also selling to U.S. factories, (x) in 1977, Bahia exporters had 85% of their tobacco crop still on hand, (xi) in 1979, there was a steady decline in tobacco output from Bahia, although cigars and wrappers were being produced in the province, (xii) in 1978, VARIG Brasilian Airlines was advertising tours of Bahia, (xiii) the word "bahia" means "bay" in spanish, (xiv) the word "bahia" is also used in referring to "bahia arrowroot" and "bahia grass," a type of pasture grass, (xv) Bahia is the old name for Salvador, the capital of Bahia province, and (xvi) Bahia forms a part of several geographical designations (namely, Bahia Island Honduras, Bahia Blanca Argentina, Bahia de Caraquez Ecuador, and Bahia Negra, Paraguay). It is on the basis of this evidence that we must determine the issues of this case.

[The TTAB determines, in accordance with the Court's opinion in *In re* Nantucket, that consumers would, upon seeing the mark "BAHIA" on cigars, make a "goods-place association"—conclude that the mark provides information about the geographic origin of the goods. Since the cigars do not come from Bahia, the mark is primarily geographically deceptively misdescriptive.]

A more perplexing question is whether "BAHIA" is a deceptive mark within the meaning of Section 2(a) of the Trademark Act. The distinction between a mark which is primarily geographically deceptively misdescriptive under Section 2(e)(2) of the Trademark Act and a geographical mark which is deceptive within the meaning of Section 2(a) of the Trademark Act is not immediately apparent from a reading of the Act. The Act's legislative history is, likewise, far from clear about the intended distinction between a mark that is to be denied registration as primarily geographically deceptively misdescriptive and one that is to be denied registration as deceptive. In fact, the legislative history suggests that at least some of the drafters perceived no distinction at all. The ambiguity in legislative intent notwithstanding, basic rules of statutory construction compel us to find that there is a distinction between a primarily geographically deceptively misdescriptive mark (which can be registered with proof of distinctiveness under section 2(f)) and a deceptive geographical mark (which is unregistrable even under the provisions of Section 2(f)).

The Board has considered a number of geographical marks alleged to be deceptive within the meaning of Section 2(a), and has, in its opinions, articulated different tests for determining whether a mark is geographically deceptive. In considering whether the mark "ITALIAN MAIDE", when applied to canned vegetables, was deceptive within the meaning of Section 2(a), the Board stated the following test:

> [T]his Board has * * * taken the position that a mark consisting of or comprising a geographical term is not deceptive under Section 2(a) unless it involves a *false assertion calculated, either planned, designed or implied to deceive the public as to the geographical origin of the goods* bearing the mark. This contemplates situations where a party applied a geographical designation to a particular product knowing that it will bestow upon the product an appearance of greater quality or sale ability not actually possessed by it *with the intention* thereby *of inducing or misleading* a particular class of consumers into purchasing this product. While such intent is often difficult to prove and especially in ex parte proceedings, intent can and has been inferred under those circumstances where a geographical area or place is well-known for the particular product as France for perfumes, Denmark for cheese, Switzerland for watches, and so forth. (emphasis ours) In re Amerise, 160 USPQ 687, 691 (TTAB 1969).

* * * The Board made a different formulation of the test for deceptiveness in a case decided at about the same time as Amerise. In deciding that the mark "SWEDEN" was not deceptive as applied to external artificial kidney units not made in Sweden, the Board distinguished the "SWEDEN" case from those cases

> * * * involving situations in which the impression created by the use of a term which has geographical significance is likely to give to the article sold thereunder an appearance of greater merit, quality or saleability not actually possessed by the product thereby inducing or misleading a particular class of consumers into purchasing this product. *In re Sweden Freezer Mfg. Co.*, 159 USPQ 246, (TTAB 1968).

In this formulation of the test, consideration of applicant's intent to deceive gives way to consideration of the "impression created by the use of the term." And, indeed, it seems to us that intent of the user of the mark should not be an element of a case of geographical deceptiveness. In the first place, establishing the intent of the user of the mark is a difficult proposition, particularly at the examination level, where the Examining Attorney is unlikely to adduce evidence of applicant's intent. Moreover, an intent test could, conceivably, lead to the incongruous result of denying registration to one party where evidence of intent to deceive is present but allowing registration of the same mark for the same goods to another party where the evidence fails to show intent to deceive.

The better approach, we believe, is to determine whether the deception is material to the purchasing decision. If so, the mark is deceptive within the meaning of Section 2(a). Probably the clearest formulation of this test was enunciated by Assistant Commissioner Daphne Leads, as follows:

> Are purchasers likely to care whether or not the product comes from the place or region which the mark identifies? If the answer is in the negative, the mark is "deceptively misdescriptive" but if the affirmative, it is "deceptive" and unregistrable under another provision of the Act. This is to say that if a locality identified by a geographical name or term is known or noted for the production of goods in the category of applicant's, or for components of such goods, and purchasers are moved by the geographical name to buy the goods in the belief that they originate in the locality name, the geographical name or term is "deceptive" as applied to the goods. Leads, "Trademarks—The Rationale of Registrability," 26 GEO. WASH. L. REV. 653, 662–63.

In embracing a "materiality" test to distinguish marks that fall within the proscription of Section 2(e)(2) from those that fall also within the proscription of Section 2(a), we are really saying no more than that we must look to the evidence that has been presented about the probable reaction of purchasers to a particular geographical term when it is applied to particular goods. If the evidence shows that the geographical area named in the mark is an area sufficiently renowned to lead purchasers to make a goods-place association but the record does not show that goods like applicant's or goods related to applicant's are a principal product of that geographical area, then the deception will most likely be found not to be material and the mark, therefore, not deceptive. On the other hand, if there is evidence that goods like applicant's or goods related to applicant's are a principal product of the geographical area named by the mark, then the deception will most likely be found material and the mark, therefore, deceptive.

It is a bit risky to suggest the kind or amount of evidence that would be sufficient to establish that goods like or related to applicant's come from a particular geographical region, but we are willing to take that risk in the attempt to give some guidance to Examining Attorneys and applicants. For us, in the ordinary case, if the record contains a concession that the area named by the mark has, as one of its principal products, applicant's goods or related goods or if the record contains a reliable gazetteer entry (or the like) to the effect that applicant's goods (or sufficiently related goods) are a principal product of the geographical area named by the mark, such evidence is sufficient to establish the materiality of the deception.

In this case, the Examining Attorney and applicant have made of record the previously-described printed publications that refer to Bahia as a source of tobacco and cigars. These materials indicate, moreover, that tobacco and cigars are important products in the Bahia region (in spite of the fact that the region may be declining as a tobacco producer, according to some of the evidence of record). We believe that, from an evidentiary standpoint, no more is required to establish that purchasers would be deceived into believing that applicant's cigars have their origin in Bahia and would be moved by that deception in deciding whether to buy applicant's cigars. We believe, then, that this record supports a finding that "BAHIA" is deceptive as applied to cigars.

* * * The refusal to register under Section 2(a) is affirmed.

Notes and Questions

1. *Deceptive marks.* The Court of Appeals for the Federal Circuit picked up on the TTAB's materiality test for section 2(a) deceptiveness in *In re* Budge Mfg. Co., Inc., 857 F.2d 773, 8 U.S.P.Q.2d 1259 (C.A.F.C. 1988). In that case the applicant had been denied registration of "Lovee Lamb" for automotive seat covers made wholly from synthetic fibers. In affirming the Board's decision, the court stated the proper test, which entailed three questions:

> (1) Is the term misdescriptive of the character, quality, function, composition or use of the goods?
>
> (2) If so, are prospective purchasers likely to believe that the misdescription actually describes the goods?
>
> (3) If so, is the misdescription likely to affect the decision to purchase?

Id., 857 F.2d at 775, 8 U.S.P.Q.2d at 1260. The court continued:

> In *ex parte* prosecution, the burden is initially on the Patent and Trademark Office (PTO) to put forth sufficient evidence that the mark for which registration is sought meets the above criteria of unregistrability. Mindful that the PTO has limited facilities for acquiring evidence—it cannot, for example, be expected to conduct a survey of the marketplace or obtain consumer affidavits—we conclude that the evidence of record here is sufficient to establish a *prima facie* case of deceptiveness. That evidence shows with respect to the three-pronged test:
>
> (1) Budge admits that its seat covers are not made from lamb or sheep products. Thus, the term LAMB is misdescriptive of its goods.
>
> (2) Seat covers for various vehicles can be and are made from natural lambskin and sheepskin. Applicant itself makes automobile seat covers of natural sheepskin. Lambskin is defined, *inter alia*, as fine-grade sheep skin. See Webster's Third New International Dictionary 639 (unabr. 1976). The board's factual inference is reasonable that purchasers are likely to believe automobile seat covers denominated by the term LAMB or SHEEP are actually made from natural sheep or lamb skins.
>
> (3) Evidence of record shows that natural sheepskin and lambskin is more expensive than simulated skins and that natural and synthetic skins have different characteristics. Thus, the misrepresentation is likely to affect the decision to purchase.

Id., 857 F.2d at 775–76, 8 U.S.P.Q.2d at 1261.

Suppose that the applicant included a disclaimer, on its label and/or in its advertising, stating that the seat covers were "simulated sheepskin." Should it then be permitted to register the "Lovee Lamb" mark? See *id.*, 857 F.2d at 776, 8 U.S.P.Q.2d at 1261.

2. *Immoral or scandalous marks.* In *In re* Old Glory Condom Corp., 26 U.S.P.Q.2d 1216 (T.T.A.B. 1993), the applicant for registration sought to register its mark for condoms which, as shown below, consisted of the words, "Old Glory Condom Corp." and a pictorial representation of a condom decorated with stars and stripes, suggesting the American flag.

The examiner had refused registration on the grounds that the mark constituted scandalous matter within the meaning of Lanham Act section 2(a). She argued that the mark was likely to offend a substantial composite of the general public because of its use of American flag imagery to promote products associated with sexual activity. On appeal, the Trademark Trial and Appeal Board reversed.

> Taking as our starting point the definitions of "scandalous" to which the Board has in previous cases looked for assistance in applying Section 2(a), we have considered whether "OLD GLORY CONDOM CORP" (and flag design) can be characterized as "[g]iving offense to the conscience or moral feelings" or "shocking to the sense of decency or propriety." If any pattern can be discerned from the most recent cases * * * where the Board or its reviewing court found marks to be scandalous [viz., a mark for newsletters comprising a photograph of a man and woman kissing and embracing in a manner appearing to expose the man's genitalia, *In re* McGinley, 660 F.2d 481, 211 U.S.P.Q. 668 (C.C.P.A.1981)], "BULLSHIT," for handbags, wallets, etc. [*In re* Tinseltown, Inc., 212 U.S.P.Q. 863 (T.T.A.B. 1981)], and the design of a defecating dog, for shirts [Greyhound Corp. v. Both Worlds Inc., 6 U.S.P.Q.2d 1635 (T.T.A.B. 1988)], that pattern seems to describe marks that convey, in words or in pictures, vulgar imagery.
>
> As applicant has asserted (and as the examining attorney seems to concede), this Office has registered many trademarks and service marks that include imagery of the American flag. While we realize that there may be citizens of this country who disapprove of *any* commercial use of the American flag or American flag imagery, such uses have been sufficiently common that there can be no justification for refusing registration of applicant's mark simply on the basis of the presence in that mark of flag imagery. Nor do we find any evidence in this case

> that convinces us that a mark containing a pictorial representation of a condom should, simply because of that fact, be refused registration as scandalous. The particular pictorial presentation featured in applicant's composite mark was not found by the examining attorney to be vulgar, nor do we find it so. The examining attorney's objection to applicant's mark seems to be directed to the mark's linking of flag imagery and a pictorial representation of a condom, each of which, in itself, she apparently finds unobjectionable. * * *

Id., at 1221. As evidence that a substantial component of the public would be offended by the applicant's mark, the examining attorney alluded to an unsuccessful proposed amendment to the U.S. Constitution to prohibit flag burning and to a comment by Chief Justice Rehnquist in a dissent that many Americans have an "almost mystical reverence" for the American flag. She also introduced printouts of several news stories describing some persons' disapproval of a video public service announcement promoting voter registration that featured rock star Madonna, scantily clad and wrapped in an American flag. The Board was unimpressed.

> We are not willing, based solely on the examining attorney's opinion, the evidence of the reaction to the Madonna video, and the unsuccessful effort to amend the U.S. Constitution to prohibit the burning of the flag, to presume that the flag imagery of applicant's mark would give offense in a manner that must be deemed "scandalous" under Section 2(a).

Id., at 1221.

Would denial of registration violate the applicant's first amendment rights? See *In re* McGinley, *supra*; Davis, *Registration of Scandalous, Immoral, and Disparaging Matter Under Section 2(a) of the Lanham Act: Can One Man's Vulgarity Be Another's Registered Trademark?* 54 OHIO ST. L.J. 331 (1993); Baird, *Moral Intervention in the Trademark Arena: Banning the Registration of Scandalous and Immoral Trademarks*, 83 TRADEMARK REP. 661 (1993).

3. *Matter which may disparage or falsely suggest a connection with persons, living or dead, institutions, beliefs, or national symbols, or bring them into contempt, or disrepute.* In Greyhound Corp. v. Both Worlds Inc., 6 U.S.P.Q.2d 1635 (T.T.A.B. 1988), which the Board cited in *Old Glory Condom*, the mark depicting a defecating dog (a greyhound) was found not only to be scandalous but also to disparage the Greyhound Bus Company, whose corporate symbol is a running greyhound. The Board explained:

> Disparagement is essentially a violation of one's right of privacy—the right to be "let alone" from contempt or ridicule. It has been defined as the publication of a statement which the publisher intends to be understood, or which the recipient reasonably should understand, as tending "to cast doubt upon the quality of another's land, chattels, or intangible things." Restatement (Second) of Torts § 629 (1977). The two elements of such a claim are (1) that the communication reasonably would be understood as referring to the plaintiff; and (2) that the communication is disparaging, that is, would be considered offensive or objectionable by a reasonable person of ordinary sensibilities.

Id. at 1639.

In University of Notre Dame Du Lac v. J.C. Gourmet Good Imports Co., Inc., 703 F.2d 1372, 217 U.S.P.Q. 505 (C.A.F.C. 1983), the University opposed Gourmet's registration of the mark "Notre Dame" with design for its imported cheese on the ground that the mark falsely suggested a connection between the cheese and the University. The TTAB dismissed the opposition, and the Court of Appeals for the Federal Circuit affirmed. The court found it unlikely that Gourmet's use of the mark would lead purchasers to think that the cheese came from or was otherwise affiliated with the University. However, such a showing was unnecessary. The drafters of section 2(a) intended to protect privacy interests. While a mark may not cause a likelihood of confusion about the source of goods or services, it might nonetheless violate another's right of privacy. The court determined that in order to demonstrate that an applicant's mark falsely suggests a connection with a person or institution, it must be shown that the mark is unmistakably associated with a particular personality or "persona." *Id.*, 703 F.2d at 1376, 217 U.S.P.Q. at 509. In this case, the court decided, such a showing could not be made.

> As the board noted, "Notre Dame" is not a name solely associated with the University. It serves to identify a famous and sacred religious figure and is used in the names of churches dedicated to Notre Dame, such as the Cathedral of Notre Dame in Paris, France. Thus, it cannot be said that the only "person" which the name possibly identifies is the University and that the mere use of NOTRE DAME by another appropriates its identity.

Id., 703 F.2d at 1377, 217 U.S.P.Q. at 509. The court suggested that its conclusion would differ if there were evidence that Gourmet had intended to identify the University with its mark. Evidence of such intent would be highly persuasive that the public would in fact make the intended false association. No such evidence, however, had been presented.

If Jimmy Buffett opposed the registration of "Margaritaville" for restaurant services under section 2(a), would he be likely to win? See Buffett v. Chi-Chi's, Inc., 226 U.S.P.Q. 428 (T.T.A.B. 1985).

Would use of the marks "Da Vinci" or "Beethoven" on products falsely suggest a connection with the famous Leonardo or Ludwig, in violation of section 2(a)? See Lucien Piccard Watch Corp. v. Since 1868 Crescent Corp., 314 F.Supp. 329, 165 U.S.P.Q. 459 (S.D.N.Y.1970) (no section 2(a) problem with the mark "Da Vinci" for jewelry because it "is scarcely likely to mislead any substantial number of purchasers into believing that Leonardo Da Vinci was in any way responsible for the design or production of the goods").

How would you evaluate the words "National Collection & Credit Control," shown with a drawing of an American eagle superimposed on an outline of the shape of the United States, for a collection agency? See *In re* National Collection & Credit Control, Inc., 152 U.S.P.Q. 200 (T.T.A.B. 1966).

4. *Geographic indications as marks for wines and spirits.* The Uruguay Round Agreements Act amended Lanham Act section 2(a), 15 U.S.C.A. § 1052(a), to prohibit registration of marks consisting of

> a geographical indication which, when used on or in connection with wines or spirits, identifies a place other than the origin of the goods and

is first used on or in connection with wines or spirits by the applicant on or after January 1, 1996.

Uruguay Round Agreements Act, Pub. L. No. 103–465 § 522, 108 Stat. 4809, 4982 (1994). This change was necessary in order to comply with Article 23 of the GATT Uruguay Round TRIPs Agreement. The Senate Report on the Uruguay Round Agreements Act explained:

> As amended, section 2 of the Trademark Act will prohibit the registration of marks for wines and spirits that contain a geographical indication which refers to a place other than where a good actually originates. "Geographical indications" are defined in TRIPs as "indications which identify a good as originating in the territory of a Member, or a region or locality in that territory, where a given quality, reputation or other characteristic of the good is essentially attributable to its geographical origin." It is intended that this definition will be applied in the context of trademark registration and that a "geographical indication" as used in this provision will be interpreted to comprise only those areas which have a reputation for being associated with the specific goods at issue. Obscure areas or those that do not have a reputation or other characteristics generally associated with wines or spirits should not be prohibited from registration.

S. REP. NO. 412, 103d Cong., 2d Sess. 226–27 (1994). Marks containing geographical indications that are registered or in use prior to January 1, 1996 may be maintained. *Id.*

What does this new statutory language prohibit that would not already have been prohibited under the existing section 2(a) language?

E. PRIOR USE OF THE MARK: LANHAM ACT SECTION 2(D)

§ 1052. (§ 2) Trademarks Registrable on Principal Register

No trademark by which the goods of the applicant may be distinguished from the goods of others shall be refused registration on the principal register on account of its nature unless it—

> * * *
>
> (d) Consists of or comprises a mark which so resembles a mark registered in the Patent and Trademark Office, or a mark or trade name previously used in the United States by another and not abandoned, as to be likely, when used on or in connection with the goods of the applicant, to cause confusion, or to cause mistake, or to deceive * * *.
>
> * * *

15 U.S.C.A. § 1052(d).

APPLICATION OF E.I. DuPONT DeNEMOURS & CO.

United States Court of Customs and Patent Appeals, 1973.
476 F.2d 1357, 177 U.S.P.Q. 563.

MARKEY, CHIEF JUDGE.

This appeal is from the decision of the Trademark Trial and Appeal Board, 166 USPQ 351 (1970), affirming a refusal to register DuPont's mark RALLY for a combination polishing, glazing and cleaning agent for use on automobiles on the basis of likelihood of confusion under section 2(d) of the Lanham Act with Horizon's registered mark RALLY for an all-purpose detergent. We reverse.

The application now before us was originally filed by Horizon. DuPont had earlier filed for registration of RALLY for a combination wax and cleaning agent for automobiles. That application was refused in view of Horizon's registration. DuPont appealed and the board affirmed.

While its appeal was pending, DuPont purchased Horizon's mark for the automobile product, the present application and the good will of that business. Because Horizon retained RALLY for all purpose detergent, an agreement designed to avoid conflict was entered into on the same day. Boundaries of use of the marks were established, permitting the sale of products "incidentally usable" in the other party's market but prohibiting any promotion as "especially suited for use in such market." DuPont's realm was the "automotive aftermarket." Horizon's encompassed the "commercial building or household market."

The examiner, aware of the assignment and agreement, nonetheless refused registration, citing Horizon's registration and describing the issue as "ruled upon" in the board's earlier decision. The board affirmed, holding:

> It is our opinion that despite any agreement between the parties the public interest cannot be ignored, and when the goods of the parties are as closely related as those here involved, their sale under the identical mark "RALLY" would be likely to result in confusion, mistake, or deception. * * * The mere fact that registrant may have precluded itself from selling an automobile cleaner under the mark "RALLY" does not overcome the likelihood of confusion as set forth in Section 2(d) of the Trademark Statute.

OPINION

* * *

We begin with interpretation of the Lanham Act as it applies here. The legislative history of the Act as a whole describes its objectives as making registration "more liberal," dispensing with "mere technical prohibitions and arbitrary provisions" and modernizing the trademark statutes "so that they will conform to legitimate present-day business practice." [S. Rep. No. 1333, 79th Cong., 2d Sess. (1946) in U.S. Code Cong. Service, 79th Cong., 2d Sess. at 174–78 (1946).] * * *

Under the statute the Commissioner must refuse registration when convinced that confusion is likely because of concurrent use of the marks of an applicant and a prior user on their respective goods.

The phrase "on account of its nature" in Sec. 2 clearly applies to the "resembles" element of Sec. 2(d). But the question of confusion is related not to the *nature* of the mark but to its *effect* "when applied to the goods of the applicant." The only *relevant* application is made in the marketplace. The words "when applied" do not refer to a mental exercise, but to all of the known circumstances surrounding use of the mark.

* * * As so often said, each case must be decided on its own facts. There is no litmus rule which can provide a ready guide to all cases.

In testing for likelihood of confusion under Sec. 2(d), therefore, the following, when of record, must be considered:

(1) The similarity or dissimilarity of the marks in their entireties as to appearance, sound, connotation and commercial impression.

(2) The similarity or dissimilarity and nature of the goods or services as described in an application or registration or in connection with which a prior mark is in use.

(3) The similarity or dissimilarity of established, likely-to-continue trade channels.

(4) The conditions under which and buyers to whom sales are made, i. e. "impulse" vs. careful, sophisticated purchasing.

(5) The fame of the prior mark (sales, advertising, length of use).

(6) The number and nature of similar marks in use on similar goods.

(7) The nature and extent of any actual confusion.

(8) The length of time during and conditions under which there has been concurrent use without evidence of actual confusion.

(9) The variety of goods on which a mark is or is not used (house mark, "family" mark, product mark).

(10) The market interface between applicant and the owner of a prior mark:

 (a) a mere "consent" to register or use.

 (b) agreement provisions designed to preclude confusion, i. e. limitations on continued use of the marks by each party.

 (c) assignment of mark, application, registration and good will of the related business.

 (d) laches and estoppel attributable to owner of prior mark and indicative of lack of confusion.

(11) The extent to which applicant has a right to exclude others from use of its mark on its goods.

(12) The extent of potential confusion, i. e., whether *de minimis* or substantial.

(13) Any other established fact probative of the effect of use.

* * *

The evidentiary elements are not listed above in order of merit. Each may from case to case play a dominant role. * * *

Applying the above criteria, and after a thorough review of the entire record, we are convinced that confusion is not likely. The agreement and assignment herein constitute far more than mere "consent." They play, in this case, a dominant role. * * *

In considering agreements, a naked "consent" may carry little weight. Absent more, the consenter may continue or expand his use. The consent may be based on ignorance or misconception of the law. The facts may show, on the other hand, that consent could exist only in the absence of any real likelihood of confusion.

The weight to be given more detailed agreements of the type presented here should be substantial. It can be safely taken as fundamental that reputable businessmen-users of valuable trademarks have no interest in *causing* public confusion. The genius of the free competitive system is the paralleling of the interest of the entrepreneur and the consuming public so far as possible. Altruism aside, it is in his *pecuniary* interest, indeed a matter of economic survival, that the businessman obtain and retain customers, the very purpose and function of a trademark, and that he avoid and preclude confusion. Millions of advertising dollars are spent daily for that precise purpose. The history of trademark litigation and the substantial body of law to which it relates demonstrate the businessman's alertness in seeking to enjoin confusion. In so doing he guards both his pocketbook and the public interest.

Thus when those most familiar with use in the marketplace and most interested in precluding confusion enter agreements designed to avoid it, the scales of evidence are clearly tilted. It is at least difficult to maintain a subjective view that confusion will occur when those directly concerned say it won't. A mere *assumption* that confusion is likely will rarely prevail against uncontroverted evidence from those on the firing line that it is not.

The parties here agreed to restrict themselves in effect to the general purpose cleaning market (Horizon) and the automobile market (DuPont). Horizon is subject to suit for breach of contract and infringement if it promotes its RALLY products for cleaning automobiles. DuPont can be sued if it promotes its RALLY products in general cleaning. The fact that the goods of one party "could be used" in the field of the other is too conjectural and too widely applicable to form the sole basis of decision, particularly where, as here, the parties have agreed to avoid the promotion of such cross-use.

The mere fact of diverse marketing emphasis alone may not in every case preclude confusion. Without more, it may well be that purchasers active in both markets and familiar with products sold under a particular mark could attribute to the same source closely related goods sold under the same mark. The agreements herein, however, considered as a whole and notwithstanding certain phrases subject to contrary interpretation, evidence that confusion will be unlikely. As we read them, the very purpose and aim of the present agreements is the avoidance of public confusion. Under provision 6 of the assignment the parties agreed "to take any further actions and execute any further agreements needed to carry out the spirit and intent of this agreement." The words of this court in a concurrent use proceeding, In re Beatrice Foods, Co., 429 F.2d 466, 57 CCPA 1302 (1970) are particularly apt:

> * * * there can be no better assurance of the absence of any likelihood of confusion, mistake or deception than the parties' promises to avoid any activity which might lead to such likelihood.

It is reasonable to conclude that experienced businessmen fully and continuously alert to each others' products, labels, trade channels and advertising and parties to the agreements before us, will be quick to act against confusion. We cannot believe that Horizon would have sold its automotive business, assigned its mark and entered into the agreement or that DuPont would have accepted and paid for the assignment and entered into the agreement, if either thought for a moment that purchasers would seriously be confused as to source. Dollars were at stake. Decisions of men who stand to lose if wrong are normally more reliable than those of examiners and judges.

We have no hesitancy in holding, therefore, under the facts of this case, that confusion is not likely to stem from concurrent use of RALLY by Horizon and DuPont on their respective goods under the terms of their agreement. Accordingly, the decision of the board must be *reversed*. * * *

Notes and Questions

1. *Prior use.* It is important to note that a "prior use" which disqualifies an applicant's mark under section 2(d) can consist of a trademark or service mark use or a use of the word, symbol or device as a trade name—the name of a business. Since a trade name, as such, cannot be registered, it is obvious that the prior user need not have registered the trade name or mark. It is sufficient that he acquired proprietary rights in the mark or trade name at common law—through use in trade and, in the case of words, symbols or devices that are not inherently distinctive, acquisition of secondary meaning—prior to the applicant. See generally Otto Roth & Co., Inc. v. Universal Foods Corp., 640 F.2d 1317, 209 U.S.P.Q. 40 (C.C.P.A.1981).

The "likelihood of confusion" standard discussed in the *DuPont* case is similar to the standard used to determine liability in infringement cases, which we will study in the next Section.

VI. RIGHTS IN MARKS

A. DIRECT INFRINGEMENT

AMF INC. v. SLEEKCRAFT BOATS

United States Court of Appeals for the Ninth Circuit, 1979.
599 F.2d 341, 204 U.S.P.Q. 808.

J. Blaine Anderson, Circuit Judge:

In this trademark infringement action, the district court, after a brief non-jury trial, found appellant AMF's trademark was valid, but not infringed, and denied AMF's request for injunctive relief.

AMF and appellee Nescher both manufacture recreational boats. AMF uses the mark Slickcraft, and Nescher uses Sleekcraft. The crux of this appeal is whether concurrent use of the two marks is likely to confuse the public. The district judge held that confusion was unlikely. We disagree and remand for entry of a limited injunction.

I. Facts

AMF's predecessor used the name Slickcraft Boat Company from 1954 to 1969 when it became a division of AMF. The mark Slickcraft was federally registered on April 1, 1969, and has been continuously used since then as a trademark for this line of recreational boats.

Slickcraft boats are distributed and advertised nationally. AMF has authorized over one hundred retail outlets to sell the Slickcraft line. For the years 1966–1974, promotional expenditures for the Slickcraft line averaged approximately $200,000 annually. Gross sales for the same period approached $50,000,000.

After several years in the boat-building business, appellee Nescher organized a sole proprietorship, Nescher Boats, in 1962. This venture failed in 1967. In late 1968 Nescher began anew and adopted the name Sleekcraft. Since then Sleekcraft has been the Nescher trademark. The name Sleekcraft was selected without knowledge of appellant's use. After AMF notified him of the alleged trademark infringement, Nescher adopted a distinctive logo and added the identifying phrase "Boats by Nescher" on plaques affixed to the boat and in much of its advertising. (See Appendix A). The Sleekcraft mark still appears alone on some of appellee's stationery, signs, trucks, and advertisements.

The Sleekcraft venture succeeded. Expenditures for promotion increased from $6,800 in 1970 to $126,000 in 1974. Gross sales rose from $331,000 in 1970 to over $6,000,000 in 1975. Like AMF, Nescher sells his boats through authorized local dealers.

Slickcraft boats are advertised primarily in magazines of general circulation. Nescher advertises primarily in publications for boat racing enthusiasts. Both parties exhibit their product line at boat shows, sometimes the same show.

* * *

IV. Factors Relevant to Likelihood of Confusion

When the goods produced by the alleged infringer compete for sales with those of the trademark owner, infringement usually will be found if the marks are sufficiently similar that confusion can be expected.[9]

9. The alleged infringer's intent in adopting the mark is weighed, both as probative evidence of the likelihood of confusion and as an equitable consideration.

When the goods are related,[10] but not competitive, several other factors are added to the calculus. If the goods are totally unrelated, there can be no infringement because confusion is unlikely.

AMF contends these boat lines are competitive. Both lines are comprised of sporty, fiberglass boats often used for water skiing; the sizes of the boats are similar as are the prices. Nescher contends his boats are not competitive with Slickcraft boats because his are true high performance boats intended for racing enthusiasts.

The district court found that although there was some overlap in potential customers for the two product lines, the boats "appeal to separate sub-markets." Slickcraft boats are for general family recreation, and Sleekcraft boats are for persons who want high speed recreation; thus, the district court concluded, competition between the lines is negligible. Our research has led us to only one case in which a similarly fine distinction in markets has been recognized, *Sleeper Lounge Co. v. Bell Manufacturing Co.*, 253 F.2d 720 (CA 9 1958). Yet, after careful review of all the exhibits introduced at trial, we are convinced the district court's finding was warranted by the evidence.

The Slickcraft line is designed for a variety of activities: fishing, water skiing, pleasure cruises, and sunbathing. The promotional literature emphasizes family fun. Sleekcraft boats are not for families. They are low-profile racing boats designed for racing, high speed cruises, and water skiing. Seating capacity and luxury are secondary. Unlike the Slickcraft line, handling capability is emphasized. The promotional literature projects an alluring, perhaps flashier, racing image; absent from the pictures are the small children prominently displayed in the Slickcraft brochures.

Even though both boats are designed for towing water skiers, only the highly skilled enthusiast would require the higher speeds the Sleekcraft promises. We therefore affirm the district court's finding that, despite the potential market overlap, the two lines are not competitive. Accordingly, we must consider all the relevant circumstances in assessing the likelihood of confusion.

V. Factors Relevant to Likelihood of Confusion

In determining whether confusion between related goods is likely, the following factors are relevant: [11]

1. strength of the mark;
2. proximity of the goods;
3. similarity of the marks;
4. evidence of actual confusion;

10. Related goods are those "products which would be reasonably thought by the buying public to come from the same source if sold under the same mark." *Standard Brands, Inc. v. Smidler*, 151 F.2d 34, 37 (CA 2 1945).

11. The list is not exhaustive. Other variables may come into play depending on the particular facts presented.

5. marketing channels used;

6. type of goods and the degree of care likely to be exercised by the purchaser;

7. defendant's intent in selecting the mark; and

8. likelihood of expansion of the product lines.

We discuss each serially.

1. Strength of the mark

A strong mark is inherently distinctive, for example, an arbitrary or fanciful mark; it will be afforded the widest ambit of protection from infringing uses. A descriptive mark tells something about the product; it will be protected only when secondary meaning is shown.[12] In between lie suggestive marks which subtly connote something about the products. Although less distinctive than an arbitrary or fanciful mark and therefore a comparatively weak mark, a suggestive mark will be protected without proof of secondary meaning.

Slickcraft is, AMF asserts, a fanciful mark and therefore entitled to wide protection. This assertion is incorrect. The issue, as we view it, is whether Slickcraft is descriptive or suggestive of appellant's boats. * * *

Although the distinction between descriptive and suggestive marks may be inarticulable, several criteria offer guidance. The primary criterion is "the imaginativeness involved in the suggestion": that is, how immediate and direct is the thought process from the mark to the particular product. From the word Slickcraft one might readily conjure up the image of appellant's boats, yet a number of other images might also follow. A secondary criterion is whether granting the trademark owner a limited monopoly will in fact inhibit legitimate use of the mark by other sellers. There is no evidence here that others have used or desire to use Slickcraft in describing their goods. Another criterion is whether the mark is actually viewed by the public as an indication of the product's origin or as a self-serving description of it. We think buyers probably will understand that Slickcraft is a trademark, particularly since it is generally used in conjunction with the mark AMF. (See Appendix A). Based on the above criteria and our reading of the district court's findings, we hold that Slickcraft is a suggestive mark when applied to boats.

Although appellant's mark is protectible and may have been strengthened by advertising, it is a weak mark entitled to a restricted range of protection. Thus, only if the marks are quite similar, and the goods closely related, will infringement be found.

12. Once secondary meaning is established, though, the protection afforded should be commensurate with the degree of consumer association proven.

2. Proximity of the goods

For related goods, the danger presented is that the public will mistakenly assume there is an association between the producers of the related goods, though no such association exists. The more likely the public is to make such an association, the less similarity in the marks is requisite to a finding of likelihood of confusion. Thus, less similarity between the marks will suffice when the goods are complementary, the products are sold to the same class of purchasers, or the goods are similar in use and function.

Although these product lines are non-competing, they are extremely close in use and function. In fact, their uses overlap. Both are for recreational boating on bays and lakes. Both are designed for water skiing and speedy cruises. Their functional features, for the most part, are also similar: fiberglass bodies, outboard motors, and open seating for a handful of people. Although the Sleekcraft boat is for higher speed recreation and its refinements support the market distinction the district court made, they are so closely related that a diminished standard of similarity must be applied when comparing the two marks.

3. Similarity of the marks

The district court found that "the two marks are easily distinguishable in use either when written or spoken." * * *

Similarity of the marks is tested on three levels: sight, sound, and meaning. Each must be considered as they are encountered in the marketplace. Although similarity is measured by the marks as entities, similarities weigh more heavily than differences.

Standing alone the words Sleekcraft and Slickcraft are the same except for two inconspicuous letters in the middle of the first syllable. To the eye, the words are similar.

In support of the district court's finding, Nescher points out that the distinctive logo on his boats and brochures negates the similarity of the words. We agree: the names appear dissimilar when viewed in conjunction with the logo, but the logo is often absent. The exhibits show that the word Sleekcraft is frequently found alone in trade journals, company stationery, and various advertisements.

Nescher also points out that the Slickcraft name is usually accompanied by the additional trademark AMF. As a result of this consistent use, Nescher argues, AMF has become the salient part of the mark indicative of the product's origin.

Although Nescher is correct in asserting that use of a housemark can reduce the likelihood of confusion, the effect is negligible here even though AMF is a well-known house name for recreational equipment. The exhibits show that the AMF mark is down-played in the brochures and advertisements; the letters AMF are smaller and skewed to one side. Throughout the promotional materials, the emphasis is on the Slickcraft name. Accordingly, we find that Slickcraft is the more conspicuous mark and serves to indicate the source of origin to the public.

Another argument pressed by Nescher is that we should disregard the common suffix "craft" and compare Slick and Sleek alone. Although these are the salient parts of the two marks, we must consider the entire mark. Craft, a generic frequently used in trademarks on boats, is not itself protectible, yet the common endings do add to the marks' similarity. The difference between Slick and Sleek is insufficient to overcome the overall visual similarity.

Sound is also important because reputation is often conveyed word-of-mouth. We recognize that the two sounds can be distinguished, but the difference is only in a small part of one syllable. In *G. D. Searle & Co. v. Chas. Pfizer & Co.*, 265 F.2d 385 (CA 7 1959), *cert. denied*, 361 U.S. 819, 80 S.Ct. 64, 4 L.Ed.2d 65 (1959), the court reversed the trial court's finding that Bonamine sounded "unlike" Dramamine, stating that: "Slight differences in the sound of trademarks will not protect the infringer." *Id.* at 387. The difference here is even slighter. * * *

Neither expert testimony nor survey evidence was introduced below to support the trial court's finding that the marks were easily distinguishable to the eye and the ear. The district judge based his conclusion on a comparison of the marks. After making the same comparison, we are left with a definite and firm conviction that his conclusion is incorrect.

The final criterion reinforces our conclusion. Closeness in meaning can itself substantiate a claim of similarity of trademarks. Nescher contends the words are sharply different in meaning. This contention is not convincing; the words are virtual synonyms.

Despite the trial court's findings, we hold that the marks are quite similar on all three levels.

4. Evidence of actual confusion

Evidence that use of the two marks has already led to confusion is persuasive proof that future confusion is likely. Proving actual confusion is difficult, however, and the courts have often discounted such evidence because it was unclear or insubstantial.

AMF introduced evidence that confusion had occurred both in the trade and in the mind of the buying public. A substantial showing of confusion among either group might have convinced the trial court that continued use would lead to further confusion.

The district judge found that in light of the number of sales and the extent of the parties' advertising, the amount of past confusion was negligible. We cannot say this finding is clearly erroneous though we might have viewed the evidence more generously.

Because of the difficulty in garnering such evidence, the failure to prove instances of actual confusion is not dispositive. Consequently, this factor is weighed heavily only when there is evidence of past confusion or, perhaps, when the particular circumstances indicate such evidence should have been available.

5. *Marketing channels*

Convergent marketing channels increase the likelihood of confusion. There is no evidence in the record that both lines were sold under the same roof except at boat shows; the normal marketing channels used by both AMF and Nescher are, however, parallel. Each sells through authorized retail dealers in diverse localities. The same sales methods are employed. The price ranges are almost identical. Each line is advertised extensively though different national magazines are used; the retail dealers also promote the lines, by participating in smaller boat shows and by advertising in local newspapers and classified telephone directories. Although different submarkets are involved, the general class of boat purchasers exposed to the products overlap.

6. *Type of goods and purchaser care*

Both parties produce high quality, expensive goods. According to the findings of fact, the boats "are purchased only after thoughtful, careful evaluation of the product and the performance the purchaser expects."

In assessing the likelihood of confusion to the public, the standard used by the courts is the typical buyer exercising ordinary caution. Although the wholly indifferent may be excluded, the standard includes the ignorant and the credulous. When the buyer has expertise in the field, a higher standard is proper though it will not preclude a finding that confusion is likely. Similarly, when the goods are expensive, the buyer can be expected to exercise greater care in his purchases; again, though, confusion may still be likely.

The parties vigorously dispute the validity of the trial court's finding on how discriminating the average buyer actually is. Although AMF presented expert testimony to the contrary, the court's finding is amply supported by the record. The care exercised by the typical purchaser, though it might virtually eliminate mistaken purchases, does not guarantee that confusion as to association or sponsorship is unlikely.

The district court also found that trademarks are unimportant to the average boat buyer. Common sense and the evidence indicate this is not the type of purchase made only on "general impressions." This inattention to trade symbols does reduce the possibilities for confusion.

The high quality of defendant's boats is also relevant in another way. The hallmark of a trademark owner's interest in preventing use of his mark on related goods is the threat such use poses to the reputation of his own goods. When the alleged infringer's goods are of equal quality, there is little harm to the reputation earned by the trademarked goods. Yet this is no defense, for present quality is no assurance of continued quality. The wrong inheres in involuntarily entrusting one's business reputation to another business; AMF, of course, cannot control the quality of Sleekcraft boats. In addition, what may be deemed a beneficial feature in a racing boat may be seen as a deficiency to a person seeking a craft for general-purpose recreation; the confused consumer may then decide, without even perusing one, that a Slickcraft boat will not suit his needs. Finally, equivalence in quality may actually contribute to the assumption of a common connection.

7. Intent

The district judge found that Nescher was unaware of appellant's use of the Slickcraft mark when he adopted the Sleekcraft name. There was no evidence that anyone attempted to palm off the latter boats for the former. And after notification of the purported infringement, Nescher designed a distinctive logo. (See Appendix A.) We agree with the district judge: appellee's good faith cannot be questioned.

When the alleged infringer knowingly adopts a mark similar to another's, reviewing courts presume that the defendant can accomplish his purpose: that is, that the public will be deceived. Good faith is less probative of the likelihood of confusion, yet may be given considerable weight in fashioning a remedy.

8. Likelihood of expansion

Inasmuch as a trademark owner is afforded greater protection against competing goods, a "strong possibility" that either party may expand his business to compete with the other will weigh in favor of finding that the present use is infringing. When goods are closely related, any expansion is likely to result in direct competition. The evidence shows that both parties are diversifying their model lines. The potential that one or both of the parties will enter the other's submarket with a competing model is strong.

VI. REMEDY

Based on the preceding analysis, we hold that Nescher has infringed the Slickcraft mark. Since Nescher's use is continuing, an injunction should have been entered. Several considerations, however, convince us that a limited injunction will suffice.

Both parties have used their trademarks for over a decade. AMF has a substantial investment in the Slickcraft name, yet a complete prohibition against appellee's use of the Sleekcraft name is unnecessary to protect against encroachment of appellant's mark, or to eliminate public confusion. Appellee has also expended much effort and money to build and preserve the goodwill of its mark.

There is little doubt both parties honestly desire to avoid confusion of their products. Nescher adopted the Sleekcraft name in good faith and has subsequently taken steps to avoid confusion. Use of the Nescher logo in all facets of the business would ensure that confusion would not occur. The exhibits, particularly the yellow pages advertisements, convince us that this is not being done.

Thus, in "balancing the conflicting interests both parties have in the unimpaired continuation of their trade-mark use," *Durox Co. v. Duron Paint Manufacturing Co.*, 4 Cir., 320 F.2d 882 at 885, and the interest the public and the trade have in avoiding confusion, we conclude that a limited mandatory injunction is warranted. Upon remand the district court should consider the above interests in structuring appropriate relief. At minimum, the logo should appear in all advertisements, signs, and promotional materials prepared either by appellee or by his retail dealers, and on all appellee's business forms except those intended for strictly internal use. A specific disclaimer of any association with AMF or the Slickcraft line seems unnecessary, nor do we think it necessary to enjoin Nescher from expanding his product line. * * *

Appendix A

Notes and Questions

1. *The Standard of Review.* There has been considerable confusion and inconsistency regarding the proper standard of review to apply when a district court's determination regarding likelihood of confusion is challenged on appeal. In *AMF*, the Court of Appeals for the Ninth Circuit stated that it would review a district court's determination *de novo* if it was based upon undisputed facts. However, when disputed facts were involved, it would apply the clearly erroneous standard to the underlying "foundational facts" and give *de novo* review to the "legal conclusion" regarding likelihood of confusion. Several years later, in Levi Strauss & Co. v. Blue Bell, Inc., 778 F.2d 1352, 1355, 228 U.S.P.Q. 346, 348 (9th Cir.1985), the court reevaluated the standard of review, and decided that the "clearly erroneous" standard was the more appropriate standard of review for the likelihood of confusion determination. While a few of the circuits continue to treat the ultimate likelihood of confusion decision as one of law, as in *AMF*, the majority of circuits today treat it as one of fact, as in *Levi Strauss,* and apply the clearly erroneous standard. See 3 J.T. McCARTHY, McCARTHY ON TRADEMARKS AND UNFAIR COMPETITION, § 23.22 (3d ed. 1992).

2. *Who must be confused, and about what?* The *AMF* opinion states that in assessing the likelihood of confusion, courts apply the standard of the typical buyer of such goods exercising ordinary caution. To find a defendant liable for trademark infringement, it must appear that a significant, or appreciable number of prospective purchasers are likely to be confused by the defendant's use of its mark. However, it is usually safe to assume that if the typical buyer exercising ordinary caution would be confused, a significant

or appreciable number of prospective purchasers would be confused. See RESTATEMENT (THIRD) OF UNFAIR COMPETITION § 20, comment g (Tentative Draft No. 2, 1990).

Courts are rarely specific about what will constitute a "significant" or "appreciable" number of prospective purchasers for purposes of infringement liability. In most cases, it would be impossible to measure the exact extent of confusion in any event. The cases do make it clear, however, that the number need not constitute the majority of potential customers for the parties' goods. Indeed, survey evidence indicating that ten or fifteen percent would be confused may be sufficient, when supported by other evidence. *Id.*

About what must this significant or appreciable number of prospective purchasers be confused? While earlier trademark law specified that they must be confused about the goods' or services' *origin*, or *source*, modern trademark law also protects against confusion as to *affiliation, connection, approval or sponsorship*. See Lindy Pen Co., Inc. v. Bic Pen Corp., 725 F.2d 1240, 1246, 226 U.S.P.Q. 17, 21 (9th Cir.1984), *cert. denied* 469 U.S. 1188, 105 S.Ct. 955, 83 L.Ed.2d 962 (1985). This broadening of the confusion standard has fostered the growing business of trademark licensing, or merchandising. For example, assume that a clothing manufacturer makes and sells tee-shirts featuring a large replica of the mark of a popular sports team on the front. Consumers, seeing the shirt in a store, may not think that the team is the *source* of the shirt, since most teams are not in the clothing sales or manufacturing business. They might, however, believe that the team has affiliated itself with the producer in some fashion, approving or sponsoring the shirt. Bringing such situations into the trademark infringement cause of action gives mark owners greater control over the use of their marks and provides lucrative opportunities to sell the right to use them. It is, of course, a question of fact in each case whether a significant number of prospective customers will understand the mark to be an indication of sponsorship or affiliation with the mark owner or merely decoration. For an excellent discussion of the present status of the law on this issue, see 2 J.T. McCARTHY, McCARTHY ON TRADEMARKS AND UNFAIR COMPETITION, § 24.03[4] (3d ed. 1992). See also Denicola, *Institutional Publicity Rights: An Analysis of the Merchandising of Famous Trade Symbols*, 75 TRADEMARK REP. 41 (1985).

The trademark law has also broadened with regard to *when* prospective customers are likely to be confused. Confusion at the point of purchase has been the traditional focus. However, assume that plaintiff manufactures and sells an expensive, prestige product, and the defendant manufactures and sells an inexpensive replica, using a similar trademark. Given the discrepancy in price and sales outlet, purchasers of the defendant's product may be unlikely to think that the product comes from the plaintiff. But after the sale, other prospective purchasers may see the defendant's product (with its mark) outside of the sales context—in the purchaser's home or on his person—and think it comes from the plaintiff. Under modern trademark law, this *post-sale* likelihood of confusion may serve as the basis for a finding of infringement. See generally, Mastercrafters Clock & Radio Co. v. Vacheron & Constantin–LeCoultre Watches, Inc., 221 F.2d 464, 105 U.S.P.Q. 160 (2d Cir.1955), *cert. denied* 350 U.S. 832, 76 S.Ct. 67, 100 L.Ed. 743 (1955). But see Nike, Inc. v. "Just Did It" Enterprises, 6 F.3d 1225, 28 U.S.P.Q.2d

1385 (7th Cir.1993). In such cases, what is the plaintiff's injury? See RESTATEMENT (THIRD) OF UNFAIR COMPETITION § 20, comment b (Tentative Draft No. 2, 1990). For criticisms of the post-sale confusion doctrine, see Ehrlich, *When Should Post–Sale Confusion Prevent Use or Registration of Marks?*, 81 TRADEMARK REP. 267 (1991).

What if the defendant's similar mark is likely to cause initial consumer confusion, when the defendant first offers to sell its product, but because of the nature of the sales process, the confusion will be dissipated prior to the actual time to purchase? Should that temporary pre-sale likelihood of confusion support a finding of infringement? What injury does it cause to the plaintiff? See Mobile Oil Corp. v. Pegasus Petroleum Corp., 818 F.2d 254, 2 U.S.P.Q.2d 1677 (2d Cir.1987); Bruzga, *Sophisticated Purchaser Defense Avoided Where Pre-sale Confusion Is Harmful*, 71 J. PAT. & TRADEMARK OFF. SOC. 32 (1989).

Most trademark infringement cases arise when a subsequent (junior) mark user creates a likelihood that purchasers will think *its* goods or services come from (or are associated with) a prior (senior) user of the mark. In some cases, however, the junior user is so much larger or more famous than the senior user, or so extensively promotes its mark, that it overshadows the senior user, leading consumers to think that *the senior user's goods come from (or are associated with) the junior user.* This is known as "reverse confusion." This reverse confusion will sustain the senior user's trademark infringement claim against the junior user. See, e.g., Big O Tire Dealers, Inc., v. Goodyear Tire & Rubber Co., 561 F.2d 1365, 195 U.S.P.Q. 417 (10th Cir.1977), *cert. dismissed* 434 U.S. 1052, 98 S.Ct. 905, 54 L.Ed.2d 805 (1978). In such cases, what is the nature of the senior user's injury? See Ameritech, Inc. v. American Information Technologies Corp., 811 F.2d 960, 1 U.S.P.Q.2d 1861 (6th Cir.1987).

For a comprehensive discussion of many of the issues raised in this note, see Allen, *Who Must Be Confused And When?: The Scope of Confusion Actionable Under Federal Trademark Law*, 81 TRADEMARK REP. 209 (1991).

3. *The multiple factor test for likelihood of confusion.* The *AMF* opinion differentiated between infringement cases in which the goods are "competitive" and those in which the goods are "related," and upheld the district court's determination that the *AMF* parties' boats were "related" goods. If the defendant's goods do not compete with the plaintiff's, why should the plaintiff be entitled to enjoin the defendant's use of a confusingly similar mark? How is the plaintiff harmed?

Every Circuit Court of Appeals has developed its own variation of the multiple factor test set forth in *AMF*. While these multiple factor tests originally were applied only in cases of *related* goods, today they routinely are applied in all infringement cases, including those involving *competing* goods. See, e.g. Lindy Pen Co. v. Bic Pen Corp., *supra*.

(1) Strength of the mark. The *AMF* court states that the "stronger" or more distinctive the mark, the greater the scope of protection it will be afforded. Why should this be the case? See RESTATEMENT (THIRD) OF UNFAIR COMPETITION § 21 and comment d (Tentative Draft No. 2, 1990).

(2) Proximity of the goods. The more similar the parties' respective goods or services, the less similar the marks must be. How should similarity of goods be measured? Do the goods perform the same function? Are the goods often used together? Are they of the same general class, so that consumers might expect that they come from the same producer? Are consumers likely to believe that lamps and light bulbs come from the same source? How about light bulbs and heavy earth moving equipment?

(3) Similarity of the marks. Courts have often admonished that the similarity of the parties' marks is not to be judged simply through a side-by-side comparison:

> The marks must be compared in the light of what occurs in the marketplace, not in the courtroom. A prospective purchaser does not ordinarily carry a sample or specimen of the article he knows well enough to call by its trade name, he necessarily depends upon the mental picture of that which symbolizes origin and ownership of the thing desired. * * * Therefore, the court must determine whether the alleged infringing mark will be confusing to the public when singly presented.

Beer Nuts, Inc. v. Clover Club Foods Co., 711 F.2d 934, 941, 221 U.S.P.Q. 209, 216 (10th Cir.1983). Indeed, "it is sufficient if one adopts a trade-name or a trade-mark so like another in form, spelling or sound that one, *with a not very definite or clear recollection as to the real trade-mark*, is likely to become confused or misled." Northam Warren Corp. v. Universal Cosmetic Co., 18 F.2d 774, 775 (7th Cir.1927) (emphasis added).

The *AMF* court discusses the "sight, sound and meaning" test, set forth in section 729 of the Restatement of Torts. As one might imagine, the "sight" test is quite subjective: given the wide variety of design, word, and device marks, there can be no uniformly applicable rule for determining when two marks "look alike." Nonetheless, especially for picture and design marks, similarity of appearance can be an extremely important factor. It may also be important in the case of foreign words. For example, are the following words confusingly similar: "Senorita," "Si Senor" and "Senioral"? See Myrurgia, S.A. v. Comptoir De La Parfumerie S.A. Ancienne Maison Tschanz, 441 F.2d 673, 169 U.S.P.Q. 587 (C.C.P.A.1971).

As the Second Circuit has observed, "[t]rademarks, like small children, are not only seen but heard." Grotrian, Helfferich, Schulz, Th. Steinweg Nachf. v. Steinway & Sons, 523 F.2d 1331, 1340, 186 U.S.P.Q. 436, 443 (2d Cir.1975). In assessing the phonetic similarity of the "Slickcraft" and "Sleekcraft" marks, the *AMF* court looked to the Seventh Circuit's opinion in G.D. Searle & Co. v. Chas. Pfizer & Co., 265 F.2d 385, 121 U.S.P.Q. 74 (7th Cir.1959), *cert. denied* 361 U.S. 819, 80 S.Ct. 64, 4 L.Ed.2d 65 (1959). The *Searle* court's opinion, which found "Bonamine" phonetically similar to "Dramamine," demonstrates one of the more scientific judicial approaches to the similarity issue:

> DRAMAMINE and BONAMINE contain the same number of syllables; they have the same stress pattern, with primary accent on the first syllable and secondary accent on the third; and the last two syllables of DRAMAMINE and BONAMINE are identical. The initial sounds of DRAMAMINE and BONAMINE ["d" and "b"] are both what are

> known as "voiced plosives," and are acoustically similar; the consonants "m" and "n" are nasal sounds and are acoustically similar. The only dissimilar sound in the two trademarks is the "r" in DRAMAMINE. Slight differences in the sound of similar trademarks will not protect the infringer.

Id., 265 F.2d at 387, 121 U.S.P.Q. at 76. How would you evaluate the phonetic similarity of the following marks:

(1) "Coca Cola" and "Cup–O'-Cola" (see Coca–Cola Co. v. Clay, 324 F.2d 198, 139 U.S.P.Q. 308 (C.C.P.A.1963));

(2) "Coca–Cola" and "Polar Cola" (see Coca–Cola Co. v. Snow Crest Beverages, Inc., 162 F.2d 280, 73 U.S.P.Q. 518 (1st Cir.1947), *cert. denied* 332 U.S. 809, 68 S.Ct. 110, 92 L.Ed. 386 (1947));

(3) "Beck's Beer" and "Ex Bier" (see Beck & Co. v. Package Distributors of America, Inc., 198 U.S.P.Q. 573 (T.T.A.B. 1978)).

Under the "meaning" prong of the Restatement test, one must consider the mental imagery evoked by the marks. For example, how would you compare a drawing of a winged horse with the word mark "Pegasus?" See Mobil Oil Corp. v. Pegasus Petroleum Corp., 818 F.2d 254, 257–58, 2 U.S.P.Q.2d 1677, 1679–80 (2d Cir.1987) (approving district court's finding that "the word 'Pegasus' evokes the symbol of the flying red horse * * *. In other words, the symbol of the flying horse and its name 'Pegasus' are synonymous.") How would you compare the word marks "Cyclone" and "Tornado" for wire fencing? See Hancock v. American Steel & Wire Co., 203 F.2d 737, 97 U.S.P.Q. 330 (1953). How about "Gravel" and "On the Rocks" for men's cologne? See Gravel Cologne, Inc. v. Lawrence Palmer, Inc., 469 F.2d 1397, 176 U.S.P.Q. 123 (C.C.P.A.1972).

Another point to bear in mind under the "meaning" test is that, under the doctrine of foreign equivalents, words from common foreign languages may be held confusingly similar to their English translation. See, e.g., *In re* American Safety Razor Co., 2 U.S.P.Q.2d 1459 (T.T.A.B. 1987) (finding "Good Morning" for shaving cream confusingly similar to "Buenos Dias" for soap). It must appear, however, that a significant number of consumers would be likely to make the translation. For a comprehensive analysis of the doctrine of foreign equivalents in this context, see 3 J.T. McCARTHY, McCARTHY ON TRADEMARKS AND UNFAIR COMPETITION, § 23.14 (3d ed. 1992).

(4) Evidence of actual confusion. As the *AMF* court notes, evidence of actual consumer confusion is not required to prove that the defendant's use of its mark causes a likelihood of consumer confusion. On the other hand, such evidence, if reliable, can be very persuasive. How might one go about proving the existence of actual confusion? See Allen, *The Role of Actual Confusion Evidence in Trademark Infringement Litigation*, 83 TRADEMARK REP. 267 (1993).

(5) Marketing channels used. Does the evidence on this factor weigh for or against a likelihood of confusion in *AMF*? Why should it matter whether the parties' goods are sold through similar retail outlets, or advertised in the same media? See RESTATEMENT (THIRD) OF UNFAIR COMPETITION § 21, comment g (Tentative Draft No. 2, 1990).

(6) Type of goods and the degree of care likely to be exercised by the purchaser. If the goods are expensive, like boats, or the purchasers are sophisticated (for example, professional purchasers or institutions), then it generally can be expected that the purchasers will devote some care and attention to selecting the goods. They are only likely to be confused by highly similar marks. By contrast, consider pickles, on sale to ordinary consumers in self-service grocery stores. As one court observed, "it has been asserted that the average purchaser undergoes, while in a supermarket, an experience not unlike that of hypnosis." Pikle–Rite Co. v. Chicago Pickle Co., 171 F.Supp. 671, 676, 121 U.S.P.Q. 128, 137 (N.D.Ill.1959). In such circumstances a much lesser degree of similarity may lead to confusion.

(7) Defendant's intent in selecting the mark. Trademark law has its origins in the tort of deceit, but the modern common-law and Lanham Act trademark causes of action do not require any showing of wrongful intent. On the other hand, as the *AMF* opinion acknowledges, evidence of an intent to confuse consumers may give rise to an inference (or in some circuits, a rebuttable presumption) that the defendant succeeded in accomplishing what she set out to do.

An intent to *copy* the plaintiff's mark is not necessarily an intent to *confuse*. For example, in Jordache Enterprises, Inc. v. Hogg Wyld, Ltd., 828 F.2d 1482, 4 U.S.P.Q.2d 1216 (10th Cir.1987), the defendants intentionally copied plaintiff's prestigious "Jordache" mark when they adopted the mark "Lardashe" for large women's jeans. The court found that their purpose in copying was to parody, not to confuse. Thus, there was no basis for inferring a likelihood of confusion under the rule stated above:

> Given the unlimited number of possible names and symbols that could serve as a trademark, it is understandable that a court generally presumes one who chooses a mark similar to an existing mark intends to confuse the public. However, where a party chooses a mark as a parody of an existing mark, the intent is not necessarily to confuse the public but rather to amuse. * * *
>
> In one sense, a parody is an attempt "to derive benefit from the reputation" of the owner of the mark, *Sicilia*, 732 F.2d at 431, if only because no parody could be made without the initial mark. The benefit to the one making the parody, however, arises from the humorous association, not from public confusion as to the source of the marks. A parody relies upon a difference from the original mark, presumably a humorous difference, in order to produce its desired effect.

Id., 828 F.2d at 1486, 4 U.S.P.Q.2d at 1219.

(8) Likelihood of expansion of the product lines. This factor is sometimes referred to as the likelihood that the senior user will "bridge the gap." As one court has explained,

> In the likelihood of confusion context, "bridging the gap" refers to two distinct possibilities. The first is that the senior user presently intends to expand his sales efforts to compete directly with the junior user; likelihood of confusion is created by the likelihood that the two products will be directly competitive. The second possibility is that, while there is no present intention to bridge the gap, consumers will assume

> otherwise and conclude, in this era of corporate diversification, that the parties are related companies.

Lambda Electronics Corp. v. Lambda Technology, Inc., 515 F.Supp. 915, 926, 211 U.S.P.Q. 75, 86 (S.D.N.Y.1981).

4. *Families of marks.* A business that uses the same prefix or suffix in a number of marks may establish a "family of marks," which effectively gives it rights in the common element itself: "A family of marks may have a synergistic recognition that is greater than the sum of each mark." Quality Inns International, Inc. v. McDonald's Corp., 695 F.Supp. 198, 212, 8 U.S.P.Q.2d 1633, 1643 (D.Md.1988). The Court of Appeals for the Federal Circuit has explained:

> A family of marks is a group of marks having a recognizable common characteristic, wherein the marks are composed and used in such a way that the public associates not only the individual marks, but the common characteristic of the family, with the trademark owner. Simply using a series of similar marks does not of itself establish the existence of a family. There must be a recognition among the purchasing public that the common characteristic is indicative of a common origin of the goods.

J & J Snack Foods Corp. v. McDonald's Corp., 932 F.2d 1460, 1462, 18 U.S.P.Q.2d 1889, 1891 (C.A.F.C. 1991).

Undoubtedly the most famous mark family is the "Mc" family, owned by the McDonald's fast food chain. McDonald's has registered numerous marks consisting of the prefix "Mc" and a generic term, such as "McMuffin," "Chicken McNuggets," etc. As a result of McDonald's tremendous volume of sales and advertising, the public has come to associate the prefix "Mc" in combination with a generic term with McDonald's, even though McDonald's has not registered or used "Mc" by itself. McDonald's has repeatedly convinced courts and the TTAB that others' use of "Mc" with the name of food items will create a likelihood of confusion. Thus, for example, in *J & J Snack Foods*, cited above, the Court of Appeals for the Federal Circuit upheld McDonald's successful opposition to J & J Snack Foods Corporation's registration of "McPretzel" for frozen soft pretzels sold in bulk to food service retailers. McDonald's business activities have not been limited to the food business, however, and neither have its trademark claims. In McDonald's Corp. v. McKinley, 13 U.S.P.Q.2d 1895 (T.T.A.B. 1989), McDonald's successfully opposed registration of "McTeddy" for teddy bears. In the *Quality Inns* case, cited above, it convinced the judge to enjoin the use of "McSleep" for economy motels. In McDonald's Corp. v. Druck and Gerner DDS, P.C., 814 F.Supp. 1127, 26 U.S.P.Q.2d 1492 (N.D.N.Y.1993), McDonald's successfully enjoined the use of "McDental" for dental services.

Note that the term "Mc" has taken on a life of its own, however. Terms such as "McNews," "McPaper," and even "McLaw" appear with some regularity in the media and common speech. Has "Mc" become generic? See *Quality Inns, supra,* 695 F.Supp. at 212, 8 U.S.P.Q.2d at 1643.

5. *The use of disclaimers.* How effective is a disclaimer, such as "not associated with * * *" likely to be as a means of avoiding consumer confusion? In most cases, courts accord little weight to use of disclaimers.

See, for example, Justice Holmes' opinion in Jacobs v. Beecham, 221 U.S. 263, 272, 31 S.Ct. 555, 556, 55 L.Ed. 729, 732 (1911):

> To call pills Beecham's pills is to call them the plaintiff's pills. The statement that the defendant makes them does not save the fraud. That is not what the public would notice or is intended to notice, and, if it did, its natural interpretation would be that the defendant had bought the original business out and was carrying it on.

Justice Holmes' observations have been demonstrated empirically in a study reported in Jacoby & Raskopf, *Disclaimers in Trademark Infringement Litigation: More Trouble Than They Are Worth?*, 76 TRADEMARK REP. 35 (1986). See also Jacoby & Szybillo, *Why Disclaimers Fail*, 84 TRADEMARK REP. 224 (1994); Radin, *Disclaimers as a Remedy for Trademark infringement: Inadequacies and Alternatives*, 76 TRADEMARK REP. 59 (1969).

6. *Trademark counterfeiting.* Trademark counterfeiting is "hard core," willful infringement. It entails intentional, knowing use of "a spurious mark which is identical with, or substantially indistinguishable from, a registered mark," 15 U.S.C.A. § 1127, on the same kind of goods or services for which the mark is registered. The problem of counterfeiting became epidemic in the late 1970's and 1980's. As one commentator has explained:

> By 1985, the United States Customs Service estimated that forty billion dollars worth of unlicensed goods reached the American market place in imports alone. High technology, when employed abroad, had made the theft of intellectual property easier and cheaper and the ability of almost anyone to copy and affix bogus trademarks to products only exacerbated this menace. Consequently, counterfeiting ranged from infringement of designer labels to crude imitations of carefully crafted, life-sustaining heart valves and crucial airplane parts threatening the public safety. After this threat became known, Congress began scrutinizing the problem more carefully and finally acknowledged that counterfeiting was an insidious crime which had ramifications to the trademark holder and the public far beyond what was readily apparent.
>
> Congress was then forced to intervene primarily because legal remedies to deter this conduct were inadequate. Counterfeiting was not a crime and many counterfeiters would simply destroy the evidence of their activity once receiving notice of the filing of a civil suit. Still, courts continued to apply notice requirements blindly without fully grasping the unique problems associated with this form of street-level commercial vandalism.
>
> Another problem in fighting counterfeiting was that judges were often influenced by the spectacle in court of a huge multinational conglomerate suing an individual wide-eyed street peddler. Consequently many did not take the cases seriously because they were shut off from the larger picture.
>
> Moreover, the picture that was playing outside the courtroom told the tale of bands of transient peddlers, "fly-by-night" distributors, and retail operators that were selling cheap knock-offs and slashing prices far below those of authentic, quality goods. Not only were they deceiving consumers and eroding the value of commercial property, but they

were thwarting the judicial process with fictitious identities, disappearing merchandise and bogus invoices. Consequently, simply proving the existence of an actionable claim against an identifiable defendant became a legal nightmare.

Bainton, *Reflections on The Trademark Counterfeiting Act of 1984: Score a Few for the Good Guys*, 82 TRADEMARK REP. 1, 3–4 (1992).[9] Congress ultimately responded to the problem by passing the Trademark Counterfeiting Act of 1984, Pub.L. No. 98–473, 98 Stat. 2178, which attempted to deter counterfeiters, provide more effective relief to legitimate mark owners, and encourage private owners to police counterfeiting by filing civil infringement suits.

Civil relief was already available against use of a counterfeit mark under Lanham Act section 1114. The Trademark Counterfeiting Act amended the Lanham Act to provide that when a defendant intentionally uses a mark, knowing it to be counterfeit, the plaintiff is entitled to recover attorney's fees and treble damages. 15 U.S.C.A. § 1117(b). It also provided for *ex parte* orders to seize goods bearing counterfeit marks, *id.*, § 1116(d), and for destruction of such goods. *Id.*, § 1118. In addition, The Trademark Counterfeiting Act amended the criminal code to provide criminal sanctions against persons who intentionally traffic or attempt to traffic in goods through use of marks they know to be counterfeit. 18 U.S.C.A. § 2320.

A mark is not counterfeit if the producer or manufacturer was authorized to apply it to the good or service at the time of production or manufacture. 15 U.S.C.A. § 1116(d)(1). Thus, dealing in "grey market" goods (defined as "trademarked goods legitimately manufactured and sold overseas and then imported into the United States outside the trademark owner's desired distribution channels") does not constitute counterfeiting. *Joint Statement on Trademark Counterfeiting Legislation,* 130 CONG. REC. 31673, 31676 (Oct. 10, 1984).

B. CONTRIBUTORY INFRINGEMENT

INWOOD LABORATORIES, INC. v. IVES LABORATORIES, INC.

United States Supreme Court, 1982.
456 U.S. 844, 102 S.Ct. 2182, 72 L.Ed.2d 606, 214 U.S.P.Q. 1.

JUSTICE O'CONNOR delivered the opinion of the Court.

This action requires us to consider the circumstances under which a manufacturer of a generic drug, designed to duplicate the appearance of a similar drug marketed by a competitor under a registered trademark, can be held vicariously liable for infringement of that trademark by pharmacists who dispense the generic drug.

I

In 1955, respondent Ives Laboratories, Inc. (Ives), received a patent on the drug cyclandelate, a vasodilator used in long-term therapy for

9. Copyright © 1992, The International Trademark Association. Excerpts reprinted with permission from 82 TMR 1, January-February, 1992, Issue 8, The Trademark Reporter®.

peripheral and cerebral vascular diseases. Until its patent expired in 1972, Ives retained the exclusive right to make and sell the drug, which it did under the registered trademark CYCLOSPASMOL. Ives marketed the drug, a white powder, to wholesalers, retail pharmacists, and hospitals in colored gelatin capsules. Ives arbitrarily selected a blue capsule, imprinted with "Ives 4124," for its 200 mg dosage and a combination blue-red capsule, imprinted with "Ives 4148," for its 400 mg dosage.

After Ives' patent expired, several generic drug manufacturers, including petitioners Premo Pharmaceutical Laboratories, Inc., Inwood Laboratories, Inc., and MD Pharmaceutical Co., Inc. (collectively the generic manufacturers), began marketing cyclandelate. They intentionally copied the appearance of the CYCLOSPASMOL capsules, selling cyclandelate in 200 mg and 400 mg capsules in colors identical to those selected by Ives.[3]

The marketing methods used by Ives reflect normal industry practice. Because cyclandelate can be obtained only by prescription, Ives does not direct its advertising to the ultimate consumer. Instead, Ives' representatives pay personal visits to physicians, to whom they distribute product literature and "starter samples." Ives initially directed these efforts toward convincing physicians that CYCLOSPASMOL is superior to other vasodilators. Now that its patent has expired and generic manufacturers have entered the market, Ives concentrates on convincing physicians to indicate on prescriptions that a generic drug cannot be substituted for CYCLOSPASMOL.[4]

The generic manufacturers also follow a normal industry practice by promoting their products primarily by distribution of catalogs to wholesalers, hospitals, and retail pharmacies, rather than by contacting physicians directly. The catalogs truthfully describe generic cyclandelate as "equivalent" or "comparable" to CYCLOSPASMOL. In addition, some of the catalogs include price comparisons of the generic drug and CYCLOSPASMOL and some refer to the color of the generic capsules. The generic products reach wholesalers, hospitals, and pharmacists in bulk containers which correctly indicate the manufacturer of the product contained therein.

A pharmacist, regardless of whether he is dispensing CYCLOSPASMOL or a generic drug, removes the capsules from the container in which he receives them and dispenses them to the consumer in the pharmacist's own bottle with his own label attached. Hence, the final consumer sees no identifying marks other than those on the capsules themselves.

3. Initially, the generic manufacturers did not place any identifying mark on their capsules. After Ives initiated this action, Premo imprinted "Premo" on its capsules and Inwood imprinted "Inwood 258."

4. Since the early 1970's, most States have enacted laws allowing pharmacists to substitute generic drugs for brand name drugs under certain conditions. * * *

II

A

Ives instituted this action in the United States District Court for the Eastern District of New York under §§ 32 and 43(a) of the Trademark Act of 1946 (Lanham Act), 60 Stat. 427, as amended, 15 U.S.C. § 1051 *et seq.* * * *.

Ives' claim under § 32, 60 Stat. 437, as amended, 15 U.S.C. § 1114, derived from its allegation that some pharmacists had dispensed generic drugs mislabeled as CYCLOSPASMOL.[8] Ives contended that the generic manufacturers' use of look-alike capsules and of catalog entries comparing prices and revealing the colors of the generic capsules induced pharmacists illegally to substitute a generic drug for CYCLOSPASMOL and to mislabel the substitute drug CYCLOSPASMOL. Although Ives did not allege that the petitioners themselves applied the Ives trademark to the drug products they produced and distributed, it did allege that the petitioners contributed to the infringing activities of pharmacists who mislabeled generic cyclandelate.

* * *

Contending that pharmacists would continue to mislabel generic drugs as CYCLOSPASMOL so long as imitative products were available, Ives asked that the court enjoin the petitioners from marketing cyclandelate capsules in the same colors and form as Ives uses for CYCLOSPASMOL. In addition, Ives sought damages pursuant to § 35 of the Lanham Act, 60 Stat. 439, as amended, 15 U.S.C. § 1117.

B

The District Court denied Ives' request for an order preliminarily enjoining the petitioners from selling generic drugs identical in appearance to those produced by Ives. * * * The Court of Appeals for the Second Circuit affirmed. To assist the District Court in the upcoming trial on the merits, the appellate court defined the elements of a claim based upon § 32 in some detail. [T]he court stated that the petitioners would be liable under § 32 either if they suggested, even by implication, that retailers fill bottles with generic cyclandelate and label the bottle with Ives' trademark or if the petitioners continued to sell cyclandelate to retailers whom they knew or had reason to know were engaging in infringing practices.

C

After a bench trial on remand, the District Court entered judgment for the petitioners. Applying the test approved by the Court of Appeals to the claim based upon § 32, the District Court found that the petitioners had not suggested, even by implication, that pharmacists should dispense generic drugs incorrectly identified as CYCLOSPASMOL.[12]

8. * * * The one retail pharmacy originally named as a defendant consented to entry of a decree enjoining it from repeating such actions.

12. The District Court also found that

In reaching that conclusion, the court first looked for direct evidence that the petitioners intentionally induced trademark infringement. Since the petitioners' representatives do not make personal visits to physicians and pharmacists, the petitioners were not in a position directly to suggest improper drug substitutions. Therefore, the court concluded, improper suggestions, if any, must have come from catalogs and promotional materials. The court determined, however, that those materials could not "fairly be read" to suggest trademark infringement.

The trial court next considered evidence of actual instances of mislabeling by pharmacists, since frequent improper substitutions of a generic drug for CYCLOSPASMOL could provide circumstantial evidence that the petitioners, merely by making available imitative drugs in conjunction with comparative price advertising, implicitly had suggested that pharmacists substitute improperly. After reviewing the evidence of incidents of mislabeling, the District Court concluded that such incidents occurred too infrequently to justify the inference that the petitioners' catalogs and use of imitative colors had "impliedly invited" druggists to mislabel. Moreover, to the extent mislabeling had occurred, the court found it resulted from pharmacists' misunderstanding of the requirements of the New York Drug Substitution Law, rather than from deliberate attempts to pass off generic cyclandelate as CYCLOSPASMOL.

* * *

Without expressly stating that the District Court's findings were clearly erroneous, and for reasons which we discuss below, the Court of Appeals concluded that the petitioners violated § 32. * * * We granted certiorari, and now reverse the judgment of the Court of Appeals.

III

A

As the lower courts correctly discerned, liability for trademark infringement can extend beyond those who actually mislabel goods with the mark of another. Even if a manufacturer does not directly control others in the chain of distribution, it can be held responsible for their infringing activities under certain circumstances. Thus, if a manufacturer or distributor intentionally induces another to infringe a trademark, or if it continues to supply its product to one whom it knows or has reason to know is engaging in trademark infringement, the manufacturer or distributor is contributorily responsible for any harm done as a result of the deceit.

It is undisputed that those pharmacists who mislabeled generic drugs with Ives' registered trademark violated § 32. However, whether these petitioners were liable for the pharmacists' infringing acts depended upon whether, in fact, the petitioners intentionally induced the pharmacists to mislabel generic drugs or, in fact, continued to supply

the petitioners did not continue to provide drugs to retailers whom they knew or should have known were engaging in trademark infringement. * * *

cyclandelate to pharmacists whom the petitioners knew were mislabeling generic drugs. The District Court concluded that Ives made neither of those factual showings.

* * *

IV

In reversing the District Court's judgment, the Court of Appeals initially held that the trial court failed to give sufficient weight to the evidence Ives offered to show a "pattern of illegal substitution and mislabeling in New York...." By rejecting the District Court's findings simply because it would have given more weight to evidence of mislabeling than did the trial court, the Court of Appeals clearly erred. Determining the weight and credibility of the evidence is the special province of the trier of fact. Because the trial court's findings concerning the significance of the instances of mislabeling were not clearly erroneous, they should not have been disturbed.

Next, after completing its own review of the evidence, the Court of Appeals concluded that the evidence was "clearly sufficient to establish a § 32 violation." In reaching its conclusion, the Court of Appeals was influenced by several factors. First, it thought the petitioners reasonably could have anticipated misconduct by a substantial number of the pharmacists who were provided imitative, lower priced products which, if substituted for the higher priced brand name without passing on savings to consumers, could provide an economic advantage to the pharmacists. Second, it disagreed with the trial court's finding that the mislabeling which did occur reflected confusion about state law requirements. Third, it concluded that illegal substitution and mislabeling in New York are neither *de minimis* nor inadvertent. Finally, the Court of Appeals indicated it was further influenced by the fact that the petitioners did not offer "any persuasive evidence of a legitimate reason unrelated to CYCLOSPASMOL" for producing an imitative product.[20]

Each of those conclusions is contrary to the findings of the District Court. An appellate court cannot substitute its interpretation of the evidence for that of the trial court simply because the reviewing court "might give the facts another construction, resolve the ambiguities differently, and find a more sinister cast to actions which the District Court apparently deemed innocent." *United States v. Real Estate Boards*, 339 U.S. 485, 495, 70 S.Ct. 711, 717, 94 L.Ed. 1007 (1950).

20. The Court of Appeals reached that conclusion despite the District Court's express finding that, for purposes of § 43(a), the capsule colors were functional. * * * By establishing to the District Court's satisfaction that uniform capsule colors served a functional purpose, the petitioners offered a legitimate reason for producing an imitative product. Nor was the Court of Appeals entitled simply to dismiss the District Court's finding of functionality as not "persuasive." If the District Court erred as a matter of law, the Court of Appeals should have identified the District Court's legal error. If the Court of Appeals disagreed with the District Court's factual findings, it should not have dismissed them without finding them clearly erroneous.

V

The Court of Appeals erred in setting aside findings of fact that were not clearly erroneous. Accordingly, the judgment of the Court of Appeals that the petitioners violated § 32 of the Lanham Act is reversed. * * *

Notes and Questions

1. *Contributory infringement.* On what basis could the district court find that the capsule colors were functional?

How would you evaluate the following facts under the standard discussed in *Inwood Labs*? X, a wholesaler, sells retailers genuine Sealy mattresses, together with foundations made by Y, who is not affiliated with Sealy. The foundations have a fabric covering or "ticking" that is identical to the Sealy mattress ticking. The foundations bear no identifying labels. The mattress and foundation combination thus give the impression of being a matched set. At X's suggestion, some of the retailers advertise the combo as a "Sealy Back–Saver and matching foundation." See Sealy, Inc. v. Easy Living, Inc., 743 F.2d 1378, 224 U.S.P.Q. 364 (9th Cir.1984).

C. MARK PARODY

CLIFFS NOTES, INC. v. BANTAM DOUBLEDAY DELL PUBLISHING GROUP, INC.

United States Court of Appeals for the Second Circuit, 1989.
886 F.2d 490, 12 U.S.P.Q.2d 1289.

FEINBERG, CIRCUIT JUDGE:

Defendant Bantam Doubleday Dell Publishing Group, Inc. appeals from an order, dated August 2, 1989, of the United States District Court for the Southern District of New York, Shirley Wohl Kram, J., enjoining defendant-appellant from distributing Spy Notes, a parody of the Cliffs Notes series of paperback books published by plaintiff-appellee Cliffs Notes, Inc. This appeal raises basic questions over application of trademark law to an allegedly infringing literary parody. For reasons given below, we vacate the injunction.

BACKGROUND

The appeal involves three principals, although only two of them are parties. The first is plaintiff-appellee, which publishes a series of study guides, known as Cliffs Notes. As many college students are aware, Cliffs Notes are condensed versions, with brief analyses, of various short stories, plays and books. The cover of a typical Cliffs Notes book lists the name of the work that is to be condensed and discussed in the pages that follow. Although appellee asserts that a variety of readers, and not just students, purchase Cliffs Notes, students apparently form the primary audience for the books. * * *

The second principal is defendant-appellant, a well-known publishing company, which publishes Spy Notes. The third principal is Spy magazine, which appellant does not publish. Spy magazine contains a mixture of journalism, humor and satire. Its purpose is to provide political and social commentary in an entertaining manner, and its style of humor is quite sharp. * * *

Although Spy magazine is not a party to this lawsuit, it played a key role as one of the two creators, along with defendant-appellant, of Spy Notes. The idea behind Spy Notes was to create a double parody. First, Spy Notes would poke fun at certain novels—Tama Janowitz's *Slaves of New York*, Brett Ellis's *Less Than Zero* and Jay McInerney's *Bright Lights, Big City*—which a Spy editor described in the district court as defining "a genre of savvy, urban novels depicting the drug abuse, promiscuity and post-adolescent angst of the 1980s." The editor further noted that "[b]ecause of their literary shortcomings and their familiarity to Spy readers, these novels were a natural target for Spy's satirical commentary." In addition, Spy Notes would satirize Cliffs Notes. Spy magazine editors thought that a study guide would provide an ideal vehicle for a parody of these works, because "[t]he flat, straightforward, academic style" of Cliffs Notes "would appear incongruous with the cool, ironic, sophisticated, urbane novels and thus greatly enhance the humor of the satire." Furthermore, "because most college graduates and students have seen or heard of" Cliffs Notes, the readers of Spy and the audience targeted for Spy Notes would be "familiar with the format and style" of Cliffs Notes.

Appellant and the Spy editors produced Spy Notes, a one-time parody of Cliffs Notes. Appellant readily admitted that it copied the prominent features of Cliffs Notes in order to make Spy Notes an effective parody. Thus, just as a Cliffs Notes book does, Spy Notes lists on the cover the works it condenses, i.e., the three novels referred to above. In addition, the cover of Spy Notes replicates the distinctive yellow color, black diagonal stripes and black lettering of Cliffs Notes, a design that is the subject of appellee's registered trademark.

At the same time, there are some important differences between the two books. (We will focus on the covers, as the district court did, because appellee's trademark protects the cover of Cliffs Notes; however, the humorous content of Spy Notes is also quite different from the serious condensation and analysis of Cliffs Notes). For example, the cover of Spy Notes, unlike that of Cliffs Notes, prominently states "A Satire" five times in bright red lettering (and the back similarly states it four times), bears the notation "A Spy Book" with the logo of Spy magazine against a bright red background, uses the word "Spy" four times, and shows a clay sculpture of New York City rather than the clay sculpture of a mountain that typically appears on Cliffs Notes. Also, the cover of Spy Notes contains red, blue and white—colors that are not used on the cover of Cliffs Notes—and bears wry notations not found on a Cliffs Notes cover, such as "All Those Other Hip Urban Novels Of The 1980s," and "Even Funnier Than The Originals." In addition, the Spy Notes cover price ($7.95) is substantially higher than that of Cliffs Notes ($3.50). Further, the cover of Spy Notes states prominently in red that it "Includes The Spy Novel–O–Matic Fiction–Writing Device!" This tool, which a prospective purchaser can inspect simply by opening Spy Notes, allows the "young, world-weary urban author" to create "16,765,056 different plot possibilities" by manipulating a card. A Cliffs Notes book contains no such obviously absurd shortcut to success. Finally, appellant plans to market Spy Notes in distinctive prepacks of 10 copies in a manner that prominently features the Spy name.

Early in July 1989, after the Spy Notes books had been bound but before the copies had been shipped to bookstores, appellee sued appellant. Appellee alleged that the cover of Spy Notes violated the Lanham Trade–Mark Act, because it would give consumers the false impression that Spy Notes was actually appellee's product. * * * Appellee sought preliminary and final injunctions against the distribution of Spy Notes, and other relief.

On August 2, 1989, the district court granted a preliminary injunction * * * [We] unanimously conclude that the preliminary injunction should not have been granted. * * *

DISCUSSION

We review the district court's grant of a preliminary injunction under an abuse of discretion standard. * * *

We start with the proposition that parody is a form of artistic expression, protected by the First Amendment. * * *

At the same time, "[t]rademark protection is not lost simply because the allegedly infringing use is in connection with a work of artistic expression." *Silverman v. CBS Inc.*, 870 F.2d 40, 49 (2d Cir.), cert. denied,—U.S.—, 109 S.Ct. 3219, 106 L.Ed.2d 569 (1989). Books are "sold in the commercial marketplace like other more utilitarian products, making the danger of consumer deception a legitimate concern that warrants some government regulation." *Rogers v. Grimaldi*, 875 F.2d 994, 997 (2d Cir.1989).

Conflict between these two policies is inevitable in the context of parody, because the keystone of parody is imitation. It is hard to imagine, for example, a successful parody of Time magazine that did not reproduce Time's trademarked red border. A parody must convey two simultaneous—and contradictory—messages: that it is the original, but also that it is *not* the original and is instead a parody. To the extent that it does only the former but not the latter, it is not only a poor parody but also vulnerable under trademark law, since the customer will be confused.

Thus, the principal issue before the district court was how to strike the balance between the two competing considerations of allowing artistic expression and preventing consumer confusion. We believe that the correct approach in this case was foreshadowed by our decision in *Rogers v. Grimaldi*, upon which appellant relies heavily. In that case, we considered a Lanham Act challenge by the actress Ginger Rogers against the producers and distributors of the film "Ginger and Fred." The movie was not about Ginger Rogers but rather about two Italian cabaret performers who imitated Ginger Rogers and Fred Astaire in their performances. Ginger Rogers contended that the title of the film created the false impression that she was the subject of the film or had endorsed it. The district court held that the title was absolutely protected against Lanham Act claims by the First Amendment. Although this court's analysis in *Rogers* differed in major respects from that of the district court, we affirmed. We noted that "[b]ecause overextension of Lanham Act restrictions in the area of titles might intrude on First Amendment values, we must construe the Act narrowly to avoid such a conflict," *id.* at 998, and went on to hold that "the Act should be construed to apply to artistic works only where the public interest in avoiding consumer confusion outweighs the public interest in free expression." *Id.* at 999.

* * *

We believe that the overall balancing approach of *Rogers* and its emphasis on construing the Lanham Act "narrowly" when First Amendment values are involved are both relevant in this case. That is to say, in deciding the reach of the Lanham Act in any case where an expressive work is alleged to infringe a trademark, it is appropriate to weigh the public interest in free expression against the public interest in avoiding consumer confusion. And just as in *Rogers*, where we said that the expressive element of titles requires more protection than the labeling of ordinary commercial products, so here the expressive element of parodies requires more protection than the labeling of ordinary commercial products. Indeed, we have said, in the context of alleged copyright infringement, that a parody is entitled "at least" to conjure up the original and can do more.

Thus, we hold that the *Rogers* balancing approach is generally applicable to Lanham Act claims against works of artistic expression, a category that includes parody. This approach takes into account the ultimate test in trademark law, namely, the likelihood of confusion "as to the source of the goods in question." At the same time, a balancing approach allows greater latitude for works such as parodies, in which expression, and not commercial exploitation of another's trademark, is the primary intent, and in which there is a need to evoke the original work being parodied.

To apply the *Rogers* approach in this case, we begin by noting the strong public interest in avoiding consumer confusion over Spy Notes. As we put it in *Rogers*, the purchaser of a book, "like the purchaser of a can of peas, has a right not to be misled as to the source of the product." *Rogers*, 875 F.2d at 997–98. But, taking into account that somewhat more risk of confusion is to be tolerated when a trademark holder seeks to enjoin artistic expression such as a parody, the degree of risk of confusion between Spy Notes and Cliffs Notes does not outweigh the well-established public interest in parody. In other words, we do not believe that there is a likelihood that an ordinarily prudent purchaser would think that Spy Notes is actually a study guide produced by appellee, as opposed to a parody of Cliffs Notes. And although the district court found a strong likelihood of confusion between the cover of Spy Notes and that of Cliffs Notes, based on its review of the eight *Polaroid* factors,[3] that determination is a legal conclusion which is reviewable by this court as a matter of law.

As indicated, we believe that the district court erred. This conclusion is based upon a number of factors. First, the district court apparently thought that the parody here had to make an obvious joke out of the cover of the original in order to be regarded as a parody. We do not see why this is so. It is true that some of the covers of the parodies brought to our attention, unlike that of Spy Notes, contain obvious visual gags.[4] But parody may be sophisticated as well as slapstick; a literary work is a parody if, taken as a whole, it pokes fun at its subject. Spy Notes surely does that, and there are sufficient reasons to conclude that most consumers will realize it is a parody. For example, a substantial portion of the potential audience for Spy Notes—i.e., college students or college-educated adults—overlaps with that for Cliffs Notes. Spy magazine, like Cliffs Notes, is widely read on some college campuses, although presumably for different reasons. As a result, the name "Spy" in the title, the notation "A Spy Book" emblazoned on the cover of Spy Notes and the use of a prepack marketing device prominently displaying the "Spy" name should alert the buyer that Spy Notes is a parody of some sort, or, at least, that it is not the same product as Cliffs Notes.

Furthermore, while the cover of Spy Notes certainly conjures up the cover of Cliffs Notes, the two differ in many respects. * * *

In addition, a Cliffs Notes book is not likely to be bought as an impulse purchase. A prospective reader of Cliffs Notes probably has a specific book in mind when going to the bookstore for a study guide. And, even if a consumer did go to a store looking for a Cliffs Notes summary of any of the three books condensed in Spy Notes, that purchaser would not find one. Appellee does not produce Cliffs Notes for these novels, and has no plans to do so. There may be a few purchasers who have been assigned to read the novels who would buy the parody thinking it is a serious work and is produced by Cliffs Notes. In view of the public interest in free expression, that slight risk should

3. [By the editor: the Second Circuit's *Polaroid* factors are similar to the eight factors that the Ninth Circuit enumerated for determining likelihood of confusion in *AMF v. Sleekcraft, supra.*] As indicated, appellee argues that the *Polaroid* factors supply the relevant standard and that the district court correctly applied them. The *Polaroid* test has its origin in cases of purely commercial exploitation, which do not raise First Amendment concerns. Thus, the *Polaroid* test is at best awkward in the context of parody, which must evoke the original and constitutes artistic expression. In such a situation, the *Polaroid* factors should be applied with proper weight given to First Amendment considerations, something the district court did not do here.

4. E.g., Sports Hallucinated for Sports Illustrated, with a floating basketball player on the cover. Cf. the National Lampoon parody of Cliffs Notes in the record, entitled Kondensed Kliffs Notes. The Kondensed Kliffs Notes version of Moby–Dick reads, in its entirety, "A whale bites off a man's leg and the man can't forget about it."

be taken in order to allow the parody to be sold. Similarly, it is conceivable, though hardly likely, that some purchaser may mistakenly think that Cliffs Notes itself produced the parody, but that small chance does not justify the injunction here. There is no requirement that the cover of a parody carry a disclaimer that it is not produced by the subject of the parody, and we ought not to find such a requirement in the Lanham Act.

The label "A Satire" is also prominently used five times on the cover (and four on the back) of Spy Notes. Appellee conceded at oral argument that "satire," for this purpose, is the same as "parody." In addition, the prepack, a major promotional tool in which the books will appear in most, although not all, bookstores, bears the legend "The Outrageous Parody from the Creators of Separated at Birth" (the latter was a very popular book authored by Spy magazine editors). These measures should alert most consumers that Spy Notes is, in fact, a parody. Moreover, even for those few readers who might be slightly confused by the cover, the most likely reaction would be to open the book. Both the title page and the copyright notice page indicate that the book is written by the editors of Spy magazine and published by appellant. The copyright notice page states, "Spy Notes is a parody of Cliffs Notes." Furthermore, the reader would encounter the Spy Novel–O–Matic Fiction–Writing Device, which is an immediate tip-off that something non-serious is afoot.[5]

Finally, with few exceptions, most Cliffs Notes are summaries of the traditional "great books," rather than contemporary works or those somewhat outside the mainstream. As indicated above, the Spy editors certainly thought that the three novels were obviously not in the former category and that the purchaser would be aware of the humor of having Cliffs Notes summarize them. Moreover, the books that Spy Notes summarizes are characterized by their spare, stripped-down prose, and uncomplicated plots. The idea of condensing them at all is something of a parody. Thus, the consumer would likely be put on notice from the first that Spy Notes was not Cliffs Notes.

In short, we believe that the district court erred as a matter of law in concluding on the record before it that there was a strong likelihood of confusion. * * *

Notes and Questions

1. *First amendment considerations.* Did the Second Circuit intend its rule in *Cliffs Notes* to apply in all trademark parody cases, or only to a subset of trademark parodies? If the latter, how did it define the subset?

In your opinion, *should* the *Cliff Notes* rule apply to all trademark parodies? For example, suppose that the defendants used the marks "Dogi-

5. By mentioning the items inside the book that would contribute to dispelling whatever risk of confusion might arise, we do not mean to suggest that a parody could copy the trademark aspects of the cover of a book without adequate indication on its own cover that it was a parody.

va" and "Cativa" for their dog and cat treats, and wrapped the treats in foil somewhat similar to the foil used to wrap the prestigious "Godiva" chocolates. Should the special first amendment considerations discussed in *Cliff Notes* come into play when the owner of the Godiva mark sues for infringement?

If so, why? Should the *Cliff Notes* rule be *limited* to trademark parodies? For example, if there is a first amendment interest in freedom of expression in the case of trademarks that parody others, why is there not a similar interest in trademarks that describe the product they identify, or trademarks that consist of words or images chosen arbitrarily? Are such marks not equally expressive?

If you do not believe that the *Cliff Notes* rule should apply to all trademark parodies, how would you define the line that differentiates those trademark parodies that are subject to special first amendment consideration and those that are not? Should it depend on whether the defendant's use of the parody was a "commercial" use? If so, how would you define "commercial?" Would the use of "Dogiva" for dog treats be commercial? Was the defendant's use in *Cliff Notes* any less so? See L.L. Bean, Inc. v. Drake Publishers, Inc., 811 F.2d 26, 1 U.S.P.Q.2d 1753 (1st Cir.1987), *cert. denied* 483 U.S. 1013, 107 S.Ct. 3254, 97 L.Ed.2d 753 (1987); Langvardt, *Protected Marks and Protected Speech: Establishing the First Amendment Boundaries in Trademark Parody Cases*, 36 VILL. L.REV. 1 (1991).

In your opinion, should first amendment considerations be factored into the determination of trademark infringement at all? If so, does the Second Circuit's *Cliff Notes* rule strike the correct balance between first amendment interests and the interest in protecting against consumer confusion? Based on the court's analysis of the likelihood of confusion issue, was it necessary for the court to rely on the special first amendment considerations it enunciated?

The degree of significance accorded to first amendment considerations varies greatly in infringement decisions involving trademark parodies. Some opinions make no reference to the first amendment at all. Those that do often treat the issue in an abbreviated fashion, with little depth of analysis. Among the decisions recognizing the relevance of first amendment considerations there is little consistency. See Langvardt, *supra*. Compare the Eighth Circuit's opinion in Mutual of Omaha Insurance Co. v. Novak, 836 F.2d 397, 5 U.S.P.Q.2d 1314 (8th Cir.1987), *cert. denied* 488 U.S. 933, 109 S.Ct. 326, 102 L.Ed.2d 344 (1988), with the Second Circuit's approach in *Cliffs Notes*. In *Mutual of Omaha*, the plaintiff had registered several marks that it used in connection with its insurance services, including the familiar head of a man wearing Native American headdress and the designation "Mutual of Omaha." The defendant, an anti-nuclear weapons activist, produced a design which featured the words "Mutant of Omaha" and depicted a side view of a feather-bonneted, emaciated human head. He initially put the design on T-shirts, along with the words "Nuclear Holocaust Insurance," and later placed it on sweatshirts, caps, buttons, and coffee mugs, as well. He offered these products for sale at retail shops, exhibitions, and fairs.

Mutual of Omaha sued, alleging trademark infringement, and the Court of Appeals upheld the district court's injunction against the defendant. The Court held that the district court did not err in finding that the similarity of defendant's design created a likelihood of confusion about whether Mutual had sponsored, endorsed, or was otherwise affiliated with the defendant's goods. In making this finding, the court relied on the usual factors for determining the likelihood of confusion, placing particular emphasis on survey results indicating that "approximately ten percent of all the persons surveyed thought that Mutual 'goes along' with [the defendant's] product." *Id.*, 836 F.2d at 400, 5 U.S.P.Q.2d at 1317.

The court rejected the defendant's argument that his use of the design was an exercise of his right of free speech, protected by the first amendment:

> Mutual's trademarks are a form of property, and Mutual's rights therein need not "yield to the exercise of First Amendment rights under circumstances where adequate alternative avenues of communication exist." Given the circumstances of this case, Mutual's property rights should not yield. The injunction our decision upholds prohibits Novak's conduct only insofar as Novak uses Mutual's marks as logos or "to market, advertise, or identify [his] services or products." Other avenues for Novak to express his views exist and are unrestricted by the injunction; for example, it in no way infringes upon the constitutional protection the First Amendment would provide were Novak to present an editorial parody in a book, magazine, or film. Because the injunction leaves open many such avenues of expression, it deprives neither Novak nor the public of the benefits of his ideas. We therefore conclude that in the circumstances of this case failure to protect Mutual's trademark rights would amount to an "unwarranted infringement of property rights," for it would "diminish [those] rights without significantly enhancing the asserted right of free speech."

Id., 836 F.2d at 402, 5 U.S.P.Q.2d at 1319 (quoting Lloyd Corp. v. Tanner, 407 U.S. 551, 567, 92 S.Ct. 2219, 2228, 33 L.Ed.2d 131 (1972)). What is the difference, for first amendment purposes, between expressing one's views on the front of a T-shirt or on a button or cap, and expressing one's views in a "book, magazine or film?" Should the existence of "alternative avenues of communication" be determinative of the defendant's first amendment interests in trademark parody cases? How were Mutual's property rights harmed? Is this approach preferable to the Second Circuit's approach in *Cliffs Notes*? See Judge Heaney's dissent in *Mutual of Omaha*:

> [T]he majority's holding sanctions a violation of Novak's first amendment rights. The T-shirts simply expressed a political message which irritated the officers of Mutual, who decided to swat this pesky fly buzzing around in their backyard with a sledge hammer (a federal court injunction).

Id., 836 F.2d at 403, 5 U.S.P.Q.2d at 1320.

Should it matter, for purposes of the first amendment analysis, that the defendant's parody places the plaintiff's mark in an unwholesome context, such as "Enjoy Cocaine" as a parody on the well-known "Enjoy Coca Cola" sign, or "Genital Electric" as a parody of General Electric? See 3 J.T.

McCARTHY, McCARTHY ON TRADEMARKS AND UNFAIR COMPETITION § 31.38[1][a] (3d ed. 1992).

2. *A likelihood of confusion.* Parody generally is not viewed as an affirmative defense in trademark infringement cases. It is often characterized as merely an assertion that confusion is unlikely. See, e.g., Anheuser–Busch, Inc. v. L. & L. Wings, Inc., 962 F.2d 316, 327, 22 U.S.P.Q.2d 1502, 1510 (4th Cir.) (Powell, J., dissenting), *cert. denied* ___ U.S. ___, 113 S.Ct. 206, 121 L.Ed.2d 147 (1992). A true parody by its nature does not seek to confuse consumers about source. If it is to work as a parody, consumers must be aware of the difference in marks, so that they can appreciate the joke that is being made. "Conjuring up" the plaintiff's mark in the public's mind is not necessarily equivalent to causing a likelihood of confusion about the source of the parties' goods or services.

D. COLLATERAL USE OF MARKS AND GRAY MARKET GOODS

CHAMPION SPARK PLUG CO. v. SANDERS

United States Supreme Court, 1947.
331 U.S. 125, 67 S.Ct. 1136, 91 L.Ed. 1386.

MR. JUSTICE DOUGLAS delivered the opinion of the Court.

Petitioner is a manufacturer of spark plugs which it sells under the trade mark "Champion." Respondents collect the used plugs, repair and recondition them, and resell them. Respondents retain the word "Champion" on the repaired or reconditioned plugs. The outside box or carton in which the plugs are packed has stamped on it the word "Champion," together with the letter and figure denoting the particular style or type. They also have printed on them "Perfect Process Spark Plugs Guaranteed Dependable" and "Perfect Process Renewed Spark Plugs." Each carton contains smaller boxes in which the plugs are individually packed. These inside boxes also carry legends indicating that the plug has been renewed.[1] But respondent company's business name or address is not printed on the cartons. It supplies customers with petitioner's charts containing recommendations for the use of Champion plugs. On each individual plug is stamped in small letters, blue on black, the word "Renewed," which at times is almost illegible.

Petitioner brought this suit in the District Court, charging infringement of its trade mark and unfair competition. The District Court found that respondents had infringed the trade mark. It enjoined them from offering or selling any of petitioner's plugs which had been repaired or reconditioned unless (a) the trade mark and type and style marks were removed, (b) the plugs were repainted with a durable grey, brown, orange, or green paint, (c) the word "REPAIRED" was stamped into the

1. "The process used in renewing this plug has been developed through 10 years continuous experience. This Spark Plug has been tested for firing under compression before packing."

"This Spark Plug is guaranteed to be a selected used Spark Plug, thoroughly renewed and in perfect mechanical condition and is guaranteed to give satisfactory service for 10,000 miles."

plug in letters of such size and depth as to retain enough white paint to display distinctly each letter of the word, (d) the cartons in which the plugs were packed carried a legend indicating that they contained used spark plugs originally made by petitioner and repaired and made fit for use up to 10,000 miles by respondent company.[2] * * *

The Circuit Court of Appeals held that respondents not only had infringed petitioner's trade mark but also were guilty of unfair competition. It likewise denied an accounting but modified the decree in the following respects: (a) it eliminated the provision requiring the trade mark and type and style marks to be removed from the repaired or reconditioned plugs; (b) it substituted for the requirement that the word "REPAIRED" be stamped into the plug, etc., a provision that the word "REPAIRED" or "USED" be stamped and baked on the plug by an electrical hot press in a contrasting color so as to be clearly and distinctly visible, the plug having been completely covered by permanent aluminum paint or other paint or lacquer; and (c) it eliminated the provision specifying the precise legend to be printed on the cartons and substituted therefor a more general one.[3] The case is here on a petition for certiorari * * *.

There is no challenge here to the findings as to the misleading character of the merchandising methods employed by respondents, nor to the conclusion that they have not only infringed petitioner's trade mark but have also engaged in unfair competition. The controversy here relates to the adequacy of the relief granted, particularly the refusal of the Circuit Court of Appeals to require respondents to remove the word "Champion" from the repaired or reconditioned plugs which they resell.

We put to one side the case of a manufacturer or distributor who markets new or used spark plugs of one make under the trade mark of another. Equity then steps in to prohibit defendant's use of the mark which symbolizes plaintiff's good will and "stakes the reputation of the plaintiff upon the character of the goods." *Bourjois & Co. v. Katzel*, 260 U.S. 689, 692, 43 S.Ct. 244, 245, 67 L.Ed. 464, 26 A.L.R. 567.

We are dealing here with second-hand goods. The spark plugs, though used, are nevertheless Champion plugs and not those of another make. There is evidence to support what one would suspect, that a used spark plug which has been repaired or reconditioned does not measure

2. The prescribed legend read:

"Used spark plug(s) originally made by Champion Spark Plug Company repaired and made fit for use up to 10,000 miles by Perfect Recondition Spark Plug Co., 1133 Bedford Avenue, Brooklyn, N.Y."

The decree also provided:

"the name and address of the defendants to be larger and more prominent than the legend itself, and the name of plaintiff may be in slightly larger type than the rest of the body of the legend."

3. "The decree shall permit the defendants to state on cartons and containers, selling and advertising material, business records, correspondence and other papers, when published, the original make and type numbers provided it is made clear that any plug referred to therein is used and reconditioned by the defendants, and that such material contains the name and address of defendants."

up to the specifications of a new one. But the same would be true of a second-hand Ford or Chevrolet car. And we would not suppose that one could be enjoined from selling a car whose valves had been reground and whose piston rings had been replaced unless he removed the name Ford or Chevrolet. *Prestonettes, Inc. v. Coty*, 264 U.S. 359, 44 S.Ct. 350, 68 L.Ed. 731, was a case where toilet powders had as one of their ingredients a powder covered by a trade mark and where perfumes which were trade marked were rebottled and sold in smaller bottles. The Court sustained a decree denying an injunction where the prescribed labels told the truth. Mr. Justice Holmes stated, "A trade-mark only gives the right to prohibit the use of it so far as to protect the owner's good will against the sale of another's product as his. * * * When the mark is used in a way that does not deceive the public we see no such sanctity in the word as to prevent its being used to tell the truth. It is not taboo." 264 U.S. at page 368, 44 S.Ct. at page 351, 68 L.Ed. 731.

Cases may be imagined where the reconditioning or repair would be so extensive or so basic that it would be a misnomer to call the article by its original name, even though the words "used" or "repaired" were added. But no such practice is involved here. The repair or reconditioning of the plugs does not give them a new design. It is no more than a restoration, so far as possible, of their original condition. The type marks attached by the manufacturer are determined by the use to which the plug is to be put. But the thread size and size of the cylinder hole into which the plug is fitted are not affected by the reconditioning. The heat range also has relevance to the type marks. And there is evidence that the reconditioned plugs are inferior so far as heat range and other qualities are concerned. But inferiority is expected in most second-hand articles. Indeed, they generally cost the customer less. That is the case here. Inferiority is immaterial so long as the article is clearly and distinctively sold as repaired or reconditioned rather than as new. The result is, of course, that the second-hand dealer gets some advantage from the trade mark. But under the rule of *Prestonettes, Inc., v. Coty*, that is wholly permissible so long as the manufacturer is not identified with the inferior qualities of the product resulting from wear and tear or the reconditioning by the dealer. Full disclosure gives the manufacturer all the protection to which he is entitled.

The decree as shaped by the Circuit Court of Appeals is fashioned to serve the requirements of full disclosure. We cannot say that of the alternatives available the ones it chose are inadequate for that purpose. * * *

Notes and Questions

1. *Use of marks in the resale of genuine goods.* Why does the plaintiff in *Champion Spark Plug* object to the defendant's use of its mark? As a practical matter, what harm can the use do to the plaintiff? Assuming that there is injury, why is the Court unwilling to prevent it?

Why does the court require that the defendant indicate clearly that it had repaired or reconditioned the plugs? In the *Prestonettes* case, discussed in *Champion*, why did the defendant have to indicate that it had rebottled the plaintiff's perfume, as long as it was the same perfume, and had not been altered? Would it constitute trademark infringement if the defendant had, in addition to transferring plaintiff's perfume to different bottles, diluted the perfume with water?

Assume that Adolph Coors Co. sells its beer only in the western states, and imposes quality control requirements on its authorized distributors to ensure that its beer remains fresh for consumers. Among other things, Coors requires its distributors to refrigerate the beer as much as possible and remove from retail stores and destroy any beer that has been on the shelf for more than 60 days after packaging. The defendant buys large quantities of Coors beer from licensed retailers in the western states, transports it to Maryland and resells it to retailers and other distributors in that state in its original packaging. Defendant advertises that it has beer for sale, including Coors, but does not represent to third persons that it is an authorized distributor of Coors. Defendant does not refrigerate the beer, and leaves it on the shelf for longer than 60 days before it is sold to the ultimate consumers. As a result, the Coors beer that Maryland consumers often get is inferior, with a deteriorated taste.

Under the principles set forth in *Champion Spark Plugs*, would the defendant be liable for trademark infringement? See Adolph Coors Co. v. A Genderson & Sons, Inc., 486 F.Supp. 131, 209 U.S.P.Q. 103 (D.Colo. 1980).

2. *The doctrine of exhaustion.* The doctrine of exhaustion underlies the reasoning in *Champion Spark Plug* and *Prestonettes*. This doctrine corresponds to the patent and copyright doctrines of first sale. The doctrine provides, essentially, that once the trademark owner permits goods bearing its mark to enter the stream of commerce, it generally cannot prevent or control resale of the goods with the mark, and truthful advertising that goods bearing that mark are for sale. The owner impliedly licenses others to further distribute the goods under the mark, as long as the use is truthful and does not confuse consumers about the immediate source of the goods. Trademark rights are thus "exhausted" as to a given good upon its first authorized sale.

1. Gray Market Goods

The doctrine of exhaustion and the question of liability for resale of genuinely marked goods lead naturally to the issue of "gray market goods" or "parallel imports," which has generated considerable litigation, particularly in the 1980s.

Gray market goods are products that are manufactured and lawfully marked abroad with trademarks identical to U.S. trademarks. While these goods are intended for sale in foreign countries, cheaper sales prices abroad and exchange rate differences sometimes make it profitable for arbitragers to buy them abroad, ship them to the United States, and sell them in competition with the entity that owns the mark in the U.S. If, for example, an importer can purchase Minolta cameras for significantly less in Taiwan than in the United States, it can ship the cameras to the United States, and sell them for less than the price charged by the U.S. entity that has registered the Minolta mark on the principal register, and still make a profit. Needless to say, this practice has not been popular with U.S. mark registrants.

While the gray market issue can arise in a variety of contexts, in K Mart Corp. v. Cartier, Inc. 486 U.S. 281, 108 S.Ct. 1811, 100 L.Ed.2d 313, 6 U.S.P.Q.2d 1897 (1988), the United States Supreme Court described three general contexts in which the issue most frequently arises:

> The prototypical gray-market victim (case 1) is a domestic firm that purchases from an independent foreign firm the rights to register and use the latter's trademark as a United States trademark and to sell its foreign-manufactured products here. * * * If the foreign manufacturer could import the trademarked goods and distribute them here, despite having sold the trademark to a domestic firm, the domestic firm would be forced into sharp intrabrand competition involving the very trademark it purchased. Similar intrabrand competition could arise if the foreign manufacturer markets its wares outside the United States, as is often the case, and a third party who purchases them abroad could legally import them. In either event, the parallel importation, if permitted to proceed, would create a gray market that could jeopardize the trademark holder's investment.
>
> The second context (case 2) is a situation in which a domestic firm registers the United States trademark for goods that are manufactured abroad by an affiliated manufacturer. In its most common variation (case 2a), a foreign firm wishes to control distribution of its wares in this country by incorporating a subsidiary here. The subsidiary then registers under its own name (or the manufacturer assigns to the subsidiary's name) a United States trademark that is identical to its parent's foreign trademark. The parallel importation by a third party who buys the goods abroad (or conceivably even by the affiliated foreign manufacturer itself) creates a gray market. Two other variations on this theme occur when an American-based firm establishes abroad a manufacturing subsidiary corporation (case 2b) or its own unincorporated manufacturing division (case 2c) to produce its U.S. trademarked goods, and then imports them for domestic distribution. If the trademark holder or its foreign subsidiary sells the trademarked goods abroad, the parallel importation of the goods competes on the gray market with the holder's domestic sales.
>
> In the third context (case 3), the domestic holder of a United States trademark authorizes an independent foreign manufacturer to use it. Usually the holder sells to the foreign manufacturer an exclusive right to use the trademark in a particular foreign location, but conditions the right on the foreign manufacturer's promise not to import its trademarked goods into the United States. Once again, if the foreign manufacturer or a third party imports into the United States, the foreign-manufactured goods will compete on the gray market with the holder's domestic goods.

Id., 486 U.S. at 286–87, 108 S.Ct. at 1815, 100 L.Ed.2d at 321.

There are two approaches that one could take in determining whether importation or sale of gray market goods constitutes an infringement of the U.S. trademark owner's rights. First, one could reason that a trademark has a separate legal existence under each country's laws, and that its proper lawful function is to symbolize the *domestic source* of the product, and that sources' reputation, consistency and good will. If the manufacturer is not the domestic source, then the mark represents whoever is—the domestic trademark owner/distributor. Another party's unauthorized importation of gray goods bearing the same mark would cause a likelihood of confusion about the immediate source of the goods, and would constitute an infringement. This is known as the "territoriality" principle. See Osawa & Co. v. B & H Photo, 589 F.Supp. 1163, 1171–72, 223 U.S.P.Q. 124, 130 (S.D.N.Y. 1984).

Alternatively, one could reason that a mark symbolizes the original manufacturer of the good, not the domestic distributor. If a good is lawfully manufactured and marked in one country, it may carry that mark lawfully wherever it goes. Subsequent resales, no matter where they occur, should not give rise to infringement liability. Concurrent domestic sales by gray market importers and the domestic mark owner will not lead to consumer confusion about the source of the good. This is known as the "universality" theory. *Id.*

Another way to approach the issue might be to ask what the scope of the doctrine of exhaustion should be. Three alternatives suggest themselves. Under alternative A, the doctrine of exhaustion would apply only within the boundaries of a country, so that a U.S. mark holder could prevent any goods originally sold abroad (by itself or others) from being resold in the U.S. without its permission. It could not, however, prevent goods which it originally sold or authorized to be sold in the United States from being resold there.

Under alternative B, the doctrine of exhaustion would apply to resales of all goods sold by or under the authority of a markholder, no matter where the original sale took place. In that case, a U.S. mark holder that originally sold its goods abroad could not prevent resales of those goods in the U.S., but could prevent domestic resales of goods originally marked and sold by other persons owning the mark abroad.

Under alternative C, the doctrine of exhaustion would apply to all goods legitimately bearing the mark, no matter where originally sold and no matter whether the original seller was the U.S. trademark owner or not. This approach seems undesirable. Apart from seeming unfair, it is inconsistent with the assumptions underlying the exhaustion doctrine. The doctrine assumes that the mark owner benefited from the original sale of the good bearing the mark, and impliedly consented, upon first sale, to subsequent resales. Alternative C would bind a U.S. mark owner to the benefit and implied promises of unrelated foreign entities.

While early case law tended to follow the universality principle, the modern debate focuses on whether an absolute or a partial territoriality principle should be applied, and on the respective merits of doctrine of exhaustion alternatives A and B.

A. Bourjois & Co., Inc. v. Katzel, 260 U.S. 689, 43 S.Ct. 244, 67 L.Ed. 464 (1923), is the key case in the development of modern gray market doctrine. In that case Bourjois, a United States company, purchased from a French powder manufacturer the manufacturer's established United States face powder business and good will, and the registered trademark "Java," under which the business had been conducted. Bourjois imported powder in bulk from the French manufacturer, packaged and sold it domestically under the "Java" mark. Bourjois and the French manufacturer were completely unrelated entities. While the French manufacturer assigned all its rights in the "Java" mark in the United States, it retained rights in the mark abroad and continued to manufacture and sell powder under the "Java" mark in other countries. The defendant bought a large quantity of the manufacturer's "Java" powder in France and imported it into the United States for sale in competition with Bourjois. The French manufacturer's packaging was similar in appearance to Bourjois'.

The district court enjoined the defendant's actions, but the Court of Appeals for the Second Circuit, applying the universality principle described above, found that Bourjois was unentitled to relief. The Supreme Court reversed the Court of Appeals, opting for the territoriality principle:

> We are of opinion that the plaintiff's rights are infringed. After the sale the French manufacturers could not have come to the United States and have used their old marks in competition with the plaintiff. That plainly follows from the statute authorizing assignments. If for the purpose of evading the effect of the transfer it had arranged with the defendant that she should sell with the old label, we suppose that no one would doubt that the contrivance must fail. There is no such conspiracy here, but apart from the opening of a door to one, the vendors could not convey their goods free from the restriction to which the vendors were subject. Ownership of the goods does not carry the right to sell them with a specific mark. It does not necessarily carry the right to sell them at all in a given place. If the goods were patented in the United States a dealer who lawfully bought similar goods abroad from one who had a right to make and sell them there could not sell them in the United States. The monopoly in that case is more extensive, but we see no sufficient reason for holding that the monopoly of a trade-mark, so far as it goes, is less complete. * * * It is said that the trade-mark here is that of the French house and truly indicates the origin of the goods. But that is not accurate. It is the trade-mark of the plaintiff only in the United States and indicates in law, and, it is found, by public understanding, that the goods come from the plaintiff although not made by it. It was sold and could only be sold with the good will of the business that the plaintiff bought. It stakes the reputation of the plaintiff upon the character of the goods. The injunction granted by the District Court was proper under sections 17 and 19 of the Trade–Mark Act. Act of February 20, 1905, c. 592 (Comp. St. §§ 9502, 9504).

Id., 260 U.S. at 691–92, 43 S.Ct. at 245, 67 L.Ed. at 466.

In reaction to the Second Circuit's opinion in *Katzel* (shortly before the Supreme Court reversed it), Congress enacted section 526 of the Tariff Act of 1922 (later reenacted in identical form as § 526 of the 1930 Tariff Act), 19 U.S.C.A. § 1526. Section 526 makes it unlawful

> to import into the United States any merchandise of foreign manufacture if such merchandise * * * bears a trademark owned by a citizen of, or by a corporation or association created or organized within, the

> United States, and registered in the Patent and Trademark Office by a person domiciled in the United States * * * unless written consent of the owner of such trademark is produced at the time of making entry.

19 U.S.C.A. § 1526(a). Under this provision, a trademark owner may have the Customs Service stop offending goods at the border or bring a private cause of action for relief. 19 U.S.C.A. § 1526(c).

The Customs Service, in promulgating regulations to implement section 526, construed that provision as prohibiting only some, not all, gray goods. 19 C.F.R. § 133.21(c) provided:

> (c) *Restrictions not applicable.* The restrictions set forth in * * * this section do not apply to imported articles when:
>
> (1) Both the foreign and the U.S. trademark or trade name are owned by the same person or business entity;
>
> (2) The foreign and domestic trademark or trade name owners are parent and subsidiary companies or are otherwise subject to common ownership or control * * *
>
> (3) The articles of foreign manufacture bear a recorded trademark or trade name applied under the authorization of the U.S. owner. * * *

In K Mart Corp. v. Cartier, Inc., 486 U.S. 281, 108 S.Ct. 1811, 100 L.Ed.2d 313, 64 U.S.P.Q.2d 1897 (1988), an association of U.S. trademark owners challenged the validity of this Customs regulation, arguing that it was inconsistent with section 526. A majority of the Court held that the exceptions set forth in subsections (c)(1) and (2) constituted reasonable constructions of the ambiguous language of section 526, and were consistent with the statute's intent. A separate majority found the third exception, subsection (c)(3), was invalid as contrary to the clear language of section 526. Thus, domestic mark registrants who are under common control or in a parent/subsidiary relationship with the foreign manufacturer are excluded from the benefits of Customs Service protection under section 526.[10]

When the U.S. mark owner and the foreign manufacturer are subject to common ownership or are in a parent/subsidiary relationship, they can be viewed as the "same person." That being the case, the original Customs Service regulation in effect implemented doctrine of exhaustion alternative B, described above. Under the original regulation, the U.S. trademark owner could not prevent resale in the U.S. of gray goods which it originally manufactured and sold abroad or which were originally manufactured and sold abroad by an unrelated foreign manufacturer under the U.S. mark owner's authorization. It could, however, prevent resales of goods originally manufactured and sold abroad by other persons, as in *Katzel.* In upholding clauses (1) and (2) of the regulation and voiding clause (3), the *K Mart* decision essentially differentiated goods marked and sold abroad by the U.S. mark owner (defined as all related companies) and goods marked and sold

10. Technically, the *K Mart* opinion only considered the reasonableness of the Customs Service's interpretation of section 526 in the regulation, for purposes of Customs assistance in stopping gray goods at the border. The Court did not itself undertake to interpret the scope of section 526 for purposes of civil suits between private parties. As a practical matter, however, the approved Customs interpretation is likely to be applied in both contexts. See, e.g., the *Weil* opinion, *infra.*

abroad by unrelated entities under the U.S. mark owner's authority. Exhaustion will apply only to goods which the U.S. mark owner manufactured and released into commerce abroad.

Turning to the three typical gray market contexts or "cases" that the *K Mart* Court identified, section 526 provides Customs Service relief against gray goods in case 1 (the *Katzel* situation) and case 3 (where the U.S. mark owner licenses an unrelated foreign manufacturer), but not in the situations described in case 2 (where the U.S. mark owner and the foreign manufacturer are related entities, and thus viewed as one person).

Deprived of a section 526 remedy, "case 2" U.S. trademark owners seeking to exclude gray goods turned to the Lanham Act, which generated the following opinion.

WEIL CERAMICS AND GLASS, INC. v. DASH

United States Court of Appeals for the Third Circuit, 1989.
878 F.2d 659, 11 U.S.P.Q.2d 1001, *cert. denied*
493 U.S. 853, 110 S.Ct. 156, 107 L.Ed.2d 114 (1989).

A. Leon Higginbotham, Jr., Circuit Judge.

On this appeal we are asked to determine the availability of trademark and tariff act protections to an American company—which is owned by the same entity that owns the foreign manufacturer of a good, but which holds a valid American trademark for the foreign manufactured good—against parallel imports or so-called "gray-market" goods. Specifically, we are asked to determine whether § 32 of the Lanham Act, 15 U.S.C. § 1114 (1982), makes damages available to the American trademark holder for trademark infringement and if § 42 of that Act, 15 U.S.C. § 1124 (1982), may be employed on behalf of the American company to prohibit the importation of gray-market goods.

This appeal also raised the question of whether § 526 of the Tariff Act, 19 U.S.C. § 1526 (1982), could be employed to preclude the importation of gray-market goods. That section has been construed by the Customs agency in its regulations as allowing the importation of gray-market goods in those cases where the American trademark holder is owned by, or owns, the foreign manufacturer of the good. See 19 C.F.R. § 133.21 (1987). [The court notes that this portion of the cited customs regulation was upheld by the Supreme Court in *K Mart*, and that this disposes of the § 526 claim.] *K Mart* is also instructive to the disposition of the Appellee/Cross–Appellant's contentions regarding §§ 42 and 32. We conclude that neither of these sections provides the relief sought and, accordingly, we will reverse the decision of the district court.

* * *

I. Background

* * * Appellee/Cross–Appellant, Weil Ceramics & Glass, Inc., ("Weil"), is the wholly owned subsidiary of Lladro Exportadora, S.A., a Spanish corporation that is a sister corporation to Lladro, S.A., which

manufactures fine porcelain in Spain.[2] The porcelain is handmade and each piece bears the trademark "LLADRO," accompanied by a flower logo.

In February 1966, Weil, a New York corporation in the business of importing and selling fine porcelain and glassware, became the exclusive distributor in the United States of Lladro porcelain. The following year Weil obtained a valid United States registration for the LLADRO trademark and continued as the exclusive distributor of the porcelain.

In 1973, Lladro, S.A. acquired 50% of Weil's stock. At that time, Weil assigned all of its rights in its United States LLADRO trademark to Lladro, S.A. In 1977, Lladro Exportadora obtained Lladro, S.A.'s shares of Weil stock, as well as the remaining 50% of Weil stock, and became the sole owner of Weil. In 1983, Lladro Exportadora assigned the United States LLADRO trademark back to Weil.

In 1982, Appellants/Cross–Appellees Jalyn Corporation and its president, Bernard Dash, (together "Jalyn"), began importing LLADRO porcelain. Jalyn legally obtained the porcelain in Spain from distributors of Lladro, S.A. and sold it in the United States without the consent of Weil. In 1984, Weil filed a complaint in the federal district court for the district of New Jersey seeking declaratory and injunctive relief against Jalyn's continued import of Lladro porcelain and money damages for trademark infringement.

[The district court granted Weil's motion for summary judgement, finding that Jalyn's use of the Lladro mark caused a likelihood of confusion, in violation of the Lanham Act. Jalyn now appeals that decision.]

III. Sections 42 and 32

Weil argues that even if § 526 does not bar importation by Jalyn of the LLADRO porcelain, § 42—which was not specifically addressed in *K Mart*—does. Moreover, Weil contends that nothing in *K Mart* precludes its recovery of damages for infringement under § 32 for Jalyn's distribution of the LLADRO porcelain in the United States. We are persuaded, however, because of the relationship that Weil has with Lladro, S.A., that the protections afforded by §§ 42 and 32 of the Lanham Act are also inapplicable.

Weil's argument on this point has two components: first, it asserts that it owns the United States LLADRO trademark independently of its foreign parent and, pursuant to the territoriality theory attributed to *Katzel*, it is entitled to the full measure of trademark protection provided by the Lanham Act. In that light, Weil contends that § 42's preclusion of goods that "copy or simulate" a trademark and that § 32's preclusion of marks that "imitate" a registered trademark are applicable—notwithstanding the fact that the goods are genuine and bear the trademark of the manufacturer—because Jalyn's importation of LLADRO porcelain

2. The specific character of the relationship between Lladro, S.A. and Weil is that they share a common parent corporation * * *.

into the United States, without Weil's permission, represents a "copying" of the registered United States trademark.

a. The "territoriality" theory

Weil's argument relies in large measure upon a theoretical concept of trademark law, attributed to the Supreme Court's decision in *Katzel*, that is the subject of significant debate in the courts * * *. [T]hat theory recognizes the separate existence of a trademark in each territory in which it has been registered. In the present case, the district court was persuaded that the theory should be available to Weil in the circumstances of this case. We do not agree.

In reaching its decision, the district court relied significantly upon the rationale of the Supreme Court's decision in *Katzel*. * * *

That case, however, does not present the same scenario as the present case. First, and perhaps most significantly, Bourjois was completely independent from the foreign manufacturer. It entered into an arms-length exchange to acquire the rights to the trademark with the clear intent that the foreign manufacturer would not market the trademarked good in the United States. Moreover, Bourjois obtained control over the quality of the product and, presumably, could have improved the quality of the product that it marketed in the United States while retaining use of the trademark. It had no control over the goods that the foreign manufacturer sold abroad which were imported into the United states and sold with the same trademark.

In the present case, no such compelling circumstances exist. Weil is not independent of the foreign manufacturer. Although it was not incorporated by Lladro, S.A., it nonetheless benefits from the corporate relationship that exits. Thus, even if Weil loses some share of its United States market to Jalyn, it nonetheless benefits from the profits it received as part of the corporate entity from which Jalyn purchased the goods abroad. Moreover, if that corporate entity decides that the profit margin from the sale of the goods to Jalyn abroad is not as significant as would be the profit margin from a United States market in which Jalyn did not compete, it has an obvious self-help mechanism: it can cease the sale to Jalyn abroad and thereby eliminate effectively its United States competition with Weil. We do not read the Lanham Act, however, to protect a foreign manufacturer—that either owns or is owned by a domestic trademark holder—from competition in the sale of its product in the United States by a domestic importer that it has supplied. Moreover, the LLADRO porcelain that Jalyn imports is *identical* to the porcelain that Weil distributes.[11] Weil has made no contention that,

11. This is the conclusion reached by the district court. The fact that it made no finding that the porcelain distributed by Jalyn and that distributed by Weil are materially different is significant to our disposition of this appeal. Weil has contended on this appeal that the porcelain imported by Jalyn was of a materially different grade and quality from the porcelain imported by Weil. If true, that fact would provide a stronger argument for Weil's claim of trademark infringement. * * * However, we cannot reach that conclusion on the findings of record, and we premise our decision pursuant to its agreement with Lladro, S.A., Weil is entitled to, and does in fact, alter the quality of the porcelain that it distributes in the United States.

In our view, the Court's conclusion in *Katzel* does not represent the establishment of a broad "territoriality theory" applicable to every instance in which a domestic company acquires the United States trademark for a foreign manufactured good. We read that decision as creating an exception to the general application of trademark law in order to protect adequately the interests of domestic trademark holders such as Bourjois.

Our conclusion is consonant with both *K Mart* and *Katzel*, and illustrates the synthesis between those Supreme Court decisions. If placed within the context of the scenarios identified by the Court in *K Mart*, *Katzel* would be described as case 1. *K Mart* clearly held that § 526 was intended to protect domestic trademark holders in that type of case and, indeed, § 526 was enacted specifically to counter the decision of the Court of Appeals for the Second Circuit in *Katzel* which had reached the opposite result. In our view, *Katzel* was intended specifically to reach the case 1 scenario and extend trademark act protection to domestic trademark holders that are truly independent of the foreign manufacturer. We do not read *Katzel* to extend beyond that circumstance. * * *

b. Goods that "copy," "simulate," "counterfeit," or "imitate"

Having concluded that *Katzel* did not create a broad territoriality principle that is applicable to every instance of parallel imports, we can more easily resolve the remainder of Weil's argument regarding § 42 and § 32. Essentially, Weil argues that our reading of § 42's prohibition of goods that "copy or simulate" a United States trademark, and of § 32's similar proscription of the commercial distribution of goods that "counterfeit" or "imitate" a valid United States trademark, should be informed by the principle attributed to *Katzel*. Accordingly, it argues, Weil's registration of the LLADRO trademark in the United States should be viewed as having created a trademark in the United States that is distinct from any other mark (even the identical mark placed by the same manufacturer) and that that mark should be accorded the full measure of United States trademark law. Weil contends, therefore, that its trademark is "copied" by *any* unauthorized use. In that light, Weil argues that, notwithstanding the fact that the porcelain imported by Jalyn is genuine and that the marks affixed to the porcelain are placed by the manufacturer just as the marks affixed to the porcelain sold by Weil, the porcelain that Jalyn imports "copies" Weil's trademark.

Because of our conclusion that nothing in *Katzel* extends the trademark act protections to the circumstances of this case, we need not attempt the strained interpretation of the language of § 42 or § 32 that

on the assumption that the porcelain imported by Jalyn was essentially identical to that imported by Weil.

Weil advocates. Our inquiry is only to discern the plain meaning of the language of those sections and, on that review, we do not reach the conclusion urged by Weil.[13]

As the starting point for our analysis, we must ascertain the appropriate definition to be given to the terms employed by § 42 and § 32 of the Lanham Act. In pertinent part § 42 provides

> that no article of imported merchandise ... which shall copy or simulate a trademark registered in accordance with the provisions of this chapter ... shall be admitted to entry at any custom house of the United States.

15 U.S.C. § 1124 (1982). Section 32(1)(a) provides that

> (1) [a]ny person who shall, without the consent of the registrant—
>
> > (a) use in commerce any reproduction, counterfeit, copy, or colorable imitation of a registered mark in connection with the sale, offering for sale, distribution, or advertising of any goods or services on or in connection with which such use is likely to cause confusion, or to cause a mistake or to deceive; ... shall be liable in a civil action by the registrant for the remedies hereinafter provided.

15 U.S.C. § 1114(1)(a) (1982). Weil urges that § 42 is applicable to provide injunctive relief against importation even if § 526 does not and that § 32 is applicable to make damages available, and to provide injunctive relief against distribution, even if neither § 526 or § 42 bar importation. It contends that "the words 'copy or simulate' are neutral terms and are only directed to the physical and visual similarity between the registered mark and the mark on the imported product." Consequently, it argues, "[w]hether or not the act of importation is a violation of § 42 depends on whether the importation is *with or without* the

13. The argument is well made that, having resolved the appropriate scope of § 526, there is nothing left to the inquiry regarding § 42. Section 526 was enacted specifically in response to the intermediate appellate court's opinion in *Katzel* with the intent to close an interstice that Congress perceived existed in the then existing trademark law and resulted in the decision by the Court of Appeals for the Second Circuit in *Katzel*. Thus, the scope of protection that Congress intended § 42 to provide is embodied in § 526. (Indeed, some commentators have suggested that, in light of the Supreme Court's subsequent decision in *Katzel*, § 526 was rendered a nullity as a redundant statement of what the trademark law already provided.) Moreover, the legislative history reflects that, by passing § 526, Congress intended not *only* to amend the customs laws but to amend the trademark law as well. In that light, the reasonable interpretation of the scope of § 526 may also be read as the reasonable interpretation of § 42. The alternate view to this interpretation is that the scope of the trademark law was extended by the Supreme Court's decision in *Katzel*, which, although decided subsequent to the passage of § 526, did not make reference to that section in its holding. (In deciding *Katzel*, the Supreme Court applied § 27 of the Trademark Act of 1905, Act of Feb. 20, 1905, ch. 592, § 27, 33 Stat. 730, which is identical to the § 42 of the present act). It is argued, therefore, that § 42 should be read with broader authority, without reference to § 526. We will assume, *arguendo*, the correctness of this view. It does not, however, affect the disposition of this case. As we have held, *supra*, *Katzel* is properly read only to apply to the case 1 circumstance. Thus, any extension of the protective authority of § 42 that *Katzel* established is limited to that scenario and, accordingly, is not applicable to the present case.

consent of the registrant." Id. We can perceive of no basis, either in the specific language of the statute or in its underlying intent that supports such a reading.

In this inquiry of statutory construction, we are assisted again by the Supreme Court's decision in *K Mart* which noted that "[i]n ascertaining the plain meaning of [a] statute, the court must look to the particular statutory language at issue, as well as [to] the language and design of the statute as a whole." *K-Mart*, 108 S.Ct. at 1817 (citing *Bethesda Hospital Ass'n v. Bowen*, 485 U.S. 399,——, 108 S.Ct. 1255, 1258, 99 L.Ed.2d 460 (1988)). In the light of these precedents, we look first to the plain language of the statute, which we do not find to be ambiguous. In our view, the language of these sections reflects Congress' intent to provide a remedy only to the domestic trademark holder who is injured by the distribution of *like* goods, which bear facsimile marks, that result in confusion to consumers or detriment to the goodwill developed by the trademark holder in the trademarked goods. "Trademark law generally does not reach the sale of *genuine* goods bearing a true mark even though such sale is without the owner's consent." NEC Electronics, 810 F.2d at 1509 (citing Monte Carlo Shirt, Inc. v. Daewoo Int'l (Am.) Corp., 707 F.2d 1054, 1057–58 & n. 3 (9th Cir.1983)).

The terms "copy," "simulate," "counterfeit" and "imitate" have readily comprehensible ordinary meanings. They are used commonly to refer to items that resemble, but are not themselves, the original or genuine artifacts. We are convinced that the Congress understood this commonly held meaning of these terms and intended to apply them literally in §§ 42 and 32. We are, therefore, unpersuaded that those sections are properly applied to the present case.

Our analysis of the "design of the statute as a whole" compels us even more to the conclusion that we have reached. * * * [W]e discern two broad policy goals that Congress sought to foster by this legislation: (1) protection against consumer deception (i.e. purchase of a good that is not what the consumer intended to purchase, but because of packaging or other deceptive imitation of the trademark appears to be the genuine trademarked good); (2) protection of the trademark holder's investment in goodwill and noteworthiness that has been generated by the holder's advertisements and quality from imitative goods over which the trademark holder has no control of quality. Sections 42 and 32 advance these policy goals but neither of the goals is undermined by the importation of genuine goods as in this case. Consumers who purchase Jalyn imported LLADRO porcelain get precisely what they believed that they were purchasing. For that same reason, Weil's investment in and sponsorship of its trademark is not adversely affected because the goodwill that stands behind its product is not diminished by an association with goods of a lesser quality.

The only "injury" that we perceive Weil endures is the uncompensated for benefit that its advertisement and promotion of the trademark confers upon Jalyn. That loss to Weil is not inconsequential or insignificant. The remedy for it, however, is not properly found in the trademark law, particularly not in this case. Moreover, as we noted earlier, that "injury" is not completely uncompensated because Weil's parent corporation profits by the sale [to] Jalyn abroad.

It is more than likely that the framers of the trademark act did not contemplate the instance in which the "source" of a trademarked good would be different from its place of manufacture. The primary concern was to protect consumers and trademark holders from spurious imitations. In *Katzel*, the Court recognized that a broader measure of protection was necessary because of the difference in "source" between the trademark holder and the manufacturer in instances in which a foreign manufacturer sells its rights in the United States trademark to a domestic company. The Court, therefore, reasonably extended the trademark protections to that circumstance. In this case, however, for all intents and purposes, the trademark holder and the manufacturer are the same and there is no reason that compels us to read anything in the language of the act and extend further the protections of the trademark act to this circumstance.[19]

* * *

V. CONCLUSION

In light of the foregoing, we will reverse the decision of the district court granting summary judgment in favor of Weil on its claim that § 42 * * * [is] correctly employed to enjoin Jalyn's importation of LLADRO porcelain. We will also reverse the decision of the district court granting summary judgment on behalf of Weil on its claim that § 32 provides damages for infringement for Jalyn's distribution of the porcelain. * * *

Notes and Questions

1. *Trademark infringement.* Under the reasoning in *Weil*, how do you know when the mark on gray goods *is* the plaintiff's mark, as opposed to a "copy," "simulation," "imitation" or "counterfeit?" Putting aside the explicit language of Lanham Act sections 32 and 42, what is the best argument that the defendant's use of the Lladro mark in this case caused a likelihood of consumer confusion?

Which of the three approaches to the scope of the doctrine of exhaustion (set forth in the note preceding *Weil*) does the plaintiff argue should apply? Which does the court appear to adopt? How does the rule in *Weil* compare

19. We are aware that our conclusion results in the seeming anomaly that the language of the trademark act will be read one way in light of the circumstances of some cases (i.e., case 1) and that that same language will be read another way in all other circumstances. This result, however, we believe is correct and mandated by the decision of the Supreme Court in *Katzel*. The seeming conflict is made scrutable, however, with the recognition that the source of the added protection to trademark holders in the case 1 scenario is *Katzel* and § 526 (as that statute has been construed by the Customs Agency)—not in a subjectively different reading given to the text of the statute.

to the case decisions interpreting section 602 of the Copyright Act, regarding the application of the first sale doctrine to imported copies and phonorecords? (See Chapter 5, § III E 2, *supra*.)

What are the economic and public policy implications of gray market goods? From a public policy perspective, should *K Mart* "case 2" U.S. trademark registrants be permitted to prohibit sale of gray market goods in the U.S.? In all circumstances? In some circumstances? Would your view differ with regard to registrants in *K Mart* "case 3" situations? "Case 1" situations? A lively debate has arisen in the law reviews concerning the economic and public policy implications of gray market goods. For a sampling of the arguments, see Steele, *Piracy and Gray Markets*, 10 HASTINGS COMM. & ENT. L.J. 1065 (1988); Allen, *Some Revisions of a Gray Market Decalogue: A Response to Messrs. Lewin and Steele*, 10 HASTINGS COMM. & ENT. L.J. 1075 (1988); Laufer, *Good Faith and Fair Dealing with the American Consumer*, [1987] COLUM. BUS. L. REV. 167; Boland, *Wrongful Assault on the Trademark System*, [1987] COLUM. BUS. L. REV. 153.

2. *Differing goods.* In *Weil*, the court stressed that the Lladro porcelain the defendant imported was identical to the porcelain the plaintiff distributed. It noted that if the plaintiff had demonstrated that the defendant's porcelain was of a materially different grade and quality, that fact would provide a stronger argument for finding trademark infringement. Several courts of appeal have found trademark infringement in gray market settings when the goods imported by the defendant differed materially from those sold by the plaintiff.

In Lever Brothers Co. v. United States, 877 F.2d 101, 11 U.S.P.Q.2d 1117 (D.C.Cir.1989), both the plaintiff and an affiliated company in the United Kingdom used the marks "Shield" for soap and "Sunlight" for dish detergent which they produced and sold in their respective countries. The soap and dish detergent each sold differed, however, in order to accommodate local tastes and conditions. For example, due to the preference for showers in the U.S., the U.S. Shield soap contained a higher concentration of coconut soap and fatty acids to generate lather quickly. Since the British preferred baths, which permit more time for lather to develop, the U.K. Shield had less of these ingredients. The U.K. Sunlight detergent was designed for water with a higher mineral content than is generally found in the U.S., and therefore did not perform as well as U.S. Sunlight in the soft water typical of U.S. metropolitan areas. Third parties imported U.K. Shield and Sunlight into the U.S. to sell in competition with the plaintiff.

The plaintiff asked the Customs Service to stop the U.K. Shield and Sunlight from entering the country, pursuant to Lanham Act section 42. The Customs service declined to do so, invoking the "common control" exception to gray market protection, 19 C.F.R. § 133.21(c)(2), which the *K Mart* decision upheld in connection with Tariff Act section 526. The plaintiff argued that Customs could make no exception under section 42 when the goods being imported differ from the goods sold by the U.S. mark registrant. It argued that "where affiliated domestic and foreign firms produce goods bearing the same trademark, but different in physical content, the foreign products 'copy or simulate' the domestic trademark, so that § 42 forbids their importation, notwithstanding the fact of affiliation." *Id.*, 887 F.2d at 103–04, 11 U.S.P.Q.2d at 1119. The court "tentatively" agreed with that view, remanding to the district court for further findings regarding legislative history and Customs' administrative practice.[11] The court noted that

> In Britain a request for "beer" will yield "bitter," a sort of ale with no exact equivalent here; an American seeking our "beer" over there must ask for "lager." Because of the differing conditions in the United States and United Kingdom, and the Lever affiliates' response to these conditions in the design of their products, Shield and Sunlight likewise have different meanings in the two countries. Thus the use of the trademarks for the UK versions in the United States is simply not truthful. The reasons that persuaded Holmes to deny relief in *Prestonettes* point toward granting it here.

Id., 877 F.2d at 108, 11 U.S.P.Q.2d at 1122. The court concluded:

> We think the natural, virtually inevitable reading of § 42 is that it bars foreign goods bearing a trademark identical to a valid U.S. trademark but physically different, regardless of the trademarks' genuine character abroad or affiliation between the producing firms. On its face the section appears to aim at deceit and consumer confusion; when identical trademarks have acquired different meanings in different countries, one who imports the foreign version to sell it under that trademark will (in the absence of some specially differentiating feature) cause the confusion Congress sought to avoid. The fact of affiliation between the producers in no way reduces the probability of that confusion; it is certainly not a constructive consent to the importation. The cases are entirely congruent with this view. * * * Thus, despite the deference we owe Customs under *Chevron*, we believe that the affiliate exception does not square with § 42.

Id., 877 F.2d at 111, 11 U.S.P.Q.2d at 1125. For an in-depth discussion of the *Lever* decision and its implications, see Davis, Lever Bros. v. United States *and the Legality of Gray Market Imports: A New Shield for United States Trademark Owners in Transnational Markets*, 28 WAKE FOREST L. REV. 571 (1993).

In denying relief in *Weil*, the court stressed that the plaintiff had the means to prevent the gray market situation of which it complained. Would the same argument be applicable in *Lever*? See *Lever*, 877 F.2d at 101, 11 U.S.P.Q.2d at 1117. Given that gray market goods provide consumers with lower price opportunities, could some other means be found to avoid confusion caused by product differences? For example, could the problem of

11. The district court ultimately found that "[n]either the legislative history of the statute nor the administrative practice of the Customs Service clearly contradicts the plain meaning of section 42." The court thus concluded that "section 42 of the Lanham Act prohibits the importation of foreign goods that bear a trademark identical to a valid United States trademark but which are physically different, regardless of the validity of the foreign trademark or the existence of an affiliation between the U.S. and foreign markholders." 796 F.Supp. 1, 5–6 (D.D.C.1992). The Court of Appeals affirmed this finding, but vacated the global injunction the district court granted as overbroad. It directed the district court to limit the injunction to the particular products at issue in the suit. 981 F.2d 1330 (D.C.Cir.1993).

product differences be more appropriately resolved by requiring full disclosure of the differences at the point of sale? See, e.g., CAL. CIV. CODE §§ 1797.8–1797.86 (West 1986).

When should gray goods be deemed "different" for purposes of the *Lever* rule? In Societe Des Produits Nestle, S.A. v. Casa Helvetia, Inc., 982 F.2d 633, 25 U.S.P.Q.2d 1256 (1st Cir.1992), the Court of Appeals for the First Circuit reasoned that the appropriate test should not be strictly limited to physical differences. Other sorts of differences, such as warranty protection or service commitments, should also be considered. *Id.*, 982 F.2d at 638 n.7, 25 U.S.P.Q.2d at 1261 n.7. The court concluded that

> when dealing with the importation of gray goods, a reviewing court must necessarily be concerned with subtle differences, for it is by subtle differences that consumers are most easily confused. For that reason, the threshold of materiality must be kept low enough to take account of potentially confusing differences—differences that are not blatant enough to make it obvious to the average consumer that the origin of the product differs from his or her expectations.
>
> * * * [T]he existence of any difference between the registrant's product and the allegedly infringing gray good that consumers would likely consider to be relevant when purchasing a product creates a presumption of consumer confusion sufficient to support a Lanham Trade–Mark Act claim.

Id., 982 F.2d at 641, 25 U.S.P.Q.2d at 1262–63. Compare Mavic, Inc. v. Sinclair Imports, Inc., 1994 WL 7703 (E.D.Pa.1994).

4. *Additional resources.* For additional reading on the issue of gray marketing, see Hiebert, *Foundations of the Law of Parallel Importation: Duality and Universality in Nineteenth Century Trademark Law*, 80 TRADEMARK REP. 483 (1990); Rubin, *Destined to Remain Grey: The Eternal Recurrence of Parallel Imports*, 26 INT'L LAW. 597 (1992); Hahm, *Gray Market Goods: Has A Resolution Been Found?*, 81 TRADEMARK REP. 58 (1991). For a comparative perspective, see Takamatsu, *Parallel Importation of Trademarked Goods: A Comparative Analysis*, 57 WASH. L. REV. 433 (1982).

2. *Competitors' Use of Marks for Comparison Purposes*

SMITH v. CHANEL, INC.

United States Court of Appeals for the Ninth Circuit, 1968.
402 F.2d 562, 159 U.S.P.Q. 388.

BROWNING, CIRCUIT JUDGE:

Appellant R. G. Smith, doing business as Ta'Ron, Inc., advertised a fragrance called "Second Chance" as a duplicate of appellees' "Chanel No. 5," at a fraction of the latter's price. Appellees were granted a preliminary injunction prohibiting any reference to Chanel No. 5 in the promotion or sale of appellants' product. This appeal followed.

The action rests upon a single advertisement published in "Specialty Salesmen," a trade journal directed to wholesale purchasers. The advertisement offered "The Ta'Ron Line of Perfumes" for sale. It gave the seller's address as "Ta'Ron Inc., 26 Harbor Cove, Mill Valley, Calif." It stated that the Ta'Ron perfumes "duplicate 100% perfect the exact scent of the world's finest and most expensive perfumes and colognes at prices that will zoom sales to volumes you have never before experienced." It repeated the claim of exact duplication in a variety of forms.

The advertisement suggested that a "Blindfold Test" be used "on skeptical prospects," challenging them to detect any difference between a well known fragrance and the Ta'Ron "duplicate." One suggested challenge was, "We dare you to try to detect any difference between Chanel #5 (25.00) and Ta'Ron's 2nd Chance. $7.00."

In an order blank printed as part of the advertisement each Ta'Ron fragrance was listed with the name of the well known fragrance which it purportedly duplicated immediately beneath. Below "Second Chance" appeared "*(Chanel #5)." The asterisk referred to a statement at the bottom of the form reading "Registered Trade Name of Original Fragrance House."

Appellees conceded below and concede here that appellants "have the right to copy, if they can, the unpatented formula of appellees' product." Moreover, for the purposes of these proceedings, appellees assume that "the products manufactured and advertised by [appellants] are *in fact* equivalents of those products manufactured by appellees." Finally, appellees disclaim any contention that the packaging or labeling of appellants' "Second Chance" is misleading or confusing.[4]

I

The principal question presented on this record is whether one who has copied an unpatented product sold under a trademark may use the trademark in his advertising to identify the product he has copied. We hold that he may, and that such advertising may not be enjoined under either the Lanham Act, 15 U.S.C. 1125(a) (1964), or the common law of unfair competition, so long as it does not contain misrepresentations or create a reasonable likelihood that purchasers will be confused as to the source, identity, or sponsorship of the advertiser's product.

* * *

The rule rests upon the traditionally accepted premise that the only legally relevant function of a trademark is to impart information as to the source or sponsorship of the product. Appellees argue that protection should also be extended to the trademark's commercially more important function of embodying consumer good will created through extensive, skillful, and costly advertising. The courts, however, have generally confined legal protection to the trademark's source identifica-

4. Appellants' product was packaged differently from appellees', and the only words appearing on the outside of appellants' packages were "Second Chance Perfume by Ta'Ron." The same words appeared on the front of appellants' bottles; the words "Ta'Ron trademark by International Fragrances, Inc., of Dallas and New York" appeared on the back.

tion function for reasons grounded in the public policy favoring a free, competitive economy.

Preservation of the trademark as a means of identifying the trademark owner's products, implemented both by the Lanham Act and the common law, serves an important public purpose.[13] It makes effective competition possible in a complex, impersonal marketplace by providing a means through which the consumer can identify products which please him and reward the producer with continued patronage. Without some such method of product identification, informed consumer choice, and hence meaningful competition in quality, could not exist.

On the other hand, it has been suggested that protection of trademark values other than source identification would create serious anticompetitive consequences with little compensating public benefit. This is said to be true for the following reasons.

The object of much modern advertising is "to impregnate the atmosphere of the market with the drawing power of a congenial symbol." Mishawaka Rubber & Woolen Mfg. Co. v. S. S. Kresge Co., 316 U.S. 203, 205, 62 S.Ct. 1022, 1024, 86 L.Ed. 1381 (1942), rather than to communicate information as to quality or price. The primary value of the modern trademark lies in the "conditioned reflex developed in the buyer by imaginative or often purely monotonous selling of the mark itself." Derring, Trademarks on Noncompetitive Products, 36 Or.L.Rev. 1, 2 (1956). To the extent that advertising of this type succeeds, it is suggested, the trademark is endowed with sales appeal independent of the quality or price of the product to which it is attached; economically irrational elements are introduced into consumer choices; and the trademark owner is insulated from the normal pressures of price and quality competition. In consequence the competitive system fails to perform its function of allocating available resources efficiently.

Moreover, the economically irrelevant appeal of highly publicized trademarks is thought to constitute a barrier to the entry of new competition into the market. "The presence of irrational consumer allegiances may constitute an effective barrier to entry. Consumer allegiances built over the years with intensive advertising, trademarks, trade names, copyrights and so forth extend substantial protection to firms already in the market. In some markets this barrier to entry may be insuperable." Papandreou, The Economic Effects of Trademarks, 44 Calif.L.Rev. 503, 508–09 (1956). High barriers to entry tend, in turn, to produce "high excess profits and monopolistic output restriction" and "probably * * * high and possibly excessive costs of sales promotion." J. Bain, Barriers to New Competition 203 (1955).

A related consideration is also pertinent to the present case. Since appellees' perfume was unpatented, appellants had a right to copy it, as

13. It also serves two substantial private interests of the owner: It protects him from diversion of sales through a competitor's use of his trademark or one confusingly similar to it; and it protects his reputation from the injury that could occur if the competitor's goods were inferior.

appellees concede. There was a strong public interest in their doing so, "for imitation is the life blood of competition. It is the unimpeded availability of substantially equivalent units that permits the normal operation of supply and demand to yield the fair price society must pay for a given commodity." American Safety Table Co. v. Schreiber, 269 F.2d 255, 272 (2d Cir.1959). But this public benefit might be lost if appellants could not tell potential purchasers that appellants' product was the equivalent of appellees' product. "A competitor's chief weapon is his ability to represent his product as being equivalent and cheaper * * *." Alexander, Honesty and Competition, 39 So.Cal.L.Rev. 1, 4 (1966). The most effective way (and, where complex chemical compositions sold under trade names are involved, often the only practical way) in which this can be done is to identify the copied article by its trademark or trade name. To prohibit use of a competitor's trademark for the sole purpose of identifying the competitor's product would bar effective communication of claims of equivalence. Assuming the equivalence of "Second Chance" and "Chanel No. 5," the public interest would not be served by a rule of law which would preclude sellers of "Second Chance" from advising consumers of the equivalence and thus effectively deprive consumers of knowledge that an identical product was being offered at one third the price.

As Justice Holmes wrote in Saxlehner v. Wagner, [216 U.S. 375, 30 S.Ct. 298, 54 L.Ed. 525 (1910),] the practical effect of such a rule would be to extend the monopoly of the trademark to a monopoly of the product. The monopoly conferred by judicial protection of complete trademark exclusivity would not be preceded by examination and approval by a governmental body, as is the case with most other government-granted monopolies. Moreover, it would not be limited in time, but would be perpetual.

Against these considerations, two principal arguments are made for protection of trademark values other than source identification.

The first of these, as stated in the findings of the district court, is that the creation of the other values inherent in the trademark require "the expenditure of great effort, skill and ability," and that the competitor should not be permitted "to take a free ride" on the trademark owner's "widespread goodwill and reputation."

A large expenditure of money does not in itself create legally protectible rights. Appellees are not entitled to monopolize the public's desire for the unpatented product, even though they themselves created that desire at great effort and expense. As we have noted, the most effective way (and in some cases the only practical way) in which others may compete in satisfying the demand for the product is to produce it and tell the public they have done so, and if they could be barred from this effort appellees would have found a way to acquire a practical monopoly in the unpatented product to which they are not legally entitled.

Disapproval of the copyist's opportunism may be an understandable first reaction, "but this initial response to the problem has been curbed in deference to the greater public good." American Safety Table Co. v. Schreiber, 269 F.2d at 272. By taking his "free ride," the copyist, albeit unintentionally, serves an important public interest by offering comparable goods at lower prices. On the other hand, the trademark owner, perhaps equally without design, sacrifices public to personal interests by seeking immunity from the rigors of competition.

Moreover, appellees' reputation is not directly at stake. Appellants' advertisement makes it clear that the product they offer is their own. If it proves to be inferior, they, not appellees, will bear the burden of consumer disapproval.[25]

The second major argument for extended trademark protection is that even in the absence of confusion as to source, use of the trademark of another "creates a serious threat to the uniqueness and distinctiveness" of the trademark, and "if continued would create a risk of making a generic or descriptive term of the words" of which the trademark is composed.

The contention has little weight in the context of this case. Appellants do not use appellees' trademark as a generic term. They employ it only to describe appellees' product, not to identify their own. They do not label their product "Ta'Ron's Chanel No. 5," as they might if appellees' trademark had come to be the common name for the product to which it is applied. Appellants' use does not challenge the distinctiveness of appellees' trademark, or appellees' exclusive right to employ that trademark to indicate source or sponsorship. For reasons already discussed, we think appellees are entitled to no more. The slight tendency to carry the mark into the common language which even this use may have is outweighed by the substantial value of such use in the maintenance of effective competition.

We are satisfied, therefore, that both authority and reason require a holding that in the absence of misrepresentation or confusion as to source or sponsorship a seller in promoting his own goods may use the trademark of another to identify the latter's goods. The district court's contrary conclusion cannot support the injunction.

* * *

Notes and Questions

1. *Use of the mark by competitors and third parties who are not reselling the originally marked product.* In *Smith*, how does the defendant's use of the "Chanel No. 5" mark harm the plaintiff? Why is the defendant's "free ride" on the plaintiff's good will an insufficient basis for granting

25. In addition, if appellants' specific claims of equivalence are false, appellees may have a remedy under 43(a) of the Lanham Act, 15 U.S.C. 1125(a) (1964), which provides a civil remedy to a person injured by "any false description or representation, including words or other symbols * * *" of goods in interstate commerce. A common-law remedy may also be available. * * *

relief? Is the trademark law's acceptance of free riding consistent with the view taken in other intellectual property doctrines?

What if the claim of equivalence in *Smith* was false? See Chanel, Inc. v. Smith, 178 U.S.P.Q. 630 (N.D.Cal.1973), *affirmed* 528 F.2d 284 (9th Cir. 1976).

Assume that the defendant makes a perfume that smells just like Yves St. Laurent's "Opium." In marketing the perfume (which is called "Omni"), the defendant uses the following slogan: "If you like Opium You'll love Omni." This slogan appears prominently on each package of Omni sold, printed in white lettering on a tab which rises vertically above the boxtop. It also appears on the retail display. Should this constitute infringement of the "Opium" trademark? See Charles of the Ritz Group Ltd. v. Quality King Distributors, Inc., 636 F.Supp. 433, 230 U.S.P.Q. 451 (S.D.N.Y.1986).

Assume that an automobile repair shop displays a sign stating: "Independent Volkswagen–Porsche Service." The owner of the Volkswagen mark for cars and for authorized service for the cars sues for trademark infringement. What is your evaluation? See Volkswagenwerk Aktiengesellschaft v. Church, 411 F.2d 350, 161 U.S.P.Q. 769 (9th Cir.1969), *opinion supplemented* 413 F.2d 1126 (9th Cir.1969).

Assume that two newspapers use the service mark/name of the musical group "New Kids on the Block" in conducting opinion surveys concerning the group. The newspapers ask fans to call a "900" telephone number and state their opinion about which New Kid is the sexiest, which is their favorite, etc. The callers are charged for the call. Profits from the calls go to charity. The newspapers later publish the results of the survey. As it happens, the New Kids themselves provide for-profit 900 number telephone services for fans to call to listen to messages from the New Kids or talk to other fans. They sue the newspapers for infringement. Is the defendants' use a legal, collateral one, or an infringement of the "New Kids" mark? What are the relevant considerations? See New Kids on the Block v. News America Publishing, Inc., 971 F.2d 302, 23 U.S.P.Q.2d 1534 (9th Cir.1992).

2. *The anti-competitive effects of marks.* Marks may be viewed as performing both an informative function and a persuasive function. In their informative function, marks identify the source of goods, and thus enable consumers to predict the goods' quality and characteristics and choose those goods that they prefer. Moreover, by enabling consumers to identify producers and reward quality through repeat patronage, marks encourage producers to provide quality goods. Marks in their informative function are clearly pro-competitive and beneficial to society as a whole. Since unauthorized use of a mark that causes a likelihood of confusion undermines the informative function of marks, courts are quick to prevent such uses.

In their persuasive function, marks provide the vehicle for persuasive advertising. While advertising can be informative, much of advertising is geared toward associating illusions of romance, success, adventure, glamour, or other desired elements of "the good life" with the mark, and contains little or no actual informative content. Consumers are assured, directly or by implication, that the woman who buys Chanel perfume will be sexy, pursued by handsome men; the man who wears Foster Grant sunglasses will appear sophisticated; the young career person who drives a Toyota automobile will successfully climb the corporate ladder; the family that eats Jello gelatin for dessert will be a happy family. Inducing consumers to associate a mark with such illusions, via advertising, greatly enhances the selling power of the mark and consumer good will for the product the mark identifies. The plaintiff in *Smith* can be characterized as seeking protection for the persuasive, rather than the informative aspect of its prestigious Chanel mark: the parties assumed for purposes of the appeal that the defendant's use did not misinform the public, it merely capitalized on the fruits of the plaintiff's persuasive advertising via the mark. Should marks be protected strictly in their persuasive function? Will doing so ultimately benefit the public?

A number of authorities have argued that persuasive advertising introduces economically irrational elements into consumer decision making and interferes with marketplace efficiency. The court in *Smith* refers to some of the arguments that have been made. How might mark advertising and promotion insulate the mark owner "from normal pressures of price and quality competition?" Will permitting the kind of mark use that occurred in *Smith* eliminate or reduce this problem? What about the argument that enjoining the defendant's use would encourage the defendant to market a new scent, which would be preferable to having two brands of the same scent? What is your assessment of the argument that the economically irrelevant appeal of highly publicized trademarks constitutes a barrier to the entry of new producers into the market? For excellent discussions of these issues see Brown, *Advertising and the Public Interest: Legal Protection of Trade Symbols*, 57 YALE L.J. 1165 (1948) (Considering "the economic waste and distortion of consumer choice growing out of large-scale persuasive advertising, it should be clear that the persuasive function of trade symbols is of dubious social utility. There seems little reason why the courts should recognize or protect interests deriving from it."); Landes & Posner, *Trademark Law: An Economic Perspective*, 30 J.L. & ECON. 265, 275 (1987) ("The hostile view of brand advertising has been largely and we think correctly rejected by economists. The fact that two goods have the same chemical formula does not make them of equal value to even the most coolly rational consumer.") 1 J.T. McCARTHY, McCARTHY ON TRADEMARKS AND UNFAIR COMPETITION § 2.14 (3d ed. 1992) ("[A]ntipathy towards 'irrational' advertising should be irrelevant in legal disputes over trademarks. If there is a problem, it should be met head on and directly debated as an issue of controlling advertising content, not used as a rationale to limit or deny trademark protection."). Assuming that you agree with the proposition that the persuasive use of marks, through advertising, has anticompetitive effects, can you identify any offsetting positive effects? See generally Economides, *The Economics of Trademarks*, 78 TRADEMARK REP. 523 (1988); Treece, *Protectibility of Product Differentiation:* Is *and* Ought *Compared*, 18 RUTGERS L. REV. 1019 (1964); McClure, *Trademarks and Unfair Competition: A Critical History of Legal Thought*, 69 TRADEMARK REP. 305 (1979).

3. *The Fair Use Defense.* The "fair use" defense, developed at common law and codified at Lanham Act section 33(b)(4), is founded on policies somewhat similar to those underlying the collateral use cases. The defense

is applicable when the plaintiff's mark is descriptive or constitutes an individual's name. It permits a defendant to use the plaintiff's mark if the defendant's use

> is a use, otherwise than as a mark, of the [defendant's] individual name in his own business, or of the individual name of anyone in privity with [the defendant], or of a term or device which is descriptive of and used fairly and in good faith only to describe the goods or services of [the defendant], or their geographic origin.

15 U.S.C.A. § 1115(b)(4). Descriptive and surname marks have two meanings: first, their original descriptive or surname meaning, and second, their acquired meaning as an indication of origin. The fair use defense clarifies that trademark law gives mark owners no right to prevent others from using their marks in their first, original descriptive or surname meaning. As Judge Leval explained in United States Shoe Corp. v. Brown Group, Inc., 740 F.Supp. 196, 15 U.S.P.Q.2d 1138 (S.D.N.Y.1990):

> When the plaintiff chooses a mark with descriptive qualities, the fair use doctrine recognizes that "he cannot altogether exclude some kinds of competing uses," particularly those which use words in their primary descriptive and non-trademark sense. * * * [T]he fact that one [candy producer] might acquire trademark rights over a descriptive identifier like "chewy" or "lemon flavored" cannot deprive society of the opportunity to be advised by other manufacturers that their candy is chewy or lemon flavored. Therefore, notwithstanding the establishment of trademark rights over a descriptive term by a showing that it has acquired secondary meaning, the statute preserves in others the right to the use of such terms "fairly and in good faith only to describe [and not to designate] the goods or services." 15 U.S.C. § 1115(b)(4). The purpose of this provision is to ensure that the according of monopoly trademark rights over descriptive marks (upon a showing of acquired secondary meaning) will not over-broadly deprive society of the use of those terms in their descriptive sense in commercial communication.

Id., 740 F.Supp. at 198–99, 15 U.S.P.Q.2d at 1140.

As the statutory language suggests, there are two important aspects to the fair use defense: First, the defendant's use must be "otherwise than as a mark," and second, the use must be fair and "in good faith." With regard to the first requirement, it is relevant to examine the placement and prominence of the mark on the defendant's packaging or in the defendant's advertisements. For example, in finding that the defendant's use of the words "dentists' choice" in advertisements for Crest toothpaste constituted a fair use of the plaintiff's registered mark, "Dentists Choice," the court emphasized that the defendant always used the words along with its "Crest" mark, prominently displayed, which indicated the source of its product. Moreover, the defendant always displayed the words "dentists' choice" in conjunction with other text, so that the words did not stand out unduly. Wonder Labs, Inc. v. Procter & Gamble Co., 728 F.Supp. 1058, 1064, 14 U.S.P.Q.2d 1645, 1649 (S.D.N.Y.1990).

The good faith provision essentially requires that the defendant use the descriptive or surname mark for the purpose of describing its goods or services and not to trade on the plaintiff's good will. Mere notice or knowledge of the plaintiff's mark is not in itself sufficient to demonstrate a lack of good faith. Evidence of knowledge, supported by additional evidence—for example, that the defendant copied the physical form or appearance of the plaintiff's mark, or used other aspects of the plaintiff's packaging or marketing concept, as well—generally would defeat a claim of good faith. See, e.g., *United States Shoe Corp., supra,* 740 F.Supp. at 199 n.3, 15 U.S.P.Q.2d at 1140 n.3.

How does a finding of fair use differ from a finding that the defendant's manner of use is unlikely to cause confusion? Substantively, is it really a separate defense? Some courts have suggested, generally in *dicta,* that it is not inconsistent to find both a fair use and a likelihood of confusion. See, e.g., Salton, Inc. v. Cornwall Corp., 477 F.Supp. 975, 988, 205 U.S.P.Q. 428, 440 (D.N.J.1979). In his influential treatise, Professor McCarthy argues the contrary: " 'fair use' should be viewed as merely one type of use which is not likely to cause confusion and hence is a 'defense' only in that sense." 1 J.T. McCARTHY, McCARTHY ON TRADEMARKS AND UNFAIR COMPETITION § 11.17[3] (3d ed. 1992). The Restatement (Third) of Unfair Competition takes a middle road:

> If the manner of use by the defendant is reasonable in light of the commercial justification for the use, the possibility or even certainty of some confusion is not sufficient to deprive the defendant of the right to use the designation in its descriptive sense. Thus, a defendant who has used a descriptive designation fairly and in good faith to describe its goods or services is not liable for infringement, even if some residual confusion remains likely. However, the extent of likely or actual confusion is an important factor in determining whether a use is fair * * *.

RESTATEMENT (THIRD) OF UNFAIR COMPETITION § 28, comment b (Tentative Draft No. 3, 1991).[12]

E. GEOGRAPHIC RIGHTS

1. *The Common–Law Rule*

SWEET SIXTEEN CO. v. SWEET "16" SHOP, INC.

United States Court of Appeals for the Eighth Circuit, 1926.
15 F.2d 920.

FARIS, DISTRICT JUDGE.

This is an action in equity for an injunction and an accounting, based on the alleged infringement of plaintiff's trade-mark and trade-name. The decree below went for defendant, and plaintiff appealed in conventional mode.

* * * In the year 1916, plaintiff began business in San Francisco, as a dealer in women's ready-to-wear clothing, under the name of Sweet

12. © 1991 by The American Law Institute. Reprinted with the permission of The American Law Institute.

Sixteen Company, a corporation. In its business and advertisements it referred to many of its garments and goods as "Sweet Sixteens," it designated its system of dealing as the "Sweet Sixteen System," and it sold many of the garments kept for sale by it at $16 per garment. In the beginning it had but one store. It prospered in such wise as that, by the year 1921, it was the owner of five stores, two in San Francisco, and the others in three other cities of the coast states, namely, Los Angeles, Portland and Seattle, and also an office and general purchasing agency in New York. It was advertising its business in divers trade journals and in the daily newspapers of the several cities in which its stores were located. Some 75 of these newspapers were daily sold and read in Utah. Its annual advertising expenditures in the year in which this suit was begun, amounted to more than $120,000. It had a very considerable mail order business, through which it sold some goods in some 12 or 15 different states, among which was the state of Utah. While the business done thus in the state of Utah was, in proportion to its total business, negligible, it was making efforts to increase it, and to this end, in the year 1921, it sent some 1,500 of its printed catalogues into that state. In the year 1922 it supplemented this selling and advertising campaign in the state of Utah by distributing therein pictures and drawings of many of the articles kept by it for sale.

Prior to 1923, and about the year 1921, it put on foot tentative plans to rent and establish a store in Salt Lake City, Utah. These plans were not consummated, however, up to April 3, 1923, when defendant started in Salt Lake City a wholly similar business, (save that it does not particularly cater to the mail order business), dealing in like merchandise, which defendant ran and operated under the name of the Sweet "16" Shop, Inc. Defendant was incorporated in the state of Utah on the 17th day of May, 1923. Prior to such incorporation, and on April 3, 1923, defendants Provol and Wrigley procured the issuance to them, as copartners, of a certificate of trade-mark from the secretary of state of the state of Utah, carrying the designation "Sweet '16' Shop." Some four days prior to the issuance of this certificate, and a like period before defendants Provol and Wrigley began business, Provol, one of the copartners, was advised by wire from plaintiff of the existence of plaintiff corporation and was warned not to use the name "Sweet 16" in defendants' business. Thereupon defendants took legal advice as to their right to use this name. While this advice was favorable to them, there is left no question in the case that defendants assumed this name with full knowledge of its use by plaintiff, if such fact shall be of controlling importance.

The record discloses fairly numerous instances wherein dealers, customers, and potential customers were misled by the similarity of names into mistaking defendants' business for that of plaintiff. * * *

[B]oth [parties] largely rely on the same cases to sustain their respective contentions. These cases are Hanover Star Milling Co. v. Metcalf, 240 U.S. 403, 36 S.Ct. 357, 60 L.Ed. 713, and United Drug Co. v. Rectanus Co., 248 U.S. 90, 39 S.Ct. 48, 63 L.Ed. 141. * * * The one decisive question here, broadly stated, is whether, on the facts, this case is within the rule announced in the above cases, or within the exceptions which plaintiff insists are clearly noted in these cases.

The brief and salient facts in the Rectanus case are that, about the year 1877, Mrs. Regis began to use the word "Rex" as a trade-mark for certain medicinal preparations made by her in Haverhill, Mass. Thereafter, through mesne assignments and continued use, this trade-mark came, about the year 1911, into the hands of the United Drug Company. During all of the years between 1877 and 1911 the sales of this medicinal preparation were confined to the New England states, with inconsiderable sales in New York, New Jersey, Canada, and Nova Scotia. In the meantime, and in the year 1889, one Rectanus, familiarly known as "Rex," began at Louisville, Ky., to use the word "Rex" as a trade-mark for another sort of medicinal preparation, which he sold and advertised in Kentucky. In 1912 the United Drug Company for the first time extended the sale of its medicines, bearing its "Rex" trade-mark, into the state of Kentucky. When it did so, and prior thereto, it had notice that the assignee of Rectanus was using the identical trade-mark in Kentucky on its medicines. These facts and all of them notwithstanding the United Drug Company sued the Rectanus Company for the infringement of its trade-mark. In the Supreme Court the decree went for defendant; the court saying, among other things, this:

> "Undoubtedly, the general rule is that, as between the conflicting claimants to the right to use the same mark, priority of appropriation determines the question. But the reason is that purchasers have come to understand the mark as indicating the origin of the wares, so that its use by a second producer amounts to an attempt to sell his goods as those of his competitor. The reason for the rule does not extend to a case where the same trade-mark happens to be employed simultaneously by two manufacturers, in different markets separate and remote from each other, so that the mark means one thing in one market, an entirely different thing in another. It would be a perversion of the rule of priority to give it such an application in our broadly extended country that an innocent party, who had in good faith employed a trade-mark in one state, and by the use of it had built up a trade there, being the first appropriator in that jurisdiction, might afterwards be prevented from using it, with consequent injury to his trade and good will, at the instance of one who theretofore had employed the same mark, but only in other and remote jurisdictions, upon the ground that its first employment happened to antedate that of the first-mentioned trader. * * *
>
> "The same point was involved in Hanover Milling Co. v. Metcalf, 240 U.S. 403, 415, 36 S.Ct. 357, 60 L.Ed. 713, where we said: 'In the ordinary case of parties competing under the same mark in the same market, it is correct to say that prior appropriation settles the question. But where two parties independently are employing the same mark upon goods of the same class, but in separate markets wholly remote the one from the other, the question of prior

appropriation is legally insignificant, unless at least it appear that the second adopter has selected the mark with some design inimical to the interests of the first user, such as to take the benefit of the reputation of his goods to forestall the extension of his trade, or the like.'

"In this case, as already remarked, there is no suggestion of a sinister purpose on the part of Rectanus or the Rectanus Company; hence the passage quoted correctly defines the status of the parties prior to the time when they came into competition in the Kentucky market. And it results, as a necessary inference from what we have said, that petitioner, being the newcomer in that market, must enter it subject to whatever rights had previously been acquired there in good faith by the Rectanus Company and its predecessor. To hold otherwise—to require Rectanus to retire from the field upon the entry of Mrs. Regis' successor—would be to establish, the right of the latter as a right in gross, and to extend it to territory wholly remote from the furthest reach of the trade to which it was annexed, with the effect not merely of depriving Rectanus of the benefit of the good will resulting from his long-continued use of the mark in Louisville and vicinity, and his substantial expenditures in building up his trade, but of enabling petitioner to reap substantial benefit from the publicity that Rectanus has thus given to the mark in that locality, and of confusing if not misleading the public as to the origin of goods thereafter sold in Louisville under the Rex mark, for, in that market, until petitioner entered it, 'Rex' meant the Rectanus product, not that of Regis."

The facts in the case of Allen & Wheeler Co. v. Hanover Star Milling Co., sub nomine Hanover Milling Co. v. Metcalf, 240 U.S. 403, 36 S.Ct. 357, 60 L.Ed. 713, are very similar to those in the Rectanus Case, supra. In the Metcalf Case, Allen & Wheeler Company had first adopted and used the trade-mark "Tea Rose," on a certain sort of flour made by it, and which it sold wholly, in that part of the United States north of the Ohio river; "while the Hanover Company had adopted 'Tea Rose' as its mark in perfect good faith with no knowledge that anybody else was using or had used those words in such a connection, and during many years it had built up and extended its trade in the southeastern territory, comprising Georgia, Florida, Alabama, and Mississippi, so that in the flour trade in that territory the mark 'Tea Rose' had come to mean the Hanover Company's flour and nothing else." The Circuit Court of Appeals held, and the Supreme Court concurred substantially in the holding, "that the right to protection in the exclusive use of a trade-mark extends only to those markets where the trader's goods have become known and identified by his use of the mark; and because of the nonoccupancy by the Allen & Wheeler Company of the Southeastern markets it had no ground of relief in equity." It need scarcely be added that the alleged infringement, above complained of, occurred in the "Southeastern markets."

Confessedly, then, the general rule is that, while the first appropriator and user of a trade-mark owns such mark and is entitled to protection by the courts in the use thereof, against subsequent users on the same class of goods, such protection will not be afforded as against a subsequent user and appropriator, who in good faith adopts and uses the mark in territory into which the goods of the first appropriator have not penetrated and have not been used or sold. [A]ppellant frankly concedes the general rule to be substantially as stated, but it urges that the instant case falls upon the facts within the exceptions held in mind by the Supreme Court * * *.

* * *

[T]he exceptions to the general rule, which appellant contends differentiate on the facts the case at bar from both the Metcalf Case and the Rectanus Case, are found in this language in the above quoted excerpts from these two opinions:

> (a) "But where two parties independently are employing the same mark upon goods of the same class, but in separate markets wholly remote the one from the other, the question of prior appropriation is legally insignificant, *unless at least it appear that the second adopter has selected the mark with some design inimical to the interests of the first user, such as to take the benefit of the reputation of his goods, to forestall the extension of his trade, or the like.*"

(Italics ours.) United Drug Co. v. Rectanus Co., 248 U.S. loc.cit. 101, 39 S.Ct. 52 (63 L.Ed. 141).

> (b) "*We are not dealing with a case where the junior appropriator of a trade-mark is occupying territory that would probably be reached by the prior user in the natural expansion of his trade, and need pass no judgment upon such a case.*"

(Italics ours.) Hanover Milling Co. v. Metcalf, 240 U.S. loc.cit. 420, 36 S.Ct. 363 (60 L.Ed. 713).

In the instant case defendants Provol and Wrigley, while they were copartners, before they organized defendant corporation and before they actually began business, had notice of plaintiff's prior adoption, appropriation, and use of the words "Sweet Sixteen" to designate its business, and as a trade-mark on the goods in which plaintiff was dealing. The trial court so found, and the facts in evidence conclusively so disclose. Not only is this conclusively shown by the telegram sent to Provol, notice to whom as a partner was notice to Wrigley, but it is corroborated by other evidence in the case, some of which is suggestive, if not sinister. For example, they saw fit to make a slight change in the manner of representing the expression "Sixteen" by the use of quoted numerals, instead of spelling the word out, as plaintiff does; before they began business, and before they had ever actually used this mark, they registered it as a trade-mark with the secretary of state of Utah. Aside from the finding of the trial court, and of the conclusive evidence of prior notice, the two latter precautions are such as would not ordinarily be taken by those who were wholly innocent of plaintiff's existence and of its use of the mark in controversy.

Apposite to the exception of prior appropriation of the field of trade and of the right to a natural expansion into such field, the facts, as already said, are that plaintiff in 1921, and some two years before defendant began business under the style complained of here, had sent some 1,500 of its catalogues into Utah and to Salt Lake City; in 1922 it supplemented these catalogues by sending into that state pictures and drawings of many of the goods kept and sold by it; and it had sold to citizens of Utah at Salt Lake City some goods and had filled some mail orders there; in all, making some six or eight sales in one or the other of the above ways. Newspapers containing its advertisements had constantly been sold in Salt Lake City for a number of years before defendants did the act here complained of. Plaintiff avers, and the evidence discloses, its intention to establish a store in Utah, and to this end it had already taken tentative steps till the acts of defendants forestalled it.

* * * Not only, we repeat, are we of the opinion that the instant case is within what seem to be the very plain exceptions to the general rule as pointed out in the above cases, but that the above facts of notice of prior use, the quantum of such use, the solicitation of trade, and the advertisements of plaintiff in the Salt Lake City territory of trade, bring the case within settled rules not at all disturbed by the above-cited leading cases. For we are dealing here with a trade-mark clearly within the category of odd and fanciful marks, and not with a mark within the public domain, in which latter the user required must be such, and so long and so expansively used, as to acquire a secondary meaning.

In a case then like the instant one, the rule laid down in the very excellent and able work of Mr. Nims, seems yet applicable:

> "In considering the question of extent of use, careful distinction must be drawn between technical and pure trade-marks and marks which are not technical, but are in the public domain. Where the name or device chosen is fanciful and may become a technical trade-mark, very slight use will, in addition to adoption create a trade-mark. * * *"

Nims, The Law of Unfair Competition and Trade–Marks, 415.

Obviously, the trade-marks under discussion in the Hanover and Rectanus Cases were likewise technical trade-marks, but in neither of the latter cases had there been any sales, advertisements of goods, or user whatever by complainants therein in the territory there in controversy. In case of a technical trade-mark as here dealt with, while there must, of course, be some user in trade in the disputed field of trade, the quantum thereof need not be large. * * * [I]t would seem to follow inevitably, that if "a single instance of user, with accompanying circumstances evidencing an intent to establish the right to a trade-mark" (Hopkins on Trade-marks), be sufficient to establish such right in San Francisco, as against an alleged infringer in that city, then six or eight instances of such use, by sales of trade-marked goods, accompanied by fairly extensive advertisements in certain newspapers circulated and read in Salt Lake City, and the distribution therein of many catalogues ought, certeris paribus, to be sufficient user, as against a subsequent appropriator, to constitute infringement by the latter in Salt Lake City.

[W]e are of opinion that the case should be reversed and remanded, with directions to grant to plaintiff the relief for which it prays. * * *

Notes and Questions

1. *The remote, good-faith user.* What policy underlies the *Rectanus/Hanover Star Milling* rule? As a practical matter, in today's world of modern communications, transportation and travel, is one still likely to encounter local, remote markets of the type involved in those cases? As you will see in the following Subsection, the Lanham Act alters the impact of the remote, good-faith user rule for registered marks. The rule still controls, however, in the case of common-law trademark and unfair competition claims, and claims for infringement of unregistered marks and unfair competition brought pursuant to Lanham Act section 43, 15 U.S.C.A. § 1125(a), which we will examine in the following Chapter.

Why, exactly, did the defendants in *Sweet Sixteen* fail to qualify as remote, good-faith users under the *Rectanus/Hanover Star Milling* rule? Were the defendants the first to use the "Sweet 16" mark in Utah? Did the defendants lack good faith? Were they not in a "remote" geographic area? Suppose that the defendants had convinced the court that they qualified as remote, good-faith first users in Utah. Does it follow under the Supreme Court's reasoning in *Rectanus* and *Hanover Star Milling* that they could enjoin the plaintiff's use of the mark in Utah?

2. *Good faith.* In order to qualify as a remote, good faith user under the *Rectanus/Hanover Star Milling* rule, a "junior" (subsequent) user must demonstrate that she had "good faith" at the time that she began her first use of the mark. Why should the junior mark user's rights turn on her state of mind?

There has been some dispute over the nature of the good faith requirement. At points, the Supreme Court in *Rectanus* and *Hanover Star Milling* spoke of a "lack of knowledge" of the senior user's mark. However, the Court also spoke of a "design inimical to the interests of the first user, such as to take the benefit of the reputation of his goods, to forestall the extension of his trade, or the like." *Hanover Star Milling*, 240 U.S. at 415, 36 S.Ct. at 361, 60 L.Ed. at 719. The majority view is that knowledge of the prior user's mark at the time the junior user commences use negates good faith. 2 J.T. McCARTHY, McCARTHY ON TRADEMARKS AND UNFAIR COMPETITION § 26.03[2] (3d ed., 1992). Indeed, in the case of registered marks, constructive knowledge of the registrant's use, imputed by the fact of registration, is sufficient to negate good faith.

A minority of case opinions and commentators have favored the "design inimical to the interests of the first user" test, suggesting that it would be possible for a junior user with knowledge of the senior user to adopt the mark in good faith. Under this view, knowledge will support an inference of bad faith, but the ultimate question is whether the junior user had the intent to benefit from the reputation or good will of the first user. See, e.g., GTE Corporation v. Williams, 904 F.2d 536, 541, 14 U.S.P.Q.2d 1971, 1975 (10th Cir.1990), *cert. denied* 498 U.S. 998, 111 S.Ct. 557, 112 L.Ed.2d 564 (1990); RESTATEMENT (THIRD) OF UNFAIR COMPETITION § 19, comment d (Tentative Draft No. 2, 1990). Which view makes the most sense?

3. *A remote area.* The fact that the senior user does no business with the mark in an area does not guarantee that the area is "remote." Given modern communications and travel, consumers may be familiar with a mark used in other parts of the country. For example, the mark of a famous department store or hotel in New York City might be well known in Omaha by virtue of national advertising, media coverage, and the travel of Omaha residents, even though the owner does no business there. If the senior user's mark is so well known in an area at the time of the junior user's first use that the junior use will lead to a likelihood of consumer confusion, then the junior use will not be deemed remote, and the *Rectanus/Hanover Star Milling* doctrine will afford no protection. See RESTATEMENT (THIRD) OF UNFAIR COMPETITION § 19 (Tentative Draft No. 2, 1990).

4. *The parties' respective territories.* The Eighth Circuit, in *Sweet Sixteen*, suggested that the plaintiff's scattered sales and advertisements in Utah might be a sufficient use to include Utah in the plaintiff's market territory prior to the date of the defendants' first use of the "Sweet 16" mark. When courts are more firmly convinced of the junior user's good faith they may not be so generous to the senior user. For example, in Sweetarts v. Sunline, Inc., 436 F.2d 705, 710, 168 U.S.P.Q. 483 (8th Cir.1971), the plaintiff, a senior user, had sold over $17,000 of its mail order candy in Idaho between 1947 and 1962, and an average of $1,285 each year more recently. The Eighth Circuit found these sales too insignificant to constitute actual market penetration of Idaho and declined to include the state in the plaintiff's market area. The court applied a four-factor test, examining the dollar value of the plaintiff's sales at the time the defendant entered the market, the number of customers compared to the population of the state, relative and potential growth of sales, and the length of time since significant sales. In announcing this four-factor test in an earlier opinion, the court had explained that "the market penetration need not be large to entitle plaintiff to protection, [but] it must be significant enough to pose the real likelihood of confusion among the consumers in that area between the products of plaintiff and the products of defendants." Sweetarts v. Sunline, Inc., 380 F.2d 923, 929, 154 U.S.P.Q. 459, 464 (8th Cir.1967).

5. *"Technical trademarks" vs. descriptive marks.* In *Sweet Sixteen*, the court made a point of stressing that it was dealing "with a trade-mark clearly within the category of odd and fanciful marks, and not with a mark within the public domain, in which latter the user required must be such, and so long and so expansively used, as to acquire a secondary meaning." Why is that relevant?

6. *The zone of natural expansion.* In *Sweet Sixteen*, the plaintiff argued that the following statement from the *Hanover Star Milling* case supported its claim: "We are not dealing with a case where the junior appropriator of a trade-mark is occupying territory that would probably be

reached by the prior user in the natural expansion of his trade * * *." 240 U.S. at 420, 36 S.Ct. at 363, 60 L.Ed. at 721. This implied exception to the general remote, good-faith user rule has served as the foundation for the somewhat dubious "zone of natural expansion" doctrine.

This doctrine may provide superior rights to the senior user in a geographic area that was not otherwise within his market territory at the time the junior user began its good faith use. To gain such rights, the senior user must demonstrate that at the time the junior user began its use in the area, it was natural and foreseeable that the senior user would expand into that area. The doctrine has been justified as giving a senior user some "breathing space" and room to expand.

Case opinions relying on the zone of natural expansion doctrine are relatively rare. A case that illustrates its application (in connection with a trade name) is Food Fair Stores, Inc. v. Lakeland Grocery Corp., 301 F.2d 156, 133 U.S.P.Q. 127 (4th Cir.1962). In 1953, the date the junior user commenced using the name "Food Fair" for a grocery store in Norfolk, Virginia, the senior user, a major grocery store chain, had over a hundred grocery stores in surrounding states operating under the name Food Fair. It had expanded to that size rapidly but steadily over 30 years. The senior user had erected a warehouse in Baltimore that would be capable of supplying Virginia stores. Based on this evidence, the court found that Norfolk was within the senior user's zone of expansion in 1953 (the date the junior user commenced using the name), and that the senior user thus had superior rights in the name there. The court noted that events taking place *after* 1953 reinforced its conclusion:

> the negotiation for a chain of stores in Newport News in 1955, the effort to buy out the defendant in 1956, and the actual opening of the plaintiff's store in 1958 give strong support to the testimony of the plaintiff that as early as 1949 when the Baltimore warehouse was opened surveys of the area were made and expansion of the business into the area was not merely possible but probable.

Id., 301 F.2d at 162. It is useful to note that alternative grounds for finding for the senior user existed in *Food Fair*: there was strong evidence of bad faith on the junior user's part, and convincing evidence that the senior user had already acquired secondary meaning in the Norfolk area in 1953, and thus that the area was already a part of the senior user's market territory. Reliance on a zone of expansion theory was thus unnecessary.

Based on the facts in *Sweet Sixteen*, would you find that Salt Lake City was within the plaintiff's natural zone of expansion? Courts that have applied the doctrine have generally defined it narrowly, confining it to areas close to the claimant's actual market territory, as it existed on the junior user's first use date. Part of their hesitance may be attributable to doubts about how to apply the doctrine. In every case of contested territory the senior user, who has moved to the junior user's trade area, can argue with hindsight that it was probable all along that it would do so. But to grant senior users superior rights based on such arguments would seriously undermine the remote, good-faith user rule. Some authorities have rejected the zone of natural expansion doctrine altogether. See, e.g., RESTATEMENT (THIRD) OF UNFAIR COMPETITION § 19, comment c (Tentative

Draft No. 2, 1990). In Raxton Corp. v. Anania Associates, Inc., 635 F.2d 924, 208 U.S.P.Q. 769 (1st Cir.1980), the Court of Appeals for the First Circuit observed that cases purporting to apply the zone of natural expansion doctrine rarely if ever relied strictly on that doctrine to bar a junior user who had adopted a mark in good faith.

> This * * * is understandable. A "natural expansion" doctrine that penalized innocent users of a trademark simply because they occupied what for them would be a largely undiscoverable path of some remote prior user's expansion strikes us as at once unworkable, unfair, and, in the light of statutory protection available today, unnecessary. Such a doctrine would have to weigh the remote prior user's intangible and unregistered interest in future expansion as more important than the subsequent user's actual and good faith use of its name. Besides involving the obvious practical difficulties of defining the "natural expansion path" of a business, this doctrine would also allow trademark owners to "monopolize markets that (their) trade ha[d] never reached." *Hanover Star Milling*, 240 U.S. at 416, 36 S.Ct. at 361.

Id., 635 F.2d at 930–31, 208 U.S.P.Q. at 775.

2. *The Lanham Act and Constructive Use and Notice*

DAWN DONUT COMPANY, INC. v. HART'S FOOD STORES, INC.

United States Court of Appeals for the Second Circuit, 1959.
267 F.2d 358, 121 U.S.P.Q. 430.

LUMBARD, CIRCUIT JUDGE.

The principal question is whether the plaintiff, a wholesale distributor of doughnuts and other baked goods under its federally registered trademarks "Dawn" and "Dawn Donut," is entitled under the provisions of the Lanham Trade–Mark Act to enjoin the defendant from using the mark "Dawn" in connection with the retail sale of doughnuts and baked goods entirely within a six county area of New York State surrounding the city of Rochester. The primary difficulty arises from the fact that although plaintiff licenses purchasers of its mixes to use its trademarks in connection with the retail sales of food products made from the mixes, it has not licensed or otherwise exploited the mark at the retail level in defendant's market area for some thirty years.

We hold that because no likelihood of public confusion arises from the concurrent use of the mark in connection with retail sales of doughnuts and other baked goods in separate trading areas, and because there is no present likelihood that plaintiff will expand its retail use of the mark into defendant's market area, plaintiff is not now entitled to any relief under the Lanham Act, 15 U.S.C.A. 1114. Accordingly, we affirm the district court's dismissal of plaintiff's complaint.

This is not to say that the defendant has acquired any permanent right to use the mark in its trading area. On the contrary, we hold that because of the effect of the constructive notice provision of the Lanham

Act, should the plaintiff expand its retail activities into the six county area, upon a proper application and showing to the district court, it may enjoin defendant's use of the mark.

* * *

Plaintiff, Dawn Donut Co., Inc., of Jackson, Michigan since June 1, 1922 has continuously used the trademark "Dawn" upon 25 to 100 pound bags of doughnut mix which it sells to bakers in various states, including New York, and since 1935 it has similarly marketed a line of sweet dough mixes for use in the baking of coffee cakes, cinnamon rolls and oven goods in general under that mark. In 1950 cake mixes were added to the company's line of products. Dawn's sales representatives call upon bakers to solicit orders for mixes and the orders obtained are filled by shipment to the purchaser either directly from plaintiff's Jackson, Michigan plant, where the mixes are manufactured, or from a local warehouse within the customer's state. For some years plaintiff maintained a warehouse in Jamestown, New York, from which shipments were made, but sometime prior to the commencement of this suit in 1954 it discontinued this warehouse and has since then shipped its mixes to its New York customers directly from Michigan.

Plaintiff furnishes certain buyers of its mixes, principally those who agree to become exclusive Dawn Donut Shops, with advertising and packaging material bearing the trademark "Dawn" and permits these bakers to sell goods made from the mixes to the consuming public under that trademark. These display materials are supplied either as a courtesy or at a moderate price apparently to stimulate and promote the sale of plaintiff's mixes.

The district court found that with the exception of one Dawn Donut Shop operated in the city of Rochester, New York during 1926–27, plaintiff's licensing of its mark in connection with the retail sale of doughnuts in the state of New York has been confined to areas not less than 60 miles from defendant's trading area. The court also found that for the past eighteen years plaintiff's present New York state representative has, without interruption, made regular calls upon bakers in the city of Rochester, N.Y., and in neighboring towns and cities, soliciting orders for plaintiff's mixes and that throughout this period orders have been filled and shipments made of plaintiff's mixes from Jackson, Michigan into the city of Rochester. But it does not appear that any of these purchasers of plaintiff's mixes employed the plaintiff's mark in connection with retail sales.

The defendant, Hart Food Stores, Inc., owns and operates a retail grocery chain within the New York counties of Monroe, Wayne, Livingston, Genesee, Ontario and Wyoming. The products of defendant's bakery, Starhart Bakeries, Inc., a New York corporation of which it is the sole stockholder, are distributed through these stores, thus confining the distribution of defendant's product to an area within a 45 mile radius of Rochester. Its advertising of doughnuts and other baked products over television and radio and in newspapers is also limited to this area. Defendant's bakery corporation was formed on April 13, 1951 and first used the imprint "Dawn" in packaging its products on August 30, 1951. The district court found that the defendant adopted the mark "Dawn" without any actual knowledge of plaintiff's use or federal registration of the mark, selecting it largely because of a slogan "Baked at midnight, delivered at Dawn" which was originated by defendant's president and used by defendant in its bakery operations from 1929 to 1935. Defendant's president testified, however, that no investigation was made prior to the adoption of the mark to see if anyone else was employing it. Plaintiff's marks were registered federally in 1927, and their registration was renewed in 1947. Therefore by virtue of the Lanham Act, 15 U.S.C.A. 1072, the defendant had constructive notice of plaintiff's marks as of July 5, 1947, the effective date of the Act.

Defendant's principal contention is that because plaintiff has failed to exploit the mark "Dawn" for some thirty years at the retail level in the Rochester trading area, plaintiff should not be accorded the exclusive right to use the mark in this area.

We reject this contention as inconsistent with the scope of protection afforded a federal registrant by the Lanham Act.

Prior to the passage of the Lanham Act courts generally held that the owner of a registered trademark could not sustain an action for infringement against another who, without knowledge of the registration, used the mark in a different trading area from that exploited by the registrant so that public confusion was unlikely. Hanover Star Milling Co. v. Metcalf, 1916, 240 U.S. 403, 36 S.Ct. 357, 60 L.Ed. 713. By being the first to adopt a mark in an area without knowledge of its prior registration, a junior user of a mark could gain the right to exploit the mark exclusively in that market.

But the Lanham Act, 15 U.S.C.A. 1072, provides that registration of a trademark on the principal register is constructive notice of the registrant's claim of ownership. Thus, by eliminating the defense of good faith and lack of knowledge, 1072 affords nationwide protection to registered marks, regardless of the areas in which the registrant actually uses the mark.

That such is the purpose of Congress is further evidenced by 15 U.S.C.A. 1115(a) and (b) which make the certificate of registration evidence of the registrant's "exclusive right to use the * * * mark in commerce." "Commerce" is defined in 15 U.S.C.A. 1127 to include all the commerce which may lawfully be regulated by Congress. These two provisions of the Lanham Act make it plain that the fact that the defendant employed the mark "Dawn," without actual knowledge of plaintiff's registration, at the retail level in a limited geographical area of New York state before the plaintiff used the mark in that market, does not entitle it either to exclude the plaintiff from using the mark in that area or to use the mark concurrently once the plaintiff licenses the mark or otherwise exploits it in connection with retail sales in the area.

Plaintiff's failure to license its trademarks in defendant's trading area during the thirty odd years that have elapsed since it licensed them to a Rochester baker does not work an abandonment of the rights in that area. We hold that 15 U.S.C.A. 1127, which provides for abandonment in certain cases of non-use,[3] applies only when the registrant fails to use his mark, within the meaning of 1127, anywhere in the nation. Since the Lanham Act affords a registrant nationwide protection, a contrary holding would create an insoluble problem of measuring the geographical extent of the abandonment. * * *

Accordingly, since plaintiff has used its trademark continuously at the retail level, it has not abandoned its federal registration rights even in defendant's trading area.

* * *

[W]e turn to the question of whether on this record plaintiff has made a sufficient showing to warrant the issuance of an injunction against defendant's use of the mark "Dawn" in a trading area in which the plaintiff has for thirty years failed to employ its registered mark.

The Lanham Act, 15 U.S.C.A. 1114, sets out the standard for awarding a registrant relief against the unauthorized use of his mark by another. It provides that the registrant may enjoin only that concurrent use which creates a likelihood of public confusion as to the origin of the products in connection with which the marks are used. Therefore if the use of the marks by the registrant and the unauthorized user are confined to two sufficiently distinct and geographically separate markets, with no likelihood that the registrant will expand his use into defendant's market,[4] so that no public confusion is possible, then the registrant is not entitled to enjoin the junior user's use of the mark.

As long as plaintiff and defendant confine their use of the mark "Dawn" in connection with the retail sale of baked goods to their present separate trading areas it is clear that no public confusion is likely.

3. 15 U.S.C.A. 1127 provides:

"A mark shall be deemed to be 'abandoned'—

"(a) When its use has been discontinued with intent not to resume. Intent not to resume may be inferred from circumstances. Nonuse for two consecutive years shall be prima facie abandonment.

"(b) When any course of conduct of the registrant, including acts of omission as well as commission, causes the mark to lose its significance as an indication of origin."

4. To sustain a claim for injunctive relief, the plaintiff need not show that the marks are actually being used concurrently in the same trading area. Since the statutory standard for the invocation of injunctive relief is the likelihood of confusion, it is enough that expansion by the registrant into the defendant's market is likely in the normal course of its business. Even prior to the passage of the Lanham Act the courts held that the second user of a mark was not entitled to exclude the registered owner of the mark from using it in a territory which the latter would probably reach in the normal expansion of his business. Certainly, under the Lanham Act, evincing a congressional purpose to afford a registrant nationwide protection, the subsequent user is not entitled to any greater immunity.

The district court took note of what it deemed common knowledge, that "retail purchasers of baked goods, because of the perishable nature of such goods, usually make such purchases reasonably close to their homes, say within about 25 miles, and retail purchases of such goods beyond that distance are for all practical considerations negligible." No objection is made to this finding and nothing appears in the record which contradicts it as applied to this case.

Moreover, we note that it took plaintiff three years to learn of defendant's use of the mark and bring this suit, even though the plaintiff was doing some wholesale business in the Rochester area. This is a strong indication that no confusion arose or is likely to arise either from concurrent use of the marks at the retail level in geographically separate trading areas or from its concurrent use at different market levels, viz. retail and wholesale in the same area.

The decisive question then is whether plaintiff's use of the mark "Dawn" at the retail level is likely to be confined to its current area of use or whether in the normal course of its business, it is likely to expand the retail use of the mark into defendant's trading area. If such expansion were probable, then the concurrent use of the marks would give rise to the conclusion that there was a likelihood of confusion.

* * *

We note not only that plaintiff has failed to license its mark at the retail level in defendant's trading area for a substantial period of time, but also that the trend of plaintiff's business manifests a striking decrease in the number of licensees employing its mark at the retail level in New York state and throughout the country. In the 1922–1930 period plaintiff had 75 to 80 licensees across the country with 11 located in New York. At the time of the trial plaintiff listed only 16 active licensees not one of which was located in New York.

The normal likelihood that plaintiff's wholesale operations in the Rochester area would expand to the retail level is fully rebutted and overcome by the decisive fact that plaintiff has in fact not licensed or otherwise exploited its mark at retail in the area for some thirty years.

Accordingly, because plaintiff and defendant use the mark in connection with retail sales in distinct and separate markets and because there is no present prospect that plaintiff will expand its use of the mark at the retail level into defendant's trading area, we conclude that there is no likelihood of public confusion arising from the concurrent use of the marks and therefore the issuance of an injunction is not warranted. *A fortiori* plaintiff is not entitled to any accounting or damages. However, because of the effect we have attributed to the constructive notice provision of the Lanham Act, the plaintiff may later, upon a proper showing of an intent to use the mark at the retail level in defendant's market area, be entitled to enjoin defendant's use of the mark. * * *

Notes and Questions

1. *The effect of registration on the Lanham Act principal register.* Why did the defendant in *Dawn Donut* not have a remote, good-faith user defense? What is the practical impact of Lanham Act section 22, 15 U.S.C.A. § 1072, on the geographic rights of registrants? Why is this result desirable?

Given the provisions of section 22, why did the court refuse to enjoin the defendant's continued use of the "Dawn" mark? What are the practical implications of the court's decision for the defendant? Of what relevance is the plaintiff's continued use of the "Dawn" mark on large bags of dough mixes in the Rochester area?

Does the rule set forth in *Dawn Donut* adequately protect the public against confusion?

Lanham Act section 22 provides nationwide priority in a mark as of the date of registration by making registration on the principal register constructive notice of the registrant's claim of ownership. 15 U.S.C.A. § 1072. Section 7(c), as amended by the Trademark Revision Act of 1988, provides:

> Contingent on the registration of a mark on the principal register provided by this chapter, the filing of the application to register such mark shall constitute constructive use of the mark *conferring a right of priority, nationwide in effect, on or in connection with the goods or services specified in the registration against any other person* except for a person whose mark has not been abandoned and who, prior to such filing—
>
> (1) has used the mark;
>
> (2) has filed an application to register the mark which is pending or has resulted in registration of the mark; or
>
> (3) has filed a foreign application to register the mark on the basis of which he or she has acquired a right of priority, and timely files an application under section 1126(d) of this title to register the mark which is pending or has resulted in registration of the mark.

15 U.S.C.A. § 1057(c) (emphasis added). Accordingly, for all registered marks whose registration is based on an application filed after the effective date of the 1988 amendments (November 16, 1989), priority is moved forward from the date of registration to the date the application to register was filed, against persons who do not fall within the three enumerated exceptions. See S. REP. NO. 515, 100th Cong., 2d Sess. 29–30 (1998).

2. *"Intermediate" junior users.* Assume that X begins using a mark in South Carolina in December, 1990. He files an application to register the mark on the principal register in December, 1992, and the mark is registered in December, 1993. Y begins using the same mark on similar products in Oregon in December, 1991, having no knowledge of X. X later decides to expand his business to Oregon. Assuming that Y continues to use the mark there, what are X's and Y's respective rights?

While X is the senior user, with nationwide priority by virtue of his registration, Y has the benefit of the "limited area defense." This defense, which is similar to the common-law good faith remote user defense, is described in Lanham Act section 33(b)(5), as amended, 15 U.S.C.A. § 1115(b)(5), which provides that "incontestable" marks [13] are subject to the following defense:

> That the mark whose use by a party is charged as an infringement was adopted without knowledge of the registrant's prior use and has been continuously used by such party or those in privity with him from a date prior to (A) the date of the constructive use of the mark established pursuant to section 1057(c) of this title, (B) the registration of the mark under this Act if the application for registration is filed before the effective date of the Trademark Law Revision Act of 1988, or (C) publication of the registered mark under subsection (c) of section 1062 of this title: *Provided, however,* That this defense or defect shall apply only for the area in which such continuous prior use is proved * * *.

Section 33(a), 15 U.S.C.A. § 1115(a), makes this same defense available against marks that are not incontestable.

Y enjoys priority in those areas in which he has continuously used the mark since before X's registration date. He may continue his use there, and may enjoin X from entering that territory, even though X has superior rights throughout the rest of the country. Note, however, that Y's territory is "frozen" to that which he occupied on the date of X's registration [14] and has occupied continuously ever since—Oregon, or if he only occupied parts of Oregon, those parts. For example, if Y had expanded his use of the mark to Idaho in 1994, he would be subject to an injunction against further use there, once X decided to enter the Idaho market with the mark. This result is dictated both by the language of section 33(a) and by the constructive notice provision in section 22.

For case opinions illustrating the application of the limited area defense, see, e.g., Burger King of Florida, Inc. v. Hoots, 403 F.2d 904, 159 U.S.P.Q. 706 (7th Cir.1968); Thrifty Rent–A–Car System, Inc. v. Thrift Cars, Inc., 831 F.2d 1177, 4 U.S.P.Q.2d 1709 (1st Cir.1987).

What if, instead of commencing use of the mark on December l, 1991, Y began use in January, 1993?

The provisions discussed above attempt to balance the conflicting interests in providing for nationwide trademark rights and accommodating the interests traditionally protected by the common-law rules. Assuming (under the first fact situation) that Y continues his use in Oregon (or the part of

13. A mark that has been in continuous use for five consecutive years following registration is eligible for incontestability status. Lanham Act section 15, 15 U.S.C.A. § 1065, sets forth the requirements and procedure for obtaining mark incontestability status. Incontestability status limits the challenges that can be made to the validity of the mark or to the registrant's right to use it. The incontestability provisions will be discussed more fully in Section VI G of this Chapter, *infra.*

14. While there has been some dispute over whether the territory is frozen as of the date of X's application or the date of his registration, see, e.g., 2 J.T. McCARTHY, McCARTHY ON TRADEMARKS AND UNFAIR COMPETITION § 26.18[2] (3d ed. 1992), the latter interpretation more nearly conforms with legislative history and the overall statutory scheme.

Oregon that he occupied at X's registration), and X expands to use the mark throughout the rest of the nation, what are the practical implications? Will X be able to advertise in the national media? See Flavor Corp. of America v. Kemin Industries, Inc., 503 F.2d 729, 183 U.S.P.Q. 401 (8th Cir.1974).

3. *When the junior user is the registrant.* Suppose that A begins using a mark in Texas in 1980 and continuously uses it in Texas thereafter. B begins using the same mark in connection with similar products in Maine in 1982, with no knowledge of A's use, and registers the mark on the principal register in 1983. B later expands her business and seeks to enter Texas with her mark. What result?

If B's registered mark has not attained incontestability status, A can rely on her senior use and enjoin B from entering Texas (or that part of Texas in which A was using the mark when B registered). Whether and to what extent A may assert superior rights beyond the geographic area that she occupied at the time of B's registration will depend on the particular circumstances of the case and a balancing of the equities. See Wiener King, Inc. v. Wiener King Corp., 615 F.2d 512, 522, 525–26, 204 U.S.P.Q. 820, 828, 830–31 (C.C.P.A.1980).

If B's mark has become incontestable, the language of Lanham Act sections 15 and 33(b), 15 U.S.C.A. §§ 1065, 1115(b), becomes relevant. Can you identify the relevant language? Assuming that A is able to demonstrate prior, continuous use of the mark, she will be able to continue using the mark on those goods for which she establishes the prior use, in those geographic areas which she occupied at the time of B's registration. She may enjoin B's use in those areas, but B will retain incontestable rights in the rest of the country. For examples of case opinions applying this principle, see Wrist–Rocket Manufacturing Co., Inc. v. Saunders Archery Co., 516 F.2d 846, 186 U.S.P.Q. 5 (8th Cir.1975), *cert. denied* 423 U.S. 870, 96 S.Ct. 134, 46 L.Ed.2d 100 (1975); Wrist–Rocket Manufacturing Co. Inc. v. Saunders Archery Co., 578 F.2d 727, 198 U.S.P.Q. 257 (8th Cir.1978); Holiday Inn v. Holiday Inns Inc., 534 F.2d 312, 189 U.S.P.Q. 630 (C.C.P.A. 1976). What policy justifies freezing A's rights when A is the senior user?

4. *Concurrent registration.* Lanham Act section 2(d), 15 U.S.C.A. § 1052(d), provides for concurrent registration when more than one party is legally entitled to use a mark. Review subsection (d). As the statutory language suggests, concurrent registration may be obtained when the PTO determines that it is appropriate in a concurrent use proceeding, or pursuant to a court determination that dual parties have a right to use the mark. The Court of Customs and Patent Appeals set forth guidelines for the PTO in making concurrent use determinations in *Application of* Beatrice Foods Co., 429 F.2d 466, 166 U.S.P.Q. 431 (1970). With regard to registration pursuant to a court determination, see Holiday Inn v. Holiday Inns, Inc., *supra.* For more information on concurrent trademark registration, see Kaul, *Concurrent Use and Registration of Trademarks*, 62 TRADEMARK REP. 581 (1972).

F. ASSIGNMENTS AND TRADEMARK ABANDONMENT

MONEY STORE v. HARRISCORP FINANCE, INC.

United States Court of Appeals for the Seventh Circuit, 1982.
689 F.2d 666, 216 U.S.P.Q. 11.

PELL, CIRCUIT JUDGE.

The Money Store, the plaintiff-appellant in this action, appeals from the district judge's cancellation of its federally registered service mark, "THE MONEY STORE," and the issuance of a permanent injunction against utilization of the mark by the plaintiff in the defendant's market area. * * *

On cross-appeal, the defendant, Harriscorp Finance, Inc. (Harriscorp), challenges the district court's holding that * * * the assignment of rights in the mark from United Bank of America (United Bank or United) to Harriscorp was ineffective because no goodwill passed pursuant to the assignment. * * *

[The plaintiff (which the court refers to as "Modern Acceptance") began using the mark "THE MONEY STORE" on January 2, 1972, at its New Jersey and Pennsylvania offices and in newspaper and radio advertisements. Plaintiff applied to register the mark on February 4, 1972, and obtained registration on April 2, 1974. The plaintiff's business increased dramatically after adoption of the mark, both in terms of the volume of business and the geographic area in which it operated under "THE MONEY STORE" mark.]

Defendant-appellee Harriscorp is a Delaware corporation. * * * In 1972, Theodore Roberts, the principal Harris executive responsible for the Harriscorp Finance retail lending project, selected "THE MONEY STORE" as his preferred name for money-lending service facilities the Bank planned to open in the metropolitan Chicago area. A trademark search conducted in mid–1973 disclosed [among other things, Modern Acceptance's pending application to register]. Because Harris found no evidence of any use of "THE MONEY STORE" in the Chicago area, it tentatively decided to use the mark.

In September 1972, Roberts learned that United Bank in Chicago was using "THE MONEY STORE" mark. United had first used the mark in August, 1972, eight months after the plaintiff's first use. In January, 1974, United assigned its rights in the mark to Harris. Although the evidence indicated that United had decided to discontinue use of the mark, it similarly indicated that United was still using "THE MONEY STORE" at the time of the assignment. In fact, at the time of the assignment, United was featuring the marks on three billboards located on major Chicago streets. The assignment recited that "for good and valuable consideration, the receipt of which is hereby acknowledged ... [the mark is assigned] together with the goodwill of the business symbolized by the mark." Harris did not acquire customer lists, real estate, receivables, accounts or any other tangible assets in return for the one dollar consideration it actually paid to United.

Having obtained the assignment from United, Harris made a final decision to use the mark and in December, 1974, Harriscorp opened three lending offices in the Chicago area utilizing the mark "THE MONEY STORE."

In January, 1975, Modern Acceptance sent Harriscorp a letter requesting it to cease and desist from using the mark. * * * In April, 1977, the plaintiff renewed its infringement claim and the instant suit was filed in August of that year.

* * *

V. Assignment From United

Harriscorp asserts the defense of a good faith junior user based on the January, 1974 assignment from United Bank. A good faith junior user is one who begins using a mark with no knowledge that someone else is already using it. The innocent junior user retains the right to use the mark in an area remote from where the senior user is operating.

United began using the mark, "THE MONEY STORE," in the metropolitan Chicago area in August, 1972, approximately eight months after the plaintiff's first use in New Jersey and Pennsylvania. United's use preceded issuance of the plaintiff's federal registration, however, by approximately twenty months. United could not be charged, therefore, with constructive knowledge of the plaintiff's use of "THE MONEY STORE" as a service mark. 15 U.S.C. § 1072 (1976). Similarly, there is no evidence that United had actual knowledge of the usage of the mark by Modern Acceptance. United therefore was a good faith junior user. This status would give United, were it still using the mark, the right to enjoin the plaintiff's use of the identical mark in the Chicago area.

Whether Harriscorp can assert the good faith junior user defense turns on three factors: (1) whether United had abandoned use of the mark at the time of the assignment; (2) whether the assignment included a transfer of goodwill; and (3) whether the assignment is invalid as a sham transaction.

Before addressing these three points, we note that the fact Harris actually paid only one dollar to United is not dispositive. The exchange of a nominal sum, like the recitation that the assignment was for "good and valuable consideration," is customary in many contracts and does not in itself make the assignment ineffective. The amount actually paid is relevant only insofar as it might indicate either that United had abandoned the mark or that no goodwill was associated with "THE MONEY STORE" mark and therefore could not be transferred pursuant to the assignment. Each of these points is discussed below.

An abandoned trademark is not capable of assignment because such a mark is subject to cancellation by the Patent Office or by the courts and is therefore invalid. 15 U.S.C. §§ 1064(c), 1119 (1976). Section 45 of the Lanham Act defines when a mark shall be deemed abandoned. The subsection relevant to United's use of "THE MONEY STORE" mark states:

> (a) When its use has been discontinued with intent not to resume. Intent not to resume may be inferred from circumstances. Nonuse for two consecutive years shall be prima facie abandonment.

15 U.S.C. § 1127 (1976). The district court found that United Bank was still using the mark at the time of the assignment and had not abandoned it. The plaintiff argues in its brief that "(a)bandonment is a matter of intent" and points to evidence suggesting that United intended to abandon use of the mark. The statutory definition makes clear, however, that abandonment requires *discontinuance of use* as well as intent to abandon. Such discontinuance of use was not found by the district court and we find nothing in the record suggesting that the court below was incorrect. * * * We conclude that the judge below correctly found that United had not abandoned the mark at the time of the assignment to Harriscorp.

The assignment conferred no rights on Harriscorp under the Lanham Act, however, unless the goodwill of the business was assigned along with the mark. 15 U.S.C. § 1060 (1976). The judge below found that no goodwill had been transferred in the assignment. First, we recognize that, although the assignment stated that the mark was assigned "together with the good will of the business symbolized by the mark," such a recitation is not necessarily dispositive.

Second, we find that it is not necessary to the continuing validity of the mark that tangible assets of the assignor pass to the assignee. * * *

It is admittedly difficult to determine when a transfer of goodwill has occurred. This is particularly so in the case of a service mark. Before turning to other cases relied upon by the parties, it is important to recognize why the common law and Lanham Act prohibitions on a transfer of a mark unassociated with any goodwill exist:

> A sale of a trademark divorced from its good will is characterized as an "assignment in gross." If one obtains a trademark through an assignment in gross, divorced from the good will of the assignor, the assignee obtains the symbol, but not the reality. Any subsequent use of the mark by the assignee will necessarily be in connection with a different business, a different good will and a different type of product. The continuity of the things symbolized by the mark is broken. Use of the mark by the assignee in connection with a different good will and different product would result in a fraud on the purchasing public, who reasonably assume that the mark signified the same things, whether used by one person or another.... The fundamental policy of consumer protection must always be kept in mind. The central purpose of the technical rules regarding the assignment of trademarks is to protect consumers and these rules were "not evolved for the purpose of invalidating all trademark assignments which do not satisfy a stereo-typed set of formalities."

Syntex Laboratories v. Norwich Pharmacal Co., 315 F.Supp. 45 (S.D.N.Y.1970), *aff'd*, 437 F.2d 566 (2d Cir.1971).

McCarthy, *Trademarks and Unfair Competition*, § 18.1, at 607.

Application of this reasoning is apparent in *Pepsico, Inc. v. Grapette Co.*, 416 F.2d 285 (8th Cir.1969). In that case, the mark "Peppy" had been used for many years on a cola-based drink. The mark was assigned to Grapette Co. Grapette acquired no tangible assets from the assignor, nor any process or formula for producing the beverage. Grapette then used the "Peppy" mark on a pepper-type beverage. The *Pepsico* court noted the possibility of public deceit if the assignment were considered valid, *id.* at 289, and stated:

> It seems fundamental that either the defendant did not acquire any "goodwill" as required by law or if it did, assuming as defendant argues the mark itself possesses "goodwill," by use of the mark on a totally different product, Grapette intended to deceive the public. Either ground is untenable to the validity of the assignment.

Id. at 290.

* * *

Perhaps the strongest case in support of Harriscorp's contention is *Hy-Cross Hatchery, Inc. v. Osborne*, 303 F.2d 947 (C.C.P.A.1962). In *Hy-Cross*, the assignor held a valid registration of the mark "HY–CROSS" and had used it for some time to identify the baby chicks that he sold. He assigned the mark, along with a recitation of goodwill. The assignor continued in the business of selling chicks. The court held that the assignment was effective, stating that "by assigning the goodwill, [the assignor] gave up the right to sell 'HY–CROSS' chicks. This had been a part of his 'business.' " *Id.* at 950.

Modern Acceptance argues that *Hy-Cross* is weak support because of then Judge Blackmun's concurrence in *Pepsico, Inc. v. Grapette Co.*, 416 F.2d 285 (8th Cir.1969). As discussed *supra*, the assignee in that case had used the mark on an entirely different type of beverage from that made by the assignor. The majority of the court had mentioned the *Hy-Cross* case, characterizing it as involving a naked assignment, but had decided the appeal on the ground that an assignment is valid only if the assignee's product has the same characteristics as that of the assignor. In his concurrence, Judge Blackmun noted that *Hy-Cross* was a peculiar case in that live baby chicks were the product of both the assignor and assignee. He read *Hy-Cross* as attaching little significance to the absence of any assignment of the chicks themselves only in that particular context. Judge Blackmun stated that he would be opposed to any broader interpretation of the *Hy-Cross* rule.

We do not believe that Judge Blackmun's concurrence casts doubt upon the applicability of *Hy-Cross* to the instant case. The circumstances in this case are also "peculiar" in that United and Harriscorp offered the identical service. A customer who was drawn first to United and later to Harriscorp because of the "MONEY STORE" mark would not be misled as to the nature of the services offered. United's use of the mark in advertising, including highly visible billboards, strongly suggests that the mark carried with it a degree of goodwill. What United gave up in assigning the mark was the right to attract customers through use of the mark. The fact that one cannot say with certainty how many customers might have gone to a Harriscorp office, rather than a United office, because they recognized the mark does not compel the conclusion that no goodwill passed with the assignment.

The cases cited by both sides of this controversy are consistent with the underlying purpose of why a transfer of goodwill is required in order for an assignment of a mark to be effective. The cases all seek to protect customers from deception and confusion. In the case of a service mark, such confusion would result if an assignee offered a service different from that offered by the assignor of the mark. Such is not the case here.

We similarly do not believe that there was a lack of continuity in the usage of the mark. The mark was utilized by Harris Bank in the short period between the assignment and the opening of the Harriscorp offices. It was used both before and after the assignment in connection with money-lending services.

One final point remains. The plaintiff claims that the assignment is ineffective because it was a sham transaction, initiated by Harris for the sole purpose of obtaining superior rights to the mark in the Chicago area. Presumably, Harris sought the assignment because it knew of the plaintiff's prior rights in the mark. Harris did in fact know of the plaintiff's pending registration and it would be naive to conclude that that knowledge was completely irrelevant to its decision to seek an assignment from United. It is also true, however, that so long as United retained any rights in the mark, that institution was itself an impediment to the defendant's usage of the mark. Obtaining the assignment from United is consistent with the defendant's documented belief that the plaintiff could not successfully assert nationwide rights in the mark, and therefore another institution was free to use the mark in the Chicago area. We do not believe that an assignment motivated at least in part by sound business judgment should be set aside as a sham transaction.

We conclude that the assignment from United to Harris was effective. The mark had not been abandoned at the time of the assignment and whatever goodwill was associated with the mark passed to the defendant pursuant to the assignment.

* * *

* * * Harriscorp is entitled * * * to assert the rights of a good faith junior user in its market area, as that area shall be determined by the district court on remand. * * *

Notes and Questions

1. *Assignment of marks.* "Unlike patents or copyrights, trademarks are not separate property rights. They are integral and inseparable ele-

ments of the goodwill of the business or services to which they pertain." Visa U.S.A., Inc. v. Birmingham Trust National Bank, 696 F.2d 1371, 1375, 216 U.S.P.Q. 649, 651 (C.A.F.C. 1982), *cert. denied* 464 U.S. 826, 104 S.Ct. 98, 78 L.Ed.2d 104 (1983). Thus, assignment of the mark alone, without the attendant good will, is meaningless in the eyes of the law and invalid. This was the rule at common law, and it is codified in Lanham Act section 10, 15 U.S.C.A. § 1060:

> A registered mark or a mark for which application to register has been filed shall be assignable with the goodwill of the business in which the mark is used, or with that part of the goodwill of the business connected with the use of and symbolized by the mark.

In determining whether a mark was assigned with the good will it represented, courts traditionally looked for evidence that assets associated with the assignor's product or business—such as plant, product formula or inventory—were assigned along with the mark. If such things were assigned, there was some assurance that the assignee would continue to offer a similar product or service under the mark. The more modern trend, as exemplified in *Money Store*, is to cast aside formulaic requirements and find a passing of good will even in the absence of such assets, as long as it is demonstrated that the assignee continued to sell goods or services of the same kind as the assignor.

As the *Money Store* opinion indicates, the main purpose of the good will requirement is to avoid consumer deception or confusion. In this sense, trademark law undertakes to guarantee the consistency of products offered under the same mark. The court in *Money Store* found that the assignee and assignor offered similar services—money lending—and thus that this purpose was fulfilled. The court did not, however, examine the specifics of the parties' respective services. For example, what if the terms under which the parties loaned money differed significantly? Should a finding to that effect lead to the conclusion that the assignment was invalid?

What, exactly, does it mean to find that the assignment of a mark is invalid? Does the invalidity, in itself, mean that the assignee may not use the mark?

What are the implications of the rule prohibiting assignments in gross for the practice of using trademarks as security for debts? See 1 J.T. McCARTHY, McCARTHY ON TRADEMARKS AND UNFAIR COMPETITION § 18.01[7] (1992).

2. *Abandonment.* Proof of "trademark abandonment" provides a defense against infringement liability as well as grounds for canceling the abandoning party's registration. 15 U.S.C.A. § 1064(3). The *Money Store* and *Dawn Donut* defendants both raised abandonment defenses based upon the first definition of abandonment set forth in Lanham Act section 45, 15 U.S.C.A. § 1127:

> A mark shall be deemed to be "abandoned" * * *
>
> (1) When its use has been discontinued with intent not to resume such use. Intent not to resume may be inferred from circumstances. Nonuse for three consecutive years shall be prima facie evidence of abandonment. "Use" of a mark means the bona fide use of such mark

> made in the ordinary course of trade, and not made merely to reserve a right in a mark.[15]

For a detailed analysis of this provision, see Radin, *Selected Issues Arising Under the Doctrine of Trademark Abandonment*, 79 TRADEMARK REP. 433 (1989).

Section 45 provides a second important basis for finding abandonment, which was also raised in *Dawn Donut*:

> A mark shall be deemed to be "abandoned" * * *
>
> (2) When any course of conduct of the owner, including acts of omission as well as commission, causes the mark to * * * lose its significance as a mark.

This second form of abandonment may arise when trademark owners license others to use their mark, but fail to supervise and control the licensees' use. The court in *Dawn Donut* explained:

> [T]he Lanham Act places an affirmative duty upon a licensor of a registered trademark to take reasonable measures to detect and prevent misleading uses of his mark by his licensees or suffer cancellation of his federal registration. * * *
>
> Prior to the passage of the Lanham Act many courts took the position that the licensing of a trademark separately from the business in connection with which it had been used worked an abandonment. The theory of these cases was that:
>
> > A trade-mark is intended to identify the goods of the owner and to safeguard his good will. The designation if employed by a person other than the one whose business it serves to identify would be misleading. Consequently, "a right to the use of a trade-mark or a trade-name cannot be transferred in gross."
>
> American Broadcasting Co. v. Wahl Co., 121 F.2d at page 413.
>
> Other courts were somewhat more liberal and held that a trademark could be licensed separately from the business in connection with which it had been used provided that the licensor retained control over the quality of the goods produced by the licensee. But even in [those cases] the court was careful to point out that naked licensing, viz. the grant of licenses without the retention of control, was invalid.
>
> The Lanham Act clearly carries forward the view of these latter cases that controlled licensing does not work an abandonment of the licensor's registration, while a system of naked licensing does. 15 U.S.C.A. 1055 provides:
>
> > "Where a registered mark or a mark sought to be registered is or may be used legitimately by related companies, such use shall inure to the benefit of the registrant or applicant for registration, and such use shall not affect the validity of such mark or of its

15. This definition provided that nonuse for *two* consecutive years would be prima facie evidence of abandonment, prior to the Uruguay Round Agreements Act, Pub. L. No. 103–465, § 521, 108 Stat. 4809, 4982 (1994), which extended the period of nonuse to three consecutive years. This amendment becomes effective on January 1, 1996.

> registration, provided such mark is not used in such manner as to deceive the public."
>
> And 15 U.S.C.A. 1127 defines "related company" to mean "any person who legitimately controls or is controlled by the registrant or applicant for registration in respect to the nature and quality of the goods or services in connection with which the mark is used."
>
> Without the requirement of control, the right of a trademark owner to license his mark separately from the business in connection with which it has been used would create the danger that products bearing the same trademark might be of diverse qualities. If the licensor is not compelled to take some reasonable steps to prevent misuses of his trademark in the hands of others the public will be deprived of its most effective protection against misleading uses of a trademark. The public is hardly in a position to uncover deceptive uses of a trademark before they occur and will be at best slow to detect them after they happen. Thus, unless the licensor exercises supervision and control over the operations of its licensees the risk that the public will be unwittingly deceived will be increased and this is precisely what the Act is in part designed to prevent. Clearly the only effective way to protect the public where a trademark is used by licensees is to place on the licensor the affirmative duty of policing in a reasonable manner the activities of his licensees.

267 F.2d at 366–67, 121 U.S.P.Q. at 436–37.[16]

Permitting controlled trademark licensing made modern franchising practices possible. Notwithstanding statutory and judicial adoption of the control requirement, the requirement is not enforced strictly and rarely leads to a finding of trademark abandonment. In *Dawn Donut*, for example, the plaintiff/registrant licensed some purchasers of its wholesale donut mixes to use the mark "Dawn" in connection with retail donut sales. In some cases it entered into written contracts with the licensees, requiring that they exclusively purchase the plaintiff's mixes and adhere to the plaintiff's directions in using the mixes. These contracts, however, contained no provisions for inspecting or otherwise ensuring that the quality control requirements were being observed. In other cases there was no written license provision governing the quality of the donuts sold under the Dawn mark. In addition, there was little evidence that the plaintiff *in fact* exercised any significant control over its licensees. The only evidence consisted of the testimony of two of the plaintiff's local sales representatives that they regularly visited their particular customers. One of them testified that "in many cases" he had an opportunity to inspect and observe the operations of customer/licensees, when he was "able to get into the shop." However, it was unclear what sort of inspection he made or how often he made it. It was also unclear whether he had sufficient technical knowledge

16. The definition of "related company," as amended by the Trademark Law Revision Act of 1988, is:

> any person whose use of a mark is controlled by the owner of the mark with respect to the nature and quality of the goods or services on or in connection with which the mark is used.

15 U.S.C.A. § 1127. This amendment clarifies that the mark owner/registrant must control use of the mark by the licensee, and not vise versa.

about the use of the plaintiff's mix to make an adequate inspection. *Id.*, 267 F.2d at 368–69, 121 U.S.P.Q. at 437–38. The majority of the court nonetheless affirmed the district court's finding that the plaintiff had not abandoned its mark through failure to control the licensees, noting that the trial judge had some "leeway in determining what constitutes a reasonable degree of supervision and control over licensees under the facts and circumstances of the particular case," and that the defendant had the burden of proof on this issue. *Id.*

Though the presence or absence of contractual provisions for control is relevant, the ultimate issue is the licensor's *actual exercise* of control over the licensees. With regard to the degree of control that the licensor must exercise, the Restatement (Third) of Unfair Competition advocates a flexible standard that takes into account consumers' likely expectations, given the particular product and circumstances. Those expectations may differ, depending on how similar the goods and services sold by the licensee are to those sold by the mark owner. The closer the goods or services, the higher the expectations of consistency. In some cases, due to a long-term relationship or the licensee's experience and expertise, the trademark owner may be justified in relying on the licensee's contractual undertaking to maintain standards, with no additional control mechanism. In other cases, where the licensee is not as reliable, or the goods or services are complex or pose particular health hazards to the public if not properly produced, the mark owner may be required to undertake a more active supervisory role. RESTATEMENT (THIRD) OF UNFAIR COMPETITION § 33, comment c (Tentative Draft No. 3, 1991). See Marks, *Trademark Licensing: Towards a More Flexible Standard,* 78 TRADEMARK REP. 641 (1988).

From a practical standpoint, why might courts hesitate to impose strong control obligations on licensors? For an argument that the licensee control requirements should be eliminated altogether, see Parks, *"Naked" Is Not a Four–Letter Word: Debunking the Myth of the "Quality Control Requirement" in Trademark Licensing*, 82 TRADEMARK REP. 531 (1992). For a contrasting view, see Bannon, *The Growing Risk of Self–Dilution*, 82 TRADEMARK REP. 570 (1992).

G. TRADEMARK INCONTESTABILITY AND IMMUNITY FROM CANCELLATION

PARK 'N FLY, INC. v. DOLLAR PARK AND FLY, INC.

United States Supreme Court, 1985.
469 U.S. 189, 105 S.Ct. 658, 83 L.Ed.2d 582.

JUSTICE O'CONNOR delivered the opinion of the Court.

[The Petitioner operates long-term parking lots near airports in several cities. It applied in 1969 to register a service mark consisting of the logo of an airplane and the words "Park 'N Fly." The registration issued in August 1971. Nearly six years later, petitioner filed an affidavit with the PTO to establish the incontestable status of the mark. As required by § 15 of the Lanham Act, as amended, 15 U.S.C. § 1065, the affidavit stated that the mark had been registered and in continuous use for five consecutive years, that there had been no final adverse decision to petitioner's claim of ownership or right to registration, and that no proceedings involving such rights were pending. Incontestable status provides, subject to the provisions of § 15 and § 33(b) of the Lanham Act, "conclusive evidence of the registrant's exclusive right to use the registered mark. . . ." § 33(b), 15 U.S.C. § 1115(b).]

[Respondent provides long-term airport parking services in Portland, Oregon, and calls its business "Dollar Park and Fly." Petitioner filed this infringement action in 1978 and requested that the court permanently enjoin the respondent from using the words "Park and Fly" in connection with its business. Among other defenses, the respondent argued that petitioner's mark was unenforceable because merely descriptive and lacking secondary meaning. See Lanham Act § 2(e), 15 U.S.C. § 1052(e).]

[The district court granted the petitioner's request for an injunction, finding that an incontestable mark could not be challenged on the grounds that it is merely descriptive. The Court of Appeals for the Ninth Circuit reversed, finding that while incontestability provides a defense against the cancellation of a mark, it may not be used offensively to enjoin another's use. Respondent could defend the infringement action by showing that the mark was merely descriptive. The Court of Appeals then determined that petitioner's mark was in fact merely descriptive, and therefore respondent should not be enjoined from using the name "Park and Fly."]

This case requires us to consider the effect of the incontestability provisions of the Lanham Act in the context of an infringement action defended on the grounds that the mark is merely descriptive. Statutory construction must begin with the language employed by Congress and the assumption that the ordinary meaning of that language accurately expresses the legislative purpose. With respect to incontestable trade or service marks, § 33(b) of the Lanham Act states that "registration shall be conclusive evidence of the registrant's exclusive right to use the registered mark" subject to the conditions of § 15 and certain enumerated defenses. Section 15 incorporates by reference subsections (c) and (e) of § 14, 15 U.S.C. § 1064.*

One searches the language of the Lanham Act in vain to find any support for the offensive/defensive distinction applied by the Court of Appeals. * * * On the contrary, § 33(b)'s declaration that the registrant has an "exclusive right" to use the mark indicates that incontestable status may be used to enjoin infringement by others. A conclusion that such infringement cannot be enjoined renders meaningless the "exclusive right" recognized by the statute. Moreover, the language in three of the defenses enumerated in § 33(b) clearly contemplates the use

* [By the editor: Section 14(c) allows cancellation of the registration of an incontestable mark under certain enumerated circumstances.]

of incontestability in infringement actions by plaintiffs. See § 33(b)(4)-(6), 15 U.S.C. § 1115(b)(4)-(6).

The language of the Lanham Act also refutes any conclusion that an incontestable mark may be challenged as merely descriptive. A mark that is merely descriptive of an applicant's goods or services is not registrable unless the mark has secondary meaning. Before a mark achieves incontestable status, registration provides prima facie evidence of the registrant's exclusive right to use the mark in commerce. § 33(a), 15 U.S.C. § 1115(a). The Lanham Act expressly provides that before a mark becomes incontestable an opposing party may prove any legal or equitable defense which might have been asserted if the mark had not been registered. Thus, § 33(a) would have allowed respondent to challenge petitioner's mark as merely descriptive if the mark had not become incontestable. With respect to incontestable marks, however, § 33(b) provides that registration is *conclusive* evidence of the registrant's exclusive right to use the mark, subject to the conditions of § 15 and the seven defenses enumerated in § 33(b) itself. Mere descriptiveness is not recognized by either § 15 or § 33(b) as a basis for challenging an incontestable mark.

* * * [A]s applied to marks that are merely descriptive, the approach of the Court of Appeals makes incontestable status superfluous. Without regard to its incontestable status, a mark that has been registered five years is protected from cancellation except on the grounds stated in §§ 14(c) and (e). Pursuant to § 14, a mark may be canceled on the grounds that it is merely descriptive only if the petition to cancel is filed within five years of the date of registration. § 14(a), 15 U.S.C. § 1064(a). The approach adopted by the Court of Appeals implies that incontestability adds nothing to the protections against cancellation already provided in § 14. The decision below not only lacks support in the words of the statute; it effectively emasculates § 33(b) under the circumstances of this case.

* * *

Nothing in the legislative history of the Lanham Act supports a departure from the plain language of the statutory provisions concerning incontestability. Indeed, a conclusion that incontestable status can provide the basis for enforcement of the registrant's exclusive right to use a trade or service mark promotes the goals of the statute. * * * National protection of trademarks is desirable, Congress concluded, because trademarks foster competition and the maintenance of quality by securing to the producer the benefits of good reputation. The incontestability provisions, as the proponents of the Lanham Act emphasized, provide a means for the registrant to quiet title in the ownership of his mark. The opportunity to obtain incontestable status by satisfying the requirements of § 15 thus encourages producers to cultivate the goodwill associated with a particular mark. This function of the incontestability provisions would be utterly frustrated if the holder of an incontestable mark could not enjoin infringement by others so long as they established that the mark would not be registrable but for its incontestable status.

Respondent argues, however, that enforcing petitioner's mark would conflict with the goals of the Lanham Act because the mark is merely descriptive and should never have been registered in the first place. * * * [This argument] is misdirected. Arguments similar to those now urged by respondent were in fact considered by Congress in hearings on the Lanham Act. * * * These concerns were answered by proponents of the Lanham Act, who noted that a merely descriptive mark cannot be registered unless the Commissioner finds that it has secondary meaning. Moreover, a mark can be challenged for five years prior to its attaining incontestable status. * * *

The dissent echoes arguments made by opponents of the Lanham Act that the incontestable status of a descriptive mark might take from the public domain language that is merely descriptive. * * * The Lanham Act allows a mark to be challenged at any time if it becomes generic, and, under certain circumstances, permits the nontrademark use of descriptive terms contained in an incontestable mark. Finally, if "monopolization" of an incontestable mark threatens economic competition, § 33(b)(7), 15 U.S.C. § 1115(b)(7), provides a defense on the grounds that the mark is being used to violate federal antitrust laws. At bottom, the dissent simply disagrees with the balance struck by Congress in determining the protection to be given to incontestable marks.

* * *

We conclude that the holder of a registered mark may rely on incontestability to enjoin infringement and that such an action may not be defended on the grounds that the mark is merely descriptive. [The Court notes that a "prior use" defense can still be made pursuant to section 33(b)(5), and that a likelihood of confusion must be demonstrated before relief against infringement can be granted, regardless of incontestability status.]

JUSTICE STEVENS, dissenting.

In trademark law, the term "incontestable" is itself somewhat confusing and misleading because the Lanham Act expressly identifies over 20 situations in which infringement of an allegedly incontestable mark is permitted.[1] Moreover, in § 37 of the Act, Congress unambiguously authorized judicial review of the validity of the registration "in any action involving a registered mark." The problem in this case arises because of petitioner's attempt to enforce as "incontestable" a mark that Congress has plainly stated is inherently unregistrable.

1. Section 33(b) enumerates seven categories of defenses to an action to enforce an incontestable mark. See 15 U.S.C. § 1115(b). In addition, a defendant is free to argue that a mark should never have become incontestable for any of the four reasons enumerated in § 15. 15 U.S.C. § 1065. Moreover, § 15 expressly provides that an incontestable mark may be challenged on any of the grounds set forth in subsections (c) and (e) of § 14, 15 U.S.C. § 1064, and those sections, in turn, incorporate the objections to registrability that are defined in §§ 2(a), 2(b), and 2(c) of the Act. 15 U.S.C. §§ 1052(a), (b), and (c).

The mark "Park 'N Fly" is at best merely descriptive in the context of airport parking. Section 2 of the Lanham Act plainly prohibits the registration of such a mark unless the applicant proves to the Commissioner of the Patent and Trademark Office that the mark "has become distinctive of the applicant's goods in commerce," or to use the accepted shorthand, that it has acquired a "secondary meaning." See 15 U.S.C. §§ 1052(e), (f). Petitioner never submitted any such proof to the Commissioner, or indeed to the District Court in this case. Thus, the registration plainly violated the Act.

The violation of the literal wording of the Act also contravened the central purpose of the entire legislative scheme. Statutory protection for trademarks was granted in order to safeguard the goodwill that is associated with particular enterprises. A mark must perform the function of distinguishing the producer or provider of a good or service in order to have any legitimate claim to protection. A merely descriptive mark that has not acquired secondary meaning does not perform that function because it simply "describes the qualities or characteristics of a good or service." No legislative purpose is served by granting anyone a monopoly in the use of such a mark.

* * *

If the registrant of a merely descriptive mark complies with the statutory requirement that prima facie evidence of secondary meaning must be submitted to the Patent and Trademark Office, it is entirely consistent with the policy of the Act to accord the mark incontestable status after an additional five years of continued use. For if no rival contests the registration in that period, it is reasonable to presume that the initial prima facie showing of distinctiveness could not be rebutted. But if no proof of secondary meaning is ever presented, either to the Patent and Trademark Office or to a court, there is simply no rational basis for leaping to the conclusion that the passage of time has transformed an inherently defective mark into an incontestable mark.

* * *

The basic purposes of the Act, the unambiguous congressional command that no merely descriptive mark should be registered without prior proof that it acquired secondary meaning, and the broad power of judicial review granted by § 37 combine to persuade me that the registrant of a merely descriptive mark should not be granted an injunction against infringement without ever proving that the mark acquired secondary meaning.

* * *

Notes and Questions

1. *The interrelationship of Lanham Act sections 14, 15, and 33(b).* To understand "incontestability," one must understand the interaction of Lanham Act sections 14, 15, and 33(b), 15 U.S.C.A. §§ 1064, 1065, and 1115(b). First, study the provisions of section 14, 15 U.S.C.A. § 1064. This section sets forth the grounds on which the registration of a mark can be cancelled.

Within the first five years of registration, a "person who believes that he is or will be damaged by the registration of a mark" may seek cancellation on any ground which would have precluded registration in the first place. After five years, the grounds for cancellation are narrowed. Those grounds that may be asserted to cancel a registration after five years are set forth in subsections (c) through (e), 15 U.S.C.A. § 1064(3)-(5).

While section 14 addresses the registration of a mark, section 15 addresses the right to use a registered mark. Review the language of section 15, 15 U.S.C.A. § 1065. Five years after registration, the registrant who complies with the "continuous use" and other requirements of the section may attain an "incontestable" right to use its mark in commerce. If the right to use the mark is incontestable, then others cannot prevent the registrant from using it in connection with the specified goods or services—except on a ground that would expose the mark to cancellation under section 14(c) and (e) and except to the extent that the registrant is infringing a valid state right predating the registration. Thus, sections 14 and 15 are "defensive" in nature. Section 14 applies to assist the registrant of five years against a petition to cancel its registration, while section 15 applies to protect an incontestable registrant against an infringement suit to enjoin the registrant's continuing use of the mark.

Subsection 33(a), as amended, provides that registration shall be

> prima facie evidence of the validity of the registered mark and of the registration of the mark, of the registrant's ownership of the mark, and of the registrant's exclusive right to use the registered mark in commerce on or in connection with the goods or services specified in the registration.

15 U.S.C.A. § 1115(a). Thus, pursuant to subsection (a), registration creates a rebuttable presumption of validity, ownership and exclusive right. While "any defense or defect" that might have been asserted in the absence of registration may still be asserted, the burden of proving the defense or defect is on the person contesting the registrant's rights.

Subsection (b) provides that "to the extent the mark has become incontestable under section 1065 of this title [Lanham Act section 15]," the presumption of validity, ownership and exclusive right set forth in subsection (a) becomes conclusive—no longer subject to challenge by others. However, subsection (b) then provides that this "conclusive evidence" is subject to a list of eight "defenses or defects" that may be asserted against the registrant. Note also that in limiting its provisions to incontestable marks, the language of subsection (b) incorporates the exceptions to incontestability set forth in section 15, which in turn incorporates the grounds for challenge "at any time" set forth in section 14(c) and (e). As the *Park 'n Fly* Court found, section 33(b) applies "offensively," to assist the registrant when it sues another for infringement. The advantage, however, is limited. As Justice Stevens points out in his dissent, there are numerous defenses available to the defendant in an infringement suit brought by the owner of an "incontestable" mark, in addition to a defense of no likelihood of confusion. Apart from the defense that the incontestable mark is merely descriptive, what additional defenses are precluded under section 33(b)? Is the term "incontestable" an accurate description of the qualifying registrant's rights?

Note that the literal language of section 33(b) suggests that proof of one of the eight enumerated defenses or defects is not a defense on the merits, but merely eliminates the conclusive evidentiary status of the incontestable registration, so that common law legal and equitable defenses may be asserted as provided under section 33(a). See *Park 'N Fly*, 469 U.S. at 199 n.6, 105 S.Ct. at 669 n.6, 83 L.Ed.2d at 591 n.6. As a technical matter, this would require that the defendant establish a defense twice: first to eliminate the conclusive effect of the incontestable registration and then to establish his defense to the infringement claim. To the extent that the section 33(b) "defenses and defects" differ from the corresponding common-law defenses, this two step procedure makes sense. Since they generally do not, the two-step procedure is duplicative in most cases. For this reason, courts usually collapse the process into one step, so that proof of the section 33(b) defense or defect serves immediately as a defense on the merits against the infringement claim. For a discussion of potential problems with this approach, see *An Analysis of Park 'N Fly: A TMR Panel*, 75 TRADEMARK REP. 180, 204–06 (1985); 3 J.T. McCARTHY, McCARTHY ON TRADEMARKS AND UNFAIR COMPETITION §§ 32.44[6], 32.45 (3d ed. 1992).

2. *The role of incontestability status in the likelihood of confusion determination.* Incontestability status does not relieve plaintiffs/registrants of the necessity of proving that the defendant's mark causes a likelihood of consumer confusion. 15 U.S.C.A. § 1115(b). The "strength" of the plaintiff's mark is an important factor in determining whether a defendant's use of the same or a similar mark is likely to create consumer confusion. See, e.g., AMF Inc. v. Sleekcraft Boats, *supra*, Section VI A. Incontestability status prevents a defendant from challenging the validity of the plaintiff's mark on the ground that it is merely descriptive. Does it also prevent an argument that because the plaintiff's mark is descriptive, it is so weak that there is no likelihood of confusion? The Circuits have split on this issue. Compare, e.g., Oreck Corp. v. U.S. Floor Systems, Inc., 803 F.2d 166, 171, 231 U.S.P.Q. 634, 638 (5th Cir.1986), *cert. denied* 481 U.S. 1069, 107 S.Ct. 2462, 95 L.Ed.2d 871 (1987) ("*Park 'N Fly* merely held * * * that an infringement action brought by the holder of an incontestable mark may not be defended on the ground that the mark is merely descriptive and therefore invalid. U.S. Floor's argument was not that Oreck's mark was invalid, but that it was not *infringed* because there was no confusion. *Park 'N Fly* says nothing to preclude this argument. Incontestable status does not make a weak mark strong.") with Dieter v. B & H Industries, 880 F.2d 322, 329, 11 U.S.P.Q.2d 1721, 1726 (11th Cir.1989), *cert. denied* 498 U.S. 950, 111 S.Ct. 369, 112 L.Ed.2d 332 (1990) ("Incontestable status is a factor to be taken into consideration in likelihood of confusion analysis. Because Dieter's mark is incontestable, then it is presumed to be at least descriptive with secondary meaning and therefore a relatively strong mark."). See Razzano, *Incontestability: Should It Be Given Any Effect in a Likelihood of Confusion Determination?*, 82 TRADEMARK REP. 409 (1992). Which approach makes more sense?

VII. REMEDIES

BRUNSWICK CORPORATION v. SPINIT REEL COMPANY

Unites States Court of Appeals for the Tenth Circuit, 1987.
832 F.2d 513, 4 U.S.P.Q.2d 1497.

McKAY, CIRCUIT JUDGE.

[Appellant Brunswick Corporation, through its Zebco division, manufactures and sells the Zebco Model 33 "closed face" spin-cast fishing reel. The Zebco Model 33 has a distinctive profile with a chrome, cone-shaped front cover, a "stubby" back cover and a black and chrome finish. Appellee Spinit Reel manufactured and sold the SR 210 closed face spin-cast reel, which was similar in appearance to the Zebco Model 33. Brunswick filed suit against Spinit under section 43(a) of the Lanham Act, 15 U.S.C.A. § 1125(a), claiming infringement of its trademark rights in the distinctive appearance of its reel. The district court found that the SR 210 violated the Lanham Act and enjoined Spinit from further manufacture of the SR 210 or anything identical or confusingly similar to the Zebco Model 33. It also ordered Spinit to recall all models of the SR 210, but declined to award Brunswick damages or attorney's fees.]

[On appeal, the court found that the reel configuration was entitled to trademark protection and that Brunswick had established a likelihood of confusion through testimony of actual confusion and a survey of potential customers. The court then turned to the issue of relief.]

Spinit argues that the injunction should be vacated because it was granted for the wrong reason and because Spinit has rectified the design problem and is not likely to repeat it. * * * Spinit asserts that it was enjoined as punishment. The court, however, explained its reasoning in the Amended Findings of Fact and Conclusions of Law: an injunction is warranted if consumers are likely to confuse a Spinit SR 210 with a Zebco 33, and consumers are likely to believe that the Spinit SR 210 is manufactured by Zebco because of the similarity of the reels. The trial court applied the appropriate test for issuing an injunction in this case. We find no basis for Spinit's claim of punishment.

* * * Spinit argues that injunctive relief is unnecessary because by drastically altering the SR 210 cover, it solved the confusion problem in the design. Regardless of whether the unfair conduct has stopped and is not likely to recur, the trial court still has the discretion to grant or deny an injunction against such conduct. The district court ruled that the two models of the SR 210 that Spinit had manufactured at the time the suit was brought were likely to confuse customers that they were made by Zebco. We find no abuse of discretion in the court's granting of an injunction.

* * *

The district court found that, although Brunswick established a legal basis for damages, it failed to establish clear proof of damages. * * *

[T]he award [of damages] is distinguishable from injunctive relief, because plaintiff bears a greater burden of proof of entitlement. Likelihood of confusion is insufficient; to recover damages plaintiff must prove it has been damaged by actual consumer confusion or deception resulting from the violation. Actual consumer confusion may be shown by direct evidence, a diversion of sales or direct testimony from the public, or by circumstantial evidence such as consumer surveys.

> Although the quantum of damages, as distinguished from entitlement, must be demonstrated with specificity, courts may engage in "some degree of speculation in computing the amount of damages, particularly when the inability to compute them is attributable to the defendant's wrongdoing."

PPX Enters. Inc. [v. Audiofidelity Enters., Inc.], 818 F.2d [266,] 271 [(2d Cir.1987)] (quoting *Burndy Corp. [v. Teledyne Indus., Inc.]*, 748 F.2d [767,] 771 [(2d Cir.1984)]).

The district court found that there was actual confusion among consumers and retailers, and that Zebco and Spinit sell reels in the same marketing channels, in direct competition with each other. Those findings support the court's determination that Brunswick established a legal basis for the recovery of damages, indicating that actual consumer confusion resulted from Spinit's violation of section 43(a). Nevertheless, by adding that Brunswick did not establish clear proof of damages, the court implies that Brunswick presented insufficient proof of actual damages. The court more likely meant that, although Brunswick established entitlement to damages, it failed to show that it suffered damages in fact.

Brunswick submitted evidence that in the fiscal year ending July 1983 sales of all Zebco spin-cast products dropped off by five percent, sales of spin-cast reels generally had decreased by six percent due to the recession. Sales for the Zebco 33, however, dropped sixteen percent. Spinit introduced testimony that the introduction of other new reels on the market might have contributed to the decrease in Zebco's sales. However, in light of the trial court's finding of actual confusion and direct competition between the reels, we are not persuaded that other reels were the sole cause of the substantial reduction in the sale of the Zebco 33. Thus, the evidence does not indicate that Brunswick failed to show it suffered any actual damages.

A defendant whose wrongful conduct has caused the difficulty in assessing damages cannot complain that the damages are somewhat speculative. Evidence of the amount of damages may be circumstantial and inexact.

> [I]n a case such as this, where the wrong is of such a nature as to preclude exact ascertainment of the amount of damages, plaintiff

> may recover upon a showing of the extent of the damages as a matter of just and reasonable inference, although the result may be only an approximation.

Bangor Punta Operations, Inc. v. Universal Marine Co., 543 F.2d [1107,] 1110–11 [(5th Cir.1976)] (quoting *Kestenbaum v. Falstaff Brewing Corp.*, 514 F.2d 690, 698 (5th Cir.1975), *cert. denied*, 424 U.S. 943, 96 S.Ct. 1412, 47 L.Ed.2d 349 (1976)).

Brunswick bases its claim for damages on the theory that Zebco lost one sale of a Model 33 as a result of each Spinit SR 210 reel sold. While this court does not necessarily believe that each Spinit sale resulted in a corresponding loss of sale by Zebco, the theory provides an upper range for an award of damages. The district court may also look to the difference in the decline of Model 33 sales as compared with the decline in sales of Zebco's other spin-cast reels. Those items of evidence provide the court a broad basis from which it may arrive at a fair, if not precise, amount with which to compensate Brunswick for wrongful infringement. We reverse the trial court's finding on damages and remand for findings of the amount of damages due.

* * *

Attorney's fees may be awarded, under certain circumstances, under the Lanham Act. Prior to 1975, the Lanham Act (15 U.S.C. §§ 1051–1127) contained no provision for the awarding of attorney's fees, and the United States Supreme Court had ruled that the judicial granting of attorney's fees was improper under the Lanham Act because the granting of fees was not contained in the language of the Act and because "Congress intended § 35 of the Lanham Act to mark the boundaries of the power to award monetary relief in cases arising under the Act." *Fleischmann Distilling Corp. v. Maier Brewing Co.*, 386 U.S. 714, 721, 87 S.Ct. 1404, 1409, 18 L.Ed.2d 475 (1967).

In 1975, Congress responded to the *Fleischmann* ruling and amended section 35 to permit "[t]he court in exceptional cases [to] award reasonable attorney fees to the prevailing party." Act of Jan. 2, 1975, Pub.L. 93–600, § 3, 88 Stat. 1955, codified as 15 U.S.C. § 1117 (1982). * * *

* * * This court has previously ruled that an exceptional case "is one in which the trademark infringement can be characterized as 'malicious,' 'fraudulent,' 'deliberate,' or 'willful.'" *VIP Foods, Inc. v. Vulcan Pet, Inc.*, 675 F.2d 1106, 1107 (10th Cir.1982); *but see USM, Inc.*, 810 F.2d at 116 (exceptional means less than "bad faith"; it means "uncommon, not run-of-the-mine"). [T]he element of being "exceptional" i.e. willful, etc., is not present in Spinit's actions. We thus rule that Brunswick is not entitled to attorney's fees under section 43(a) of the Lanham Act.

* * *

Notes and Questions

1. *Lanham Act remedies.* Registration on the Lanham Act principal register offers several important advantages to trademark owners: the constructive notice and use provisions for establishing priority in the United States; the six-month "grace" period for filing foreign registration applications pursuant to the Paris Convention; U.S. Customs assistance in excluding infringing imports at the border; prima facie evidence of mark validity and the registrant's ownership and exclusive right to use; as well as incontestability status. Another valued feature of the Lanham Act is its generous remedy provisions. Unlike the Act's other advantageous features, however, the Lanham Act remedies are available both for owners of registered marks and for owners of unregistered marks claiming infringement pursuant to Lanham Act section 43(a), 15 U.S.C.A. § 1125(a).

Apart from injunctive relief, which is authorized in section 34, 15 U.S.C.A. § 1116, Lanham Act section 35(a) provides:

> * * * [T]he plaintiff shall be entitled, subject to the provisions of sections 1111 [notice requirements] and 1114 [limitations on the liability of printers and publishers], and subject to the principles of equity, to recover (1) defendant's profits, (2) any damages sustained by the plaintiff, and (3) the costs of the action. * * * In assessing profits the plaintiff shall be required to prove defendant's sales only: defendant must prove all elements of cost or deduction claimed. In assessing damages the court may enter judgment, according to the circumstances of the case, for any sum above the amount found as actual damages, not exceeding three times such amount. If the court shall find that the amount of the recovery based on profits is either inadequate or excessive the court may in its discretion enter judgment for such sum as the court shall find to be just, according to the circumstances of the case. Such sum in either of the above circumstances shall constitute compensation and not a penalty. The court in exceptional cases may award reasonable attorney fees to the prevailing party.

15 U.S.C.A. § 1117(a). Special, enhanced remedies are provided for counterfeiting cases, including mandatory treble damages and attorney fees, 15 U.S.C.A. § 1117(b), and *ex parte* seizure of goods bearing counterfeit marks, 15 U.S.C.A. § 1116(d).[17] For a discussion of the special counterfeiting remedies, see Bainton, *Reflections on the Trademark Counterfeiting Act of 1984: Score a Few for the Good Guys*, 82 TRADEMARK REP. 1 (1992).

2. *Injunctive relief.* Since monetary damages are difficult to determine and inadequate to compensate a plaintiff for continuing infringement, permanent injunctions against further infringement are granted as a matter of course once infringement is found. As the *Brunswick* court observes, only a *likelihood* of confusion, not actual confusion, need be demonstrated.

Preliminary injunctions may also be granted in proper cases. The Circuit Courts of Appeals have varied in their enunciation of the standards for imposing preliminary injunctions, but factors commonly emphasized

17. By virtue of the definition of "counterfeit," these remedies are only available to owners of registered marks.

include the likelihood that the plaintiff will succeed on the merits; whether the plaintiff will suffer irreparable injury in the absence of preliminary relief; the respective hardship a preliminary injunction will pose to each party; and the public interest. See RESTATEMENT (THIRD) OF UNFAIR COMPETITION § 35 (Tentative Draft No. 3, 1991).

3. *Actual damages.* The *Brunswick* opinion illustrates the problems plaintiffs may encounter in establishing actual damages. Did the court hold the plaintiff to different standards for proving the *fact* of damage and the specific *amount* of damage? If so, does this make sense? Do the standards of proof imposed by the court provide adequate safeguards for defendants? Is there sufficient guidance for the district court? How should the district court proceed in determining a specific damage amount on remand in *Brunswick*? Would it make more sense to impose a "reasonable royalty" measure of damages as a default standard for use when the plaintiff is unable to prove the specific amount of its loss with certainty, as is done in patent law? Or should Congress enact a provision for statutory damages, as it has in the Copyright Act? What other means of measuring damages might a court adopt? Apart from lost sales, what items of pecuniary loss might be subject to recovery as actual damages? See RESTATEMENT (THIRD) OF UNFAIR COMPETITION § 36(2) (Tentative Draft No. 3, 1991).

Note the Lanham Act's provision for notice of registration in section 29, 15 U.S.C.A. § 1111. A registrant who fails to give such notice is prohibited from recovering either damages or profits unless it can demonstrate that the defendant had actual notice of the registration. What are the implications of this provision for plaintiffs with unregistered marks, such as the plaintiff in *Brunswick*?

4. *The defendant's profits.* An accounting for profits may be ordered if the "defendant is unjustly enriched, if the plaintiff sustained damages from the infringement, or if an accounting is necessary to deter a willful infringer from doing so again." W.E. Bassett Co. v. Revlon, Inc., 435 F.2d 656, 664, 168 U.S.P.Q. 1, 7 (2d Cir.1970). The Court of Appeals for the Ninth Circuit has explored the various rationales underlying the profits remedy:

> There appear to be two distinct views as to the basis for awarding an accounting of profits. The majority of cases seem to view an accounting of profits by the defendant as a method of shifting the burden of proof as to damages for lost or potentially lost sales from the plaintiff to the defendant. The minority view, which is apparently the more recent trend, bases the accounting of profits on the equitable concepts of restitution and unjust enrichment. The rationale behind this view, as expressed in Monsanto Chemical Co. v. Perfect Fit Products Mfg. Co., 349 F.2d 389 (2d Cir.1965), the leading case in this trend, is that the infringer has taken the plaintiff's property as represented by his trade-mark and has utilized this property in making a profit, and that if permitted to retain the profit, the infringer would be unjustly enriched.
>
> Those courts which utilize an accounting of profits as a means of compensating the plaintiff for sales which he has lost as a result of his customers being diverted to the infringer, have, as a result of this

premise, required that there be competition between the parties before this recovery can be granted. Clearly, if there is no competition, there can be no diversion of customers. It does not necessarily follow, however, that just because there is no direct competition an accounting of profits can serve no reasonable end.

The legislative history of the Lanham Act expressly states the purpose of the Act:

> "This bill, as any other proper legislation on trade-marks, has as its object the protection of trade-marks, securing to the owner the good will of his business and protecting the public against spurious and falsely marked goods. The matter has been approached with the view of protecting trade-marks *and making infringement and piracy unprofitable*."

S.Rep. No. 1333, 79th Cong., 2d Sess. 1–2 (1946). * * *

Earlier in our country's history it may have been necessary to copy both the trade-mark and the product of another in order to obtain a free ride on the good reputation of that product and its maker. In such an instance requiring direct competition between the parties as a prerequisite to the granting of an accounting of profits would have been both just and logical. This, however, is the age of television and mass communications. Fortunes are spent in publicizing a name, often with only slight reference to the real utility of the product. The theory behind this modern advertising is that once the name or trade-mark of a product is firmly associated in the mind of the buying public with some desired characteristic—quality, social status, etc.—the public will buy that product. * * *

Although courts will protect this psychological value of the trade-mark by means of an injunction against infringement, even where the products are of different descriptive qualities and are, therefore, not in competition, those courts which treat an accounting solely as a method of compensating for the diversion of customers fail to fully effectuate the policies of the Act. Such courts are neither "securing to the owner the good will of his business (nor) protecting the public against spurious and falsely marked goods."

These courts are protecting the trademark owner from only the most obvious form of damages—the diversion of sales, and are not in fact providing protection to the value of the good will built up in the trade-mark itself. No recognition is given to the possibility that customers who believe that they are buying a product manufactured by the plaintiff—whether such product is competitive or non-competitive—may be so unhappy with that product that they will never again want to buy that product or any other product produced by the same manufacturer, who they believe to be the plaintiff. Nor do these opinions recognize that, even if the infringing product is of higher quality than that bearing the registered trade-mark, the trade-mark registrant has been deprived of his right to the exclusive use and control of the reputation of his product.

> It should also be noted that although the granting of an injunction, upon the finding that a confusion of source may exist between the trade-marked product and the infringing product, protects the public from buying this particular falsely marked product from this particular infringer in the future, it does not necessarily protect them from similar future acts of commercial piracy by the same party. To accomplish this, the courts must, as was recognized in the legislative history of the Act quoted above, make acts of trade-mark infringement, or at the very least acts of deliberate trade-mark piracy, unprofitable. As the court in *Monsanto,* supra, recognized, it is possible for a party to adopt a deliberate business pattern of trade piracy—selling his product under the trade-mark of one reputable company until enjoined and then merely adopting the trade-mark of another company and continuing his fraudulent activities. * * *
>
> Thus, it must be determined if the concept of unjust enrichment, utilized "subject to the principles of equity," will properly serve to effectuate the policies of the Lanham Act. It would seem that it would. The utilization of this concept will not of course make an accounting of profits automatic. Situations will exist where it would be unduly harsh to grant such recovery. Cases exist where the infringement is entirely innocent; where rather than attempting to gain the value of an established name of another, the infringer has developed what he imagined to be a proper trade name only to find out later that his name caused confusion as to the source of, and therefore infringed, a product with a registered trade-mark. In such a case an injunction fully satisfies both the policy of the Act and the equities of the case.

Maier Brewing Co. v. Fleischmann Distilling Corp., 390 F.2d 117, 121–23, 157 U.S.P.Q. 76, 79–81 (9th Cir.1968), *cert. denied* 391 U.S. 966, 88 S.Ct. 2037, 20 L.Ed.2d 879, 157 U.S.P.Q. 720 (1968). Should the accounting for profits remedy always be limited to cases in which the defendant intentionally or willfully infringed?

Section 35(a) provides that "[i]n assessing profits the plaintiff shall be required to prove defendant's sales only; defendant must prove all elements of cost or deduction claimed." What sorts of costs and deductions might the defendant successfully assert in order to reduce the amount it must pay? See RESTATEMENT (THIRD) OF UNFAIR COMPETITION § 37, comments d, g, and h (Tentative Draft No. 3, 1991); Bussert & Davis, *Calculating Profits under Section 35 of the Lanham Act: A Practitioner's Guide*, 82 TRADEMARK REP. 182 (1992).

In some cases courts permit a plaintiff to recover both its actual damages and the defendant's profits, though they are careful not to permit the plaintiff to recover twice for the same loss. In what sorts of settings would imposing both forms of recovery be most appropriate? When would it be most likely to lead to double recovery? See RESTATEMENT (THIRD) OF UNFAIR COMPETITION § 36, comment c (Tentative Draft No. 3, 1991).

For a survey of the courts' application of the accounting remedy, see Barber, *Recovery of Profits under the Lanham Act: Are the District Courts Doing Their Job?* 82 TRADEMARK REP. 141 (1992).

Chapter Seven

UNFAIR COMPETITION

I. INTRODUCTION

> The theoretic basis [of unfair competition law] is obscure, but the birth and growth of this branch of the law is clear. It is a persuasive example of the law's capacity for growth in response to the ethical, as well as the economic needs of society. As a result of this broad background, the legal concept of unfair competition has evolved as a broad and flexible doctrine with a capacity for further growth to meet changing conditions.
>
> There is no complete list of the activities which constitute unfair competition.

Dior v. Milton, 9 Misc.2d 425, 430–31, 155 N.Y.S.2d 443, 451, 110 U.S.P.Q. 563, 566 (1956), *affirmed* 2 A.D.2d 878, 156 N.Y.S.2d 996, 113 U.S.P.Q. 210 (1st Dept. 1956).

The law of unfair competition has deep roots in tort doctrine, and particularly in the law of deceit. In its earliest stages, this body of law consisted solely of a cause of action against misrepresentations about the source of goods or services. This "misrepresentation of source" branch of the law of unfair competition often is called "passing off" or "palming off." Courts later recognized causes of action for a merchant's misrepresentations about other aspects of goods or services than their source. The common-law false advertising cause of action rectifies a competitor's misrepresentations about the nature or characteristics of its own goods or services, when the plaintiff can demonstrate resulting harm to the plaintiff's business good will. The common-law commercial disparagement cause of action redresses a defendant's misrepresentations about the nature or character of the plaintiff's goods or services.

Each of these three causes of action remains available to competitors under state common law or by virtue of state statutes that have codified and modernized the original common-law causes of action. In addition, the Lanham Act, section 43(a), has provided a federal cause of action which parallels common-law passing off, false advertising and commercial disparagement. 15 U.S.C.A. § 1125(a). Because the Lanham Act version modernizes and expands these doctrines, and provides the same liberal remedies as are available for infringement of registered marks, the federal cause of action has become very popular and has tended to eclipse the state causes of action.

In some instances, the law of unfair competition has departed from its origins in the law of deceit, embracing instead a rationale more nearly tracking trespass or conversion. First, state courts have adopted and developed the controversial unfair competition doctrine of "misappropriation," originally implemented by the United States Supreme Court in International News Service v. Associated Press, as pre-*Erie Railroad* federal common law. The misappropriation doctrine may recognize a property right in the product of one's skill and labor, and prevent others from taking that product in a manner that constitutes "free-riding," or "reaping where they have not sewn." Second, the doctrine of trademark dilution, created primarily through state legislation, expands rights in trademarks beyond the traditional boundaries of trademark law, explicitly recognizing property rights in the persuasive (as opposed to the informative) function of marks. The law of trademark dilution protects the selling power of a plaintiff's strong mark by preventing others from using it, regardless of whether their goods or services are similar to the plaintiff's and regardless of whether their use is likely to mislead or confuse consumers.

There is no federal counterpart to the misappropriation and dilution doctrines. Indeed, in 1988, Congress rejected attempts to amend Lanham Act section 43(a) to create a federal cause of action for trademark dilution.

While the five causes of action discussed above do not comprise the whole of the modern law of unfair competition, they comprise the bulk of it, and will be the focus of this Chapter.

Notes and Questions

1. *International Considerations.* Article 10bis of the Paris Convention provides:

> 1. The countries of the Union are bound to assure to nationals of such countries effective protection against unfair competition.
>
> 2. Any act of competition contrary to honest practices in industrial or commercial matters constitutes an act of unfair competition.
>
> 3. The following in particular shall be prohibited:
>
> (1) all acts of such a nature as to create confusion by any means whatever with the establishment, the goods, or the industrial or commercial activities, of a competitor;
>
> (2) false allegations in the course of trade of such a nature as to discredit the establishment, the goods, or the industrial or commercial activities, of a competitor;
>
> (3) indications or allegations the use of which in the course of trade is liable to mislead the public as to the nature, the manufacturing process, the characteristics, the suitability for their purpose, or the quantity, of the goods.

Paris Convention for the Protection of Industrial Property, March 20, 1883, as most recently revised at Stockholm on July 14, 1967, 21 U.S.T. 1629, 828 U.N.T.S. 107.

Lanham Act section 44, 15 U.S.C.A. § 1126, implements the United States' treaty obligations with regard to protection against unfair competition. Review section 44(g)-(i). On its face, it could be interpreted to authorize federal unfair competition suits involving strictly domestic parties, as well as those involving foreign parties, and to encompass a broader array of unfair acts than the more limited provisions of section 43(a). While many have advocated such an interpretation, see, e.g., Wolf, *"Effective Protection Against Unfair Competition" Under Section 44 of the Lanham Act*, 82 TRADEMARK REP. 33 (1992), most courts have declined to interpret section 44 as providing a general federal cause of action for unfair competition. See, e.g. L'Aiglon Apparel, Inc. v. Lana Lobell, Inc., 214 F.2d 649, 102 U.S.P.Q. 94 (3d Cir.1954). Rather, section 44 has been interpreted to provide federal jurisdiction for reciprocal claims of unfair competition by and against those foreign nationals identified in section 44(b). The substantive scope of the unfair competition claim that may be brought pursuant to section 44 remains largely unexplored. See Wolf, *supra*; Derenberg, *Federal Unfair Competition Law at the End of the First Decade of the Lanham Act: Prologue or Epilogue?*, 32 N.Y.U. L. REV. 1029, 1055–65 (1957). As you proceed through this Chapter, consider whether it would be desirable to provide greater federal protection against unfair competition than that provided under section 43(a), and if so, how this should be achieved.

For examples of how other countries protect against unfair competition, see D.C. THOMPSON (ed.), UNFAIR COMPETITION: SOME COMPARATIVE ASPECTS OF THE LAWS OF THE UNITED STATES, GERMANY, FRANCE AND THE UNITED KINGDOM (1966); Comments, *Symposium: Selected Business Torts in Civil and Common Law Systems*, 53 TUL. L. REV. 164 (1978).

2. *Additional resources.* The leading treatises on Unfair Competition are J.T. McCARTHY, McCARTHY ON TRADEMARKS AND UNFAIR COMPETITION (3d ed. 1992), and R. CALLMANN, THE LAW OF UNFAIR COMPETITION, TRADEMARKS AND MONOPOLIES (L. Altman 4th ed. 1981 & Supp.). The new Restatement (Third) of Unfair Competition is also an invaluable resource. For information about the law of unfair competition in each individual state, see U.S. TRADEMARK ASSN. (ed.), STATE TRADEMARK AND UNFAIR COMPETITION LAW (1988). For in-depth treatment of Lanham Act section 43(a), see 1 J. GILSON, TRADEMARK PROTECTION AND PRACTICE (1991); C.E. McKENNEY & G.F. LONG, FEDERAL UNFAIR COMPETITION: LANHAM ACT § 43(a) (1989).

II. PASSING OFF

"Passing off" occurs when a business makes a false representation that is likely to cause consumers to believe that its business, product or service is or is affiliated with that of the plaintiff. That false representation may take a number of different forms. For example, a defendant may show a prospective purchaser a photograph of the plaintiff's product, falsely telling the purchaser that this is her own product. A defendant who sells "knock-offs" of plaintiff's product may expressly tell the buyer at the point of sale that his product is "the original."[1] In addition, a defendant may use a mark, trade name (business name), packaging, employee uniform, or building decor that is confusingly similar to the plaintiff's.

As you can see, trademark infringement falls within the broad spectrum of behavior constituting passing off. At an earlier time there were some perceived differences between a claim of "trademark infringement" and a "passing off" claim. Because of the unfair competition claim's origins in the law of deceit, early case opinions required proof that the defendant *intended* to deceive consumers before imposing liability. At one point in time, a showing of intent was required for "passing off" claims, but not for "technical trademark" infringement. Modern decisions have cast aside this intent requirement across the board. See RESTATEMENT (THIRD) OF UNFAIR COMPETITION § 4, comments b, d (Tentative Draft No. 1, 1988).

Today the purposes and rules underlying common-law trademark infringement and passing off claims are essentially the same. See Note, *Unfair Competition*, 53 HARV. L. REV. 1289, 1296–1301 (1940). Thus, the touchstone for recovery for passing off, as for determining trademark infringement, is proof that the defendant's actions created a likelihood of consumer confusion about the identity or commercial affiliation of the defendant or the source or sponsorship of its goods or services. RESTATEMENT (THIRD) OF UNFAIR COMPETITION § 4, comment c (Tentative Draft No. 1, 1988). Likewise, both types of claims are limited by the rules requiring that generic words and functional product features remain in the public domain. See Chapter 6, § V B1 & C, *supra*. Passing off claims involving the use of confusingly similar trade dress or trade names entail the same rules regarding priority and the geographic rights of the parties as common-law trademark claims. See Chapter 6, §§ III, VI E, *supra*. The primary difference between a claim that an unregistered trademark has been infringed and other kinds of passing off claims is its potential scope. In addressing a specific claim of trademark infringement, the court focuses primarily on the mark to which the plaintiff claims exclusive rights. By contrast, in other passing off claims, the court may consider the total impression created by a combination of elements, which may or may not include the parties' respective marks. See, e.g., Jean Patou, Inc. v. Jacqueline Cochran, Inc., 201 F.Supp. 861, 133 U.S.P.Q. 242 (S.D.N.Y.1962), *affirmed* 312 F.2d 125, 136 U.S.P.Q. 236 (2d Cir.1963).

Because of the way that the law of unfair competition evolved, terminology can be confusing. Writers sometimes use the terms "passing off" and "palming off" to refer to the earlier, more narrow intentional tort, and the term "unfair competition," to refer to the more modern, non-intentional cause of action for acts creating a likelihood of consumer

1. Passing off may also occur when a merchant represents that the products or services of one competitor are those of another. This would occur, for example, when a restaurant defendant fills orders for a brand of cola manufactured by X with a brand manufactured by Y without notifying consumers.

confusion. This usage is problematic because, as discussed above, modern "unfair competition" encompasses much more than misrepresentations about source. As used in this Chapter (and in many other places, including the new Restatement (Third) of Unfair Competition), the terms "passing off" and "palming off" refer to the modern *branch* of unfair competition law which prohibits misrepresentations which lead to a likelihood of consumer confusion concerning source or affiliation, regardless of the defendant's intent.

As noted in the prior Section, Lanham Act section 43(a) provides a federal cause of action for passing off. As amended in 1989, section 43(a) provides:

> (a)(1) Any person who, on or in connection with any goods or services, or any container for goods, uses in commerce any word, term, name, symbol, or device, or any combination thereof, or any false designation of origin, false or misleading description of fact, or false or misleading representation of fact, which—
>
> (A) is likely to cause confusion, or to cause mistake, or to deceive as to the affiliation, connection, or association of such person with another person, or as to the origin, sponsorship, or approval of his or her goods, services, or commercial activities by another person, or
>
> (B) in commercial advertising or promotion, misrepresents the nature, characteristics, qualities, or geographic origin of his or her or another person's goods, services, or commercial activities,
>
> shall be liable in a civil action by any person who believes that he or she is or is likely to be damaged by such act.

15 U.S.C.A. § 1125(a).[2] While this provision encompasses the entire spectrum of common-law passing off claims, the majority of section 43(a) passing off cases have entailed infringement of unregistered common-law

2. The amendments resulted from the Trademark Law Revision Act of 1988, Pub. L. No. 100–667, 102 Stat. 3935. Prior to the 1989 amendment, the statutory language was as follows:

> (a) Any person who shall affix, apply, or annex, or use in connection with any goods or services, or any container or containers for goods, a false designation of origin, or any false description or representation, including words or other symbols tending falsely to describe or represent the same, and shall cause such goods or services to enter into commerce, and any person who shall with knowledge of the falsity of such designation of origin or description or representation cause or procure the same to be transported or used in commerce or deliver the same to any carrier to be transported or used, shall be liable to a civil action by any person doing business in the locality falsely indicated as that of origin or the region in which said locality is situated, or by any person who believes that he is likely to be damaged by the use of any such false description or representation.

While the case law had construed this language to provide a federal cause of action for passing off and for false advertising, the construction was an awkward one. The amendments were intended to conform the statutory language to the case law interpretation and to provide a cause of action for product disparagement, as well. S. REP. NO. 515, 100 Cong., 2nd Sess. 40–41 (1988).

marks, trade dress and trade names. Section 43(a) has proven popular in the past three decades, not only because of the perceived advantages of federal jurisdiction but also because the Lanham Act makes the same liberal remedies available for actions under section 43(a) as are available for infringement of registered marks. 15 U.S.C.A. § 1117.[3] Moreover, state trade dress infringement claims have been preempted to some extent by federal law. See Chapter 9, *infra*. Litigants have sought to avoid preemption by claiming trade dress infringement under section 43(a). The federal case law interpreting and applying section 43(a) tends to track the state common law of passing off, but, of course, the federal courts are not bound by state decisions.

TWO PESOS, INC. v. TACO CABANA, INC.

United States Supreme Court, 1992.
___ U.S. ___, 112 S.Ct. 2753, 120 L.Ed.2d 615, 23 U.S.P.Q.2d 1081.

JUSTICE WHITE delivered the opinion of the Court.

The issue in this case is whether the trade dress [1] of a restaurant may be protected under § 43(a) of the Trademark Act of 1946 (Lanham Act), 60 Stat. 441, 15 U.S.C. § 1125(a) (1982 ed.), based on a finding of inherent distinctiveness, without proof that the trade dress has secondary meaning.

I

Respondent Taco Cabana, Inc., operates a chain of fast-food restaurants in Texas. The restaurants serve Mexican food. The first Taco Cabana restaurant was opened in San Antonio in September 1978, and five more restaurants had been opened in San Antonio by 1985. Taco Cabana describes its Mexican trade dress as

> a festive eating atmosphere having interior dining and patio areas decorated with artifacts, bright colors, paintings and murals. The patio includes interior and exterior areas with the interior patio capable of being sealed off from the outside patio by overhead garage doors. The stepped exterior of the building is a festive and vivid color scheme using top border paint and neon stripes. Bright awnings and umbrellas continue the theme.

3. The Lanham Act does not make other advantages of registration on the principal register, including the presumption of validity, incontestability status, constructive use and constructive notice, available for unregistered marks.

1. The District Court instructed the jury: " '[T]rade dress' is the total image of the business. Taco Cabana's trade dress may include the shape and general appearance of the exterior of the restaurant, the identifying sign, the interior kitchen floor plan, the decor, the menu, the equipment used to serve food, the servers' uniforms and other features reflecting on the total image of the restaurant." 1 App. 83–84. The Court of Appeals accepted this definition and quoted from *Blue Bell Bio-Medical v. Cin-Bad, Inc.*, 864 F.2d 1253, 1256 (CA5 1989): "The 'trade dress' of a product is essentially its total image and overall appearance." It "involves the total image of a product and may include features such as size, shape, color or color combinations, texture, graphics, or even particular sales techniques." *John H. Harland Co. v. Clarke Checks, Inc.*, 711 F.2d 966, 980 (CA11 1983).

In December 1985, a Two Pesos, Inc., restaurant was opened in Houston. Two Pesos adopted a motif very similar to the foregoing description of Taco Cabana's trade dress. Two Pesos restaurants expanded rapidly in Houston and other markets, but did not enter San Antonio. In 1986, Taco Cabana entered the Houston and Austin markets and expanded into other Texas cities, including Dallas and El Paso, where Two Pesos was also doing business.

In 1987, Taco Cabana sued Two Pesos in the United States District Court for the Southern District of Texas for trade dress infringement under § 43(a) of the Lanham Act, 15 U.S.C. § 1125(a) (1982 ed.), and for theft of trade secrets under Texas common law. The case was tried to a jury, which was instructed to return its verdict in the form of answers to five questions propounded by the trial judge. The jury's answers were: Taco Cabana has a trade dress; taken as a whole, the trade dress is nonfunctional; the trade dress is inherently distinctive; the trade dress has not acquired a secondary meaning in the Texas market; and the alleged infringement creates a likelihood of confusion on the part of ordinary customers as to the source or association of the restaurant's goods or services. Because, as the jury was told, Taco Cabana's trade dress was protected if it either was inherently distinctive or had acquired a secondary meaning, judgment was entered awarding damages to Taco Cabana. In the course of calculating damages, the trial court held that Two Pesos had intentionally and deliberately infringed Taco Cabana's trade dress.

The Court of Appeals ruled that the instructions adequately stated the applicable law and that the evidence supported the jury's findings. In particular, the Court of Appeals rejected petitioner's argument that a finding of no secondary meaning contradicted a finding of inherent distinctiveness.

In so holding, the court below followed precedent in the Fifth Circuit. In *Chevron Chemical Co. v. Voluntary Purchasing Groups, Inc.*, 659 F.2d 695, 702 (CA5 1981), the court noted that trademark law requires a demonstration of secondary meaning only when the claimed trademark is not sufficiently distinctive of itself to identify the producer; the court held that the same principles should apply to protection of trade dresses. The Court of Appeals noted that this approach conflicts with decisions of other courts, particularly the holding of the Court of Appeals for the Second Circuit in *Vibrant Sales, Inc. v. New Body Boutique, Inc.*, 652 F.2d 299 (1981), cert. denied, 455 U.S. 909, 102 S.Ct. 1257, 71 L.Ed.2d 448 (1982), that § 43(a) protects unregistered trademarks or designs only where secondary meaning is shown. We granted certiorari to resolve the conflict among the Courts of Appeals on the question whether trade dress which is inherently distinctive is protectible under § 43(a) without a showing that it has acquired secondary meaning. We find that it is, and we therefore affirm.

II

The Lanham Act was intended to make "actionable the deceptive and misleading use of marks" and "to protect persons engaged in ...

commerce against unfair competition." § 45, 15 U.S.C. § 1127. Section 43(a) prohibits a broader range of practices than does § 32, which applies to registered marks, but it is common ground that § 43(a) protects qualifying unregistered trademarks and that the general principles qualifying a mark for registration under § 2 of the Lanham Act are for the most part applicable in determining whether an unregistered mark is entitled to protection under § 43(a).

* * * In order to be registered, a mark must be capable of distinguishing the applicant's goods from those of others. Marks are often classified in categories of generally increasing distinctiveness; following the classic formulation set out by Judge Friendly, they may be (1) generic; (2) descriptive; (3) suggestive; (4) arbitrary; or (5) fanciful. *See Abercrombie & Fitch Co. v. Hunting World, Inc.*, 537 F.2d 4, 9 (CA2 1976). The Court of Appeals followed this classification and petitioner accepts it. The latter three categories of marks, because their intrinsic nature serves to identify a particular source of a product, are deemed inherently distinctive and are entitled to protection. * * *

Marks which are merely descriptive of a product are not inherently distinctive. When used to describe a product, they do not inherently identify a particular source, and hence cannot be protected. However, descriptive marks may acquire the distinctiveness which will allow them to be protected under the Act. Section 2 of the Lanham Act provides that a descriptive mark that otherwise could not be registered under the Act may be registered if it "has become distinctive of the applicant's goods in commerce." §§ 2(e), (f), 15 U.S.C. §§ 1052(e), (f). This acquired distinctiveness is generally called "secondary meaning." The concept of secondary meaning has been applied to actions under § 43(a).

The general rule regarding distinctiveness is clear: an identifying mark is distinctive and capable of being protected if it *either* (1) is inherently distinctive *or* (2) has acquired distinctiveness through secondary meaning. It is also clear that eligibility for protection under § 43(a) depends on nonfunctionality. It is, of course, also undisputed that liability under § 43(a) requires proof of the likelihood of confusion.

The Court of Appeals determined that the District Court's instructions were consistent with the foregoing principles and that the evidence supported the jury's verdict. Both courts thus ruled that Taco Cabana's trade dress was not descriptive but rather inherently distinctive, and that it was not functional. None of these rulings is before us in this case, and for present purposes we assume, without deciding, that each of them is correct. In going on to affirm the judgment for respondent, the Court of Appeals, following its prior decision in *Chevron*, held that Taco Cabana's inherently distinctive trade dress was entitled to protection despite the lack of proof of secondary meaning. It is this issue that is before us for decision, and we agree with its resolution by the Court of Appeals. There is no persuasive reason to apply to trade dress a general requirement of secondary meaning which is at odds with the principles generally applicable to infringement suits under § 43(a). * * *

Petitioner argues that the jury's finding that the trade dress has not acquired a secondary meaning shows conclusively that the trade dress is not inherently distinctive. The Court of Appeals' disposition of this issue was sound:

> Two Pesos' argument—that the jury finding of inherent distinctiveness contradicts its finding of no secondary meaning in the Texas market—ignores the law in this circuit. While the necessarily imperfect (and often prohibitively difficult) methods for assessing secondary meaning address the empirical question of current consumer association, the legal recognition of an inherently distinctive trademark or trade dress acknowledges the owner's legitimate proprietary interest in its unique and valuable informational device, regardless of whether substantial consumer association yet bestows the additional empirical protection of secondary meaning.

Although petitioner makes the above argument, it appears to concede elsewhere in its briefing that it is possible for a trade dress, even a restaurant trade dress, to be inherently distinctive and thus eligible for protection under § 43(a). Recognizing that a general requirement of secondary meaning imposes "an unfair prospect of theft [or] financial loss" on the developer of fanciful or arbitrary trade dress at the outset of its use, petitioner suggests that such trade dress should receive limited protection without proof of secondary meaning. Petitioner argues that such protection should be only temporary and subject to defeasance when over time the dress has failed to acquire a secondary meaning. This approach is also vulnerable for the reasons given by the Court of Appeals. If temporary protection is available from the earliest use of the trade dress, it must be because it is neither functional nor descriptive but an inherently distinctive dress that is capable of identifying a particular source of the product. Such a trade dress, or mark, is not subject to copying by concerns that have an equal opportunity to choose their own inherently distinctive trade dress. To terminate protection for failure to gain secondary meaning over some unspecified time could not be based on the failure of the dress to retain its fanciful, arbitrary, or suggestive nature, but on the failure of the user of the dress to be successful enough in the marketplace. This is not a valid basis to find a dress or mark ineligible for protection. The user of such a trade dress should be able to maintain what competitive position it has and continue to seek wider identification among potential customers.

This brings us to the line of decisions by the Court of Appeals for the Second Circuit that would find protection for trade dress unavailable absent proof of secondary meaning, a position that petitioner concedes would have to be modified if the temporary protection that it suggests is to be recognized. In *Vibrant Sales, Inc. v. New Body Boutique, Inc.*, 652 F.2d 299 (1981), the plaintiff claimed protection under § 43(a) for a product whose features the defendant had allegedly copied. The Court of Appeals held that unregistered marks did not enjoy the "presumptive source association" enjoyed by registered marks and hence could not qualify for protection under § 43(a) without proof of secondary meaning.

The court's rationale seemingly denied protection for unregistered but inherently distinctive marks of all kinds, whether the claimed mark used distinctive words or symbols or distinctive product design. The court thus did not accept the arguments that an unregistered mark was capable of identifying a source and that copying such a mark could be making any kind of a false statement or representation under § 43(a).

This holding is in considerable tension with the provisions of the Act. If a verbal or symbolic mark or the features of a product design may be registered under § 2, it necessarily is a mark "by which the goods of the applicant may be distinguished from the goods of others," and must be registered unless otherwise disqualified. Since § 2 requires secondary meaning only as a condition to registering descriptive marks, there are plainly marks that are registrable without showing secondary meaning. These same marks, even if not registered, remain inherently capable of distinguishing the goods of the users of these marks. Furthermore, the copier of such a mark may be seen as falsely claiming that his products may for some reason be thought of as originating from the plaintiff.

Some years after *Vibrant*, the Second Circuit announced in *Thompson Medical Co. v. Pfizer Inc.*, 753 F.2d 208 (CA2 1985), that in deciding whether an unregistered mark is eligible for protection under § 43(a), it would follow the classification of marks set out by Judge Friendly in *Abercrombie & Fitch*, 537 F.2d, at 9. Hence, if an unregistered mark is deemed merely descriptive, which the verbal mark before the court proved to be, proof of secondary meaning is required; however, "[s]uggestive marks are eligible for protection without any proof of secondary meaning, since the connection between the mark and the source is presumed." 753 F.2d, at 216. The Second Circuit has nevertheless continued to deny protection for trade dress under § 43(a) absent proof of secondary meaning, despite the fact that § 43(a) provides no basis for distinguishing between trademark and trade dress.

The Fifth Circuit was quite right in *Chevron*, and in this case, to follow the *Abercrombie* classifications consistently and to inquire whether trade dress for which protection is claimed under § 43(a) is inherently distinctive. If it is, it is capable of identifying products or services as coming from a specific source and secondary meaning is not required. This is the rule generally applicable to trademark, and the protection of trademarks and trade dress under § 43(a) serves the same statutory purpose of preventing deception and unfair competition. There is no persuasive reason to apply different analysis to the two. * * *

It would be a different matter if there were textual basis in § 43(a) for treating inherently distinctive verbal or symbolic trademarks differently from inherently distinctive trade dress. But there is none. The section does not mention trademarks or trade dress, whether they be called generic, descriptive, suggestive, arbitrary, fanciful, or functional. Nor does the concept of secondary meaning appear in the text of § 43(a). Where secondary meaning does appear in the statute, 15 U.S.C. § 1052

(1982 ed.), it is a requirement that applies only to merely descriptive marks and not to inherently distinctive ones. We see no basis for requiring secondary meaning for inherently distinctive trade dress protection under § 43(a) but not for other distinctive words, symbols, or devices capable of identifying a producer's product.

Engrafting onto § 43(a) a requirement of secondary meaning for inherently distinctive trade dress also would undermine the purposes of the Lanham Act. Protection of trade dress, no less than of trademarks, serves the Act's purpose to "secure to the owner of the mark the goodwill of his business and to protect the ability of consumers to distinguish among competing producers. National protection of trademarks is desirable, Congress concluded, because trademarks foster competition and the maintenance of quality by securing to the producer the benefits of good reputation." *Park' N Fly v. Dollar Park and Fly, Inc.*, 469 U.S. [189], at 198, 105 S.Ct. [658], at 663, [83 L.Ed.2d 582 (1985)] citing S.Rep. No. 1333, 79th Cong., 2d Sess., 3–5 (1946). By making more difficult the identification of a producer with its product, a secondary meaning requirement for a nondescriptive trade dress would hinder improving or maintaining the producer's competitive position.

Suggestions that under the Fifth Circuit's law, the initial user of any shape or design would cut off competition from products of like design and shape are not persuasive. Only nonfunctional, distinctive trade dress is protected under § 43(a). The Fifth Circuit holds that a design is legally functional, and thus unprotectible, if it is one of a limited number of equally efficient options available to competitors and free competition would be unduly hindered by according the design trademark protection. This serves to assure that competition will not be stifled by the exhaustion of a limited number of trade dresses.

On the other hand, adding a secondary meaning requirement could have anticompetitive effects, creating particular burdens on the start-up of small companies. It would present special difficulties for a business, such as respondent, that seeks to start a new product in a limited area and then expand into new markets. Denying protection for inherently distinctive nonfunctional trade dress until after secondary meaning has been established would allow a competitor, which has not adopted a distinctive trade dress of its own, to appropriate the originator's dress in other markets and to deter the originator from expanding into and competing in these areas.

As noted above, petitioner concedes that protecting an inherently distinctive trade dress from its inception may be critical to new entrants to the market and that withholding protection until secondary meaning has been established would be contrary to the goals of the Lanham Act. Petitioner specifically suggests, however, that the solution is to dispense with the requirement of secondary meaning for a reasonable, but brief period at the outset of the use of a trade dress. If § 43(a) does not require secondary meaning at the outset of a business' adoption of trade dress, there is no basis in the statute to support the suggestion that such a requirement comes into being after some unspecified time.

III

We agree with the Court of Appeals that proof of secondary meaning is not required to prevail on a claim under § 43(a) of the Lanham Act where the trade dress at issue is inherently distinctive, and accordingly the judgment of that court is affirmed.

Notes and Questions

1. *Trade dress infringement.* What justification might exist for always requiring that trade dress have secondary meaning? Should it matter what kind of trade dress is involved?

a. The nature of "trade dress." While some trade dress is registered as a mark, section 43(a) has become an especially important vehicle for trade dress infringement claims. What exactly is "trade dress?" The term originally was understood primarily to refer to product packaging, but it came to encompass nonfunctional product features, as well. As the district court in *Two Pesos* noted, trade dress now is understood to include the "total image" of a product or service, which may include visual aspects as well as sales techniques. In Hartford House, Ltd. v. Hallmark Cards, Inc., 846 F.2d 1268, 6 U.S.P.Q.2d 2038 (10th Cir.1988), *cert. denied* 448 U.S. 908, 109 S.Ct. 260, 102 L.Ed.2d 248 (1988), the court found enforceable trade dress rights in the overall "look" of the plaintiff's line of greeting cards. This "look" consisted of

> 1. A two-fold card containing poetry on the first and third pages.
>
> 2. Unprinted surfaces on the inside three panels.
>
> 3. A deckle edge on the right side of the first page.
>
> 4. A rough-edge stripe of color, or wide stripe, on the outside of the deckle edge of the first page.
>
> 5. A high-quality, uncoated, and textured art paper for the cards.
>
> 6. Fluorescent ink for some of the colors printed on the cards.
>
> 7. Lengthy poetry, written in free verse, typically with a personal message.
>
> 8. Appearance of hand-lettered calligraphy on the first and third pages with the first letter of the words often enlarged.
>
> 9. An illustration that wraps around the card and is spread over three pages, including the back of the card.
>
> 10. The look of the cards primarily characterized by backgrounds of soft colors done with air brush blends or light watercolor strokes, usually depicting simple contrasting foreground scenes superimposed in the background.

Id., 846 F.2d at 1270, 6 U.S.P.Q.2d at 2040. The court explained that its ruling did not grant the claimant, Blue Mountain,

> exclusive rights in an artistic style or in some concept, idea, or theme of expression. Rather, it is Blue Mountain's specific artistic expression, in

> combination with other features to produce an overall Blue Mountain look, that is being protected. This protection does not extend the protection available under trademark law and does not conflict with the policy of copyright law.

Id., 846 F.2d at 1274, 6 U.S.P.Q.2d at 2043. Study the Court's description of Taco Cabana's trade dress in *Two Pesos.* Could it be argued that this trade dress constitutes a "concept, idea, or theme of expression?" Why should it matter? How might one draw the line between protectible trade dress and concepts or themes?

Could an artist prevent others from imitating his distinctive artistic style in works of fine art pursuant to section 43(a)? See Romm Art Creations Ltd. v. Simcha International, Inc., 786 F.Supp. 1126, 22 U.S.P.Q.2d 1801 (E.D.N.Y.1992). Could a rock band claim its performing style as trade dress? See Cesare v. Work, 36 Ohio App.3d 26, 520 N.E.2d 586 (1987). Could software producers rely on a trade dress infringement claim to prevent others from copying their programs' "look and feel?" See Kellner, *Computer User Interfaces: Trade Dress Protection for "Look and Feel,"* 84 TRADEMARK REP. 337 (1994).

b. Determining inherent distinctiveness. While the Supreme Court's *Two Pesos* opinion establishes that inherently distinctive trade dress can be protected in the absence of secondary meaning, it offers little guidance in determining when trade dress is inherently distinctive. The district court instructed the jury that "to be found inherently distinctive, the trade dress must not be descriptive." *Two Pesos,* ___ U.S. at ___, 112 S.Ct. at 2756 n.3, 120 L.Ed.2d at 622 n.3. Does this mean that anything not "descriptive" is inherently distinctive? When is trade dress descriptive? Is Mexican-style restaurant decor descriptive of Mexican cuisine? Could it be argued that whenever trade dress is designed to create a favorable "image" for a product (e.g., "modern," "upscale," "elegant," "youthful," "sexy") that trade dress is descriptive? See Turtle Wax, Inc. v. First Brands Corp., 781 F.Supp. 1314, 1322, 22 U.S.P.Q.2d 1013, 1020 (N.D.Ill.1991).

In Paddington Corp. v. Attiki Importers & Distributors, Inc., 996 F.2d 577, 27 U.S.P.Q.2d 1189 (2d Cir.1993), the Second Circuit, chastened by the Supreme Court's ruling in *Two Pesos*, undertook to determine when trade dress is inherently distinctive. The court described the trade dress before it, for imported Greek ouzo, as follows:

> No. 12 Ouzo is sold in a clear glass bottle with a large label on its side and a second, smaller label on its neck. Both labels are red, white, and black. The large label consists of a white background, inside of which is a rectangle consisting of a white top half and a red lower half, bordered by a thin black line. In the white half, there is a small "No" and a very large "12" in black block letters made to resemble a stencilled number on a crate or barrel. In the red lower half the word "ouzo" appears in white block letters with black shadowing, under which the word "Kaloyannis" is found in small, thin black letters, along with some other information in fine print. The neck label mirrors the large label in layout, except that a circle is used in place of the rectangle. The overall appearance of the bottle is simple, even stark.

Id., 996 F.2d at 581, 27 U.S.P.Q.2d at 1191. Turning to the issue of classification, the court observed:

> In Chevron Chemical Co. v. Voluntary Purchasing Groups, Inc., 659 F.2d 695 (5th Cir.1981), *cert. denied*, 457 U.S. 1126, 102 S.Ct. 2947, 73 L.Ed.2d 1342 (1982), relied on heavily by the Court in *Two Pesos*, the Fifth Circuit determined that the plaintiff's bottles and packaging were inherently distinctive, noting that "the possible varieties of advertising display and packaging are virtually endless." Since the choices that a producer has for packaging its products are, as the Fifth Circuit noted, almost unlimited, typically a trade dress will be arbitrary or fanciful and thus inherently distinctive, and the only real question for the courts will be whether there is a likelihood of confusion between the products, provided, of course, the trade dress is not functional.
>
> However, where it is the custom of an industry to package products in a particular manner, a trade dress in that style would be generic and therefore not inherently distinctive. For example, packaging lime-flavored soda in green twelve-ounce cans is so common in the soft drink industry that such packaging probably is not inherently distinctive, although without the industry practice green cans would be either suggestive or arbitrary and therefore inherently distinctive. Descriptive trade dresses also are not inherently distinctive. In Blau Plumbing, Inc. v. S.O.S. Fix–It, Inc., 781 F.2d 604, 609 (7th Cir.1986), the court found that an advertisement for a sewer service company containing four boxes labeled north, south, east, and west, each containing the locations and phone numbers of different branches of the company within that area of the city, was a trade dress descriptive of the company's ability to service the entire city. Similarly, a trade dress featuring an illustration of a shining car on a bottle of car wax likely would be descriptive.
>
> Trade dresses often utilize commonly used lettering styles, geometric shapes, or colors, or incorporate descriptive elements, such as an illustration of the sun on a bottle of suntan lotion. While each of these elements individually would not be inherently distinctive, it is the combination of elements and the total impression that the dress gives to the observer that should be the focus of a court's analysis of distinctiveness. If the overall dress is arbitrary, fanciful, or suggestive, it is inherently distinctive despite its incorporation of generic or descriptive elements. One could no more deny protection to a trade dress for using commonly used elements than one could deny protection to a trademark because it consisted of a combination of commonly used letters of the alphabet.
>
> The No. 12 Ouzo bottle is inherently distinctive. There is no evidence in the record of any industry practice of using a design like the one that appears on the bottle's labels. There is nothing descriptive about the bottle and label design that conveys anything about its particular contents, except for the use of the trademark "No. 12 Ouzo," * * * and the fact that the bottle is of a style such that it indicates to the observer that it contains a liquid that probably is potable. The tone and layout of the colors, the style and size of the lettering, and, most important, the overall appearance of the bottle's labeling, are undeni-

ably arbitrary. They were selected from an almost limitless supply of patterns, colors and designs. Since the No. 12 trade dress is arbitrary, and therefore protectible under the Lanham Act, the secondary meaning analysis is unnecessary * * *.

Id., 996 F.2d at 583–84, 27 U.S.P.Q.2d at 1193.

What if the court finds that the individual elements of the plaintiff's trade dress are commonplace in the industry, but that no product possesses those same elements in combination? Does this compel a finding that the trade dress is inherently distinctive? The district court in Turtle Wax, Inc. v. First Brands Corp., *supra*, rejected such an argument:

> [S]uch a rule essentially would extend trade dress protection to every new compilation of elements in a particular field and would run afoul of the [tenet in Seabrook Foods, Inc. v. Bar–Well Foods Ltd., 568 F.2d 1342 (C.C.P.A.1977)] that a trade dress is not unique and distinctive if it merely refines common forms of ornamentation utilized in a particular field of goods. Presumably, it could be said about the trade dress of any new product that no competitive product combines precisely the same elements in its trade dress * * * However, that fact alone does not make the product's trade dress inherently distinctive. Any other rule essentially would require a finding of inherent distinctiveness whenever a new product enters the market.

Id., 781 F.Supp. at 1321, 22 U.S.P.Q.2d at 1019.

Given the above, how would you evaluate the distinctiveness of the trade dress in *Two Pesos*?

How should the distinctiveness of product configurations, as opposed to product packaging, be evaluated? In Duraco Products, Inc. v. Joy Plastic Enterprises, Ltd., 40 F.3d 1431, 1448–50, 32 U.S.P.Q.2d 1724, 1738–39 (3d Cir.1994), the Court of Appeals for the Third Circuit described the circumstances in which a product's configuration may be considered inherently distinctive:

> These circumstances are characterized by a high probability that a product configuration serves a virtually exclusively identifying function for consumers—where the concerns over "theft" of an identifying feature or combination or arrangement of features and the cost to an enterprise of gaining and proving secondary meaning outweigh concerns over inhibiting competition, and where consumers are especially likely to perceive a connection between the product's configuration and its source. We conclude that, to be inherently distinctive, a product feature or a combination or arrangement of features, i.e., a product configuration, for which Lanham Act protection is sought must be (i) unusual and memorable; (ii) conceptually separable from the product; and (iii) likely to serve primarily as a designator of origin of the product.
>
> For a product configuration to have the capacity to distinguish goods in a consumer's mind—the first prerequisite for inherent distinctiveness—it must be unusual and memorable. It must partake of a unique, individualized appearance, so that a consumer informed of all the options available in the market could reasonably rely on it to identify a source. * * *
>
> Moreover, unless the trade dress is memorable—that is, striking or unusual in appearance, or prominently displayed on the product packaging, or otherwise somehow to be impressed upon the minds of consumers, so that it is likely to be actually and distinctly remembered—it cannot serve as a designator of origin. * * *
>
> But the uniqueness of a product configuration is not enough by itself to make the configuration inherently distinctive. To be inherently distinctive, a product configuration must also be conceptually separable

from the product, so that a consumer will recognize its symbolic (signifying) character. * * *

[T]he configuration for which protection is sought must not appear to the consumer as a mere component, or the essence, of the product gestalt, but rather must appear as something attached (in a conceptual sense) to function in actuality as a source designator—it must appear to the consumer to act as an independent *signifier* of origin rather than as a component of the good.

Third, to be inherently distinctive, it must be likely that the product configuration will primarily serve as a designator of the source of the product. If the configuration itself, separate from the product, is likely to serve some substantial purpose other than as a designation of origin—that is, besides to set it apart from other sources' products in consumers' minds—then it cannot be inherently distinctive, but must acquire secondary meaning before becoming entitled to protection against copying. In this regard, a source's intent in adopting the particular configuration is highly probative.

In Stuart Hall Co., Inc. v. Ampad Corp., 51 F.3d 780, 34 U.S.P.Q.2d 1428 (8th Cir.1995), the Eighth Circuit rejected the *Duraco* standard, holding that no distinction should be made between product configuration and packaging.

c. Determining functionality. In its opinion in *Two Pesos*, the Court of Appeals approved the district court's instruction on functionality:

Even if the trade dress is made up of individual elements, **some of which serve a functional purpose,** the trade dress may be protectible so long as the combination of these individual elements which define Taco Cabana's trade dress is arbitrary. On the other hand, if you find that Taco Cabana's trade dress as a whole **must be used by others in order to compete** in the Mexican fast-food restaurant business, then you should find that Plaintiff's trade dress is functional and not protectible.

[T]he inquiry into whether Taco Cabana's trade dress is functional or non-functional **should not be addressed to whether individual elements fall within the definition, but whether the whole collection of elements taken together are functional or non-functional**.

Taco Cabana Intern., Inc. v. Two Pesos, Inc., 932 F.2d 1113, 1119, 19 U.S.P.Q.2d 1253, 1257 (5th Cir.1991). The Fifth Circuit holds that "a design is legally functional, and thus unprotectible, if it is one of a limited number of equally efficient options available to competitors and free competition would be unduly hindered by according the design trademark protection." See *Two Pesos*, ___ U.S. at ___, 112 S.Ct. at 2760, 120 L.Ed.2d at 627–28. In light of this, how would you evaluate the functionality of Taco Cabana's trade dress?

d. Infringement of trade dress. The central inquiry in a section 43(a) trade dress infringement suit is whether the defendant is passing off his goods or services as those of the plaintiff by employing trade dress that is so similar to the plaintiff's that it causes a likelihood of consumer confusion.

In determining the likelihood of confusion, the overall trade dress of the products must be considered: "it is the 'combination of features as a whole rather than a difference in some of the details which must determine whether the competing product is likely to cause confusion in the mind of the public.'" Perfect Fit Industries, Inc. v. Acme Quilting Co., 618 F.2d 950, 955, 205 U.S.P.Q. 297, 302 (2d Cir.1980). Courts typically consider the same factors in evaluating likelihood of confusion as they do in registered trademark infringement suits. Thus, the similarity of the trade dress, the similarity of the parties' goods or services, the defendant's intent, evidence of actual confusion, the similarity of retail outlets and purchasers, the strength of the trade dress, and the sophistication of potential purchasers may all be relevant. See, e.g. Chevron Chemical Co. v. Voluntary Purchasing Groups, Inc., 659 F.2d 695, 703, 212 U.S.P.Q. 904, 908 (5th Cir.1981), *cert. denied* 457 U.S. 1126, 102 S.Ct. 2947, 73 L.Ed.2d 1342 (1982). See Chapter 6, § VI A.

2. *Trade names.*

> Trademarks and trade names are technically distinct. Trade names are symbols used to distinguish companies, partnerships and businesses. Trade names symbolize the reputation of a business as a whole. In contrast, trademarks and service marks are designed to identify and distinguish a company's goods and services.

Accuride International, Inc. v. Accuride Corp., 871 F.2d 1531, 1534, 10 U.S.P.Q.2d 1589, 1591 (9th Cir.1989). Though trade name infringement litigation has focused primarily on profit-seeking businesses, other entities, such as charitable organizations, educational institutions, and fraternal groups may also avail themselves of trade name protection.

The same rationales exist for protecting trade names as for protecting trademarks and service marks: protection of a business' trade name prevents infringers from unfairly appropriating its identity and good will, and jeopardizing its reputation. Trade name protection may encourage businesses to invest in quality by insuring the opportunity to reap the benefits of the favorable reputation that such investment generates. Also, of course, prevention of trade name infringement protects consumers from confusion.

The common law traditionally has protected trade names under the same basic principles as trade marks, and Lanham Act section 43(a) continues this tradition. Accordingly, trade names must satisfy the same standards of distinctiveness as marks—they typically are categorized in the same way: generic, descriptive, suggestive, arbitrary or fanciful. Moreover, the same standard of infringement—a likelihood of consumer confusion—applies. The same basic rules regarding geographic rights and priority apply as for unregistered marks. See Chapter 6, §§ III, VI E1.

What, if any impact do state statutes governing incorporation and registration of corporate names have on rights in trade names? Exclusive rights in trade names, like exclusive rights in trade marks, are obtained through use of the name in the ordinary course of business. Registration or incorporation under a name pursuant to state corporate statutes, in the absence of use, generally gives no exclusive right in the name in an infringement suit against others. In some states, however, persons incorporating or registering under a name receive indirect trade name protection through statutory provisions precluding businesses from registering or incorporating under a name that is deceptively similar to that of a corporation already authorized to transact business in that state. See RESTATEMENT (THIRD) OF UNFAIR COMPETITION § 12 comment c (Tentative Draft No. 2, 1990). In most states, however, the fact that the state has accepted registration of a name does not shield the registrant against infringement liability to a senior user. *Id.*

A trade name, in itself, may not be registered on either of the Lanham Act registers. Of course, a business that uses a word or symbol both as its trade name and as a mark for its goods or services may register the word or symbol in the latter capacity. Note that a defendant's unauthorized use of a plaintiff's trade name as a mark may infringe the plaintiff's rights in the name, if the use leads to a likelihood of confusion. Indeed, prior continuing use of a word or symbol as a trade name may prevent another from registering a confusingly similar word or symbol as a mark under Lanham Act section 2(d). 15 U.S.C.A. § 1052(d). See Chapter 6, § V E, *supra.*

3. *Reverse passing off.* Assume that X acquires products manufactured and sold by Y, replaces Y's trademark with his own, and sells the products to his customers. This scenario is sometimes called "reverse passing off." See RESTATEMENT (THIRD) OF UNFAIR COMPETITION § 5 (Tentative Draft No. 1, 1988). Should X be liable to Y? Is Y harmed? If so, in what way? See RESTATEMENT (THIRD) OF UNFAIR COMPETITION, *supra*; Freedman, *Reverse Passing Off: A Great Deal of Confusion*, 83 TRADEMARK REP. 305 (1993). If you believe that liability should be imposed, what, specifically, should Y be required to prove? What if X merely removes Y's mark and makes no representations to his customers regarding the manufacture of the products? Should he be liable?

What if A, an actor, performs in a movie. B, a distributor, removes A's name from the movie credits, substitutes C's name in its place, and proceeds to distribute the movie. Is your analysis the same as in the prior scenario? See Smith v. Montoro, 648 F.2d 602, 211 U.S.P.Q. 775 (9th Cir.1981).

III. FALSE ADVERTISING

ELY–NORRIS SAFE CO. v. MOSLER SAFE CO.

United States Court of Appeals for the Second Circuit, 1925.
7 F.2d 603, *reversed on other grounds*
273 U.S. 132, 47 S.Ct. 314, 71 L.Ed. 578 (1927).

The jurisdiction of the District Court depended upon diverse citizenship, and the suit was for unfair competition. The bill alleged that the plaintiff manufactured and sold safes under certain letters patent, which had as their distinctive feature an explosion chamber, designed for protection against burglars. Before the acts complained of, no one but the plaintiff had ever made or sold safes with such chambers, and, except for the defendant's infringement, the plaintiff has remained the only manufacturer and seller of such safes. By reason of the plaintiff's efforts the public has come to recognize the value of the explosion chamber and to wish to purchase safes containing them. Besides infringing the patent, the defendant has manufactured and sold safes without a chamber, but with a metal band around the door, in the same place where the plaintiff put the chamber, and has falsely told its customers that this band was employed to cover and close an explosion chamber. Customers have been thus led to buy safes upon the faith of the representation, who in fact wished to buy safes with explosion chambers, and would have done so, but for the deceit.

The bill prayed an injunction against selling safes with such metal bands, and against representing that any of its safes contained an explosion chamber. From the plaintiff's answers to interrogatories it appeared that all the defendant's safes bore the defendant's name and address, and were sold as its own. Furthermore, that the defendant never gave a customer reason to suppose that any safe sold by it was made by the plaintiff.

HAND, CIRCUIT JUDGE (after stating the facts as above).

This case is not the same as that before Mr. Justice Bradley in New York & Rosendale Co. v. Coplay Cement Co. (C.C.) 44 F. 277, 10 L.R.A. 833. The plaintiffs there manufactured cement at Rosendale, N.Y., but it did not appear that they were the only persons making cement at that place. There was no reason, therefore, to assume that a customer of the defendant, deceived as to the place of origin of the defendant's cement, and desiring to buy only such cement, would have bought of the plaintiffs. It resulted that the plaintiffs did not show any necessary loss of trade through the defendant's fraud upon its own customers. * * *

American Washboard Co. v. Saginaw Mfg. Co., 103 F. 281 (C.C.A. 6), 43 C.C.A. 233, 50 L.R.A. 609, was, however, a case in substance like that at bar, because there the plaintiff alleged that it had acquired the entire output of sheet aluminum suitable for washboards. It necessarily followed that the plaintiff had a practical monopoly of this metal for the articles in question, and from this it was a fair inference that any customer of the defendant, who was deceived into buying as an aluminum washboard one which was not such, was a presumptive customer of the plaintiff, who had therefore lost a bargain. This was held, however, not to constitute a private wrong, and so the bill was dismissed.

* * *

We must concede, therefore, that on the cases as they stand the law is with the defendant, and the especially high authority of the court which decided American Washboard Co. v. Saginaw Mfg. Co., supra, makes us hesitate to differ from their conclusion. Yet there is no part of the law which is more plastic than unfair competition, and what was not reckoned an actionable wrong 25 years ago may have become such today. We find it impossible to deny the strength of the plaintiff's case on the allegations of its bill. As we view it, the question is, as it always is in such cases, one of fact. While a competitor may, generally speaking, take away all the customers of another that he can, there are means which he must not use. One of these is deceit. The false use of another's name as maker or source of his own goods is deceit, of which the false use of geographical or descriptive terms is only one example. But we conceive that in the end the questions which arise are always two: Has the plaintiff in fact lost customers? And has he lost them by means which the law forbids? The false use of the plaintiff's name is only an instance in which each element is clearly shown.

In the case at bar the means are as plainly unlawful as in the usual case of palming off. It is as unlawful to lie about the quality of one's wares as about their maker; it equally subjects the seller to action by the buyer. * * * The reason, as we think, why such deceits have not been regarded as actionable by a competitor, depends only upon his inability to show any injury for which there is a known remedy. In an open market it is generally impossible to prove that a customer, whom the defendant has secured by falsely describing his goods, would have bought of the plaintiff, if the defendant had been truthful. Without that, the plaintiff, though aggrieved in company with other honest traders, cannot show any ascertainable loss. He may not recover at law, and the equitable remedy is concurrent. The law does not allow him to sue as a vicarious avenger of the defendant's customers.

But, if it be true that the plaintiff has a monopoly of the kind of wares concerned, and if to secure a customer the defendant must represent his own as of that kind, it is a fair inference that the customer wants those and those only. Had he not supposed that the defendant could supply him, presumably he would have gone to the plaintiff, who alone could. At least, if the plaintiff can prove that in fact he would, he shows a direct loss, measured by his profits on the putative sale. If a tradesman falsely foists on a customer a substitute for what the plaintiff alone can supply, it can scarcely be that the plaintiff is without remedy, if he can show that the customer would certainly have come to him, had the truth been told.

Yet that is in substance the situation which this bill presents. It says that the plaintiff alone could lawfully make such safes, and that the defendant has sold others to customers who asked for the patented kind. It can make no difference that the defendant sold them as its own. The sale by hypothesis depended upon the structure of the safes, not on their maker. To be satisfied, the customer must in fact have gone to the plaintiff, or the defendant must have infringed. Had he infringed, the plaintiff could have recovered his profit on the sale; had the customer gone to him, he would have made that profit. Any possibilities that the customers might not have gone to the plaintiff, had they been told the truth, are foreclosed by the allegation that the plaintiff in fact lost the sales. It seems to us * * * that, if this can be proved, a private suit will lie.

Notes and Questions

1. *The common-law cause of action for false advertising.* Prior to the Second Circuit's *Mosler* opinion, the cause of action for unfair competition had consisted almost exclusively of relief for misrepresentations about the source of goods or services. As the *Mosler* court suggests, the courts had

strongly resisted expanding the law to provide redress for other misrepresentations a competitor might make about his own goods or services. The court in the *American Washboard* case, cited in *Mosler*, summarized the reasons:

> [The private cause of action for passing off] is not based upon fraud or imposition upon the public, but is maintained solely for the protection of the property rights of the complainant. It is true that in these cases it is an important factor that the public are deceived, but it is only where this deception induces the public to buy the goods as those of complainant that a private right of action arises. * * *
>
> If the doctrine contended for by complainant in this case was to be carried to its legitimate results, we should, as suggested by Mr. Justice Bradley in the case of New York & R. Cement Co. v. Coplay Cement Co., (C.C.) 44 Fed. 277, open a Pandora's box of litigation. A person who undertook to manufacture a genuine article could suppress the business of all untruthful dealers, although they were in no wise undertaking to pirate his trade. Says Mr. Justice Bradley:
>
> > The principle for which counsel for complainant contends would enable any crockery merchant of Dresden or elsewhere interested in the particular trade to sue a dealer of New York or Philadelphia who should sell an article as Dresden china, when it is not Dresden china. * * * A dry-goods merchant selling an article of linen as Irish Linen could be sued by all the haberdashers of Ireland and all the linen dealers of the United States.

American Washboard Co. v. Saginaw Mfg. Co., 103 Fed. 281, 285–86 (6th Cir.1900).

Why does the Court of Appeals for the Second Circuit decide to permit the plaintiff's cause of action in *Mosler*? As a practical matter, how broad is the *Mosler* exception to the general rule?

On certiorari, the Supreme Court reversed the Second Circuit. Mosler Safe Co. v. Ely–Norris Safe Co., 273 U.S. 132, 47 S.Ct. 314, 71 L.Ed. 578 (1927). The Court explained:

> The Circuit Court of Appeals held that if, as it took it to be alleged, the plaintiff had the monopoly of explosion chambers and the defendant falsely represented that its safes had such chambers, the plaintiff had a good case * * *.
>
> At the hearing below all attention seems to have been concentrated on the question passed upon and the forcibly stated reasons that induced this Court of Appeals to differ from that for the Sixth Circuit. But, upon closer scrutiny of the bill than seems to have been invited before, it does not present that broad and interesting issue. The bill alleges that the plaintiff has a patent for an explosion chamber as described and claimed in said Letters Patent; that it has the exclusive right to make and sell safes containing such an explosion chamber * * *. It then is alleged that the defendant is making and selling safes with a metal band around the door at substantially the same location as the explosion chamber of plaintiff's safes, and has represented to the public that the said metal band was employed to cover or close an explosion chamber by reason of which the public has been led to

> purchase defendant's said safes as and for safes containing an explosion chamber, such as is manufactured and sold by the plaintiff herein. * * *
>
> It is consistent with every allegation in the bill and the defendant in argument asserted it to be a fact, that there are other safes with explosion chambers beside that for which the plaintiff has a patent. The defendant is charged only with representing that its safes had an explosion chamber, which, so far as appears, it had a perfect right to do if the representation was true. If on the other hand the representation was false as it is alleged sometimes to have been, there is nothing to show that customers had they known the facts would have gone to the plaintiff rather than to other competitors in the market, or to lay a foundation for the claim for a loss of sales. The bill is so framed as to seem to invite the decision that was obtained from the Circuit Court of Appeals, but when scrutinized is seen to have so limited its statements as to exclude the right to complain.

Id., 273 U.S. at 133–34, 47 S.Ct. at 314–15, 71 L.Ed. at 579–80. Given the reason for the reversal, the Second Circuit's substantive rule continued to be persuasive and ultimately gained general acceptance.

What (if any) justifications exist for making a cause of action for false advertising more readily available to competitors? See RESTATEMENT (THIRD) OF UNFAIR COMPETITION § 2, comment a (Tentative Draft No. 1, 1988). Compare BeVier, *Competitor Suits for False Advertising Under Section 43(a) of the Lanham Act: A Puzzle in the Law of Deception*, 78 VA. L. REV. 1 (1992), with McChesney, *Deception, Trademark Infringement, and the Lanham Act: A Property–Rights Reconciliation*, 78 VA. L. REV. 49 (1992), and Schechter, *Additional Pieces of the Deception Puzzle: Some Reactions to Professor BeVier*, 78 VA. L. REV. 57 (1992).

JOHNSON & JOHNSON v. CARTER–WALLACE, INC.

United States Court of Appeals for the Second Circuit, 1980.
631 F.2d 186, 208 U.S.P.Q. 169.

MANSFIELD, CIRCUIT JUDGE:

Johnson & Johnson ("Johnson"), manufacturer of Johnson's Baby Oil and Johnson's Baby Lotion, appeals from a judgment of the United States District Court for the Southern District of New York, entered by Judge Constance Baker Motley, dismissing at the end of the plaintiff's case during a non-jury trial its suit for injunctive relief brought under § 43(a) of the Lanham Act, 15 U.S.C. § 1125(a), against Carter–Wallace ("Carter"), the manufacturer of NAIR, a leading depilatory product. Because we believe Johnson's showing on the required elements of its false advertising claim was sufficient to withstand a motion to dismiss, we reverse and remand for further proceedings.

Johnson's claim arises out of Carter's use of baby oil in NAIR and its advertising campaign regarding that inclusion. In 1977, Carter added baby oil to its NAIR lotion and initiated a successful advertising campaign emphasizing this fact. NAIR is sold in a pink plastic bottle with the word "NAIR" written in large, pink letters. A bright turquoise-blue banner, open at both ends, contains the words "with baby oil." In addition to its packaging of NAIR, Carter's television advertisements emphasize that NAIR contains baby oil.[2]

Alleging that Carter is making false claims for NAIR with baby oil * * *, plaintiff filed the instant suit for injunctive relief under § 43(a) of the Lanham Act, 15 U.S.C. § 1125(a), and under New York's common law of unfair competition. * * * Johnson's false representation claim alleges that Carter's "NAIR with baby oil" campaign falsely represents to consumers that the baby oil in NAIR has [a] moisturizing and softening effect on the skin of the user. While recognizing that Carter's advertising makes no explicit claims for its product, Johnson alleges that this claim is implicit in the manner in which NAIR has been marketed. It contends that these false claims have unfairly dissuaded consumers from using its products in favor of NAIR with baby oil.

* * *

In dismissing Johnson's false advertising claim, the trial court did not reach either the question of whether Carter advertises or implies in its advertising that baby oil as an ingredient in NAIR has a moisturizing and softening effect, or the issue of whether such a claim is false. Instead, its dismissal was "granted on the ground that [Johnson] failed to carry its burden of proving damage or the likelihood of damage." Just what that burden is and what evidence will satisfy it, are the central issues in this appeal.

Discussion

Prior to the enactment of § 43(a) of the Lanham Act, false advertising claims were governed by the common law of trade disparagement. Under the common law, liability was generally confined to "palming-off" cases where the deceit related to the origin of the product. *Ely-Norris Safe Co. v. Mosler Safe Co.*, 7 F.2d 603 (2d Cir.1925), *revd. on other grounds*, 273 U.S. 132, 47 S.Ct. 314, 71 L.Ed. 578 (1926). In these cases the offending product was foisted upon an unwary consumer by deceiving him into the belief that he was buying the plaintiff's product (normally an item with a reputation for quality). Other instances of false advertising were safe from actions by competitors due to the difficulty of satisfying the requirement of proof of actual damage caused by the false claims. In an open market it is normally impossible to prove

2. The court has viewed samples of Carter's television advertisements. Carter's commercials all featured several young women dancing and singing while dressed in clothing that revealed their legs. A typical audio portion of these commercials is as follows:

"Who's got Baby Oil?

Nair's got Baby Oil.

If you're a baby goil, Nair with Baby Oil.

Nair with Baby Oil.

It takes off the hair so your legs feel baby-smooth.

And Nair's baby-soft scent smells terrific, baby.

Who's got Baby Oil?

Nair's got Baby Oil.

Soft-smelling Nair with Baby Oil.

Nair, for baby-smooth legs."

that a customer, who was induced by the defendant through the use of false claims to purchase the product, would have bought from the plaintiff if the defendant had been truthful.

The passage of § 43(a) represented a departure from the common law * * * and from the need to prove actual damages as a prerequisite for injunctive relief. This departure marked the creation of a "new statutory tort" intended to secure a market-place free from deceitful marketing practices. The new tort, as subsequently interpreted by the courts, differs from the common law action * * * in two important respects: (1) it does not require proof of intent to deceive, and (2) it entitles a broad range of commercial parties to relief.

The broadening of the scope of liability results from a provision in § 43(a) allowing suit to be brought "by any person who believes that he is or is likely to be damaged by the use of any false description or representation." 15 U.S.C. § 1125(a). Whether this clause is viewed as a matter of standing to sue, or as an element of the substantive claim for relief, certain bounds are well established. On the one hand, despite the use of the word "believes," something more than a plaintiff's mere subjective belief that he is injured or likely to be damaged is required before he will be entitled even to injunctive relief. On the other hand, as the district court in this case recognized, a plaintiff seeking an injunction, as opposed to money damages, need not quantify the losses actually borne. What showing of damage in between those two extremes will satisfy the statute is the subject of the instant dispute.

Johnson claims, in effect, that once it is shown that the plaintiff's and the defendant's products compete in a relevant market and that the defendant's ads are false, a likelihood of damage sufficient to satisfy the statute should be *presumed* and an injunction should issue "as a matter of course." The district court, in contrast, drew the line as follows: "Of course, J & J (Johnson) need not quantify its injury in order to obtain injunctive relief. But J & J must at least prove the existence of some injury caused by Carter." The court had said that "J & J has failed to prove that its loss of sales was in any way caused by NAIR's allegedly false advertising."

Both the case law and the policy behind § 43(a) indicate that the district court's construction of the statute placed too high a burden on the plaintiff in this case. To require a plaintiff to "prove the existence of some injury caused by" the defendant, is to demand proof of actual loss and specific evidence of causation. Perhaps a competitor in an open market could meet this standard with proof short of quantified sales loss, but it is not required to do so. The statute demands only proof providing a reasonable basis for the belief that the plaintiff is likely to be damaged as a result of the false advertising. The correct standard is whether it is *likely* that Carter's advertising has caused or will cause a loss of Johnson sales, not whether Johnson has come forward with specific evidence that Carter's ads actually resulted in some definite loss of sales. Contrary to Johnson's argument, however, the likelihood of injury and causation will not be presumed, but must be demonstrated. If such a showing is made, the plaintiff will have established a reasonable belief that he is likely to be damaged within the meaning of § 43(a) and will be entitled to injunctive relief, as distinguished from damages, which would require more proof. We believe that the evidence offered by Johnson, though not overwhelming, is sufficient to prove a likelihood of damage from loss of sales.

Initially, we find that Johnson has shown that it and Carter are competitors in a relevant market. Although Johnson's Baby Oil and Lotion do not compete with NAIR in the narrower depilatory market, they do compete in the broader hair removal market. NAIR is used for hair removal by depilation. Johnson's Baby Lotion has been promoted as a substitute for shaving cream and is used for removal of hair by shaving. Also, both of Johnson's products are used as skin moisturizers after shaving or after the use of depilatories. Such indirect competitors may avail themselves of the protection of § 43(a); the competition need not be direct. Moreover, Carter's advertising campaign itself, by its emphasis on baby oil, directly links the depilation and the moisturizer markets. Johnson's stake in the shaving market gives it a "reasonable interest to be protected against the alleged false advertising." 1 R. Callmann, Unfair Competition, Trademarks and Monopolies, § 18.2(b) at 625 (3d ed. 1967).

To prove a likelihood of injury Johnson must also show a logical causal connection between the alleged false advertising and its own sales position. This it has done with specific evidence. It has shown that large numbers of consumers in fact use its baby lotion for shaving and its baby oil as an after-shave and after-depilation moisturizer. Carter's "NAIR with baby oil" campaign affects both markets. First, NAIR's share of the hair removal market has increased since its baby oil advertising began. For each new depilatory user, a corresponding decline in the use of shaving products such as oils and lotions appears probable. Second, the use of baby oil after depilation is likely to be reduced if, as Johnson contends, Carter's advertising conveys to consumers the idea that NAIR's baby oil has a moisturizing and softening effect and leads the consumer to believe that use of a second, post-depilation, moisturizer is unnecessary. Of course, if Carter's ads are truthful, then its gains at Johnson's expense are well earned. If false, however, the damage to Johnson is unfair.

Johnson's case is supported by more than just the above logic. First, sales of its baby oil have in fact declined. Second, a consumer witness testified at trial that she switched from use of baby oil by shaving to NAIR because it was advertised as containing baby oil. Third, Johnson introduced surveys indicating that some people, after viewing NAIR ads, thought they would not have to use baby oil if they used NAIR. Together, Johnson's evidence was enough to prove a likelihood of competitive injury resulting from the NAIR advertising.

That much of the decline in Johnson's Baby Oil sales may be due to competition from lower priced baby oils, does not save Carter. * * * Further, the possibility that the total pecuniary harm to Johnson might be relatively slight does not bar injunctive relief.

Finally, Johnson's inability to point to a definite amount of sales lost *to Carter* (a failure which would bar monetary relief) does not preclude injunctive relief. Likelihood of competitive injury sufficient to warrant a § 43(a) injunction has been found in the absence of proof of actual sales diversion in numerous cases. Although the overall likelihood of harm to the plaintiff from the defendant's ads in some of these cases was perhaps greater than here, * * * there was little or even no evidence of any actual sales losses to the defendant. * * *

Sound policy reasons exist for not requiring proof of actual loss as a prerequisite to § 43(a) injunctive relief. Failure to prove actual damages in an injunction suit, as distinguished from an action for damages, poses no likelihood of a windfall for the plaintiff. The complaining competitor gains no more than that to which it is already entitled—a market free of false advertising.

While proof of actual diversion of sales is not required for a § 43(a) injunction to issue, proof that the advertising complained of is in fact false is essential. This issue, though briefed by parties in this case, is not before the court at this time. The district court did not reach the question for purposes of determining whether permanent relief should issue. Since the action was dismissed at the close of the plaintiff's case, Carter was afforded no opportunity to introduce additional evidence answering the plaintiff on this point. Johnson, having shown that it is likely to be damaged by Carter's advertising, must prove that the NAIR advertising was false before being entitled to injunctive relief under the Lanham Act. Should the district court find that the defendant's advertising conveys a false message, irreparable injury for the purpose of injunctive relief would be present for the very reason that in an open market it is impossible to measure the exact amount of Johnson's damages.

Accordingly, this cause is reversed and remanded for further proceedings in conformity with this opinion.[5]

Notes and Questions

1. *Section 43(a) standing.* The statutory language creating the false advertising cause of action, as amended, provides:

5. The record discloses strong evidence, including Carter's internal documents, admissions of its chief executive, independent expert opinion, and consumer surveys, that Carter's advertising of "NAIR with baby oil," some of which we viewed upon argument, is perceived as informing the public that the baby oil in NAIR has moisturizing benefits, leaving the skin smoother and softer than it would be without the oil. Indeed, from our review of the record and viewing of the NAIR advertisements the purpose and effect of the latter clearly appears to have been to lead consumers to believe that if they used NAIR with baby oil they would gain benefits from the product in the form of a moisturizing or softening effect not realized when baby oil is absent. Upon remand, therefore, the essential issue will be whether the presence of baby oil in NAIR does in fact have such a moisturizing or softening effect.

> (a)(1) Any person who, on or in connection with any goods or services, or any container for goods, uses in commerce * * * any false or misleading description of fact, or false or misleading representation of fact, which—
>
> * * *
>
> (B) in commercial advertising or promotion, misrepresents the nature, characteristics, qualities, or geographic origin of his or her or another person's goods, services, or commercial activities,
>
> shall be liable in a civil action by any person who believes that he or she is or is likely to be damaged by such act.

15 U.S.C.A. § 1125(a).

Unlike its common-law predecessor, the section 43(a) false advertising cause of action is intended to benefit consumers, at least indirectly, as well as competitors. As the Sixth Circuit has explained:

> Protecting consumers from false or misleading advertising * * * is an important goal of the statute and a laudable public policy to be served. * * * [C]ompetitors have the greatest interest in stopping misleading advertising, and a private cause of action under section 43(a) allows those parties with the greatest interest in enforcement, and in many situations with the greatest resources to devote to a lawsuit, to enforce the statute rigorously.

Coca–Cola Co. v. Procter & Gamble Co., 822 F.2d 28, 31, 3 U.S.P.Q.2d 1364, 1367 (6th Cir.1987). The legal community was slow to recognize and exploit the breadth of the new statutory provision. Though section 43(a) was enacted in 1946, its use did not become prevalent until the 1970's and 80's. For a sketch of the history and development of section 43(a) in the courts, see Bauer, *A Federal Law of Unfair Competition: What Should Be the Reach of Section 43(a) of the Lanham Act?*, 31 U.C.L.A. L. REV. 671 (1984).

As interpreted today, section 43(a) eliminates the requirement, imposed at common law, that a false advertising plaintiff demonstrate direct, actual loss of customers resulting from the defendant's allegedly false advertisement. On the other hand, the court refuses to presume a likelihood of injury and causation from the falsity of the advertising and the fact that the parties compete. The *Johnson* court holds that the plaintiff must demonstrate a "reasonable basis for the belief that the plaintiff is likely to be damaged as a result of the false advertising." Given what the court accepts as an adequate demonstration of likelihood of injury, is the requirement meaningful? Is the standard set forth in *Johnson* too liberal? If so, what should the standard be? On the other hand, if part of the purpose of section 43(a) is to protect consumers from false advertising, why require a plaintiff to demonstrate even a likelihood of injury to itself? See generally BeVier, *Competitor Suits for False Advertising Under Section 43(a) of the Lanham Act: A Puzzle in the Law of Deception*, 78 VA. L. REV. 1 (1992).

In McNeilab, Inc. v. American Home Products Corp., 848 F.2d 34, 6 U.S.P.Q.2d 2007 (2d Cir.1988), the defendant, manufacturer of Advil pain reliever, advertised that "like Tylenol, Advil doesn't give me minor [occasional] stomach upset." Plaintiff, the manufacturer of Tylenol, sued, alleging section 43(a) false advertising, and obtained a preliminary injunction.

On appeal, the defendant challenged the district court's finding that "where false or misleading advertising in violation of the Lanham Act is shown, irreparable harm is presumed." In upholding the finding, the Second Circuit distinguished the *Johnson* decision:

> *Johnson & Johnson* involved misleading, non-comparative commercials which touted the benefits of the product advertised but made no direct reference to any competitor's product. The injury in such cases accrues equally to all competitors; none is more likely to suffer from the offending broadcasts than any other. The Lanham Act, however, only authorizes actions by one "who believes that he is or is likely to be damaged." 15 U.S.C.§ 1125(a). Thus, we required some indication of actual injury and causation to satisfy Lanham Act standing requirements and to ensure a plaintiff's injury was not speculative.
>
> This case, by contrast, presents a false comparative advertising claim. Thus, the concerns voiced in * * * *Johnson & Johnson* regarding speculative injury do not arise. A misleading comparison to a specific product necessarily diminishes that product's value. By falsely implying that Advil is as safe as Tylenol in all respects, AHP deprived McNeil of a legitimate competitive advantage and reduced consumers' incentive to select Tylenol rather than Advil. This is analogous to a Lanham Act trademark dispute. An infringing mark, by its nature, detracts from the value of the mark with which it is confused. In that context, we recently confirmed that irreparable harm will be presumed. Consequently, the district court did not err in presuming harm from a finding of false or misleading advertising.

Id., 848 F.2d at 38, 6 U.S.P.Q.2d at 2010.

The plaintiffs in both *Johnson* and *McNeilab* sought injunctive relief, and the court held that they could obtain it without demonstrating actual injury or the extent of their injury. As the *Johnson* court suggests, a plaintiff seeking damages would have a greater burden of proof. If the plaintiff seeks actual damages based on its lost sales, it must demonstrate actual customer reliance on the false advertisement. Parkway Baking Co. v. Freihofer Baking Co., 255 F.2d 641, 117 U.S.P.Q. 426 (3d Cir. 1958). Damages may be recovered for injuries other than lost sales, however. For example, the plaintiff might seek profits lost on sales at reduced prices necessitated by the false advertising; the costs of completed advertising to respond to the defendant's offending ads; or quantifiable harm to the plaintiff's reputation, to the extent that completed corrective advertising has not repaired that harm. See ALPO Petfoods, Inc. v. Ralston Purina Co., 913 F.2d 958, 969, 16 U.S.P.Q.2d 1081, 1089–90 (D.C.Cir.1990).

While section 43(a) makes no restriction on its face, the Second and Third Circuits have held that defrauded consumers have no standing to sue for false advertising. See Serbin v. Ziebart International Corp., 11 F.3d 1163, 28 U.S.P.Q.2d 1881 (3d Cir.1993); Colligan v. Activities Club of New York, Ltd., 442 F.2d 686, 170 U.S.P.Q. 113 (2d Cir.1971), *cert. denied* 404 U.S. 1004, 92 S.Ct. 559, 30 L.Ed.2d 557 (1971). In the course of drafting and enacting the Trademark Law Revision Act of 1988, the House Judiciary Committee recommended that Congress expressly amend section 43(a) to provide consumers with standing. H.R. REP. NO. 1028, 100th Cong., 2d

Sess. 33 (1988). Congress, however, declined to adopt the recommendation. Assuming that their standing were established, is it likely that many consumers would avail themselves of the section 43(a) cause of action?

2. *False or misleading descriptions or representations of fact.* The generally accepted elements of a section 43(a) false advertising claim for injunction include: 1) A defendant's false or misleading statement of fact in advertising about its own product; 2) the statement actually deceived or had the capacity to deceive a substantial segment of the audience; 3) the deception was material, in that it was likely to influence the purchasing decision; 4) the defendant caused its goods to enter interstate commerce; and 5) the plaintiff has been or is likely to be injured as a result. Skil Corp. v. Rockwell International Corp., 375 F.Supp. 777, 183 U.S.P.Q. 157 (N.D.Ill. 1974).

A statement may be explicitly false or implicitly false and misleading in this context. A growing body of case law has focused on the proper method of analyzing the alleged falsity of a statement. The Court of Appeals for the Second Circuit set forth the framework for the analysis in Coca–Cola Co. v. Tropicana Products, Inc., 690 F.2d 312, 317, 216 U.S.P.Q. 272, 276–77 (2d Cir.1982):

> When a merchandising statement or representation is literally or explicitly false, the court may grant relief without reference to the advertisement's impact on the buying public. When the challenged advertisement is implicitly rather than explicitly false, its tendency to violate the Lanham Act by misleading, confusing or deceiving should be tested by public reaction.

In *Tropicana*, the defendant's television advertisement showed American Olympic athlete Bruce Jenner squeezing an orange while saying "It's pure, pasteurized juice as it comes from the orange." The advertisement then showed Jenner pouring the fresh-squeezed juice into a Tropicana carton while the audio stated "It's the only leading brand not made with concentrate and water." Plaintiff, the maker of Minute Maid orange juice, brought suit for section 43(a) false advertising, and sought a preliminary injunction. The court of appeals found the advertisement literally or explicitly false:

> [T]he squeezing-pouring sequence in the Jenner commercial is false on its face. The visual component of the ad makes an explicit representation that Premium Pack is produced by squeezing oranges and pouring the freshly-squeezed juice directly into the carton. This is not a true representation of how the product is prepared. Premium Pack juice is heated and sometimes frozen prior to packaging. Additionally, the simultaneous audio component of the ad states that Premium Pack is "pasteurized juice as it comes from the orange." This statement is blatantly false—pasteurized juice does not come from oranges. Pasteurization entails heating the juice to approximately 200 degrees Fahrenheit to kill certain natural enzymes and microorganisms which cause spoilage. Moreover, even if the addition of the word "pasteurized" somehow made sense and effectively qualified the visual image, Tropicana's commercial nevertheless represented that the juice is only

> squeezed, heated and packaged when in fact it may actually also be frozen.

Id., 690 F.2d at 318, 216 U.S.P.Q. at 276. Since the ad was false on its face, there was no need to consider how consumers would perceive it. The court of appeals ultimately found that the plaintiff had demonstrated a likelihood of success on the merits.

When is a statement is literally true, it may still serve as the basis for section 43(a) false advertising liability if misleading, or implicitly false. Otherwise, "clever use of innuendo, indirect intimations, and ambiguous suggestions could shield the advertisement from scrutiny precisely when protection against such sophisticated deception is most needed." American Home Products Corp. v. Johnson & Johnson, 577 F.2d 160, 165, 198 U.S.P.Q. 132, 137 (2d Cir.1978). Pursuant to the *Tropicana* rule, the truth or falsity of such advertisements must be tested by the reactions of the public. The plaintiff must provide evidence—usually in the form of consumer surveys or other market research—demonstrating that the relevant consumers understood the ad to convey the alleged false message. See Johnson & Johnson * Merck Consumer Pharmaceuticals Co. v. Smithkline Beecham Corp., 960 F.2d 294, 297–98, 22 U.S.P.Q.2d 1362, 1365 (2d Cir. 1992).

In *Smithkline*, the district court had relied upon consumer survey results to reject the plaintiff's argument that the defendant's advertisement had a misleading impact. On appeal, the plaintiff argued that the district court failed sufficiently to consider factors other than consumer survey evidence, such as "1) the general 'commercial context' or sea of information in which consumers are immersed; 2) the defendant's intent to harness public misperception; 3) the defendant's prior advertising history; and 4) the sophistication of the advertising audience." *Id.* The court of appeals rejected the challenge. It explained:

> Appellant's criticism of the district court's findings misconstrues the proper role of consumer survey evidence in the analysis of implied falsehood claims. Generally, before a court can determine the truth or falsity of an advertisement's message, it must first determine what message was actually conveyed to the viewing audience. Consumer surveys supply such information. "Once the meaning to the target audience has been determined, the court, as the finder of fact, must then judge whether the evidence establishes that they were likely to be misled." Nikkal Indus., Ltd. v. Salton, Inc., 735 F.Supp. 1227, 1235 (S.D.N.Y.1990).
>
> Three of the factors * * *, commercial context, defendant's prior advertising history, and sophistication of the advertising audience, only come into play, if at all, during the latter part of the court's analysis. In a particular case, these factors may shed some light on whether the challenged advertisement contributed to the meaning that was ultimately gleaned by the target audience. In other words, in determining whether an advertisement is likely to mislead or confuse, the district court may consider these factors after a plaintiff has established "that a not insubstantial number of consumers," Coca–Cola Co., 690 F.2d at 317, hold the false belief allegedly communicated in the ad.

Absent such a threshold showing, an implied falsehood claim must fail. This follows from the obvious fact that the injuries redressed in false advertising cases are the result of public deception. Thus, where the plaintiff cannot demonstrate that a statistically significant part of the commercial audience holds the false belief allegedly communicated by the challenged advertisement, the plaintiff cannot establish that it suffered any injury as a result of the advertisement's message. Without injury there can be no claim, regardless of commercial context, prior advertising history, or audience sophistication.

However, we have held that "where a plaintiff adequately demonstrates that a defendant has intentionally set out to deceive the public," and the defendant's "deliberate conduct" in this regard is of an "egregious nature," a presumption arises "that consumers are, in fact, being deceived." Resource Developers, Inc. v. Statue of Liberty–Ellis Island Foundation, Inc., 926 F.2d 134, 140 (2d Cir.1991). This presumption, which may be engendered by the expenditure "of substantial funds in an effort to deceive consumers and influence their purchasing decisions," relieves a plaintiff of the burden of producing consumer survey evidence that supports its claim. *Id.* (quoting U–Haul Int'l, Inc. v. Jartran, Inc., 793 F.2d 1034, 1041 (9th Cir.1986)). In such a case, once a plaintiff establishes deceptive intent, "the burden shifts to the defendant to demonstrate the absence of consumer confusion." Resource Developers, *supra*. * * *

Id., 960 F.2d at 298–99, 22 U.S.P.Q.2d at 1366.

A "statistically significant portion of the commercial audience" may be considerably less than 50% of the audience. To the extent that advertising conveys useful information to members of the audience who were not deceived, is imposition of liability in such cases in the public interest? See RESTATEMENT (THIRD) OF UNFAIR COMPETITION § 2, comment d (Tentative Draft No. 1, 1988).

3. *Other approaches to regulating false advertising.* The Federal Trade Commission is empowered to prevent "unfair or deceptive acts or practices" in or affecting interstate commerce. 15 U.S.C.A. § 45. Armed with both rulemaking and adjudicatory powers, the F.T.C. has played an important role in policing false advertising. The agency is strictly concerned with the general public interest, and acts directly, in its own capacity to prevent and remedy fraud on consumers. The Federal Trade Commission Act provides no means for private enforcement of its provisions, and no forum or vehicle to resolve private disputes among competitors. For an analysis of F.T.C. false advertising activities, see Sullivan & Marks, *The FTC's Deceptive Advertising Policy: A Legal and Economic Analysis*, 64 OR. L. REV. 593 (1986).

Is public agency intervention needed in order to control false advertising, or is private litigation, via section 43(a) and state provisions sufficient? See Best, *Controlling False Advertising: A Comparative Study of Public Regulation, Industry Self–Policing, and Private Litigation*, 20 GA. L. REV. 1 (1985).

A number of states have enacted "Little F.T.C. Acts," patterned after the federal act, and after the Unfair Trade Practices and Consumer Protection Act, developed by the Federal Trade Commission and published by the Council of State Governments in 1967. Unlike the federal provision, in addition to government agency regulation, many of these state statutes authorize private consumer causes of action to enforce their provisions against errant businesses engaged in false advertising. Some of the statutes are broad enough to accommodate suits by competitors, as well. For a comprehensive list of these state statutes, see RESTATEMENT (THIRD) OF UNFAIR COMPETITION § 1, Statutory Note (Tentative Draft No. 1, 1988).

The Uniform Deceptive Trade Practices Act, promulgated by the National Conference of Commissioners on Uniform State Laws in 1964 (revised in 1966), was "designed to bring state law up to date by removing undue restrictions on the common law action for deceptive trade practices." *Id.*, Prefatory Note. Section 3 of the Act provides that a "person *likely to be damaged* by a deceptive trade practice of another" may obtain injunctive relief. (Emphasis added.) This relief is "in addition to remedies otherwise available against the same conduct under the common law or other statutes." *Id.* "Deceptive trade practices" for purposes of the Act include passing off, false advertising and commercial disparagement. *Id.*, § 2. Approximately 12 states have adopted the Act. They are identified in RESTATEMENT (THIRD) OF UNFAIR COMPETITION § 2, Statutory Note (Tentative Draft No. 1, 1988). For additional information about the Uniform Act, see Dole, *The Uniform Deceptive Trade Practices Act: Another Step Toward a National Law of Unfair Trade Practices*, 51 MINN. L. REV. 1005 (1967).

NOTE: "FILLING THE GAPS" WITH SECTION 43(a)

Because of its flexibility and reach, section 43(a) has often been employed to protect private interests omitted from the protection of other intellectual property doctrines, or to provide an alternative to other intellectual property causes of action. For example, authors may turn to section 43(a) for protection of their literary characters, for whom copyright protection has been uncertain. Unauthorized use of a literary character may falsely suggest sponsorship by or affiliation with the character's creator or copyright owner. See, e.g., Walt Disney Co. v. Powell, 698 F.Supp. 10, 9 U.S.P.Q.2d 1234 (D.D.C.1988), *affirmed in part, vacated in part* 897 F.2d 565, 14 U.S.P.Q.2d 1160 (D.C.Cir.1990). Likewise, section 43(a) may protect against use of confusingly similar titles for works of authorship, which generally are not protected by copyright. See 1 J.T. McCARTHY, McCARTHY ON TRADEMARKS AND UNFAIR COMPETITION, §§ 10.02–10.06 (3d ed., 1992).

Section 43(a)'s protection of trade dress may serve as an alternative to a design patent or copyright for an article's appearance, providing rights against copying in some cases when neither of the other doctrines would afford relief. Moreover, section 43(a) may be used as an alternative to the common-law right of publicity cause of action, to protect a celebrity's interest in controlling commercial exploitation of his or her identity. The right of publicity will be discussed in the next Chapter. As you proceed through the cases in that Chapter, you should consider how a section 43(a) claim might have been used to vindicate the plaintiffs' interests.

Section 43(a) has also played a vital role in the vindication of moral rights. Recall that the United States is required to protect the moral rights of attribution and integrity as a member of the Berne Convention. See Chapter 5, § III H, *supra*. In each of the following situations consider how a section 43(a) claim might be framed to vindicate what is essentially a moral right of attribution:

— Lamothe, Jones and Crosby co-authored two songs while they were members of a band called Mac Meda. Mac Meda later dissolved, and Crosby joined a new band called RATT. At this point, Crosby and another member of RATT licensed the two songs to licensees who released recordings of the songs and published the songs in sheet music form. Both the recordings and the sheet music attributed the songs to Crosby, giving no credit to Lamothe or Jones. See Lamothe v. Atlantic Recording Corp., 847 F.2d 1403, 7 U.S.P.Q.2d 1249 (9th Cir.1988).

Would your analysis change if it appeared that Crosby altered the songs after leaving Mac Meda and only licensed use of the altered versions? See Cleary v. News Corp., 30 F.3d 1255, 31 U.S.P.Q.2d 1760 (9th Cir.1994).

— Ken Follett, while still relatively unknown, edited the English translation of a French book about a famous bank robbery for publication in Britain. Follett went beyond normal editing, restructuring the story, enhancing the writing style, developing the characters and filling in gaps. The published British edition credited the French author only on the cover, and credited the French author, followed by "with Ken Follett," on the title page. After Follett became a best-selling novelist, an American edition was readied for publication, which highlighted Follett's name, reducing the original French author to a secondary role. Only Follett's name appeared on the spine of the book. At that point, Follett did not wish to have principle authorship attributed to him. See Follett v. Arbor House Publishing Co., 497 F.Supp. 304, 208 U.S.P.Q. 597 (S.D.N.Y.1980).

In Gilliam v. American Broadcasting Companies, Inc., 538 F.2d 14, 192 U.S.P.Q. 1 (2d Cir.1976), the British comedy group Monty Python wrote scripts for television programs, which were subsequently filmed by the BBC. Under its agreement with the BBC, Monty Python retained considerable editorial control over the scripts. After filming, the BBC licensed ABC to show the programs in the United States. In the course of airing a 90–minute special featuring three of the 30–minute programs, ABC made substantial unauthorized changes: in order to make time for commercials and to remove "offensive or obscene matter," ABC cut out 24 of the original 90 minutes. Appalled at the "mutilation" of the programs, Monty Python sued ABC, alleging copyright infringement and a violation of section 43(a), and sought a preliminary injunction against further broadcasts. The court's decision with regard to the copyright claim is set forth in Chapter 5, § III H, *supra*. The court of appeals found a likelihood of success on the merits of the section 43(a) claim, as well:

> American copyright law, as presently written, does not recognize moral rights or provide a cause of action for their violation, since the law seeks to vindicate the economic, rather than the personal, rights of authors. Nevertheless, the economic incentive for artistic and intellec-

tual creation that serves as the foundation for American copyright law cannot be reconciled with the inability of artists to obtain relief for mutilation or misrepresentation of their work to the public on which the artists are financially dependent. Thus courts have long granted relief for misrepresentation of an artist's work by relying on theories outside the statutory law of copyright, such as contract law, * * * or the tort of unfair competition. Although such decisions are clothed in terms of proprietary right in one's creation, they also properly vindicate the author's personal right to prevent the presentation of his work to the public in a distorted form. Here, the appellants claim that the editing done for ABC mutilated the original work and that consequently the broadcast of those programs as the creation of Monty Python violated the Lanham Act § 43(a), 15 U.S.C. § 1125(a). This statute, the federal counterpart to state unfair competition laws, has been invoked to prevent misrepresentations that may injure plaintiff's business or personal reputation, even where no registered trademark is concerned. It is sufficient to violate the Act that a representation of a product, although technically true, creates a false impression of the product's origin. See Rich v. RCA Corp., 390 F.Supp. 530 (S.D.N.Y.1975) (recent picture of plaintiff on cover of album containing songs recorded in distant past held to be a false representation that the songs were new).

These cases cannot be distinguished from the situation in which a television network broadcasts a program properly designated as having been written and performed by a group, but which has been edited, without the writer's consent, into a form that departs substantially from the original work. "To deform his work is to present him to the public as the creator of a work not his own, and thus makes him subject to criticism for work he has not done." Roeder, *The Doctrine of Moral Right*, 53 HARV. L. REV. 554, 569 (1940). In such a case, it is the writer or performer, rather than the network, who suffers the consequences of the mutilation, for the public will have only the final product by which to evaluate the work. Thus, an allegation that a defendant has presented to the public a "garbled," distorted version of plaintiff's work seeks to redress the very rights sought to be protected by the Lanham Act, 15 U.S.C. § 1125(a), and should be recognized as stating a cause of action under that statute. * * * We find that the truncated version at times omitted the climax of the skits to which appellants' rare brand of humor was leading and at other times deleted essential elements in the schematic development of a story line. We therefore agree with Judge Lasker's conclusion that the edited version broadcast by ABC impaired the integrity of appellants' work and represented to the public as the product of appellants what was actually a mere caricature of their talents. We believe that a valid cause of action for such distortion exists and that therefore a preliminary injunction may issue to prevent repetition of the broadcast prior to final determination of the issues.

Id., 538 F.2d at 24–25, 192 U.S.P.Q. at 9.

Which moral right did the *Gilliam* court vindicate—the right of attribution or the right of integrity? For purposes of the section 43(a) claim, is there any way that ABC might have shown the edited programs and avoided liability? See *id.*, 538 F.2d at 26–27, 192 U.S.P.Q. at 11 (Judge Gurfein concurring).

For further discussion of the role of section 43(a) in the vindication of moral rights, see Verbit, *Moral Rights and Section 43(a) of the Lanham Act: Oasis or Illusion?* 78 TRADEMARK REP. 579 (1988); Pinover, *The Rights of Authors, Artists and Performers Under Section 43(a) of the Lanham Act*, 83 TRADEMARK REP. 38 (1993).

IV. COMMERCIAL DISPARAGEMENT

U.S. HEALTHCARE, INC. v. BLUE CROSS OF GREATER PHILADELPHIA

United States Court of Appeals for the Third Circuit, 1990.
898 F.2d 914, 14 U.S.P.Q.2d 1257, *cert. denied*
498 U.S. 816, 111 S.Ct. 58, 112 L.Ed.2d 33 (1990).

SCIRICA, CIRCUIT JUDGE.

* * *

I. FACTS AND PROCEDURAL HISTORY

These cross appeals arise from a comparative advertising war between giants of the health care industry in the Delaware Valley—U.S. Healthcare on the one side and Blue Cross/Blue Shield on the other. The thrust of these claims is that each side asserts the other's advertising misrepresented both parties' products.

[Blue Cross/Blue Shield offers "traditional" medical insurance coverage, in which the subscriber has freedom in choosing hospitals and health care providers. U.S. Healthcare is a health maintenance organization, generically known as an "HMO." Generally, HMO subscribers choose a primary health care provider from the HMO network, who coordinates their health care services and determines when hospital admission or treatment from a specialist is required. Usually, subscribers are not covered for services obtained without this permission or from providers outside this network. Blue Cross/Blue Shield lost some of its market share to U.S. Healthcare and other HMOs, and in an attempt to regain it, introduced a new product that it called "Personal Choice," known generically as a preferred provider organization or "PPO." PPO insurance provides subscribers with a network of health care providers and hospitals, and generally covers subscribers only for services obtained from the network providers and administered at the network hospitals. Subscribers must obtain permission to receive treatment from providers outside the network, and in such instances receive at most only partial coverage.]

[In July 1986, Blue Cross/Blue Shield launched a comparative advertising campaign calculated to introduce its Personal Choice product and to promote its products at the expense of HMO products. The campaign ran for about six months at a cost of approximately $2.175 million. Blue Cross/Blue Shield's eight print advertisements compared the features of

HMO and Personal Choice. Seven of the eight represented that with HMO, the subscriber selects a "primary care physician" who, in turn, must give permission before HMO will provide coverage for examination by a specialist. The eighth print advertisement simply stated that with Personal Choice, the subscriber may be examined by a specialist whenever he chooses, without "permission." After describing HMO's referral procedure, however, three of the eight print advertisements—as well as a brochure—said the following:

> You should also know that through a series of financial incentives, HMO encourages this doctor to handle as many patients as possible without referring to a specialist. When an HMO doctor does make a specialist referral, it could take money directly out of his pocket. Make too many referrals, and he could find himself in trouble with HMO.

One of the print advertisements and the brochure also featured a senior citizen under the banner heading "Your money or your life," juxtaposed with Blue Cross/Blue Shield's description of "The high cost of HMO Medicare."]

[Of the seven television advertisements run by Blue Cross/Blue Shield, four mentioned HMO only in the closing slogan common to all seven of the ads: "Personal Choice. Better than HMO. So good, it's Blue Cross and Blue Shield." The fifth featured an indignant "everyman," who simply stated "I resent having to ask my HMO doctor for permission to see a specialist," after which a spokesperson extolled the benefits of Personal Choice without reference to HMO until, again, the closing slogan. The sixth featured a cab driver who said, "I don't like those HMO health plans. You get one doctor, no choice of hospitals," after which a shopper told him about the virtues of Personal Choice—again, without reference to HMO until the closing slogan. The seventh television advertisement featured a grief-stricken woman who said, "The hospital my HMO sent me to just wasn't enough. It's my fault." The implication of the advertisement was that some tragedy had befallen the woman because of her choice of health care.]

[The three radio advertisements of Blue Cross/Blue Shield compared the features of HMO and Personal Choice. All represented that HMO limits choice of hospitals and physicians and requires plan permission to see a specialist. They also stated that Personal Choice provides unlimited choice of network hospitals and physicians and affords unrestricted access to specialists.]

[U.S. Healthcare responded to Blue Cross/Blue Shield's promotional campaign by launching its own advertising campaign at the cost of $1.255 million. Some of U.S. Healthcare's advertisements merely highlighted the positive characteristics of its own product, but others were "anti-Blue Cross." One print advertisement simply showed a comparative list of the features available under HMO and Personal Choice, with a banner heading that read "It's your choice." Two others explained that under Personal Choice, the number of hospitals available to the subscriber was limited and, moreover, that many Personal Choice doctors did not have admitting privileges at even those few. One of these advertisements ran under a banner heading of "When it Comes to Being Admitted to a Hospital, There's Something Personal Choice May Not Be Willing to Admit;" the other ran under a banner heading of "If You Really Look Into 'Personal Choice,' You Might Have a Better Name For It."]

[One television advertisement showed a person flipping through the Hospitals and Physicians Directory of Personal Choice, pointing out the "gray area" of physicians without admitting privileges—essentially making the same point as the two print advertisements. In another, solemn music played as the narrator listed the shortcomings of Personal Choice and the camera panned from a Personal Choice brochure resting on the pillow of a hospital bed to distraught family members standing at bedside. The advertisement closed with a pair of hands pulling a sheet over the Personal Choice brochure.]

[In the present suit, U.S. Healthcare asserted, among other things, a § 43(a) Lanham Act claim, commercial disparagement and defamation against Blue Cross/Blue Shield. Blue Cross/Blue Shield counterclaimed on the same theories of liability. The jury deadlocked on U.S. Healthcare's claims, and returned a verdict against Blue Cross/Blue Shield on its counterclaims. Later, Blue Cross/Blue Shield filed a motion under Fed.R.Civ.P. 50(b) requesting the court to direct entry of judgment in its favor with regard to U.S. Healthcare's claims, on the grounds that the advertisements were entitled to heightened constitutional protection under the first amendment, and that U.S. Healthcare had not met the applicable standard of proof set forth in *New York Times Co. v. Sullivan*, 376 U.S. 254, 84 S.Ct. 710, 11 L.Ed.2d 686 (1964). The district court granted the motion. The district court held that because the objects of the advertisements were "public figures," and because the matters in the advertisements were "community health issues of public concern," heightened constitutional protections attached to the advertising speech. In order to prevail on their respective claims of Lanham Act violation, commercial disparagement and defamation, both parties must prove by clear and convincing evidence: (1) that the other side published the advertisements with knowledge or with reckless disregard of their falsity, and (2) that the advertisements were false. The court concluded that neither side had made the necessary showing.]

[The court of appeals reversed, for the reasons set forth below.]

II. THE ACTIONABLE CLAIMS AND COUNTERCLAIMS UNDER APPLICABLE SUBSTANTIVE FEDERAL AND STATE LAW

We note initially that federal law governs the substantive issues of the parties' Lanham Act claims, while Pennsylvania law governs the commercial disparagement [and] defamation * * * claims. Although the district court granted the Rule 50(b) motions on constitutional grounds, we must first determine whether the statements are actionable under the substantive law governing the case before addressing whether the

First Amendment prohibits the imposition of liability, since a determination of the former may obviate the need to examine the latter. * * *

1. Section 43(a) of the Lanham Act.

Section 43(a) of the Lanham Act, 15 U.S.C. § 1125(a) (1988), which was recently amended, creates a cause of action for any false description or representation of a product. This proscription extends to misleading descriptions or representations. "While it has been stated that a failure to disclose facts is not actionable under § 43(a), it is equally true that a statement is actionable under § 43(a) if it is affirmatively misleading, partially incorrect, or untrue as a result of failure to disclose a material fact." 2 J. McCarthy, *Trademarks and Unfair Competition* § 27:7B (2d ed. 1984).

The pre-amendment version, which controlled when the district court considered the matter, applied only to statements made by a defendant about its own products, not to statements about the plaintiff's products. As amended, however, § 43(a) encompasses statements made by a defendant about "his or her *or another person's* " products. 15 U.S.C. 1125(a) (emphasis added).[9]

When analyzing a challenged advertisement, the court first determines what message is conveyed. Sometimes this determination may be made from the advertisement on its face. Nonetheless, "[c]ontext can often be important in discerning the message conveyed." *Plough, Inc. v. Johnson & Johnson Baby Prods. Co.*, 532 F.Supp. 714, 717 (D.Del.1982).

After determining the message conveyed, the court must decide whether it is false or misleading. Mere puffing, advertising " 'that is not deceptive for no one would rely on its exaggerated claims,' " is not actionable under § 43(a). *Toro Co. v. Textron, Inc.*, 499 F.Supp. 241, 253 n. 23 (D.Del.1980) (quoting 1 R. Callmann, *Unfair Competition, Trademarks and Monopolies* § 19.2(b)(2) (3d ed. 1967 & 1979 Supp.)). If the advertisement is literally true, the plaintiff "must persuade the court that the persons 'to whom the advertisement is addressed' would find that the message received left a false impression about the product." *Id.* at 251. Finally, establishing lack of substantiation of defendant's claim is insufficient without also establishing falsity or deception.

The plaintiff must also show that defendant's misrepresentation is " 'material, in that it is likely to influence the purchasing decision.' " *Id.* at 251. However, "there is no requirement that the falsification

9. This court must "apply the law in effect at the time it renders its decision, unless doing so would result in manifest injustice or there is statutory direction or legislative history to the contrary." *Bradley v. School Bd. of Richmond*, 416 U.S. 696, 711, 94 S.Ct. 2006, 2016, 40 L.Ed.2d 476 (1974). Although there is no statutory direction, the legislative history, which states that the amendment is intended "to make clear that misrepresentations about another's products are as actionable as misrepresentations about one's own," would appear to support retroactive application of the new provision. S.Rep. No. 515, 100th Cong., 2d Sess. 40, *reprinted in* 1988 U.S.Code Cong. & Admin.News 5577, 5603. Having considered the parties, the nature of their rights and the impact on those rights of this change in law, we perceive no threat of manifest injustice and shall apply the provision as it now is written.

occur wilfully and with intent to deceive." *Parkway Baking Co. v. Freihofer Baking Co.*, 255 F.2d 641, 648 (3d Cir.1958).

Next, § 43(a) requires that the defendant use the false or misleading description or representation "in commerce." 15 U.S.C. § 1125(a). The commerce requirement has been broadly interpreted.

Finally, § 43(a) provides a remedy to one who "is or is likely to be damaged by [the false or misleading description or representation]." 15 U.S.C. § 1125(a). To recover damages, a plaintiff must show that the "falsification [or misrepresentation] actually deceives a portion of the buying public." *Parkway Baking*, 255 F.2d at 648. "This does not place upon the plaintiff a burden of proving detailed individualization of loss of sales. Such proof goes to quantum of damages and not to the very right to recover." *Parkway Baking*, 255 F.2d at 648. * * *

3. Commercial Disparagement.

A commercially disparaging statement—in contrast to a defamatory statement—is one "which is intended by its publisher to be understood or which is reasonably understood to cast doubt upon the existence or extent of another's property in land, chattels or intangible things, or upon their quality, ... if the matter is so understood by its recipient." *Menefee v. Columbia Broadcasting Sys., Inc.*, 458 Pa. 46, 54, 329 A.2d 216 (1974) (quoting Restatement of Torts § 629 (1938)). In order to maintain an action for disparagement, the plaintiff must prove 1) that the disparaging statement of fact is untrue or that the disparaging statement of opinion is incorrect; 2) that no privilege attaches to the statement; and 3) that the plaintiff suffered a direct pecuniary loss as the result of the disparagement.

The distinction between actions for defamation and disparagement turns on the harm towards which each is directed. An action for commercial disparagement is meant to compensate a vendor for pecuniary loss suffered because statements attacking the quality of his goods have reduced their marketability, while defamation is meant to protect an entity's interest in character and reputation. In *Menefee*, the Pennsylvania Supreme Court made the following observation:

> One of the most important purposes for which liability for the publication of matter derogatory to another's personal reputation is imposed is to enable the person defamed to force his accuser into open court so that the accusation, if untrue, may be branded as false by the verdict of a jury. The action for disparagement has no such purpose and cannot be used merely to vindicate one's title to or the quality of one's possessions....

Id. (quoting Restatement of Torts introductory note to Chapter 28).

Given the similar elements of the two torts, deciding which cause of action lies in a given situation can be difficult. The Court of Appeals for the Eighth Circuit gave the following time-honored explanation of when impugnation of the quality of goods crosses the line from disparagement of products to defamation of vendors:

> [W]here the publication on its face is directed against the goods or product of a corporate vendor or manufacturer, it will not be held libelous per se as to the corporation, unless by fair construction and without the aid of extrinsic evidence it imputes to the corporation fraud, deceit, dishonesty, or reprehensible conduct in its business in relation to said goods or product.

National Ref. Co. v. Benzo Gas Motor Fuel Co., 20 F.2d 763, 771 (8th Cir.), *cert. denied*, 275 U.S. 570, 48 S.Ct. 157, 72 L.Ed. 431 (1927).

An examination of state court decisions indicates that Pennsylvania law tracks the National Refining distinction. *See, e.g.*, * * * *Will v. Press Publishing Co.*, 309 Pa. 539, 544, 164 A. 621 (1932) (defamation action lay for accusation that plaintiff did not pay accounts of his business, as words implied dishonesty); *Pfeifly v. Henry*, 269 Pa. 533, 535, 112 A. 768 (1921) (defamation action lay for statement that plaintiff miller dishonestly weighed flour he sold) * * *.

B. The Actionable Construction of the Advertisements

From the record before us, both U.S. Healthcare and Blue Cross/Blue Shield have taken a broad approach to this litigation, each complaining about all of the advertisements in the other's comparative campaign. Not all of the advertisements are actionable under all of the theories alleged. Therefore, we make the following rulings on which advertisements could be found actionable by a jury under the standards we have outlined.

First, we consider as a group three of Blue Cross/Blue Shield's television advertisements, which appear to be mere identification pieces containing no substantive information. They feature actors stating either their trust in Blue Cross/Blue Shield, or their preference for Personal Choice over HMO. Additionally, they all feature the slogan "Better than HMO. So good, it's Blue Cross and Blue Shield." This strikes us as the most innocuous kind of "puffing," common to advertising and presenting no danger of misleading the consuming public. Consequently, we find that no cause of action lies with regard to these three advertisements.

[In its second ruling, the court notes that those ads describing the advertiser's own services and making no reference to the other party's could only be actionable under the "false advertising" prong of Lanham Act section 43(a).]

Third, we consider as a group the bulk of the advertisements, which either compare the competing health plans on one or more points, or simply criticize the competitor's health plan without detailed exposition of the advertiser's own competing plan. Because they may contain misrepresentations beyond puffing, a cause of action may lie under the Lanham Act, even for those advertisements that focus exclusively on the competitor's health plan. In addition, as these advertisements all make representations about the competitor's product, a cause of action may lie for commercial disparagement with respect to any of them. None of these, however, could be said to impute to the competitor by fair construction any "fraud, deceit, dishonesty, or reprehensible conduct." *National Refining Co.*, 20 F.2d at 771. Consequently, no cause of action for defamation will lie with regard to these. * * *

We believe the remaining advertisements are capable of defamatory meaning. These include, first, the Blue Cross/Blue Shield advertisements that suggest HMO primary care physicians have a financial interest in not referring patients to specialists and, indeed, that HMO makes reprisals against those primary care physicians who make too many referrals. These advertisements imply that U.S. Healthcare, the people who run it, and the doctors who are employed by it, all place personal profit above adequate health care. Such an implication goes beyond the comparative quality of HMO health care to suggest reprehensible conduct by U.S. Healthcare and its employees in the conduct of their business.

Also capable of defamatory meaning is Blue Cross/Blue Shield's "Distraught Woman" advertisement. Her statement that "The hospital my HMO sent me to just wasn't enough," matched with her grief-stricken demeanor, suggests she has suffered some tragedy because of HMO's substandard care. The suggestion that U.S. Healthcare chose to send her to a hospital that could not adequately treat her problem goes beyond the product itself to impute reprehensible conduct to the corporation. Indeed, the scare tactic is the point of the commercial.

Finally, we find U.S. Healthcare's "Critical Condition" television commercial to be capable of a defamatory construction as well. As a dirge plays, the narrator lists the shortcomings of Personal Choice while the camera pans from a Personal Choice brochure resting on the pillow of a hospital bed to distraught family members standing around the bed. At the end of the advertisement, a pair of hands pulls a sheet over the Personal Choice brochure. We do not believe the depiction of a distressing death scene in a health insurance commercial is an uncalculated association. Again, we believe a scare tactic was the intent and, more to the point, a jury could find the commercial suggests Blue Cross/Blue Shield knowingly provides health care so substandard as to be dangerous.

As to this final group of advertisements, no action for commercial disparagement will lie because the statements are directed at the vendor, not his goods. Nonetheless, Lanham Act claims may lie. * * *

III. First Amendment Principles and the Standard of Proof in Claims Arising From a Comparative Advertising Campaign

Having determined that some of the advertisements may be actionable under federal and state law, we must now consider whether the First Amendment affects the standard of proof. As we have already noted, the district court held that under *New York Times Co. v. Sullivan et seq.* each party must prove as to each claim, by clear and convincing evidence, that the other party acted with actual malice—that is, with knowledge that the advertisement was false or with reckless disregard of whether it was false or not. In so holding, the court rejected U.S. Healthcare's argument that the advertisements were commercial speech and thereby entitled to less constitutional protection. The district court viewed the comparative advertising campaign giving rise to this litigation as a "dispute ... about how best to deal with spiraling medical costs," and concluded that, "[t]o characterize the advertisements in this case as mere commercial speech ignores the fact that, at their core, they are instruments in a debate between two providers of public health care 'intimately involved in the resolution of important public questions.' "

In arguing that the district court erred in applying heightened evidentiary standards to any of its claims, U.S. Healthcare maintains that the *New York Times* standard is "not mandated where, as here, false commercial speech is at issue." * * *

B. Rules and Conceptual Framework

Most speech is protected by the First Amendment. "Under the First Amendment there is no such thing as a false idea. However pernicious an opinion may seem, we depend for its correction not on the conscience of judges and juries but on the competition of other ideas." *Gertz [v. Robert Welch, Inc.*], 418 U.S. [323,] 339–40, 94 S.Ct. [2997,] 3006–[70, 41 L.Ed.2d 789] (1974). Even false statements of fact are insulated from liability in some situations. * * *

Although speech is generally protected, the Supreme Court has "long recognized that not all speech is of equal First Amendment importance. It is speech on 'matters of public concern' that is 'at the heart of the First Amendment's protection.' " *Dun & Bradstreet*, 472 U.S. at 758–59, 105 S.Ct. at 2944–45. Such speech * * * requires heightened constitutional protection in the defamation context. * * *

[The court reviews the *New York Times* and related rules regarding the standard of proof for "public" and "private" plaintiffs suing media defendants for defamation.]

In arriving at these rules, the [Supreme] Court articulated the conceptual framework underlying its decisions. *New York Times*, the Court explained, represents an accommodation between the state interest in protecting the reputations of individuals and the First Amendment interest in safeguarding freedom of speech. * * *

In evaluating these competing interests, the Court has determined that the state has only a "limited" interest in compensating public persons for injury to reputation by defamatory statements, but has a "strong and legitimate" interest in compensating private persons for the same injury. The Court has provided a two-fold explanation for the discrepancy in the extent of the state interests. First, because public officials and public figures enjoy "greater access to the channels of effective communication and hence have a more realistic opportunity to counteract false statements than private individuals," the states have a greater interest in protecting private persons whose relative lack of "self-help" remedies render them "more vulnerable to injury." *Gertz*, at 344, 94 S.Ct. at 3009. Second, the state has a stronger interest in protecting the reputations of private individuals because, unlike public persons, they have not voluntarily placed themselves in the public eye.

On the other side of the coin, the "type of speech involved" also affects the way in which the "balance is struck," by varying the weight of the First Amendment interest. "[S]peech on 'matters of public concern' ... is 'at the heart of the First Amendment's protection.'" *Dun & Bradstreet*, 472 U.S. at 758–59, 105 S.Ct. at 2944–45. The Court has determined that "speech of private concern," such as a credit report for business, is of less First Amendment importance, in the same way that utterances labeled "commercial speech" are "less central to the interests of the First Amendment," *id.* at 757–59, 105 S.Ct. at 2944–45.

C. Application of the Rules and Conceptual Framework

At the outset, we note that it is of no consequence that the defendants (and counterclaim defendants) here are not members of the broadcast and print media. Although the Supreme Court has not finally settled whether "non-media" defendants should receive protections identical to those afforded "media" defendants, this court has so far declined to limit the protections of the *New York Times* standard to media defendants only * * *.

In addition, we do not limit our consideration of the applicability of the *New York Times* standard to the parties' claims for defamation alone. The Supreme Court has already applied a similar analysis to other torts, such as intentional infliction of emotional distress. * * *

We next turn to assessing the relative weight of the First Amendment interests in this case. * * * Our appraisal of these interests depends on whether the speech at issue can properly be characterized as commercial speech. "There is no longer any room to doubt that what has come to be known as 'commercial speech' is entitled to the protection of the First Amendment, albeit to protection somewhat less extensive than that afforded 'noncommercial speech.'" *Zauderer v. Office of Disciplinary Counsel*, 471 U.S. 626, 637, 105 S.Ct. 2265, 2274, 85 L.Ed.2d 652 (1985). If the speech here is commercial speech, then it likely does not mandate heightened constitutional protection.[21]

* * *

Before proceeding further, we must consider what qualifies as "commercial speech." Since deciding *New York Times*, the Supreme Court has provided substantial guidance. Commercial speech may be broadly defined as expression related to the economic interests of the speaker and its audience, generally in the form of a commercial advertisement for the sale of goods and services. The Supreme Court has cited three factors to consider in deciding whether speech is commercial: (1) is the speech an advertisement; (2) does the speech refer to a specific product

21. Although we can "contemplate public controversies arising from commercial conduct" that might necessitate a different result, *Bruno & Stillman, Inc. v. Globe Newspaper Co.*, 633 F.2d 583, 590–91 (1st Cir.1980), we do not find that here.

or service; and (3) does the speaker have an economic motivation for the speech. *Bolger v. Youngs Drug Prods. Corp.*, 463 U.S. 60, 66–67, 103 S.Ct. 2875, 2879–80, 77 L.Ed.2d 469 (1983). An affirmative answer to all three questions provides "strong support" for the conclusion that the speech is commercial. Stated succinctly, the "commercial speech doctrine rests heavily on 'the common sense distinction between speech proposing a commercial transaction . . . and other varieties of speech.' " *Zauderer v. Office of Disciplinary Counsel*, 471 U.S. 626, 637, 105 S.Ct. 2265, 2274, 85 L.Ed.2d 652 (1985) (quoting *Ohralik v. Ohio State Bar Ass'n*, 436 U.S. 447, 455–56, 98 S.Ct. 1912, 1918–19, 56 L.Ed.2d 444 (1978)). The Court has elaborated on the reasons why commercial speech receives less than heightened protection. First, commercial speech generally makes a different contribution to the exposition of ideas.[24] * * *

Second, commercial speech tends to be more durable than other types of speech. As the commercial speaker has an economic self-interest in dissemination, there is little likelihood of the speech being chilled by proper regulation. This attribute, the Court concluded, "may make it less necessary to tolerate inaccurate statements for fear of silencing the speaker." *Virginia Pharmacy Bd.*, 425 U.S. at 772 n. 24, 96 S.Ct. at 1381 n. 24 * * *.

Third, commercial speakers have extensive knowledge of both their market and their own products. Consequently, they are uniquely situated to evaluate the truthfulness of their speech. * * *.

The fourth reason is extrinsic. "To require a parity of constitutional protection for commercial and noncommercial speech alike could invite dilution, simply by a leveling process, of the force of the [First] Amendment's guarantee with respect to the latter kind of speech." *Ohralik*, 436 U.S. at 456, 98 S.Ct. at 1918.

In this case, affirmative answers to all three prongs of the *Bolger* test provide "strong support" for our conclusion that the statements here are commercial in nature. First, there is no question that they are advertisements; they were disseminated as part of an expensive, professionally run promotional campaign. Second, the speech specifically refers to a product; it touts the relative merits of Personal Choice (or U.S. Healthcare's HMO) over competing products. Third, the desire for revenue motivated the speech; the record contains abundant evidence that Blue Cross/Blue Shield launched the promotional campaign in order to recoup its share of the health insurance market. * * * Similarly, protection of its new market share motivated U.S. Healthcare's speech. In short, "common sense" informs us that the statements here propose a commercial transaction, and thus differ from other types of speech.

24. At the same time, we recognize that commercial speech "is indispensable to the proper allocation of resources in a free enterprise system [and therefore] to the formation of intelligent opinions as to how that system ought to be regulated or altered." *Virginia Pharmacy Bd.*, 425 U.S. at 765, 96 S.Ct. at 1827. Moreover, as we have noted, we can envision advertising that would address public issues in such a way as to necessitate heightened protection.

Even more importantly, we find it significant that the advertisements have all of the characteristics that the Supreme Court has identified in the commercial speech cases as making speech durable, not susceptible to "chill." Consequently, they do not require the heightened protection we extend to our most valuable forms of speech. Because the thrust of all of the advertisements is to convince the consuming public to bring its business to one of these health care giants rather than the other, there is no doubt that the advertisements were motivated by economic self-interest. Furthermore, given the size of the health care market in the Delaware Valley—Blue Shield virtually shouts about the hundreds of millions of dollars at stake—we believe it would have to be a cold day before these corporations would be chilled from speaking about the comparative merits of their products. * * *

In addition, these are advertisements for products and services in markets in which U.S. Healthcare and Blue Cross/Blue Shield deal—and, presumably, know more about than anyone else. The facts upon which the advertisements are based—comparative price, procedures, and services offered—are readily objectifiable. These advertisements were precisely calculated, developed over time and published only when the corporate speakers were ready. Consequently, the advertisements were unusually verifiable.

Finally, while the speech here does discuss costs and consequences of competing health insurance and health care delivery programs, some of the advertisements capable of defamatory meaning here add little information and even fewer ideas to the marketplace of health care thought. The expression in these advertisements "differs markedly from ideological expression because it is confined to the promotion of specific . . . services." *Virginia Pharmacy Bd.*, 425 U.S. at 780, 96 S.Ct. at 1835. * * * And to the extent that the advertisements are false statements of fact, of course, the speech has no constitutional value at all.

It is important to note that we do not have a situation in which a corporation addresses an issue of public concern involving a competitor, but does so with speech that is neither commercial nor chill resistant. We simply recognize here, as the Court has in a similar context, that "[a] company has the full panoply of protections available to its direct comments on public issues, so there is no reason for providing similar protection when such statements are made in the context of commercial transactions." *Bolger*, 463 U.S. at 68, 103 S.Ct. at 2881.

* * *

Therefore, while the speech here is protected by the First Amendment, we hold that the First Amendment requires no higher standard of liability than that mandated by the substantive law for each claim. The heightened protection of the actual malice standard is not "necessary to give adequate 'breathing space' to the freedoms protected by the First Amendment." *Hustler Magazine, Inc. v. Falwell*, 485 U.S. 46, 56, 108 S.Ct. 876, 882, 99 L.Ed.2d 41 (1988).

Having concluded that the speech here is commercial speech that does not warrant heightened constitutional protection, we nonetheless proceed to consideration of the nature and weight of the state's interest in compensating individuals for injuries resulting from each of the distinct torts alleged. We have previously discussed the state and federal interests implicated. As we shall see in this case, however, traditional defamation analysis is not well suited to strike the proper balance between the state and federal interests and First Amendment values in the context of commercial speech.

In weighing the state interest, we must look to the status of the claimants. As we have noted, the Court has determined that the state has only a "limited" interest in compensating public persons for injury to reputation but has a "strong and legitimate" interest in compensating private persons for the same injury. Contending that the actual malice standard applies because a public figure is implicated, Blue Cross/Blue Shield argues that the following factors render U.S. Healthcare a "public figure": it has voluntarily exposed itself to public comment on the issues involved in this dispute; it is a contributor to the ongoing debate concerning health care insurance; it is among the nation's largest providers of HMO-type insurance coverage; it markets its products extensively and aggressively, and has a substantial annual advertising budget; and it frequently and consistently asserts the advantages of its method of health care financing and delivery, and has done so in advertisements, press releases, professional journals, newspapers, magazines and speeches before public assemblies. These activities, Blue Cross/Blue Shield submits, "constitute a voluntary effort to influence the consuming public." Similar statements can be made regarding Blue Cross/Blue Shield.

Gertz identified three classes of public figures: those who achieve such stature or notoriety that they are considered public figures in all contexts; those who become public figures involuntarily, but these are "exceedingly rare"; and those who are deemed public figures only within the context of a particular public dispute. *Id.* at 345, 94 S.Ct. at 3009. The Court defined the last group, limited purpose public figures, as individuals who voluntarily "thrust themselves to the forefront of particular public controversies in order to influence the resolution of the issues involved." *Id.*

[The court determines that the relevant question in this case is whether the parties are limited purpose public figures.]

Under traditional defamation analysis, the parties' considerable access to the media and their voluntary entry into a controversy are strong indicia that they are limited purpose public figures. Indeed, inflexible application of these factors would warrant a finding of public figure status and facilitate a finding of heightened constitutional protection. Nonetheless, we hold that these corporations are not public figures for the limited purpose of commenting on health care in this case.

As noted, *Gertz* defines the limited purpose public figure as one who has "thrust [himself] to the forefront of particular public controversies in order to influence the resolution of the issues involved." 418 U.S. at 345, 94 S.Ct. at 3009. Although some of the advertisements touch on matters of public concern, their central thrust is commercial. Thus, the parties have acted primarily to generate revenue by influencing customers, not to resolve "the issues involved."

While discerning motivations of the speaker is often difficult, we have a more fundamental reason for declining to find limited purpose public figure status in this case. The express analysis in *Gertz* is not helpful in the context of a comparative advertising war. Most products can be linked to a public issue. And most advertisers—including both claimants here—seek out the media. Thus, it will always be true that such advertisers have voluntarily placed themselves in the public eye. It will be equally true that such advertisers have access to the media. Therefore, under the *Gertz* rationale, speech of public concern that implicates corporate advertisers—i.e., typical comparative advertising—will always be insulated behind the actual malice standard. We believe a corporation must do more than the claimants have done here to become a limited purpose public figure under *Gertz*.

In summary, we conclude that the speech at issue does not receive heightened protection under the First Amendment. Because this speech is chill-resistant, the *New York Times* standard is not, as we have noted, "necessary to give adequate 'breathing space' to the freedoms protected by the First Amendment." *Hustler Magazine, Inc. v. Falwell*, 485 U.S. 46, 56, 108 S.Ct. 876, 882, 99 L.Ed.2d 41 (1988). Therefore, the standard of proof needed to establish the substantive claims is that applicable under federal and state law.

For these reasons, we hold that the district court erred in applying the *New York Times* standard to the claims in this case and in directing entry of judgment under Fed.R.Civ.P. 50(b). Accordingly, we will reverse the judgment of the district court and remand for proceedings consistent with this opinion. * * *

Notes and Questions

1. *The common-law commercial disparagement claim.* The common-law cause of action for commercial disparagement has many alternative names, including product disparagement, trade libel, slander of title, and injurious falsehood. As the *U.S. Healthcare* opinion suggests, the cause of action is closely related to the law of libel and slander, though the causes of action are directed to different interests: libel and slander protect the plaintiff's personal interest in reputation, while commercial disparagement protects commercial, economic interests.

The greatest hurdle that common-law commercial disparagement plaintiffs must overcome is the "special damages" requirement. In order to satisfy the special damages requirement, the commercial disparagement plaintiff must plead and prove actual, specific economic harm. Some courts have held that proof of special damages requires detailed evidence of individual transactions and specific customers lost as a result of the disparaging publication. See, e.g., Testing Systems, Inc. v. Magnaflux Corp., 251 F.Supp. 286, 290, 149 U.S.P.Q. 129, 132 (E.D.Pa.1966). Other courts have been somewhat more liberal. See, e.g., Trenton Mutual Life & Fire Ins. Co. v. Perrine, 23 N.J.L. 402 (Sup. Ct. 1852) (court accepts evidence of a general loss of business when the plaintiff demonstrates that it is impossible to prove specific losses because of the nature of his business). Some jurisdictions have imposed the pleading and proof of special damages as a prerequisite both for a damages award and for injunctive relief, see R. CALLMANN, THE LAW OF UNFAIR COMPETITION, TRADEMARKS AND MONOPOLIES § 11.33 (L. Altman 4th ed. 1981 & Supp.), while others are more lenient with respect to suits for injunctions. See, e.g., Systems Operations, Inc. v. Scientific Games Development Corp., 414 F.Supp. 750, 193 U.S.P.Q. 222 (D.N.J.1976), *reversed on other grounds* 555 F.2d 1131 (3d Cir.1977). The special damages requirement might have been met more readily long ago, when businesses and the communities they served were small and the plaintiff was likely to know his customers personally. In today's large, complex and impersonal marketplace, a strict special damages requirement may prove impossible to satisfy. See Testing Systems, Inc., *supra*. See generally, Hayden, *A Goodly Apple Rotten at the Heart: Commercial Disparagement in Comparative Advertising as Common–Law Tortious Unfair Competition*, 76 IOWA L. REV. 67, 97–99 (1990).

The precise elements of the commercial disparagement cause of action may differ from one jurisdiction to the next. The Court of Appeals for the Third Circuit, in *U.S. Healthcare,* finds that under Pennsylvania law, the commercial disparagement plaintiff must prove three elements:

> 1) that the disparaging statement of fact is untrue or that the disparaging statement of opinion is incorrect; 2) that no privilege attaches to the statement; and 3) that the plaintiff suffered a direct pecuniary loss as the result of the disparagement.

Should a defendant be held liable for stating an "incorrect" *opinion* about the plaintiff's goods or services? How does one determine whether a statement is one of fact or one of opinion? The court finds that some of Blue Cross/Blue Shield's alleged disparaging statements were mere "puffery," and thus not actionable. What is "puffing," and why should it not support a disparagement claim?

Why must a disparaging statement be false or incorrect? Why not have a cause of action for truthful disparagement? For example, suppose that the defendant told consumers that the plaintiff's product had been designed by an ax murderer. While true, the fact is totally irrelevant to the quality of the product and is highly prejudicial. Should the law condone such competitive behavior? See R. CALLMANN, *supra*, at §§ 11.04, 11.14.

Consider the Restatement (Second) of Torts definition of the disparagement cause of action, which it calls "injurious falsehood:"

> One who publishes a false statement harmful to the interests of another is subject to liability for pecuniary loss resulting to the other if

(a) he intends for publication of the statement to result in harm to interests of the other having a pecuniary value, or either recognizes or should recognize that it is likely to do so, and

(b) he knows that the statement is false or acts in reckless disregard of its truth of falsity.

RESTATEMENT (SECOND) OF TORTS § 623A (1976).[4] Note that the Restatement adds intent and knowledge requirements that had not been included in the First Restatement's treatment of the subject. See RESTATEMENT OF TORTS §§ 624–629 (1938). These requirements were added partly due to concerns that strict liability or liability based on negligence might prove unconstitutional under the first amendment, see *id.*, comment c, and partly due to concerns that the earlier approach (deleting requirements of intent and knowledge) had been predicated on a false analogy to cases of personal defamation. See Prosser, *Injurious Falsehood: The Basis of Liability*, 59 COLUM. L. REV. 425 (1959). In light of the Third Circuit's opinion in *U.S. Healthcare*, were the constitutional concerns necessary?

In 1988, Congress amended Lanham Act section 43(a) to encompass false descriptions and representations of fact concerning "another person's goods, services, or commercial activities." Courts are likely to construe the new federal cause of action for commercial disparagement to dispense with detailed proof of special damages and intent requirements imposed at state law, as they did in the case of false advertising claims.

The Uniform Deceptive Trade Practices Act has also undertaken to update the common law of commercial disparagement. Like section 43(a), section 2(a)(8) of the Uniform Act rests liability on *false or misleading statements of fact* that disparage the goods, services or business of another. Section 3(a) provides: "A person likely to be damaged by a deceptive trade practice of another may be granted an injunction against it under the principles of equity and on terms that the court considers reasonable. Proof of monetary damage, loss of profits, or intent to deceive is not required." For further discussion of the Uniform Act, see Note, *Disparagement Under the Uniform Deceptive Trade Practices Act*, 51 IOWA L. REV. 1066 (1966).

2. *Acts constituting disparagement.* Disparaging statements may be communicated directly or indirectly, and through a wide variety of conduct. The key to liability is a finding that the defendant's words or conduct conveyed a disparaging message to third persons. How would you evaluate the following conduct?

(a) The defendant retailer acquires from third parties irregular fabrics ("seconds") produced by the plaintiff in a prior season. It sells them as though they were the plaintiff's current, best quality fabrics. Defendant advertises that the goods are "fine quality * * * the world's best," and claims that it "shopped for the identical fabrics in seven of the principal shops in Greater New York" and found the current price for plaintiff's

4.

fabrics at those shops to be much higher than its own. See Cheney Bros. v. Gimbel Bros., 280 Fed. 746 (S.D.N.Y.1922).

(b) Defendant's radio program represents that it plays the nine or ten most popular songs of the week in the relative order of their popularity, based upon the results of a nationwide survey. The plaintiff, a music publisher, alleges that the defendant's weekly selections are not made in good faith as the result of a an accurate survey, and that the defendants have omitted plaintiff's songs which were, in fact, among the most popular, or have placed them in the wrong order of popularity. See Advance Music Corp. v. American Tobacco Co., 296 N.Y. 79, 70 N.E.2d 401, 71 U.S.P.Q. 279 (1946).

3. *First amendment issues.* The *New York Times* rule was a compromise which the Supreme Court reached upon balancing two competing interests in libel cases: the state's interest in protecting a plaintiff's reputation from defamatory statements versus the first amendment interest in free, unchilled speech. The Court found that when a private plaintiff was involved, the state interest weighed sufficiently to permit recovery for libel, as long as the state did not impose strict liability. When the plaintiff was a public figure, the state interest was less weighty, and the first amendment interest more weighty, so that the plaintiff would have to demonstrate actual malice before recovering. In disparagement cases, the interest to be weighed against first amendment interests is not personal reputation but a private economic interest, and the state's interest in maintaining a deceit-free marketplace. Should that make a difference? Is an economic interest more or less "weighty" than the interest in personal reputation?

Did the court in *U.S. Healthcare* find that the speech's status as commercial speech was enough to justify rejecting an actual malice standard of proof, or was it necessary for the court to find that the plaintiff was not a public figure, as well? Why did the court find that the parties were not public figures in this case? If a plaintiff has thrust itself to the forefront of a public controversy, should it matter for first amendment purposes whether its motivation was to influence the resolution of the issues involved or to promote its commercial interests? What are the implications of considering the plaintiff's motivations?

Did the *U.S. Healthcare* court find that the *Gertz* test for limited public figure status was satisfied in this case but irrelevant in the comparative advertising context, or that the *Gertz* test for limited public figure status was not satisfied? If the former, why was it irrelevant? If the court held that the *Gertz* test was unsatisfied, what more, besides voluntarily placement in the public eye and media access, did the *Gertz* test demand? How would you resolve the public figure status of the parties in this case? As a general matter, should the "public figure" status of corporations be judged under the same standards as the public figure status of an individual? See Fetzer, *The Corporate Defamation Plaintiff as First Amendment "Public Figure": Nailing the Jellyfish,* 68 IOWA L. REV. 35 (1982). For criticisms of the *U.S. Healthcare* decision, see Ulin, *First Amendment Crossroads—Extending Constitutional Defamation Protection to Commercial Speech: A Critique of* U.S.

Healthcare, Inc. v. Blue Cross of Greater Philadelphia *and Some Suggestions*, 39 U.C.L.A. L. REV. 633 (1992).

Suppose that Consumers Union, which tests products and reports the test results in its magazine, tested X Company's product and disparaged it in the resulting magazine article. Could X Company state a cause of action under section 43(a)?. Note that in the Trademark Law Revision Act of 1988, Congress amended section 43(a) not only expressly to include commercial disparagement claims but also to restrict all false advertising and disparagement claims to misrepresentations of fact in "commercial advertising or promotion." Pub. L. No. 100–667, 102 Stat. 3935 (1988). Representative Kastenmeier explained: "Because section 43(a) will now provide a kind of commercial defamation action, the reach of the section specifically extends only to false and misleading speech that is encompassed within the 'commercial speech' doctrine developed by the United States Supreme Court." 134 CONG. REC. H1042 (daily ed. Oct. 19, 1988) (statement of Rep. Kastenmeier). For a detailed discussion of when a defendant's representations constitute "commercial advertising or promotion" under section 43(a), see Gordon & Breach, Science Publishers, S.A. v. American Institute of Physics, 859 F.Supp. 1521, 32 U.S.P.Q.2d 1705 (S.D.N.Y.1994).

In the hypothetical situation above, assume that X Company brought a common-law commercial disparagement claim. Should the *New York Times* rule apply? In Bose Corp. v. Consumers Union of United States, Inc., 508 F.Supp. 1249 (D.Mass.1981), *reversed on other grounds* 692 F.2d 189 (1st Cir.1982), *affirmed* 466 U.S. 485, 104 S.Ct. 1949, 80 L.Ed.2d 502 (1984), the district court found it applicable, so that the plaintiff must prove actual malice on Consumers Union's part. In that case, Consumers Union had tested Bose's new design stereo speakers and reported to its readers that "individual instruments heard through the Bose system * * * tended to wander about the room." The court found the statement disparaging.

The court concluded that Bose was a public figure for a limited range of issues. Rejecting the suggestion that corporations should always be considered public figures for purposes of statements about their products or services, the court applied the fact-specific test set forth in Bruno & Stillman, Inc. v. Globe Newspaper Co., 633 F.2d 583 (1st Cir.1980), for determining whether the plaintiff had "thrust itself into the vortex of a public controversy and this rendered itself a public figure." *Id.*, 508 F.Supp. at 1272. First, the court considered whether a public controversy existed, and if so, whether it preceded the alleged disparagement. In this case, the court found that

> [b]y creating a new design for the Bose 901 and then emphasizing that unique design in its extensive promotional campaign, the plaintiff precipitated discussion about the relative merits of the Bose 901 and other loudspeaker systems. Because other loudspeaker manufacturers and reviewers for nationally published magazines were involved, the "controversy" was necessarily public rather than private. Thus, this case presents a situation where "persons actually were discussing some specific question"—the relative merits of the Bose 901 and conventional loudspeaker systems—and a "reasonable person would have expected

> persons beyond the immediate participants in the dispute to feel the impact of its resolution." Waldbaum v. Fairchild Publications, Inc., 627 F.2d 1287, 1297, *cert. denied,* 449 U.S. 898, 101 S.Ct. 266, 66 L.Ed.2d 128 (1980). * * * The defendant by its publication of the Article, did not create the public controversy. It simply added its voice to the chorus that was already discussing the merits of various loudspeaker systems. Thus, in the present case there was a "public controversy" that preceded the publication of the allegedly disparaging remarks.

Id. at 1273. The court then turned to the nature and extent of the plaintiff's participation in the controversy giving rise to the disparagement. In this case, the participation was extensive. Bose actually precipitated the controversy by using a market strategy that emphasized the unconventional design of the Bose 901 speakers. Indeed, the court noted, the "extent of the plaintiff's advertising alone might very well justify a holding that the plaintiff is a public figure." *Id.* at 1273. In addition, Bose had actively sought to have reviewers test and review the speakers and then incorporated the reviews into its advertising brochures. These actions clearly invited public attention and comment. *Id.*

Finally, the court noted that two other factors emphasized in *Gertz* militated in favor of finding that Bose was a public figure: First, Bose had extensive access to the media, and thus was in a better position than a private individual to counteract the effects of the false statements. Second, under the facts of the case, Bose had voluntarily assumed the increased risk of disparaging falsehood by virtue of its conduct, which generated controversy. *Id.* at 1274. For all these reasons, Bose was a public figure, at least with respect to the limited issues of the characteristics and quality of the Bose 901 speakers. The court then found that Bose had succeeded in demonstrating that Consumers Union acted with actual malice in publishing the disparaging statement.

Bose did not challenge the finding that the *New York Times* rule applied to its claim. Thus, on appeal, the only issue was whether Bose had succeeded in demonstrating actual malice. The Court of Appeals for the First Circuit found that it had not, and reversed. 692 F.2d 189 (1st Cir.1982). The Supreme Court affirmed the court of appeals. 466 U.S. 485, 104 S.Ct. 1949, 80 L.Ed.2d 502 (1984). Neither court found it necessary to determine whether the *New York Times* rule should apply in product disparagement cases, or to review Bose's status as a public figure.

Assuming that the Consumers Union article was not commercial speech, what would happen if a competitor of Bose quoted the disparaging aspects of the article in its advertising? Would the competitor's actions constitute commercial speech, as defined in *U.S. Healthcare*? If so, would it make sense to find that the actual malice standard would not apply in a suit against the competitor, even though it applied in a suit against Consumers Union?

V. MISAPPROPRIATION

BOARD OF TRADE OF CITY OF CHICAGO v. DOW JONES & CO., INC.

Supreme Court of Illinois, 1983.
98 Ill.2d 109, 74 Ill.Dec. 582, 456 N.E.2d 84.

GOLDENHERSH, JUSTICE:

Defendant, Dow Jones & Company, Inc., appealed from the judgment of the circuit court of Cook County entered in favor of plaintiff, the Board of Trade of the City of Chicago, in its action for declaratory judgment. Plaintiff sought a declaration that its offering of a commodity futures contract utilizing the Dow Jones Industrial Average as the underlying commodity would not violate defendant's legal or proprietary rights. The appellate court reversed and we allowed plaintiff's petition for leave to appeal.

[Defendant publishes the Wall Street Journal and maintains the Dow Jones News Service, through which it distributes financial news to subscribers.] It produces several stock market indexes, the Dow Jones Industrial Average, Transportation Average, and Utilities Average, which are computed on the basis of the current prices of stocks of certain companies selected by defendant's editorial board.

The financial news furnished by defendant is disseminated * * * to brokerage houses, banks, financial institutions, individual investors, and others who are interested in stock market news. * * * Plaintiff has a "Subscription Agreement" under which it pays defendant for its News Service and is allowed to compute and display the Dow Jones Averages on plaintiff's trading floor on a continuous, "real time" basis.

Plaintiff is the oldest and largest commodities exchange market in the United States. * * * All commodities exchanges in the United States are regulated by the Commodities Futures Trading Commission (CFTC), and no exchange may trade a futures contract until the CFTC approves the futures contract and designates the exchange as a contract market for that contract.

A futures contract is a contract traded on a commodities exchange which binds the parties to a particular transaction at a specified future date. A stock index futures contract is a futures contract based upon the value of a particular stock market index. Dr. James H. Lorie, stipulated by the parties to be an expert, called by plaintiff, testified that these contracts have been traded since February 1982. At the time of trial they were traded on the Kansas City Board of Trade based on the Value Line Average, on the Chicago Mercantile Exchange based on the Standard & Poor's 500 Stock Index and on the New York Futures Exchange based on the New York Stock Exchange Composite Index. He stated that their "overriding purpose is the management of risk." Unlike other futures contracts, no underlying commodity exists to be delivered at the future date, but rather the transaction is settled by the delivery of a certified promissory note in lieu of cash. * * *

Plaintiff, desiring to be designated as a contract market for stock index futures contracts, devoted more than two years to developing its own index to be used as the basis for its stock index futures contract. During the greater part of this period, the Securities and Exchange Commission (SEC) and the CFTC were in a dispute concerning which agency had jurisdiction to regulate stock index futures contracts. In December 1981, the two Federal agencies agreed on the scope of their respective jurisdiction and on recommendations to Congress for regulatory legislation. They agreed that the CFTC would regulate trading in stock market index contracts and that such trading would be permitted only if the contracts were based on widely known and well-established stock market indexes. This jurisdictional agreement effectively precluded CFTC approval of a contract based on the index developed by plaintiff.

On February 26, 1982, plaintiff submitted an application to the CFTC asking that it be designated as a contract market for Chicago Board of Trade Portfolio Futures Contracts. The application proposed the use of three indexes, the stock market index, transport index, and the electric index portfolio contracts. * * * No mention of the Dow Jones name appeared in the application, but the stocks used in each of the indexes were identical to those used in the Dow Jones averages. In a draft proposal to the CFTC for trading "CBT indexes," the Dow Jones averages stock lists were cut out of the Wall Street Journal and pasted into the proposals. The CFTC advised plaintiff that the CBT indexes were not just similar to, but were identical to the Dow Jones averages and that this should be explicitly stated in its application. On May 7, 1982, plaintiff amended its application to state that the CBT indexes were identical to Dow Jones averages and that when Dow Jones changed a component stock or revised the divisor, plaintiff would make the same change so that the CBT indexes would remain identical to the Dow Jones averages. Plaintiff also added a disclaimer to the application disclaiming any association with Dow Jones. On May 13, the CFTC approved plaintiff's use of the stock market index portfolio contract, but did not rule concerning the use of the transportation or utility index portfolio contracts.

* * *

Plaintiff argues that the appellate court's holding erroneously expands the tort of misappropriation and that its decision contravenes public policy. Citing * * * *International News Service v. Associated Press* (1918), 248 U.S. 215, 39 S.Ct. 68, 63 L.Ed. 211, plaintiff argues that competitive injury is a fundamental prerequisite essential to a finding of misappropriation. * * * It argues that it has done nothing immoral or unethical but has merely created a "new product" which is "outside the primary market which the producer of the original product originally set out to satisfy * * *." (See J. Rahl, *The Right to "Appro-*

priate" Trade Values, 23 Ohio St. L.J. 56, 62–63 (1962).) Finally, plaintiff argues that the appellate court's decision is against public policy in that it grants what amounts to a common law patent monopoly to defendant which permits it to exclude others from using its product for any purpose "regardless of whether the producer is being injured or intends to exploit the product itself."

Defendant responds that the tort of misappropriation should be flexible so that, by carefully tailoring their misappropriation to avoid the strict rules of the tort, "enterprising pirates" cannot avoid the application of the doctrine. * * * [D]efendant argues that under the doctrine of misappropriation direct competition is not essential to tort liability. Defendant argues that plaintiff seeks to exploit defendant's reputation for accuracy and impartiality without compensating it for its good will. Finally, in response to plaintiff's argument that the appellate court's opinion is against public policy, defendant argues that the appellate court's opinion is consistent with public policy in that it maintains the incentive for the creation of intellectual property. Defendant argues that if its rights in the averages are not protected, there will be a diminished incentive for it to continue to provide the averages. Defendant points out that it does not seek to monopolize the production of stock indexes and that plaintiff is free to develop its own, but that it desires to protect its rights in the averages which it created and continues to produce.

* * *

The doctrine of misappropriation as a form of unfair competition was first enunciated by the Supreme Court in *International News Service v. Associated Press* (1918), 248 U.S. 215, 39 S.Ct. 68, 63 L.Ed. 211. In that case, INS was copying news stories from bulletin boards of members of AP and transmitting the fresh news contained on those bulletin boards to its own members. Thus, INS could obtain information collected by AP at great expense and transmit this information to its midwestern and west coast members, who could then print the news at the same time as the competing AP members or, in some instances, earlier. In affirming the decree enjoining the practice the majority opinion suggested that without the revenues derived from this exclusive, timely presentation of the news, AP or other news services would not have sufficient incentive to continue performing their services.

The tort of misappropriation was recognized in Illinois for the first time in *Capitol Records, Inc. v. Spies* (1970), 130 Ill.App.2d 429, 264 N.E.2d 874. There the defendant purchased records and magnetic tapes sold by the plaintiff and recorded them on magnetic tapes. He then sold these re-recordings to his customers. A disclaimer was placed on the cassette tapes disclaiming any relationship between the defendant and plaintiff or the recorded artists. Defendant was able to sell his product at a lesser price than plaintiff since he avoided the costs of contracting with the performers, producing the master recordings, paying royalty fees, and advertising. * * * [T]he court reasoned that the manner of competition was "unfair" since the defendant was able to compete on equal terms by avoiding those costs normally associated with producing such recordings. Underlying the court's reasoning is the premise that the plaintiff's pecuniary reward for producing its intangible product would be severely reduced if other competitors could avoid production costs by merely waiting until a record became popular and then recording the work for resale.

Competing with the policy that protection should be afforded one who expends labor and money to develop products is the concept that freedom to imitate and duplicate is vital to our free market economy. Indeed, when the doctrine of misappropriation was first enunciated, Justice Brandeis recognized this competing policy:

> "He who follows the pioneer into a new market, or who engages in the manufacture of an article newly introduced by another, seeks profits due largely to the labor and expense of the first adventurer; but the law sanctions, indeed encourages, the pursuit." (*International News Service v. Associated Press* (1918), 248 U.S. 215, 259, 39 S.Ct. 68, 79, 63 L.Ed. 211, 229 (Brandeis, J., dissenting)).

Similarly, Professor Rahl reasons:

> "Substantial similarity of alternatives can come about in only one of two ways—by independent development or by imitation. While there are many instances of simultaneous independent innovation, our economy would still be in the Dark Ages if this were the only circumstance under which competing alternatives could be offered. Imitation is inherent in any system of competition and it is imperative for an economy in which there is rapid technological advance." Rahl, *The Right to "Appropriate" Trade Values*, 23 Ohio St. L.J. 56, 72 (1962).

In balancing the factors that should determine which of the competing concepts should prevail, it appears unlikely that an adverse decision will cause defendant to cease to produce its averages or that the revenue it currently receives for the distribution of those averages will be materially affected. Defendant correctly asserts that it will lose its right to prospective licensing revenues in the event that in the future it elects to have its name associated with stock index futures contracts, but reliance upon the existence of a property right based upon the ability to license the product to prospective markets which were not originally contemplated by the creator of the product is somewhat "circular."

Alternatively, holding that plaintiff's use of defendant's indexes in the manner proposed is a misappropriation may stimulate the creation of new indexes perhaps better suited to the purpose of "hedging" against the "systematic" risk present in the stock market.

Whether protection against appropriation is necessary to foster creativity depends in part upon the expectations of that sector of the business community which deals with the particular intangible. If the creator of an intangible product expects to be able to control the licensing or distribution of the intangible in order to profit from his effort, and similarly those who would purchase the product expect and are willing to pay for the use of the intangible, a better argument can be made in favor of granting protection. The record shows that the plaintiff sought to develop its own index prior to the CFTC's requirement that the contracts be based on well-known, well-established indexes. It then offered defendant 10 cents per transaction, which it estimated would be somewhere between $1 million and $2 million per year, for the use of its name and averages. While there appears to be some dispute as to whether this offer of payment was primarily for the use of defendant's name or for the use of the averages, the offer of money is relevant to the extent that it acknowledges the value of the association of defendant's name and good will with the averages it produces.

To hold that defendant has a proprietary interest in its indexes and averages which vests it with the exclusive right to license their use for trading in stock index futures contracts would not preclude plaintiff and others from marketing stock index futures contracts. The extent of defendant's monopoly would be limited, for as defendant points out, there are an infinite number of stock market indexes which could be devised. As one commentator notes, the effect of granting a "monopoly" at the base of the production pyramid is much less objectionable than granting a monopoly at the top of the pyramid:

> "Social cost assumes more manageable size and so less significance near the base of the pyramid. Exclusive rights in a special kind of typewriter key are far less objectionable than a monopoly in the lever, because far less is swept into the monopolist's control." *Developments In the Law: Competitive Torts*, 77 Harv.L.Rev. 888, 938 (1964).

We conclude that the possibility of any detriment to the public which might result from our holding that defendant's indexes and averages may not be used without its consent in the manner proposed by plaintiff are outweighed by the resultant encouragement to develop new indexes specifically designed for the purpose of hedging against the "systematic" risk present in the stock market.

We have considered plaintiff's contention that defendant has failed to prove that the proposed use of the averages would cause it injury. The publication of the indexes involves valuable assets of defendant, its good will and its reputation for integrity and accuracy. Despite the fact that plaintiff's proposed use is not in competition with the use defendant presently makes of them, defendant is entitled to protection against their misappropriation.

* * *

For the reasons stated, the judgment of the appellate court is affirmed.

SIMON, JUSTICE, dissenting:

The majority opinion fairly identifies the general approach to the common law tort of misappropriation. In order to determine whether that tort will lie we must balance Dow Jones' interest in preventing the use of its average by the Board of Trade against society's interest in the widest use and dissemination of intellectual property. Obviously, both interests are important and require fair consideration in the balancing process. Unless the creators of intellectual property have some protection against the appropriation of their ideas by others they will be discouraged from producing them; on the other hand, unless society can demand that the owners of intellectual property allow it to be appropriated by people who have developed novel and productive uses for it, the pace of innovation will slow.

I would allow the Board of Trade to use the Dow Jones Averages for its stock market futures contracts. The majority errs, in part, because it has failed to place enough emphasis on the unfettered access to ideas in the public domain, a privilege which is essential to our free market economy. * * *

The common law tort of misappropriation has been limited to cases where intellectual property, lawfully obtained, is used in direct competition with the person who created it. * * * The competitive-injury requirement has a sound basis in policy, for it allows the tort of misappropriation to protect the creators of intellectual property against actual injury to their business, but at the same time it allows for suitable reward for people who develop novel uses for information and ideas that are freely obtained from the public domain.

In this case the circuit court found that Dow Jones would not suffer any competitive injury if the Board of Trade used the Dow Jones index for its futures contracts. * * * Moreover, the circuit court decree ensured that Dow Jones' good will would not be diminished through the Board of Trade's use of the index. The circuit court's decree required that all contracts, advertising, and promotional activity relating to the Board of Trade's stock market futures index contain express disclaimers of any sponsorship or association with Dow Jones.

Dow Jones claims that it will suffer the loss of future licensing revenues if we hold that the Board of Trade may freely use the Dow Jones' index in its futures contracts. At trial, however, Dow Jones pleaded and presented testimony claiming that it had no interest or expectation in licensing its name or index for use in stock market futures. Even if Dow Jones changed this position in the future, nothing in the circuit court decree would prevent it from licensing its name to sponsor a stock market futures index in competition with the one to be offered by the Board of Trade. Moreover, as the majority opinion admits, it is somewhat circular to base a finding of competitive injury on the ability to license the index to prospective markets when those licenses have no value unless we find in this action that Dow Jones has a property right in its index under the tort of misappropriation.

Dow Jones has no more than an inchoate interest in the Board of Trade's use of its index, but the majority's opinion converts that interest into a property right. The majority is swayed by what it sees as "unjust" enrichment—the Board of Trade's plan to earn a profit by the free use of an idea developed by Dow Jones at considerable cost. I do not regard this use as "unjust" in the least. The Board of Trade proposed to use information that Dow Jones had freely allowed the public to acquire in a business that Dow Jones has not shown the slightest interest in pursuing. If "unjust enrichment" has become the only element for the tort of misappropriation in Illinois, I fear that there will be few commercial ideas and little information left in the public domain. I view the proper elements of the tort of misappropriation to be a combination of unjust enrichment and competitive injury. Although the former feature may be present in this case, neither the majority opinion nor Dow Jones reveals where to find the latter feature.

UNITED STATES GOLF ASSOCIATION v. ST. ANDREWS SYSTEMS, DATA–MAX, INC.

United States Court of Appeals for the Third Circuit, 1984.
749 F.2d 1028, 224 U.S.P.Q. 646.

BECKER, CIRCUIT JUDGE.

This appeal * * * arises from a lawsuit brought by appellant, the United States Golf Association ("U.S.G.A."), the governing body of amateur golf in the United States. The U.S.G.A. has developed a system for deriving the "handicaps" of amateur golfers, the core of which is a mathematical formula. Appellee Data–Max, Inc., d/b/a St. Andrews Systems, markets small computers that are programmed to calculate a golfer's handicap based on the U.S.G.A. formula. The U.S.G.A. brought this suit to enjoin Data–Max from using its formula as the basis for its computerized handicap system.

The U.S.G.A. bases its claim for an injunction on two theories. The first is that the use of the U.S.G.A. formula by Data–Max amounts to a "false designation of origin," and thus violates both section 43(a) of the Lanham Act, 15 U.S.C. § 1125(a), and the New Jersey common law against unfair competition. The second theory is that the use of the formula is a "misappropriation" under the doctrine of *International News Service v. Associated Press*, 248 U.S. 215 (1918), as that doctrine has been adopted by New Jersey. * * *

We conclude that the U.S.G.A. handicap formula is "functional," and thus that the U.S.G.A. cannot enjoin the use of the formula either under section 43(a) of the Lanham Act or under state law on the basis of any association in the public mind between the formula and the U.S.G.A. We also conclude that the U.S.G.A.'s claim does not fall within the "misappropriation" doctrine as it has been adopted by the State of New Jersey, largely because in using the formula Data–Max will not compete directly with the U.S.G.A., and thus will not interfere with the economic incentives of the U.S.G.A. to maintain and update its handicap formula. * * *

I. Facts and Procedural History

The U.S.G.A. has been the governing body of amateur golf in the United States since 1894. It seeks to promote the game of golf by numerous means, including the establishment of rules and regulations for play, the promotion of amateur tournaments, and the regulation of its member golf clubs. Among the services that the U.S.G.A. provides to amateur golfers is a "handicap" formula that allows golfers of different skill levels to compete with each other on an equal basis. The U.S.G.A. handicap system takes account of the difficulty of the course on which a round is played and provides "safeguards" against the inflation of handicaps by excluding particularly bad holes and by counting only the best ten of a golfer's last twenty rounds.

[The U.S.G.A. has developed the handicap formula over a period of eighty years, regularly refining and improving it.]

Data–Max was incorporated in 1980 for the purpose of providing golfers, primarily those who do not belong to U.S.G.A.-member clubs, with "instant handicaps." A computer program to calculate a handicap based on the U.S.G.A. formula is central to the products and services that Data–Max offers. Data–Max has sold or leased its computer to U.S.G.A.-member golf clubs, which use the computer in calculating handicaps.[2] Data–Max also markets a subscription telephone handicap service, which enables a golfer to call in a new score and immediately receive an updated handicap, and a computer that enables a golfer to directly enter a new score and receive an updated handicap.

* * *

II. Discussion

* * *

C. *The Misappropriation Claim*

The doctrine of "misappropriation," which is a distinct branch of the law of unfair competition, originated with the Supreme Court's decision in *International News Service v. Associated Press*, 248 U.S. 215, 39 S.Ct. 68, 63 L.Ed. 211 (1918) ("*I.N.S.*"). The doctrine has been applied to a variety of situations in which the courts have sensed that one party was dealing "unfairly" with another, but which were not covered by the three established statutory systems protecting intellectual property: copyright, patent, and trademark/deception as to origin. The doctrine has also been the subject of considerable scholarly attention. Application of the misappropriation doctrine requires courts to contend with the basic problem of the law of intellectual property: balancing the

2. The U.S.G.A. has no objection to this aspect of Data–Max's business, since the handicap is ultimately provided by a member golf club. The U.S.G.A. objects to an unauthorized organization, such as Data–Max, providing handicaps derived by means of the U.S.G.A. formula directly to golfers.

rights of the creator of ideas or information to exploit them for commercial gain against the public's right to free access to those ideas. Concomitantly, the dilemma posed by the doctrine can best be viewed as an attempt to provide the necessary incentives to the creators of intellectual property without unnecessarily restricting the public's free access to information.[12] The *I.N.S.* case illustrates the problem.

I.N.S., which was barred for political reasons by British censors from cabling its reports of the First World War to the United States, provided war coverage to the readers of its papers by buying early editions of A.P. papers and either copying or paraphrasing the A.P. reports in its own later editions. A.P. objected to this use of its stories, even though the stories were not copyrighted and even though A.P. had no protectible interest in the underlying facts it was reporting. The Court came down on the side of protecting A.P.'s investment of "labor, skill, and money" in reporting the news, against I.N.S.'s right to take that information and use it in direct competition with A.P. The Court noted that without such protection, A.P. would have little incentive to invest in newsgathering.

The language of the *I.N.S.* opinion is very broad, and courts have struggled over the years to define the limits of the doctrine. The Second Circuit, under the leadership of Judge Learned Hand, sought to limit *I.N.S.* to its facts, because of the broad implications of the doctrine for limiting the use of copying in commercial competition. * * * The doctrine survived, however, in the context of factual situations very close to that of I.N.S. * * *

After the Supreme Court's decision in *Erie Railroad v. Tompkins*, 304 U.S. 64, 58 S.Ct. 817, 82 L.Ed. 1188 (1939), misappropriation became a question of state, rather than federal law. * * * [S]ome state courts took a more expansive view of the scope of the misappropriation doctrine in the post-*Erie* era.

A federal aspect to the problem of the scope of the misappropriation doctrine was reintroduced by the Supreme Court's decisions in *Sears, Roebuck & Co. v. Stiffel Co.*, 376 U.S. 225, 84 S.Ct. 784, 11 L.Ed.2d 661 (1964), and *Compco Corp. v. Day–Brite Lighting, Inc.*, 376 U.S. 234, 84 S.Ct. 779, 11 L.Ed.2d 669 (1964). The Court held that the decision by Congress to exclude certain types of intellectual property from protection

12. The dilemma can also be framed in terms of balancing the natural right of a producer in the fruits of his or her labor against the public's access right. The constitutional provision authorizing copyrights and patents, and the statutes implementing it, are based on the "incentive" theory, in contrast to continental systems that are based on a "natural rights" theory. *I.N.S.*, however, explicitly recognized that the creator's interest is rooted in the "labor, skill and money" which has been devoted to the creation. Professor Baird believes there is little practical difference between relying on the "incentive" theory and relying on the "natural rights" theory. Baird, *Common Law Intellectual Property and the Legacy of International News Service v. Associated Press*, 50 U.Chi.L.Rev. 411, 420–21 (1983). In our view, using the incentive theory to define the limits of misappropriation is more appropriate, since it is based on a "social" interest (incentives for creation) which can be balanced against another social interest (free access), while the natural rights theory requires a balancing of incommensurables.

under the patent and copyright laws was a policy decision that the societal interest in free access to those ideas outweighed the need to provide incentives for their production, and that state law doctrines which protected such intellectual property were preempted by that policy decision. Subsequent decisions of the Supreme Court have made clear, however, that the misappropriation doctrine has not been completely eviscerated. The Court has not rejected the *Sears-Compco* doctrine, nor has it clearly defined where the power of the states to protect interests in intellectual property ends, and where the realm of federal preemption begins. The problem before us, therefore, is to apply the misappropriation doctrine as we believe the New Jersey courts would apply it, in light of the limitations which we believe federal preemption places on the permissible scope of state-law protection for intellectual property.

[The court notes the decision in *Board of Trade v. Dow Jones, supra,* as well as that in Standard & Poor's Corp. v. Commodity Exchange, Inc., 683 F.2d 704 (2d Cir.1982). In the latter case, the Second Circuit, applying New York law, upheld a preliminary injunction against the Commodities Exchange ("Comex"), which was using the Standard & Poor's 500 ("S & P 500") as the basis of its stock index futures contract without Standard & Poor's authorization. Standard & Poor's had licensed another entity to create a stock market index future based on the S & P 500.]

This case is similar to the stock market index cases in a number of significant respects. As in the stock market index cases, the plaintiff here is seeking to exclude a rival from using a formula it has derived for commercial gain. The formulas in all three cases serve useful functions—in the stock market cases, the index is designed to track the general movement of the stock market; in this case, the formula is designed to indicate a golfer's level of competence. None of these formulas, however, is unique to its function. As a result of their creators' efforts, the respective formulas are generally accepted by the public as reliable means of performing their respective functions. Although the plaintiffs spend some time and effort updating their formulas, and also compute results by means of their formulas, the primary value of the results produced are not their inherent value in performing the underlying functions, but rather in the fact that they enable the public to discuss the underlying matters (*i.e.*, the direction of the stock market or the ability of golfers) by means of a common set of terms.

In determining whether the misappropriation doctrine should be applied in this case, however, we must keep in mind the basic policies that underlie the doctrine and its limits. In *I.N.S.*, the Court based its conclusion in substantial part on the fact that I.N.S. was using information which A.P. had developed in direct competition with A.P. in its primary market, the sale of newspapers. I.N.S.'s activity, if not checked, could have destroyed A.P.'s incentive to create the information involved, and this would not only have harmed A.P. but also would have left the public without the information. If, on the other hand, I.N.S. had used the information in a different manner—for instance, in writing a story on American correspondents covering the war—the use of A.P.'s information would not have affected A.P.'s incentive to gather the information. Although A.P. might have been better off if it had exclusive rights to such derivative uses of its information, providing legal protection might also harm the public, since A.P. might never have produced the story about correspondents covering the war. Indirect competition of this sort—use of information in competition with the creator outside of its primary market—falls outside the scope of the misappropriation doctrine, since the public interest in free access outweighs the public interest in providing an additional incentive to the creator or gatherer of information.

The competition in this case is indirect. The U.S.G.A. is not in the business of selling handicaps to golfers, but is primarily interested in the promotion of the game of golf, and in its own position as the governing body of amateur golf. The handicap formula was developed to further these two goals. A member of a golf club who obtains his handicap through his club does not pay for that service, and the U.S.G.A. is not directly affected by the number of official handicaps the clubs calculate each year or by the number of golfers who obtain handicaps. Data–Max, on the other hand, is in the business of providing "instant handicaps" to golfers, either by selling or leasing its computers to golf clubs, or by providing handicaps directly to golfers who cannot obtain "instant handicaps" through their clubs. The U.S.G.A. does not object to the sale or lease of Data–Max's computers, and does not attempt to provide the direct services which Data–Max provides to golfers. Thus, it is inconceivable that Data–Max's business will interfere with the U.S.G.A.'s incentive to maintain or update the handicap formula.

The absence of direct competition with the producer's primary use of the information was not viewed as dispositive by either the Illinois Supreme Court in *Dow Jones* or the Second Circuit in *Standard & Poor's*. The court in *Dow Jones* concluded that direct competition was unnecessary, and the court in *Standard & Poor's* found "direct competition" between S & P and Comex, even though the competition was outside S & P's primary market. Neither of these cases makes a persuasive argument for dispensing with the "direct competition" requirement. Since direct competition has generally been seen as necessary to a finding of misappropriation, and since it properly balances the competing concerns of providing incentives to producers of information while protecting free access, we believe that New Jersey would require direct competition in a misappropriation case, absent a substantial justification for making an exception.

A possible justification for dispensing with the direct competition requirement in this case, which was also present in *Dow Jones* and *Standard & Poor's*, is the fact that the information involved is so closely associated with the creator and has so little intrinsic value that the use of the information by the competitors is really an attempt to trade on the "good will" of the creator, and thus should be prohibited. The fact that the U.S.G.A. formula, like those involved in the stock market cases, is only one of a potentially large number of possible approaches to the underlying problem (quantifying the ability of golfers to enable them to compete with (and bet with) other golfers on an equitable basis) reduces the cost to the public of recognizing proprietary rights in the formula. The presence of so many alternatives also indicates that the primary value to Data–Max of using the U.S.G.A. formula is the public acceptance that the U.S.G.A. has built up for it over the years. This public acceptance could be characterized as part of the U.S.G.A.'s "good will." We must determine, therefore, whether the New Jersey courts would interpret the misappropriation doctrine in such a way as to dispense with the "direct competition" requirement on the facts of this case.

We conclude that, at least on the facts of this case, New Jersey would not dispense with the requirement of direct competition.[23] The public acceptance of the U.S.G.A.'s handicap formula stems from the golfing public's desire to have a uniform system of quantifying recent performances in a way that will allow equitable competition among golfers of differing abilities. The U.S.G.A., in furtherance of its role as the governing body of amateur golf, has provided such a system and, in the absence of a better system, the public has apparently accepted it. Under this state of affairs, the emergence of a single standard becomes largely a function of the need for uniformity. To require Data–Max to use a different formula would effectively destroy its ability to provide a handicapping service, since the U.S.G.A. formula is widely accepted by the golfing public. The purpose of a handicap is comparison between golfers, and handicaps based on different formulas cannot be readily compared.

Because the U.S.G.A. formula is the equivalent of an "industry standard" for the golfing public, preventing other handicap providers from using it would effectively give the U.S.G.A. a national monopoly on the golf handicapping business. Where such a monopoly is unnecessary to protect the basic incentive for the production of the idea or information involved, we do not believe that the creator's interest in its idea or information justifies such an extensive restraint on competition. This case provides a good example of why such a restraint would harm the golfing public. Data–Max has expended time and creative energy in devising its own products and services. It has not only created the program used to calculate handicaps by computer, but has devised a handicapping service which improves on that provided by the U.S.G.A., at least to the extent that Data–Max provides a golfer with a fresh handicap faster than the U.S.G.A. does. In addition, the U.S.G.A. has not been completely deprived of the opportunity to be compensated for its "good will" in connection with the handicap formula. To the extent that the approval of the U.S.G.A. would enhance the value of "instant handicaps," the U.S.G.A. has an opportunity, if it wishes to exercise it, of

23. We further note that expanding the misappropriation doctrine in such a way that it might give the creator of a particular idea or piece of information that has been made public a permanent monopoly over its commercial use could raise problems of preemption under the *Sears-Compco* doctrine.

offering either Data–Max or other companies the use of the U.S.G.A. name in marketing its products and services.

* * *

Notes and Questions

1. *The misappropriation cause of action.* As the opinions in *Board of Trade* and *United States Golf* suggest, the *I.N.S.* case is generally acknowledged to be the source of the misappropriation doctrine. That case is reprinted in Chapter 1, *supra.*

The classic elements of the misappropriation cause of action are: 1) the plaintiff has invested time, money, skill or labor to create something; 2) the defendant has appropriated that something in a manner than can be characterized as "reaping where it has not sown" or taking a free ride off the plaintiff's effort; and 3) the plaintiff has suffered injury as a result. See 1 J.T. McCARTHY, McCARTHY ON TRADEMARKS AND UNFAIR COMPETITION § 10.25 (3d ed. 1992). It seems fairly clear that the first two elements are satisfied in both *Board of Trade* and *United States Gulf.* Is the third element satisfied in *Board of Trade*? If so, how? If not, is the court essentially saying that injury is not necessary? Did the court substitute another consideration in place of injury? If so, what was the substituted consideration?

2. *The purpose of the misappropriation doctrine.* In *Board of Trade,* what does the Illinois Supreme Court appear to view as the purpose of the misappropriation doctrine? Is it to enforce basic standards of commercial morality—to prevent parties from "reaping where they have not sown"? Is reaping where one has not sown inherently immoral or unfair? Under the specific circumstances of the *Board of Trade* case, was the Board of Trade's action in taking the stock index immoral or unfair?

Is the purpose of the misappropriation doctrine to provide a flexible means of promoting public policy? If so, what is the public policy? How was it promoted by a finding of misappropriation in *Board of Trade*? Do you agree with the Illinois Court's balancing of the potentially conflicting policy interests?

Is the purpose of the misappropriation doctrine to protect business good will? Did the court in *United States Golf* find that the defendant was not taking the plaintiff's good will, or that the taking of good will under the circumstances was not sufficient to justify granting relief? If the latter, what were the circumstances the court found influential? Under what, if any, circumstances might the court have found that the appropriation of a plaintiff's good reputation and public acceptance justified misappropriation relief?

In National Football League v. Governor of Delaware, 435 F.Supp. 1372, 195 U.S.P.Q. 803 (D.Del.1977), the court grappled with the implications of taking good will in the absence of competition. In that case, the Delaware State Lottery instituted lottery games based on participants' predictions of the scores generated in National Football League ("NFL") games. The lottery tickets listed teams by city names (e.g., Tampa), rather than trade name or mark (Buccaneers). The NFL sued to enjoin the lottery games, alleging a number of legal theories, including misappropriation. In evaluating this claim, the court acknowledged that the plaintiffs had made a great investment in developing public acceptance and popularity, and that the defendant lottery intended to capitalize on the NFL popularity and reputation when it chose NFL games as the subject matter of its lottery. The defendants conceded that in making this election they expected to generate revenue which would not be generated from betting on a less popular pastime. The court observed:

> It is undoubtedly true that defendants seek to profit from the popularity of NFL football. The question, however, is whether this constitutes wrongful misappropriation. I think not.
>
> We live in an age of economic and social interdependence. The NFL undoubtedly would not be in the position it is today if college football and the fan interest that it generated had not preceded the NFL's organization. To that degree it has benefited from the labor of others. The same, of course, can be said for the mass media networks which the labor of others have developed.
>
> What the Delaware Lottery has done is to offer a service to that portion of plaintiffs' following who wish to bet on NFL games. It is true that Delaware is thus making profits it would not make but for the existence of the NFL, but I find this difficult to distinguish from the multitude of charter bus companies who generate profit from servicing those of plaintiffs' fans who want to go to the stadium or, indeed, the sidewalk popcorn salesman who services the crowd as it surges towards the gate.
>
> While courts have recognized that one has a right to one's own harvest, this proposition has not been construed to preclude others from profiting from demands for collateral services generated by the success of one's business venture. General Motors' cars, for example, enjoy significant popularity and seat cover manufacturers profit from that popularity by making covers to fit General Motors' seats. The same relationship exists between hot dog producers and the bakers of hot dog rolls. But in neither instance, I believe, could it be successfully contended that an actionable misappropriation occurs.
>
> The NFL plaintiffs, however, argue that this case is different because the evidence is said to show "misappropriation" of plaintiffs' "good will" and "reputation" as well as its "popularity". To a large extent, plaintiffs' references to "good will" and "reputation" are simply other ways of stating their complaint that defendants are profiting from a demand plaintiffs' games have generated. To the extent they relate to a claim that defendants' activities have damaged, as opposed to appropriated, plaintiff's good will and reputation, I believe one must look to other lines of authority to determine defendants' culpability. In response to plaintiffs' misappropriation argument, I hold only that defendants' use of the NFL schedules, scores and public popularity in the Delaware Lottery does not constitute a misappropriation of plaintiffs' property.

Id., 435 F.Supp. at 1378, 195 U.S.P.Q. at 806.

In light of your evaluation of the purposes of the misappropriation cause of action, should relief be limited to cases in which the parties compete? If so, how strictly would you define competition? For example, would you consider the parties in *United States Golf* to be competitors for this purpose?

3. *The interface between the misappropriation cause of action and other intellectual property doctrines.* In *Board of Trade*, the plaintiff argued that a finding of misappropriation would essentially grant Dow Jones a common-law patent in its stock index. Is that true? If so, would application of the state common law of misappropriation undermine Congress' purposes in setting strict standards for patents, which the stock index is unlikely to meet? In *United States Golf*, the court found that the plaintiff's handicap formula was "functional," and thus could not be protected under the law of passing off. Under those circumstances, would it be appropriate to grant property rights in the formula under the law of misappropriation, even if the parties were competitors? For that matter, in a classic trademark infringement setting, could a trademark owner obtain relief without proving a likelihood of confusion by simply pleading that the defendant "misappropriated" its trademark? See Denicola, *Trademarks as Speech: Constitutional Implications of the Emerging Rationales for the Protection of Trade Symbols*, [1982] WISC. L. REV. 158, 166–81. Taken to its logical extremes, the doctrine of misappropriation is so broad that it could be used to circumvent the carefully drawn limitations of other causes of action, essentially overrunning them. Putting aside the issues of federal preemption, which we will examine in Chapter 9, *infra*, is this worrisome? When faced with this reality, courts have tended to be conservative in applying the misappropriation doctrine. They have tended to avoid applications that would undermine the careful balances that legislative bodies and courts have drawn in connection with other intellectual property causes of action. See, e.g., 1 J.T. McCARTHY, McCARTHY ON TRADEMARKS AND UNFAIR COMPETITION § 10.34[2] (3d ed. 1992).

The new Restatement (Third) of Unfair Competition goes further. It would eliminate misappropriation altogether as an independent cause of action for the taking of intangible trade values, regardless of whether the parties are competitors. RESTATEMENT (THIRD) OF UNFAIR COMPETITION § 38 (Tentative Draft No. 4, 1993). The drafters explain in comment b:

> Protection against the misappropriation of intangible trade values provides an incentive to invest in the creation of intangible assets and prevents the potential of unjust enrichment that may result from the appropriation of an investment made by another. However, the recognition of exclusive rights in intangible trade values can restrain competition and impede access to valuable information. Unlike appropriations of physical assets, an appropriation of information or other intangible assets does not ordinarily deprive the originator of simultaneous use. The recognition of exclusive rights may thus deny to the public the full benefits of valuable ideas and innovations by limiting their distribution and exploitation. In addition, the principle of unjust enrichment does not demand restitution of every gain derived from the efforts of others. A small shop, for example, may freely benefit from the customers attracted by a nearby department store, a local manufacturer may

benefit from increased demand attributable to the promotional efforts of a national manufacturer of similar goods, and a newspaper may benefit from reporting on local athletic teams. Similarly, the law has long recognized the right of a competitor to copy the successful products and methods of others absent an infringement of patent, copyright, or trademark rights. On the other hand, unrestricted appropriation of intangible assets can threaten the originator's incentive to invest in continued production of the asset. Achieving a proper balance between protection and access is often a complicated and difficult undertaking. Because of the complexity and indeterminacy of the competing interests, exclusive rights in intangible trade values such as ideas, innovations, and information have been created primarily through legislation. The common law of unfair competition has generally recognized rights against the appropriation of intangible trade values only when the recognition of such rights is supported by additional interests that justify protection, and then only when the scope of the resulting rights can be clearly defined. The protection of trade secrets, for example, reflects the established interests in preserving confidential relationships and physical security. Protection against an appropriation of the commercial value of a person's identity implicates interests in privacy, reputation, and personal autonomy. Absent such additional interests, the common law has resisted the recognition of a general right to prevent the appropriation of information and other intangible commercial assets.

The patent and copyright statutes illustrate the intricacy required to harmonize the competing public and private interests that are implicated in the recognition of exclusive rights in intangible trade values. Both statutes contain elaborate mechanisms designed to achieve an appropriate balance between the interests in protection and access. * * *

The rule stated in this Section limits common law liability for misappropriation to cases involving an appropriation of trade secrets, an appropriation of the commercial value of another's identity, or an appropriation of a work of authorship that is not fixed in a tangible medium of expression and is thus protectible under common law copyright. Although courts have occasionally utilized the *INS* decision to grant relief on an ad hoc basis against commercial appropriations in other contexts, they have not articulated coherent principles for its application. It is clear that no general rule of law prohibits the appropriation of a competitor's ideas, innovations, or other intangible assets once they become publicly known. In addition, the federal patent and copyright statutes now preempt a considerable portion of the domain in which the common law tort might otherwise apply. The better approach, and the one most likely to achieve an appropriate balance between the competing interests, does not recognize a residual common law tort of misappropriation.[5]

5. © 1993, The American Law Institute. Reprinted with the permission of The American Law Institute.

A number of thought-provoking law review articles have been written about this controversial cause of action. See, e.g., Handler, *Unfair Competition*, 21 IOWA L. REV. 175 (1936); Callmann, *He Who Reaps Where He Has Not Sown: Unjust Enrichment in the Law of Unfair Competition*, 55 HARV. L. REV. 595 (1942); Baird, *Common Law Intellectual Property and the Legacy of* International News Service v. Associated Press, 50 U. CHI. L. REV. 411 (1983); Paepke, *An Economic Interpretation of the Misappropriation Doctrine: Common Law Protection for Investments in Innovation*, 2 HIGH TECH. L.J. 55 (1987); Raskind, *The Misappropriation Doctrine as a Competitive Norm of Intellectual Property Law*, 75 MINN. L. REV. 875 (1991); Gordon, *On Owning Information: Intellectual Property and the Restitutionary Impulse,* 78 VA. L. REV. 149 (1992).

VI. TRADEMARK DILUTION

WEDGWOOD HOMES, INC. v. LUND

Supreme Court of Oregon, 1983.
294 Or. 493, 659 P.2d 377, 222 U.S.P.Q. 446.

ROBERTS, JUSTICE.

This case presents for our consideration the extent of protection of trademarks and names provided by ORS 647.107, Oregon's antidilution statute. The statute provides:

> "Likelihood of injury to business reputation or of dilution of the distinctive quality of a mark registered under ORS 647.015, or a mark valid at common law, or a trade name valid at common law, shall be a ground for injunctive relief notwithstanding the absence of competition between the parties or the absence of confusion as to the source of goods or services."

Plaintiff, Wedgwood Homes of Portland, Inc., and its wholly owned subsidiary, Wedgwood Homes, Inc., sought to enjoin defendant from using "Wedgwood" in its assumed business names, Wedgwood Downs and Wedgwood Place. At trial plaintiff attempted to prove common law unfair competition as well as dilution of its trade name pursuant to ORS 647.107. We accept the facts as found by the trial court and Court of Appeals. Plaintiff has failed to show a likelihood of consumer confusion of the identities of plaintiff and defendant. Its cause of action for unfair competition therefore fails. The trial court nonetheless granted an injunction finding a likelihood of injury to business reputation or dilution of the distinctive quality of plaintiff's name under the statute. The Court of Appeals affirmed. We review to determine if there was "dilution" of the "distinctive quality" of plaintiff's name. The statute does not define either term. Neither this court nor the Court of Appeals has had occasion to construe the statute.

"Distinctive" is a term often used in the common law of trademarks. To qualify as a trademark a symbol must be "so distinctive that it is capable of performing the function of identifying and distinguishing the goods which bear the symbol." 1 J. McCarthy, Trademarks and Unfair

Competition § 3:1 (1973). Marks are considered distinctive if they comprise coined words invented for the sole purpose of identifying a product or if they are arbitrary marks, existing words applied to a product in an unexpected and nondescriptive fashion. A mark may also become distinctive by acquiring a secondary meaning * * *.

We realize that the distinctiveness adequate to identify the origin of a product may be different from the distinctive quality deserving of protection from dilution. To this extent, the fact that a plaintiff may possess a distinctive tradename only begins our inquiry. The meaning of "distinctive quality" must take shape within the confines of the interests sought to be protected by the antidilution statute.

Traditionally, trademarks were the method by which the public identified a product's source. In modern times, trademarks have assumed a marketing function:

> "The protection of trade-marks is the law's recognition of the psychological function of symbols. If it is true that we live by symbols, it is no less true that we purchase goods by them. A trade-mark is a merchandising short-cut which induces a purchaser to select what he wants, or what he has been led to believe he wants. The owner of a mark exploits this human propensity by making every effort to impregnate the atmosphere of the market with the drawing power of a congenial symbol. Whatever the means employed, the aim is the same—to convey through the mark, in the minds of potential customers, the desirability of the commodity upon which it appears. Once this is attained, the trade-mark owner has something of value. If another poaches upon the commercial magnetism of the symbol he has created, the owner can obtain legal redress."

Mishawaka Rubber & Woolen Manufacturing Co. v. S.S. Kresge Co., 316 U.S. 203, 205, 62 S.Ct. 1022, 1024, 86 L.Ed. 1381 (1942).

The antidilution statutes [6] developed out of the growing recognition that trademarks now surpass the traditional identity role. "[T]he trademark functions on three different levels—as an indication of origin or ownership, as a guarantee of constancy, and as a medium of advertisement." 3 R. Callmann, The Law of Unfair Competition, Trademarks and Monopolies § 65 (3d ed. 1969). A mark may possess independent protectible value to the extent that it acquires advertising and selling power.

In the context of dilution, the protectible quality of a mark has been defined as the mark's power to evoke images of the product, that is, its favorable associational value in the minds of consumers. This attribute

6. Massachusetts enacted the first antidilution statute in 1947. Act of May 2, 1947, ch. 307, § 7a, 1947 Mass. Acts 300 (current version at Mass.Gen.Laws Ann. ch. 110B, § 12 (West 1982–83)). Since then 19 other states have enacted such statutes. Most of them, like Oregon, have adopted the language of the Model State Trademark Bill.

may be developed in a variety of ways: long use, consistent superior quality instilling consumer satisfaction, extensive advertising.

In application the existence of the mark's distinctive quality must be proven by demonstrating what the mark signifies to the consuming public. If the mark has come to signify plaintiff's product in the minds of a significant portion of consumers and if the mark evokes favorable images of plaintiff or its product it possesses the distinctive quality of advertising value—consumer recognition, association and acceptance,—and will be entitled to protection from dilution.

Plaintiff has been engaged for the past 25 years in the development, construction and marketing of single and multiple family residential real estate in eastern Washington County. Plaintiff's substantial advertising programs seek to promote the quality, styling and flair of plaintiff's residential construction. Defendant has maintained dormitory style housing for the elderly in two retirement apartment complexes in eastern Washington County since 1977.

The trial court found that after 25 years' use plaintiff had established a secondary meaning in its name. Defendant does not dispute this conclusion but argues that the antidilution statute should be limited to marks which are coined, unique or truly famous. Relying on legislative history defendant contends that only the most distinctive marks deserve the enhanced protection afforded by ORS 647.107, and that because plaintiff's name is neither coined, unique nor nationally famous the statute should not be invoked on plaintiff's behalf.

We reject defendant's argument that the protection of the antidilution statute should apply to coined and unique words alone. As we have noted, marks may become distinctive in three ways: by use of coined words, by use of arbitrary words, or by acquisition of secondary meaning.

In light of the nature of the distinctive quality we have defined there is no reason to assume, as defendant's argument implies, that only coined marks possess advertising value. When first coined a mark will likely have no commercial value at all. Distinctive quality develops over time as consumer recognition and association is instilled. Moreover, defendant cannot dispute that a mark which has become distinctive through the acquisition of secondary meaning could be entitled to protection from dilution. Among examples of marks covered by the statute is Tiffany, a jewelry trademark, which acquired its distinctiveness through secondary meaning. *Tiffany & Co. v. Boston Club, Inc.*, 231 F.Supp. 836 (D.Mass.1964).[9] It is our opinion that protection may be extended regardless of the manner by which a trademark becomes distinctive.

Likewise, we reject defendant's suggestion that the statute be limited to nationally famous marks. We see no reason why marks of national

9. Defendant, relying on legislative history, asserts that only "truly famous" names such as Tiffany are entitled to antidilution protection. Tiffany was among the trademarks referenced during hearings before enactment of the antidilution statute as an example of a name to be protected by the antidilution statute.

renown should enjoy protection while local marks should not. A small local firm may expend efforts and money proportionately as great as those of a large firm in order to establish its mark's distinctive quality. In both situations the interest to be protected and the damage to be prevented are the same. In summary, it is not the manner by which distinctiveness is acquired nor the span of a mark's notoriety but rather the degree of advertising value the mark has gained which determines the applicability of ORS 647.107.

At trial plaintiff demonstrated, by means of survey evidence, a high association between the words "Wedgwood" and "Homes" in the minds of consumers. Plaintiff has established that its name, Wedgwood, evokes its product, homes, in the minds of a large portion of the public where it does business. Plaintiff further showed that such an association was a positive one. The trial court observed, "Wedgwood Homes is a well recognized name in [eastern Washington County] which approaches a high degree of local fame." We recognize that this association has commercial value to plaintiff. For purposes of the antidilution statute plaintiff has demonstrated that its name possesses distinctive quality.

We must now resolve what dilution is and whether it occurred or was likely to occur in this case.

In *Pignons S.A. de Mecanique de Precision v. Polaroid Corporation*, 657 F.2d 482, 494–95 (1st Cir.1981), the court illustrated the three situations where dilution may arise. The term may refer to injury to the value of the mark caused by actual or potential consumer confusion. It may also be applied to injury caused by use which detracts from the reputation associated with plaintiff's mark. Finally it may encompass any diminution in the uniqueness and individuality of the mark resulting from defendant's use of a similar mark.

The first definition is inapplicable because our statute recognizes an action for dilution "notwithstanding the absence of confusion as to the source of goods or services."

An action for potential detraction from or tarnishment of the reputation associated with plaintiff's mark may be recognized in our statute as "likelihood of injury to business reputation" or it may be encompassed within the meaning of dilution. We need not address that issue here. Although plaintiff attempted to show unfavorable associations cast upon its product's reputation by what plaintiff characterized as the inferior construction and design of defendant's buildings, the trial court found that such unfavorable associations were not proven.[10]

10. We recognize that unfavorable associations may be enjoined. For example, in *Dallas Cowboys Cheerleaders, Inc. v. Pussycat Cinema, Ltd.*, 604 F.2d 200 (2d Cir. 1979), plaintiff successfully enjoined a pornographic film depicting performers in the costume of its cheerleaders. The court reasoned that it would be "hard to believe that anyone who had seen defendants' sexually depraved film could ever thereafter disassociate it from plaintiff's cheerleaders. This association results in confusion which has a 'tendency to impugn [plaintiff's services] and injure plaintiff's business reputation * * *,' " 604 F.2d at 205, citing *Coca-Cola Company v. Gemini Rising, Inc.*, 346

We are left, then, with the third definition of dilution, a diminution in the uniqueness and individuality of the mark caused by another's use of the same or similar mark. We must consider whether a form of dilution is cognizable which does not depend on the relative quality of defendant's product or the undesirability of its association with plaintiff's product. We are persuaded that it is.

Where tradename owners have created a favorable association between their name and their product, they possess a valuable marketing tool. This aura of recognition enhances the value of plaintiff's name. Subsequent use of the name with a nonrelated product broadens the associations linking name and product in the minds of consumers of plaintiff's product and diminishes the specific association plaintiff seeks to foster. "[U]nrelated use erodes selling power by destroying the automatic identification of the trademark with the original product and the favorable images created by advertising." Greiwe, *Antidilution Statutes: A New Attack on Comparative Advertising*, 72 Trademark Rep. 178, 186 (1982). A second use may therefore be prevented by means of the antidilution statute.

We are aware of instances of judicial reluctance to apply antidilution statutes literally. Some courts refuse to issue injunctive relief because likelihood of confusion is not present, despite statutory language to the contrary. Other courts have refused to apply the statute where confusion exists, or where competition exists. We are persuaded, however, in light of the interest sought to be protected by the law and the very language of the statute, that ORS 647.107 protects this plaintiff's tradename.

Allied Maintenance Corporation v. Allied Mechanical Trades, Inc., 42 N.Y.2d 538, 542, 399 N.Y.S.2d 628, 630, 369 N.E.2d 1162, 1164 (1977), defined dilution as "the whittling away of an established trademark's selling power and value through its unauthorized use by others upon dissimilar products." The court distinguished the rationale for the dilution statute from the common law actions of trademark infringement and unfair competition:

> "The evil which the Legislature sought to remedy was not public confusion caused by similar products or services sold by competitors, but a cancer-like growth of dissimilar products or services which feeds upon the business reputation of an established distinctive trade-mark or name. * * * The harm that section 368–d [the New York antidilution statute] is designed to prevent is the gradual whittling away of a firm's distinctive trade-mark or name."

42 N.Y.2d at 544, 399 N.Y.S.2d at 632, 369 N.E.2d at 1165–66.

F.Supp. 1183, 1189 (EDNY 1972). In *Chemical Corp. of America v. Anheuser–Busch, Inc.*, 306 F.2d 433, 437 (5th Cir. 1962), cert. denied, 372 U.S. 965, 83 S.Ct. 1089, 10 L.Ed.2d 129 (1963), an insecticide manufacturer's slogan "where there's life—there's bugs" was held to create "a peculiarly unwholesome association of ideas" with plaintiff's slogan "where there's life—there's Bud."

In *R.G. Barry Corp. v. Mushroom Makers, Inc.*, 108 Misc.2d 113, 436 N.Y.S.2d 927, 931, aff'd 85 A.D.2d 544, 444 N.Y.S.2d 922 (1981), the court in denying defendant's summary judgment motion in opposition to plaintiff's antidilution claim observed: "Justice Felix Frankfurter termed the result of association of a name with a product through use and advertising 'commercial magnetism.' *Mishawaka Rubber & Woolen Mfg. Co. v. S.S. Kresge Co.*, 316 U.S. 203, 205, 62 S.Ct. 1022, 1024, 86 L.Ed. 1381. The anti-dilution statute was designed to prevent poaching on that commercial value of a distinctive trademark."

In Augusta National, Inc. v. Northwestern Mutual Life Ins. Co., 193 USPQ 210 (SD Ga. 1976), the court explained how dilution would occur if defendant were permitted to use "Masters" in its golf tournament "Ladies Masters at Moss Creek Plantation."

> "If the suspect name is used there is reasonable certainty that the value of plaintiff's mark will be eroded; a little now, more later, until the 'magic' of the Masters [Golf Tournament] will be mortally dissipated if not completely dispelled."

193 USPQ at 222.

We hold that where a tradename possesses the distinctive quality of favorable associational value a second use may be enjoined under the statute whenever this is proven to be necessary in order to prevent the diminution of plaintiff's name as an advertising tool among consumers of plaintiff's product. In the case before us plaintiff has established that its name possesses the distinctive quality of positive associational value with its product. To a significant percentage of the consuming public of eastern Washington County, Wedgwood connotes homes. Defendant's use of the name in connection with retirement apartments expands the associations consumers are likely to connect with the name and thereby reduces the name's effectiveness in identifying and advertising plaintiff's product. On these facts plaintiff has adequately demonstrated dilution of the distinctive quality of its name.

The decision of the Court of Appeals is affirmed.

Notes and Questions

1. *The dilution cause of action.* What is the purpose of the dilution cause of action? Given the expansion of the trademark infringement cause of action to encompass confusion about sponsorship and affiliation, how much does the dilution cause of action add? See Moskin, *Dilution or Delusion: The Rational Limits of Trademark Protection*, 83 TRADEMARK REP. 122 (1993). Does protecting against dilution in the absence of a likelihood of confusion promote any public interest, or is it solely a benefit for trademark owners?

The dilution cause of action was created primarily through legislative enactment. Massachusetts enacted the first antidilution statute in 1947. Since then, at least 24 other states have adopted similar statutes.[6] Most of

6. A list of these state statutes can be found in RESTATEMENT (THIRD) OF UNFAIR COMPETITION § 25, Statutory Note (Tentative Draft No. 2, 1990).

these statutes, including the Oregon statute set forth in *Wedgwood*, resemble Section 12 of the U.S. Trademark Association's Model State Trademark Bill (1964).

As the *Wedgwood* opinion suggests, for many years, courts were skeptical, even hostile, to the antidilution statutes, and reluctant to apply them literally. What might explain this reaction? See Pattishall, *The Dilution Rationale for Trademark–Trade Identity Protection, Its Progress and Prospects*, 71 NW. U. L. REV. 618 (1976). Some courts construed the antidilution statutes to require proof of likelihood of confusion, or wrongful intent on the defendant's part, despite clear statutory language to the contrary. See, e.g., Girl Scouts of United States v. Personality Posters Mfg. Co., 304 F.Supp. 1228, 1233, 163 U.S.P.Q. 505, 509 (S.D.N.Y.1969). Others suggested that the antidilution statutes did not apply when the parties' goods competed or a likelihood of confusion might be found to exist. See, e.g., Edgewater Beach Apartments Corp. v. Edgewater Beach Management Co., Inc., 12 Ill.App.3d 526, 299 N.E.2d 548, 179 U.S.P.Q. 555 (1973). That trend to limit or avoid the statutes has gradually dissipated, and courts have begun to embrace them literally. For a detailed history of the development of the dilution cause of action, see Handler, *Are the State Antidilution Laws Compatible With the National Protection of Trademarks?*, 75 TRADEMARK REP. 269 (1985); Shire, *Dilution Versus Deception—Are State Antidilution Laws an Appropriate Alternative To the Law of Infringement?*, 77 TRADEMARK REP. 273 (1987).

2. *The distinctiveness standard.* As the *Wedgwood* opinion suggests, the case opinions have established two basic issues for resolution in a trademark dilution case: first, is the mark "distinctive," and second, if it is, is there a likelihood of dilution?

How does the *Wedgwood* court define the "distinctiveness" requirement of dilution law?

Though the statutory language may not expressly require it, most jurisdictions have limited dilution protection to marks or trade names that are particularly strong and well known, due to concerns about the anticompetitive consequences of extending antidilution protection to all marks and trade names, across the board. See, e.g., Accuride International, Inc. v. Accuride Corp., 871 F.2d 1531, 10 U.S.P.Q.2d 1589 (9th Cir.1989). Thus, often more is required than the level of "distinctiveness" necessary to obtain ownership rights in a mark or to register it.

How would you measure a trade name or mark's "fame" or "distinctiveness" for purposes of determining whether it is entitled to dilution protection? The Restatement (Third) of Unfair Competition suggests that the mark will be sufficiently "distinct" if it "retains its source significance when encountered outside the context of the goods or services with which it is used by the trademark owner." RESTATEMENT (THIRD) OF UNFAIR COMPETITION § 25, comment e (Tentative Draft No. 2, 1990). For example, if people think "a source of cameras" when they hear or see the word "Kodak," even in a context other than sale of cameras, the mark is sufficiently distinctive. *Id.* If the mark only evokes a source association when used in connection with the goods or services it identifies, then it is not sufficiently distinctive. *Id.* How would you go about making this finding of fact? Could you devise a list of factors that would be relevant to the determination, to introduce method and uniformity to the measurement process? See *id.*

Some case opinions have required that the trade name or mark enjoy national fame, while others, like *Wedgwood*, have rejected the notion that the name or mark's fame must be national in scope. What are the practical implications of the *Wedgwood* position? For example, what if the defendant had been a nationwide retailer wishing to use the word "Wedgwood" as a mark for a consumer product throughout the nation? Should the court grant the plaintiff's request for injunction against use of the mark in eastern Washington County, Oregon?

What if the mark's fame is limited to a particular segment of the national population, rather than to the general population of a particular geographic region? For example, most lawyers (and law students) and accountants are very familiar with the mark "Lexis" for computerized legal research services, but the general public is not. Should the owner of the Lexis mark for computerized legal research services be entitled to prevent use of a similar mark for a general consumer item, like an automobile, wherever there are lawyers or accountants? See Mead Data Central, Inc. v. Toyota Motor Sales, U.S.A. Inc., 875 F.2d 1026, 10 U.S.P.Q.2d 1961 (2d Cir.1989). What if, instead of a car, the defendant wished to use the similar mark to identify its legal process serving service?

3. *A likelihood of dilution.* The antidilution statutes recognize and redress three forms of injury. First, actionable injury may occur when the defendant's use of a similar mark or name causes a likelihood of consumer confusion about the source, affiliation or sponsorship of the defendant's product or service. This branch of dilution essentially duplicates trademark infringement. Second, dilution injury may occur when the defendant's use of a similar mark or name diminishes or whittles away the individuality and uniqueness of the mark or name and the strong public association the plaintiff has developed between the mark or name and itself. We will refer to this branch as "diminution" dilution, although it is also sometimes called "blurring," as well. Third, dilution injury may occur when the defendant's use of a similar mark or name "tarnishes" the plaintiff's mark or name by placing it in an "unwholesome" context or in a context that is "out-of-keeping with plaintiff's high-quality image." Jordache Enterprises, Inc. v. Hogg Wyld, Ltd., 828 F.2d 1482, 1490, 4 U.S.P.Q.2d 1216, 1223 (10th Cir.1987). We will focus on the diminution and tarnishment branches here.

a. Diminution. Few courts have enunciated clear criteria for determining when a defendant's use diminishes or "blurs" a plaintiff's mark. The U.S. Court of Appeals for the Second Circuit has stated that

> there must be some mental association between plaintiff's and defendant's marks. "[I]f a reasonable buyer is not at all likely to link the two uses of the trademark in his or her own mind, even subtly or subliminally, then there can be no dilution. * * * [D]ilution theory presumes *some kind of mental association* in the reasonable buyer's mind between the two party's [sic] use of the mark."

Mead Data Central, Inc. v. Toyota Motor Sales, U.S.A., Inc., 875 F.2d 1026, 1031, 10 U.S.P.Q.2d 1961, 1965–66 (2d Cir.1989) (quoting 2 J.T. McCARTHY, McCARTHY ON TRADEMARKS AND UNFAIR COMPETITION, § 24.13 at 213–14 (2d ed. 1984)). As the Restatement explains, the buyer must recognize "that a mark once associated with the plaintiff is now also in use as an identifying symbol by others." RESTATEMENT (THIRD) OF UNFAIR COMPETITION § 25, comment f (Tentative Draft No. 2, 1990). What kinds of evidence would be relevant to determine whether the necessary mental association is likely?

Clearly, the similarity of the marks would be an important consideration. How similar must the defendant's mark be in order to dilute? Should dilution relief extend beyond the use of identical marks? In *Mead Data Central*, the Second Circuit (applying the New York antidilution statute) held that the marks must be "substantially similar," and held that there was no substantial similarity between the plaintiff's mark, "Lexis," and the defendant's mark "Lexus." The court explained that the two marks were visually distinct and that professional television and radio announcers making advertisements would enunciate the difference in their second syllables. *Mead Data Central, supra,* 875 F.2d at 1026, 10 U.S.P.Q.2d at 1964–65. Compare Polaroid Corp. v. Polaraid, Inc., 319 F.2d 830, 138 U.S.P.Q. 265 (7th Cir.1963), where the Court of Appeals for the Seventh Circuit (applying the Illinois antidilution statute) found that the defendant's use of "Polaraid" for the installation of refrigeration and heating systems diluted the plaintiff's mark "Polaroid" for cameras.

What other factors might be relevant in determining whether the defendant's use dilutes? In *Mead Data Central, supra*, 875 F.2d at 1035, 10 U.S.P.Q.2d at 1968–69, Judge Sweet, in his concurrence, suggested that courts should entertain the following considerations: similarity of the products covered by the marks; sophistication of consumers; predatory intent; renown of the senior mark; and renown of the junior mark. Why are these factors relevant? See RESTATEMENT (THIRD) OF UNFAIR COMPETITION, *supra,* § 25, comment f. Compare Simonson, *How and When Do Trademarks Dilute: A Behavioral Framework to Judge "Likelihood" of Dilution*, 83 TRADEMARK REP. 149 (1993).

Is a mark intended to parody the plaintiff's mark likely to diminish or blur it? In Jordache Enterprises, Inc. v. Hogg Wyld, Ltd., 828 F.2d 1482, 4 U.S.P.Q.2d 1216 (10th Cir.1987), the defendants marketed their size large jeans for women under the mark "Lardashe." The Court of Appeals for the Tenth Circuit found that the mark was a parody of the plaintiff's prestigious "Jordache" mark for women's jeans, and rejected the claim that its use diminished or blurred the plaintiff's mark under the New Mexico antidilution statute:

> [T]he district court found that "[b]ecause of the parody aspect of Lardashe, it is not likely that public identification of JORDACHE with the plaintiff will be eroded; indeed, parody tends to increase public identification of a plaintiff's mark with the plaintiff." * * * We hold these findings are not clearly erroneous.

Id., 828 F.2d at 1489–90, 4 U.S.P.Q.2d at 1224.

Is it appropriate to assume that use of a well-known mark by others does in fact diminish the selling power of the mark? For arguments questioning this assumption, see Welkowitz, *Reexamining Trademark Dilution*, 44 VAND. L. REV. 531 (1991).

b. Tarnishment. Under the tarnishment branch of dilution, the plaintiff's claim is not simply that the defendant's use will diminish the distinctiveness of its mark or name, but rather that it will actively impair the selling power and allure of the plaintiff's mark or name through negative or unsavory association. In the *Jordache* case, *supra*, the Tenth Circuit recognized two ways in which a defendant's use might tarnish a plaintiff's mark. First, "[a] mark can be tarnished if it is used in an unwholesome context." *Id.*, 828 F.2d at 1490, 4 U.S.P.Q.2d at 1223. For example, in Coca–Cola Co. v. Gemini Rising, Inc., 346 F.Supp. 1183, 1189, 175 U.S.P.Q. 56, 61 (E.D.N.Y.1972), the court found that the defendant's use of the distinctive red-and-white script design of the Coca–Cola trademark on a poster admonishing viewers to "Enjoy Cocaine" was likely to tarnish the Coca–Cola mark. Likewise, in Eastman Kodak Co. v. Rakow, 739 F.Supp. 116, 15 U.S.P.Q.2d 1631 (W.D.N.Y.1989), the defendant comedian's use of the stage name "Kodak" in comedy routines featuring crude language and raunchy jokes about bodily functions and sex tarnished the camera and film company's wholesome "Kodak" mark. Compare Tetley, Inc. v. Topps Chewing Gum, Inc., 556 F.Supp. 785, 794, 217 U.S.P.Q. 1128, 1135 (E.D.N.Y. 1983) ("Petley Flea Bags" does not tarnish "Tetley Tea Bags").

Second, the plaintiff's mark may be tarnished through a defendant's "use in a context which, while not inherently 'unwholesome,' is out-of-keeping with plaintiff's high-quality image." *Jordache, supra,* 828 F.2d at 1490, 4 U.S.P.Q.2d at 1224 (quoting 2 J. McCARTHY, McCARTHY ON TRADEMARKS AND UNFAIR COMPETITION § 24:13(E) at 222 (2d ed. 1984)). Perhaps the best known example of this second form of tarnishment is Steinway & Sons v. Robert Demars & Friends, 210 U.S.P.Q. 954 (C.D.Cal. 1981). In that case, the court found that the defendants' adoption of the mark "Stein–Way" for their clip-on handles for beer cans tarnished the prestigious "Steinway" mark for pianos. According to the court:

> Defendants' use of the designation STEIN–WAY in connection with its business and on its products, unless enjoined, will associate or tend to associate plaintiff's high quality pianos and plaintiff's business and cultural activities with defendants' inexpensive, mass-produced products and with the retail liquor stores, supermarkets and similar merchandising concerns which sell defendants' products. Such association will inevitably tarnish plaintiff's reputation and image with the public of manufacturing and/or sponsoring only products and activities of taste, quality and distinction.

Id. at 961.

Which kind of tarnishment did the plaintiff claim in *Wedgwood*? Why did the court reject the claim?

4. *Criticisms of the dilution doctrine.* The dilution doctrine had its genesis in a law review article in which the author, Frank Schechter, condemned as "archaic" the notion that trademarks function solely to indicate "source of origin." Rather, Schechter argued that the "*creation*

and retention of custom, rather than the designation of source, is the primary purpose of the trademark today." Schechter, *The Rational Basis of Trademark Protection*, 40 HARV. L. REV. 813, 822 (1927). Schechter stated four principles:

> (1) that the value of the modern trademark lies in its selling power; (2) that this selling power depends for its psychological hold upon the public, not merely upon the merit of the goods upon which it is used, but equally upon its own uniqueness and singularity; (3) that such uniqueness or singularity is vitiated or impaired by its use upon either related or non-related goods and (4) that the degree of its protection depends in turn upon the extent to which, through the efforts or ingenuity of its owner, it is actually unique and different from other marks.

Id., at 831. Schechter urged the creation of a property right in trademarks which would protect against the "gradual whittling away or dispersion of the identity and hold upon the public mind of the mark or name by its use upon non-competing goods." *Id.*, at 825.

Schechter's arguments won the support of others, and eventually led to passage of antidilution statutes in a number of jurisdictions, as described in note 1, above. There have, however, been a number of criticisms of the dilution doctrine and the rationale that underlies it. See, e.g., Middleton, *Some Reflections on Dilution*, 42 TRADEMARK REP. 175, 178–79 (1952) ("The trade-mark owner complaining of dilution, like the dress designer deploring the copyist, is seeking some means for protecting property in an idea embodied in a catchy word, an original design; but under our constitution this can be done, if at all, only by invoking the patent or copyright laws * * *. [T]rademark rights have nothing to do with property in ideas.")

One line of criticism essentially views the dilution cause of action as a means of promoting and protecting "persuasive advertising." The desirability of the cause of action then turns on the social desirability of persuasive advertising. In a 1948 Yale Law Journal article, Professor Ralph Brown distinguished between "informative" advertising and "persuasive" advertising, finding the latter unworthy of promotion through adoption of a dilution cause of action.

> The buying public submits to a vast outpouring of words and pictures from the advertisers, in which, mingled with exhortations to buy, is a modicum of information about the goods offered. * * * To the extent that the blandishments of sellers inform buyers what is to be bought, and at what price, advertising undoubtedly helps to quicken the stream of commerce.
>
> Most advertising, however, is designed not to inform, but to persuade and influence. What is the occasion for such tremendous outlays on persuasion and influence in a well-ordered economic system? If we consider first the total stream of production and consumption, persuasive advertising seems only to consume resources that might be put to better use producing more goods and services. It does not increase total demand; it only increases wants. Effective demand arises, not from what we would like to have, but from the purchasing power of the community created by its productive power. We consume what we produce, and no more. Considering the economic welfare of the commu-

> nity as a whole, to use up part of the national product persuading people to buy product A rather than product B appears to be a waste of resources.

Brown, *Advertising and the Public Interest: Legal Protection of Trade Symbols*, 57 YALE L. J. 1165, 1168–69 (1948). Professor Brown then argued that persuasive advertising can be anticompetitive in effect, permitting advertisers to differentiate their products from the similar products of their competitors in the public mind, thus carving out a separate market in which a modicum of monopoly power can be exercised through manipulation of demand, price, and output. *Id.*, at 1171–1175. Brown considered and rejected the argument that advertising, by increasing the volume of sales, leads to greater economic efficiency. *Id.*, at 1175–77. He likewise considered and rejected arguments that the profits generated by the anticompetitive aspects of advertising lead to greater investment of capital. *Id.*, at 1177–80. He then turned to freedom-of-choice arguments:

> Defenders of the institution [of persuasive advertising] have two additional lines of defense. The first is that persuasive advertising creates a cluster of values, no less real because they are intangible. The second, related to the first, argues that the sovereign consumer has made a free election between those values and the austerities of price competition. * * *
>
> What are the intangible values? One is said to be the assurance of reliability, because the advertiser wants to build up repeat sales, and cannot afford to sell patently unsatisfactory goods. Admitting, for the sake of getting on, that unadvertised brands offer a greater opportunity for "hit-and run" frauds, the difficulty with this contention is that the hope of continued custom is quite unrelated to the magnitude of persuasive advertising. Nothing more than information as to source is necessary for the consumer to be able to repeat a satisfactory purchase.
>
> Other values derive from the proposition that cheapness is not enough. The buyer of an advertised good buys more than a parcel of food or fabric; he buys the pause that refreshes, the hand that has never lost its skill, the priceless ingredient that is the reputation of its maker. All these may be illusions, but they cost money to create, and if the creators can recoup their outlay, who is the poorer? Among the many illusions which advertising can fashion are those of lavishness, refinement, security, and romance. Suppose the monetary cost of compounding a perfume is trivial; of what moment is this if the ads promise, and the buyer believes, that romance, even seduction, will follow its use? The economist, whose dour lexicon defines as irrational any market behavior not dictated by a logical pecuniary calculus, may think it irrational to buy illusions; but there is a degree of that kind of irrationality even in economic man; and consuming man is full of it.
>
> The taint of irrationality may be dispelled by asserting flatly that the utility of a good, that is, its capacity to satisfy wants, is measured exactly by what people will pay for it. If, as is undeniably the case, consumers will pay more for an advertised brand than for its unheralded duplicate, then consumers must get more satisfaction out of the advertised brand. The nature of the satisfaction is of concern only to the

moralist. Though this argument can easily be pushed to absurdity—suppose it was to the interest of the advertisers to consume half the national product in persuasion?—it seems plausible if it is based on the dogma of consumer autonomy. Then anyone who questions the untrammelled use of influence by the seller and its uncoerced acceptance by the buyer is at best a Puritan, at worst a Fascist. The debate seems to end in a defense of freedom, for the advertiser as well as for the consumer.

But does the sovereign consumer have real freedom of choice? The first requisite of choice is an adequate presentation of alternatives. The classical economists who enthroned the consumer never dreamed that he would make his decisions under a bombardment of stupefying symbols. He should be informed, and willing to pay the necessary price for information. But the most charitable tabulations reveal relatively little information in advertising directed to consumers outside the classified columns and local announcements. National advertising is dominated by appeals to sex, fear, emulation, and patriotism, regardless of the relevance of those drives to the transaction at hand. The purchase of many advertised articles, then, has a raw emotional origin. Many others are compelled by the endless reiteration of the advertisers' imperative: eat lemons, drink milk, wear hats. Pseudo-information fills any gaps. It takes many forms. There is the bewildering manipulation of comparatives and superlatives; "No other soap washes cleaner"; "the world's most wanted pen." In the atomic age, precise scientific data are helpful. Bayer Aspirin tells us that the tablet dissolves in two seconds. Whether the analgesic effect is then felt in one hour or two hours will no doubt be explained in time. Buick lists among its features such well-understood engineering terms as "Dynaflow Drive, Taper-thru Styling, Vibra–Shielded Ride, Hi–Posed Fire-ball Power." The reader, after ten minutes with a magazine or the radio, can select his own examples of the types of influence that are thought to move the sovereign consumer.

The foundation of free choice, to repeat, is an adequate presentation of alternatives. Admittedly, many choices, for example in politics or religion, are presented under a smoke screen of exaggeration and emotion. But there are usually at least two sides to the argument. The choice between one highly advertised dentifrice and another is, in important respects, no choice at all. It cannot register a decision to support or reject institutional arrangements which, as has been shown, contribute to monopolistic waste of resources; it cannot reflect a preference to get more or less for one's money, to take an illusion or leave it. It is only a choice between one illusion or another. * * *

Id., at 1180–83. Do you agree with Professor Brown's analysis of the value of persuasive advertising? How would you describe the link between protection against trademark dilution and promotion and protection of persuasive advertising? Is Professor Brown's connection of the two an accurate one?

5. *A federal cause of action for dilution?* The Trademark Law Revision Act of 1988, as originally proposed, would have amended Lanham Act section 43(a) to provide a federal cause of action for dilution, but the dilution

provisions ultimately were deleted. Pub. L. No. 100–667, 102 Stat. 3935. As proposed, the amendment would have protected against dilution of "famous" registered marks, and made federal registration an absolute defense against state dilution claims. See S. REP. NO. 515, 100th Cong., 2nd Sess. 41–43 (1988).

Should there be a federal cause of action for dilution? For arguments in favor of a federal law, see Gilson, *A Federal Dilution Statute: Is It Time?*, 83 TRADEMARK REP. 108 (1993); Muller, *A Position of Advocacy In Support of Adoption of a Preemptive Federal Antidilution Statute*, 83 TRADEMARK REP. 175 (1993). For arguments against, see Port, *The Unnatural Expansion of Trademark Rights: Is A Federal Dilution Statute Necessary?*, 18 SETON HALL LEGIS. J. 433 (1994); Handler, *Are the State Antidilution Laws Compatible with the National Protection of Trademarks?*, 75 TRADEMARK REP. 269 (1985).

6. *First amendment considerations.* In L.L. Bean, Inc. v. Drake Publishers, Inc., 811 F.2d 26, 1 U.S.P.Q.2d 1753 (1st Cir.1987), *cert. denied* 483 U.S. 1013, 107 S.Ct. 3254, 97 L.Ed.2d 753 (1987), the defendant "adult erotic entertainment" magazine published a two-page article entitled "L.L. Bea*m*'s Back–To–School–Sex–Catalog." (Emphasis added.) The article was labelled on the magazine's contents page as "humor" and "parody." The article displayed a facsimile of L.L. Bean's trademark and featured pictures of nude models in sexually explicit positions using "products" that were described in a crudely humorous fashion. L.L. Bean sought relief on a number of grounds, and the district court granted its motion for summary judgement on a trademark dilution "tarnishment" theory, enjoining further publication of the parody. The question on appeal was whether the injunction violated the first amendment. The Court of Appeals for the First Circuit found that it did, and reversed.

> The district court believed that if a noncommercial parody "would result in images of impurity in the minds of [consumers] . . . [s]uch connotations would obviously tarnish the affirmative associations the mark had come to convey." It thus read the anti-dilution statute as granting a trademark owner the unfettered right to suppress the use of its name in any context, commercial or noncommercial, found to be offensive, negative or unwholesome. As one commentator has pointed out, there are serious first amendment implications involved in applying anti-dilution statutes to cover noncommercial uses of a trademark:
>
>> Famous trademarks offer a particularly powerful means of conjuring up the image of their owners, and thus become an important, perhaps at times indispensable, part of the public vocabulary. Rules restricting the use of well-known trademarks may therefore restrict the communication of ideas.... If the defendant's speech is particularly unflattering, it is also possible to argue that the trademark has been tarnished by the defendant's use. The constitutional implications of extending the misappropriation or tarnishment rationales to such cases, however, may often be intolerable. Since a trademark may frequently be the most effective means of focusing attention on the trademark owner or its product, the

> recognition of exclusive rights encompassing such use would permit the stifling of unwelcome discussion.

Denicola, *Trademarks as Speech*, 1982 Wis.L.Rev. at 195–96.

> * * * Neither the strictures of the first amendment nor the history and theory of anti-dilution law permit a finding of tarnishment based solely on the presence of an unwholesome or negative context in which a trademark is used without authorization. Such a reading of the anti-dilution statute unhinges it from its origins in the marketplace. * * *
>
> * * * The Constitution is not offended when the anti-dilution statute is applied to prevent a defendant from using a trademark without permission in order to merchandise dissimilar products or services. Any residual effect on first amendment freedoms should be balanced against the need to fulfill the legitimate purpose of the anti-dilution statute. * * *
>
> * * * [T]he instant defendant used plaintiff's mark solely for non-commercial purposes. Appellant's parody constitutes an editorial or artistic, rather than a commercial, use of plaintiff's mark. The article was labelled as "humor" and "parody" in the magazine's table of contents section; it took up two pages in a one-hundred-page issue; neither the article nor appellant's trademark was featured on the front or back cover of the magazine. Drake did not use Bean's mark to identify or promote goods or services to consumers; it never intended to market the "products" displayed in the parody. * * *
>
> If the anti-dilution statute were construed as permitting a trademark owner to enjoin the use of his mark in a noncommercial context found to be negative or offensive, then a corporation could shield itself from criticism by forbidding the use of its name in commentaries critical of its conduct. * * *
>
> * * * Trademark parodies, even when offensive, do convey a message. The message may be simply that business and product images need not always be taken too seriously; a trademark parody reminds us that we are free to laugh at the images and associations linked with the mark. The message also may be a simple form of entertainment conveyed by juxtaposing the irreverent representation of the trademark with the idealized image created by the mark's owner. While such a message lacks explicit political content, that is no reason to afford it less protection under the first amendment.

Id., 811 F.2d at 30–34, 1 U.S.P.Q.2d at 1756–59. Does the first amendment *always* prevent recovery for dilution tarnishment in non-commercial settings? See Anheuser–Busch, Inc. v. Balducci Publications, 28 F.3d 769, 31 U.S.P.Q.2d 1296 (1994) (expressly rejecting this suggestion).

Compare the Second Circuit's approach to trademark parody in Dallas Cowboys Cheerleaders, Inc. v. Pussycat Cinema, Ltd., 604 F.2d 200, 203 U.S.P.Q. 161 (2d Cir.1979). In that case, the defendant showed a pornographic film in which the heroine, dressed in a uniform strikingly similar to that worn by the plaintiff's cheerleaders, engaged in graphic sexual activities. The Second Circuit, which characterized the film as "gross and revolting," found that the plaintiff had trademark rights in the cheerleader uniforms and purported to find confusion of sponsorship or approval. The court upheld a preliminary injunction against the defendant's further use of the uniform, expressly rejecting the defendant's first amendment objections:

> Plaintiff's trademark is in the nature of a property right, and as such it need not "yield to the exercise of First Amendment rights under circumstances where adequate alternative avenues of communication exist." * * * [T]here are numerous ways in which defendants may comment on "sexuality in athletics" without infringing plaintiff's trademark * * *.

Id., 604 F.2d at 206, 203 U.S.P.Q. at 165–66 (quoting Lloyd Corp. v. Tanner, 407 U.S. 551, 92 S.Ct. 2219, 33 L.Ed.2d 131 (1972)). The First Circuit, in *L.L. Bean*, rejected the *Dallas Cowboys* opinion as precedent:

> [W]e do not think the court fully assessed the nature of a trademark owner's property rights. A trademark is a form of intellectual property; the Supreme Court case [*Lloyd Corp. v. Tanner*] relied upon by the Dallas Cowboys Cheerleaders court involved a shopping center. The first amendment issues involved in this case cannot be disposed of by equating the rights of a trademark owner with the rights of an owner of real property * * *.

L.L. Bean, supra, 811 F.2d at 29, 1 U.S.P.Q.2d at 1755.

Should a mark owner have a "diminution" or "whittling away" dilution cause of action to prevent generic uses of its mark by noncommercial defendants such as the media or dictionary publishers? Compare Wolf, *Trademark Dilution: The Need for Reform*, 74 TRADEMARK REP. 311 (1984), with RESTATEMENT (THIRD) OF UNFAIR COMPETITION § 25, comment i (Tentative Draft No. 2, 1990).

For additional reading about the first amendment implications of dilution relief, see Denicola, *supra*; Comment, *Trademark Parody: A Fair Use and First Amendment Analysis*, 72 VA. L. REV. 1079 (1986).

Chapter Eight

THE RIGHT OF PUBLICITY

I. THE NATURE AND PURPOSE OF THE RIGHT OF PUBLICITY

HAELAN LABORATORIES, INC. v. TOPPS CHEWING GUM, INC.

United States Court of Appeals for the Second Circuit, 1953.
202 F.2d 866, *cert. denied* 346 U.S. 816, 74 S.Ct. 26.
98 L.Ed. 343 (1953).

FRANK, CIRCUIT JUDGE.

After a trial without a jury, the trial judge dismissed the complaint on the merits. The plaintiff maintains that defendant invaded plaintiff's exclusive right to use the photographs of leading baseball-players. * * *

1. So far as we can now tell, there were instances of the following kind:

(a). The plaintiff, engaged in selling chewing-gum, made a contract with a ball-player providing that plaintiff for a stated term should have the exclusive right to use the ball-player's photograph in connection with the sales of plaintiff's gum; the ball-player agreed not to grant any other gum manufacturer a similar right during such term; the contract gave plaintiff an option to extend the term for a designated period.

(b). Defendant, a rival chewing-gum manufacturer, knowing of plaintiff's contract, deliberately induced the ball-player to authorize defendant, by a contract with defendant, to use the player's photograph in connection with the sales of defendant's gum either during the original or extended term of plaintiff's contract, and defendant did so use the photograph.

Defendant argues that, even if such facts are proved, they show no actionable wrong, for this reason: The contract with plaintiff was no more than a release by the ball-player to plaintiff of the liability which, absent the release, plaintiff would have incurred in using the ball-player's photograph, because such a use, without his consent, would be an invasion of his right of privacy under Section 50 and Section 51 of the New York Civil Rights Law; this statutory right of privacy is personal, not assignable; therefore, plaintiff's contract vested in plaintiff no "property" right or other legal interest which defendant's conduct invaded.

Both parties agree, and so do we, that, on the facts here, New York "law" governs. And we shall assume, for the moment, that, under the

New York decisions, defendant correctly asserts that any such contract between plaintiff and a ball-player, in so far as it merely authorized plaintiff to use the player's photograph, created nothing but a release of liability. On that basis, were there no more to the contract, plaintiff would have no actionable claim against defendant. But defendant's argument neglects the fact that, in the contract, the ball-player also promised not to give similar releases to others. If defendant, knowing of the contract, deliberately induced the ball-player to break that promise, defendant behaved tortiously.

* * *

2. The foregoing covers the situations where defendant, by itself or through its agent, induced breaches. But in those instances where [another party] induced the breach, we have a different problem; and that problem also confronts us in instances * * * where defendant, "with knowledge of plaintiff's exclusive rights," used a photograph of a ball-player without his consent during the term of his contract with plaintiff.

With regard to such situations, we must consider defendant's contention that none of plaintiff's contracts created more than a release of liability, because a man has no legal interest in the publication of his picture other than his right of privacy, i.e., a personal and non-assignable right not to have his feelings hurt by such a publication.

A majority of this court rejects this contention. We think that, in addition to and independent of that right of privacy (which in New York derives from statute), a man has a right in the publicity value of his photograph, *i.e.*, the right to grant the exclusive privilege of publishing his picture, and that such a grant may validly be made "in gross," *i.e.*, without an accompanying transfer of a business or of anything else. Whether it be labelled a "property" right is immaterial; for here, as often elsewhere, the tag "property" simply symbolizes the fact that courts enforce a claim which has pecuniary worth.

This right might be called a "right of publicity." For it is common knowledge that many prominent persons (especially actors and ball-players), far from having their feelings bruised through public exposure of their likenesses, would feel sorely deprived if they no longer received money for authorizing advertisements, popularizing their countenances, displayed in newspapers, magazines, busses, trains and subways. This right of publicity would usually yield them no money unless it could be made the subject of an exclusive grant which barred any other advertiser from using their pictures.

We think the New York decisions recognize such a right.

* * *

* * * [P]laintiff, in its capacity as exclusive grantee of a player's "right of publicity," has a valid claim against defendant if defendant used that player's photograph during the term of plaintiff's grant and with knowledge of it. It is no defense to such a claim that defendant is

the assignee of a subsequent contract between that player and [a third party], purporting to make a grant to [the third party] or its assignees. For the prior grant to plaintiff renders that subsequent grant invalid during the period of the grant (including an exercised option) to plaintiff, but not thereafter. [5]

* * *

LUGOSI v. UNIVERSAL PICTURES

Supreme Court of California, 1979.
25 Cal.3d 813, 160 Cal.Rptr. 323, 603 P.2d 425,
205 U.S.P.Q. 1090.

* * *

BIRD, CHIEF JUSTICE, with JUSTICES TOBRINER and MANUEL, dissenting.

* * *

Although Bela Lugosi died more than 20 years ago, his name still evokes the vivid image of Count Dracula, a role he played on stage and in motion pictures. So impressed in the public's memory, the image of Lugosi as Dracula was profitably marketed by defendant Universal Pictures, which had employed Lugosi to portray Count Dracula in the motion picture *Dracula*. Specifically, Universal Pictures concluded licensing agreements which authorized the use of Lugosi's likeness in his portrayal of Count Dracula in connection with the sale of numerous commercial merchandising products.

Plaintiffs, beneficiaries under Bela Lugosi's will, commenced this action for damages and an injunction against further licensing of Lugosi's likeness on the ground that such use was unauthorized and infringed on their interest in controlling the commercial use of Lugosi's likeness. This case thus presents the novel question in California of the nature and scope of an individual's interest in controlling the commercial exploitation of his or her likeness. I conclude that Universal Picture's licensing of Lugosi's image was unauthorized and infringed on Lugosi's proprietary interest in his likeness. * * *

II. THE RIGHT OF PUBLICITY

The fundamental issue in this case is the nature of Lugosi's right to control the commercial exploitation of his likeness. The trial court found Universal's licensing agreements constituted a tortious interference with Lugosi's proprietary or property interest in the commercial use of his likeness, an interest which had descended to plaintiffs. Universal asserts that Lugosi's interest is protected only under the rubric of the right of privacy. Since that right is personal and ceased with Lugosi's death, plaintiffs cannot recover damages based on Universal's conduct. Accordingly, the critical question is whether an individu-

5. Since plaintiff asserts that, in all instances, defendant acted with knowledge of plaintiff's contracts, we need not consider whether and how far defendant would be liable to plaintiff, absent such knowledge, when, during the term of plaintiff's contract, defendant used a player's photograph without inducing a breach of that contract.

al's interest in the commercial use of his likeness is protected solely as an aspect of the right of privacy or whether additional or alternative protection exists.

A. *Privacy or Publicity*

The common law right of privacy creates a cause of action for "an interference with the right of the plaintiff ... 'to be let alone.'" (Prosser, *Privacy* (1960) 48 Cal.L.Rev. 383, 389.) "The gist of the cause of action in a privacy case is ... a direct wrong of a personal character resulting in injury to the feelings.... The injury is mental and subjective. It impairs the mental peace and comfort of the person and may cause suffering much more acute than that caused by a bodily injury." (*Fairfield v. American Photocopy Equipment Co.* (1955) 138 Cal.App.2d 82, 86–87, 291 P.2d 194, 197.) Since the right of privacy developed to protect an individual from certain injuries to his feelings and assaults on his peace of mind, he need not suffer any injury to his property, business or economic interests as a prerequisite to initiating a suit for an invasion of privacy.

The appropriation of an individual's likeness for another's commercial advantage often intrudes on interests distinctly different than those protected by the right of privacy. Plaintiffs in this case have not objected to the manner in which Universal used Lugosi's likeness nor claimed any mental distress from such use. Rather, plaintiffs have asserted that Universal reaped an economic windfall from Lugosi's enterprise to which they are rightfully entitled.

Today, it is commonplace for individuals to promote or advertise commercial services and products or, as in the present case, even have their identities infused in the products. Individuals prominent in athletics, business, entertainment and the arts, for example, are frequently involved in such enterprises. When a product's promoter determines that the commercial use of a particular person will be advantageous, the promoter is often willing to pay handsomely for the privilege. As a result, the sale of one's persona in connection with the promotion of commercial products has unquestionably become big business.

Such commercial use of an individual's identity is intended to increase the value or sales of the product by fusing the celebrity's identity with the product and thereby siphoning some of the publicity value or good will in the celebrity's persona into the product. This use is premised, in part, on public recognition and association with that person's name or likeness, or an ability to create such recognition. The commercial value of a particular person's identity thus primarily depends on that person's public visibility and the characteristics for which he or she is known.

Often considerable money, time and energy are needed to develop one's prominence in a particular field. Years of labor may be required before one's skill, reputation, notoriety or virtues are sufficiently developed to permit an economic return through some medium of commercial promotion. For some, the investment may eventually create considerable commercial value in one's identity.

In this context, the marketable product of that labor is the ability of a person's name or likeness to attract the attention and evoke a desired response in a particular consumer audience. That response is a kind of good will or recognition value generated by that person. While this product is concededly intangible, it is not illusory.

An unauthorized commercial appropriation of one's identity converts the potential economic value in that identity to another's advantage. The user is enriched, reaping one of the benefits of the celebrity's investment in himself. The loss may well exceed the mere denial of compensation for the use of the individual's identity. The unauthorized use disrupts the individual's effort to control his public image, and may substantially alter that image. The individual may be precluded from future promotions in that as well as other fields. Further, while a judicious involvement in commercial promotions may have been perceived as an important ingredient in one's career, uncontrolled exposure may be dysfunctional. As a result, the development of his initial vocation—his profession—may be arrested. Finally, if one's identity is exploited without permission to promote products similar to those which the individual has already endorsed, the unauthorized use resembles unfair competition. While the product which first used the celebrity paid for the privilege of trading on his publicity value, the second product has secured a costless endorsement. The simultaneous presence in the market of these competing products may cause the latter to be mistaken for the former and will probably diminish the value of the endorsement.

Accordingly, the gravamen of the harm flowing from an unauthorized commercial use of a prominent individual's likeness in most cases is the loss of potential financial gain, not mental anguish.[11] The fundamental objection is not that the commercial use is offensive, but that the individual has not been compensated. Indeed, the representation of the person will most likely be flattering, since it is in the user's interest to project a positive image. The harm to feelings, if any, is usually minimal.

The individual's interest thus threatened by most unauthorized commercial uses is significantly different than the personal interests protected under the right of privacy. Recognition of this difference has prompted independent judicial protection for this economic interest. The individual's interest in the commercial value of his identity has been

11. This is not to suggest that commercial misappropriations of one's likeness may not inflict noneconomic injuries. Commercial misappropriations may injure a person's feelings in several ways. First, the person may find any commercial exploitation undesirable and offensive. Second, while certain commercial uses may be acceptable or even desirable, a particular use may be distressing. Third, other individuals, unaware that the use is unauthorized, may disparage one who would sell their identity for that purpose, thereby inducing embarrassment, anger or mental distress. Further, any unauthorized use infringes on one's effort to control the public projection of one's identity, including the desire for solitude and anonymity.

regarded as proprietary in nature and sometimes denominated a common law "right of publicity." This right has won increasing judicial recognition, as well as endorsements by legal commentators.

The right of publicity has been regarded as "the right of each person to control and profit from the publicity values which he has created or purchased." (Nimmer, *The Right of Publicity (1954),* 19 Law & Contemp. Prob. 203, 216.) * * *

Further, there is a broader social objective implicit in according judicial protection to the right of publicity, analogous to the policies underlying copyright and patent law. The Supreme Court recently described the purpose of granting copyright protection as encouraging "people to devote themselves to intellectual and artistic creation ...," and thereby secure the benefits of such labors for the entire society. (*Goldstein v. California* (1973) 412 U.S. 546, 555, 93 S.Ct. 2303, 2309, 37 L.Ed.2d 163.) Similarly, providing legal protection for the economic value in one's identity against unauthorized commercial exploitation creates a powerful incentive for expending time and resources to develop the skills or achievements prerequisite to public recognition and assures that the individual will be able "to reap the reward of his endeavors...." (*Zacchini v. Scripps–Howard Broadcasting Co.*, (1977) 433 U.S. 562, 573, 97 S.Ct. 2849, 2856, 53 L.Ed.2d 965.) While the immediate beneficiaries are those who establish professions or identities which are commercially valuable, the products of their enterprise are often beneficial to society generally. Their performances, inventions and endeavors enrich our society, while their participation in commercial enterprises may communicate valuable information to consumers. [19]

The reasons for affording independent protection for the economic value in one's identity are substantial and compelling, as attested by the increasing number of jurisdictions which have done so. I am similarly persuaded that an individual's right of publicity is entitled to the law's protection.

19. One commentator has suggested a related benefit which may flow from recognizing an individual's right of publicity: "The use of celebrities' names and pictures appears to be a characteristic of advertising. Advertisers would probably continue to use celebrities' pictures even if they knew that other advertisers could freely make similar use of the same names and pictures. In other words, if free use of names and pictures developed, they would probably continue to attract the consumer's attention, provoke emulation, and, perhaps, suggest sponsorship. If society chooses to allow uses of names and likenesses in advertising, it might prefer that consumers not be misled about the willingness of a celebrity to associate himself with a product or service. It might give celebrities a cause of action for unconsented uses of names and likenesses in furtherance of that objective. Similarly, society might decide that the 'emulating' behavior of consumers would channel itself more acceptably if the persons emulated had some control over the decision to link their names and likenesses with particular products. Indeed, persons whose personalities attract consumers might find that coercing advertisers to forego some forms of undesirable advertising behavior advances their interests. Allowing individuals to control the advertising use of their personalities could thus provide a private law mechanism for advertising regulation." (Treece, *Commercial Exploitation of Names, Likenesses, and Personal Histories*, (1973) 51 Texas L.Rev. 637, 647, fn. omitted.)

The common law can readily accommodate judicial recognition of the right of publicity. " 'The rules of the common law are continually changing and expanding with the progress of the society in which it prevails. It does not lag behind, but adapts itself to the conditions of the present so that the ends of justice may be reached.' " (*Johnston v. 20th Century–Fox Film Corp.* (1947) 82 Cal.App.2d 796, 815, 187 P.2d 474, 485–86.) Specifically, this court has long recognized that the concept of "property" is not static but changes to accommodate creative developments and novel legal relationships. * * *

Universal argues that judicial recognition of an independent right of publicity is unnecessary in light of the adequate protection afforded under the common law right of privacy. However, the interest at stake in most commercial appropriation cases is ill-suited to protection under the umbrella of the right of privacy. First, the *raison d'etre* of the common law right of privacy is protection against assaults on one's feelings; an unauthorized commercial appropriation usually precipitates only economic loss, not mental anguish. Second, since the representation of the individual is often flattering, substantial linguistic acrobatics are required to construct a privacy claim on the ground that the use is offensive to a reasonable person. Third, if information about a person is already in the public domain, there can be no claim for an invasion of privacy; to that extent, the right of privacy has been waived. Yet it is publicity which frequently creates value in the individual's identity. To deny a claim for damages for commercial misappropriation because the claimant is prominent is to deny the right to the very individuals to whom the right is most valuable. Fourth, if treated as an aspect of privacy, the use of one's identity for commercial purposes may not be assigned because privacy is a personal, nonassignable right. Such a limitation precludes transferring this economic interest, thereby substantially diminishing its value. In short, conforming a claim for the misappropriation of the commercial value in one's identity to the requirements of the right of privacy requires a procrustean jurisprudence.

B. The Scope of the Right of Publicity

The parameters of the right of publicity must now be considered. This case presents two questions: (1) whether the right extends to the likeness of an individual in his portrayal of the fictional character; and (2) whether the right dies with the individual or may be passed to one's heirs or beneficiaries.

Because the right protects against the unauthorized commercial use of an individual's identity, the right clearly applies to the person's name and likeness. However, such protection would appear to be insufficient because many people create public recognition not only in their "natural" appearance but in their portrayal of particular characters. Charlie Chaplin's Little Tramp, Carroll O'Connor's Archie Bunker and Flip Wilson's Judge and Geraldine exemplify such creations. Substantial publicity value exists in the likeness of each of these actors in their character roles. The professional and economic interests in controlling the commercial exploitation of their likenesses while portraying these characters are identical to their interests in controlling the use of their own "natural" likenesses. Indeed, to the extent one's professional endeavors have focused on the development of one or more particular character images, protection for one's likeness in the portrayal of those characters may well be considerably more important than protection for the individual's "natural" appearance. Hence, there appears to be no reason why the right of publicity should not extend to one's own likeness while portraying a particular fictional character.[26]

Lugosi's likeness in his portrayal of Count Dracula is clearly such a case. Many men have portrayed Count Dracula in motion pictures and on stage. However, the trial court found that Universal did not license the use of an undifferentiated Count Dracula character, but the distinctive and readily recognizable portrayal of Lugosi as the notorious Transylvanian count. Universal thereby sought to capitalize on the particular image of Lugosi in his portrayal of Count Dracula and the public recognition generated by his performance. Such use is illustrative of the very interests the right of publicity is intended to protect. Hence, Lugosi had a protectible property interest in controlling unauthorized commercial exploitation of *his* likeness in his portrayal of Count Dracula.

Recognizing Lugosi's legitimate interest in controlling the use of his portrayal of Count Dracula limits neither the author's exploitation of the novel Dracula[27] nor Universal's use of its copyrighted motion picture. Lugosi only agreed to allow Universal to make limited use of his likeness in their 1930 contract. Further, Lugosi's right certainly does not prohibit others from portraying the character Count Dracula. Consequently, nothing established herein suggests that any of the individuals involved in contemporary cinematic or theatrical revivals of Count Dracula's nocturnal adventures have violated Lugosi's right of publicity. The only conduct prohibited is the unauthorized commercial use of *Lugosi's likeness* in his portrayal of Count Dracula. To the extent that Universal or another seeks such use, that right can be secured by contract.

[The dissent then argues that the right of publicity is descendible.]

Notes and Questions

1. *The right of publicity and the right of privacy.* The *Haelan* opinion coined the term "right of publicity," and was the first judicial opinion to

26. This protection extends only to the individual's likeness—a representation or image of the person while portraying the particular character. Nothing herein is intended to extend protection to the idea for the character or to the character itself. Nothing in the right of publicity prohibits another person, for example, from developing and playing a sympathetic tramp character similar to the one portrayed by Chaplin.

27. This case does not present the question of the relative rights of the novel's copyright holder and Lugosi and his heirs in commercial exploitations of Lugosi's likeness in his portrayal of Count Dracula. However, it should be noted that the trial court found that the novel Dracula has always been in the public domain in the United States due to the author's failure to comply with a requirement of the copyright law in existence when the novel was published.

recognize the right as a distinct cause of action, separate from the invasion of privacy claim. Professor Melville Nimmer pursued the distinction in his influential article, *The Right of Publicity*, 19 L. & CONTEMP. PROB. 203 (1954). In 1960, Professor William Prosser published his famous article, *Privacy*, 48 CAL. L. REV. 383 (1960), which provided the definitive description of the privacy cause of action, but may have diffused recognition of the type of claim asserted in *Haelan* and *Lugosi* as a cause of action distinct from the law of privacy.

In his article, Professor Prosser divided the privacy cause of action into four categories: 1) "intrusion upon the plaintiff's seclusion or solitude, or into his private affairs;" 2) "public disclosure of embarrassing private facts about the plaintiff;" 3) "publicity which places the plaintiff in a false light in the public eye;" and 4) "appropriation, for the defendant's advantage, of the plaintiff's name or likeness." *Id.* at 389. The fourth, "appropriation," category encompassed the situation in which a defendant makes an unauthorized use of a plaintiff's name or likeness to advertise or sell a product.

In the "appropriation" category, the plaintiff's injury is likely to differ, depending on whether she is a private person or a celebrity. In the case of the private plaintiff, the victim may experience mental distress at seeing her name or likeness on the label of products or plastered on billboards, and wish to assert a "right to be let alone." Her damage consists of injury to a personal interest: her sense of dignity and mental tranquility. As Judge Frank notes in *Haelan*, a celebrity, such as a baseball player or an actress, may suffer a different kind of injury, primarily economic in nature. This sets the celebrity's claim apart from all the other "privacy" claims falling within Professor Prosser's four categories. While Prosser himself appeared to recognize the differing interests, his decision to include the celebrity's claim within his fourth "privacy" category (and the subsequent Restatement (Second) of Torts' adoption of his framework, RESTATEMENT (SECOND) OF TORTS §§ 652A (1977)), may have led some litigants and courts to overlook the important distinction between the interests being asserted by the celebrity "appropriation" claimant and other right to privacy claimants.

Overlooking the distinction may lead to findings that are difficult to justify conceptually. For example, by analogy to rights of privacy, some authorities have indicated that the right of publicity cannot be assigned, devised or passed by intestate succession. A much stronger argument can be made for alienability of an economic interest, such as the right of publicity, than of a personal "right to be left alone." The issue of transfer will be explored in more depth below.

Today, the relationship between the invasion of privacy and right of publicity causes of action remains unsettled. Some jurisdictions appear to view the celebrity's economic injury claim as encompassed within the "privacy" cause of action, while others recognize it as a separate and distinct cause of action, known as the "right of publicity." Many states have yet to make their position clear. Those jurisdictions that continue to view the celebrity's economic injury claim as a privacy claim may differ in the extent to which they apply rules and reasoning developed in the context of personal privacy claims to vindicate celebrities' economic interests. The uncertainty pervading the right of publicity cause of action has lead one court to liken it to a "haystack in a hurricane." Ettore v. Philco Television Broadcasting Corp., 229 F.2d 481, 485, 108 U.S.P.Q. 187, 190 (3d Cir.1956), *cert. denied* 351 U.S. 926, 76 S.Ct. 783, 100 L.Ed. 1456 (1956). See Ausness, *The Right of Publicity: A "Haystack in a Hurricane,"* 55 TEMP. L. Q. 977 (1982); Halpern, *The Right of Publicity: Commercial Exploitation of the Associative Value of Personality*, 39 VAND. L. REV. 1199 (1986).

While some jurisdictions draw their "right of publicity" cause of action from the common law, others have enacted statutes which encompass a right of publicity claim. See, e.g., CAL. CIV. CODE §§ 990, 3344 (West Supp. 1993); FLA. STAT. ANN. § 540.08 (West 1988); MASS. GEN. LAWS ANN. ch. 214, § 3A (West 1989); N.Y. CIV. RIGHTS LAW §§ 50–51 (McKinney Supp. 1992). The language of these statutes varies greatly, and may place restraints on assertion of the cause of action that would not exist in the more flexible common law. While some states, such as California, recognize a common-law cause of action that coexists with the statutory cause of action, others, such as New York, have held that the statute supersedes any common-law cause of action.

While the U.S. Court of Appeals in *Haelan*, sitting in diversity, found that New York would recognize a common-law right of publicity apart from its "privacy" statute, the New York courts had not actually done so. Many years later, in Stephano v. News Group Publications, Inc., 64 N.Y.2d 174, 485 N.Y.S.2d 220, 474 N.E.2d 580 (1984), the New York Court of Appeals held that claims for economic injuries arising from unauthorized commercial use of a person's likeness were subsumed under the State's privacy statute, and that no common law right of publicity existed in New York.

Sections 50 and 51 of the New York Civil Rights Law provide that any person or business who uses a living person's name, portrait or picture for advertising purposes or for purposes of trade without written consent will be liable to the person so exploited. The *Stephano* court noted that sections 50 and 51 were enacted to protect privacy interests. Nonetheless, the statutory language literally encompassed the economic injury claim of a celebrity, and would provide the sole avenue for relief. In rejecting *Haelan's* interpretation of New York law, the New York Court of Appeals conceptually reunited the privacy and publicity causes of action which the *Haelan* court had attempted to distinguish. The ramifications of this decision are not yet clear in New York, which (as a major media and entertainment center) is a key state for developing right of publicity law. Of course, the *Haelan* decision has been highly influential in other states, and the *Stephano* court's decision, based on the state's unique statutory provision, need not undercut that influence.

For an exhaustive survey of all the relevant state statutes, as well as examples of foreign approaches to the right of publicity, see J.T. McCARTHY, THE RIGHTS OF PUBLICITY AND PRIVACY ch. 6 (1993).

2. *The relationship of the right of publicity to other causes of action.* The right of publicity is closely related to several legal doctrines in addition to the law of privacy. To begin, do you see a relationship with the unfair competition cause of action for misappropriation? How would you describe the relationship?

The right of publicity is also closely related to the unfair competition doctrines of passing off, trademark dilution, and false advertising. One or more of these causes of action might be pleaded in the alternative to a right of publicity claim in many fact settings. How would you articulate the relationship? What elements differentiate each of these unfair competition causes of action from the right of publicity claim?

What is the relationship between the right of publicity and copyright? What are the key differences? The similarities are strongest in cases in which the plaintiff claims that the defendant appropriated his identity by taking his creation or performance, which is closely linked with his identity. The most famous case involving such a claim is Zacchini v. Scripps–Howard Broadcasting Co., 433 U.S. 562, 97 S.Ct. 2849, 53 L.Ed.2d 965 (1977).

In *Zacchini*, the plaintiff made his living by performing a human cannonball act in which he was shot from a cannon into a net 200 feet away. Each performance took about 15 seconds. While plaintiff was performing at a fair ground, a television reporter filmed his entire act without his permission. Defendant television station broadcast the film over the evening news, along with a favorable commentary. Plaintiff brought suit for damages. The Ohio Supreme Court found the plaintiff's right of publicity would have been violated, except that the defendant was protected from liability by the first amendment. On certiorari, the United States Supreme Court found that the first amendment did not in fact shield the defendant from liability. With regard to the right of publicity cause of action, the Supreme Court stated:

> The broadcast of a film of petitioner's entire act poses a substantial threat to the economic value of that performance. As the Ohio court recognized, this act is the product of petitioner's own talents and energy, the end result of much time, effort, and expense. Much of its economic value lies in the "right of exclusive control over the publicity given to his performance"; if the public can see the act free on television, it will be less willing to pay to see it at the fair. The effect of a public broadcast of the performance is similar to preventing petitioner from charging an admission fee. "The rationale for [protecting the right of publicity] is the straightforward one of preventing unjust enrichment by the theft of good will. No social purpose is served by having the defendant get free some aspect of the plaintiff that would have market value and for which he would normally pay." Moreover, the broadcast of petitioner's entire performance, unlike the unauthorized use of another's name for purposes of trade or the incidental use of a name or picture by the press, goes to the heart of petitioner's ability to earn a living as an entertainer. Thus, in this case, Ohio has recognized what may be the strongest case for a "right of publicity" involving, not the appropriation of an entertainer's reputation to enhance the attractiveness of a commercial product, but the appropriation of the very activity by which the entertainer acquired his reputation in the first place.
>
> Of course, Ohio's decision to protect petitioner's right of publicity here rests on more than a desire to compensate the performer for the time and effort invested in his act; the protection provides an economic

incentive for him to make the investment required to produce a performance of interest to the public. This same consideration underlies the patent and copyright laws long enforced by this Court. As the Court stated in Mazer v. Stein, 347 U.S. 201, 219, 74 S.Ct. 460, 471, 98 L.Ed. 630 (1954):

> The economic philosophy behind the clause empowering Congress to grant patents and copyrights is the conviction that encouragement of individual effort by personal gain is the best way to advance public welfare through the talents of authors and inventors in "Science and useful Arts." Sacrificial days devoted to such creative activities deserve rewards commensurate with the services rendered.

These laws perhaps regard the "reward to the owner [as] a secondary consideration," United States v. Paramount Pictures, 334 U.S. 131, 158, 68 S.Ct. 915, 929, 92 L.Ed. 1260 (1948), but they were "intended definitely to grant valuable, enforceable rights" in order to afford greater encouragement to the production of works of benefit to the public. Washingtonian Publishing Co. v. Pearson, 306 U.S. 30, 36, 59 S.Ct. 397, 400, 83 L.Ed. 470 (1939). The Constitution does not prevent Ohio from making a similar choice here in deciding to protect the entertainer's incentive in order to encourage the production of this type of work.

Id., 433 U.S. at 575–77, 97 S.Ct. at 2857–58, 53 L.Ed.2d at 976–77.

3. *The underlying justifications for a right of publicity.* The California Supreme Court's majority opinion in *Lugosi* accepted that Lugosi had a right of publicity during his lifetime (though it did not explore the scope of that right in any depth), but held that the right did not descend to Lugosi's heirs upon his death.

Justice Bird's dissent reviews the numerous justifications that have been given for the right of publicity cause of action. Which do you find most convincing? Do you find the incentive rationale persuasive? What about the concern that unauthorized use of a plaintiff's identity on products similar to products actually endorsed by the plaintiff may cause consumer confusion? Does the possibility that other causes of action may be available to vindicate these interests affect your evaluation of the need for the right of publicity cause of action?

What is your response to the following:

> The rationales underlying the recognition of a right of publicity are generally less compelling than those that justify rights in trademarks or trade secrets. The commercial value of a person's identity often results from success in endeavors such as entertainment or sports that afford their own substantial rewards. Any additional incentive attributable to the right of publicity may have only marginal significance. In some cases the commercial value associated with a person's identity is largely fortuitous or otherwise unrelated to any investment made by the individual, thus diminishing the weight of the property and unjust enrichment rationales. In addition, the public interest in avoiding false suggestions of endorsement or sponsorship can be pursued through the

> cause of action for deceptive marketing. Thus, courts may be properly reluctant to adopt a broad construction of the publicity right.

RESTATEMENT (THIRD) OF UNFAIR COMPETITION § 46, comment c (Tentative Draft No. 4, 1993).[1]

Compare the following observation from a leading authority on the right of publicity:

> While several rationales or reasons have been argued to support the right of publicity, the one that appeals the most to me is the simplest and most obvious. It is the natural right of property justification. It is an appeal to first principles of justice. Each and every human being should be given control over the commercial use of his or her identity. Perhaps nothing is so strongly intuited as the notion that my identity is mine—it is my property, to control as I see fit. Put simply, my identity is "me." The existence of a legal right to control identity would seem to be essential to any civilized society.

McCarthy, *Public Personas and Private Property: The Commercialization of Human Identity*, 79 TRADEMARK REP. 681, 685 (1989).[2] See generally J.T. McCARTHY, THE RIGHTS OF PUBLICITY AND PRIVACY, ch. 2 (1993).

How would you evaluate the dissent's argument that Lugosi's right of publicity should extend beyond his "natural" likeness to encompass his likeness in portraying Count Dracula? Should it matter how similar or different the likeness is to the plaintiff's "natural" likeness? What if the portrayal involves use of a face mask or heavy make-up? Should it matter whether the plaintiff designed the mask or make-up? What if the plaintiff's appearance in portraying the fictitious character matches a description of the fictitious character written into the original novel or screen play? Might it be difficult, in some cases, to prove whether the defendant has identified the actor in his portrayal of the role or the role itself?

Consider Justice Mosk's view of the issue, set forth in his opinion concurring with he majority:

> We are not troubled by the nature of Lugosi's right to control the commercial exploitation of *his* likeness. That right has long been established. The issue here is the right of Lugosi's successors to control the commercialization of a likeness of a dramatic character—i.e., Count Dracula—created by a novelist and portrayed for compensation by Lugosi in a film version produced by a motion picture company under license from the successor of the novelist. * * *
>
> Bela Lugosi was a talented actor. But he was an actor, a practitioner of the thespian arts; he was not a playwright, an innovator, a creator or an entrepreneur. As an actor he memorized lines and portrayed roles written for him, albeit with consummate skill. * * *
>
> Merely playing a role under the foregoing circumstances creates no inheritable property right in an actor, absent a contract so providing.

1. © 1993, The American Law Institute. Reprinted with the permission of The American Law Institute.

2. © 1989, J. Thomas McCarthy. Reprinted by permission of the copyright owner.

> Indeed, as the record discloses, many other actors have portrayed the same role * * *. Thus neither Lugosi during his lifetime nor his estate thereafter owned the exclusive right to exploit Count Dracula any more than Gregory Peck possesses or his heirs could possess common law exclusivity to General MacArthur, George C. Scott to General Patton, James Whitmore to Will Rogers and Harry Truman, or Charlton Heston to Moses.
>
> I do not suggest that an actor can never retain a proprietary interest in a characterization. An original creation of a fictional figure played exclusively by its creator may well be protectible. Thus, Groucho Marx just being Groucho Marx, with his moustache, cigar, slouch and leer, cannot be exploited by others. Red Skelton's variety of self-devised roles would appear to be protectible, as would the unique personal creations of Abbot and Costello, Laurel and Hardy and others of that genre. * * *
>
> Here it is clear that Bela Lugosi did not portray himself and did not create Dracula, he merely acted out a popular role that had been garnished with the patina of age, as had innumerable other thespians over the decades. His performance gave him no more claim on Dracula than that of countless actors on Hamlet who have portrayed the Dane in a unique manner.

Id., 25 Cal.3d at 825–26, 603 P.2d at 432, 160 Cal.Rptr. at 330, 205 U.S.P.Q. at 1097 (Mosk, J., concurring). Compare McFarland v. Miller, 14 F.3d 912, 29 U.S.P.Q.2d 1586 (3d Cir.1994) (a court should consider whether the public has come to associate the actor with the character he has portrayed. "Where an actor's screen persona becomes so associated with him that it becomes inseparable from the actor's own public image, the actor obtains an interest in the image which gives him standing to prevent mere interlopers from using it without authority.").

II. THE SCOPE OF THE RIGHT OF PUBLICITY

WHITE v. SAMSUNG ELECTRONICS AMERICA, INC.

United States Court of Appeals for the Ninth Circuit, 1992.
971 F.2d 1395, 23 U.S.P.Q.2d 1583, *cert. denied*
___ U.S. ___, 113 S.Ct. 2443, 124 L.Ed.2d 660 (1993).

GOODWIN, SENIOR CIRCUIT JUDGE:

This case involves a promotional "fame and fortune" dispute. In running a particular advertisement without Vanna White's permission, defendants Samsung Electronics America, Inc. (Samsung) and David Deutsch Associates, Inc. (Deutsch) attempted to capitalize on White's fame to enhance their fortune. White sued, alleging infringement of various intellectual property rights, but the district court granted summary judgment in favor of the defendants. We affirm in part, reverse in part, and remand.

Plaintiff Vanna White is the hostess of "Wheel of Fortune," one of the most popular game shows in television history. An estimated forty million people watch the program daily. Capitalizing on the fame which her participation in the show has bestowed on her, White markets her identity to various advertisers.

The dispute in this case arose out of a series of advertisements prepared for Samsung by Deutsch. The series ran in at least half a dozen publications with widespread, and in some cases national, circulation. Each of the advertisements in the series followed the same theme. Each depicted a current item from popular culture and a Samsung electronic product. Each was set in the twenty-first century and conveyed the message that the Samsung product would still be in use by that time. By hypothesizing outrageous future outcomes for the cultural items, the ads created humorous effects. For example, one lampooned current popular notions of an unhealthy diet by depicting a raw steak with the caption: "Revealed to be health food. 2010 A.D." Another depicted irreverent "news"-show host Morton Downey Jr. in front of an American flag with the caption: "Presidential candidate. 2008 A.D."

The advertisement which prompted the current dispute was for Samsung video-cassette recorders (VCRs). The ad depicted a robot, dressed in a wig, gown, and jewelry which Deutsch consciously selected to resemble White's hair and dress. The robot was posed next to a game board which is instantly recognizable as the Wheel of Fortune game show set, in a stance for which White is famous. The caption of the ad read: "Longest-running game show. 2012 A.D." Defendants referred to the ad as the "Vanna White" ad. Unlike the other celebrities used in the campaign, White neither consented to the ads nor was she paid.

Following the circulation of the robot ad, White sued Samsung and Deutsch in federal district court under: (1) California Civil Code § 3344; (2) the California common law right of publicity; and (3) § 43(a) of the Lanham Act, 15 U.S.C. § 1125(a). The district court granted summary judgment against White on each of her claims. White now appeals.

I. Section 3344

White first argues that the district court erred in rejecting her claim under section 3344. Section 3344(a) provides, in pertinent part, that "[a]ny person who knowingly uses another's name, voice, signature, photograph, or likeness, in any manner, ... for purposes of advertising or selling, ... without such person's prior consent ... shall be liable for any damages sustained by the person or persons injured as a result thereof."

White argues that the Samsung advertisement used her "likeness" in contravention of section 3344. In *Midler v. Ford Motor Co.*, 849 F.2d 460 (9th Cir.1988), this court rejected Bette Midler's section 3344 claim concerning a Ford television commercial in which a Midler "sound-alike" sang a song which Midler had made famous. In rejecting Midler's claim, this court noted that "[t]he defendants did not use Midler's name or anything else whose use is prohibited by the statute. The voice they used was [another person's], not hers. The term 'likeness' refers to a visual image not a vocal imitation." *Id.* at 463.

In this case, Samsung and Deutsch used a robot with mechanical features, and not, for example, a manikin molded to White's precise features. Without deciding for all purposes when a caricature or impressionistic resemblance might become a "likeness," we agree with the district court that the robot at issue here was not White's "likeness" within the meaning of section 3344. Accordingly, we affirm the court's dismissal of White's section 3344 claim.

II. Right of Publicity

White next argues that the district court erred in granting summary judgment to defendants on White's common law right of publicity claim. In *Eastwood v. Superior Court,* 149 Cal.App.3d 409, 198 Cal.Rptr. 342 (1983), the California court of appeal stated that the common law right of publicity cause of action "may be pleaded by alleging (1) the defendant's use of the plaintiff's identity; (2) the appropriation of plaintiff's name or likeness to defendant's advantage, commercially or otherwise; (3) lack of consent; and (4) resulting injury." *Id.* at 417, 198 Cal.Rptr. 342 (citing Prosser, Law of Torts (4th ed. 1971) § 117, pp. 804–807). The district court dismissed White's claim for failure to satisfy *Eastwood's* second prong, reasoning that defendants had not appropriated White's "name or likeness" with their robot ad. We agree that the robot ad did not make use of White's name or likeness. However, the common law right of publicity is not so confined.

The *Eastwood* court did not hold that the right of publicity cause of action could be pleaded only by alleging an appropriation of name or likeness. *Eastwood* involved an unauthorized use of photographs of Clint Eastwood and of his name. Accordingly, the *Eastwood* court had no occasion to consider the extent beyond the use of name or likeness to which the right of publicity reaches. That court held only that the right of publicity cause of action "may be" pleaded by alleging, *inter alia,* appropriation of name or likeness, not that the action may be pleaded *only* in those terms.

The "name or likeness" formulation referred to in *Eastwood* originated not as an element of the right of publicity cause of action, but as a description of the types of cases in which the cause of action had been recognized. The source of this formulation is Prosser, *Privacy*, 48 Cal.L.Rev. 383, 401–07 (1960), one of the earliest and most enduring articulations of the common law right of publicity cause of action. In looking at the case law to that point, Prosser recognized that right of publicity cases involved one of two basic factual scenarios: name appropriation, and picture or other likeness appropriation.

Even though Prosser focused on appropriations of name or likeness in discussing the right of publicity, he noted that "[i]t is not impossible that there might be appropriation of the plaintiff's identity, as by impersonation, without the use of either his name or his likeness, and that this would be an invasion of his right of privacy." *Id.* at 401, n.

155. [1] At the time Prosser wrote, he noted however, that "[n]o such case appears to have arisen." *Id.*

Since Prosser's early formulation, the case law has borne out his insight that the right of publicity is not limited to the appropriation of name or likeness. In *Motschenbacher v. R.J. Reynolds Tobacco Co.*, 498 F.2d 821 (9th Cir.1974), the defendant had used a photograph of the plaintiff's race car in a television commercial. Although the plaintiff appeared driving the car in the photograph, his features were not visible. Even though the defendant had not appropriated the plaintiff's name or likeness, this court held that plaintiff's California right of publicity claim should reach the jury.

In *Midler*, this court held that, even though the defendants had not used Midler's name or likeness, Midler had stated a claim for violation of her California common law right of publicity because "the defendants ... for their own profit in selling their product did appropriate part of her identity" by using a Midler sound-alike. *Id.* at 463–64.

In *Carson v. Here's Johnny Portable Toilets, Inc.*, 698 F.2d 831 (6th Cir.1983), the defendant had marketed portable toilets under the brand name "Here's Johnny"—Johnny Carson's signature "Tonight Show" introduction—without Carson's permission. The district court had dismissed Carson's Michigan common law right of publicity claim because the defendants had not used Carson's "name or likeness." In reversing the district court, the sixth circuit found "the district court's conception of the right of publicity ... too narrow" and held that the right was implicated because the defendant had appropriated Carson's identity by using, *inter alia*, the phrase "Here's Johnny." *Id.* at 835–37.

These cases teach not only that the common law right of publicity reaches means of appropriation other than name or likeness, but that the specific means of appropriation are relevant only for determining whether the defendant has in fact appropriated the plaintiff's identity. The right of publicity does not require that appropriations of identity be accomplished through particular means to be actionable. It is noteworthy that the *Midler* and *Carson* defendants not only avoided using the plaintiff's name or likeness, but they also avoided appropriating the celebrity's voice, signature, and photograph. The photograph in *Motschenbacher* did include the plaintiff, but because the plaintiff was not visible the driver could have been an actor or dummy and the analysis in the case would have been the same.

Although the defendants in these cases avoided the most obvious means of appropriating the plaintiffs' identities, each of their actions directly implicated the commercial interests which the right of publicity is designed to protect. As the *Carson* court explained:

> [t]he right of publicity has developed to protect the commercial interest of celebrities in their identities. The theory of the right is

1. Under Professor Prosser's scheme, the right of publicity is the last of the four categories of the right to privacy. Prosser, 48 Cal.L.Rev. at 389.

> that a celebrity's identity can be valuable in the promotion of products, and the celebrity has an interest that may be protected from the unauthorized commercial exploitation of that identity.... If the celebrity's identity is commercially exploited, there has been an invasion of his right whether or not his "name or likeness" is used.

Carson, 698 F.2d at 835. It is not important *how* the defendant has appropriated the plaintiff's identity, but *whether* the defendant has done so. *Motschenbacher*, *Midler*, and *Carson* teach the impossibility of treating the right of publicity as guarding only against a laundry list of specific means of appropriating identity. A rule which says that the right of publicity can be infringed only through the use of nine different methods of appropriating identity merely challenges the clever advertising strategist to come up with the tenth.

Indeed, if we treated the means of appropriation as dispositive in our analysis of the right of publicity, we would not only weaken the right but effectively eviscerate it. The right would fail to protect those plaintiffs most in need of its protection. Advertisers use celebrities to promote their products. The more popular the celebrity, the greater the number of people who recognize her, and the greater the visibility for the product. The identities of the most popular celebrities are not only the most attractive for advertisers, but also the easiest to evoke without resorting to obvious means such as name, likeness, or voice.

Consider a hypothetical advertisement which depicts a mechanical robot with male features, an African–American complexion, and a bald head. The robot is wearing black hightop Air Jordan basketball sneakers, and a red basketball uniform with black trim, baggy shorts, and the number 23 (though not revealing "Bulls" or "Jordan" lettering). The ad depicts the robot dunking a basketball one-handed, stiff-armed, legs extended like open scissors, and tongue hanging out. Now envision that this ad is run on television during professional basketball games. Considered individually, the robot's physical attributes, its dress, and its stance tell us little. Taken together, they lead to the only conclusion that any sports viewer who has registered a discernible pulse in the past five years would reach: the ad is about Michael Jordan.

Viewed separately, the individual aspects of the advertisement in the present case say little. Viewed together, they leave little doubt about the celebrity the ad is meant to depict. The female-shaped robot is wearing a long gown, blond wig, and large jewelry. Vanna White dresses exactly like this at times, but so do many other women. The robot is in the process of turning a block letter on a game-board. Vanna White dresses like this while turning letters on a game-board but perhaps similarly attired Scrabble-playing women do this as well. The robot is standing on what looks to be the Wheel of Fortune game show set. Vanna White dresses like this, turns letters, and does this on the Wheel of Fortune game show. She is the only one. Indeed, defendants themselves referred to their ad as the "Vanna White" ad. We are not surprised.

Television and other media create marketable celebrity identity value. Considerable energy and ingenuity are expended by those who have achieved celebrity value to exploit it for profit. The law protects the celebrity's sole right to exploit this value whether the celebrity has achieved her fame out of rare ability, dumb luck, or a combination thereof. We decline Samsung and Deutch's invitation to permit the evisceration of the common law right of publicity through means as facile as those in this case. Because White has alleged facts showing that Samsung and Deutsch had appropriated her identity, the district court erred by rejecting, on summary judgment, White's common law right of publicity claim.

[The court also reversed the district court's grant of summary judgement against White's Lanham Act § 43(a) claim.]

IV. The Parody Defense

In defense, defendants cite a number of cases for the proposition that their robot ad constituted protected speech. The only cases they cite which are even remotely relevant to this case are *Hustler Magazine v. Falwell*, 485 U.S. 46, 108 S.Ct. 876, 99 L.Ed.2d 41 (1988), and *L.L. Bean, Inc. v. Drake Publishers, Inc.*, 811 F.2d 26 (1st Cir.1987). Those cases involved parodies of advertisements run for the purpose of poking fun at Jerry Falwell and L.L. Bean, respectively. This case involves a true advertisement run for the purpose of selling Samsung VCRs. The ad's spoof of Vanna White and Wheel of Fortune is subservient and only tangentially related to the ad's primary message: "buy Samsung VCRs." Defendants' parody arguments are better addressed to non-commercial parodies.[3] The difference between a "parody" and a "knock-off" is the difference between fun and profit.

V. Conclusion

In remanding this case, we hold only that White has pleaded claims which can go to the jury for its decision.

3. In warning of a first amendment chill to expressive conduct, the dissent reads this decision too broadly. This case concerns only the market which exists in our society for the exploitation of celebrity to sell products, and an attempt to take a free ride on a celebrity's celebrity value. Commercial advertising which relies on celebrity fame is different from other forms of expressive activity in two crucial ways.

First, for celebrity exploitation advertising to be effective, the advertisement must evoke the celebrity's identity. The more effective the evocation, the better the advertisement. If, as Samsung claims, its ad was based on a "generic" game-show hostess and not on Vanna White, the ad would not have violated anyone's right of publicity, but it would also not have been as humorous or as effective.

Second, even if some forms of expressive activity, such as parody, do rely on identity evocation, the first amendment hurdle will bar most right of publicity actions against those activities. In the case of commercial advertising, however, the first amendment hurdle is not so high. *Central Hudson Gas & Electric Corp. v. Public Service Comm'n of New York*, 447 U.S. 557, 566, 100 S.Ct. 2343, 2351, 65 L.Ed.2d 341 (1980). Realizing this, Samsung attempts to elevate its ad above the status of garden-variety commercial speech by pointing to the ad's parody of Vanna White. Samsung's argument is unavailing. Unless the first amendment bars all right of publicity actions—and it does not, *see Zacchini v. Scripps–Howard Broadcasting Co.*, 433 U.S. 562, 97 S.Ct. 2849, 53 L.Ed.2d 965 (1977)—then it does not bar this case.

ALARCON, CIRCUIT JUDGE, concurring in part, dissenting in part:

* * *

In each of the federal cases relied upon by the majority, the advertisement affirmatively represented that the person depicted therein was the plaintiff. In this case, it is clear that a metal robot and not the plaintiff, Vanna White, is depicted in the commercial advertisement. The record does not show an appropriation of Vanna White's identity.

In *Motschenbacher*, a picture of a well-known race driver's car, including its unique markings, was used in an advertisement. Although the driver could be seen in the car, his features were not visible. The distinctive markings on the car were the only information shown in the ad regarding the identity of the driver. These distinctive markings compelled the inference that Motschenbacher was the person sitting in the racing car. We concluded that "California appellate courts would ... afford legal protection to an individual's proprietary interest in his own identity." *Id.* at 825. (Emphasis added). Because the distinctive markings on the racing car were sufficient to identify Motschenbacher as the driver of the car, we held that an issue of fact had been raised as to whether his identity had been appropriated.

In *Midler v. Ford Motor Co.*, 849 F.2d 460 (9th Cir.1988), a singer who had been instructed to sound as much like Bette Midler as possible, sang a song in a radio commercial made famous by Bette Midler. A number of persons told Bette Midler that they thought that she had made the commercial. Aside from the voice, there was no information in the commercial from which the singer could be identified. We noted that "[t]he human voice is one of the most palpable ways identity is manifested." *Id.* at 463. We held that, "[t]o impersonate her voice is to pirate her identity," *id.*, and concluded that Midler had raised a question of fact as to the misappropriation of her identity.

In *Carson v. Here's Johnny Portable Toilets, Inc.*, 698 F.2d 831 (6th Cir.1983), the Sixth Circuit was called upon to interpret Michigan's common-law right to publicity. The case involved a manufacturer who used the words, "Here's Johnny," on portable toilets. These same words were used to introduce the star of a popular late-night television program. There was nothing to indicate that this use of the phrase on the portable toilets was not associated with Johnny Carson's television program. The court found that "[h]ere there was an appropriation of Carson's identity," which violated the right to publicity. *Id.* at 837.

The common theme in these federal cases is that identifying characteristics unique to the plaintiffs were used in a context in which they were the only information as to the identity of the individual. The commercial advertisements in each case showed attributes of the plaintiff's identities which made it appear that the plaintiff was the person identified in the commercial. No effort was made to dispel the impression that the plaintiffs were the source of the personal attributes at issue. The commercials affirmatively represented that the plaintiffs were involved. *See, e.g., Midler* at 462 ("The [Motschenbacher] ad suggested that it was he.... In the same way the defendants here used an imitation to convey the impression that Midler was singing for them."). The proper interpretation of *Motschenbacher*, *Midler*, and *Carson* is that where identifying characteristics unique to a plaintiff are the only information as to the identity of the person appearing in an ad, a triable issue of fact has been raised as to whether his or her identity as been appropriated.

The case before this court is distinguishable from the factual showing made in *Motschenbacher*, *Midler*, and *Carson*. It is patently clear to anyone viewing the commercial advertisement that Vanna White was not being depicted. No reasonable juror could confuse a metal robot with Vanna White.

The majority contends that "the individual aspects of the advertisement ... [v]iewed together leave little doubt about the celebrity the ad is meant to depict." It derives this conclusion from the fact that Vanna White is "the only one" who "dresses like this, turns letters, and does this on the Wheel of Fortune game show." In reaching this conclusion, the majority confuses Vanna White, the person, with the role she has assumed as the current hostess on the "Wheel of Fortune" television game show. A recognition of the distinction between a performer and the part he or she plays is essential for a proper analysis of the facts of this case. As is discussed below, those things which Vanna White claims identify her are not unique to her. They are, instead, attributes of the role she plays. The representation of those attributes, therefore, does not constitute a representation of Vanna White.

Vanna White is a one-role celebrity. She is famous solely for appearing as the hostess on the "Wheel of Fortune" television show. There is nothing unique about Vanna White or the attributes which she claims identify her. Although she appears to be an attractive woman, her face and figure are no more distinctive than that of other equally comely women. She performs her role as hostess on "Wheel of Fortune" in a simple and straight-forward manner. Her work does not require her to display whatever artistic talent she may possess.

The majority appears to argue that because Samsung created a robot with the physical proportions of an attractive woman, posed it gracefully, dressed it in a blond wig, an evening gown, and jewelry, and placed it on a set that resembles the Wheel of Fortune layout, it thereby appropriated Vanna White's identity. But an attractive appearance, a graceful pose, blond hair, an evening gown, and jewelry are attributes shared by many women, especially in Southern California. These common attributes are particularly evident among game-show hostesses, models, actresses, singers, and other women in the entertainment field. They are not unique attributes of Vanna White's identity. Accordingly, I cannot join in the majority's conclusion that, even if viewed together, these attributes identify Vanna White and, therefore, raise a triable issue as to the appropriation of her identity.

The only characteristic in the commercial advertisement that is not common to many female performers or celebrities is the imitation of the "Wheel of Fortune" set. This set is the only thing which might possibly lead a viewer to think of Vanna White. The Wheel of Fortune set, however, is not an attribute of Vanna White's identity. It is an identifying characteristic of a television game show, a prop with which Vanna White interacts in her role as the current hostess. To say that Vanna White may bring an action when another blond female performer or robot appears on such a set as a hostess will, I am sure, be a surprise to the owners of the show. * * *

[T]he fact that an actor or actress became famous for playing a particular role has, until now, never been sufficient to give the performer a proprietary interest in it. I cannot agree with the majority that the California courts, which have consistently taken a narrow view of the right to publicity, would extend law to these unique facts.

* * *

WHITE v. SAMSUNG ELECTRONICS AMERICA, INC.

United States Court of Appeals for the Ninth Circuit, 1993.
989 F.2d 1512, 26 U.S.P.Q.2d 1362.

* * *

The petition for rehearing is DENIED and the suggestion for rehearing en banc is REJECTED.

KOZINSKI, CIRCUIT JUDGE, with whom CIRCUIT JUDGES O'SCANNLAIN and KLEINFELD join, dissenting from the order rejecting the suggestion for rehearing en banc.

I

Saddam Hussein wants to keep advertisers from using his picture in unflattering contexts. Clint Eastwood doesn't want tabloids to write about him. Rudolf Valentino's heirs want to control his film biography. The Girl Scouts don't want their image soiled by association with certain activities. George Lucas wants to keep Strategic Defense Initiative fans from calling it "Star Wars." Pepsico doesn't want singers to use the word "Pepsi" in their songs. Guy Lombardo wants an exclusive property right to ads that show big bands playing on New Year's Eve. Uri Geller thinks he should be paid for ads showing psychics bending metal through telekinesis. Paul Prudhomme, that household name, thinks the same about ads featuring corpulent bearded chefs. And scads of copyright holders see purple when their creations are made fun of.

Something very dangerous is going on here. Private property, including intellectual property, is essential to our way of life. It provides an incentive for investment and innovation; it stimulates the flourishing of our culture; it protects the moral entitlements of people to the fruits of their labors. But reducing too much to private property can be bad medicine. Private land, for instance, is far more useful if separated from other private land by public streets, roads and highways. Public parks, utility rights-of-way and sewers reduce the amount of land in private hands, but vastly enhance the value of the property that remains.

So too it is with intellectual property. Overprotecting intellectual property is as harmful as underprotecting it. Creativity is impossible without a rich public domain. Nothing today, likely nothing since we tamed fire, is genuinely new: Culture, like science and technology, grows by accretion, each new creator building on the works of those who came before. Overprotection stifles the very creative forces it's supposed to nurture.

The panel's opinion is a classic case of overprotection. Concerned about what it sees as a wrong done to Vanna White, the panel majority erects a property right of remarkable and dangerous breadth: Under the majority's opinion, it's now a tort for advertisers to *remind* the public of a celebrity. Not to use a celebrity's name, voice, signature or likeness; not to imply the celebrity endorses a product; but simply to evoke the celebrity's image in the public's mind. This Orwellian notion withdraws far more from the public domain than prudence and common sense allow. It conflicts with the Copyright Act and the Copyright Clause. It raises serious First Amendment problems. It's bad law, and it deserves a long, hard second look.

* * *

III

* * * Intellectual property rights aren't like some constitutional rights, absolute guarantees protected against all kinds of interference, subtle as well as blatant. They cast no penumbras, emit no emanations: The very point of intellectual property laws is that they protect only against certain specific kinds of appropriation. I can't publish unauthorized copies of, say, *Presumed Innocent*; I can't make a movie out of it. But I'm perfectly free to write a book about an idealistic young prosecutor on trial for a crime he didn't commit. So what if I got the idea from *Presumed Innocent*? So what if it reminds readers of the original? Have I "eviscerated" Scott Turow's intellectual property rights? Certainly not. All creators draw in part on the work of those who came before, referring to it, building on it, poking fun at it; we call this creativity, not piracy.

The majority isn't, in fact, preventing the "evisceration" of Vanna White's existing rights; it's creating a new and much broader property right, a right unknown in California law. It's replacing the existing balance between the interests of the celebrity and those of the public by a different balance, one substantially more favorable to the celebrity. Instead of having an exclusive right in her name, likeness, signature or voice, every famous person now has an exclusive right to *anything that reminds the viewer of her*. After all, that's all Samsung did: It used an inanimate object to remind people of White, to "evoke [her identity]." [17]

17. Some viewers might have inferred White was endorsing the product, but that's a different story. The right of publicity isn't aimed at or limited to false endorse-

Consider how sweeping this new right is. What is it about the ad that makes people think of White? It's not the robot's wig, clothes or jewelry; there must be ten million blond women (many of them quasi-famous) who wear dresses and jewelry like White's. It's that the robot is posed near the "Wheel of Fortune" game board. Remove the game board from the ad, and no one would think of Vanna White. *See* Appendix. But once you include the game board, anybody standing beside it—a brunette woman, a man wearing women's clothes, a monkey in a wig and gown—would evoke White's image, precisely the way the robot did. It's the "Wheel of Fortune" set, not the robot's face or dress or jewelry that evokes White's image. The panel is giving White an exclusive right not in what she looks like or who she is, but in what she does for a living.[18]

This is entirely the wrong place to strike the balance. Intellectual property rights aren't free: They're imposed at the expense of future creators and of the public at large. Where would we be if Charles Lindbergh had an exclusive right in the concept of a heroic solo aviator? If Arthur Conan Doyle had gotten a copyright in the idea of the detective story, or Albert Einstein had patented the theory of relativity? If every author and celebrity had been given the right to keep people from mocking them or their work? Surely this would have made the world poorer, not richer, culturally as well as economically. This is why intellectual property law is full of careful balances between what's set aside for the owner and what's left in the public domain for the rest of us: The relatively short life of patents; the longer, but finite, life of copyrights; copyright's idea-expression dichotomy; the fair use doctrine; the prohibition on copyrighting facts; the compulsory license of television broadcasts and musical compositions; federal preemption of overbroad state intellectual property laws; the nominative use doctrine in trademark law; the right to make soundalike recordings. All of these diminish an intellectual property owner's rights. All let the public use something created by someone else. But all are necessary to maintain a free environment in which creative genius can flourish.

The intellectual property right created by the panel here has none of these essential limitations: No fair use exception; no right to parody; no idea-expression dichotomy. It impoverishes the public domain, to the

ments; that's what the Lanham Act is for. Note also that the majority's rule applies even to advertisements that unintentionally remind people of someone. California law is crystal clear that the common-law right of publicity may be violated even by unintentional appropriations.

18. Once the right of publicity is extended beyond specific physical characteristics, this will become a recurring problem: Outside name, likeness and voice, the things that most reliably remind the public of celebrities are the actions or roles they're famous for. A commercial with an astronaut setting foot on the moon would evoke the image of Neil Armstrong. Any masked man on horseback would remind people (over a certain age) of Clayton Moore. And any number of songs—"My Way," "Yellow Submarine," "Like a Virgin," "Beat It," "Michael, Row the Boat Ashore," to name only a few—instantly evoke an image of the person or group who made them famous, regardless of who is singing.

* * *

detriment of future creators and the public at large. Instead of well-defined, limited characteristics such as name, likeness or voice, advertisers will now have to cope with vague claims of "appropriation of identity," claims often made by people with a wholly exaggerated sense of their own fame and significance. Future Vanna Whites might not get the chance to create their personae, because their employers may fear some celebrity will claim the persona is too similar to her own. The public will be robbed of parodies of celebrities, and our culture will be deprived of the valuable safety valve that parody and mockery create.

Moreover, consider the moral dimension, about which the panel majority seems to have gotten so exercised. Saying Samsung "appropriated" something of White's begs the question: *Should* White have the exclusive right to something as broad and amorphous as her "identity"? Samsung's ad didn't simply copy White's schtick—like all parody, it created something new. True, Samsung did it to make money, but White does whatever she does to make money, too; the majority talks of "the difference between fun and profit," 971 F.2d at 1401, but in the entertainment industry fun is profit. Why is Vanna White's right to exclusive for-profit use of her persona—a persona that might not even be her own creation, but that of a writer, director or producer—superior to Samsung's right to profit by creating its own inventions? Why should she have such absolute rights to control the conduct of others, unlimited by the idea-expression dichotomy or by the fair use doctrine?

To paraphrase only slightly *Feist Publications, Inc. v. Rural Telephone Service Co.*, — U.S. ——, ——, 111 S.Ct. 1282, 1289–90, 113 L.Ed.2d 358 (1991), it may seem unfair that much of the fruit of a creator's labor may be used by others without compensation. But this is not some unforeseen byproduct of our intellectual property system; it is the system's very essence. Intellectual property law assures authors the right to their original expression, but encourages others to build freely on the ideas that underlie it. This result is neither unfair nor unfortunate: It is the means by which intellectual property law advances the progress of science and art. We give authors certain exclusive rights, but in exchange we get a richer public domain. The majority ignores this wise teaching, and all of us are the poorer for it.

* * *

VI

Finally, I can't see how giving White the power to keep others from evoking her image in the public's mind can be squared with the First Amendment. Where does White get this right to control our thoughts? The majority's creation goes way beyond the protection given a trademark or a copyrighted work, or a person's name or likeness. All those things control one particular way of expressing an idea, one way of referring to an object or a person. But not allowing *any* means of reminding people of someone? That's a speech restriction unparalleled in First Amendment law.

What's more, I doubt even a name-and-likeness-only right of publicity can stand without a parody exception. The First Amendment isn't just about religion or politics—it's also about protecting the free development of our national culture. Parody, humor, irreverence are all vital components of the marketplace of ideas. The last thing we need, the last thing the First Amendment will tolerate, is a law that lets public figures keep people from mocking them, or from "evok[ing]" their images in the mind of the public.[29]

The majority dismisses the First Amendment issue out of hand because Samsung's ad was commercial speech. So what? Commercial speech may be less protected by the First Amendment than noncommercial speech, but less protected means protected nonetheless. *Central Hudson Gas & Elec. Corp. v. Public Serv. Comm'n*, 447 U.S. 557, 100 S.Ct. 2343, 65 L.Ed.2d 341 (1980). And there are very good reasons for this. Commercial speech has a profound effect on our culture and our attitudes. Neutral-seeming ads influence people's social and political attitudes, and themselves arouse political controversy. "Where's the Beef?" turned from an advertising catchphrase into the only really memorable thing about the 1984 presidential campaign. Four years later, Michael Dukakis called George Bush "the Joe Isuzu of American politics."

In our pop culture, where salesmanship must be entertaining and entertainment must sell, the line between the commercial and noncommercial has not merely blurred; it has disappeared. Is the Samsung parody any different from a parody on Saturday Night Live or in Spy Magazine? Both are equally profit-motivated. Both use a celebrity's identity to sell things—one to sell VCRs, the other to sell advertising. Both mock their subjects. Both try to make people laugh. Both add something, perhaps something worthwhile and memorable, perhaps not, to our culture. Both are things that the people being portrayed might dearly want to suppress.

Commercial speech is a significant, valuable part of our national discourse. The Supreme Court has recognized as much, and has insisted that lower courts carefully scrutinize commercial speech restrictions, but the panel totally fails to do this. The panel majority doesn't even purport to apply the *Central Hudson* test, which the Supreme Court devised specifically for determining whether a commercial speech restriction is valid. The majority doesn't ask, as *Central Hudson* requires,

29. The majority's failure to recognize a parody exception to the right of publicity would apply equally to parodies of politicians as of actresses. Consider the case of Wok Fast, a Los Angeles Chinese food delivery service, which put up a billboard with a picture of then-L.A. Police Chief Daryl Gates and the text "When you can't leave the office. Or won't." (This was an allusion to Chief Gates's refusal to retire despite pressure from Mayor Tom Bradley.) Gates forced the restaurant to take the billboard down by threatening a right of publicity lawsuit.

See also Samsung Has Seen the Future: Brace Yourself, Adweek, Oct. 3, 1988, at 26 (ER 72) (Samsung planned another ad that would show a dollar bill with Richard Nixon's face on it and the caption "Dollar bill, 2025 A.D...," but Nixon refused permission to use his likeness).

whether the speech restriction is justified by a substantial state interest. It doesn't ask whether the restriction directly advances the interest. It doesn't ask whether the restriction is narrowly tailored to the interest. These are all things the Supreme Court told us—in no uncertain terms—we must consider; the majority opinion doesn't even mention them.

* * *

VII

For better or worse, we *are* the Court of Appeals for the Hollywood Circuit. Millions of people toil in the shadow of the law we make, and much of their livelihood is made possible by the existence of intellectual property rights. But much of their livelihood—and much of the vibrancy of our culture—also depends on the existence of other intangible rights: The right to draw ideas from a rich and varied public domain, and the right to mock, for profit as well as fun, the cultural icons of our time. In the name of avoiding the "evisceration" of a celebrity's rights in her image, the majority diminishes the rights of copyright holders and the public at large. In the name of fostering creativity, the majority suppresses it. Vanna White and those like her have been given something they never had before, and they've been given it at our expense. I cannot agree.

APPENDIX

Vanna White

Ms. C3PO?

Notes and Questions

1. *Identifying the plaintiff.* The *White* case addresses the issue of *how* the plaintiff was identified. There seemed little question that she had in fact been identified to the public through the defendant's ad, by virtue of the combination of the robot's dress, hair, jewelry and the Wheel of Fortune setting.

Obviously the defendant's use must invoke the plaintiff's identity before a right of publicity cause of action will lie. Thus, for example, if a photograph of the plaintiff has been used, a person viewing the photograph should be able to identify the plaintiff without special visual aids. See, e.g.,

CAL. CIV. CODE § 3344(b) (West 1993). Likewise, if the plaintiff's name has been used, it must appear from the total context that the plaintiff, rather than someone else, is being identified. See, e.g., Hooker v. Columbia Pictures Industries, Inc., 551 F.Supp. 1060 (N.D.Ill.1982) (finding that use of "T.J. Hooker" for a fictitious television policeman did not identify T.J. Hooker the woodcarver). The issue of identifiability ultimately is an issue of fact. While the common law does not appear to impose an intent requirement, evidence that the defendant in fact did intend to identify the plaintiff may support a finding that he succeeded in doing so. See RESTATEMENT (THIRD) OF UNFAIR COMPETITION § 46, comment d (Tentative Draft No. 4, 1993).

How many people must be able to identify the plaintiff? While most right of publicity plaintiffs are "celebrities," celebrity status is not mandatory. See, e.g., RESTATEMENT, *supra,* § 46, comment d ("The identity of even an unknown person may possess commercial value. Thus, an evaluation of the relative fame of the plaintiff is more properly relevant to the determination of appropriate relief"). Should a different (lower) standard of identifiability be applied in the case of non-celebrity plaintiffs? See J.T. McCARTHY, THE RIGHTS OF PUBLICITY AND PRIVACY § 3.4 (1993).

The majority in *White* holds that the means by which a defendant appropriates or "evokes" the plaintiff's identity is not determinative. Is this broad rule consistent with the purposes of the publicity cause of action identified in Justice Bird's dissent in *Lugosi*? Does the result in the *White* case promote those purposes? Does the majority rule reach the right balance in accommodating the conflicting interests identified in Judge Kozinski's dissent to the denial of rehearing? If you answer to any of these questions is no, how would you alter the rule? Should the cause of action be restricted to appropriation of the plaintiff's name or likeness? If so, would use of a plaintiff's nickname suffice? See Hirsch v. S.C. Johnson & Sons, Inc., 90 Wisc.2d 379, 280 N.W.2d 129, 205 U.S.P.Q. 920 (1979). How about a cartoon characterization? See Ali v. Playgirl, Inc., 447 F.Supp. 723, 206 U.S.P.Q. 1021 (S.D.N.Y.1978). What about a photograph of a look-alike? See Onassis v. Christian Dior–New York, Inc., 122 Misc.2d 603, 472 N.Y.S.2d 254 (1984), *affirmed* 110 A.D.2d 1095, 488 N.Y.S.2d 943 (1985). Putting aside the issue of the descendability of rights, what if the defendant used a bad Elvis impersonator in its ad, who very clearly was not Elvis, or even Elvis returned from the dead?

What if the defendant evoked the plaintiff's identity, but included a disclaimer in the advertisement making it clear that the image or sound being projected was not, in fact, the plaintiff, and that plaintiff was not in any way associated with the advertiser? Would this be sufficient to avoid liability under the majority view in *White*? Under Judge Alarcon's view? Should it be?

2. *Commercial use and the first amendment.* The advertisement in *White* undoubtedly was "commercial speech." As Judge Kozinski notes in his dissent, while commercial speech receives a lower level of first amendment protection than other varieties of speech, it nonetheless is subject to some protection. Should the first amendment have protected Samsung's use of White's identity in its ad? If not, is there any case in which the first

amendment should shield a defendant who has used a plaintiff's identity in commercial advertising? How about the case of the Chinese restaurant advertisement invoking Police Chief Gates, described in Judge Kozinski's footnote 29? Should a political figure ever have a right of publicity cause of action?

A right of publicity cause of action arises when the defendant makes a commercial use, or "use in trade," of the plaintiff's identity. It is usually easy to demonstrate that a defendant's use is a commercial one, since a broad range of activity qualifies: in addition to using an identity to advertise products, using it on merchandise for sale, as in *Lugosi*, or in connection with the rendition of services satisfies the requirement. Indeed, even unauthorized use of the plaintiff's identity to solicit contributions to non-profit charitable organizations may qualify. See RESTATEMENT (THIRD) OF UNFAIR COMPETITION § 47, comment a (Tentative Draft No. 4, 1993). It is important to note that the range of uses constituting "commercial use" or "use in trade" for purposes of the right of publicity is broader than "commercial speech," as that concept has been defined for first amendment purposes. Thus, the right of publicity might be violated by speech that is entitled to the fullest degree of first amendment protection. The *Zacchini* case (discussed *supra*) illustrates that even in such cases, the first amendment may not prohibit the right of publicity claim.

In *Zacchini*, the Ohio Supreme Court had held that the defendant's broadcast of the plaintiff's human cannonball act on the evening news was privileged under the first amendment, so that the plaintiff's right of publicity claim must be dismissed. The United States Supreme Court agreed that the first amendment was applicable in its full force, but reversed the Ohio court's judgment that it immunized the defendant from suit. The Court observed:

> The Ohio Supreme Court held that respondent is constitutionally privileged to include in its newscasts matters of public interest that would otherwise be protected by the right of publicity, absent an intent to injure or to appropriate for some nonprivileged purpose. If under this standard respondent had merely reported that petitioner was performing at the fair and described or commented on his act, with or without showing his picture on television, we would have a very different case. But petitioner is not contending that his appearance at the fair and his performance could not be reported by the press as newsworthy items. His complaint is that respondent filmed his entire act and displayed that film on television for the public to see and enjoy. This, he claimed, was an appropriation of his professional property.

433 U.S. at 569, 97 S.Ct. at 2854, 53 L.Ed.2d at 972. In finding that the first amendment did not prohibit the right of publicity claim, the Court stressed several considerations, in addition to the fact that the defendant had broadcast the plaintiff's entire 15–second act. First, the state had an important interest in encouraging its residents to engage in creative activities for the entertainment of others. Second, the defendant's broadcast interfered with the plaintiff's ability to make a living as an entertainer. Moreover, permitting the suit would not deprive the public: the plaintiff did not seek to enjoin the broadcast of his performance, but only to recover

damages as payment for the defendant's use of it. The Court explained: "The Constitution no more prevents a State from requiring respondent to compensate petitioner for broadcasting his act on television than it would privilege respondent to film and broadcast a copyrighted dramatic work without liability to the copyright owner." *Id.*, 433 U.S. at 575, 97 S.Ct. at 2857, 53 L.Ed.2d at 975–76. The Court thus balanced the first amendment interests against the interests of the state and of the plaintiff, taking into account the severity of the impact that permitting recovery would have on the public interest.

How does the first amendment apply to right of publicity claims in "non-commercial speech" contexts other than news reporting? It is clear that the author of an unauthorized biographical work is privileged to use her subject's name, likeness, and other aspects of identity in the biography. See, e.g., Rosemont Enterprises, Inc. v. Random House, Inc., 58 Misc.2d 1, 294 N.Y.S.2d 122 (1968), *affirmed* 32 A.D.2d 892, 301 N.Y.S.2d 948 (1969). Likewise, the first amendment prevents other persons mentioned in the biography, such as the subject's family, friends or business associates, from asserting a claim. See, e.g., Meeropol v. Nizer, 560 F.2d 1061, 195 U.S.P.Q. 273 (2d Cir.1977), *cert. denied* 434 U.S. 1013, 98 S.Ct. 727, 54 L.Ed.2d 756 (1978). What if the work is not strictly biography, but contains some fictitious elements, such as invented dialogue and incidents? Should that make a difference?

Entertainment, as well as news, enjoys full first amendment protection. That being the case, assume that an Elvis Presley impersonator performs a concert. Would the first amendment protect him in a right of publicity suit brought by Elvis' successors in interest? The issue arose in Estate of Elvis Presley v. Russen, 513 F.Supp. 1339, 211 U.S.P.Q. 415 (D.N.J.1981). In *Russen*, the defendant produced "The Big El Show," which was patterned after an actual Elvis Presley stage show, though on a lesser scale. In addition to an Elvis impersonator, who sang songs that Elvis made popular, imitated Elvis' appearance, dress, movements, singing voice and style, the show featured a band that used the same name as the real Elvis' band, and opened in a similar fashion to real Elvis stage show openings. The defendant advertised the show with a photograph of the impersonator which was indistinguishable from the real Elvis, and with statements such as: "Reflections on a Legend ... A Tribute to Elvis Presley" and "Looks and Sounds LIKE THE KING."

After finding, under New Jersey law, that Elvis' right of publicity descended to his estate on his death, the court turned to the issue of whether The Big El Show infringed that right, finding, ultimately, that it did.

> [T]he purpose of the portrayal in question must be examined to determine if it predominantly serves a social function valued by the protection of free speech. If the portrayal mainly serves the purpose of contributing information, which is not false or defamatory, to the public debate of political or social issues or of providing the free expression of creative talent which contributes to society's cultural enrichment, then the portrayal generally will be immune from liability. If, however, the portrayal functions primarily as a means of commercial exploitation, then such immunity will not be granted.

* * * In general, in determining whether a plaintiff's right of publicity can be invoked to prevent a defendant's activity, the courts have divided along the lines set out above. In cases finding the expression to be protected, the defendant's activity has consisted of the dissemination of such information as "thoughts, ideas, newsworthy events, ... matters of public interest," *Rosemont Enterprises, Inc. v. Random House, Inc.*, 58 Misc.2d 1, 6, 294 N.Y.S.2d 122, 129 (Sup.Ct. 1968), *aff'd mem.*, 32 App.Div.2d 892, 301 N.Y.S.2d 948 (1969), and fictionalizations. The importance of protecting fictionalizations and related efforts as against rights of publicity was explained by Chief Justice Bird of the California Supreme Court:

> Contemporary events, symbols and people are regularly used in fictional works. Fiction writers may be able to more persuasively, more accurately express themselves by weaving into the tale persons or events familiar to their readers. The choice is theirs. No author should be forced into creating mythological worlds or characters wholly divorced from reality. The right of publicity derived from public prominence does not confer a shield to ward off caricature, parody and satire. Rather, prominence invites creative comment.

Guglielmi v. Spelling–Goldberg Productions, 25 Cal.3d 860, 869, 160 Cal.Rptr. 352, 358, 603 P.2d 454, 460 (Bird, C.J., concurring).

On the other hand, most of those cases finding that the right of publicity, or its equivalence, prevails have involved the use of a famous name or likeness predominantly in connection with the sale of consumer merchandise or "solely 'for purposes of trade—*e.g.*, merely to attract attention' [without being artistic, informational or newsworthy]." *Ali v. Playgirl, Inc.*, 447 F.Supp. 723, 727, 728–29 (S.D.N.Y.1978). In these cases, it seems clear that the name or likeness of the public figure is being used predominantly for commercial exploitation, and thus is subject to the right of publicity. As the court in *Palmer v. Schonhorn* noted, "While one who is a public figure or is presently newsworthy may be the proper subject of news or informative presentation, the privilege does *not extend to commercialization of his personality through a form of treatment distinct from the dissemination of news or information.*" 96 N.J.Super. 72, 78, 232 A.2d 458 (Ch.1967) (emphasis added by Palmer court).

In the present case, the defendant's expressive activity, THE BIG EL SHOW production, does not fall clearly on either side. Based on the current state of the record, the production can be described as a live theatrical presentation or concert designed to imitate a performance of the late Elvis Presley. The show stars an individual who closely resembles Presley and who imitates the appearance, dress, and characteristic performing style of Elvis Presley. The defendant has made no showing, nor attempted to show, that the production is intended to or acts as a parody, burlesque, satire, or criticism of Elvis Presley. As a matter of fact, the show is billed as "A TRIBUTE TO ELVIS PRESLEY." In essence, we confront the question of whether the use of the likeness of a famous deceased entertainer in a performance mainly designed to imitate that famous entertainer's own past stage performances is to be considered primarily as a commercial appropriation by the imitator or show's producer of the famous entertainer's likeness or as a valuable contribution of information or culture. After careful consideration of the activity, we have decided that although THE BIG EL SHOW contains an informational and entertainment element, the show serves primarily to commercially exploit the likeness of Elvis Presley without contributing anything of substantial value to society. In making this decision, the court recognizes that certain factors distinguish this situation from the pure commercial use of a picture of Elvis Presley to advertise a product. In the first place, the defendant uses Presley's likeness in an entertainment form and, as a general proposition, "entertainment ... enjoys First Amendment protection." *Zacchini v. Scripps–Howard Broadcasting Co.*, 433 U.S. 562, 578, 97 S.Ct. 2849, 2859, 53 L.Ed.2d 965 (1977). However, entertainment that is merely a copy or imitation, even if skillfully and accurately carried out, does not really have its own creative component and does not have a significant value as pure entertainment. As one authority has emphasized:

> The public interest in entertainment will support the sporadic, occasional and good-faith imitation of a famous person to achieve humor, to effect criticism or to season a particular episode, but it does not give a privilege to appropriate another's valuable attributes on a continuing basis as one's own without the consent of the other.

Netterville, "Copyright and Tort Aspects of Parody, Mimicry and Humorous Commentary," 35 S.Cal.L.Rev. 225, 254 (1962).

In the second place, the production does provide information in that it illustrates a performance of a legendary figure in the entertainment industry. Because of Presley's immense contribution to rock 'n roll, examples of him performing can be considered of public interest. However, in comparison to a biographical film or play of Elvis Presley or a production tracing the role of Elvis Presley in the development of rock 'n roll, the information about Presley which THE BIG EL SHOW provides is of limited value.

This recognition that defendant's production has some value does not diminish our conclusion that the primary purpose of defendant's activity is to appropriate the commercial value of the likeness of Elvis Presley. * * *

Russen, 513 F.Supp. at 1355–61, 211 U.S.P.Q. at 432–37.

Is the court saying that determination of first amendment protection in cases such as *Russen* depends upon a judicial evaluation of the value, creativity and informational content of the defendant's material? If so, what are the ramifications of this? Is there any way to avoid it?

Based on what the court says, what result if the defendant's show had consisted of a number of different acts impersonating a variety of rock and roll stars?

Should it make any difference whether the imitated celebrity is alive or dead? See J.T. McCARTHY, *supra*, § 8.16[B][5]; RESTATEMENT

(THIRD) OF UNFAIR COMPETITION § 46, comment h, § 47, comment d (Tentative Draft No. 4, 1993).

In determining whether the first amendment protects expression in a right of publicity suit, courts have sometimes engaged in an analysis analogous to the fair use defense analysis used in copyright infringement cases. See Chapter 5, § IV, *supra*. See, e.g., Groucho Marx Productions, Inc. v. Day and Night Co., 523 F.Supp. 485, 212 U.S.P.Q. 926 (S.D.N.Y.1981), *reversed on other grounds* 689 F.2d 317, 216 U.S.P.Q. 553 (2d Cir.1982). Why should the copyright fair use doctrine be relevant?

3. *Descendability*. As the *Haelan* opinion suggests, the transferability, and particularly the descendability of the right of publicity to a celebrity's beneficiaries or next of kin, has posed some difficulties. The problem stems from the traditional link between the right of publicity and the right of privacy, discussed above. Because privacy rights are personal in nature, and protect the holder's interest in dignity, reputation, and peace of mind, they end upon his death. This fact has led some jurisdictions to hold that publicity rights die with the holder, as well. See, e.g., Reeves v. United Artists, 572 F.Supp. 1231, 222 U.S.P.Q. 541 (N.D. Ohio 1983), *affirmed* 765 F.2d 79 (6th Cir.1985).

The majority of jurisdictions to consider the question, however, have reasoned that since the right of publicity primarily protects economic, rather than personal rights, it should be treated like other economic rights, such as copyrights and trademarks, which are descendible. Some jurisdictions have reached this result through judicial opinion, see, e.g., Martin Luther King, Jr. Center for Social Change, Inc. v. American Heritage Products, Inc., 250 Ga. 135, 296 S.E.2d 697, 216 U.S.P.Q. 711 (1982), while others have enacted statutes to that effect. See, e.g., TEX. PROP. CODE ANN. § 26.004 (Vernon 1993). Does continuation of publicity rights after the holder's death appreciably further the purposes of the cause of action? Are there convincing arguments that could be made against descendability? Some jurisdictions, while recognizing that a person's right of publicity may descend, have suggested that it will only descend if the person "exploited" it during his lifetime. See, e.g., Lugosi v. Universal Pictures, 25 Cal.3d 813, 160 Cal.Rptr. 323, 603 P.2d 425, 205 U.S.P.Q. 1090 (1979). What is the justification for such a rule? What constitutes "exploitation?" The trend appears to be against imposing such a requirement.

Once it is determined that a right of publicity descends, the question arises whether it has any durational limit. For example, if a drawing of Ben Franklin were used in an advertisement, would his descendants have a cause of action? Should they? Or should some cut-off be devised? The majority in *Lugosi* recognized this problem and cited the difficulty in "judicially selecting an appropriate durational limitation" as a justification for finding that the right is not descendible. *Lugosi*, *supra*, 25 Cal.3d at 824 n.8, 160 Cal.Rptr. at 329 n.8, 603 P.2d at 431 n.8. In her dissent, Justice Bird agreed that the duration of the right should be limited, but argued that this should pose no barrier to finding that the right descends:

> The fixing of the precise date for the termination of the right of publicity is inherently a policy decision, one that the Legislature may be best able to determine. However, in the absence of legislative action, a

> limit must be prescribed. In fashioning common law rights and remedies in the past, this court has often considered federal and state statutory schemes for guidance. Since the right of publicity recognizes an interest in intangible property similar in many respects to creations protected by copyright law, that body of law is instructive. The Copyright Act of 1976 provides that a copyright in new works shall be recognized during the author's life and for 50 years thereafter. That period represents a reasonable evaluation of the period necessary to effect the policies underlying the right of publicity. Therefore, I would hold that the right of publicity should be recognized during the subject's life and for 50 years thereafter.

Id., 25 Cal.3d at 847, 160 Cal.Rptr. at 344–45, 603 P.2d at 446–47 (Bird, C.J., dissenting). Several state legislatures appear to have found Justice Bird's reasoning persuasive, for they have limited statutory post mortem publicity rights to 50 years. See, e.g., NEV. REV. STAT. § 598.984 (Michie 1991). A few states, however, have deviated from this approach. Oklahoma, for example, recognizes the post mortem right for 100 years, OKLA. STAT. ANN. tit. 12, § 1448 (West 1993), while Tennessee recognizes a right for ten years and however long thereafter the right continues to be commercially exploited. TENN. CODE ANN. § 47–25–1104 (1988). This lack of uniformity may make national marketing campaigns more difficult.

For further discussion of the descendability issue, see Felcher & Rubin, *The Descendability of the Right of Publicity: Is There Commercial Life after Death?*, 89 YALE L. J. 1125 (1980); Sims, *Right of Publicity: Survivability Reconsidered*, 49 FORDHAM L. REV. 453 (1981); Hoffman, *The Right of Publicity: Heirs' Right, Advertisers' Windfall, or Courts' Nightmare*, 31 DePAUL L. REV. 1 (1981).

4. *Remedies.* Injunctions against further infringement are standard in right of publicity actions, since damages frequently are inadequate to remedy a plaintiff's interest in controlling or developing her own public image, and may be difficult to measure even when appropriate. Moreover, commercial exploitation of the plaintiff's identity is often a continuing wrong. Preliminary injunctions may also be available, but courts' sensitivity to granting prior restraints on speech may preclude this remedy, especially in cases falling outside of the "commercial speech" context. See RESTATEMENT (THIRD) OF UNFAIR COMPETITION § 48 (Tentative Draft No. 4, 1993).

Monetary damages generally consist of the fair market value of the use of the plaintiff's identity. This value may be determined through evidence of what "comparable" personalities receive for "comparable" commercial uses of their identities, or through evidence of what plaintiff herself has received for licensing similar uses in the past. If the plaintiff is able to demonstrate that the defendant's use injured her ability to capitalize on her identity in the future (for example, by associating her with shabby products, thus decreasing demand for her future product endorsements), she may be able to recover for this projected loss of income, as well. In some jurisdictions the defendant's profit may be recovered, to the extent that it exceeds the plaintiff's loss, and punitive damages may be permitted in particularly egregious cases. See J.T. McCARTHY, THE RIGHTS OF PUBLICITY AND PRIVACY §§ 11.8 & 9 (1993).

5. *References.* The McCarthy Treatise, cited above, is the leading treatise on the right of publicity. See also II P. GOLDSTEIN, COPYRIGHT PRINCIPLES, LAW AND PRACTICE § 15.17–21 (1989). Lisa Lawrence has provided a comprehensive research guide in the field which covers statutes and case opinions, law review and other periodical articles. Lawrence, *The Right of Publicity: A Research Guide*, 10 HASTINGS COMM. & ENT. L.J. 143 (1987). For a multidisciplinary approach to the right of publicity, see J. GAINES, CONTESTED CULTURE (1991).

Part Five

CONCLUDING CONSIDERATIONS

Chapter Nine

FEDERAL–STATE RELATIONS

I. SUPREMACY CLAUSE PREEMPTION

SEARS, ROEBUCK & CO. v. STIFFEL CO.

United States Supreme Court, 1964.
376 U.S. 225, 84 S.Ct. 784, 11 L.Ed.2d 661, 140 U.S.P.Q. 524.

MR. JUSTICE BLACK delivered the opinion of the Court.

The question in this case is whether a State's unfair competition law can, consistently with the federal patent laws, impose liability for or prohibit the copying of an article which is protected by neither a federal patent nor a copyright. The respondent, Stiffel Company, secured design and mechanical patents on a "pole lamp"—a vertical tube having lamp fixtures along the outside, the tube being made so that it will stand upright between the floor and ceiling of a room. Pole lamps proved a decided commercial success, and soon after Stiffel brought them on the market Sears, Roebuck & Company put on the market a substantially identical lamp, which it sold more cheaply, Sears' retail price being about the same as Stiffel's wholesale price. Stiffel then brought this action against Sears in the United States District Court for the Northern District of Illinois, claiming in its first count that by copying its design Sears had infringed Stiffel's patents and in its second count that by selling copies of Stiffel's lamp Sears had caused confusion in the trade as to the source of the lamps and had thereby engaged in unfair competition under Illinois law. * * *

The District Court, after holding the patents invalid for want of invention, went on to find as a fact that Sears' lamp was "a substantially exact copy" of Stiffel's and that the two lamps were so much alike, both in appearance and in functional details, "that confusion between them is likely, and some confusion has already occurred." On these findings the court held Sears guilty of unfair competition, enjoined Sears "from unfairly competing with (Stiffel) by selling or attempting to sell pole lamps identical to or confusingly similar to" Stiffel's lamp, and ordered an accounting to fix profits and damages resulting from Sears' "unfair competition."

The Court of Appeals affirmed. That court held that, to make out a case of unfair competition under Illinois law, * * * Stiffel had only to prove that there was a "likelihood of confusion as to the source of the products"—that the two articles were sufficiently identical that customers could not tell who had made a particular one. Impressed by the "remarkable sameness of appearance" of the lamps, the Court of Appeals upheld the trial court's findings of likelihood of confusion and some actual confusion, findings which the appellate court construed to mean confusion "as to the source of the lamps." The Court of Appeals thought this enough under Illinois law to sustain the trial court's holding of unfair competition, and thus held Sears liable under Illinois law for doing no more than copying and marketing an unpatented article. * * *

Before the Constitution was adopted, some States had granted patents either by special act or by general statute, but when the Constitution was adopted provision for a federal patent law was made one of the enumerated powers of Congress because, as Madison put it in *The Federalist* No. 43, the States "cannot separately make effectual provision" for either patents or copyrights. That constitutional provision is Art. I, § 8, cl. 8, which empowers Congress "To promote the Progress of Science and useful Arts, by securing for limited Times to Authors and Inventors the exclusive Right to their respective Writings and Discoveries." Pursuant to this constitutional authority, Congress in 1790 enacted the first federal patent and copyright law, and ever since that time has fixed the condition upon which patents and copyrights shall be granted. These laws, like other laws of the United States enacted pursuant to constitutional authority, are the supreme law of the land. When state law touches upon the area of these federal statutes, it is "familiar doctrine" that the federal policy "may not be set at naught, or its benefits denied" by the state law. *Sola Elec. Co. v. Jefferson Elec. Co.*, 317 U.S. 172, 173, 176, 63 S.Ct. 172, 173, 87 L.Ed. 165 (1942). This is true, of course, even if the state law is enacted in the exercise of otherwise undoubted state power.

The grant of a patent is the grant of a statutory monopoly; indeed, the grant of patents in England was an explicit exception to the statute of James I prohibiting monopolies. Patents are not given as favors, as was the case of monopolies given by the Tudor monarchs, but are meant to encourage invention by rewarding the inventor with the right, limited to a term of years fixed by the patent, to exclude others from the use of his invention. During that period of time no one may make use, or sell the patented product without the patentee's authority. But in rewarding useful invention, the "rights and welfare of the community must be fairly dealt with and effectually guarded." *Kendall v. Winsor*, 21 How. 322, 328, 16 L.Ed. 165 (1859). To that end the prerequisites to obtaining a patent are strictly observed, and when the patent has issued the limitations on its exercise are equally strictly enforced. To begin with, a genuine "invention" or "discovery" must be demonstrated "lest in the constant demand for new appliances the heavy hand of tribute be laid on each slight technological advance in an art." *Cuno Engineering Corp. v. Automatic Devices Corp.*, 314 U.S. 84, 92, 62 S.Ct. 37, 41, 86 L.Ed. 58 (1941). Once the patent issues, it is strictly construed. It cannot be used to secure any monopoly beyond that contained in the patent, the patentee's control over the product when it leaves his hands is sharply limited, and the patent monopoly may not be used in disregard of the antitrust laws. Finally, and especially relevant here, when the patent expires the monopoly created by it expires, too, and the right to make the article—including the right to make it in precisely the shape it carried when patented—passes to the public.

Thus the patent system is one in which uniform federal standards are carefully used to promote invention while at the same time preserving free competition. Obviously a State could not, consistently with the Supremacy Clause of the Constitution, extend the life of a patent beyond its expiration date or give a patent on an article which lacked the level of invention required for federal patents. To do either would run counter to the policy of Congress of granting patents only to true inventions, and then only for a limited time. Just as a State cannot encroach upon the federal patent laws directly, it cannot, under some other law, such as that forbidding unfair competition, give protection of a kind that clashes with the objectives of the federal patent laws.

In the present case the "pole lamp" sold by Stiffel has been held not to be entitled to the protection of either a mechanical or a design patent. An unpatentable article, like an article on which the patent has expired, is in the public domain and may be made and sold by whoever chooses to do so. What Sears did was to copy Stiffel's design and to sell lamps almost identical to those sold by Stiffel. This it had every right to do under the federal patent laws. That Stiffel originated the pole lamp and made it popular is immaterial. "Sharing in the goodwill of an article unprotected by patent or trade-mark is the exercise of a right possessed by all—and in the free exercise of which the consuming public is deeply interested." *Kellogg Co. v. National Biscuit Co.*, 305 U.S. [111] at 122, 59 S.Ct. [109] at 115 [, 83 L.Ed. 73 (1938)]. To allow a State by use of its law of unfair competition to prevent the copying of an article which represents too slight an advance to be patented would be to permit the State to block off from the public something which federal law has said belongs to the public. The result would be that while federal law grants only 14 or 17 years' protection to genuine inventions, States could allow perpetual protection to articles too lacking in novelty to merit any patent at all under federal constitutional standards. This would be too great an encroachment on the federal patent system to be tolerated.

Sears has been held liable here for unfair competition because of a finding of likelihood of confusion based only on the fact that Sears' lamp was copied from Stiffel's unpatented lamp and that consequently the two looked exactly alike. Of course there could be "confusion" as to who had manufactured these nearly identical articles. But mere inability of the public to tell two identical articles apart is not enough to support an injunction against copying or an award of damages for copying that which the federal patent laws permit to be copied. Doubtless a State may, in appropriate circumstances, require that goods, whether patented or unpatented, be labeled or that other precautionary steps be taken to prevent customers from being misled as to the source, just as it may protect businesses in the use of their trademarks, labels, or distinctive dress in the packaging of goods so as to prevent others, by imitating such markings, from misleading purchasers as to the source of the goods. But because of the federal patent laws a State may not, when the article is unpatented and uncopyrighted, prohibit the copying of the article itself or award damages for such copying. The judgment below did both and in so doing gave Stiffel the equivalent of a patent monopoly on its unpatented lamp. That was error, and Sears is entitled to a judgment in its favor.

COMPCO CORP. v. DAY–BRITE LIGHTING, INC.

United States Supreme Court, 1964.
376 U.S. 234, 84 S.Ct. 779, 11 L.Ed.2d 669, 140 U.S.P.Q. 528.

MR. JUSTICE BLACK delivered the opinion of the Court.

As in *Sears, Roebuck & Co. v. Stiffel Co.*, the question here is whether the use of a state unfair competition law to give relief against the copying of an unpatented industrial design conflicts with the federal patent laws. Both Compco and Day–Brite are manufacturers of fluorescent lighting fixtures of a kind widely used in offices and stores. Day–Brite in 1955 secured from the Patent Office a design patent on a reflector having cross-ribs claimed to give both strength and attractiveness to the fixture. Day–Brite also sought, but was refused, a mechanical patent on the same device. After Day–Brite had begun selling its fixture, Compco's predecessor began making and selling fixtures very similar to Day–Brite's. This action was then brought by Day–Brite. One count alleged that Compco had infringed Day–Brite's design patent; a second count charged that the public and the trade had come to associate this particular design with Day–Brite, that Compco had copied Day–Brite's distinctive design so as to confuse and deceive purchasers into thinking Compco's fixtures were actually Day–Brite's, and that by doing this Compco had unfairly competed with Day–Brite. The complaint prayed for both an accounting and an injunction.

The District Court held the design patent invalid; but as to the second count, while the court did not find that Compco had engaged in any deceptive or fraudulent practices, it did hold that Compco had been guilty of unfair competition under Illinois law. The court found that the overall appearance of Compco's fixture was "the same, to the eye of the ordinary observer, as the overall appearance" of Day–Brite's reflector, which embodied the design of the invalidated patent; that the appearance of Day–Brite's design had "the capacity to identify [Day–Brite] in the trade and does in fact so identify [it] to the trade"; that the concurrent sale of the two products was "likely to cause confusion in the trade"; and that "[a]ctual confusion has occurred." On these findings the court adjudged Compco guilty of unfair competition in the sale of its fixtures, ordered Compco to account to Day–Brite for damages, and enjoined Compco "from unfairly competing with plaintiff by the sale or attempted sale of reflectors identical to, or confusingly similar to" those made by Day–Brite. The Court of Appeals held there was substantial evidence in the record to support the District Court's finding of likely confusion and that this finding was sufficient to support a holding of unfair competition under Illinois law. Although the District Court had not made such a finding, the appellate court observed that "several choices of ribbing were apparently available to meet the functional needs of the product," yet Compco "chose precisely the same design used by the plaintiff and followed it so closely as to make confusion likely." A design which identifies its maker to the trade, the Court of Appeals held, is a "protectible" right under Illinois law, even though the design is unpatentable. * * *

To support its findings of likelihood of confusion and actual confusion, the trial court was able to refer to only one circumstance in the record. A plant manager who had installed some of Compco's fixtures later asked Day–Brite to service the fixtures, thinking they had been made by Day–Brite. There was no testimony given by a purchaser or by anyone else that any customer had ever been misled, deceived, or "confused," that is, that anyone had ever bought a Compco fixture thinking it was a Day–Brite fixture. All the record shows, as to the one instance cited by the trial court, is that both Compco and Day–Brite fixtures had been installed in the same plant, that three years later some repairs were needed, and that the manager viewing the Compco fixtures—hung at least 15 feet above the floor and arranged end to end in a continuous line so that identifying marks were hidden—thought they were Day–Brite fixtures and asked Day–Brite to service them. Not only is this incident suggestive only of confusion *after* a purchase had been made, but also there is considerable evidence of the care taken by Compco to prevent customer confusion, including clearly labeling both the fixtures and the containers in which they were shipped and not selling through manufacturers' representatives who handled competing lines.

Notwithstanding the thinness of the evidence to support findings of likely and actual confusion among purchasers, we do not find it necessary in this case to determine whether there is "clear error" in these findings. They, like those in *Sears, Roebuck & Co. v. Stiffel Co.*, were based wholly on the fact that selling an article which is an exact copy of another unpatented article is likely to produce and did in this case produce confusion as to the source of the article. Even accepting the findings, we hold that the order for an accounting for damages and the injunction are in conflict with the federal patent laws. Today we have held in *Sears, Roebuck & Co. v. Stiffel Co.* that when an article is unprotected by a patent or a copyright, state law may not forbid others to copy that article. To forbid copying would interfere with the federal policy, found in Art. I, § 8, cl. 8, of the Constitution and in the implementing federal statutes, of allowing free access to copy whatever the federal patent and copyright laws leave in the public domain. Here Day–Brite's fixture has been held not to be entitled to a design or mechanical patent. Under the federal patent laws it is, therefore, in the public domain and can be copied in every detail by whoever pleases. It is true that the trial court found that the configuration of Day–Brite's fixture identified Day–Brite to the trade because the arrangement of the ribbing had, like a trademark, acquired a "secondary meaning" by which that particular design was associated with Day–Brite. But if the design is not entitled to a design patent or other federal statutory protection, then it can be copied at will.

As we have said in *Sears*, while the federal patent laws prevent a State from prohibiting the copying and selling of unpatented articles, they do not stand in the way of state law, statutory or decisional, which requires those who make and sell copies to take precautions to identify their products as their own. A State of course has power to impose liability upon those who, knowing that the public is relying upon an original manufacturer's reputation for quality and integrity, deceive the public by palming off their copies as the original. That an article copied from an unpatented article could be made in some other way, that the design is "nonfunctional" and not essential to the use of either article, that the configuration of the article copied may have a "secondary meaning" which identifies the maker to the trade, or that there may be "confusion" among purchasers as to which article is which or as to who is the maker, may be relevant evidence in applying a State's law requiring such precautions as labeling; however, and regardless of the copier's motives, neither these facts nor any others can furnish a basis for imposing liability for or prohibiting the actual acts of copying and selling. * * *

Since the judgment below forbids the sale of a copy of an unpatented article and orders an accounting for damages for such copying, it cannot stand.

Notes and Questions

1. *The scope and impact of Sears and Compco.* The *Sears* and *Compco* decisions caused a considerable stir, since they appeared to curtail a well established tradition of state law protection against the copying of distinctive, non-functional product features which created a likelihood of consumer confusion. A number of commentators criticized the decisions and speculated about their scope. See, e.g., Symposium, *Product Simulation: A Right or a Wrong?*, 64 COLUM. L. REV. 1178 (1964). While lower courts initially applied the decisions strictly to preempt state unfair competition causes of action, subsequent Supreme Court decisions (set forth below), which seemed to retreat from the hard-line view set forth in *Sears* and *Compco*, encouraged them to find ways to distinguish *Sears* and *Compco* and uphold the state claims. See, e.g., Ideal Toy Corp. v. Plawner Toy Mfg. Corp., 685 F.2d 78, 216 U.S.P.Q. 102 (3d Cir.1982). How might one distinguish *Sears* and *Compco* in order to uphold state unfair competition protection of product features?

The Court had to decide in *Sears* and *Compco* whether enforcement of the state law would frustrate accomplishment of Congress' purposes in enacting the patent and copyright laws. What does the Court view Congress' purposes to be?

Did the *Sears* and *Compco* cases involve functional or nonfunctional product features? Does it matter for purposes of the Court's opinions?

Did the Court view the defendants' intent as a relevant consideration? Should it be?

Of what, if any relevance is the fact that the Lanham Act prevents copying of distinctive, non-functional product features that cause a likelihood of consumer confusion?

Could the language and reasoning of *Sears* and *Compco* be interpreted to preempt other state intellectual property causes of action? For example, what are the apparent implications of *Sears* and *Compco* for state trade secret claims? For state misappropriation and dilution causes of action? How about state right of publicity claims, or claims for undeveloped ideas?

GOLDSTEIN v. CALIFORNIA

United States Supreme Court, 1973.
412 U.S. 546, 93 S.Ct. 2303, 37 L.Ed.2d 163, 178 U.S.P.Q. 129.

MR. CHIEF JUSTICE BURGER delivered the opinion of the Court.

We granted certiorari to review petitioners' conviction under a California statute [California Penal Code § 653h] making it a criminal offense to "pirate" recordings produced by others.

* * *

I

Petitioners were engaged in what has commonly been called "record piracy" or "tape piracy"—the unauthorized duplication of recordings of performances by major musical artists. Petitioners would purchase from a retail distributor a single tape or phonograph recording of the popular performances they wished to duplicate. The original recordings were produced and marketed by recording companies with which petitioners had no contractual relationship. At petitioners' plant, the recording was reproduced on blank tapes, which could in turn be used to replay the music on a tape player. The tape was then wound on a cartridge. A label was attached, stating the title of the recorded performance—the same title as had appeared on the original recording, and the name of the performing artists.[4] After final packaging, the tapes were distributed to retail outlets for sale to the public, in competition with those petitioners had copied.

[Petitioners made no payments for the use of the performances, the recordings or the artists' names or record titles.]

The challenged California statute forbids petitioners to transfer any performance fixed on a tape or record onto other records or tapes with

4. An additional label was attached to each cartridge by petitioners, stating that no relationship existed between petitioners and the producer of the original recording or the individuals whose performances had been recorded. Consequently, no claim is made that petitioners misrepresented the source of the original recordings or the manufacturer of the tapes.

the intention of selling the duplicates, unless they have first received permission from those who, under state law, are the owners of the master recording. Although the protection afforded to each master recording is substantial, lasting for an unlimited time, the scope of the proscribed activities is narrow. No limitation is placed on the use of the music, lyrics, or arrangement employed in making the master recording. Petitioners are not precluded from hiring their own musicians and artists and recording an exact imitation of the performance embodied on the master recording. Petitioners are even free to hire the same artists who made the initial recording in order to duplicate the performance. In essence, the statute thus provides copyright protection solely for the specific expressions which compose the master record or tape.

* * * [P]etitioners claim that the state statute interferes with the implementation of federal policies inherent in the federal copyright statutes. According to petitioners, it was the intention of Congress, as interpreted by this Court in *Sears, Roebuck & Co. v. Stiffel Co.*, and *Compco Corp. v. Day–Brite Lighting*, to establish a uniform law throughout the United States to protect original writings. As part of the federal scheme, it is urged that Congress intended to allow individuals to copy any work which was not protected by a federal copyright. Since § 653h effectively prohibits the copying of works which are not entitled to federal protection, petitioners contend that it conflicts directly with congressional policy and must fall under the Supremacy Clause of the Constitution. * * *

We note at the outset that the federal copyright statutes to which petitioners refer were amended by Congress while their case was pending in the state courts. In 1971, Pub.L. 92–140, 85 Stat. 391, 17 U.S.C. §§ 1(f), 5(n), 19, 20, 26, 101(e), was passed to allow federal copyright protection of recordings. However, § 3 of the amendment specifically provides that such protection is to be available only to sound recordings "fixed, published, and copyrighted" on and after February 15, 1972, and before January 1, 1975, and that nothing in Title 17, as amended is to "be applied retroactively or (to) be construed as affecting in any way any rights with respect to sound recordings fixed before" February 15, 1972. The recordings which petitioners copied were all "fixed" prior to February 15, 1972. Since, according to the language of the amendment, Congress did not intend to alter the legal relationships which govern these recordings, the amendments have no application in petitioners' case.

[In the omitted section, the Court rejects arguments that the states relinquished all power to regulate in the pertinent field.]

III

Our conclusion that California did not surrender its power to issue copyrights does not end the inquiry. We must proceed to determine whether the challenged state statute is void under the Supremacy Clause. No simple formula can capture the complexities of this determination; the conflicts which may develop between state and federal action are as varied as the fields to which congressional action may apply. "Our primary function is to determine whether, under the circumstances of this particular case, [the state] law stands as an obstacle to the accomplishment and execution of the full purposes and objectives of Congress." *Hines v. Davidowitz*, 312 U.S., 52, 67, 61 S.Ct. 399, 404, 85 L.Ed. 581 (1941). We turn, then, to federal copyright law to determine what objectives Congress intended to fulfill.

By Art. I, § 8, cl. 8, of the Constitution, the States granted to Congress the power to protect the "Writings" of "Authors." These terms have not been construed in their narrow literal sense but, rather, with the reach necessary to reflect the broad scope of constitutional principles. While an "author" may be viewed as an individual who writes an original composition, the term, in its constitutional sense, has been construed to mean an "originator," "he to whom anything owes its origin." *Burrow-Giles Lithographic Co. v. Sarony*, 111 U.S. 53, 58, 4 S.Ct. 279, 281, 28 L.Ed. 349 (1884). Similarly, although the word "writings" might be limited to script or printed material, it may be interpreted to include any physical rendering of the fruits of creative intellectual or aesthetic labor. Thus, recordings of artistic performances may be within the reach of Clause 8.

While the area in which Congress *may* act is broad, the enabling provision of Clause 8 does not require that Congress act in regard to all categories of materials which meet the constitutional definitions. Rather, whether any specific category of "Writings" is to be brought within the purview of the federal statutory scheme is left to the discretion of the Congress. The history of federal copyright statutes indicates that the congressional determination to consider specific classes of writings is dependent, not only on the character of the writing, but also on the commercial importance of the product to the national economy. As our technology has expanded the means available for creative activity and has provided economical means for reproducing manifestations of such activity, new areas of federal protection have been initiated.[17]

Petitioners contend that the actions taken by Congress in establishing federal copyright protection preclude the States from granting similar protection to recordings of musical performances. According to petitioners, Congress addressed the question of whether recordings of

17. The first congressional copyright statute, passed in 1790, governed only maps, charts, and books. In 1802, the Act was amended in order to grant protection to any person "who shall invent and design, engrave, etch or work . . . any historical or other print or prints. . . ." Protection was extended to musical compositions when the copyright laws were revised in 1831. In 1865, at the time when Mathew Brady's pictures of the Civil War were attaining fame, photographs and photographic negatives were expressly added to the list of protected works. Again in 1870, the list was augmented to cover paintings, drawings, chromos, statuettes, statuary, and models or designs of fine art.

In 1909, Congress agreed to a major consolidation and amendment of all federal copyright statutes. A list of 11 categories of protected works was provided. * * *

Since 1909, two additional amendments have been added. In 1912, the list of categories in § 5 was expanded specifically to include motion pictures. * * *

Finally, in 1971, § 5 was amended to include "sound recordings." * * *

performances should be granted protection in 1909; Congress determined that any individual who was entitled to a copyright on an original musical composition should have the right to control to a limited extent the use of that composition on recordings, but that the record itself, and the performance which it was capable of reproducing were not worthy of such protection. In support of their claim, petitioners cite the House Report on the 1909 Act, which states:

> "It is not the intention of the committee to extend the right of copyright to the mechanical reproductions themselves, but only to give the composer or copyright proprietor the control, in accordance with the provisions of the bill, of the manufacture and use of such devices." H.R.Rep.No. 2222, 60th Cong., 2d Sess., 9 (1909).

To interpret accurately Congress' intended purpose in passing the 1909 Act and the meaning of the House Report petitioners cite, we must remember that our modern technology differs greatly from that which existed in 1909. * * *

* * * The section of the House Report cited by petitioners was intended only to establish the limits of *the composer's* right; composers were to have no control over the recordings themselves. Nowhere does the report indicate that Congress considered records as anything but a component part of a machine, capable of reproducing an original composition or that Congress intended records, as *renderings of original artistic performance*, to be free from state control.

Petitioners' argument does not rest entirely on the belief that Congress intended specifically to exempt recordings of performances from state control. Assuming that no such intention may be found, they argue that Congress so occupied the field of copyright protection as to pre-empt all comparable state action. This assertion is based on the language of 17 U.S.C. §§ 4 and 5, and on this Court's opinions in *Sears, Roebuck & Co. v. Stiffel Co.*, and *Compco Corp. v. Day-Brite Lighting.*

Section 4 of the federal copyright laws provides:

> "The works for which copyright may be secured under this title shall include all the writings of an author." 17 U.S.C. § 4.

Section 5, which lists specific categories of protected works, adds:

> "The above specifications shall not be held to limit the subject-matter of copyright as defined in section 4 of this title...." 17 U.S.C. § 5.

Since § 4 employs the constitutional term "writings," it may be argued that Congress intended to exercise its authority over all works to which the constitutional provision might apply. However, in the more than 60 years which have elapsed since enactment of this provision, neither the Copyright Office, the courts, nor the Congress has so interpreted it. The Register of Copyrights, who is charged with administration of the statute, has consistently ruled that "claims to exclusive rights in mechanical recordings ... or in the performances they reproduce" are not entitled to protection under § 4. 37 CFR § 202.8(b) (1972). With one early exception, American courts have agreed with this interpretation; and in 1971, prior to passage of the statute which extended federal protection to recordings fixed on or after February 15, 1972, Congress acknowledged the validity of that interpretation. Both the House and Senate Reports on the proposed legislation recognized that recordings qualified as "writings" within the meaning of the Constitution, but had not previously been protected under the federal copyright statute. In light of this consistent interpretation by the courts, the agency empowered to administer the copyright statutes, and Congress itself, we cannot agree that § 4 and 5 have the broad scope petitioners claim.

Sears and Compco, on which petitioners rely, do not support their position. In those cases, the question was whether a State could, under principles of a state unfair competition law, preclude the copying of mechanical configurations which did not possess the qualities required for the granting of a federal design or mechanical patent. * * *

In regard to mechanical configurations, Congress had balanced the need to encourage innovation and originality of invention against the need to insure competition in the sale of identical or substantially identical products. The standards established for granting federal patent protection to machines thus indicated not only which articles in this particular category Congress wished to protect, but which configurations it wished to remain free. The application of state law in these cases to prevent the copying of articles which did not meet the requirements for federal protection disturbed the careful balance which Congress had drawn and thereby necessarily gave way under the Supremacy Clause of the Constitution. No comparable conflict between state law and federal law arises in the case of recordings of musical performances. In regard to this category of "Writings," Congress has drawn no balance; rather, it has left the area unattended, and no reason exists why the State should not be free to act.

IV

* * * The California statutory scheme evidences a legislative policy to prohibit "tape piracy" and "record piracy," conduct that may adversely affect the continued production of new recordings, a large industry in California. Accordingly, the State has, by statute, given to recordings the attributes of property. No restraint has been placed on the use of an idea or concept; rather, petitioners and other individuals remain free to record the same compositions in precisely the same manner and with the same personnel as appeared on the original recording.

In sum, we have shown that § 653h does not conflict with the federal copyright statute enacted by Congress in 1909. Similarly, no conflict exists between the federal copyright statute passed in 1971 and the present application of § 653h, since California charged petitioners only with copying recordings fixed prior to February 15, 1972. Finally, we have concluded that our decisions in *Sears* and *Compco*, which we reaffirm today, have no application in the present case, since Congress has indicated neither that it wishes to protect, nor to free from protection, recordings of musical performances fixed prior to February 15, 1972.

* * * Until and unless Congress takes further action with respect to recordings fixed prior to February 15, 1972, the California statute may be enforced against acts of piracy such as those which occurred in the present case.

* * *

MR. JUSTICE MARSHALL, with whom MR. JUSTICE BRENNAN and MR. JUSTICE BLACKMUN join, dissenting.

* * * Ordinarily, the failure to enumerate "sound recordings" in § 5 would not be taken as an expression of Congress' desire to let free competition reign in the reproduction of such recordings, for, because of the realities of the legislative process, it is generally difficult to infer from a failure to act any affirmative conclusions. But in *Sears* and its companion case, *Compco Corp. v. Day–Brite Lighting, Inc.*, the Court determined that with respect to patents and copyrights, the ordinary practice was not to prevail. In view of the importance of not imposing unnecessary restraints on competition, the Court adopted in those cases a rule of construction that, unless the failure to provide patent or copyright protection for some class of works could clearly be shown to reflect a judgment that state regulation was permitted, the silence of Congress would be taken to reflect a judgment that free competition should prevail. I do not find in *Sears* and *Compco* a limitation on that rule of construction to general classes that Congress has enumerated although, of course, on the facts of those cases only items in such classes were involved; rather, the broadest language was used in those cases.[3] Nor can I find in the course of legislation sufficient evidence to convince me that Congress determined to permit state regulation of the reproduction of sound recordings. For, whenever technological advances made extension of copyright protection seem wise, Congress has acted promptly. This seems to me to reflect the same judgment that the Court found in *Sears* and *Compco*: Congress has decided that free competition should be the general rule, until it is convinced that the failure to provide copyright or patent protection is hindering "the Progress of Science and useful Arts."

The business of record piracy is not an attractive one; persons in the business capitalize on the talents of others without needing to assess independently the prospect of public acceptance of a performance. But the same might be said of persons who copy "mechanical configurations." Such people do provide low-cost reproduction that may well benefit the public. In light of the presumption of *Sears* and *Compco* that congressional silence betokens a determination that the benefits of competition outweigh the impediments placed on creativity by the lack of copyright protection, and in the absence of a congressional determina-

3. It bears noting that in *Sears, Roebuck & Co. v. Stiffel Co.*, the Court repeatedly referred to the patent and copyright statutes as if the same rules of interpretation applied to both.

tion that the opposite is true, we should not let our distaste for "pirates" interfere with our interpretation of the copyright laws. I would therefore hold that, as to sound recordings fixed before February 15, 1972, the States may not enforce laws limiting reproduction.

Notes and Questions

1. *The Goldstein opinion.* What rule does the *Goldstein* court provide regarding supremacy clause preemption? Is it consistent with the Court's opinion in *Sears* and *Compco*? Does the *Goldstein* opinion narrow or modify *Sears* and *Compco*? If so, how?

Is the *Goldstein* decision consistent with the article I, § 8, cl. 8 provision, which specifies that Congress may only grant exclusive rights to authors and inventors *"for limited times?"*

What if the California statute had prevented the copying for sale of something that clearly was included within the scope of the Copyright Act as it then existed—for example, works of literature? Would the statute be preempted under *Goldstein*? If so, why?

For interesting discussions of the implications of the *Goldstein* decision, see Brown, *Publication and Preemption in Copyright Law: Elegiac Reflections on Goldstein v. California*, 22 U.C.L.A. L. REV. 1022 (1975); Abrams & Abrams, *Goldstein v. California: Sound, Fury, and Significance*, [1975] SUP. CT. REV. 147.

KEWANEE OIL CO. v. BICRON CORP.

United States Supreme Court, 1974.
416 U.S. 470, 94 S.Ct. 1879, 40 L.Ed.2d 315, 181 U.S.P.Q. 673.

MR. CHIEF JUSTICE BURGER delivered the opinion of the Court.

We granted certiorari to resolve a question on which there is a conflict in the courts of appeals: whether state trade secret protection is pre-empted by operation of the federal patent law. * * *

I

Harshaw Chemical Co., an unincorporated division of petitioner, is a leading manufacturer of a type of synthetic crystal which is useful in the detection of ionizing radiation. In 1949 Harshaw commenced research into the growth of this type crystal and was able to produce one less than two inches in diameter. By 1966, as the result of expenditures in excess of $1 million, Harshaw was able to grow a 17–inch crystal, something no one else had done previously. Harshaw had developed many processes, procedures, and manufacturing techniques in the purification of raw materials and the growth and encapsulation of the crystals which enabled it to accomplish this feat. Some of these processes Harshaw considers to be trade secrets.

The individual respondents are former employees of Harshaw who formed or later joined respondent Bicron. While at Harshaw the individual respondents executed, as a condition of employment, at least one agreement each, requiring them not to disclose confidential information or trade secrets obtained as employees of Harshaw. Bicron was formed in August 1969 to compete with Harshaw in the production of the crystals, and by April 1970, had grown a 17–inch crystal.

Petitioner brought this diversity action in United States District Court for the Northern District of Ohio seeking injunctive relief and damages for the misappropriation of trade secrets. The District Court, applying Ohio trade secret law, granted a permanent injunction against the disclosure or use by respondents of 20 of the 40 claimed trade secrets until such time as the trade secrets had been released to the public, had otherwise generally become available to the public, or had been obtained by respondents from sources having the legal right to convey the information.

The Court of Appeals for the Sixth Circuit held that the findings of fact by the District Court were not clearly erroneous, * * * [and that] the District Court properly applied Ohio law relating to trade secrets. Nevertheless, the Court of Appeals reversed the District Court, finding Ohio's trade secret law to be in conflict with the patent laws of the United States. The Court of Appeals reasoned that Ohio could not grant monopoly protection to processes and manufacturing techniques that were appropriate subjects for consideration under 35 U.S.C. § 101 for a federal patent but which had been in commercial use for over one year and so were no longer eligible for patent protection under 35 U.S.C. § 102(b).

We hold that Ohio's law of trade secrets is not preempted by the patent laws of the United States, and, accordingly, we reverse.

II

* * *

The subject of a trade secret must be secret, and must not be of public knowledge or of a general knowledge in the trade or business. This necessary element of secrecy is not lost, however, if the holder of the trade secret reveals the trade secret to another "in confidence, and under an implied obligation not to use or disclose it." *Cincinnati Bell Foundry Co. v. Dodds*, 10 Ohio Dec.Reprint 154, 156, 19 Weekly Law Bull. 84 (Super.Ct.1887). These others may include those of the holder's "employees to whom it is necessary to confide it, in order to apply it to the uses for which it is intended." *National Tube Co. v. Eastern Tube Co.*, 3 Ohio C.C.R., n.s., [459,] 462 [(1902) aff'd., 69 Ohio St. 560, 70 N.E. 1127 (1903)]. Often the recipient of confidential knowledge of the subject of a trade secret is a licensee of its holder.

The protection accorded the trade secret holder is against the disclosure or unauthorized use of the trade secret by those to whom the secret has been confided under the express or implied restriction of nondisclosure or nonuse. The law also protects the holder of a trade secret against disclosure or use when the knowledge is gained, not by the owner's volition, but by some "improper means," Restatement of Torts § 757(a), which may include theft, wiretapping, or even aerial reconnaissance. A trade secret law, however, does not offer protection against discovery by fair and honest means, such as by independent invention, accidental disclosure, or by so-called reverse engineering, that is by starting with the known product and working backward to divine the process which aided in its development or manufacture.

Novelty, in the patent law sense, is not required for a trade secret. * * * However, some novelty will be required if merely because that which does not possess novelty is usually known; secrecy, in the context of trade secrets, thus implies at least minimal novelty.

The subject matter of a patent is limited to a "process, machine, manufacture, or composition of matter, or . . . improvement thereof," 35 U.S.C. § 101, which fulfills the three conditions of novelty and utility as articulated and defined in 35 U.S.C. §§ 101 and 102, and nonobviousness, as set out in 35 U.S.C. § 103. If an invention meets the rigorous statutory tests for the issuance of a patent, the patent is granted, for a period of 17 years * * *. This protection goes not only to copying the subject matter, which is forbidden under the Copyright Act, 17 U.S.C. § 1 et seq., but also to independent creation.

III

The first issue we deal with is whether the States are forbidden to act at all in the area of protection of the kinds of intellectual property which may make up the subject matter of trade secrets.

* * * In the 1972 Term, in *Goldstein v. California*, we held that the cl. 8 grant of power to Congress was not exclusive and that, at least in the case of writings, the States were not prohibited from encouraging and protecting the efforts of those within their borders by appropriate legislation. * * *

Just as the States may exercise regulatory power over writings so may the States regulate with respect to discoveries. States may hold diverse viewpoints in protecting intellectual property relating to invention as they do in protecting the intellectual property relating to the subject matter of copyright. The only limitation on the States is that in regulating the area of patents and copyrights they do not conflict with the operation of the laws in this area passed by Congress, and it is to that more difficult question we now turn.

IV

The question of whether the trade secret law of Ohio is void under the Supremacy Clause involves a consideration of whether that law "stands as an obstacle to the accomplishment and execution of the full purposes and objectives of Congress." *Hines v. Davidowitz*, 312 U.S. 52, 67, 61 S.Ct. 399, 404, 85 L.Ed. 581 (1941). We stated in *Sears, Roebuck & Co. v. Stiffel Co.*, that when state law touches upon the area of federal statutes enacted pursuant to constitutional authority, "it is 'familiar doctrine' that the federal policy 'may not be set at naught, or its benefits denied' by the state law. This is true, of course, even if the state law is enacted in the exercise of otherwise undoubted state power."

The laws which the Court of Appeals in this case held to be in conflict with the Ohio law of trade secrets were the patent laws passed by the Congress in the unchallenged exercise of its clear power under Art. I, § 8, cl. 8, of the Constitution. The patent law does not explicitly endorse or forbid the operation of trade secret law. However, as we have noted, if the scheme of protection developed by Ohio respecting trade secrets "clashes with the objectives of the federal patent laws," *Sears, Roebuck & Co. v. Stiffel Co., supra*, then the state law must fall. To determine whether the Ohio law "clashes" with the federal law it is helpful to examine the objectives of both the patent and trade secret laws.

The stated objective of the Constitution in granting the power to Congress to legislate in the area of intellectual property is to "promote the Progress of Science and useful Arts." The patent laws promote this progress by offering a right of exclusion for a limited period as an incentive to inventors to risk the often enormous costs in terms of time, research, and development. The productive effort thereby fostered will have a positive effect on society through the introduction of new products and processes of manufacture into the economy, and the emanations by way of increased employment and better lives for our citizens. In return for the right of exclusion—this "reward for inventions,"—the patent laws impose upon the inventor a requirement of disclosure. To insure adequate and full disclosure so that upon the expiration of the 17–year period "the knowledge of the invention enures to the people, who are thus enabled without restriction to practice it and profit by its use," *United States v. Dubilier Condenser Corp.*, 289 U.S. 178, 187, 53 S.Ct. 554, 77 L.Ed. 1114 (1933), the patent laws require that the patent application shall include a full and clear description of the invention and "of the manner and process of making and using it" so that any person skilled in the art may make and use the invention. When a patent is granted and the information contained in it is circulated to the general public and those especially skilled in the trade, such additions to the general store of knowledge are of such importance to the public weal that the Federal Government is willing to pay the high price of 17 years of exclusive use for its disclosure, which disclosure, it is assumed, will stimulate ideas and the eventual development of further significant advances in the art. The Court has also articulated another policy of the patent law: that which is in the public domain cannot be removed therefrom by action of the States.

> "[F]ederal law requires that all ideas in general circulation be dedicated to the common good unless they are protected by a valid patent." *Lear, Inc. v. Adkins*, 395 U.S., at 668, 89 S.Ct., at 1910.

The maintenance of standards of commercial ethics and the encouragement of invention are the broadly stated policies behind trade secret law. * * *

Having now in mind the objectives of both the patent and trade secret law, we turn to an examination of the interaction of these systems of protection of intellectual property—one established by the Congress and the other by a State—to determine whether and under what circumstances the latter might constitute "too great an encroachment on the federal patent system to be tolerated." *Sears, Roebuck & Co. v. Stiffel Co.*

As we noted earlier, trade secret law protects items which would not be proper subjects for consideration for patent protection under 35 U.S.C. § 101. As in the case of the recordings in *Goldstein v. California*, Congress, with respect to nonpatentable subject matter, "has drawn no balance; rather, it has left the area unattended, and no reason exists why the State should not be free to act." *Goldstein v. California, supra*, 412 U.S., at 570, 93 S.Ct. at 2316.

Since no patent is available for a discovery, however useful, novel, and nonobvious, unless it falls within one of the express categories of patentable subject matter of 35 U.S.C. § 101, the holder of such a discovery would have no reason to apply for a patent whether trade secret protection existed or not. Abolition of trade secret protection would, therefore, not result in increased disclosure to the public of discoveries in the area of nonpatentable subject matter. Also, it is hard to see how the public would be benefitted by disclosure of customer lists or advertising campaigns; in fact, keeping such items secret encourages businesses to initiate new and individualized plans of operation, and constructive competition results. This, in turn, leads to a greater variety of business methods than would otherwise be the case if privately developed marketing and other data were passed illicitly among firms involved in the same enterprise.

Congress has spoken in the area of those discoveries which fall within one of the categories of patentable subject matter of 35 U.S.C. § 101 and which are, therefore, of a nature that would be subject to consideration for a patent. Processes, machines, manufactures, compositions of matter and improvements thereof, which meet the tests of utility, novelty, and nonobviousness are entitled to be patented, but those which do not, are not. The question remains whether those items which are proper subjects for consideration for a patent may also have available the alternative protection accorded by trade secret law.

Certainly the patent policy of encouraging invention is not disturbed by the existence of another form of incentive to invention. In this respect the two systems are not and never would be in conflict. Similarly, the policy that matter once in the public domain must remain in the public domain is not incompatible with the existence of trade secret protection. By definition a trade secret has not been placed in the public domain.

The more difficult objective of the patent law to reconcile with trade secret law is that of disclosure, the *quid pro quo* of the right to exclude. We are helped in this stage of the analysis by Judge Henry Friendly's opinion in *Painton & Co. v. Bourns, Inc.*, 442 F.2d 216 (CA2 1971). There the Court of Appeals thought it useful, in determining whether inventors will refrain because of the existence of trade secret law from applying for patents, thereby depriving the public from learning of the invention, to distinguish between three categories of trade secrets:

> "(1) the trade secret believed by its owner to constitute a validly patentable invention; (2) the trade secret known to its owner not to be so patentable; and (3) the trade secret whose valid patentability is considered dubious." *Id.*, at 224.
>
> * * *

As to the trade secret known not to meet the standards of patentability, very little in the way of disclosure would be accomplished by abolishing trade secret protection. * * *

Even as the extension of trade secret protection to patentable subject matter that the owner knows will not meet the standards of patentability will not conflict with the patent policy of disclosure, it will have a decidedly beneficial effect on society. Trade secret law will encourage invention in areas where patent law does not reach, and will prompt the independent innovator to proceed with the discovery and exploitation of his invention. Competition is fostered and the public is not deprived of the use of valuable, if not quite patentable, invention.

Even if trade secret protection against the faithless employee were abolished, inventive and exploitive effort in the area of patentable subject matter that did not meet the standards of patentability would continue, although at a reduced level. Alternatively with the effort that remained, however, would come an increase in the amount of self-help that innovative companies would employ. * * * Security precautions necessarily would be increased, and salaries and fringe benefits of those few officers or employees who had to know the whole of the secret invention would be fixed in an amount thought sufficient to assure their loyalty. Smaller companies would be placed at a distinct economic disadvantage, since the costs of this kind of self-help could be great, and the cost to the public of the use of this invention would be increased. * * *

Another problem that would arise if state trade secret protection were precluded is in the area of licensing others to exploit secret processes. The holder of a trade secret would not likely share his secret with a manufacturer who cannot be placed under binding legal obligation to pay a license fee or to protect the secret. The result would be to hoard rather than disseminate knowledge. Instead, then, of licensing others to use his invention and making the most efficient use of existing manufacturing and marketing structures within the industry, the trade secret holder would tend either to limit his utilization of the invention, thereby depriving the public of the maximum benefit of its use, or engage in the time-consuming and economically wasteful enterprise of constructing duplicative manufacturing and marketing mechanisms for the exploitation of the invention. The detrimental misallocation of resources and economic waste that would thus take place if trade secret protection were abolished with respect to employees or licensees cannot be justified by reference to any policy that the federal patent law seeks to advance.

Nothing in the patent law requires that States refrain from action to prevent industrial espionage. In addition to the increased costs for protection from burglary, wire-tapping, bribery, and the other means used to misappropriate trade secrets, there is the inevitable cost to the basic decency of society when one firm steals from another. A most fundamental human right, that of privacy, is threatened when industrial espionage is condoned or is made profitable; the state interest in denying profit to such illegal ventures is unchallengeable.

The next category of patentable subject matter to deal with is the invention whose holder has a legitimate doubt as to its patentability. The risk of eventual patent invalidity by the courts and the costs associated with that risk may well impel some with a good-faith doubt as to patentability not to take the trouble to seek to obtain and defend patent protection for their discoveries, regardless of the existence of trade secret protection. Trade secret protection would assist those inventors in the more efficient exploitation of their discoveries and not conflict with the patent law. In most cases of genuine doubt as to patent validity the potential rewards of patent protection are so far superior to those accruing to holders of trade secrets, that the holders of such inventions will seek patent protection, ignoring the trade secret route. For those inventors "on the line" as to whether to seek patent protection, the abolition of trade secret protection might encourage some to apply for a patent who otherwise would not have done so. For some of those so encouraged, no patent will be granted and the result

> "will have been an unnecessary postponement in the divulging of the trade secret to persons willing to pay for it. If (the patent does issue), it may well be invalid, yet many will prefer to pay a modest royalty than to contest it, even though Lear allows them to accept a license and pursue the contest without paying royalties while the fight goes on. The result in such a case would be unjustified royalty payments from many who would prefer not to pay them rather than agreed fees from one or a few who are entirely willing to do so." *Painton & Co. v. Bourns, Inc.*, 442 F.2d, at 225.

The point is that those who might be encouraged to file for patents by the absence of trade secret law will include inventors possessing the chaff as well as the wheat. * * * Some of the chaff may not be thrown out. This Court has noted the difference between the standards used by the Patent Office and the courts to determine patentability. * * * More [invalid] patents would likely issue if trade secret law were abolished. Eliminating trade secret law for the doubtfully patentable invention is thus likely to have deleterious effects on society and patent policy which we cannot say are balanced out by the speculative gain which might result from the encouragement of some inventors with doubtfully patentable inventions which deserve patent protection to come forward and apply for patents. There is no conflict, then, between trade secret law and the patent law policy of disclosure, at least insofar as the first two categories of patentable subject matter are concerned.

The final category of patentable subject matter to deal with is the clearly patentable invention, i.e., that invention which the owner believes to meet the standards of patentability. It is here that the federal interest in disclosure is at its peak; these inventions, novel, useful and nonobvious, are "the things which are worth to the public the embarrassment of an exclusive patent." *Graham v. John Deere Co.*, 383 U.S. [1,] at 9, 86 S.Ct. [684] at 689 [, 15 L.Ed.2d 545] (1966) (quoting Thomas Jefferson). The interest of the public is that the bargain of 17 years of exclusive use in return for disclosure be accepted. If a State, through a system of protection, were to cause a substantial risk that holders of patentable inventions would not seek patents, but rather would rely on the state protection, we would be compelled to hold that such a system could not constitutionally continue to exist. In the case of trade secret law no reasonable risk of deterrence from patent application by those who can reasonably expect to be granted patents exists.

Trade secret law provides far weaker protection in many respects than the patent law. While trade secret law does not forbid the discovery of the trade secret by fair and honest means, *e.g.*, independent creation or reverse engineering, patent law operates "against the world," forbidding any use of the invention for whatever purpose for a significant length of time. The holder of a trade secret also takes a substantial risk that the secret will be passed on to his competitors, by theft or by breach of a confidential relationship, in a manner not easily susceptible of discovery or proof. Where patent law acts as a barrier, trade secret law functions relatively as a sieve. The possibility that an inventor who believes his invention meets the standards of patentability will sit back, rely on trade secret law, and after one year of use forfeit any right to patent protection, 35 U.S.C. § 102(b), is remote indeed.

Nor does society face much risk that scientific or technological progress will be impeded by the rare inventor with a patentable invention who chooses trade secret protection over patent protection. The ripeness-of-time concept of invention, developed from the study of the many independent multiple discoveries in history, predicts that if a particular individual had not made a particular discovery others would have, and in probably a relatively short period of time. If something is to be discovered at all very likely it will be discovered by more than one person. Even were an inventor to keep his discovery completely to himself, something that neither the patent nor trade secret laws forbid, there is a high probability that it will be soon independently developed. * * *

We conclude that the extension of trade secret protection to clearly patentable inventions does not conflict with the patent policy of disclosure. * * *

Our conclusion that patent law does not pre-empt trade secret law is in accord with prior cases of this Court. Trade secret law and patent law have co-existed in this country for over one hundred years. Each has its particular role to play, and the operation of one does not take away from the need for the other. Trade secret law encourages the development and exploitation of those items of lesser or different invention than might be accorded protection under the patent laws, but which items still have an important part to play in the technological and scientific advancement of the Nation. Trade secret law promotes the sharing of knowledge, and the efficient operation of industry; it permits the individual inventor to reap the rewards of his labor by contracting with a company large enough to develop and exploit it. Congress, by its silence over these many years, has seen the wisdom of allowing the States to enforce trade secret protection. Until Congress takes affirmative action to the contrary, States should be free to grant protection to trade secrets.

* * *

MR. JUSTICE DOUGLAS, with whom MR. JUSTICE BRENNAN concurs, dissenting.

Today's decision is at war with the philosophy of *Sears, Roebuck & Co. v. Stiffel Co.*, and *Compco Corp. v. Day–Brite Lighting, Inc.* * * * We held that when an article is unprotected by a patent, state law may not forbid others to copy it, because every article not covered by a valid patent is in the public domain. Congress in the patent laws decided that where no patent existed, free competition should prevail; that where a patent is rightfully issued, the right to exclude others should obtain for no longer than 17 years, and that the States may not "under some other law, such as that forbidding unfair competition, give protection of a kind that clashes with the objectives of the federal patent laws."

The product involved in this suit, sodium iodide synthetic crystals, was a product that could be patented but was not. Harshaw the inventor apparently contributed greatly to the technology in that field by developing processes, procedures, and techniques that produced much larger crystals than any competitor. These processes, procedures, and techniques were also patentable; but no patent was sought. * * *

The District Court issued a permanent injunction against respondents, ex-employees, restraining them from using the processes used by Harshaw. By a patent which would require full disclosure Harshaw could have obtained a 17–year monopoly against the world. By the District Court's injunction, which the Court approves and reinstates, Harshaw gets a permanent injunction running into perpetuity against respondents. In *Sears*, as in the present case, an injunction against the unfair competitor issued. We said: "To allow a State by use of its law of unfair competition to prevent the copying of an article which represents too slight an advance to be patented would be to permit the State to block off from the public something which federal law has said belongs to the public. The result would be that while federal law grants only 14 or 17 years' protection to genuine inventions, States could allow perpetual protection to articles too lacking in novelty to merit any patent at all under federal constitutional standards. This would be too great an encroachment on the federal patent system to be tolerated." 376 U.S., at 231–232, 84 S.Ct. at 789.

The conflict with the patent laws is obvious. The decision of Congress to adopt a patent system was based on the idea that there will be much more innovation if discoveries are disclosed and patented than there will be when everyone works in secret. * * *

From the findings of fact of the lower courts, the process involved in this litigation was unique, such a great discovery as to make its patentability a virtual certainty. Yet the Court's opinion reflects a vigorous activist antipatent philosophy. My objection is not because it is activist. This is a problem that involves no neutral principle. The Constitution in Art. I, § 8, cl. 8, expresses the activist policy which Congress has enforced by statutes. It is that constitutional policy which we should enforce, not our individual notions of the public good.

I would affirm the judgment below.

Notes and Questions

1. *The Kewanee decision*. What general rule can you distill from the *Kewanee* decision? Is the rule consistent with the *Goldstein* decision? Is it consistent with *Sears* and *Compco*? Compare Goldstein, *Kewanee Oil Co. v. Bicron Corp.: Notes on a Closing Circle*, [1974] SUP. CT. REV. 81, with Heald, *Federal Intellectual Property Law and the Economics of Preemption*, 76 IOWA L. REV. 959 (1991).

When the Court determines that trade secret law does not withdraw matter from the public domain, does it conceive of "the public domain" in the same way that it did in *Sears* and *Compco*?

The *Kewanee* Court identifies three public policies that Congress sought to promote in enacting the patent laws. Are these three policies equivalent to the public policy goal that the Court described in *Sears* and *Compco*? If not, does the *Kewanee* Court take the *Sears* and *Compco* policy concern into account in evaluating the impact of the trade secret laws?

Do you agree with the Court's assumption that, because of its weaker protection, the trade secret cause of action will not deter patent applications for clearly patentable inventions? See Stern, *A Reexamination of Preemption of State Trade Secret Law After Kewanee*, 42 GEO. WASH. L. REV. 927, 946–48 (1974). Do you agree with the Court's assumption that the "ripeness of time concept of invention" will minimize any loss of disclosure caused by the availability of trade secret protection? See Stern, *supra*, at 950. If you disagree with the Court's assumptions in these matters, were the assumptions crucial to the result? Could the Court still have justified reaching the result that it did?

From a practical standpoint, does the result in *Kewanee* make sense?

2. *The Aronson case: state contract protection for inventive ideas*. Five years after *Kewanee*, the Burger Court again addressed the preemption issue. In Aronson v. Quick Point Pencil Co., 440 U.S. 257, 99 S.Ct. 1096, 59 L.Ed.2d 296 (1979), Aronson applied for a patent for her new form of

keyholder, and while the application was pending, she negotiated a contract with Quick Point for the manufacture and sale of the keyholder. Quick Point agreed to pay Aronson a royalty of 5% of the selling price in return for "the exclusive right to make and sell keyholders of the type shown" in the patent application. The agreement further provided that if Aronson's patent application was rejected, the royalties would be reduced to 2 1/2%. Apart from a provision giving Quick Point the right to cancel the agreement whenever the volume of sales failed to meet expectations, the agreement contained no limit on its duration.

Quick Point commenced manufacturing and selling the key holders, which proved to be a considerable success. When the PTO ultimately rejected Aronson's patent application, Quick Point reduced the royalty payments, as provided in the agreement, but continued manufacturing the keyholder and paying Aronson for the next fourteen years. While sales continued to be good, competitors, who were not bound to pay royalties to Aronson, began to sell the keyholder in competition with Quick Point. In 1975, Quick Point filed for a declaratory judgement, asserting that it was not obligated to pay royalties because the royalty agreement was unenforceable. Quick Point asserted that the state law which might otherwise make the contract enforceable was preempted by federal patent law. The Supreme Court rejected the argument.

The Court noted that the parties clearly contracted with full awareness of the possibility that a patent might not issue. The court continued:

> In this as in other fields, the question of whether federal law pre-empts state law involves a consideration of whether that law "stands as an obstacle to the accomplishment and execution of the full purposes and objectives of Congress." *Hines v. Davidowitz*, 312 U.S. 52, 67 [, 61 S.Ct. 399, 404, 85 L.Ed. 581] (1941). If it does not, state law governs.
>
> In *Kewanee Oil Co.*, we reviewed the purposes of the federal patent system. First, patent law seeks to foster and reward invention; second, it promotes disclosure of inventions, to stimulate further innovation and to permit the public to practice the invention once the patent expires; third, the stringent requirements for patent protection seek to assure that ideas in the public domain remain there for the free use of the public.
>
> Enforcement of Quick Point's agreement with Mrs. Aronson is not inconsistent with any of these aims. Permitting inventors to make enforceable agreements licensing the use of their inventions in return for royalties provides an additional incentive to invention. Similarly, encouraging Mrs. Aronson to make arrangements for the manufacture of her keyholder furthers the federal policy of disclosure of inventions; these simple devices display the novel idea which they embody wherever they are seen.
>
> Quick Point argues that enforcement of such contracts conflicts with the federal policy against withdrawing ideas from the public domain and discourages recourse to the federal patent system by allowing states to extend "perpetual protection to articles too lacking in novelty to merit any patent at all under federal constitutional stan-

dards," *Sears, Roebuck & Co. v. Stiffel Co.*, 376 U.S. 225, 232, 84 S.Ct. 784, 789, 11 L.Ed.2d 661 (1964).

We find no merit in this contention. Enforcement of the agreement does not withdraw any idea from the public domain. The design for the keyholder was not in the public domain before Quick Point obtained its license to manufacture it. In negotiating the agreement, Mrs. Aronson disclosed the design in confidence. Had Quick Point tried to exploit the design in breach of that confidence, it would have risked legal liability. It is equally clear that the design entered the public domain as a result of the manufacture and sale of the keyholders under the contract.

Requiring Quick Point to bear the burden of royalties for the use of the design is no more inconsistent with federal patent law than any of the other costs involved in being the first to introduce a new product to the market, such as outlays for research and development, and marketing and promotional expenses. For reasons which Quick Point's experience with the Aronson keyholder demonstrate, innovative entrepreneurs have usually found such costs to be well worth paying.

Finally, enforcement of this agreement does not discourage anyone from seeking a patent. Mrs. Aronson attempted to obtain a patent for over five years. It is quite true that had she succeeded, she would have received a 5% royalty only on keyholders sold during the 17–year life of the patent. Offsetting the limited terms of royalty payments, she would have received twice as much per dollar of Quick Point's sales, and both she and Quick Point could have licensed any others who produced the same keyholder. Which course would have produced the greater yield to the contracting parties is a matter of speculation; the parties resolved the uncertainties by their bargain.

No decision of this Court relating to patents justifies relieving Quick Point of its contract obligations. We have held that a state may not forbid the copying of an idea in the public domain which does not meet the requirements for federal patent protection. *Compco Corp. v. Day–Brite Lighting, Inc.*; *Sears, Roebuck & Co. v. Stiffel Co.* Enforcement of Quick Point's agreement, however, does not prevent anyone from copying the keyholder. It merely requires Quick Point to pay the consideration which it promised in return for the use of a novel device which enabled it to pre-empt the market.

* * *

Enforcement of the royalty agreement here is also consistent with the principles treated in *Brulotte v. Thys Co.*, 379 U.S. 29, 85 S.Ct. 176, 13 L.Ed.2d 99 (1964). There, we held that the obligation to pay royalties in return for the use of a patented device may not extend beyond the life of the patent. The principle underlying that holding was simply that the monopoly granted *under a patent* cannot lawfully be used to "negotiate with the leverage of that monopoly." The Court emphasized that to "use that leverage to project those royalty payments beyond the life of the patent is analogous to an effort to enlarge the

> monopoly of the patent ...." *Id.*, at 33, 85 S.Ct., at 179. Here the reduced royalty which is challenged, far from being negotiated "with the leverage" of a patent, rested on the contingency that no patent would issue * * *.
>
> No doubt a pending patent application gives the applicant some additional bargaining power for purposes of negotiating a royalty agreement. The pending application allows the inventor to hold out the hope of an exclusive right to exploit the idea, as well as the threat that the other party will be prevented from using the idea for 17 years. However, the amount of leverage arising from a patent application depends on how likely the parties consider it to be that a valid patent will issue. Here, where no patent ever issued, the record is entirely clear that the parties assigned a substantial likelihood to that contingency, since they specifically provided for a reduced royalty in the event no patent issued within five years.
>
> This case does not require us to draw the line between what constitutes abuse of a pending application and what does not. It is clear that whatever role the pending application played in the negotiation of the 5% royalty, it played no part in the contract to pay the 2 1/2 royalty indefinitely.

Id., 440 U.S. at 262–65, 99 S.Ct. at 1099–1101, 59 L.Ed.2d at 302–04. Is it likely that the Court would reach the same result if Aronson depended on a quasi-contract (contract implied in law) theory or on the "property" theory of idea law to recover for Quick Point's use of her inventive idea, rather than on an express contract? How might the Court's analysis differ? See Barrett, *The "Law of Ideas" Reconsidered*, 71 J. PAT. & TRADEMARK OFF. SOC. 691, 726–737 (1989). What if the contract Aronson was seeking to enforce was a "shrink-wrap" license accompanying all copies of a computer program offered for sale to the public, which prohibited reverse engineering of the program as a means of protecting the program's trade secrets? Would the Court's preemption analysis be likely to differ from that in the *Aronson* case? See Rice, *Public Goods, Private Contract and Public Policy: Federal Preemption of Software License Prohibitions against Reverse Engineering*, 53 U. PITT. L. REV. 543 (1992).

Under the rule set forth in the *Brulotte* decision, if Aronson had gotten a patent, her royalties contract with Quick Point would have become unenforceable when the patent expired. See, e.g., *Pitney Bowes v. Mestre*, 701 F.2d 1365, 218 U.S.P.Q. 987 (11th Cir.1983), *cert. denied* 464 U.S. 893, 104 S.Ct. 239, 78 L.Ed.2d 230 (1983). Moreover, under *Lear, Inc. v. Adkins*, 395 U.S. 653, 89 S.Ct. 1902, 23 L.Ed.2d 610, 162 U.S.P.Q. 1 (1969), if Aronson had gotten a patent and Quick Point, as licensee, had successfully challenged its validity, Quick Point would have been relieved from liability for royalties, notwithstanding the contract. See Chapter 3, § IG2, *supra*. That being the case, why should Aronson be entitled to enforce the contract in perpetuity under the facts of the case?

BONITO BOATS, INC. v. THUNDER CRAFT BOATS, INC.

United States Supreme Court, 1989.
489 U.S. 141, 109 S.Ct. 971, 103 L.Ed.2d 118, 9 U.S.P.Q. 1847.

JUSTICE O'CONNOR delivered the opinion of the Court.

We must decide today what limits the operation of the federal patent system places on the States' ability to offer substantial protection to utilitarian and design ideas which the patent laws leave otherwise unprotected. * * * In this case, the Florida Supreme Court * * * struck down a Florida statute which prohibits the use of the direct molding process to duplicate unpatented boat hulls, finding that the protection offered by the Florida law conflicted with the balance struck by Congress in the federal patent statute between the encouragement of invention and free competition in unpatented ideas. [W]e now affirm the judgment of the Florida Supreme Court.

I

In September 1976, petitioner Bonito Boats, Inc. (Bonito), a Florida corporation, developed a hull design for a fiberglass recreational boat which it marketed under the trade name Bonito Boat Model 5VBR. Designing the boat hull required substantial effort on the part of Bonito. A set of engineering drawings was prepared, from which a hardwood model was created. The hardwood model was then sprayed with fiberglass to create a mold, which then served to produce the finished fiberglass boats for sale. The 5VBR was placed on the market sometime in September 1976. There is no indication in the record that a patent application was ever filed for protection of the utilitarian or design aspects of the hull, or for the process by which the hull was manufactured. The 5VBR was favorably received by the boating public, and "a broad interstate market" developed for its sale.

In May 1983, after the Bonito 5VBR had been available to the public for over six years, the Florida Legislature enacted Fla.Stat. § 559.94 (1987). The statute makes "[i]t ... unlawful for any person to use the direct molding process to duplicate for the purpose of sale any manufactured vessel hull or component part of a vessel made by another without the written permission of that other person." § 559.94(2). The statute also makes it unlawful for a person to "knowingly sell a vessel hull or component part of a vessel duplicated in violation of subsection (2)." § 559.94(3). Damages, injunctive relief, and attorney's fees are made available to "[a]ny person who suffers injury or damage as the result of a violation" of the statute. § 559.94(4). The statute was made applicable to vessel hulls or component parts duplicated through the use of direct molding after July 1, 1983. § 559.94(5).

On December 21, 1984, Bonito filed this action in the Circuit Court of Orange County, Florida. The complaint alleged that respondent here, Thunder Craft Boats, Inc. (Thunder Craft), a Tennessee corporation, had violated the Florida statute by using the direct molding process to duplicate the Bonito 5VBR fiberglass hull, and had knowingly sold such duplicates in violation of the Florida statute. * * * Respondent filed a motion to dismiss the complaint, arguing that under this Court's decisions in *Sears, Roebuck & Co. v. Stiffel Co.*, and *Compco Corp. v. Day–Brite Lighting, Inc.*, the Florida statute conflicted with federal patent law and was therefore invalid under the Supremacy Clause of the Federal Constitution. The trial court granted respondent's motion, and a divided Court of Appeals affirmed the dismissal of petitioner's complaint.

On appeal, a sharply divided Florida Supreme Court agreed with the lower courts' conclusion that the Florida law impermissibly interfered with the scheme established by the federal patent laws. The majority read our decisions in *Sears* and *Compco* for the proposition that "when an article is introduced into the public domain, only a patent can eliminate the inherent risk of competition and then but for a limited time." * * *

II

* * *

From their inception, the federal patent laws have embodied a careful balance between the need to promote innovation and the recognition that imitation and refinement through imitation are both necessary to invention itself and the very lifeblood of a competitive economy. * * *

* * * To qualify for protection, a design must present an aesthetically pleasing appearance that is not dictated by function alone, and must satisfy the other criteria of patentability. [The Court describes the limitations on patentability posed by the novelty, statutory bar and nonobviousness provisions of 35 U.S.C.A. §§ 102 and 103.]

* * * Taken together, the novelty and nonobviousness requirements express a congressional determination that the purposes behind the Patent Clause are best served by free competition and exploitation of either that which is already available to the public or that which may be readily discerned from publicly available material. See *Aronson v. Quick Point Pencil Co.*, 440 U.S. 257, 262, 99 S.Ct. 1096, 1099, 59 L.Ed.2d 296 (1979) ("[T]he stringent requirements for patent protection seek to ensure that ideas in the public domain remain there for the use of the public").

The applicant whose invention satisfies the requirements of novelty, nonobviousness, and utility, and who is willing to reveal to the public the substance of his discovery and "the best mode ... of carrying out his invention," is granted "the right to exclude others from making, using, or selling the invention throughout the United States," for a period of 17 years. The federal patent system thus embodies a carefully crafted bargain for encouraging the creation and disclosure of new, useful, and nonobvious advances in technology and design in return for the exclusive right to practice the invention for a period of years. * * *

The attractiveness of such a bargain, and its effectiveness in inducing creative effort and disclosure of the results of that effort, depend almost entirely on a backdrop of free competition in the exploitation of unpatented designs and innovations. The novelty and nonobviousness requirements of patentability embody a congressional understanding, implicit in the Patent Clause itself, that free exploitation of ideas will be the rule, to which the protection of a federal patent is the exception. Moreover, the ultimate goal of the patent system is to bring new designs and technologies into the public domain through disclosure. State law protection for techniques and designs whose disclosure has already been induced by market rewards may conflict with the very purpose of the patent laws by decreasing the range of ideas available as the building blocks of further innovation. The offer of federal protection from competitive exploitation of intellectual property would be rendered meaningless in a world where substantially similar state law protections were readily available. To a limited extent, the federal patent laws must determine not only what is protected, but also what is free for all to use. * * *

Thus our past decisions have made clear that state regulation of intellectual property must yield to the extent that it clashes with the balance struck by Congress in our patent laws. * * * We have long held that after the expiration of a federal patent, the subject matter of the patent passes to the free use of the public as a matter of federal law. * * * Where the public has paid the congressionally mandated price for disclosure, the States may not render the exchange fruitless by offering patent-like protection to the subject matter of the expired patent. * * *

In our decisions in *Sears, Roebuck & Co. v. Stiffel Co.*, and *Compco Corp. v. Day–Brite Lighting, Inc.*, we found that publicly known design and utilitarian ideas which were unprotected by patent occupied much the same position as the subject matter of an expired patent. * * *

The pre-emptive sweep of our decisions in *Sears* and *Compco* has been the subject of heated scholarly and judicial debate. Read at their highest level of generality, the two decisions could be taken to stand for the proposition that the States are completely disabled from offering any form of protection to articles or processes which fall within the broad scope of patentable subject matter. Since the potentially patentable includes "anything under the sun that is made by man," *Diamond v. Chakrabarty*, 447 U.S. 303, 309, 100 S.Ct. 2204, 2207, 65 L.Ed.2d 144 (1980), the broadest reading of *Sears* would prohibit the States from regulating the deceptive simulation of trade dress or the tortious appropriation of private information.

That the extrapolation of such a broad pre-emptive principle from *Sears* is inappropriate is clear from the balance struck in *Sears* itself. The *Sears* Court made it plain that the States "may protect businesses in the use of their trademarks, labels, or distinctive dress in the packaging of goods so as to prevent others, by imitating such markings, from misleading purchasers as to the source of the goods." *Sears, supra*, 376 U.S., at 232, 84 S.Ct., at 789. Trade dress is, of course, potentially the subject matter of design patents. Yet our decision in *Sears* clearly indicates that the States may place limited regulations on the circumstances in which such designs are used in order to prevent consumer confusion as to source. Thus, while *Sears* speaks in absolutist terms, its conclusion that the States may place some conditions on the use of trade dress indicates an implicit recognition that all state regulation of potentially patentable but unpatented subject matter is not *ipso facto* pre-empted by the federal patent laws.

What was implicit in our decision in *Sears*, we have made explicit in our subsequent decisions concerning the scope of federal pre-emption of state regulation of the subject matter of patent. Thus, in *Kewanee Oil Co. v. Bicron Corp.*, we held that state protection of trade secrets did not operate to frustrate the achievement of the congressional objectives served by the patent laws. Despite the fact that state law protection was available for ideas which clearly fell within the subject matter of patent, the Court concluded that the nature and degree of state protection did not conflict with the federal policies of encouragement of patentable invention and the prompt disclosure of such innovations.

Several factors were critical to this conclusion. First, because the public awareness of a trade secret is by definition limited, the Court noted that "the policy that matter once in the public domain must remain in the public domain is not incompatible with the existence of trade secret protection." *Id.*, at 484, 94 S.Ct., at 1887. Second, the *Kewanee* Court emphasized that "[t]rade secret law provides far weaker protection in many respects than the patent law." *Id.*, at 489–490, 94 S.Ct., at 1889–1890. This point was central to the Court's conclusion that trade secret protection did not conflict with either the encouragement or disclosure policies of the federal patent law. The public at large remained free to discover and exploit the trade secret through reverse engineering of products in the public domain or by independent creation. Thus, the possibility that trade secret protection would divert inventors from the creative effort necessary to satisfy the rigorous demands of patent protection was remote indeed. Finally, certain aspects of trade secret law operated to protect non-economic interests outside the sphere of congressional concern in the patent laws. As the Court noted, "[A] most fundamental human right, that of privacy, is threatened when industrial espionage is condoned or is made profitable." *Id.*, at 487, 94 S.Ct., at 1889. There was no indication that Congress had considered this interest in the balance struck by the patent laws, or that state protection for it would interfere with the policies behind the patent system.

* * *

At the heart of *Sears* and *Compco* is the conclusion that the efficient operation of the federal patent system depends upon substantially free trade in publicly known, unpatented design and utilitarian conceptions. In *Sears*, the state law offered "the equivalent of a patent monopoly," in the functional aspects of a product which had been placed in public commerce absent the protection of a valid patent. While, as noted above, our decisions since *Sears* have taken a decidedly less rigid view of the scope of federal pre-emption under the patent laws, we believe that the *Sears* Court correctly concluded that the States may not offer patent-like protection to intellectual creations which would otherwise remain unprotected as a matter of federal law. Both the novelty and the nonobviousness requirements of federal patent law are grounded in the notion that concepts within the public grasp, or those so obvious that they readily could be, are the tools of creation available to all. They provide the baseline of free competition upon which the patent system's incentive to creative effort depends. A state law that substantially interferes with the enjoyment of an unpatented utilitarian or design conception which has been freely disclosed by its author to the public at large impermissibly contravenes the ultimate goal of public disclosure and use which is the centerpiece of federal patent policy. Moreover, through the creation of patent-like rights, the States could essentially redirect inventive efforts away from the careful criteria of patentability developed by Congress over the last 200 years. We understand this to be the reasoning at the core of our decisions in *Sears* and *Compco*, and we reaffirm that reasoning today.

III

We believe that the Florida statute at issue in this case so substantially impedes the public use of the otherwise unprotected design and utilitarian ideas embodied in unpatented boat hulls as to run afoul of the teaching of our decisions in *Sears* and *Compco*. It is readily apparent that the Florida statute does not operate to prohibit "unfair competition" in the usual sense that the term is understood. The law of unfair competition has its roots in the common-law tort of deceit: its general concern is with protecting *consumers* from confusion as to source. While that concern may result in the creation of "quasi-property rights" in communicative symbols, the focus is on the protection of consumers, not the protection of producers as an incentive to product innovation. * * *

With some notable exceptions, including the interpretation of the Illinois law of unfair competition at issue in *Sears* and *Compco*, the common-law tort of unfair competition has been limited to protection against copying of nonfunctional aspects of consumer products which have acquired secondary meaning such that they operate as a designation of source. The "protection" granted a particular design under the law of unfair competition is thus limited to one context where consumer confusion is likely to result; the design "idea" itself may be freely exploited in all other contexts.

In contrast to the operation of unfair competition law, the Florida statute is aimed directly at preventing the exploitation of the design and utilitarian conceptions embodied in the product itself. The sparse legislative history surrounding its enactment indicates that it was intended to create an inducement for the improvement of boat hull designs. * * * To accomplish this goal, the Florida statute endows the original boat hull manufacturer with rights against the world, similar in scope and operation to the rights accorded a federal patentee. Like the patentee, the beneficiary of the Florida statute may prevent a competitor from "making" the product in what is evidently the most efficient manner available and from "selling" the product when it is produced in that fashion. The Florida scheme offers this protection for an unlimited number of years to all boat hulls and their component parts, without regard to their ornamental or technological merit. Protection is available for subject matter for which patent protection has been denied or has expired, as well as for designs which have been freely revealed to the consuming public by their creators.

* * *

That the Florida statute does not remove all means of reproduction and sale does not eliminate the conflict with the federal scheme. In essence, the Florida law prohibits the entire public from engaging in a form of reverse engineering of a product in the public domain. This is clearly one of the rights vested in the federal patent holder, but has never been a part of state protection under the law of unfair competition or trade secrets. * * * The duplication of boat hulls and their component parts may be an essential part of innovation in the field of hydrodynamic design. Variations as to size and combination of various elements may lead to significant advances in the field. Reverse engineering of chemical and mechanical articles in the public domain often leads to significant advances in technology. If Florida may prohibit this particular method of study and recomposition of an unpatented article, we fail to see the principle that would prohibit a State from banning the use of chromatography in the reconstitution of unpatented chemical compounds, or the use of robotics in the duplication of machinery in the public domain.

* * * Given the substantial protection offered by the Florida scheme, we cannot dismiss as hypothetical the possibility that it will become a significant competitor to the federal patent laws, offering investors similar protection without the *quid pro quo* of substantial creative effort required by the federal statute. The prospect of all 50 States establishing similar protections for preferred industries without the rigorous requirements of patentability prescribed by Congress could pose a substantial threat to the patent system's ability to accomplish its mission of promoting progress in the useful arts.

* * *

* * * In [both *Sears* and *Kewanee*], state protection was not aimed exclusively at the promotion of invention itself, and the state restrictions on the use of unpatented ideas were limited to those necessary to promote goals outside the contemplation of the federal patent scheme. Both the law of unfair competition and state trade secret law have

coexisted harmoniously with federal patent protection for almost 200 years, and Congress has given no indication that their operation is inconsistent with the operation of the federal patent laws.

Indeed, [by virtue of Congress' passage of Lanham Act § 43(a) and its explicit statutory safeguards for trade secret information provided to federal agencies] there are affirmative indications from Congress that both the law of unfair competition and trade secret protection are consistent with the balance struck by the patent laws. * * * The case for federal pre-emption is particularly weak where Congress has indicated its awareness of the operation of state law in a field of federal interest, and has nonetheless decided to "stand by both concepts and to tolerate whatever tension there [is] between them." *Silkwood v. Kerr–McGee Corp.*, 464 U.S. 238, 256, 104 S.Ct. 615, 625, 78 L.Ed.2d 443 (1984). The same cannot be said of the Florida statute at issue here, which offers protection beyond that available under the law of unfair competition or trade secret, without any showing of consumer confusion, or breach of trust or secrecy.

* * *

Congress has considered extending various forms of limited protection to industrial design either through the copyright laws or by relaxing the restrictions on the availability of design patents. Congress explicitly refused to take this step in the copyright laws, and despite sustained criticism for a number of years, it has declined to alter the patent protections presently available for industrial design. It is for Congress to determine if the present system of design and utility patents is ineffectual in promoting the useful arts in the context of industrial design. By offering patent-like protection for ideas deemed unprotected under the present federal scheme, the Florida statute conflicts with the "strong federal policy favoring free competition in ideas which do not merit patent protection." *Lear, Inc. v. Adkins*, 395 U.S. [653], 656, 89 S.Ct. [1902], 1903 (1969). We therefore agree with the majority of the Florida Supreme Court that the Florida statute is preempted by the Supremacy Clause, and the judgment of that court is hereby affirmed.

Notes and Questions

1. *The Bonito Boats decision.* In your opinion, does the Court successfully reconcile *Sears* and *Compco* with the more recent *Goldstein, Kewanee,* and *Aronson* decisions? After *Bonito Boats*, what factors appear to be the most important in determining whether state causes of action for intellectual property will be preempted under the supremacy clause?

The Florida plug molding statute did not prohibit all copying or use of the protected boat hulls. In *Kewanee* and *Aronson* the Court found the fact that the state laws at issue precluded only some uses to be an important factor. Why not in *Bonito Boats*?

In *Kewanee*, the court stressed that the trade secret laws operated to protect the interest in privacy, a non-economic interest outside the sphere of congressional concern in the patent laws. Did the Florida plug molding statute not protect any comparable additional interest? In Interpart Corp. v. Italia, 777 F.2d 678, 228 U.S.P.Q. 124 (C.A.F.C. 1985), the Court of Appeals for the Federal Circuit, in upholding a California anti-plug molding statute against preemption claims, stressed that the statute prevented "unscrupulous competitors" from using a method of copying which the state considered "unfair." Why did the Supreme Court in *Bonito Boats* not credit the state's interest in preventing marketplace conduct that it deems unfair?

What is the justification for anti-plug molding provisions? Do they benefit the public, or only the manufacturers of boat hulls? Is the *Bonito Boats* Court's evaluation of this issue a factor in its decision? Are you convinced by the Court's arguments that the anti-plug molding statute, by preventing a form of reverse engineering, may impair innovation in the field of aquadynamic design? See Heald, *Federal Intellectual Property Law and the Economics of Preemption*, 76 IOWA L. REV. 959, 985–88 (1991).

After *Bonito Boats*, may the states apply their unfair competition laws to enjoin the copying of distinctive, nonfunctional product features when the copying leads to a likelihood of consumer confusion? See RESTATEMENT (THIRD) OF UNFAIR COMPETITION § 16, comment c (Tentative Draft No. 2, 1990).

For additional analysis of the *Bonito Boat* decision, see Shipley, *Refusing To Rock the Boat: The* Sears/Compco *Preemption Doctrine Applied to* Bonito Boats v. Thunder Craft, 25 WAKE FOREST L. REV. 385 (1990).

2. *The status of other state causes of action.* Some commentators believed that *Sears* and *Compco* sounded a death knell for the misappropriation cause of action, and some courts did find misappropriation claims preempted thereafter. See, e.g., Columbia Broadcasting System, Inc. v. DeCosta, 377 F.2d 315, 153 U.S.P.Q. 649 (1st Cir.1967), *cert. denied* 389 U.S. 1007, 88 S.Ct. 565, 19 L.Ed.2d 603 (1967). In *DeCosta*, the plaintiff, who had originated the "Paladin" character, brought a misappropriation claim against CBS, arguing that the network had stolen his character for its television series, "Have Gun Will Travel." The district court found for the plaintiff, but the Court of Appeals for the First Circuit reversed, finding the misappropriation claim preempted:

> Congress has established a procedural scheme of [copyright] protection by notice and registration. The necessary implication of this approach, we conclude, is that absent compliance with the scheme, the federal policy favoring free dissemination of intellectual creations prevails. Thus, if a "writing" is within the scope of the constitutional clause, and Congress has not protected it, whether deliberately or by unexplained omission, it can be freely copied.

Id., 377 F.2d at 318–19, 153 U.S.P.Q. at 653.

In other cases, courts rejected preemption challenges to misappropriation claims. Compare, for example, Pottstown Daily News Publishing Co. v. Pottstown Broadcasting Co., 247 F.Supp. 578, 147 U.S.P.Q. 414 (E.D.Pa. 1965), in which the defendant, a radio station, used news gathered by the plaintiff newspaper in its daily news broadcasts, thus avoiding the cost of gathering its own news:

> The Copyright Act permits copyright protection against exact reproduction but such protection does not preclude the public from using the factual content of a news account. Therefore since the Copyright Act would not prevent the defendant from using plaintiff's news items as a basis for its newscasts, we think that the state unfair competition laws can afford such protection.

Id., 247 F.Supp. at 582, 147 U.S.P.Q. at 418. The court argued that construing *Sears* and *Compco* to prevent a misappropriation remedy would lead to highly inequitable results.

Given the ensuing Supreme Court decisions, and particularly *Bonito Boats*, how would you approach the question of whether a misappropriation claim is preempted? For an examination of some of the issues, see Abrams, *Copyright, Misappropriation, and Preemption: Constitutional and Statutory Limits of State Law Protection*, [1983] SUP. CT. REV. 509.

How would you evaluate a supremacy clause preemption challenge to a state trademark dilution claim? Do the state anti-dilution statutes frustrate Congress' purposes in enacting the Lanham Act? Compare United States Jaycees v. Commodities Magazine, Inc., 661 F.Supp. 1360, 2 U.S.P.Q.2d 1119 (N.D.Iowa 1987) (finding preemption because the anti-dilution law conflicts "with one of the major goals of the Lanham Act—uniformity"), with Plasticolor Molded Products v. Ford Motor Co., 713 F.Supp. 1329, 11 U.S.P.Q.2d 1023 (C.D.Cal.1989), *vacated after settlement* 767 F.Supp. 1036, 18 U.S.P.Q.2d 1975 (C.D.Cal.1991) (rejecting argument that "because the dilution statute dispenses with the requirement of proving a likelihood of confusion, it is preempted by the Lanham Act or, to the extent that the dilution statute purports to prohibit the copying of functional features, the federal patent law"). Like the courts, commentators have provided mixed views. Compare Handler, *Are the State Anti-dilution Laws Compatible with the National Protection of Trademarks?*, 75 TRADEMARK REP. 269 (1985), and Heald, *Federal Intellectual Property Law and the Economics of Preemption*, 76 IOWA L. REV. 959 (1991) (both suggesting the possibility of preemption); with Welkowitz, *Preemption, Extraterritoriality, and the Problem of State Antidilution Laws*, 67 TULANE L. REV. 1 (1992), and Van Slyke, *State Laws against Trademark Dilution: Why They Should Not Be Preempted by the Lanham Act*, 83 TRADEMARK REP. 197 (1993) (both rejecting preemption).

Might a right of publicity claim be preempted? See Shipley, *Publicity Never Dies; It Just Fades Away: The Right of Publicity and Federal Preemption*, 66 CORNELL L. REV. 673 (1981).

II. STATUTORY PREEMPTION: COPYRIGHT ACT SECTION 301

MAYER v. JOSIAH WEDGWOOD & SONS, LTD.

United States District Court, Southern District of New York, 1985.
601 F.Supp. 1523, 225 U.S.P.Q. 776.

LEISURE, DISTRICT JUDGE:

This case concerns a dispute over a Christmas tree ornament. Rather than fostering peace and harmony in the holiday spirit, the ornament has instead led to litigation.

The ornament consists of a small round cameo made of blue jasper-ware (dull gloss china), embossed with a white snowflake in bas-relief, and mounted in gold. It is surrounded by three alternating perpendicular concentric gold bands, with a small eye hook at the top, presumably for hanging. This ornament was offered for sale in the United States during the 1982 Christmas season by Josiah Wedgwood & Sons, Inc. [Josiah Wedgwood & Sons, Inc. ("JWS Inc.") is the sister corporation of JWS Ltd., the named defendant, which manufactured the ornament.]

This case is now before me on defendant's motion for summary judgment. For the reasons set forth below, that motion should be granted.

I. Facts

The plaintiff, Sandra Mayer, is an artist. Her work, including snowflake designs, has been sold to museums and art houses. Her snowflake designs are a product of her own "interpretation" of what is found in nature. * * * No federally registered copyright was obtained for any of her work, though she did place a copyright notice on at least some of her creations. The design at issue here, however, had no such copyright notice.

In late 1978 or early 1979, Mayer met with Roy Moyer, a representative of the United Nations Children's Fund (UNICEF), and offered to contribute this design to UNICEF for use in a Christmas card to be issued by UNICEF. UNICEF accepted her offer and for the 1979 holiday season marketed a greeting card featuring Mayer's snowflake, which was embossed on the cover. The back of the card acknowledged Mayer's contribution, but contained no copyright notice.

At about the same time, Mayer began exploring possibilities for commercial exploitation of her snowflake. She engaged the services of one Emil ("Sam") Polk, president of a company called Latama, Inc. It was proposed that a Christmas plate be manufactured, featuring Mayer's design. In an effort to bring the plan to fruition, Polk approached James Fulks, Vice President–Marketing of JWS Inc., to explore possibilities for a deal. Negotiations began, and in December 1978, Mayer submitted to JWS Inc. through Polk an embossed print of the snowflake design.

[JWS Inc. then conferred with JWS Ltd., in England, which would manufacture the proposed plate.] It is clear from the correspondence between the two Wedgwood companies that by October 25, 1979, the Polk project was considered unfeasible and thus would not be going forward.

At this point the evidence presented to me becomes unclear. Mayer testified at deposition that she does not remember requesting return of her print. However, in a letter dated July 27, 1983, Catherine Adamczyk, Corporate Secretary of JWS Inc., wrote to Mayer's attorney, Ms. Liebert, that the print had been returned to Polk in 1979. I have no evidence from Polk or anyone else as to where the print is now. * * *

On February 22, 1984, Mayer filed suit against JWS Ltd. Her complaint states two causes of action. The first alleges that JWS Ltd. converted her design to its own use, and the second alleges unfair competition. She seeks damages for the alleged conversion and an accounting and payment to her of all profits earned by JWS Ltd. on sales of the allegedly infringing Christmas ornament. * * *

III. Preemption

When Congress revised the copyright laws in 1976, it specifically provided for preemption of all state rights equivalent to those within the scope of federal copyright law. 17 U.S.C. § 301. Under § 301, federal preemption takes hold once three conditions are met: the work is the type of work protected by the copyright laws; the right asserted is equivalent to a right protected by federal copyright law; and the January 1, 1978 cutoff date is met. When these three conditions converge, the state law right of action is preempted.

A. *The time element*

The preemption provision of § 301 by its terms does not apply to state law rights and remedies as to "any cause of action arising from undertakings commenced before January 1, 1978." It is quite clear from the language and background of § 301(a) that Congress meant to exclude from preemption only those cases in which the cause of action arose before January 1, 1978. Section 301(a) provides that federal law governs all rights in covered works, "whether created before or after [January 1, 1978]." Thus, the deadline applies to the cause of action, not to the work of authorship. The legislative history of the copyright law revision of 1976 reinforces this conclusion. Thus, although the statute is susceptible to a reading which would exclude from preemption causes of action in which the work in issue was created before 1976, by reading "undertaking" to refer to the works of authorship, such a reading is clearly erroneous in light of the congressional intent.

In this case, the work from which the dispute arose was created before January 1, 1978. The causes of action, though, arose later. Plaintiff's papers place the time in December 1978 when Mayer gave her print to Polk for submission to Wedgwood. Hence, any infringement of her rights necessarily occurred later, and in any event after January 1, 1978. Thus, Mayer's cause of action is within the temporal scope of § 301 preemption.

B. *Subject matter of copyright*

A state law action covering "subject matter that does not come within the subject matter of copyright as defined by sections 102 and 103 ..." is not preempted by § 301. 17 U.S.C. § 301(b)(1). In general terms, that subject matter is "original works of authorship fixed in any tangible medium of expression," 17 U.S.C. § 102(a), including "compilations and derivative works," 17 U.S.C. § 103(a). Section 102(a) lists several examples of protectible works, among which is "pictorial, graphic and sculptural works." 17 U.S.C. § 102(a)(5).

Mayer's snowflake design clearly is within the subject matter of the copyright laws. Indeed, Mayer's attorney had at one time considered adding to the complaint a copyright claim, but later abandoned the idea, apparently because no such claim could be stated due to the design's entry into the public domain with its publication in the UNICEF card.[15] Thus, the second condition of preemption under § 301 is met in this case.[16]

C. Nature of the right

Section 301, while preempting state law as to rights equivalent to copyright, specifically preserved nonequivalent state law rights. 17 U.S.C. § 301(b)(3). Thus, the issue to be determined here is whether actions for conversion and the misappropriation branch of unfair competition protect rights that are "equivalent" to those protected by federal copyright law. Because Congress did not define equivalence in the statute, I turn now to the legislative history and case law development of § 301.

1. Legislative History. Section 301 as enacted describes the preempted rights generically, that is, as those rights "equivalent" to copyright. Earlier drafts of § 301, however, contained examples of the types of actions that § 301 did not aim to preempt. At the time it was submitted to the House, § 301(b)(3) preserved state law actions pertaining to

> activities violating legal or equitable rights that are not equivalent to any of the exclusive rights within the general scope of copyright

15. The fact that a work has entered the public domain does not itself remove causes of action respecting that work from the scope of § 301's preemptive provisions. As the House Report states,

> if a work fits within one of the general subject matter categories of sections 102 and 103, the bill prevents the States from protecting it even if it fails to qualify for federal statutory copyright because . . . it has fallen into the public domain.

House Report at 131, U.S.Code Cong. & Admin.News 1976, p. 5747.

16. Federal copyright law does not protect ideas, 17 U.S.C. § 102(b). Rather, it protects only the author's particular expression of those ideas. Thus, state laws that protect ideas, as distinct from their expression, are without the subject matter of copyright and therefore not preempted under § 301.

In this case, Mayer is seeking to protect her right to use her snowflake design from appropriation by JWS Ltd. She does not—indeed, realistically no one can—claim rights in the *idea* of using snowflake designs on Christmas items. Thus, her reliance on *Werlin v. Reader's Digest Ass'n, Inc.*, 528 F.Supp. 451 (S.D.N.Y.1981), for the proposition that § 301 does not preempt misappropriation and quasi-contract claims is misplaced. In *Werlin*, Judge Ward held simply that Reader's Digest was liable for using plaintiff's story idea, though it did not use plaintiff's story, and that the actions for Reader's Digest's use of plaintiff's *idea* were not preempted. Here, by contrast, Mayer is complaining of use by JWS Ltd. of her design itself, not the idea of using a snowflake design for Christmas items.

> as specified by section 106, including rights against *misappropriation* not equivalent to any of such exclusive rights, breaches of contract, breaches of trust, trespass, *conversion*, invasion of privacy, defamation, and deceptive trade practices such as passing off and false representation.

House Report at 24 (emphasis added). Thus, both causes of action Mayer is suing upon were mentioned among those excluded from § 301 preemption. Moreover, it seems that no inference as to Congress's intent may be drawn from the fact that the illustrative list was dropped from the statute as it finally was enacted. In a detailed discussion of this point, Nimmer points out that "[i]t seems clear that the amendment which caused such deletion was not intended substantively to alter Section 301(b)(3) as regards those examples." 1 M. Nimmer, *The Law of Copyright* § 1.01[B][3] at 1–14.3 (1984). Thus, it may appear that conversion and misappropriation claims have not been preempted.

In this case, however, the prior draft is of no aid to plaintiff. It is quite clear from the House Report that "conversion" in the draft refers to a cause of action to vindicate possessory rights in chattels.[17] Plaintiff here obviously means something else. Her conversion claim alleges that JWS Ltd. converted her snowflake design by reproducing it on the Christmas ornament, causing her damage of at least $100,000. It is not reasonable to think that the print itself was worth such a large amount of money. Indeed, Mayer testified that besides her investment of perhaps 15 hours of her time, she incurred a total of approximately $125 in out-of-pocket expenses to create the design at issue in this case. Thus, Mayer is not suing to vindicate her right to the physical print which was given to defendant. It is plain that what Mayer is suing for is the deprivation of the rights flowing from the labor and expertise which she embodied in the snowflake.

The misappropriation claims preserved by the statute are only those "not equivalent to any such exclusive rights." The draft language thus is circular. It is apparent, though, that Congress recognized that, in at least some instances, misappropriation claims would be preempted. Noting that " 'misappropriation' is not *necessarily* synonymous with copyright infringement," House Report at 132, U.S.Code Cong. & Admin.News 1976, p. 5748 (emphasis added), the House Report used an example of an unpreempted misappropriation action—*International News Serv. v. Associated Press*, 248 U.S. 215, 39 S.Ct. 68, 63 L.Ed. 211 (1918) (*"INS"*). In *INS*, defendant was found to have taken the facts reported in plaintiff's transmissions of "hot news" and used them in its own competing news service. The other example advanced was of sanctions imposed on one who improperly invades another's computerized data base and gains access to the data. Both these examples involve subject matter other than copyright, specifically the facts and data as

17. Nothing contained in section 301 precludes the owner of a *material embodiment* of a copy ... from enforcing a claim of conversion against one who takes possession of the copy ... without consent.

House Report at 133.

opposed to their expression. Thus, the House Report states that "a cause of action labelled as 'misappropriation' is not preempted if it is in fact based neither on a right within the general scope of copyright ... nor on a right equivalent thereto." House Report at 132, U.S.Code Cong. & Admin.News 1976, p. 5748. It is thus not surprising that the House Report considered misappropriation to survive preemption. The tort it had in mind was not equivalent to copyright infringement.

The misappropriation branch of unfair competition under New York law, however, is arguably a somewhat different tort, one that the House Report did not directly consider. Although it traces its roots to *INS*, the New York misappropriation tort has grown much broader. It is now a fact-oriented action, providing relief from all types of "commercial immorality," *Metropolitan Opera Ass'n v. Wagner–Nichols Recorder Corp.*, 199 Misc. 786, 101 N.Y.S.2d 483 (Sup.Ct.1950), *aff'd*, 279 A.D. 632, 107 N.Y.S.2d 795 (1951). Generally, it protects against a defendant's competing use of a valuable product or idea created by the plaintiff through investment of time, effort, money and expertise.

Thus, the legislative history of § 301 gives no direct guidance as to the contours of preemption in this case. Accordingly, I turn now to the cases dealing with the scope of § 301's preemptive effect in this case.

2. Case law. Section 301 has been applied by various courts to preempt a wide range of actions. *See, e.g., Harper & Row, Publishers, Inc. v. Nation Enters.*, 501 F.Supp. 848 (S.D.N.Y.1980) (conversion and tortious interference with contractual relations), *aff'd*, 723 F.2d 195 (2d Cir.1983), *cert. granted*,—U.S.——, 104 S.Ct. 2655, 81 L.Ed.2d 362 (1984); *Warner Bros. v. American Bdcstg. Cos., Inc.*, 720 F.2d 231 (2d Cir.1983) (unfair competition/misappropriation); *Crow v. Wainwright*, 720 F.2d 1224 (11th Cir.1983) (crime of dealing in stolen property) * * *. It is important, however, to focus on the facts of each case and the particular rights the plaintiff seeks to protect. Courts have found that state law torts similar to those found in the cases above to be preempted, often even sharing the same names, in fact survive § 301. * * * The test for preemption was well-stated by Nimmer in his classic treatise.

> [A] right which is "equivalent to copyright" is one which is infringed by the mere act of reproduction, performance, distribution or display.... If under state law the act of reproduction, performance, distribution or display, ... will *in itself* infringe the state created right, then such right is preempted. But if other elements are required, in addition to or instead of, the acts of reproduction, performance, distribution or display, in order to constitute a state created cause of action, then the right does not lie "within the general scope of copyright," and there is no preemption.

Nimmer, *supra* at 1–11–12. The prevailing test may be referred to as the "extra element" test. That extra element, however, must be one which changes the nature of the action so that it is *qualitatively* different from a copyright infringement claim. Elements such as awareness or intent, which alter the action's scope but not its nature, will not save it from preemption under § 301. Thus, the issue here is whether Mayer's conversion and misappropriation claims contain an "extra element" which qualitatively distinguishes the actions and their underlying rights from those addressed by copyright law.

The conversion claim fails on its own terms. Count I of the complaint alleges that Mayer "possessed the right to use, sell, assign or reproduce [the] design" and that JWS Ltd. "wrongfully converted plaintiff's snowflake design to its own use and benefit by reproducing said design on a 1982 Wedgwood Christmas ornament." Thus, the rights asserted are clearly the same as those protected by § 106 of the copyright law, and the act constituting the alleged violation of plaintiff's rights corresponds exactly to the act necessary for a copyright infringement. I have not been shown, nor am I aware of any, extra element of the conversion claim that would save it. Thus, even assuming that plaintiff may assert a claim for conversion of an intangible property right under New York law, that claim is preempted here.

As for misappropriation, Mayer asserts that there is in fact an extra element that will save the action from preemption—commercial immorality. But it is hard to see how this is an extra element. In this case, the alleged misappropriation of Mayer's time, talent and effort is by the reproduction of the product of her time, talent and effort, i.e. the snowflake design. That is precisely the type of misconduct the copyright laws are designed to guard against. To call such conduct immoral adds nothing. "Commercial immorality" appears to be merely a judgmental label attached to odious business conduct, not an extra element.

If, however, it is an extra element, it is not the type that would save the action from preemption. It is an extra element in the same sense that awareness and intent are: it alters the *scope* of the action but not its nature. That is, it would permit the action to go forward when the infringing conduct is immoral, but not when it is not immoral. The basic act which constitutes the infringement of plaintiff's rights, however, is the same as that of copyright. The claimed use rights are identical as well. Thus, the cause of action asserted here is not qualitatively different from one for copyright infringement, and accordingly it is preempted.

* * *

Notes and Questions

1. *Preemption of state law.* Why did Congress wish to preempt state causes of action that emulate copyright? What is the relationship of section 301 preemption to supremacy clause preemption, discussed in the prior section? In *Wedgwood*, the court suggests that ideas and facts contained within copyrightable works are not copyrightable subject matter for purposes of section 301, so that state laws providing rights in ideas or facts are not subject to preemption under that section. Does it necessarily follow that such state laws should also survive a supremacy clause challenge? Might

state protection of ideas and facts frustrate accomplishment of Congress' purpose to strike the proper balance between what should be protected and what should be left in the public domain?

What, if any, effect does section 301 have on federal causes of action providing rights equivalent to copyright in copyrightable subject matter? See 17 U.S.C.A. § 301(d).

2. *The subject matter of copyright.* Section 301 only preempts state causes of action to the extent that they protect "works of authorship that are fixed in a tangible medium of expression and come within the subject matter of copyright as specified by sections 102 and 103" of the Copyright Act. 17 U.S.C.A. § 301(a). The "subject matter" issue has posed relatively few difficulties. There is general agreement that section 301 preempts state causes of action protecting works that fall within the general subject matter set forth in sections 102 and 103 (for example, literary works, musical works, pictorial, graphic or sculptural works) but fail to qualify for copyright due to insufficient originality, a failure to provide proper copyright notice or expiration of their term of protection.

The language of section 102(b), however, has raised some questions. Section 102(b) provides: "In no case does copyright protection for an original work of authorship extend to any idea, procedure, process, system, method of operation, concept, principle, or discovery, regardless of the form in which it is described, explained, illustrated, or embodied in such work." Suppose that a plaintiff brings a state cause of action to prevent the defendant from taking ideas, facts ("discoveries") or principles employed or described in the plaintiff's copyrightable literary work. Could the claim be preempted under section 301? A number of courts addressing the issue have, like the *Wedgwood* court, interpreted the statutory language of section 102(b) to place ideas, facts, methods of operation, etc., outside the scope of copyrightable subject matter, so that the states are free to protect them in such circumstances. Could you construct an argument to the contrary? See Harper & Row, Publishers, Inc. v. Nation Enterprises, 723 F.2d 195, 200 (2d Cir.1983), *reversed on other grounds* 471 U.S. 539, 105 S.Ct. 2218, 85 L.Ed.2d 588, 225 U.S.P.Q. 1073 (1985).

Assuming that section 301 would not preempt a state cause of action to prevent the copying of facts or ideas employed in the plaintiff's copyrightable work, would the first amendment permit it? See 1 M. NIMMER & D. NIMMER, NIMMER ON COPYRIGHT, § 1.01[B][2][b] & [c] (1991).

3. *Legal or equitable rights equivalent to the exclusive rights of copyright.* The second branch of the section 301 preemption test has given the courts greater difficulty than the first. The "extra element" test, set forth in the *Wedgwood* opinion, is the most widely adopted approach to determining whether the state right at issue is "equivalent" to the exclusive rights of copyright.

The *Wedgwood* court notes that in order to avoid preemption, the "extra element" in the state cause of action must render the state right "qualitatively different" from the copyright cause of action. Only extra elements that alter the "nature" (as opposed to the "scope") of the action will do this. The court mentions awareness and intent as extra elements which would only alter the scope of the action. Do you agree that an extra element of "commercial immorality" falls into the same category? See Nash v. CBS, Inc., 704 F.Supp. 823, 833, 10 U.S.P.Q.2d 1026, 1034 (N.D.Ill.1989), *affirmed* 899 F.2d 1537, 14 U.S.P.Q.2d 1755 (7th Cir.1990). If not, would you find that the alleged extra element of "commercial immorality" differentiates misappropriation sufficiently from copyright to avoid section 301 preemption? How would you enunciate the difference between elements that alter the scope and elements that alter the nature of a cause of action?

Assume that X brings a trade secret action against Y, a former employee who has started a competing business, alleging that Y is incorporating large parts of X's trade secret computer program into the program Y's new company has developed for sale. X alleges that Y's actions violate a confidentiality agreement that Y signed when he first entered X's employ and gained access to X's program. Would the trade secret claim be preempted? It seeks redress for the unauthorized reproduction of a computer program, which is copyrightable subject matter. To prevail in his trade secret action, however, X must demonstrate that the program was a trade secret and that Y breached a duty of confidentiality—elements beyond what would be required to demonstrate copyright infringement. Does the imposition of these "extra elements" render the state trade secret claim "qualitatively different" from the copyright infringement claim? Courts have generally found that it does. See, e.g., Brignoli v. Balch Hardy & Scheinman, Inc., 645 F.Supp. 1201 (S.D.N.Y.1986).

How would you evaluate breach of contract claims in which the alleged breach consists of a defendant's reproduction, adaptation, public distribution, performance or display of copyrightable subject matter, in violation of express terms of the contract? Contract plaintiffs must demonstrate the "extra element" of a bargained-for exchange, which need not be demonstrated in copyright infringement actions. Courts have generally found that this extra element renders the claim "qualitatively" different from copyright infringement. See, e.g., *Brignoli, supra.*

State claims for passing off whose facts entail the unauthorized reproduction, adaptation, public distribution, performance or display of copyrightable subject matter also are usually upheld. See, e.g., Donald Frederick Evans and Associates, Inc. v. Continental Homes, Inc., 785 F.2d 897, 914, 229 U.S.P.Q. 321, 333 (11th Cir.1986) (Passing off claims entail the extra elements of deceptive or fraudulent conduct by a competitor and a likelihood of consumer confusion. "Rather than going to the question of copying in the manufacture of a product, unfair competition goes to the question of marketing.") How would you evaluate a trademark dilution claim for purposes of section 301?

How would you evaluate a right of publicity claim, when the alleged violation consisted of copying copyrightable subject matter? Compare Baltimore Orioles, Inc. v. Major League Baseball Players Ass'n, 805 F.2d 663, 231 U.S.P.Q. 673 (7th Cir.1986), *cert. denied* 480 U.S. 941, 107 S.Ct.1593, 94 L.Ed.2d 782 (1987), with Apigram Publishing Co. v. Factors Etc., Inc., 1980 WL 2047 (N.D. Ohio 1980).

Of course, as the *Wedgwood* court suggests, each case is determined on its specific facts, the court's evaluation of the essence of the plaintiff's allegations, and the applicable state jurisdiction's interpretation of the state cause of action at issue. A plaintiff cannot escape section 301 preemption merely by adopting the label of a separate state cause of action, when the substance of his claim is essentially copyright infringement. For example, in Motown Record Corporation v. George A. Hormel & Co., 657 F.Supp. 1236, 3 U.S.P.Q.2d 1124 (C.D.Cal.1987), the plaintiffs owned the copyright in the hit song "Baby Love," which had been made popular by The Supremes, and trademark rights in The Supremes. The defendants ran a commercial advertisement for Hormel's "Dinty Moore" beef stew featuring three young African–American women with bouffant hair and sequined formal gowns singing "Dinty Moore, My Dinty Moore," to the tune of "Baby Love." The plaintiffs brought suit, alleging a number of state law claims, including unfair competition and violation of a California right of publicity statute which prohibited use of a person's name, voice, signature, photograph or likeness in advertising or selling without permission. The court found both these claims preempted. In their unfair competition claim the plaintiffs alleged, among other things, that the defendants' deliberate broadcast of the advertisement falsely implied that the song and the image of The Supremes were utilized with the plaintiffs' permission. The defendants argued that this claim was preempted because its gravamen was "nothing more than the alleged taking of plaintiffs' intellectual property." *Id.*, 657 F.Supp. at 1239, 3 U.S.P.Q.2d at 1126–27. The court agreed that the unfair competition claim was not qualitatively different from copyright infringement, stating that the "essence of plaintiffs complaint is derived from defendants alleged unauthorized use of a copyrighted work. The additional allegation that the use falsely implied permission was not sufficient to change the nature of the claim." *Id.*, 657 F.Supp. at 1240, 3 U.S.P.Q.2d at 1127.

Likewise the court found the additional element of use in commercial advertising insufficient to save the statutory right of publicity claim. In this particular case, the court noted, the claim revolved around the unauthorized use of the copyrighted song, "Baby Love." There might be no right of publicity claim without the unauthorized use of the song, since the song served to identify the Supremes. The court recognized that the statute might not always be preempted, but given the unique nature of this plaintiff's complaint, the basic act which constituted the alleged infringement of the right of publicity—the unauthorized use of plaintiffs' composition—was the same as the act of copyright infringement. *Id.*, 657 F.Supp. at 1240–41, 3 U.S.P.Q.2d at 1128.

4. *Special exceptions to section 301 preemption.* Section 301 specifically leaves state common-law copyright intact for some types of works. First, the statutory language makes it clear that the states are free to provide copyright protection for works that are unfixed. Thus, for example, the states may provide rights for strictly oral compositions, or improvised works of music, choreography or drama that are never preserved in a tangible copy or phonorecord.

Second, section 301(c) specifically preserves state protection of sound recordings fixed prior to February 15, 1972, the date on which federal copyright was first made available for sound recordings. Since the amendment extending federal copyright to sound recordings did not encompass works fixed prior to its effective date, such works would be completely unprotected unless state record piracy laws were preserved. Section 301(c) preserves them for pre-February 15, 1972 sound recordings, as long as the cause of action arises before February 15, 2047. Causes of action arising on or after that date are preempted, to avoid the possibility of perpetual state protection.

5. *The additions of the Visual Artists Rights Act.* Prior to 1990, federal copyright law provided no explicit protection for moral rights. Under section 301, state moral rights laws could only be preempted if they were "equivalent" to the economic rights set forth in section 106 of the Copyright Act. One could argue that state "rights of integrity," prohibiting alteration of copyrightable works may be equivalent to the section 106(2) exclusive right to adapt a copyrighted work in some cases, and thus preempted. But see Wojnarowicz v. American Family Association, 745 F.Supp. 130, 136, 17 U.S.P.Q.2d 1337, 1341 (S.D.N.Y.1990) (New York Artists' Authorship Rights Act claim "requires proof of elements not required to prove copyright infringement, namely (a) the artwork must be altered, defaced, mutilated or modified; (b) the altered, defaced, mutilated or modified artwork must be attributed to the artist, or displayed in such circumstances as to be reasonably understood to be his work; and (c) this attribution must be reasonably likely to damage the artist's reputation.")

In 1990, Congress enacted the Visual Artists Rights Act ("VARA"), which provided, in a new section 106A, rights of attribution and integrity for a limited class of "works of visual art." See *supra*, Chapter 5, § III H. VARA also amended section 301 to preempt state rights "that are equivalent to any of the rights conferred by section 106A with respect to works of visual art to which the rights conferred by section 106A apply." 17 U.S.C.A. § 301(f)(1). Congress further provided, however, that state rights or remedies would not be preempted with respect to "activities violating legal or equitable rights which extend beyond the life of the author." 17 U.S.C.A. § 301(f)(2). See Gorman, *Visual Artists Rights Act of 1990*, 38 J. COPYRIGHT SOC. 233, 239–41 (1991).

6. *Parallel provisions and additional sources.* The Semiconductor Chip Protection Act of 1984, which provides federal rights in mask works, states that its provisions

> [S]hall preempt the laws of any State to the extent those laws provide any rights or remedies with respect to a mask work, which are equivalent to those rights or remedies provided by this chapter, except that such preemption shall be effective only with respect to actions filed on or after January 1, 1986.
>
> * * * [N]othing in this chapter shall detract from any rights of a mask work owner, * * * with respect to any mask work first commercially exploited before July 1, 1983.

17 U.S.C.A. § 912(c) & (d). See *supra*, Chapter 5, § II D 4. For an analysis of these provisions, see II P. GOLDSTEIN, COPYRIGHT PRINCIPLES, LAW AND PRACTICE § 15.34 (1989); J. DRATLER, INTELLECTUAL PROPERTY LAW: COMMERCIAL, CREATIVE, AND INDUSTRIAL PROPERTY, § 8.06[5][d] (1991).

Two excellent sources for information about section 301 of the Copyright Act are II P. GOLDSTEIN, COPYRIGHT PRINCIPLES, LAW AND PRACTICE ch. 15 (1989); and I M.B. NIMMER & D. NIMMER, NIMMER ON COPYRIGHT ch. 1 (1994).

*

Index

References are to Pages

References are to Pages

References are to Pages

References are to Pages

†

0-314-06126-6

90000

9 780314 061263